BUILDING AMERICA'S FIRST UNIVERSITY

BUILDING AMERICA'S FIRST UNIVERSITY

AN HISTORICAL and ARCHITECTURAL GUIDE to THE UNIVERSITY of PENNSYLVANIA

GEORGE E. THOMAS *and* DAVID B. BROWNLEE

•••••••••••••••••••••••••••••

UNIVERSITY OF PENNSYLVANIA PRESS

PHILADELPHIA

Publication of this volume was assisted by generous grants from the office of the Executive Vice President of the University of Pennsylvania, the division of Facilities Services, the department of Campus Services, the Martin Meyerson Publication Fund, and Franklyn L. Rodgers.

10 9 8 7 6 5 4 3 2 1

Published by
University of Pennsylvania Press
Philadelphia, Pennsylvania
19104-4011

Designed by John Baxter, Acme Design Company

Library of Congress Cataloging-in-Publication Data
Thomas, George E.
 Building America's first university : an historical and architectural guide to the University of Pennsylvania / George E. Thomas and David B. Brownlee.
  p. cm.
 Includes bibliographical refernces and index.
 ISBN 0-8122-3515-0 (alk. paper)
 1. University of Pennsylvania—Buildings—History. I.Brownlee, David Bruce. II. Title.
LD4531.T56 1999
378.748'11—dc21   *99-39838*
                    CIP

CONTENTS

ACKNOWLEDGMENTS

EVERY PROJECT has its moment of birth. In the case of this publication there were at least two starting points. *Building America's First University: An Historical and Architectural Guide to the University of Pennsylvania* has been a joint effort with David Brownlee, who wrote most of the initial text to the guide portion nearly a decade ago. Some years later I began augmenting the guide portion, noting changes of status and new additions to the campus as well as beginning to weave in material on the persons associated with the buildings. This in turn led to the idea of an architectural history accompanying the guide, the result of which is the present volume. We have each reviewed the other's work, but we take responsibility for our own materials. As always, my work with David has been collegial and enjoyable, punctuated with good meals and good fellowship.

During the fall of 1995 I began to write the introductory historical chapters to provide an historical context for the decisions and values that give Penn's buildings their special qualities. This most recent part of the project was precipitated by research on Houston Hall and Irvine Auditorium in preparation for the Perelman Quadrangle project. It became clear that Houston Hall, the dormitory quadrangle, and Franklin Field all were opened in the year and a half between spring 1895 and fall 1896, making it appropriate to celebrate Penn's late nineteenth-century renaissance. More than any other moment, the end of the nineteenth century marked the period when Penn "got a life." It has retained that vitality ever since.

Nearly a century after Provost Harrison's great projects, the modern renewal of the University campus began under Martin Meyerson with the Landscape Action Master Plan. The realization that beautiful was good marketing led in turn to the restoration of the old University Library, College Hall, and Logan Hall under Sheldon Hackney and now continues with the Perelman Quadrangle under the Rodin administration.

This project owes much to the operations side of the University and would not have been completed without the interest of Dean Emeritus G. Holmes Perkins, University Trustee Walter G. Arader, Penn's Director of Facilities Planning and now University Architect Titus B. Hewryk, and then Vice President for Facilities Arthur Gravina. For a decade Titus Hewryk skillfully guided the University Facilities Planning Department from the era of urban renewal toward a reasoned dialogue about the values of past and present. Art Gravina's commitment to quality is a recognizable hallmark of recent campus projects. Their perception of the value of Penn's historic buildings paralleled the transformation of the institution's attitudes about itself, and their leadership has resulted in the preservation and restoration of the buildings that are the stars of this history. Without their efforts Penn would not be nearly so attractive and this project might never have been pursued. Penn's treasures, from the revitalized Franklin Field on the east to the restored Evans Building on the west, are an important contribution to the national architectural heritage.

As the 1990s end, Penn has embarked on a great adventure, testing its belief that institutions such as the University should use their talents where they are best suited while hiring outside talent to provide specialized services such as real estate management. Under Executive Vice President John Fry a new team will work with representatives of Trammell Crow Company to serve the University's future. Vice President for Operations Omar Blaik and Tom Lussenhop, Managing Director for Real Estate, have the opportunity to make this new venture a success. Their support of this project confirms their commitment to the University's future.

Earlier research on other campus projects solved other pieces of this vast puzzle that a two-and-a-half-century-old institution becomes. The material on the Victorian campus draws heavily on research undertaken in the late 1980s for the restoration of the old University Library. That work was encouraged by Robert Venturi and his able associate David Marohn. Their obvious affection and admiration for Furness's work led to the publication of *Frank Furness: The Complete Works* (1991). More recent work with Venturi, Scott Brown and Associates on other areas of the campus led to studies of the scientific precinct for the Institute for Advanced Science and Technology and the Perelman Quadrangle. Their professional and intellectual interests energized these studies and contributed to this larger project.

Another piece of this undertaking was supported by the Graduate School of Fine Arts for its Centennial celebration in 1990. In that year, with the support of Dean Lee Copeland, I worked with Ann Strong on a history of the Graduate School of Fine Arts, published as *The Book of the School: 100 Years.* That work was the basis for an exhibition organized by Penn's Architectural Archives and its gifted and enthusiastic director Julia Moore Converse. Through that project I learned of the impact of the Graduate School of Fine Arts on the physical evolution of the modern campus. It is not a coincidence that Penn was transformed in the 1890s after Warren Laird arrived on campus, and that it was again reborn in the 1950s with the deanship of G. Holmes Perkins. For Julia, whose infectious enthusiasm carries all along with her, for Holmes, whose cutting insights always made him a great critic, and for Martin Meyerson, who as president emeritus continues to serve his University, my utmost thanks for reviewing the text.

So vast a group of images as have been amassed for this history required many collaborators. The University Archives have opened their files for many of the historic views; their collection includes photographs by the leading architectural photographers of the past generation including Lawrence Williams and Frank Ross. Over the past two years, Lewis Tanner took important color views that add much to the book. Each has graciously provided the use of their images, adding much to the project, while also reducing the days that I have spent with view camera and film bag. To them my gratitude is boundless. My work has been ably assisted by the staff of the University Archives, who have pointed out sources, found files, urged me forward, and provoked much additional thought. Gail Pietzyk survived an autumnal migration of students, guiding them toward valuable research on the University; Curtis Ayers provided astute observations on Penn's basketball and football teams while finding and then copying materials with indefatigable good will; Mark Frazier Lloyd, the director of the University Archives and Records Center, read and reread the text and offered important comments, testing my ideas against his own research over a decade as director of the Archives. The value of this history reflects their many contributions. To all of them, sincere thanks are due.

I acknowledge with affection and pleasure the years of reading, editing, commenting, and encouraging that my dear wife Emily Cooperman has provided. In so many ways, it has been Emily who has made it possible for me to have the time to produce this study. As my colleague in our joint consulting practice, she has pushed the importance of landscape and setting, focused ideas and served as the ideal critic. My debt to her is boundless.

It is with delight that I remember the work of my students in Urban Studies 272 course in the fall of 1995. They researched the early trustees and those at the end of the nineteenth century, and each studied a campus building, searching for the purpose, pedagogical values, donors, significant faculty and students, and the like. Their efforts added significantly to the completeness of this project and made it all the more pleasurable. I have thanked these students for the research they did in notes on the buildings they studied. Engineering student Dana Royer's wonderful comparative paper on Ivy League trustees bril-

liantly and clearly differentiated between the Ivy colleges, leading in turn to our understanding of the differences between Penn and Harvard, Yale, and Princeton, as represented by the professions of the trustees.

Finally, I call attention to the special work of Josh Gottheimer, who worked with admirable intensity and thoroughness on the details and many of the larger questions during the spring and summer of 1996. In that same year Josh managed simultaneously to research issues for this book while working on the Clinton reelection campaign, attending classes, and serving as president of the Interfraternity Council. He is the best tribute to the leadership and potential of the University fraternity system. He made many contributions on a wide range of issues, from the role of the Moravians in shaping Franklin's college to the continuing value of the fraternity and sorority system. Students like Josh keep teaching fresh and exciting. It is to Penn's undergraduates exemplified by Josh that this book is dedicated.

Hurrah for the Red and the Blue!

GET

PREFACE

Building America's First University tells the story of the University of Pennsylvania, a story that begins with Benjamin Franklin's transcendent notion that learning ought not to be restricted to a single leading religion or class. Rather than looking back toward classical learning, Franklin set his College's course toward the world of the present and the future by focusing on modern languages, the natural sciences, and contemporary literature. His goals were soon reflected in the addition of a course in medicine, the first in the New World, and, by the end of the century, a course in law. This broader definition of education was celebrated after the American Revolution when the College was renamed the University of Pennsylvania, the first American institution to carry that all-encompassing title. In the intervening centuries, Franklin's vision has become the model of American higher education.

Since its founding the University has adapted to reflect the values of the community that has supported it, charting a course between innovation and convention. These changes are evident in the architecture and character of the three campuses that have been its home. From Franklin's adaptation of a nonsectarian chapel as the institution's first quarters to Frank Furness's innovative University Library and Louis Kahn's momentous Richards Medical Research Laboratory, Penn's buildings can be seen as evidence of the evolving intentions of the University's leaders.

Building America's First University is organized into two complementary sections. Five chapters tell the history of the University, with the last three devoted to the evolution of the present campus. The historical chapters weave together the often conflicting interests and goals of trustees, administrators, alumni, and students that have shaped the institution of today. The history serves as prologue to the second half of the book, which presents the campus in the form you see now—two hundred and fifty years after Benjamin Franklin wrote his *Proposals for the Education of Youth in Pensilvania*. Coming at the end of forty years of massive growth, this is the first comprehensive architectural history of the University since the early twentieth century.

I

George E. Thomas

CHAPTER ONE

AN AWAKENING OF CONSCIOUS VIGOR

The Transforming Moment

THE EVENING OF January 2, 1896 began a fiercely cold winter week that ended with high temperatures in the teens and Philadelphia's Schuylkill River sufficiently frozen for ice skating. As if to contest with the icy grip of winter, the golden oak doors of Houston Hall were opened for the first time to the members of the University of Pennsylvania revealing a great oak-beamed hall dotted with massive oak Morris chairs and leather-covered benches artfully arranged in casual groupings.[1] Oriental carpets formed scattered pools of richly patterned color on its oak floors and at each end of the room, great Gothic stone fireplaces roared with flames and warmed the heart of the University community.[2] After the singing of the collegiate song "Ben Franklin," and a round of opening speeches, the guests toured the building, finding a swimming pool in the basement, billiard tables to provide gentlemanly amusement in the west wing of the first floor, and a quiet reading room in the eastern end. A theater seating 300 filled the upper levels of the eastern gabled wing, and a handsome dining hall occupied the western end of the second floor. Here, for the first time, Penn's students could enjoy each other's company in their own club in the heart of the campus.

Houston Hall's opening gave life to the campus and to the University.[3] Its designers were Penn students selected on the basis of a competition that was open to the present students and recent graduates of the

University's Department of Architecture. No longer would the University of Pennsylvania be known chiefly for its professional and graduate schools; instead, with the nation's first student union at its center, Penn would join the national movement that blended historical architecture and academic pageantry into a romantic and emotional experience that celebrated the transition from youth to maturity. "Collegiate" was about to become an adjective in the national vocabulary, and college life would step onto center stage of a culture that was discovering the joys of what Theodore Roosevelt called "the strenuous life."

That it took Pennsylvania's leaders a century and a half after its founding to understand the importance of the physical setting of the University should not be surprising to any who know of the hand-to-mouth beginnings of most American colleges. It has been a rare case when the founding of a college and the construction of its initial buildings have produced that rich fusion of architecture, memorial structures, and sculptures set in a landscape that are the constituent elements of a memorable campus.[4] To be sure, some English colleges, such as Nicholas Hawksmoor's splendid early eighteenth-century quadrangle at All Souls College, Oxford or William Butterfield's mid-nineteenth-century Victorian polychromed campus for Keble College, also at Oxford, were instantly recognized as important artistic achievements. But these groupings were the culminations of centuries of design traditions rooted in monastic communities that formed the basis for the residences, refectories, and meeting rooms of the ancient colleges.

In the United States, which lacked the design tradi-

Fisher Fine Arts Library spires, 1991. GET.

tion rooted in the ecclesiastical past of these earlier colleges, there were few obvious architectural models. Thomas Jefferson's "academical village" for the University of Virginia, set on its iconic green and framed by the low buildings in front of the Rotunda, was—and is—a convincing aesthetic whole, but it was all the more rare for its success.[5] More commonly, colleges in the New World began as utilitarian and economical structures whose architectural style changed to represent the evolving political and cultural values of the new nation, resulting in architectural stews with little consistency and less unity of flavor. For these early American colleges, the setting offered little more than was suggested by its designation as a "yard" (the term used for a farmer's fenced-in field). Indeed, the word "campus" would not become common until the last

Hall of Houston Hall, 1897. Photo: Rau Art Studio. UPA.

quarter of the nineteenth century, when the maturation of collegiate life finally made the setting as important a part of the college as the classroom instruction.[6]

A Word on Names

Reflecting the two and a half centuries of its history, the University of Pennsylvania has carried different names that denote its historical eras. The institution began as the Academy and Charitable School of Philadelphia, to which was appended the College of Philadelphia in 1755. The next change of name, in 1779 from College of Philadelphia to University of the State of Pennsylvania, reflected the addition of professional courses in medicine and law and designated the new chartering agency of the state after the dissolution of the Tory-dominated institution during the Revolution. It also made the institution the first in the United States to be so called. The title was shortened to the University of Pennsylvania in 1791 when the resuscitated College and the University of the State of Pennsylvania were reunited by act of legislature. While the institution's leaders were careful to use its full name on stationery and legal documents well into the middle of the nineteenth century, the American habit of informality quickly led to various contractions of the name, the most common of which is now "Penn." This choice might be presumed to have been driven by modern advertising dicta that prefer names of five letters or fewer beginning with consonants and including doubled letters, but in fact the custom reaches well back into the last century when the alumni frequently referred to their University as "Old Penn." The first song book, *Songs of the University of Pennsylvania* (1879), includes numerous examples of this usage or the even more colloquial Penn—doubtless for the greater ease of fitting the name into lyrics.[7]

By the 1970s the University administration's use of "Penn" was so common that it might have been supposed that the Board of Trustees had officially renamed the institution to commemorate one of its early founders, Thomas Penn, son of William Penn, the founder of the Commonwealth of Pennsylvania. This shift of name occurred at the moment when a remarkably successful prank issue of the *Daily Pennsylvanian* reported in banner headlines that the University trustees had finally decided to re-christen the institution for its great founder Benjamin Franklin, on the grounds that many of the other Ivy League schools such as Harvard, Yale, Brown, and Cornell were named for their founders.[8] Henceforth it would be Benjamin Franklin University, or Franklin U for short, with the sports teams carrying the nickname the "Bens." The success of the prank was evident from news stories in the local media and outrage from trustees who felt they had been overlooked in the decision-making. Clearly, a nerve had been touched! The proper title

The Green, University of Virginia, c. 1910. Hegeman and Peets, Civic Art, *1922.*

remains the University of Pennsylvania, which continues to appear on diplomas and other official documents, but it is Penn—not for the commonwealth's founder or his son who provided funds, but as a familiar abbreviation of Pennsylvania—that is the University's most common name as the twentieth century ends.

Throughout this book, care has been taken to use the name that reflects the usage appropriate to the historical era. Academy and Charitable School or the longer College, Academy and Charitable School of Philadelphia refer to the pre-1779 institution. University of the State of Pennsylvania is reserved for the Revolutionary era institution; University of Pennsylvania is used after 1791. Modern usage is such that the University of Pennsylvania sounds impossibly formal, so Penn is used familiarly and interchangeably with the longer and more formal title, it is hoped without too much confusion for the reader.

The Rise of the Modern College

In 1872 the University of Pennsylvania left its home in the old center of Philadelphia on Ninth Street for its new campus in West Philadelphia. The move across the Schuylkill River to the western suburbs coincided with the moment when the social and architectural

University of Pennsylvania at Henley-on-Thames, 1910. UPA

norms of America's colleges were metamorphosed after the Civil War.[9] When the first surge of college foundations began on this side of the Atlantic at the end of the seventeenth century, Americans were separated from Britain's ancient universities by an arduous voyage across the Atlantic Ocean. Unlike the great European universities that grew out of monastic and court communities, college study in the American colonies typically reflected the utilitarian needs of the New World. Training was emphasized over scholarship, providing what Daniel Boorstin has termed "higher education in place of higher learning."[10] Colleges from New England to Virginia and soon even west of the Appalachians found their peculiarly American mission of transmitting and diffusing training rather than the traditional European universities' purpose of the advancement of learning among an elite class.

Because the costs of American colleges were relatively lower than those of their European counterparts, and because of the relatively open social structure in the American colonies and later the United States, the student body of the typical American college reflected a broader social spectrum. The democratization of higher education was further encouraged by the late eighteenth-century federal land grants that led to such state-affiliated colleges as Dartmouth and the University of Pennsylvania. It has been customary to celebrate the number of American colleges as an example of national diversity, but their increasing numbers were also a liability, causing most American colleges to remain small in population and limited in resources, at best pale imitations of the ancient European colleges and universities.

In the second half of the nineteenth century, as the American labor force shifted from rural farming and small-town crafts to urban commerce and manufacturing, the apprenticeship system that had trained professionals and craftsmen alike gave way to new types of schooling. Accelerating technological and social changes, byproducts of industrialization, encouraged the establishment of new forms of higher education, particularly technical schools, which conveyed the torrents of new information that shaped modern work. These institutions provided credentials that became one of the criteria for employment.[11] By the 1850s and 1860s, more forward-looking colleges added technical courses, generally referred to as the sciences, to the classical curriculum, the so-called liberal arts, to enable them to compete with the technological institutes.

The rising tide of higher education soon crossed boundaries of gender, race, and social class. By the mid-nineteenth century, the Elmira Female College, Mount Holyoke Seminary, and Vassar College had been founded to provide advanced education for young women. Simultaneous with the arrival of women on campuses, the children of the rapidly growing middle classes broadened the spectrum of students who would attend college. Each generation has introduced new aspirants to upward mobility in the national rite of passage of the college years.

As the student population of American colleges changed, the typical curriculum changed as well, with the most important changes occurring in the 1870s. Post-Civil War America was already awash in the first flood of modern media, which graphically described in lurid text and vivid artists' sketches the events of the Civil War, the Indian wars, and western expansion. By

contrast, college studies were removed from the passions of the day. Lectures and books were the tools that transmitted received knowledge from the past as part of a largely passive educational system whose teaching practices were not far removed from those of the medieval universities. In an era speeded up by engineering and applied research, and instantaneously connected to faraway places by the telegraph and the telephone, most colleges were as out of touch with the spirit of the age as the sailing ship or the covered wagon. In the 1870s and 1880s, at Harvard University under Charles Eliot, at the University of Pennsylvania under Charles Stillé and later William Pepper, Jr., M.D., and at other American institutions, education was revitalized by the elective system, which enabled students to tailor the curriculum to fit their interests. Simultaneously, academic disciplines were reshaped by a new ideal, the search for new knowledge that was both stimulated by and a consequence of the new industrial culture. Rooted in scientific method, the new empiricism took a variety of forms on American campuses. Laboratory training and library research vied with design courses in architectural studios and metalwork in mechanical engineering shops, each mimicking the modern world of work. The laboratories and large research libraries that became common on American campuses in the 1870s and 1880s represented the fruits of these new ideals. The University of Pennsylvania was shaped by each of these movements, selecting students from the economic and social strata of the region, adding courses from the world of work, and eventually building the libraries and laboratories that would give its campus the appearance of a red brick factory for learning.

College Life

The transformation of the curriculum and the growth of the student body soon led to sweeping changes in the design of colleges.[12] This occurred when the vast wealth of post-Civil War America was applied to the honorific donation of new buildings and sometimes of entire colleges. These spectacular gifts were spurred by a new generation of institutional leaders who applied their increasing financial and spatial resources to the turn-of-the-century concept that ennobled the college campus as the setting for a new and significant stage of youth.[13] This new idea—fundamentally a prolonging of adolescence in a special setting for training—was but one of the effects of industrialization, which transformed all the nation's fundamental social structures. Home, work, and recreation were all reshaped by the rising pressures of the age; schooling by contrast was given more time and space and blossomed into a new lifestyle for its participants.

That the idealization of college life was more than a regional phenomenon restricted to the northeastern

Roy D. Bassett (1908), "At 'Em Now Pennsylvanyer! Spirit of '76." From Punch Bowl *III, 1907. UPA.*

"AT 'EM NOW PENNSYLVANYER! SPIRIT OF '76!"

United States is proved by the similar architectural forms, student activities, academic rituals, and collegiate experiences that appeared nearly simultaneously in the colleges and universities of the old northeast, the industrial heartland, the then largely rural south, and the still new west. By the 1890s colleges in every corner of the restored Union shared the new glamor.[14] There can be little doubt that the new system of education prospered because it was housed in seductive architectural forms that were manifestations of the new values. But, while there have always been motivated students, new educational systems and even new buildings have rarely been so seductive that the majority of prospective students would flock to experience them. For most of the new recruits, the choice of college was made because of the excitement of extracurricular activities rather than the substance of coursework. Paralleling the elective system that could be tailored to fit students' individual interests was the rise of American intercollegiate sports. Rowing and cricket matches between American collegiate student teams were first organized in the 1860s, imitating the collegiate sports that provided competitive outlets for the English upper classes. Around the nation's Centennial, college football became a national passion; Penn played its first intercollegiate game in 1876, which because of its link to the Centennial of the American Revolution made the "Spirit of '76" one of the rallying cries of the University into the twentieth century.

Simultaneously, and again based on English models, American college leaders began to encourage the establishment of traditions and rituals that gave each college class an identity, enriching the bonds of student life. Novels about college life recalled the literary form of British prep-school novels such as *Tom Brown's School Days.* Penn undergraduate life was described in Arthur Hobson Quinn's *Pennsylvania Stories* (1899), which celebrated prowess on the football field, fraternal spirit, and loyalty to the University as the greatest of manly virtues.[15] In a manner familiar to all who have participated in the search for the perfect college, the

Exterior of Houston Hall, looking north, 1900.
Photo: R. Newell and Son. UPA.

••••••••••••••••••••••••••••••••••

popular novels marketed the experience of the university far more than they described the education.

Soon, as success bred success, most American colleges, whether the older institutions of the east or the
new land grant schools of the west, supplemented
their regimen of lectures with the multi-vitamin of
academic rituals, from Convocation and Baccalaureate
to football games and formal galas. These activities
took place in the new settings of the dormitory, the
student union, the football stadium, the theater or the
landscaped campus. As the nineteenth century ended,
older institutions such as Columbia University and
the University of Pennsylvania built new campuses,
while new universities, such as the University of
Chicago in the midwest and Stanford University on
the west coast, constructed imposing complexes that
were intended to look as if they had been built over

centuries. These splendid new campuses reflected the
romance of history set within pastoral green landscapes that contrasted with the industrial society that
supported them. By 1900 the packaging of sports
facilities, student clubs, and campus conveyed the
institution to most students and to the public.

Architecture as Historical Evidence

When the golden oak doors of Houston Hall opened
to the public for the first time in the winter of 1896,
several men were certainly present. The University
provost, Charles Custis Harrison, the initiator of the
project, was the principal speaker at the dedication; the
Dean of the College, George Fullerton, was present, as
was the supervising architect, Frank Miles Day, himself an earlier graduate of the University. Members of
the Houston family, the donors of the project, were in
attendance as well. Presumably Milton B. Medary
(attended 1890, class of 1894) and William C. Hays
(Ar 1893), the winners of the student competition for

the design of the building, were given tickets of admission, too, though they were not mentioned in the accounts of the opening.[16]

Who selected these students and their mentor to design Houston Hall and why these men were chosen to design the building is an important part of the history of the University. It would be easy enough to state that the young students won the commission for the "best" design, and that they were assigned to work with faculty member Frank Miles Day, but that begs the question why their design was preferred. For that matter, why Day was selected as the advisor rather than another architect, such as the Hewitt brothers (who were at that time Houston's favored designers), brings to the fore the meanings later historians can read from the patterns of architectural patronage of an institution.

The selection of architects as campus designers tells much about the character of the institution and its leaders because, until the 1950s, the choice of the architects at most American universities was usually made by the donor or by a committee of trustees. Reflecting their personal commissions for home, office, and other institutions, Penn's benefactors made the University in the image of their personal world. Like more conventional forms of portraiture, architecture meets specific functional requirements while also exemplifying the goals and values of the institution through its manifestation as a work of art. Architecture expresses the intentions and expectations of the client through the medium of another person, the architect, so the potential for mixed messages is ever present. As in the case of the choice of an artist for a portrait, many of the underlying requirements of the client are resolved simply by the process of selection, usually based on knowledge of previous buildings and previous connections. Does the artist or architect produce work that is pleasing to the patron? Do the works project the image the patron intends? Because the leaders who selected design professionals viewed architecture from their institutional perspective rather than from the perspective of contemporary design,

their choices tended toward conservatism. Precedent ruled.

The architectural history of University of Pennsylvania is as telling as its corporate minutes, describing in brick, stone, steel, and concrete the values and goals of its leadership. Because of the physical and capital costs of buildings, and because of their role as manifestations and, broadly speaking, as representations of the institution that are expected to exist well into the foreseeable future, campus projects are usually reviewed, negotiated, and modified in a complex dialogue between the architect and the client. This process of selection shaped Penn's campus as it shaped the other great universities of the nation, typically making important buildings at universities the highest achievement of a select circle of local architects whose numbers were restricted by the difficulty of transportation and the closed circle of patronage of most college boards of trustees.

This dependence on local architects and the resulting local character of most colleges began to change with the rise of a national culture reflected in a growing national architectural press. In the 1890s architectural publications first trumpeted the breakdown of regionalism by publishing the work of a small cadre of architects whose practices transcended the parochialism of the Civil War generation. Architecture quickly became a commodity that conveyed prestige, and a new link was forged in the chain that bound the growing consumer culture and the great colleges and universities. By 1900 McKim, Mead and White from New York, Philadelphians Cope and Stewardson and Frank Miles Day, and Bostonians Ralph Adams Cram and landscape architects the Olmsted Brothers were among a handful of firms whose collegiate practices spanned the nation.

After World War II, air travel turned architectural practices into vagabondage for celebrity architects. High-signature design came to dominate the collegiate architectural scene as institutions from around the country vied with each other to "collect" the works of Richard Neutra, Eero Saarinen, Paul Rudolph, and,

Academic procession through Quad for dedication of Evans Dental School, 1915. Photo: F. Paul Menzen. UPA.

••••••••••••••••••••••••••••••••••••••

more recently, Venturi, Scott Brown and Associates, Michael Graves, and Robert Stern. As a result of these changes, architectural practices and the college campuses on which the new superstars now work transcend regional boundaries and reflect the national and global ambitions of the institutions.

The design of Houston Hall was part of this rapidly evolving national pattern that began reshaping of colleges across the nation at the end of the nineteenth century. Having served on the University board for a generation, Provost Harrison had a clear idea how he intended to reshape the campus, away from its Victorian roots toward the more conventional English Collegiate Gothic that was suddenly fashionable on American campuses because it represented the new aspirations of higher education. In Philadelphia, two firms could be counted on for historically accurate designs of the sort that gave instant credibility—Cope and Stewardson, who were already working on the designs for the University's new dormitory quadrangles, and Frank Miles Day the valedictorian of the class of 1883, who had taken the courses of the University's earlier architectural program taught by Thomas Richards. Perhaps most tellingly, it was Day who had recently been the victor in an architectural competition for the Art Club on South Broad Street

that became the local model for the new urban club. There, instead of following the regional convention of red brick Victorian, he had proposed a limestone and tan brick Venetian palazzo that reflected the rising national awareness of European history. Day would be the advisor to the Houston Hall project.

Unfortunately, we do not have the drawings for the winning entry by Medary and Hays or those of their competitors to confirm the reasons for the choice made by the national jury assembled by the new Professor of Architecture Warren Powers Laird to judge the competition. But even so there is important evidence that can be gleaned from their victory. Both victors had studied in the University's architectural program after it had been reconfigured toward the Beaux-Arts curriculum by Laird, who had also been placed in charge of the development of the campus. The method of the young architects—like the campus architecture that typified the Harrison era—adapted historical precedent to modern purpose. In the case of the University student club, the young designers selected as their model the Peacock Inn at Rowley, Yorkshire, a much-admired source whose architectural style evoked the future direction of the Harrison campus and whose original purpose was not unlike that required by the competition. Moreover, the chosen material, Wissahickon schist or "Chestnut Hill stone," would have been especially favored by the Houstons, whose great mansion Druim Moir and their surrounding real estate developments made extensive use of the material. Thus the design for the student union reflected the personal taste of the donor and the aspirations of the provost, while serving as a pedagogically sound model for students in Penn's architecture program. It won because it met many more requirements than style, size, and cost.

Form and Content: The Role of Leadership in the Shaping of Penn's Campus

Just as Penn's campus is a story of the values of its trustees, who often chose its architects, the campus architecture is also a record of the leadership of its

provosts (the original title given to the institution's leaders) and later its presidents. Each architectural era of the present campus has been stamped with the personalities and values of the activist provosts and presidents, making it possible to "read" the remnants of their campuses and thus to organize this history by their administrations. The first modern provost, Charles Stillé, headed the University from 1868 until 1880. The "Moses" who led the University to its new home in West Philadelphia from the heart of the old downtown, he envisioned a renewed and enlarged institution whose buildings, for reasons of economy rather than preference, would have the utilitarian character of the new land-grant universities that had sprung up across the United States with the passage of the Morrill Land Grant Act.[17] Stillé's College and Logan Halls, erected in the odd but engaging green serpentine stone and piled up in Gothic buttresses and pinnacles, remain Penn's physical and spiritual core.

When the provostship passed to William Pepper, Jr., M.D. in 1880, the fundamental compositional principles of individual buildings set in the midst of a green carried over from Stillé's campus. However, the structure of the University was radically altered from

Campus looking west, 1890. UPA.

the old unified division of knowledge of arts and sciences that would have been familiar to the first provost, William Smith, to the modern departmentalized institution that denoted the rise of separate and distinct academic disciplines on the model of contemporary European universities. New buildings represented these new divisions, and, instead of the striking green structures of Stillé's campus, most of the new buildings of the Pepper campus were as red as his own name suggested. Pepper's greatest contributions were his comprehension of the possibilities of the methods and goals of modern education and his desire to raise Penn's aspirations. This ambition was demonstrated by his charge to the building committee of the new University Library to produce "the best college library in America." During the Pepper years, red brick, terra cotta, sandstone, and tile were shaped in original forms that befitted their use as libraries, laboratories, power plants, and the myriad other facilities of a modern university. As in a modern factory, each use was particularized and was largely independent of other buildings so that future changes could be accommodated. Reflecting the increasing dominance of the engineering culture of the industrial city that was the University's home, Pepper forged the links that bonded the University to the dynamic forces of the modern world.

Penn owes its present appearance principally to the marketing genius of Charles Custis Harrison, provost between 1894 and 1910. In the heyday of Howard Pyle's and Maxfield Parrish's medievalizing illustrations for the national magazines of the day, Harrison turned toward the romance of the past as the packaging of the campus that could spark Penn's renaissance. Harrison's architects who recreated the nostalgic collegiate architecture of the preindustrial age were Frank Miles Day and the partnership of Walter Cope and John Stewardson, all of whom were then serving on the new faculty of the School of Architecture. Their architectural talents transformed Harrison's guiding vision into the red brick, late medieval style architecture based on the buildings of Oxford and Cambridge that even now, a century later, embodies the University to the public.

After World War II, first politician Harold Stassen (1948–53) and then Gaylord Harnwell (1953–70), by training a physicist, turned the University toward the modern architecture practiced by its renowned architectural school under the direction of Dean G. Holmes Perkins.[18] More recently, Martin Meyerson (1970–81), by training a city planner, was president during the years that Penn's setting was reshaped from the raw diagram left by the 1960s urban renewal project to the present landscaped park; it was under Meyerson that Penn became a global institution represented by works and deeds as well as by its ever more diverse student population.[19] And it is certainly no coincidence that the tenure of historian Sheldon Hackney (1981–93) was marked by the restoration of many of the historic buildings of Penn's central campus, including the old University Library and College Hall. At present, under Judith Rodin (1994–), the historic center of the University is being adapted to the future needs of a new century and a new millennium, with Houston Hall and Irvine Auditorium being reconfigured to make them once again a center for undergraduate life.

The Rise of Penn Pride

Penn's physical transformation had its roots in the change of spirit that began in 1872 with the move to West Philadelphia under Provost Stillé. Its new attitude was immediately made visible with the selection by the Philomathean Society of college colors—the now familiar red and blue that graced enameled tints on the cover of the cornerstone of College Hall and later the patterned slate of the mansard roof and the paving of the original floor of its front porch. In 1873 the first ivy plaque was installed on the north front of College Hall, beginning Penn's tradition of celebrating its history. This custom continues each spring with the planting of ivy and the installation of a student-designed plaque on an important campus landmark. These new festivals of institutional awareness were soon followed by the publication of yearbooks and magazines, and in turn were accompanied

••

1875 Ivy Day plaque, north facade of College Hall. GET.

by the composition of sentimental college songs arranged for the rich harmonies of the bass registers of male glee clubs. For the first time since the eighteenth century, the collegiate experience at Penn was principally aimed at the undergraduates instead of the students of such graduate courses as medicine, law, and business.

During Provost Harrison's tenure in the 1890s, as the children of the first generation of Penn's West Philadelphia campus graduates reached college age, alumni associations were founded to foster institutional allegiance. Soon a flood of University publications were aimed at furthering the bonds of college life. In 1896 the first issue of Penn's *Alumni Register* carried an article by Philip H. Goepp (L 1888) praising the publication of a new University songbook, *Pennsylvania Songs*, and ascribing its publication to the rising sense of self esteem:

A symptom, or is it rather an effect, of the great awakening of conscious vigor in the University, is the new book of *Pennsylvania Songs*, edited by a committee of her graduates and undergraduates.[20]

Particularly singled out was "Hail Pennsylvania" by Edgar M. Dilley (C 1897), which it was hoped would "fill the place with Pennsylvania given at Cambridge to 'Fair Harvard.'" (As an aside, it was sneeringly remarked that Harvard's hymn was set to an Irish melody, while Penn's new anthem, it was gleefully noted, was "set to the Russian hymn.")[21] Invidious collegiate competition could even to be found in the heritage of the music! Some of these new songs were written for specific football games and were handed out as flyers at the game. For example, "The Red and Blue," by Henry Clarkson Westervelt (M 1898) and William J. Goeckel (L 1896), first appeared in such a flyer for the 1896 Harvard game.

Despite its new alumni organizations, athletic teams, and student associations, Penn was at a disadvantage in the "awakening of conscious vigor" that was occurring at other American colleges. Having moved from its earlier sites on the east side of Philadelphia, it lacked both the historic buildings softened by the genteel patina of age and the tree-shaded canopy over central greens that gave a more finished appearance to the settings of peer institutions. Philadelphia's national status had also changed. It was no longer the nation's most sophisticated city, the generating center of national architectural design, or the national capital. It had become a massive beehive of industry whose honeycomb cells were the endless blocks of workers' row houses that contrasted with the small neighborhoods of the elite. By the 1890s Penn was surrounded by industry to the north and east, and portions of its campus looked like the industrial complexes that dominated the Philadelphia economy. Early photographs of the University's West Philadelphia setting attest to the daunting rawness of the scene. The first buildings of the new campus, College Hall, Logan Hall, the now demolished Hare Laboratory, the University Library, and the nondescript clapboarded frame shed that functioned as a dining hall, stood in barren grass stubble, interrupted here and there by the staccato rhythm of twiglike trees. Lacking too were the floral beds and flowering shrubbery that were the typical finishing touches of post-Civil War landscaping.

Except for the front steps of College Hall and the entrance hall of the new University Library, designated the "Conversation Hall," there were few places for undergraduates to gather, let alone eat, perform, or play. In his autobiography, *On the Edge of Evening* (1946), long-time English professor Cornelius Weygandt (C 1891) made no mention of undergraduate pleasures.[22] Student amusements such as the first football games were played behind College Hall, where Houston Hall now stands. Undergraduates played in street clothes, before chapel, making the aroma of perspiration-soaked wool a vivid memory of early graduates. In the generally treeless campus of Stillé's and Pepper's tenures, there were no cooling groves for

••••••••••••••••••••••••••••••••••••••

"Pennsylvania Songs for the Harvard Game, November 21, 1896." UPA.

Pennsylvania Songs

FOR THE

Harvard Game, November 21, 1896.

AND THE BLOW ALMOST KILLED HARVARD.

Fair Harvard came to Franklin Field
  One chill day in November,
And tried to teach us how to play,
  Perhaps you may remember.
Their backs did all that men could do
  To drive the leather forward,
But they couldn't beat the Red and Blue
  And the blow almost killed Harvard!

Since then two years have passed away,
  And once again we meet her,
And five to three the dollars say
  That good old Penn will beat her!
Just wait until the game is through,
  You'll read upon the score board
"The victors wear the Red and Blue
  And the blow almost killed Harvard!"

Let Morice kick a goal or two
  And Minds go through the centre;
'Twill be a tiny hole indeed
  That Gelbert cannot enter!
And throughout all the land to-night
  The story will go forward
That Penn has hit the Crimson line
  And the blow almost killed Harvard!
                  '94.

Tune: "THE NEW BULLY."

Have you seen that new football team, that's just come to town,
They have come down to Franklin Field, old Pennsy for to
  down,
And to drag the Red and Blue upon the ground;
Oh! the Indians came down here, with their ax in their hand,
And vowed that they would surely swipe old Pennsy from this
  land,
But our good team work was more than they could stand.

CHORUS.

When we put the Crimson, down, down, down,
When we put the Crimson, down, down, down,
When we put the Crimson down,
Then a single Harvard rooter won't be found.

Although we like old Harvard and she would like to score,
That's something that our team has vowed she would permit
  no more,
Since she's learned to regulate a football war;
So every member of the team, brace up and be a man,
And put up Pennsy team-work, as only Pennsy can,
And then we all may sing upon this plan.

CHORUS.

We have put the Crimson down, down, down,
We have put the Crimson down, down, down,

THE RED AND BLUE.

Come all ye loyal classmen, now in hall and campus through,
Lift up your hearts and voices for the royal Red and Blue.
Fair Harvard has her crimson, old Yale her colors too;
But for old Pennsylvania she wears the Red and Blue.

CHORUS.

Hurrah, hurrah, Pennsylvania! Hurrah for the Red
  and the Blue!
Hurrah, hurrah, hurrah, hurrah, hurrah for the Red
  and Blue!

One color's in the blushing rose, the other tints the clouds,
And when together both disclose we're happy as the gods.
We ask no other emblem, no other sign to view;
We only ask to see and cheer our colors Red and Blue.
                  —CHORUS.

How often when on fields of sport we've seen our boys go
    through,
The very air is rent in twain with cheers for Red and Blue.
We knew that victory then was ours, all else we might eschew,
If only we could wave and sing our colors Red and Blue.
                  —CHORUS.

Tune: "MARCHING THROUGH GEORGIA."

Oh, come ye jolly sons of Penn and make the welkin ring,
Raise ye up your voices and a song of triumph sing,
Let old Johnny know that on the gridiron Penn is king,
  While we go marching thro' Harvard!

CHORUS.

Hurrah! Hurrah! We're in to-day to win.
Hurrah! Hurrah! We'll pocket Harvard's tin.
Our team was never better, so let's raise a joyous din
  While we go marching through Harvard!

Oh, we all remember well the game of Ninety-four,
And the score of last year, too, but now we'll make it more.
Three times in succession, boys, we'll lay them on the floor,
  While we go marching thro' Harvard!

Pennsy's team has got the nerve, to-day they'll do or die.
Down the field they'll rush the ball or know the reason why,
Touchdown after touchdown on the score-board they'll lay by,
  While we go marching through Harvard!

We can trust our valiant team to hold up Pennsy's fame,
For they'll give those Harvard men some pointers on the game,
Which will make them sorry that to Franklin Field they came,
  While we go marching through Harvard!

US AND JOHNNY HARVARD.

Raise the good old tune again with hearts and voices stout;
If Johnny Harvard's mamma doesn't know her boy is out,
She'll learn we're taking care of him when Cambridge hears

conversation and recreation in the spring and fall. And, apart from Frank Furness's largely symbolic fireplace in the new library reading room, there was no central hearth for students to gather around in the winter. Though Penn had its songs and its Ivy Day festivals, it still had the appearance of a workplace, differing in detail but not in functional utility from the foundries and manufactories of the industrial city that surrounded and supported it.

Against the background of utilitarian planning that had heretofore typified the University, the announcement in 1894 of a competition among architectural students for the design of Houston Hall signaled more than the intention of meeting student needs for on-campus eating and recreation.[23] Simultaneous with the beginning of the Houston Hall project came the announcement of the intention to build a group of undergraduate dormitories, now familiar to generations of Penn students as "the Quad"; this was followed by the first efforts at landscaping the campus, initiated by Mrs. Charles C. Harrison, the wife of the new provost. Another year would see the construction of the first phase of Franklin Field. With the undefeated football teams of 1895 and 1896 and the song book of 1896, Pennsylvania had something to sing about— and the songs to sing. From the late 1890s on, the festivals of undergraduate life, academic, dramatic, musical, and athletic, have been as much a part of the University calendar as fall convocation and winter and spring examinations. Penn's increasingly heated rivalries with Princeton, Harvard, Yale, and Cornell bespoke the earlier evolution of undergraduate life on those campuses.

By 1900 college life at the University of Pennsylvania was far closer to the vital present than it was to the lifeless institution of the mid-nineteenth century. With these shifts of purpose, Penn began to incorporate those special details of setting and style that first broadened the experience of its students and since then have gladdened the hearts and the memories of her alumni. These were the great gifts of the 1890s to Penn's future.

Earlier Guides and Histories

The transformation of the campus that began in the 1890s is noteworthy for another reason. A generation earlier, when the nation's Centennial celebration brought millions of visitors to Philadelphia, few of the numerous guidebooks to the city took note of the University of Pennsylvania's campus or its architecture. The later evidence of off-campus clubs and fraternities across the Schuylkill where students resided with their families demonstrated that, into the 1890s, the campus had not become the focus of student culture. The few organized extracurricular activities took place off-campus in city theaters and suburban cricket clubs and thus were only peripherally associated with the institution. As a result there are few surviving accounts of life on Penn's early campuses, suggesting that the undergraduate years were remembered with fondness by few if any of its students.[24] In direct proportion to its metamorphosis under Provost Harrison came a series of guides and illustrated books that celebrated the transformed campus and the delights of college life.

Of these early guides, the most complete was *The University of Pennsylvania Illustrated*, written in 1897 by Professor of History John Bach McMaster.[25] His historical overview was accompanied by a *Sketch of Franklin Field* by football star and later trustee H. Laussat Geyelin (C 1877), who is remembered in the annals of Penn sports as the first to wear the Red and Blue colors to victory in an athletic contest. As European immigrants flooded into the United States at the end of the nineteenth century, social and class consciousness again reared its head, causing antediluvian institutions to celebrate their history as evidence of their elite origins and hence of their significance. Because of the new importance placed on institutional antiquity, McMaster's text began with an idealized perspective of the first campus, the "Academy and Charity School and Dormitories" that stood on Fourth Street. This antique image was followed by a view of the house built for the President of the United States on Ninth Street that became the University home in

1801. No other American university could claim such roots! Next came a perspective of William Strickland's 1829 design for the College and the Medical School that replaced the President's House and served as the campus until 1872. This was the College of memory for many of Penn's alumni, including then-Provost Charles Harrison, who had graduated from the old campus in 1862.

The 1897 history is also noteworthy for its chronological overview by Professor McMaster, which asserted that Penn had been founded in 1740, thereby specifically advancing its faculty in academic processions ahead of rival Princeton, and also incidentally ahead of Columbia.[26] This seemingly obvious question

••••••••••••••••••••••••••••••••••••••

Prepublication flyer for Francis Newton Thorpe, The University of Pennsylvania, 1745–1791–1891. *UPA.*

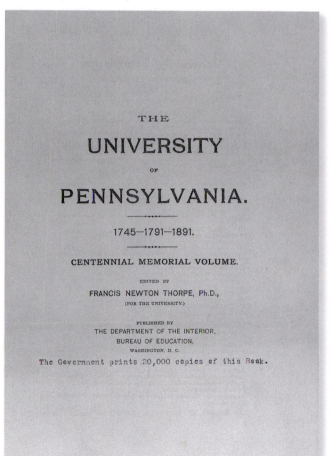

of Penn's founding date has been the subject of a century-long controversy because position in academic processions is usually determined by the antiquity of the attending institutions, based on the belief that age rather than originality is evidence of significance. In the mid-1890s two schools of thought on the topic of Penn's age developed, leading to a ridiculous situation. The group who adhered to the conventional date of 1749 prepared to celebrate the 150th anniversary of the University, while the other group would have completed their celebrations several years before—had they realized that there was an argument, albeit slender, for 1740.[27] The former group, which accepted 1749 or 1750 as the date of founding, based their claims on the publication date of Franklin's *Proposals Relating to the Education of Youth in Pensilvania* (1749) or the actual purchase of the real estate and building, which occurred on 1 February 1750.[28] The latter group eventually championed the now accepted date of 1740, using the establishment of the Whitefield Charity School and its supposed continuity through the intermediary of Franklin as the basis for the claim. That this new claim was rooted in the developing rivalry with Princeton University is apparent from the memoirs of Samuel Whitaker Pennypacker (L 1866), trustee and later governor of the state, who remarked:

> Before I became trustee, the University always traced its origin to a pamphlet written by Franklin in 1749, but I succeeded in proving that it really began with a charity school for which a building was erected in 1740, thus adding nine years to its life at the other end and *making it antedate Princeton.* Since my presentation of proofs to the trustees the catalogues have all borne the date of 1740. (Emphasis added)[29]

Ever since 1893, when this argument was made, 1740 has been used on the seal on Penn's buildings, even though College Hall carries large shields emblazoned with the dates 1755 (the year of the first college charter) and 1872 (the year the new West Philadelphia campus opened).

In John Bach McMaster's publication, illustrations of the campus, especially the splendid bird's-eye perspective of the projected campus (reproduced here as an endpaper) were accompanied by photographs of the new University Library and the older College Hall and the Medical School, as well as the quadrangle framed by the new Houston Hall and the rears of the earlier buildings. Despite the fall from grace of the early Victorian style of the original buildings, College Hall was the subject of several exterior views as well as a photograph of the interior of its chapel, then the setting of the college's academic rituals and the principal shared space of the entire college. And, as if to prove to parents that Penn students did study, there were three views of the new University Library, including the reading room with its new lone electric light bulb hanging from the ceiling four stories above.

As could be expected, the most popular subjects for the photographer were the newer buildings. There were half a dozen interiors of Houston Hall and a similar number of views of the more theatrical aspects of the dormitory quadrangle, which had immediately become the quintessential setting for undergraduate life. For those who thought of Penn as old-fashioned, a captive of the conservative Philadelphia elite, these photographs demonstrated its up-to-date allegiance to the national taste for the English academic Gothic style, metamorphosed by its architects from the stone of suburban colleges to urban brick. Of classroom interiors there were no photographs—but the new Franklin Field was illustrated by three architectural perspectives and two plans of the field house. There was even a photograph of the 1896 Penn-Cornell game in the old wooden grandstands across Spruce Street from the Wistar Institute. That nearly half of the views would be devoted to student life was to be expected; the glorification of adolescent male activities was the usual focus of such illustrated campus handbooks and of popular collegiate fiction such as the Yale-centered Frank Merriwell series.

Of the guide genre, *The University of Pennsylvania Illustrated* (1906) was the handsomest campus history until now.[30] Within its red and blue covers were numerous views of the major public interior and exterior spaces of the campus—and even less history. Selling the excitement of the activities rather than the hard facts of the curriculum effectively marketed the institution. The more serious tone of *Pennsylvania: A Glimpse of the University*, published by the General Alumni Society in 1914, was perhaps intended to reassure parents that their children were getting the education for which they paid. It opened with a ponderous foreword by Provost Edgar Fahs Smith (a chemist), which proved that scientists were less familiar than businessmen with marketing principles:

Our University began its career as a Charity School, under the guidance of godly, self-sacrificing men and women. Its earliest lesson was in the field of *service*.[31]

Following this dreary text was a photo with the caption "After Chapel" showing students in academic robes leaving Houston Hall. Sprinkled among conventional campus views were interiors of the engineering and medical laboratories, the law library, and other places were the work of the institution occurred. But the serious tone of the introduction was quickly offset by views of student dramatic groups, athletic events, and the "Big Men" on campus. There was even a discussion of the bowl fights and other events unique to Penn's undergraduate experience; these fights were sanctioned by the University administration based on centuries-old customs of hazing at English public schools where they formed a rite of passage into membership in an elite group. At Penn, pants fights and hall fights between freshmen and sophomores were succeeded by battles within schools. First-year architecture students, for example, fought upperclassmen for the right to wear the architect's smock; other schools had flour fights and other contests. These fights were allowed, even encouraged, on the grounds

Bowl fight, 1904. Photo: S. M. Ely. UPA.

that "no injuries, other than minor bruises, are ever reported. They are in no way brutal or dangerous and on the other hand, tend to develop manliness and courage."[32] In 1916, two years after the publication of that reassuring text, one battle resulted in a student's death from suffocation; the class battles were officially ended immediately—though minor "fights" continued into the 1920s and were a first-semester staple of the *Pennsylvanian*, which covered the stories as important campus news.[33] Massive wooden bowls and other emblems of those contests survive in Houston Hall and in the University Archives. In the intervening years, University students continued to find other ingenious ways to vent excess energies, including the anarchical spring riots given the name of "Rowbottom," after the hapless but studious student whose name, called late at night by his night-owl roommate, provoked brickbats and shrieks from disturbed dormmates. Rowbottoms continued into the post-World War II era, when, after a particularly destructive night, they too were ended by administrative fiat.[34]

Another important group of publications about the campus was written by University Recorder George E. Nitzsche and entitled variously *Official Guide: University of Pennsylvania* (1906) or *Philadelphia and Its Great University* (1918). These were published by the University in several editions and featured the architecture of the campus—the author's particular hobby-horse—providing a clear and detailed history of the buildings, memorials, portraits, and other physical artifacts of the campus. The development of the Gothic campus in these years no doubt accounted for the success of these architectural guides. The bicentennial of the University motivated Cornell M. Dowlin's *University of Pennsylvania of Today* (1940). It focused on the academic departments, the faculty, and the events that had occurred within the buildings of the campus. Organized chronologically by school and program, it gave precedence to the male dominion of the old school, but offered hints at the changes that had begun with the establishment in 1933 of the College of Liberal Arts for Women.

In the more than half a century since Dowlin's book, the campus has been transformed in its physical scale and architectural character. From its modest size in 1940, the campus has nearly tripled in area and its built space has grown tenfold, reflecting a rising enrollment that constitutes the bulk of a University community of more than 30,000—more than the entire population of the city of the Revolution when Penn was founded. Changes of a different sort have remade the student body, the faculty, and the administration. Women now make up half the undergraduates, and in a metamorphosis which would have been impossible to predict as recently as a generation ago, but which Benjamin Franklin would surely have appreciated, Penn's first home-grown leader in half a century is Judith Rodin (CW 1966). While there have been numerous departmental and institutional histories, many associated with the University's 250th anniversary, which was celebrated in 1990, there has been no overview of the campus or its architecture, a gap we intend to close with this publication.

Like all great institutions, Penn's history is rich in strong individuals and marked by landmark buildings where professors taught, researched, wrote, and shaped the modern world. Though many of those professors are gone, the campus, its buildings, and its spaces make Penn's history tangible. This guide is intended as a history of that campus as it is recorded in its buildings

and open spaces, with an eye directed toward planning and design more than toward pedagogy. Such a book necessarily responds to the points of interest to its own era, but, in the case of an institution such as a great university, it also must meet the expectations of those who share a proprietary feeling for the place of their own experiences. Undergraduates remember their haunts and places of amusement with special feeling and typically freeze the institution into their four years; graduate students may recall their classmates as well as faculty who were their mentors—or tormentors; faculty and administrators share a longer perspective of the institution. Still, like the blind men and the elephant, these groups each hold to their own perspective. The institution is the sum of their experiences, but it is also the product of the intentions of its executives, the trustees, the faculty, and, last but certainly not least, its students.

For each generation the University of Pennsylvania has been different. Different music streams through the memories of each generation, from hip-hop and rap to the Beatles and rock and roll to big bands and before. Different images fill the mind's eye—1960s sit-ins at College Hall vie with the old grads' memories of Rowbottoms and bowl fights before World War I. But there are unifying memories as well: Spring Flings and Hey Days, football games and basketball champions, convocations and graduations and the events of the academic year that fill out each class's unique yet conventional history. Although the West Philadelphia campus is the University's third site, after more than a century it is now the setting of

••••••••••••••••••••••••••••••••••••••

President Judith Rodin (W 1966). Photo: Tommy Leonardi.

memory for all its living sons and daughters.

The maturation of the University that began with the opening of Houston Hall has quickened in the last generation, making the Penn campus one of the showplaces of Philadelphia and the nation. As much as the University owes to the late nineteenth-century provosts and board members who recognized the importance of nurturing undergraduate fellowship, it owes an equal debt to more recent planners, architects, and landscape designers who have continued the enrichment of the campus begun a century ago. The present restoration of the buildings of the central campus and the affirmation of the importance of the undergraduate experience in the Perelman Quadrangle offer an appropriate moment to celebrate the contribution of the planners, architects, and landscape architects who have shaped the University of Pennsylvania's campus. These men and women, from Thomas Richards, Frank Furness, and Walter Cope and John Stewardson to Louis I. Kahn, Ian McHarg, Sir Peter Shepheard, Laurie Olin, Denise Scott Brown, and Robert Venturi among others, are celebrated throughout these pages. Their work mirrors the culture of the last century and a quarter, an age of science and progress, as well as of learning and nostalgia. Across the campus is the evidence of the flaming arc of modernism that erupted in Furness's architecture of the last century, was transformed by European interpretations after World War II, and as the century ends, has reverted toward the historicism of the late nineteenth century. In that time, Penn's campus has been a laboratory of the experiments of architects working to express the values of an institution that has itself been transformed while remaining true to its founder's ideals.

CHAPTER TWO

FIRST STEPS:
THE OLD CITY CAMPUSES

From Academy to University—Origins

FROM ITS BEGINNINGS, the University of Pennsylvania has mirrored the special circumstances of Philadelphia.[1] Founded in William Penn's religiously tolerant community under the leadership of nonsectarian Benjamin Franklin, the new college reflected the diversity of the "City of Brotherly Love," Penn's name for the chief community in his commonwealth. William Penn was a member of the Religious Society of Friends, or as they are commonly known, Quakers. Pennsylvania was originally established as a haven for that group. That sect placed no special value on houses of worship, called their buildings "meeting houses," and valued the inner light of each individual (whether a member of their sect or not), making Philadelphia a haven of religious freedom. So open was Philadelphia that it was considered remarkable to eighteenth-century visitors such as Swedish naturalist Pehr Kalm, who wrote:

> Everyone who acknowledges God to be the Creator, preserver and ruler of all things, and teaches or undertakes nothing against the state or against the common peace, is at liberty to settle, stay and carry on his trade, be his religious principles ever so strange. And he is so well secured by the laws, both as to person and property, and enjoys such liberties that a citizen here may, in a manner, be said to live in his house like a king. It would be difficult to find anyone who could wish for and obtain greater freedom.[2]

Kalm recounted the numerous congregations of the city including "the English established church" (Anglicans), "the Swedish church," Quakers, Anabaptists, German Lutherans, German Reformed (Calvinists), Moravians, Presbyterians and New Light Presbyterians, and Roman Catholics. (He missed the Methodist and Jewish congregations, which had yet to build their own buildings.) Each group had its own distinctive place of worship, making Philadelphia unusual in an age when religion was allied with statecraft. The hybrid vigor of so many different ethnic and religious groups in Philadelphia must have been a strong factor in attracting young Benjamin Franklin from Boston in 1723. Half a century after Franklin's arrival and a quarter of a century after the visit of Kalm, the diversity of the Quaker City made it the logical gathering place for the Continental Congress. Here were the dissenters' meeting houses, synagogues, and churches, reflecting major and minor denominations and sects that

....

Charles Willson Peale, Benjamin Franklin. *Pennsylvania Academy of the Fine Arts.*

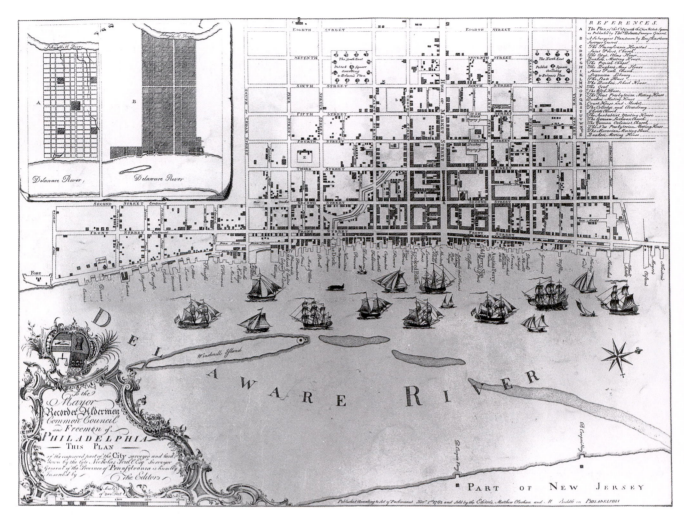

were excluded or even outlawed in other regions of the American colonies. Because the dominant Quakers had no ministers, there was no need to establish a seminary, so Franklin was able to found the Academy and Charitable School and later the College of Philadelphia to serve the many peoples of the city. As a result, the institution founded by Franklin has never been affiliated with a single religious denomination, and there have been no separate buildings specifically erected on a Penn campus to serve as church or chapel.

The Quaker City

When the charter of the College of Philadelphia was granted in 1755, William Penn's capital city was less than 75 years old. More than half a century younger

Nicholas Scull, "A Map of the Improved Part of the City of Philadelphia," 1766. Historical Society of Pennsylvania.

than New York and Boston, the Quaker City rapidly became the chief metropolis of the American colonies, a hub of commerce, transportation, and law, and a center for a comfortable and sophisticated population of nearly 15,000. The 2500 brick houses of the city were tightly clustered within four or five blocks of the Delaware River front, then the chief highway from Great Britain into the American heartland.[3] Philadelphia's plan took the open form of a grid, recalling Roman planned communities. Its major avenues, Broad and High Streets, were planned to intersect at the center of a rectangle midway between the two rivers that defined its site. By the early eighteenth century, a courthouse and markets occupied the center of High (later renamed Market) Street at Second Street. Near the new village center were built the Great Meeting House and the Almshouse of the Quakers, and the Anglican Christ Church. With markets at each end and at its center and important institutions nearby, Second Street became the chief avenue of the city, paralleling the port facilities of the river front three blocks to the east. As Penn's Professor Anthony Garvan

••••••••••••••••••••••••••••••••••••

Title page, Benjamin Franklin, Proposals Relating to the Education of Youth in Pensilvania, *1749. UPA.*

PROPOSALS

RELATING TO THE

EDUCATION

OF

YOUTH

IN

PENSILVANIA.

PHILADELPHIA:
Printed in the Year, M.DCC.XLIX.

observed, Philadelphia would have looked very much like late medieval English market towns such as Amersham in Buckinghamshire, with church, state, and market buildings in close proximity.[4]

Despite the cosmopolitan appearance of Philadelphia, academies and colleges were noticeably lacking.[5] Because the worship of the Society of Friends required no clergy, Quakers placed little value on the foundation of institutions of higher education whose usual function was the provision of ministers for the dominant sect in a region. Instead, Philadelphia offered its residents little more than primary schools associated with various church and national groups and William Penn's chartered secondary school. William Penn himself had attended Oxford University, where he encountered George Fox's teachings, but his comments on all but the most practical forms of higher education gave little support to the founding of a college or university in his commonwealth:

> [Universities are] . . . places for idleness, looseness, prophaneness, prodigality and gross ignorance.

> We pursue false knowledge and mistake education extremely.[6]

However, in a letter to his wife on the education of his children, Penn advocated the type of practical education that anticipated Franklin's College of the next century:

> Let their learning be liberal. Spare no cost, for by such parsimony all is lost that is saved, but let it be useful knowledge such as is consistent with truth and godliness, not cherishing a vain conservation or an idle mind; but ingenuity mixed with industry is good for the body and mind too. I recommend the useful parts of measuring, surveying, dialing, navigation; but agriculture is especially in my eye.[7]

Higher education found support in other regions of the American colonies, in New England, which had been settled by better-educated colonists from East Anglia, and in Virginia, whose culture looked toward London. Both regions established colleges in the seventeenth century, with Harvard being established within a generation of the Pilgrims' landing at Plymouth. Lacking the support of Pennsylvania's founder or his descendants, it was Boston-born Benjamin Franklin who, three generations after the founding of the commonwealth, proposed the academy and charitable school to which was soon appended the college.[8]

The Academy and Charitable School of Philadelphia

In later years Benjamin Franklin recalled that he had first conceived the idea of a local college in 1743, but the press of other affairs kept him from pursuing the task.[9] Six years later, in 1749, Franklin published his essay, *Proposals Relating to the Education of Youth in Pensilvania*, which proposed the establishment of an academy that would train leaders for the growing city and in turn lead to the demand for a college of the sort already established in New England and Virginia. According to his tract, the academy's courses would be taught in modern English rather than the Greek and Latin of contemporary advanced education; the curriculum was to be aimed toward subjects that would be useful to the modern world of business and commerce: modern languages, geology, and geography as well as natural history. The institution Franklin conceived was unusual, for its goal was the education of a governing and business class rather than the training of clergymen as was the case in most American colleges. More than a century earlier, the Puritan founders of Harvard College had recorded as their goal, "to advance learning, and perpetuate it to Posterity, dreading to leave an illiterate Ministry to the Churches."[10] Yale was founded to meet similar goals by New England Congregationalists, who feared (rightly, as it turned out) that intellectual Harvard might become so free-thinking that it would depart from its Puritan roots. To the south, the charter of the College of William and Mary required that its head be the leader of the Anglican Church in Virginia. A generation after Philadelphia's Academy was established, the College of Rhode Island (now Brown University) was founded by a Baptist Association (from Philadelphia) to provide ministers, with the requirement that its leader and the majority of its board be Baptists. The president of King's College (now Columbia) was required by its charter to be of the Anglican faith, while the College of New Jersey (now Princeton University) was founded as a New Light Presbyterian seminary.[11] Franklin's idea for a nonsectarian and practical academy drew immediate interest in Philadelphia, and soon he was engaged in organizing a board of trustees.

The Original Board

In Philadelphia, Franklin's Academy and Charitable School of Philadelphia was unusual in seeking support from most of the religious groups of the growing city. To that end, the "Constitutions of the Publick Academy in the City of Philadelphia" drawn up by Franklin and Pennsylvania Attorney General Tench Francis made no attempt to link the Academy to any single religious denomination. Franklin's selections to the Board of Trustees were first and foremost members of the activist elite of the city, those who could afford to support the new institution financially until its future was secure, and who could take the necessary time from their work to attend meetings, raise funds, and superintend the institution.[12] The board's members included leading Quakers such as James Logan and Richard Stretell, as well as several who had recently converted from Quakerism to Anglicanism (mainly because they had been read out of their Quaker meetings for various causes). William Allen, Joseph Turner, and William Shippen, M.D. were Presbyterians; Franklin was an avowed nonsectarian if not an agnostic; most if not all the remainder were Anglicans. The diversity of the new Academy board was an astute political move by Franklin to ensure that no one denomination would dominate.

Analyzed quantitatively, the Board of the Academy

was an accurate barometer of Philadelphia's evolving elite and a testament to the social mobility of the era.[13] Perhaps not surprising in view of the newness of the city, three-quarters of the new trustees were born outside Pennsylvania; half were from the British Isles and a quarter, including Franklin, were from other American colonies. In work, nearly half (ten) were merchants, many of whom had inherited wealth and might be considered the elite of the community. Nearly as many were representatives of the growing professional classes, five lawyers and four medical doctors, but, in sharp contrast to the New England colleges, there was only one clergyman. Two, Franklin and Syng, were "mechanics," the group most predisposed to identify with the colonies rather than with the mother country; the remaining two had been principally employed in municipal government. Only James Logan could be said to be a Philadelphia gentleman. Membership on the Philadelphia Common Council was the greatest point of similarity among the trustees, providing a link between fifteen of the original twenty-four board members.[14] As a group, all were activists accustomed to the rough and tumble politics of the city. Selected at the moment when the city's social and political hierarchy was in flux as Quakers, having lost their majority in their community, began to shun government, the board represented the future course of the city toward a new, largely Anglican elite.

Franklin picked several members of the new board for their symbolic importance to the entire community. The best known of this group was James Logan, the aging but "weighty Friend" who had been William Penn's secretary and colonial administrator and was the strongest remaining link to the original values of the proprietor. When Logan died shortly after the board was established, he was immediately replaced by his son-in-law, the equally weighty Friend Isaac Norris II. Initially, at least, the board included Friends and Anglicans, merchants and professionals, native Philadelphians and new (but wealthy) immigrants. Because it was hoped that support would be gained from the present Proprietors, Penn's children (who

had abandoned their Quaker roots), the trustees also included the contemporary representative of the Proprietors, the Anglican clergyman Richard Peters. And whenever members of Penn's family were in Pennsylvania they were also proffered a position on the board. The varied religious and personal backgrounds of the trustees and faculty surely represented Franklin's effort to avoid the dominance of the institution by any one group and distinguished Philadelphia's Academy and Charitable School and later its College from all other American institutions of higher education before the Revolution.

Early Architectural Decisions

The diverse backgrounds and allegiances of the board also hint at the reasons behind the initial decisions that shaped the college and they were soon reflected in the peculiar appearance of its home. The first significant issue was whether to accept James Logan's generous offer of a plot of land for the new Academy and Charitable School adjacent to his own private library on Sixth Street across from the State House. Such a location would have placed the new academy near the center of power in the city and the commonwealth, and, with Logan's library, would have offered a resource unequaled in the American colonies. By not accepting the Logan gift, Franklin and his board served notice that their institution would not be a captive of the old Quaker gentry or of the new elite whose neighborhoods were nearby.

While Franklin was organizing the new school, he was simultaneously a member of the nonsectarian board that managed a chapel, the "New Building" that had been erected to house the congregation of the flamboyant preacher George Whitefield, a follower of the founder of English Methodism, John Wesley. In contrast to the distant and ritualized Anglican service, evangelical Methodists were part of the so-called Great Awakening that assaulted the hierarchical church using fiery preaching to reach the heart as much as the intellect. Whitefield had taken "the call" to the American colonies, preaching far and wide to immense

Pierre Eugène Du Simitière, Old Academy and Charity School, c. 1770. Black chalk on paper. Library Company of Philadelphia.

••

crowds in open squares or in churches.[15] When the Presbyterians, who had welcomed him on an earlier visit, refused him the use of their church because of their fear of his popularity, a group of Philadelphians built the largest structure in the city for his use. However, rather than settle in Philadelphia as the builders had hoped, Whitefield continued to preach throughout the colonies. Lacking his presence, the organization that built the chapel fell on hard times and was unable to finish paying for the building or to establish and run the charity school that had been promised as a part of the institution.[16] Franklin quickly led the new board of the Academy and Charitable School toward his preferred approach, the purchase of the chapel and property on Fourth Street, thereby turning two problems into a single solution.[17] Though we might see a conflict of interest in Franklin's actions,

the nonsectarian antecedents of the New Building met Franklin's intention of charting a course among the various groups of the city. Franklin's board of the Academy shared the diversity of the board of the New Building, though obviously lacking the Moravians, Lutherans, and other Germans who were not interested in an Academy whose courses would be taught in English and not in German.

The New Building

Because of its initial purposes, the Academy and Charitable School's new building differed in appearance from those of the New England and Virginia colleges that looked across the Atlantic to English academic precedent for their designs. Instead of relying on architectural forms developed to serve English church and state, the origins of the elevation and the plan of the New Building lay in the ecclesiastical architecture of the various nonconforming sects which had been attracted to William Penn's Quaker City and which dotted the city with their unusual and typically highly identifiable buildings. In the case of the Whitefield chapel, there are several documents that provide insight into its special meaning. The most important of these is a simple line drawing by a French visitor, Pierre Eugène Du Simitière.[18] His elevation shows the long east facade divided by a belt course conventionally used to mark the stories of a building, and interrupted near the center of the long facade by a two-story, gable-roofed entrance portico. This element was probably intended to serve as an outside pulpit, accessed from the internal gallery, from which Whitefield could address a crowd in the yard of the building. With the odd proportions of the facade and the absence of the typical ennobling architectural details of English churches, the New Building contrasted with the robust Georgian style of nearby Christ Church but had the advantage of representing the dissenting culture of the various peoples who made Philadelphia their home.

That the design of the New Building was purposeful rather than merely provincial is apparent from other works by its architect, Edmund Woolley.[19] A decade before, he had a principal role in the design of the Pennsylvania State House, better known as Independence Hall, the most ambitious group of government buildings in the American colonies north of Williamsburg.[20] There, for a more sophisticated clientele of lawyers, many of whom had trained in London, he demonstrated his awareness of the sculptural forms and broader, classically-based proportions of the urbane Georgian style. For Whitefield's hall, however, Woolley reverted to the tall volumes and spare architectural details that were more in keeping with the late Gothic and provincial architecture that survived in

England into the first part of the eighteenth century. These qualities served to represent the values of the religious dissenters, many of whom came from rural backgrounds and were suspicious of continent-influenced classicism. The most prominent features of the building were the tall roof and the narrow entrance wing that were derived from the pre-Georgian forms of the English midlands. These features gave the building an appearance not unlike the much older Gloria Dei (Old Swedes') Church, dedicated in 1700, that still stands at Christian Street and Delaware Avenue in the neighborhood originally settled by Swedes.[21]

Though no view of the interior of the New Building survives, letters from Franklin and other sources provide clear evidence of both its original appearance and its later configuration after it had been modified to serve the Academy and later the College. In one letter, Franklin compared the future home of the Academy and Charitable School to the dimensions of London's Westminster Hall and termed it a "great and lofty hall," implying that it was a single clear-span space without interruption by nave arcades or colonnades. Franklin described its purchase and the projected alterations in a letter of February 1751 as

the house that was built for itinerant preaching, which stands on a large lot of ground capable of receiving more buildings to lodge scholars if it should come to be a regular college. The house is one hundred feet long and seventy wide, built of brick, very strong and sufficiently high for three lofty stories. I suppose the building did not cost less than two thousand pounds; but we bought it for seven hundred seventy-five pounds, eighteen shillings, eleven pence and three farthings; though it will cost us three and perhaps four hundred more to make the partitions and floors and fit up the rooms."[22]

To even a casual observer, the building must have seemed unusual because it was not oriented in the fashion of contemporary Anglican churches, with the main door on the west and the apse on the east at opposite ends of the long axis of the building. Instead, it was built on a north-south axis. This orientation was not the consequence of the shape of the property, which could have held the building in the traditional direction had that been preferred. Moreover, the absence of a separate volume for the apse and the off-center entrance on the east side probably indicated a pulpit on the opposite west wall in the manner of the Presbyterian and Baptist churches and Methodist chapels that were beginning to appear in England and were already familiar in the mid-Atlantic colonies. The conscious avoidance of orientation and the cross-axial plan immediately distinguished the building from conventional edifices of the Church of England.[23] And, unlike contemporary English churches, whose principal exterior feature was the spired tower at the west facade, the principal architectural feature of the New Building was the great volume of its roof, perhaps denoting the potential for a second story gallery if crowds warranted that additional construction.

Exterior Alterations

The changes necessary to transform the building from a church to a school were directed by Franklin, who had recently sold his printing business and thus had the necessary free time to supervise the project. To meet its new purposes, the building had to be converted from preaching hall to the multiple spaces required for its new role as academy, charitable school, and eventually college. On the exterior, the most obvious change to the building was the addition of a modest belfry at the south end. This was also designed by Edmund Woolley, but was executed by Robert Smith, a master builder recently arrived from Scotland.[24] As Franklin knew from simultaneously assisting Christ Church with the lottery that funded its new spire, towers and belfries attested to the aspirations and sense of well-being of a community.[25] Pehr Kalm confirmed the importance of steeples as gauges of the significance of the institution by reporting on those of the city. According to Kalm, the first belfry of Christ

Church, before the addition of the present tower designed by Robert Smith, was "small, insignificant"; the German Lutheran church's was termed "little"; the new tower of the "Town Hall" (the State House) was described as the "greatest ornament of the town."[26] Thus, far from being an affectation, the academy's new belfry symbolized the conversion of the building to its new task and the growing urbanity of the city. For the

••••••••••••••••••••••••••••••••••••••

Nicholas Scull and George Heap, detail of "East Prospect of the City of Philadelphia," 1756. Library Company of Philadelphia. (College spire is no. 3.)

economizing trustees of the Academy and Charitable School of Philadelphia, working from Edmund Woolley's drawings, Smith built a small, plain, square-based structure that was closer to the belfry and spire of the courthouse that stood at Second and Market Streets rather than to the baroque spires published by James Gibbs in *A Book of Architecture*.[27] Presumably to meet structural requirements rather than for aesthetic considerations, the new tower was placed almost out of view on the south end of the building, where it could be supported by the masonry of the south wall, rather than in the center of the roof, where it would be supported only by the trusses of the roof-framing. Surmounted by a short spire and vane, it was an economical and utilitarian addition to an adapted building.

Soon the belfry housed the fire bell that had been commissioned from English bell-maker Thomas Lester by the Union Fire Company (another Franklin foundation) with the assistance of the Hand-in-Hand Company. Lacking a tower, the fire companies were persuaded by the ever-resourceful Franklin to offer the bell to the Academy, which had a belfry but no bell.[28] There it rang for classes while also signaling fire alarms until the institution moved to Ninth Street in 1801. The Fire Company then demanded the return of its bell to hang it in nearby St. James Episcopal Church, where it could resume its double duties.

Woolley also made the plans for the insertion of a floor that created a second story hall, designed the subdivisions of the first floor to create separate class-rooms for the boys' and girls' rooms for the charity school and a larger room for the academy, and added the internal partitions at the south end that formed a corridor providing access to both the massive stair to the upper level and the playground on the west side of the building. After it had been modified for College use with the addition of a full second story and a third level gallery, the New Building was closer to the model of the German Lutheran churches, such as nearby St. Michael's on Appletree Street, which provided an upper room for worship and a lower story for offices

and other functions. Montgomery described the plan as follows:

> The entrance opened into a large hall, on either side large class rooms, that to the north being occupied by the Charity School. The western half of the first floor was occupied by the large school room, about ninety by thirty-five feet, in the center of which was a platform [probably the original preaching platform]. . . . The hall here turned to the South between the large room and the front classroom, and then to the west, opening out into the play ground, about one hundred feet by fifty. . . . In this side hall [along the south end of the building] arose a heavy stair case with a solid balustrade . . . and which on a turn opened into a large upper hall covering the width of the building and about ninety feet of its length. Across the south end, over the stairway, was a gallery, and the rostrum was against the north wall.[29]

Because the initial renovations were not completed in time, the first classes at the Academy began in January 1751 in trustee William Allen's warehouse at Second and Arch Streets, moving to the Fourth Street location on 16 September 1751, after a year of construction.

Ultimately the building's original architectural appearance, one rooted in the culture of dissent, was appropriate to Franklin's goals. The call for liberty that would be made at Woolley's Independence Hall in 1776 was anticipated in Woolley's Academy Hall a generation earlier. When the Reverend Richard Peters addressed the opening of the new Academy on 7 January 1751, he took as his theme the biblical verse, "And ye shall know the truth, and the truth shall make you free."[30] Its location also spoke of the meaning of the institution. When the Academy opened its doors in 1751, it stood at a bustling corner of a city, rooting the institution not in a quiet village or suburb as at Cambridge and Princeton, but in the center of Philadelphia, near Franklin's house. Here, near the heart of the city, was stimulation, the sounds and actions of labor and trade—a real world rather than an ivory tower. Instead of the conventional English academic cloisters in a quiet village, Franklin had established his Academy in and of the city.

One of the first visitors to the new institution was the previously mentioned Pehr Kalm, who visited the city in 1748 and again in 1750, soon after the purchase of the New Building. He reported that the new institution in the old Whitefield chapel was "destined to become the seat of higher learning, or to express myself in more exact terms, to be a college. The young men here are taught only those things which they learn in our common schools and gymnasia; but in time such lectures are intended to be given as are usual in real universities."[31] Thus the institution was initially to function in a preparatory role not unlike the colleges and academies that were beginning to flourish in Britain and on the continent, but with the implicit intention, as Kalm reported, that it would soon grant the bachelor's degree.[32]

The College and a Changing Board

The original nonsectarian board chose a diverse faculty that included Presbyterian minister Francis Alison, who was instructor in logic and languages, and Baptist minister and scientist, Ebenezer Kinnersley, collaborator with Franklin on his electrical experiments, who taught English and oratory.[33] (In its dependence on clergymen for its teachers, the new academy was typical of the eighteenth century, when few professions except for the clergy required college training.) When the College was established as an adjunct to the Academy and Charitable School, it was deemed appropriate to find a conventionally trained leader. To serve that role, Franklin was persuaded to hire William Smith, a Scots-born Anglican clergyman who attracted Franklin's attention with his writings about an imaginary "College of Mirania" whose curriculum balanced practical education with traditional academic courses and thus seemed to fit with Franklin's conception of the new institution.[34]

In his *Proposals* of 1749, Franklin had stated as his goals, "As to their studies, it would be well if they could be taught everything that is useful and everything that is ornamental; but art is long and their time is short. It is therefore proposed that they learn those things that are likely to be most useful and most ornamental."[35] This utilitarian formula continued in 1755, when the College's new provost, William Smith, published the curriculum for the three years of attendance. While the customary attention was paid to the classical texts in the original Latin and Greek, in a remarkable shift from conventional colleges a third of the subject matter was devoted to the sciences of the modern world. The second period of each day for the first-year students was devoted to mathematics, algebra, geometry, and trigonometry; the first and second periods of second-year students were devoted to the practical application of first-year mathematics in problems of surveying and navigation and to the broad topics of natural philosophy (physics). The second period of the third year was devoted to chemistry, natural history (botany and zoology), and astronomy. The significance of the curriculum is clear from Frederick Rudolph's remark that a new secular curriculum flourished in the "urban coastal cities of Philadelphia and New York [where] institutions of learning were developing that were prepared to state their purposes in the broadest most secular terms." As proof, Rudolph cited Penn's Provost William Smith's observation that "Thinking, Writing and Acting Well . . . is the grand aim of a liberal education."[36]

In 1755, when the College was added to the Academy, a new charter vested day-to-day operations in the faculty and permitted a secret ballot for the selection of the various offices of the board. These changes resulted in Franklin's loss of control of the institution. So long as hands had been raised, Franklin's position was sure; in the new climate of secrecy, he was replaced as president of the board by the Proprietor's representative Richard Peters.[37] Though most of the original trustees continued on the new board, the replacements augured more change. The new members were almost invariably Anglicans; many had been educated

Gilbert Stuart, Provost William Smith. *UPA.*

••

in England, and most were more closely connected by social affiliation as well as culture with the mother country. Though the College's initial course under Provost Smith included studies directed toward the modern world, under his direction the curriculum soon turned toward a more conventional classical education rooted in the traditional education for clergy. Fortunately for the future of the institution, the goals of Franklin regularly returned to the fore, establishing the direction of Penn and other modern universities.[38]

Architectural Changes: The New College

The selection of Scotsman and English-trained builder Robert Smith for the next round of building activities in 1755 coincided with the appointment of William Smith as provost and the simultaneous withdrawal of the original Quakers from the board of trustees. Robert Smith later served as the architect for Franklin's

house in its interior court off High Street and was allied with fellow mechanics Franklin and Syng as a member of the Revolutionary Committee of Safety, for whom he devised harbor barriers against the British fleet. His selection as the architect for the new round of alterations to the New Building, while Edmund Woolley was still active, hints at new allegiances for the changing and ever more elite board. In his first project for the trustees, Robert Smith was commissioned to design modifications to the upper room by the addition of a gallery which the Trustees' Minutes describe as being "on three sides similar to Mr Tennent's building" (the new Robert Smith-designed Presbyterian Church at Third and Arch Street completed in 1752).[39] The same building program called for a platform at the far end of the great auditorium for the accommodation of the trustees, a pattern of separation and elevation of the trustees that was repeated more than a century later with the design of the private trustees' stairs to the raised platform of the second-story Chapel in the 1871 College Hall. At the same time, Smith also added what must have been a bizarre composition of circular and square windows in the gable ends to increase light in the room. They were presumably necessitated by the insertion of the galleries, which would have blocked light from the second tier of windows along the sides of the building.

Robert Smith's work for the College of Philadelphia was part of an important segment of his professional practice.[40] In 1753 he had designed the College of New Jersey's Nassau Hall, which, though much modified by Victorian rebuilding, still stands on Princeton's campus; the following year he planned the house for that college's president. In 1770, for a group of Philadelphia Baptists, the peripatetic Smith drew the plans for the College of Rhode Island's new building in Providence. Between those projects, Smith designed two buildings for the College of Philadelphia, the so-called New College, in 1764 and, a decade later, the provost's residence at the corner of Fourth and Arch Streets. Beginning with his initial work on the interior, the trustees of the College of Philadelphia gave the preeminent college architect of the day his first work in that field.

The College in a Changing City

The College Hall, as the great auditorium of the New Building was called, became a vital part of the life of the institution and of the city; now it is the name given to the central building of the present campus. Undergraduates gathered in the great room for Anglican morning prayer and there too occurred the major celebrations of college life. The "college hall" became a new center of the cultural life of the city as well, offering plays and concerts in the evening performed by its students and graduates such as Francis Hopkinson (C 1757).[41] By 1760 one of the first organs in the city was installed in the auditorium of the college building; contemporary accounts of the first graduation reported that the organ was played by Hopkinson with "a bold and masterly Hand"; it ornamented the ceremonies of the college and for other

events as well.[42] Two years after the installation of the organ, the hall was the scene of the presentation of an ode to the "late gracious Sovereign George II, written and set to Music in a very grand and masterly Taste by Francis Hopkinson, Esq. A.M., of the College in this city."[43] In Quaker Philadelphia, music, especially that played on an organ, was suspected of betraying leanings toward Roman Catholicism (in 1757, the only other organ in the city was in St. Joseph's Roman Catholic Church) and thus may have been a cause of concern for some. Its purchase by the college suggests the continuing independent course followed by the college in its early years. In the 1790s the hall was the site of Charles Willson Peale's introductory lectures on natural history, and, in keeping with the original grant to Whitefield, Presbyterians, Unitarians, Universalists, and others continued to hold their religious services in the great college hall.

Buildings and Setting

In 1762 Provost Smith traveled to England to raise funds to enlarge the young institution's facilities. During its first years in operation, the College's trustees had acquired additional lands in the vicinity of the school, eventually resulting in the ownership of the eastern quarter of the block that also contained the Christ Church burial ground. In those early years, the growth of the student body had been remarkable. At the outset, the Academy and Charitable School began with only 17 students in attendance but there were 146 students at the end of the first year.[44] Two years later 226 scholars were crammed into the New Building; nearly a quarter came from neighboring states with some even from foreign countries. In 1757, three years after the collegiate charter was received, a class of seven were awarded the first bachelor's degrees. Though most of the students were taking preparatory courses in the Academy and not the College, the success of Franklin's foundation was apparent.

By 1761 a committee concluded that, based on the rapid growth and the likelihood of attracting students from distant lands, the institution was losing students because there were no dormitories. The trustees decided to "have some additional Buildings erected on the Ground belonging to the Academy that might hold a number of the Scholars that came from other Provinces and the West Indies and put them upon a collegiate way of living, as is done at Jersey and New York Colleges."[45] Ever on the lookout for ways to spread the costs of their new institution to the widest possible base, the board proposed that a public lottery be held to raise money for "some necessary lodging Rooms to accommodate the Elder part of the Youth that come from abroad; and partly to rebuild the Charity Schools that are in ruinous condition."

Though lotteries were generally illegal in Pennsylvania, they were tolerated in some instances when the goal was the public good. Lotteries enabled members of a generally divided city to cross social and cultural boundaries to support institutions that were of importance to the community. For example, as noted earlier, in Philadelphia lotteries had helped pay for the steeple of Christ Church and had been used to raise support for the College. Tellingly, the lottery plan was rejected, presumably because some groups in the city already viewed the college as being in the control of one sect, the Anglicans.

The College trustees called again on architect Smith, this time to produce a plan that would provide separate quarters for the Charity School and its younger students in a separate building while also providing housing for those students from outside the city. Smith's initial design called for two buildings on opposite sides of the yard, framing the college and forming a composition that would have been like the Harvard campus as it had existed for two generations since the completion of Stoughton College in 1720. In 1762, with the provost overseas raising funds and some doubt as to his ultimate success, the committee on the additions to the college reached a decision to begin only one of the two new structures:

We are therefore of the Opinion that Workmen should now be agreed with to go on in the ensuing Summer with one half of the Buildings contained in the Plan formerly given to us by Mr Robert Smith which will be 70 feet long by 30 wide, and will have on the Ground Floor two Charity Schools, with a Kitchen and a Dining Room, and in the upper Stories Sixteen Lodging Rooms, with cellar beneath the whole, which by an Estimate given to us may be executed for £1500.[46]

The north block was constructed in time for the 1764 school year. It housed fifty students in its dormitory on the upper levels, while the Charity School met on the main floor.[47] Despite the completion of the "New College" on the north and the refurbishing of the old Whitefield building on the west, the grounds of the college remained treeless and bare. It would be another generation before trees were finally planted—just before the removal of the institution to the President's House on Ninth Street.[48]

Unlike the awkward proportions and forms of the original building, Smith's dormitory displayed the new urbane discipline of the English Georgian style. The stories of the building were separated by beltcourses and diminished in height in accord with classical proportions; the fenestration was regular and the facades were symmetrical (see figure, page 28). Like a regimental tie, these traits communicated allegiance to Proprietor, Crown, and Anglican church, the groups whose funds had been solicited to help pay for the New College, as the building was called.[49] In large measure, Smith's design for the New College and later for the provost's house reflected the continuing allegiance of the mercantile elite to Britain, an allegiance that was reflected in their great houses such as Cliveden in Germantown or Mount Pleasant in Fairmount Park, which relied on similar English sources.

Soon there would be hard evidence of the College's change of course from Franklin's original direction, for the published appeals by which Provost Smith sought gifts from English churchmen and gentry were phrased with an ethnocentric zeal that both undid the ecumenism of the original faculty and board and increasingly challenged the core values of Penn's city of tolerance.[50] Simultaneously, in his reports on the progress of the fund-raising, Provost Smith noted that the English Quakers gave no assistance and that the Dissenters he approached were less supportive than he professed to hope. As Smith carefully tallied the gifts by name, it was immediately apparent that most support for the college came from members of the Church of England.[51] The implications of Smith's fund-raising were confirmed by a letter to the college from the Archbishop of Canterbury demanding that, because of this support, the college henceforth should ensure that "all such as are designed for Clergymen of our Church will be instructed by a Professor of Divinity who is a Member of our Church; which may surely be done without giving offense to Persons of other Denominations."[52] In a letter from the archbishop and from the Proprietors Thomas and Richard Penn (by then members of the Church of England), the board was instructed that, because gifts had been given based on representations by Smith that the College was a seminary, any future board should reflect the present strength of Anglicans instead of the former ecumenical basis.[53] Henceforth, while the College purported to serve the diverse community of Philadelphia, its leadership would usually be drawn from its much smaller Anglican community (which after the Revolution was renamed the Episcopal Church).[54] Even as the Stamp Act was enraging American colonists, control of Philadelphia's College by the English church was being exerted that would bring about the downfall of the College during the Revolution.

Those events were in the future, and into the 1770s the College complex continued to grow. In 1774 architect Smith was asked to provide plans for a three-story brick residence contiguous with the campus at the corner of Fourth and Arch Streets for Provost Smith, who had been commuting by horseback from his unusual semi-octagonal home (nicknamed Smith's Folly) in East Falls near the Schuylkill River.[55] The first campus was completed just as the Revolution began, leaving a clear representation of the values of the trustee groups that had commissioned its buildings The economy of adapting the Whitefield chapel attested to the pragmatism of Franklin, but the later selection of Robert Smith as the college's architect demonstrated the rise to dominance of the Anglican mercantile upper class that increasingly controlled Philadelphia. These divergent architectural directions would represent the dual nature of the institution for much of the next century.

The Revolution, Closure, and Rebirth

In the summer of 1777, the turmoil of the Revolution made it necessary to cease academic operations. After a brief rebirth, the college charter was annulled by the city's Revolutionary leaders on the grounds that too many of board members were Tory sympathizers. In 1779 an act of legislature reestablished the school as the "University of the State of Pennsylvania," denoting in its new name both the added course in medicine that had been taught at the College for a decade and the new sponsor of the institution. Its board again represented the multiple sects of the community, including for the first time, two Germans, a group that had not been represented on the original board. Ministers from each denomination in the community, including a Roman Catholic priest, sat ex officio on its board, and a German language school was added so that German-speaking youths could be educated. Diversity is not an entirely twentieth-century idea! With Presbyterian minister Dr. John Ewing as provost, the university was for the moment as revolutionary as the new nation.[56]

The growth of the college was mirrored by the special needs of the medical school, which soon required its own facility for teaching and demonstrations. This led to a split in the campus with the acquisition of a separate medical building several blocks from the original campus. A building on Fifth Street below Sansom Street and across from the State House was given by the city to the university and was adapted to its new purpose by Drs. William Shippen and Casper Wistar. The enormous cupola on the roof

Drawn & Engraved by W. Birch & Son.   *Published by R. Campbell & Cᵒ Nᵒ 30 Chesnut Street Philadᵃ 1799*

LIBRARY and SURGEONS HALL, in Fifth Street PHILADELPHIA.

William Russell Birch, "Library and Surgeons Hall, in Fifth Street Philadelphia." Plate 13 from The City of Philadelphia . . . as it appeared in the Year 1800. *UPA*

••••••••••••••••••••••••••••••••••••

lighted the dissecting amphitheater, "Anatomical Hall," anticipating the form and function of the central pavilion of Pennsylvania Hospital by a quarter of a century. Courses in chemistry were taught by Dr. James Woodhouse in the chemistry labs in the first floor of the building.[57]

After the Revolution had ended and peace had returned, Provost Smith, who had retained possession of the provost's residence, successfully petitioned the state legislature for the return of the College property to the resuscitated College, leaving the University of the State of Pennsylvania without a home. When the College regained control of its buildings, the university leaders were forced to rent rooms from the American Philosophical Society; for two years both institutions were in operation but without the resources adequately to support either. On 30 September 1791, in response to an overture by the University, the College agreed to merge with the University under the new name University of Pennsylvania.

Drawn & Engraved by W. Birch & Son.   Published by R. Campbell & Cº. Nº 30, Chesnut Street Philadª. 1799.

THE HOUSE *intended for the* PRESIDENT *of the* UNITED STATES,

in Ninth Street PHILADELPHIA.

The Ninth Street Campus

As the eighteenth century ended, the University faced for the first time the dual dilemmas of a constricted campus and a changing neighborhood.[58] The trustees turned away from their first site by purchasing at auction the mansion on the west side of Ninth Street that had been erected between 1792 and 1797 as the house for the President of the United States.[59] It was never occupied by the president, initially because of the constitutional requirement that he accept no remuneration other than his salary, and later because of the removal of the federal government to Washing-

William Russell Birch, "The House intended for the President of the United States, in Ninth Street Philadelphia." Plate 19 from The City of Philadelphia . . . as it appeared in the Year 1800. *UPA*

ton, D.C.[60] The vacant mansion had been a source of injury to the self-esteem of the city and a powerful reminder of the loss of both the state and federal governments.

William Birch's well-known engraving proves that the house was worthy of both the purpose for which it was built and that to which it was adapted. One of the largest and handsomest urban houses of its era in the nation, it was principally the design of William Williams, son-in-law of the late Robert Smith and one of the leading architect-builders of the city in the decades after the Revolution. Williams's advertisement in the *Pennsylvania Packet* for 4 January 1773 emphasized his debt to English sources, which contributed to his success in Philadelphia:

William Williams, a native of this city, where he was regularly bred to the business of HOUSE CARPENTRY, BEGS leave to inform his friends, and the public, that having lately returned from London, where he has for some time studied ARCHITECTURE in its various branches, he proposes carrying on the business of House Carpentry in the most useful and ornamental manner, as is now executed in the city of London and most parts of England; and humbly hopes to give the highest satisfaction to such as shall be pleased to employ him, in the new, bold, light and elegant taste, which has lately been introduced by the great architect [Robert Adam] of the Adelphi Buildings at Ducham Yard; and which is now universally practiced all over Britain.[61]

Brick in construction and essentially square in plan, the subtly modulated facade of the President's house was enlivened by a projecting center on the front and recessed center on the sides, the whole generously overlaid with marble pilasters and crowned by an elaborate cornice and balustrade. These, along with the recessed Palladian windows that enlivened the corner pavilions of the main floor, reflected Williams's incorporation of motifs from Robert Adam's London work and contrasted with the generally simple fenestration of colonial and federal buildings in Philadelphia. A central cupola crowned by an immense eagle (one of the first to represent the new republic) could be seen behind the balustrade that crowned the wall, hinting at a grand central double stair that rose up through the core of the house.

A University committee examined the house and concluded that what was appropriate for the President's House could not directly meet the needs of the University.[62] In 1800 Benjamin Henry Latrobe (1764–1820), newly arrived from Britain, offered the trustees free plans to make the necessary changes for its conversion.[63] The trustees' program called for the President's House to contain housing for four professors and the master of the charity school (as a means of saving on salaries as well as guaranteeing their presence at the college), as well as the necessary quarters for both the boys' and girls' divisions of the charity school and the College. To raise funds for the renovation, Latrobe immediately proposed mortgaging the future growth of the institution by subdividing the north and south ends of the property, which fronted on Market and Chestnut Streets, for sale or for rent.

To meet the spatial needs of the schools, Latrobe initially proposed the dramatic step of removing the mansion's central feature, the handsome double stair that rose beneath a skylight in the center of the mansion. The resulting multistory circular central hall, Latrobe suggested, could become a chapel and assembly room.[64] The oval parlor on the west side (perhaps remembered in the later Oval Office of the White House in Washington, D.C.), he proposed to keep intact for the provost's office. In the end, Latrobe found that the removal of the stair made it impossible to link the third floor effectively to the lower stories, so he left that level vacant, thereby not providing the required apartments for three of the professors in the building.[65] An unsigned contemporary drawing in the University Archives depicts the "Second Floor" (the main floor) of the Ninth Street building as it eventually functioned. The stair was removed according to the Latrobe plan, but the assembly room (which doubled as chapel) was not placed in the vacated stairwell; instead, the college hall was inserted into a long gallery on the south side. Small staircases within the larger rooms on the perimeter provided for private connections between the upper and lower stories, while the central hall remained simply for circulation.

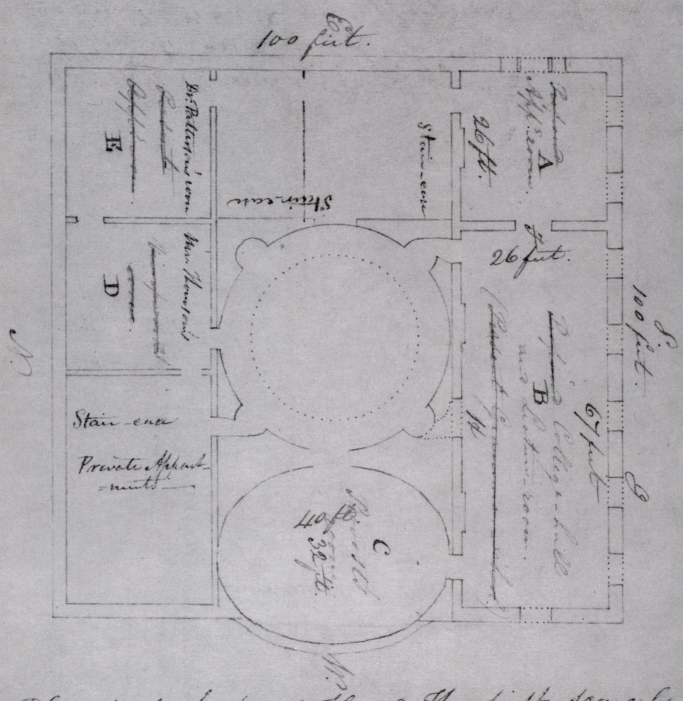

Front on Ninth Street.

100 feet.

A — 26 ft

26 feet

100 feet

Staircase

Staircase

Dr. Patterson's Private Office

E

D

Staircase

Private Apartments

Room B College Hall and Lecture room

C 40 ft 32 ft

67 feet

S.

N.

This Plan is of the Second Floor. The first scarcely ___s from it in its arrangement. The room under A is ___ry. Those under B and C are appropriated to the gram___ ___.

If, as appears likely, this drawing accurately represents Latrobe's plan, in an odd way it told much about the values of the leaders of the institution. On the exterior the building was sophisticated and urbane, a setting appropriate to the capital city of the new nation. Within, it must have been a disappointing hash of subdivided and altered spaces that served the needs of its occupants but did little to ennoble the institution. After more than a year of construction, the building received its new occupants in March 1802, beginning seven decades of university history on Ninth Street.

Accompanying the renovations to the President's House, the University petitioned to be relieved of the task of operating the boys' and girls' charitable school, an obligation it had incurred with the purchase of the original Whitefield building. The state courts, however, rebuffed the plea, so the charitable school was maintained in the old dormitory that had been built as the New College on Fourth Street, while the adjacent provost's house and a portion of the original academy building were eventually sold to the Union Methodist congregation. The old campus served the University once again in 1829, when it was determined to demolish and replace the President's House with purpose-built structures for the Medical School and the College. During the year of construction, the original buildings once again housed the University.[66] Sentiment and even the potential of future utility could not save Penn's past forever; by 1833, after a generation of using Penn's original building, the Methodist congregation demolished their portion of the nearly century-old relic and built a new brick church. Ten years later the Charitable School was moved again, to a small building that was constructed off a tiny alley in the middle of the Fourth Street block, and the then superannuated "New College" was also replaced by the new warehouses and lofts of industrializing Philadelphia.[67] By the Civil War, the shift of the neighborhood toward

....

"The plan of the Second Floor." Unsigned drawing for the Ninth Street building. UPA.

industry and commerce so reduced the number of students as to make it inappropriate to continue the Charitable School.[68] The final act of the Academy and Charitable School was written in 1876, when, with the principal of a new gift that was intended to support the graduate education of women, Penn was finally permitted to close the Academy and Charitable School accounts.

During the first three decades of the nineteenth century, the President's mansion alone housed the college. Given the ongoing management difficulties of the dormitory in the New College, it was not surprising that dormitories were not part of the new campus. Had it been desired, there would have been room for students in residence, because Latrobe's plan left the entire third floor of the President's House vacant. However, for the next century, as the University strayed from Franklin's vision, the much reduced undergraduate population mostly lived at home, while a few boarded in the city. The "collegial" life of other institutions that had encouraged the construction of the New College ended at Penn, not to reappear for nearly a century.

Despite its new location and facilities, the College languished. At the outset of his tenure in 1813, Provost Frederick Beasley suggested reforms that would have added a fourth year to the course of study and set admission standards that could be satisfied by students of at least fifteen years of age who were capable of meeting certain academic requirements. Anticipating the concerns of Provost Stillé half a century later, Beasley warned that "some prompt and efficient measures must be resorted to, in order to raise the College from the present state of depression and decay, and infuse some new life and vigor into it."[69] Beasley's tenure ended in disarray when the trustees fired the entire faculty in 1827. The following year, many of the changes suggested by Beasley were initiated when a new provost, the Reverend William H. DeLancey, took office and for the first time made the claim that the provost should have a seat on the board of trustees.[70]

The Medical School

Ironically, as the University population fell, the Medical School's rapid growth required extensive new facilities. While the College turned toward the conventional education of northern schools, medical education picked up the fallen banner of Franklin's pragmatism that was better suited to the intellectual climate of Philadelphia. For more than half a century, the Medical School grew until it vastly overshadowed the diminutive College. The Medical School soon required more space than could be found in the President's mansion; by 1805 the medical course's lecture and demonstration method of teaching necessitated a large auditorium, which was provided in an addition. Designed by Latrobe at the suggestion of Samuel Mickle Fox, director of the Bank of Pennsylvania (a previous Latrobe client), it relied on the same classicizing vocabulary and palette of red brick and Pennsylvania blue marble as the President's mansion, but was clearly different in its aesthetic directions.[71] While the simple Adamesque volume of the President's house masked the interior spaces, Latrobe's carefully proportioned volumes denoted the various interior functions. Its skylighted dome described an operating amphitheater similar to that of the contemporary Pennsylvania Hospital. Anticipating modern design in its rejection of history in favor of description, Latrobe's addition set the course for later Penn architects such as Frank

Benjamin Henry Latrobe, Medical School of the University of Pennsylvania, c. 1810. UPA.

Furness, Louis I. Kahn, and eventually Robert Venturi.

Despite the originality of Latrobe's building, within a decade it too was outgrown by the medical program. With Latrobe long since removed from Philadelphia and his reputation damaged by the failure of his waterworks for the city, the opportunity fell to a Latrobe student, William Strickland (1788–1855), to enlarge his master's work. Strickland's 1817 project extended the building twenty feet on the south side to provide additional seating for the growing student body. The resulting auditorium continued to be the chief facility of the school, but the addition came at the expense of loss of the clarity of Latrobe's design.[72] As with the original alterations to the President's House, the University campus continued to respond to the needs of the moment, reflecting the short-term vision of its leadership.

The Strickland Campus

By 1828, even with Latrobe's and Strickland's additions, the continuing growth of the Medical School forced the trustees to consider a new solution. A committee of trustees asked William Strickland, by then the leading architect in Philadelphia after

Latrobe's departure for Washington, D.C., to provide new quarters.[73] Strickland suggested demolishing the by then outdated and outgrown Medical Hall and constructing a new building in its place. This new building, it was estimated, would cost $23,750, including the fittings for the anatomical and chemical departments, with an additional 5 percent fee to the architect.[74]

In spring 1829, after the carnage of the two years previous when the entire arts faculty had been fired, and fearing the loss of status if the college remained in the old building while the growing Medical School was housed in spacious new quarters, the Faculty of

William Strickland, Plan for Additions to Medical School, 1817. UPA.

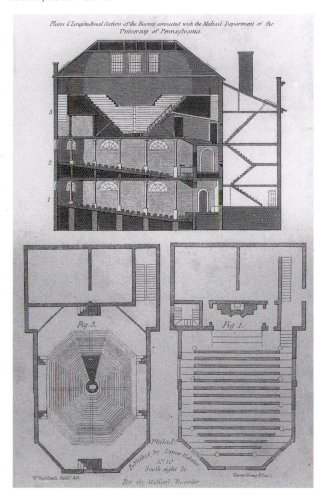

Arts requested a new building for the College. Strickland responded with a matching building separated by a yard from the Medical School. These buildings and the intervening yard were described shortly after their completion:

College and Medical Hall
These buildings were erected on the site of the old University of Pennsylvania. They are each 85 feet front on Ninth Street, by 112 deep. The space between them is about 80 feet, and occupied as a grass plot and shrubbery, surrounded by a paved walk, and enclosed by an iron railing, which extends along the buildings. The College Hall contains a chapel 82 by 40 feet: Recitation rooms, Philosophical, Chemical, and other lecture rooms, &c.

In the Medical Hall, are an anatomical museum, several dissecting rooms, lecture rooms, &c. The buildings are of brick, rough cast, in imitation of Gniess. These buildings command an imposing appearance, are quite an ornament to the city.[75]

Strickland's design of symmetrical buildings whose principal facades were of ruled and jointed stucco subdivided by slender pilasters recalled both the William Williams design for the President's House (and in fact reused its pilasters) and the facade of William Thornton's Library Company of Philadelphia of two generations before on Fifth Street. In contrast to Strickland's designs in the fashionable, massive, marble Greek Revival style of such new federal buildings as the Second Bank of the United States and the U.S. Naval Asylum, civic architecture funded by the descendants of the old Whig culture continued to reflect the delicate proportions and English character of Robert Adam's mid-eighteenth-century design. This choice of style for the new University buildings signified the board's continuing allegiance to old Philadelphia values, and as the account below of the reuse of the pilasters from the old building demonstrates, of their continuing thrift. The removal from these buildings was mourned by those who did not understand that the University's future lay with the industrialists and manufacturers who were transforming the city. Into the twentieth century, Edward Cheyney's views were typical:

> From a purely artistic point of view these two buildings were the most satisfactory of all the outward forms the University has taken. Plain, but of the classic style . . . they had a simplicity and a unity that have been impossible of attainment in the later rapid and diversified growth.[76]

A century after the Strickland buildings were constructed, the *General Magazine and Historical Chronicle* published accounts of the campus by several members of the class of 1862 (whose illustrious members included two provosts, William Pepper, Jr., M.D. and Charles Custis Harrison). George Budd, another member of the class, described the by then decrepit College Building with more sarcasm than affection:

> They were large buildings, of brick, plastered and painted or rough cast of a colour somewhat yellow: and were faced with pillars of marble taken from the old edifice.
> The Chapel is a large room capable of seating five hundred people. It is very plain but neat . . . . The room is a wretched one to speak in. The faculty room is a handsomely furnished apartment, with a table large enough to accommodate the whole faculty who meet here, and try delinquent students. These faculty trials are rather arbitrary tribunals, and scarcely any evidence is admitted in favor of the accused.
> The Library contains a good assortment of old works of no value, and is never used, despite what the Catalogue says of its being open "two hours daily." It is chiefly used as a meeting room for the trustees. Frazer's lecture room is very large, and has arm chairs in lieu of benches. It is in it that oral examinations take place. In all the rooms, the seats

rise one over another, on steps. The janitor's room was a favorite loafing place for the students, but it was poorly furnished, being uncarpeted and unpapered. Still it was a pleasant place, and Momus reigned within its limits. The other recitation rooms were plain and unpretending, being uncarpeted, and their furniture consisting of benches for students, a chair and table for the professor, and occasionally a book case. The Society (Philo and Zelo) halls are now very handsomely fitted up at the expense of their members. A flight of stairs from the third story of the building leads to the loft which is very spacious, and on the roof is a platform whence Frazer and Kendall sometimes take observations with the college telescope. The students never enjoy this advantage.[77]

Charles Harrison's contemporary recollections of student life on Ninth Street were colored by his own actions as Provost of the University, but they afford a picture of the sterile atmosphere of a college where the needs of the students were largely unimportant:

> There were no athletic teams, and physical exercise was limited to cricket and what was then called town ball [an antecedent to modern football], the former being then as now, a most scientific and gentlemanly game to a number of the student body.
> The number of professors was small, five or six in all, but their reputation was very high.
> We met at ten o'clock and adjourned at a quarter after one o'clock, there being therefore three hours of instruction or recitation daily, excepting upon Saturday. On the five days of the week we had opening and closing "worship," as it was then called, and on Saturday we had but two hours of instruction or recitation with opening worship, but not with closing "worship."[78]

In 1868 Penn's first instructor in architecture, Thomas Webb Richards, was asked to study the possibilities of adapting the buildings to the needs of the

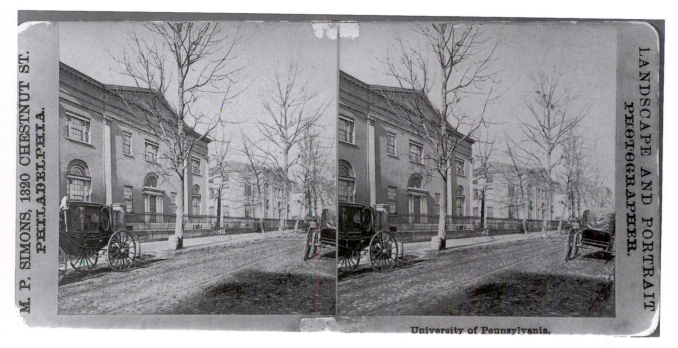

University of Pennsylvania, c. 1860. Photo: M. P. Simons. UPA.

••

post-Civil War institution. Just as the area of Fourth and Arch had become congested, commercial, and a source of temptation to students by the 1790s, by the end of the Civil War Ninth and Market was no longer a quiet suburban edge of the nation's capital. Instead, it was near the administrative and financial centers of an immense industrial city that was producing vast wealth for a new generation of engineers and industrialists trained at Penn before the Civil War. Other uses could be found for Penn's valuable piece of land on Ninth Street; shortly after taking over as Provost, Charles Janeway Stillé proposed a new campus on the west side of the Schuylkill. Three years later, after proving that the old buildings were unsuited to the future of the University, Richards would design new buildings for a site across the Schuylkill.

With the move across the Schuylkill River, Penn's era in the red city of the Revolution ended, but much that had originally characterized the downtown University would remain in the spirit of the nonsectarian and intensely practical institution. Although Penn has moved twice, it has preserved emblems of its early history. The cornerstone of the House for the President of the United States, "erected when the people of Pennsylvania were happily free of debt," was reinstalled first in the chapel of the 1829 buildings, then in the tower of the University Library, later in the corridor of College Hall, and now in the restored Room 200 of College Hall, the successor to the college halls of Franklin's College on Fourth Street and the President's House, and the Strickland buildings on Ninth Street. Together with other plaques and trophies, these objects link the University to its origins in Franklin's city of Revolution. Bronze plaques to the University's early sons who played roles in the Revolution are displayed in the stairwell of Houston Hall. Elsewhere on campus, a bronze George Whitefield strikes an impassioned (and one presumes typical pose) in the dormitory quadrangle; the young Franklin strides in front of the athletic fields; an older, more mature Franklin is enthroned in front of College Hall; and an aged but genial Franklin sits on a park bench at the corner of 36th Street and watches the bustle of his University, which has grown larger than the entire city he knew.

CHAPTER THREE

INDUSTRIAL PHILADELPHIA: THE ROOTS OF THE MODERN UNIVERSITY

Philadelphia and Its University Before the Civil War

IN THE DECADE before the Civil War, the Revolutionary city that had given birth to Benjamin Franklin's College of Philadelphia was a distant memory. Its eighteenth-century landmarks were begrimed by coal soot and its role as a generator of the national culture had been lost to New York and Boston. In place of the national city of the end of the eighteenth century arose a larger and equally potent city poised between its mercantile and commercial past and its industrial future. Since the founding of the College, the built-up portion of the city had expanded from its eighteenth-century boundaries between the framing rivers and Vine and South Streets. The growing and industrializing city stretched along the Delaware River from the shipyards at Washington Avenue on the south to the giant grain warehouses of Port Richmond and Frankford on the north, while residential and industrial development extended west to the railyards on the west bank of the Schuylkill. Although Philadelphia retained its small, distinct neighborhoods, in population it was second only to New York, and it continued the rapid growth of most northern cities.

Provost Charles Janeway Stillé. Frontispiece,
Reminiscences of a Provost, 1860–1880. *UPA.*

In 1854, to satisfy political ambition, the borders of the city and county were merged, making Philadelphia the nation's largest city in terms of area and nearly doubling its population. But this growth added little to its metropolitan vigor. Most of Philadelphia's new citizens remained industrial villagers, dependent on mills for their existence and no more urbane or literate after their change in status than before. Frustrated by their loss of control over the old city, the children and grandchildren of the Signers of the Declaration of Independence retired to their suburban estates, abandoning their responsibilities to the city and its institutions. Control of the city was left to politicians, who contested for the soul of the city with a new generation of industrialists and capitalists. After the Civil War the children of the retired gentry, many of whom had served with distinction in the Union cause, returned to the city, battled for its reform, and reshaped its institutions. From their new neighborhoods around Rittenhouse Square, these new yet old Philadelphians directed the renewal of the University.[1]

The University of Pennsylvania's home remained Strickland's modest Adamesque buildings on Ninth Street that denoted its ties to the fading heritage of the old elites. Rather than serving the needs of its growing industrial city, it had become an ossified agent of Whig Philadelphia. With Philadelphia's decline as a generating center of the national culture and the lack of involvement of its original supporters, the University lost its national and regional standing. Although its faculty continued to attract distinguished scholars, by the 1860s its enrolled students numbered fewer than one hundred and the College of the University of Pennsylvania was smaller than suburban Swarthmore and Haverford Colleges, both of which had large campuses to ensure their future expansion. In 1840, in an effort to rekindle the spark of regional higher education, the Commonwealth, at the urging of the city, had given the capacity to grant degrees to Central High School and to the Girard College, an orphanage! A century after Penn opened, newly founded institutions, some little more than high schools, were its rivals.

Grudging changes began at the University. In 1850 a curriculum in the sciences was proposed but not funded. Two years later, a gift from the Cresson family enabled the staffing of the curiously named Department of Mines, Arts and Manufactures. Subjects included civil and mechanical engineering, drawing (a prerequisite for mechanical drawing and architecture), geology, and other subjects that would serve the industries of the city. The 1854 University catalog announced that the Bachelor of Science degree would be given to students who had taken all the courses offered in mathematics, natural philosophy, and chemistry and two modern languages. For the first time a university student could receive a degree without having taken examinations in the classical languages and literature. However, because the arts faculty refused to accept the qualifications of the scientific faculty, a separate division was formed, establishing the future structure of the University that would be reflected in its later buildings.

Overshadowed by the commercial blocks of the industrial and commercial downtown, the University of Pennsylvania was limited by its site and constricted by the lack of vision of its leaders. When the Morrill Act of 1862 established federal land grants for education, the trustees of the University of Pennsylvania petitioned (unsuccessfully) to be Pennsylvania's state university. At the end of the Civil War, Penn was in desperate straits; it was realistically described by its new provost, Charles Stillé, as "a small and local institution." In his memoirs Stillé later recalled:

> . . . so little hold had the University on public confidence, that for more than eighty years previous to my election it had received but one donation or legacy, that of Mr. Elliott Cresson of $5,000, the income of which was to be devoted to aid in the instruction of drawing, an instruction by the way not given in the University. The number of undergraduates had been for many years less than a hundred, and everyone seemed discouraged and hopeless—dry rot was everywhere.[2]

The Provostship of Charles Janeway Stillé

Charles Janeway Stillé's election as provost in 1868 marked the beginning of the University's renewal. Appointed professor of English two years before, Stillé was only the third non-clergyman to lead the University and the first secular leader who was anything more than a caretaker.[3] Based on what he knew of other successful American colleges, the new provost argued that "The college has been just what its President, with full power has made it."[4] Asserting that the board members could not be cognizant of all the pressing issues of the college, Stillé proclaimed that "All this must be the work of one man, the live energetic head who knows what is needed, what is possible to accomplish."[5] At Penn however, the provost was not the president of the board but "a servant to it." Though Stillé ultimately was forced to resign over the same point a decade later, he turned the University toward its future.[6]

In a letter of 26 September 1868 to the head of the Board of Trustees, the new provost, having surveyed his paltry kingdom, remarked on the overcrowding that resulted from the popularity of the new scientific courses, which required that even the library, the faculty room, and the room set aside for the School of

Arts be turned into recitation spaces. With a growing student population, Stillé had been forced to double classes into two sections, which in turn made the old University building untenable. In that situation, he closed his remarks with a diatribe on the University's setting:

> I need not enlarge upon the unsuitable character of the present recitation rooms, nor upon the vile neighborhood growing viler every day which surrounds the University, nor upon the vast influence which new and appropriate buildings would exercise upon the general prosperity of the University.[7]

Because industry had become the foundation of the economy of the region, Stillé proposed that a separate scientific school be built on a new campus to train skilled engineers and scientists for the great workplaces of the city. In this idea he joined the movement toward the elective system that would reshape American colleges, to the dismay of those who viewed education as being a badge of elite status as opposed to a useful tool. Philadelphian Sydney George Fisher's distress at President Charles Eliot's inaugural address at Harvard hints at the difficulties that would be faced by Stillé:

> Read among other things the address of Mr. Ch. W. Eliot on his inauguration sometime ago as President of Harvard College. Do not like it. It is hard, dry, practical, Yankee of the utilitarian sort, in thought & sentiment & not well written. There is no genial love of letters in it, no liberal views, no elegance of style, no indications of refined & cultivated taste. The colleges of the country are sinking in tone, lower & lower, in accordance with the opinion & manners of the people—I mean what is considered even the best educated portion of the people. Practical ability, physical science, knowledge that may promote success in the real & absorbing interest of all—making money—are now immensely prized & preferred to literature, philoso-

phy & art. Parents wish to see their sons successful men of business, not scholars and gentlemen, & to gratify this desire the colleges are reducing their standard of excellence & admitting the natural sciences to the foremost place among the studies prescribed.[8]

Unlike Fisher, who remained rooted in the past, Stillé, like Franklin before him and like his contemporary Charles Eliot of Harvard, saw the future of college education in its ability to integrate studies about the present with the study of the past. Perhaps as background for taking the position as provost, Stillé read Matthew Arnold's *Schools and Universities on the Continent* (1868), which provided an overview of systems of education and the goals of curriculum as a goad to changing the English universities. Though Arnold's interpretation remained mired in the classism of Great Britain, still it was clear that change was coming. With the problems of funding the enlarged institution, how jealous Stillé must have been to read Arnold's accounts of the public funding of Germany's schools. Nonetheless, Stillé proposed a new agenda for the University:

> . . . it cannot be disguised any longer that it is *the modern spirit*, especially in the form in which it has been developed in this country, which is now the open enemy of the old system of college education. There is clearly no lack of interest in the higher forms of culture, but a distrust of and discontent with the sort of culture, as specially inapplicable to many of our needs, which the old system was designed to promote. . . . we are told by Mr. Matthew Arnold . . . there spreads a growing disbelief in Latin and Greek . . . and a growing disposition to make modern languages and natural sciences take their place.[9]

Acting on his own initiative, Stillé put into motion events that led toward the new campus. Because the gift from the Cresson family required instruction in drawing, Stillé consulted with Henry Morton (C1857), who had been personal secretary of trustee William Sellers when Sellers was president of the Franklin Institute. Morton later served as the first president of the Stevens Institute of Technology. At Penn as an undergraduate, he had helped translate the Rosetta Stone, then studied law, and finally settled on the sciences as his own field of interest. Morton recommended architect Thomas Webb Richards, a graduate of the Franklin Institute's program in architectural design and later an instructor in the same program, to teach drawing and design at the University.

Thomas Richards and his brother, the marine artist William Trost Richards, were the orphaned children of a Philadelphia tailor. Both had taken advantage of the opportunities the city offered for upward mobility. The two brothers studied architecture and art respectively at night, while working in related trades in one of the booming businesses of the day: William as a designer of brass gas lamps and chandeliers for Archer, Warner and Miskey, Thomas at the great lighting manufacturer Cornelius and Baker. Years later, Richards specified Cornelius and Baker's products for lighting the new College Buildings.

After training in the architectural course at the Franklin Institute, where he encountered Henry Morton, Richards entered the office of Philadelphia architect and popular author of pattern books Samuel Sloan. He was later employed by Calvert Vaux, who pioneered the polychromatic Victorian Gothic in New York. During the Civil War he designed military hospitals, learning some of the new principles of hygienic design, ventilation, washable surfaces, and so on, but this specialty led to no important commissions. Because of the circumstances of his family, Richards began his career with no strong base of clients from the usual circle of family and social connections that sustained the practices of most young architects of the era.[10] Despite the local building boom after the Civil War, his lack of clients caused his career to founder; at the moment that he signed on to teach architecture at Penn, he was debating whether to turn

to his other interest, photography, for employment.[11]

Stillé set Richards to work on a survey of the Strickland buildings to demonstrate that they could not meet the immediate and future needs of the College. The architect's report was resounding agreement. Simultaneous with Richards's appointment, a trustee suggested that the University ask the city to give or sell to it a large tract of land to the rear of the Philadelphia Almshouse. In the 1820s the growth of the city had forced the Almshouse from Tenth Street next to Pennsylvania Hospital to a new site on the west bank of the Schuylkill River, where its managers purchased a large plot of ground and built a Greek revival building also designed by William Strickland. After the Civil War, Penn's leaders hoped that a portion of the property could become the new site for the University while the remainder could be sold to create funds that would be needed for new buildings.[12] The hostility between the new populist leaders of the enlarged city and the University was revealed in their refusal to cooperate with this scheme. Ultimately the University did acquire a portion of the Almshouse property for slightly below market rate, but with no additional land to sell, and lacking financial resources of its own, it again appeared stymied.

New Trustee Leadership

A decade earlier, Penn's Board of Trustees might not have been prepared to take the risk of purchasing a new site and building a new campus, but during the 1860s and early 1870s new leaders receptive to change had begun to supplant the old, conservative, mercantile and clergy-based board. As was true for most local boards of the era, the University of Pennsylvania's post-Civil War trustees came from engineering and industry or from the allied scientific professions, particularly medicine. Unlike the boardsmen of institutions in financial centers such as New York, these were not merely experts in the amassing of capital. Fairman Rogers, trained as a civil engineer, had solved the problem of compass deviation in iron ships for the Navy and served as an engineer for the Union Army during his summer vacations from teaching at Penn. John Henry Towne headed great iron foundries and endowed the University's scientific school. William Pepper, Jr., M.D., who succeeded Stillé as provost, was a medical doctor with an interest in research science. William Sellers, head of the board after the Civil War, was the premier mechanical engineer of his day, designing and manufacturing the great machines that made Philadelphia the world capital of heavy industry. During his presidency of the Franklin Institute, Sellers pushed American industry toward standardization of parts, creating enormous efficiencies that fueled Philadelphia's prosperity until the end of the century. The remaining key trustees, Frederick Fraley and John Welsh, were drawn from the old mercantile culture. In later years Welsh's reputation for probity

and his hard work as its treasurer salvaged the Centennial Exhibition of 1876. When the citizens of Philadelphia paid tribute to Welsh's efforts on behalf of the fair with an immense cash gift, Welsh used those funds to establish the Welsh Professorship in English Literature and History. Welsh's personal financial guarantee and his pledge to raise money, as well as his connections to the Grant administration, ultimately gave Penn's board the courage to begin the building of a new University.

After considerable debate that included the possible removal of the University to a rural setting far removed from the evils of the city (a theme that would come up again just before and again after World War I), the trustees supported the move to a new site in West Philadelphia. For the second time, the University abandoned the buildings of its past. The availability of open land alone would not have encouraged the

••••••••••••••••••••••••••••••••••••••

The Woodlands, looking northwest, 1973. GET.

Woodland Terrace, 1973. GET.

move had not engineering and technological innovations of the early nineteenth century made possible great bridges that spanned the Schuylkill. These maintained Penn's link to Center City, where most of its students, faculty, and trustees still lived.

The suburb of West Philadelphia into which the University moved had been a part of the County of Philadelphia from William Penn's original purchase. It became a separate township in 1844 and remained so until the Act of Incorporation of 1854 joined the region to the city. In the same decade the city was criss-crossed by the steel tracks of horse-drawn streetcars, whose added efficiency and economy led to a new market for housing in the suburbs, dramatically expanding the built area of the city and for the first time creating geographically distinct, class-based neighborhoods. Soon the old estates that had overlooked the Schuylkill River valley were subdivided for houses,

or, in the case of the great Woodlands estate, for a cemetery. By the 1860s the region was one of Philadelphia's handsomest neighborhoods, the home of the Drexels and other captains of finance and industry. For the next half century West Philadelphia remained a suburb, distinguished from the built-up portions of Center City by broad, tree-lined streets and handsome villas. In marked contrast to its expansion in the 1960s, the University was viewed as an extension of elite Philadelphia and was welcomed to this setting.

Charles Stillé's Green Campus

With the acquisition of the new site, Stillé, on his own initiative and without consulting his board, asked Thomas Richards to sketch an alternate building at a

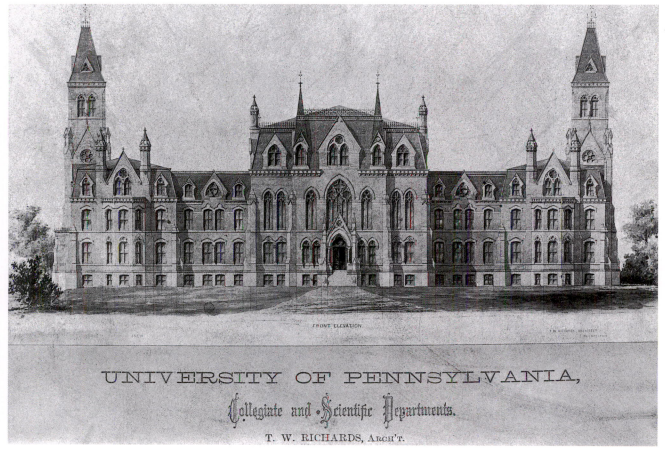

FRONT ELEVATION.

UNIVERSITY OF PENNSYLVANIA,
Collegiate and Scientific Departments.
T. W. RICHARDS, ARCH'T.

Thomas W. Richards, Front elevation, University of
Pennsylvania, Collegiate and Scientific Departments,
1872. Photograph of lost original. UPA.

new site, though with the admonition that cost would
be an important issue. Stillé left no record of the
reasoning behind his decision to use Richards as
campus architect, although, from Stillé's concern about
cost, it seems likely that Richards was selected because
he was on the University faculty and could be expected to provide architectural services at a lower fee.
Because this was the type of step that would have been
appropriate had Stillé indeed been the president of the
institution, his decision forced his board's hand.

We know little about Stillé's own architectural
views other than his recorded delight with the first of
Richards's schemes. Unfortunately, no images exist of
the first drawings, but some sense of the provost's

personal preference may be drawn from the fact that
the College Buildings and his own home on St. James
Street were built of the same green serpentine and
ornamented with similar Gothic detail. In making his
workplace at the University and his home in the same
style and materials, he followed the example of Nicholas Biddle. Biddle's home, Andalusia, and later Girard
College (whose board Biddle chaired) were designed
in the Greek Revival style by Thomas Ustic Walter,
mimicking his workplace in the Parthenon-based Second Bank of the United States. In any event, Stillé
enthused over the first plan by Richards, which he
described as "far more beautiful than what we finally
adopted."[13] Indicating that he rather than the trustees
was in charge of the design process, Stillé warned
Richards that cost would be a critical factor in whether
the board proceeded with the new building. Stillé
commented:

I do not think that the Board would be justified, nor do I believe that they have the slightest intention in the present state of their funds of expending more than $50,000 in the erection of buildings. They know that the best public schools have in no case cost more than $50,000. . . . This of course excludes all ideas of ornament, but I should be satisfied with the [utilitarian] effect of some of the public [i.e., land grant] schools.[14]

In an unexpected turn that probably represented an effort to regain control of the planning process, the trustees surprised the provost by quadrupling the budget, but they also invited other leading city architects to compete for the commission Stillé had promised Richards. Those invited were John McArthur, the recent victor in the competition for City Hall, James H. Windrim, designer of the new Masonic Temple, Frazer, Furness and Hewitt, victors in the Pennsylvania Academy of the Fine Arts competition, as well as other important members of the profession such as Addison Hutton, Samuel Sloan, and Henry A. Sims. However, the newly founded American Institute of Architects barred its members from trying to wrest commissions from each other, and when the other architects found that the job had been more or less promised to Richards all except Windrim declined to compete. Windrim

••

Thomas W. Richards, Perspective, University of Pennsylvania, Medical Department. Engraving, c. 1874. UPA.

was not part of old Philadelphia society and thus did not have the logical access to elite commissions, nor was he a member of the American Institute of Architects. To make certain that his man won, Stillé coached Richards with a letter prior to the board meeting of 20 July 1870:

I hope you will not hesitate to explain in person to W. Sellers and to Mr. Fraley (before the meeting of the committee) what you consider its [Richards's plan] essential advantages. I wish you would point out especially how it provides for light & air as essential to such a building and also . . . a certain general largeness and roominess about the halls & passages. I am personally most desirous that its different parts should not be squeezed together. It may be that this may be attempted by Windrim with a view to greater economy, and this is a point that you must be ready to meet.[15]

Even to prove their point to Stillé about who ran the institution, the Board of Trustees could not stomach the alternative of hiring an architect from outside their circle. With coaching from Stillé, Richards was awarded the commission.

For the central building Richards proposed a dazzling multi-towered and spired Gothic structure built of brilliant green serpentine stone from West Chester, trimmed with yellow sandstone and purple brownstone, accented with red pointing, and finished with blue slates on the mansard roof. As for Oxford University's Natural History Museum of the previous decade by Deane and Woodward, local stone would celebrate the natural history of the region, while carved ornament, finials, and towers would reflect the connection with the Gothic style of the great English schools such as William Butterfield's Rugby School (1860) and Keble College (1866).

The cornerstone for Stillé's new multipurpose College building was laid in June 1871, but another dark cloud loomed. Although the board had authorized construction, it had not raised the funds necessary to pay for it. Eventually trustee John Welsh came to the University's rescue by arranging the sale of the old site to the federal government for a new Federal Building and Post Office. The funds raised by this route covered the costs of construction, but left no endowment to ensure the future of the University. Still, the effects of the new buildings were immediately felt. The student body quickly surpassed the hundred or so that some members of the board had announced were all that Philadelphia could reasonably be expected to provide, and for the first time Stillé could report that "there seemed to be some pride in the University on the part of the public."[16]

Soon the University went even deeper into debt to build the new Medical Hall (now Logan Hall) and the University Hospital, but those building afforded space for important new programs. For these buildings the University once again turned to the state for assistance, establishing the idea that health-related costs should receive public funding. With the removal of Medicine from College Hall, the Towne Scientific School could be established; in 1878, with the completion of the Hare Medical Laboratory, room was found for a dental program in the Medical Hall.[17] Over the next decade, other programs including engineering and architecture were incubated in College Hall. Under Stillé, Penn had returned to Franklin's pragmatic goal of a college that taught its students the useful and ornamental skills aimed toward "the several Professions for which they are intended."[18] The future course of the University was established.

Campus Planning: The Richards Years

For most of the nineteenth century, costs had forced the designers of American colleges to ignore the Jeffersonian model of an entire University built to a predetermined plan. Instead, new buildings were typically sited as required by hierarchy and by use, usually without regard for earlier planning. Over the course of the century, styles of collegiate architecture changed with the ideals and values of each generation. Georgian robustness gave way to the flat and attenuated

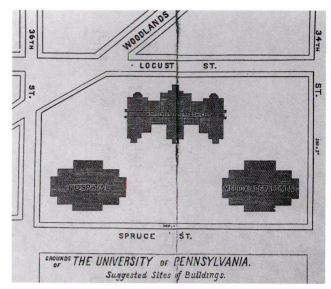

"Grounds of the University of Pennsylvania: Suggested Sites of Buildings," c. 1874. UPA.

forms of the early Republic; soon Grecian porticos were in turn succeeded by imposing French mansards of the Second Empire and then by towered collegiate Gothic quadrangles and Beaux-Arts colonnades. All these styles were rooted in imported architectural fashions that paralleled the acquisitiveness of American culture as it gathered the treasures of the world, first in the homes of its entrepreneurs and later in its great museums. While they provide immediate cues about the era that built them, their variety typically further eroded whatever unity a college might evoke.

Because Penn was at a new site, its first group of buildings could be united by style and materials. Despite the continuity of detail of the buildings of the Stillé campus, historians have assumed that their arrangement was as unplanned as most of its contemporary institutions. However, a tiny engraved plan of the West Philadelphia campus in the University Archives and a Centennial-era description of the campus hint that the facts may be otherwise. The plan probably dates from 1872, when funds were being raised for the new University Hospital and Medical School. According to the drawing, these medical facilities were to be placed on the same block as College Hall but were to face Spruce Street toward the rear of the property. This scheme would have given the hospital and the medical school a unified front, but would have once again put the University in a position where further expansion was nearly impossible. Further confirmation of a single overarching plan is found in a description of the campus in a Centennial guide to Philadelphia, which referred to the campus as "a complete square of Gothic structures devoted to various uses, all in connection with the University," suggesting that other buildings were planned for the unbuilt corner sites.[19] More important for the future of the institution, Richards sited College Hall off center in the triangular lot acquired from the city, facing the main streets of the city. With the college departments and administration in the College Buildings and the medical school in the Medical Building, the subdivision of the earlier Ninth Street campus was repeated on the new campus. But, by facing the Medical School toward 36th Street and simplifying its form, Richards stressed the new hierarchy in which College Hall and the College would be central in the growing institution.

Almost immediately after the completion of College Hall and the Medical School, Richards was asked to design a new building for the campus that marked the ever-bolder vision of the University trustees. Penn's westward move had separated the institution from Pennsylvania Hospital at Eighth and Pine Streets, which had long provided clinical experience for its students. If the Medical School was to join the westward move with the University, the medical faculty demanded that the new campus include a hospital of practice to serve the faculty and students. The resulting Hospital of the University of Pennsylvania was the first university-owned hospital in the nation.[20] This building was placed on the far side of Spruce Street toward 34th Street, where it could be linked to the existing Philadelphia Almshouse, which provided many of the subjects who were the basis of teaching. Downwind of the prevailing breezes and separated from the growing College by Spruce Street, Penn's hospital and medical center have become the center of

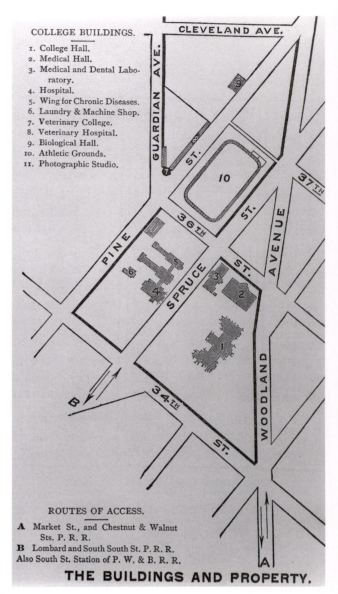

1885 *University plan as shown in the* Catalogue and Announcements of the University of Pennsylvania, 1885–6. *UPA.*

an immense medical campus that now covers several city blocks and once again rivals the rest of the University in size.[21] With the construction of the new hospital, the Board of Trustees of the University put into action a plan to lengthen the course of instruction in the medical school, with the particular goal of uniting the medical faculty and the hospital staff "so as to secure that harmony of action which is necessary to success."[22] New clinical professorships were established in Surgery, Medicine, and Diseases of Women and Children. Dr. William Pepper, Jr. became Professor of Clinical Medicine.

In 1878 Richards placed the final building of the Stillé campus, the Robert Hare Medical Laboratory at the corner of 36th and Spruce Streets where Williams Hall now stands. With its roofline punctuated by myriad ventilator stacks, it was the first laboratory building on Penn's campus to express its function through its architectural design. Its location, adjacent to the medical school, established the planning principle that still shapes the campus, namely, that facilities should be located by proximity to other related programs. Because three times as many students were enrolled in medical classes as in the College, the medical school had been the recipient of the largest facilities of the University, but on the new campus there was room for growth for the entire institution. Moreover, the resulting collegiate group offered more than a simple functional arrangement of buildings on an irregular property. Although the three buildings of the main campus block typified the Victorian planning approach of individual buildings placed on a lawn, their enclosure of space anticipated the future course of campus planning of quadrangles and large ensembles of buildings.

Richards's Buildings

The buildings of the Stillé years were united by color (green serpentine stone), style (Academic Gothic), and, despite the towers and Gothic pinnacles, economy. Functionally planned with few spatial or decorative grace notes on their interiors, they reflected the cost-consciousness that typified the Stillé years. In College Hall, the absence of carved paneling and massive carved beams in the chapel is particularly telling, while the simple surfaces of the interior offices, classrooms, and corridors denote as much the values of Penn's trustees as the financial constraints of the early years. Still, with red and blue tiles on the floor of the

entrance portico, red and blue slate in the roof, and red and blue encaustic on the cornerstone, College Hall marked the first official use of Pennsylvania's future colors.

Taken chronologically, the buildings of the Stillé era reflected the major issues that affected college education in the nineteenth century. In their size they accommodated the increasing numbers of students. Their large windows and roof vents and chimneys indicated a rising awareness of the importance of hygienic design. The presence of specialized classrooms marked the supplanting of the old lecture-based educational system by the new experience-based teaching that relied on libraries, laboratories, and other buildings. In these new buildings students could practice the new skills of the utilitarian era that Matthew Arnold had predicted would shape future colleges.

College Hall, or the College Buildings, as the first structure was originally known, represented by its plural name the collegiate subdivisions of the central administration and the continuing division between the arts in the west wing and the sciences in the east. To emphasize their separateness, each of these functions was placed in a distinct block that was given identity by a separate entrance and a distinguishing architectural feature, with towers for the two schools at each end and a projecting Gothic baldachin for the main entrance in the central administration block. The central block contained administrative offices, with the library in the projecting rear wing. The assembly room, which doubled as a chapel, was indicated on the exterior by large pointed windows on the second floor above the entrance. Because education still was largely passively received through lectures, the wings containing the separate schools were devoted to lecture rooms that served as recitation rooms for the arts and demonstration rooms for the sciences. Small labs and other rooms for individual work by the science professors were placed adjacent to science classrooms, continuing the idea of the solitary worker—a sort of St. Jerome's cell that characterized the

College Hall, looking southeast, c. 1872. UPA.
Chapel in College Hall, c. 1888. UPA.

••

scientist's laboratory from the middle ages until the late nineteenth century. In the fashion of the English Gothic Revival of the time, the exterior massing reflected the issues of the interior plan, and variations in fenestration suggested the different types of interior space.

In the light of Stillé's letter to Richards before the board selected its architect, several features of the design are noteworthy. At the rear of the building, on the south side, giant windows lighted the stairs through which the light then streamed across the broad corri-

Hospital of the University of Pennsylvania, looking south, c. 1888. Photo: William Rau. UPA.

dor toward the front of the building. Cast iron elements woven into the fabric of the building pointed to the arriving industrial culture. Most visible are the cast iron columns in the original main entrance hall, the iron treads and balusters of the stairs, and the cast iron piers that frame the windows in the central corridor that are lighted by the oversized Gothic windows in the south wall. On the upper levels, large iron brackets reduce the span of ceiling timbers in the large classrooms. It is likely that the use of the new material announced a contribution to the design from the trustee who was placed in charge of the project, engineer William Sellers, who according to the Trustees' Minutes had "thoroughly studied" every aspect of its plan and construction.[23]

The newly understood possibilities of hygienic design were evidenced by the skylines of College Hall and all Richards's later buildings. These buildings were punctuated by a remarkable array of chimneys,

ventilator stacks, and other roof-level structures that enlivened their silhouettes while giving each something of the character of an apartment house. The year before Penn's new buildings were designed, Lehigh College in Bethlehem, Pennsylvania had been swept by respiratory diseases that forced the college to close temporarily. The ventilator shafts of Penn's buildings were intended to promote health by ensuring a continuous flow of fresh air into each classroom. This feature reflected the growing understanding of the possibilities of hygienic design, which originated first in hospital architecture and soon spread to other public facilities.

The new Hospital of the University of Pennsylvania reflected these ideas as well. Its pavilion plan, with a narrow central wing linked by corridors to planned outer wings, afforded ample ventilation and light. Reflecting in part Richards's experience as a designer of Civil War military hospitals and anticipating the later focus on hygienic design of the Johns Hopkins Hospital in Baltimore, it was Philadelphia's first postwar hospital to take into account the new discoveries about germ theory. Of greater importance for the future of medical education were the laboratories that were built in the basement of the building. These were the fruits of Dr. William Pepper's European tour as research for the design of the hospital, reflecting in particular his visit to state-supported medical research institutions in Germany. The presence of laboratories for clinical research in the hospital demonstrated his growing belief in the value of scientific process as a basis for medical training and treatment, in contrast to the old lecture system that had dominated medical education in Europe and America. From these labs would grow an immense cluster of laboratories that have come to characterize Penn's modern approach to education.

The use of laboratories as a general teaching tool would become the norm at Penn by the end of the 1870s, but it was not yet the practice when the new Medical Hall was constructed. Because Civil War-era medical education continued to rely on demonstration-based teaching, much of the volume of the Medical School's new home was taken up with large amphitheaters. These were represented on the exterior by oversized windows that denoted the multistory auditoriums, which filled the entire rear of the building, while their extent was suggested by the buttresses that subdivided the east facade. Thomas Eakins's painting of the Agnew Clinic captures the drama of Dr. Agnew in one of the amphitheaters, surrounded by his peers and students, who are straining to catch every nuance of word and every gesture of action (see color plate 2). That the Medical School required such facilities attests to the continuing size and importance of its program. During the Civil War the vast majority of doctors on both sides had graduated from Philadelphia's medical schools. After the Civil War,

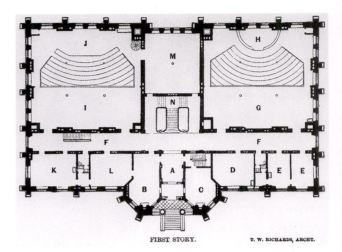

Thomas W. Richards, Medical School, first-floor plan, c. 1874. UPA.

despite losing southern students, the Medical School continued to graduate an of average three times as many students as the College.[24]

The Hare Medical Laboratory, Richards's last building on the main campus, continued the use of serpentine stone and Victorian Gothic details of his earlier work.[25] In its purpose, however, the new building marked a revolutionary shift toward learning by doing that soon would transform education at Penn. A spring 1878 letter from Fairman Rogers (C 1853) to his fellow trustee John Welsh, who was then overseas as the American Ambassador to the Court of St. James, makes it apparent that the trustees understood the implications of the new building:

As the new medical instruction introduces more chemistry and adds laboratory practice, it is absolutely necessary to have more laboratory accommodation. . . . We have decided, therefore, to erect a building 150 by 40 on the ground to the south of the Medical Building. . . . The second and third floor will be for the laboratories and will be entered from the [uphill] basement floor of the Medical Hall. . . . The fourth story which is in the roof will be occupied by Physilogical and Histological rooms. . . . The new building will be of green stone, like the rest, finished with brick on the inside without plastering and will be simple so as to keep the cost down.[26]

Henceforth medical education would include laboratory training as a major component of schooling. It should not be concluded that each student became a sophisticated researcher; rather, students were taught basic methods of analysis that eventually served their medical training. More advanced training was still several years in the future.

Within the decade of the 1880s, a new Graduate School would be founded at Penn to enable advanced students to pursue the goal of the new technocratic world, the search for "new knowledge." A new University Library would provide research space and an enlarged collection of books so that all University students could be exposed to the principles of independent research, and laboratory-based teaching would

••

Hare Medical Laboratory, looking northeast, c. 1885. UPA.

affect all the sciences. Penn would return to its eighteenth-century heritage of experience-based education. But, before these fundamental changes swept the University, Stillé would lose his battle with the trustees for control of the institution. It would take the next two provosts, both from backgrounds of wealth, the first from the medical field, and the second from business, who had already served as trustees, to place the final authority for the institution's direction in the hands of one leader.

The Pepper "Poem in Red"

In 1880, after leading the University to its new campus and guiding it for twelve years, Stillé resigned when he could not persuade the Board of Trustees to give him day-to-day control of the institution. The following year, William Pepper, Jr., M.D. (1843–1898, C 1862, M 1864), long an activist in the public affairs of the city and a member of the Board of Trustees, accepted the position as provost. Unlike Stillé, who was intellectually attuned to history and culture, Pep-

per, a laboratory-trained scientist and medical doctor, was drawn from the ranks of the new professional culture. With a stronger mandate that finally made the provost the head of the board, though still with the caveat "when the governor was not present," Pepper began the expansion of the institution beyond its old duality of college and medical school.[27] During his fourteen years as provost, Pepper added programs in business, engineering, dentistry, and the sciences, which soon paralleled the rise of the new elective curriculum that enabled undergraduates to customize their education. The particularization and separation of academic programs had originated on the continent and were gradually adapted to the American educational system in the years after the Civil War. At Penn under Provost Pepper, that specialization would be revealed in separate buildings for the new programs. And, just as important for the future of the institution, under Dr. Pepper's leadership the Medical School turned from its proprietary origins, owned and controlled by its faculty, to a school that for the first time was controlled by the University.

With William Pepper as its leader, the University was soon colored by the values of the engineers and manufacturers who had rejuvenated the Board of Trustees. Unlike leaders in mercantile and commercial New York and academic and literary Boston, both of which remained closely linked to Europe and dependent on its cultural forms, Philadelphia's elite ran foundries and factories and found art in their experience-based culture. This gulf between the cultures of the learned northeast and the experience-based mid-Atlantic regions was not new. Daniel Boorstin had observed similar differences between the colonial Puritans and Quakers:

Within the ample frame of English Puritanism, New England Puritans required that men attend to their books, but Pennsylvania Quakers with equal earnestness urged men to attend to experience.[28]

·······································
Provost William Pepper, c. 1881. Photo: Maynen. UPA.

Even at the end of the nineteenth century this difference in approach was sufficiently alive to foster cultural conflict between the values and expectations of Philadelphia and other northern cities.[29] In aesthetics, this difference was most obvious in the continual choice of Frank Furness as the architect for the institutions, industries, commercial buildings, and factories of the Quaker City—to the dismay of critics from other cities, especially Boston and New York, where the new, history-based architecture had become the accepted mode of design.[30] The effects of the same values also shaped the regional expectations about the nature and appropriateness of various careers. When William Henry Furness, a Unitarian minister and father of architect Frank Furness, described engineer Evans Rogers, father of trustee Fairman Rogers, as "very solid in his character [who] . . . has got his money not by speculation but by 17 years devoted to his business as a hardware merchant," he was conferring the highest praise that a Philadelphian could give.[31] In Philadelphia business meant real work, the production of objects, not the will-o'-the-wisp of profits obtained through financial manipulation. After the Civil War Penn's Board of Trustees were increasingly drawn from the world of work.

Beyond their obvious role in selecting architects and shaping the appearance of the campus along the lines of their businesses, Philadelphia boardsmen, whose resources were tied up in their industries, took a different course from the capitalists of New York in running and funding the University. This would have significant consequences for Penn's future. Instead of building the University's endowments, Philadelphia boardsmen made up any deficits of the programs that they oversaw from the profits of their industries. So long as their industries prospered, annual support would carry each program and the University would not need a large endowment. As a corollary of this practice, Penn's emphasis was on the applied sciences and the application of the new knowledge to manufacturing and engineering, setting it apart from its peer institutions in the northeast.

Architectural Selection in the Pepper Era

Though Pepper retained Thomas Richards as Professor of Architecture, during his tenure as provost Penn's architectural future was turned over to the architects who had transformed the city in the previous decade. But, where Stillé had been happy to use one architect and to have one aesthetic mask for the University, Pepper, shaped by the rising professional culture, took the route of hiring consultants to advise trustee committees on the theory that each field was evolving so rapidly that no architect could be expected to know more than his special niche of the craft. This approach could be observed in the building dearest to Pepper and the first important commission of his provostship, an extension to the University Hospital. Dr. Pepper himself had overseen the hospital's design during the Stillé years, and it remained the center of his interest during his tenure as provost. To set the tone of his tenure, Pepper brought in John Shaw Billings, M.D. to serve as consultant for the new hospital buildings. After serving as a military surgeon and observing a link between the design of hospitals and mortality during the Civil War, Billings had guided the design of the new hygienic hospital constructed for the Johns Hopkins University, giving him an important reputation in the field of hospital design. The large windows and exterior vents of the Gibson Wing of the hospital represented Billings's input. G. W. and W. D. Hewitt masked those features behind a conventional Queen Anne facade, producing a handsome work of design that gave the hospital a more contemporary appearance than Richards's academic Gothic building of the previous decade to which it was attached.

Unlike Stillé, who had attempted an end run around the board in his selection of an architect for College Hall, Provost Pepper usually appears to have left the choice of designer to the trustees most interested in the building. This approach was beneficial for fund-

•••••••••••••••••••••••••••••••••

Henry C. Gibson Wing for Chronic Diseases, looking southeast c. 1885. Photo: Gutekunst. UPA.

raising and in many cases brought important regional architects to the campus. Some choices were obvious. The Wilson Brothers, the premier architecture and engineering firm in the nation, whose technical innovations in construction anticipated by a decade the structural systems if not the form of Chicago School high rises, were selected to design the power plant and the adjacent engineering school building. Presumably they were chosen by William Sellers.[32] Collins and Autenrieth had been the family architects for Henry Charles Lea for two generations, designing his Walnut Street home, as well as numerous stores and business buildings. In 1890 they designed the Lea Institute of Hygiene, later Smith Hall, and again at Pepper's urging used John Shaw Billings as their consultant on the design.[33] Similarly, the Hewitts were the favorites of the Gibsons, having designed their huge Wynnewood mansion, a speculative row on Powelton Avenue, a downtown office block, and the hospital addition. And it can certainly be argued that Frank Furness was chosen as the architect of the new University Library because of his connection to the chairman of the building committee—his brother Horace!

These architects shared important characteristics. All were from Philadelphia, and all had a wide range of experience, far beyond most college architects of the era. As might have been expected in Philadelphia, all had experience designing industrial buildings and thus would have been familiar with the new ideas that were beginning to affect design. Richards had even worked in a factory and would have been aware of the potential for congestion at stairs and in corridors, factors that were taken into account in his design of College Hall. As Lindy Biggs points out in *The Rational Factory*, industrial buildings had become part of the equation in improving productivity, causing their designers to conceive of them in mechanical terms and even to consider them as machines.[34] During the Pepper years, Penn's buildings would draw on this new approach, departing from convention in the process in large measure because the University's board came from the same industrial culture and, as will be shown below, were accustomed to the idea that function should be expressed through form.

Pepper's Board: Agent of Change

Judged against the standard of the architecture of Penn's peer institutions, the University of Pennsylvania's buildings were strikingly different. The cause of this gulf is apparent when the makeup of Penn's board during the Pepper administration is compared with those of its peer institutions. At the end of Provost Pepper's term, Penn's twenty-four board members were chiefly drawn from engineering, industry, and the new professional community: six were engineers, five were medical doctors, five were manufacturers, three were lawyers, and one was an architect. Most served on the boards of the giant industries that dominated the city. Only four members of Penn's board were clergymen. By contrast, in 1900 the largest professional groups on Harvard University's board were theologians, academics, and lawyers, men culturally attuned to look backward, with no engineers, industrialists, or businessmen in their group. Similarly, Yale's board was still composed mostly of Congregational ministers, with no engineers, scientists, or businessmen, and Princeton's board was nearly equally divided among lawyers, ministers, and academics, again with no engineers or scientists. The greatest point of similarity of these boards was the relative parochialism in their make-up, with members typically graduates of the institution and residents of nearby communities. Penn differed from the others again in that it had the lowest proportion of Penn alumni board members—probably because many of the engineers and businessmen on its board had not attended college at all.[35]

The distribution of students in the various academic departments of these universities reflected the orientation of their respective boards. During the decade between 1885 and 1893, the ratio of Bachelor of Arts and Bachelor of Science degrees awarded to Penn students was nearly the reverse of those at Yale

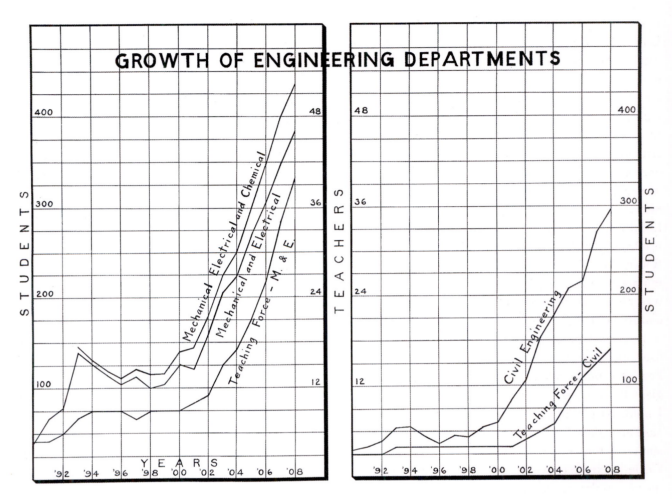

GROWTH OF ENGINEERING DEPARTMENTS

Growth of Engineering Departments, 1892–98. UPA.

and Princeton. Two-thirds of Penn's students received the science degree, while at Yale and Princeton the vast majority received arts degrees. At Harvard, fewer than 2 percent of undergraduates attended the engineering school, while at Penn half were enrolled in engineering courses. When business and dentistry students are included in the professional courses, Penn's proportion of liberal arts students was less than a third of the undergraduate population. In the New England colleges, the liberal arts curriculum remained the core program.

Furness and the Engineering Culture

Penn's core trustees—engineers, scientists, physicians, and businessmen—were Frank Furness's principal clients. It is therefore not surprising that Furness became the chief architect of the campus during Pepper's tenure. In part, Frank Furness became the University's architect because of his own connections to the powers of the city who sat on the University's board. The son of the city's leading Unitarian minister, William Henry Furness, he was also the brother of Shakespearian scholar, University lecturer, and University trustee Horace Howard Furness (who in turn had married the sister of trustee Fairman Rogers). But Furness had another link to the University trustees. Rarely has any architect so closely comprehended the values and opportunities of his own society and been able to express them as Furness did after the Civil War.

In the mid-1880s the board turned several of the new University projects over to Furness because his designs reflected the value system of Philadelphia's industrial culture, which they represented. After a decade of the cautious Gothic of Thomas Richards, the University was fortunate in its choice. After nearly three-quarters of a century of bitter denunciations by critics and historians, Furness's work is now championed as innovative architecture that forms a part of the genealogy of modern design via his student Louis Sullivan, who in turn taught Frank Lloyd Wright. Locally George Howe learned in Furness's office and was a mentor for Louis Kahn, who in turn would teach Robert Venturi. A good case can be made that an important wing of modern architecture in America was rooted in Furness's response to the industrial culture he served.

In earlier buildings in Philadelphia, Furness had used exposed iron trusses on the exterior of the Pennsylvania Academy of the Fine Arts, threaded giant tie-rods through iron bolts on the sides of the Undine Barge Club, and built public waiting rooms of steel and glass for the Baltimore and Ohio Railroad station on the banks of the Schuylkill. From the outset, Furness demonstrated his belief in the importance of the present by incorporating the materials of modern industry throughout his early works. But more directly connected to the Philadelphia industrial culture was Furness's ability to make buildings "out of his head," in his pupil Louis Sullivan's phrase. This approach, which represented function through form, linked his design method to an approach that had evolved among Philadelphia mechanical engineers before the Civil War. Certainly by the 1850s and perhaps earlier, designers in Philadelphia's machine shops and architectural studios had established a modern "organic" basis for design for machine tools and locomotives, the chief products of the giant factories of the city. Indeed, the phrases by which the functional values of modern design are still identified first appeared in Philadelphia publications on manufacturing. This quality was frequently ascribed by

critics from outside Philadelphia to a rejection of artistic values rooted in some surviving Quaker anti-aesthetic. It is more likely that Philadelphians, who were exposed by their occupations to the progressive values of the industrial culture, saw in functional or organic design the direct expression of the forces of the modern world.[36]

Furness would have been exposed to these ideas for most of his life. By the 1850s, local manufacturing publications and railroad journals described a regional aesthetic based on values developed in the city's machine shops. Edward Freedley commented in *Philadelphia and Its Manufactures* that the Philadelphia origins of machinery was obvious to knowledgeable observers because of its design:

> The machine work executed in the leading establishments of Philadelphia, we may remark in conclusion, is distinguished by certain characteristics, which enable a competent judge to pronounce with confidence upon the source of its construction, or in other words to detect a Philadelphia-made machine by the "earmarks." Excellence of material, solidity, an admirable fitting of the joints, *a just proportion and arrangement of the parts, and a certain thoroughness and genuineness*, are qualities that pervade the machine work executed in Philadelphia, and distinguish it from all other American-made machinery.[37] (my emphasis)

Linking concepts of genuineness with ideas about form and proportion, Freedley implied a distinct regional approach that typified the work of local machine designers.

Nearly a generation later, in 1876, the British judges at the Centennial Exhibition reached similar conclusions about the aesthetic means and intentions of the Philadelphia engineers who designed the locomotives exhibited by the Baldwin Locomotive Works:

> The painting and general finish of the engine is planned with a view to quiet and harmonious effect,

and is based upon the principle that the purpose for which a locomotive is used does not admit of any merely ornamental devices: but that its beauty, so far as it may have any, should depend upon *good proportions and thorough adaptation of the various parts to their uses.*[38] (my emphasis)

The same judges especially singled out for praise the machine work of William Sellers (a leading Penn trustee from the 1860s), enthusing that his display was

remarkable [for] . . . originality, without parallel in the past history of international exhibits. Besides it is thoroughly national in its characteristics. Every piece is worthy of an award, each one being of the highest standard in its particular class. The na-

tional characteristics included the nice fitting and precision, *the beautiful outlines that are imparted to each structure by the correct proportions that have been worked out in the determining of strength and form and the disposal of material to take full share of the duty.*[39] (my emphasis)

What overseas judges viewed as American qualities were in fact Philadelphia qualities.[40] Sellers stated as his own rule of thumb that a "machine looks right if it is right," implying a direct relationship between form and function. Philadelphia's role in the develop-

••••••••••••••••••••••••••••••••••••••
William Sellers and Co., "Planing Machine." Masterpieces of the International Exposition, *vol. 3 (1880), p. 18.*

ment of the modern aesthetic was still remembered by British engineers well into the twentieth century. Joseph Roe's appraisal in 1915 of Sellers as one of the great innovators in machine design was quoted half a century later by W. H. Mayall:

> Almost from the first, Sellers cut loose from the accepted designs of the day. He was among the first to realize that red paint, beads and mouldings and architectural embellishments were false in machine design. He introduced the "machine-gray" paint which has become universal, made the machine follow the functions to be performed.[41]

Thus, half a century before the Bauhaus and International Modernism swept Europe, ideas central to modern aesthetics were to be found in the products of the machine shop culture of Philadelphia where they were observed by European visitors to the Centennial and transplanted across the Atlantic.

The phrases that defined the nineteenth-century Philadelphia approach to industrial design could have been written in the twentieth century: "a just proportion and arrangement of the parts, and a certain thoroughness and genuineness"; "beauty, so far as it may have any, should depend upon good proportions and thorough adaptation of the various parts to their uses"; "beautiful outlines that are imparted to each structure by the correct proportions that have been worked out in the determining of strength and form and the disposal of material to take full share of the duty." Each represented the idea that form and function were related. That such ideas would be rooted in the machine culture of Philadelphia was no accident, for here there was the necessary combination of a literate and widely read cultural elite who shaped mechanical engineering and industrial production in the progressive environment of the scientific age.

Frank Furness responded to the forces of the present as developed by Philadelphia industrialists because he had been exposed to the progressive ideals of his father's closest friend, Ralph Waldo Emerson. Nearly two generations before the Centennial, Emerson had staked out the position that the United States would and should develop its own architecture that would represent its evolving culture by expressing the forces of modern industry and the variety of nature.[42] Because of the city's unusual industry-based elite, this idea reached fruition in Philadelphia in the generations after the Civil War far more than in any of the other east coast cities. Sustained by the Quaker value system that encouraged its members to engage in useful and tangible work, Philadelphia industrialists were at home in the modern world of machines and engineering. For Furness and the equally important but more engineering-oriented Wilson Brothers, regional design came to be rooted in the dynamizing forces of industry and a new machine-based aesthetic more than in the collective memory of conventional culture.

Furness's Penn Commissions

Between 1885 and 1892, Furness's firm designed the new Veterinary Hospital on an unopened portion of Pine Street behind the University of Pennsylvania Hospital (1885, demolished 1902), the new morgue for the hospital, the University Library (1888), and the designs for a new Alumni Auditorium (1892), which if executed would have spared future Penn generations both Horace Trumbauer's Irvine Auditorium of 1926 and Meyerson Hall. Furness's revolutionary approach to design was immediately apparent in the new Veterinary Hospital. Instead of the compact and symmetrical forms of conventional hospitals, Furness combined stone, brick, and steel into functionally expressive volumes that represented the multiple tasks of the building. In the case of a veterinary hospital, these included stables for large animals, offices, and an oversized operating amphitheater with a retractable skylight and a horseshoe-shaped operating table. Instead of forcing an illogical symmetry onto the plan of the building, Furness brought these elements together with the same discordance of forms—and the same expression of function—that mechanical engi-

Veterinary Hospital, c. 1885. UPA.

••

neers were giving to contemporary locomotives and other great machines.

The University Library

Where the Veterinary Hospital and the morgue were on the periphery of the campus, behind the hospital, the new University Library took center stage on the main campus. It was central to Pepper's belief in the importance of the new experience-based means of training that was appearing in German Universities, and nearly simultaneously in the more advanced medical schools—including Penn. In 1874, during Stillé's tenure, Dr. Pepper had helped design Penn's teaching hospital—the world's first—in conjunction with a medical school, where its faculty served as staff. Four years later, laboratory practice had been added to the medical curriculum in the Hare Building. By the early 1880s Penn students were calling for a full-time librarian, so that they could "use the librarian, which by the way is as important as using the library."[43] In 1883

a report signed by the new librarian, James G. Barnwell, Provost Pepper, and chairman of the library committee Horace Howard Furness asked the Philadelphia business community to assist in enlarging the University Library collections, as a "record of the busy work of the world today, and within the walls of a library, it should be garnered, where students can use it and learn the methods of original investigations and research."[44] These new materials and its host of new users quickly overwhelmed the single room set aside for library purposes in College Hall.

In 1887 Frank Furness's brother Horace was asked to chair the new Library Committee.[45] The formation of a separate Library Committee to serve as the planning and decision-making group followed the usual practice of Penn's Board of Trustees, placing the project in the hands of the trustees who were most involved with it. The Board's use of committees for

Furness, Evans and Co., sketch of Alumni Auditorium.
Photozincograph, 9 May 1890. UPA.

executive purposes marked its ongoing direction of the day-to-day activities of the University. The Library Committee was charged with gathering information that would be turned over to an architect selected by its members, "before the architect selected is asked to do any designing." The design, in other words, was to be kept under the control of the committee, rather than left to the aesthetic decisions by the architect.[46] In the same meeting, when the committee adopted its policy on design, it immediately recommended that the chairman's brother Frank be hired as architect.[47] That the University's business would be conducted behind the private doors of its trustees, or that it would award important projects without competition to a family member or close business associate of the committee chairman or the donor, violates the standards of our age. But, in nineteenth-

century Philadelphia and other American cities, nepotism was described as "a form of paternal pride in all successful institutions."[48] Fortunately, the results justified the means.

As for other projects that deeply concerned Pepper, the University began the library project by hiring the principal consultants of the day, Melvil Dewey of the Columbia University Library Bureau and the recent inventor of the Dewey Decimal System of cataloging, and Justin Winsor, head librarian of the nation's largest academic collection at Harvard. With their advice, Furness provided plans that delighted Dewey, who reported in a letter to Pepper:

The plans I sketched with Mr. Furness late that evening, seem to me better than any college library has yet adopted. I should like to see your building by all odds the best model for similar institutions to follow and it will be a great pleasure if I can be of any service in that direction.[49]

The Poetry of the Present

When Penn's new library was completed, professional librarians immediately judged it to be the most successful building of its kind in the United States. Despite the lack of practicality of historical formalism for the modern library, most American architects were simultaneously turning toward the historicism of McKim, Mead and White's white classicism or Henry Hobson Richardson's granite Romanesque. By contrast, Furness's University Library was designed in the fiery red brick of industrial Philadelphia and at first glance seemed to have more in common with the picturesque Gothic of the past than the symmetrical volumes of contemporary Beaux-Arts classicism. As a result, the fundamental originality of Furness's design was missed by hostile contemporary critics—and by most later historians as well.

Like the earlier Veterinary Hospital, the library was a conflation of towers, chimneys, skylighted rooms, and foundry-like clerestoried halls that recalled the

Furness, Evans and Co., "Design of the Library, University of Pennsylvania Library," 1888. Ink on linen. Architectural Archives.

•••••••••••••••••••••••••••••••••••••••

mills of Philadelphia in the direct expression of their various purposes. More remarkable was the plan. With its generous entrance hall and broad stair leading to the upper level auditorium, and its axis of entrance leading directly to the main doors and through to the card catalog, the library plan was conceived along lines of production rather than the conventions of public space. In a similar fashion, the librarians' side of the building was planned so that new books were brought in from the street at the northeast corner, proceeded south through the cataloging department (one wall of which was the card catalog, whose drawers could be pulled from either the librarians' or the public's side), before finally reaching the book stack. The stack was designed to be extendable, giving the library the self-adjusting character of Philadelphia

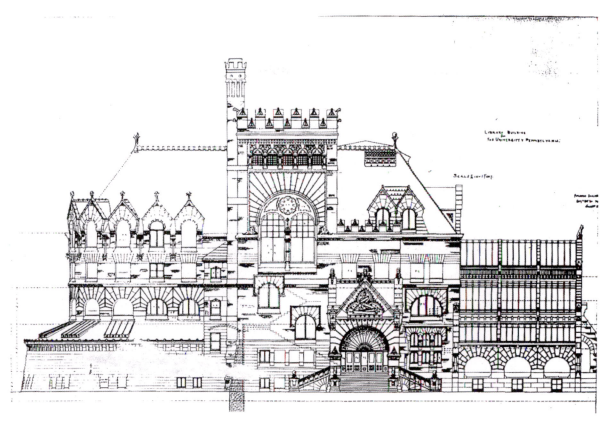

Furness, Evans and Co., west elevation, University
Library, 1888. Ink on linen. Negative of lost photostat.
G. Thomas collection, Architectural Archives.

••••••••••••••••••••••••••••••••••••••

machines! By solving the problem of the growth of the collection that overwhelms most library buildings even today, Furness created one of the seminal masterpieces of his time. An industrial iconography of gearlike crockets, piston-like columns, and sawblade-like brackets overlay the tough mass-produced materials of the building, celebrating the industrial might of the Philadelphia region. Though there are hints of history in its gargoyles, and students quickly noted its similarity to the architect's contemporary train stations, it functioned superbly as the University Library, surviving a tenfold increase in the number of books and an eightfold increase in students before it was finally replaced in the 1960s.[50]

That the library was a reflection of conviction rather than an aberration is evident from other com-missions of the Pepper years. While the library was under construction, the University hired the Wilson Brothers, the nation's preeminent architecture/engineering firm of the day, to build a power plant to the south of the library, where Irvine now stands. It also was of red brick with a raised clerestory for light and ventilation like a great machine assembly room, to which was attached a towering industrial smokestack that gave the 34th Street side of the campus the appearance of a giant foundry. Adjacent to the power plant, the same architects designed a massive brick engineering laboratory that looked like a typical industrial office block tucked against its mill or foundry. It was attached to the power plant so that Penn's engineering students could use its machinery for investigations (providing evidence that students were either more trustworthy or less imaginative than later generations). There was no clearer evidence of the type of practical education that was being sought for Penn's students.

Other science buildings that dated from the Pepper years were in the same vein. Collins and Autenrieth's Lea Institute of Hygiene stood across 34th Street from the new library, which was of red brick with terra cotta ornament and a roofline that bristled with ventilators and ducts. At its dedication, its director, John Shaw Billings, M.D., found merit in its simplicity as an expression of its purpose as "a workshop of the future." He noted that, unlike earlier buildings of the campus, it was "planned from within outward, which is why it looks like a laboratory and not a castle."[51] Its close proximity to the engineering laboratories across the street formed the basis for the growth of a science precinct on the east side of the campus. The new Biology Hall that was intended to serve the medical students was of a similarly utilitarian appearance, and was located near the medical and veterinary facilities, reinforcing the location of the life sciences on the south side of the campus.

In 1894, when the University of Pennsylvania's leadership passed from a scientist to a financier and businessman, Furness was fired and replaced as campus architect by the firm of Cope and Stewardson. Their designs in the more conventional Academic Gothic mode became Penn's twentieth-century image, marking Philadelphia's shift toward the national main-

....

Power Plant and Engineering School, looking northwest, c. 1892. UPA.

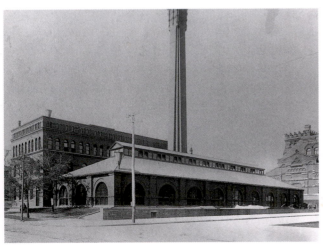

stream of historically-based design. Albert Kelsey (C 1895), a veteran of Furness's office who had continued to maintain contact with another Furness pupil, Louis Sullivan, was outraged at the shift of direction.[52] Noting that Penn's first graduates had been among the leaders of the American Revolution, he asked about the effects such historicism might have on the young students working with "x-ray light" in modern labs of the campus "But what inspiration might they not impart if they reflected the poetry of the present as well as they suggest the romance of an alien past!" At the end of the century, as historical eclecticism came to dominate American architectural practice, buildings such as these in the heart of its campus gave Penn an industrial appearance that prompted attacks by effete critics from the centers of history and cultural continuity with Europe. Among the kindest descriptions that the library received was a "fortified greenhouse than which nothing more grotesque could be imagined."[53] It would be half a century before the library was appreciated again. In 1957, when Louis Sullivan's student Frank Lloyd Wright visited Penn to see the library, he proclaimed, "It is the work of an artist."[54]

Pepper's Contribution

Penn's hiring of Frank Furness and the Wilson Brothers reflected the values of Philadelphia's post-Civil War leadership and its relation to the progressive engineering and industrial culture from which they came. There can be no doubt that it was the Pepper era that laid the foundation in research and applied science that came to characterize the University and was reflected in what can be seen as an experimental and pragmatically modern architecture. William Pepper, Jr., M.D. wrote his own credit line: "After the days of Benjamin Franklin, the University went to sleep. It slept in peace till I came one hundred years after. When I came it woke up and there was trouble—and there has been trouble ever since."[55] Under Provost Harrison, many of the thirteen departments founded during Pepper's provostship received new buildings, while the facilities that enlivened the campus—the

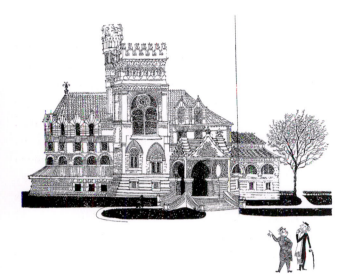

Alfred Bendiner showing Frank Lloyd Wright the old "Penn Library." Bendiner's Philadelphia, *p. 14.*

student dormitory, the student union, and Franklin Field—also were constructed. But each of those structures would be designed by architects from a new generation whose values were shaped by the national culture rather than by the industrial world that was already losing out in attracting the children of the post-Civil War engineers to its factories and workshops.

The last work of the Civil War generation on the campus was a memorial to Provost Pepper that was erected adjacent to the west wing of the University Museum and has since been moved to the rear of College Hall. Although Provost Harrison had already shifted to a new generation of architects, Pepper's statue was the work of Karl Bitter, a sculptor who had worked with Frank Furness on the Broad Street Station and on the office building for Provost Harrison's partner, William West Frazier, Furness's fellow cavalry officer in the Rush's Lancers of three decades earlier. Bitter's piece is somberly elegiac, depicting Pepper in weighty academic robes, head sinking toward his chest but with his hand raised in one final

command. It was an appropriate memorial to a generation that believed in its ability to shape its own future through its effort.

On the statue's base is a list of Pepper's achievements that is as astonishing now as it must have been when it was first cast in bronze. Pepper had established thirteen departments and programs that spanned the contemporary realm of human endeavor. Listed in Francis Newton Thorpe's *Benjamin Franklin and the University of Pennsylvania*, they were the Department of Finance and Economy (the Wharton School), 1881; the Department of Philosophy (Graduate), 1883; the Department (School) of Veterinary Medicine, 1882; the Department (School) of Biology, 1883; the Department of Physical Education, 1883; the Department of Archaeology and Paleontology, 1889; the Department (School) of Hygiene, 1891; the Department for Women (Graduate School), 1891; the School of American History and Institutions, 1891; the School of Architecture, 1891; the School for Nurses in the University Hospital, 1888; the Veterinary Hospital, 1883; the Marine Laboratory at Sea Isle City, 1891; and, finally, the Wistar Institute, 1891. Also listed were the new University Library, the Free Museum of Science and Art, and the city's Commercial Museum and the Free Library system—all of which Pepper found time to supervise from the provost's office while he continued to run his own professional practice.[56] The University had been transformed by William Pepper's guiding vision. That Pepper and Stillé had hired local architects who had served the industrial culture was telling. As leaders of the University of Pennsylvania in the heady years after the Centennial, they had hired Furness and the Wilson Brothers because their buildings represented the independent industry-based work-culture that dominated in Philadelphia and thus were the appropriate visage for Philadelphia's University.

Chas. C. H

THE ACADEMIC STAGE: HARRISON'S VISION

The Past and the Present

Although William Pepper and Charles Custis Harrison were both born into old Philadelphia families and graduated from the University of Pennsylvania in the same class of 1862, in their personalities and in their worlds of work they were very nearly opposites. Where Pepper had been a skilled scientist, a professional, a theoretician about education, and a leader of Philadelphia's reform movement, Harrison was an adept businessman and a skilled politician who curried favors and donations from all sides of an increasingly fragmented city. Above all, in an age of great showmen from P. T. Barnum to Teddy Roosevelt, Harrison was the greatest showman to lead Penn since Franklin.

Charles Custis Harrison had other assets. Like Pepper, he was independently wealthy and had been a board member before he became acting provost. He had been a founder of the Franklin Sugar Company, turning it into the nation's largest refiner of sugar and one of the principal businesses of Philadelphia. But, as the head of his own business, he was also used to

....

Provost Charles Custis Harrison, 1905. Photo: Haeseler. UPA.

making his own decisions. In his "Autobiography" Harrison proudly recalled firing Frank Furness, who had been the campus architect during the 1880s. Describing Furness as "intensely interested in his own architectural views," Harrison stated that "as I was obliged to raise the money, I would like architects with whom I could work happily."[1] So long as Harrison was provost, he would function like the president of a closely held corporation. His vision would provide the direction for the University, and his choices would define the style and appearance of the campus.

Few American college leaders knew the institution that they would head more intimately than Harrison. He had attended the University when it was lodged in its small Whig structures on Ninth Street and graduated at the head of his class in 1862. Unlike most of his predecessors as provost, who had been trained for the ministry or for a career in education, his life was rooted in business. Harrison's role at Penn began in 1876, when, without his prior knowledge, he was elected a trustee of the University. In 1886, after the death of John Welsh, he was appointed head of the Committee on Ways and Means, making him aware of the urgent financial needs of the institution. After selling the Franklin Sugar Company in 1892, Harrison was asked to serve as acting provost while the board sought a

The past & the present
1898
Mr Pepper ?
Chas Harrison } Provost of University of Pen

*Frank Furness, "The Past and the Present," sketch of
Provosts Harrison and Pepper, c. 1895. Private collection.
Roy D. Bassett, "Punch Bowl Portraits—Our Santa
Claus."* Punchbowl *III, December 1907. UPA.*

••••••••••••••••••••••••••••••••••••

replacement for retiring Provost Pepper. It was a
position to which he quickly warmed.[2] Over the next
generation he would pour vast sums of his personal
wealth into the University while relying also on his
acquaintance with the leaders of Philadelphia industry, whose resources he carefully recorded in his "little
black book," the information in which became the basis
for him to pry additional gifts for his University.

Harrison soon saw that for the University to grow
it had to escape its parochial limits by reaching out

beyond the ever-diminishing aristocracy of the old
mercantile elite and the early industrial meritocracy
to the new financiers whose self-aggrandizement
troubled old Philadelphians. Old Philadelphia had an
undisguised contempt for the newly wealthy, but
Harrison made them a prime objective of his fund-
raising. Harrison's embrace of the *nouveaux riches*,
many of whom had made wealth through their political connections, incurred the contempt of Lincoln
Steffens, who in his muckraking series *The Shame of the
Cities* labeled Philadelphia "corrupt and contented."
Steffens singled out for criticism a certain unnamed
provost "who declined to join the revolt" against the
corrupt political machine of Matthew Quay.[3] There is
no evidence that Harrison ever flinched from the
disagreeable aspects of his duty as provost. Creating
new boards for organizations such as the Free Museum of Science and Art, he brought the newly wealthy
into the circle of University leadership. Simultaneously,
he worked out deals with the city to swap land for full
scholarships for poor but able scholars, marking the
beginning of the end of Penn as a clublike institution
of the old elite.

The Evolving University Community

Even as Harrison reached out to the larger community of Philadelphia, the makeup of Penn's student
body was beginning its slow, steady turn toward the
diverse international population of the present. This is
not to say that Penn suddenly became a model of
cultural diversity on the modern order, one whose
members completely embraced the broad spectrum of
Philadelphia's population. Though immensely different from what it had been before the Centennial, the
University of Pennsylvania remained an institution
that was very much a part of nineteenth-century
America. Just as that era's triumphs became part of
Penn's heritage, so too did its faults. Though the
success of the region's industrial culture made it easy
to overlook, in the background lurked the dangers of
class separation and discrimination. These problems
were visible in the social fragmentation of Philadel-

OUR SANTA CLAUS

phia's neighborhoods as well as in its institutions.

Throughout most of the nineteenth century, the University, like its peer institutions across the nation, was largely under the control of a single elite class who maintained their power and status by controlling membership. Class consciousness and its consequences have been a pervasive theme of the historical interpretation of the city from the middle of the nineteenth century. It forms the central intrigue of Philip Barry's *A Philadelphia Story* and was the crux of the crisis in Christopher Morley's *Kitty Foyle*. Class was central to the interpretation of the city in Nathaniel Burt's *Perennial Philadelphians* and E. Digby Baltzell's portrait of *Philadelphia Gentlemen*. Early cracks in the monolithic social class structure at Penn were observed by Cornelius Weygandt (C 1891), a long-time professor of English at the University. Many years after graduating from Penn, he mused on the changing undergraduate population, its reflection of the ever-evolving city, and its implications for teaching:

It was in the early 1880's that the old order in America began to be changed by the coming in of southern and eastern Europeans.

At college most of the boys were of the old stock. We had no Italians in my class, no Slavs, no Greeks, no Armenians, and but one Russian Jew, Feldman, a man older than most of us and of exceptional ability. We were mostly sons of people in fairly comfortable circumstances. There were a few boys from poor families whose brains had won them scholarships. There was a solidarity of knowledge and of experience and of prejudices such as is far to seek in any American university today. We had nearly all of us been brought up on the King James version of the Bible, Mother Goose, *Pilgrim's Progress*, *Paradise Lost* and Shakespeare. We were much easier to teach than the classes of today [1946], classes in which there is no common denominator of culture.[4]

Weygandt was only partly correct in his memory of the members of his class. Certainly many of his class-

mates, including most who were his circle of friends, were from "old stock." Their names are woven through the tapestry of old Philadelphia history and appear as street names and on the rosters of old Philadelphia clubs: Ashhurst, Roberts, Catherwood, Griscom, McKean, White, Wood, and Yarnall are among the familiar surnames and ancestral middle names that dotted his class.[5] Identifiable by their fraternal affiliations with Delta Phi, Delta Psi, Psi Upsilon, and Zeta Psi, they form a distinct and important subgroup of the class of 1891 as recorded in the University of Pennsylvania's *General Alumni Catalogue* of 1917. At the end of the century, these private fraternity houses enabled the wealthy elite to maintain barriers of isolation between themselves and the changing University community.[6] Also among the student body of Weygandt's era were members of the city's new intelligentsia, including Horace Howard Furness's son Horace Jr., and there was even a Benjamin Franklin (though he was no relation to the original and had first attended with the class of 1884).

But despite Weygandt's claims Arthur Feldman was far from being the only member of a minority subgroup in his class—he was but one of many students who came from different backgrounds from those of the traditional Penn students. Baron Hisaya Iwasaki returned to Tokyo and applied his Science degree to building Japan's industrial base.[7] Samuel Clifford Boston was listed in the *General Alumni Catalogue* as the "First Colored graduate in Biology," but was also noted for his athletic contributions as "quarterback, Biology football team; centrefield baseball." He received his M.D. from the University in 1898 and worked in the emerging field of public health; according to the *General Alumni Catalogue* his original research had identified "a new Hydra (red) on under surface of water-lily leaves; also found a parasite in the intestine of the common red house roach."[8] Though Jews had been discriminated against by many portions of American and Philadelphia society, they had found a safe haven in the University from its eighteenth-century beginnings. In the class of 1891 there were more Jews than were apparently known to or remembered by Weygandt. Most notable was certainly Jules Mastbaum, whose collection of Rodin sculptures now graces the Benjamin Franklin Parkway and who became the great impresario of movie palaces in Philadelphia in the early twentieth century while also serving on the board of the Horn and Hardart Automat Company.

Weygandt also overlooked the nineteen women who received certificates in 1891 from the University. Many excelled at Penn, including Josephine Ancona, who would win a scholarship in 1894 and graduate with a B.S. in 1895. Emma Boone, Mary Schively, and Mary Smith took courses that later led to medical degrees from Woman's Medical College; Catharine Stevens received "1st prize junior yr, best anatomical preparations." Others studied and later taught music. Many of these women were members of the Kappa Gamma sorority and must have had an obvious presence on the campus during Weygandt's term. Indeed, women received more than 10 percent of the degrees and certificates awarded by Penn in 1891.

By the last decade of the nineteenth century, Penn's student body was closer in its mix of students to that of the present than it was to the pre-Civil War roster, but the architectural setting was less accommodating to these changes. Women were excluded from most of the male-dominated recreational facilities; it would be another generation before social facilities of any type were established for women. The first fraternities had been built in the vicinity of the campus in the 1890s, but with the exception of Psi Upsilon's Japanese baron their members were closer in social background to the Board of Trustees than to the city or the evolving student body. Fraternities segregated by class, race, and religion. With the admission of a broader class of students to the University, the wealthier elites used private resources to build houses where they were able to maintain their social hierarchy and separateness; the few fraternities that accepted minorities lacked resources to build their own houses until the twentieth century.[9]

Marketing the University

In industrial and still Quaker-leaning Philadelphia, the University had attained local prominence by producing skilled and capable engineers, doctors, and lawyers. Apart from its professional schools Penn still had little to distinguish itself from nearby and slightly smaller colleges such as Swarthmore and Haverford. Nor had Penn made the changes necessary to be perceived as a great national institution. Harrison resolved to change this. As a businessman he was prepared for the new role of the college leader as chief marketer, and he could see that marketing a college was a tricky business. In the previous decade Provost Pepper had demanded the best university library in the nation and had been rewarded with a two-page spread in *Harper's Weekly*—the equivalent of a cover story in today's *Time* or *Newsweek*. A few years later, when Harrison invited President McKinley to speak at Penn's University Day on Washington's birthday, long a special occasion at the University, the cover of *Harper's* depicted a view of the rear ends of horses carrying the mounted officers of the First City Troop drawn up to greet McKinley at the porch of the University Library.[10] The trick, as Harrison well knew from marketing sugar, was to keep the product on the nation's front pages, and to do that the University had to produce front-page news. The president's visit was such an event, but it could hardly be orchestrated every year.

Harrison realized that in America nothing succeeds like success—but success was maddeningly hard to schedule. In the Stillé and Pepper years, learned lectures and symposia had enlarged the University's circle. The new provost may have suspected that research and invention by the faculty alone would not attract regular coverage in the popular press, and it too was unpredictable. The desired acclaim would come from the aspects of the University that interested the rest of the city, outside academic circles. Under Harrison, the University reached out to this public with the pageants and festivals of college life. To accomplish this, Harrison first built athletic fields

WRECK OF THE "MAINE."—ZOLA TRIAL.—SPANISH NAVY.

HARPER'S WEEKLY

JOURNAL OF CIVILIZATION

Vol. XLII.—No. 2150.
Copyright, 1898, by Harper & Brothers.
All Rights Reserved.

NEW YORK, SATURDAY, MARCH 5, 1898.

TEN CENTS A COPY.
FOUR DOLLARS A YEAR.

WASHINGTON'S BIRTHDAY CELEBRATION AT THE UNIVERSITY OF PENNSYLVANIA, PHILADELPHIA.
PRESIDENT McKINLEY'S RECEPTION AT THE LIBRARY BUILDING.—[SEE PAGE 235.]

and a student union and then helped create the events that filled them. Though there were certainly other needs on the campus, Harrison's initial project laid the foundations for the nation's greatest urban football stadium, Franklin Field. On its opening day in April 1895, it housed the Penn Relays, to this day the nation's premier amateur track event. Harrison's decision to make sports central to the University was appropriate to an era when college football even preoccupied the nation's presidents. As one educator at the end of the century put it, it was common knowledge that every

> boy wishes to enter the college that has the strongest foot-ball team. It is not a young ladies' game, and it has driven the milksop out of American college life. The American college that tries to live without games like foot-ball is working against serious difficulties.[11]

A decade later, at the dedication of Penn's Towne Engineering Building, the creator of the principles of scientific management, Frederick Winslow Taylor, used football as a model for the type of training and teamwork that was the framework for modern business. Comparing education to football, and the student's advisor to the coach, Taylor suggested that the goal-oriented training of athletics was one of

> the most useful elements in the college course, for two reasons: First, because they are actuated by a truly serious purpose, and second because they are there given, not the elective idea of doing what they want to, but co-operation of the same general character which they will be called upon to practice in after life.[12]

In a blue-collar city, athletics provided an obvious

••••••••••••••••••••••••••••••••••••••

"Washington's Birthday Celebration at the University of Pennsylvania, Philadelphia." Cover, Harper's Weekly, 5 March 1898. UPA.

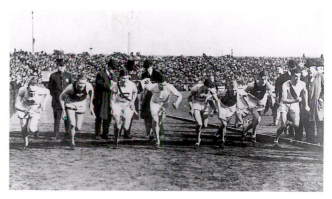

Penn Relays, April 1895. UPA.

••••••••••••••••••••••••••••••••••••••

route to attract attention, with victories fueling the city's newfound glow of affection for Penn. During the mid-1890s Penn football teams won thirty-five games in a row with the 1895 team winning all their games by a combined score of 480 to 24, provoking *Harper's Weekly* (a New-York dominated publication) to charge that Penn had devised

> a professional method of preparing her football eleven ... [because] Pennsylvania cares less for the spirit of the contest and more for the victory than any other of the colleges.[13]

After a generation of losses to the teams of Harvard, Yale, and Princeton, there was a certain irony in the surfacing of this claim only after Penn had finally trounced Princeton. Penn's athletic association leaders responded to the charges:

> Our medical advisors, as well as our Faculty Committee believe that the men are safer physically and better students as well as better football players for limiting rather than abolishing this preliminary [practice] period.
>
> We think moreover, that the game itself, as developed in this country, has a value to the whole student body, as encouraging and fostering manly attributes, which justifies this slight extension of the football season as a means of promoting the scientific character of the game.[14]

A Sculptor of the Gridiron

HEISMAN PREDICTS WINNER FOR PENN

Former Coach of Red and Blue Has Praise for Lou Young

Penn should put a formiable football team on the field during the coming season. John W. Heisman, former head coach at Franklin Field, and now mentor of the Washington and Jefferson team, voiced this opinion yesterday at the Camden Armory, where he was a judge of track events at the second annual indoor meet of the New Jersey division of the Pennsylvania Railroad.

"I expect Lou Young to produce a fine team," Heisman said. "He has the personality, the spirit is there and there are a number of good players back from last year in addition to the material from an excellent freshman team.

"Young is an earnest, hard worker, indefatigable and should get the results with the combination of veterans and freshman. Prospects are unusually bright for Franklin Field. I cannot wish anything but the best of success for Young, who was a great help to me while I was coaching at the University."

All Set for Action

The former Red and Blue tutor, beam-

Winnie King, "A Sculptor of the Gridiron," cartoon of John W. Heisman, 1923. UPA.

Signed by George Wharton Pepper, John C. Bell, J. William White, M.D., and H. Laussat Geyelin, all former athletes, devoted alumni, and avid students of the game, it denoted the rise of the culture of athletics and its domination by interested alumni. It would be these men who shaped the alumni boards and who drove many of the initiatives of the early twentieth-century University.

As football became the great fall spectacle of American colleges, Harrison assembled a football power led by coach George W. Woodruff (L 1895), who had played on the Yale teams of late 1880s. Under Woodruff's "scientific" coaching Penn soared. Another graduate of the law school was John W. Heisman (L 1892), who was permitted to play on the varsity football team in 1890 and 1891 because Penn made no distinction between graduate and undergraduates for intercollegiate athletic competition, a situation that would continue into the twentieth century. Heisman went on to a career in coaching that brought him back to the University in the 1920s, and of course it is his name that is now on the New York Athletic Club's trophy for the best college football player of the year. Penn's domination of the turn-of-the-century game is evident from the selection of another Penn player, John Outland (M 1902), as the namesake for the Maxwell Club's Outland Trophy for the premier line-

Franklin Field, looking east, Thanksgiving Day, 1926. Photo: Berry and Homer. UPA.

••••••••••••••••••••••••••••••••••••

man in the game. In the early twentieth century, as the modern Olympic movement got underway, it was Penn athletes who won the gold medals for the United States—including a memorable gold by Truxton Hare (C 1901) in the 1900 Tug of War. The growth of Franklin Field and the sports complex attests to the importance of athletics at the turn of the last century.

Changing of the Guard: Trustees

Just as Harrison represented a new type of individually powerful provost, his Board of Trustees was also evolving toward the character of the modern board,

which is less regional and represents a broader cross-section of American achievement. Though the trustees at the end of the Harrison era were typically drawn from Philadelphia professions and industry as they had been half a century before, an increasing number had attended the University on its new West Philadelphia campus, had participated in the new rituals of Ivy Days, had worn the red and blue in sporting events, had joined fraternities, and were true Penn men.[15] Like their predecessors, most lived in the vicinity of Rittenhouse Square, and the majority were Episcopalians, Republicans, and members of old Philadelphia clubs such as the Rittenhouse and Philadelphia Clubs. But, unlike the early Pepper boards, more of Harrison's twentieth-century appointees were lawyers, doctors, and financiers rather than engineers and manufactur-ers. By national standards they were still doers as opposed to speculators or theologians, but some were dependent on inherited wealth and as a group they had less contact with Philadelphia industry. In 1916 a board member, William Augustus Redding (L 1876), would be selected to represent the New York alumni; soon thereafter he was one of the founders of New York's University of Pennsylvania Alumni Associa-tion, which established New York's University of Pennsylvania Club.

In 1927 the board membership of twenty-four (as originally prescribed by Franklin), was enlarged to forty, and new ten-year term and alumni memberships were added to the old trustee-for-life category. An Executive Committee was empowered to oversee de-velopment, property, and finance and to act for the entire board between meetings. Eight committees were established for oversight of the various Univer-sity programs including fine arts, the law school, teacher training, engineering, medicine, and the lib-eral arts.[16] So that the Executive Committee could meet as frequently as required, its members tended to be Philadelphians, maintaining local control even though outsiders were admitted to the board. Simul-taneously, the new committee structure made the liberal arts college but one of many competing inter-ests for University support. By that change, the Col-lege was once again diminished at the expense of the graduate and professional schools.[17]

In their affection for the University, for its new customs, and above all for its sporting establishment, the new board reflected Provost Harrison's perspec-tive on marketing the University. Joined together by the bond of competition, the trustees became a lobby-ing and fund-raising group for expansion of the ath-letic community. Over the next quarter of a century, leading up to the Depression, the athletic campus would grow faster than any other division of the campus with Franklin Field rising in three phases (1895, 1915, 1922) to a size that eventually made it the largest double-decked stadium in the world. With

Weightman Hall (1903), the J. William White Train-ing House (1903–5), the Hutchinson Gymnasium (1925), and the Palestra (1925), as well as various land-intensive sports fields, Penn's investment in ath-letics was immense and a true barometer of the board's interest. In a world of predatory capitalism, affiliation with an institution that was triumphant on the field of sport was a badge of honor in the University clubs that were established in the hearts of America's great cities in the early twentieth century.

Building a Campus

With new sports facilities under construction, Harrison next turned his attention to building his vision of the University. The organization of the University Mu-seum had been begun by Provost Pepper, who pro-posed to place its collections in an upper room of the new library. After University archaeological expedi-tions made spectacular finds in the Middle East, plans were developed to build the world's largest anthropo-logical museum on land acquired from the city on the east side of Penn's campus. The new building's con-struction was led by Provost Harrison, who, anticipat-ing Daniel Burnham's battle cry for planning cities, "Make no little plans," proclaimed, "it was easier dealing with large men to do large things than small ones."[18] The drawings his team of architects produced for the new museum were for a building that would have been the largest museum in the world, some three times larger than the present complex. Despite his ambitions, Harrison was enough of a pragmatist to suggest planning the building "in such a way that portions might be erected from time to time, each portion being complete in itself."

Harrison continued in the same vein with the am-bitious scheme for the University dormitories, which eventually stretched for blocks but began as a small triangle at 38th Street. While the dorms were being planned, Harrison held a student competition to de-sign the nation's first student union (see Chapter 1) which, in another public relations coup, was judged by the premier architects of the day. These buildings became the focus of the celebrations that filled the calendar of college life, keeping the University in the public eye.

The choice of architects for these projects was another matter. Harrison's own offices in Philadelphia and his mansion in the country were both designed by Frank Furness, but while late twentieth-century scholars value Furness's architecture, critics trained in the history-based methods of the Beaux-Arts at the end of the nineteenth century were horrified at his free design. As architectural training and taste turned toward the revival of historical forms and style, Furness's

•••••••••••••••••••••••••••••••••••

Franklin Building, 12th Street, looking east, 1894–95. The office building, designed for Harrison by Furness, Evans and Co., was demolished c. 1940. Historical Society of Pennsylvania.

original work based on the machine aesthetic and, by extension, the works of most Philadelphia's post-Civil War architects were mauled by one critic after another. Ralph Adams Cram, the patriarch of New England designers, summarized the national view of Philadelphia's architectural history in one sentence:

> Blessed with an early architecture of the various best type developed on this continent, it sank first to a condition of stolid stupidity almost unparalleled, then produced at a bound a group of men of abundant vitality [the Furness generation], but the very worst taste ever recorded in art.[19]

In another publication, Cram singled out Furness for contempt:

> Consider two buildings, for example, chosen almost at random: the library of the University of Pennsylvania and the Unitarian Meeting House in Chestnut Street. At first, one sees only inflexible, unvarying bad taste. Well, the bad taste is there, all one could possibly claim, but besides this is something else that is even more radical and demands our sympathy, or at all events our considerate recognition, and this is Personality.[20]

Continuing, Cram conceded that in the case of the "Furnissic [sic] revolt," there was significance:

> . . . let us remember this: that its founder and its disciples tried to be something besides cheap copyists, tracing their working drawings from Vignola or Letarouilly or Welby Pugin; they tried to be live Americans, not dead archaeologists; they sought for vitality, originality, personal and ethnic expression. . . . If God had given them taste they would have succeeded beyond belief.

Still, Cram held out hope for the architects of the Quaker City, for he ended his capsule history of Philadelphia architecture with the following line:

... then [Philadelphia] amazed everyone by flashing on the world a small circle of architects whose dominant quality was exquisite and almost impeccable taste.

This "small circle of architects" were the subjects of biographical articles in the *Architectural Record*, beginning with Wilson Eyre, continuing with Cope and Stewardson, and following with Frank Miles Day.[21] Not coincidentally, they were the core of the University's new architectural faculty, which had replaced the one-man program taught by Thomas Richards from 1868 until 1890. This new faculty was first led by Theophilus Parsons Chandler, who headed the school while the search was underway for a new professor of architecture to lead the school. That search found Warren Powers Laird, trained in Paris's Ecole des Beaux-Arts, who headed the school for the next forty years. When Harrison replaced Pepper as provost, he turned to Laird for advice on the architecture of the campus. Laird must have made the point that what appealed to Philadelphians of the industrial culture was inexplicable to critics in the taste-making centers of the nation, and hence that Penn's architecture must join the national mainstream of historicizing design.

For the first architecturally important commission of the new era of leadership, the board of the Free Museum of Science and Art (now known as the University Museum), turned the design over to a committee of the new junior architecture faculty, Eyre, Day, and Cope and Stewardson. Under Harrison, these men, particularly Day for the athletic campus and Cope and Stewardson for the academic and residential campus, would be the architects for Penn's future. For Philadelphia there could have been no better choice, for their firms shared a professional genealogy that led back to the giants of the previous generation: Walter Cope had studied the historicizing design process in Chandler's office; John Stewardson had gained his love of color and his flair for original detail in Furness's firm; and Day had studied at Penn and

later in England, reinforcing ties between Philadelphia gentlemen and their English roots.

Gothic or Classic, Brick or Marble: The Battle of the Styles

As important as the selection of the architects of the campus was the choice of its style. Now, at the close of the twentieth century, the battle of the styles between classical and Gothic design for campus buildings is largely forgotten, but at the time when Beaux-Arts training was beginning to dominate architectural education it was the first order of business. At Penn this battle was fought over the design of the museum. Surviving drawings show the University Museum rendered both in the chaste, classical, white marble of the Beaux Arts with Pantheon-like domes and in the brick of North Italy that was the ultimate choice. Given Cope and Stewardson's contemporary Italianate design for the Harrison Chemistry Laboratory on 34th Street (where 1973 Chemistry now stands) and the Flemish gables of the Dental School by Edgar Seeler, the *patron* or chief design instructor of the Department of Architecture's atelier, both in red brick, it must have seemed likely that Penn would continue as a brick university—but with forms and details recalling various historical eras rather than the organic design inspired by the machine culture of the Furness generation.

In fact, the choice of brick was not so preordained as it might have seemed, for Cope and Stewardson simultaneously were given the commission to design dormitories in the Academic Gothic mode similar to their work at Bryn Mawr College. The architects' earliest drawings for the elevations of the dormitory quadrangle show the broken range stonework of their brilliant dormitories at Bryn Mawr and Princeton. While fund-raising for the dormitories continued, several smaller projects went into construction on campus including the student union and the contemporary private project for the Psi Upsilon fraternity by

Dean Warren P. Laird, c. 1895. Photo: Haeseler. UPA.

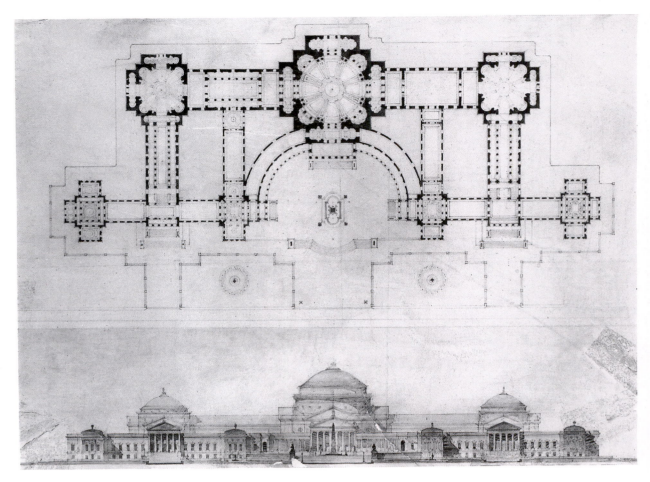

the Hewitt Brothers. Based on the assumption that the University would shift to stone for the dormitories, these new projects were built using the local gray schist of the dormitory renderings. In fact, construction had already begun on the dormitories in the gray broken-range stone when John Stewardson, while on a trip to England, sent back a watercolor of the "Backs of St. John's College, Cambridge," which demonstrated the merits of urban brick over suburban stone for Penn's campus.[22] This was the turning point. Recalling the precedent of the colonial city, the Harrison campus would be built in brick and limestone, in styles reflecting the English architecture of the sixteenth and seventeenth centuries, establishing the dominant character of the campus until the Depression. This choice was in line with Ralph Adams Cram's assessment of the goals of the younger Philadelphia archi-

Wilson Eyre, Jr., Cope and Stewardson, and Frank Miles Day, proposed classical scheme for the University Museum, 1895. Watercolor and ink. Architectural Archives.

••••••••••••••••••••••••••••••••••••

tects: "The Philadelphia group has stood and is standing for nationality, for ethnic continuity, and for the impulses of Christian civilization."[23] Such smug ethnocentrism typified the leadership of Penn and of most other American universities until the end of World War II.[24]

We know little about the reasoning behind Harrison's final decision on campus style and material, but it seems likely that the Academic Gothic met the provost's criteria by being in accord with both the contemporary national taste and elite Philadelphia's long love affair with things English. This was so pronounced that when British arts and crafts architect

Wilson Eyre, Jr., Cope and Stewardson, and Frank Miles Day, executed scheme for the University Museum, 1896. Charcoal and pencil. Architectural Archives.

••••••••••••••••••••••••••••••••••••

C. R. Ashbee visited the Philadelphia area in 1900 he remarked with surprise on the "Anglo-mania" of the region.[25] Walter Cope provided his own personal justification for working in the Gothic style when he was awarded the commission for Washington University in St. Louis in 1899:

Broadly speaking—the architecture of today may be divided into two styles: the Gothic and the Classic. With the former we would, for the purposes of this discussion, include such modifications of pure Gothic as were introduced during the Fifteenth and Sixteenth centuries, without material change in Gothic principles of construction or composition. By Classic, we mean the purer type of that style, which has come to be known as "Monumental," such architecture as we are familiar with in our great government buildings, or in those of the World's Fair in Chicago. It is useless to discuss which of these two styles is the most beautiful. We assume that their claims in this respect, broadly speaking are equal—but it is in place to compare those qualities in which each bear directly on the question before you—the choice of the most appropriate style for an American University.

The Greeks rejected the arch because they said it never rests, and this feeling of the Greeks is the key note of every classic building. Classic architecture expresses completion, finality, perfection; Gothic Architecture expresses aspiration, growth, development. To the beholder, the Classic says: This is the sum—Here is perfection—Do not aspire further. The Gothic says to him: Reach higher— Spread outward and upward—There are no limitations. Now, when we consider what a University is, can there be any doubt which of these two styles better answers of its idea?[26]

Campus Planning: The Cope and Stewardson Years

The character of Provost Stillé's campus was established by the buildings designed by Thomas Richards, each of which was more or less symmetrical and freestanding. Separated from each other, and facing different streets, they were rather like large sculptures arrayed on a green lawn, related to each other by materials, detail, and proximity. Though most of the buildings of Provost Pepper's years shifted toward a fiery red brick and more expressive form that represented interior function, their independent placement amidst green lawns continued the practices that typified most Victorian American campuses.

For centuries English colleges were designed in a tradition that was based on the foundation of English higher education in monastic communities. There church cloister, chapel, refectory, and housing were typically built as a rectangle of structures that separated the college from the outside world while framing private interior spaces. The character of Penn's central campus had already largely been determined when Cope and Stewardson were first hired, so they did not have free rein to develop an interconnected campus on the Oxford-Cambridge model. At other sites, where they had the opportunity to plan the entire campus, as they did at Washington University, or when they were called in early in the process, as at Bryn Mawr College, their preference was for a nearly continuous wall of buildings enclosing interior space. At those schools, the perimeter walls, interrupted by archways that focus views on vistas and landmarks bound together a University fabric that would not be "disfigured by later additions." The increasing urban-

Rockefeller Hall, Bryn Mawr College, 1977. Designed by Cope and Stewardson. GET.

ization of West Philadelphia soon caused Cope and Stewardson to propose constructing new buildings along the perimeter of campus sites, thereby enclosing interior yards. In this approach they anticipated the direction that John R. Freeman, president of the Manufacturers Mutual Fire Insurance Company, would suggest for his alma mater MIT's new campus which was eventually designed along his suggested lines by Welles Bosworth.[27] Because of limited funds, Freeman suggested a "factory plan" that might have been offered by an industrial engineer. Instead of separate buildings, he proposed multiple departments in a single connected building. Noting that most college architecture was unsuccessful because it was designed for monumentality rather than function, Freeman suggested a different design strategy:

I studied the problem from the point of view of an industrial engineer, who plans his buildings *from the inside*, and first of all arranges things with a view to moving the raw materials along the lines of least resistance.[28]

Over the next three decades many of Cope and Stewardson's buildings, including the University Museum, the dormitory quadrangles, the Veterinary Hospital, and finally Bennett Hall, would surround space. However, instead of working from the factory model, Cope and Stewardson's elevations if not their plans were based on English medieval buildings. When Paul Cret and Warren Laird were asked to review campus planning directions in the early twentieth century, they too preferred the linear, space-enclosing approach, establishing it as a principle of campus design, but again not to create efficiencies, but for privacy and picturesqueness of effect. That approach remained the norm on the Penn campus until the neo-Victorian modernists of the 1950s (who would have hated that term as much as they hated Victorian architecture) returned to the earlier principles of original and non-historical designs scattered as free-standing sculptures on the campus albeit on a vastly larger scale.

After working in a north Italian brick early Renaissance mode for the Harrison Chemistry Laboratory, Cope and Stewardson turned to the Academic Gothic for the University dormitories. This vast building finally returned Penn to the collegial way of life that it had abandoned a century before. A report on the proposed dormitory system, signed and probably written by Harrison, recounted the difficulties that Penn's lack of dormitories caused students of three decades earlier when he was a student:

Those students from a distance found such boarding places as they could in the neighborhood of the old site on Ninth Street. Many establishments were devoted exclusively to their use, and there was a certain—not always salutary—charm in the Bohemian side of the medical student's life, while attending lectures in Philadelphia. For the rest, the students of the University came decorously every morning from their parent's homes on Walnut Street or from far-off Germantown and were safely home by candle-light. And if now and then a man came from the interior of the state, or from some

southern state, it was only because he had friends in Philadelphia with whom he could find a safe and real home.[29]

To make it possible for non-Philadelphians to join the University community, Harrison's solution was to shift to the English College system which offered additional benefits that simple accommodation:

There is in the Hall life of the former [the English universities] something which has been hitherto lacking in our University, and that is something which has been needed to give full tone to the University career.

It is not a question so much of lecture rooms and laboratories; it is of his home while at the University. Around him are the traditions of centuries; for in this Hall lived and studied men who went forth to win fame that reflected honor upon their college. It is a vital part of the educational apparatus.[30]

For the dormitories Cope and Stewardson took their preferred course of framing spaces with quadrangles of buildings, creating picturesque vistas framed by archways. That vast building began a small triangular court at 38th Street and Woodland Avenue and gradually extended eastward toward the campus center. The Quad, as the building has been known since its beginning, by its theatricality, conveyed the enlarged scope and purpose of the University. College was more than classes—it was extracurricular activities as well. Embellished by niches and archways, oriels and towers, given delight by a rich array of sculpted bosses (generally mistakenly called gargoyles), and accented by such treasures of sculpture as Alexander Stirling Calder's miniature bronze of a scholar and a football player, these buildings came to represent undergraduate life at Penn. They remained the "men's dorms," a bastion of male privilege, long after women were admitted to full standing in the University. For architectural critics such as Montgomery Schuyler, they were a triumph—albeit florid for his taste:

Architecturally, quite as much as educationally, places of residence are necessary to the fulfillment of the college idea as well as places of instruction. It is these domestic or monastic buildings, compounded "of the cloister and the hearth," which give to collegiate architecture the cloistral character which we find so delightful in it, and which is carried to its perfection in the degenerated and "collegiate" architecture of England. For the architectural fulfillment of the collegiate idea in Philadelphia, no luckier choice could have been made than that of Messrs. Cope & Stewardson.[31]

While the dormitories were under construction it was decided to move the Law School from its location in the old city court building on Independence Square. It had remained there because most of the faculty were active lawyers whose offices were downtown; its removal to a new building at 34th and Chestnut Streets marked a change from the old proprietary system in which the teachers were paid directly by students to a system in which the University was in control. For the Law School Cope and Stewardson continued the red brick and white stone color scheme but changed style, both to establish a special identity for the law school and to link it to the seventeenth-century British heritage of our modern legal codes. Their other buildings—the Towne Engineering School, the medical and zoology laboratories, and the Veterinary School—

are identifiable by the common architectural palette of brick with limestone trim, with stylistic details derived from the late sixteenth to the late seventeenth century before English architecture was overrun by continental sources. Only in the plans of the Towne Engineering Building and the Medical Laboratory are there traces of the industrial culture. Both were megastructures that incorporated classrooms, offices, auditoria, and laboratories and shop spaces organized as two parallel volumes linked at the ends and centers, framing interior courts that provided north-facing light on the order of industrial buildings. But these industrial characteristics were masked by the trappings of English late medieval design that linked them to the larger campus.

Together these buildings gave Penn the unified appearance that characterized most modern institutions of higher learning in the United States, such as Stanford on its Shepley, Rutan, and Coolidge campus, Columbia on its McKim, Mead, and White classical campus, and Berkeley planned on Emile Bernard's great axial scheme. Although Stewardson died in 1896 in an ice skating accident and Cope was felled by a stroke in 1902, their office continued to work at Penn, though with waning vitality, into the 1920s. Under the name Stewardson (John's brother Emlyn, C

Cope and Stewardson, perspective of Residence Halls, 1895. UPA.

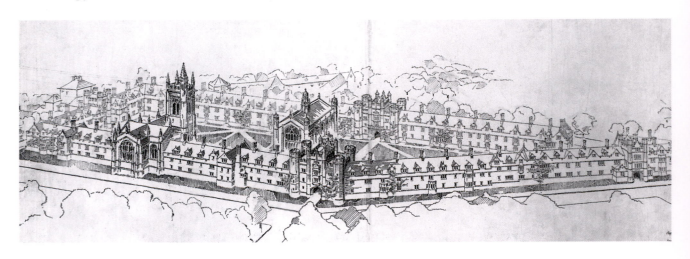

1884) and Page, the firm continued to contribute to the campus's development, designing buildings such as Bennett Hall, the Anatomy-Chemistry Wing extension of the Medical Laboratories, and the ongoing construction of the Quad, while consulting with other architects such as John T. Windrim on the Dental School.

As Harrison's tenure came to an end, an American magazine, the *Independent*, published a series of articles on American higher education that were gathered together in a book, *Great American Universities*.[32] Precipitated by a study by the Carnegie Foundation for the Advancement of Teaching that ranked the top fourteen American universities based on the amount spent on instruction, it painted a generally flattering picture of the University of Pennsylvania.[33] Singled out for attention were the new buildings of the campus and the unified effect that they created. Still, there were clear deficiencies: less was spent on instruction at Penn than at any of the other great universities with the exception of the University of Minnesota. Worse, unlike all its peers, Penn was charging more in tuition than it spent on instruction (though this probably was skewed by the number of scholarship students that resulted from the land grants from the city).[34] Finally, it was clear that Penn's endowment was not keeping up with those of its fellow private institutions, a deficiency it was suggested could be resolved by receiving state aid.

The deaths of Cope and Stewardson freed the University to hire other architects, but with few exceptions the new construction continued the themes they had established. Brockie and Hastings' new hospital buildings, Windrim's Dental Hall, and Horace Trumbauer's White Training House persisted in the English design and brick and limestone or terra cotta trim. A design subplot developed on the east end of the campus in connection with Franklin Field and Weightman Hall. There the broad mortar joints and paired bricks that imitated Roman brick followed the example of the University Museum across South Street. In the case of Franklin Field, north Italian detail is also evident in its cornice, further linking the two sides of the street. The sports buildings became the last link to industrial culture, though not on their exteriors, which, like the rest of the campus looked to history. Their vast interiors were spanned by light steel trusses of the sort that typified twentieth-century mills. Unadorned and tough, they were a fitting counterpart to the male world of athletics. Franklin Field's unadorned reinforced concrete structure speaks of the same values.

Fraternities

Penn's first fraternities began at the Ninth Street campus, where Delta Psi was founded in 1849 and was followed by Delta Phi. In 1888 Delta Psi was also the first to build its own residential house, a mini-palazzo designed by Wilson Eyre, Jr. constructed across the Schuylkill on 22nd Street in the elite Rittenhouse neighborhood. So long as most students commuted home to Rittenhouse Square, Delta Psi's location placed the fraternity closer to the evening activities of the city. Similar attitudes caused the Mask and Wig Club to build its club house and small theater (another Wilson Eyre design), in the midst of the cluster of daytime bohemian clubs east of Broad Street.

With the opening in 1896 of the dormitory quadrangles and Houston Hall, West Philadelphia became the focus of campus life, which led in turn to the construction of a wave of new fraternity buildings, followed by clubs such as the Christian Association. Fraternities were quickly romanticized by authors such as Arthur Hobson Quinn (C 1894) in *Pennsylvania Stories* (1899), celebrating the bonds of friendship fostered by small elite units in the midst of the ever-growing institution; however, the social legacy of many of these organizations continues to be a thorny issue in the life of the University. More than a few of the fraternities established their houses as a setting for an elite caste who would not be forced to live in the dormitories and whose selection process could ensure the perpetuation of their caste. By the twentieth century, the University so supported the system that it differentiated between "A" and "B" fraternities, the former being reserved for the old elite groups and the latter admitting Jews and blacks. The University even published A and B lists of eligible freshmen according to religious affiliation! Thus, even while the campus was coalescing, forces within the University administration fostered and encouraged invidious distinction. Not surprisingly, in the 1920s many of the members of these same elite fraternities became leading advocates of the move of the college from West Philadelphia to Valley Forge.[35]

Because these allied organizations wished to be identified as part of Penn, they typically followed the historicizing Gothic mode of the Cope and Stewardson campus. As a group the purpose-built fraternity buildings have typically been modest in size, following the conventions of the region's domestic architecture, but several have been distinguished designs. Many of these buildings have been incorporated into the campus as it has expanded, serving new University functions; others were demolished during later campus expansion. Psi Upsilon, the first purpose-built house on the Penn campus, set the tone. Designed by the Hewitt Brothers, it was based on the new, more academic version of Gothic that would characterize the future campus; its interior reduced the scale but kept the elements of the men's clubs of the day. Later Gothic buildings such as Phi Gamma Delta by Mellor (Ar 1904) and Meigs followed the model of Rittenhouse Square mansions by placing a large room on the front where its denizens could look down Locust Street; the entrance was recessed in a small court so it would not block the view. The free Arts and Crafts style of the early twentieth century produced at least one masterpiece, Folsom and Stanton's now-demolished Phi Sigma Kappa of 1916, which betrayed the influences of Price and McLanahan's Rose Valley architecture and Eyre's University Museum.[36] Other buildings, such as Bissell and Sinkler's Phi Kappa Sigma, Robert Rhodes McGoodwin's Phi Delta Theta, and Theodore Epps's Kappa Sigma, adhered to the dominant brick and limestone of the campus but, under the impetus of

Philadelphia's rediscovery of its own past, drifted toward the fashionable Colonial Revival.

The Campus After Harrison

Until World War II, the Harrison formula based on English collegiate architecture held with one notable exception that suggests that under Provost Edgar Fahs Smith and his successors, the trustees gradually regained control of the architectural selection process. Although Irvine Auditorium, by Horace Trumbauer, was built in the familiar brick and stone, its style was based on the insistent verticalism and delicate detail of French rather than English Gothic! This choice reflected early twentieth-century theory rooted in the highly personal evaluation of *Mont-Saint-Michel and Chartres* by Bostonian Henry Adams. Departing from ethnic heritage as a basis for criticism and resorting simply to the direct appeal to emotion, Adams established a new theoretical paradigm that gave to French Gothic the highest cultural and aesthetic honors in western art. The flamboyance of Irvine Auditorium's styling also reflected the earlier preference of trustee John C. Bell (L 1884), who had hired Trumbauer for his own house on Locust Street and who ensured that his personal architect was chosen for the auditorium. Not coincidentally, Penn's trustees had been exposed to the new French taste in their homes in Chestnut Hill's French Village, while the ever-increasing verticality of the urban architecture of modern cities gave the French verticalism preference over the horizontal, earth-hugging English styles.

The architecture school also contributed an important new element to the commentary on the campus; aesthetes who had been trained in the new historicism soon applied their training to criticism of the earlier architecture of the campus. In "A Stroll Out Spruce Street," George Cunney (C 1917) was harsh in his review of Penn's architecture:

And now we come to the Library.

Oh, Library what have you not been called? Seas of opprobrium have washed over you year in and year out since first you were seen of men, yet here you stand as staunch and tight as the day of your dedication.

The style is Pidgin Byzantine embellished with advanced delirium tremens motifs. It is built of rusticated red sandstone, lachrymose red brick, brilliant red faience and ornate red terra cotta. It has a roof of Spanish tile ridged with livid green copper. The eaves are ornamented with terra cotta gondola prows and the roof is profuse with sturdy little plants or shrubs.[37]

With such criticism it was no wonder that during the 1930s Robert Rhodes McGoodwin, himself the personal choice of the Houston family, began screening the old University Library behind an English Gothic skin—a process that was fortunately arrested by the Great Depression.

A Larger Vision: The Cret Plan

Under Harrison Penn had once more doubled its population and quadrupled its area. Its campus stretched from the east end of Franklin Field at 30th Street to the Veterinary School at 39th Street, and its fraternities and affiliated organizations filled the triangle above Woodland Avenue west to 40th Street. The old Victorian principle of proximity had created precincts devoted to medicine on the south, sports to the east, residence to the west, and the academic campus in the center. Still, anomalies could be found; for example, dentistry was removed from the medical and science portion of the campus to the site of donor Thomas Evans's former home at 40th Street while biology remained within the medical complex instead of moving to the east science precinct where the sciences of the college were located.

In 1910, after sixteen years headed by businessman Harrison, the University turned for leadership to the vice-provost, Professor of Chemistry Edgar Fahs Smith (1910–20). Little more than half a century after the liberal arts faculty had rejected the new scientific faculty, a scientist led the University. Smith had done

pioneering work in electrochemistry and was an important link with regional industry. In one of his first important decisions, he asked Dean Warren Laird and architect Paul Philippe Cret, the professor of design in the architecture program, to produce a plan to direct the future growth of the University. In preparing their 1913 report, Cret and Laird were joined by the Boston-based planning firm of the Olmsted Brothers who were the principal campus planners of the time. Entitled *Report to the Board of Trustees of the University of Pennsylvania upon Future Development of Buildings and Grounds and the Conservation of Surrounding Territory*, their report was a warning of the dangers of further unplanned growth:

> Upon one very serious aspect of present conditions we would lay especial stress, namely the total disintegration—or lack of organization—of the University's physical growth. The first request of efficiency is system, but this fact, so long ago and so universally accepted in the administrative functions of American universities seemed to have no recognition in its physical counterpart—the grouping of buildings. Thus at the University of Pennsylvania, as in practically every other institution of its time, growth has proceeded without plan and through mere accretion advancing step by step through marginal enlargements, into every increasing confusion.[38]

Calling for new principles of growth in which space would be "enclosed by buildings and not employed to surround them," it further recommended that the central campus be "planned exclusively for pedestrians; . . . having ample space for planting of grass plats." The spaces that characterized the dormitory quadrangles were to typify the Penn campus of the future— but with a difference. Where Cope and Stewardson's Quad was unashamedly picturesque, the new plan would bring Beaux-Arts axial grandeur to Penn in the manner of modern university campuses from Columbia to Stanford.

Paul P. Cret, 1903 (above). UPA.
Provost Edgar Fahs Smith, c. 1910 (right). UPA.

••

Cret and Laird envisioned yet another doubling of the campus, which they believed should take place to the north. In an imaginative scheme to resolve the problems caused by the city's east-west streets, they proposed an elevated central axis or pedestrian mall that would bridge the viaduct of Walnut Street and the smaller Sansom Street. Aimed toward Chestnut Street to the rear of the Law School, its principal features were a broad, tree-lined walk that linked a large open square at the north end of the main axis to stairs leading down to the College Hall green at the south.

The diagonal intersection of Walnut Street and Woodland Avenue would be recast as an immense street-level traffic circle appropriate to the scale of the enlarged University, while new quarters for the Graduate School buildings would be constructed where Bennett Hall now stands. Future growth for the Graduate School could be extended either east along Walnut or, preferably, south along 34th Street. Bennett Hall's beveled facade with east and south wings permitting expansion in either direction reflects the continuing force of these ideas.[39]

Despite the Cret/Laird plan, University growth slowed dramatically under Smith and succeeding provosts. On the western campus, the science buildings along Hamilton Walk were completed; the Medical School was enlarged with the Anatomy/Chemistry wing to the south; the eastern range of the dormitories were constructed according to Cope and Stewardson's 1890s plan. On the east, the east wing and great rotunda of the University Museum were constructed; Franklin Field was rebuilt and then double-decked; and, in the 1920s, the Palestra and Hutchinson Gymnasium were built. These projects each marked extensions of the ideas of the Harrison campus, but none moved beyond the central idea of the turn-of-the-century designers and, with the sole exception of the angled plane of Bennett Hall's facade, none made any steps toward the new plan.

The University of Pennsylvania— at Valley Forge?

One reason building slowed at Penn in the 1920s was the decade-long love affair of a large portion of the alumni with the idea of moving the University yet again, to a new site in Valley Forge near the site of the encampment of Washington's Revolutionary army. The potential for an independent college in small residential houses like those of Yale was first raised in a speech by trustee George Wharton Pepper (C 1877, L 1889) at an Alumni Association dinner in Wilmington, Delaware in 1920. During the next decade Philadelphia was preoccupied with the Sesquicentennial of

American independence, choosing for its exhibit a recreation of Philadelphia's eighteenth-century High Street. It was a vision of the future as past that did not augur well for the University or the city. Within a few years, the powerful appeal to the imagination of a country campus elevated the alumni to near equality with the trustees and the administration in shaping the future of the institution.

Through the pages of the *General Magazine and Historical Chronicle*, the battle was waged. The magazine's editor, H. Mather Lippincott (C 1897), and others wrote on "The Problem of a College in a City" and illustrated their conclusions with bucolic scenes of the campuses of Princeton, Haverford, Dartmouth, and Williams—all primarily undergraduate male colleges that had at most a small graduate division.[40] By the mid-1920s, Alumni Association president Henry Woolman (C 1898) had purchased the 175-acre Cressbrook Farm and was prepared to offer it to the University as the new home of the undergraduate college. Simultaneously, the state of Pennsylvania commemorated the 150th anniversary of Washington's troops' encampment at Valley Forge by the purchase of much of the Revolutionary site. Penn's undergraduate college could be a part of national history, while its

business and professional schools would remain in the city on the old site.

Because of the trustees' power to control committees and to coopt the opposition by bringing its leaders onto the board, the board inevitably managed to maintain control of the University. The trustees had been advised confidentially by F. J. Kelley, Dean of College Administration of the University of Minnesota, of the dangers and costs of operating two campuses, but even so they were also caught up in the romance of the idea of the college at Valley Forge.[41] In April 1929 the University accepted the gift of the Cressbrook Farm from Woolman, who previously had been elevated to the Board of Trustees.[42] Six months later, the onset of the great Depression brought an end to the possibility of immediate construction, but for another generation the idea of the Valley Forge campus would be regularly advanced, sometimes to cheer the alumni, sometimes to threaten the city if the University did not get its way on land acquisitions or other matters. The idea was finally put to rest in a board meeting of 22 May 1959, when it was resolved "That the proposal to establish a College of Liberal Arts near Valley Forge is hereby abandoned."[43]

Motives assessed from a distance of several generations are often judged with modern biases, but the dream of the Valley Forge campus certainly expressed desires that were both escapist and elitist, paralleling the contemporary retreat to rural residences of many of the trustees. For the University it probably constituted another grasp for power by the alumni and trustees who regarded themselves as "old Penn," and who, a century after the removal of the federal government to Washington, D.C. and Andrew Jackson's destruction of the power of the Philadelphia-based Second Bank of the United States, were still brooding over those losses. The escapist idea also pointed to changes in the city that supported the University.

A comparison of the two world's fairs held in Philadelphia makes apparent the changed perspective of the city. The 1876 Centennial Exhibition was planned at the moment that the University was moving to

Warren Powers Laird and Paul P. Cret, "Plan of a High Level Mall," c. 1920. From Laird, "Records of a Consulting Practice." University of Pennsylvania Fine Arts Library, Rare Book Room.

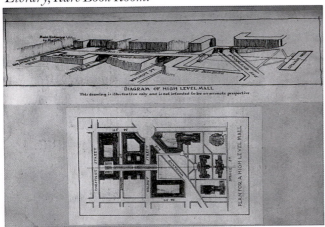

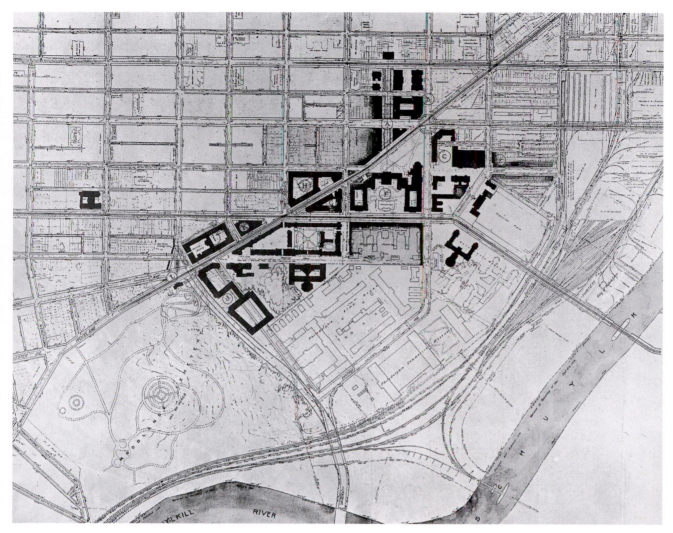

Paul P. Cret, Olmsted Brothers, "Suggested Developments in the Vicinity of Woodland Ave." Map 1, Report to the Board of Trustees of the University of Pennsylvania Upon the Future Development of Buildings, *1913.*

••

West Philadelphia. Its themes were technology and the future; at its center was an immense Corliss engine that powered the exhibits in the various buildings and exposed Europeans and Americans to the sounds and dynamism of the new industrial age. The enlarged University fairly reflected these same themes. When Penn was considering moving to Valley Forge, planners of the Sesquicentennial of 1926 focused that

exhibit on the past; at its center was a reconstructed version of Old High Street and a giant electrified Liberty Bell. Clearly, the past-oriented Philadelphia of the 1920s was a very different city from the center of innovation of half a century before. More alarming was the rise to prominence of the idea of "secular stagnation," which claimed that the world economy was essentially mature and that Philadelphia industry would run along for as long as the republic endured.[44] A few years later a new Franklin Institute would be constructed on the Benjamin Franklin Parkway, but, instead of being a center for the dissemination of new technology, it would be transformed into a museum of the recent past. Those changes would affect the future

of the region and its greatest institution. Henceforth the nation's perspective on Philadelphia would be of a city living in the past.

Some of the factors causing this change were obvious. Industrialization had made the city a less pleasant place to live, while the automobile enabled the wealthy to live year round in the western suburbs. Simultaneously the children of Philadelphia business leaders had abandoned the engineering curriculum of Penn for the liberal arts of Princeton and Yale, and if they

Cressbrook Farm, Valley Forge, Pennsylvania, c. 1929. Photo: Rittase.

•••

returned to the city many of them found new careers in medicine, banking, law, and the corporate professions. In the past Philadelphia manufacturers had been deeply involved with their businesses: many, such as William Sellers, had lived within a few blocks of work so that they could return to work at a moment's notice. By contrast merchants and professionals usually did not live over the shop, living instead in the new downtown, later in the railroad suburbs, and by the 1920s in even more remote automobile suburbs. Thus Penn's trustees anticipated the post–World War II changes in the city by their increasingly distant residences and their lack of connection to their city.

There was another point of conflict for the trustees who still represented old Philadelphia. The city was changing rapidly and Penn was changing with it. Though the *Pennsylvanian* published articles such as "Tradition Persists," about undergraduate descendants of Signers of the Declaration of Independence and of Franklin, which sought to prove Penn's ongoing links to its noble history, at every corner of the campus there were signs of change that threatened the old order.[45] How better to exclude women, the children of recent immigrants, and others who would not have been in attendance a generation or two earlier than to move to the distant suburbs? An article entitled "Evils of Women" in the *Gazette* concluded that Valley Forge was the means by which the College could be returned to being a true single-sex college that would compare favorably with Harvard, Princeton, and Yale.[46] Had Penn moved to the suburbs, and had the Depression, World War II, and other forces not intervened, the student body might have been reconstituted according to its nineteenth-century elite male heritage—and the modern University would not have arrived for many years.

Franklin's Daughters: Women at Penn

In addition to the conflict over the location of the University, seeds for further change had been planted at the end of William Pepper's tenure and continued to be nurtured during the Harrison and Smith years. At the end of the nineteenth century various gifts were accepted that were intended to make it possible for women to be educated at Penn. Simultaneously, in 1876, the Charity School, which had educated girls and boys from its inception in 1751, was formally disbanded on the grounds that women were allowed to take courses at the University. Later women were

permitted to receive degrees in scattered programs, beginning with the Towne Scientific School and the History Department in the 1870s, the Medical School in 1878, and the Law School in 1881. The local success of Bryn Mawr College, the previous establishment of Radcliffe College using Harvard's faculty in 1879 and Barnard College using Columbia's faculty in 1889, along with such coeducational institutions as Swarthmore, again brought the topic of women's education to the fore. By the late 1880s many women were engaged in study at Penn in such disparate fields as anatomy, chemistry, and music, leading to certificates—the University's device for avoiding the awarding of degrees. In 1892 under Pepper, a Graduate Department for Women was opened in two of the row houses that had been given by Colonel Joseph Bennett at the corner of 34th and Walnut Streets, the site of the present Bennett Hall. The graduate program was soon augmented by courses in education which were aimed at women and which led in 1914 to a School of Education. There women prepared for careers in teaching, while others took the "College Collateral Course" as a means of receiving a Penn bachelor's degree.[47]

In 1924 Bennett Hall was built on the site of the proposed Graduate School to house the women's programs. With its own student union in the basement, its own school store, a library on the second floor for the education program, a gymnasium for women's physical education on the fourth floor, academic offices and classrooms, it functioned for women as College Hall had for the University in 1872. It would take the economic catastrophe of the Depression before women were admitted to most of the University in the separate and nearly equal College of Liberal Arts for Women established in 1933. Even then, in Edward Potts Cheyney's hostile account, women were at the University "as it were on sufferance. The College, the oldest and most characteristic part of the University, that which is best known to the public and which largely gives tone to the whole institution, is strictly masculine."[48]

As the 1930s began, for the first time since the mid-

34th and Walnut Streets, looking southeast, c. 1900. UPA.
Bennett Hall, Women's Union, c. 1950. UPA.

••••••••••••••••••••••••••••••••••

nineteenth century, even with the admission of women to most of its programs, Penn was shrinking, its numbers of students falling off. The consequences of the economic collapse on the industries that supported the University were drastic. Programs were dropped, faculty positions were eliminated, buildings deteriorated. In the face of the obstacles that confronted them, that women held onto their goal of admission was remarkable. From the mid-1930s, quotas limited their numbers in courses and they were typically taught in separate courses—supposedly to avoid distracting the men. The College for Women would continue as a separate division into the 1960s before finally being absorbed into the University. Despite the hostility of its leaders, more than two centuries after the founding of the University Benjamin Franklin's goal of providing education to both sexes was again the policy of the institution.

CHAPTER FIVE

TOWARD A MODERN UNIVERSITY

Redevelopment and Renewal

FOR THE PHILADELPHIA REGION, the end of World War II brought on an Indian summer of false prosperity. The city's population surged above 2 million, cresting at nearly 2.25 million in the mid-1950s. Most men in the city still were employed in the heavy manufacturing industries that had been the base of the regional economy since the nineteenth century. Unlike Europe's cities, many of which had been bombed and largely destroyed during the war, Philadelphia's industrial base remained strong, but its factories relied on aging technologies and work systems devised before World War I. The core of Philadelphia survived, too, as a darkened, earthbound brick Victorian relic, at odds with the soaring brilliance of New York's Art Deco skyscrapers of the 1920s and the cool, white, rectilinear abstractions of modern design in rebuilding Europe.

At the University of Pennsylvania, within the concrete structure of a converted piano factory, the foundations for the future were being laid with the construction, under a contract from the United States Army Ordnance Division, of a thirty-ton electronic machine that employed 18,000 vacuum tubes and occupied 1500 cubic feet, the volume of a good-sized truck. ENIAC, as the machine was known, was 1000 times faster than any previous calculator and held the potential for almost miraculous increases in efficiency. In 1961, when Penn scientists celebrated its fifteenth anniversary, its landmark importance already was apparent to Detlev Bronk, a former member of Penn's faculty who had become president first of Johns Hopkins and afterward of the Rockefeller Institute for Medical Research. Reflecting on the computer, Bronk saw it heralding a new age:

> This period in which we now live and in which we possess new forces, new extensions of our senses, new mental powers with which to seek knowledge and shape the patterns of our life and environments, could be another of the great ages of the world.[1]

While ENIAC was being built at Penn's Moore School of Electrical Engineering, the still-energized federal government that had made the United States the "arsenal of democracy" during World War II was producing a broad variety of programs intended gradually to return millions of troops to civilian life. Federal urban renewal programs calling for the demolition and reconstruction of America's urban centers resulted in modern office centers such as Philadelphia's Penn Center. Federal initiatives for highways and homebuilding stimulated new automobile-linked suburbs that encouraged an exodus from American cities. Outside Philadelphia, the suburbs of the city grew as old estates were subdivided for new tract housing. The surge of new building projects transformed Philadelphia as well. The Schuylkill Expressway provided an automobile link between Center City and the western suburbs along the old Main Line of the Pennsylvania Railroad, while the city's new downtown arose on the site of the Railroad's Broad Street Station.

Despite the invention of ENIAC at Penn and the political, social, spatial, and economic forces that were transforming the city, in the three-quarters of a cen-

Aerial photo of campus, looking northeast, c. 1940. UPA.

tury since the nation had celebrated its Centennial in Fairmount Park Philadelphia had fallen from the center of national attention. In 1963 in the introduction to *The Perennial Philadelphians*, Nathaniel Burt remarked on the city's cultural and intellectual isolation:

> There used to be a time when people didn't really believe in Philadelphia. . . . Of course they knew there was such a city. They sometimes passed through it on the train. Otherwise it was just a statistic and so safely ignored.
>
> It was neither exciting like Manhattan, quaint like Boston, nor picturesque and glamorous like the South and West. It was not even conspicuously awful like the Midwest. It was, in fact, like some forbidden Oriental city. John Gunther in *Inside U.S.A.* quotes J. David Stern, publisher in the forties of the now defunct Philadelphia *Record*, as saying that "Philadelphia was the most Chinese city in the United States."[2]

Though it was on the east coast at the center of the nation's rail transport systems, the continued focus of Philadelphia on manufacturing isolated it from the international centers of Boston, New York, and Washington, D.C. In fact, many changes in the region had been missed by the national press. The war had infused a new generation of leaders into Philadelphia businesses, overturning the old leadership hierarchy of the Quaker City. After World War II, under the direction of city planner Edmund Bacon, Philadelphia's renewal of its Center City made it a national urban success story. With locally-born Grace Kelly on the nation's movie screens and later with her story-book wedding to Monaco's Prince Rainier, and with political reform led by Philadelphian patrician Joseph Clark, the city was again an acknowledged fact in the nation's consciousness—stimulating Digby Baltzell's scholarly analysis of the city's elite, *Philadelphia Gentlemen* (1957) and Burt's witty and insightful *Perennial Philadelphians*. Tellingly, many of the city's new leaders were raised and educated outside the city. Planner

Edmund Bacon (Cranbrook Academy and Cornell University), architect Vincent Kling (East Orange, N.J. and Columbia University), lawyer and later reform mayor Richardson Dilworth (Pittsburgh and University of Virginia), the new president of the University of Pennsylvania, Minnesota's ex-governor Harold Stassen, and his new Dean of the School of Fine Arts, G. Holmes Perkins (Cambridge and Harvard University) had in common their status as outsiders. They and others would challenge Philadelphia's insularity, dragging the city toward the national mainstream.[3]

In 1947 Philadelphia's Director of City Planning, Edmund Bacon, in conjunction with German-born Oscar Stonorov and a council of corporate leaders, produced the "Better Philadelphia Exhibition" that attracted half a million visitors to the Gimbel's department store in downtown Philadelphia. Using the device of a giant model of the city, constructed so that portions of the old city could be overlaid with the possibilities of the future, Bacon was the impresario of change. In the model the old portions of the city were as dark as the soot-blackened buildings of the industrial city, while the new was as bright as the crystalline glass office towers of European modernism. Bacon proposed demolishing the Victorian city core and replacing it with a glittering cluster of light-toned, International Style office towers that would house the offices required by the transition of the city's economic base from industry to service and finance. Philadelphia's historic eighteenth-century neighborhoods would be restored; new neighborhoods would be created and linked by a network of highways that would serve the automobile. Center City, the university neighborhoods, and the river fronts would be rehabilitated.[4] Working from the presumption that Philadelphia would soon be a city of 3,000,000 people, Bacon planned for a city whose best years lay ahead.[5]

Penn's Future

Despite the new ferment in the city, after a decade of the Great Depression and six years of world war,

Penn's trustees were again faced with a daunting present. As it had been on its Ninth Street site after the Civil War, the University was land-locked, surrounded by rail lines and the planned Schuylkill Expressway on the east, by Philadelphia General Hospital and the Woodlands Cemetery on the south, and by changing residential communities and growing institutions such as Drexel Institute on the north and west. The old families, who had formerly lived in the residential neighborhood around the University because of its convenience to the downtown, had moved to the western Main Line suburbs, and most of their houses

had been converted to apartments to meet housing shortages as the nation mobilized during World War II. Instead of being known as the home of the Drexels, Felses, and other distinguished families, West Philadelphia was reduced to a battleground fought over by the University, the remaining largely Irish middle-class residents, and African-American families who had moved north for industrial jobs before and during World War II.[6]

The University in the 1940s

Between 1929 and 1949 new construction on the campus nearly ceased. From the completion of Irvine Auditorium in 1928 to the end of World War II, the

ENIAC, 1946. UPA.

only realized projects were the 1940 Chemistry Building by Paul Cret and two minor projects by the Houston's family architect, Robert Rhodes McGoodwin, who designed the new wings of Houston Hall and added a room on the front of the old library for Horace Howard Furness, Jr.'s Shakespeare collection. The latter addition was intended as the first stage of wrapping the outdated Victorian-styled building in modern collegiate Gothic that would link the library to the adjacent Irvine Auditorium. As the Depression deepened, attendance dropped across the entire University; Penn's lack of an endowment forced the elimination of programs such as landscape architecture in the School of Fine Arts.

Penn's leaders and the institution itself were ill-prepared for the whirlwind of change that would assault American universities and colleges in the mid-1940s. During the first years after the end of the war, millions of men and women would return to civilian life through the doors of colleges and universities, their attendance paid for by provisions in the Serviceman's Readjustment Act of 1944, the so-called "G. I. Bill." The millions of dollars that flooded American higher education further hastened the democratization of education that had begun at Penn in previous generations with the city scholarship program.

After extensive experimentation on the possibilities of gauging intelligence and using such tests as an element in their admissions process, American colleges began a slow but steady turn away from their historic roots as hereditary fiefdoms, ruled and populated by the descendants of those who had gone before, to a new system of selection that stressed merit over social class and economic clout.[7] More fully reflecting the broadest promise of equal opportunity implied in the U. S. Constitution, selection by talent increased prestige if the student body and faculty were drawn from the entire nation rather than from a parochial base.[8] Beginning in 1926, Penn had required that its applicants take the standardized test of the College Entrance Examination Board; with its city scholarship students, Penn's student body began to anticipate

the future, though divisions of economic and social classes were painfully obvious to many of the city students.[9] Simultaneously, women at Penn continued their slow advance against the grudging acceptance of alumni. During World War II women had been free to use most of the campus, but with the return of male students Houston Hall was again closed to women except for one room on the first floor and women were not permitted to use the front entrance to College Hall. The Quad remained a bastion of male residence, and women generally were kept on the periphery of the University with separate classes and separate residences. When, in 1957, it was decided to build a new dormitory for women, the first proposal would have placed women as far as possible from the main campus, in the vicinity of 40th and Walnut Streets; later, when an apartment complex project at 33rd and Walnut fell through, Hill House was constructed on the east side of the campus, in the vicinity of Bennett Hall, where the women's program was centered.[10] Separate classes continued to be held for women so that the male students wouldn't be distracted; separate yearbooks continued after the war, as did separate honor groups and separate alumni reunions.[11] A collection of notes assembled about the history of women at Penn in the *Gazette* in 1957 makes it obvious that being a Penn coed had never been easy and continued to require additional efforts than were expected of the male students:

1900—Dean Penniman excuses women from chapel because of "the indignation manifested by senior men because about twenty-five of the women, for whom no place has been reserved at chapel, have presumed to take their seats in the senior section."

1933—"Words of Wisdom," in *1933 Frosh Handbook*, "Simple and inconspicuous clothing become the college woman" and "Pennsylvania Women do not join football parades. You are coming to a university old in tradition. Help build tradition for women; don't be a destroyer of old things."[12]

At Penn, as elsewhere, separate wasn't equal. Women's Ivy Day plaques were placed only on Bennett Hall until the construction of Hill House provided a second women's building.[13] During the academic year 1965–66, future University president Judith Rodin negotiated the merger of the women's and men's student government which took place with the 1966–67 school year. Coeds finally were fully accepted as members of the University community in the late 1960s and early 1970s—when most of the other Ivies were first considering accepting women or had decided to merge their separate women's colleges into the male institution.[14] At Penn the final boundaries fell in 1970 with the opening of the new high-rise undergraduate residences, when all dormitory rooms including the Quad and Hill Hall were placed in a pool for housing that was open to all students. Simultaneously, organizations such as the Sphinx Senior Society began to admit women to membership.[15] After nearly a century on campus, the barriers to women were finally removed.

Those changes were still a generation in the future. In the late 1940s the tentative acceptance of women that had begun during the Depression was crushed by the general desire of returning students, aging faculty, and alumni trustees to return to the good old days of the prewar status quo. At least on the surface, the University of the late 1940s remained devoted to the successful values of Provost Harrison's era, supporting its big-time football program that played a national schedule including the service academies and teams from the Big Ten. One 1940s graduate recalled autumn Saturdays at Penn:

> ...if you weren't in Franklin Field on a game day, on this part of the campus [at 36th and Walnut] or even further west, you could hear the roar of the crowd; you'd get up early in the morning, at seven o'clock, and already the policemen would be at the intersections directing traffic, the program vendors would be already on the street corners selling programs. . . . Even that early in the morning the

> excitement would be building up. . . . After the game, they always played the carillon in Irvine Auditorium, and as you came out of Franklin Field you heard them playing the Penn songs.
>
> Sixty thousand, seventy thousand people, being on television, in those days Penn was on every Saturday.[16]

Into the 1950s a party atmosphere prevailed at Penn that made the Penn-Cornell game the big event of the city's Thanksgiving Day but lowered Penn's standing among the great universities of the land.

First Steps Toward the Modern University

For the University's first campus development plans for the postwar period, Penn's leaders once again turned to its architectural faculty and alumni. Although the new plan coincided with the 1947 Better Philadelphia Exhibition, there could hardly have been a greater contrast between the plans advanced by the city and those of the University architectural advisors. In 1913, when architecture professor Paul Cret and Dean Laird had developed Penn's first master plan, its faculty had been national leaders in the fields of planning and design.[17] By 1948, Penn's aging Beaux-Arts-trained faculty were out of touch with the revolutionary architectural theories that had toppled the design faculties at Harvard, North Carolina, and Illinois and would transform their profession over the next decade. Penn's 1948 campus plan was developed by University architectural graduates Sydney Martin (Ar 1907, also a University trustee), James Edmunds (Ar 1912), James Kellum Smith (Ar 1918), John Harbeson (Ar 1910), and Grant M. Simon (Ar 1911). With the exception of the slightly younger Smith, all had studied with Paul Cret before he departed for Europe—for World War I military service! They prepared a plan that proposed demolishing the old University Library and Logan Hall and the Hare Laboratory, the aging Victorian buildings that had been objects of scorn during their schooling before World War I.[18] In place of those relics from Penn's past would rise a campus framed by three- and four-story buildings in the red brick and light stone trim of the 1890s but vaguely *moderne* in styling.

The question of the appropriate style for America's universities and colleges had been a topic of interest in architectural journals for nearly a generation. In 1931 the editors of the *Architectural Forum* devoted an issue to that topic in an attempt to reconcile the remarkable transformations of teaching and subject matter in American colleges and universities since the end of the century with the historical styles that cloaked the buildings in which these changes were occurring. Introducing the topic, the magazine's editor, Kenneth K. Stowell, argued that the greatest need for college and University buildings of the present was for "flexibility so that the buildings may be changed to serve the changing educational methods with the least possible demolition and rebuilding." At the end of the issue, he summarized the strategies available to college planners:

> They might choose to . . . erect a permanent monument which will serve the needs of the present; to erect a durable building so constructed as to be flexible in use and easily added to; [to] erect a modern building of materials having some salvage value with the idea that it may be replaced after a period of fifteen or twenty years. This might be done in frank acknowledgment that there is a possibility that both methods and materials of construction will have changed so much in that period as to make this the wise course.

He concluded that, because of costs and the peculiar situation of most universities, "building committees in colleges and universities are more apt to adopt the second course."[19]

On the question of what approach should be taken to style, Stowell was more certain:

> The growing idea of architectural unity through the adoption of a style serves as a brake on those who would adopt the third course. The older colleges have passed through periods of styles, each new building being added in the then current architectural fashion—of old Colonial or American Georgian, Richardsonian Romanesque, Victorian Gothic, and then perhaps a return to adaptations of the styles of the original buildings. Such heterogeneous collections have not been found pleasing even though they have given an historical record, and the tendency at present is to establish definitely a style in the interests of coherence and unity. It does leave an opportunity for the newer colleges to erect thoroughly modern buildings, but few have availed themselves of this opportunity, evidently feeling that the "modern" of to-day is transitional and that the safer course is to follow the venerable style precedent of older institutions.

The *Forum* editors selected other authors with different perspectives to comment on the discussion. Taking the conventional point of view that historical styles were most appropriate was C. Howard Walker, formerly of the Penn fine arts faculty and later a professor at Harvard. His flowery prose gave a hint as to why the Beaux-Arts educational system collapsed in the midst of the Depression:

> It may be reasonably inferred that buildings already in existence in any and all periods . . . will have created and used so-called styles which have in them architectural expression of value at all times for work of the same kind. Their use today is not merely traditional but results from certain solutions which accord with present conditions.
>
> Standardization [modernism], if I may be permitted to change the metaphor, cuts its way through this fascinating, intriguing jungle of opportunity in a narrow swath, safe behind a steam roller. Standardization, the mechanism of the paid accountant, sees little of the flowers of the jungle, hears few of its birds, or knows little of its byways.
>
> Art is a Beloved Vagabond, who can be a beggar

or a king, but is not regally clothed in tailor-made garments.[20]

Architect and campus planner Frederick Ackerman took a middle-of-the-road course, differentiating between the situation of the academy with its long-term perspective and the commercial world:

In urban centers, business deals with the changing processes of life by destruction and replacement of buildings. This method of dealing with changing events and values is accepted without question; and the rate at which destruction and replacement takes place constitutes a scale by which we measure progress. The financial structure of the educational institution, however, not only precludes, but is likely to continue to preclude, the adoption of such a plan of action. Durability and permanence call for

an architectural expression more deeply rooted in reason than the extremes of fashion which pass in a day.[21]

Ironically, as Yale underwent the great surge of Gothic cloister-building that has come to characterize its campus, the *Forum* editors selected a Yale undergraduate as the advocate of modern styles. William Harlan Hale, editor of the humor magazine *The Harkness Hoot*, wrote "Old Castles for New Colleges" as an assault on the rampant historicism that he termed "girder Gothic."[22]

America's Coming of Age implies not only a bigger navy, a closer railroad net, and a larger population total per square mile, but also a new consciousness of cultural aims. Men who made hundreds of millions out of America's physical growth now donate tens of millions to establish America's mental maturity. It has become a sign of enlightenment to provide funds for erecting a college library, a dormitory or a monumental tower which exalts the

....

Architects' Committee, University of Pennsylvania Campus Master Plan, *1948, "Plan of Development." UPA.*

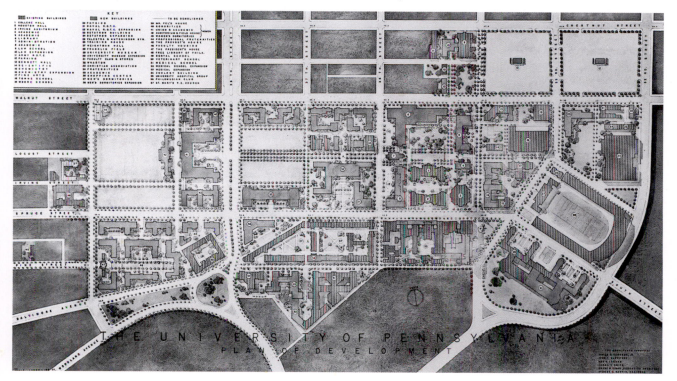

estate of learning and advertises the assets of the favored institution.

Intentions have been of the best; while taste, however, frequently has been of the worst. The overwealthy retired magnate, conceiving a sudden passion for culture, is less likely to turn over a million dollars to be used simply and efficiently than to devote that million to the erection of a magnificent edifice, luxuriously furnished and gorgeously decorated, as a memorial to his generosity. His tendency is to get as much personal glory as possible out of his million dollars.

Thus, our colleges are likely to become museums of gilt and glory rather than workplaces of simplicity and directness.

In the house plans of Yale and Harvard lay great opportunities for the construction of the best-fitted types of residential structures. Almost limitless funds were at hand, and the plans were so extensive that a unity of many buildings was envisaged. Some observers dreamed of modern designs—of bold, clear shapes as suggested by the Dessau Bauhaus, the Weissenhof settlement, or other European community developments. Rash visionaries fondly hoped that here the trappings of antiquity might be dropped, and a bold path be struck toward the formulation of a new style. They thought that academic leadership might mean artistic or cultural leadership.

Hale's conclusion anticipated the cry of the modernists who soon shaped most campuses:

Hundreds of institutional buildings hide their proper life and function under a garment stolen from the past. . . . Life is possible only in a living style. . . . A race of men who are sound and fearless can only be reared with difficulty in a world of buildings that are false and cowardly.

Three decades earlier, Penn grad and veteran of Frank Furness's office Albert Kelsey had made a simi-

lar assault on Cope and Stewardson's Academic Gothic buildings at Penn, asking what effect the architectural rejection of the present had on students working with x-ray light in the nearby science laboratories. But until the Depression and World War II undermined the foundations of the borrowed culture, Penn like its peer institutions adhered to Cope and Stewardson's late English Gothic in a palette of brick and limestone.

In 1948, after two decades of no building, the question of style preoccupied the University planners and trustees. The committee of architects advised the University leaders to take the modern direction, reporting:

> Some trustees were at first of the opinion that a traditional style of architecture should be adopted for all our future buildings. It was found that only here in the United States . . . had college buildings been designed in anything but a contemporary style.[23]

In fact the architects' historical argument was false but went unchallenged. British Victorian Gothic revivals and French Second Empire classical revivals had long shaped the design of academic buildings in Europe; many collegiate buildings in the United States were based on them including Thomas Richards's William Butterfield-like Gothic revival of College Hall. Cope and Stewardson's various interpretations of English history for Penn could as easily have been designed for a contemporary English university. In any event, with the triumph of scientific progressivism in the aftermath of World War II, the trend of the architectural profession toward the seemingly objective and rational antihistorical style of modern architecture was ratified at Pennsylvania as elsewhere. Even though the designers of Penn's new campus had long been under the sway of Beaux-Arts historicism, they were quick to adapt to the new stylistic currents

••

Architects' Committee, University of Pennsylvania Campus Master Plan, *1948, bird's-eye perspective. UPA.*

and to adopt the arguments of the new theoreticians of modernism.

Unlike the younger architects and editors who took over the professional journals in the 1930s, Penn's planning team, trained before World War I, sought a middle ground that would harmonize with the Cope and Stewardson campus by continuing the use of brick trimmed with light stone for the low-rise buildings. This formula was described as a goal of the 1948 master plan and was immediately ratified by the Board of Trustees. The centerpiece of the scheme was a 30-story limestone-clad skyscraper designed in the set-back massing of the RCA tower of Rockefeller Center, which was to stand on the vacated intersection of 36th and Locust Streets. Intended as a "Cathedral of Learning" like the University of Pittsburgh's 1920s skyscraper (by the Philadelphia firm of Day and Klauder), it was to be a visual sign of Penn's renewed vigor.

At first glance the 1948 scheme was hopelessly mired in the Beaux-Arts past. The new axis toward the proposed tower was forced; the asymmetrical brick buildings, overlaid with regularly spaced external column-like piers derived from early twentieth-century classicism, were insipid in conception, while their lack of ornament and detail reflected the more obvious characteristics of contemporary architecture but missed its subtlety. Fortunately much that the planners proposed never happened. The old University Library, Logan Hall, and most of the smaller Victorian buildings have survived, and most of these buildings have since been restored, notably enriching the campus. Careful examination of the planning portions of the 1948 scheme finds much of merit. In the aerial perspective published in the *Gazette* the north-south numbered streets between 34th and 40th Streets were largely eliminated, as was Locust Street, creating oversized "super-blocks" that excluded the automobile, asserting the pedestrian space of the campus over the urban grid. The plan's authors also recognized the new realities of the emerging campus. Penn had not acquired the lands to the north that were to be the basis of the central mall of the 1913 Cret plan;

instead it had been acquiring properties to the west along Locust and Spruce Streets. By 1948 the new Dietrich Hall of the Wharton School was designed and under construction on the 3600 block of Locust Street, establishing the Locust Street–Smith Walk corridor as the future campus spine. As a part of the new master plan, a War Memorial Flagpole was erected to serve as the eastern terminus of a walk system that was to cross the campus along the route of Locust Street.[24]

Thus the 1948 plan succeeded in two important regards: first it provided a vision of campus growth on the present site that once again caused the trustees to decide not to proceed with the Valley Forge site; and second, it turned the direction of Penn's future expansion away from the north-south axis of the Cret plan to the east-west axis of the modern University. The University of Pennsylvania could remain on its 1870s campus, benefiting from its established canopy of trees and from the buildings that represented nearly half the University's history.

Harold Stassen's Presidency

In response to Philadelphia's and Penn's continuing fall from the national scene, Penn's board looked outside their usual channels to select Harold Stassen (1948–53) as its first non-Philadelphian leader since William Smith in 1755. A decade earlier Stassen had been the "boy wonder" governor of Minnesota; his close loss in the run for the 1948 Republican nomination for the U.S. presidency caused many to view him as a sure winner in 1952.[25] By selecting Stassen as their president, members of Penn's board hoped that it would keep the University in the national spotlight during a short presidency that would end with Stassen and many Penn faculty and board members in positions of power in Washington.[26] The achievements of Stassen's presidency at Penn have been downplayed by later historians and by the institution itself largely because of his outsider roots, his nonacademic background that led to conflicts with faculty, his short-term status, and later his seemingly perpetual and quixotic pursuit of the presidency of the United States. Just as outsiders had transformed the center of Philadelphia, it would take an outsider such as Stassen to initiate change at the University.[27] Under Stassen, Penn came to be thought of as an acceptable alternative to the other great eastern American universities. James Michener (a Swarthmore graduate) caught the quickening of the spirit of the University in 1950:

Years ago an ambitious family would have hesitated at the idea of sending a son to the University of Pennsylvania. Princeton was a must. But now the

Harold Stassen with football team and former President McClelland, 1948. Photo: Jack Snyder. UPA.

scions of the old families attend Penn and live at home to cut expenses.[28]

After initially accommodating the football establishment, Stassen's Athletic Director Jeremiah Ford pushed Penn toward the unthinkable step of deemphasizing big-time football so that it could join an "Ivy League" of ancient east coast colleges and universities. The University's standing would be elevated by Penn's athletic association with those schools. Stassen also began a national search for academic stars who could enliven Penn's schools, and by enlarging the University administration he set the stage for the type of presidency Stillé had envisioned eighty years before.[29] Though Penn had changed the name of its leader from

G. Holmes Perkins with Louis I. Kahn and students, 1958. Photo: Jules Schick. UPA.

••••••••••••••••••••••••••••••••••

provost to president nearly twenty years before, Stassen was the first to take full advantage of the meaning of the title.

For the future of the campus, no appointment of Stassen's was more significant than a new dean of the School of Fine Arts. Attesting to the powers of the free-wheeling presidency he inherited, Stassen formed a committee independent of the faculty of the School of Fine Arts who met secretly with candidates for the deanship at New York's Century Club. After interviewing several candidates, they recommended G. Holmes Perkins, who had been a graduate and then a faculty member at Harvard's School of Architecture. With Stassen's blank check to hire new faculty, Perkins was convinced to move to Philadelphia.[30] The new dean was committed to the values of modern architecture as it had evolved in Europe between the two wars, but he himself had been taught by the generation who revered Henry Adams's *Mont-Saint-Michel and*

Chartres; the fruits of his hybrid education would appear in the faculty he assembled at Penn. Perkins selected a young faculty with an interest in teaching and practice. Many of them would leave their mark on the campus and on the American profession, including Robert Geddes, Ian McHarg, Romaldo Giurgola, Robert Venturi, and Denise Scott Brown.[31] The relative youth of this faculty was complemented by a smattering of mature teachers with broader perspectives, notably critic and cultural historian Lewis Mumford, architect and philosopher Louis I. Kahn, and later landscape architect and planner Sir Peter Shepheard. Together, in great rambling discussions that began in design studios, continued into faculty meetings, and spilled over into architectural juries, these men shaped the core of what is best about the appearance of the University of the present.

Perkins would also leave his mark on the city. During the war he had been the director of the Urban Development Division of the National Housing Agency, a position that gave him a broad overview of national urban policy. On his arrival at Penn, Perkins was quickly placed on the University planning councils as well as on the City Planning Commission. His activist stance caused many of his faculty to become involved in the reshaping of Philadelphia even before they had the opportunity to reshape their own institution.

The Harnwell Years

Perkins's partner in the transformation of the campus was not the soon to depart Stassen but Gaylord P. Harnwell, whose seventeen-year tenure as president (1953–70) was the longest of any of the modern University leaders. Trained at Haverford College and Princeton University in physics, he had served as department chair at Penn and proved to be a masterful leader. During the war he, like Perkins, had been recruited by the federal government. Harnwell was

••••••••••••••••••••••••••••••••••

Gaylord P. Harnwell with model of campus development, 1968. Photo: Frank Ross. UPA.

selected to work with the west coast team that developed sonar, for which he received the Medal of Merit and the Order of the British Empire. With Harnwell's background in modern physics and Perkins's allegiance to the ideals and values of modern design, Penn once again had a close fit between contemporary design principles that expressed the modern industrial culture and institutional leadership, recalling the Pepper-Furness decade of the 1880s. Their scheme for campus renewal manifested the institutional and cultural changes that were initiated during Harnwell's term in office.

The delay between Gaylord P. Harnwell's accession to the presidency in 1953 and the actual planning and reconstruction of the campus at the end of the decade was one of the side effects of the collapse of Philadelphia's industrial base. During the 1950s increasing competition from new factories located in the rebuilt industrial complexes of Europe and the Pacific rim, often using technologies pioneered in Philadelphia, proved disastrous for the regional economy. By the 1960s even the region's foundation industries, such as the Pennsylvania Railroad, were faltering. Emblematic of the effects of the changing economic climate of the city were the means by which the University acquired its first main-frame computer and the different means by which it obtained its solid-state successor six years later. In 1957 Harnwell, like earlier generations of Penn leaders, looked to Philadelphia industrialists for capital and assistance for the acquisition of a main-frame computer. The Remington Rand Corporation, which had acquired the commercial rights to the computer from its Penn inventors, gave a UNIVAC I to the University.[32] Only six years later, when solid-state computer technology had reached the market, Penn was forced to depend for assistance on federal government agencies rather than its earlier industrial sources. Within less than a generation after the end of World War II, Philadelphia industrialists were no longer able to fund the University's growth. In the future, Penn would depend for capital on sources outside the immediate Philadelphia

region. Much of this new funding would come from federal sources as University researchers studied social, economic, and scientific issues. In 1964 for the first time the University received more funding from research than from tuition.[33]

The new funding sources brought other changes that transformed the University during the Harnwell years. When industry was the principal supporter of research, the vast majority of graduate students were part-time and were drawn from local businesses. In the 1960s federal and foundation support for research produced numerous full-time fellowships that reversed the proportion of part- and full-time students. Simultaneously, the numbers of graduate students rose from fewer than a hundred at the turn of the century to the thousands of the present-day university. The numbers of faculty and researchers rose correspondingly, transforming the character of the institution from a sleepy university with a powerhouse football team and a few good undergraduate departments, notably History and English, to a modern university with an emphasis on advanced research.

The nature of the research funded by the federal government changed, too. Much of the research was classified work for the Department of Defense. As campus unrest over the Vietnam War expanded, students and faculty debated whether the genie of classified research could be contained. The battle lines were clear. For Harnwell, who had led wartime research teams and who needed outside sources of funding, freedom to conduct research was an academic right whose morality should be judged by the individual researcher. For other members of the faculty, Harnwell's laissez faire approach was amoral at best. The battle raged across the campus with student demonstrations and faculty debate. In the fall of 1965, while acknowledging the University's need for federal, foundation, and industrial support, the University Senate debated the appropriateness of classified research on campus and resolved that:

It is the obligation of a faculty member to make

freely available to his colleagues and to the public the significant results he has achieved in the course of his inquiries...the freedom of inquiry shall never be abrogated, and except when a national emergency has been declared by the President of the United States, and then only in circumstances that require it, the obligation to disseminate freely the results of such inquiry shall not be abrogated.[34]

In the atmosphere of distrust represented by the debate over classified research, much of the unity that had characterized the University was lost. In its place would come greater involvement by students who questioned, challenged, and battled with administrators and ultimately shaped the present institution.

A Broader Board for a National University

The collapse of Philadelphia's industrial economy precipitated a changing of the guard on the Board of Trustees of the University. In the early twentieth century Penn already had begun seeking trustees from beyond the city, but after World War II a concerted effort was made to draw board membership that represented the University's turn toward a national and international constituency. As the industries of the city failed, fewer and fewer local executives were viewed as potential candidates for the board. Like Franklin's first Board of Trustees, Penn's modern board accurately reflects the varied backgrounds of the University's community of students and faculty and attests to its standing among the great universities of the world. Still, into the 1970s, despite the increasing diversity of the board members, the leaders continued to be locally born, Penn-educated, and chiefs of Philadelphia-based corporations and businesses. More recently, the board has reflected the success of Wharton graduates in the New York financial markets. Under their guidance Penn's endowments have grown, further reducing the University's dependence on local industry.

With trustees drawn from the entire nation and the world, it has no longer been possible (or desirable) for the entire board to oversee the day-to-day activities of the University. This is not to say that the trustees no longer serve important roles. Members with particular expertise have continued to provide counsel for the University departments, mirroring the old committee system of the earlier board. For the campus and the School of Fine Arts, notable architects such as Sydney Martin (Ar 1907), Bruce Graham (Ar 1948), and Eugene Kohn (Ar 1954, GAr 1957) have served on oversight committees, while trustees with expertise in real estate and commercial development, such as Walter G. Arader (W 1942) and Myles Tanenbaum (W 1952, L 1957), have served with distinction on committees that have overseen campus development.

To replace the leadership provided by the board before World War II, Harnwell enlarged the University central administration and restructured it with separate departments given responsibility for specific tasks. The administration became a bureaucracy not unlike the enlarged federal government that had emerged under the Roosevelt administration and had become the model for other universities as well. The new bureaucratic structure of the University was reflected in campus planning. No longer was planning principally the mandate of the dean of the School of Fine Arts as had been the case ever since the arrival of Warren Powers Laird in 1891. In 1959 a University Planning Office was established as a branch of the central administration; the following year, Harold Taubin, a protégé of G. Holmes Perkins, was selected to head the planning office.[35]

University Redevelopment District Planning

The previous system of knitting new buildings into an existing campus one by one was inadequate to handle the University's postwar expansion. With Penn hemmed in on the north, east, and south, future growth had to occur on privately held land to the west. In ordinary times, private ownership of land would have permitted only piecemeal expansion based on the negotiated sale of individual properties, but the 1949 Urban Renewal Act offered government agencies a means of cutting the Gordian knot that limited the transformation of cities and restricted institutional growth. While Penn was forming its planning department, City Planning Commission director Edmund Bacon certified a University Redevelopment Area as part of the city's urban renewal program. For the first time since Penn moved west in 1871, it was possible for its planners to design in bold strokes. The academic and residential campuses of the present University are largely the results of this planning.

The first stages of this plan began somewhat tentatively with the closing of Locust Street between 37th and 36th Streets in 1963. Two years later the construction of a new trolley tunnel under a corner of Drexel's campus and south along 36th Street to the vacated route of Woodland Avenue permitted the removal of the trolleys from Woodland Avenue, leading to its closing between 34th and 38th Streets to create the first superblock of the main campus. Most of these spaces remained unlandscaped, but Ian McHarg, the leading proponent of sustainable design on the School of Fine Arts faculty, drew plans for a sequence of small parks above the trolley route under Woodland Avenue between the Wharton School and the Wistar Institute that suggested the potential richness of the campus. Together these projects aimed University expansion west and pointed the way toward pedestrian walkways separated from vehicular traffic modeled on the forward-looking residential planning at Radburn, New Jersey and Greenbelt, Maryland.[36]

Planning for University City

In 1960 the planning office undertook a multiyear master plan that was intended to guide development until 1966. Instead of focusing on single buildings within the limits of the University, the plan looked at much of West Philadelphia as far west as 50th Street and as far north as Powelton. Under the rubric "University City," the region (to the concern of many who lived there) was viewed from the perspective of the future expansion of Penn, Drexel, and the smaller

Philadelphia College of Pharmacy and Science and the College of Osteopathy. The University's master plan called for housing a larger portion of students on campus, for expanding academic facilities, and for encouraging faculty to live in the residential neighborhoods in the immediate vicinity of the campus through the use of innovative mortgage guarantees.[37] The impact of the University's new planning office was immediately apparent in the constant dust and noise of construction activity that transformed a large area of West Philadelphia from 33rd Street to 40th Street.

During the first half of the twentieth century, in Great Britain and later in the United States, regional planning had evolved as a counter to the individual goals of speculative development. Penn's postwar planners had to deal with the large scale of urban renewal and with the automobile's seemingly insatiable demand for space. The plan that emerged for the campus paralleled the ideas of modern town planning. Across America work remained concentrated in downtowns while shopping was relocated along highways creating modern shopping centers; institutions and residences were pushed toward the suburban periphery. Penn followed a similar formula, as Locust Walk became an internal pedestrian spine connecting the sports and academic centers on the east with the bedroom suburbs of the dormitories to the west. Commerce was restricted to a University-built shopping mall midway between the two centers. Taking a cue from suburban office parks, the main facade of the proposed library was turned inward toward the campus and away from the street and the city. Departmental groupings such as Psychology and Education were shaped around their own courtyards while other buildings such as the McNeil Social Sciences Building were created around an interior court.

An Architectural Laboratory
Instead of a Museum

Though it was the 1948 master plan and the subsequent 1960–61 development plan that provided the

David Rittenhouse Laboratory, looking north, 1954. UPA.

framework for institutional growth, to the casual observer the changing styles and new materials of buildings have signaled Penn's directions after World War II. For the initial round of post-World War II buildings such as the Wharton School's Dietrich Hall on Locust Street, the old palette of red brick and light stone trim was modified toward a modern style in accordance with the 1948 plan. Although Penn planners had initially diagnosed the need for additional dormitory space, new classrooms, and a central library, the priority given to laboratories reflected the growing national concern about national leadership in scientific research during the Cold War. As a result, the first fruits of the collaboration between University leadership under President Harnwell and Dean Perkins and his faculty were the laboratory buildings which announced the architectural themes of the next decade. Two of these labs, the David Rittenhouse Laboratory (1954) and the Pender wing that linked the Moore School to the Towne Building (1956), were erected on the east side of the campus in the developing science precinct, while the third, the Alfred Newton Richards laboratory (1957), was

constructed in the medical school campus.

The earliest of these new buildings, the David Rittenhouse Laboratory, was the work of James Edmunds, who had served on the architectural master planning board of 1948. In the forward-looking spirit of the new era of science, Edmunds proposed reddish-orange instead of the customary deep red brick, steel instead of wood sash, and cold white marble instead of the warm tones of Penn's limestone trim. This new palette of materials (later slightly modified toward orange and adopted by adjacent Drexel University for its technology-oriented campus) was arranged in forms that were unmistakably modern. Since the 1890s Penn had followed the model of Cope and Stewardson's Cambridge-based mask over buildings of varying functions, but during the Harnwell years nonhistorical design became the rule. New technology-driven laboratories might be expected to be up-to-date, even innovative in representing function; by the 1960s every corner of the Penn campus was affected by modernism. Modernism was the rule not only for parking garages and other new design problems, but also for the central library, undergraduate and graduate housing, faculty club, and classroom buildings, in short, the entire range of buildings of the growing University. Although in the 1930s it had been pro-

posed that some temporary buildings such as laboratories might be constructed in modern materials, by
the late 1950s, Penn, like its peer institutions, was
looking forward.[38]

Peers as Patrons: Selection and Design in the 1960s

At Penn the modernists' confrontation with the rejected Academic Gothic uniform threatened to make
the new campus a patchwork of construction systems
and materials. To be sure there was precedent, for Yale
also had abandoned its historical forms and unified
palette for the diverse modes and materials of the
present. At Yale there were important Philadelphia
connections, notably the Dean of the School of Architecture, Philadelphian George Howe, whose 1931
Philadelphia Savings Fund Society (PSFS) skyscraper
on Market Street had become a classic of American
modernism. He had brought his architectural associate Louis I. Kahn to the Yale architecture faculty and
in 1953 had persuaded Yale to retain Kahn as the
architect for an addition to the existing art gallery.
Writing a decade after it was commissioned, with
buildings in the new style at every corner of the Yale
campus, Jonathan Barnett understood the seminal
importance of Kahn's work:

> Yale's first major building after the war, the exten-
> sion of the University art gallery completed in
> 1953, provided an unusually clear test case for
> modern architecture. The original building, de-
> signed in a style officially designated as Lombardic
> Romanesque, represented two-fifths of a projected
> structure now impossible to complete because of
> prohibitive costs. In a situation fraught with possi-
> bilities for compromise, the University proceeded
> to erect a building that has become famous as an
> example of uncompromising intellectual rigor; it is
> the work of Louis I. Kahn, then teaching at Yale. .
> . . Kahn's name was suggested by the late George
> Howe, at that time the chairman of the department
> of Architecture, who thus did much to put Yale on

the course that has been followed so successfully
ever since.[39]

Of equal significance was Barnett's conclusion that
"The art gallery extension was more a product of the
policy of the School of Art and Architecture than the
University itself."

Penn's campus was the result of similar forces, in
particular the influence of the new dean on President
Harnwell, but with a significant difference: the "old
boy" network still found a way to affect the awarding
of commissions. At Penn as at Yale, an important
agent of change was the revised selection process for
designers. Heretofore most of the architectural commissions for the campus had gone to designers selected by the donor or the provost (or in instances such
as Irvine Auditorium by an interested trustee). This
process tended to produce conservative designs that
reflected the often conventional taste of those outside
of the design field. Beginning in the mid-1950s, the
architects of Penn's expansion were selected by an
advisory committee headed by Dean Perkins. It included trustee Sydney Martin, who had led the design
team for the 1948 master plan and headed the architectural firm of Martin, Stewart and Noble, and Roy
Larson of Harbeson, Hough, Livingston and Larson,
successors to Paul Cret's firm. J. Roy Carroll of Carroll,
Grisdale and Van Alen also joined the committee from
time to time. These firms were preapproved by the
Pennsylvania General State Authority (GSA) on the
grounds that they were easy to deal with, making
them eligible to work on state-funded projects. Original design was not the highest priority. As projects
were proposed that would be funded by the GSA—for
the Social Sciences complex, the central library, the
Fine Arts Building, and later laboratories such as the
Laboratory for Research on the Structure of Matter,
the extension to the David Rittenhouse Laboratory,
and the administration's Franklin Building—the work
was parceled out more or less in rotation among the
three firms.[40] The fact that the GSA was an outside
agency with no long-term vision for the University

was not taken into account, nor was the question whether the impoverished designs would be detrimental to the future of the institution. After 1963, when the state announced that henceforth GSA would provide not grants but loans the University would have to repay, the quality of publicly-funded buildings fell even lower. Not coincidentally, none of the GSA-funded buildings are cherished in the present.

Nowhere was the failure of publicly-funded projects to arrive at high architectural quality that would prove of lasting value more evident than in the dormitories of the late 1960s. Initially, the University had intended to fund its new dormitories from its General Fund. Studies undertaken during the 1960s established principles of small college houses of 300 students with a density of fewer than 150 students per acre; each house would have faculty residents and separate dining rooms to encourage collegiality. In a reversal of the old plans that had placed women on the far west border of the University, the men's dormitories were to be built between 39th and 40th Streets and the women's residences were to be built on the east, near Bennett Hall.[41] University planners determined that men would continue to dominate the institution by maintaining a ratio of four men to one woman. Architects were commissioned to produce studies and eventually working drawings for the new low-rise men's dormitories, but the project stalled in the late 1960s when it became apparent that the University's $93,000,000 fund drive would fall far short of its goal. Pennsylvania Higher Education Facilities Authority funds that could be borrowed for housing would not meet the projected costs of the low-rise house system. To bring the same number of students onto campus for lower costs, the University commissioned a new team of architects and planners headed by Dean Perkins and the Department of Architecture's professor of design, Mario Romañach, to design a cluster of high-rise dormitories.

Recalling Le Corbusier's revolutionary towers of "Radiant City" planning that had been the new idea when they were in school in the 1920s, the architects placed high-rise towers off the center of three of the four blocks while reserving the northeast quadrant for a group of existing Victorian and turn-of-the-century mansions, where it was intended that the University president ultimately would live. These new towers shared the scale and vocabulary of modern housing projects, abandoning the low-rise dormitory formula that had served the University for more than half a century. Constructed in the drab tans and grays of architectural concrete and unadorned by ornament other than the plastic elements of their massing, with broad sheets of glass that denoted lobbies and lounges, they capped the transformation of the campus of the Harnwell years.[42] The myths that have developed about their supposed origins as NASA wind tunnels and the continuing legend about their temporary status are proofs that they have not been favorites among the undergraduate community.

The University had greater freedom in selecting architects for projects that were funded through the University's General Fund.[43] For those projects, Dean Perkins and Sydney Martin sought designers who would bring distinction to the University. The trustees insisted on one remaining control. The architect had to be a University of Pennsylvania graduate (or, later, a member of its faculty), presumably to ensure that there was some awareness of the Penn culture. Instead of viewing the future through the lens of the past, as committees of trustees had done when they chose the architects, the new selection process run by design professionals chose designers of interest to the profession rather than to the alumni. Henceforth Penn's design committee would no longer select the same architects who were being hired by the trustees for their homes and their workplaces, as had been the case since the late eighteenth century. Architecture selected by architects proved to be dramatically different from the designs that had been selected in previous decades by trustees.

Working from the principle that good design was more important than the old standard of the visual unity of the campus, Perkins sought innovative designers who would add to the prestige of the University. In some instances he proposed architects who were working at peer institutions, but he was also careful to find commissions for the rising stars of the Penn faculty. This was sometimes managed by subterfuge. In one instance, Perkins offered trustee Sydney Martin the opportunity to select the designer for either the Alfred Newton Richards Medical Research Laboratories or the new women's dormitory, thereby hoping to get an important non-Penn architect for the remaining building. Perkins was astonished when Martin selected Eero Saarinen, who had no known Penn connection, for Hill Hall, leaving Perkins free to select Penn grad and faculty member Louis I. Kahn for the research laboratory. Martin confided to Perkins that a Penn graduate who worked in Saarinen's office would be the firm representative at Penn, and that this was good enough for him.[44] By teaming a Philadelphia office with Richard Neutra, it was possible to bring that aging pioneer modernist to the Penn campus for the Graduate Towers. In another instance, Perkins let it be known that if Geddes, Brecher and Qualls, all young members of his faculty from other architectural schools, would add a recent Penn graduate to their practice, then they too would be eligible for a Penn commission. By adding Warren Cunningham (Ar 1949) to their office, they received a future partner—and the Pender Laboratory project.

Before 1950 Penn's West Philadelphia campus buildings had all been designed by native Philadelphians; henceforth important commissions would go to architects of national repute, wherever they were based. Given their varied backgrounds and interests, it was no wonder that Penn's new buildings were as disparate as they were. Saarinen used fiery-red cull-bricks to surround an interior Italian courtyard for Hill Hall; Neutra's graduate housing adapted the contemporary vocabulary of architectural concrete and glass for the undergraduate towers while reverting stylistically toward the early twentieth-century constructivist idiom of contrasting transparency and solidity. Mitchell/Giurgola overlaid the expressive concrete frame of their first parking garage on Walnut Street with a purplish brick screen wall. The coffee-colored brick of Geddes, Brecher, Qualls and Cunningham's

••••••••••••••••••••••••••••••••••••••

Louis I. Kahn, sketch of Richards Medical Research Laboratory. Architectural Archives.

Stouffer Triangle contrasted with the Quad's red brick, while Bower and Fradley's Vance Hall and Vincent Kling's Annenberg Center and Small Animal Hospital for the Veterinary School epitomized the brown decade of the 1970s in their brownish tinted brick. Mirroring the diversity of post-World War II America, Penn's campus was no longer a static continuation of themes of ancient European colleges; joining the new culture of the modern world that ranged from Walt Whitman to Jack Kerouac, the campus reflected the present.

Penn was not alone in choosing cutting-edge designers. Its post-1955 architecture was part of a larger rejection by the architectural profession of the design principles of the Beaux Arts that affected every great American university, no matter how rigid its existing architectural frames. On McKim, Mead and White's symmetrical brick and limestone Georgian-styled campus for Columbia University and Cope and Stewardson's pink granite and limestone Gothic-styled campus for Washington University in St. Louis, symmetry of form and axiality of plan were discarded as arbitrary and not conforming to the organic reality of modern life. At such eastern institutions as Princeton and Yale Universities and Bryn Mawr College, Louis Kahn, Eero Saarinen, Paul Rudolph, Minoru Yamasaki, and other modernists discarded the historic palette of materials and details, replacing them with scaleless modern materials. At Penn, where the green serpentine stone Victorian Gothic campus of Provost Stillé had been supplanted by the red-brick realism of Provost Pepper's campus, which in turn had given way to Provost Harrison's brick and limestone English campus, the variety of the new fit with the old with surprisingly felicitous results. Indeed, given the variations of Penn's past campus, the momentary unity of the Cope and Stewardson era may have been an aberration while the architecture of the 1870s to 1880s and the 1950s to 1990s may be more representative of the realism that is central to the character of the institution. In any event, there was method in these changes, for the new buildings, visible from the bridges and highways that are the principal entrances to the modern city, made it clear, that like Bacon's renewed downtown, Penn had wholeheartedly and confidently embraced the modern world.

The Philadelphia School Architects at Penn

While Penn was bringing nationally-known architects to its campus, it was also commissioning young members of the fine arts faculty to test their ideas about campus planning. By the late 1950s, under the influence of Kahn, most of the faculty had turned toward the descriptive and expressive realism that characterized the so-called "Philadelphia School" of design. In 1961, in a seminal article on this contextual and functionally expressive architecture, Jan Rowan asserted that under Perkins "a new design renaissance that might prove as important . . . as the Chicago School" was centered in the Graduate School of Fine Arts.[45] Although the style has been principally associated with Louis Kahn, the first project on campus to show its characteristics was by faculty members Geddes, Brecher, and Qualls, who designed the Pender Laboratory as a link between the Moore School and the Towne Building. There, instead of simply reversing the norms of campus design as had occurred at David Rittenhouse Laboratory, the new lab shared features of the historic architecture of its setting in the contextual use of Flemish bond brick panels and front retaining walls that flanked a precast concrete frame whose columns interlocked with a three-dimensional web of girders and beams.

The following year Louis Kahn was awarded the commission to design the Alfred Newton Richards Medical Research Building. His complex and revealing design acknowledged and responded to the context of the Cope and Stewardson dormitory quadrangle across Hamilton Walk while also expressing the various functions within the building in a way that recalled Furness's Library of seventy years earlier. The Richards laboratory was immediately recognized as a modern masterpiece. In 1961, the year the first wing was completed, it was the subject of an exhibit at

New York's Museum of Modern Art. Hailed by Wilder Green as "the single most consequential building constructed in the United States since the war," more than any single structure it epitomized the Philadelphia School and gave the University's Graduate School of Fine Arts national and international prominence.[46]

That the Philadelphia School would arise at Penn in the late 1950s was fitting. Despite the dominance of the Beaux-Arts system of design at Penn's School of Fine Arts from 1900 until 1940, young architects with eyes to see in Philadelphia must have noticed the myriad nonclassical designs from the age of engineering that gave the city its special character. Frank Furness's library stood in the heart of the campus and for many years housed Kahn's architectural studio; two of Furness's railroad stations were still in service in Center City; his banks still dominated Bankers' Row in the old city. Those structures must have always made it apparent to young architects that there were other avenues to nonhistorical design than the simplistic formulas of European Modernism taught in many American universities. On the Penn faculty, Lewis Mumford was a powerful advocate of the idea that Americans had contributed to the development of modern architecture and would continue to contribute to its future. This was the central thesis of Mumford's *Roots of Contemporary Architecture*, the textbook of American critical writings Mumford selected and edited for his course at Penn. As Mumford's years at Penn drew to a close, Robert Venturi taught architectural theory and turned his course notes into *Complexity and Contradiction in Architecture*, which became the manifesto of the late twentieth century. Drawing on the intellectual ferment within the faculty and the strengths of their historic campus and city, Penn's architectural faculty established an original mode of design that enriched the campus for a decade with buildings that demand attention because of their evocative expression of their internal functions and their

•••••••••••••••••••••••••••••••••

Walnut Street looking west from 36th Street, c. 1960.
UPA.

subtle adjustment to context. Few campuses have been blessed with so many examples of the best of modern design by the masters of the Philadelphia School. Louis I. Kahn, Robert Geddes, Ehrman Mitchell and Romaldo Giurgola, and John Bower and more recently Robert Venturi and Denise Scott Brown have continued to carry the banner of provocative, communicative, and contextually responsive design into the 1990s.

It was also not a coincidence that the Philadelphia school reached its peak at Penn during the years when the University was led by a scientist, Gaylord P. Harnwell. Like Provost Pepper three-quarters of a century earlier, Harnwell was comfortable with the challenge of the present and like his nineteenth-century predecessor, he was able to delegate authority. Penn's modern architecture reflected the poetry of the discordant present just as Furness's architecture of the 1870s and 1880s had resonated with the values of the booming industrial city during the provostship of William Pepper. In 1970, as the Harnwell presidency drew to a close, there seemed to be a major construction project at every corner of the campus. At 36th, 37th, and 39th Streets sidewalks and paving were disappearing, while along 38th Street whole rows of buildings were being demolished to widen it into a broad north-south connector. The rows of Victorian suburban houses framed by those streets were soon being cleared for the undergraduate dormitories, the Class of 1920 Commons, and the open spaces around them. On the eastern campus, late nineteenth-century buildings such as the Hare Laboratories and the John Harrison Laboratory of Chemistry were demolished for new classroom buildings and modern laboratories. Along Walnut Street, where Grand's Restaurant (now remembered for its giant Robert Venturi-designed teacup sign) and Cy's Penn Lunch had fueled students before exams and where the Onion, the Deck, and Smokey Joe's had provided solace afterward, and along Spruce Street, where Pagano's pizzeria, Mackrides's shoe repair shop, and Joseph Bank's Clothiers had served generations of Penn students, sites were cleared

for the new academic support facility (3401 Walnut Street), for Vance Hall for Wharton's graduate division, and for additional dormitories.

The demolition of the old setting corroborated the true extent of change that was sweeping the entire University. However, the failure of the 1960s development campaign stifled many of the initiatives of the Meyerson presidency that followed, forcing Penn's

••••••••••••••••••••••••••••

Martin Meyerson, 1970. Photo: Frank Ross. UPA.
Campus Development Plan, 1961. Architectural Archives.

trustees once again to consider privately whether to affiliate with the state to ensure the flow of public dollars. The loss of quality in design that the GSA-funded buildings represented indicated the perils of that approach, and it was quickly rejected. The pretense of a separate, parallel women's college finally ended with the decision to admit men and women in equal proportions and to grow into a national rather than a regional institution. In the meantime, Penn had so completely adhered to the principles of the Ivy League that its football team found a nearly perma-

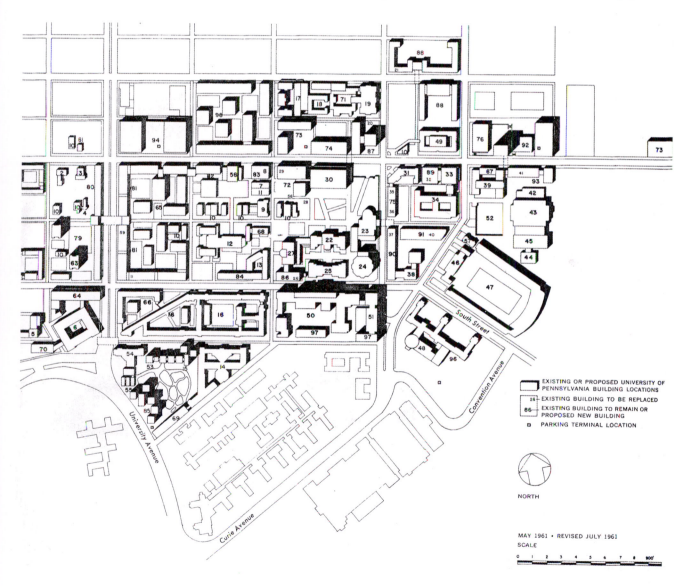

EXISTING OR PROPOSED UNIVERSITY OF PENNSYLVANIA BUILDING LOCATIONS

EXISTING BUILDING TO BE REPLACED

EXISTING BUILDING TO REMAIN OR PROPOSED NEW BUILDING

PARKING TERMINAL LOCATION

NORTH

MAY 1961 • REVISED JULY 1961
SCALE

nent position in the basement of the league. The roar of the crowd switched from Saturday to Sunday, when Philadelphia Eagles fans shook the campus with their cheers. For those who strolled from Franklin Field to their parked automobiles, it was clear that Penn was no longer the "Old Penn" of inheritance and privilege.

Recent Years and the Landscape Master Plan

By the late 1970s, the volume of Penn's buildings and the acreage of its campus had once again doubled. Nearly 30,000 students, faculty, and staff worked and lived in a campus that stretched from 32nd Street to the rear of the Palestra to the west side of 40th Street beyond the Dental School, and from the rear of Drexel south of Chestnut Street to Civic Center Boulevard. Penn's new president, Martin Meyerson, was especially suited for the tasks of the 1970s. Trained as a city planner at Harvard, Meyerson had worked with Edmund Bacon in Philadelphia's city planning office before joining Perkins's faculty. After various teaching posts and the presidency of the State University of New York at Buffalo, he returned to Philadelphia in 1970 to serve as the University's president.

Under Harnwell Penn had become an immense institution, but its sudden growth had outstripped the landscape that dated back to the efforts of Provost Harrison's wife in the 1890s. It was an awkward time. The interstices between buildings was too frequently merely unbuilt space, and the walks and roads were leftovers as well. The diagonal *allée* of poplars across the central campus remained from the former route of Woodland Avenue from 34th to 36th Streets; the curbs had been removed but the old street was still revealed in the strips of macadam walkways. Other walks paid homage to the ghosts of removed buildings. New mud paths across the sparse lawns denoted changing needs that were not met by the old walks. The new campus was immense but disjointed; like the campus Harrison had inherited in the 1890s, it lacked the connecting tissue of walks, monuments, trees. Still, within the campus there were areas of beauty that hinted at what could be. Cope and Stewardson's elm-shaded Smith

Walk between 33rd and 34th Streets and Hamilton Walk along the south side of the dormitory quad offered a late Victorian scheme of trees ordered like columns within a nave of red brick walls. George Patton's Locust Walk, which replaced Locust Street with a Persian carpet of brick and stone, and Ian McHarg's linked small squares along the route of Woodland Avenue were examples of good modern design. But these small jewels were overwhelmed by the functional and utilitarian character of most of the campus.

The disjointed appearance of the main campus was especially grating to Penn's next dean of the Graduate School of Fine Arts, Sir Peter Shepheard, whose particular specialty was the forming of urban landscapes. In 1975, at the request of Penn's renamed Department of Facilities Planning, the Center for Environmental Design was created to work on a campus landscape development plan. Directed by Dean Shepheard, the center consisted of faculty in the Landscape program of the Graduate School of Fine Arts, particularly Laurie Olin, Rolf Sauer, Leslie Sauer, Carol Franklin, Colin Franklin, and Narendra Juneja. Several had studied with Ian McHarg, and all were concerned with the rigorous application of ecological principles within a strong design framework. Together they produced a plan that focused not on further growth, but on knitting together elements that were functionally related but dis-integrated. The drafters of the plan reported that Penn's campus

was besieged by multimillion dollar buildings, each with its own peculiar problems. There had been a kind of functional breakdown of the campus overall, so much so that it became questionable whether the University plan was indeed operating. For the 1961 master plan had created a plethora of new problems, perhaps more devastating in human terms than the initial chaotic growth that it was supposed to have governed. The campus pedestrian and ve-

••••••••••••••••••••••••••••••••••••

Sir Peter Shepheard on campus, 1978. Photo: Fred Sacks. UPA.

hicular systems had become a maze of conflicts. The open space had been reduced, or its character so altered, that there was now inadequate space for private retreat, casual recreation, and even competitive sports. The rich edges of the campus had all but disappeared, with the intimate mix of housing, shops, and city life usurped by massive single-use, University controlled buildings, Worst of all, it seemed that the very life, balance and identity of the campus was being lost.[47]

To be effective, the campus had to be more than merely the setting for the University. Rather, it must become "a city, an ideal city of ideal and communal life" whose function was to bring people together for learning. Working from a premise similar to that of Cope and Stewardson three-quarters of a century earlier, the new team of planners observed that "the campus is the largest and most intricate 'room' of the University," and sought to make it special. Shepheard and his associates Laurie Olin and the future principals of Andropogon Associates advanced the novel idea that the appearance of the University was in many ways as important as the classroom education.

  For the first time since Provost Harrison, attention was paid to the campus as setting. Not surprisingly, the models found by the modern planners were the surviving fragments of Cope and Stewardson's landscapes from the end of the last century, Hamilton Walk behind the dormitory quadrangles, the garden courtyard of the University Museum, and Smith Walk between Hayden Hall and the Towne Building. The first fruits of this new vision were the spaces that now form Blanche Levy Park, the renamed central campus. A similar approach that separates pedestrian from vehicular traffic, establishes tree-shaded walkways, and light dappled lawns has since been expanded west along Locust Walk and the old bed of 37th Street. As important as the Landscape Development Plan's contribution to the Penn setting, however was its contribution to the future of the region. Drawing on their collegial experience, two of the principal landscape

firms of the region Andropogon Associates and the Olin Partnership were formed. Their work on campus continues to enliven its outdoor rooms.

The Hyper-University

During the presidency of Sheldon Hackney (1980–93), as the nation's historic preservation movement came of age, Penn began caring for and restoring the buildings of its central campus. In part this change in attitude reflected the softening effects of age; in part it reflected the contrast between the human scale of the old campus with the larger scale of modern buildings. Certainly too, Robert Venturi's *Complexity and Contradiction in Architecture* had sensitized the design professions to the expressive values of architecture from eras other than the present. By the 1970s the Philadelphia Museum of Art had organized a major exhibit on Frank Furness, while his Centennial-era landmark, the Pennsylvania Academy of the Fine Arts, was being restored under the direction of Hyman Myers (GAr 1965). When the new walkways and grass lawns of the central campus were finished, it was suddenly apparent that Penn had much to like about itself. The interweaving of new with old had created juxtapositions such as Furness's red library against the green serpentine of College Hall. Trumbauer's French Irvine Auditorium was an effective landmark at the corner of 34th Street. Buildings that were hated had come to be loved. More revolutionary was the direction of new buildings on the campus such as Robert Venturi's Institute for Advanced Science and Technology. Designed to complement rather than conflict with the historic campus while remaining challenging in its expression of tasks and siting, it offers a much-needed antidote to the often banal contextualism of much of recent design on the campus. A century from now, this lab may be serving another purpose—but it should still be interesting.[48]

  Penn's love affair with its historic buildings is neither an aberration nor an affectation. It is the logical outcome of one hundred and twenty five years of campus building in West Philadelphia. A quarter of

Sheldon Hackney, c. 1986. UPA.

••

a century after laying the corner stone of College Hall in 1871, Penn opened the doors of Houston Hall. A century after the opening of Houston Hall, the serpentine facades of College and Logan Halls have been restored and Frank Furness's old University Library has been restored to its astonishing exterior color with its great five-story reading room once again open to its skylight. Simultaneously, University trustees and planners have embraced the core values of the Harrison years, preferring for new construction the rich palette of red brick and light stone advocated in

1895 by John Stewardson to unify the campus and at the same time create precincts unified by function. The future bodes well for Penn's historic buildings. A century after its opening, Venturi, Scott Brown and Associates have developed a plan by which Houston Hall will be restored as a part of the Perelman Quadrangle, functionally linking the University's hearth with a modified and acoustically improved Irvine Auditorium and a restored Logan Hall to keep the center of the campus alive and vital.

More significant for the future of the institution have been the initiatives of the Rodin years that have turned the University outward toward its community. Penn's multiyear plans of the 1960s caused many long-time neighbors to fear that their community would suffer from the pressures of urban redevelopment.[49] A former neighborhood resident, Sister Mary Ann Craig, recalled, "Because we were aware that Penn always had 'plans' for our area, life took on a 'provisional' quality for all of us. How long would we stay? Who knew? One thing was sure: One day, in some five-year plan our homes and neighborhood would cease to exist. This caused not only depressed property values but also a sense of disconnection from the responsibility to take root and seriously plan our lives together as neighbors."[50] As a result of the extent of change, many residents sold out to a new group of landlords who saw the economic potential of the student real estate market. The new student market, though lucrative, was a mixed blessing, replacing a stable resident base with transient and less experienced undergraduates. Lacking the standards of homeowners, absentee landlords no longer attended to the niceties of flower planting, house-painting, trash removal, and cleanup that make communities pleasant. Retailing aimed entirely at undergraduates and the lowest common denominator seemed to rule in the selection of restaurants, shops and movies. With the city school system continuing to decline, faculty and staff members who had been attracted to the neighborhood for its convenience and its rich stock of housing, as well as its remarkable transportation connections to the region, began to move out, making the neighborhoods of the University as far west as 48th Street a student quarter.

By the early 1990s, there were signs of stress in every area of University City. Students had begun to cross the Schuylkill in search of housing in safe neighborhoods; the undergraduate and graduate high-rise dormitories had so many vacancies that rooms were being rented to Drexel students. Vacant apartments and storefronts indicated a neighborhood on the decline. Under President Rodin, a series of initiatives were taken to reverse the community decline. Vacancies in the superblock dormitories were viewed as signals of larger campus problems that demanded a broad response rather than simply requiring students to live in the dorms. Unfortunately, the high-rise towers had never fostered the type of community facilitated by the Cope and Stewardson dormitory quadrangle. Indeed, given the track record of high-rise housing for less sophisticated tenant groups, this might have been anticipated. Beginning in the 1950s, critics had analyzed the problems of "skyscraper Utopias of Le Corbusier and Gropius" and found them wanting for public housing. It should not have been a great leap to see that they were equally unsuited for undergraduates in their first unsupervised residential experience.[51] Jane Jacobs's hymn to the value of the street and the anonymity of the high-rise of 1961, *The Death and Life of Great American Cities*, should have been an even more forceful warning about the potential problems that the high-rise dormitories posed. When the buildings first opened in 1970, students who left their doors open on the assumption that they were living in a dorm were victimized by crimes that ranged from the minor to the serious. Over three decades, the buildings proved difficult to manage and were usually the last choice behind the quad, off-campus housing, and even the tiny rooms of Hill House.

Solutions to the problems of Superblock overlapped with the goal of the Rodin administration to foster the undergraduate experience. Centered in Penn's 21st Century Project for the Undergraduate Experience, a University committee looked at the issues of campus housing. For the high-rises, options were explored from demolition or radical redesign to modest renovation. After much discussion, it was determined to rethink the goals of the high-rises, re-integrating them into a comprehensive scheme that would return to the original goals of the 1960s planners who had proposed small college houses. In the final plan, college houses with faculty masters and graduate residents will foster academic and social goals that will link students and faculty while also providing advising and academic support. In the coming years, additional planning studies will look at replacing the underutilized windy plains around the high rises with a denser and more urban streetscape perhaps mixing commerce and housing.

Surveys of the campus revealed inadequate retail and restaurant spaces, and the supposedly "temporary" University bookstore of the 1960s had an air of frowzy permanence. Working in partnership with an outside developer, the University proposed to solve many of the commercial issues with a block-long hotel, the Inn at Penn, above a base of shops and a handsome University bookstore that would occupy the site of a parking lot (where Pagano's Pizzeria had formerly stood) stretching from 36th to 37th Street and north to Sansom Street. While the architectural forms, especially the corner tower toward the central campus are derived from postmodern shopping malls, the overlay of red brick and limestone trim links the building to recent University design. To give presence to the Inn's main Sansom Street entrance, the great plaza of the Graduate Towers was cut out to make a north drive from Chestnut Street. The previous bookstore site was in turn conveyed to the Wharton School for an imposing classroom building that will serve undergraduate and graduate instruction. Designed by New Yorker's Kohn, Pederson and Fox, it is energetic in its description of the multiple functions housed within its vast bulk.

Other projects were developed to reach out toward

the University neighborhood. Penn revised and enhanced its innovative 100 percent mortgage program of the 1960s, adding incentives that would help new residents restore and upgrade the historic housing of University City. Small shopping centers on the western perimeter of the campus were acquired by the University and redesigned and renamed. An important addition to the Dental School by Bohlin, Cywinski, Jackson acknowledges the style of Windrim's historic Dental School while adding commercial space to the Locust Street front to reinforce the shopping center along 40th Street which is intended to become the main street of the University neighborhood. To create a magnet that would draw the region to share in the riches of University City, the University has announced that the down-at-the-heels movie complex on 40th Street would become Robert Redford's first east-coast Sundance Theater with multiple small screens showing contemporary films. Additional retail along 40th Street, including a modern upscale grocery store is aimed at the residents of the enlarging community. With these changes, it is anticipated that Penn's neighborhood will lose its provisional quality and become a true University City, serving University faculty, staff, and students, as well as others who appreciate the possibilities of a cosmopolitan community set in a handsome Victorian suburb with remarkable transit connections to the city and the entire east coast.

Though these changes quickly brought new residents, the core issue of the community at the end of the twentieth century remains the same as it was in the 1960s—the neighborhood schools. Starved for funds for most of the twentieth century, the city's school system has been a principal disincentive for neighborhood residence since World War II.[52] For those able to afford it, the city's numerous private schools have long offered first-rate schooling but for junior faculty and staff, the choice has been to leave the community for the suburbs. Faced with this fact, the University leadership has again reached out to the public school system as it did for a time in the 1960s, proposing to create a University-public school partnership in a

Kindergarten through Eighth Grade school on the site of the Episcopal seminary at 42nd and Locust Streets. Taking the University of Chicago Laboratory School as its model, this project will be central to the community-building process.

Two hundred and fifty years ago, in 1749, Benjamin Franklin wrote his *Proposals Relating to the Education of Youth in Pensilvania*. A century and a half later the University was galvanized into life on its West Philadelphia campus by Provost Harrison's vision of a student-centered institution in a rich architectural setting. As the twentieth century ends, the Penn campus has taken on a hyper-reality, its hues the saturated colors of *Architectural Digest* photographs, and its events over scaled like a Technicolor Pan-a-Vision spectacle. Still, the University is not an ivory tower divorced from the real world; like Franklin's original College of Philadelphia, Penn remains a part of its city, offering to its sons and daughters the varied textures and experiences of urban America. The sculptures of Franklin scattered across the campus, from the youthful Franklin in front of Franklin Field on the east to the genial, aging Franklin on his bench on the west, demonstrate Penn's link to its founder. Franklin remains an appropriate symbol of the University for, historically, Penn has been most stimulating in those periods when it most closely mirrored his 1749 ideal. In the 1750s Penn served men and women from up and down the east coast and as far as the near islands of the Caribbean in the Charitable School, the Academy and the College with a diverse curriculum taught by an ecumenical faculty; in the 1870s and 1880s, Provosts Stillé and Pepper linked the University to the modern world of industry and engineering and gave it an architectural image shaped by architects who valued the poetry of the present. Again in the modern world, from the moment ENIAC was invented on the campus to the presidency of Judith Rodin, who now seeks to build a diverse and attractive community around the institution, Penn has succeeded as it has met Franklin's challenge of service to the modern world.

THE Pennsylvania GAZETTE
MARCH, 1973

COLLEGE HALL

CAMPUS LEGENDS

EVERY CAMPUS has its legends that center on buildings that in appearance, form, or plan apparently defy logic and therefore need special explanation. Not surprisingly, many of these stories reappear from campus to campus, suggesting that to undergraduates the basic explanations of most campus oddities are the same: administrative economy (read cheapness) or special interests (read favoritism). From tales about the origin of the stones of College Hall to the supposedly temporary nature of the reinforced concrete dormitory towers of Superblock, the University of Pennsylvania is no exception. Campus legends are a form of undergraduate speculation about the student's world; passed on from generation to generation, the stories acquire a life of their own that transcends the events and even the concepts that spawned them, defying research and logic with the same tenacity of their subjects. This is as it should be, for the myths and legends of the campus are manifestations of undergraduate interest even as they are attempts to explain and celebrate special features that differentiate their campus from other colleges.

••••••••••••••••••••••••••••••••••••

Charles Addams, "Addams Family go to Penn," Penn-sylvania Gazette (March 1973). UPA.

After all, other universities and colleges may have Victorian Gothic old main halls, but how many are built of the green serpentine stone of Penn's College Hall? How many other universities and colleges have a library that looks more like a giant machine than a classically inspired library? How many other colleges have an auditorium that makes the auditory function nearly impossible? With the successful model of the quadrangle in the midst of the campus, how are the high-rise concrete dormitories to be explained except as a temporary aberration? All these buildings and more have been the subject of legends.

The Date of the Founding of the University

No single fact has been the subject of more obfuscation, interpretation, and cogitation than the date of the founding of the University. The east tower of College Hall bears the date 1755, the year when the charter of the college was granted; it is this date that outside scholars and critics such as Montgomery Schuyler and Paul Turner have used to locate the University in the chronology of American colleges. Zealous Penn advocates seeking to advance the University in that chronology could have selected an earlier date of 1743 based on Franklin's own reports that it was then that he first advanced the idea of an Academy to Proprietor's representative Richard Peters. However, because Franklin admitted that he did not pursue the issue at that time, no one in the eighteenth or nineteenth century suggested it for the official date of the University's founding—though, based on the preliminary cover of Francis Newton Thorpe's University history, at least one effort was made to push Penn's founding to 1745. Certainly 1749, when Franklin wrote his *Proposals,* or 1750, when the Franklin-led board purchased the Whitefield Church and began alterations to its new building, would seem to be conservative and responsible dates representing the moment when the institution had passed from thought into actuality.

When Penn officials first sought to establish the earliest date of the institution, their customary choice was the year 1749 when Franklin published his *Proposals Relating to the Education of Youth in Pensilvania.* After receiving a positive response to this publication, he began his fund-raising and organizing efforts that led to the Board of Trustees and a short time later to the actual Academy; this date was used by Provost Smith in his eulogy for Franklin in 1791 and was used by the University on seals and catalogs until 1893. To be sure, 1749 might be considered a bit exaggerated in that no courses were actually taught at the Academy and Charitable School until 1751, but, under ordinary circumstances either 1749 or 1750 would certainly be a date that would stand the test of intercollegiate scrutiny.

In the late nineteenth century more than a few American colleges searched their records to establish the earliest possible date of founding, and many were aggressive in their choice, reflecting the first rousing of intercollegiate rivalries. In 1893 historian and faculty member John Bach McMaster, trustee Samuel Pennypacker, and recent graduate Francis Newton Thorpe devised a rationalization to push Penn's date of founding back all the way to 1740. This was accomplished by claiming that Franklin had taken over the charter of the Whitefield New Building *and its attendant charity school,* and thus that the date of the ac-

quired organization could be adopted as Penn's own.[1] Such piggy-backing of founding dates was not uncommon in corporate practice of the day as magazines, banks, and a host of other organizations used the date of the oldest portion of the corporate family tree as the basis for determining their age. America had come of age, and antique was in—especially when such manipulation put Penn ahead of Princeton University in academic processions. To be sure, there was one important problem with the 1740 date—the Whitefield group never opened their school. Hence, if teaching rather than the promise of holding classes is the criterion, the 1740 date is implausible.[2]

Penn is not alone in such shenanigans. Paul Turner's sequence of American colleges foundations begins with Harvard (1636), William and Mary (1693), Yale (1701), the College of New Jersey (later Princeton, 1746), King's College (later Columbia, 1754), and finally Penn, using the date of its receipt of the College charter of 1755. Turner is from Stanford University and may not have understood the depths or strengths of the currents of the river of controversy into which he waded. Indeed, it is the only charitable interpretation of Turner's chronology, which, to judge from his apparent lack of contact with Pennsylvania representatives, depended almost entirely on potentially (presumably) prejudiced Princeton sources, as evidenced by the acknowledgments of his book.[3]

In any event, Turner's chronology made the error of using different standards for the colleges in question. Because of the relatively large gaps in dates between the founding of Harvard University and the College of William and Mary, their position in the chronology is absolute, though William and Mary advocates have advanced their starting date several years forward by using the date of their charter (1693) rather than the date of actual opening, which occurred in 1700, only a year ahead of Yale's foundation. Princeton dates its beginnings to a charter granted in 1746 that resulted in a Presbyterian seminary whose various sites included Elizabeth and Newark before finally settling in Princeton in 1753, by which time the

Academy and Charitable School of Philadelphia had been offering classes for two years and had been in the planning stage for several years before that date. Columbia University has traditionally taken the most conservative starting point by using the date when King's College opened its doors in 1754, a year before the College of Philadelphia was granted its charter but three years after Franklin's Academy had begun offering classes.

By William and Mary's standard of a date when planning began, Penn might legitimately choose the 1743 or 1749 date; by Columbia's standard of the date of opening, Penn was founded in January 1751; by the Princeton standard of the continuation of an earlier institution, perhaps Penn's corporate takeover of the Whitefield Charity School provides a reasonable use of the 1740 date. Lacking a clear standard for the founding of an institution—it is difficult to establish an absolute chronology of American colleges—as it also has been in Europe. And even then there is the apples and oranges comparison of whether the products of these institutions were truly serving preparatory or college students, as could certainly be claimed of several colleges including the College of Philadelphia until its college charter was granted in 1755, the date chosen by Turner.[4]

Although there has been more than a little sleight-of-hand in the process of determining the date, and though it has always been clear from Samuel Pennypacker's history that the entire purpose of his research was aimed at Princeton University, undergraduate historians have resolved the solution of the conflict by claiming that the use of the earliest possible date was required by an act of Pennsylvania's legislature. This act was supposed to have been prompted by the University's loyal sons, who required that henceforth Penn must use the earlier date on its seals and official documents.[5] There is no evidence, however, that this act of legislation ever occurred.

The Legend of the Free Stone

With few exceptions, campus legends have apparently simply risen to consciousness as the occasion warrants. Tellingly, these tales are not products of the initial period of construction of the buildings that are their subjects, when they would have been easy to refute. For example, although College Hall and the other green buildings of the campus were certainly the first buildings of the present campus to demand scrutiny, the myths relating to those buildings were undoubtedly invented well after they were constructed, appearing when later buildings were built of brick and the decaying green buildings suddenly looked old and odd.

Thus it must have been in the 1880s or 1890s, when most of Penn's new construction had shifted to brick, that Penn students for the first time began to speculate on how and why this strange stone, which was already disintegrating in the acid rain of Philadelphia, had been selected for the campus buildings. An answer was quickly offered, one that was rooted in the collegians' fundamental mistrust of administrative motive that is at the core of many legends. According to one long-standing tradition, a trustee's farm near West Chester was overlain with a vein of this strange green stone, and wishing to rid himself of this material he offered it to the University for free for its new buildings. Always on the lookout to save a few dollars, the University grasped the opportunity, and the green campus resulted.

The story has the ring of truth, recalling the era in the 1870s when the trustees commissioned the buildings of the new campus without raising the funds for their construction or support. It would certainly also ring true in the 1880s and early 1890s, when the University was heavily in debt for those new buildings. And there is something to the story that expresses the hand-me-down character of most underfunded institutions of nineteenth-century Philadelphia. Every college and university has furniture and other objects that were given, one suspects, because they were out of fashion. However, in the 1870s, when Thomas Richards was in charge of campus planning, serpentine stone, with its brilliant green tints was a popular building material across the entire city. On Logan Square, James H. Windrim's new Academy of Natural History was built of green serpentine in the late 1860s, as were several churches in Powelton (all since refaced because of the deterioration of the stone). Serpentine facades brightened the facades of numerous town houses in the Rittenhouse Square area, including Provost Stillé's own house on St. James Street. In the case of Penn's green stone, it is clear from the popularity of the material in the 1860s and 1870s, and from the delight contemporary architects (influenced by John Ruskin) found in the richness and variety of nature, that the use of serpentine was planned and not forced on an unwilling institution.

Other stories about College Hall also have a basis in fact, recording vanished elements of the building. Persistent legends of underground tunnels between College Hall and Logan Hall, "large enough to drive a wagon through," probably were based on steam tunnels from the era when the University's power plant on the site of Irvine Auditorium produced steam that could be used for heating as a byproduct of the generation of electricity. And it was certainly a fact that on the east end a ramp led to the basement stable for the University horse that was called on to haul trash and other items. Other stories abound of secret passages within College Hall's walls. These perhaps were derived from the private stairs that enabled trustees to reach the chapel room without being subjected to the noise and crowding of the main stairs.

The Myth of the Addams Family in the Attic of College Hall

A century after its construction, College Hall was the subject of another legend, one rooted in the popular culture of television and the artistic gifts of a favorite son, cartoonist Charles Addams, who attended the School of Fine Arts in the 1930s. With *The Addams Family* a popular television show and Addams's grotesquely humorous *New Yorker* cartoons in the public eye, it was easy enough to observe his delight in towered Gothic facades. Knowing of his time at the University, many deduced that various buildings in the University neighborhood, including the now demolished Blanchard Hall at 36th and Walnut Streets and eventually College Hall itself, were Addams's remembered muse. Despite his repeated denials, the story lives on, now encouraged by his well-known cover for the *Gazette* with the Addams family posing in front of College Hall. Clearly, a little knowledge is a dangerous thing.

The Library as Roadblock and the Reused Railroad Station

The next building of the campus to become the subject of mythmaking was Frank Furness's University Library. With its red brick, red sandstone, red terra cotta, red tile, and red copper arranged in distinct masses to describe every interior function, it stood out from the symmetrical green serpentine Academic Gothic buildings of the earlier campus, and it turned its back on 34th Street, facing College Hall. Had later American architecture followed the Furness manner, there might not have been any legends about the building, but within a few years after its completion architectural taste changed dramatically toward Beaux-Arts classicism or Gothic historicism. Two legends quickly followed, the earlier of which reflected the library's unusual composition that juxtaposed disparate volumes to describe interior functions. An explanation for Penn's unusual library was required and, as usual, was quickly found in the fertile imaginations of Penn's undergraduates.

In the 1880s Furness had pioneered functional expressionism in literally hundreds of buildings dotted across the landscape of the city, including the new Baltimore & Ohio Railroad Station on the east bank of the Schuylkill River at Chestnut Street. It exemplified Furness's expressionism with a vengeance, with the passenger waiting rooms and offices at the bridge level of Chestnut Street and a concourse and train shed along the tracks at grade level. The similarity of the reading rooms and offices of the library juxtaposed against the train-shed-like extendable bookstack was obvious. Was it not likely that Furness had an old railroad station plan lying around his office, and when the library project came along simply modified the station to library use? This legend, like most of the others, has its germ of truth. Furness did apply his modern approach to developing a plan from the facts of the program, and he was not averse to distinguishing the separate and distinct functions of the "people" part of the building from the book storage areas. However, the record of the planning of the building, with the assistance of Justin Winsor and the high praise of Melvil Dewey, makes it clear that the building was carefully thought out to meet the functional requirements of a college library, though with Furness's modern method and use of materials. Like his railroad stations, the building reflected the values of the machine culture of Philadelphia industrialists, but it was always intended to be a library.

In unwritten chronicles it is typically difficult to establish the exact moment when stories were invented, but often it is possible to find historical events that stimulated undergraduate imaginations. One story that seeks to explain the siting of the building across the axis of (unopened) Locust Street may have been triggered by the modern emphasis on Smith Walk as the major cross-campus link. How could the University have made the howling mistake of locating its library, and especially a building that for most of its history was perceived as a red eyesore, across the route of Locust Street? In fact, for most of the University's West Philadelphia years, Smith Walk was only important for one block between 33rd and 34th Streets. Until it was closed in the late 1950s to create Locust Walk, Locust Street to the west of Woodland Avenue was a narrow urban street, lined with cars, and of no more importance than any other street. Indeed, for much of the twentieth century Penn intended to grow north-south with its main axis aimed at College Hall and paid little attention to its east-west axis.

This northward axis lost importance with the rise to prominence of Smith Walk in the 1960s, after the 3600 block of Locust Street was converted into a pedestrian walkway and Woodland Avenue was removed from the center of the campus. Then it occurred to someone that the placement of the library blocked the direct path of Locust Walk through the campus. If this were not simply a grievous mistake, it must have represented the University's attempt to ensure that Locust Street could not pass through the campus, thereby ensuring that the northern triangle of space would remain in the University's possession. However, the first plans for the library show that it was originally intended to be built on the site now occupied by the Wistar Institute, and it was only redesigned for the present site when the Wistar gift was received. Presumably Penn was more concerned about holding onto the triangle of space below Woodland Avenue than about blocking the progress of Locust Street!

Irvine, or a Parent's Revenge

That most curious of Penn spaces, Irvine Auditorium, has been the subject of the most widespread myth, one that is transmitted to every undergraduate who walks the campus. Its acoustical liabilities are a product of the soaring space that demonstrated the force of the black holes of outer space even before they were discovered. How a reasonable architect could make such an error as to produce a design in which it was impossible to hear was incomprehensible—especially for an auditorium. Obviously the University had been forced to accept this incompetent scheme at the wish of some donor. But why a donor would want such a silly design could not be imagined—unless the donor or someone dear to him had designed the building! The explanation was obvious. In the distant past, a student who was enamored with Mont Saint Michel had been given the design problem of an auditorium. To the horror of the faculty, he had transformed the island crowned by a Gothic church into an auditorium. The faculty promptly and properly flunked him and demanded that he be drummed from the corps of architects. However, his father, a University trustee (or sometimes it is the architectural student himself, returned to the University after success in another

Horace Trumbauer, first scheme for Irvine Auditorium, 1926. UPA.

field), was determined to avenge this insult to the family honor. Pulling out his checkbook, he decided to make a gift to his alma mater of its most needed facility. The University was ecstatic and announced that they would call Cope and Stewardson or Frank Miles Day for the design. But no! The donor pulled out of his briefcase his son's crumpled and failed project. "Build this," he said and Penn of course did.[6] Combining the core myths of institutional cheapness and willingness to succumb to favoritism, the story has been a favorite. Once, however, when the author told this story to a group of alumni, a growling voice in the back of the group responded, "That's not true! My firm designed it." Mortified, my question came back, "And what firm was that?" "Horace Trumbauer" was the reply. Later research confirmed the truth, but the story deserves to live on. After all, how else to explain the acoustics?[7]

Additional research proves that the root of Irvine's problems was the interference of trustees rather than architectural incompetence. According to acousticians, the chief difficulty of the design is its square plan, which makes for strong, multiple echoes. The preliminary designs for the auditorium were in fact for a conventional rectangular hall, running either north-south toward the recently extended Duhring Wing of the library or east-west toward Houston Hall. Prudent trustees concluded that such a plan would interfere if either building needed to be enlarged (as indeed happened with Houston Hall and almost happened with the library). The result was a nearly square site, which is at the root of the horrific acoustics.

Throughout the course of Irvine's design development, further trustee interference made things progressively worse. To make the hall as long as possible on the nearly square site, the architect's original scheme had called for a short stage and no entrance lobbies. Trustee John C. Bell, who supervised the project, demanded lobbies and a stage, further shortening the hall. The great height of the room, into which much of the sound disappears, was also an afterthought. With a new bridge across the Schuylkill making South Street a major entrance to the University, a great spire on top of the auditorium would help celebrate this new entrance to the campus. And, with the added opportunity of providing a location for the vast organ built for the recently closed Sesquicentennial Exposition, the new tower would be functional as well. Clearly most of Irvine's problems resulted from the interference of the client rather than the fault of the architect.

Women's Needs Are Less Than Men's: Hill Hall's Small Rooms

Most of the recent buildings have yet to develop their complement of myths, but given the number of build-

ings that deviate from the norms of the Penn campus there is a high degree of certainty that myths will develop. While dormitory rooms are rarely palatial, Hill Hall is notable for the miniaturization of its rooms, which are far and away the smallest of the campus's accommodations. In the age of scientific rationalism, students assumed that there must have been some reason for this decision. Surely behavioral scientists had studied the issue of women's housing needs. They must have found that boys require more space than girls. Logically, if one were to design a dormitory for women, scientific study would support making their rooms smaller than comparable rooms for men—hence Hill Hall.

Of course Penn planners and architects had relied on no such study because no study of this sort was ever done. In fact, Hill Hall was originally designed to be a larger complex composed of four nearly independent houses. Each of those sections would have its own elevator block and the rooms would mainly be singles. Later, for reasons of economy, while the building was still being designed, the entire project was made smaller, three of the elevator cores were removed, and the rooms were converted to doubles. It was economy, not behavioral science, that ruled Penn's planners.

The Temporary High-Rises

Of Penn's recent buildings, it was the high-rise dormitories of Superblock that were almost immediately singled out for attention. In a university blessed with the great example of the Cope and Stewardson dormitory quadrangle, how was it possible to make such a mistake in residential design? Certainly no responsible party could have proposed these giant tombstone-like buildings that towered over West Philadelphia. There must be a reason! Of course! Surely these public housing project-like towers must not have been intended as permanent housing. They were temporary, and when their mortgage was paid off they would be torn down and replaced with something more suitable like the designs that had previously been developed for the same site. This certainly sounds like

a plausible explanation, but in fact their speedy demolition is not likely. Such tall dormitory buildings were the rage a few years ago at Harvard University, where José Luis Sert designed similar residences. Indeed, these became a standard dormitory type at colleges across the nation. But for anyone who has seen the difficulty of demolishing reinforced concrete buildings the probable longevity of these buildings must be apparent. They will be a part of Penn's skyline for the foreseeable future, but it is to be hoped that the myth of their imminent removal will continue to enliven the discussion of undergraduates who have puzzled over the green stone of College Hall, the odd form of the old Library, the abysmal acoustics of Irvine, and the contrast between the success of the Quad and the lack of delight of Superblock.

The NASA Wind Tunnel

Even if these giant buildings were permanent, certain physical peculiarities of the group demanded explanation. Anyone who has walked through Superblock in the winter cannot have failed to notice the wind gusts that howl down the walls of the buildings and blast across the stony pavements, whirling trash in the air before whistling out onto the streets that surround the block. Surely so perfect a wind tunnel must have a story behind it—but what organization or agency could need so large a wind tunnel? Obviously no one in Philadelphia would have a need for such a facility—but who else might?

In the 1960s and early 1970s much research on space travel was being funded by the government, including the question whether to develop a reusable space vehicle. Penn in the 1960s was a center of government-sponsored research, some of it secret, that resulted in battles between various wings of the faculty and between the administration and the undergraduates. In an era of suspicion, some Cold-War government project might be the cause. In an age

....

Interior of Hill Hall room, c. 1960. Photo: Lawrence Williams. UPA.

when computer modeling had yet to achieve prominence, and when wind tunnels remained a tool for testing of prototypes, some bright undergraduate decided that this was in fact the answer. Perhaps some sort of giant wind tunnel had been designed—one with a profitable side, such as a giant apartment complex whose buildings could generate immense winds that could test space vehicles. How such a structure had ended up at Penn was more difficult to explain, but, given an answer such as a NASA project, a hypothesis could surely be found that would fill the holes. Perhaps Penn had accepted the federal plans as part of some secret program. Of course! That was it! It was just another instance of the University's insatiable desire for economy, even if it meant that every undergraduate who ventured into the square risked being blown across the campus.

The Lost Pyramid

How quickly new legends develop can be seen in the instant legend that developed during the preliminary planning of the Perelman Quadrangle. Working from fragmentary published reports in the *Daily Pennsylvanian* on the various strands of the design that were to bring together activities in College Hall, Houston Hall, Irvine Auditorium, Logan Hall, and Williams Hall, and with an awareness that some form of glass roof was to cover some part of the project (in fact a part of Williams's courtyard), undergraduate imagination boldly strode to the next step. A giant glass pyramid on the order of I. M. Pei's imaginative redesign of the Louvre courtyard would link the buildings—a fitting landmark for late twentieth-century Penn. Fortunately for the opportunity to lunch outside in spring and fall, there was no such scheme. The invention of the story took less than a month between the first reports on the project to the trustees and the development of the first undergraduates' enhanced account.

Missing Legends

Because legends tend to be temporary, most are lost, surviving only in the memories of undergraduates

Kneedler, Mirick and Zantzinger, design for Under-graduate Men's Residence, 1964. UPA.
Superblock, 1970. UPA.

••••••••••••••••••••••••••••••••••

who create them, spread them, or believe them. It is surprising, however, that no myths have been discovered about other buildings on campus that should have elicited some comment. Do no lost souls prowl the towers of the Quad? Have no deranged patients lurked outside the hospital awaiting the doctor or the student who erred in an operation? Did no Quasimodo mourn the loss of the missing bell towers of College Hall? Does no track star who missed the bell because of a late bus haunt the dressing rooms of Franklin Field? As new buildings continue to rise on Penn's campus, Penn undergraduates will continue to rise to the challenge of explaining the unexplainable, thereby adding to the store of legends, and enriching the University's future history.

II

Gazetteer

David B. Brownlee and George E. Thomas

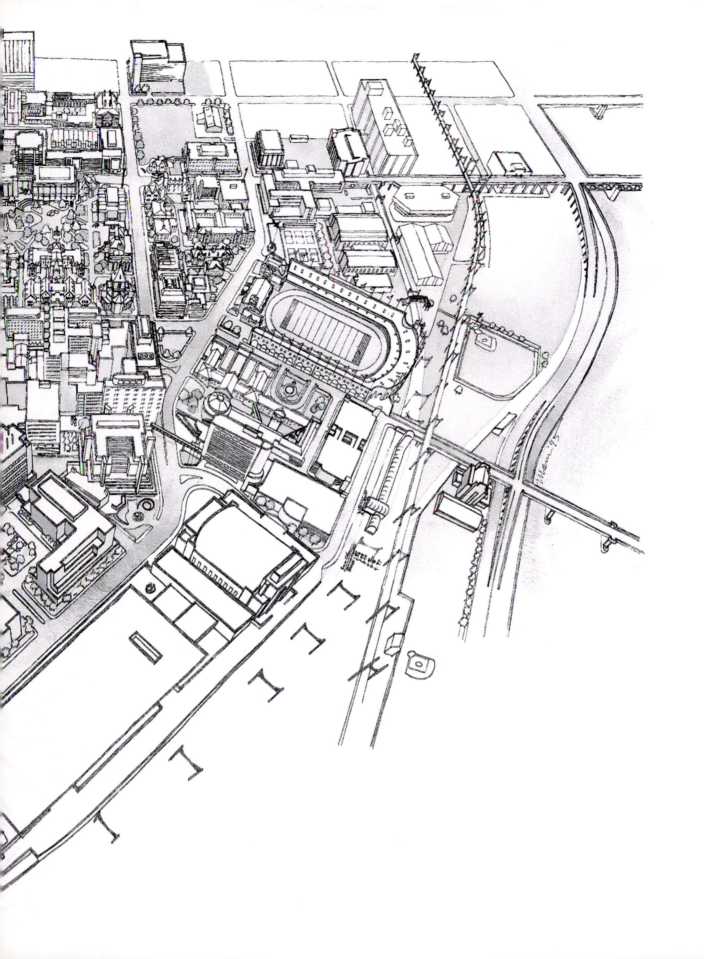

THE CENTRAL CAMPUS

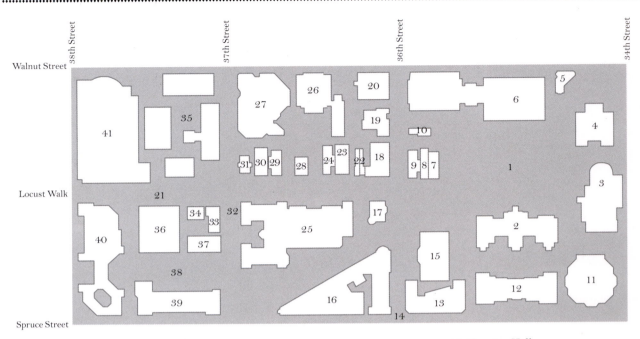

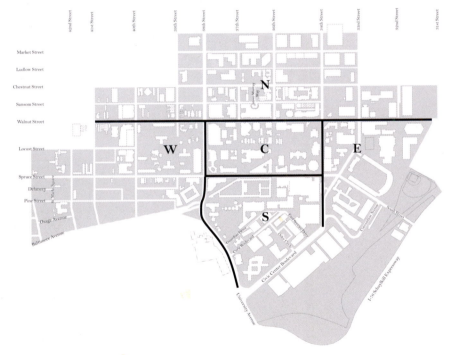

12. Houston Hall
13. Williams Hall
14. Class of 1893 Gate
15. Logan Hall
16. Wistar Institute
17. Psi Upsilon
18. Christian Association
19. Hillel Foundation
20. Skinner Hall
21. Locust Walk
22. 3609 Locust Walk
23. Veranda
24. Phi Gamma Delta
25. Steinberg-Dietrich Hall
26. Annenberg School
27. Annenberg Center
28. Delta Phi
29. Delta Psi
30. Colonial Penn Center
31. Locust House
32. Ben Franklin on Campus
33. Phi Delta Theta
34. Kappa Sigma
35. Social Sciences Quad
36. McNeil Building
37. Lauder-Fischer Hall
38. Shearson Lehman Hutton Quad
39. Vance Hall
40. Steinberg Center
41. Huntsman Hall

Central Campus
1. Blanche Levy Park
2. College Hall
3. Fisher Fine Arts Library
4. Meyerson Hall
5. Jaffe History of Art Building
6. Van Pelt Library
7. Sweeten Alumni Center
8. 3537 Locust Walk
9. Phi Kappa Sigma
10. Alpha Chi Rho
11. Irvine Auditorium

THE CENTRAL CAMPUS

Blanche Levy Park. 1977: Sir Peter Shepheard, Laurie Olin, Andropogon Associates and others. (Color Plate 7)

The central campus is the chief monument to Provost Charles Janeway Stillé, under whose leadership Penn moved to West Philadelphia from its Ninth Street site. After a century of expedient landscape design, Sir Peter Shepheard, dean of the Graduate School of Fine Arts (1971–79), was given the task of transforming the old campus green into an appropriate setting for the core of the University. Working from the existing strengths of large trees and important buildings that served to set off their own zones, Shepheard knit together the major pedestrian walks in red brick and blue stone curbed with light-toned granite. Given its own identity from the name of its benefactor, Blanche Paley Levy, the campus green is now a significant and handsome landscape. A bronze plaque in front of the statue of Franklin commemorates her gift.

The central campus is accented with numerous statues representing the University's history. On the axis in front of College Hall is John J. Boyle's aging and genial *Benjamin Franklin* (1899, moved to the present site 1939), which was originally designed to stand in front of the U. S. Post Office at Ninth Street. In the rear of College Hall is Karl Bitter's curiously pensive, seated and robed figure of Provost William Pepper (1895, moved to the present site 1980). Of the more recent sculpture acquisitions, the favorite is unquestionably Claes Oldenburg's *Split Button* (1981), in the small plaza in front of Van Pelt Library, which functions as both landmark and children's slide. It is joined on the east side of the campus by Alexander Calder's red steel, elephant-like *Jerusalem Stabile* (1979) in the

Blanche Levy Park, central campus, looking northwest, 1997. GET.

Blanche Levy Park, central campus, looking toward Van Pelt Library, 1997. GET.

••••••••••••••••••••••••••••••••••

brick courtyard between Furness and Meyerson Hall. To the north of Meyerson Hall is Robin Friedenthal's geometrical minimalist piece *Black Forest* (1983, installed 1984). On the far side of the central campus is Tony Smith's black steel, ironic anti-triumphal portal entitled *We Lost* (1966, installed 1975). Adjacent to the south facade of the Dietrich wing of the library is David Lindquist's brushed stainless steel *Peace Symbol* (1967, fabricated in permanent material and reinstalled, 1970), a relic of the decade of student activism of the 1960s. Alexander Archipenko's *King Solomon* (1968, installed 1985) stands watch on the 36th Street walk, opposite the Hillel Foundation. Many of these modern pieces were acquired as a part of Philadelphia's requirement that 1 percent of the cost of projects in redevelopment areas go to art; others have been the gifts of generous donors.

COLLEGE HALL. 1870–73: Thomas Webb Richards. Exterior restoration, 1990–97: Marianna M. Thomas Architects and the Clio Group, Inc. Interior restoration and adaptive renovations, 1998: David Polk Architects; John Q. Lawson Architects.[1] (Color plate 3)

The commission for the first building of the new suburban campus was awarded to the University's first instructor of architectural drafting, Thomas Richards, who was soon promoted to Professor of

Drawing and Architecture, a position he held between 1874 and 1891. The lively, syncopated composition bears the characteristic hybrid ornament of the period, with polychromatic Gothic stonework supporting mansard roofs borrowed from the French Renaissance. All the college functions were housed here at first, including the library in the south wing on axis with the main entrance; the west wing was assigned to the liberal arts, the east wing to the sciences. Later the architectural courses occupied the third floor. Towers originally rose at both ends of the building (their truncated bases remain); one of them contained the bell now in Houston Hall. Richards also designed Logan Hall, the Hare Laboratories (demolished to

••••••••••••••••••••••••••••••••••

Blanche Levy Park, Karl Bitter, Statue of Provost William Pepper, Jr., M.D., 1895. Rear of College Hall, formerly adjacent to University Museum. GET.

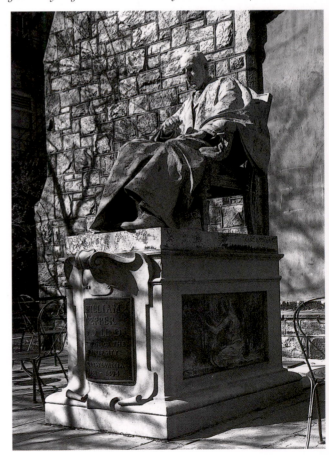

College Hall during restoration, looking south, 1997. GET.

••••••••••••••••••••••••••••••••••••

build Williams), and the original hospital building. All were constructed of green serpentine stone from Chester County, an unusual material that has proved to be very susceptible to damage by airborne pollutants. Restoration of the exterior began in 1990 under the direction of Marianna M. Thomas (GAr 1972), who has also handled the restoration of the main entrance corridor.

The corridors of College Hall form a portrait gallery of the University. On the first floor are portraits of the first provost, William Smith (after the original by Gilbert Stuart) and Thomas Sully's handsome portrait of Professor Henry Hope Reed, the American editor of William Wordsworth; in the president's office are notable eighteenth-century portraits of University founders, an oval of Franklin by J. F. de L'Hospital, Charles Willson Peale's portrait of

America's great eighteenth-century astronomer and later trustee David Rittenhouse, and Sully's mid-nineteenth-century representation of John Andrews. On the second floor opposite Room 200 is the immense portrait by Louis Hasselbusch of Provost Edgar Fahs Smith in his laboratory (1922). Room 200, the old chapel, contains other relics of the history of the University, including the plaque for the John Welsh Professorship, the Thomas Richards-designed Civil War Memorial Plaque and the cornerstone from the house built for the President of the United States and occupied as the University's second home from 1801 until 1829.

In the rear of College Hall is a portrait bust of nineteenth-century chemist Charles Lennig by John J. Boyle (1900).

Jerome and Anne Fisher FINE ARTS LIBRARY and ARTHUR ROSS GALLERY (originally University Library and Museum), 220 South 34th Street.

College Hall and University Library, c. 1890. UPA

1888–91: Frank Furness, of Furness, Evans and Co. Duhring Wing, 1916: Furness, Evans and Co. Henry C. Lea Reading Room, 1923: Furness, Evans and Co. Horace Howard Furness Shakespeare Library, 1931: Robert Rhodes McGoodwin (Ar 1907, GAr 1912). Restoration and adaptive reuse, 1986–91: Venturi, Scott Brown and Associates, the Clio Group, Inc. and Marianna M. Thomas Architects. (Color Plates 5, 6)

The shift toward research rather than lecture-based teaching required more books and space than could be provided in the small library in College Hall, compelling the University to build a separate library building. In 1887 a committee of the University trustees, chaired by Shakespearian scholar Horace Howard Furness, called for the construction of the "best college library in America," a charge they met by hiring consultants Melvil Dewey (the inventor of the Dewey Decimal System) and Harvard's librarian Justin Winsor, who, in association with architect Frank Furness, developed the original conceptual design. Furness produced a plan that was a model of functional logic presented in an expressive envelope that

contrasted the architectural reading rooms with the industrial character of the train-shed-like bookstack. He devised an exceptionally powerful exterior whose mixed stylistic elements are bound together by a single, unifying color (red) and a great swath of quarry-faced masonry that sweeps around the building at ground level. The glass-roofed and -floored, iron-framed stack was only the second such in the United States. Its original capacity was 100,000; like a great self-adjusting machine, it was designed to be lengthened southward as the collection grew. On the upper floor, reached by a ceremonial stair, Furness placed a great auditorium and an exhibition hall for the University's museum. The museum moved into its own building in 1899 and the library quickly moved upward, invading the museum's former precinct. In the 1960s and 1970s the auditorium space served as the design studio of Penn's celebrated professor of modern architecture Louis I. Kahn. That use is perpetuated in the restored building as the studio for the Design of the Environment program.

In 1914–15 the Furness office added the Duhring Wing to the south, extending the stacks in a different form but along the same direction as originally planned. The height of the great reading room was halved in 1922 when a floor was inserted to create more working space upstairs. In 1923–24 the Furness firm added the Henry C. Lea Reading Room on the 34th Street side to house Lea's private library, removed from his house and reinstalled in its exact form in the new addition. In 1931 Robert Rhodes McGoodwin built the Horace Howard Furness Shakespeare Reading Room on the west front to house Horace's extensive Shakespeare library, one of the glories of the University collection of books. When the Van Pelt Library was built the interior fittings of the Lea and Furness rooms were moved to the sixth floor of the new building. The old library building was assigned to the Graduate School of Fine Arts and was renamed by the trustees at the suggestion of Dean Perkins for its architect Frank Furness; the Duhring Wing was converted into offices. In the 1960s the Lea reading room and the present periodical reading rooms were painted austere, modern white to house the Institute of Contemporary Art, which Dean Perkins hoped would bring cutting-edge art to the city. Among its most notorious exhibits was that of Andy Warhol, which

College Hall Chapel during use as architectural studio, c. 1915. UPA.

••

turned into one of the first "happenings" of the 1960s, forcing the artist and friends to exit via the roof!

After the removal of its original fittings to Van Pelt Library, the Shakespeare Reading Room became the meeting room of the Board of Trustees, a role it served until 1980, when it was converted into the Arthur Ross Gallery. The Postmodern design was the work of Marco Frascari of the Architecture Department; the simultaneous restoration of the stairhall was directed by Hyman Myers (GAr 1965). Because the original stair lamps had been discarded, new bronze lamps were fabricated as a metalworking studio led by Professor of Fine Arts Robert Engman.

In 1985 the building was listed as a National Historic Landmark; at that time the University retained Venturi, Rauch and Scott Brown, in association with Marianna M. Thomas Architects and restoration consultants the Clio Group, Inc., to plan and supervise its restoration. Under their direction the exterior was cleaned, restoring it to its original vibrant red; the interior floor that had subdivided the great main Reading Room was removed; the original bookstacks were replaced with a fireproof concrete system; and modern building systems were installed. Renamed for Anne Fisher (W 1973) and Jerome Fisher, who supported the restoration, Frank Furness's great library

••

Thomas Webb Richards, plan of second story, University of Pennsylvania Collegiate and Scientific Departments. Ink on paper. Architectural Archives.

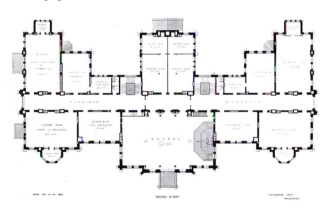

again is a vital part of the University's future.

In the stairhall is a carved Gothic memorial panel designed by John P. B. Sinkler (Ar 1898) in honor of Theophilus Parsons Chandler, the first director of the Department of Architecture (1890–91). Under the stair is the spectacular rendering of the facade of Santa Maria in Civita Castellana, submitted as part of his study requirements by Paris-prize winner and Penn professor Harry Sternfeld (GAr 1911), who depicted himself as a monk in the doorway.

••

Fisher Fine Arts Library, main reading room, c. 1895. UPA.

Fisher Fine Arts Library, looking east, 1990. GET.

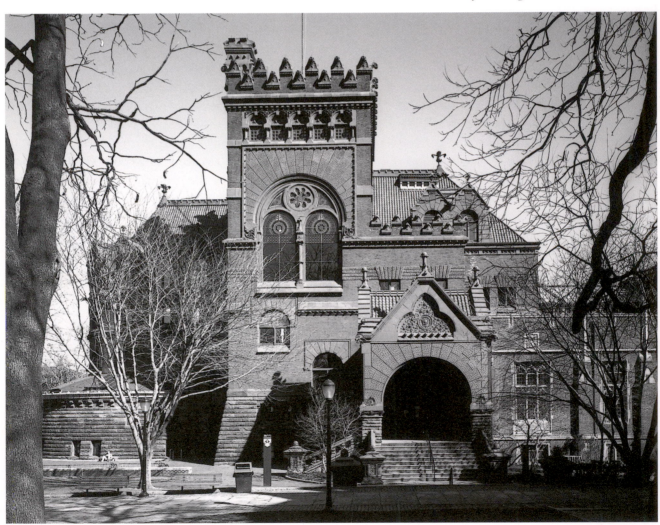

The **Kroiz Gallery and the Architectural Archives** in the basement of the Fisher Fine Arts Library are entered from the small plaza on the northeast corner off 34th Street, though there is an elevator link as well. The Architectural Archives form one of the treasures of the campus. Gathered here are the drawings and office materials of Louis I. Kahn (Ar 1924) and other notable modern Philadelphia architects as well as important collections of such nineteenth-century luminaries as Frank Furness, Wilson Eyre, Jr., Walter Cope, John Stewardson, and Frank Miles Day (C 1883). Small changing exhibits are noted on the bulletin board at the stair to the Archives; permanent installations include the structural models of Robert LeRicolais and a sampling from the collection including the riotously humorous drawings of Paul Cret's student Alfred Bendiner (GAr 1927).

MEYERSON HALL, 210 South 34th Street. 1965–68: Stewart, Noble, Class, and Partners.[2]

The Fine Arts program was long housed in the

••••••••••••••••••••••••••••••••••••

Furness, Evans and Co., south elevation, University of Pennsylvania Library, 1888. Ink on linen. Photocopy of lost photostat of lost original. George E. Thomas Collection, Architectural Archives.
Fisher Fine Arts Library, Horace Howard Furness Reading Room, 1990. GET.

building that was erected as the Dental Hall (now Hayden Hall). The first scheme for the new home of the Graduate School of Fine Arts would have located it in an addition to the Duhring Wing of the Furness Building extending nearly to Irvine Auditorium. Fortunately that scheme proved impossible because of fire codes. A second site was approved to the north of the old University Library. Initially it was presumed that the new building would be the work of Louis Kahn, the leading light of the architectural faculty. Conflicts with state funding agencies over Kahn's Richards Laboratories resulted in the selection of University trustee Sydney Martin's firm; it was hoped that Kahn would somehow be the designer sub rosa, a position he refused. The building was intended to include skylit studios, basement classrooms, and offices, as well as a large, central exhibition space for the Institute of Contemporary Art, which had been housed in the Furness Building.

Like the buildings of other nationally important architectural programs, including Paul Rudolph's Art and Architecture Building at Yale and Joseph Esherick's Wurster Hall at Berkeley, Meyerson Hall is a disappointing home for one of the nation's greatest architecture programs of the twentieth century. Its painful parody of Kahn's paradigm of central "served" spaces and peripheral "servant" functions is a constant reminder of his absence as architect. However, Meyerson

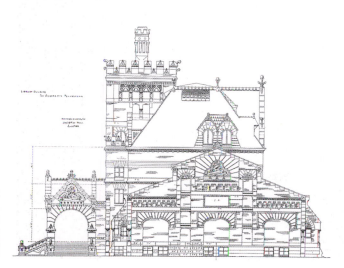

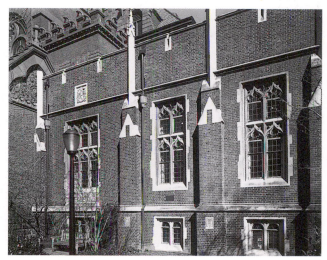

is enlivened by a corrugated roofline that brings to mind the industrial skylights of early twentieth-century factories, and on the east and west by massive *brise-soleils*, another modern motif said to reflect the ideas of Romaldo Giurgola.

In 1983 the building was named to honor President Emeritus Martin Meyerson. City planner Meyerson joined the celebrated faculty assembled by Dean G. Holmes Perkins after his arrival in 1951. That group included ecologist Ian McHarg, landscape architect Sir Peter Shepheard, city planner Edmund Bacon, and architects Louis I. Kahn, Robert Venturi, and Romaldo Giurgola. Together they shaped the so-called "Philadelphia School" of contextual designers who influenced their respective professions in the 1960s and 1970s.

In the dean's office are trophies from the history of the School of Fine Arts, including Wayman Adams's immense portrait of Warren Powers Laird, dean from 1891 until 1930, which formerly hung in the great drafting room in Hayden Hall, and a gigantic Beaux-Arts rendering of a tiny Italian oratory of S. Bernardino by Laird's successor as dean, George Koyl (1932–50). Also present are two oversized framed sketches by Le Corbusier, who visited the school in the 1960s. With the removal of the Institute of Contemporary Art to its new building, the central gallery provides exhibit space for student and faculty shows.

ELLIOT AND ROSLYN JAFFE HISTORY OF ART BUILDING (originally Phi Delta Theta), 3405 Woodland Walk. 1900: Oswin Shelly. Adaptive restoration and extensions, 1990: Tony Atkin (GAr 1974).[3]

The former diagonal route of Woodland Avenue across the campus is echoed in the oblique facade of the

••

Meyerson Hall, looking north from Fisher Fine Arts Library entrance, 1990. GET.

*1. Aerial perspective of University of Pennsylvania
Master Plan, 1963, rendering by George C. Rudolph,
color photograph of lost rendering. UPA.*

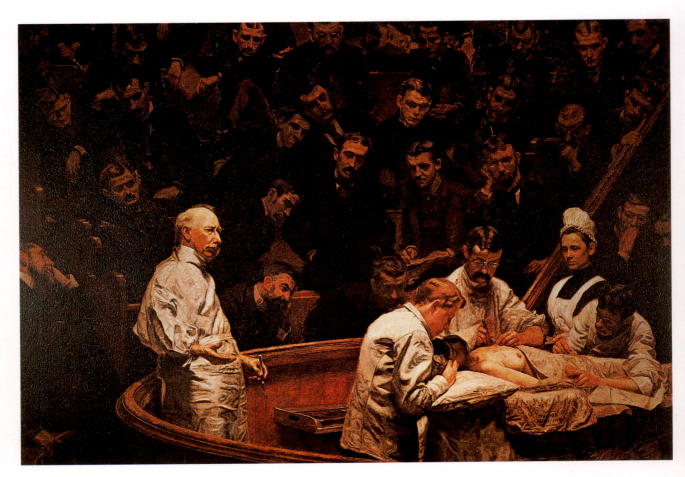

2. Thomas Eakins, The Agnew Clinic, *1889. Oil on canvas. Courtesy University of Pennsylvania School of Medicine.*

3. College Hall during restoration, looking south; with John J. Boyle's Benjamin Franklin, *bronze on granite base, 1899. GET.*

4. Logan Hall after restoration, looking northeast, 1997.
Photo: Lewis Tanner.

5. *Fisher Fine Arts Library after restoration, looking west,*
1990. GET.

*6. Fisher Fine Arts Library after restoration, main
reading room, 1990. Photo: Matt Wargo. Courtesy
Venturi, Scott Brown and Associates, Architects.
7. The Green and the "Castle," looking southwest, 1997.
Photo: Lewis Tanner.*

8. *Shearson, Lehman, Hutton Quadrangle, looking west, 1997. GET.*

9. University Museum, looking southwest, 1997. GET.

*10. University Museum, architects' model of Collections
Wing and landscaped courtyard, 1998. Courtesy Atkin,
Olshin, Lawson-Bell and Associates, Architects.*

11. Dormitory Quadrangles, looking northwest, 1997.
Photo: Lewis Tanner.

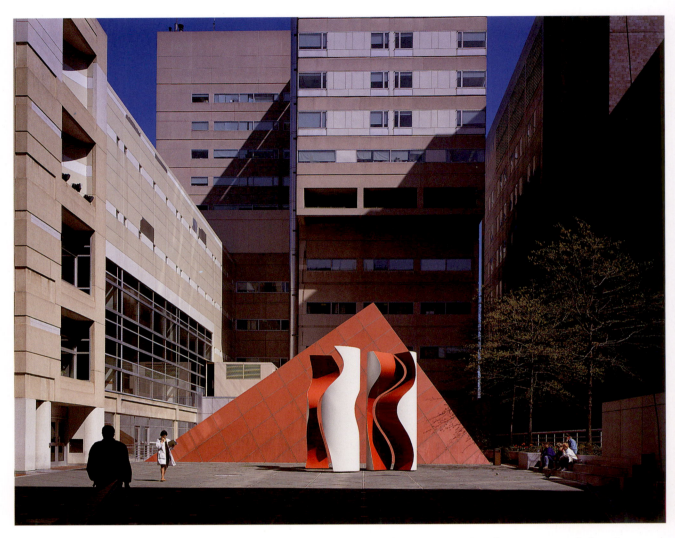

12. Robert Engman, Quadrature, *enameled steel.*
Medical Education Quadrangle, looking west, 1997.
Photo: Lewis Tanner.
13. Alexander Lieberman, Covenant, *enameled steel.*
Superblock, looking west, 1997. Photo: Lewis Tanner.

14. *Roy and Diana Vagelos Laboratories, looking south-west, 1997. Photo: Matt Wargo. Courtesy Venturi, Scott Brown and Associates.*

15. *The Penn Club, dining rooms, 1994. Copyright © 1995
Durston Saylor. Courtesy H. Durston Saylor, Inc.*

16. *Penn Club Grill Murals, Max Mason, "Penn 23–Harvard 21," "College Green," "Boat House Row," Max Mason, 1992. Oil on canvas. Courtesy Max Mason.*

Elliot and Roslyn Jaffe History of Art Building, looking north, 1997. GET.

••••••••••••••••••••••••••••••••••

building that houses the History of Art department. Designed by a young Penn alumnus (C 1894) in the English late medieval style Cope and Stewardson had established for the new dormitories, the Phi Delta Theta house embraced the new University image. Its eastern bay alludes to the west tip of the dormitory quadrangles at the opposite end of the campus and was later echoed by Thomas, Martin and Kirkpatrick's Zeta Psi across Walnut Street. The University purchased the building when Phi Delta Theta moved to larger quarters on Fraternity Row in 1924. Over the years it housed the offices of the General Alumni Society, the University Endowment Committee, Recorder, Alumni Records, and Placement Service. While the building served as the Placement Office, E. Craig Sweeten steered Wharton Graduate student Elliot Jaffe (W 1949) toward a position at Macy's Department Stores; he returned to the University as a trustee and member of the History of Art Visiting Committee, and his gift restored and enlarged the building. Along the former party wall at the west end, Tony Atkin's office has added a larger-scaled classroom wing that mediates with some success between the old fraternity and the adjacent library.

CHARLES PATTERSON VAN PELT LIBRARY, 3420 Walnut Street. 1960-62: Harbeson, Hough, Livingston, and Larson. Sculpted panel at entrance to library, *The Family of Man* by Constantine Nivolo. Renovations and interior design, 1997–98: BLT Architects.

John Harbeson (Ar 1910), William Hough (Ar 1911), William Livingston (Ar 1919), and Roy Larson (Ar 1923) formed the early corps of Paul Cret's office, which handled most of the campus planning before and after World War I. Renamed Harbeson, Hough, Livingston and Larson and more recently H2L2, the firm continued in that role after Cret's death, sketching the zoned campus of the post-World War II years. The cornerstone of the new campus that abolished Woodland Avenue and turned Locust Street into a pedestrian zone, Van Pelt frames one side of the newly regularized College Hall Green. Insistent concrete verticals lend a measure of Athenian dignity to an otherwise lackluster design. The same architects were

••••••••••••••••••••••••••••••••••

Charles Patterson Van Pelt Library, looking west, 1963. Photo: Courtland V. D. Hubbard; courtesy H2L2 Architects.

also responsible for the Dietrich Graduate Library (1965–67), which serves as a westward extension of Van Pelt and contains the Lippincott Library of the Wharton School. The original private library of Henry Charles Lea (by Collins and Autenrieth, c. 1880) and the interior fittings of Robert Rhodes McGoodwin's medievalizing addition of 1931 to the old University Library for Horace Howard Furness's Shakespeare collection were reinstalled on the sixth floor. The special collections elevator lobby and gallery is lined with excellent English linenfold paneling from a fifteenth-century house in Chester, England, provided by trustee Robert Dechert, Esq. (Col. 1916)

Scattered throughout the building are casts and copies of classical busts that once occupied plinths in the rotunda reading room of the old Furness-designed library across the campus. A first floor gallery contains changing exhibits drawn from University collections. In the lounge between the two parts of the library is the Orrery, a clockwork representation of the solar system, the second designed and made in 1771 by University trustee and professor David Rittenhouse. The College of New Jersey purchased Rittenhouse's first orrery despite the contention of the leaders of Philadelphia's College that they already had agreed to its purchase. The Governor of Pennsylvania ordered a meeting of the Trustees and declared it his

Charles Patterson Van Pelt Library, Henry Charles Lea Reading Room, moved from University Library, 1963, previously in home of Henry Charles Lea. UPA.
Charles Patterson Van Pelt Library, Horace Howard Furness Reading Room, moved from University Library, 1963. UPA.
E. Craig Sweeten Alumni House, looking northwest, 1995. GET.

opinion that the College "ought to have the *first* Orrery, and not the second—even if the second should be better." Competition with Princeton is nothing new! The College finally purchased the second orrery; apparently the first is no longer in existence. The splendid Chippendale-style orrery case by Parnell Gibbs and John Folwell is one of the triumphs of Philadelphia cabinetry. Beginning in 1782 this testament to Philadelphia skill was depicted on the seal of the University. Among the treasures of the Rare Book Room on the sixth floor are Thomas Cole's *Indian Sacrifice*, Henry Inman's glorious portrait of William Wordsworth, and Beatrice Fenton's elegant bronze *Pan with Sundial.*

E. CRAIG SWEETEN ALUMNI CENTER (originally Delta Tau Delta), 3533–35 Locust Walk. 1914: Elliston P. Bissell, John P. B. Sinkler, and Marmaduke

Tilden. Interior reconstruction, 1960s, Hamilton, Murphy and Garrison. Adaptive rehabilitation, 1981–82: Dagit/Saylor.

Bissell (Ar 1893), Sinkler (Ar 1898), and Tilden (Harvard 1903) provided Delta Tau Delta with a tiny but handsome Elizabethan home, complete with carving in the manner initiated in Pennsylvania by Cope and Stewardson, with whom Bissell had worked. A disastrous fire led to the reconstruction of much of the interior in the late 1960s (architects Hamilton, Murphy, Garrison) and in turn led to the building's being taken over by the University. The razing of Beta Theta Pi next door gave new importance to the house's nondescript east facade, and the remodeling of the building for the alumni center by Dagit/Saylor added a bay window, topped by a flagpole, to exploit that new exposure. E. Craig Sweeten (W 1937), honored in the naming of the building, was Senior Vice President for Development of the University.

A group of small buildings in the familiar histor-icizing detail and brick turn the corner at 36th Street. These include **3537 Locust Walk**, which contains the Jerome Fisher Program in Management and Technology (formerly Delta Upsilon, and before that Kappa Alpha), 1913: Lester Kintzing (Ar 1900). Now University offices, this former fraternity was enlivened by adding a Tudor facade to an existing late nineteenth-century house. Adjacent to the west is **Phi Kappa Sigma**, 3539 Locust Walk, designed in 1909–11 by Elliston P. Bissell and John P. B. Sinkler. This earlier work by the architects of the Sweeten Center (and members of Penn's Alpha chapter of Phi Kappa Sigma) adopts a refined classical idiom. The fine second-floor loggia overlooks what was once a trolley-filled urban street. Psi chapter of Tri Delta Society was formed at Penn in 1986 and is occupying the building on a

••

3537 Locust Walk, looking northeast, 1998. GET.
Phi Kappa Sigma, looking northwest, 1996. GET.
Alpha Chi Rho, looking east, 1995. GET.

temporary lease. To the north on 36th Street is **Alpha Chi Rho**, 219 South 36th Street, 1916: Alfred B. Kister (Ar 1910). Unlike the more flamboyant fraternity houses of the period this quiet neo-Tudor building with subdued detail would have been a fine addition to a suburban tree-shaded street but runs the risk of being lost against the bulk of the library to its north. The Phi chapter is the oldest active chapter of Alpha Chi Rho and has been on the Penn campus since 1896.

WILLIAM B. IRVINE AUDITORIUM, 3401 Spruce Street. 1926–32: Horace Trumbauer. Renovations and restoration, Venturi, Scott Brown and Associates, 1995–99.[4]

Doubtless thanks to Henry Adams's written homage, *Mont-Saint-Michel and Chartres* (1913), Penn's Mont Saint Michel rises with the same concatenation of masses above a Gothic auditorium that originally seated 2300. Named for its donor, city Treasurer William B. Irvine, it was designed by Horace Trumbauer, the architect of choice of parvenu Philadelphians. Severe externally, but lushly painted in a movie-palace version of English medieval decor within, Irvine is a noble building.

Many of its long-noted acoustical problems derived from modifications during construction that added the soaring upper tower to serve as a sounding chamber for the vast, 11,000-pipe organ built for the Sesquicentennial Exhibition, which was acquired as a gift of publisher Cyrus Curtis in 1928. Designed by Philadelphia's leading organists, the great instrument was constructed by the Austin Organ Company and was referred to as the "Organists' Organ." In 1995 Irvine

••••••••••••••••••••••••••••••••••••

Irvine Auditorium, looking northwest, 1974. GET. Horace Trumbauer, perspective of Irvine Auditorium. Photograph of lost original, charcoal on coarse paper. UPA.

Irvine Auditorium, looking south from stage, c. 1987.
Courtesy Curtis Organ Society.

was included in the Perelman Quadrangle project. The architects, Venturi, Scott Brown and Associates, were charged with adaptively restoring and modifying the building with the aim of achieving reasonable acoustics while preserving the aesthetic character of the great room.

HOUSTON HALL, 3405 Spruce Street. 1894–96: William C. Hays (Ar 1893) and Milton B. Medary (C 1894), with Frank Miles Day and Brother. Commons Room and John Houston Lounge added 1936: Robert Rhodes McGoodwin (Ar 1907). Interior renovations, 1980: Venturi, Rauch and Scott Brown. Restoration, 1995–99: Venturi, Scott Brown and Associates.

Hays had just received his B.S. from Penn and Medary had only recently dropped out of Penn's degree program when they won first and second places respectively in the competition to build the first student union in America. The competition was organized by Professor of Architecture Warren P. Laird and was judged by a national jury that included William Mead of McKim, Mead and White and others. They were dazzled by the young architects' Spanish scheme, but acceded to Provost Harrison's vision of a unified Gothic campus and recommended the alternate English design based on the Peacock Inn at Rowley. The chief responsibility for the exterior was assigned to Medary, while Frank Miles Day, in whose office both men worked, was appointed to oversee the project. Many of the details of Houston Hall and its H-shaped plan were derived from English late medieval practice, but there are touches that speak of the return of classicism, like the shaped gable over the Spruce Street entrance. Inside, the building provided an extraordinary array of amenities: a reading nook, small

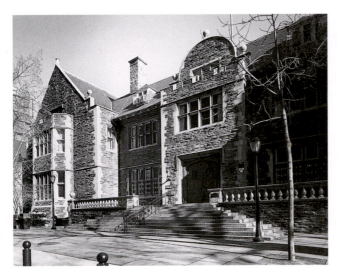

theater, gymnasium, swimming pool, and a bowling alley. While the athletic functions have been moved elsewhere, the wonderful hammer-beamed theater remains on the second floor and the building still possesses a turn-of-the-century, clubby atmosphere. It is at its best in the winter when fires are burning in the fireplaces of the great hall.

With the addition of the wings in the 1930s, the east room served for a time as the freshman dining commons; it is balanced by a handsome parlor at the west end, originally dedicated to Revolutionary War doctor and Medical School graduate John Houston (M 1769) and since renamed the Bodek Lounge. A case of memorabilia including Dr. Houston's saber ornaments the lounge. Both rooms were added by Robert McGoodwin with such skill that they are often confused with the original design. The ground floor was updated by Venturi, Rauch, and Scott Brown in 1980, when they also refurbished the basement corridor as a miniature commercial strip, complete with neon, of the kind Venturi, Denise Scott Brown and Steven Izenour celebrated in *Learning from Las Vegas* (1972). In later years, administrative offices occupied progressively more space. These have been removed as part of the restoration of Houston Hall as the centerpiece of the Perelman Quadrangle.

Houston Hall contains several handsome portraits, the most notable of which is by Cecilia Beaux of Henry Howard Houston, Jr. (C 1878), in whose memory the building was dedicated. The 1872 bell that tolled the hours for two generations from the tower of College Hall is now on a handsome stand, though removed from its familiar position of many years in the center of the great hall.

EDWIN B. AND LEONORE R. WILLIAMS HUMANITIES AND LANGUAGE HALL, 36th and Spruce Streets. 1972: Nolen, Swinburne, and Associates. Courtyard skylight and alterations for Perelman Quadrangle by Venturi, Scott Brown and Associates, 1995–99.[5]

Williams Hall was built by the Commonwealth as part of the University's rapid expansion of the 1960s and 1970s. Professor of Romance Languages Edwin Williams, who served as the Dean of the Graduate School of Arts and Sciences and Provost of the University, and his wife Leonore were the honorees for the building, which provides humanities classrooms and office space for language departments. Cupping a small courtyard within a tall, ruggedly detailed mass of brown brick, Williams aspires to recapture the sense of enclosure and collegiate security Cope and

••••••••••••••••••••••••••••••••••••••

Houston Hall, Spruce Street facade, looking northwest, 1997. GET.
Houston Hall, Commons Room, 1995. GET.

Houston Hall, Billiards Room, c. 1896. UPA.

••••••••••••••••••••••••••••••••••••

Stewardson achieved in the Quadrangle. The building occupies the site of Thomas Richards's rather austere, mansarded Robert Hare Laboratories (1877–78), which introduced laboratory training to medical students, marking the beginning of the new medical curriculum. As the 1990s end, the courtyard is being infilled with a glass vestibule and study space as a complement to the Perelman Quadrangle, by Venturi, Scott Brown and Associates.

CLASS OF 1893 MEMORIAL GATE, 3400 block of Spruce Street. 1900: Elliston P. Bissell and William C. Hays.

The Memorial Gate was designed by two members of the class of 1893. Its design, in the familiar red brick and limestone trim, followed the model of Cope and Stewardson's gate across Hamilton Walk adjacent to the west end of the dormitories. Its iron arch bears a motto that could have been that of the University: "Inveniemus viam aut faciemus"—"We shall find a way or we shall make one."

LOGAN HALL (originally Medical Hall), 249 South 36th Street. 1873–74: Thomas W. Richards. Reconstruction after 1919 fire, McIlvain and Roberts. Exterior restoration, 1988–95: Marianna M. Thomas Architects. Interior renovations, 1995–98: Venturi, Scott-Brown and Associates.[6]

Thomas Richards's other surviving serpentine building, Logan Hall, is more compactly composed than College Hall, and the Gothic detail possesses more of what a nineteenth century critic would have called "muscularity." The entrance porch with its stout columns is especially impressive. The facades denoted the dual nature of the building; on the front the small windows designated classrooms and offices while the large multistory windows on the rear lit the large auditoria where most teaching occurred.

••••••••••••••••••••••••••••••••••••••

Logan Hall, looking southeast, 1998 (right). GET.
Edwin B. and Leonore R. Williams Humanities and Language Hall, looking northeast, 1995. GET.
Class of 1893 Memorial Gate, looking north, before 1914. UPA.

The change in the medical curriculum from lecture to practice led in 1906 to the replacement of the Medical Hall with the new Medical Laboratories (now the John Morgan Building) on Hamilton Walk. After housing the medical school for a quarter of a century, the building became the second home of the Wharton School, the nation's first school of business. To memorialize this new purpose, the building was renamed for James Logan, William Penn's colonial secretary and a founding trustee of the College of Philadelphia. Slightly damaged by fire in 1888, the entire north wing was burned on 31 October 1919. This disaster spurred a reconstruction of the building for use by the Wharton School, which gave up plans to build immediately on the eventual site of Dietrich Hall, even though Cope and Stewardson had prepared a design. The rear half of the building, which contained two, 300-seat medical amphitheaters, was rebuilt by McIlvain and Roberts (Charles McIlvain Ar 1890). Its concrete frame was faced with cast stone blocks with a serpentine aggregate surface, leaving only the cast-iron stair of the central hall and the severe ruled plaster walls of the main cross corridors to suggest the character of the original interior. The top two floors were devoted to the Lippincott Library that served the business school.

When the Wharton School departed for Dietrich Hall, Logan Hall passed to the Faculty of Arts and Sciences. Recent planning by Venturi, Scott Brown and Associates incorporates part of the building into the Perelman Quadrangle. The first floor contains the offices of the College and serves as a focus for undergraduate education, while academic departments including Philosophy, Classical Studies, and the History and Sociology of Science share the upper floors.

WISTAR INSTITUTE OF ANATOMY, 36th and Spruce Streets. 1892–94, 1897: George W. Hewitt and William D. Hewitt. Addition, 1975: Mansell, Lewis and Fugate.

The oldest independent biomedical research institute in the United States, the Wistar Institute was founded by General Isaac Wistar to house the ana-

tomical specimen collection of his uncle Dr. Caspar Wistar. It was built adjacent to the Medical School because it was the donor's intention that it should be affiliated with the University. The general entrusted the design to George W. and William D. Hewitt, who had worked with Frank Furness a generation earlier. The Hewitts created a restrained classical building whose form represented the iron skeleton within; its exterior of yellow brick enlivened with terra cotta ornament was another of the freestyle designs of the Pepper campus. At the north end, the originally acute corner of the 36th Street-Woodland Avenue intersection was filled with a tall semicircular bay. A remarkable ferrous frame is everywhere visible on the inside,

••

Wistar Institute of Anatomy and Biology, Spruce Street facade, looking northeast, 1995 (right). GET.
Wistar Institute of Anatomy and Biology, 36th Street facade, looking northwest, 1974. GET.

Psi Upsilon, looking west, 1991. GET.

●●

especially around the soaring skylighted stairhall. The splendid pierced iron stair celebrates the modern age with the same vigor as the University Library stair by Furness across the campus. Before its recent modernization, the early fireproof construction of brick arches on steel beams carrying the floors was visible in the great exhibition hall which occupied the south half of the main floor. The steel frame construction has ensured sufficient flexibility to accommodate modern changes in research methods and laboratory design, so that Wistar continues to serve its original mission more than a century after its opening.

In 1897 the Hewitts built an addition on the west, fronting on Woodland Avenue, giving it a second major street front and creating an engaging series of volumes from flat to polygonal to round at the corner. The large western addition was built by Mansell, Lewis, and Fugate in 1975 on the foundations of a printing plant for the Institute, designed by Magaziner, Eberhard and Harris in 1932.

PSI UPSILON (The Castle), 300 South 36th Street. 1897: George W. Hewitt and William D. Hewitt. Restoration 1991: Steege, Crimm. (Color Plate 7)

Because William Hewitt's son John (C 1899) was a member of the Tau chapter which had been founded in

Psi Upsilon, great hall, 1991. GET.

••••••••••••••••••••••••••••••••••••

1891, the Hewitts were selected to design the University's first on-campus, purpose-built fraternity house. Designed at the moment when Cope and Stewardson's initial plans for the dormitory quadrangles were underway, Psi Upsilon was an older Victorian architect's response to their Academic Gothic style, resulting in a rather stolid and symmetrical building. Its castellated pretensions project little of the Furnessian vigor with which the Hewitts had infused their own earlier medievalizing work. The house possesses some of the fraternity system's best preserved interiors, particularly the low-beamed main

hall. Later alterations by alumnus H. Bartol Register (Ar 1910), of the well-known firm Tilden, Register, and Pepper, brought the dining room into a 1920s mode. Alumni have included Owen J. Roberts (C 1895, L 1898), justice of the United States Supreme Court, as well as a remarkable group of architects, notably William Hough (Ar 1911), one of Paul Cret's first employees and later partner in Harbeson, Hough, Livingston and Larson. Also among this group was Francis Keally (Ar 1916), designer of Oregon's State Capitol and the Trylon and Perisphere of the New York World's Fair of 1939. The building was restored by alumni Paul Steege (Ar 1973) and Walter Crimm (Ar 1980) in 1991.

CHRISTIAN ASSOCIATION, 3601 Locust Walk. 1927–29: Walter H. Thomas, Sydney Martin, and Donald M. Kirkpatrick.[7]

Dating from the era when Penn was still strongly stratified by class, religion, and ethnic origins, the "CA" was intended to serve Protestant students, but remains private property. It is the work of three alumni, Walter H. Thomas (Ar 1899), Sydney Martin (Ar 1907, and later a University trustee) and Donald Kirkpatrick (Ar 1911), the winner of a national competition for the Paris Prize. Their strong Beaux-Arts leanings were much more obvious in the stripped classicism of the heating plant they built on South Street (now the Hollenback Center) than in their Zeta Psi house or in this building—the last of Pennsylvania's truly distinguished neo-medieval designs. Their first published sketches show a design in the Lombard Romanesque style that was then the rage, but it was soon changed to imitate a miniature Elizabethan mansion in accord with current campus architecture. It possesses a wealth of finely scaled and executed detail, much of it carved in situ in the open-pored French limestone. There are many reminiscences of Edwin Lutyens's beautiful early work, as in the adroit composition of the minor entrance on Locust Walk. Inside, the firm provided a handsome common room on the ground floor (now a restaurant open to the public) and a 350-seat Memorial Auditorium (honoring the sacrifices of University men in the First World War) at the rear of the second floor. The restaurant and a cafeteria in the basement (also open to the public) now replace the three dining rooms of the original plan.

HILLEL FOUNDATION (originally Delta Sigma Phi), 202 South 36th Street. 1925: Arthur E. Davis., Jr (Newark, N.J.). Additions, 1983–85: GBQC Architects.

The small neo-Tudor Hillel Building was enlarged with a Postmodern addition that makes abstracted allusions to the towered forms and academic Gothic style of the original structure.

JAMES M. SKINNER HALL (FINE ARTS STUDIOS), 200 South 36th Street. 1957–59: Hatfield, (Ar 1929), Martin (Ar 1926), and White (Ar 1925).

A mannerly building that was built as the faculty club, Skinner Hall is given dignity by the use of marble

•••••••••••••••••••••••••••••••••••

James M. Skinner Hall, looking northwest, 1995. GET.
Hillel Foundation, looking northwest, 1995. GET.
Christian Association, looking north, 1995 (right). GET.

panels below the windows. It is entered from a quiet Japanese-influenced garden into a multi-story stairhall. Wood paneling hints at the collegiate character abandoned by contemporary architecture in the 1950s, while later alterations have tempered the original stridently antiseptic modernism. A western addition by the same firm in 1966–68 contained a large second-floor dining room with a bay window. James Skinner (T 1911) was president of Philco Corporation and a University trustee. With the move of the Faculty Club to Sansom Common, Skinner Hall has been adapted to house the Fine Arts Studios.

Locust Walk, 3600 and 3700 blocks of former Locust Street. 1957: George Patton, landscape architect.

The 1948 master plan envisioned the removal of

Locust Walk, looking west from 37th Street, 1996. GET.
••

many of the streets of the campus and their replacement with tree-shaded walkways. The first to be closed was the 3600 block of Locust Street. With its patterned brick and stone pavement and bordering shade trees, the walk provided a look into the future for the campus. It is now the site of numerous sculptures and objects including the *Lindemann Fountain*, a granite basin with bronze dome by Delia Bentivoglio (M.L.A. 1978) and Robert Lundgren (M.L.A. 1982).

3609–11 LOCUST WALK, ca. 1868.

This pair of brownstones survives from a row that once extended to the corner of 36th Street. The mansard roofs echo the popular forms of Second

Empire Paris, and the dry, incised detailing of the doorheads is usually called neo-grec, after the French avant-garde architectural movement of the mid-nineteenth century. These features appeared here as soon as the first wave of French-trained Americans returned to practice in the United States and were quickly incorporated into pattern books, many of which were written by Samuel Sloan, who was active in West Philadelphia before the Civil War. Sloan is a likely possibility as the architect of the buildings. They house University offices.

THE VERANDA (originally Phi Sigma Kappa), 3615 Locust Walk. 1951: Abraham Levy (Ar 1920)

The Veranda is a spirited if somewhat naive design

•••••••••••••••••••••••••••••••••••••

The Veranda (formerly Phi Sigma Kappa), looking north, 1995. GET.

3609–11 Locust Walk, looking northwest, 1995. GET.

whose strident asymmetry and hovering cantilevered slabs belatedly recall the exuberant *moderne* of the 1930s. A huge multipurpose hall stretches from the front to the back on the ground floor. The Mu chapter of Phi Sigma Kappa was established in 1900; the move to their present purpose-built modern house was occasioned by the construction of Dietrich Hall across Locust Street on the site of the chapter's previous home.

PHI GAMMA DELTA, 3619–21 Locust Walk. 1913–14: Walter Mellor and Arthur I. Meigs.

The architecture of Mellor (Ar 1904) and Meigs (Princeton 1903) easily conjures up images of monied life in the sunny decades before the Great Depression. Their only work at Penn, Phi Gamma Delta is a most sophisticated design that creates a small, sheltered forecourt (a welcome feature in the days before Locust Walk was created) beside the medieval great hall. The hall's towering leaded window advances nearly to the street. Penn's Beta chapter of Phi Gamma Delta was established in 1882.

STEINBERG-DIETRICH HALL, 3620 Locust Walk. Dietrich Hall, 1949-50: McKim, Mead and White. Steinberg Hall, 1980-82: Warner, Burns, Toan and Lunde. Pergola: Hanna/Olin.

Built to house the Wharton School (which had been

located in Logan Hall), Dietrich Hall was designed in a hybrid *moderne* manner in Penn's red brick and light stone, by McKim, Mead, and White, who were led at that time by James Kellum Smith (Ar 1918). Its somewhat old-fashioned civility was swept away in the 1980s building program that gutted Dietrich and inserted Steinberg Hall in what had been a courtyard. As rebuilt, the school turns inward onto an atrium that contains the original Dietrich facade as well as the 1950 dedication wall. The blank Locust Street facade would have been even bleaker, had not the Campus Design Committee insisted on changes. The result is the wisteria-draped pergola based on Greene and Greene's California work, which landscape architects Robert Hanna and Laurie Olin skillfully inserted between the building and the pedestrian axis of the campus. The original McKim, Mead and White building was dedicated to D. Wellington Dietrich by Daniel (W 1924) and H. Richard Dietrich (W 1930). The new facade bears the name of Saul Steinberg (W 1959), University trustee and head of the Reliance Group.

••

Phi Gamma Delta, looking north, 1995. GET.
Steinberg-Dietrich Hall, looking southwest, 1995. GET.
McKim, Mead and White, "Birdseye view of the Wharton School of Finance and Commerce, University of Pennsylvania." Photo of lost original. Earl Purdy, del. c. 1949. UPA.

The massive bronze *Reclining Figure* by Henry Moore (1982, installed 1984) in the Steinberg-Dietrich Hall court is on loan from Mr. and Mrs. Jeffrey H. Luria.

ANNENBERG SCHOOL FOR COMMUNICATION, 3620 Walnut Street. 1962: Alfred Easton Poor (M.Arch 1924). Additions, 1982–84: Mitchell [B.Arch '48]/Giurgola Architects. North additions, 1998–99: MGA Partners.

Publisher and later ambassador to Great Britain, Walter Annenberg was the Maecenas of the Annenberg School for Communication and principal donor of many of the facilities that place it among the elite programs of the nation. Poor's 1962 design gave the Annenberg School a serene limestone building with a vast, glass-faced lobby that contains Sam Maitin's (B.F.A. 1951) brightly hued construction *Celebration* (1976, enlarged in 1985) and José de Rivera's *Construction 66* (1959, installed 1963). A splendid bronze tensile structure by Henry Bertoia, entitled *Homage to Performing Art* (1975), is suspended in the main lobby. Twenty years after the completion of the building, the south facade disappeared behind Romaldo Giurgola's immensely sophisticated extension. Giurgola created a serene piazza atop a suite of underground classrooms, framed by a boldly symmetrical main facade and a new east wing. A restrained limestone-clad design that nonetheless incorporates a surprising

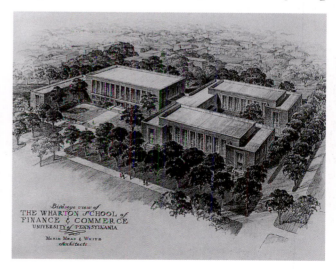

amount of colored stonework, ordered by axes and echoing geometries, the new Annenberg facade manifests a measure of the undisguised classicism that has returned to contemporary architecture.

ANNENBERG CENTER, 3680 Walnut Street. 1971: Vincent Kling and Associates.

The flyloft of the Zellerbach Theater, largest of the center's three halls (972 seats), rises above this strongly massed building like a signboard. Its brown brick, unornamented masses were hallmarks of the Kling firm's 1970s work on campus, including the Veterinary School additions at 39th and Pine Streets. Inside, the large lobby also serves the Harold Prince (C 1948) and Studio Theaters (250 and 125 seats respectively). The overall severity of the design perhaps uncon-

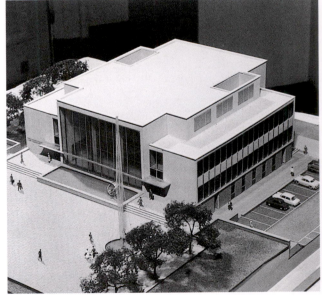

Annenberg School for Communication, looking northwest, 1996. GET.
Annenberg School for Communication, photograph of architect's model, 1962. UPA.
Annenberg Center, looking west, 1995. GET.

••••••••••••••••••••••••••••••••••••••

sciously reiterates the theatrical truth that "the Play's the Thing."

DELTA PHI (St. Elmo), 3627 Locust Walk. 1959: Wright, Andrade, and Amenta.

A genteel compromise with modernism, the present Delta Phi house replaces a rather robust design whose concatenated gables rose at 3453 Woodland Avenue. The old house was demolished for the construction of Van Pelt Library. The Eta chapter of the St. Elmo Club

was the first fraternity founded on the Penn campus, being established in 1849 when the campus was still on its Ninth Street site. In 1980 the organization broke new ground by becoming the first coed fraternity on campus.

DELTA PSI (St. Anthony Hall), 3637 Locust Walk. 1907–10: Cope and Stewardson.

Delta Psi dates from the period after the deaths of Walter Cope and John Stewardson, when the firm was run by Emlyn Stewardson (C 1884), John's younger brother, with Scottish-born and English-trained James P. Jamieson as chief designer. The house is an unexpectedly rectangular version of the English late medieval style the firm also adopted for the Quadrangle. Its hard edges and tiny pediments whisper of the coming

Renaissance. Penn's Delta chapter of St. Anthony Hall was also founded in 1849, making it the second fraternity associated with the Ninth Street campus. In 1888 it was the first fraternity to have its own purpose-built house, a Wilson Eyre Jr. palazzo on 22nd Street across the Schuylkill. With the shift to the residential campus in West Philadelphia, Delta Psi built the present Locust Street house.

COLONIAL PENN CENTER (originally Phi Kappa Psi), 3641 Locust Walk. 1904–5: Frank Rommel with Francis A. Gugert. Renovated 1973: Eshbach, Glass, Kale and Associates.

Phi Kappa Psi presents a powerful, freely medieval

Delta Phi, looking northwest, 1995. GET.
Delta Psi, looking northwest, 1985 (right). GET.

image, dark red in color and strongly punctuated by repeated gables and a fenestrated arcade on the ground floor. Rommel (Ar 1897) and Gugert (attended Towne School in 1891–93 but graduated with the class of 1895) were both members of the fraternity. Its interior drew on the fashionable Mission Style, with a remarkable frieze of murals around the dining room in the fashion of Maxfield Parrish. The building was renovated for the Leonard Davis Institute of Health Economics in 1973 by Eshbach, Glass, Kale, and Associates.

Colonial Penn Center, Locust Walk facade, looking north, c. 1908. UPA.

Locust House, Locust Walk, looking northwest, 1998. GET.

Benjamin Franklin on Campus, *intersection of 37th Street and Locust Walk, 1997. GET.*

••••••••••••••••••••••••••••••••••

LOCUST HOUSE, 3643 Locust Walk. ca. 1870. Renovations and new porch, 1996–97: Voith & McTavish Architects.

A modest Second Empire twin that was for a time home to Theta Chi, it is now the Penn Women's Center and other offices. It is characteristic of the smaller suburban houses built during the period when Penn moved to West Philadelphia. After being largely dismantled by its residents, the building was acquired by the University and adapted to the purpose of bringing women on to what had essentially been an all-male preserve of Locust Walk.

BENJAMIN FRANKLIN ON CAMPUS, 37th and Locust Walks. 1987: George W. Lunden.

A gift of the class of 1962, this piece has gained immediate acceptance as a setting for photographs.

PHI DELTA THETA, 3700 Locust Walk. 1924–25: Robert McGoodwin (Ar 1907, GAr 1908).

After a generation at 34th and Walnut Streets, the Zeta chapter of Phi Delta Theta, founded in 1883, acquired an important corner site at 37th and Locust Streets and joined the rapidly growing Fraternity Row. Unlike the fraternity's first Gothic building, the new house was designed in the Colonial Revival style that was fashionable as the nation's Sesquicentennial drew near. The ambitious portico reflects McGoodwin's education at the Ecole des Beaux-Arts and his office training with Horace Trumbauer, Philadelphia's master of the grand gesture.

KAPPA SIGMA 3706 Locust. 1923: Theodore Epps (Ar 1919).

Securely and confidently neo-Georgian, the Alpha Epsilon chapter of Kappa Sigma (Penn's chapter was founded in 1892) is graced with a massive doorway whose overlarge pediment recalls some of the lively but ill-proportioned detailing of the style as it was practiced two hundred years earlier in London's Lincoln's Inn. It is the work of a Penn grad who served as the editor of the Boston-based journal *Home-Building* in the 1920s.

Social Sciences Quadrangle. 1965–66: Harbeson, Hough, Livingston and Larson.

Phi Delta Theta, looking southwest, 1987. GET.
Kappa Sigma, looking southwest, 1995. GET.
Social Sciences Quadrangle, looking north, 1995. GET.

••••••••••••••••••••••••••••••••••••

The Social Sciences Complex was one of the big plans of the Harnwell era. The repetitious pilaster-like piers that unify the group recall the same architects' Van Pelt Library and doubtless represent the roots of their education in the Beaux-Arts orders of Paul Cret's atelier at Penn. The real interest of the group, however, is as it suggests the character of the campus if the 1948 plan had been put into effect. Early photographs emphasize the serenity of the courtyard removed from the street while the interior lounge that

was intended to serve the entire group recalls the community-building idealism that shaped the rhetoric of Philadelphia School modernists.

The most interesting building of the group is **Stiteler Hall**, at 208 South 37th Street (1965–66), which, befitting its more public role, is the most expressive of the Social Sciences group. Irregular, corrugated concrete faces of the lecture halls peek out from beneath the overhang of the second floor. The lounge with its folded roof juts into the courtyard of the complex and provides the one piece of visual energy in the ensemble. The donor, Frederick Stiteler, was not an alumnus, but a West Philadelphia neighbor and a "long friend of the University." The **Psychology**

McNeil Building, interior court, 1971 (left). Frank Ross.
McNeil Building, looking northwest, 1995. GET.
Lauder-Fischer Building, looking northwest, 1995. GET.

••••••••••••••••••••••••••••••••••••

Laboratory Building at 3720 Locust Walk (1965–66) has faint echoes of the articulation of Kahn's Richards Building, restrained by the overall order of the building. Its lack of large windows reflects the function of the building as a laboratory. The **Graduate School of Education** (3700 Walnut Street) and the **Caster Building** (3715 Locust Walk) are simple framing parentheses to the more dynamic buildings on the east and west, suggesting a hierarchy. Caster is the home of the Graduate School of Social Work and was named in 1973 for Reading, Pennsylvania businessman Harold Caster and his sisters.

ROBERT McNEIL BUILDING, 3718 Locust Walk. 1964–70: Ballinger Company.

The McNeil Building is the largest of the classroom and office buildings constructed to serve the social sciences during the Harnwell expansion. It is entered from its ends and turns its myriad oriels toward Locust Walk, but its principal feature is the large atrium space that fills the center of the building on the upper floors. Named for pharmaceutical magnate Robert L. McNeil, Jr. (whose company invented Tylenol), it is the work of one of Philadelphia's oldest architectural firms, Ballinger Company, that was founded three-quarters of a century earlier and established a reputation for important innovations in industrial design which are here recalled in the vast interior space.

LAUDER-FISCHER HALL, 37th Street and Locust Walk. 1988–90: Davis and Brody.

Lou Davis (Ar 1949) and Brody, better known for their innovative air structure for the United States Pavilion at the Kyoto World's Fair and for high-rise housing in New York City, here venture a muscular Postmodern design for the Wharton School. A continuous glass strip window in the modern idiom below the green slate roof contrasts with the obvious historicism of the Flemish bond brickwork of the facade. On its south elevation, a projecting bay and overscaled limestone trim recall the American Beaux-Arts of the 1920s. The support of the Lauder family has been instrumental in the transformation of the business campus; the Joseph Lauder Institute of Management and International Studies, is joined with the Arthur Fischer (W 1952, Wharton Overseer) Real Estate program.

SHEARSON LEHMAN HUTTON QUAD-RANGLE, between 37th and 38th Streets below Locust Walk. 1991: Hanna-Olin Ltd. (Color Plate 8)

The handsome green enlivens the interior spaces of the Wharton campus and provides a setting for the events of the surrounding Wharton School. The same designers were responsible for the adjacent Class of '62 Walk on the vacated 37th Street.

Shearson, Lehman, Hutton Quadrangle, looking west, 1995. GET.
Vance Hall, looking southeast, 1975. GET.

••••••••••••••••••••••••••••••••••••••

VANCE HALL, 37th and Spruce Streets. 1971–72: Bower and Fradley.

In 1968, John Bower (Ar 1953) and Frederick Fradley began a project to house Penn's main-frame computer

in a centralized facility. During its gestation period, miniaturization began the reduction of computers from behemoths requiring individual structures to the familiar desk-top tool. So as not to lose the investment, the building was adapted to house the graduate programs of the Wharton School. Much of the facade was based on the requirements of early computers. Vance Hall turns its glass face northward to dissipate heat, while its south wall is screened by a skillfully integrated *brise-soleil*. The particular vocabulary of brick and glass is obviously derived from James Stirling's Engineering Building at Leicester University in England, one of the most celebrated Brutalist buildings of the 1960s; its rounded glass corner towers perhaps allude to Gropius's Bauhaus; and its particularized forms proved Louis Kahn's continuing influence. How-

Vance Hall, north corridor, 1973. Photo: Lawrence S. Williams. Courtesy H2L2 Architects.
Steinberg Conference Center, looking northeast, 1999. GET.
Steinberg Conference Center, looking southwest, 1999. GET.

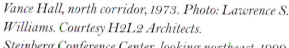

ever, the jagged, aggressive technophilia of the English building has been diluted and its wild skyline tamed. Vance Hall carries the name of Henry T. Vance (W 1927), a University trustee and head of Vance, Sandero and Co. of Boston.

STEINBERG CONFERENCE CENTER and ARESTY CORPORATE CENTER, 38th and Spruce Streets. 1988: The Hillier Group.

The Steinberg Conference Center's towered 38th Street entrance and small interior court on the diagonal pedestrian passage at the corner of Spruce Street were derived from Cope and Stewardson's masterful Quad. But the shift of hue from red and white to brown-red and tan with teal blue windows links the exterior to the trendy commercial architecture of 1980s corporate campuses. Penn's first encounter with

Postmodernism appropriately serves as the conference center and in-house hotel of the Wharton School. Whether it will prove as timeless as the Quad is for the future to determine. It carries the name of Saul Steinberg (W 1959) who has been a Wharton and University trustee and a generous supporter of multiple University programs.

JON M. HUNTSMAN HALL, 38th Street and Locust Walk. 1998– : Kohn Pederson Fox Associates.

This site was for many years occupied by the University Bookstore, demolished in 1999 for the Wharton Classroom building. The tripartite program of undergraduate and graduate classrooms with a tower for faculty offices is expressed in the massing of the building. Within, new forms of classrooms are designed to pull students into the conversation of the class. Kohn Pederson Fox Associates have redesigned the skyline of Philadelphia in a cluster of tall buildings on the west side of City Hall, and with this structure build a presence on the campus where Eugene Kohn (Ar 1953, GAr 1957) and Sheldon Fox (Ar 1953) were students.

THE EAST CAMPUS

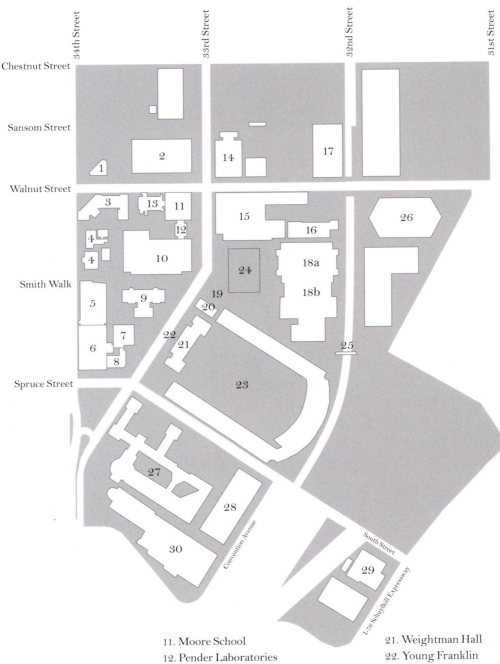

East Campus

1. Zeta Psi
2. Hill College House
3. Bennett Hall
4. Music and Morgan Buildings
5. Vagelos Laboratories
6. 1973 Chemistry Laboratories
7. 1958 Chemistry Laboratories
8. Cret Chemistry Building
9. Hayden Hall
10. Towne Building

11. Moore School
12. Pender Laboratories
13. Moore Graduate Center
14. Laboratory for Research on the Structure of Matter
15. Rittenhouse Laboratories
16. Tandem Accelerator Laboratory
17. Walnut Street Garage
18. Palestra and Hutchinson Gymnasium
19. All Wars Memorial
20. White Training House

21. Weightman Hall
22. Young Franklin
23. Franklin Field
24. Lott Tennis Courts
25. Bower Field Bridge
26. Class of 1923 Ice Rink
27. University Museum
28. Museum Garage
29. Hollenback Center
30. Penn Tower (South Campus)

THE EAST CAMPUS

THE EAST CAMPUS slowly evolved out of open space at the rear of the Blockley Almshouse, the mid-nineteenth-century William Strickland-designed poorhouse of the city of Philadelphia, which later became basis for the Philadelphia General Hospital. In the late 1880s Provost William Pepper began to encourage related institutions to locate adjacent to the University on the public lands. Within a few years, however, their buildings were acquired by the ever-expanding Penn. Locust Street was drawn on city plans but it was never opened east of 34th Street. Instead, in the early twentieth century, it was landscaped into a handsome, elm-shaded walk by Cope and Stewardson in association with their project for the Towne Building. When the statue of Edgar Fahs Smith, the former provost and professor of chemistry, by faculty member R. Tait McKenzie, was installed (1926) at the 34th Street end, the walk gained a focus that gave the name to Smith Walk. The War Memorial added in 1950 provides a sculptural terminus for the east end. Other sculptures in the precinct include the standing figure of chemist John Harrison (1773–1833) by Lynn Jenkins (1934, moved 1997), the founder of the Harrison Chemical Works. Harrison was the first American to synthesize sulfuric acid, which served as the basis for the fortune that helped pay for the Harrison Chemistry lab and for the alterations to convert the Dental School into the Harrison Fine Arts building. The statue originally faced Spruce Street adjacent to the flank of the Harrison lab but was moved to the rear of the chemistry complex with the construction of 1973 Chemistry. The handsome park between the buildings of the Institute for Advanced Science and Technology (IAST) has been designed by the Olin Partnership.

ZETA PSI, 3337 Walnut Street. 1909: Walter H. Thomas, C. Wharton Churchman, and John Molitor.

Like the former Phi Delta Theta house (now the Jaffe History of Art Building) on the opposite corner of Walnut and 34th Streets, Zeta Psi responds with a triangular plan to the route of the now vanished Woodland Avenue. The detail, especially around the door, is somewhat more florid than Cope and Stewardson's contemporary work, prefiguring the same firm's later Christian Association Building. The polygonal corner bay is filled by a great sitting room

Zeta Psi, looking northeast, 1997. GET.

on the ground floor with a library above. Churchman (Certificate of Architectural Proficiency 1899) was a member of Zeta Psi . Thomas (Ar 1899) continued his studies in Paris. Molitor served as Philadelphia's City Architect between 1923 and 1928.

HILL COLLEGE HOUSE, 3333 Walnut Street. 1960: Eero Saarinen and Associates.[1]

Built as a women's dormitory to serve the students whose academic headquarters was across the street in Bennett Hall, Hill House is now a coed College House. One of the last designs of Eero Saarinen, it is a building full of the historical allusions the architect loved—a mighty medieval fortress of crudely formed brick, surrounded by a moat, entered by a bridge, and crowned by a modern version of a Victorian cornice. Inside, the secure courtyard of the castle is trans-

Hill College House, looking northeast, 1976. GET.
Hill College House, interior courtyard, c. 1961. Lawrence Williams.

••

formed into a luminous, skylit atrium into which the residents may look out from many vantages. In its brilliant white surfaces and interior balconies, the atrium recalls the Italian hill towns that inspired other Saarinen dormitories of the era. The great atrium dining room has been ornamented since 1973 with N. C. Wyeth's *Apotheosis of Franklin* (1926), a highly colored exercise in mythmaking by one of the masters of the Brandywine School.

The building's implicit criticism of modernism's abstraction fell on hospitable soil at Penn, where Louis Kahn's Richards Building was then under construction. Robert Venturi, it should be noted, worked for a

Bennett Hall, looking east, 1998. GET
Bennett Hall, looking southwest, 1995. GET

while in Saarinen's office. Kevin Roche (who succeeded as leader of Saarinen's firm) prepared a project for a second women's dorm, which was to be placed on Hill Field to the north, in 1963, but was never constructed. Hill House is named for Robert Hill (C 1889), whose gift was used to buy the land. It replaced the Hannah E. Sergeant Hall (demolished 1975), an apartment building (1900) on the northeast corner of 34th and Chestnut Streets, which the University purchased in 1924 to serve as its first women's residence.

BENNETT HALL, 3340 Walnut Street. 1923–25: Stewardson and Page. Alterations, 1966: Suer, Livingston and Demas[2]

Constructed to serve the growing educational demands placed on the University by the admission of women undergraduates, Bennett Hall became the home of the College of Liberal Arts for Women, founded in 1933. It is on the site of properties which Joseph Bennett, a Philadelphia clothing manufacturer whose wealth derived from making Civil War uni-

forms, gave to the University to encourage the education of women. Bennett's will provided an endowment with the expectation that "a new building should be erected covering the site of the houses included in his gift to the University." By 1924 the fund was sufficient to begin construction. In addition to classrooms, Bennett also housed the School of Education (then largely composed of women) and the Maria Hosmer Penniman Library, devoted to education, which filled the great two-story hall above the main entrance (now converted into a lecture room and lounge). There was even room for a women's student union in the basement and a gymnasium at the east end of the fourth floor (now divided into offices). George Page's rather dispirited Tudor design with a *moderne* flair compares poorly with his contemporary work in the Quadrangle, but its beveled facade was part of a larger Paul Cret-designed scheme to form a plaza at 34th and

Walnut Streets that was to become the main entrance to the campus. In 1966, following the elimination of the distinction between the College and the College for Women, Bennett Hall was adapted to provide classrooms and offices for the English department.

MUSIC AND MORGAN BUILDINGS (formerly the north and south wings of the Randall Morgan Laboratory of Physics; built as the Foulke and Long Institute for Orphan Girls of Soldiers and Firemen), 201 and 205 South 34th Street. 1890–92: Cope and Stewardson. North wing renovations, 1967–69: Alexander Ewing and Associates.

••••••••••••••••••••••••••••••••••••

Music and Morgan Buildings, looking south, 1991. GET.

The University purchased the buildings of a short-lived girls' orphanage in 1900 and converted them into physics laboratories because they were located in the area that was becoming the science precinct. They are the campus's only surviving representatives of the many buildings designed by Cope and Stewardson in this restrained Italian mode. (Among the demolished examples of their work in this style were the John Harrison Laboratory of Chemistry, also on 34th Street, the Pepper Clinical Research Laboratory, and the Piersol wing of the Hospital.) Low roofs and wide eaves with excellent brickwork—much of it molded—were hallmarks of Cope and Stewardson's early works. In 1900 the buildings were renamed the Randall Morgan Laboratory for the Penn graduate (C 1873, A.M.

Roy and Diana Vagelos Laboratories, looking southeast, 1998. GET.

••••••••••••••••••••••••••••••••••••

1876) and financier who supported the conversion of these buildings for the Physics Department. At the Centennial Exhibition, it was a Penn Physics professor, George Barker, who demonstrated Alexander Graham Bell's telephone to the public, and the University's first Ph.D. was awarded in 1889 to a student in the Physics Department. Beginning in the 1930s, the Morgan Laboratory was headed by nuclear physicist Gaylord P. Harnwell, who would serve as Penn's president. For a time, a Van de Graaff generator or "atom smasher" was operated in the rear of Morgan. The north wing later housed the nursing program; it was then transferred to the Music Department, for whom Alexander Ewing and Associates built the rear annex in 1967–69 and replaced the interiors.

ROY AND DIANA VAGELOS LABORATORIES OF THE INSTITUTE FOR ADVANCED SCIENCE AND TECHNOLOGY, 215 South 34th Street. 1991–97: Venturi, Scott Brown and Associates with Payette Associates (Color Plate 14)

The IAST stands midway between 1973 Chemistry, the Towne Building, and Hayden Hall, physically and symbolically linking the disciplines within the applied sciences precinct. This, among the newest of Penn's science laboratories, is an essay in the colors of

the old campus, based largely on Furness's University Library across the street, and Edgar Seeler's Dental Hall (now Hayden Hall) to the east. Unlike Louis Kahn's complex massing of the different functions of the Alfred Newton Richards Medical Research Laboratories, the Vagelos Laboratories are housed in a simple rectangular volume denoting the repetitive laboratory units within. The articulated north end contains conference rooms and other more public spaces overlooking Smith Walk. The north lobby contains terra cotta panels salvaged from Smith Hall (the Lea Laboratory of Hygiene, 1891) that stood on the site until 1995. Designed by Collins and Autenrieth, the Lea family architects, with design guidance by Dr. John Shaw Billings, the nation's leading exponent of public health, it later housed chemistry labs and more recently fine arts studios. Board of Trustees chairman Roy Vagelos (C 1950), president of the Merck Corporation, shepherded this project through its evolution. He and his wife were the lead donors of the building that now bears their names.

1973 CHEMISTRY LABORATORIES, 34th and Spruce Streets. 1969–73: Ballinger Company with Harbeson, Hough, Livingston and Larson.

The present sedate building of brick and reinforced

••••••••••••••••••••••••••••••••••••

1973 Chemistry Laboratories, looking northeast, 1995. GET.

*1958 Chemistry Laboratories, looking northwest, 1994.
GET.*

••••••••••••••••••••••••••••••••••

concrete replaces Cope and Stewardson's John
Harrison Laboratory of Chemistry (1893–94), a building quite like their Morgan Labs in its references to
the brick architecture of Italy of the fourteenth and
fifteenth centuries. For the present structure, a noted
industrial firm brought the massive, vibration-proof
concrete frame to the surface, sheathing it with the
contextual Flemish bond brickwork that typifies most
of Penn's more recent architecture. In the first floor
lobby are memorials of the history of the Chemistry
program, the most notable being the portrait of John
Harrison, grandfather of Provost Harrison, by Mary
Jean Peale, another member of the ubiquitous Peale
family of artists. Its splendid Italianate frame is a
memento of the Italian details of Cope and Stewardson's
Harrison Chemistry Building. Hanging in the well
that links the upper and lower lobbies is Robert
Engman's cast aluminum *After Iyengar* (1977).

1958 CHEMISTRY LABORATORIES, 33rd above
Spruce Street. 1958–59: Harbeson, Hough, Livingston
and Larson. Alterations, 1980s: Ellenzweig, Moore
and Associates.

The 1958 addition to the chemistry laboratories
reflected the shift toward the prosaic, repetitive spaces
of modern design over the expressionistic character of
the same firm's earlier 1940 building. The designer in
charge of this project was Elizabeth Rottenberg (Ar
1936), Penn's first woman architecture graduate. The
present building is the result of alterations in the
1980s by Ellenzweig, Moore and Associates that reduced the glare of natural light through the oversized
windows with panels that overlie the exterior with a
calico-like pattern. The skyline of stainless steel ex-
hausts recalls Paris's Pompidou Center and identifies
the enterprise of science as a progressive undertaking.

CRET CHEMISTRY BUILDING, 33rd and Spruce
Streets. 1940: Paul P. Cret.

The oldest surviving wing of the chemistry lab
complex is the only building on campus by Paul Cret,
who was the Professor of Design in the School of Fine
Arts from 1903 until 1929. Erected in 1940, it is a far

••••••••••••••••••••••••••••••••••

Cret Chemistry Building, looking northwest, 1991. GET.

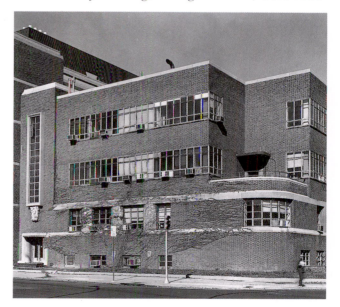

less classical building than the early career of its French-trained architect would suggest. Indeed, the curve with which it inserts itself into its corner site at 33rd and Spruce Streets and the horizontal strips of windows are reminiscent of such modernist or (perhaps more properly) *moderne* buildings as Howe and Lescaze's Philadelphia Savings Fund Society, but the traditional limestone and brick idiom links the building to the remainder of the campus. Cret's austere modern stairhall is the only surviving example of prewar architecture at the University that avoided historical allusions. An elegantly scripted limestone plaque to George Rosengarten in the same stairhall suggests the tensions in architecture and the arts as the opening salvos of World War II were being fired.

Hayden Hall, looking south, 1896. UPA.
Hayden Hall, dental hall, c. 1898. UPA.
Hayden Hall, detail, looking south, 1994. GET.

••••••••••••••••••••••••••••••••••

HAYDEN HALL (originally Dental Hall), 240 South 33rd Street on Smith Walk. 1894–96: Edgar V. Seeler. Alterations 1958: Geddes, Brecher and Qualls.[3]

Edgar V. Seeler (MIT, 1890) had just returned from the Ecole des Beaux-Arts in Paris when Penn hired him to teach architecture. Shortly afterward he was commissioned to design a new home for the dental program, which until then had shared space in the Medical School. His model was H. H. Richardson's Sever Hall at Harvard, which Seeler certainly had studied while attending MIT. Sever's robust pair of

entrance-flanking bays are repeated facing Smith Walk. Seeler eschewed the Romanesque reminiscences with which Richardson seeded his design in favor of a more conventional Queen Anne vocabulary complete with shaped gables. His floor plan took full advantage of the bays, which contained classrooms on the first floor and small amphitheaters off the hall of practice on the upper level.

The entire north-facing second floor, measuring 50 by 180 feet, was originally filled with dental chairs. In 1915 the chairs were replaced by drafting tables when the dental school moved to its new quarters at 40th and Spruce Streets. Rechristened the Fine Arts Building, the great dental hall of practice was converted into the drafting room of the atelier; here Penn

Towne Building, looking northwest, 1995. GET.

••

produced four Rome Prize winners in a row during the early tenure of Paul Cret as Professor of Design. During the tenancy of the modern School of Fine Arts, led by G. Holmes Perkins, the grand central stair was removed and replaced with a large room that could be used for school juries. Constructed in 1958, this space was among the first projects of faculty members Geddes, Brecher, and Qualls. Here architects Louis Kahn, Romaldo Giurgola, and Robert Venturi, urbanist Lewis Mumford, ecologist Ian McHarg, and other stars of the school's many departments jousted with one another and their students in the open discussions that enlivened the school.

With the departure of Fine Arts to Meyerson Hall, Geology, the last of the sciences still housed at College Hall, found its home in the science precinct. The building was renamed once again, this time for geologist Ferdinand Hayden, who headed the Federal Survey of the Territories after the Civil War. His explorations led to the designation of the Yellowstone region as the first National Park. In 1971 John Sabatino converted the old teaching amphitheater in the south wing into offices by the insertion of floors, but a bit of the old skylight that once lighted the operating table is still visible in the ceiling. The building has recently been ceded to the School of Engineering and Applied Science with the intention of converting the great vaulted dental hall into a center for information systems (a library).

TOWNE BUILDING, 220 South 33rd Street on Smith Walk. 1903–6: Cope and Stewardson.[4]

Built for the Scientific School that was renamed to honor the gift of Philadelphia industrialist, trustee, and donor John Henry Towne, the Towne Building was the largest of the four new buildings for schools with which Cope and Stewardson decentralized the University's educational plant in the first decade of the twentieth century. For the Towne Building, the style was derived from the seventeenth-century classicism of England, with two entrance pavilions topped by baroque segmental pediments. The broad interior corridors are floored and faced with marble, with light

••

Towne Building, interior of machine shop, 1907. UPA.

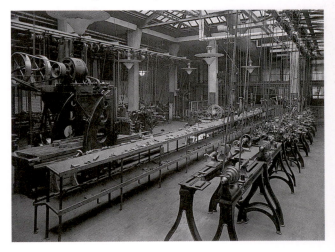

Towne Building, looking northeast, 1907. UPA.

"borrowed" through transoms illuminating the corridors. Beyond the marble corridors, the interior light courts were roofed with light industrial steel trusses and housed vast machine shops of the sort common to Philadelphia industry, where students could get hands-on experience in the type of work that they would supervise. These rooms have since been replaced by more prosaic computer labs.

The dedicatory address for the new building was given by Frederick Winslow Taylor, the father of "Scientific Management," who proclaimed: "The largest possibility, and one which does not exist for, and cannot be created by any other American University, lies in the opportunity for bringing your students in close touch and personal contact with the men who are working in and managing the great industrial establishments of Philadelphia." Though most of those

great industries are now closed, Towne remains the principal building of the School of Engineering and Applied Science.

The second-floor corridor contains portraits of the men who shaped the school, including William M. Hunt's portrait of donor John Henry Towne. Two presidents of the Pennsylvania Railroad are included in this group: J. Edgar Thompson and Thomas Scott. Machine maker and engineer William Sellers, whose tenure as trustee marked the rise of engineering at Penn, and industrialist, J. Vaughan Merrick, the chief donor for the building and a fellow trustee, are also here. Among portraits of faculty, there is a handsome image of Fairman Rogers, Professor of Civil Engineering, now remembered as an advocate of the painting of Thomas Eakins and the architecture of Frank Furness, and a portrait of Professor Edgar Marburg, whose work in materials testing for Sellers led to the founding of the American Society for the Testing of

Materials. At Towne's Lesley Testing Laboratory, funded by Robert Lesley (Hon. A.M. 1908), Marburg established the industrial standards for structural steel and reinforced concrete that made Philadelphia a center for concrete construction.

ALFRED F. MOORE SCHOOL OF ELECTRICAL ENGINEERING (originally Pepper Musical Instrument factory), 200 South 33rd Street. 1909: George S. Morris and Richard Erskine. Alterations, 1923–24, Paul Cret. Upper floor added, 1940: Alfred Bendiner. [5]

A bequest from the estate of electrical manufacturer Alfred Fitler Moore in honor of his parents enabled the electrical engineering department of the Towne School to become a separate school in 1923. It continued to share the Towne Building until 1924, when Alfred Bendiner of the Paul Cret office adapted

Alfred F. Moore School of Electrical Engineering, looking southwest, 1991. GET.

Harold E. Pender Laboratories, looking west, 1991. GET.

the adjacent factory for its new use. With little more than new classical door frames to denote the change in purpose, the effect is surprisingly felicitous. At the dedication, which was timed to coincide with the 40th convention of the American Institute of Electrical Engineers, it was confidently predicted that Moore would become "the greatest school of its kind in America." The rugged reinforced concrete construction of the original factory permitted the addition of a third floor in the 1940s by Bendiner, who by then was practicing independently. Under Dean Harold Pender, the Moore School shifted from applied to theoretical sciences and by the early 1930s emphasized mathematics and feedback control systems. Here, in February 1946, ENIAC, the first large-scale electronic computer, blinked to life, beginning the modern computer age. A museum dedicated to the invention of the computer was opened here for the fiftieth anniversary of the public unveiling of the new technology. The Moore School is now rejoined with the Towne School to form the School of Engineering and Applied Science.

HAROLD E. PENDER LABORATORIES, 33rd Street. 1957–60: Geddes, Brecher, Qualls and Cunningham.

The first of two Moore School additions by Geddes, Brecher, Qualls and Cunningham, the Pender Labs (named for the Moore School's first dean, Harold Pender, who shifted Penn's electrical engineering program from applied to theoretical research) linked the former instrument factory with the Towne Building along 33rd Street. The precast reinforced concrete frame both articulates the facade and provides clear span interior spaces, while the flanking panels of Flemish bond brickwork echo the colors and textures of the adjoining Moore and Towne Buildings in an early contextual design. Built before Kahn's Richards Building, this is the first campus landmark to reflect the principles of the Philadelphia School of architectural design.

••••••••••••••••••••••••••••••••••••

Moore School Graduate Research Center, looking southwest, 1991. GET.

MOORE SCHOOL GRADUATE RESEARCH CENTER, Walnut Street. 1966: Geddes, Brecher, Qualls and Cunningham.

For their second addition, on the Walnut Street side of the Moore building, the same architects adopted an alternative solution, screening and minimizing their work behind a curtain wall of dark reflective glass. Massive polygonal piers containing vertical circulation and services rephrase the Philadelphia School vocabulary in the sculptural massing of the mid-1960s. The west-facing windows are set in angled reveals, minimizing the intrusion of the afternoon sun.

LABORATORY FOR RESEARCH ON THE STRUCTURE OF MATTER, 3231 Walnut Street. 1962: Martin, Stewart, Noble, and Class.

An ungainly design whose ventilator stacks are concealed in exterior piers that seem to echo meaninglessly the forms of the Richards Building, the building is like the David Rittenhouse Laboratory in rejecting the University's typical palette of materials. Tawny pebble-surfaced concrete, dark glass, brown brick, and bright blue metal members transform it into a kind of harlequin. Federal research funds aimed at breaking through the "materials barrier" made the LRSM possible and created the first interdisciplinary research setting of the type that is increasingly common in the sciences.

DAVID RITTENHOUSE LABORATORIES, 209 South 33rd Street. 1952–54: Office of James R. Edmunds. Additions, 1964–67: Carroll, Grisdale and Van Alen.

One of the University's first postwar buildings, DRL turned its back on the traditional campus red brick and limestone, using orange brick, marble, and stainless steel to distance the modern University from the historicism of the past. It was initially proposed that it be named for Franklin, but it eventually memorialized David Rittenhouse, Philadelphia's premier early mathematician and astronomer and the designer

*Laboratory for Research on the Structure of Matter,
looking northeast, 1985. GET.*
*David Rittenhouse Laboratory extension, looking north-
west, 1990. GET.*

••••••••••••••••••••••••••••••••••••••

of the Orrery (see Van Pelt Library). Riding the crest
of post–World War II optimism about the contribution of the sciences, this marked a commitment of
resources to the sciences that significantly enlarged
the science precinct and allowed the Physics Department to quit Morgan Hall.

A broad, sun-filled corridor, brightened with brilliantly toned tiles, runs along the south side of the
building. It gives access to a row of large lecture
rooms, with the laboratories rising above them. The
new wing turns an active face toward Walnut Street,

David Rittenhouse Laboratory, looking northeast, 1990.
GET.

Tandem Accelerator Laboratory, looking south, 1995.
GET.

••

with angular projections counterbalanced by deep,
smoothly curved window reveals. Its deep red brick
walls trimmed in limestone and concrete mark a
return to the customary palette of the historic campus,
although with fenestration that is presumably intended to describe interior functions in the manner of
the Victorian rather than the Cope and Stewardson
sensibility.

Numerous minor buildings dot the eastern science
precinct. The **Tandem Accelerator Laboratory** hides

below the Walnut Street Bridge to the rear of David Rittenhouse Laboratory, Designed with *moderne* details, it was the work of Martin, Stewart, and Noble with United Engineers in 1961 with an addition in 1965–66. Another adjunct to the science precinct is the understated **Edison Building** adjacent to the LRSM on Walnut Street. This nondescript laboratory housed a project funded by the Edison Electric Company.

GARAGE, 3201 Walnut Street. 1964: Mitchell/ Giurgola.

Giurgola's celebrated expressionist exposure of this building's huge trusses owes more than a little to Kahn's visionary but largely unrealized experiments with structure in the 1950s when both were on the Penn architecture faculty. Giurgola contrasts this exhibition of structure with a nearly blank street facade, whose subtle angularity derived from the internal auto ramps bespeaks another quite un-Kahnian aspect of his architecture.

PALESTRA AND SYDNEY EMLEN HUTCHINSON GYMNASIUM, 220 South 32nd Street. 1926–28: Day and Klauder.[6]

The University's emphasis on athletics and the

••••••••••••••••••••••••••••••••••••••

Garage, looking northeast, 1978. GET.

Sydney Emlen Hutchinson Gymnasium, looking southeast, 1995. GET.

••••••••••••••••••••••••••••••••••••••

power of the Athletic Association are evident in the construction in the 1920s of two facilities that made the sports grouping the largest portion of the campus (during that era). The commission for a larger gymnasium, a swimming pool, and an "indoor stadium" (as the Palestra was called) was awarded to Charles Klauder, also the architect of Franklin Field. Huge utilitarian structures, they were given vaguely Georgian facades, the details of which (notably the quoins) have been smoothed by the forces of modernity. Both were projects of the alumni-led Council on Athletics, the Hutchinson Gymnasium is named for financier Sydney Hutchinson (C 1888), a trustee, former football and baseball player for the University, and chairman of the Council on Athletics.

The Palestra is a name that is uniquely Penn's. Several names, including Colosseum, Arena, and Ephebeum, were suggested for the indoor stadium; eventually Palestra was suggested by Professor of Greek William Bates, taking the name of the place where Greek athletes prepared for competition. For a

Palestra, looking northeast, 1995. GET.
Palestra, interior, c. 1930. UPA.

generation it housed the Big Five, the unique city conference of Philadelphia basketball powers: Penn, LaSalle, St. Joseph's, Temple, and Villanova. The Big Five Hall of Fame remains in the entrance lobby. The lobby is also ornamented with a pair of handsome bas reliefs of football, one depicting a field goal and the other a plunge into the line, both by R. Tait McKenzie in 1924. The Palestra has been the home of Penn's great basketball teams of the 1970s and 1980s, including its Final Four team of 1978 and the Ivy Champions of the 1990s.

ALL WARS MEMORIAL TO PENN ALUMNI,
33rd Street, end of Smith Walk. 1951–52: Grant Simon, architect, Charles Rudy, sculptor.

Memorial in character, monumental in intention, and combining architecture and sculpture in a harmonious synthesis, the All Wars Memorial epitomized the Beaux-Arts system of planning that ruled Penn's designers in the first half of the twentieth century. Paid for by Walter Annenberg and designed by Grant Simon, one of Penn's pre-World War I Paris Prize winners, it was intended as the eastern terminus of the great axis that would proceed westward through the site of the Furness Library to a new skyscraper office tower at 36th Street. As this was being designed, a new dean of Fine Arts, G. Holmes Perkins, and a new value system were about to take over Penn's planning. In the end, instead of being the beginning of the 1948 Master Plan, it marked the end of Beaux-Arts design at the University.

J. WILLIAM WHITE TRAINING HOUSE, 231
South 33rd Street. 1905–7: Horace Trumbauer.[7]

In 1904 the founder and chairman of the Department of Physical Education, J. William White, M.D., promised the construction of "a training house and dormitory for those members of the student body who . . . represent the University in competitive games." For that facility, the University turned to Horace Trumbauer, who produced an elegant, domestic-scale composition in the style suggested by Weightman Hall. It provided twenty-six bedrooms along with dining and living rooms, enabling the University to segregate Penn's semiprofessional athletes from the general student body while denoting their special status and purpose—the triumph of the University's sports teams. For a time the building also served as the student infirmary. The dedication to White (1850–1916, M 1871, Gr 1871) attests to the Rooseveltian energy of Penn's chair of Clinical Surgery, coauthor of

••••••••••••••••••••••••••••••••••••

All Wars Memorial to Penn Alumni, looking northwest, 1995. GET.

J. William White Training House, looking northeast, 1995. GET.

••••••••••••••••••••••••••••••••••••

The American Text-Book of Surgery, and physician to the Penn football team.[8]

WEIGHTMAN HALL, 235 South 33rd Street. 1903–
4: Frank Miles Day and Brother.[9]

Day designed the University's first purpose-built gymnasium, a powerfully-massed, twin-towered building of mixed classical and medieval detail that fills the mouth of the stadium. Its two outer wings provide entrances into handsome oak-paneled stair halls. The center of the building contains a 150- by 75-foot gymnasium on its upper floor, while beneath it was a 100- by 30-foot swimming pool that replaced the first campus swimming pool in the basement of Houston Hall. Funded by alumni and named for Dr. William Weightman, Jr., an 1867 graduate of the medical school who willed Penn $50,000 for "enhancing physical education and athletics," the new gymnasium en-

abled the University to improve the health of its students and maintain parity with other eastern universities.

YOUNG BENJAMIN FRANKLIN, plaza in front of Weightman Hall. 1914: R. Tait McKenzie.

As an emblem for the sports campus, McKenzie depicted the youthful Franklin as he might have appeared just after his arrival in Philadelphia in 1723. Though it is more a costume piece than most of

••

Weightman Hall, looking northwest, 1995. GET.
Weightman Hall, interior, c. 1905. UPA.
Young Benjamin Franklin, *looking south, c. 1915. UPA.*

[222]

McKenzie's works, which usually celebrate the athlete in action, it is in keeping with the period's love of detail which carried over to the adjacent buildings. The base was designed by the Frank Miles Day office.

FRANKLIN FIELD, 33rd and Spruce Streets. 1922 and 1925: Day and Klauder; Gavin Haddin and Horace Campion, associated engineers.[10]

When the University's first playing fields at 36th and Spruce Streets were taken over by the eastern end of the Dormitory Quadrangles in the 1890s, athletics facilities were relocated to 33rd Street. At first only a cinder track with a wooden grandstand on the south side was provided. These facilities were dedicated on 20 April 1895, with the first running of the Intercollegiate and Interscholastic Relays, the inaugural "Penn Relays." In 1903–5 a low horseshoe stadium seating 20,000 was built by Frank Miles Day and Brother; it was in turn demolished to make way for the present structure. This colossal building was designed by Charles Klauder, whom Day had taken on as a partner and who continued to practice under the

·····································

Franklin Field, looking northwest, 1995. GET.

name Day and Klauder for a decade after Day's death in 1918. The lower stands, of reinforced concrete faced with brick, were erected in 1922. The upper stands, whose arcade, mounted atop that of the lower stands, gives the stadium its resemblance to the Colosseum, were built of steel and concrete only four years later. Completed for $500,000, it was quickly paid for from ticket sales, as the average attendance rose to 60,000! Augmented by seating on the track and temporary stands in front of Weightman Hall, the stadium could seat 84,000 spectators for a big game. Franklin Field continues to house the Penn Relays, the premier amateur track event in the nation. During much of the twentieth century it was also the home of powerhouse Penn football teams, coached by the likes of George Woodruff, John Heisman, and George Munger, with players such as John Outland and Chuck Bednarik, who returned to play on his home turf as a member of the NFL champion Philadelphia Eagles of 1961.

Other sports facilities are less monumental but not less beloved to their users. In front of Franklin Field and the Palestra are the **Lott Tennis Courts**, designed in 1966–70 by George C. Patton. They were named in honor of H. Hunter Lott (C 1936), a tennis

Bower Field Bridge, looking east, 1995. GET.

champion at the University and a long-time supporter of its athletic programs. At the rear of Hutchinson Gymnasium are the **Ringe Squash Courts**, designed in 1959 and added to in 1967 by Paul Monaghan. They are named for Thomas B. Ringe (C 1923, L 1926), who was president of the class of 1923. The principal baseball field of the University, Bower Field, can be seen from the Schuylkill Expressway. It is reached by a handsome tubular steel truss bridge, designed by Peter McCleary of the Graduate School of Fine Arts Faculty. To the north of Bower Field is the **Levy Tennis Pavilion**, which houses indoor courts in a functional building constructed in 1973 of prefab panels from designs of Thalheimer and Weitz. The building's name honors Robert P. Levy, University trustee and loyal alumnus (C 1952) who has been a long-time supporter of Penn's racquet sports.

CLASS OF 1923 ICE RINK, 32nd and Walnut Streets. 1970: Robert C. McMillan Associates.

The rink is a tough reinforced concrete building whose mighty boat-shaped roof suggests that the architect was familiar with Eero Saarinen's Ingalls Ice Hockey Rink at Yale, a similarly allusive but more biomorphic building nicknamed the "Yale Whale."

Lott Tennis Courts, looking southeast, 1991. GET.

Class of 1923 Ice Rink , looking west, 1985. GET.

••••••••••••••••••••••••••••••••••••••

UNIVERSITY OR PENNSYLVANIA MUSEUM OF ARCHAEOLOGY AND ANTHROPOLOGY

(Free Museum of Science and Art), 3260 South Street. 1895–99: Wilson Eyre, Jr.; Cope and Stewardson; and associated architects (later additions, see text). (Color Plates 9, 10). Sculpted figures by Alexander Stirling Calder.[11]

In 1888 an expedition funded by Philadelphians and sponsored by the University set off to explore the ancient site of Nippur in what is now Iraq; as a part of its agreement, the University proposed to build a fireproof structure to house any findings. The collections were first displayed on the upper stories of the new University Library. Vast discoveries soon overwhelmed the available space in the library, leading to the decision to build a new facility. Designed by an extraordinary team of Philadelphia's most talented young architects, all of whom were teaching in Warren Laird's architecture faculty, the University Museum was envisioned to enframe three courtyards (representing the primitive cultures of Asia and Oceania, the Americas, and Africa)—two like the present entrance court, with a larger courtyard between them. Three enormous rotundas (representing Greece, Rome, and Mesopotamia) were to rise behind

the; later campus plans show the courtyards repeated to the south, making a total of six courtyards in a vast building! Less than half of this scheme was achieved, but the effect is nevertheless remarkable. With its vaguely oriental gateway and grave Italian Romanesque exteriors, all ornamented in colored tile and an astonishing variety of Renaissance and Mannerist-inspired sculpture, the museum is the largest American example of Arts and Crafts aesthetic libertarianism. The interiors are more reserved, as befits a setting for the great archaeological treasures transferred from the upper floors of the library.

In 1912–15 the first of the three intended rotundas was built on the axis of the courtyard. A splendid, almost sublime exercise in brickwork and Gustavino tile vaulting, it contains the large Harrison Auditorium in its basement. After a long hiatus, work was resumed according to a revised plan by Charles Z. Klauder, Day's former partner, who built the Coxe Memorial Wing (home of the Egyptian collections) in 1926 and the Sharpe Wing, intended as the main facade of the yet-to-be-completed central court, in

•••••••••••••••••••••••••••••••••••••

University Museum, looking southwest, 1975. GET.
Wilson Eyre, Jr., University Museum, perspective of full plan, c. 1900. Ink and watercolor on paper. Architectural Archives.
University Museum, Harrison Auditorium, c. 1915. Photo: Charles Sheeler. UPA.

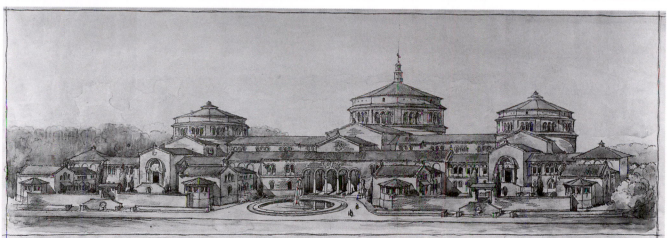

1929. Its jazzy green tiled cornice conveys a hint of the spirit of the Roaring '20s and denotes its later date. The front gate posts bear figures facing into the courtyard (and toward the south light) as suggested by their maker, sculptor Alexander Stirling Calder. They represent the four continents from which collec-

••••••••••••••••••••••••••••••••••••••

University Museum, Academic Wing, looking south, 1985. GET.

University Museum, Collections Wing, photograph of architect's model. Courtesy Atkin, Olshin, Lawson-Bell and Associates.

Garage, looking southwest, 1985. GET.

tions are drawn—Africa, Asia, North America, and Europe. An elegant fountain by the same artist enlivens the courtyard.

Nothing more was built until 1968–71, when Ehrman Mitchell (Ar 1948) and Romaldo Giurgola added the academic wing containing a new library, classrooms, and offices behind the Sharpe Wing. Their work, which repeated the roof shapes of the older building and even its tiled covering, was hailed as one of the principal examples of "contextualism"—a rallying cry for Postmodernists. A new collections wing will soon complete the main courtyard. Designed by Atkin, Olshin, Lawson-Bell and Associates, it will takes its cues from the original design.

The collections are as remarkable as the building. Especially notable are the early finds from Mesopotamia, including the lapis-lazuli and gold "Ram in a Thicket" and the astonishing Bull's Head Harp.

GARAGE, 3200 South Street. 1968: Mitchell/ Giurgola.

The firm responsible for the new wing of the museum also built the adjacent garage, which stands on the site originally intended for the museum's third courtyard. Although the precast structural members are clearly articulated, there is much less constructional expression here than in their earlier garage on Walnut Street (see above). The over-scaled "ear" of the stair enclosure on the top floor salutes the Ghibelline cornice of Franklin Field across Spruce Street.

HOLLENBACK CENTER (originally University Power Plant), 3000 South Street. 1923–25: Walter Thomas, Sydney E. Martin, and Donald M. Kirkpatrick. Renovations, 1968: Clemmer and Groll.

Built to replace the power plant by the Wilson Brothers that stood on the site of Irvine Auditorium, the coal-burning facility is a sober example of the simplified classicism that flourished in the 1920s. Treating paired bricks as a unit creates an uncommon oversized, industrial-scale "common" bond. The building once had a 250-foot stack that replaced the simi-

larly great stack of the earlier power plant as a monument. Because the University now buys its steam from Philadelphia Electric, in 1968 it commissioned Leon Clemmer (Ar 1951) and Groll to adapt the boiler building for the physical education and ROTC programs. At that time it was renamed in honor of William "Big-Bill" Hollenback (D 1908), the All-American star of Penn's undefeated 1908 football team.

••••••••••••••••••••••••••••••••••••

Hollenback Center, looking southwest, 1995. GET.
University Power Plant, looking southeast, c. 1930. UPA.

THE SOUTH CAMPUS

Spruce Street

Hamilton Walk

38th Street
37th Street
36th Street
34th Street

Guardian Drive
Curie Boulevard
University Avenue
Osler Circle
East Service Drive
Civic Center Boulevard

South Campus

1. The Quad
2. Class of 1873 Gate
3. Stouffer Triangle
4. Leidy Laboratory
5. Richards and Goddard Laboratories
6. Biology Gardens
7. Kaplan Wing
8. Mudd Laboratory
9. Morgan Building
10. Johnson Pavilion

11. Stemmler Hall
12. Maloney Pavilion
13. Rhoads Pavilion
14. Gates Pavilion
15. Dulles and Agnew Pavilion
16. White Building
17. Ravdin Institute
18. Silverstein Pavilion
19. Penn Tower (see East Campus, # 30)
20. Founders Wing
21. Nursing Education Building

22. Blockley Hall
23. The Consortium
24. Children's Hospital
25. Wood Center
26. Children's Seashore House
27. Abramson Laboratories
28. Gray Foundation/Clinical Research
    Building
29. Stellar-Chance Laboratories
30. Health Care Campus Garage
31. Biomedical Research Building II

THE SOUTH CAMPUS

**DORMITORY QUADRANGLES, "THE QUAD,"
now Community, Goldberg, Spruce, and Ware
College Houses**, 36th to 38th Streets and Spruce
Street to Hamilton Walk. 1894–1912: Cope and
Stewardson. 1912–29: Stewardson and Page. 1945–
59: Trautwein and Howard. Alterations, 1978–87:
Davis and Brody, with John Milner Associates.[1] Alter-
ations, 1998–2003, Ewing Cole Cherry Brott. (Color
Plate 11)

In 1892 Provost William Pepper solicited designs
for Penn's first dormitories since quitting its Fourth
Street site in 1800. Several local firms submitted
plans, including Addison Hutton, who proposed a
great oval encompassing the 3700 block of Spruce
Street. The dormitories became a fact during Provost
Charles Harrison's tenure. He raised $100,000 of the
first $250,000 by consulting his "little black book" and
persuading many of Philadelphia's old families to
sponsor a unit or "house." The design was turned over
to two of the young faculty members of the architecture department, Walter Cope and John Stewardson,
who had already established their reputation for academic design with their innovative work at Bryn
Mawr College.

In 1896 John Stewardson cabled home from England to suggest that the new dormitories he and his
partner were designing for Penn be built in the palette
of red brick and limestone of St. John's College Cambridge, rather than the gray stone they had adopted
for Bryn Mawr (and would later use at Princeton).
Those more vibrant, urban materials bring the great
complex of undergraduate housing to life. Although
never provided with the chapel and permanent dining
hall that were first planned, the quadrangles nevertheless offer a wonderful contrast of visual experiences. Entrance is obtained through the Tudor Memo-

rial Tower into the Upper Quad, whose buildings were
largely erected in 1894–96. Here, as everywhere in the
dorms, students' rooms originally opened off stair-
ways in the manner of Oxford and Cambridge colleges. The small units of the dormitories were planned
as houses and named for donors, breaking down the
otherwise overwhelming scale of the building.

For the architectural vocabulary, the transitional
style between the late middle ages and early English
Renaissance was adopted. Cope and Stewardson fash-
ioned from these ingredients a ragged skyline of

*Dormitory Quadrangles, Memorial Tower, looking south,
1991. GET.*

dormers, towers, and chimneys that accurately reflects the small-scale subdivision of the residences. The stone-trimmed brick of St. John's College, Cambridge was the specific model for many of their facades. At the far western end of the complex, beyond a classical triple arcade, lies the intimate "Little Quad," which looks out onto Hamilton Walk.

After the deaths of John Stewardson in 1896 and Walter Cope in 1902, the design of the dormitories remained with the same firm. Their successors retained the name of Cope and Stewardson, but the office was headed by Stewardson's brother Emlyn with James P. Jamieson as chief designer. Passing through the Palladian archway from the northeast corner of the triangular Upper Quad into the "Big Quad," or "Lower Quad" one encounters the line of dormitories that the successor firm built eastward down Spruce

••

Dormitory Quadrangles, Upper Quad, looking toward Provosts' Tower, 1975. GET.

Street as the first decade of the twentieth century passed. By 1908 work had progressed to Birthday House (a gift to Provost Harrison from his wife) and the Mask and Wig House (erected by the University's dramatic society) at the corner of 36th Street. Turning the corner, the architects added a second great Tudor gateway, Provosts' Tower, in 1910. The gate dominated the "East Quad," whose eastern range is Graduate House, built to provide graduate students with the same amenities offered to undergraduates.

Jamieson left the firm in 1912 to manage the office's work at St. Louis's Washington University, and in that year Emlyn Stewardson joined forces with a new design partner, George Page, to establish the firm of Stewardson and Page. Page was responsible for the more flamboyantly detailed circle of dormitories which defines the south and west sides of the East Quad and shapes the diminutive south or "Baby" Quad, completed by 1929. The shared facade which Magee and Ashhurst Houses turn to the Big Quad is an unusually formal, symmetrical composition, with twin shaped gables and slender Ionic pilasters. The remaining gaps in the south ranges of the Upper and Big Quad were filled in 1954, when Trautwein and Howard completed the perimeter in a bland but still palatable version of collegiate Gothic. By that time the plan to add a dining hall to the complex had been abandoned, leaving the exterior gate towers as the principal landmarks of Cope and Stewardson's masterpiece. The interiors were modernized by New Yorkers Davis and Brody, who replaced the sophisticated turn-of-the-century rooms with New York loft simplicity between 1979 and 1987 and interconnected the separate houses with internal corridors.

Three sculptures enliven the quad. In the upper quad is R. Tait McKenzie's heroic figure of The Rev-

••

Dormitory Quadrangles, East Quad and Provosts' Tower, c. 1915. GET.
Dormitory Quadrangles, "Little Quad," looking north, 1995. GET.
Dormitory room, c. 1900. UPA.

erend George Whitefield (commissioned for the bicentennial of his birth in 1914, installed in 1919), whose advocacy of education led to the founding of the Charity School and recalls the University's past. At the far end is Lynn Jenkins's seated figure of Provost Harrison (1925) on a base by Horace Trumbauer, commemorating the leader who transformed undergraduate life at the end of the nineteenth century. Diminutive by contrast, but elegantly situated in the arcade leading to the big quad is Alexander Stirling Calder's youthful bronze of a scholar and a football player, which was given in 1900 by the class of 1892 to accent a wall fountain.

CLASS OF 1873 GATE, 38th Street and Hamilton Walk. 1898: Frederick Mann and Cope and Stewardson.

The first of the memorial gates, this was intended to mark the west edge of campus. It commemorated

the first class to have spent two years at the West Philadelphia site.

STOUFFER TRIANGLE, 38th and Spruce Streets. 1968–72: Geddes, Brecher, Qualls and Cunningham.

Woodland Avenue was closed to motor traffic in 1957, but the campus will forever bear signs of its diagonal route. Designed by three early members of the Perkins faculty, Stouffer fills the triangular site left between the Woodland Avenue facade of the Quadrangle and Spruce Street. Its small bays, stepped roofline, and mixture of brown brick and tawny concrete echo the textures of its neo-medieval neighbor with some success; with modern irony, the architects reversed the great punctuating towers, varying their

•••••••••••••••••••••••••••••••••••••

Dormitory Quadrangles and Class of 1873 Gate, looking east, c. 1900. UPA.

Stouffer Triangle, looking west, 1995. GET.
Stouffer Triangle, looking west, 1973. Frank Ross, UPA.

••••••••••••••••••••••••••••••••••

roofline with depressions. A shopping arcade in the ground floor introduces a real medieval mixture of Jane Jacobs-inspired residential and commercial usage. The dormitory rooms and a large dining commons are entered from the sheltered side of the building. The dining facility has expanded to occupy what was originally a bowling alley in the basement. Its namesake is University donor Vernon J. Stouffer (W 1923), who headed Stouffer Foods Corporation.

LEIDY LABORATORY OF BIOLOGY (originally Zoological Laboratory Building), Hamilton Walk and 38th Street. 1910–11: Cope and Stewardson.

The rhythm of buildings along present-day Hamilton Walk is largely determined by two buildings that are no longer there, Furness's Veterinary Hospital, which stood to the east where the John Morgan Building now stands, and the front wing of Frederick Mann's Botanical Hall, the Vivarium. Its rear wing was incorporated into the back of the present Leidy Laboratory, determining its position. Leidy Laboratory was named to commemorate the Professor of Anatomy and director of the graduate department of biology, Joseph Leidy (1823–1891) who was considered the most prominent naturalist of his time. Like much of the later work of Cope and Stewardson, the

Leidy Lab building is more classical than medieval, with a firm rectangular profile, dominant horizontal string courses, and an alternating rhythm of triangular and segmental pediments above the second-floor windows. Despite the newfound order, the Renaissance is still an infant in much of this work, which is full of idiosyncratic ornament and numerous medieval recollections, like the stone mullions that recall their Tudor forebears. James P. Jamieson, a Scot trained in art school at London's South Kensington, was the firm's chief designer when this building came into being.

ALFRED NEWTON RICHARDS MEDICAL RESEARCH LABORATORY AND GODDARD LABORATORIES (Goddard was originally the Biology Building), Hamilton Walk. 1957–61 and 1961–64: Louis I. Kahn.[2]

Louis Kahn quit the architectural faculty at Yale University in 1957 to join the Penn faculty; in that year he began the design of Penn's first postwar medical research building. This laboratory building was Kahn's first internationally acclaimed work and was termed by Wilder Green "the single most consequential building" erected since World War II. Unlike the parallelopideds of contemporary modernism, Richards raises three brick and concrete towers to offer good fellowship to the neo-Tudor of the adjacent Quadrangle. It was Kahn's respect for locale, and for the specifics of the human demands that lie behind any architectural problem, that set his ideology apart from the universalizing abstraction of earlier modernists. Rough where the International Style was smooth, vertical where it was reposeful, irregular where it was uniform, and colored where it was monochromatic, Kahn's architecture celebrated these striking visual alternatives.

The Richards Laboratory part of the complex (the two western towers of the Goddard Labs were built to a slightly simplified design as part of a planned second phase) was conceived as the workplace for laboratory teams, each of which would be accommodated on an unpartitioned 40-foot-square tower floor. These great open spans were achieved by the use of prestressed Vierendeel concrete trusses. The tower floors seem to be suspended from the smaller, windowless towers that flank them, but it is actually the system of easily overlooked concrete columns that do the work, while the small brick towers contain fire stairs and an exceptionally elaborate ventilating system. Thus this is not a design shaped by structural rationalism in the ordinary sense of that word. It is, however, Kahn's highly rational hierarchy of what he called "served"

Alfred Newton Richards Medical Research Laboratory, architect's aerial perspective, looking north, 1957. Graphite and ink on paper. Architectural Archives.
Alfred Newton Richards Medical Research Laboratory, looking north, 1962. Photo: Frank Ross. UPA.

and "servant" spaces that defines the relationship between the central working areas and the peripherally placed auxiliary rooms. These ideas exerted enormous influence, and the visual signature of the Richards building, a broken roofline of brick towers that rise between concrete piers, can be found replicated all over the campus and around the world. Richards and Goddard stand on the site of the John M. MacFarlane Hall of Botany (originally the Biology Building), erected in 1884 with a third story added in 1887.

The initial portion of the building was named for Professor of Pharmacology and Vice President of the University for Medical Affairs Alfred Newton Richards, who during World War II had been instrumental in initiating large-scale production of penicillin for the armed forces and had furthered research on sulfa drugs and on blood plasma. Of Richards, it was claimed with only the slightest touch of hyperbole, "It is doubtful if anyone connected with this institution since Benjamin Franklin has done so much to add luster to its reputation in the scientific world." The later and slightly simpler west wing bears the name of Dr. David Goddard, a bioscientist, who was consid-

Leidy Laboratory of Biology, looking southwest, 1997. GET.

ered the architect of Penn's second renaissance in the biological sciences and served as provost during the Harnwell presidency.

BIOLOGY GARDENS, rear of Richards Medical Research Laboratory. Circa 1890: John Muirhead MacFarlane, Professor of Botany.

There are few more enchanting spots on the campus than the Biology Gardens at the rear of the Richards complex. They were located here to serve the original Biology Building, which stood on the

••••••••••••••••••••••••••••••••••••••

Biology Pond, looking north with Biology Building on right and Vivarium on left, c. 1900. UPA.

Biology Pond, looking northwest, c. 1970. Photo: Frank Ross. UPA.

Richards site on Hamilton Walk. As an adjunct to that program, a garden and greenhouses were constructed for the propagation of botanical specimens. Although the original regular grid of plantings has long since disappeared, the lily pond with its schools of goldfish remains, as do several historic tree specimens including an immense gingko, a bald cypress, and a sequoia.

FLORENCE AND DAVID KAPLAN MEMORIAL WING, behind Leidy Laboratory. 1959–60: Louis I Kahn. Additions, 1963–64: Vreeland and Schlesinger

In 1960 Louis Kahn began the design for the Biology Services Building, standing behind the Leidy Labs, as a separate laboratory for the study of the behavior of cells. Although its second floor was added by Timothy Vreeland and Frank Schlesinger in 1964,

....

Florence and David Kaplan Memorial Wing, looking northwest, 1995. GET.

Seeley G. Mudd Biological Research Laboratory, looking west, 1995. GET.

....

the expressed slab, T-windows, cantilevered corners, and expressionistic vent stack are derived from the vocabulary Kahn was simultaneously developing for the Richards labs. It bears the name of the Philadelphia founder of the Penn Fruit Company, which pioneered the large-scale supermarket in Philadelphia in the 1950s.

SEELEY G. MUDD BIOLOGICAL RESEARCH LABORATORY, 38th Street below Hamilton Walk. 1984–86: Carlos Vallhonrat, designer, Francis, Cauffman, Wilkinson and Pepper.

The palette of dark red brick skin with light-toned horizontal accents originates in Kahn's Richards laboratory, but the materials no longer are the construction itself; rather, they are a descriptive metaphor for structure. Instead of bringing the concrete floor slab to the surface as an element of facade articulation, limestone bands represent the floor slabs and blue stone lines represent wall panels and outline the windows. Formal symmetry has replaced functional expressionism in a Postmodern homage to the Penn titans of the 1950s. In 1931, when bacteriology was separated from the School of Hygiene and returned to the Medical School, it was organized into a separate department under the direction of Dr. Mudd.

JOHN MORGAN BUILDING, MEDICAL LABO-RATORIES BUILDING (formerly the Laboratories of Pathology, Physiology, and Pharmacology), Hamilton Walk. 1902–4: Cope and Stewardson. Anatomy-Chemistry addition, 1928: Stewardson and Page.[3] (Color Plate 2)

Between 1900 and 1907 the University dedicated new buildings for four of its schools—medicine, law, engineering, and veterinary medicine. Unlike the muscular and assertive Tudor of a decade before in the dormitory quadrangles, this generation of Cope and Stewardson's Penn work was dressed in the polychromed and ornamented planar surfaces of the English Renaissance. Here the minute early Renaissance pilasters of the central tower lack tectonic substance, and in the manner of their English sources they are ornamental only, an appliqué—indeed, they seem to have less work to do than the balusters that crown the parapet! The marble-lined interior corridors lead the visitor to no great public spaces, although there is a noble if somewhat spartan stairhall at the rear of the building, outside the great amphitheater wing. The original building offered no accommodation for the anatomy and chemistry departments of the school, which remained in the Hare Medical Laboratory. These had to wait until 1928 for the construction of the Anatomy-Chemistry Wing by Stewardson and Page.

••••••••••••••••••••••••••••••••••

John Morgan Building, main stair with Agnew Clinic, *c. 1910. UPA.*

John Morgan Building, looking southwest, 1997. GET.

••

The new labs, half of whose cost was borne by the Rockefeller Foundation, were attached to the rear of the amphitheater. At the same time a mezzanine was inserted above the amphitheater to enlarge the already overcrowded library.

The medical school, the first in the colonies, was founded in 1765 by two graduates of the University of Edinburgh, John Morgan (in whose honor the building was renamed) and William Shippen, accounting for the Scottish thistle in the seal of the school. From Shippen (Washington) through D. Hayes Agnew (Garfield) to I. S. Ravdin (Eisenhower), Penn professors watched over the health of the nation's presidents.

The talents of the medical faculty are recalled in a host of memorials. Here for example, hangs Thomas Eakins's superb group portrait, *The Agnew Clinic* (1889, Color Plate 2), depicting Dr. D. Hayes Agnew, the celebrated surgeon who brought asepsis to Penn's operating theater. His youthful dark-haired assistant in the foreground is Dr. J. William White, who succeeded Agnew as the chief of Penn's surgery program. On the same landing are two bas-reliefs (1908 and 1909 respectively) by Penn faculty member R. Tait McKenzie of Samuel Jackson and of Nathaniel

Chapman (1780–1853), physician, essayist, and Professor of Clinical Practice in 1816–53.

ROBERT WOOD JOHNSON PAVILION, Hamilton Walk and 36th Street. 1965–69: Ewing, Cole, Erdman and Eubank, Architects.

Connected to the John Morgan building by a low entrance pavilion, this simple brick-clad, background building bears an enormous workload in Penn's medical education, containing classrooms, offices, and the medical library that fills its several basements.

EDWARD STEMMLER HALL, MEDICAL EDUCATION BUILDING, Hamilton Walk. 1976–78: Geddes, Brecher, Qualls and Cunningham.

Beginning in the late 1960s, Penn flirted with noncontextual modernism for the high-rise dormito-

••

Robert Wood Johnson Pavilion, looking east, 1997. GET.

[245]

ries and for many of the buildings of the medical campus. This light-toned design for the Medical School is more ambitious, springing across Hamilton Walk to place a lounge on the north side of the walkway. The bridging wing contains study carrels, department offices, and a microwave laboratory. Flexible loft spaces with clear spans of 70 feet are provided in the main block. The multicolored exterior forecasts the vocabulary used by the same architects on a much larger scale in the Franklin Plaza Hotel.

MARTIN MALONEY MEMORIAL PAVILION,

36th and Spruce Streets. 1928–29: Marmaduke Tilden, H. Bartol Register, and George W. Pepper.[4]

Tilden, while a member of another partnership, had already built the fraternity that is now the Sweeten Center when this large commission came his way; his 1920s partnership with H. B. Register (Ar 1910, GAr 1914) and George Pepper (C 1916, Ar 1919) also pro-

Edward Stemmler Hall, looking east, 1997. GET. Martin Maloney Memorial Pavilion, looking southwest, 1985. GET.

duced 30th Street Post Office and several of the city's better known 1920s skyscrapers, including 1616 Walnut Street, which are suggestive of the derivation of this building. Maloney is Penn's only Art Deco structure, its floral panels and accentuated pier-caps unobtrusively speaking that exotic commercial language which was perhaps intended to describe the modernity of medical practice, while the materials recall the collegiate architecture of the University. For many years, it was the most imposing building of the hospital skyline. The modern character was appropriate to its donor, Martin Maloney, an Irish immigrant who had arrived in Philadelphia in 1873 and made his fortune in the electrification of the city. Additional funds were provided by RCA President Eldridge R. Johnson. It stands on the site of Cope and Stewardson's

SC-12b. Martin Maloney Memorial Pavilion, entrance lobby, 1929. UPA.

••••••••••••••••••••••••••••••••••

William Pepper Laboratory of Clinical Medicine (1894–97), a dark brick building of Italian detailing that was very like the same firm's contemporary Foulke and Long Institute (now the Morgan and Music Buildings) and Harrison Chemistry Laboratory on 34th Street. A portion of the ornamental frieze of the Pepper Lab is preserved inside the Gates Pavilion.

JONATHAN EVANS RHOADS PAVILION, 37th Street and Hamilton Walk. 1993–95: Robert D. Lynn,

Associates, design architect, Payette Associates, laboratory designers.

The stone-veneered, hotel-like lobbies and flashy facade denote the modern super-hospital in the age of consumerism—and are in striking contrast to the dignified member of the Society of Friends in whose honor it is named. The mannerist variations on Flemish bond brickwork that typify those used throughout the medical complex are here overlaid with vertical ornamental piers that were presumably intended to relate to the Art-Deco of the adjacent Maloney Building. Dr. Rhoads, a twentieth-century renaissance man, has continued for more than half a century on the

Jonathan Evans Rhoads Pavilion, looking southeast, 1998. GET.

Thomas Sovereign Gates Pavilion, looking southwest, 1995. GET.

Crothers Dulles Hospital and D. Hayes Agnew Memorial Pavilion, looking southeast, 1995. GET.

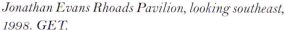

surgical faculty of the University. Among his many services to the University, he served as provost during Harnwell's presidency. In a new courtyard at the rear of Rhoads stands the terra cotta portal of Cope and Stewardson's Maternity Hospital (1897).

THOMAS SOVEREIGN GATES MEMORIAL PAVILION, 3400 block of Spruce Street. 1950–53: Schmidt, Garden, and Erikson.[5]

The Gates Pavilion, Maloney's enormous neighbor, makes an astonishing effort to place the facade design of a modern hospital within a recognizable historical framework. It is not as ungainly as it might

be, for the prodigious oriels and linked windows do more than one might expect to enliven what could be an otherwise monotonous perforated facade. The skillful overlay of historic detail on a modern slab perhaps attests to Erikson's training in Cret's studio at Penn (Ar 1910). The vast building bears the name of financier Thomas Sovereign Gates (C 1893, L 1898) who had served as President of the University and later as chairman of its Board of Trustees. His bust, by Evelyn Longman Batchelder (1941, installed 1964), appears in a small niche in the center of the vast facade. During his presidency, Gates envisioned the transformation of the hospital into the medical center that is now the core of the vast medical empire south of the University.

The Gates Memorial Pavilion was inserted as the new face for the hospital in front of the then surviving nineteenth- and early twentieth-century wings. The earliest of these buildings was designed in the green serpentine of College Hall by Thomas Webb Richards,

the architect of the original campus. The administrative block, once the centerpiece of the ward blocks that lined Spruce Street, stood at the east end of Gates. Each building turned a gable with a traceried window toward the street; these were flanked by tourelles and backed by steep mansard roofs.

CROTHERS DULLES HOSPITAL AND D. HAYES AGNEW MEMORIAL PAVILION, 3400 block of Spruce Street. 1939–41: Marmaduke Tilden, H. Bartol Register, and George W. Pepper.

The hospital turned again to the architects of the Maloney Pavilion when Cope and Stewardson's D. Hayes Agnew Surgical Pavilion (1894–97) was damaged by fire in February 1937. Tilden, Register, and Pepper incorporated the old building's ward wing in the rear into the new building, but built a tall, new streetside block in a polished red and white neo-Georgian idiom (they flirted no more with the *moderne*). Half of the new building retains the name of the great surgeon D. Hayes Agnew, while the other half honors

••••••••••••••••••••••••••••••••••

J. William White Memorial Building, looking southwest, 1985. GET.
I. S. Ravdin Institute and entire Hospital of University of Pennsylvania, looking southwest, 1991. GET.
I. S. Ravdin Institute, postmodern entrance, looking southwest, 1998. GET.

Crothers Dulles. In recent years, additional stories have been added above the cornice but continuing the original architectural style.

J. WILLIAM WHITE MEMORIAL BUILDING, 34th and Spruce Streets. 1913–22: Arthur H. Brockie and Theodore M. Hastings.

Brockie (Ar 1895) and Hastings did a good deal of hospital work for the University, but this, their largest building, was delayed first by World War I and then by budgetary concerns. Even then it represents only a tenth of the projected length, which according to their 1916 plans was to reach all the way to 36th Street. The second building on campus named for surgeon, J. William White (the other is the training house in the sports complex), this portion of the hospital was built to serve the surgical needs of the hospital, all of which were accommodated behind a facade which endeavored to harmonize with Cope and Stewardson's original Clinical Building, further west on Spruce Street. The massing is nearly Georgian in proportion and blankness of wall, but the verticality, the strapwork ornament, and the huge, bulbous finials at the corners are more Jacobean in character. The White Building replaced the main block of Addison Hutton's gambrel-roofed Home for Nurses (1891) and caused the rear wing of the nurses' residence to be moved south along 34th Street, where it stood until it was demolished for

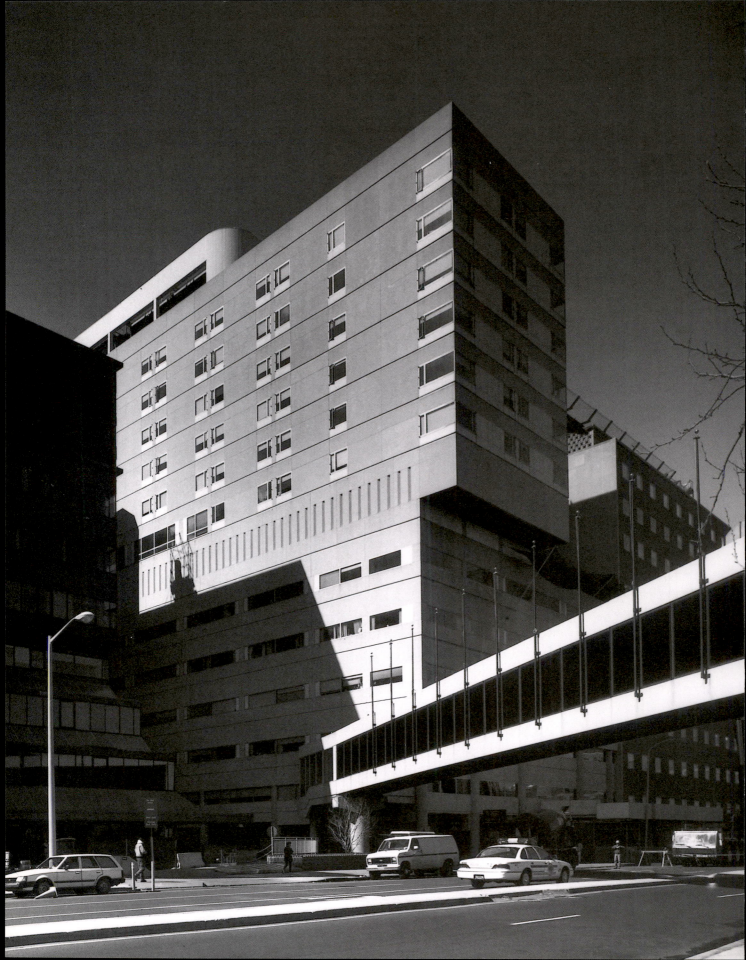

Silverstein Pavilion, looking northwest, 1995. GET.
David W. Devons Medical Imaging Center and Quadrature, *looking east, 1994. GET.*
Penn Tower, 1995. GET.

••••••••••••••••••••••••••••••••••••••

the Ravdin Institute, leading in turn to the construction of English House.

I. S. RAVDIN INSTITUTE, 34th Street. 1958–63: Schmidt, Garden, and Erikson. Additions, 1973: Dagit Associates. Facade additions, 1997: The Architects Collaborative.

Seven floors of this planar-faced minimalist building comprise patients' rooms; the other space is devoted to surgery and services. Dr. Isador S. Ravdin, Harrison Professor of Surgery, was commissioned as a general and led the World War II Pennsylvania medical contingent in south Asia that "reduced the mortality of our troops to a record unequaled by any nation in the annals of war." The building was expanded by Dagit Associates in 1973, while its Postmodern portico and lobby were among the last works of the Architects Collaborative, the Cambridge-based firm founded by Walter Gropius, which dissolved during its construction.

LOUIS SILVERSTEIN PAVILION, 34th Street. 1976–78: Geddes, Brecher, Qualls and Cunningham.

The largest component of the hospital contains patients' rooms and a new emergency room, all wrapped in a sleek tan skin. The handsome plaza behind Silverstein, named for T. G. Miller, is a 1986 work of landscape architects Hanna/Olin, Ltd. Penn's version of I. M. Pei's Louvre pyramid forms the background to Robert Engman's *Quadrature* (see below) and serves as a sculptural accent to the courtyard. Its brown tile base is crowned by a red-brown cap of enameled metal, accented by an off-center ventilator cutout. The David W. Devons Medical Imaging Center occupies the space below the plaza. To the south is the William H. Donner Center for Radiology (1955–59, Schmidt, Garden, and Erikson).

PENN TOWER (formerly Hilton Hotel) 34th and Civic Center Boulevard. 1972–74: Geddes, Brecher, Qualls and Cunningham

Of all the Philadelphia School members, Geddes, Brecher, Qualls and Cunningham remained closest to the European character of modern design, rigorously

distinguishing between building skin as plane and structure as engineered frame. The resulting architecture is often one of elegant subtlety that in this case manages to elevate even a developer's hotel commissioned for the Bicentennial. A vertical column of windows on the north facade denotes the elevator bank which provides views of the University Museum and Franklin Field while the curving corners add a sculptural touch that emphasizes the otherwise simple structural frame. The building continues as a hotel, but, connected via bridge to the University Hospital, it also provides outpatient service rooms and doctors' offices.

FOUNDERS WING, Hamilton Walk. 1985–87: GBQC Architects. (Color Plate 12)

   GBQC's (the more recent name for Geddes, Brecher, Qualls and Cunningham) handsome reversal of Penn's usual masonry formula of red field and light trim brightens and lightens the immense bulk of this 220 bed, 23 operating theater addition to the hospital

complex, which stands on the site of the original wing of Thomas Richards's University Hospital. Concrete aggregate surfaces are highlighted by red tile bands interspersed with panels of tan and brown tile. The L plan enframes a large courtyard named T. G. Miller Plaza, on one side of which is Robert Engman's enameled steel sculpture *Quadrature* (1984, installed 1986). Its four white and orange-brown shapes appear to have been carved out of each other, implying a unified form.

The Nursing and Medical campuses include several less distinguished buildings, among which is what is now the **Nursing Education Building**, on Curie Boulevard. Built in 1968–70 from designs by Morton L. Fishman Associates as the Tri-institutional Nursing Education Building, it provided classrooms for a joint nursing program shared by Penn, Philadelphia General Hospital, and Presbyterian Hospital. The brown brick and pedestrian detailing obscure the clichéd use of such Philadelphia School motifs as the entrance

Founders Wing, looking north, 1995. GET.
Nursing Education Building, looking west, 1995. GET.
Blockley Hall, looking northwest, 1995. GET.
The Consortium, Philadelphia Center for Health Care
Sciences, looking northeast, 1995. GET.

••

tucked under the volume of the building and the expression of interior functions by the contrast between bays and flat wall sections. Another refugee from the past is **Blockley Hall**, which stands on Guardian Drive. Designed in 1963–64 by Supowitz and Demchick, it was built as a nurses' dormitory for the now vanished Philadelphia General Hospital. With the closing of PGH, this building was purchased by the University and converted to office use. Its name is derived from the great seventeenth-century Warner estate on this site that was named for his ancestral home in Blockley, England. "Blockley" became the common name for the Philadelphia Almshouse, the forerunner of Philadelphia General Hospital. Portions of the almshouse property were sold by the city

for the University's first West Philadelphia buildings. The architects, David Supowitz (Ar 1916) and Israel Demchick (Ar 1915), were classmates at South Philadelphia High School and again at Penn; after World War II they formed a partnership that designed many of the movie houses of the new automobile suburbs at the northern end of the city. The "floating cornice" and vertical registers of windows link the building to the classicism of Paul Cret, modified by the intervening International Style.

Philadelphia Center for Health Care Sciences

Nowhere is the dramatic growth of the medical campus in the last decade of the twentieth century more apparent than along Civic Center Boulevard. In two generations of growth since the demolition of Philadelphia General Hospital, the entire site has been covered with buildings whose bright colors and historicizing surface patterns denote their construction in the age of Postmodernism. The Philadelphia Center for Health Care Sciences contains elements of

Children's Hospital, looking west, 1974. GET.

the Hospital of the University of Pennsylvania (HUP), Children's Hospital of Philadelphia (CHOP), and allied institutions including the Children's Seashore House. The now demolished PGH was a group of twentieth-century buildings designed in the Colonial Revival style by city architect Philip Johnson (1868–1933, the Philadelphia politico rather than the guru of International modernism). All that remains of that immense property are the handsome brick and wrought iron fences and the **Consortium** at 451 University Avenue, the last remaining building of the Philadelphia General Hospital. Constructed in 1912, its mass and weight contrast with the postmodern behemoths that have arisen around it.

CHILDREN'S HOSPITAL OF PHILADELPHIA, Civic Center Boulevard and 34th Street. 1974: Harbeson, Hough, Livingston, and Larson, associated with William A. Amenta.

Like the University, Children's Hospital is now at its third site. Its first location was on 22nd Street below Walnut Street; later it moved south to 18th and Fitzwater Streets to a hospital designed by Stewardson and Page. While the dark tile and smoked glass give the building a tough, Brutalist exterior appearance, the interior is very different. All functions are clustered around a vast central atrium with a children's play area beside a splashing fountain and a McDonald's restaurant. Children's Hospital was the first such institution founded on the North American continent, and it quickly established a link with the University Hospital and Medical School. Children's Hospital and more recently the Children's Seashore House have made this an internationally known center for pediatric medicine. Dr. C. Everett Koop, the familiar bearded, genial U.S. surgeon general during the Reagan presidency, was for many years a leading member of the staff of Children's Hospital.

The **Richard D. Wood Center of Children's Hospital**, on Osler Boulevard, is a 1989 work by Ballinger and Co. Within, Sam Maitin (B.F.A 1951) has constructed a brilliantly colored bas-relief mural to brighten the lobby (1991). The Wood Center provides

ambulatory patient facilities for Children's Hospital. Wood, the descendent of an old Quaker manufacturing family, transformed his family's small dairy in Wawa, Pennsylvania into the region's Wawa Markets. Sharing the entrance court is **Children's Seashore House**, designed in 1989 by GBQC Architects. It is the successor to an ocean-front villa built by a late Victorian organization founded in 1872 for therapeutic pediatric care. Bright colors and roof garden play areas confirm its purpose. The most recent building in this complex is the **Leonard and Madlyn Abramson Pediatric Research Laboratories of Children's Hospital**, which occupies a prominent location at Civic Center Boulevard and Osler Avenue. Designed in 1994–96 by Ellenzweig Associates of Boston, it is named for the founder of U.S. Healthcare, a pioneering health maintenance organization (HMO). The light palette of this high-rise laboratory denotes its connection to Children's Hospital. A handsome blond wood lobby with a freestanding spiral stair is inscribed with

....

Children's Hospital, atrium, 1974. GET.
Richard D. Wood Center of Children's Hospital, looking northeast, 1995. GET.

Children's Seashore House, looking northeast, 1995. GET.

a quotation from Dr. William Osler, the pioneering public health advocate who led the battle against tuberculosis; his first teaching position was at the University of Pennsylvania's Medical School (1884–89).

SEYMOUR GRAY RESEARCH FOUNDATION FOR MOLECULAR MEDICINE-CLINICAL RESEARCH BUILDING, Curie Boulevard and Osler Circle. 1988–90: Venturi, Rauch and Scott Brown.

Penn's extension into the Philadelphia Center for Health Care Sciences is evident in a group of buildings that reflect the University color scheme. Unlike Kahn's expressive but complex particularization of functions in the Richards Medical Research Laboratories, the Venturi office's response to the functional requirements of laboratories resulted in an uncomplicated rectangular volume with a vast array of ventilating equipment on the top. This flexible plan permits lab groups to shrink and expand with the workload, responding to a common criticism of Kahn's building. In a site of many separate institutions, Venturi marks

identity with a metamorphosis of Penn's conventional red and white into a giant mosaic with the subtle tonality of an oriental carpet. Oversized red-brown and tan-brown stretchers are accented with persimmon and blue-black headers in a striking variation on the Flemish bond of Cope and Stewardson's campus. The base is a brownish granite that combines all the hues of the brick; the top is a pearly gray metal, emblazoned with the overscaled seal of the University, recalling Venturi and Scott-Brown's seminal study of highway scale design in *Learning from Las Vegas*.

Other University laboratories share the growing medical campus. Most have adapted some form of the Flemish bond brickwork and red and white coloration to designate their affiliation with the University. The **Stellar-Chance Laboratories** on Guardian Drive are

Leonard and Madlyn Abramson Pediatric Research Laboratories of Children's Hospital, looking northwest, 1996. GET.
Seymour Gray Research Foundation for Molecular Medicine-Clinical Research Building, looking northeast, 1995 (below). GET.

the 1992–94 work of BLT Associates in association with Earl Walls & Associates, laboratory planners. It stands atop a chiller plant, previously designed by BLT Associates. The name jointly honors Professor of Psychology and later Provost Eliot Stellar and Professor of Biochemistry and Biophysics Britton Chance. The familiar oversized decorative grills, bold limestone moldings, and panels of Flemish bond brickwork are links to other recent BLT projects, including the multistory **Center for Health Care Sciences Garage** (1989) across Curie Avenue. This Postmodern mode contrasts with BLT's earlier Kahnian vocabulary seen in Vance Hall and International House. The capstone to the Health Care Campus is the **Biomedical Research Building II** that faces Osler Circle. It is the design of Perkins and Will & Associates with Francis, Cauffman, Wilkinson and Pepper, and when completed in 1999 it was Penn's largest building, containing 384,000 square feet. The medical research, medical school, and hospital facilities will again rival the size of the University as they did for much of the nineteenth century!

••••••••••••••••••••••••••••••••••••••

Philadelphia Center for Health Care Sciences Garage, looking northeast, 1995. GET.
Stellar-Chance Laboratories, looking north, 1996. GET.
Biomedical Research Building II, looking northwest, 1999 (far right). GET.

THE NORTH CAMPUS

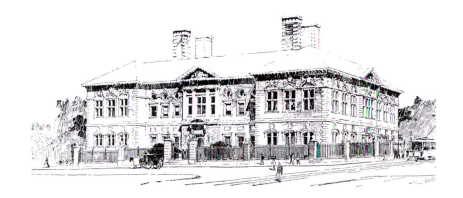

Market Street — *Ludlow Street* — *Chestnut Street* — *Sansom Street* — *Walnut Street*

41st Street — 40th Street — 39th Street — 38th Street — 37th Street — 36th Street — 34th Street

Steve Murray Way

North Campus

1. Sansom Common
2. The Block
3. Lewis Hall
4. Law School Addition
5. Tanenbaum Hall
6. English House
7. Kings Court
8. West Philadelphia Title and Trust
9. Franklin Building
10. Bookstore and Inn
11. Gimbel Gymnasium
12. Walnut Street Garage
13. Ralston House
14. Sansom Place
15. Institute of Contemporary Art
16. University Lutheran Church
17. International House
18. Iron Gate Theater
19. Greenfield Center
20. St. Agatha and St. James Church
21. Cathedral Church of the Saviour
22. Tau Epsilon Phi
23. Sigma Alpha Mu
24. Sigma Nu
25. Sigma Delta Tau

26. Delta Tau Delta
27. 3931-33 Walnut Street
28. Atlas Storage
29. Pi Beta Phi
30. Delta Upsilon
31. Kappa Alpha Theta
32. Alpha Phi
33. Bell Telephone Exchange
34. St. Leonard's Court
35. Chestnut Hall
36. Church of Latter Day Saints
37. Literacy Research Center
38. Hamilton Court
39. 3401 Walnut Street
40. Institute for Scientific Information
41. 3440 Market Street
42. Monell Center
43. 3508 Market Street
44. Gateway Building
45. Greater Atlantic Healthcare Building
46. 3600 Market Street
47. 3624 Market Street
48. 3665 Market Street
49. Kuljian Building
50. National Board of Medical Examiners

THE NORTH CAMPUS

SANSOM COMMON: THE SHOPPES AT PENN AND THE GEORGE FUNDERBERG INFORMATION CENTER, 3401 Walnut Street. 1985-87: GBQC Architects[1]

Too many compromises rarely make great architecture, as is proven by the academic support building at 34th and Walnut Streets. It is the result of a decade of conflict and contention among university planners, local community groups, and those who ran the small businesses that had made Walnut and Sansom Streets the chief centers of local entrepreneurship. Initial University schemes called for an eleven-story behemoth complete with movie theaters, two stories of parking, two stories of shops, and seven stories of academic offices. That project was reduced to a more manageable scale. At street level the building is a campus-oriented version of a shopping mall with conventional shop windows framed by brick quoining. The carefully detailed and articulated limestone and varied shapes of the blue glass windows of the upper office levels imply specific functions in the manner of the fenestration of Furness's University Library. Here, however, the varied windows light flexible loftlike interiors, marking the decline of Philadelphia School functional expressionism to surface mannerism.

The interior food court, by David Slovic, encircles a ring of tables with an indoor marketplace of interesting foods. In warm months diners spill out onto a rear courtyard on Moravian Street behind the Victorian houses of Sansom Street. At the 34th Street corner, the Funderberg Information Center serves as Penn's front door. Here is where to find out what is happening on campus. The Center is named for George Funderberg (GAr 1916), who for many years operated a local real estate practice and preached the importance of open housing policies and the merits of living in University City.

"The Block", 3400 block of Sansom Street. Circa 1870.

Built in the first years after the Civil War, this brownstone, Second Empire row denoted the trend toward urban density west of the Schuylkill. For most of its history the row housed Penn faculty and other congenial sorts including Mme. Helena Petrova Blavatsky, a founder of the United Order of Theosophists, who lived at 3420. In the 1960s the antiseptic planning theory of the urban renewal era collided with radical restaurateur and architecture school student Elliot Cook, who advanced the theories of Jane Jacobs's urbanism in his Moravian Restaurant (named for the rear alley, Moravian Street). A decade-long battle ensued, resulting in the preservation of the block and a notable Redevelopment Authority agreement that turned the buildings of the block over to tenants who

Sansom Common: the Shoppes at Penn, looking northwest, 1996. GET.

had been removed from Walnut Street. The result is a street that teems with life, a mini-town square that attracts students and faculty alike to a rich array of restaurants and shops.

WILLIAM DRAPER LEWIS HALL (LAW SCHOOL), 100 South 34th Street. 1899–1900: Cope and Stewardson.[2]

For the Law School, Cope and Stewardson produced their grandest and most classical work at the University of Pennsylvania, closely modeled on Christopher Wren's garden facade at Hampton Court Palace. The design was intended to recall the England of the late seventeenth century, when the modern English law code was established. Rondels, inscribed with the names of great legal thinkers from Edward I through to modern American justices, represent mileposts in the history of the law. The warm character of the exterior contrasts with the huge and rather chilly marble-lined stairhall, but it returns in the two great upstairs reading rooms of the Biddle Law Library: Sharswood Hall at the south end and McKean Hall at the north (now divided into two classrooms). In these rooms the carved and molded vegetal ornament has been based on the work of Grinling Gibbons, Wren's brilliant sculptor.

After the initial eighteenth-century lectures on law

•••••••••••••••••••••••••••••••••••••••

"The Block," looking southwest, 1996. GET.

by James Wilson, law instruction was largely turned over to practicing attorneys who were paid on a per capita basis. That proprietary system continued with the reconstitution of the law school in 1850 under Dean George Sharswood, who was one of the preeminent jurists of his day. William Draper Lewis, for whom the building is named, advocated the creation of a full-time faculty and was instrumental in moving the Law School to the West Philadelphia campus from its previous home in the shadows of Independence Hall.

To the rear of Lewis Hall is the **Law School Addition**, 3420–40 Chestnut Street, 1956–59 and 1960–62 by Carroll, Grisdale, and Van Alen. The first enlargement to the Law School provided dormitories (1956–59, demolished 1992 for Tanenbaum Hall), a dining commons, and lecture rooms, gathered around an internal courtyard—a private space much appreciated on an urban campus. Within is *Hseih-Chai*, a bronze dragon beast by famed animal sculptor Henry Mitchell (1962). The planar exterior brick walls are relieved by concrete segmentally headed arches that nod ever so slightly toward Cope and Stewardson's adjacent segmental pediments of the Law School. The interior court contains a fountain installed by the Friends of Rebecca Fordham in 1966.

NICOLE E. TANENBAUM HALL, 3440 Chestnut Street and Sansom Street. 1992–94: Davis and Brody[3]

The newest piece of the Law School is Tanenbaum Hall, which stands on the site of the Law School dormitories. It continues the recent strategy of contextual and largely sympathetic design in the central campus; however, the tension between its planar surfaces and the ambiguous overlay of Postmodern Flemish bond brickwork lead to the conclusion that the architects' values remain based on the convictions of post-World War II Modernism, which are reflected in

•••••••••••••••••••••••••••••••••••••••

William Draper Lewis Hall, looking northwest, 1975. GET.
William Draper Lewis Hall, main stair, 1903. UPA.
William Draper Lewis Hall, reading room, 1903. UPA.

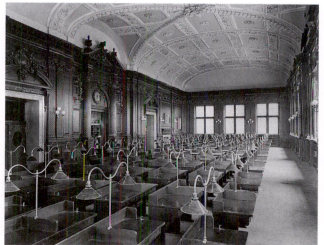

the corner windows and the simple cubic massing of the building. A decade of Postmodernism has reestablished the importance of detail, creating a firmer link between the past and present, here most obviously in the use of the bulls-eye windows above the entrances that recall features of Lewis Hall. This project was chaired by Penn trustee Myles Tanenbaum (W 1952, L 1957), who, as the principal donor, named the building as a memorial to his daughter.

ENGLISH HOUSE, 3446 Chestnut Street. 1958–60: Schmidt, Garden, and Erikson. Renovations, 1991: MGA Partners.[4]

Despite its name, this is not a residence where one would find students discussing Shakespeare or Milton. It was built as a home for nurses by the architect of many of the hospital's newer buildings (Carl Erikson, Ar 1910) and was named for its donor, Mrs. Chancellor English. Derived from Le Corbusier's Unités d'Habitation, this glass-faced slab with a Mediterranean roof deck on top and *pilotis* below was intended to keep nursing students living near the hospital while separating them from the University coeds. The fragmentation of the complex into its separate functions recalls Le Corbusier's United Nations Complex of the previous decade. In recent years it has become part of an undergraduate College House. The hallmark Postmodern shallow arc of the new entrance bay and flat limestone piers that sheath the new common rooms and dining hall are the work of MGA Partners (successors to Mitchell/Giurgola Architects).

KINGS COURT, 3450 Chestnut Street. 1912–15: Frank R. Watson and Samuel Huckel.

Built as an apartment building for local developer Clarence Siegel, Kings Court has the type of continuous window bays that were popularized by Chicago architects. In the 1920s Siegel developed the neighborhood west of Penn as an the automobile suburb that he called Garden Court. Kings Court was purchased by the University for nurses' housing in 1961 and adapted for that purpose by Francis, Cauffman, Wilkinson and Pepper in the same year. It has been joined with English House to form Kings Court/English College House.

WEST PHILADELPHIA TITLE AND TRUST COMPANY, 3557–59 Walnut Street. 1925: Paul A. Davis, M. Edmunds Dunlap, and W. Pope Barney. Eastern additions, 1927: McIlvain and Roberts.

This diminutive skyscraper, now owned by the University, combines the ahistorical ornamentalism of Art Deco with some hints of the "stripped classi-

••

Law School Addition, looking northwest, 1995. GET.
Nicole Tanenbaum Hall, looking south, 1996. GET.

cism" that found favor among those architects of the 1920s who fancied themselves progressives but not revolutionaries. Architectural sculpture by Philadelphia's principal early twentieth-century architectural stone carver, Joseph Bass, enlivens the lower walls. Davis (Ar 1894) was one of those responsible for bringing Paul Cret to teach at the University, and it was under Cret that Barney studied (Ar 1912, GAr 1913). The original building was only three bays wide but was doubled in width two years later.

••

Kings Court, looking southeast, 1996. GET.
English House, looking northwest, 1996. GET.

FRANKLIN BUILDING, 3415 Walnut Street. 1964–67: Carroll, Grisdale, and Van Alen.

Carroll, Grisdale, and Van Alen gave Pennsylvania's administrators a tough-looking quasi-industrial office building, with two massive piers on each face and a huge top-floor machinery space (complete with a hayloft-style exterior door and projecting I-beam hoist). The formula owes something to Kahn and perhaps to the PSFS Building as well. The Franklin Building is attached to an older annex at the rear (1923, with third story added in 1927) that housed a small factory. It took the place of rows of tiny Civil War-era trinity houses, built for the factory workers who worked in the giant plants along the railroad tracks on the west bank of the Schuylkill.

••

West Philadelphia Title and Trust Company, looking northeast, 1985. GET.
Franklin Building, looking northeast, 1995. GET.

Sansom Common: University Bookstore and the Inn at Penn, looking northwest, 1996, architect's perspective. Courtesy Elkus/Manfredi, Architects, Ltd.

••

SANSOM COMMON, 3601 Walnut Street. 1996–99: Elkus/Manfredi Architects Ltd.

Sansom Common marks Penn's efforts to cure some of the ills of its community by encouraging retail and economic development around the campus. It has two principal anchors, the University Bookstore, which opens toward the campus through a corner tower, and the Inn at Penn, an on-campus hotel, as well as restaurants, shops, and other facilities intended to enrich campus life. One of the largest buildings of the entire campus, it adheres to the color schemes that have typified the University for most of the century. Despite the model of Cope and Stewardson's dormitory quadrangles, where vast scale is handled deftly by subdividing the facade into small units that are spiced with small but engaging carvings, Sansom Common has little but its shop fronts to connect with the pedestrian.

BERNARD F. GIMBEL GYMNASIUM, 3701 Walnut Street. 1966–68: Stewart, Noble, Class, and Partners.[5]

Gimbel Gymnasium is named for Bernard F. Gimbel (W 1907), the grandson of the founder of Gimbel Brothers Department Stores and a Penn wrestler, heavyweight boxing champion, and football player. Its

Bernard F. Gimbel Gymnasium, swimming pool, c. 1970.
Frank Ross, UPA.
Bernard F. Gimbel Gymnasium, looking northeast, 1996.
GET.

••

location, separated from the spots campus to the east,
denoted the westward move of the University in the
1960s under President Harnwell; with new student
residences west of 38th Street, this location was more
central to the modern campus. The nubbly brick
facade recalls the texture of Saarinen's Hill House, but
the historicist allusion here is classical, with a notional
pediment surmounting a kind of portico on the Walnut Street front that perhaps recalls the architects'
Beaux-Arts training in the Cret atelier before World

Garage, looking northeast, 1997. GET.
Ralston House, looking north, 1996. GET.

••

War I. The same architects were responsible for Meyerson Hall and the Laboratory for Research on the Structure of Matter.

Inside, there are the predictable swimming pool and gym but also the unexpected Lloyd P. Jones Gallery, devoted to the work of Penn's talented twentieth-century sculptor R. Tait McKenzie, M.D. McKenzie, after training as a physician, learned to sculpt as a tool for teaching anatomy. At Penn he served simultaneously as a professor in the University's Physical Education, Medical, and Fine Arts programs. McKenzie's best work shows athletes in competition and finds lyrical form in moments of explosive effort. Other works by McKenzie dot the campus, including the Young Franklin on 33rd Street, Provost Smith at the head of Smith Walk, and the dynamic George Whitefield in the Quad. Contrasting with the sure detail of McKenzie's work are several pieces by his student Joseph Brown, who continued as a sports artist, providing the giant figures of athletes outside Philadelphia's Veterans Stadium.

Among the minor buildings of the north campus is the **Garage** at 38th and Walnut Streets, which was constructed in 1994 from designs of BLT Architects. In this instance the building contains a chiller plant for the north campus. The odd cylindrical corner stair tower with overhanging corrugated metal awnings is harder to place. Perhaps it is a bit of Russian constructivism visiting after the end of the Cold War. First floor shops continue the commercial presence along Walnut Street. **Ralston House** at 3615 Chestnut Street dates from 1889 and is the work of the Wilson Brothers. Despite the originally horrific Victorian name, "The Home for Indigent Widows," the design was collegiate, recalling the romanticization of history of A. W. N. Pugin's *Contrasts.* The building has been shorn of the ranks of rooftop chimneys that originally signaled the presence of a fireplace in every room, bringing warmth and dignity to its residents. A modern wing by Cope and Lippincott, with Lee and Thaete was constructed in 1980. It is now operated by the University as geriatric housing and medical offices.

SANSOM PLACE (formerly Graduate Towers), 3600 block of Chestnut Street. 1970: Richard and Dion Neutra (Bellante, Clauss, Miller, and Nolan, collaborating architects).

For their late date, Neutra's four Graduate Towers evince an unusually straightforward modernism. But after all they were designed by one of the men who, nearly half a century before, first brought the International Style to America. Especially dramatic are the freestanding elevator towers that rise between each

spaces of its program. The Institute of Contemporary Art was formed in 1963 at the direction of G. Holmes Perkins, then dean of the School of Fine Arts, as an antidote to the staid Philadelphia art world. "Devoted to the examination and presentation of international activities in the visual arts," its goal was "to intensify concern for and enlarge understanding of current thinking of this field within the University and the community at large." The ICA was housed first in the rear spaces of the old University Library (now Fisher Fine Arts Library) and later in the center gallery of Meyerson Hall. As Perkins hoped, the ICA has sponsored the avant garde and happenings, from Clifford Still's abstract expressionist paintings to Andy Warhol's still-remembered vanishing act through the roof of the Furness building, and from Christo's pyramid of Gulf oil barrels to Robert Mapplethorpe's now notorious exhibit, "The Perfect Moment."

pair of apartment slabs and are connected to the residential units by glass-walled passages that read as transparent in the late afternoon sun. The effect is like that of Russian Constructivist architecture in the 1920s. The eastern pair of towers has been renamed Nichols House in honor of Roy Nichols, professor of history and later dean of the Graduate School of Arts and Sciences. The buildings originally were linked by a plaza atop a below grade garage. This amenity was removed to create Steve Murray Way, the new street that provides a view of the north facade of Sansom Common to Chestnut Street.

INSTITUTE OF CONTEMPORARY ART, 118 South 36th Street. 1990–91: Adèle Naudé Santos and Jacobs/Wyper Architects, associated architects.[6]

Nuzzled up against the south wall of the Graduate Towers is this tough play on Le Corbusier and Richard Meier by former head of the Department of Architecture Adèle Santos. A strident cacophony of industrial materials, commercial lettering, and deconstructivist fenestration, its exterior is a representation of the

UNIVERSITY LUTHERAN CHURCH OF THE INCARNATION, 37th and Chestnut Streets. 1969: Pietro Belluschi, with Alexander Ewing and Associates.

Here, as in his many other church designs, Belluschi

••••••••••••••••••••••••••••••••••••

Graduate Towers, Nichols House, looking east, 1970. Photo: Frank Ross. UPA.
Graduate Towers, looking west, 1997. GET.

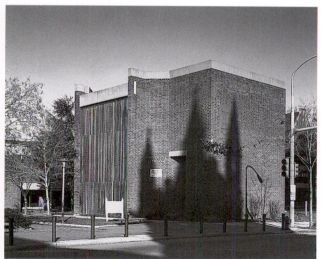

Institute of Contemporary Art, looking northwest, 1996. GET.

University Lutheran Church of the Incarnation, looking northeast, 1996. GET.

••

manipulates modern forms and a Greek cross plan in order to recall the traditional imagery of worship. Within, the sanctuary is lit by a wall of leaded glass set between deep wood strips that lights the lower levels of the space while the upper levels dissolve into darkness that recalls the mystery of Byzantium. A separate, smaller block to the rear contains the church offices, recalling the similar distinction of functions in Frank Lloyd Wright's Unitarian Unity Chapel.

INTERNATIONAL HOUSE, 3701 Chestnut Street. 1968–70: Bower and Fradley.

With its internal shopping street and vigorously sculpted facade of poured-in-place concrete, John Bower's design pays homage to Le Corbusier's several Unités d'Habitation. The building holds its own very effectively in the now crowded University City sky-line. Its architects were selected in a competition, largely because of their ability to integrate the program requirements of private suites for students with shared common spaces, thereby mandating a sense of community. This was an important theme of the day at Penn's architecture school and one that Louis Kahn explored at Bryn Mawr's Erdman Hall. The building's form denotes the various housing opportunities, ranging from single rooms on the upper levels to suites in the deeper base, while the emphasis on the character of the construction and the exterior expression of internal functions are hallmarks of the Philadelphia School architecture of the 1960s.

IRON GATE THEATER, formerly Tabernacle United Church, 37th and Chestnut Streets. 1883–86: Theophilus P. Chandler.

Designed by the architect who directed the University's architecture school during its first year (1890–91), Tabernacle is a beamy, auditorium-plan church enriched by a glory of angels at the ends of the

International House, looking northwest, 1975. GET.
Albert M. Greenfield Intercultural Center, looking southeast, 1996. GET.
Iron Gate Theater, Tabernacle Church, looking southeast, 1994. GET.

•••••••••••••••••••••••••••••••••••••

hammerbeams of the great wood trusses. A large school and office wing was added by the same architects to the rear (1890). The parsonage stands at the southeast corner of the property, joined by an elegant bit of cloister arcading that suggests in its delicacy of touch the reasons Chandler was asked to serve as the director of the School of Architecture. This design, academic in detail and free in form and plan, shows Chandler at his most willfully Gothic, with his French training apparent only in the surprisingly symmetrical plan. The decline of the church's congregation led to the acquisition of the building by the University for adaptation as a theater; the congregation continues to use some of the building space.

ALBERT M. GREENFIELD INTERCULTURAL CENTER, 3708 Chestnut Street. Circa. 1850. Alterations 1982–84: Cecil Baker and Associates.[7]

This Italianate villa is surely the oldest building in the neighborhood and once stood alone on its splendid hilltop. Its present use was initiated after a 1978 takeover of the Franklin Building by the Black Students League,

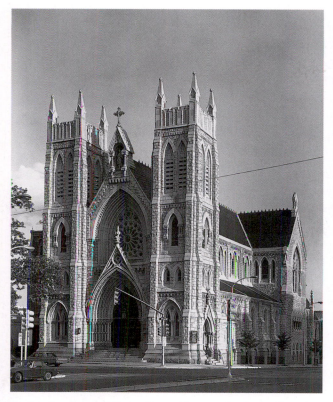

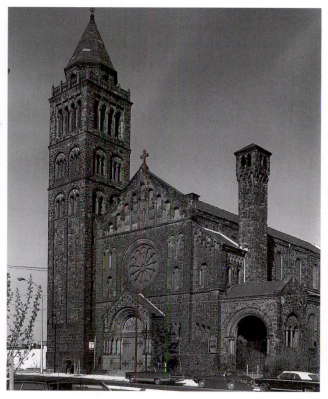

Saint Agatha and Saint James Roman Catholic Church, nave, 1975. GET.
Saint Agatha and Saint James Roman Catholic Church, looking southeast, 1975. GET.
Church of the Saviour, looking northeast, 1975. GET.

••

which led to the creation of the Intercultural Center, whose funds were derived from a much earlier donation by real estate mogul Albert M. Greenfield.

SAINT AGATHA AND SAINT JAMES ROMAN CATHOLIC CHURCH (originally St. James), 38th and Chestnut Streets. 1881–87: Edwin F. Durang.

Designed by Philadelphia's premier late nineteenth-century Roman Catholic architect, St. James is a miniature cathedral in plan, complete with twin-towered facade, apsed choir, transepts, and a circular baptistery. Durang's detail is often feisty. In the case of St. James, the north facade was originally constructed with differing towers, one round and the other square in plan. The present symmetry is the result of a

rebuilding in 1930. The interior is vibrantly painted with images of saints recalling the polychromy of Italy; the crossing and nave columns are cast iron, painted to imitate polished stone. Adjacent to the church is the **Newman Center** at 3730 Chestnut Street, constructed in 1969 from plans of Albert and Daniel Dagit, Associates. For much of the twentieth century the Dagit family dominated Catholic architecture in the Philadelphia region, producing masterpieces such as the Byzantine-domed St. Francis de Sales on Springfield Avenue. The listless modernism of the Newman Center would seem more at home in suburbia.

CATHEDRAL CHURCH OF THE SAVIOUR (Episcopal), 38th and Ludlow Streets. 1902–6: Charles M. Burns.

In 1889 Burns replaced an older church by Samuel Sloan with a new building that was in turn destroyed by fire in 1902. Burns then designed the present building, which recalls the general Italian Romanesque

Church of the Saviour, nave, 1975. GET.
Tau Epsilon Phi, looking north, 1995. GET.
Sigma Alpha Mu, looking northwest, 1995. GET.

••••••••••••••••••••••••••••••••••••

character of its predecessor but with the addition of a grand tower and an extraordinary hammerbeam roof over the nave. The apse is decorated with a glorious cycle of murals painted by Edwin Blashfield, commissioned to honor the memory of Anthony J. Drexel, whose family worshiped here. The carved altar by R. Tait McKenzie is a World War I memorial, an *ara pacis* of modern soldiers. The leaded glass windows were repaired and lighted by film stars Jeanette MacDonald and Nelson Eddy, who, before they found fame in Hollywood, were residents of the neighborhood and members of the choir. In 1992 the Church of the Saviour was designated as the Cathedral of the Episcopal Diocese of Philadelphia.

WEST OF 38TH STREET

West of the divide created by the enlargement of

38th Street in the 1970s are remains of the mixed residential and institutional neighborhood that evolved before the Civil War along the streetcar lines that extended west from Center City. These neighborhoods recall the flavor of the region before Penn's 1960s expansion. Early in the twentieth century, some of the large properties were demolished and replaced by apartment buildings that even now form the skyline north of the University.

Tau Epsilon Phi at 3805 Walnut Street is part of a row of twin houses built in 1889 and attributed to Frank Furness. Like the other buildings of the group, it is missing its original front porch with its massive turned wood posts and knee-braces. The porch was renovated in 1992 by Becker-Winston Architects (respectively Ar 1971 and 1972). The Rho chapter of Tau Epsilon Phi was established on the campus in 1921. **Kappa Delta** is part of the same row; most of original Furness detail of the exterior has unfortunately been stripped away, including its projecting front bay, but some of the original detail survives within. The **Psy-**

cornices and the cupola. The classical porch, French windows, wrought iron gate, and other details associated with the colonial revival are the work of Baker and Dallett in 1904 and 1912. The Beta Rho chapter, established at Penn in 1894, is the fraternity's longest continually active chapter.

During the Centennial decade of the 1870s, most of the minor vacant lots were infilled with mansarded brownstone twins such as **Lambda Chi Alpha**, formerly **Lambda Phi Epsilon**, at 3829 Walnut Street.

Sigma Delta Tau, 3833–35 Walnut Street, is similar in detail and was fully restored in 1993. Houses such as these typified the solid middle-class lifestyle sustained by the city's remarkable mix of industry, commerce, and finance. Beta chapter of Sigma Delta Tau sorority was founded in 1920; in 1987 it merged with Alpha Zeta, a campus social club. Just to the north at 130–32 South 39th Street is **Delta Tau Delta**, designed by Willis G. Hale, Furness's chief rival for visual pyrotechnics. Hale was the architect of choice for the north Philadelphia developers who owned the

••

Sigma Nu, looking north, 1995. GET.
Lambda and Sigma Delta Tau, looking northwest, 1996. GET.

chology Building at 3815 Walnut Street is a grisly disfigurement of another part of the group. The screen is the work of H. C. Stevens in 1959, who followed the anti-Victorian lead of Edward Durrell Stone's refacing of his own New York brownstone townhouse. Originally, these buildings were part of a symmetrical composition of four pairs; 3801–3 was demolished for the widening of 38th Street along with a subsidiary row from the same project that stood on 38th Street.

To the west at 3817 Walnut Street is **Sigma Alpha Mu**, a Civil War-era house that is strikingly less well preserved than its contemporary mid-nineteenth-century neighbor next door. It houses the Theta chapter, which has been active at Penn since 1914. An exceptionally fine Italianate house of the kind that established Walnut and Chestnut Streets as West Philadelphia's most prestigious nineteenth-century addresses, **Sigma Nu** (3819 Walnut Street) preserves much of the handsome original woodwork that embellishes the

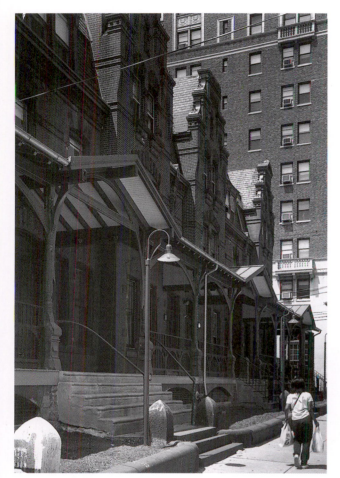

Delta Tau Delta, looking north, 1987. GET.
3931–33 Walnut Street, looking north, 1987. GET.

••

streetcar lines and controlled much of the real estate development in west and north Philadelphia. Contemporary sociologist Thorstein Veblen coined the phrase "conspicuous consumption" to describe buildings of this sort that epitomized the new consumer culture with motif piled on motif in a remarkable array of materials. Delta Tau Delta and its neighbors were built as part of a larger project that included immense houses lining Walnut Street (all of which are demolished), these townhouses on 39th Street, and smaller row houses on Sansom Street. Despite the economic hierarchy of the block, porch fronts for all designated the shared suburban experience.

The site of the University Mall on the 3900 block

of Walnut Street was formerly occupied by an immense Presbyterian church and a row of huge four-story twin houses designed by Willis Hale for William Weightman. Something of the former character of the street can be told by the surviving twin brownstone at **3931–33 Walnut Street**, designed in 1887 by William Decker, Jr. The western half of this ambitious Queen Anne twin, with shaped gables and a corner turret, contains University offices.

4015 WALNUT STREET (originally Atlas Storage). 1926: George Kingsley.

This former storage warehouse is an exuberant exercise in polychromatic terra cotta classicism by New York architects whose specialty was secure storage for shorebound summer vacationers. Here in its windowless recesses the student editors of the *Daily*

Pennsylvanian toil in subterranean-like offices, producing the city's fourth largest daily paper.

The north side of Walnut Street is also part of the westward course of the Greek organizations. **Pi Beta Phi** occupies 4027 Walnut Street, a post-Civil War house. The Iota chapter of this sorority was founded at Penn in 1992 and, after residing at 3916 Spruce Street, moved to its new house in 1996. The Italianate bracketed cornice of **Delta Upsilon** at 4035 Walnut Street gives away the pre-Civil War date of construction of this former twin house. Penn's chapter of Delta Upsilon was founded in 1888; Delta Upsilon terminated activities in 1972 but was revived again in 1990. Another in this group of suburban houses is **Kappa Alpha Theta** at 4039 Walnut Street. The sorority was first chartered at Penn in 1919, but was recolonized in

••••••••••••••••••••••••••••••••••••

4015 Walnut Street, looking northwest, 1994. GET.
Pi Beta Phi, looking northeast, 1995. GET.
Delta Upsilon, looking north, 1995. GET.

1988 when the Nu Delta social club merged into the sorority. **Alpha Phi** at 4045 Walnut Street occupies the more prestigious corner location was the largest of these pre-Civil War suburban houses. It now houses the Eta Iota chapter of the sorority, which arrived on campus in 1988.

Chestnut Street West of 38th Street

The **Bell Telephone Exchange** at 3810 Chestnut Street was the home of the EVergreen exchange. Designed in 1923 by John T. Windrim, it has a handsome Georgian facade that borrows from Peter Harrison's Market House (1762) in Newport, Rhode Island. The limestone columns on the second story demonstrate the civic virtues of pre-World War II utility buildings.

Saint Leonard's Court at 3819–33 Chestnut Street was converted from a small Catholic private school for girls housed in a pair of existing Centennial-period brownstone mansions; later additions, notably the

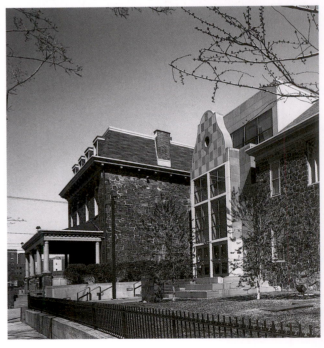

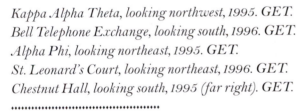

Kappa Alpha Theta, looking northwest, 1995. GET.
Bell Telephone Exchange, looking south, 1996. GET.
Alpha Phi, looking northeast, 1995. GET.
St. Leonard's Court, looking northeast, 1996. GET.
Chestnut Hall, looking south, 1995 (far right). GET.

••••••••••••••••••••••••••••••••••••

convent building on the east with its incised lintels and cantilevered colonnetted cornice, suggest the hand of Edwin Forrest Durang, the architect of St. Agatha and St. James Roman Catholic Church a block to the east. The post-Venturi facade on 39th Street serves as the new front door when the school was converted to offices by C. Stanley Runyan for Sheward-Henderson Architects in 1986. It now provides offices for the University.

The **Chestnut Hall Apartments** at 39th and Chestnut Streets was originally the Hotel Pennsylvania, a handsome, triple-slab hotel with Robert Adam-in-

Chestnut Hall, entrance hall, 1988. GET.
Chestnut Hall, University Credit Union, 1985. Courtesy
Graydon Wood for Clio Group, Inc.

••••••••••••••••••••••••••••••••••

spired detail from plans of Clarence Wunder. Built in the era when Penn football had a national following and Fred Waring's Pennsylvanians played for the crowds that came for home games, it is now University-owned apartments. The offices of the University Credit Union were refitted in a thoroughly Postmodern way and the neo-Adam lobbies were restored by William Becker in 1983–84. Horace Trumbauer's

French Gothic city house for James Connelly at 3910 Chestnut Street (1896) was the long-time home of the Original House of Pagano, a fondly remembered Italian restaurant. Acquired by the University, it is now occupied by the **Literacy Research Center**.

The **Church of Jesus Christ of Latter Day Saints** at 3913 Chestnut Street was designed in 1985 by Davis, Poole, and Sloan. Its low silhouette and insistent horizontals are more Prairie School than urban Philadelphia. At 39th and Chestnut Streets is **Hamilton Court**, which was based on a fifteenth-century Venetian palazzo, the Ca d'Oro. With its reflecting pool out

Church of Jesus Christ of Latter Day Saints, looking northeast, 1997. GET.
Literacy Research Center, looking southeast, 1996. GET.
Hamilton Court Apartments, looking southwest, 1996 (right). GET.

••••••••••••••••••••••••••••••••••••

front and roof gardens above, Hamilton Court must have seemed like a corner of Venice in West Philadelphia. It was designed in 1901 by Milligan and Webber, the chief architects of apartment houses of turn-of-the century Philadelphia.

UNIVERSITY CITY SCIENCE CENTER

The north edge of the campus is occupied by the University City Science Center. It is the result of the creative partnership formed in the 1950s between the Philadelphia City Planning Commission under its executive director, Edmund Bacon, and the University of Pennsylvania through its dean of the School of Fine Arts, G. Holmes Perkins, who also chaired the commission. A consortium of regional colleges and

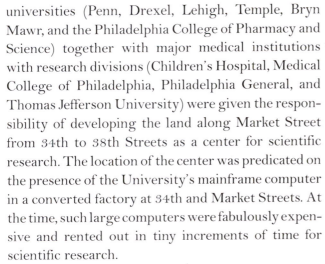

universities (Penn, Drexel, Lehigh, Temple, Bryn Mawr, and the Philadelphia College of Pharmacy and Science) together with major medical institutions with research divisions (Children's Hospital, Medical College of Philadelphia, Philadelphia General, and Thomas Jefferson University) were given the responsibility of developing the land along Market Street from 34th to 38th Streets as a center for scientific research. The location of the center was predicated on the presence of the University's mainframe computer in a converted factory at 34th and Market Streets. At the time, such large computers were fabulously expensive and rented out in tiny increments of time for scientific research.

The master plan provided for twenty-story office towers at the corners of each block, framing low-rise loft-type incubator buildings for start-up businesses. In the intervening three decades, many of the smaller buildings have been built, but only one tower was constructed, the so-called Gateway Building at 36th

and Market Streets. The buildings share a palette of brown brick (presumably intended to differentiate the center from the red and orange bricks of the two main institutional sponsors, neighboring Penn and Drexel). The utilitarian drabness was offset to some extent by sculptures and interior murals, a requirement of the Redevelopment Authority's "One Percent for Art" program. After Venturi's reinterpretation of the loft buildings as "decorated shed," other architects have followed their lead in creating more interesting facades that transcend the context.

The University's former computing center, **3401 Market Street**, was built in 1922 to house the printing plant of Stephen Green and Co. from plans of Clarence Wunder, an industrial architect. Until the late 1960s, Market Street in West Philadelphia was a central cog in the great industrial machine that was Philadelphia. Along its length, candy manufacturers such as Croft and Allen vied with hardware suppliers, printing plants, and transportation-related businesses in a band

3401 Market Street, looking northeast, 1996. GET.
3440 Market Street, looking southwest, 1996. GET.
Institute for Scientific Information, looking northwest, 1996. GET.
Monell Chemical Senses Center and 3508 Market Street, looking southwest, 1996. GET.
Gateway Building, looking northwest, 1996. GET.

of three- and four-story industrial buildings that divided residential districts to the north and south. The Green Printing Company shows the influence of such regional protomodernists as Price and McLanahan in the expressed frame punctuated by pier caps that articulate the roofline. After World War II, this building was acquired by the University for its main-frame computer.

The **Institute for Scientific Information (ISI)** at 3501 Market Street was a 1978 essay in high-signature, low-cost design by Venturi, Rauch and Scott-Brown. Using the required drab-toned brick of the Science Center uniform as base color, the architects overlaid a polychromatic tile checkerboard pattern on the upper stories that strives to achieve formality through color and pattern alone. The angled plane at the entrance is ornamented with giant enameled tile flowers that recall the firm's 1977 highway-scaled showroom for Best Products. The resulting counterpoint of curved forms and grid continues the explora-

tion of pattern that has preoccupied their office since the Oberlin Art Museum additions. This highway-scaled "Decorated Shed" competes for attention in the fashion of the best American commercial architecture. In the entry lobby, Jennnifer Bartlett's mural *In the Garden* is painted on vinyl tiles that coalesce into an abstract mosaic of color.

Most of the other buildings of the Science Center are loft buildings for science. **3440 Market Street** by Levinson, Lebowitz and Zaprauskis (1981–83) reinterprets the Venturi decorated shed paradigm with an overlay of bay-defining metal panels on an otherwise plain box. The lobby is enlivened by an illusionistic tunnel created by tapestries designed by Minnesota textile artist Jean Nordlund; the decorative tiles are by Farley Tobin, who trained with the Moravian Tile Works in Doylestown, Pennsylvania. The drab **Monell Chemical Senses Center** at 3500 Market Street is a 1970 design by Ewing, Cole, Erdman, Eubank that reverses the elements of the earlier, adjacent building by the same architects. Arlene Love's gilded fiberglass *Face Fragment* graphically hints at the scientific research that is the focus of the building's tenants. **3508 Market Street** was the first new building constructed in the Science Center in 1968. Its architects, again Ewing, Cole, Erdman, Eubank, responded to the then-hostile environs of Market Street with a facade that was more fortress-like than were its later neighbors. The largest and least interesting building of the center is the sole skyscraper, Nowicki and Polillo's **Gateway Building** at 36th and Market Streets (1973). In 1998–99 it was the subject of an extensive redesign by Ueland, Junker, McCauley, Nicholson.

More recent buildings have been more engaging. The **Greater Atlantic Healthcare Building** at 3550 Market Street was constructed in 1985–87 by Levinson, Zaprauskis Associates. It occupies one of the corner sites intended for the twenty-story office towers. To maintain some semblance of the master plan's intended framing of the block, this building projects forward over the sidewalk to create a covered arcade, a planning motif of the period. The facade is enlivened by Jeffrey Marin's sculpted panels inspired by Japanesque pictographs of natural forces. More mannered is **3600 Market Street**, designed in 1988 by the Vitetta Group. By lopping the corner, 3600 provides views toward the trolley tunnel and the rears of buildings along Chestnut Street, proving that too much design

is as bad as too little. The cavetto cornice gives the upper levels of the building a vaguely Egyptian image that contrasts with the earthy base. Two sculptures ornament the site. In the small entrance plaza is a 1988 bronze by Masayuki Kama depicting Dr. Hideyo Noguchi (1876–28), a renowned Japanese researcher who spent several years at Penn in the first years of the twentieth century. He led the attack on syphilis and died of yellow fever in Africa. Above it looms the splendid *Refractive Light Spire* by James Carpenter, installed in 1989. In the lobby is the Esther Klein Gallery, a venue for small changing art exhibits in the Science Center. The adjacent **3624 Market Street**, by Day and Zimmerman, Architects (predecessors to the Vitetta Group) was one of the earliest buildings of the center, constructed in 1972. It proves the Venturi reversal of the modern dictum that sometimes "Less is a bore." The small plaza in front of this bland piece of background architecture is enlivened by James Lloyd's bronze globe-like sculpture entitled *Untitled*. The entrance lobby is dominated by Edith Neff's nostalgic commemoration of the streetscapes of the rapidly disappearing Powelton neighborhoods north of Mar-

Greater Atlantic Healthcare Building, looking southeast, 1996. GET.
3624 Market Street, looking southwest, 1996. GET.
3600 Market Street, looking southeast, 1996. GET.

ket Street. For a time in the 1970s, during his professorship at the University, noted futurist Buckminster Fuller had his offices here.

3665 Market Street, built between 1996-98 from designs by B Five Studio, is a sprightly neo-Victorian building with patterned brick and exposed steel lintels above the first floor openings. It recalls the small-scale turn of the century buildings that once lined Market Street. Adjacent to it is the **University City Science Center Parking Garage** that was designed and built in 1994–95 from plans by GBQC Architects. Russian constructivism overlays the facade of this otherwise utilitarian structure. Across Market Street is **Founders' Plaza**. Built in 1976 on the closed right-of-way of 37th Street, it contains a dedicatory plaque listing the founders of the Science Center and Timothy Duffield's (M.L.A. 1975) 1976 fiberglass, resin, and acrylic sculpture, *Dream of Sky*. Bordering the plaza on the west is Bower and Fradley's **Kuljian Building** of 1973. It was the first building to break out of the box formula of the earlier Science Center buildings, turning toward the direction the architects had explored for Vance Hall. Here the poured-in-place reinforced concrete frame structure is revealed at the base but screened at the

3665 Market Street, looking northeast, 1997. GET.
Kuljian Building, formerly Otis Elevator Building,
looking southwest, 1994. GET.
National Board of Medical Examiners, looking west,
1995. Courtesy GBQC Architects (right).

upper levels. The original tenant was Otis Elevator; presently the building houses an engineering office.

The western end of the Science Center is anchored by the **National Board of Medical Examiners** at 3750 Market Street. Built in 1993–94, it is another work by GBQC Architects. The architects used Minnesota dolomite, the yellow stone of the Philadelphia Museum of Art, for trim, with green-tinted windows that contrast with the Science Center's usual brown brick. Architectural character is derived from a peculiar juxtaposition of 1920s sci-fi and Bauhaus details. The advancing corner with sheltered walkway repeats the motif of the earlier Greater Atlantic Building and continues the planning formula of the original master plan. The rear opens onto a handsome landscaped garden enlivened by the double-functioning security fence that forms the frame for Roy Wilson's splendid *Wind Helix* sculpture of 1994.

THE WEST CAMPUS

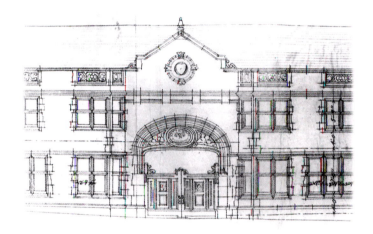

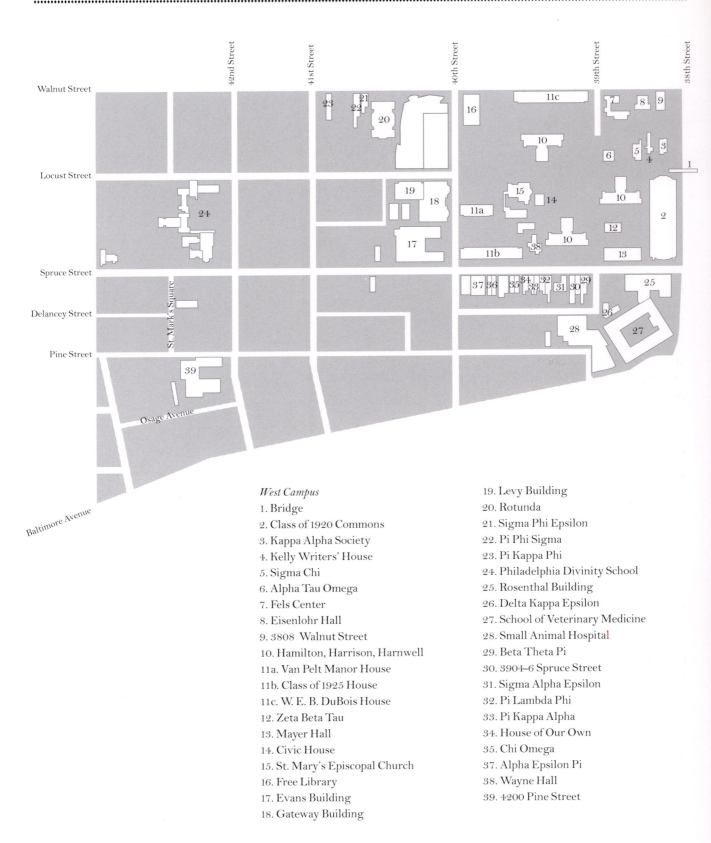

West Campus

1. Bridge
2. Class of 1920 Commons
3. Kappa Alpha Society
4. Kelly Writers' House
5. Sigma Chi
6. Alpha Tau Omega
7. Fels Center
8. Eisenlohr Hall
9. 3808 Walnut Street
10. Hamilton, Harrison, Harnwell
11a. Van Pelt Manor House
11b. Class of 1925 House
11c. W. E. B. DuBois House
12. Zeta Beta Tau
13. Mayer Hall
14. Civic House
15. St. Mary's Episcopal Church
16. Free Library
17. Evans Building
18. Gateway Building

19. Levy Building
20. Rotunda
21. Sigma Phi Epsilon
22. Pi Phi Sigma
23. Pi Kappa Phi
24. Philadelphia Divinity School
25. Rosenthal Building
26. Delta Kappa Epsilon
27. School of Veterinary Medicine
28. Small Animal Hospital
29. Beta Theta Pi
30. 3904–6 Spruce Street
31. Sigma Alpha Epsilon
32. Pi Lambda Phi
33. Pi Kappa Alpha
34. House of Our Own
35. Chi Omega
37. Alpha Epsilon Pi
38. Wayne Hall
39. 4200 Pine Street

THE WEST CAMPUS

BRIDGE, Locust Street and 38th Street. 1971: Eshbach, Pullinger, Stevens and Bruder, Associates with Perkins and Romanach.

A massive poured-in-place reinforced concrete arched bridge hurls Locust Walk across the divide of 38th Street toward the residential campus. The style of the bridge and the immense buildings of Superblock fall into the category termed Brutalism—a pun on the French *beton brut* (for reinforced concrete) and the toughness of exposed concrete, but the architects worked in a bit of whimsy paralleling the arc of the bottom of the concrete with the arc of the top of the railing.

CLASS OF 1920 COMMONS AND GARAGE, 3800 Locust Walk. 1971: Eshbach, Pullinger, Stevens and Bruder with Perkins and Romanach Architects and Planners. Alterations, 1986–89: Research Planning Associates with Maria Romanach.

This tough poured-in-place reinforced concrete building with tall, slope-topped skylight shafts, came from the Eshbach office, though the Le Corbusian massing of the side elevation with the expressed stairs recalls earlier work by Romanach. Its two functions of parking and dining hall are distinctly differentiated by the contrast between the open grid of the garage and the solid walls of the Commons. Within, the great dining hall has the strengths and weaknesses of its era with the hardness of its material being offset by the

dramatic lighting that recalls Kahn's top-lighted spaces at Bryn Mawr College's Erdman Hall. The obtrusive air conditioning machinery and the Postmodern, shiny, enameled metal-clad north entrance were more recent alterations.

Superblock from 38th Street, looking west, 1997. GET.

KAPPA ALPHA SOCIETY, 3803 Locust Walk. 1851–55: Samuel Sloan.

A rare survivor of the streetcar suburb that the University invaded in the 1870s, this small Gothic villa was built on speculation for S. A. Harrison, a major developer of Victorian West Philadelphia. Gothic associations with the idea of the Christian home were part of the sentimentalization of the Victorian age. Kappa Alpha claims the title of the nation's oldest fraternity; its Beta Chapter was established at Penn in 1913. Adjacent and part of the same development is the **Kelly Writers House** at 3805 Locust Walk, also by

Class of 1920 Commons and garage, looking northwest, 1995. GET.
Samuel Sloan, Architect, sketch for English Gothic style house, 1851–52. Samuel Sloan, The Model Architect.
Kelly Writers House, looking north, c. 1900. UPA.

••••••••••••••••••••••••••••••••••••

Sloan. Built at the same time as Kappa Alpha, also for S. A. Harrison, it was enlarged by Edgar Hoffman of the Furness, Evans and Co. office in 1916. It has been recently adapted from its long-time role as the Chaplain's home to serve as a center for creative writing on campus.

SIGMA CHI (originally Anthony Drexel, Jr. House), 3809 Locust Street. 1884: Thomas Roney Williamson.

The Drexel House is a sophisticated Queen Anne design with the variety of materials, textures, and colors that mark the style. Its architect was trained in the Philadelphia office of James P. Sims that also produced Wilson Eyre, Jr. As a youth, Williamson toured the west and in a confrontation with Indians was scalped and left for dead; his death, some three decades after the incident, was blamed on his wounds! The house was part of the Drexel family compound, with the adjacent George W. Childs Drexel House

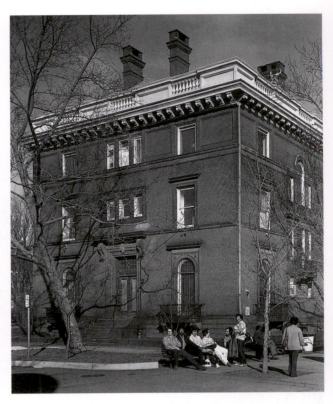

and, at 39th and Walnut Streets (where Fels now stands), the site of the now-demolished Italianate mansion for the patriarch of the family, Anthony J. Drexel. Drexel was the senior partner of J. P. Morgan and the principal financier of the nation in the late nineteenth century. Sigma Chi is the most flamboyant of the group and marks the regional transition away from the Victorian individualism of Furness toward the historicism of the end of the nineteenth century. Within, a wonderful leaded glass partition is one of the glories of the house. The Pi Phi Chapter was established at Penn in 1875, shortly after the University moved to West Philadelphia.

ALPHA TAU OMEGA (originally George W. Childs Drexel House), 225 South 39th Street. 1891: Wilson Brothers.

Alpha Tau Omega is squarer and more purely classical than its Queen Anne neighbor, making it closer in character to McKim, Mead and White's neo-Georgian work. Built for a Drexel son, the mansion

Sigma Chi, looking northeast, 1975. GET.
Alpha Tau Omega, looking northwest, 1985. GET.
Fels Center for Government, looking southeast, 1985. GET.

••••••••••••••••••••••••••••••••••••

was the design of the Wilson Brothers, the family's favorite architects and the premier architect-engineers of their day. For the Drexel family, the architects designed their bank at Fifth Street and their Institute (now Drexel University), for which Joseph Wilson also helped define the mission of the school and designed the curriculum. For the Penn campus, the Wilson Brothers designed its first power plant and engineering buildings on the site of Irvine Auditorium. The Tau Chapter was founded at Penn in 1881.

SAMUEL FELS CENTER OF GOVERNMENT (originally Samuel Fels House), 3814 Walnut Street. 1907–9: Frank E. Newman and James R. Harris. Office wing addition, 1956: W. Pope Barney and Roy Banwell.

A vigorous neo-Georgian building, the Fels house dates from Walnut Street's last period as a prestigious

residential address before the automobile turned the east-west streets into highways. This was the home of industrialist Samuel Fels, whose Fels Naphtha soaps were a nationally known product at the end of the nineteenth century. His interest in supporting utopian communities and activist community groups led to the founding of the Fels Center, the purpose of which was the training of city managers with the skills needed to manage the modern metropolis. The office wing is the work two Penn grads, W. Pope Barney (Ar 1912) and Roy Banwell (Ar 1917). Their first design (a drawing for which is in the Architectural Archives) followed the model of their teacher, Paul Cret, in

merging modern motifs with Georgian symmetry, but their eventual solution was more conventional.

EISENLOHR HALL (President's House) (originally Otto Eisenlohr House), 3812 Walnut Street. 1910–11: Horace Trumbauer. Restoration; 1979–80: Dagit/Saylor.

The home of cigar manufacturer Otto Eisenlohr is much indebted to the classicism of seventeenth-century France, and Trumbauer was undoubtedly much

••

President's House, formerly Eisenlohr Hall, looking south, 1994. GET.

indebted for its design to Julian Abele (Ar 1902), who had returned from France to work in Trumbauer's office in 1906. The interior is divided by a vast, cool, T-shaped hallway that provides access to the major spaces and to the handsome stair. Most of the entertaining rooms are similarly restrained, but the dining room is paneled with warm, dark wood. Restored by Dagit/Saylor, Eisenlohr has been the home of the president of the University since 1981. It was donated to the University by Josephine Eisenlohr and is named in her honor.

3806–8 WALNUT STREET. 1898–89: W. Frisbey Smith

A pair of dark brick twins of the highest class, by a developer's architect who was also active on Spruce Street, these were characteristic of the houses along the major streets of West Philadelphia at the end of the nineteenth century. The pilasters and rich detailing of the facade denotes the transition from the brick Queen Anne style of the 1880s toward the Beaux-Arts classicism of its neighbor to the west.

HIGH-RISES (HAMILTON COLLEGE HOUSE, HARRISON COLLEGE HOUSE, HARNWELL COLLEGE HOUSE), 3800 Locust Walk. 1968–72: Eshbach, Pullinger, Stevens, and Bruder, with Perkins and Romanach.

In 1967, after a decade of planning, designs for low-rise dormitory quadrangles were scrapped because of costs. In their place, Dean of the Graduate School of Fine Arts G. Holmes Perkins prepared the site plan for the Superblock complex of high-rise and low-rise dormitories on what had been four separate city blocks. The mixture of tall and short buildings in a parklike setting owes much to the early 1920s Radiant City planning schemes of Le Corbusier, but the Brutalist architectural vocabulary is more up-to-date. Perkins

3806–8 Walnut Street, looking southeast, 1988. GET.
Hamilton College House, Harrison College House,
Harnwell College House, looking north, 1987. GET.

was the designer of the high rises—marvelously strong buildings that fill the horizon for motorists approaching the city from the west. The top floor lounges are cantilevered beyond the lower facades and the advanced plane of their glazed faces is carried to the ground by two towering bays. The effect recalls El Lissitzky's "Cloud Prop" skyscraper projects of the 1920s. Inside, residents are provided not with dormitory rooms but with true apartments, designed to lure the students back from the student apartments that had proliferated around the campus. The top floor lounges are splendid rooms with views of the entire region. Hanging from the ceiling of the lobby of Hamilton College House is Rafael Ferrer's *Kayak Magnetic North*, a magnetized steel kayak that points north. It was the gift of the Class of 1948. Charles Ross's *Two Prisms* (1977) was installed in the lobby of Harrison College House. The names are drawn from the region's distant past (Hamilton, the late eighteenth-century estate holder of the area), the near past

(Harnwell, the University president during the great leap forward that produced these buildings), and Harrison (not the provost of the 1890s but a twentieth-century donor).

Alexander Lieberman's **Covenant** (1975) is building-sized in scale and forms a triumphal arch in steel tubes that frames the westward extension of Locust Walk through Superblock and vies with the high-rise dorms for visual interest (see Color Plate 13).

LOW-RISES (W. E. B. DUBOIS COLLEGE HOUSE, VAN PELT MANOR HOUSE, CLASS OF 1925 HOUSE), 3900 Walnut Street, 3909 Spruce Street, 3940 Locust Walk. 1970–72: Eshbach, Pullinger, Stevens, and Bruder, with Perkins and Romanach.

The low-rise dormitories were designed by Mario Romanach, a professor in the Department of Architecture. Their combination of concrete slabs and brick walls, punctuated by towers and other picturesque incidents, closely resembles the English Brutalist James

••

Class of 1925 House, looking north, 1995. GET.
Van Pelt College House, looking northeast, 1995. GET.

Zeta Beta Tau, looking northeast, 1995. GET.
Harold C. Mayer Hall, looking northwest, 1995. GET.

••••••••••••••••••••••••••••••••••••••

Stirling's apartment building at Ham Common of 1955–58. The three buildings are now college houses devoted to special themes of study or lifestyle. W. E. B. DuBois College House commemorates the African-American scholar whose research for *The Philadelphia Negro* was conducted as an Associate in Sociology in 1896–89. Van Pelt Manor House recalls the important donations of Charles Patterson Van Pelt. In 1987 the Class of 1925 house was distinguished by a new entrance designed by Marco Frascari of the School of Fine Arts. The last two named houses have been combined to form Gregory College House.

ZETA BETA TAU, 250 South 39th Street. 1929: Edwin L. Rothschild.

A fine example of the restrained Gothicism of the period between the wars, Zeta Beta Tau now stands adrift of its former streetscape in Superblock. Its side facades explicate its internal subdivisions in a very rational way while its street front pays homage to the Academic Gothic of earlier fraternities. Rothschild (Ar 1916) was a member of the fraternity and the son of the faculty advisor. Penn's Theta Chapter arrived on the campus in 1907.

HAROLD C. MAYER HALL, 3817 Spruce Street. 1964–65: Eshbach, Pullinger, Stevens, and Bruder.

The 1963 master plan's solution for campus dormitories (see Color Plate 1) shows two low-rise alternatives: an evocative and intricate plan by Kneedler, Mirick, and Zantzinger and an economical scheme of simple blocks whose chief advantage was the interior courtyards they framed. This building is an example of the later design that was a forerunner of the low-rises that frame the remainder of Superblock. The heart of the design was the intended contrast between the low-rises, framing and controlling space, and the soaring high-rise towers. As originally built, Mayer was less drab, with blue and yellow panels below the windows. These were replaced in the 1980s. It is named for Harold C. Mayer (W 1915), a senior partner in the New York investment firm of Bear Stearns and Co. and a University trustee.

CIVIC HOUSE, 3914 Locust Walk. Circa 1850.

Another Gothic villa from the mid-nineteenth-century streetcar suburb, the Civic House is a contemporary of the Harrison houses at 3803 and 3805 Locust Walk. For most of its history it served as the rectory for the adjacent St. Mary's Church. In its present role it fosters links between University students and the community around them.

ST. MARY'S EPISCOPAL CHURCH, 3916 Locust Walk. 1871–73: Thomas W. Richards. Parish house, 1897: George Nattress. Spire, 1907: Herbert J. Wetherill.

St. Mary's was the neighborhood parish church for Hamilton Village, an early nineteenth-century development project of William Hamilton, the owner of the Woodlands estate to the south. Though it was designed after the village had been incorporated into the city, St. Mary's retains a modicum of rural informality, offering a gauge of the suburban neighborhood into which the University moved. It and the Christian

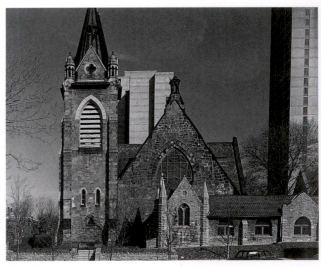

Civic House, looking north, 1995. GET.
Saint Mary's Episcopal Church, looking west, 1972. GET.

Association to the east are the last privately owned buildings on the main campus. Presumably Richards was selected for this project because of his success in the competition for the new University buildings. Its tower was constructed and a spire added in 1907 from plans of Herbert J. Wetherill (Ar 1895); the spire was removed in 1973. A magnificent altar imported from Italy was installed in 1890, when the chancel was remodeled and the west porch was added by Charles M. Burns, a graduate of the College before the Civil War. The attached parish building, now used for a school, recalls the rural-vernacular-inspired work of C. F. A. Voysey in its simple massing and roof forms. It was added in 1897 by George Nattress, Burns's long-time assistant.

FREE LIBRARY, WEST PHILADELPHIA BRANCH, 3948–50 Walnut Street. 1904–5: Clarence C. Zantzinger and Charles L. Borie.

Alumni of Penn's architecture program, Zantzinger (Ar 1895) and Borie (C 1892, awarded 1897) established one of the most important practices in early twentieth-century Philadelphia. Their West Philadelphia Library, paid for by the Carnegie program, is a serene terra cotta building whose classical detail is wonder-

Free Library of Philadelphia, West Philadelphia Branch, looking southeast, 1994. GET.

fully inventive. Note especially the rows of shelved books worked into the entablature. In more recent years Martin, Stewart and Noble replaced the north end with a glass wall, unintentionally anticipating Postmodern complexities, but without the irony. It may face demolition.

THOMAS W. EVANS MUSEUM AND DENTAL INSTITUTE (SCHOOL OF DENTISTRY), 4015 Spruce Street. 1912–15: John T. Windrim, in consultation with Cope and Stewardson.

When Dr. Thomas W. Evans died in Paris in 1897, he had amassed an enormous fortune, the fruit of the years he spent supplying "pain-free" (anaesthetized) dental care to the wealthiest patients in Europe. His will directed that his money be sent to his native

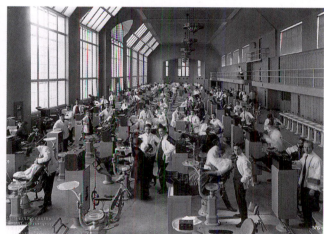

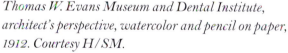

Thomas W. Evans Museum and Dental Institute,
architect's perspective, watercolor and pencil on paper,
1912. Courtesy H/SM.
Thomas W. Evans Museum and Dental Institute, looking
northeast, 1985. GET.
Thomas W. Evans Museum and Dental Institute,
entrance hall, 1916. UPA.
Thomas W. Evans Museum and Dental Institute, hall of
practice, 1916. UPA.

Philadelphia to found a museum (for his eclectic collection of art and memorabilia) joined with a dental institute. The French courts prevented much of his fortune from leaving the country, but $1.75 million did

reach Philadelphia, where a society was created to fulfill the terms of his bequest. The society consulted the Cope and Stewardson firm, who in 1910 prepared a design for the site occupied by Evans's house at 40th and Spruce Streets. The society soon recognized that their funds would not permit them to accomplish all that Evans's will stipulated, so they entered into an agreement to join forces with the Dental School at the University. Although their building on Smith Walk was less than twenty years old, the dental faculty gladly abandoned it for the present structure, for which Cope and Stewardson acted as consultants to John T. Windrim. The result is a building whose details are colder than Cope and Stewardson would have produced by themselves, but one of great presence. The Tudor tower provides entrance into a stairway that rises into a convincing medieval great hall. The museum originally occupied the rooms to the right of the main entrance, with the library located above the main doorway in rooms overlooking Spruce Street. The north wing was filled with clinics, which at first derived almost all their light from an enormous battery of north-facing windows, just as they had in the school's former building. In recent years, to meet accessibility requirements, the main entrance was shifted to the side courtyard. It is accented by Ernest Shaw's *Shongun XII* (1983).

In 1999 construction began for the **Gateway Building** for the School of Dental Medicine at the corner of 40th and Locust Streets. Designed by architects Bohlin, Cywinski, Jackson, it adheres to the University's customary palette of materials of brick and light stone

••••••••••••••••••••••••••••••••••••

Leon Levy Oral Health Sciences Building, looking northwest, 1993. GET.

trim, with bays and secondary articulation intended to relate to the historic Evans Building, but with a simplification appropriate to the late twentieth-century date. The Gateway Building will incorporate a multi-level lobby that will become the principal public entrance to the Dental School. Jane Jacobs's urbanism is reflected in the decision to add commercial space on Locust Street to continue the retail development along 40th Street. On the upper levels are clinical teaching and practice spaces as well as offices for the staff.

LEON LEVY ORAL HEALTH SCIENCES BUILDING (CENTER FOR ORAL HEALTH RESEARCH), 4010 Locust Street. 1969–70: Francis (Ar 1943), Cauffman, Wilkinson, and Pepper (Ar 1948).

The Levy Building's rugged features and jagged skyline, as well as its concatenation of brick towers and reinforced concrete piers, reinterpret Kahn's Richards Building, but with a less picturesque plan that permits more workable laboratories. Here too, much attention was devoted to ventilation, as the huge air intakes above the Locust Street sidewalk attest. Its namesake, Dr. Leon Levy, was a graduate of the School of Dentistry and a frequent benefactor of school programs.

THE ROTUNDA, formerly First Church of Christ Scientist, 4012 Walnut Street. 1911: Carrère and Hastings.

An exceptionally interesting work by one of the nation's leading firms of classical architects, the First Church simulates a central-plan early Christian building that had been reclad in the garb of the Renaissance. It speaks of Italy in every detail. It was purchased in 1995 by the University, and plans are underway for its development.

More fraternities and sororities have established houses west of 40th Street. **Sigma Phi Epsilon** at 4028 Walnut Street occupies a handsome neo-Georgian house, designed in 1900 by Walter Smedley, a well-known Quaker architect. It should be compared with

First Church of Christ Scientist, looking southwest, 1994. GET.

Sigma Phi Epsilon, looking southwest, 1994. GET.

••••••••••••••••••••••••••••••••

4017 Walnut Street. Penn's Delta chapter was established in 1904. To the west is **Pi Phi Sigma** at 4032 Walnut Street. It was built in 1898 by William Kimball, son-in-law of the Clark family, whose mansion occupied the entire 4200 block between Locust and Spruce Streets where the divinity school now stands. This sorority occupies half of a classical twin house of unusual pretensions. Notable are the giant pilasters,

carryovers from the Queen Anne of the previous decade. The Nu chapter of this sorority was established at Penn in 1926. **Pi Kappa Phi** at 4040 Walnut Street was designed in 1895 by Angus Wade, a disciple of Willis Hale. At the end of the century, Philadelphia developers wavered between the flamboyant conspicuous consumption of Hale and the more cautious classicism of the new generation of academically trained designers. This is of the former variety. The Eta Nu chapter was the first new fraternity to arrive on Penn's campus in seven decades when it was established in 1993.

PHILADELPHIA DIVINITY SCHOOL, 42nd to 43rd and Locust to Spruce Streets. 1919–60: Clarence C. Zantzinger, Charles L. Borie, and Milton B. Medary.

This perfect, jewel-like campus is one of Philadel-

Pi Phi Sigma, looking southwest, 1994. GET.
Pi Kappa Phi, looking southeast, 1994. GET.
Philadelphia Divinity School, looking northwest, 1978. GET.

••

phia's architectural treasures. The buildings were purchased by the University following the decision of the Episcopal Church to combine the divinity school with its sister institution in Cambridge, Massachusetts. Although one may regret that the architects' original plan for filling the entire city block with intimate quadrangles (as shown in a model preserved in the Architectural Archives) was not completed, the parklike setting that frames the few executed buildings contributes enormously to their effectiveness. The William Bacon Stevens Library, at the north side of the site, was the first structure to be built (1921–22).

It was followed in 1924–26 by the tall, narrow St. Andrew's Collegiate Chapel, placed on the highest ground of the campus. The chapel's seating plan—with congregants facing each other across the central aisle—follows the model of European collegiate chapels. The attached deanery and the faculty houses at the southwest corner of the site were built at the same time in a style based on the domestic architecture of the Cotswolds. After World War II, the school's only quadrangle (albeit an incomplete one) was created behind the chapel. The block of buildings that forms

....

Philadelphia Divinity School, nave, 1985. GET.
Philadelphia Divinity School, looking northwest, 1985. GET.
Delta Kappa Epsilon, looking east, 1985. GET.
Gladys Rosenthal Building, looking south, 1995. GET.

its west side was built in two phases (1951, 1955); the later, south part of the block is a wonderfully effective, roof-dominated design. In 1960 the library was extended to form a northern enframement for the space. The three principal members of the original firm were all Penn alumni: Zantzinger (Ar 1895), Borie (C 1892, Ar 1897), and Medary (attended classes 1890ff). Borie was a founding member of the Mask and Wig Club. The grave of John Haviland, Philadelphia's great Greek Revivalist, lies south of the chapel, having been transported from the yard of the original St. Andrew's Episcopal Church Haviland had designed on South Eighth Street.

For a generation the site was used by a private neighborhood school; at the time of publication, the University has formed a partnership with the School District of Philadelphia to establish a public school that will be supported by the resources of the University.

South of Spruce Street

GLADYS HALL ROSENTHAL BUILDING, 3800 Spruce Street. 1963: Paul Monaghan and Forrest.

A modest building of utilitarian modernity linked to the rear to Cope and Stewardson's old Veterinary School building, it was funded by the Benjamin Rosenthal Foundation. The small park to the west is the site of the former Phi Sigma Delta, whose attractive 1920s house had to be demolished in 1981 after sustaining structural damage at the hands of its inmates.

DELTA KAPPA EPSILON, 307 South 39th Street. 1927: Harry Sternfeld, associated with John I. Bright.

Harry Sternfeld (Ar 1911, GAr 1914, Paris Prize, and for many years a Professor of Design in the School of Fine Arts) was one of Penn's most talented early twentieth-century architectural alumni. He is best remembered for his *moderne* commercial buildings of the 1920s and 1930s, but for Delta Kappa Epsilon he created a subdued medieval design whose V-plan slips into its awkward site. Penn's chapter was founded in 1898.

SCHOOL OF VETERINARY MEDICINE, 325
South 39th Street. 1902–13: Cope and Stewardson.

The School of Veterinary Medicine first opened in 1884 in a Frank Furness-designed building on Hamilton Walk. In 1901 the school was moved to a temporary building on the present site to make way for the new laboratories of the Medical School. Cope and Stewardson designed the new quarters in another variant on their favorite conflation of late medieval and early Renaissance English architecture. The work progressed in phases, with the four sides completed in 1907, 1909, 1911, and 1913. The west wing, pierced by an entrance arch broad enough to permit the arrival of ambulances and large animals, contained the administrative offices and the library; the south wing, along Woodland Avenue, housed the hospital; the north and east wings were occupied by laboratories.

SMALL ANIMAL HOSPITAL, 3900 Delancey
Street. 1978–81: Vincent Kling Partnership.

The newest of the veterinary facilities, the Small Animal Hospital is attached to the old building by a bridge across what was once 39th Street. Like his Annenberg Center, Kling's design is composed of crisply punctuated brown brick masses, but there is less sculptural interest here. At the entrance is a painted steel sculpture by Billie Lawless, aptly titled *Life Savers* (1982). On this site formerly stood the Convent of the Good Shepherd (John Deery and Edwin Durang, 1880), a mansarded building acquired by the University in 1958 for use by the now defunct School of Allied Medical Professions.

Most of the buildings along the 3900 block of Spruce Street are now devoted to University-related functions. At the corner is **Beta Theta Pi**, 3900–3902 Spruce Street, an elegant Federal Revival twin house constructed in 1899 by developers Wendell and Smith and altered into a fraternity by James Khruly and Associates. Founded at Penn in 1889, the Gamma

••••••••••••••••••••••••••••••••••

School of Veterinary Medicine, looking west, 1976. GET.
Small Animal Hospital, looking south, 1996. GET.
Beta Theta Pi, looking southwest, 1992. GET.

3904–6 Spruce Street, looking southwest, 1992. GET.
Sigma Alpha Epsilon, looking southwest, 1992. GET.
Pi Lambda Phi, looking southwest, 1992. GET.

chapter of the fraternity formerly inhabited a fine neo-Georgian house at 3529 Locust Street, built for it in 1922 by Savery, Scheetz, and Savery. That building was demolished when the present Blanche Levy Park was created, causing the fraternity to move west to its present location. Next door is **3904–6 Spruce Street**, which was built in 1900. It is an unusual Tudor twin in the manner of Cope and Stewardson's Academic Gothic of the campus. One half of this building now houses the Alpha Epsilon chapter of Alpha Chi Omega, a sorority that was first established in 1919 and reestablished in 1990. Becker/Winston Architects supervised its renovation in 1993. **Sigma Alpha Epsilon** at 3908 Spruce Street was built in 1893 and altered for its present use by brother William Steele (C 1911) in 1922 and again in 1927. Built as a private home, its composition and varied ornament reflect the possibilities open to Philadelphia's Free Style classicists in the late

nineteenth century. The fraternity's Theta Chapter opened at Penn in 1901.

The adjacent group of buildings were built as a row of high-style townhouses, developed by William Weightman from an 1890 design by Willis Hale, the flamboyant architect of north Philadelphia's *nouveau riche* entrepreneurs. The facade of **Pi Lambda Phi** at 3914 Spruce reveals its long history. Details of the original design are apparent on the side elevation. It was modernized in 1928, when the reticent and beautifully detailed French limestone facade was added from designs of Andrew C. Borzner (C 1910) The insensitive fire tower is a much more recent "improvement." The Zeta chapter was founded at Penn in

1912. **Pi Kappa Alpha** at 3916 Spruce Street was refaced in 1965 in the heyday of anti-Victorian sentiment. The local chapter of Pi Kappa Alpha is a new colony of a fraternity that was on the campus until 1992. Its redesigned facade respects the domestic scale of its older neighbors, while totally obscuring the detail of the Weightman row. **House of Our Own** at 3920 Spruce Street and its neighbor to the west are the best preserved parts of Hale's wonderfully parvenu row. 3920 has been an alternative bookstore since the early 1970s. Like another, now demolished Hale-designed row for Weightman on the 100 block of South 39th Street, this group demonstrated the merits of the more-is-more school of design for upwardly mobile Philadelphians at the end of the nineteenth century.

The twin house at 3926 Spruce Street that is the home of **Chi Omega** was built in 1899 from plans by

W. Frisbey Smith, who specialized in work for developers who were infilling West Philadelphia. A prepossessing Queen Anne townhouse that typified the streetcar suburb of the time, it was designed for the same West Philadelphia developer who built 3808–10 Walnut Street. Unfortunately much of its pressed-metal ornamentation is now aluminum-clad. The Beta Alpha chapter of Chi Omega was established at Penn in 1919. To the west is **Phi Kappa Psi** at 3932–34 Spruce Street in a double house of the sort that was fashionable in West Philadelphia around 1885, and in the style often associated with the Hewitt brothers. Much of Frank Furness resounds in the building's unconventional detail. This fraternity was founded at Penn in

••

Pi Kappa Alpha, looking southwest, 1992. GET.
House of Our Own, looking southwest, 1992. GET.
Chi Omega, looking southwest, 1992. GET.

1877 and formerly occupied 3641 Locust Walk, now Colonial Penn Center.

The last fraternity house on the block is **Alpha Epsilon Pi** at 3940 Spruce Street. There seems to be a fragment of a large Italianate house contained within this much-altered structure. Most of the present-day facade of the house with its tall front windows was added by Frank Hahn (T 1900) in 1922. Penn's Gamma chapter of the fraternity was founded in 1919. The house was savagely modernized in 1962 by Thalheimer and Weitz and was more sympathetically updated with the addition of a screening front trellis by William Becker (Ar 1971) that recalls the Hanna/Olin pergola in front of Dietrich Hall.

Phi Kappa Psi, looking southwest, 1992. GET.
Alpha Epsilon Pi, looking southwest, 1992. GET.
Wayne Hall, looking north, 1978.
Wayne Hall, detail of conservatory, looking north, 1978. GET.

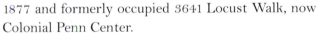

WAYNE HALL (originally Joseph D. Potts House), 3905 Spruce Street. Circa 1876: Wilson Brothers.

This is a wonderfully vibrant Victorian house whose refacing for iron merchant Joseph Potts gives it an abundance of polychromy and wide-ranging eclecticism that were rare in domestic work. The polychromed and molded brick skin and the projecting bays on each side envelop a mid-nineteenth-century Italianate sub-

Wayne Hall, looking north, 1883. Wilson Brothers,
Catalog of the Work of the Wilson Brothers, *1883.*
4200 Pine Street, looking south, 1995. GET.

••

urban house. Its details and color suggest the broad influence of Frank Furness's 1870s work on his peers in Philadelphia. The original roof of the Moorish iron solarium at the southeast corner has been removed, as has the porch that once infilled the el at the southwest corner. Acquired by the University in 1960, it is now the home of WXPN, Penn's radio station.

4200 PINE STREET (formerly Marie Eisenlohr residence). 1904: Horace Trumbauer. Addition, 1972: William Edward Frank.

Trumbauer's first house for a member of the Eisenlohr family looked toward the more conventional French Beaux-Arts sources that had inspired the mid-phase of his career. The cool, understated brick exterior with limestone trim contrasts with the hot brick of the adjacent twin houses by the Hewitt Brothers to the south on 42nd Street and marked the arrival of a new generation of entrepreneurs in West Philadelphia. By the end of the decade, the automobile would direct future construction of great houses toward the western suburbs, ending the half century of suburban development along the streetcar lines. After World War II, the house was adapted to the needs of the American College of Physicians. In 1972 their growth required the addition of the rear office building, which was designed by William Edward Frank who had continued Trumbauer's practice. The complex now houses University offices including those of the University of Pennsylvania Press.

OFF CAMPUS

OFF CAMPUS

THE UNIVERSITY OF PENNSYLVANIA is represented by a remarkable assortment of buildings that are scattered far beyond the limits of the campus. Some, such as the Mask and Wig Club, reflect the customs of the Victorian era when most University students lived in Center City and built their nighttime clubs near their homes. Others, such as the Boat Club, were located among buildings of similar use along the Schuylkill. More recently, the University has acquired important properties by gift.

2016 SPRUCE STREET. Circa 1865: attributed to Samuel Sloan. Alterations 1971: Louis I. Kahn.

After World War II Penn's presidents resided in suburban Chestnut Hill, a tradition resisted by urbanist Martin Meyerson, who preferred a setting closer to the University in the heart of the city. The University acquired a handsome Civil War-era brownstone with a central entrance, tall windows, and crowning mansard. Kahn's work was modest, simplifying the deteriorating brownstone of the facade and inserting an elegant, light-filled corner pavilion in the rear.

MASK AND WIG CLUB, 310 South Quince Street. 1894: Wilson Eyre Jr.

Built as a Lutheran chapel for the African American residents of the small houses near Broad Street, the structure was converted into a stable and later served as a pathology lab for Jefferson College students before being acquired by Penn's undergraduate theater society. As the downtown moved westward from the old city to Broad Street, Quince and Camac Streets became the site of numerous small clubs. The club contains two remarkable rooms, the handsome small theater for student performances and Eyre's notable Rathskeller clubroom, decorated with a replica of the *Old King Cole* mural by Maxfield Parrish that originally graced the room. The mural was sold in the

2016 Spruce Street, looking south, 1982. GET.

1990s. Parrish painted a second version for the Knickerbocker Hotel in New York; it has since been moved to the St. Regis Hotel, where it is the focus of the King Cole Bar. Caricatures of members cover the walls, continuing a late nineteenth-century tradition of undergraduate organizations.

CENTER FOR JUDAIC STUDIES, 416–20 Walnut Street. 1992–93: GBQC Architects.

This Postmodern addition to the neighborhood of

••••••••••••••••••••••••••••••••••••••

Mask and Wig Club, looking northwest, 1994 (left). GET.
Mask and Wig Club, club room, c. 1900. UPA.
Mask and Wig Club, theater, c. 1900. UPA
Center for Judaic Studies, looking south, 1997. GET.

Independence Hall takes its stylistic cues of Flemish bond brickwork, gabled roofs, and small-paned windows from the traditional architecture of the region. A splendid library looks out over the side garden. It is another of the many gifts of Walter Annenberg to his alma mater.

KNAUER HOUSE, "Man Full of Trouble Tavern," 127–29 Spruce Street. Restoration, 1962: W. Nelson Anderson (Ar 1955).

The present building was constructed before the Revolution as two small houses, but the oval basement built of round river stones may be evidence of an even earlier structure on the site. The segmentally-headed windows and handmade bricks are evidence of the

early construction, as are the cove cornice below the gambrel roof which gave this early tavern its popular name, the Cove Cornice House. The interior contains several handsome paneled walls from the eighteenth century, as well as a recreated historic bar of the tavern on the first floor. The house was restored by the Knauer Foundation for Historic Preservation and was given to the University by Virginia Knauer, Penn alumna, trustee and Secretary of Commerce in the

••

Knauer House, looking north, 1996. GET.
University Boat Club, looking northeast, 1974. GET.

University Boat Club, looking north, c. 1890. UPA.
Morris Arboretum, Rose Garden toward Morris resi-
dence, c. 1950. UPA.

••

Reagan administration. It will be used as living quarters for visiting faculty.

UNIVERSITY BOAT CLUB, Kelly Drive. Circa
1875: attributed to Thomas W. Richards. Additions,
1980: Francis, Cauffman, Wilkinson, and Pepper.

Among the earliest of the surviving boat houses on
the Schuylkill, the University Boat Club is the oldest
of the University's off-campus facilities. It has been
almost entirely encased in bland additions whose size
attests to the continuing vitality of Penn's rowing
tradition; the original vertical-boarded gable ends are
evidence of the original Victorian building. From this
club have rowed Olympians.

MORRIS ARBORETUM, 100 Northwestern Av-
enue, Chestnut Hill. Original house and stable, 1887:
Theophilus P. Chandler. David Pepper house, 1893:
Wilson Eyre Jr. Landscape restoration, 1978–present:
Andropogon Associates, Ltd. (Carol Franklin M.L.A.
1965, Colin Franklin M.L.A. 1967, Leslie Sauer, Rolf
Sauer Ar 1971).

At the end of the nineteenth century, John and
Lydia Morris created an important arboretum on their
Chestnut Hill property in the northwest corner of the
city. They deeded the arboretum to the University on

the condition that their great gray stone mansion by
T. P. Chandler be demolished; unfortunately the anti-
Victorian sentiment of the era caused the University
to follow through with this plan. The landscape and its
collections remained to become an important part of
the teaching and study facilities of the University. In
the 1970s director William Klein envisioned a restored and significantly more active arboretum, and
he turned to Andropogon Associates, whose approach
to sustainable design had been developed under Ian
McHarg in the Penn landscape program. The old
carriage house was adapted into a study center, original structures and landscape portions were researched
and restored, and new features were added with an eye
to preserving the original features and spaces. Now
designated as the official arboretum of the Commonwealth of Pennsylvania, it is one of the treasures of the
region.

New Bolton Farm, parlor, 1987. GET.
New Bolton Farm, looking northwest, 1987. GET

••••••••••••••••••••••••••••••••••

NEW BOLTON FARM, 382 West Street Road, Kennett Square, Pennsylvania.

New Bolton Farm takes its name from the Bucks County property, Bolton Farm, given to Penn by Effingham B. Morris, president of the Girard Trust Company, which for some time served as the large animal center for the School of Veterinary Medicine. The original farm was replaced by the present location, which is among the most historic in Chester County. Here settled the Caleb Pusey family after constructing the earliest mill in Pennsylvania in part-

New Bolton Farm, Clinical Building, looking north, 1975. Photo: Lawrence Williams. UPA.
Penn Club, New York, looking southwest, 1994. Copyright © 1995 Durston Saylor. Courtesy H. Durston Saylor, Inc.

••••••••••••••••••••••••••••••••••••••

nership with the Proprietor, William Penn. The farm includes an early settlement house of the Pusey family, now the rear wing of a tenant house on the property, as well as a slightly later eighteenth-century house that was skillfully enlarged in the 1920s by R. Brognard Okie (Ar 1897). Pennsylvania bank barns complement the historic landscape. Adjacent are modern residences and classrooms. The Kline Center is by Ewing, Cole, Erdman and Eubank (1973). The Clinical Building is the work of Vincent Kling Associates (1975) and contains operating amphitheaters and other buildings that serve the modern instructional purpose.

THE PENN CLUB, 44th Street, New York. 1900: Tracy and Swartwout. Adaptive restoration architect, Helpern Architects, 1988–93. Interior design, Bennett (W 1962) and Judith Weinstock (CW 1962) historical themes, George E. Thomas, Ph.D. (Gr. 1975), the Clio Group, Inc.

Built as the Yale Club, the Penn Club is superbly located on a street of clubhouses, across from the New York Yacht Club and the Harvard Club, in the heart of the city. Its red brick and limestone façade was part of a cohort of palatial residential buildings of the region—but fortunately also relates to the Penn's palette of colors. The building housed a U.S. Army facility

during World War II and later was the home of Truro College, a rabbinical school, before being acquired by the University. The main floor is the site of the handsome Franklin Room, or parlor, whose theme is announced by a cast of R. Tait McKenzie's *Young Franklin*, who serves as greeter. With portraits from the University collections on its walls, books by faculty authors in its library, and medallions of the principal donors in the cornice, it is very much a Penn space. In the lower level Penn Grill are murals of the academic year—the Penn-Harvard game of 1985, the Green in winter, and Boathouse Row in spring—by Max Mason (M.F.A. 1884). (Color Plate 16) Dining rooms on the second floor recall the era of the provosts in an eighteenth-century detailed room and the modern era of the presidents of the University. A health club on the upper level is named after the Palestra and takes as its theme the University sports programs. At that level, a balcony, ornamented with a cast of R. Tait McKenzie's *Oarsmen Carrying a Shell* provides views of New York City to the north.

NOTES

Chapter 1: An Awakening of Conscious Vigor

1. The opening was reported in the *Pennsylvanian* 12, 62 (3 January 1896): 1, col. 1; as well as in the *Philadelphia Inquirer*, 3 January 1896.

2. The *Philadelphia Inquirer*, 8 January 1896, p. 1, reported high temperatures in the teens with lows around 0; two days earlier it was reported "Coldest Day of Winter" (6 January, 1896, p. 3, col. 2). In a terrible irony, within a week of the opening of Houston Hall, John Stewardson, the young architect whose work gave color and character to the new campus, was reported to have drowned in an ice-skating accident on the Schuylkill River.

3. George E. Thomas, "William C. Hays," and "Houston Hall," in Ann Strong and George E. Thomas, *The Book of the School: 100 Years* (Philadelphia: Graduate School of Fine Arts, 1991), pp. 52–53.

4. The design of American college campuses has been the subject of numerous publications in the twentieth century. The most accessible is Paul Venable Turner, *Campus: An American Planning Tradition* (Cambridge, Mass.: MIT Press, 1984); earlier accounts that are contemporary with much of Penn's planning include Charles Z. Klauder and Herbert C. Wise, *College Architecture in America and Its Part in the Development of the Campus* (New York: Charles Scribner's Sons, 1929); and George Edgell, *The American Architecture of To-day* (New York: Charles Scribner's Sons, 1928).

5. The University of Virginia's seminal role in American college planning is acknowledged by Philadelphians Klauder and Wise; the most important critical view is a series of articles by American critic Montgomery Schuyler, "Architecture of American Colleges," *Architectural Record* 27–30 (1909–12). Penn is treated in Schuyler, "The Architecture of American Colleges, V: University of Pennsylvania, Girard, Haverford, Lehigh and Bryn Mawr Colleges," *Architectural Record* 28 (July–December 1910): 183ff.

6. *Oxford English Dictionary.* "Campus" was used in reference to the setting of Princeton College as early as 1779, but was not used again until the nineteenth century.

7. Edited by H. A. Clarke, Professor of Music and director of the Glee Club, this rare publication marked the removal of the University to its new West Philadelphia site and the developing pleasures of the campus and the collegial way of life.

8. In 1926 Provost Josiah Harmer Penniman proposed that the undergraduate male college be named for Benjamin Franklin and other divisions carry the names of illustrious founders or graduates. This was clearly a ruse to keep women in a lesser status as their diploma would carry another name. *Pennsylvanian* 42 (27 February 1926): 1, col. 2

9. Daniel J. Boorstin, *The Americans: The Colonial Experience* (New York: Vintage Books, 1958). "Educating the Community," pp. 171–88 offers an overview of the contrast between the centralized English higher education and the decentralized American "blurring of the distinction between college and university [that] helped break educational monopolies."

10. Boorstin, p. 178.

11. For an account of the changing work environment and its impact on education during the mid-nineteenth century, see Monte A. Calvert, *The Mechanical Engineer in America, 1830–1910* (Baltimore: Johns Hopkins University Press, 1967).

12. For a contemporary architect's comments on early campuses, see Aymar Embury II, "The New University of Colorado Buildings, Boulder, Colo.," *Architectural Forum* 31, 3 (September 1919): 71.

13. The establishment of major athletic conferences such as the Big Ten in 1895, the founding of Penn's Penn Relays in the same year, and the contemporary architectural transformation of many American colleges represented by the construction of major new dormitory groups in the same decade denotes the dispersion of the idea of the modern college campus across the nation at the end of the nineteenth century.

14. Henry Seidel Canby, *American Memoir* (Boston: Houghton Mifflin, 1947) provides a loving account of college experience of the time in "Part Two, Alma Mater," pp. 133–245.

15. Philadelphia: Penn Publishing Company, 1899.

16. Harrison and Fullerton spoke and Day made a brief address, but the principal donor, Henry Houston, was not present for the dedication of the Cecilia Beaux portrait of his son Henry Howard Houston Jr. (C 1878) to whom the building was dedicated. *Pennsylvanian* 12, 62 (3 January 1896): 1, col. 1.

17. Sponsored in 1862 by Senator Justin Morrill of Vermont, the land grant bill provided 30,000 acres of land per congressional representative for each state in the Union for endowing mechanical and agricultural colleges. Thomas H. Johnson, *Oxford Companion to American History* (New York: Oxford University Press, 1966), p. 545.

18. Perkins's career is treated in Ann L. Strong, "The Perkins Years," in Strong and Thomas, pp. 130–51.

19. A brief overview of Meyerson's career is contained in Ann L. Strong, "Martin Meyerson," in Strong and Thomas, pp. 166–67.

20. Philip H. Goepp, "Pennsylvania Songs," *Alumni Register* 1, 4 (December 1896): 14–15. The full title is *Pennsylvania Songs—A Collection of College Songs, Glees, and Choruses, arranged by a committee of graduates and undergraduates* (Philadelphia: Avil Publishing, 1896).

21. Edgar M. Dilley, "How Hail Pennsylvania Came to be Written," *Pennsylvania Gazette* 36, 8 (May 1938): 239.

22. Cornelius Weygandt (C 1891), later a professor of English at the University, made no mention of undergraduate amusements at Penn, remarking only that he went to the University instead of Haverford because he could return home more readily from West Philadelphia to Germantown. *On the Edge of Evening: The Autobiography of a Teacher and Writer Who Holds to the Old Ways* (New York: G.P. Putnam's Sons, 1946), pp. 46–56.

23. For an account of the process of the competition see Warren Powers Laird, "Records of a Consulting Practice" vol. 62 (unpublished typescript, Rare Book Room, Fisher Fine Arts Library, University of Pennsylvania), pp. 1–4.

24. Examples of student accounts at the original campus on Fourth Street include Alexander Graydon, *Memoirs of a Life Chiefly Passed in Pennsylvania* (Harrisburg, Pa.: John Wyeth, 1811), p. 28, quoted in Thomas Harrison Montgomery, *A History of the University of Pennsylvania* (Philadelphia: George W. Jacobs & Co., 1900), p. 124, which describes the hazing of the early Academy students by older boys; Weygandt, *On the Edge of Evening*, provides a detailed account of his early life in Philadelphia, but gives no details on his undergraduate years at Penn. See also H. Mather Lippincott, "Early Undergraduate Life," *General Magazine and Historical Chronicle* 38, 3 (April 1926): 316–19.

25. John Bach McMaster, *The University of Pennsylvania Illustrated* (Philadelphia: J. B. Lippincott, 1897). McMaster's account, "A Short History of the University of Pennsylvania," began "The history of the University begins in 1740 . . ."

26. The question of date rose to prominence in the late 1880s, after Provost Pepper's return from Harvard's celebration of its 250th anniversary. At Pepper's instigation, a Penn graduate student, Francis Newton Thorpe, suggested that Penn was older than 1749, the commonly used date. Newton edited a collection of essays and accounts of the various programs of the University, *Benjamin Franklin and the University of Pennsylvania* (Washington, D.C., Government Printing Office, 1893). It used the 1740 date in several sections, including one written by Judge Pennypacker (pp. 234–35). As is evidenced by the flyer for his publication (UPA), Thorpe at first tried the date 1745, a date independent from the

1743 date when Franklin claimed to have first conceived of the institution. This had the advantage of preceding Princeton's 1746 while retaining Franklin's role as founder. By 1893 when the book was finally published, he had been "convinced" by Judge Pennypacker and John Bach McMaster to use the 1740 date. Penn's vault ahead of Princeton was known to critics as well; when Montgomery Schuyler published his series of articles on "Architecture of American Colleges" he led off with the history of Penn's choice of date. "It is set forth in the 'Official Guide' to the university that Pennsylvania, at least that 'the college' thereof, is 'third oldest in America,' whereas we are taking it as the fifth." Schuyler, "Architecture of American Colleges, V," p. 183. The subject is complicated by the "apples and oranges" nature of the claims for dating of many colleges. Columbia, for example, uses its opening for classes as its date of founding; William and Mary uses 1693, the date of its royal charter.

27. The new date was first used in the 1893–94 *University of Pennsylvania Catalogue*, which was published three years after the putative 150th anniversary. In 1899 Harrison made no mention of the 150th anniversary of the 1749 date.

28. The most widely available discussion of the early buildings is William Turner, "The Charity School, the Academy, and the College," in *Historic Philadelphia from the Founding until the Nearly Nineteenth Century*, ed. Luther Eisenhart, Transactions of the American Philosophical Society 43, part 1 (Philadelphia, American Philosophical Society, 1953), pp. 179–86.

29. Samuel Whitaker Pennypacker, *The Autobiography of a Pennsylvanian* (Philadelphia: John C. Winston Co., 1918), p. 152. Mark Frazier Lloyd points out the "History" files in the General Files section of the Archives, in the early 1890s, when the case for 1740 is put forward. Essentially Thorpe, Pennypacker, and McMaster rely on one another for corroboration of their chosen date. Correspondence in the same files proves Penn's claim to be the first American university.

30. George E. Nitzsche, *University of Pennsylvania Illustrated* (Philadelphia: for the University of Pennsylvania, 1906).

31. Lippincott, H. Mather, ed. *Pennsylvania: A Glimpse of the University: Its history, equipment and advantages with some account of its requirements* (Philadelphia: General Alumni Society, 1914).

32. Ibid.

33. For an account of the class wars see Andrew R. Becker and Michelle Woodson, "Rites of Passage: Student Traditions and Class Fights," *A Pennsylvania Album; Undergraduate Essays on the 250th Anniversary of the University of Pennsylvania*, ed. Richard Slator Dunn and Mark Frazier Lloyd (Philadelphia: University of Pennsylvania, 1990), pp. 31–37. For an earlier summary see Ralph Morgan, "History and Recollections of Class Fights at the University," *General Magazine and Historical Chronicle* 38, 3 (April 1926): 300–306. There are numerous reports in the *Pennsylvanian;* see, for

example, 43, 57 (1 December 1926): 3 reported on a "flour fight" between freshman and sophomores that "was marked by a lack of injuries" there having been only one compound fracture of a student's leg. The *Pennsylvanian* 45, 75 (11 January 1929): 1. col. 1 ran an article entitled "Sophomore Architects Defeat Junior's in Smock Battle." Photographs of the various battles are collected in the Photographs Collection, Box 48, Fights, Smock, University of Pennsylvania Archives

34. Rowbottoms originated shortly after the opening of the dormitories, when the carefree roommate of Joseph Rowbottom (T 1913) would yell outside their window to be let into the locked building. The hullabaloo would awaken other undergraduates, who would throw various objects. Later undergraduates called the name to signal the first outbursts of spring fever.

Chapter 2: First Steps

1. This chapter depends on the numerous histories of the University of Pennsylvania that have been published in the twentieth century. These include Martin Meyerson and Dilys Pegler Winegrad, *Gladly Learn and Gladly Teach: Franklin and His Heirs at the University of Pennsylvania 1740–1976* (Philadelphia: University of Pennsylvania Press, 1978); Edward Potts Cheyney, *History of the University of Pennsylvania, 1740–1940* (Philadelphia: University of Pennsylvania Press, 1940); Thomas Harrison Montgomery, *A History of the University of Pennsylvania from its Foundation to A.D. 1770 . . .* (Philadelphia: George W. Jacobs & Co., 1900). Modern research on many issues can be found in Richard Slator Dunn and Mark Frazier Lloyd, eds., *A Pennsylvania Album: Undergraduate Essays on the 250th Anniversary of the University of Pennsylvania* (Philadelphia: University of Pennsylvania, 1990). I have used Daniel J. Boorstin, *The Americans: The Colonial Experience* (New York: Vintage Books, 1958) and Frederick Rudolph, *The American College and University: A History* (New York: Knopf, 1961) as the background for much of this overview of the relationship of the College of Philadelphia to the developments in American higher education.

2. Pehr Kalm, *Travels in North America*, trans. John R. Forster (London, 1770; reprint New York: Dover, 1987), p. 33.

3. The best early description of the city is in James Mease, M.D., *The Picture of Philadelphia* (Philadelphia: B & T Kite, 1811). Maps and views of the eighteenth-century city have been gathered by Martin Snyder, *City of Independence: Maps and Views of Philadelphia Before 1800* (New York: Praeger Publishers, 1975).

4. Anthony N. B. Garvan, "Proprietary Philadelphia as Artifact," in *The Historian and the City*, ed. Oscar Handlin and John Burchard (Cambridge, Mass.: Harvard University Press, 1963), pp. 177ff.

5. The Religious Society of Friends supported grammar schools but no colleges until the founding of Haverford College in the 1830s. Their educational values are discussed in David Hackett Fischer, *Albion's Seed: Four British Folkways in America* (New York: Oxford University Press, 1989), pp. 536ff. Digby Baltzell in *Philadelphia Gentlemen: The Making of a National Upper Class* (New York: Free Press, 1958), *Puritan Boston and Quaker Philadelphia: Two Protestant Ethics and the Spirit of Class Authority and Leadership* (New York: Free Press, 1979), pp. 140–42, and elsewhere addresses the value placed on education by later Philadelphians.

6. William Penn's views on education are quoted in Fischer, *Albion's Seed*, p. 537.

7. William Penn, *A Letter from William Penn to His Wife and Children* (London, 1761), quoted in Fischer, *Albion's Seed*, p. 537.

8. The truism that Quakers valued facts over hypotheses is developed by Boorstin, p. 307. Similar conclusions were reached by Baltzell, *Puritan Boston and Quaker Philadelphia*, p. 240, and also by Fischer, p. 534.

9. Benjamin Franklin, *Autobiography*, in *Benjamin Franklin's Autobiography*, ed. Larzer Ziff (New York: Holt, Rinehart and Winston, 1959), p. 105.

10. Elwood C. Cubberly, ed., "The First Rules for the Government of Harvard College," quoted in William C. Turner, "The College, Academy, and Charitable School of Philadelphia: The Development of a Colonial Institution of Learning" (Ph.D. dissertation, University of Pennsylvania, 1952), p. 7.

11. For a summary of theocratic colleges, see Rudolph, *The American College and University*, pp. 3–22.

12. The College Board included many who were shortly identified with the new class of Proprietary Gentry, that is, those tied economically, socially, and through kinship to the Penn family. See Stephen Brobeck, "Revolutionary Change in Colonial Philadelphia: The Brief Life of the Proprietary Gentry," *William and Mary Quarterly* 3rd. ser. 33 (1976): 410–34.

13. Gary B. Nash, *The Urban Crucible: The Urban Seaports and the Origins of the American Revolution* (Cambridge, Mass.: Harvard University Press, 1986), and Sam Bass Warner, *Philadelphia: The Private City* (Philadelphia: University of Pennsylvania Press, 1966, rev. ed. 1987) offer complementary images of social class and personal economies in the developing American colonies of the eighteenth century.

14. Among the members of the early board who were involved with local politics were Thomas Lawrence (Mayor), William Allen (Recorder), Joseph Turner, William Plumstead*, and Robert Strettell* (Aldermen), Benjamin Franklin, Thomas Hopkinson, John Inglis, Samuel McCall, Jr., Thomas Bond*, Phineas Bond,* William Shippen, Tench Francis, Thomas Lawrence, and William Coleman* (Common Councilmen). Those whose names are followed by an asterisk also shared the distinction of having been read out of Quaker Meeting. Babcock, p. 420.

15. Franklin in his *Autobiography* gives a remarkable account of Whitefield's voice and his ability to persuade, recounting his own experience of moving back through a crowd to test whether ancient generals could have harangued many thousands of troops, and concluding from Whitefield's power of voice that they could have. As he gradually listened to the sermon, Franklin resolved to give more and more of the coin in his pocket. Franklin, *Autobiography* (New York: Holt, Rinehart and Winston, 1959), pp. 102–3.

16. Franklin remembered that he was placed on the board after its Moravian member had quit. Each of the city's principal churches had been represented on the board, including an Anglican, a Baptist, and a Presbyterian. Each not wishing to have one of the denominations represented by two members, Franklin was selected as nonsectarian. Franklin, *Autobiography*, p. 114.

17. A fragment of a note in Franklin's hand suggests that his first intention was for the Academy to modify and then to rent the building for a period of time. For that scheme two rooms would have been created on each of the two stories on the south end of the building, presumably leaving the remainder of the building for the use of the Whitefield group. *The Papers of Benjamin Franklin*, ed. Leonard Larabee, vol. 3 (New Haven, Conn: Yale University Press, 1965), p. 436.

18. An account of Pierre Eugène Du Simitière can be found in Snyder, *City of Independence*, pp. 84–85.

19. Woolley is discussed by Beatrice Garvan, "Edmund Woolley" in *Philadelphia: Three Centuries of American Art*, ed. Darrell Sewell (Philadelphia: Philadelphia Museum of Art, 1975), p. 40.

20. Sandra L. Tatman and Roger W. Moss, *Biographical Dictionary of Philadelphia Architects, 1700–1930* (Boston: G. K. Hall, 1985), p. 882.

21. For an account of Old Swedes' Church, see Beatrice Garvan, "Gloria Dei, Old Swedes'" Church," in *Philadelphia: Three Centuries of American Art*, ed. Sewell, pp. 11–13.

22. The letter was directed to Jared Eliot and is quoted in Montgomery, pp. 122–23. The board voted £200 for the task, but the work eventually cost nearly three times that amount, nearly doubling the cost of the building and forcing the board to leave the auditorium unfinished until 1755.

23. The form of the building, with its entrance in the center of the side and its large upper level windows, was very much like the mid-eighteenth-century Baptist meeting house in Old Amersham, Buckinghamshire, Great Britain.

24. Tatman and Moss, pp. 741–43.

25. Kalm's description (p. 21) of Christ Church in 1750 is evidence of the value placed on spires, both for signifying location of important urban institutions—churches were the center of record-keeping—and for representing the ambition of their members.

26. Kalm, pp. 23–25. Had he visited a few years later, the skyline would have been more in keeping with that of the Scull and Heap view of the city. A year after the construction of the steeple for the Academy, Robert Smith received the architectural commission to design the splendid, multi-stage tower of Christ Church, which he in turn immediately topped with his design for the spire of the Second Presbyterian Church on Arch Street.

27. James Gibbs's *A Book of Architecture* (London: n.p., 1728) was widely available in the American colonies.

28. The bell's history is summarized in "President Harnwell Recalled the History of the Bell," *University of Pennsylvania Gazette* 61, 3 (December 1962): 17–18. Additional funds were raised by the Hand-in-Hand Company to purchase the bell; when the University moved to Ninth Street, the Union Company demanded the return of its bell; after much conflict, it was retrieved and turned over to St. James Episcopal Church, whose new building had a belfry that could sound the alarm in the northern neighborhoods. It thus did double duty again, for church and fire, until 1869, when it was moved west with the church to its new location at 22nd and Walnut Streets. In the meantime, a new University Bell was cast for the new College Hall in 1872; after the removal of College Hall's towers, it is now in Houston Hall. When St. James Church was demolished in 1945, its members offered the bell to the university. It rang for the dedication of Van Pelt Library, where it is now displayed. A more detailed account is in Turner, diss., pp. 161–68.

29. Montgomery, *A History of the University of Pennsylvania from its Foundation to A.D. 1770* (pp. 123–24).

30. John 8:32, King James version. The sermon was published under the title "A Sermon on Education wherein Some Account is given of the Academy Established in the City of Philadelphia. Preached at the opening thereof on the Seventh Day of January 1750–1 By the Reverend Richard Peters," as noted in Montgomery, pp. 139–40. The quote is noted in Provost William Smith's "Account of the College and Academy," *American Magazine*, October 1758, pp. 630ff, republished in Montgomery, p. 520.

31. Kalm, pp. 25–26 The text was originally published in 1753–61 and was based on a journey that lasted from 5 August 1748 until 1750. Descriptions must have been edited with information from later visits. For instance, the account of the Academy is part of his description of Philadelphia in 1748, but it includes information about the purchase by Franklin's board in 1750.

32. Research by Josh Gottheimer on another source that may have influenced Franklin finds an article by the University Recorder, George E. Nitzsche, "Moravian Towns in Pennsylvania—Exceptional Field for Modern Writers of Fiction," *Pennsylvania-German Magazine* 12, 6 (June 1911): 321ff. Nitzsche suggests (p. 322) that Franklin's school that educated boys and girls with an emphasis on the courses for the modern world might have been derived from Moravian education. See also Daniel Gilbert, "Moravian Colleges

and Universities," in *Religious Higher Education in the United States: A Source Book*, ed. Thomas C. Hunt and James C. Carper (New York: Garland, 1966), p. 174. Gilbert makes the point that Moravian educators had already made the turn toward modern curriculum because the Moravian Church "preached a doctrine of preparing everyone—men and women—over their entire lifetime for any and all vocations to which the Lord had called them." A Moravian girls' academy met in Philadelphia's Germantown in 1742. Franklin's hostility toward Moravians, expressed in his account of his being placed on the board of the Whitefield Academy, might seem to suggest that he was not likely to have imitated Moravian schooling. However, it must be remembered that Franklin's Moravian predecessors had joined the Whitefield charity school project, presumably because it met their general requirements. Certainly, it is fair to say that these new ideas were alive in Pennsylvania because of the tolerance of the Quaker community.

33. Turner, diss., p. 182.

34. Montgomery includes a lengthy biography of William Smith as well as excerpts of his *A General Idea of the College of Mirania* (New York: J. Parker and W. Weyman, 1753).

35. Franklin, *Proposals Relating to the Education of the Youth in Pensilvania* (1749; reprint Philadelphia: University of Pennsylvania Press, 1931), p. 11.

36. Rudolph, p. 12.

37. The overthrow of Franklin and his conflict with Provost Smith has been downplayed in early histories of the University, which have supported Smith and the Anglophile history of the institution. Cheyney in particular advances the Tory/Proprietor cause and is most circumspect about what can only be viewed as Smith's indiscretions, which included slandering Franklin with his claim that Professor Kinnersley had in fact made the discoveries about electricity. There can, however, be no doubt that Franklin knew who was doing the instigating and for what purpose. In a letter to Kinnersley dated 28 July 1759, Franklin reports that changes at the Academy had been "privately preconcerted in a cabal, without my knowledge or participation, and accordingly carried into execution. The scheme of public parties made it seem requisite to lessen my influence wherever it could be lessened. The Trustees had reaped the full advantage of my head, hands, heart and purse in getting through the first difficulties of the design, and when they thought they could do without me they laid me aside." Quoted in *Pennsylvania Magazine of History and Biography* 13 (1889): 247–48 and republished in *The Papers of Benjamin Franklin*, ed. Larabee, vol. 8, p. 416.

38. Turner (diss. p. 18) credits the "main innovations" in curriculum "with Benjamin Franklin and William Smith at the College of Philadelphia, where practical training and the study of English began to be admitted along with the classical courses." See also Rudolph, p. 12.

39. Turner (pp. 171–72) cites Board of Trustees' Minutes for 30 June 1755, which describe the proposed balcony by comparing it to Tennent's church.

40. *Dictionary of American Biography* 17: 335–36; Beatrice Garvan, "Robert Smith," in Sewell, pp. 31–32; Tatman and Moss, pp. 741–43.

41. Albert Frank Gegenheimer, *William Smith, Educator and Churchman, 1727–1803* (Philadelphia: University of Pennsylvania Press, 1943), pp. 95–123.

42. Hopkinson's life is treated in Montgomery, pp. 296–301, and his organ playing is described, p. 297.

43. Montgomery, pp. 346, 349.

44. The beginning class was remarkable, including future cleric Jacob Duché, Francis Hopkinson, John Morgan the future founder of the Medical School, and, for a period of time, artist Benjamin West. W. J. Maxwell, comp., *General Alumni Catalogue of the University of Pennsylvania* (Philadelphia: University of Pennsylvania Alumni Association, 1917).

45. Board of Trustees Minutes, for meeting of 10 March 1761, cited in Montgomery, p. 354.

46. Board of Trustees Minutes, for meeting 28 November 1761, cited in Montgomery, pp. 355–56.

47. Within a year, it was proposed to increase the number of students living in the building to sixty, to remove the girls' portion of the charity school as "unbecoming and indecent," and to add a resident steward. Board of Trustees Minutes for 11 September 1764, cited in Montgomery, pp. 444–45.

48. Student accounts of hazing date to the earliest years and suggest that English battles for entry were common. On p. 124 Montgomery cites Alexander Graydon, *Memoirs of a Life, &c*, p. 28 and quotes his account of his first fight, p. 353.

49. Report of the Committee on Ways and Means for Improving the State of the Academy, 28 November 1761, cited in Montgomery, pp. 355ff. "We therefore most heartily recommend to the Trustees to take this Matter into their immediate and most serious Consideration and to engage some proper person to go over to England with all convenient Expedition." Montgomery, p. 357.

50. That Franklin was aware of the potential consequences of the change toward dominance by the Anglicans is clear from a letter of Smith referring to a report that Franklin had referred to the College as "a narrow, bigoted institution, put into the hands of the Proprietary party as an engine of government" (Montgomery, p. 396). Smith's prejudice against the Quakers and their German allies was prompted or at least exacerbated by his having been thrown into gaol on the grounds that he had caused a letter to be published in the German newspaper. There he spent several

months of the late winter and spring of 1758. Montgomery, pp. 324ff.

51. Montgomery, p. 418, quoting Smith, 11 February 1764.

52. Archbishop Thomas Secker to Reverend Richard Peters, quoted in Montgomery, p. 419.

53. Montgomery, p. 424. George B. Wood, M.D., *Early History of the University of Pennsylvania from its origin to the Years 1827*, 3rd ed. (Philadelphia: J. B. Lippincott, 1896), pp. 76–84 finds a less confrontational meaning in the letter from Archbishop Secker, but also reported that it formed the principal reason for the Revolutionary councils to close the College.

54. As a part of this fundraising, Smith was required by the Anglican benefactors abroad to enact an Act of Catholicity, which required that the current proportions of the board, then largely Church of England, be maintained in perpetuity. The College of Philadelphia had lost most of its Quaker board men when Smith (ordained by the Church of England) was appointed as provost; in the future, it would remain functionally in the control of the church's successors until the appointment of provost Stillé in 1868. As a result, the College lost the benefit of the diversity of the city—and for more than a century it was the captive of a tiny proportion of the city's populace.

55. The provost's house is described and the original contracts are published (pp. 49–51) in H. Mather Lippincott, "The Provosts," *Alumni Register* 38, 1 (October 1925): 44–61.

56. Provost Ewing's career is discussed in Wood, pp. 118–23.

57. Turner, diss., p. 186; see also Edgar Fahs Smith, *The Life of Robert Hare: An American Chemist (1781–1858)* (Philadelphia: J. B. Lippincott, 1917), pp 5–6.

58. Reports to the trustees cited crowding, the need for extensive repairs, and the difficulty of scheduling in the buildings on Fourth Street. Minutes of the Board of Trustees. See Meeting 5 December 1797 (vol. 5, p. 174), on problems with scheduling and the same subject and repairs being made, Meeting 19 June 1797 (vol. 5, p. 169).

59. Dennis C. Kurjack, "Who Designed the President's House?" *Journal of the Society of Architectural Historians* 12 (May 1953): 27–28; Tatman and Moss, pp. 854–56.

60. The house is discussed in Wood, pp. 133–40.

61. Tatman and Moss, p. 854.

62. The same meeting of the Trustees of 10 April 1801 (vol. 5, p. 233) reported on the decision to move the schools to the President's House that had recently been purchased, and the appointment of a "Committee to make Repairs, Alterations and Improvements, Trustees."

63. See Benjamin Henry Latrobe, *The Correspondence and Miscellaneous Papers of Benjamin Henry Latrobe, 1805–10*, ed. John C. Van Horne and Lee W. Formwalt (New Haven, Conn.: Yale University Press for the Maryland Historical Society, 1984–88), 2: p. 82.

64. Latrobe is the subject of a considerable publishing industry; for a brief history see David Orr in Sewell, pp. 187–88; also Talbot Hamlin, *Benjamin Henry Latrobe* (New York: Oxford University Press, 1955), pp. 194–85.

65. The *Report of the Committee Appointed to Provide for the Payment of the President's House* (Philadelphia, Printed for Z. Poulson, 1801), contains Latrobe's report on the building, dated 19 December 1800. He proposed that the ground floor should contain the boys' and girls' rooms for the charity school along with its separate kitchens and rooms for the master and mistress, the office of the resident professor, and the library, which would also contain the apparatus collection. In that room the trustees could meet. Latrobe proposed adding a porch "erected before the door to screen the room from the weather" (p. 8). The main floor would contain the room for the master of the Charity school. Latrobe suggested the "circular room in the center of the building is at present incumbered [sic] by a flight of double stairs, in every respect badly contrived and constructed, and perfectly unnecessary to the purpose of the University. I propose that they be entirely removed. When they are taken down, the railing of the gallery and the entablature must be completed" (where they had not been constructed because of the stair). The English and the Latin schools and the provost's class were to be on the main floor as well, along with the professor's apartment (pp. 8–10).

66. The fate of the original college buildings is discussed in Wood, pp 12–13; see also Thompson Westcott, *The Historic Mansions and Buildings of Philadelphia* (Philadelphia: Porter and Coates, 1877), pp. 169–70.

67. The provost's house alone survived into the twentieth century, much altered; the entire campus is now the site of a hotel.

68. Wood, p. 12 (note).

69. Beasley's tenure is practically ignored in Wood, perhaps because of the rancor with which it was ended in 1828 along with the dismissal of the entire faculty (pp. 123, 169–70). A fair interpretation of the events is given in C. Seymour Thompson, "The Provostship of Dr. Beasley: 1813–1828, Part I," *General Magazine and Historical Chronicle* 33, 1 (October 1930): 79–93. Beasley is quoted p. 81.

70. This demand would continue until 1880, when Provost Pepper was finally granted board membership. For DeLancey, the board agreed that he could sit in when matters pertaining to the college were discussed. DeLancey soon resigned. See Thompson, "The Provostship of Dr. Beasley, 1813–1828, Part II," *General Magazine and Historical Chronicle* 33, 2 (January 1931): 176ff.

71. Hamlin, pp. 194–96.

72. Proposal from William Strickland to the Medical School, 3 May 1817. University of Pennsylvania Archives.

73. Agnes Addison Gilchrist, *William Strickland of Philadelphia: Architect and Engineer, 1788–1855* (Philadelphia: University of Pennsylvania Press, 1950). Strickland in turn taught Thomas Ustick Walter, the architect of the dome and wings of the Capitol. The national practice of these classicists denoted Philadelphia's continuing dominance of the new nation's culture into the 1850s.

74. Gilchrist, p. 80. The chemistry department, headed by Robert Hare (1781–1858), was among the earliest associated with a university and marked Penn's continuing practical turn.

75. Thomas Porter, *Picture of Philadelphia from 1811 to 1831* (Philadelphia: Robert Desilver, 1831), p. 10.

76. Cheyney, p. 229. What he would have said about the developments of the late 1960s can only be imagined!

77. George Davis Budd, "Four Years at the University of Pennsylvania," *General Magazine and Historical Chronicle* 31, 3 (April 1929): 345–96. The description of the buildings is pp. 389–91, It seems likely that the pilasters were in fact taken from the old President's House, though there is always the chance that this is an early student myth. There were enough pilasters (eight) to serve both buildings. Such would provide another example of the thrift of the trustees—and their willingness to be ruled by the past.

78. Charles C. Harrison, "The Class of '62," *Alumni Register* 27, 8 (May 1925): 510–15.

Chapter 3: Industrial Philadelphia

1. For the post-Civil War reform movement in Philadelphia, see George E. Thomas, "Frank Furness's Red City: The Patronage of Reform," in Thomas et al., *Frank Furness: The Complete Works* (New York: Princeton Architectural Press, 1991), pp. 53ff.

2. Charles Janeway Stillé, *Reminiscences of a Provost, 1866–1880* (Philadelphia: privately printed, 1880), p. 7.

3. Stillé provides an overview of his tenure from his own point of view; his career is detailed in the *Dictionary of American Biography.*

4. Stillé developed this theme in *Reminiscences of a Provost.*

5. Stillé, *Reminiscences of a Provost*, p. 19.

6. The story of Stillé's battle with the trustees for control is partly recounted in *Reminiscences of a Provost* and reported by Martin Meyerson and Dilys Pegler Winegrad, *Gladly Learn and Gladly Teach: Franklin and His Heirs at the University of Pennsylvania, 1740–1976* (Philadelphia: University of Pennsylvania Press, 1978), pp. 100–106.

7. Charles J. Stillé to Frederick Fraley, 26 September 1868, University of Pennsylvania Archives.

8. Sidney George Fisher, *A Philadelphia Perspective: The Diary of Sidney George Fisher Covering the Years 1834–1871*, ed. Nicholas Wainwright (Philadelphia: Historical Society of Pennsylvania, 1967), p. 555.

9. Charles Stillé, Provost, "The New University Building," *Penn Monthly* 1 (November 1870): 401–9; the quote is on p. 406.

10. Richards's career is surveyed in George E. Thomas, "Thomas W. Richards," in Ann Strong and George E. Thomas, *The Book of the School: 100 Years* (Philadelphia: Graduate School of Fine Arts, 1991), pp. 1–17.

11. Thomas, "The Richards Years: Mining . . . and other kindred subjects," Strong and Thomas, *The Book of the School*, pp. 7–8.

12. This scheme is eerily like the gift of land that the College trustees negotiated from the Penn family, which the trustees proposed to sell immediately to create an endowment. In the 1860s the University sought a grant of land from the city almshouse property, a portion of which could be sold to create an endowment. The city eventually sold a smaller piece to the University for slightly less than market value, but again it did not provide the bonanza hoped for by the University trustees.

13. Stillé, *Reminiscences of a Provost*, p. 24.

14. Stillé to Richards, 28 February 1870, University of Pennsylvania Archives, Richards collection.

15. Stillé to Richards, 16 July 1870, University of Pennsylvania Archives, Richards collection.

16. Stillé, *Reminiscences of a Provost*, p. 31.

17. Unlike the schools of medicine and law, which relied on untenured faculties who were paid directly by their students, the new dental faculty were salaried like the other appointed professors. This shift was the first step toward bringing the professional schools under the control of the University.

18. Franklin, *Proposals Relating to the Education of Youth in Pensilvania* (1749, reprint Philadelphia: University of Pennsylvania Press, 1931), p. 11.

19. Richard Magee, *Magee's Centennial Guide of Philadelphia* (Philadelphia: n.p., 1876), p. 63. An unidentified site plan shows an early stage with College Hall in its present location but with the Medical School and Hospital arrayed on the north side of Spruce Street, presumably facing south. This plan would have put the Medical School on an equal footing with the hospital, and in the end would have seriously compromised Penn's future. University of Pennsylvania Archives, Iconography files.

20. At the core of the new building was a research laboratory for Pepper and his colleagues. During the Centennial Exhibition, Pepper organized the medical department, again leading him to study evolving medical practice overseas. Pepper and a committee

of University trustees made important contributions toward the reform of American medical education. See Fairman Rogers, chairman, *Report of the Special Committee on the Medical Department of the University of Pennsylvania* (Philadelphia: 1876); see also *Dictionary of American Biography*.

21. The University School of Medicine has been the subject of several histories, the most recent being David Cooper III and Marshall Ledger, *Innovation and Tradition at the University of Pennsylvania School of Medicine* (Philadelphia: University of Pennsylvania Press, 1990); an earlier but still useful history is George W. Corner, *Two Centuries of Medicine: A History of the School of Medicine of the University of Pennsylvania* (Philadelphia: J. B. Lippincott, 1965).

22. Rogers, *Report of the Special Committee*, p. 9.

23. Stillé, *Reminiscences of a Provost*, p. 24.

24. See W. J. Maxwell, *General Alumni Catalogue of the University of Pennsylvania 1917* (Philadelphia: Alumni Association, 1917), which lists alumni by class. In 1871 there were 120 medical graduates and 36 graduates from the College; in 1874, with the new building completed the number of graduates nearly doubled to 62. These numbers are in accord with accounts of the medical school of half a century before, when the college students in attendance were fewer than 100 and the medical school was more than 450. See George B. Wood, *Early History of the University of Pennsylvania from its Origins to the Year 1827* (Philadelphia: J. B. Lippincott, 1896) p. 196, n.

25. The Hare Medical Laboratory was named for Robert Hare, who taught chemistry at the University beginning in 1818 and was widely regarded as one of the leading scientists of the age. See Edgar Fahs Smith, *The Life of Robert Hare: An American Chemist* (Philadelphia: J. B. Lippincott Co., 1917).

26. Welsh, *Letters of John Welsh, Envoy Extraordinary and Minister Plenipotentiary to the Court of St. James*, ed. Edward Lowber Stokes (Philadelphia: Harris and Partridge, 1937), pp. 72–73.

27. "William Pepper Jr., M.D.," *Dictionary of American Biography*.

28. Daniel Boorstin, *The Americans: The Colonial Experience* (New York: Vintage Books, 1959), p. 307.

29. The regional factionalism of American scholarship is apparent in Joseph Leidy's reaction on learning of his election to the National Academy of Sciences, which continued to ignore the contributions of Leidy's fellow faculty member Ferdinand Hayden. According to Leidy, the Academy was "an illiberal clique, based on Plymouth Rock." Quoted in Meyerson and Winegrad, *Gladly Learn and Gladly Teach*, p. 89.

30. The idea of separate work cultures is now well understood. See Monte A. Calvert, *The Mechanical Engineer in America, 1830–1910* (Baltimore: Johns Hopkins University Press, 1967) which provides a broad account of the evolving profession and its approach to education. This useful study was pointed out to me by a Cornell-trained mechanical engineer, Harris Cooperman, my father-in-law and adviser on engineering matters. Furness designed more than 800 commissions in a forty year career. See Thomas et al., *Frank Furness: The Complete Works*.

31. Elizabeth Geffen, *Philadelphia Unitarianism, 1796–1861* (Philadelphia: University of Pennsylvania Press, 1961), p. 149.

32. Wilson Brothers & Co., *A Catalogue of Work Executed* (Philadelphia: J. B. Lippincott, 1885) provides a list of the industrial work of the firm in its first decade.

33. Collins and Autenrieth are the subject of a 1981 Master's Thesis at the University of Delaware by Jane K. Schweizer, "Collins and Autenrieth, Architects in Victorian Philadelphia."

34. Lindy Biggs, *The Rational Factory: Architecture, Technology, and Work in America's Age of Mass Production* (Baltimore: Johns Hopkins University Press, 1996), pp. 48–53.

35. I am indebted for this method of comparing institutions to Dana Royer, whose Urban Studies 272 final paper, "University of Pennsylvania in the 1890s: The Blue-Collar Ivy," developed an important perspective on Penn's standing among its peer institutions with a comparative overview of late nineteenth-century trustees and students.

36. Elizabeth Johns's insightful study *Thomas Eakins: The Heroism of Modern Life* (Princeton, N.J.: Princeton University Press, 1983) finds similar modern qualities in Eakins's choice of subjects and his approach to them.

37. Edward Freedley, *Philadelphia and Its Manufactures* (Philadelphia: Edward Young Co., 1858), p. 328.

38. Francis A. Walker, ed., *United States Centennial Commission, International Exhibition 1876, Reports and Awards* (Washington, D.C.: Government Printing Office, 1880), 6: 236.

39. Walker, *Reports and Awards*, 7: 14.

40. The different goals of Philadelphia manufacturers is analyzed in Philip Scranton, *Endless Novelty: Specialty Production and American Industrialization, 1865–1925* (Princeton, N.J.: Princeton University Press, 1997), p. 33.

41. Joseph Roe in 1915, quoted by L. T. C. Rolt, *Tools for the Job*, quoted in W. H. Mayall, *Machines and Perception in Industrial Design* (London: Studio Vista, 1968), p. 15.

42. See George E. Thomas, "The Flowering of an American Architecture," in Thomas et al., *Frank Furness: The Complete Works*, pp. 13–51.

43. *University Magazine* 8, 15 (20 April 1883): 197–98.

44. James G. Barnwell, William Pepper, Horace Howard Furness, flyer, John Clarke Sims Scrapbook 1 (1883–86): 50, University of Pennsylvania Archives. Noting that one man's "rubbish" was

another man's history, the University requested business records and the day to day materials of business as a way to build a collection that would serve the new business school.

45. Thomas et al. *Frank Furness: The Complete Works*, discusses the Emersonian links to Furness and the meaning of his architecture.

46. Addison Hutton's design for the Ridgway Library of 1878 on South Broad Street memorialized the continuing love affair of the Whig leadership of the city with the Greek revival of half a century earlier. Hutton's building was so functionally catastrophic that such control may have seemed warranted. Within two years it had been supplanted by a new library, by Furness, at 13th and Locust Streets.

47. At the same Board of Trustees meeting, 5 April 1887, the Board acted to direct the Library Committee headed by Horace Howard Furness to research and seek out the best possible plans by competition, and in the next resolution retained Frank Furness as the architect. Trustees' Minutes, vol. 1882–92, p. 304.

48. Ernest Earnest, *Silas Weir Mitchell: Novelist and Physician* (Philadelphia: University of Pennsylvania Press, 1950), p. 113.

49. Melvil Dewey to William Pepper, Jr., M.D., ms. 20 April 1888, University of Pennsylvania Archives, box 21, General Files 1888, folder, Library. Talcott Williams published a preliminary sketch plan in "Plans for the Library of the University of Pennsylvania," *Library Journal* (13 August 1888): 237–43. It shows an inverted variant of the final design intended for the present site of the Wistar Institute. When the Wistar family agreed to fund their anatomical institute, the library was shifted to its present site when Pepper persuaded the city to provide the land along 34th Street.

50. The library was well received as the best and most efficient plan of its day; see Talcott Williams, "New Library of the University of Pennsylvania," *Harper's Weekly* 35, 1794 (14 February 1891): 124.

51. John Shaw Billings, "Opening Exercises of the Institute of Hygiene," 22 February 1892, University of Pennsylvania Archives, General Files, Hygiene.

52. Albert Kelsey, *The Architectural Annual* (Philadelphia: Architectural Annual, 1901), p. 179.

53. Huger Elliot, "Architecture in Philadelphia and a Coming Change," *Architectural Record* 23 (April 1908): 294ff. The reference to Furness is p. 294; Penn's new campus is described positively, pp. 302–7.

54. Albert Bendiner, *Bendiner's Philadelphia* (New York: A. S. Barnes and Co., 1964), pp. 40–41.

55. Charles Franklin Thwing, "William Pepper," in *Friends of Men: Being a Series of Guides, Philosophers, and Friends* (New York: Macmillan, 1933), pp. 368–69.

56. Pepper's contribution is described in Francis Newton Thorpe, *Benjamin Franklin and the University of Pennsylvania* (Washington, D.C.: Government Printing Office, 1893), pp. 195–200.

Chapter 4: The Academic Stage

1. Harrison's memoirs exist in two forms in the University Archives, an earlier version written in the early twentieth century entitled "Autobiography," which includes the account of Furness's personality in the section "Flotsam and Jetsam," and a later version entitled "Memoirs," which includes the account of Frank's brother Horace Howard Furness attacking Harrison for firing Furness when he could look at "a poem in bricks." "Memoirs," p. 40, University of Pennsylvania Archives.

2. Ellis Paxon Oberholtzer, "Charles C. Harrison," steel plate supplement to *Philadelphia, Pictorial and Biographical* (Philadelphia: S. J. Clarke Publishing Co., 1911), pp. 35ff. The text repeats much of the autobiographical sketch of Harrison cited previously and suggests that the details were largely gathered from Harrison.

3. Lincoln Steffens, *Shame of the Cities* (1904, reprint New York: Hill and Wang, 1957), p. 148. A generation later, when William C. Bullitt wrote the roman à clef *It's Not Done* (New York: Harcourt Brace, 1926), Harrison was again attacked for betraying his class by raising funds for the University from Peter Widener and John Wanamaker. Another view along the same line is found in an unidentified newspaper clipping (probably from the *Public Ledger* dated 3/8/11) in the Harrison biographical file, which reported that a Dr. Henry W. Cattell had described the former provost as a "gangster of gangsters" in an article on the February 1911 *Medical Notes and Queries* because of his selection of certain trustees.

4. Cornelius Weygandt, *On the Edge of Evening: The Autobiography of a Teacher and Writer Who Holds to the Old Ways* (New York: G. P. Putnam's Sons, 1946), pp. 55–56.

5. Each of these families was represented in the class of 1891.

6. *Greek Lettermen of Philadelphia* (p. 166) provides an account of Tau Chapter of Psi Upsilon being the first fraternity to acquire a house and, a few years later, to build a new house designed for the purpose.

7. Even if he was from Japan, royalty being royalty, he was admitted into Zeta Psi.

8. W. P. Mayall, comp., *General Alumni Catalogue of the University of Pennsylvania, 1917* (Philadelphia: University of Pennsylvania Alumni Association, 1917), p. 125. See also Marvin P. Lyon, "Blacks at Penn, Then and Now," in *A Pennsylvania Album: Undergraduate Essays on the 250th Anniversary of the University of Pennsylvania*, ed. Richard Slator Dunn and Mark Frazier Lloyd, pp. 43ff. The first modern black graduate, James Brister, graduated in 1881 with a D.D.S.

9. Lyon, "Blacks at Penn," p. 46. The first black sorority on campus was founded in 1913; the first black fraternity followed in 1920.

10. Harrison pulled off the coup of McKinley's presence days after the bombing of the U.S.S. *Maine* in Havana because he had raised $500,000 for McKinley's presidential campaign, an immense sum. In later years, Harrison persuaded Roosevelt and Taft to make similar visits—presumably to repay similar debts. "Autobiography," pp. 26–32.

11. Austin O'Malley, "Catholic Collegiate Education in the United States," *Catholic World* 67 (April 1898): 297.

12. Frederick Winslow Taylor's speech was reprinted in the *Proceedings of the Dedication of the New Building for the Engineering Department, October 19, 1906* (Philadelphia: University of Pennsylvania, 1906), pp. 16–25. His comparison of football to undergraduate education is found on pp. 23–24.

13. *Harper's Weekly*, 24 October 1896, reported in the *Alumni Gazette* 1, 4 (December 1896): 11–13.

14. Ibid., p. 11.

15. The partial list of trustees that follows includes, first, the year and school if they graduated from Penn, with some of their activities, and second, in brackets, the year they were placed on the board. It indicates two key groups, those from the mid-1870s, the first classes to attend the new campus for all of their years, and the mid-1880s, the first classes to have the full range of sports and activities. Charles C. Harrison (C 1862), Zeta Psi, Philomathian [1876]; Wharton Barker (C 1866) [1880]; Morris Lewis (C 1871, Gr. 1874, M 1874) [1896]; Joseph Rosengarten (C 1852, Gr. 1856); Zelosophic [1896]; Randall Morgan (M 1870, Gr. 1872) [(1896]; Samuel Houston (C 1887), Delta Psi, varsity football, [1898]; James Levering Jones (L 1875) [1901]; Robert Le Conte (C 1885, Med. 1888), Delta Psi [1903]; J. Bertram Lippincott (C 1878), Philomathian [1903]; Arthur Lapham Church (C 1878) Delta Psi [1905]; George Harrison Frazier (C 1887) [1906]; John Cadwalader (C 1862), Delta Phi, Philomathian Society [1910]; Charles Borie, Jr. (C 1892), Zeta Psi [1910]; Edward T. Stotesbury [1910]; Effingham B. Morris (C 1875, Law. 1878), Phi Kappa Sigma, College Boat Club [1911]; George Wharton Pepper (C 1887; Law 1889, Hon. 1907), Zeta Psi, valedictorian, varsity football, cricket and track; ed. *Pennsylvanian*, spoonman [1911]; John C. Bell (L 1884) played on 1882–84 football team [1911]; Samuel G. Dixon (M 1886) [1911]; Morris Lewis Clothier [1911]; Richard A. Fullerton Penrose [1911]; William A. Redding (L 1876) [1916]; David Milne (C 1881, Gr. 1884), Philomathian, College Boat Club [1917]; and Hampton Carson (C 1871, L 1874), Philomathian [1917].

16. The revised "Rules and Statutes of the University of Pennsylvania" were published in the Trustees' Minutes, vol. A-20, pp. 398a ff. This lists the new boards of each school.

17. The changing of the board was the subject of numerous articles in the *Gazette* during the fall of 1927. See especially "Trustees Increased to 40 Members," *Gazette* 26, 6 (11 November 1927): 129ff.; "Court Approves Petition to Amend Charter," 26, 11 (6 January 1927): 273.

18. Free Museum of Arts and Sciences, Building Committee minutes, October 1893, General Files, University of Pennsylvania Archives.

19. Ralph Adams Cram, "The Work of Messrs Frank Miles Day and Brother," *Architectural Record* 15, 3 (May 1904): 397.

20. Ibid., p. 398.

21. The *Architectural Record* series began with Julian Millard, "The Work of Wilson Eyre," 14, 4 (October 1903): 280-325, and continued with three articles by Ralph Adams Cram: "A New Influence in the Architecture of Philadelphia—Horace Trumbauer," 15, 2 (February 1904): 93–123; "The Work of Messrs. Frank Miles Day and Brother," 15, 3 (May 1904): 397–421; and "The Work of Cope and Stewardson," 15, 5 (November 1904): 407–38.

22. The water color perspective was in the possession of Thomas Pym Cope, Walter Cope's son, at Lincoln, Massachusetts in 1978.

23. Ralph Adams Cram, "The Work of Cope and Stewardson," *Architectural Record* 15, 5 (November 1904): 413.

24. As an example, see the University Day lecture, 22 February 1922 by Sir Arthur Currie, "The Anglo Saxon Ideals of Washington," *Alumni Register*, 24, 6 (March 1922): 343ff.

25. C. R. Ashbee, "Memoirs," ms. vol. 1 (for November, 1900), pp. 210ff., Victoria and Albert Museum, London. Ashbee also visited Provost Harrison of the University of Pennsylvania, and remarked on the contrast between Swarthmore and Bryn Mawr. He quoted M. Carey Thomas, Bryn Mawr College's dean, as referring to Swarthmore as "the 'Matrimonial Agency,'" and reported that at Bryn Mawr "marriage is discouraged, and indeed the life is made so comfortable, interesting and luxurious, that I can understand girls staying on permanently as many do, under the autocratic rule of Miss. Thomas" (p. 210).

26. Walter Cope, 4 November 1899, "Brief" to the Board of Washington University, explaining the victorious competition submission, original typescript in Washington University Archives. For the history of the Washington University competition see Buford Pickens and Margaretta J. Darnell, *Washington University in St. Louis: Its Design and Architecture* (St. Louis: Washington University, 1978).

27. The Bosworth plan is clearly the result of John R. Freeman's approach, see note 26, but is described by Paul Venable Turner, *Campus: An American Planning Tradition* (Cambridge, Mass.: MIT Press, 1984), p. 196, pl. 203 for its Beaux-Arts trappings. The buildings were of reinforced concrete factory construction with a veneer of limestone and columns to give a conventional appearance.

28. Lindy Biggs, *The Rational Factory: Architecture, Technology, and Work in America's Age of Mass Production* (Baltimore: Johns Hopkins University Press, 1996), pp. 53–54, quotes John R. Freeman, "Planning the New Technology."

29. Charles C. Harrison et al., *University of Pennsylvania: The Dormitory System* (Philadelphia: Edward Stern & Co., 1895), pp. 4–5.

30. Ibid., p. 10.

31. Montgomery Schuyler, "The Architecture of American Colleges," *Architectural Record* 27–30 (1909–12); "V. University of Pennsylvania, Girard, Haverford, Lehigh and Bryn Mawr Colleges," 28 (July–December, 1910): 183ff.

32. Edwin E. Slosson, *Great American Universities* (New York: Macmillan, 1910). Slosson, the editor of the *Independent*, made a 14-week journey to study Harvard, Yale, Columbia, Princeton, Cornell, Chicago, Pennsylvania, Stanford, and Johns Hopkins among the private institutions and Michigan, Minnesota, Wisconsin, California, and Illinois among the state-funded universities. The articles were published between January 1909 and March 1910. Clearly, ranking of institutions is not a new idea.

33. Penn was treated in Slosson, *Great American Universities*, chap. 9, pp. 344–71.

34. The relative expenditures on education and per student are treated in a table on p. ix, which placed Johns Hopkins and Princeton lower in total expenditures, but with far fewer students, while the disparity between tuition and costs per student is in a table on p. x.

35. Much of the research on the early fraternity system that informs this section was undertaken by Josh Gottheimer (C 1997), who was president of the Interfraternity Council during the year 1996 and is a member of Alpha Epsilon Pi. His work has been invaluable in this publication; his belief in the potential for positive value of the fraternity system is evident in the breadth of his efforts on its behalf.

36. Donald Folsom was a member of the fraternity and attended the University in the class of 1907; his partner William M. Stanton graduated with a Bachelor of Architecture in 1914 with a Master's in 1916.

37. George A. Cunney, "A Stroll Out Spruce Street," *General Magazine and Historical Chronicle* 32, 1 (October 1929): 66.

38. Paul P. Cret, Warren P. Laird, Olmsted Brothers, *Report to the Board of Trustees of the University of Pennsylvania Upon the Future Development of Buildings and Grounds and the Conservation of Surrounding Territory* (Philadelphia: privately published, 1913), p. 7.

39. Ibid., pp. 13–14.

40. H. Mather Lippincott, "The Problem of a College in a City," *General Magazine and Historical Chronicle* 28 (July 1926): 437ff. See also Robert E. Spiller, "The Valley Forge Project," *General Magazine and Historical Chronicle* 29 (4 July 1927): 457ff. The latter lists two of the leading colonial revival architects of Penn's era, H. Brognard Okie (C 1897) and G. E. Brumbaugh (Ar 1913), on the committee on the "physical aspects."

41. F. J. Kelley, "Report to the Valley Forge Committee of the Trustees of the University of Pennsylvania December 1 1926," typescript, University of Pennsylvania Archives.

42. *Gazette* 27, 24 (12 April 1929): 556.

43. The Valley Forge project was the subject of Robert Goshorn, "The Valley Forge Project of the University of Pennsylvania," *Tredyffrin Easttown History Club Quarterly* 24, 1 (Jan. 1986): 17–34. A copy is in the University of Pennsylvania Archives, Box 55 UPA 9.4. Martin Meyerson recalls that even during his presidency Valley Forge would be raised as a possibility whenever there was an outbreak of crime in West Philadelphia; comments on draft 4/7/96.

44. Herbert T. Webster, ed., *1850–1950: A Century of Service: Spring Garden Institute* (Philadelphia: Spring Garden Institute, 1950), p. 161.

45. "Tradition Persists, " *Pennsylvanian* 33, 3 (April 1931): 431 reported the presence of Edward Hopkinson III, a descendant of Francis Hopkinson of the first graduating class and a signer of the Declaration of Independence, and George Willing Pepper, son of Benjamin Franklin Pepper, the fourth generation of Peppers who in that lineage included Provost William Pepper, Jr.

46. *Gazette* 27, 10 (14 December 1928): 247.

47. Dr. Althea Hottel, "The Women of Pennsylvania," *Gazette* 55, 6 (February 1957): 8ff. provides an overview of the presence of women students, beginning with "Master Dove's English Grammar for Women."

48. Edward Potts Cheyney, *History of the University of Pennsylvania, 1740–1940* (Philadelphia: University of Pennsylvania Press, 1940), p. 408.

Chapter 5: Toward a Modern University

1. Detlev Bronk, speech at fifteenth anniversary dinner of ENIAC, *Gazette* 60, 2 (November 1961): 23.

2. Nathaniel Burt, *The Perennial Philadelphians: The Anatomy of an American Aristocracy* (Boston: Little Brown and Co. 1963), p. 3.

3. For a lengthier overview of the period with a Penn flavor, see Ann L. Strong and George E. Thomas, *The Book of the School: 100 Years* (Philadelphia: Graduate School of Fine Arts, 1991), pp. 131ff.

4. The design for the new downtown attracted national attention to Philadelphia. However, regional industries continued practices of nearly a century which had led it to international prominence but by 1950 were outdated. In 1946 the computer, the great tool

of the next era of work, was invented in Philadelphia, at the University of Pennsylvania's Moore School of Electrical Engineering, but, because Philadelphia industry continued to prosper with its nineteenth-century practices, its leaders were slow to adapt the computer to their businesses. The consequences for the next half century have been disastrous.

5. Philadelphia Chapter, American Institute of Architects, "Challenge 1950," *A.I.A. Yearbook, 1950* (Philadelphia: American Institute of Architects, 1950).

6. The University concern about the deterioration of its neighborhood is evident in a series of planning documents beginning with the 1960–61 University Development Plan, prepared by the University Planning Office, Taubin Papers, University of Pennsylvania Archives. In the early 1960s, mortgage assistance plans, and University sponsored building projects such as the University Mews at 46th Street brought young faculty into the neighborhood.

7. "[James Bryant] Conant's main interest was in expanding higher education to the point that it would become a new American opportunity structure, to replace the vanished frontier. Every year testing would find the few hundred most promising youths, wherever they might be, and route them to schools like Harvard and Princeton. But this was only the first stage of Conant's plan. What he really wanted was to see the more democratic state universities expand to the point where they would set practically everybody on the path to success and the Ivy league would become nearly irrelevant." Nicholas Lemann, "The Structure of Success in America, " *Atlantic Monthly* 276, 2 (August, 1995): 41ff; "The Great Sorting," *Atlantic Monthly* 276, 3 (September 1995):88.

8. Howard Goodman, "In a War of the Ivies, Penn Recruiters Blitz the World," *Philadelphia Inquirer*, 27 November 1995, p. 1, col. 1.

9. *Pennsylvanian* 42, 131 (29 March 1926): 1. Lemann, "The Structure of Success" (p. 46) makes the case that the exam was primarily intended as a means of forcing the leading private schools to cover certain topics and to adequately prepare their students for higher education, rather than as a means of selection.

10. "Women's Quadrangle to be Built: Wanted $1,000,000," *Gazette* 55, 6 (February 1957): 14.

11. The first unified class reunion occurred in 1951 when the class of 1941 invited the coeds to join them in their tenth reunion. Althea Hottel, "The Women of Pennsylvania," *Gazette* 55, 6 (February 1957): 8.

12. "The Women Wrote it Down," *Gazette* 55, 6 (February 1957): 29–30.

13. According to research assistant Josh Gottheimer, separate women's plaques were placed on the walls of the women's facilities from 1926 until 1961, after which date men and women competed to design one plaque.

14. Unlike the male domination of the eighteenth-century members of the modern Ivy League, Cornell University began as a post-Civil War land-grant institution that accepted women beginning in 1872. Yale and Princeton went coed in 1969, Brown followed in 1971, and Dartmouth accepted women in 1972. Radcliffe and Harvard merged in 1975, while Columbia was only fully opened to women in 1983.

15. The decision of the Sphinx Society to admit women made the *New York Times*, 7 February 1971, p. 47, col. 1. On 17 January 1971, p. 61, col. 2, there was a story about the decision of President Meyerson to open all aspects of the University to women. The College for Women was finally merged into the College of Arts and Sciences in 1975.

16. Mike Huber, former director of Alumni Affairs, recounted in Harold Taubin, "Campus Planning, Prolog," version of 9 August 1988, typescript, p. 8, Taubin papers, University of Pennsylvania Archives.

17. The 1913 Plan has been discussed earlier; the so-called "Bicentennial Plan" was developed in 1940 by Paul Cret but did not excite much interest because of the war. See Sydney Martin, "Architectural Elements of the New Campus," *General Magazine and Historical Chronicle* (Winter 1952): 65.

18. Martin, "Architectural Elements," pp. 65–78.

19. Kenneth K. Stowell, "The Editor's Forum: Collegiate Architecture," *Architectural Forum* 55, 6 (June 1931): 689. Stowell's editorial followed up on his comments earlier in the same issue, "Education's New Demands," pp. 650ff.

20. C. Howard Walker, "Expression and the College Style," *Architectural Forum* 55, 6 (June 1931): 653–55.

21. Frederick Ackerman, "The Planning of Colleges and Universities" *Architectural Forum* 55, 6 (June 1931): 691ff. The same issue illustrates the women's dormitories which Ackerman had designed for Cornell that closely resembled the academic Gothic of Frank Miles Day at Princeton.

22. William Harlan Hale, "Old Castles for New Colleges," *Architectural Forum* 55, 6 (June 1931): 729–31.

23. Martin, "Architectural Elements," p. 67.

24. Officially entitled the *All Wars Memorial to Penn Alumni*, it was the 1951 work of sculptor Charles Rudy. The base and the surrounding plaza were designed by Grant Simon. Installed in December 1952, the memorial was a gift of Walter Annenberg.

25. Stassen is ignored in most recent University publications ranging from Martin Meyerson and Dilys Winegrad, *Gladly Learn and Gladly Teach: Franklin and His Heirs at the University of Pennsylvania, 1740–1976* (Philadelphia: University of Pennsylvania Press, 1976) to *A Pennsylvania Album: Undergraduate Essays on the 250th Anniversary of the University of Pennsylvania*, ed. Richard Slator Dunn and Mark Frazier Lloyd (Philadelphia: University of

Pennsylvania, 1990). In 1962 Nathaniel Burt (p. 554) only noted Stassen's later run as a Republican mayoral candidate against the reform Democrats, ignoring his tenure as University president.

26. Other universities tried the same strategy. In 1948 former General of the Armies Dwight Eisenhower became president of Columbia University. He wrested the GOP nomination from Stassen in 1952.

27. This is not the place for a full reappraisal of Stassen's contribution, but it continues to be downplayed. See James Bessen,"The Modern Urban University," in Dunn and Lloyd, *A Pennsylvania Album*, pp. 53ff. Skipping from Franklin to the 1940s, it gives the honor for Penn's modern development to President Harnwell. Harnwell's roots in the academic community undoubtedly gave him an edge in dealing with his faculty, but it is also clear that Stassen's outsider status enabled him to make many needed changes in the University. Lloyd argues that it was Stassen's continuing highhandedness that drove the faculty to create the Faculty Senate, the basis of its modern independence.

28. James Michener, "The Main Line," *Holiday* (April 1950): 34–57, quote p. 39.

29. The debate of whether to join the Ivy League is recounted in "Controversy," *Gazette* 50, 4 (December 1951): 22. By that fall all the old schools except Cornell had dropped Penn in football because of Penn's perceived overemphasis, recalling the controversy over Penn's success in the 1890s. Undergraduates surveyed agreed that it was more important to maintain Ivy ties. Tellingly, alumni were not surveyed. The following March, the *Gazette* reported that Penn had signed the Ivy League agreement, the net result of which was that athletics were to be controlled by each school's academic authorities and that spring and summer training would be prohibited. In an understatement, Penn's Athletic Director Franny Major noted that "Of course it will require a major adjustment from the coaching point of view." *Gazette* 52, 7 (March 1952): 28. There had been no true Ivy League before this date, the name having been invented by a *New York Herald Tribune* columnist to typecast games played by the old eastern universities. Robert Harron, "How the Ivy League Got Its Name," *Gazette* 60, 5 (February 1962): 26.

30. Interview with G. Holmes Perkins, 3 October 1995. His father had attended Penn (C 1894), but moved to New England where he raised his family.

31. Perkins's early faculty went on to transform American architectural education. Geddes was later dean at Princeton; Giurgola was dean at Columbia. Other early notables included Blanche Lemko Van Ginkel, later dean at the University of Toronto, David Crane, dean at Rice, and William Wheaton, dean at UCLA. See Ann L. Strong, "The Perkins Years," in Strong and Thomas, *The Book of the School*, pp. 147–48.

32. The computer at Penn was the subject of an article on "ENIAC: Fifteenth Anniversary of a Computer," *Gazette* 60, 2 (November 1961): 16ff. The funding issues are discussed in Board of Trustees Minutes, Executive Committee, 14 December 1962, vol. 28, p. 177 and Executive Committee, 19 June 1968, vol. 32, p. 9. The Atomic Energy Commission helped with the Physics Department's purchase of an IBM 360/65 and the United States Department of Health helped the Medical School purchase a PDP-6 computer.

33. David R. Goddard, "Annual Report of the Office of the Provost," *Annual Report of the University, 1963–64* (typescript, University of Pennsylvania Archives) describes the growth of the graduate schools and the new sources of funding, pp. 1–14. Goddard, "Annual Report of the Office of the Provost," *Annual Report of the University, 1964–65*, p. 6 (typescript, University of Pennsylvania Archives), noted that for the first time full-time graduate students outnumbered part-time students. The numbers on University research grants are compiled in "Office of Projects Research and Grants," 2, pp. 615–22, with particular note to Table IV, p. 618.

34. University of Pennsylvania, Faculty Senate resolution, 10 November 1965, "News from the University," *Almanac* 12, 3 (December. 1965): 2

35. The "University Development Plan" was a requirement of city Redevelopment Authority policy; the first was completed in 1960–61; it was revised in 1963 and again in 1966. For a history of University planning during this period, see the Taubin papers, University of Pennsylvania Archives. The 1963 plan proposed a campus building coverage ratio of 50 percent with a floor area ratio of 150 percent (p. 6); it recognized the value of preservation, calling for "harmonious juxtaposition of different architectural eras in the University's development. The architecture of the University is meant to portray continuity over the centuries, to link the past with the future' (p. 7).

36. This type of planning that excluded cars from the campus is based on the earlier work of Penn's planning graduates Frederick Bigger (C 1903) and Henry Wright (C 1901). See George E. Thomas, "Henry Wright" and "Radburn, N.J." in Strong and Thomas, *The Book of the School*, pp. 64–65.

37. University Development Plan, 1963, Taubin Papers, University of Pennsylvania Archives (pp. 6–18) discusses the general goals of the University.

38. Jonathan Barnett, "The New Collegiate Architecture at Yale," *Architectural Record* (April 1962): 125ff. Barnett had been an undergraduate at Yale and then returned as an architecture student. His research turned up William Hale's piece in *Architectural Forum* (see note 22) but stated that by the 1960s, the formal and spatial merits of the Rogers quadrangles were apparent even if the historicism no longer met contemporary taste.

39. Barnett, p. 126.

40. Sources of funding for projects are listed in the University Development Plan, pp. 53ff. For Phase I, GSA funding was to be

sought for Fine Arts (Meyerson), Main Library (Van Pelt), Graduate Library (Dietrich), Medical School (Johnson), Social Sciences Center (McNeil), Veterinary School additions (Rosenthal), and the Sciences classrooms (David Rittenhouse additions). The University General Fund would be used for Annenberg, Biology (Goddard), Law School (Roberts), Museum expansion (Kress Wing), Materials Sciences expansion (LRSM), Nursing (Tri-State Facility), Wharton expansion (Vance), and Parking facilities (3301 Walnut and Museum). Phase II funding including GSA projects for Administration and General Services (Franklin), Gymnasium (Gimbel), Chemistry (1973), Hare Replacement (Williams), Research, general engineering (Moore additions), Social Sciences expansion (McNeil), while the General Fund would handle the Annenberg Center, Squash Courts (Ringe), Dental Addition (Levy), Faculty Club addition and Wharton expansion, and so on. The Trustees Minutes for 19 January 1962, vol. 1961–64, pp. 54–55, stated, "In the past few years, the University has looked to Dean Perkins, Mr. Sydney E. Martin, and Mr. Roy F. Larson for advice on architectural matters. Mr. J. Roy Carroll has been invited on occasion to serve on this group. In view of the fact that the firms of Messrs. Martin, Larson and Carroll have all been assigned architectural projects at the University, it would appear appropriate for the University to revise its arrangements for the next few years. In the future, Dean Perkins will be asked to engage consultants appropriate to the particular matter in question, and the Design Review Committee will cease to function as a standing committee."

41. University Development Plan, 1963, p. 17.

42. Low-rise dormitories had been studied for more than a decade, culminating with a project for handsome vaguely modern clusters each housing 256 students, a number arrived at by scientific study. Framing enclosed courts, they would have carried on the character and scale of the Quad—and by all accounts would have been more successful. They were abandoned because of cost. For plans and perspectives of the proposed low-rise project by Kneedler, Mirick and Zantzinger, see Philadelphia Chapter of the A.I.A., *AIA66 Yearbook* (1966): 28, 29.

43. See University Development Plan, 1963 and note 40 above. Initially, the University planned to build its dormitories from private funds as well, but when the $93,000,000 fund drive of the 1960s fell short, the dormitories of Superblock were also built with public monies.

44. Interview with G. Holmes Perkins, 3 October 1995.

45. Jan C. Rowan, "The Philadelphia School," *Progressive Architecture* 42 (April 1961): 130–63.

46. Wilder Green, "Louis I. Kahn, Architect: Richards Medical Research Building," *Museum of Modern Art Bulletin* 28, 1 (1961).

47. Peter Shepheard et al., *Landscape Development Plan* (Philadelphia: University of Pennsylvania, 1977), p. 29.

48. Robert Venturi's goals for the laboratory can be gauged in *Iconography and Electronics upon a Generic Architecture: A View from the Drafting Room* (Cambridge, Mass.: MIT Press, 1996), pp. 219–26. The preservation controversy the IAST engendered is the subject of "The Preservation Game at Penn: An Emotional Response," pp. 145–48.

49. Much of this story is told in the Harold Taubin papers, University of Pennsylvania Archives. Confirmation was found in a letter to the editor of the *Philadelphia Inquirer* by Sister Mary Ann Craig, "Growing up Near Penn," 12 May 1998, 1, p. 13.

50. Sister Mary Ann Craig, "Growing up Near Penn."

51. Catherine Bauer, "Clients for Housing: The Low-Income Tenant," *Progressive Architecture* (May 1952): 61–64.

52. For a summary of the recent history of the Philadelphia schools, see Jon S. Birger, "Race, Reaction, and Reform: The Three Rs of Philadelphia School Politics, 1965–1971," *Pennsylvania Magazine of History and Biography* 120, 3 (1996): 163–216.

Epilogue

1. Samuel Whitaker Pennypacker, *The Autobiography of a Pennsylvanian* (Philadelphia: John C. Winston Co., 1918), p. 152.

2. This was clear to Thomas Montgomery (p. 112), who ascertained that no teaching had taken place in the Whitefield building and thus discredited the 1740 date. *A History of the University of Pennsylvania, from Its Foundation to A.D. 1770 . . .* (Philadelphia: George W. Jacobs & Co., 1900).

3. Paul Venable Turner, *Campus: An American Planning Tradition* (Cambridge, Mass.: MIT Press, 1984), pp. 17-49.

4. Provost Smith in his Eulogium on Franklin used the 1749 date. Montgomery, *A History of the University of Pennsylvania*, p. 114.

5. Montgomery is clear that the date change first appeared on the 1893–94 catalogue. p. 112.

6. An earlier variant is recounted by David Umansky, "Rise, Fall of a U. of P. Campus Legend," *Philadelphia Inquirer*, 19 August 1970, p. 23.

7. Similar stories abound at other colleges, suggesting that blame can be spread even beyond administrators.

Central Campus

1. Research on College Hall was undertaken by Alexander Berkett as a part of the requirements for Urban Studies 272, fall 1995.

2. Research on Meyerson Hall was undertaken by Amber Cohen as part of the requirement for Urban Studies 272, fall 1995.

3. Research on the Jaffe Building was undertaken by Talia Braude as part of the requirement for Urban Studies 272, fall 1995.

4. Research on Irvine Auditorium was undertaken by Jeffrey Rosenbaum as part of the requirement for Urban Studies 272, fall 1995.

5. Research on Williams Hall was undertaken by Jeremy Zweig as part of the requirement for Urban Studies 272, fall 1995.

6. Research on Logan Hall was undertaken by Elizabeth Beidler as part of the requirement for Urban Studies 272, fall 1995.

7. *The Pennsylvanian* Photo Supplement, Saturday, 24 January 1926.

East Campus

1. Research on Hill Hall was undertaken by Abby Close as part of the requirements for Urban Studies 272, fall 1995.

2. Research on Bennett Hall and women's facilities was undertaken by Jeff Pokras as part of the requirements for Urban Studies 272, fall 1995.

3. Research on Hayden Hall was undertaken by Kathryn McCarthy as part of the requirements for Urban Studies 272, fall 1995.

4. Research on the Towne Building was undertaken by Colin Evans as part of the requirements for Urban Studies 272, fall 1995.

5. Research on the Moore School was undertaken by Jason Rabin as part of the requirements for Urban Studies 272, fall 1995.

6. Research on Hutchinson Gymnasium and the Palestra were undertaken by Kyle Andeer and Amy Malerba as part of the requirements for Urban Studies 272, fall 1995.

7. Research on the J. William White Training House was undertaken by Scott Ford as part of the requirements for Urban Studies 272, fall 1995.

8. Agnes Repplier, *J. William White, M.D.: A Biography* (Boston and New York: Houghton Mifflin Company, 1919).

9. Research on Weightman Hall was undertaken by Alexandra Caccavella as part of the requirements for Urban Studies 272, fall 1995.

10. Research on Franklin Field was undertaken by Adam Barrist as part of the requirements for Urban Studies 272, fall 1995.

11. Research on the Free Museum of Science and Art was undertaken by Sarah Firestone as part of the requirements for Urban Studies 272, fall 1995.

South Campus

1. Research on the Quad was undertaken by Dana Royer as part of the requirements for Urban Studies 272, fall 1995.

2. Research on the Alfred Newton Richards Medical Research Laboratory was undertaken by Corrie Rosen as part of the requirements for Urban Studies 272, fall 1995.

3. Research on the Medical Laboratories was undertaken by Dinakar Shenbagamurthi as part of the requirements for Urban Studies 272, fall 1995.

4. Research on the Maloney Building was undertaken by Jordan Greenbaum as part of the requirements for Urban Studies 272, fall 1995.

5. Research on the Gates Pavilion was undertaken by Yasushi Komatsu as a part of the requirements for Urban Studies 272, fall 1995.

North Campus

1. Research on 3401 Walnut Street was undertaken by Lawren Callahan as part of the requirements for Urban Studies 272, fall 1995.

2. Research on Lewis Hall was undertaken by Adam Hillegers as part of the requirements for Urban Studies 272, fall 1995.

3. Research on Tannenbaum Hall was undertaken by Josh Gottheimer as part of the requirements for Urban Studies 272, fall 1995.

4. Research on English House was undertaken by Lisa Yelen as part of the requirements for Urban Studies 272, fall 1995.

5. Research on Gimbel Gymnasium was undertaken by Michael Huang as part of the requirements for Urban Studies 272, fall 1995.

6. Research on the ICA building was undertaken by Amy Krissman as part of the requirements for Urban Studies 272, fall 1995.

7. Research on the Greenfield Intercultural Center was undertaken by Gloria Lee as part of the requirements for Urban Studies 272, fall 1995.

BIBLIOGRAPHY

General

Ackerman, Frederick. "The Planning of Colleges and Universities." *Architectural Forum* 55 (June 1931): 691ff.

Arnold, Matthew. *Schools and Universities on the Continent.* 1868. Ed. R. H. Super. Ann Arbor: University of Michigan Press, 1964.

Baltzell, E. Digby. *Philadelphia Gentlemen: The Making of a National Upper Class.* New York: Free Press, 1958. Reprint Philadelphia: University of Pennsylvania Press, 1979.

——. *Puritan Boston and Quaker Philadelphia: Two Protestant Ethics and the Spirit of Class Authority and Leadership.* New York: Free Press, 1979.

Barnett, Jonathan. "The New Collegiate Architecture at Yale." Building Types Study 305, "College Buildings." *Architectural Record* 131 (April 1962): 125ff.

Bauer, Catherine. "Clients for Housing: The Low-Income Tenant." *Progressive Architecture* (May 1952): 61–64.

Bendiner, Albert. *Bendiner's Philadelphia.* New York: A. S. Barnes, 1964.

Biggs, Lindy. *The Rational Factory: Architecture, Technology, and Work in America's Age of Mass Production.* Baltimore: Johns Hopkins University Press, 1996.

Birch, William Russell. *The City of Philadelphia . . . as it appeared in the Year 1800.* 1800. Reprint as *Birch's Views of Philadelphia.* Philadelphia: University of Pennsylvania Press, 1983.

Birger, Jon S. "Race, Reaction, and Reform: The Three Rs of Philadelphia School Politics, 1965–1971." *Pennsylvania Magazine of History and Biography* 120, 3 (1996): 163–216.

Boorstin, Daniel J. *The Americans: The Colonial Experience.* New York: Vintage Books, 1958.

Brobeck, Stephen. "Revolutionary Change in Colonial Philadel-

phia: The Brief Life of the Proprietary Gentry." *William and Mary Quarterly* 3rd ser. 33 (1976): 410–34.

Bullitt, William C. *It's Not Done.* New York: Harcourt Brace, 1926.

Burt, Nathaniel. *The Perennial Philadelphians: The Anatomy of an American Aristocracy.* Boston: Little, Brown, 1963. Reprint Philadelphia: University of Pennsylvania Press, 1999.

Calvert, Monte A.. *The Mechanical Engineer in America, 1830–1910.* Baltimore: Johns Hopkins University Press, 1967.

Canby, Henry Seidel. *American Memoir.* Boston: Houghton Mifflin, 1947.

Cram, Ralph Adams. "A New Influence in the Architecture of Philadelphia—Horace Trumbauer." *Architectural Record* 15, 5 (November 1904): 407–38.

——. "The Work of Cope and Stewardson." *Architectural Record* 15, 5 (November 1904): 407–38.

——. "The Work of Messrs. Frank Miles Day and Brother." *Architectural Record* 15, 3 (May 1904): 397ff.

Earnest, Ernest Penney. *S. Weir Mitchell: Novelist and Physician.* Philadelphia: University of Pennsylvania Press, 1950.

Edgell, George. *The American Architecture of To-day.* New York: Charles Scribner's Sons, 1928.

Elliot, Huger. "Architecture in Philadelphia." *Architectural Record* 23 (April 1908): 294ff.

Embury, Aymar II. "The New University of Colorado Buildings, Boulder, Colo." *Architectural Forum* 31, 3 (September 1919): 71.

Fischer, David Hackett. *Albion's Seed: Four British Folkways in America.* New York: Oxford University Press, 1989.

Fisher, Sydney George. *A Philadelphia Perspective: The Diary of Sydney George Fisher Covering the Years 1834–1871.* Ed. Nicholas Wainwright. Philadelphia: Historical Society of Pennsylvania, 1967.

Franklin, Benjamin. *Autobiography.* Reprint in *Benjamin Franklin's Autobiography,* ed. Larzer Ziff. New York: Holt, Rinehart, and Winston, 1959.

Fisher Fine Arts Library after restoration, main reading room, 1990. Photo: Matt Wargo. Courtesy Venturi, Scott Brown and Associates, Architects.

—. *The Papers of Benjamin Franklin*. 33 vols. Ed. Leonard W. Larabee. New Haven, Conn.: Yale University Press, 1959–97.

Freedley, Edwin T. *Philadelphia and Its Manufactures: A Hand-book Exhibiting* . . . . Philadelphia: Edward Young Co., 1858.

Fries, Sylvia Doughty. *The Urban Idea in Colonial America*. Philadelphia: Temple University Press, 1977.

Furness, Horace Howard. *F. R. [Fairman Rogers], 1833–1900*. Philadelphia: privately printed, 1903.

Garvan, Anthony N. B. "Proprietary Philadelphia as Artifact." In *The Historian and the City*, ed. Oscar Handlin and John Burchard. Cambridge, Mass.: Harvard University Press, 1963. 177ff.

Garvan, Beatrice. "Benjamin Henry Latrobe." In *Philadelphia: Three Centuries of American Art*, ed. Darrell Sewell. Philadelphia: Philadelphia Museum of Art, 1976.

—. "Edmund Woolley." In *Philadelphia: Three Centuries of American Art*, ed. Darrell Sewell. Philadelphia: Philadelphia Museum of Art, 1976.

—. "Gloria Dei, Old Swedes' Church." In *Philadelphia: Three Centuries of American Art*, ed. Darrell Sewell. Philadelphia: Philadelphia Museum of Art, 1976.

—. "Robert Smith." In *Philadelphia: Three Centuries of American Art*, ed. Darrell Sewell. Philadelphia: Philadelphia Museum of Art, 1976.

Geffen, Elizabeth. *Philadelphia Unitarianism, 1796–1861*. Philadelphia: University of Pennsylvania Press, 1961.

Gibbs, James. *A Book of Architecture, Containing Designs of Buildings and Ornaments*. London: n.p., 1728.

Gilbert, Daniel. "Moravian Colleges and Universities." In *Religious Higher Education in the United States: A Source Book*, ed. Thomas C. Hunt and James C. Carper. New York: Garland, 1966.

Gilchrist, Agnes Addison. *William Strickland, Architect and Engineer, 1788–1854*. Philadelphia: University of Pennsylvania Press, 1950. Reprint New York: Da Capo Press, 1969.

Hale, William Harlan. "Old Castles for New Colleges." *Architectural Forum* 55 (June 1931).

Hamlin, Talbot. *Benjamin Henry Latrobe*. New York: Oxford University Press, 1955.

Hegemann, Werner and Elbert Peets. *The American Vitruvious: An Architects' Handbook of Civic Art*. New York: Architectural Book Publishing Co., 1922.

Johns, Elizabeth. *Thomas Eakins: The Heroism of Modern Life*. Princeton, N.J.: Princeton University Press, 1983.

Johnson, Thomas H. *The Oxford Companion to American History*. New York: Oxford University Press, 1966.

Kalm, Pehr. *Peter Kalm's Travels in North America*. Trans. John Reinhold Forster. London: T. Lowndes, 1770. Reprint New York: Dover, 1987.

Kelsey, Albert. *The Architectural Annual*. Vol. 1. Philadelphia: Architectural Annual, 1901.

Klauder, Charles Z. and Herbert C. Wise. *College Architecture in America and Its Part in the Development of the Campus*. New York: Charles Scribner's Sons, 1929.

Kurjack, Dennis C. "Who Designed the President's House?" *Journal of the Society of Architectural Historians* 12 (May 1953): 27–28.

Latrobe, Benjamin Henry. *The Correspondence and Miscellaneous Papers of Benjamin Henry Latrobe*. 3 vols. Ed. John C. Van Horne and Lee W. Formwalt. New Haven, Conn.: Yale University Press for the Maryland Historical Society, 1984–88.

Lemann, Nicholas. "The Great Sorting." *Atlantic Monthly* 276, 3 (September 1995): 88ff.

—. "The Structure of Success in America." *Atlantic Monthly* 276, 2 (August 1995): 41ff.

Magee, Richard. *Magee's Centennial Guide of Philadelphia*. Philadelphia: n.p., 1876.

Mayhall, W. H. *Machines and Perception in Industrial Design*. London: Studio Vista, 1968.

Mease, James. *The Picture of Philadelphia . . . as it is in 1811*. Philadelphia: B & T. Kite, 1811. Reprint New York: Arno Press, 1970.

Michener, James. "The Main Line." *Holiday* (April 1950): 34–57.

Millard, Julian. "The Work of Wilson Eyre," *Architectural Record* 14, 4 (October 1903): 280–325.

Nash, Gary B. *The Urban Crucible: The Northern Seaports and the Origins of the American Revolution*. Cambridge, Mass.: Harvard University Press, 1986.

Nitzsche, George E. "Moravian Towns in Pennsylvania—Exceptional Field for Modern Writers of Fiction." *Pennsylvania-German Magazine* 12, 6 (June 1911): 321ff.

O'Gorman, James F. *The Architecture of Frank Furness*. Philadelphia: Philadelphia Museum of Art, 1973.

O'Gorman, James F., Jeffrey A. Cohen, George E. Thomas, and G. Holmes Perkins. *Drawing Toward Building: Philadelphia Architectural Graphics 1734–1986*. Philadelphia: University of Pennsylvania Press, 1986.

O'Malley, Austin. "Catholic Collegiate Education in the United States." *Catholic World* 67 (April 1898): 297.

Penn, William. *A Letter from William Penn to His Wife and Children.* London, 1761. Reprint Frankford, Pa.: Joseph Sharpless, 1812.

Pennypacker, Samuel Whitaker. *The Autobiography of a Pennsylvanian.* Philadelphia: John C. Winston Co., 1918.

Pepper, William. *Higher Medical Education, the True Interest of the Public and of the Profession.* Philadelphia: J. B. Lippincott, 1894.

Philadelphia Chapter, American Institute of Architects. "Challenge 1950." *A.I.A. Yearbook* (1950).

—. "Kneedler, Mirick and Zantzinger." *AIA66 Yearbook* (1966): 28, 29.

Pickens, Buford and Margaretta J. Darnell. *Washington University in St. Louis: Its Design and Architecture.* St. Louis: Washington University, 1978.

Porter, Thomas. *Picture of Philadelphia from 1811 to 1831.* Philadelphia: Robert Desilver, 1831.

Pugin, A. W. N. *Contrasts.* 2nd ed. London, 1841. Reprint New York: Humanities Press, 1969.

Repplier, Agnes. *J. William White, M.D.: A Biography.* Boston and New York: Houghton Mifflin, 1919.

Rowan, Jan C. "The Philadelphia School." *Progressive Architecture* 42 (April 1961): 130–63.

Rudolph, Frederick. *The American College and University: A History.* New York: Knopf, 1962.

Scharf, J. Thomas and Thompson Westcott. *History of Philadelphia, 1609–1884.* 3 vols. Philadelphia: L. H. Everts, 1884.

Schuyler, Montgomery. "The Architecture of American Colleges." *Architectural Record* 27–30 (1909–12).

Schweizer, Jane K. "Collins and Autenrieth, Architects in Victorian Philadelphia." Master's thesis, University of Delaware, 1981.

Scranton, Philip. *Endless Novelty: Specialty Production and American Industrialization, 1865–1925.* Princeton, N.J.: Princeton University Press, 1997.

Sewell, Darrell, ed. *Philadelphia: Three Centuries of American Art.* Philadelphia: Philadelphia Museum of Art, 1976.

Slosson, Edwin E. *Great American Universities.* New York: Macmillan, 1910.

Snyder, Martin P. *City of Independence: Maps and Views of Philadelphia Before 1800.* New York: Praeger, 1975.

Steffens, Lincoln. *The Shame of the Cities.* 1904. Reprint New York: Hill and Wang, 1957.

Stowell, Kenneth K. "The Editor's Forum." *Architectural Forum* 55 (June 1931): 689.

—. "Education's New Demands." *Architectural Forum* 55 (June 1931): 650ff.

Tatman, Sandra L. and Roger W. Moss. *Biographical Dictionary of Philadelphia Architects, 1700–1930.* Boston: G. K. Hall, 1985.

Thomas, George E. "The Flowering of an American Architecture." In *Frank Furness: The Complete Works,* ed. Thomas, Michael J. Lewis, and Jeffrey A. Cohen. New York: Princeton Architectural Press, 1991. Rev. ed. 1996. 13–51.

Thomas, George E., Michael J. Lewis, and Jeffrey A. Cohen. *Frank Furness: The Complete Works.* New York: Princeton Architectural Press, 1991. Rev. ed. 1996.

Turner, Paul Venable. *Campus: An American Planning Tradition.* Cambridge, Mass.: MIT Press, 1984.

Venturi, Robert. *Complexity and Contradiction in Architecture.* New York: Museum of Modern Art, 1966.

—. *Iconography and Electronics Upon a Generic Architecture: A View from the Drafting Room.* Cambridge, Mass.: MIT Press. 1996

Venturi, Robert, Denise Scott Brown, and Steven Izenour. *Learning from Las Vegas: The Forgotten Symbolism of Architectural Form.* Cambridge, Mass.: MIT Press, 1972.

Von Moos, Stanislaus. *Venturi, Rauch & Scott Brown: Buildings and Projects.* Trans. David Antal. New York, Rizzoli, 1987.

Walker, C. Howard. "Expression and the College Style." *Architectural Forum* 55 (June 1931): 653ff.

Walker, Francis A., ed. *United States Centennial Commission, International Exhibition 1876.* Vols. 5–10, *Reports and Awards.* Washington, D.C.: Government Printing Office, 1880.

Warner, Sam Bass. *The Private City: Philadelphia in Three Periods of Its Growth.* Philadelphia: University of Pennsylvania Press, 1966. Rev. ed. 1987.

Webster, Herbert T., ed. *1850–1950: A Century of Service: Spring Garden Institute.* Philadelphia: Spring Garden Institute.

Weigley, Russell F., ed. *Philadelphia: A 300-Year History.* New York, W. W. Norton, 1982.

Welsh, John. *Letters of John Welsh, Envoy Extraordinary and Minister Plenipotentiary to the Court of St. James.* Ed. Edward Lowber Stokes. Philadelphia: Harris and Partridge, 1937.

Westcott, Thompson. *The Historic Mansions and Buildings of Philadelphia.* Philadelphia: Porter and Coates, 1877.

Weygandt, Cornelius. *On the Edge of Evening: The Autobiography of a Teacher and Writer Who Holds to the Old Ways.* New York: G. P. Putnam's Sons, 1946.

Wilson Brothers & Co. *A Catalogue of Work Executed.* Philadelphia: J. B. Lippincott, 1885.

University of Pennsylvania-Related

Becker, Andrew R. and Michelle Woodson. "Rites of Passage: Student Traditions and Class Fights." In *A Pennsylvania Album: Undergraduate Essays on the 250th Anniversary of the University of Pennsylvania*, ed. Richard Slator Dunn and Mark Frazier Lloyd. Philadelphia: University of Pennsylvania, 1990. 31–37.

Bessen, James. "The Modern Urban University." In *A Pennsylvania Album: Undergraduate Essays on the 250th Anniversary of the University of Pennsylvania*, ed. Richard Slator Dunn and Mark Frazier Lloyd. Philadelphia: University of Pennsylvania, 1990. 53ff.

Billings, John Shaw, M.D. "Opening Exercises of the Institute of Hygiene, 22 February 1892." University of Pennsylvania Archives, General Files, Hygiene.

Bronk, Detlev. Speech "ENIAC Fifteenth Anniversary of a Computer." Fifteenth Anniversary Dinner of ENIAC. *Gazette* 60, 2 (November 1961): 23.

Budd, George Davis. "Four Years at the University of Pennsylvania." *General Magazine and Historical Chronicle* 31, 3 (April 1929): 345–96.

Cheyney, Edward Potts. *History of the University of Pennsylvania, 1740–1940.* Philadelphia: University of Pennsylvania Press, 1940.

Clarke, H. A., ed. *Songs of the University of Pennsylvania.* Philadelphia: Glee Club, 1879.

Cooper, David Y. III and Marshall A. Ledger. *Innovation and Tradition at the University of Pennsylvania School of Medicine: An Anecdotal Journey.* Philadelphia: University of Pennsylvania Press, 1990.

Corner, George W. *Two Centuries of Medicine: A History of the School of Medicine, University of Pennsylvania.* Philadelphia: J. B. Lippincott, 1965.

Craig, Sister Mary Ann. "Growing up Near Penn." Letter to *Philadelphia Inquirer*, 12 May 1998, 1, p. 13.

Cunney, George A. "A Stroll Out Spruce Street." *General Magazine and Historical Chronicle* 32, 1 (October 1929): 66.

Currie, Sir Arthur. "The Anglo Saxon Ideals of Washington." *Alumni Register* 24, 6 (March 1922): 343ff.

Dilley, Edgar M. "How Hail Pennsylvania Came to be Written." *Pennsylvania Gazette* 36, 8 (May 1938): 239.

Dowlin, Cornell M. *The University of Pennsylvania of Today, Its Buildings, Departments & Work.* Philadelphia: University of Pennsylvania Press, 1940.

Dunn, Richard Slator and Mark Frazier Lloyd, eds. *A Pennsylvania Album: Undergraduate Essays on the 250th Anniversary of the University of Pennsylvania.* Philadelphia: University of Pennsylvania, 1990.

Franklin, Benjamin. *Proposals Relating to the Education of Youth in Pensilvania.* 1749. Reprint Philadelphia: University of Pennsylvania Press, 1931.

Gegenheimer, Albert Frank. *William Smith, Educator and Churchman, 1727–1803.* Philadelphia: University of Pennsylvania Press, 1943.

Goddard, David. "Annual Report of the Office of the Provost." *Annual Report of the University, 1963–64.* Typescript, University of Pennsylvania Archives.

——. "Annual Report of the Office of the Provost." *Annual Report of the University, 1964–65.* Typescript, University of Pennsylvania Archives.

Goodman, Howard. "In a War of the Ivies, Penn Recruiters Blitz the World." *Philadelphia Inquirer*, 27 November 1995, p. 1, col. 1.

Goshorn, Robert. "The Valley Forge Project of the University of Pennsylvania." *Tredyffrin Easttown History Club Quarterly* 24, 1 (January 1986): 17–34.

Graydon, Alexander. *Memoirs of a Life, Chiefly Passed in Pennsylvania . . .* Harrisburg, Pa.: John Wyeth, 1811.

Harrison, Charles Custis. "Autobiography." Papers, 1854–1943. University of Pennsylvania Archives.

——. "The Class of '62." *General Magazine and Historical Chronicle* (1927–28): 341.

——. "Memoirs." Papers, 1854–1943. University of Pennsylvania Archives.

Harrison, Charles Custis et al. *University of Pennsylvania: The Dormitory System.* Philadelphia: Edward Stern & Co., 1895.

Harron, Robert. "How the Ivy League Got Its Name." *Gazette* 60, 5 (February 1962): 26.

Hottel, Althea. "The Women of Pennsylvania." *Gazette* 55, 6 (February 1957): 8ff.

Kelley, F. J. "Report to the Valley Forge Committee of the Trustees of the University of Pennsylvania December 1 1926." Typescript, University of Pennsylvania Archives.

Laird, Warren Powers. "Records of a Consulting Practice." Typescript. Rare Book Room, Fisher Fine Arts Library, University of Pennsylvania.

Lippincott, Horace Mather. "Early Undergraduate Life," *General Magazine and Historical Chronicle* 38, 3 (April 1926): 316–19.

——. "The Problem of a College in a City." *General Magazine and Historical Chronicle* 28 (July 1926): 437ff.

——. "The Provosts." *Alumni Register* 38, 1 (October 1925): 44–61.

—, ed. *Pennsylvania: A Glimpse of the University: Its History, Equipment, and Advantages with Some Account of Its Requirements.* Philadelphia: General Alumni Society, 1914.

Lyon, Marvin P., Jr. "Blacks at Penn, Then and Now." In *A Pennsylvania Album: Undergraduate Essays on the 250th Anniversary of the University of Pennsylvania*, ed. Richard Slator Dunn and Mark Frazier Lloyd. Philadelphia: University of Pennsylvania, 1990. 43ff.

Martin, Sydney. "Architectural Elements of the New Campus." *General Magazine and Historical Chronicle* 20 (Winter 1952): 65.

Maxwell, W. J. *General Alumni Catalogue of the University of Pennsylvania, 1917.* Philadelphia: University of Pennsylvania Alumni Association, 1917.

McMaster, John Bach. *The University of Pennsylvania Illustrated.* Philadelphia: J. B. Lippincott, 1897.

Meyerson, Martin and Dilys Pegler Winegrad. *Gladly Learn and Gladly Teach: Franklin and His Heirs at the University of Pennsylvania, 1740–1976.* Philadelphia: University of Pennsylvania Press, 1978.

Montgomery, Thomas Harrison. *A History of the University of Pennsylvania, from Its Foundation to A.D. 1770 . . . .* Philadelphia: George W. Jacobs & Co., 1900.

Morgan, Ralph. "History and Recollections of Class Fights at the University." *General Magazine and Historical Chronicle* 38, 3 (April 1926): 300–306.

Nitzsche, George E. *University of Pennsylvania Illustrated.* Philadelphia: For the University of Pennsylvania, 1906.

Oberholtzer, Ellis Paxon. "Charles C. Harrison." *Philadelphia Pictorial and Biographical Steel Plate Supplement.* Philadelphia: S. J. Clarke Publishing Co., 1911.

Pennsylvania Songs: A Collection of College Songs, Glees, and Choruses Generally in Use Among Students and Alumni. Arranged by a committee of graduates and undergraduates. Philadelphia: Avil Printing Company, 1896.

Pennypacker, Samuel Whitaker. *The Origin of the University of Pennsylvania in 1740.* Philadelphia: Press of Edward Stern, 1899.

Peters, Richard. "A Sermon on education. Wherein some account is given of the Academy, established in the city of Philadelphia. Preach'd at the opening thereof on the seventh day of January 1750–1. By the Reverend Mr. Richard Peters." Philadelphia: B. Franklin and D. Hall, 1751.

Quinn, Arthur Hobson. *Pennsylvania Stories.* Philadelphia: Penn Publishing Company, 1899.

Report of the Committee Appointed to Provide for the Payment of the President's House, &c. Philadelphia: Printed for Z. Poulson, 1801.

Royer, Dana. "The University of Pennsylvania in the 1890s: The Blue-Collar Ivy." Paper, Urban Studies 272, University of Pennsylvania, 1975.

Salsburg, David. "The True Story Behind Irvine Auditorium." *Daily Pennsylvanian*, 27 February 1950.

Schuyler, Montgomery. "The Architecture of American Colleges V. University of Pennsylvania, Girard, Haverford, Lehigh, and Bryn Mawr Colleges." *Architectural Record* 28 (July–December 1910): 183ff.

Smith, Edgar Fahs. *The Life of Robert Hare: An American Chemist (1781–1858).* Philadelphia: J. B. Lippincott, 1917.

Smith, William. "Account of the College and Academy." *American Magazine*, October 1758.

—. *A General Idea of the College of Mirania . . . .* New York: J. Parker and W. Weyman, 1753.

Spiller, Robert E. "The Valley Forge Project." *General Magazine and Historical Chronicle* 29, 4 (July 1927): 457ff.

Stillé, Charles Janeway. "The New University Building." *Penn Monthly* 1870.

—. *Reminiscences of a Provost, 1866–1880.* Philadelphia: privately printed, 1880.

Strong, Ann and George E. Thomas. *The Book of the School: 100 Years.* Philadelphia: Graduate School of Fine Arts, 1991.

—. "The Perkins Years." In Ann Strong and George E. Thomas, *The Book of the School: 100 Years.* Philadelphia: Graduate School of Fine Arts, 1991.

Taubin, Harold. "Campus Planning, Prolog." 9 August 1988, typescript, p. 8. Taubin papers, UPA.

Taylor, Frederick Winslow. Address. *Proceedings of the Dedication of the New Building for the Engineering Department, October 19, 1906.* Philadelphia: University of Pennsylvania, 1906. 16–25.

Thomas, George E. "Henry Wright." In Ann Strong and George E. Thomas, *The Book of the School: 100 Years.* Philadelphia: Graduate School of Fine Arts, 1991. 1–17.

—. "Houston Hall." In Ann Strong and George E. Thomas, *The Book of the School: 100 Years.* Philadelphia: Graduate School of Fine Arts, 1991. 52–53.

—. "The Poetry of the Present." In Edward R. Bosley, *University of Pennsylvania Library: Frank Furness.* London: Phaidon Press, 1996. 4–5.

—. "Radburn, N. J." In Ann Strong and George E. Thomas, *The Book of the School: 100 Years.* Philadelphia: Graduate School of Fine Arts, 1991. 1–17.

—. "The Richards Years—Money and Other Relative Subjects." In Ann Strong and George E. Thomas, *The Book of the School: 100 Years*. Philadelphia: Graduate School of Fine Arts, 1991.

—. "Thomas W. Richards." In Ann Strong and George E. Thomas, *The Book of the School: 100 Years*. Philadelphia: Graduate School of Fine Arts, 1991. 1–17.

—. "William C. Hays." In Ann Strong and George E. Thomas, *The Book of the School: 100 Years*. Philadelphia: Graduate School of Fine Arts, 1991. 52–53.

Thompson, C. Seymour. "The Provostship of Dr. Beasley: 1813–1828." Part I. *General Magazine and Historical Chronicle* 33, 1 (October 1930): 79–93; Part II, 33, 2 (January 1931): 176ff.

Thorpe, Francis Newton. *Benjamin Franklin and the University of Pennsylvania*. Washington D.C.: Government Printing Office, 1893.

Thwing, Charles Franklin. "William Pepper." In *Friends of Men: Being a Second Series of Guides, Philosophers and Friends*. New York: Macmillan, 1933. 368–69.

"Tradition Persists." *Pennsylvanian* 33, 3 (April 1931): 431.

"Trustees Increased to 40 Members." *Gazette* 26, 6 (11 November 1927).

Turner, William C. "The College, Academy, and Charitable School of Philadelphia: The Development of a Colonial Institution of Learning." Ph.D. dissertation, University of Pennsylvania, 1952.

-----. "The Charity School, the Academy, and the College," In *Historic Philadelphia from the Founding Until the Nearly Nineteenth Century*, ed. Luther Eisenhart. Transactions of the American Philosophical Society 43, part 1. Philadelphia: American Philosophical Society, 1953. 179–86.

Umansky, David. "Rise, Fall of a U. of P. Campus Legend." *Philadelphia Inquirer*, 19 August 1970, p. 23.

Williams, Talcott. "Plans for the Library of the University of Pennsylvania." *Library Journal* (13 August 1888): 237–43.

—. "New Library of the University of Pennsylvania." *Harper's Weekly*, 14 February 1891.

"Women's Quadrangle to be Built: Wanted $1,000,000." *Gazette* 55, 6 (February 1957): 8.

"The Women Wrote It Down." *Gazette* 55, 6 (February 1957): 29–30.

Wood, George B. *Early History of the University of Pennsylvania, from Its Origin to the Year 1827*. 3rd ed. Philadelphia: J. B. Lippincott, 1896.

University of Pennsylvania Master Plans

Adelman, Collins, and Dutot. "Open Space and Beautification Program, University City, Philadelphia." 1966. Typescript, Taubin Papers, University of Pennsylvania Archives.

Architects' Committee. *University of Pennsylvania Campus Master Plan*, 1948.

Center for Environmental Design and Planning. "A Master Plan for the Campus." *Almanac* supplement, 17 May 1988.

Cret, Paul P., Warren P. Laird, Olmsted Brothers. *Report to the Board of Trustees of the University of Pennsylvania Upon the Future Development of Buildings and Grounds and the Conservation of Surrounding Territory*. Philadelphia: Privately published, 1913.

Davis and Brody. University of Pennsylvania Master Plan. 1979

Philadelphia City Planning Office. "University City Core Plan." 1966.

Shepheard, Peter et al. *Landscape Development Plan*. Philadelphia: University of Pennsylvania, 1977.

University of Pennsylvania. Bicentennial Plan. 1940

University of Pennsylvania Planning Office. "University of Pennsylvania Development Plan." 1961, 1963, 1966.

INDEX

General Index

Numbers in **boldface** indicate primary descriptions.

Modern Physics

FOURTH EDITION

Paul A. Tipler

Formerly of Oakland University

Ralph A. Llewellyn

University of Central Florida

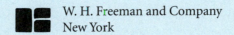

W. H. Freeman and Company
New York

Publisher:	*Susan Finnemore Brennan*
Project Editor:	*Mary Louise Byrd*
Cover Designer:	*Vicki Tomaselli*
Text Designer:	*Nancy Singer*
Illustration Coordinator:	*Bill Page*
Illustrations:	*Burmar Technical Corporation*
Photo Editor PM:	*Nicole Villamora*
Production Coordinator:	*Paul W. Rohloff*
Media and Supplements Editor:	*Brian Donnellan*
Editorial Assistant:	*Eileen McGinnis*
Marketing Manager:	*Mark Santee*
Composition:	*Progressive Information Technologies*
Manufacturing:	*Quebecor World Printing*

Library of Congress Cataloging-in-Publication Data

Tipler, Paul Allen, 1933–
   Modern physics / Paul A. Tipler, Ralph A. Llewellyn—4th ed.
     p.   cm.
   Includes bibliographical references and index.
   ISBN 0–7167–4345–0 (EAN: 9780716743453)
     1.Physics.   I. Llewellyn, Ralph A.   II. Title

QC21.3 .T56 2002   2002072054
530—dc21   CIP

Printed in the United States of America

Fourth printing

W. H. Freeman and Company
41 Madison Avenue, New York, NY 10010

About the cover: The head-on collision of two bare gold nuclei, each traveling at 99.99 percent of the speed of light, produces thousands of particles whose trajectories were recorded by the STAR detector at Brookhaven National Laboratory's Relativistic Heavy Ion Collider (RHIC). [*Courtesy of Brookhaven National Laboratory, STAR experiment.*]

Abbreviations for Units

A	ampere	keV	kilo-electron volts
Å	angstrom (10^{-10} m)	L	liter
atm	atmosphere	m	meter
Btu	British thermal unit	MeV	mega-electron volts
Bq	becquerel	min	minute
C	coulomb	mm	millimeter
°C	degree Celsius	ms	millisecond
cal	calorie	N	newton
Ci	curie	nm	nanometer (10^{-9} m)
cm	centimeter	rev	revolution
eV	electron volt	R	roentgen
°F	degree Fahrenheit	Sv	seivert
fm	femtometer, fermi (10^{-15} m)	s	second
G	gauss	T	tesla
Gy	gray	u	unified mass unit
g	gram	V	volt
H	henry	W	watt
h	hour	Wb	weber
Hz	hertz	y	year
J	joule	μm	micrometer (10^{-6} m)
K	kelvin	μs	microsecond
kg	kilogram	μC	microcoulomb
km	kilometer	Ω	ohm

Some Useful Combinations

$hc = 1.9864 \times 10^{-25}$ J·m $= 1239.8$ eV·nm

$\hbar c = 3.1615 \times 10^{-26}$ J·m $= 197.33$ eV·nm

Bohr radius $a_0 = \dfrac{4\pi\varepsilon_0\hbar^2}{m_e e^2} = 5.2918 \times 10^{-11}$ m

$ke^2 = 1.440$ eV·nm

Fine structure constant $\alpha = \dfrac{e^2}{4\pi\varepsilon_0\hbar c} = 0.0072974 \approx \dfrac{1}{137}$

$kT = 2.5249 \times 10^{-2}$ eV $\approx \frac{1}{40}$ eV at $T = 293$ K

Contents

The 📘 icon indicates material that appears only on the Web site: www.whfreeman.com/modphysics4e

The ✳ icon indicates material of high interest to students.

Preface

This new edition of *Modern Physics* brings to the fore the discoveries and developments that have augmented modern physics during the opening years of the twenty-first century and continues to respond to the numerous helpful suggestions that were offered by the users of the previous editions. As the term *modern physics* has evolved to mean the physics of the modern era—relativity and quantum theory— we have preserved the historical and cultural flavor and carefully maintained the mathematical level of the third edition. We have continued, indeed enhanced, the flexibility for instructors to match the book to a wide variety of teaching modes, including both one- and two-semester courses and media-enhanced courses.

Features

The successful features of the third edition have been retained. Among them are the following:

- The logical structure—beginning with an introduction to relativity and quantization and following with applications—has been continued. Opening the book with relativity has been endorsed by the overwhelming majority of reviewers.
- As with the third edition, we have put great effort into the problem sets, resulting in the greatest quantity and variety you'll find. The end-of-chapter problems are separated into sets based on difficulty, with the Level I (easiest) ones grouped by chapter section.
- The first edition's *Instructor's Solutions Manual* with solutions, not just answers, to all end-of-chapter problems was the first such aid to accompany a physics (and not just a modern physics) textbook, and that leadership has been continued in this edition. The *Instructor's Solutions Manual (ISM)* is available in print or on CD for those adopting *Modern Physics,* Fourth Edition, for their classes. A paperback *Student's Solution Manual* containing one-quarter of the solutions is also available.
- We have continued the use of real data in figures, photos of real people and apparatus, and short quotations by many scientists who were key participants in the development of modern physics. These features, along with the Notes at the end of each chapter, bring to life many events in the history of science and help

counter the too-prevalent view among students that physics is a dull, impersonal collection of facts and formulas.

- We have continued to use many examples in every chapter. As before, we use combined quantities such as hc, $\hbar c$, and ke^2 in eV · nm to simplify many numerical calculations.
- The summaries and reference lists at the end of every chapter have been retained, including the two-column format of the former that improves its clarity.
- Questions for discussion and review at the ends of various sections continue to appear throughout the new edition.
- EXPLORING sections, identified by an atom icon ⊗ and dealing with related topics of high student interest, are distributed throughout the text.
- The book's Web site, containing Chapter 14, "Astrophysics and Cosmology," and the MORE sections, and enthusiastically endorsed by both students and instructors, has been significantly improved. MORE sections are indicated by an icon 📖 and a brief description. Both the MORE sections and Chapter 14 are provided in Adobe Acrobat® for easy download and printing.

New Features

Several new features have been added for the fourth edition. Among them:

- We have added or modified numerous sections and paragraphs that reflect discoveries and advances that have been made in modern physics since the previous edition. Among these are neutrino oscillations, gravity wave experiments, and dark energy. Responding to users and reviewers, we have also added a new section on magnetism to Chapter 10.
- More than 15 percent of the over 700-plus end-of-chapter problems are new or modified from the previous edition.
- The *Instructor's Solutions Manual*, containing solutions to all end-of-chapter problems is now available on a CD to instructors adopting the text.
- The book's site on the World Wide Web has been expanded to become even more helpful to instructors and students. In addition to Chapter 14 and 30-plus MORE sections, it now has a "Physics in the Twenty-first Century" section, updated frequently by the authors, to keep users better informed about what is happening in modern physics *now*. Located at http://www.whfreeman.com/modphysics4e, it may be directly accessed by students or linked by instructors to their own course home pages.
- The instructor's side of the Web site and the Instructor's Resource CD include about 50 percent of the figures from the text in PowerPoint®. This enables the examination of figure details on individual computer screens and large-screen projection in multimedia classrooms. Given the accuracy of the actual data diagrams, measurements can be made directly from the projected images for in-class examples and calculations.
- A new MORE section, "How Transistors Work," has been added to those located on the Web site to amplify, extend, and provide examples of selected material in the book.
- Chapter 14, "Astrophysics and Cosmology," located on the book's Web site, has been thoroughly revised. Extensive use is made of the dramatic, high-resolution color imagery available from the many observatories throughout the world and the Hubble Space Telescope. Chapter 14 is designed according to specifications of the text and is provided in Adobe Acrobat® for color or black-and-white printing. The outline of this chapter is included in the printed book's table of contents.

Organization and Coverage

This edition, as the earlier ones, is divided into two parts: Part 1, "Relativity and Quantum Mechanics: The Foundations of Modern Physics," and Part 2, "Applications." We continue to open Part 1 with the two relativity chapters. This location for relativity is firmly endorsed by users and reviewers. The rationale is that this arrangement avoids separation of the foundations of quantum mechanics in Chapters 3 through 8 from its applications in Chapters 9 through 14. The two-chapter format for relativity provides instructors the flexibility to cover only the basic concepts or to go deeper into the subject. Chapter 1 covers the basics of special relativity and includes discussions of several paradoxes, such as the twin paradox and the pole-in-the-barn paradox, that never fail to excite student interest. Relativistic energy and momentum are covered in Chapter 2, which concludes with an expanded qualitative section on general relativity that emphasizes experimental tests. Because the relation $E^2 = p^2c^2 + (mc^2)^2$ is the main result needed for the later applications chapters, it is possible to omit this chapter without disturbing continuity. Chapters 3 through 7 have been updated with several improved explanations and new diagrams. Many quantitative topics are included as MORE sections on the Web site. Examples of these are the derivation of Compton's equation (Chapter 3), the details of Rutherford's alpha scattering theory (Chapter 4), the graphical solution of the finite square well (Chapter 6), the excited states and spectra of two-electron atoms (Chapter 7), and an analysis of how bipolar transistors work (Chapter 10). The section on "The Schrödinger Equation for Two (or More) Particles" has been moved from Chapter 6 to Chapter 7 at the suggestion of several reviewers. Chapter 8, "Statistical Physics," which completes Part 1, uses the quantum statistics chapter of the first edition as its core. The kinetic theory material in the second chapter of that edition is a MORE section, serving as an introductory review for classical statistics. The comparisons of classical and quantum statistics are illustrated with several examples, and Chapter 8, unlike other chapters in Part 1, is arranged to be covered briefly and qualitatively, if desired. This chapter, like Chapter 2, is not essential to the understanding of those in Part 2 and may be used by instructors as an application chapter or omitted without loss of continuity.

Preserving the approach used in the previous edition, in Part 2 the ideas and methods discussed in Part 1 are applied to the study of molecules, solids, nuclei, particles, and the cosmos. Chapter 9 ("Molecular Structure and Spectra") is a broad, detailed discussion of molecular bonding and the basic types of lasers. Chapter 10 ("Solid-State Physics") includes sections on the quantum Hall effect and high-temperature superconductivity. A new Section 10–7 on magnetism has been added and material on the operation of transistors has been moved to a MORE section on the Web site. Chapter 11 ("Nuclear Physics") focuses on nuclear properties and the structure of nuclei; it contains a new discussion of the neutrino mass experiments. Discussion of the semiempirical mass formula continues as a topic in a MORE section. Fission, fusion, and applications of nuclear reactions are the focus of Chapter 12, which includes a new discussion of accelerator mass spectrometry and particle-induced x-ray emission elemental analysis. The interactions of particles and radiation with matter and a discussion of radiation dosage continue as MORE sections. The material on particle physics, Chapter 13, has been revised to reflect the advancements of that field since the previous edition. The emphasis is on qualitatively discussing the fundamental particle interactions, conservation laws, and the standard model. Finally, an extensively revised Chapter 14 ("Astrophysics and Cosmology") examines the current observations of stars and galaxies and qualitatively integrates our discussions of quantum mechanics, atoms, nuclei, particles, and relativity to explain our present

understanding of the universe. It includes several new EXPLORING sections. Located with deliberate and symbolic intent on the book's Web site, this location enables us to include some of the beautiful color imagery available from today's remarkable telescopes and to update the chapter's contents between revisions.

New Coverage

Research over the past quarter century has added abundantly to our understanding of our world, enhanced the links from physics to virtually every other discipline, and measurably improved the tools and devices that enrich life. Here are just a few of the new topics covered in *Modern Physics*, Fourth Edition, that reflect 25 years of physics research.

- **The search for the Higgs boson** has shifted into high gear at Brookhaven's Relativistic Heavy Ion Collider and at CERN with construction of the Large Hadron Collider. (Chapter 13)
- **The neutrino mass problem** appears to be solved by measurements from the Super Kamiokande and SNO neutrino detectors. (Chapters 2 and 11)
- **The spin of the proton** may include contributions from virtual strange quarks. (Chapter 11)
- **The Bose-Einstein condensates**, that suggest that atomic lasers and super-atomic clocks are in our future, have been joined by **Fermi-Dirac condensates**. (Chapter 8)
- It now appears that a mysterious **dark energy** accounts for as much as 70 percent of the mass of the universe. (Chapter 14)
- **Scanning tunneling and atomic force microscopes** can image individual atoms, and probes can put the atoms where we want them. (Chapter 10)
- **High-temperature superconductors have reached > 130 K with doped fullerenes now competing with cuprates for high-T_c records**, but we still don't know why they work. (Chapter 10)
- **Gravity waves from space** may soon be detected by the Large Interferometric Gravitational Observatory. (Chapter 2)
- **Adaptive-optics telescopes, large baseline arrays, and the improved Hubble telescope** are providing new views of deeper into space of the very young universe, revealing that the expansion is speeding up. (Chapter14)
- **Giant Rydberg atoms**, made accessible by research on tunable dye lasers, are now of high interest and may provide the first direct test of the correspondence principle. (Chapter 4)
- **The search for new elements has reached $Z = 114$ and possibly 116**, tantalizingly near the edge of the "island of stability." (Chapter 11)

Many more new discoveries and developments are to be found throughout the fourth edition of *Modern Physics*.

Some Teaching Suggestions

This book is designed to serve well in either one- or two-semester courses. The chapters in Part 2 are independent of one another and can be covered in any order, with the exception that Chapter 12 is best preceded by Chapter 11. Some possible one-semester courses might consist of:

- Part 1, Chapters 1, 3, 4, 5, 6, 7; and Part 2, Chapters 11, 13
- Part 1, Chapters 3, 4, 5, 6, 7, 8; and Part 2, Chapters 9, 10

- Part 1, Chapters 1, 2, 3, 4, 5, 6, 7; and Part 2, Chapter 9
- Part 1, Chapters 1, 3, 4, 5, 6, 7; and Part 2, Chapters 11, 13, 14

Possible two-semester courses might be made up of:

- Part 1, Chapters 1, 3, 4, 5, 6, 7; and Part 2, Chapters 9, 10, 11, 12, 13, 14
- Part 1, Chapters 1, 2, 3, 4, 5, 6, 7, 8; and Part 2, Chapters 9, 10, 11, 12

There is tremendous potential for individual student projects and extra-credit assignments based on the EXPLORING or, in particular, the MORE sections. The latter will encourage students to search for related sources on the web.

Acknowledgments

Many people contributed to the success of the earlier editions of this book and many more have helped with the development of the fourth edition. We owe our thanks to them all. Those who reviewed all or parts of this book, offering suggestions for the fourth edition, include the following:

Prescriptive Reviewers:
Darin Acosta, University of Florida
Wei Cui, Purdue University
Ronald E. Jodoin, Rochester Institute of Technology
Edward R. Kinney, University of Colorado at Boulder
Robert Pompi, SUNY at Binghamton
Warren Rogers, Westmont College
Nitin Samarth, The Pennsylvania State University
Martin A. Sanzari, Fordham University
Earl E. Scime, West Virginia University
Gil Shapiro, University of California at Berkeley
Paul Tipton, University of Rochester
Edward A. Whittaker, Stevens Institute of Technology

Developmental Reviewers:
Jeeva Anandan, University of South Carolina
David A. Bahr, Bemidji State University
David P. Carico, California Polytechnic State University at San Luis Obispo
David Church, University of Washington
Wei Cui, Purdue University
Snezana Dalafave, The College of New Jersey
Richard Gass, University of Cincinnati
David Gerdes, University of Michigan
Robert Pompi, SUNY at Binghamton
George Rutherford, Illinois State University
K. Thad Walker, University of Wisconsin at Madison

Focus Group Participants (January 2001, AAPT, San Diego, CA):
Gordon Aubrecht, Ohio State University
Patricia C. Boeshaar, Drew University
Mark Hollabaugh, Normandale Community College
John L. Hubisz, North Carolina State University
Paul D. Lane, University of St. Thomas
Fernando J. López-López, Southwestern College

Dan MacIsaac, Northern Arizona University
Larry Solanch, Georgia College & State University
Francis M. Tam, Frostburg State University
Stephen Yerian, Xavier University
Dean Zollman, Kansas State University

All offered valuable suggestions for improvements and we appreciate their help.

We also thank the reviewers of the third edition. Their comments significantly influenced and shaped the fourth edition, as well. They were Bill Bassichis, Texas A&M University; Brent Benson, Lehigh University; H. J. Biritz, Georgia Institute of Technology; Patrick Briggs, The Citadel; David A. Briodo, Boston College; Tony Buffa, California Polytechnic State University at San Luis Obispo; Duane Carmony, Purdue University; Ataur R. Chowdhury, University of Alaska at Fairbanks; Bill Fadner, University of Northern Colorado; Ron Gautreau, New Jersey Institute of Technology; Charles Glashauser, Rutgers—The State University of New Jersey; Roger Hanson, University of Northern Iowa; Gary G. Ihas, University of Florida; Yuichi Kubota, University of Minnesota; David Lamp, Texas Tech University; Philip Lippel, University of Texas at Arlington; A. E. Livingston, University of Notre Dame; Steve Meloma, Gustavus Adolphus College; Benedict Y. Oh, The Pennsylvania State University; Paul Sokol, The Pennsylvania State University; Thor F. Stromberg, New Mexico State University; Maurice Webb, University of Wisconsin at Madison; and Jesse Weil, University of Kentucky.

In addition, we give a special thanks to all those physicists and students from around the world who took time to send us kind words about the third edition and offer suggestions for improvements.

Finally, though certainly not least, we are grateful for the support, encouragement, and patience of our families throughout the project. We especially want to thank Mark Llewellyn for his preparation of the·*Instructor's Solutions Manual* and the *Student's Solutions Manual* and for his numerous helpful suggestions from the very beginning of the project, as well as Brian Donnellan for his imaginative work on the Web site. Finally, to Susan Brennan, our publisher, and Mary Louise Byrd, our project editor, at W. H. Freeman and Company, goes our sincerest appreciation for their skill, understanding, and support in bringing it all together.

Paul A. Tipler, Berkeley, California
Ralph A. Llewellyn, Oviedo, Florida

MODERN PHYSICS

Part 1

Relativity and Quantum Mechanics: The Foundations of Modern Physics

The earliest recorded systematic efforts to assemble knowledge about motion as a key to understanding natural phenomena were those of the ancient Greeks. Set forth in sophisticated form by Aristotle, theirs was a natural philosophy (i.e., physics) of explanations deduced from assumptions rather than experimentation. For example, it was a fundamental assumption that every substance had a "natural place" in the universe. Motion then resulted when a substance was trying to reach its natural place. Time was given a similar absolute meaning, as moving from some instant in the past (the creation of the universe) toward some end goal in the future, its natural place. The remarkable agreement between the deductions of Aristotelian physics and motions observed throughout the physical universe, together with a nearly total absence of accurate instruments to make contradictory measurements, enabled acceptance of the Greek view for nearly 2000 years. Toward the end of that time a few scholars had begun to deliberately test some of the predictions of theory, but it was the Italian scientist Galileo Galilei who, with his brilliant experiments on motion, established for all time the absolute necessity of experimentation in physics and, coincidentally, initiated the disintegration of Aristotelian physics. Within 100 years Isaac Newton had generalized the results of Galileo's experiments into his three spectacularly successful laws of motion, and the natural philosophy of Aristotle was gone.

With the burgeoning of experimentation, the following 200 years saw a multitude of major discoveries and a concomitant development of physical theories to explain them. Most of the latter, then as now, failed to survive increasingly sophisticated experimental tests, but by the dawn of the twentieth century Newton's theoretical explanation of the motion of mechanical systems had been joined by equally impressive laws of electromagnetism and thermodynamics as expressed by Maxwell, Carnot, and others. The remarkable success of these laws led many scientists to believe that description of the physical universe was complete. Indeed, A. A. Michelson, speaking to scientists near the end of the nineteenth century, said, "The grand underlying principles have been firmly established . . . the future truths of physics are to be looked for in the sixth place of decimals."

Such optimism (or pessimism, depending on your point of view) turned out to be premature, as there were already vexing cracks in the foundation of what we now refer to as classical physics. Two of these were described by Lord Kelvin, in his famous Baltimore Lectures in 1900, as the "two clouds" on the horizon of twentieth-century physics: the failure of theory to account for the radiation spectrum emitted by a blackbody and the inexplicable results of the Michelson-Morley experiment. Indeed, the breakdown of classical physics occurred in many

different areas: the Michelson-Morley null result contradicted Newtonian relativity; the black-body radiation spectrum contradicted predictions of thermodynamics; the photoelectric effect and the spectra of atoms could not be explained by electromagnetic theory; and the exciting discoveries of x rays and radioactivity seemed to be outside the framework of classical physics entirely. The development of the theories of quantum mechanics and relativity in the early twentieth century not only dispelled Kelvin's "dark clouds," they provided answers to all of the puzzles listed here and many more. The applications of these theories to such microscopic systems as atoms, molecules, nuclei, and fundamental particles and to macroscopic systems of solids, liquids, gases, and plasmas have given us a deep understanding of the intricate workings of nature and have revolutionized our way of life.

In Part 1 we discuss the foundations of the physics of the modern era, relativity theory and quantum mechanics. Chapter 1 examines the apparent conflict between Einstein's principle of relativity and the observed constancy of the speed of light and shows how accepting the validity of both ideas led to the special theory of relativity. Chapter 2 concerns the relations connecting mass, energy, and momentum in special relativity and concludes with a brief discussion of general relativity and some experimental tests of its predictions. In Chapters 3, 4, and 5 the development of quantum theory is traced from the earliest evidences of quantization to de Broglie's hypothesis of electron waves. An elementary discussion of the Schrödinger equation is provided in Chapter 6, illustrated with applications to one-dimensional systems. Chapter 7 extends the application of quantum mechanics to many-particle systems and introduces the important new concepts of electron spin and the exclusion principle. Concluding the development, Chapter 8 discusses the wave mechanics of systems of large numbers of identical particles, underscoring the importance of the symmetry of wave functions. Beginning with Chapter 3, the chapters in Part 1 should be studied in sequence because each of Chapters 4 through 8 depends on the discussions, developments, and examples of the previous chapters.

Chapter *1* Relativity I

The relativistic character of the laws of physics began to be apparent very early in the evolution of classical physics. Even before the time of Galileo and Newton, Nicolaus Copernicus[1] had shown that the complicated and imprecise Aristotelian method of computing the motions of the planets, based on the assumption that Earth was located at the center of the universe, could be made much more simple and accurate if it were assumed that the planets move about the sun instead of Earth. Although Copernicus did not publish his work until very late in life, it became widely known through correspondence with his contemporaries and helped pave the way for acceptance a century later of the heliocentric theory of planetary motion. While the Copernican theory led to a dramatic revolution in human thought, the aspect that concerns us here is that it did not consider the location of Earth to be special or favored in any way. Thus, the laws of physics discovered on Earth could apply equally well with any point taken as the center—i.e., the same equations would be obtained regardless of the origin of coordinates. This invariance of the equations that express the laws of physics is what we mean by the term *relativity*.

We will begin this chapter by investigating briefly the relativity of Newton's laws and then concentrate on the theory of relativity as developed by Albert Einstein (1879–1955). The theory of relativity consists of two rather different theories, the special theory and the general theory. The special theory, developed by Einstein and others in 1905, concerns the comparison of measurements made in different frames of reference moving with constant velocity relative to each other. Contrary to popular opinion, the special theory is not difficult to understand. Its consequences, which can be derived with a minimum of mathematics, are applicable in a wide variety of situations in physics and engineering. On the other hand, the general theory, also developed by Einstein (around 1916), is concerned with accelerated reference frames and gravity. Although a thorough understanding of the general theory requires more sophisticated mathematics (e.g., tensor analysis), a number of its basic ideas and important predictions can be discussed at the level of this book. The general theory is of great importance in cosmology and in understanding events that occur in the vicinity of very large masses (e.g., stars), but is rarely encountered in other areas of physics and engineering. We will devote this chapter entirely to the special theory (often referred to as *special relativity*) and discuss the general theory in the final section of Chapter 2, following the sections concerned with special relativistic mechanics.

1-1 The Experimental Basis of Relativity

Classical Relativity

Galileo was the first to recognize the concept of acceleration when, in his studies of falling objects, he showed that the rate at which the velocity changed was always constant, indicating that the motion of the falling body was intimately related to its *changing* velocity. It was this observation, among others, that Newton generalized into his second law of motion:

$$\mathbf{F} = m\frac{d\mathbf{v}}{dt} = m\mathbf{a} \qquad\qquad \textbf{1-1}$$

where $d\mathbf{v}/dt = \mathbf{a}$ is the acceleration of the mass m and $\mathbf{F}$ is the net force acting on it. (Recall that letters and symbols printed in boldface type are vectors.) Newton's first law of motion, the law of inertia, is also implied in Equation 1-1: the velocity of an object acted upon by no net force does not change; i.e., its acceleration is zero.

Frames of Reference   An important question regarding the laws of motion, one that concerned Newton himself and one that you likely studied in first-year physics, is that of the reference frame in which they are valid. It turns out that they work correctly only in what is called an *inertial reference frame,* a reference frame in which the law of inertia holds.[2] Newton's laws of motion for mechanical systems are *not* valid in systems that accelerate relative to an inertial reference frame; i.e., an accelerated reference frame is not an inertial reference frame. Figures 1-1 and 1-2 illustrate inertial and noninertial reference frames.

Galilean Transformation   Newton's laws brought with them an enormous advance in the relativity of the laws of physics. The laws are *invariant,* or unchanged, in reference systems that move at constant velocity with respect to an inertial frame. Thus, not only is there no special or favored position for measuring space and time, there is no special or favored velocity for inertial frames of reference. All such frames are equivalent. If an observer in an inertial frame S measures the velocity of an object to be $\mathbf{u}$ and an observer in a reference frame S' moving at constant velocity $\mathbf{v}$ in the $+x$ direction with respect to S measures the velocity of the object to be $\mathbf{u}'$, then $\mathbf{u}' = \mathbf{u} - \mathbf{v}$, or, in terms of the coordinate systems in Figure 1-3 (page 5),

$$u'_x = u_x - v \qquad u'_y = u_y \qquad u'_z = u_z \qquad\qquad \textbf{1-2}$$

If we recall that $u'_x = dx'/dt$, $u_x = dx/dt$, and so forth, then, integrating each of the Equations 1-2, the *velocity transformation* between S and S', yields Equations 1-3, the *Galilean transformation of coordinates:*

$$x' = x - vt \qquad y' = y \qquad z' = z \qquad\qquad \textbf{1-3}$$

assuming the origins of S and S' coincided at $t = 0$. Differentiating Equations 1-2 leads to

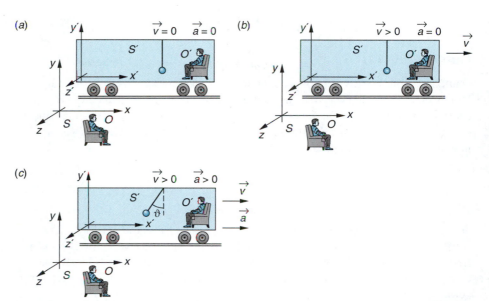

Fig. 1-1 A mass suspended by a cord from the roof of a railroad boxcar illustrates the relativity of Newton's second law $\mathbf{F} = m\mathbf{a}$. The only forces acting on the mass are its weight $m\mathbf{g}$ and the tension $\mathbf{T}$ in the cord. (*a*) The boxcar sits at rest in *S*. Since the velocity $\mathbf{v}$ and the acceleration $\mathbf{a}$ of the boxcar (i.e., the system S') are both zero, both observers see the mass hanging vertically at rest with $\mathbf{F} = \mathbf{F}' = 0$. (*b*) As S' moves in the $+x$ direction with $\mathbf{v}$ constant, both observers see the mass hanging vertically, but moving at $\mathbf{v}$ with respect to O in S and at rest with respect to the S' observer. Thus, $\mathbf{F} = \mathbf{F}' = 0$. (*c*) As S' moves in the $+x$ direction with $\mathbf{a} > 0$ with respect to S, the mass hangs at an angle $\theta > 0$ with respect to the vertical. However, it is still at rest (i.e., in equilibrium) with respect to the observer in S', who now "explains" the angle θ by adding a pseudoforce F_p in the $-x'$ direction to Newton's second law.

$$a'_x = \frac{du'_x}{dt} = \frac{du_x}{dt} = a_x \qquad a'_y = \frac{du'_y}{dt} = \frac{du_y}{dt} = a_y \qquad a'_z = \frac{du'_z}{dt} = \frac{du_z}{dt} = a_z \qquad \textbf{1-4}$$

and the conclusion that $\mathbf{a}' = \mathbf{a}$. Thus, we see that $\mathbf{F} = m\mathbf{a} = m\mathbf{a}' = \mathbf{F}'$ in Figure 1-3 and Figure 1-1*b* and, indeed, in every situation where the relative velocity $\mathbf{v}$ of the reference

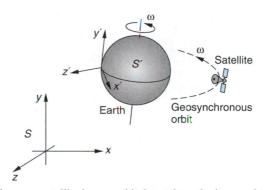

Fig. 1-2 A geosynchronous satellite has an orbital angular velocity equal to that of Earth and, therefore, is always located above a particular point on Earth; i.e., it is at rest with respect to the surface of Earth. An observer in *S* accounts for the radial, or centripetal, acceleration $\mathbf{a}$ of the satellite as the result of the net force $\mathbf{F}_G$. For an observer O' at rest on Earth (in S'), however, $\mathbf{a}' = 0$ and $\mathbf{F}'_G \neq m\mathbf{a}'$. To explain the acceleration being zero, observer O' must add a pseudoforce $\mathbf{F}_p = -\mathbf{F}_G$.

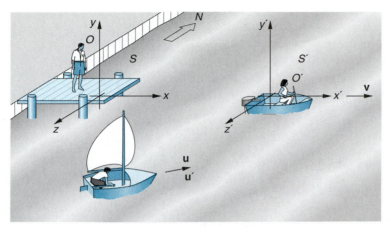

Fig. 1-3 The observer in S on the dock measures $\mathbf{u}$ for the sailboat's velocity. The observer in S' (in the motorboat) moving at constant velocity $\mathbf{v}$ with respect to S measures $\mathbf{u}'$ for the sailboat. The invariance of Newton's equations between these two systems means that $\mathbf{u}' = \mathbf{u} - \mathbf{v}$.

frames is constant. Constant relative velocity $\mathbf{v}$ of the frames means that $d\mathbf{v}/dt = 0$; hence the observers measure identical accelerations for moving objects and agree on the results when applying $\mathbf{F} = m\mathbf{a}$. Note that S' is thus also an inertial frame and neither frame is preferred or special in any way. This result can be generalized as follows:

> Any reference frame which moves at constant velocity with respect to an inertial frame is also an inertial frame. Newton's laws of mechanics are invariant in all reference systems connected by a Galilean transformation.

The second of the preceding statements is the *Newtonian principle of relativity*. Note the tacit assumption in the foregoing that the clocks of both observers keep the same time, i.e., $t' = t$.

EXAMPLE 1-1 **Velocity of One Boat Relative to Another** What will a person in the motorboat in Figure 1-3 measure for the velocity of the sailboat? The motorboat is sailing due east at 3.0 m/s with respect to the dock. The person on the dock measures the velocity of the sailboat as 1.5 m/s toward the northeast. The coordinate system S is attached to the dock and S' is attached to the motorboat.

Solution

1. The magnitude of the sailboat's velocity $\mathbf{u}'$ is given by:

$$u' = \sqrt{u_x'^2 + u_y'^2 + u_z'^2}$$

2. The components of $\mathbf{u}'$ are given by Equations 1-2 with $v = 3.0$ m/s, $u_x = 1.5 \cos 45°$, $u_y = 0$, and $u_z = -1.5 \sin 45°$:

$$u_x' = 1.5 \cos 45° - 3.0$$
$$u_y' = 0$$
$$u_z' = -1.5 \sin 45°$$

3.   Substituting these into **u′** above yields:

$$u' = \sqrt{(3.76 \text{ m}^2/\text{s}^2 + 1.13 \text{m}^2/\text{s}^2)}$$
$$= 2.2 \text{ m/s}$$

4.   The direction of **u′** relative to north (the $-z$ axis) is given by:

$$\theta' = \tan^{-1}(u'_x/u'_z)$$

5.   Substituting from above:

$$\theta' = \tan^{-1}(-1.94/-1.06)$$
$$= 61° \text{ west of north}$$

Remarks: *Note that the observers in S and S′ obtain different values for the speed and direction of the sailboat. It is the equations that are invariant between inertial systems, not necessarily the numbers calculated from them. Since neither reference frame is special or preferred, both results are correct!*

Speed of Light

In about 1860 James Clerk Maxwell discovered that the experimental laws of electricity and magnetism could be summarized in a consistent set of four concise mathematical statements, the Maxwell equations, one consequence of which was the prediction of the possibility of electromagnetic waves. It was recognized almost immediately, indeed by Maxwell himself, that the Maxwell equations did not obey the principle of Newtonian relativity, i.e., the equations were not invariant when transformed between inertial reference frames using the Galilean transformations. That this is the case can be seen by considering Figure 1-4, which shows an infinitely long wire with a uniform negative charge density λ per unit length and a point charge q located a distance y_1 above the wire. The wire and charge are at rest in the S frame. A second reference frame S' moves at constant speed v in the $+x$ direction with respect to S. An observer at rest in S' sees the wire and charge q moving in the $-x'$ direction at speed v. The observers in S and S' thus have *different forms* for the electromagnetic force acting on the point charge q near the wire, implying that Maxwell's equations are not invariant under a Galilean transformation.

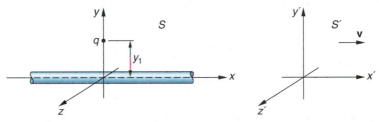

Fig. 1-4 The observers in S and S' see identical electric fields $2k\lambda/y_1$ at a distance $y_1 = y'_1$ from an infinitely long wire carrying uniform charge λ per unit length. Observers in both S and S' measure a force $2kq\lambda/y_1$ on q due to the line of charge; however, the S' observer measures an additional force $-\mu_0\lambda v^2 q/(2\pi y_1)$ due to the magnetic field at y'_1 arising from the motion of the wire in the $-x'$ direction. Thus, the electromagnetic force does not have the same form in different inertial systems, implying that Maxwell's equations are *not* invariant under a Galilean transformation.

A fair question at this point would be, Why does anyone care that Maxwell's electromagnetic laws are not invariant between inertial systems the way Newton's laws of mechanics are? Scientists of the time probably *wouldn't* have cared a great deal, except that Maxwell's equations predict the existence of electromagnetic waves whose speed would be a particular value $c = 1/(\mu_0\epsilon_0)^{1/2} = 3.00 \times 10^8$ m/s. The excellent agreement between this number and the measured value of the speed of light[3] and between the predicted polarization properties of electromagnetic waves and those observed for light provided strong confirmation of the assumption that light was an electromagnetic wave and, therefore, traveled at speed c.[4]

That being the case, it was postulated in the nineteenth century that electromagnetic waves, like all other waves, propagated in a suitable material medium. Called the *ether,* this medium filled the entire universe including the interior of matter. (The Greek philosopher Aristotle had first suggested that the universe was permeated with "ether" 2000 years earlier.) It had the inconsistent properties, among others, of being extremely rigid (in order to support the stress of the high electromagnetic wave speed) while offering no observable resistance to motion of the planets, which was fully accounted for by Newton's law of gravitation. The implication of this postulate is that a light wave, moving with velocity **c** with respect to the ether, would, according to the classical transformation (Equations 1-2), travel at velocity $\mathbf{c'} = \mathbf{c} + \mathbf{v}$ with respect to a frame of reference moving through the ether at **v**. This would require that Maxwell's equations have a different form in the moving frame so as to predict the speed of light to be c', instead of $c = 1/(\mu_0\epsilon_0)^{1/2}$. That would in turn reserve for the ether the status of a favored or special frame for the laws of electromagnetic theory. It should then be possible to design an experiment that would detect the existence of the favored frame.

The problem with the ether postulate at the time it was made was not that it became a favored frame of reference for Maxwell's equations (Newton had postulated a similar status for the "fixed stars" for the laws of mechanics), but that, unlike the media through which other kinds of waves moved (e.g., water, air, solids), it offered no other evidence of its existence. Many experiments were performed to establish the existence of the ether, but nearly all of them suffered from the same serious limitation.

Let's use Fizeau's classic measurement of the speed of light to illustrate that limitation (see Figure 1-5). The time t for the light beam to make a round trip (wheel to mirror back to wheel) is $2L/c$; therefore, the speed of light would be

$$c = \frac{2L}{t}$$

However, the motion of Earth relative to the ether at some speed v (unknown) would affect the time measured in an "out and back" terrestrial measurement of the light's speed, such as Fizeau's. If Earth moves toward the right in Figure 1-5 at speed v, then in the outbound leg the speed of light relative to the laboratory is $c' = c - v$ and in the return leg $c' = c + v$. The round-trip time t is then

$$t = \frac{L}{c - v} + \frac{L}{c + v} = \frac{2Lc}{c^2 - v^2} = \frac{2L}{c}\frac{1}{1 - \dfrac{v^2}{c^2}}$$

1-5

$$= \frac{2L}{c}\left(1 - \frac{v^2}{c^2}\right)^{-1} \approx \frac{2L}{c}\left(1 + \frac{v^2}{c^2} + \dots\right)$$

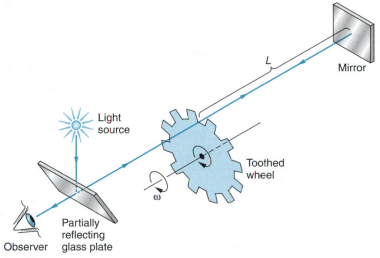

Fig. 1-5 Fizeau measured the speed of light in 1849 by aiming a beam of light at a distant mirror through the gap between two teeth in a wheel, in effect changing the light beam into pulses. A light pulse traveling at speed c would take $2L/c$ seconds to go from the wheel to the mirror and back to the wheel, If, during that time, rotation of the wheel moved a tooth into the light's path, the observer could not see the light. But if the angular velocity ω were such that the pulse arrived back at the wheel coincident with the arrival of the next gap, the observer saw the light.

where the term $(1 - v^2/c^2)^{-1}$ has been expanded using the binomial expansion in powers of the small quantity v^2/c^2 (see Appendix B4) and only the first two terms have been retained. Although the speed of Earth relative to the ether was unknown, one could reasonably expect that at some season of the year it should be at least equal to Earth's orbital speed around the sun, about 30 km/s. Thus, the maximum observable effect would only be of the order of $v^2/c^2 = (3 \times 10^4/3 \times 10^8)^2 = 10^{-8}$, or about 1 part in 10^8. The experimental accuracy of Fizeau's measurement was too poor by a factor of about 10^4 to detect this small an effect. A large number of experiments intended to detect the effect of Earth's motion on the propagation speed of light were proposed, but for all of them except one the accuracy possible with the apparatus available was, like Fizeau's, insufficient to detect the small effect. The one exception was the experiment of Michelson and Morley.[5]

EXAMPLE 1-2 Earth's Orbital Speed Determine Earth's average orbital speed with respect to an inertial frame of reference attached to the center of the sun. The mean value of Earth's orbit radius R is 1.496×10^8 km.

Solution

1. The average orbital speed is given in terms of the orbital circumference C and the time required to complete one orbit:

$$v = C/t$$

2. The circumference is given in terms of the orbit radius R. The mean value of R is a convenient unit of length used for distances within the solar system; it is called the *astronomical unit* (AU).

$$C = 2\pi R$$
$$= 2\pi(1.496 \times 10^8 \text{ km})$$
$$= 9.40 \times 10^8 \text{ km}$$

3. Earth travels a distance equal to C in $t = 1 \text{ y} = 3.16 \times 10^7 \text{ s}$. The average speed is then given by:

$$v = \frac{9.40 \times 10^8 \text{ km}}{3.16 \times 10^7 \text{s}}$$
$$= 29.8 \text{ km/s}$$

QUESTIONS

1. What would the relative velocity of the inertial systems in Figure 1-4 need to be in order for the S' observer to measure no net electromagnetic force on the charge q?

2. Discuss why the very large value for the speed of the electromagnetic waves would imply that the ether be rigid, i.e., have a large bulk modulus.

The Michelson-Morley Experiment

All waves that were known to nineteenth-century scientists required a medium in order to propagate. Surface waves moving across the ocean obviously require the water. Similarly, waves move along a plucked guitar string, across the surface of a struck drumhead, through Earth after an earthquake, and, indeed, in all materials acted upon by suitable forces. The speed of the waves depends on the properties of the medium and is derived *relative to the medium.* For example, the speed of sound waves in air, i.e., their absolute motion relative to still air, can be measured. The Doppler effect for sound in air depends not only on the relative motion of the source and listener, but also on the motion of each relative to still air. Thus, it was natural for scientists of that time to expect the existence of some material like the ether to support the propagation of light and other electromagnetic waves *and* to expect that the absolute motion of Earth through the ether should be detectable, despite the fact that the ether had not been observed previously.

Michelson realized that, although the effect of Earth's motion on the results of any "out and back" speed of light measurement, such as shown generically in Figure 1-6, would be too small to measure directly, it should be possible to measure v^2/c^2 by

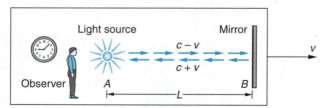

Fig. 1-6 Light source, mirror, and observer are moving with speed v relative to the ether. According to classical theory, the speed of light c, relative to the ether, would be $c - v$ relative to the observer for light moving from the source toward the mirror and $c + v$ for light reflecting from the mirror back toward the source.

Page 107.

The numbers in column z of the preceding table are thus translated:

3 = good
2 = fair
1 = poor

These numbers do not however, represent the relative weights.

Mean result	299728
Correction for temp. (2.51)	+12
Velocity of Light in air	299740
✳ Correction for vacus	+88
Velocity of Light in vacus	299828 Kilo-
meters per second.	
✳ Should be	+80

Albert A. Michelson made the first accurate measurement of the speed of light. Above, in his own handwriting, is the value as recorded on page 107 of his laboratory records of the 1878 experiment. (*Below*) Michelson in his laboratory. [*Courtesy of American Institute of Physics, Niels Bohr Library.*]

a difference measurement, using the interference property of the light waves as a sensitive "clock." The apparatus that he designed to make the measurement is called the *Michelson interferometer*. The purpose of the Michelson-Morley experiment was to measure the speed of light relative to the interferometer (i.e., relative to Earth), thereby detecting Earth's motion through the ether and, thus, verifying the latter's existence. To illustrate how the interferometer works and the reasoning behind the experiment, let us first describe an analogous situation set in more familiar surroundings.

EXAMPLE 1-3 A Boat Race Two equally matched rowers race each other over courses as shown in Figure 1-7a. Each oarsman rows at speed c in still water; the current in the river moves at speed v. Boat 1 goes from A to B, a distance L, and back. Boat 2 goes from A to C, also a distance L, and back. A, B, and C are marks on the riverbank. Which boat wins the race, or is it a tie? (Assume $c > v$.)

Solution

The winner is, of course, the boat that makes the round trip in the shortest time, so to discover which boat wins we compute the time for each. Using the classical velocity transformation (Equations 1-2), the speed of 1 relative to the ground is $(c^2 - v^2)^{1/2}$, as shown in Figure 1-7b; thus the round-trip time t_1 for boat 1 is

$$t_1 = t_{A \to B} + t_{B \to A} = \frac{L}{\sqrt{c^2 - v^2}} + \frac{L}{\sqrt{c^2 - v^2}} = \frac{2L}{\sqrt{c^2 - v^2}}$$

$$= \frac{2L}{c\sqrt{1 - \frac{v^2}{c^2}}} = \frac{2L}{c}\left(1 - \frac{v^2}{c^2}\right)^{-1/2} \approx \frac{2L}{c}\left(1 + \frac{1v^2}{2c^2} + \ldots\right) \qquad \textbf{1-6}$$

(a)

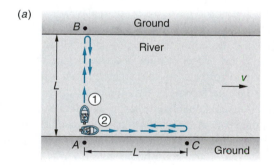

(b)

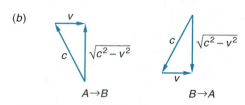

$A \to B$ $B \to A$

Fig. 1-7 (a) The rowers both row at speed c in still water. (See Example 1-3.) The current in the river moves at speed v. Rower 1 goes from A to B and back to A, while rower 2 goes from A to C and back to A. (b) Rower 1 must point the bow upstream so that the sum of the velocity vectors $\mathbf{c} + \mathbf{v}$ results in the boat moving from A directly to B. His speed relative to the banks (i.e., points A and B) is then $(c^2 - v^2)^{1/2}$. The same is true on the return trip.

where we have again used the binomial expansion. Boat 2 moves downstream at speed $c + v$ relative to the ground and returns at $c - v$, also relative to the ground. The round-trip time t_2 is thus

$$t_2 = \frac{L}{c + v} + \frac{L}{c - v} = \frac{2Lc}{c^2 - v^2}$$

$$= \frac{2L}{c} \frac{1}{1 - \dfrac{v^2}{c^2}} \approx \frac{2L}{c}\left(1 + \frac{v^2}{c^2} + \ldots\right) \qquad \textbf{1-7}$$

which, you may note, is the same result that we obtained in our discussion of the speed-of-light experiment (Equation 1-5).

The difference Δt between the round-trip times of the boats is then

$$\Delta t = t_2 - t_1 \approx \frac{2L}{c}\left(1 + \frac{v^2}{c^2}\right) - \frac{2L}{c}\left(1 + \frac{1}{2}\frac{v^2}{c^2}\right) \approx \frac{Lv^2}{c^3} \qquad \textbf{1-8}$$

The quantity Lv^2/c^3 is always positive; therefore, $t_2 > t_1$ and the rower of boat 1 has the faster average speed and wins the race.

The Results   Michelson and Morley carried out the experiment in 1887, repeating with a much improved interferometer an inconclusive experiment that Michelson alone had performed in 1881 in Potsdam. The path length L on the new interferometer (see Figure 1-8) was about 11 m, obtained by a series of multiple reflections. Michelson's interferometer is shown schematically in Figure 1-9a (page 14). The field of view seen by the observer consists of parallel alternately bright and dark interference bands, called *fringes,* as illustrated in Figure 1-9b. The two light beams in the interferometer are exactly analogous to the two boats in Example 1-3, and Earth's motion through the ether was expected to introduce a time (phase) difference as given by Equation 1-8. Rotating the interferometer through 90° doubles the time difference and changes the phase, causing the fringe pattern to shift by an amount ΔN. An improved system for rotating the apparatus was used in which the massive stone slab on which the interferometer was mounted floated on a pool of mercury. This dampened vibrations and enabled the experimenters to rotate the interferometer without introducing mechanical strains, both of which would cause changes in L, and hence a shift in the fringes. Using a sodium light source with $\lambda = 590$ nm and assuming $v = 30$ km/s (i.e., Earth's orbital speed), ΔN was expected to be about 0.4 of the width of a fringe, about 40 times the minimum shift (0.01 fringe) that the interferometer was capable of detecting.

To Michelson's immense disappointment, and that of most scientists of the time, the expected shift in the fringes did not occur. Instead, the shift observed was only about 0.01 fringe, i.e., approximately the experimental uncertainty of the apparatus. With characteristic reserve, Michelson described the results thus:[6]

The actual displacement [of the fringes] was certainly less than the twentieth part [of 0.4 fringe], and probably less than the fortieth part. But since the displacement is proportional to the square of the velocity, the relative velocity of the earth and the ether is probably less than one-sixth the earth's orbital velocity and certainly less than one-fourth.

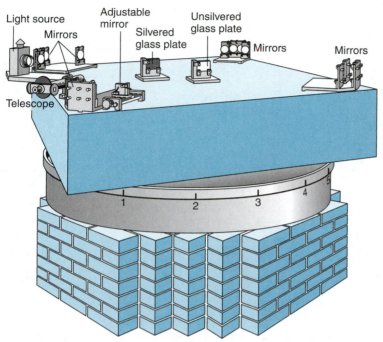

Light source
Mirrors
Adjustable mirror
Silvered glass plate
Unsilvered glass plate
Mirrors
Mirrors
Telescope

1   2   3   4   5

Fig. 1-8 Drawing of Michelson-Morley apparatus used in their 1887 experiment. The optical parts were mounted on a sandstone 5 ft square slab, which was floated in mercury, thereby reducing the strains and vibrations during rotation that had affected the earlier experiments. Observations could be made in all directions by rotating the apparatus in the horizontal plane. [*From R. S. Shankland, "The Michelson-Morley Experiment." Copyright © November 1964 by Scientific American, Inc. All rights reserved.*]

Michelson and Morley had placed an upper limit on Earth's motion relative to the ether of about 5 km/s. From this distance in time it is difficult for us to appreciate the devastating impact of this result. The then accepted theory of light propagation could not be correct, and the ether as a favored frame of reference for Maxwell's equations was not tenable. The experiment was repeated by a number of people more than a dozen times under various conditions and with improved precision, and no shift has ever been found. In the most precise attempt, the upper limit on the relative velocity was lowered to 1.5 km/s by Georg Joos in 1930 using an interferometer with light paths much longer than Michelson's. Recent, high-precision variations of the experiment using laser beams have lowered the upper limit to 15 m/s.

Michelson interferometers with arms as long as 4 km are currently being used in the search for gravity waves. See Section 2-5.

More generally, on the basis of this and other experiments, we must conclude that Maxwell's equations are correct and that the speed of electromagnetic radiation is the same in all inertial reference systems independent of the motion of the source relative to the observer. This invariance of the speed of light between inertial reference frames means that there must be some relativity principle that applies to electromagnetism as well as to mechanics. That principle cannot be Newtonian relativity, which implies the dependence of the speed of light on the relative motion of the source and observer. It follows that the Galilean transformation of coordinates between inertial frames cannot be correct, but must be replaced with a new coordinate transformation whose application preserves the invariance of the laws of electromagnetism. We then expect that the fundamental laws of mechanics, which were consistent with the old Galilean transformation, will require modification in order to be invariant under the new transformation. The theoretical derivation of that new transformation was a cornerstone of Einstein's development of special relativity.

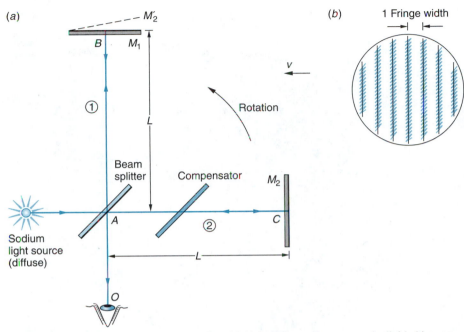

(a)

(b)   1 Fringe width

Fig. 1-9 Michelson interferometer. (*a*) Yellow light from the sodium source is divided into two beams by the second surface of the partially reflective beam splitter at *A*, at which point the two beams are exactly in phase. The beams travel along the mutually perpendicular paths 1 and 2, reflect from mirrors M_1 and M_2, and return to *A*, where they recombine and are viewed by the observer. The compensator's purpose is to make the two paths of equal optical length, so that the lengths *L* contain the same number of light waves, by making both beams pass through two thicknesses of glass before recombining. M_2 is then tilted slightly so that it is not quite perpendicular to M_1. Thus, the observer *O* sees M_1 and M_2', the image of M_2 formed by the partially reflecting second surface of the beam splitter, forming a thin wedge-shaped film of air between them. The interference of the two recombining beams depends on the number of waves in each path, which in turn depends on (1) the length of each path and (2) the speed of light (relative to the instrument) in each path. Regardless of the value of that speed, the wedge-shaped air film between M_1 and M_2' results in an increasing path length for beam 2 relative to beam 1, looking from left to right across the observer's field of view; hence, the observer sees a series of parallel interference fringes as in (*b*), alternately yellow and black from constructive and destructive interference, respectively.

More

A more complete description of the *Michelson-Morley experiment,* its interpretation, and the results of very recent versions can be found on the home page: www.whfreeman.com/modphysics4e   See also Figures 1-10 through 1-12 here, as well as Equations 1-9 through 1-12.

1-2 Einstein's Postulates

In 1905, at the age of 26, Albert Einstein published several papers, among which was one on the electrodynamics of moving bodies.[11] In this paper, he postulated a more general principle of relativity which applied to both electrodynamic and mechanical

laws. A consequence of this postulate is that absolute motion cannot be detected by any experiment. We can then consider the Michelson apparatus and Earth to be at rest. No fringe shift is expected when the interferometer is rotated 90°, since all directions are equivalent. The null result of the Michelson-Morley experiment is therefore to be expected. It should be pointed out that Einstein did not set out to explain the Michelson-Morley experiment. His theory arose from his considerations of the theory of electricity and magnetism and the unusual property of electromagnetic waves that they propagate in a vacuum. In his first paper, which contains the complete theory of special relativity, he made only a passing reference to the experimental attempts to detect Earth's motion through the ether, and in later years he could not recall whether he was aware of the details of the Michelson-Morley experiment before he published his theory.

The theory of special relativity was derived from two postulates proposed by Einstein in his 1905 paper:

Postulate 1.   The laws of physics are the same in all inertial reference frames.

Postulate 2.   The speed of light in a vacuum is equal to the value c, independent of the motion of the source.

Postulate 1 is an extension of the Newtonian principle of relativity to include all types of physical measurements (not just measurements in mechanics). It implies that no inertial system is preferred over any other; hence, absolute motion cannot be detected. Postulate 2 describes a common property of all waves. For example, the speed of sound waves does not depend on the motion of the sound source. When an approaching car sounds its horn, the frequency heard increases according to the Doppler effect, but the speed of the waves traveling through the air does not depend on the speed of the car. The speed of the waves depends only on the properties of the air, such as its temperature. The force of this postulate was to include light waves, for which experiments had found no propagation medium, together with all other waves whose speed *was* known to be independent of the speed of the source. Recent analysis of the light curves of gamma-ray bursts that occur near the edge of the observable universe have shown the speed of light to be independent of the speed of the source to a precision of one part in 10^{20}.

Although each postulate seems quite reasonable, many of the implications of the two together are surprising and seem to contradict common sense. One important implication of these postulates is that every observer measures the same value for the speed of light independent of the relative motion of the source and observer. Consider a light source S and two observers R_1, at rest relative to S, and R_2, moving toward S with speed v, as shown in Figure 1-13a. The speed of light measured by R_1 is $c = 3 \times 10^8$ m/s. What is the speed measured by R_2? The answer is *not* $c + v$, as one would expect based on Newtonian relativity. By postulate 1, Figure 1-13a is equivalent to Figure 1-13b, in which R_2 is at rest and the source S and R_1 are moving with speed v. That is, since absolute motion cannot be detected, it is not possible to say which is really moving and which is at rest. By postulate 2, the speed of light from a moving source is independent of the motion of the source. Thus, looking at Figure 1-13b, we see that R_2 measures the speed of light to be c, just as R_1 does. This result, that all observers measure the same value c for the speed of light, is often considered an alternative to Einstein's second postulate.

This result contradicts our intuition. Our intuitive ideas about relative velocities are approximations that hold only when the speeds are very small compared with the

(a)

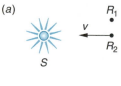

(b)

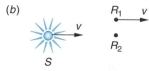

Fig. 1-13 (*a*) Stationary light source S and a stationary observer R_1, with a second observer R_2 moving toward the source with speed v. (*b*) In the reference frame in which the observer R_2 is at rest, the light source S and observer R_1 move to the right with speed v. If absolute motion cannot be detected, the two views are equivalent. Since the speed of light does not depend on the motion of the source, observer R_2 measures the same value for that speed as observer R_1.

Albert Einstein in 1905, at the time of his greatest productivity. [*Courtesy of Lotte Jacobi.*]

speed of light. Even in an airplane moving at the speed of sound, it is not possible to measure the speed of light accurately enough to distinguish the difference between the results c and $c + v$, where v is the speed of the plane. In order to make such a distinction, we must either move with a very great velocity (much greater than that of sound) or make extremely accurate measurements, as in the Michelson-Morley experiment, and when we do, we will find, as Einstein pointed out in his original relativity paper, that the contradictions are "only apparently irreconcilable."

Events and Observers

In considering the consequences of Einstein's postulates in greater depth, i.e., in developing the theory of special relativity, we need to be certain that meanings of some important terms are crystal clear. First, there is the concept of an *event*. A physical event is something that happens, like the closing of a door, a lightning strike, the collision of two particles, your birthday, or the explosion of a star. Every event occurs at some point in space and at some instant in time, but it is very important to recognize that events are independent of the particular inertial reference frame that we might use to describe them. Events do not "belong" to any reference frame.

Events are described by *observers* who do belong to particular inertial frames of reference. Observers could be people (as in Section 1-1), electronic instruments, or other suitable recorders, but for our discussions in special relativity we are going to be very specific. Strictly speaking, the observer will be an array of recording clocks located throughout the inertial reference system. It may be helpful for you to think of the observer as a person who goes around reading out the memories of the recording clocks or receives records that have been transmitted from distant clocks, but always keep in mind that in reporting events such a person is strictly limited to summarizing the data collected from the clock memories. The travel time of light precludes him from including in his report distant events that he may have seen by eye! It is in this sense that we will be using the word *observer* in our discussions.

Each inertial reference frame may be thought of as being formed by a cubic three-dimensional lattice made of identical measuring rods (e.g., meter sticks) with a recording clock at each intersection as illustrated in Figure 1-14. The clocks are all identical, and we, of course, want them all to read the "same time" as one another at any instant, i.e., they must be *synchronized*. There are many ways to accomplish synchronization of the clocks, but a very straightforward way, made possible by the second postulate, is to use one of the clocks in the lattice as a standard, or *reference clock*. For convenience we will also use the location of the reference clock in the lattice as the coordinate origin for the reference frame. The reference clock is started with its indicator (hands, pointer, digital display) set at zero. At the instant it starts it also sends out a flash of light that spreads out as a spherical wave in all directions. When the flash from the reference clock reaches the lattice clocks 1 m away (notice that in Figure 1-14 there are six of them, two of which are off the edges of the figure), we want their indicators to read the time required for light to travel 1 m ($= 1/299{,}792{,}458$ s). This can be done simply by having an observer at each clock set that time on the indicator and then having the flash from the reference clock start them as it passes. The clocks 1 m from the origin now display the same time as the reference clock, i.e., they are all synchronized. In a similar fashion, all of the clocks throughout the inertial frame can be synchronized, since the distance of any clock from the reference clock can be calculated from the space coordinates of its position in the lattice and the initial setting of its indicator will be the corresponding travel time for the reference light flash. This procedure can be used to synchronize the

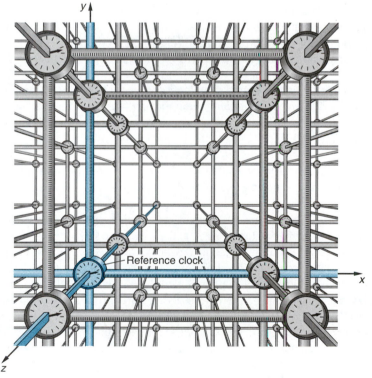

Fig. 1-14 Inertial reference frame formed from a lattice of measuring rods with a clock at each intersection. The clocks are all synchronized using a reference clock. In this diagram the measuring rods are shown to be 1 m long, but they could all be 1 cm, 1 μm, or 1 km as required by the scale and precision of the measurements being considered. The three space dimensions are the clock positions. The fourth spacetime dimension, time, is shown by indicator readings on the clocks.

clocks in any inertial frame, *but* it does not synchronize the clocks in reference frames that move with respect to one another. Indeed, as we shall see shortly, clocks in relatively moving frames cannot in general be synchronized with one another.

When an event occurs, its location and time are recorded instantly by the nearest clock. Suppose that an atom located at $x = 2$ m, $y = 3$ m, $z = 4$ m in Figure 1-14 emits a tiny flash of light at $t = 21$ s on the clock at that location. That event is recorded in space and in time, or, as we will henceforth refer to it, the *spacetime* coordinate system with the numbers (2,3,4,21). The observer may read out and analyze these data at his leisure, within the limits set by the information transmission time (i.e., the light travel time) from distant clocks. For example, the path of a particle moving through the lattice is revealed by analysis of the records showing the particle's time of passage at each clock's location. Distances between successive locations and the corresponding time differences enable the determination of the particle's velocity. Similar records of the spacetime coordinates of the particle's path can, of course, also be made in any inertial frame moving relative to ours, but to compare the distances and time intervals measured in the two frames requires that we consider carefully the relativity of simultaneity.

Relativity of Simultaneity

Einstein's postulates lead to a number of predictions regarding measurements made by observers in inertial frames moving relative to one another that initially seem very strange, including some that appear paradoxical. Even so, these predictions have been experimentally verified; and nearly without exception, every paradox is resolved by an understanding of the *relativity of simultaneity*, which states that

> Two spatially separated events simultaneous in one reference frame are not simultaneous in any other inertial frame moving relative to the first.

A corollary to this is that

> Clocks synchronized in one reference frame are not synchronized in any other inertial frame moving relative to the first.

What do we mean by simultaneous events? Suppose two observers, both in the inertial frame S at different locations A and B, agree to explode bombs at time t_0 (remember, we have synchronized all of the clocks in S). The clock at C, equidistant from A and B, will record the arrival of light from the explosions at the same instant, i.e., simultaneously. Other clocks in S will record the arrival of light from A or B first, depending on their locations, but after correcting for the time the light takes to reach each clock, the data recorded by each would lead an observer to conclude that the explosions were simultaneous. We will thus define two events to be simultaneous in an inertial reference frame if the light signals from the events reach an observer halfway between them at the same time as recorded by a clock at that location, called a local clock.

Einstein's Example   To show that two events which are simultaneous in frame S are not simultaneous in another frame S' moving relative to S, we use an example introduced by Einstein. A train is moving with speed v past a station platform. We have

observers located at A', B', and C' at the front, back, and middle of the train. (We consider the train to be at rest in S' and the platform in S.) We now suppose that the train and platform are struck by lightning at the front and back of the train and that the lightning bolts are simultaneous in the frame of the platform (S; Figure 1-15a). That is, an observer located at C halfway between positions A and B, where lightning strikes, observes the two flashes at the same time. It is convenient to suppose that the lightning scorches both the train and the platform so that the events can be easily located in each reference frame. Since C' is in the middle of the train, halfway between the places on the train which are scorched, the events are simultaneous in S' only if the clock at C' records the flashes at the same time. However, the clock at C' records the flash from the front of the train before the flash from the back. In frame S, when the light from the front flash reaches the observer at C', the train has moved some distance toward A, so that the flash from the back has not yet reached C', as indicated in Figure 1-15b. The observer at C' must therefore conclude that the events are not simultaneous, but that the front of the train was struck before the back. Figures 1-15c and 1-15d illustrate, respectively, the subsequent simultaneous arrival of the flashes at C and the still later arrival of the flash from the rear of the train at C'. As we have discussed, all observers in S' on the train will agree with the observer at C' when they have corrected for the time it takes light to reach them.

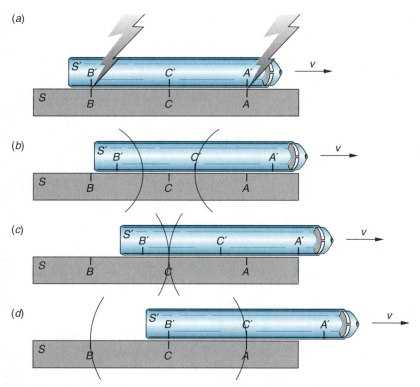

Fig. 1-15 Lightning bolts strike the front and rear of the train, scorching both the train and the platform, as the train (frame S') moves past the platform (system S) at speed v. (a) The strikes are simultaneous in S, reaching the C observer located midway between the events at the same instant as recorded by the clock at C as shown in (c). In S' the flash from the front of the train is recorded by the C' clock, located midway between the scorch marks on the train, before that from the rear of the train (b and d, respectively). Thus, the C' observer concludes that the strikes were not simultaneous.

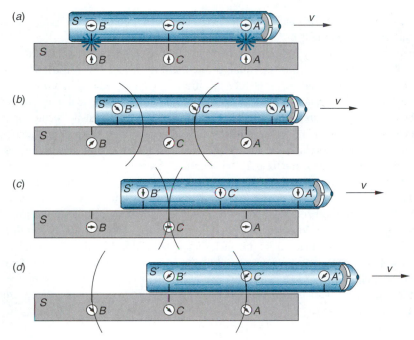

Fig. 1-16 (*a*) Light flashes originate simultaneously at clocks *A* and *B*, synchronized in *S*. (*b*) The clock at *C'*, midway between *A'* and *B'* on the moving train, records the arrival of the flash from *A* before the flash from *B* shown in (*d*). Since the observer in *S* announced that the flashes were triggered at t_0 on the local clocks, the observer at *C'* concludes that the local clocks at *A* and *B* did not read t_0 simultaneously; i.e., they were not synchronized. The simultaneous arrival of the flashes at *C* is shown in (*c*).

The corollary can also be demonstrated with a similar example. Again consider the train to be at rest in *S'*, which moves past the platform, at rest in *S*, with speed *v*. Figure 1-16 shows three of the clocks in the *S* lattice and three of those in the *S'* lattice. The clocks in each system's lattice have been synchronized in the manner that was described earlier, but those in *S* are not synchronized with those in *S'*. The observer at *C* midway between *A* and *B* on the platform announces that light sources at *A* and *B* will flash when the clocks at those locations read t_0 (Figure 1-16*a*). The observer at *C'*, positioned midway between *A'* and *B'*, notes the arrival of the light flash from the front of the train (Figure 1-16*b*) *before* the arrival of the one from the rear (Figure 1-16*d*). Observer *C'* thus concludes that, if the flashes were each emitted at t_0 on the local clocks, as announced, then the clocks at *A* and *B* are not synchronized. All observers in *S'* would agree with that conclusion after correcting for the time of light travel. The clock located at *C* records the arrival of the two flashes simultaneously, of course, since the clocks in *S* are synchronized (Figure 1-16*c*). Notice, too, in Figure 1-16 that *C'* also concludes that the clock at *A* is ahead of the clock at *B*. This is important, and we will return to it in more detail in the next section.

QUESTIONS

3. In addition to that described above, what would be another possible method of synchronizing all of the clocks in an inertial reference system?

4. In the demonstration of the validity of the corollary, how do observers at *A'* and *B'* reach the same conclusion as the observer at *C'* regarding the synchronization of the clocks at *A* and *B*?

1-3 The Lorentz Transformation

We now consider a very important consequence of Einstein's postulates, the general relation between the spacetime coordinates x, y, z, and t of an event as seen in reference frame S and the coordinates x', y', z', and t' of the same event as seen in reference frame S', which is moving with uniform velocity relative to S. For simplicity we shall consider only the special case in which the origins of the two coordinate systems are coincident at time $t = t' = 0$ and S' is moving, relative to S, with speed v along the x (or x') axis and with the y' and z' axes parallel, respectively, to the y and z axes, as shown in Figure 1-17. As we discussed earlier, the classical Galilean coordinate transformation is

$$x' = x - vt \qquad y' = y \qquad z' = z \qquad t' = t \qquad \textbf{1-3}$$

which expresses coordinate measurements made by an observer in S' in terms of those measured by an observer in S. The inverse transformation is

$$x = x' + vt' \qquad y = y' \qquad z = z' \qquad t = t'$$

and simply reflects the fact that the sign of the relative velocity of the reference frames is different for the two observers. The corresponding classical velocity transformation was given in Equation 1-2 and the (invariant) acceleration transformation in Equation 1-4. (For the rest of the discussion we shall ignore the equations for y and z, which do not change in this special case of motion along the x and x' axes.) These equations are consistent with experiment as long as v is much less than c.

It should be clear that the classical velocity transformation is not consistent with the Einstein postulates of special relativity. If light moves along the x axis with speed c in S, Equation 1-2 implies that the speed in S' is $u'_x = c - v$ rather than $u'_x = c$. The Galilean transformation equations must therefore be modified to be consistent with Einstein's postulates, but the result must reduce to the classical equations when v is much less than c. We shall give a brief outline of one method of obtaining the relativistic transformation which is called the *Lorentz transformation*, so named because of its original discovery by H. A. Lorentz.[12] We assume the equation for x' to be of the form

$$x' = \gamma (x - vt) \qquad \textbf{1-13}$$

where γ is a constant which can depend upon v and c but not on the coordinates. If this equation is to reduce to the classical one, γ must approach 1 as v/c approaches 0. The inverse transformation must look the same except for the sign of the velocity:

$$x = \gamma (x' + vt') \qquad \textbf{1-14}$$

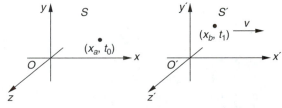

Fig. 1-17 Two inertial frames S and S' with the latter moving at speed v in $+x$ direction of system S. Each set of axes shown is simply the coordinate axes of a lattice like that in Figure 1-14. Remember, there is a clock at each intersection. A short time before the times represented by this diagram O and O' were coincident and the lattices of S and S' were intermeshed.

With the arrangement of the axes in Figure 1-17, there is no relative motion of the frames in the y and z directions; hence $y' = y$ and $z' = z$. However, insertion of the as yet unknown multiplier γ modifies the classical transformation of time, $t' = t$. To see this, we substitute x' from Equation 1-13 into Equation 1-14 and solve for t'. The result is

$$t' = \gamma \left[t + \frac{(1 - \gamma^2)}{\gamma^2} \frac{x}{v} \right] \qquad \text{1-15}$$

Now let a flash of light start from the origin of S at $t = 0$. Since we have assumed that the origins coincide at $t = t' = 0$, the flash also starts at the origin of S' at $t' = 0$. The flash expands from *both* origins as a spherical wave. The equation for the wave front according to an observer in S is

$$x^2 + y^2 + z^2 = c^2 t^2 \qquad \text{1-16}$$

and according to an observer in S' it is

$$x'^2 + y'^2 + z'^2 = c^2 t'^2 \qquad \text{1-17}$$

where both equations are consistent with the second postulate. Consistency with the first postulate means that the relativistic transformation that we seek must transform Equation 1-16 into Equation 1-17, and vice versa. For example, substituting Equations 1-13 and 1-15 into 1-17 results in Equation 1-16, *if*

$$\gamma = \frac{1}{\sqrt{1 - \dfrac{v^2}{c^2}}} = \frac{1}{\sqrt{1 - \beta^2}} \qquad \text{1-18}$$

where $\beta = v/c$. Notice that $\gamma = 1$ for $v = 0$ and $\gamma \to \infty$ for $v = c$. How this is done is illustrated in Example 1-4.

EXAMPLE 1-4 Relativistic Transformation Multiplier γ Show that γ must be given by Equation 1-18, if Equation 1-17 is to be transformed into Equation 1-16 consistent with Einstein's first postulate.

Solution
Substituting Equations 1-13 and 1-15 into 1-17 and noting that $y' = y$ and $z' = z$ in this case yield

$$\gamma^2 (x - vt)^2 + y^2 + z^2 = c^2 \gamma^2 \left[t + \frac{1 - \gamma^2}{\gamma^2} \frac{x}{v} \right]^2 \qquad \text{1-19}$$

To be consistent with the first postulate, Equation 1-19 must be identical to 1-16. This requires that the coefficient of the x^2 term in Equation 1-19 be equal to 1, that of the t^2 term equal to c^2, and that of the xt term equal to 0. Any of those conditions can be used to determine γ and all yield the same result. Using, for example, the coefficient of x^2, we have from Equation 1-19 that

$$\gamma^2 - c^2\gamma^2 \frac{(1 - \gamma^2)^2}{\gamma^4 v^2} = 1$$

which can be rearranged to

$$-c^2 \frac{(1 - \gamma^2)^2}{\gamma^2 v^2} = (1 - \gamma^2)$$

Canceling $1 - \gamma^2$ on both sides and solving for γ yield

$$\gamma = \frac{1}{\sqrt{1 - \dfrac{v^2}{c^2}}}$$

With the value for γ found in Example 1-4, Equation 1-15 can be written in a somewhat simpler form, and with it the complete Lorentz transformation becomes

$$x' = \gamma(x - vt) \qquad y' = y$$
$$t' = \gamma\left(t - \frac{vx}{c^2}\right) \qquad z' = z \tag{1-20}$$

and the inverse

$$x = \gamma(x' + vt') \qquad y = y'$$
$$t = \gamma\left(t' + \frac{vx'}{c^2}\right) \qquad z = z' \tag{1-21}$$

with

$$\gamma = \frac{1}{\sqrt{1 - \beta^2}}$$

EXAMPLE 1-5 **Transformation of Time Intervals** The arrivals of two cosmic ray μ mesons (muons) are recorded by detectors in the laboratory, one at time t_0 at location x_a and the second at time t_1 at location x_b in the laboratory reference frame, S in Figure 1-17. What is the time interval between those two events in system S' which moves relative to S at speed v?

Solution
Applying the time coordinate transformation from Equation 1-20,

$$t_1' - t_0' = \gamma\left(t_1 - \frac{vx_b}{c^2}\right) - \gamma\left(t_0 - \frac{vx_a}{c^2}\right) \tag{1-22}$$

$$t_1' - t_0' = \gamma(t_1 - t_0) - \frac{\gamma v}{c^2}(x_b - x_a)$$

We see that the time interval measured in S' depends not just on the corresponding time interval in S, but also on the spatial separation of the clocks in S that measured the interval. This result should not come as a total surprise, since we have already discovered that, although the clocks in S are synchronized with each other, they are not synchronized for observers in other inertial frames.

Special Case 1

If it should happen that the two events occur at the same location in S, i.e., $x_a = x_b$, then $(t_1 - t_0)$, the time interval measured on a clock located at the events, is called the *proper time interval*. Notice that, since $\gamma > 1$ for all frames moving relative to S, the proper time interval is the *minimum* time interval that can be measured between those events.

Special Case 2

Does there exist an inertial frame for which the events described above would be measured to be simultaneous? Since the question has been asked, you probably suspect that the answer is yes, and you are right. The two events will be simultaneous in a system S'' for which $t''_1 - t''_0 = 0$, i.e., when

$$\gamma (t_1 - t_0) = \frac{\gamma v}{c^2} (x_b - x_a)$$

or when

$$\beta = \frac{v}{c} = \left(\frac{t_1 - t_0}{x_b - x_a} \right) c \qquad \text{1-23}$$

Notice that $(x_b - x_a)/c = $ time for a light beam to travel from x_a to x_b; thus we can characterize S'' as being that system whose speed relative to S is that fraction of c given by the time interval between the events divided by the travel time of light between them.

While it is possible for us to get along in special relativity without the Lorentz transformation, it has an application that is quite valuable: it enables the spacetime coordinates of events measured by the measuring rods and clocks in the reference frame of one observer to be translated into the corresponding coordinates determined by the measuring rods and clocks of an observer in another inertial frame. As we will see in Section 1-4, such transformations lead to some startling results.

Relativistic Velocity Transformations

The transformation for velocities in special relativity can be obtained by differentiation of the Lorentz transformation, keeping in mind the definition of the velocity. Suppose a particle moves in S with velocity $\mathbf{u}$ whose components are $u_x = dx/dt$, $u_y = dy/dt$, and $u_z = dz/dt$. An observer in S' would measure the components $u'_x = dx'/dt'$, $u'_y = dy'/dt'$, $u'_z = dz'/dt'$. Using the transformation equations, we obtain

$$dx' = \gamma(dx - v\,dt) \qquad dy' = dy$$

$$dt' = \gamma\left(dt - \frac{v\,dx}{c^2}\right) \qquad dz' = dz$$

from which we see that u_x' is given by

$$u_x' = \frac{dx'}{dt'} = \frac{\gamma(dx - v\,dt)}{\gamma\left(dt - \dfrac{v\,dx}{c^2}\right)} = \frac{(dx/dt - v)}{1 - \dfrac{v}{c^2}\dfrac{dx}{dt}}$$

or

$$u_x' = \frac{u_x - v}{1 - \dfrac{vu_x}{c^2}} \qquad\qquad \textbf{1-24}$$

and, if a particle has velocity components in the y and z directions, it is not difficult to find the components in S' in a similar manner.

$$u_y' = \frac{u_y}{\gamma\left(1 - \dfrac{vu_x}{c^2}\right)} \qquad u_z' = \frac{u_z}{\gamma\left(1 - \dfrac{vu_x}{c^2}\right)}$$

Remember that this form of the velocity transformation is specific to the arrangement of the coordinate axes in Figure 1-17. Note, too, that when $v \ll c$, i.e., when $\beta = v/c \approx 0$, the relativistic velocity transforms reduce to the classical velocity addition of Equation 1-2. Likewise the inverse velocity transformation is

$$u_x = \frac{u_x' + v}{\left(1 + \dfrac{vu_x'}{c^2}\right)} \qquad u_y = \frac{u_y'}{\gamma\left(1 + \dfrac{vu_x'}{c^2}\right)} \qquad u_z = \frac{u_z'}{\gamma\left(1 + \dfrac{vu_x'}{c^2}\right)} \qquad \textbf{1-25}$$

EXAMPLE 1-6 Relative Speeds of Cosmic Rays Suppose that two cosmic ray protons approach Earth from opposite directions as shown in Figure 1-18a. The speeds relative to Earth are measured to be $v_1 = 0.6c$ and $v_2 = -0.8c$. What is

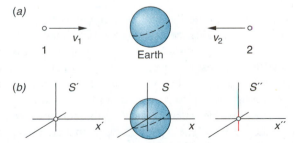

Fig. 1-18 (a) Two cosmic ray protons approach Earth from opposite directions at speeds v_1 and v_2 with respect to Earth. (b) Attaching an inertial frame to each particle and Earth enables one to visualize the several relative speeds involved and apply the velocity transformation correctly.

Earth's velocity relative to each proton, and what is the velocity of each proton relative to the other?

Solution

Consider each particle and Earth to be inertial reference frames S', S'', and S with their respective x axes parallel, as in Figure 1-18b. With this arrangement $v_1 = u_{1x} = 0.6c$ and $v_2 = u_{2x} = -0.8c$. Thus, the speed of Earth measured in S' is $v'_{Ex} = -0.6c$ and the speed of Earth measured in S'' is $v''_{Ex} = 0.8c$.

To find the speed of proton 2 with respect to proton 1, we apply Equation 1-24 to compute u'_{2x}, i.e., the speed of particle 2 in S'. Its speed in S has been measured to be $u_{2x} = -0.8c$, where the S' system has relative speed $v_1 = 0.6c$ with respect to S. Thus, substituting into Equation 1-24, we obtain

$$u'_{2x} = \frac{-0.8c - (0.6c)}{1 - (0.6c)(-0.8c)/c^2} = \frac{-1.4c}{1.48} = -0.95c$$

and the first proton measures the second to be approaching (moving in the $-x'$ direction) at $0.95c$.

The observer in S'' must of course make a consistent measurement, i.e., find the speed of proton 1 to be $0.95c$ in the $+x''$ direction. This can be readily shown by a second application of Equation 1-24 to compute u''_{1x}.

$$u''_{1x} = \frac{0.6c - (-0.8c)}{1 - (0.6c)(-0.8c)/c^2} = \frac{1.4c}{1.48} = 0.95c$$

QUESTIONS

5. The Lorentz transformation for y and z is the same as the classical result: $y = y'$ and $z = z'$. Yet the relativistic velocity transformation does not give the classical result $u_y = u'_y$ and $u_z = u'_z$. Explain.

6. Since the velocity components of a moving particle are different in relatively moving frames, the *directions* of the velocity vectors are also different, in general. Explain why the fact that observers in S and S' measure different directions for a particle's motion is not an inconsistency in their observations.

Spacetime Diagrams

The relativistic discovery that time intervals between events are not the same for all observers in different inertial reference frames underscores the four-dimensional character of spacetime. With the diagrams that we have used thus far, it is difficult to depict and visualize on the two-dimensional page events that occur at different times, since each diagram is equivalent to a snapshot of the spacetime at a particular instant. Showing events as a function of time typically requires a series of diagrams, such as Figures 1-15 and 1-16; but even then our attention tends to be drawn to the space coordinate systems, rather than the events, whereas it is the *events* that are fundamental. This difficulty is removed in special relativity with a simple yet powerful graphing method called the *spacetime diagram*. (This is just a new name given to the t versus x graphs that you first began to use when you discussed motion in introductory physics.) On the spacetime diagram we can graph both the space and time coordinates of many events in

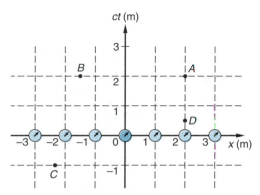

Fig. 1-19 Spacetime diagram for an inertial reference frame S. Two of the space dimensions (y and z) are suppressed. The units on both the space and time axes are the same, meters. A meter of time means the time required for light to travel 1 meter, i.e., 3.3×10^{-9} s.

one or more inertial frames, albeit with one limitation. Since the page offers only two dimensions for graphing, we suppress, or ignore for now, two of the space dimensions, in particular y and z. With our choice of the relative motion of inertial frames along the x axis, $y' = y$ and $z' = z$ anyhow. (This is one of the reasons we made that convenient choice a few pages back, the other reason being mathematical simplicity.) This means that for the time being we are limiting our attention to one space dimension and to time, i.e., to events that occur, regardless of when, along one line in space. Should we need the other two dimensions, e.g., in a consideration of velocity vector transformations, we can always use the Lorentz transformation equations.

In a spacetime diagram the space location of each event is plotted along the x axis horizontally and the time is plotted vertically. From the three-dimensional array of measuring rods and clocks in Figure 1-14, we will use only those located on the x axis as in Figure 1-19. (See, things are simpler already!) Since events that exhibit relativistic effects generally occur at high speeds, it will be convenient to multiply the time scale by the speed of light (a constant), which enables us to use the same units and scale on both the space and time axes, e.g., meters of distance and meters of light travel time.[13] The time axis is, therefore, c times the time t in seconds, i.e., ct. As we will see shortly, this choice prevents events from clustering about the axes and enables the straightforward addition of other inertial frames into the diagram.

As time advances, notice that in Figure 1-19 each clock in the array moves vertically upward along the dotted lines. Thus, as events $A, B, C,$ and D occur in spacetime, one of the clocks of the array is at (or very near) each event when it happens. Extending our previous definition a bit, the clock located at each event records *proper time.* (See Example 1-5.) In the figure, events A and D occur at the same place ($x = 2$ m), but at different times. The time interval between them measured on clock 2 is the proper time, since clock 2 is located at *both* events. Events A and B occur at different locations, but at the same time (i.e., simultaneously in this frame). Event C occurred before the present ($ct = 0 =$ present), since $ct = -1$ m.

Worldlines in Spacetime   Particles moving in space trace out a line in the spacetime diagram called the *worldline* of the particle. The worldline is the "trajectory" of the particle on a ct versus x graph. To illustrate, consider four particles moving in space (not spacetime), as shown in Figure 1-20a, which shows the array of synchronized clocks on the x axis and the space trajectories of four particles, each starting at $x = 0$ and moving at some constant speed, during 3 m of time. Figure 1-20b shows the worldline for each of the particles in spacetime. Notice that constant speed means that the worldline has

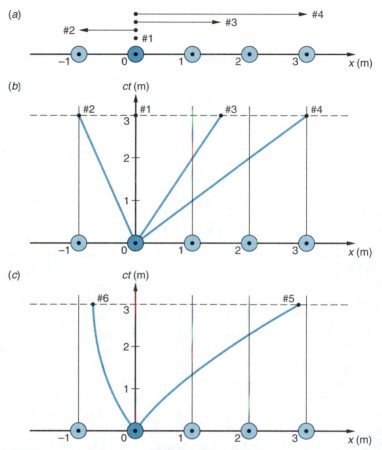

Fig. 1-20 (*a*) The space trajectories of four particles with various constant speeds. Note that particle 1 has a speed of zero and particle 2 moves in the −*x* direction. The worldlines of the particles are straight lines. (*b*) The worldline of particle 1 is also the *ct* axis, since that particle remains at *x* = 0. The constant slopes are a consequence of the constant speeds. (*c*) For accelerating particles 5 and 6 [not shown in (*a*)], the worldlines are curved, the slope at any point yielding the instantaneous speed.

constant slope; i.e., it is a straight line (slope = $\Delta t/\Delta x = 1/(\Delta x/\Delta t) = 1/\text{speed}$). That was also the case when you first encountered elapsed time versus displacement graphs in introductory physics. Even then, you were plotting spacetime graphs and drawing worldlines! If the particle is accelerating—either speeding up as particle 5 in Figure 1-20*c*, or slowing down, like particle 6—the worldlines are curved. Thus, the worldline is the record of the particle's travel through spacetime, giving its speed (= 1/slope) and acceleration (= 1/rate at which the slope changes) at every instant.

EXAMPLE 1-7 Computing Speeds in Spacetime Find the speed *u* of particle 3 in Figure 1-20.

Solution

The speed $u = \Delta x/\Delta t = 1/\text{slope}$ where we have $\Delta x = 1.5 - 0 = 1.5$ m and $\Delta ct = c \cdot \Delta t = 3.0 - 0 = 3.0$ m (from Figure 1-20). Thus, $\Delta t = (3.0/c) = (3.0/3.0 \times 10^8) = 10^{-8}$ s and $u = 1.5 \text{ m}/10^{-8} \text{ s} = 0.5c$.

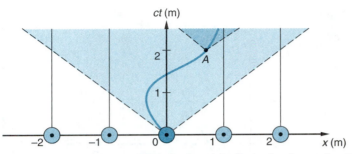

Fig. 1-21 The speed-of-light limit to the speeds of particles limits the slopes of worldlines for particles that move through $x = 0$ at $ct = 0$ to the shaded area of spacetime, i.e., to slopes < -1 and $> +1$. The dashed lines are worldlines of light flashes moving in the $-x$ and $+x$ directions. The curved worldline of the particle shown has the same limits at every instant. Notice that the particle's speed = 1/slope.

The speed of particle 4, computed as shown in Example 1-7, turns out to be c, the speed of light. (Particle 4 is a light pulse.) The slope of its worldline $\Delta(ct)/\Delta x = 3$ m/3 m = 1. Similarly, the slope of the worldline of a light pulse moving in the $-x$ direction is -1. Since relativity limits the speed of particles with mass to less than c, as we will see in Chapter 2, the slopes of worldlines for particles that move through $x = 0$ at $ct = 0$ are limited to the larger shaded triangle in Figure 1-21. The same limits to the slope apply at every point along a particle's worldline, such as point A on the curved spacetime trajectory in Figure 1-21. This means that the particle's possible worldlines for times greater than $ct = 2$ m must lie within the heavily shaded triangle.

Analyzing events and motion in inertial systems that are in relative motion can now be accomplished more easily than with diagrams such as Figures 1-15 through 1-18. Suppose we have two inertial frames S and S' with S' moving in the $+x$ direction of S at speed v as in those figures. The clocks in both systems are started at $t = t' = 0$ (the present) as the two origins $x = 0$ and $x' = 0$ coincide, and, as before, observers in each system have synchronized the clocks in their respective systems. The spacetime diagram for S is, of course, like that in Figure 1-19, but how does S' appear in that diagram, i.e., with respect to an observer in S? Consider that, as the origin of S' (i.e., the point where $x' = 0$) moves in S, its worldline is the ct' axis, since the ct' axis is the locus of all points with $x' = 0$ (just as the ct axis is the locus of points with $x = 0$). Thus, the slope of the ct' axis as seen by an observer in S can be found from Equation 1-20, the Lorentz transformation, as follows:

$$x' = \gamma (x - vt) = 0 \qquad \text{for} \qquad x' = 0$$

or

$$x = vt = (v/c)(ct) = \beta ct$$

and

$$ct = (1/\beta)x$$

which says that the slope (in S) of the worldline of the point $x' = 0$, the ct' axis, is $1/\beta$. (See Figure 1-22a.)

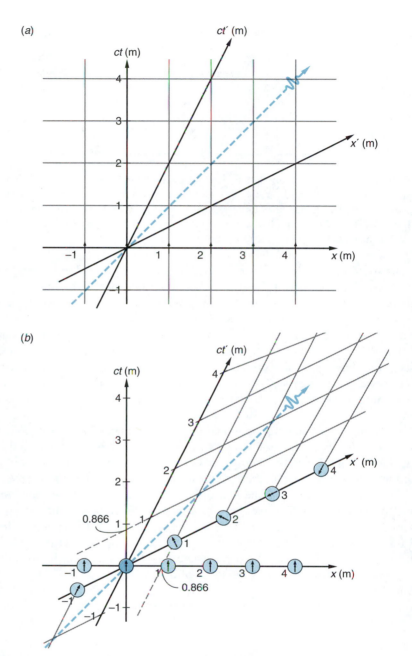

Fig. 1-22 (*a*) Spacetime diagram of S showing S' moving at speed $v = 0.5c$ in the $+x$ direction. The diagram is drawn with $t = t' = 0$ when the origins of S and S' coincided. The dashed line shows the worldline of a light flash that passed through the point $x = 0$ at $t = 0$ heading in the $+x$ direction. Its slope equals 1 in both S and S'. The ct' and x' axes of S' have slopes of $1/\beta = 2$ and $\beta = 0.5$, respectively. (*b*) Calibrating the axes of S' as described in the text allows the grid of coordinates to be drawn on S'. Interpretation is facilitated by remembering that (*b*) shows the system S' as it is observed in the spacetime diagram of S.

In the same manner, the x' axis can be located using the fact that it is the locus of points for which $ct' = 0$. The Lorentz transformation once again provides the slope:

$$t' = \gamma\left(t - \frac{vx}{c^2}\right) = 0$$

or

$$t = \frac{vx}{c^2} \quad \text{and} \quad ct = \frac{v}{c}x = \beta x$$

Thus, the slope of the x' axis as measured by an observer in S is β, as shown in Figure 1-22a. Don't be confused by the fact that the x axes don't look parallel anymore. They are still parallel in *space,* but this is a *spacetime* diagram. It shows motion in both space and time. For example, the clock at $x' = 1$ m in Figure 1-22b passed the point $x = 0$ at about $ct = -1.5$ m as the x' axis of S' moved both upward and to the right in S. Remember, as time advances, the array of synchronized clocks and measuring rods that are the x axis also moves upward, so that, for example, when $ct = 1$, the origin of S' $(x' = 0, ct' = 0)$ has moved $vt = (v/c)ct = \beta ct$ to the right along the x axis.

QUESTION

7. Explain how the spacetime diagram in Figure 1-22b would appear drawn by an observer in S'.

EXAMPLE 1-8 Simultaneity in Spacetime Use the train-platform example of Figure 1-16 and a suitable spacetime diagram to show that events simultaneous in one frame are not simultaneous in a frame moving relative to the first. (This is the corollary to the relativity of simultaneity that we first demonstrated in the previous section using Figure 1-16.)

Solution

Suppose a train is passing a station platform at speed v and an observer C at the midpoint of the platform, system S, announces that light flashes will be emitted at clocks A and B located at opposite ends of the platform at $t = 0$. Let the train, system S', be a rocket train with $v = 0.5c$. As in the earlier discussion, clocks at C and C' both read 0 as C' passes C. Figure 1-23 shows this situation. It is the spacetime equivalent of Figure 1-16.

Two events occur: the light flashes. The flashes are simultaneous in S, since both occur at $ct = 0$. In S', however, the event at A occurred at ct' (A') (see Figure 1-23), about 1.2 ct' units *before* $ct' = 0$, and the event at B occurred at ct' (B'), about 1.2 ct' units *after* $ct' = 0$. Thus, the flashes are not simultaneous in S' and A occurs before B, as we also saw in Figure 1-16.

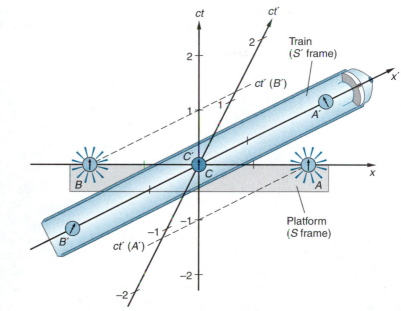

Fig. 1-23 Spacetime equivalent of Figure 1-16, showing the spacetime diagram for the system *S* in which the platform is at rest. Measurements made by observers in *S'* are read from the primed axes.

Exploring

Calibrating the Spacetime Axes

By calibrating the coordinate axes of *S'* consistent with the Lorentz transformation we will be able to read the coordinates of events and calculate space and time intervals between events as measured in both *S* and *S'* directly from the diagram, in addition to calculating them from Equations 1-20 and 1-21. The calibration of the *S'* axes is straightforward and is accomplished as follows. The locus of points, e.g., with $x' = 1$ m, is a line parallel to the *ct'* axis through the point $x' = 1$, $ct' = 0$, just as we saw earlier that the *ct'* axis was the locus of those points with $x' = 0$ through the point $x' = 0$, $ct' = 0$. Substituting these values into the Lorentz transformation for x', we see that the line through $x' = 1$ m intercepts the *x* axis, i.e., the line where $ct = 0$, at

$$x' = \gamma(x - vt) = \gamma(x - \beta ct)$$

$$1 = \gamma x \qquad \text{or} \qquad x = \frac{1}{\gamma} = \sqrt{1 - \beta^2}$$

1-26

or, in general,

$$x = x'\sqrt{1 - \beta^2}$$

In Figure 1-22*b*, where $\beta = 0.5$, the line $x' = 1$ m intercepts the *x* axis at $x = 0.866$ m. Similarly, if $x' = 2$ m, $x = 1.73$ m; if $x' = 3$ m, $x = 2.60$ m; and so on.

The ct' axis is calibrated in a precisely equivalent manner. The locus of points with $ct' = 1$ m is a line parallel to the x' axis through the point $ct' = 1$, $x' = 0$. Using the Lorentz transformation, the intercept of that line with the ct axis (where $x = 0$) is found as follows:

$$t' = \gamma\,(t - vx/c^2)$$

which can also be written as

$$ct' = \gamma\,(ct - \beta x) \qquad\qquad \textbf{1-27}$$

or $ct' = \gamma ct$ for $x = 0$. Thus, for $ct' = 1$, $1 = \gamma ct$ or $ct = (1 - \beta^2)^{1/2}$ and, again, in general, $ct = ct'(1 - \beta^2)^{1/2}$. The $x' \cdot ct'$ coordinate grid is shown in Figure 1-22b.

Notice in Figure 1-22b that the clocks located in S' are *not* found to be synchronized by observers in S, even though they are synchronized in S'. This is exactly the conclusion that we arrived at in the discussion of the lightning striking the train and platform. In addition, those with positive x' coordinates are behind the S' reference clock and those with negative x' coordinates are ahead, the difference being greatest for those clocks farthest away. This is a direct consequence of the Lorentz transformation of the time coordinate—i.e., when $ct = 0$ in Equation 1-27, $ct' = -\gamma\beta x$. Note, too, that the slope of the worldline of the light beam equals 1 in S', as well as in S, as required by the second postulate.

1-4 Time Dilation and Length Contraction

The results of correct measurements of the time and space intervals between events do not depend upon the kind of apparatus used for the measurements or on the events themselves. We are free therefore to choose any events and measuring apparatus that will help us understand the application of the Einstein postulates to the results of measurements. As you have already seen from previous examples, convenient events in relativity are those that produce light flashes. A convenient clock is a *light clock,* pictured schematically in Figure 1-24. A photocell detects the light pulse and sends a

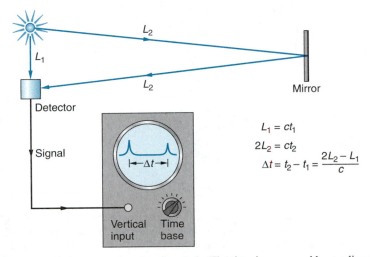

$$L_1 = ct_1$$
$$2L_2 = ct_2$$
$$\Delta t = t_2 - t_1 = \frac{2L_2 - L_1}{c}$$

Fig. 1-24 Light clock for measuring time intervals. The time is measured by reading the distance between pulses on the oscilloscope after calibrating the sweep speed.

voltage pulse to an oscilloscope, which produces a vertical deflection of the oscilloscope's trace. The phosphorescent material on the face of the oscilloscope tube gives a persistent light that can be observed visually, photographed, or recorded electronically. The time between two light flashes is determined by measuring the distance between pulses on the scope and knowing the sweep speed. Such a clock, which can easily be calibrated and compared with other types of clocks, is often used in nuclear physics experiments. Although not drawn as in Figure 1-24, the clocks used in explanations in this section may be thought of as light clocks.

Time Dilation (or Time Stretching)

We first consider an observer A' at rest in frame S' a distance D from a mirror, also in S', as shown in Figure 1-25a. He triggers a flash gun and measures the time interval $\Delta t'$ between the original flash and the return flash from the mirror. Since light travels with speed c, this time is $\Delta t' = (2D)/c$.

We now consider these same two events, the original flash of light and the returning flash, as observed in reference frame S, with respect to which S' is moving to the right with speed v. The events happen at two different places, x_1 and x_2, in frame S because between the original flash and the return flash observer A' has moved a horizontal distance $v\Delta t$, where Δt is the time interval between the events measured in S. In Figure 1-25b, a space diagram, we see that the path traveled by the light is longer in S than in S'. However, by Einstein's postulates, light travels with the same speed c in frame S as it does in frame S'. Since it travels farther in S at the same speed, it takes longer in S to reach the mirror and return. The time interval between flashes in S is thus longer than it is in S'. We can easily calculate Δt in terms of $\Delta t'$. From the triangle in Figure 1-25c, we see that

$$\left(\frac{c\,\Delta t}{2}\right)^2 = D^2 + \left(\frac{v\,\Delta t}{2}\right)^2$$

or

$$\Delta t = \frac{2D}{\sqrt{c^2 - v^2}} = \frac{2D}{c}\,\frac{1}{\sqrt{1 - v^2/c^2}}$$

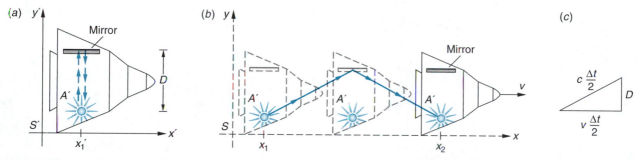

Fig. 1-25 (*a*) Observer A' and the mirror are in a spaceship at rest in frame S'. The time it takes for the light pulse to reach the mirror and return is measured by A' to be $2D/c$. (*b*) In frame S, the spaceship is moving to the right with speed v. If the speed of light is the same in both frames, the time it takes for the light to reach the mirror and return is longer than $2D/c$ in S because the distance traveled is greater than $2D$. (*c*) A right triangle for computing the time Δt in frame S.

Using $\Delta t' = 2D/c$, we have

$$\Delta t = \frac{\Delta t'}{\sqrt{1 - v^2/c^2}} = \gamma \Delta t' = \gamma \tau \qquad \textbf{1-28}$$

where $\tau = \Delta t'$ is the *proper time interval* that we first encountered in Example 1-5. Equation 1-28 describes *time dilation*; i.e., it tells us that the observer in frame S always measures the time interval between two events to be longer (since $\gamma > 1$) than the corresponding interval measured on the clock located at both events in the frame where they occur at the same location. Thus, observers in S conclude that the clock at A' in S' runs slow, since that clock measures a smaller time interval between the two events. Notice that the faster S' moves with respect to S, the larger is γ, and the slower the S' clocks will tick. It appears to the S observer that time is being stretched out in S'.

Be careful! The *same* clock must be located at each event for $\Delta t'$ to be the proper time interval τ. We can see why this is true by noting that Equation 1-28 can be obtained directly from the inverse Lorentz transformation for t. Referring again to Figure 1-25 and calling the emission of the flash event 1 and its return event 2, we have that

$$\Delta t = t_2 - t_1 = \gamma \left(t_2' + \frac{vx_2'}{c^2} \right) - \gamma \left(t_1' + \frac{vx_1'}{c^2} \right)$$

$$\Delta t = \gamma (t_2' - t_1') + \frac{\gamma v}{c^2} (x_2' - x_1')$$

or

$$\Delta t = \gamma \Delta t' + \frac{\gamma v}{c^2} \Delta x' \qquad \textbf{1-29}$$

If the clock that records t_2' and t_1' is located at the events, then $\Delta x' = 0$. If that is not the case, however, $\Delta x' \neq 0$ and $\Delta t'$, though certainly a valid measurement, is not a proper time interval. Only a clock located *at* an event *when* it occurs can record proper time.

EXAMPLE 1-9 Spatial Separation of Events Two events occur at the same point x_0' at times t_1' and t_2' in S', which moves with speed v relative to S. What is the spatial separation of these events measured in S?

Solution

1. The location of the events in S is given by the Lorentz inverse transformation Equation 1-21:

$$x = \gamma (x' + vt')$$

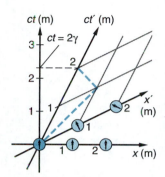

Fig. 1-26 Spacetime diagram illustrating time dilation. The dashed line is the worldline of a light flash emitted at $x' = 0$ and reflected back to that point by a mirror at $x' = 1$ m. $\beta = 0.5$.

2. The spatial separation of the two events $\Delta x = x_2 - x_1$ is then:

$$\Delta x = \gamma(x_0' + vt_2') - \gamma(x_0' + vt_1')$$

3. The $\gamma x_0'$ terms cancel:

$$\Delta x = \gamma v(t_2' - t_1') = \gamma v \Delta t'$$

4. Since $\Delta t'$ is the proper time interval τ, Equation 1-28 yields:

$$\Delta x = v\gamma\tau = v\Delta t$$

5. Using the situation in Figure 1-26 as a numerical example, where $\beta = 0.5$ and $\gamma = 1.15$, we have:

$$\Delta x = \gamma \frac{v}{c} \Delta(ct') = (1.15)(0.5)(2)$$

$$= 1.15 \text{ m}$$

EXAMPLE 1-10 The Pregnant Elephant[14] Elephants have a gestation period of 21 months. Suppose that a freshly impregnated elephant is placed on a spaceship and sent toward a distant space jungle at $v = 0.75c$. If we monitor radio transmissions from the spaceship, how long after launch might we expect to hear the first squealing trumpet from the newborn calf?

Solution

1. In S', the rest frame of the elephant, the time interval from launch to birth is $\tau = 21$ months. In the Earth frame S, the time interval is Δt_1, given by Equation 1-28:

$$\Delta t_1 = \gamma\tau = \frac{1}{\sqrt{1 - \beta^2}}\tau$$

$$= \frac{1}{\sqrt{1 - (0.75)^2}}(21 \text{ months})$$

$$= 31.7 \text{ months}$$

2. At that time the radio signal announcing the happy event starts toward Earth at speed c, but from where? Using the result of Example 1-9, since launch the spaceship has moved Δx in S given by:

$$\Delta x = \gamma v\tau = \gamma\beta c\tau$$

$$= (1.51)(0.75)(21c \cdot \text{months})$$

$$= 23.8c \cdot \text{months}$$

where $c \cdot$ month is the distance light travels in one month.

3. Notice that there is no need to convert Δx into meters, since our interest is in how long it will take the radio signal to travel this distance in S. That time is Δt_2, given by:

$$\Delta t_2 = \Delta x / c$$
$$= 23.8 c \cdot \text{months} / c$$
$$= 23.8 \text{ months}$$

4. Thus, the good news will arrive at Earth at time Δt after launch where:

$$\Delta t = \Delta t_1 + \Delta t_2$$
$$= 31.7 + 23.8$$
$$= 55.5 \text{ months}$$

Remarks: This result, too, is readily obtained from a spacetime diagram. Figure 1-27 illustrates the general appearance of the spacetime diagram for this example, showing the elephant's worldline and the worldline of the radio signal.

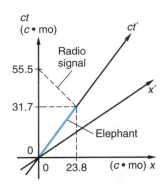

Fig. 1-27 Sketch of the spacetime diagram for Example 1–10. $\beta = 0.75$. The colored line is the worldline of the pregnant elephant. The worldline of the radio signal is the dashed line at 45° toward the upper left.

QUESTION

8. You are standing on a corner and a friend is driving past in an automobile. Both of you note the times when the car passes two different intersections and determine from your watch readings the time that elapses between the two events. Which of you has determined the proper time interval?

The time dilation of Equation 1-28 is easy to see in a spacetime diagram such as Figure 1-26, using the same round trip for a light pulse used above. Let the light flash leave $x' = 0$ at $ct' = 0$ when the S and S' origins coincided. The flash travels to $x' = 1$ m, reflects from a mirror located there, and returns to $x' = 0$. Let $\beta = 0.5$. The dotted line shows the worldline of the light beam, reflecting at $(x' = 1, ct' = 1)$ and returning to $x' = 0$ at $ct' = 2$ m. Note that the S observer records the latter event at $ct > 2$ m; i.e., the observer in S sees the S' clock running slow.

Experimental tests of the time dilation prediction have been performed using macroscopic clocks, in particular, accurate atomic clocks. In 1975, C. O. Alley conducted a test of both general and special relativity in which a set of atomic clocks were carried by a U.S. Navy antisubmarine patrol aircraft while it flew back and forth over the same path for 15 hours at altitudes between 8000 m and 10,000 m over Chesapeake Bay. The clocks in the plane were compared by laser pulses with an identical group of clocks on the ground. (See Figure 1-14 for one way such a comparison might be done.) Since the experiment was primarily intended to test the gravitational effect on clocks predicted by general relativity (see Section 2-5), the aircraft was deliberately flown at the rather sedate average speed of 270 knots (140 m/s) = $4.7 \times 10^{-7} c$ so as to minimize the time dilation due to the relative speeds of the clocks. Even so, after deducting the effect of gravitation as predicted by general relativity, the airborne clocks lost an average of 5.6×10^{-9} s due to the relative speed during the 15-hour flight. This result agrees with the prediction of special relativity, 5.7×10^{-9} s to within 2 percent, even at this low relative speed. The experimental results leave little basis for further debate as to whether traveling clocks of all kinds lose time on a round trip. They do.

Length Contraction

A phenomenon closely related to time dilation is *length contraction*. The length of an object measured in the reference frame in which the object is at rest is called its *proper length* L_p. In a reference frame in which the object is moving, the measured length parallel to the direction of motion is shorter than its proper length. Consider a rod at rest in the frame S' with one end at x_2' and the other end at x_1' as illustrated in Figure 1-28. The length of the rod in this frame is its proper length $L_p = x_2' - x_1'$. Some care must be taken to find the length of the rod in frame S. In this frame, the rod is moving to the right with speed v, the speed of frame S'. The length of the rod in frame S is *defined* as $L = x_2 - x_1$, where x_2 is the position of one end at some time t_2, and x_1 is the position of the other end *at the same time* $t_1 = t_2$ as measured in frame S. Since the rod is at rest in S', t_2' need not equal t_1'. Equation 1-20 is convenient to use to calculate $x_2 - x_1$ at some time t because it relates x, x', and t, whereas Equation 1-21 is not convenient because it relates x, x', and t':

$$x_2' = \gamma\,(x_2 - vt_2) \qquad \text{and} \qquad x_1' = \gamma\,(x_1 - vt_1)$$

Since $t_2 = t_1$, we obtain

$$x_2' - x_1' = \gamma\,(x_2 - x_1)$$

$$x_2 - x_1 = \frac{1}{\gamma}\,(x_2' - x_1') = \sqrt{1 - \frac{v^2}{c^2}}\,(x_2' - x_1')$$

or

$$L = \frac{1}{\gamma}\,L_p = \sqrt{1 - \frac{v^2}{c^2}}\,L_p \qquad\qquad \textbf{1-30}$$

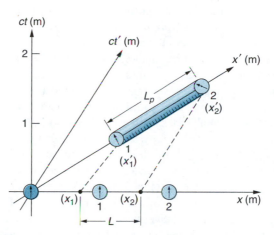

Fig. 1-28 A measuring rod, a meterstick in this case, lies at rest in S' between $x_2' = 2$ m and $x_1' = 1$ m. System S' moves with $\beta = 0.62$ relative to S. Since the rod is in motion, S must measure the locations of the ends of the rod x_2 and x_1 simultaneously in order to have made a valid length measurement. L is obviously shorter than L_p. By direct measurement from the diagram (use a millimeter scale) $L/L_p = 0.78 = 1/\gamma$.

Thus the length of a rod is smaller when it is measured in a frame with respect to which it is moving. Before Einstein's paper was published, Lorentz and FitzGerald had independently shown that the null result of the Michelson-Morley experiment could be explained by assuming that the lengths in the direction of the interferometer's motion contracted by the amount given in Equation 1-30. For that reason, the length contraction is often called the *Lorentz-FitzGerald contraction.*

EXAMPLE 1-11 **Speed of S′** A stick that has a proper length of 1 m moves in a direction parallel to its length with speed v relative to you. The length of the stick as measured by you is 0.914 meter. What is the speed v?

Solution

1. The length of the stick measured in a frame relative to which it is moving with speed v is related to its proper length by Equation 1-30:

$$L = \frac{L_p}{\gamma}$$

2. Rearranging to solve for γ:

$$\gamma = \frac{L_p}{L}$$

3. Substituting the values of L_p and L:

$$\gamma = \frac{1 \text{ m}}{0.914 \text{ m}} = \frac{1}{\sqrt{1 - v^2/c^2}}$$

4. Solving for v:

$$\sqrt{1 - v^2/c^2} = 0.914$$
$$1 - v^2/c^2 = (0.914)^2 = 0.835$$
$$v^2/c^2 = 1 - 0.835 = 0.165$$
$$v^2 = 0.165c^2$$
$$v = 0.406c$$

It is important to remember that the relativistic contraction of moving lengths occurs only parallel to the relative motion of the reference frames. In particular, observers in relatively moving systems measure the same values for lengths in the y and $y′$ and in the z and $z′$ directions perpendicular to their relative motion. The result is that observers measure different shapes and angles for two- and three-dimensional objects. (See Example 1-12 and Figures 1-29 and 1-30.)

EXAMPLE 1-12 The Shape of a Moving Square Consider the square in the $x'y'$ plane of S' with one side making a 30° angle with the x' axis as in Figure 1-30a. If S' moves with $\beta = 0.5$ relative to S, what are the shape and orientation of the figure in S?

Solution

The S observer measures the x components of each side to be shorter by a factor $1/\gamma$ than those measured in S'. Thus, S measures

$$A = [\cos^2 30 + \sin^2 30/\gamma^2]^{1/2} A' = 0.968A'$$
$$B = [\sin^2 30 + \cos^2 30/\gamma^2]^{1/2} B' = 0.901B'$$

Since the figure is a square in S', $A' = B'$. In addition, the angles between B and the x axis and between A and the x axis are given by, respectively,

$$\theta = \tan^{-1}\left[\frac{B'\sin 30}{B'\cos 30/\gamma}\right] = \tan^{-1}\left[\gamma\frac{\sin 30}{\cos 30}\right] = 33.7°$$

$$\phi = \tan^{-1}\left[\frac{A'\cos 30}{A'\sin 30/\gamma}\right] = \tan^{-1}\left[\gamma\frac{\cos 30}{\sin 30}\right] = 63.4°$$

Thus, S concludes from geometry that the interior angle at vertex 1 is not 90°, but $180° - (63.4° + 33.7°) = 82.9°$ —i.e., the figure is not a square, but a parallelogram whose shorter sides make 33.7° angles with the x axis! Its shape and orientation in S are shown in Figure 1-30b.

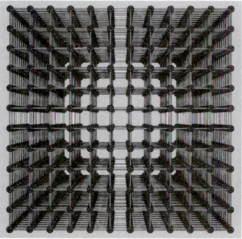
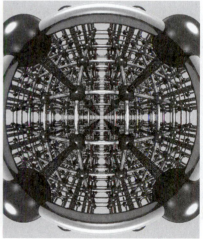

(a)   (b)

Fig. 1-29 The appearance of rapidly moving objects depends on both length contraction in the direction of motion and the time when the observed light left the object. (a) The array of clocks and measuring rods that represents S' as viewed by an observer in S with $\beta = 0$. (b) When S' approaches the S observer with $\beta = 0.9$, the distortion of the lattice becomes apparent. This is what an observer on a cosmic ray proton might see as it passes into the lattice of a cubic crystal such as NaCl. [*P.-K. Hsiung, R. Dunn, and C. Cox. Courtesy of C. Cox, Adobe Systems, Inc., San Jose, CA.*]

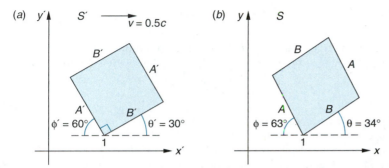

Fig. 1-30 Length contraction distorts the shape and orientation of two- and three-dimensional objects. The observer in S measures the square shown in S' as a rotated parallelogram.

Muon Decay

An interesting example of both time dilation and length contraction is afforded by the appearance of muons as secondary radiation from cosmic rays. Muons decay according to the statistical law of radioactivity:

$$N(t) = N_0 e^{-t/\tau} \qquad \textbf{1-31}$$

where N_0 is the original number of muons at time $t = 0$, $N(t)$ is the number remaining at time t, and τ is the mean lifetime (a proper time interval), which is about 2 μs for muons. Since muons are created (from the decay of pions) high in the atmosphere, usually several thousand meters above sea level, few muons should reach sea level. A typical muon moving with speed $0.998c$ would travel only about 600 m in 2 μs. However, the lifetime of the muon measured in Earth's reference frame is increased according to time dilation (Equation 1-28) by the factor $1/(1 - v^2/c^2)^{1/2}$, which is 15 for this particular speed. The mean lifetime measured in Earth's reference frame is therefore 30 μs, and a muon with speed $0.998c$ travels about 9000 m in this time. From the muon's point of view, it lives only 2 μs, but the atmosphere is rushing past it with a speed of $0.998c$. The distance of 9000 m in Earth's frame is thus contracted to only 600 m in the muon's frame, as indicated in Figure 1-31.

It is easy to distinguish experimentally between the classical and relativistic predictions of the observations of muons at sea level. Suppose that we observe 10^8 muons at an altitude of 9000 m in some time interval with a muon detector. How many would we expect to observe at sea level in the same time interval? According to the nonrelativistic prediction, the time it takes for these muons to travel 9000 m is $(9000 \text{ m})/0.998c \approx 30$ μs, which is 15 lifetimes. Substituting $N_0 = 10^8$ and $t = 15\tau$ into Equation 1-31, we obtain

$$N = 10^8 e^{-15} = 30.6$$

We would thus expect all but about 31 of the original 100 million muons to decay before reaching sea level.

According to the relativistic prediction, Earth must travel only the contracted distance of 600 m in the rest frame of the muon. This takes only 2 μs = 1τ. Therefore the number of muons expected at sea level is

Experiments with muons moving near the speed of light are performed at many accelerator laboratories throughout the world despite their short mean life. Time dilation results in much longer mean lives relative to the laboratory, providing plenty of time to do experiments.

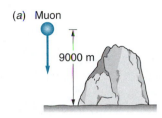

(a) Muon

9000 m

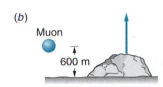

(b)

Muon

600 m

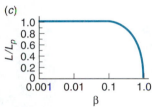

(c)

Fig. 1-31 Although muons are created high above Earth, and their mean lifetime is only about 2 μs when at rest, many appear at Earth's surface. (a) In Earth's reference frame, a typical muon moving at $0.998c$ has a mean lifetime of 30 μs and travels 9000 m in this time. (b) In the reference frame of the muon, the distance traveled by Earth is only 600 m in the muon's lifetime of 2 μs. (c) L varies only slightly from L_p until v is of the order of $0.1c$. $L \rightarrow 0$ as $v \rightarrow c$.

$$N = 10^8 e^{-1} = 3.68 \times 10^7$$

Thus relativity predicts that we would observe 36.8 million muons in the same time interval. Experiments of this type have confirmed the relativistic predictions.

The Spacetime Interval

We have seen earlier in this section that time intervals and lengths (= space intervals), quantities that were absolutes, or invariants, for relatively moving observers using the classical Galilean coordinate transformation, are not invariants in special relativity. The Lorentz transformation and the relativity of simultaneity lead observers in inertial frames to conclude that lengths moving relative to them are contracted and time intervals are stretched, both by the factor γ. The question naturally arises: Is there *any* quantity involving the space and time coordinates that is invariant under a Lorentz transformation? The answer to that question is yes, and as it happens, we have already dealt with a special case of that invariant quantity when we first obtained the correct form of the Lorentz transformation. It is called the *spacetime interval*, or usually just the *interval*, Δs, and is given by

$$(\Delta s)^2 = (c\Delta t)^2 - [\Delta x^2 + \Delta y^2 + \Delta z^2] \qquad \textbf{1-32}$$

or, specializing it to the one-space-dimensional systems that we have been discussing,

$$(\Delta s)^2 = (c\Delta t)^2 - (\Delta x)^2 \qquad \textbf{1-33}$$

It may help to think of Equations 1-32 and 1-33 like this:

$$[\text{interval}]^2 = [\text{separation in time}]^2 - [\text{separation in space}]^2$$

The interval Δs is the only measurable quantity describing pairs of events in spacetime for which observers in all inertial frames will obtain the same numerical value. The negative sign in Equations 1-32 and 1-33 implies that $(\Delta s)^2$ may be positive, negative, or zero depending on the relative sizes of the time and space separations. With the sign of $(\Delta s)^2$ nature is telling us about the causal relation between the two events. Notice that whichever of the three possibilities characterizes a pair for one observer, it does so for all observers, since Δs is invariant. The interval is called *timelike* if the time separation is the larger and *spacelike* if the space separation predominates. If the two terms are equal, so that $\Delta s = 0$, then it is called *lightlike*.

Timelike Interval   Consider a material particle[15] or object, e.g., the elephant in Figure 1-27, that moves relative to S. Since no material particle has ever been measured traveling faster than light, particles always travel less than 1 m of distance in 1 m of light travel time. We saw that to be the case in Example 1–10, where the time interval between launch and birth of the baby was 31.7 months on the S clock, during which time the elephant had moved a distance of 23.8 $c \cdot$ months. Equation 1-33 then yields $(c\Delta t)^2 - (\Delta x)^2 = (31.7c)^2 - (23.8c)^2 = (21.0c)^2 = (\Delta s)^2$ and the interval in S is $\Delta s = 21.0 \ c \cdot$ months. The time interval term being the larger, Δs is a timelike interval and we say that material particles have *timelike worldlines*. Such worldlines

lie within the shaded area of the spacetime diagram in Figure 1-21. Note that in the elephant's frame S' the separation in space between the launch and birth is zero and Δt is 21.0 months. Thus $\Delta s = 21.0\ c \cdot$ months in S', too. That is what we mean by the interval being invariant: observers in both S and S' measure the same number for the separation of the two events in spacetime.

The proper time interval τ between two events can be determined from Equation 1-33 using space and time measurements made in *any* inertial frame, since we can write that equation as

$$\frac{\Delta s}{c} = \sqrt{(\Delta t)^2 - (\Delta x/c)^2}$$

Since $\Delta t = \tau$ when $\Delta x = 0$—i.e., for the time interval recorded on a clock in a system moving such that the clock is located at each event as it occurs—in that case

$$\sqrt{(\Delta t)^2 - (\Delta x/c)^2} = \sqrt{\tau^2 - 0} = \tau = \frac{\Delta s}{c} \qquad \textbf{1-34}$$

Notice that this yields the correct proper time $\tau = 21.0$ months in the elephant example.

Spacelike Interval   When two events are separated in space by an interval whose square is greater than the value of $(c\Delta t)^2$, then Δs is called *spacelike*. In that case it is convenient for us to write Equation 1-33 in the form

$$(\Delta s)^2 = (\Delta x)^2 - (c\Delta t)^2 \qquad \textbf{1-35}$$

so that, as with timelike intervals, $(\Delta s)^2$ is not negative.[16] Events that are spacelike occur sufficiently far apart in space and close together in time that no inertial frame could move fast enough to carry a clock from one event to the other. For example, suppose two observers in Earth frame S, one in San Francisco and one in London, agree to each generate a light flash at the same instant, so that $c\Delta t = 0$ m in S and $\Delta x = 1.08 \times 10^7$ m. For *any* other inertial frame $(c\Delta t)^2 > 0$ and we see from Equation 1-35 that $(\Delta x)^2$ must be greater than $(1.08 \times 10^7)^2$ in order that Δs be invariant. In other words, 1.08×10^7 m is as close in space as the two events can be in any system; consequently, it will not be possible to find a system moving fast enough to move a clock from one event to the other. A speed greater than c, in this case infinitely greater, would be needed. Notice that the value of $\Delta s = L_p$, the proper length. Just as with the proper time τ, measurements of space and time intervals in any inertial system can be used to determine L_p.

Lightlike (or Null) Interval   The relation between two events is *lightlike* if Δs in Equation 1-33 equals zero. In that case

$$c\Delta t = \Delta x \qquad \textbf{1-36}$$

and a light pulse that leaves the first event as it occurs will just reach the second as it occurs.

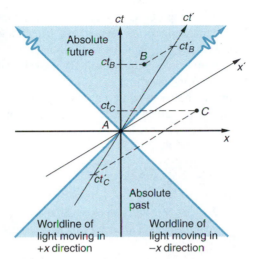

Fig. 1-32 The relative temporal order of events for pairs characterized by timelike intervals, such as *A* and *B,* is the same for all inertial observers. Events in the upper shaded area will all occur in the future of *A*; those in the lower shaded area occurred in *A*'s past. Events whose intervals are spacelike, such as *A* and *C,* can be measured as occurring in either order, depending on the relative motion of the frames. Thus, *C* occurs after *A* in *S,* but before *A* in *S'.*

The existence of the lightlike interval in relativity has no counterpart in the world of our everyday experience, where the geometry of space is Euclidean. In order for the distance between two points in space to be zero, the separation of the points in each of the three space dimensions must be zero. However, in spacetime the interval between two events may be zero, even though the intervals in space and time may individually be quite large. Notice, too, that pairs of events separated by light-like intervals have both the proper time interval and proper length equal to zero, since $\Delta s = 0$.

Things that move at the speed of light[17] have lightlike worldlines. As we saw earlier (see Figure 1-22), the worldline of light bisects the angles between the *ct* and *x* axes in a spacetime diagram. Timelike intervals lie in the shaded areas of Figure 1-32 and share the common characteristic that their relative order in time is the same for observers in all inertial systems. Events *A* and *B* in Figure 1-32 are such a pair. Observers in both *S* and *S'* agree that *A* occurs *before B,* although they of course measure different values for the space and time separations. Causal events, i.e., events that depend upon or affect one another in some fashion, such as your birth and that of your mother, have timelike intervals. On the other hand, the temporal order of events with spacelike intervals, such as *A* and *C* in Figure 1-32, depends upon the relative motion of the systems. As you can see in the diagram, *A* occurs before *C* in *S,* but *C* occurs first in *S'.* Thus, the relative order of pairs of events is absolute in the shaded areas, but elsewhere may be in either order.

QUESTION

9. In 1987 light arrived at Earth from the explosion of a star (a supernova) in the Large Magellanic Cloud, a small companion galaxy to the Milky Way, located about 170,000 $c \cdot y$ away. Describe events that together with the

explosion of the star would be separated from it by (*a*) a spacelike interval, (*b*) a lightlike interval, and (*c*) a timelike interval.

EXAMPLE 1-13 **Characterizing Spacetime Intervals** Figure 1-33 is the spacetime diagram of a laboratory showing three events, the emission of light from an atom in each of three samples.

1. Determine whether the interval between each of the three possible pairs of events is timelike, spacelike, or lightlike.
2. Would it have been possible in any of the pairs for one of the events to have been caused by the other? If so, which?

Solution

1. The spacetime coordinates of the events are:

event	ct	x
1	2	1
2	5	9
3	8	6

and for the three possible pairs 1 and 2, 2 and 3, and 1 and 3 we have

pair	$c\,\Delta t$	Δx	$(c\,\Delta t)^2$	$(\Delta x)^2$	
1 & 2	5−2	9−1	9	64	spacelike
2 & 3	8−5	6−9	9	9	lightlike
1 & 3	8−2	6−1	36	25	timelike

2. Yes, event 3 may possibly have been caused by either event 1, since 3 is in the absolute future of 1, or event 2, since 2 and 3 can just be connected by a flash of light.

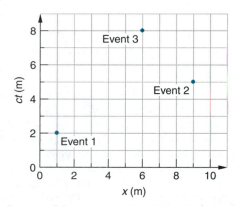

Fig. 1-33 A spacetime diagram of three events whose intervals Δs are found in Example 1-13.

1-5 The Doppler Effect

In the Doppler effect for sound the change in frequency for a given velocity v depends on whether it is the source or receiver that is moving with that speed. Such a distinction is possible for sound because there is a medium (the air) relative to which the motion takes place, and so it is not surprising that the motion of the source or the receiver relative to the still air can be distinguished. Such a distinction between motion of the source or receiver cannot be made for light or other electromagnetic waves in a vacuum as a consequence of Einstein's second postulate; therefore, the classical expressions for the Doppler effect cannot be correct for light. We will now derive the relativistic Doppler effect equations that are correct for light.

Consider a light source moving toward an observer or receiver at A in Figure 1-34a at velocity v. The source is emitting a train of light waves toward receivers A and B while approaching A and receding from B. Figure 1-34b shows the spacetime diagram of S,

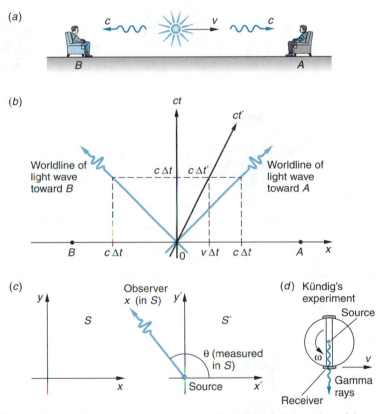

Fig. 1-34 Doppler effect in light, as in sound, arises from the relative motion of the source and receiver; however, the independence of the speed of light on that motion leads to different expressions for the frequency shift. (a) A source approaches observer A and recedes from observer B. The spacetime diagram of the system S in which A and B are at rest and the source moves at velocity v illustrates the two situations. (b) The source located at $x' = 0$ (the x' axis is omitted) moves along its worldline, the ct' axis. The N waves emitted toward A in time Δt occupy space $\Delta x = c\Delta t - v\Delta t$, whereas those headed for B occupy $\Delta x = c\Delta t + v\Delta t$. In three dimensions the observer in S may see light emitted at some angle θ with respect to the x axis as in (c). In that case a transverse Doppler effect occurs. (d) Kündig's apparatus for measuring the transverse Doppler effect.

the system in which A and B are at rest. The source is located at $x' = 0$ (the x' axis is not shown), and, of course, its worldline is the ct' axis. Let the source emit a train of N electromagnetic waves in each direction beginning when the S and S' origins were coincident. First, let's consider the train of waves headed toward A. During the time Δt over which the source emits the N waves, the first wave emitted will have traveled a distance $c\Delta t$ and the source itself a distance $v\Delta t$ in S. Thus, the N waves are seen by the observer at A to occupy a distance $c\Delta t - v\Delta t$ and, correspondingly, their wavelength λ is given by

$$\lambda = \frac{c\Delta t - v\Delta t}{N}$$

and the frequency $f = c/\lambda$ is

$$f = \frac{c}{\lambda} = \frac{cN}{(c - v)\Delta t} = \frac{1}{1 - \beta} \frac{N}{\Delta t}$$

The frequency of the source in S', called the *proper frequency,* is given by $f_0 = c/\lambda' = N/\Delta t'$, where $\Delta t'$ is measured in S', the rest system of the source. The time interval $\Delta t' = \tau$ is the proper time, since the light waves, in particular the first and the Nth, are all emitted at $x' = 0$; hence $\Delta x' = 0$ between the first and the Nth in S'. Thus, Δt and $\Delta t'$ are related by Equation 1-28 for time dilation, so $\Delta t = \gamma \Delta t'$. Thus, when the source and receiver are moving toward each other, the observer A in S measures the frequency

$$f = \frac{1}{1 - \beta} \frac{f_0 \Delta t'}{\Delta t} = \frac{f_0}{1 - \beta} \frac{1}{\gamma} \qquad \textbf{1-37}$$

or

$$f = \frac{\sqrt{1 - \beta^2}}{1 - \beta} f_0 = \sqrt{\frac{1 + \beta}{1 - \beta}} f_0 \qquad \text{(approaching)} \qquad \textbf{1-38}$$

This differs from the classical equation only in the addition of the time dilation factor. Note that $f > f_0$ for the source and observer approaching one another. Since for visible light this corresponds to a shift toward the blue part of the spectrum, it is called a *blueshift.*

The use of Doppler radar to track weather systems is a direct application of special relativity.

Suppose the source and receiver are moving away from one another, as for observer B in Figure 1-34b. Observer B, in S, sees the N waves occupying a distance $c\Delta t + v\Delta t$, and the same analysis shows that observer B in S measures the frequency

$$f = \frac{\sqrt{1 - \beta^2}}{1 + \beta} f_0 = \sqrt{\frac{1 - \beta}{1 + \beta}} f_0 \qquad \text{(receding)} \qquad \textbf{1-39}$$

Notice that $f < f_0$ for the observer and source receding from one another. Since for visible light this corresponds to a shift toward the red part of the spectrum, it is called a *redshift.* It is left as a problem for you to show that the same results are obtained when the analysis is done in the frame in which the source is at rest.

In the event that $v \ll c$ (i.e., $\beta \ll 1$), as is often the case for light sources moving on Earth, useful (and easily remembered) approximations of Equations 1-38 and 1-39 can be obtained. Using Equation 1-38 as an example and rewriting it in the form

$$f = f_0 (1 + \beta)^{1/2} (1 - \beta)^{-1/2}$$

the two quantities in parentheses can be expanded by the binomial theorem to yield

$$f = f_0 \left(1 + \frac{1}{2}\beta - \frac{1}{8}\beta + \ldots \right)\left(1 + \frac{1}{2}\beta + \frac{3}{8}\beta^2 + \ldots \right)$$

Multiplying out and discarding terms of higher order than β yield

$$f/f_0 \approx 1 + \beta \qquad \text{(approaching)}$$

and, similarly,

$$f/f_0 \approx 1 - \beta \qquad \text{(receding)}$$

and $|\Delta f/f_0| \approx \beta$ in both situations, where $\Delta f = f_0 - f$.

EXAMPLE 1-14. Rotation of the Sun The sun rotates at the equator once in about 25.4 days. The sun's radius is 7.0×10^8 m. Compute the Doppler effect that you would expect to observe at the left and right edges (limbs) of the sun near the equator for light of wavelength $\lambda = 550$ nm $= 550 \times 10^{-9}$ m (yellow light). Is this a redshift or a blueshift?

Solution
The speed of limbs $v =$ (circumference)/(time for one revolution) or

$$v = \frac{2\pi R}{T} = \frac{2\pi (7.0 \times 10^8) \text{ m}}{25.4 \text{ d} \cdot 3600 \text{ s/h} \cdot 24 \text{ h/d}} = 2000 \text{ m/s}$$

$v \ll c$, so we may use the approximation equations. Using $\Delta f/f_0 \approx \beta$ we have $\Delta f \approx \beta f_0 = \beta c/\lambda_0 = v/\lambda_0$ or $\Delta f \approx 2000/550 \times 10^{-9} = 3.64 \times 10^9$ Hz. Since $f_0 = c/\lambda_0 = (3 \times 10^8 \text{ m/s})/(550 \times 10^{-9}) = 5.45 \times 10^{14}$ Hz, Δf represents a fractional change in frequency of β, or about one part in 10^5. It is a redshift for the receding limb, a blueshift for the approaching one.

Doppler Effect of Starlight

In 1929, E. P. Hubble became the first astronomer to suggest that the universe is expanding.[18] He made that suggestion and offered a simple equation to describe the expansion on the basis of measurements of the Doppler shift of the frequencies of light emitted toward us by distant galaxies. Light from distant galaxies is always shifted toward frequencies lower than those emitted by similar sources nearby. Since the general expression connecting the frequency f and wavelength λ of light is $c = f\lambda$, the shift corresponds to longer wavelengths. As noted above, the color red is on the longer-wavelength side of the visible spectrum (see Chapter 4), so the

redshift is used to describe the Doppler effect for a receding source. Similarly, *blueshift* describes light emitted by stars, typically stars in our galaxy, that are approaching us.

Astronomers define the redshift of light from astronomical sources by the expression $z = (f_0 - f)/f$, where f_0 = frequency measured in the frame of the star or galaxy and f = frequency measured at the receiver on Earth. This allows us to write $\beta = v/c$ in terms of z as

$$\beta = \frac{(z + 1)^2 - 1}{(z + 1)^2 + 1} \qquad\qquad \textbf{1-40}$$

Equation 1-39 is the appropriate one to use for such calculations, rather than the approximations, since galactic recession velocities can be quite large. For example, the quasar 2000-330 has a measured $z = 3.78$, which implies from Equation 1-40 that it is receding from Earth at $0.91c$.

EXAMPLE 1-15 Redshift of Starlight The longest wavelength of light emitted by hydrogen in the Balmer series (see Chapter 4) has a wavelength of $\lambda_0 = 656$ nm. In light from a distant galaxy, this wavelength is measured as $\lambda = 1458$ nm. Find the speed at which the galaxy is receding from Earth.

Solution

1. The recession speed is the v in $\beta = v/c$. Since $\lambda > \lambda_0$, this is a redshift and Equation 1-39 applies:

$$f = \sqrt{\frac{1 - \beta}{1 + \beta}} f_0$$

2. Rewriting Equation 1-39 in terms of the wavelengths:

$$\sqrt{\frac{1 - \beta}{1 + \beta}} = \frac{f}{f_0} = \frac{\lambda_0}{\lambda}$$

3. Squaring both sides and substituting values for λ_0 and λ:

$$\frac{1 - \beta}{1 + \beta} = \left(\frac{\lambda_0}{\lambda}\right)^2 = \left(\frac{656 \text{ nm}}{1458 \text{ nm}}\right)^2 = 0.202$$

4. Solving for β:

$$1 - \beta = (0.202)(1 + \beta)$$
$$1.202\beta = 1 - 0.202 = 0.798$$
$$\beta = \frac{0.798}{1.202} = 0.664$$

5. The galaxy is thus receding at speed v, where:

$$v = c\beta = 0.664c$$

Exploring

Transverse Doppler Effect

Our discussion of the Doppler effect in Section 1-5 involved only one space dimension wherein the source, observer, and direction of the relative motion all lie on the *x* axis. In three space dimensions, where they may not be colinear, a more complete analysis, though beyond the scope of our discussion, makes only a small change in Equation 1-37. If the source moves along the positive *x* axis, but the observer views the light emitted at some angle θ with the *x* axis, as shown in Figure 1-34c, Equation 1-37 becomes

$$f = \frac{f_0}{\gamma} \frac{1}{1 - \beta \cos \theta} \qquad \textbf{1-37}a$$

When θ = 0, this becomes the equation for the source and receiver approaching, and when θ = π it becomes that for them receding. Equation 1-37a also makes the quite surprising prediction that even when viewed perpendicular to the direction of motion, where θ = π/2, the observer will still see a frequency shift, the so-called *transverse Doppler effect*, $f = f_0/\gamma$. Note that $f < f_0$, since γ > 1. It is sometimes referred to as the second-order Doppler effect. It is the result of time dilation of the moving source.

Following a suggestion first made by Einstein in 1907, Kündig in 1962 made an excellent quantitative verification of the transverse Doppler effect.[19] He used 14.4-keV gamma rays emitted by a particular isotope of Fe as the light source (see Chapter 11). The source was at rest in the laboratory, on the axis of an ultracentrifuge, and the receiver (an Fe absorber foil) was mounted on the ultracentrifuge rim, as shown in Figure 1-34d. Using the extremely sensitive frequency measuring technique called the Mössbauer effect (see Chapter 11), Kündig found a transverse Doppler effect in agreement with the relativistic prediction within ±1 percent over a range of relative speeds up to about 400 m/s.

1-6 The Twin Paradox and Other Surprises

The consequences of Einstein's postulates—the Lorentz transformation, relativistic velocity addition, time dilation, length contraction, and the relativity of simultaneity—lead to a large number of predictions which are unexpected and even startling when compared with our experiences in a macroscopic world where β ≈ 0 and geometry obeys the Euclidean rules. Still other predictions seem downright paradoxical, with relatively moving observers obtaining equally valid but apparently totally inconsistent results. This chapter concludes with the discussion of a few such examples that will help you hone your understanding of special relativity.

Twin Paradox

Perhaps the most famous of the paradoxes in special relativity is that of the twins, or, as it is sometimes called, the clock paradox. It arises out of the time dilation

(Equation 1-28) and goes like this. Homer and Ulysses are identical twins. Ulysses travels at a constant high speed to a star beyond our solar system and returns to Earth while his twin Homer remains at home. When the traveler Ulysses returns home, he finds his twin brother much aged compared to himself—in agreement, we shall see, with the prediction of relativity. The paradox arises out of the contention that the motion is relative and either twin could regard the other as the traveler, in which case each twin should find the other to be younger than he and we have a logical contradiction—a paradox. Let's illustrate the paradox with a specific example. Let Earth and the destination star be in the same inertial frame S. Two other frames S' and S'' move relative to S at $v = +0.8c$ and $v = -0.8c$, respectively. Thus $\gamma = 5/3$ in both cases. The spaceship carrying Ulysses accelerates quickly from S to S', then coasts with S' to the star, again accelerates quickly from S' to S'', coasts with S'' back to Earth, and brakes to a stop alongside Homer.

It is easy to analyze the problem from Homer's point of view on Earth. Suppose, according to Homer's clock, Ulysses coasts in S' for a time interval $\Delta t = 5$ y and in S'' for an equal time. Thus Homer is 10 y older when Ulysses returns. The time interval in S' between the events of Ulysses' leaving Earth and arriving at the star is shorter because it is proper time. The time it takes to reach the star by Ulysses' clock is

$$\Delta t' = \frac{\Delta t}{\gamma} = \frac{5 \text{ y}}{5/3} = 3 \text{ y}$$

Since the same time is required for the return trip, Ulysses will have recorded 6 y for the round trip and will be 4 y younger than Homer upon his return.

The difficulty in this situation seems to be for Ulysses to understand why his twin aged 10 y during his absence. If we consider Ulysses as being at rest and Homer as moving away, Homer's clock should run slow and measure only $3/\gamma = 1.8$ y, and it appears that Ulysses should expect Homer to have aged only 3.6 y during the round trip. This is, of course, the paradox. Both predictions can't be right. However, this approach makes the incorrect assumption that the twins' situations are symmetrical and interchangeable. They are not. Homer remains in a single inertial frame, whereas Ulysses *changes* inertial frames, as illustrated in Figure 1-35a, the space-time diagram for Ulysses' trip. While the turnaround may take only a minute fraction of the total time, it is absolutely essential if the twins' clocks are to come together again so that we can compare their ages (readings).

A correct analysis can be made using the invariant interval Δs from Equation 1-33 rewritten as

$$\left(\frac{\Delta s}{c}\right)^2 = (\Delta t)^2 - \left(\frac{\Delta x}{c}\right)^2$$

where the left side is constant and equal to $(\tau)^2$, the proper time interval squared, and the right side refers to measurements made in any inertial frame. Thus Ulysses, along each of his worldlines in Figure 1-35a, has $\Delta x = 0$ and, of course, measures $\Delta t = \tau = 3$ y, or 6 y for the round trip. Homer, on the other hand, measures

$$(\Delta t)^2 = (\tau)^2 + \left(\frac{\Delta x}{c}\right)^2$$

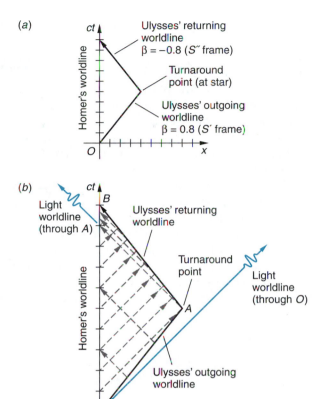

Fig. 1-35 (*a*) The spacetime diagram of Ulysses' journey to a distant star in the inertial frame in which Homer and the star are at rest. (*b*) Divisions on the *ct* axis correspond to years on Homer's clock. The broken lines show the paths (worldlines) of light flashes transmitted by each twin with a frequency of one/year on his clock. Note the markedly different frequencies at the receivers.

and since $(\Delta x/c)^2$ is always positive, he always measures $\Delta t > \tau$. In this situation $\Delta x = 0.8c\Delta t$, so

$$(\Delta t)^2 = (3 \text{ y})^2 + (0.8c\Delta t/c)^2$$

or

$$(\Delta t)^2(0.36) = (3)^2$$

$$\Delta t = \frac{3}{0.6} = 5 \text{ y}$$

or 10 y for the round trip, as we saw earlier. The reason that the twins' situations cannot be treated symmetrically is because the special theory of relativity can predict the behavior of accelerated systems, such as Ulysses at the turnaround, provided that in the formulation of the physical laws we take the view of an inertial, i.e., unaccelerated, observer such as Homer. That's what we have done. Thus, we cannot do the same analysis in the rest frame of Ulysses' spaceship because it does not remain in an inertial frame during the round trip; hence, it falls outside of the special theory, and no paradox arises. The laws of physics can be reformulated so as to be invariant for accelerated observers, which is the role of general relativity (see Chapter 2), but the result is the same: Ulysses returns younger that Homer by just the amount calculated.

EXAMPLE 1-16 Twin Paradox and the Doppler Effect This example, first suggested by C. G. Darwin,[20] may help you understand what each twin sees during Ulysses' journey. Homer and Ulysses agree that once each year, on the anniversary of the launch date of Ulysses' spaceship (when their clocks were together), each twin will send a light signal to the other. Figure 1-35*b* shows the light signals each sends. Homer sends 10 light flashes (the *ct* axis, Homer's worldline, is divided into 10 equal intervals corresponding to the 10 years of the journey on Homer's clock) and Ulysses sends 6 light flashes (each of Ulysses' worldlines is divided into 3 equal intervals corresponding to 3 years on Ulysses' clock). Note that each transmits his final light flash as they are reunited at *B*. Although each transmits light signals with a frequency of 1 per year, they obviously do not receive them at that frequency. For example, Ulysses sees no signals from Homer during the first 3 years! How can we explain the observed frequencies?

Solution

The Doppler effect provides the explanation. As the twins (and clocks) recede from each other, the frequency of their signals is reduced from the proper frequency f_0 according to Equation 1-39, and we have

$$\frac{f}{f_0} = \sqrt{\frac{1 - \beta}{1 + \beta}} = \sqrt{\frac{1 - 0.8}{1 + 0.8}} = \frac{1}{3}$$

which is exactly what both twins see (refer to Figure 1-35*b*): Homer receives 3 flashes in the first 9 years and Ulysses 1 flash in his first 3 years; i.e., $f = (1/3) f_0$ for both.

After the turnaround they are approaching each other and Equation 1-38 yields

$$\frac{f}{f_0} = \sqrt{\frac{1 + \beta}{1 - \beta}} = \sqrt{\frac{1 + 0.8}{1 - 0.8}} = 3$$

and again this agrees with what the twins see: Homer receives 3 flashes during the final (10th) year and Ulysses receives 9 flashes during his final 3 years; i.e., $f = 3f_0$ for both.

QUESTION

10. The different ages of the twins upon being reunited are an example of the relativity of simultaneity that was discussed earlier. Explain how that accounts for the fact that their biological clocks are no longer synchronized.

More

It is the relativity of simultaneity that is responsible for the age difference between the twins, not their different accelerations. This is readily illustrated in *The Case of the Identically Accelerated Twins,* which can be found on the home page: www.whfreeman.com/modphysics4e   See also Figure 1-36 here.

The Pole and Barn Paradox

An interesting problem involving length contraction developed by E. F. Taylor and J. A. Wheeler[22] involves putting a long pole into a short barn. One version goes as follows. A runner carries a pole 10 m long toward the open front door of a small barn 5 m long. A farmer stands near the barn so that he can see both the front and the back doors of the barn, the latter being a closed swinging door, as shown in Figure 1-37*a*. The runner carrying the pole at speed *v* enters the barn and at some instant the farmer sees the pole completely contained in the barn and closes the front door, thus putting a 10-m pole into a 5-m barn. The minimum speed of the runner *v* that is necessary for the farmer to accomplish this feat may be computed from Equation 1-30, giving the relativistic length contraction $L = L_p/\gamma$, where L_p = proper length of the pole (10 m) and L = length of the pole measured by the farmer, to be equal to the length of the barn (5 m). Therefore, we have

$$\gamma = \frac{1}{\sqrt{1 - v^2/c^2}} = \frac{L_p}{L} = \frac{10}{5}$$

$$1 - v^2/c^2 = (5/10)^2$$

$$v^2/c^2 = 1 - (5/10)^2 = 0.75$$

$$v = 0.866c \quad \text{or} \quad \beta = 0.866$$

A paradox seems to arise when this situation is viewed in the rest system of the runner. For him the pole, being at rest in the same inertial system, has its proper length of 10 m. However, the runner measures the length of the barn to be

$$L = L_p/\gamma = 5\sqrt{1 - \beta^2}$$

$$L = 2.5 \text{ m}$$

How can he possibly fit the 10-m pole into the length-contracted 2.5-m barn? The answer is that he can't, and the paradox vanishes, but how can that be? To understand the answer, we need to examine two events—the coincidences of both the front and back ends of the pole, respectively, with the rear and front doors of the barn—in the inertial frame of the farmer and in that of the runner.

These are illustrated by the spacetime diagrams of the inertial frame *S* of the farmer and barn (Figure 1-37*b*) and that of the runner *S'* (Figure 1-37*c*). Both diagrams are drawn with the front end of the pole coinciding with the front door of the barn at the instant the clocks are started. In Figure 1-37*b* the worldlines of the barn doors are, of course, vertical, while those of the two ends of the pole make an angle $\theta = \tan^{-1}(1/\beta) = 49.1°$ with the *x* axis. Note that in *S* the front of the pole reaches the rear door of the barn at $ct = 5$ m/0.866 = 5.8 m *simultaneously* with the arrival of the back end of the pole at the front door; i.e., at that instant in *S* the pole is entirely contained in the barn.

In the runner's rest system *S'* it is the worldlines of the ends of the pole that are vertical, while those of the front and rear doors of the barn make angles of 49.1° with the $-x'$ axis (since the barn moves in the $-x'$ direction at *v*). Now we see that the rear door passes the front of the pole at $ct' = 2.5$ m/0.866 = 2.9 m, but the front door of the barn doesn't reach the rear of the pole until $ct' = 10$ m/0.866 = 11.5 m. Thus the first of those two events occurs *before* the second, and the runner never sees the pole entirely contained in the barn. Once again, the relativity of simultaneity is the

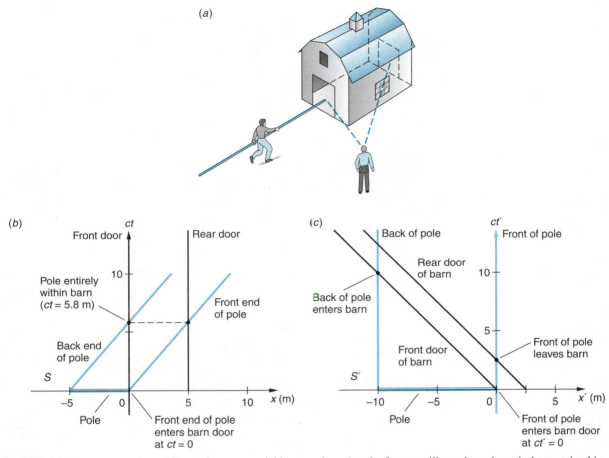

Fig. 1-37 (*a*) A runner carrying a 10-m pole moves quickly enough so that the farmer will see the pole entirely contained in the barn. The spacetime diagrams from the point of view of the farmer's inertial frame (*b*) and that of the runner (*c*). The resolution of the paradox is in the fact that the events of interest, shown by the large dots in each diagram, are simultaneous in *S*, but not in *S'*.

key—events simultaneous in one inertial frame are not simultaneous when viewed from another inertial frame.

QUESTION

11. Suppose that the barn's back wall was made from armor-plate steel and had no door. What would the farmer and the runner see then?

Headlight Effect

We have made frequent use of Einstein's second postulate asserting that the speed of light is independent of the source motion for all inertial observers; however, the same is not true for the *direction* of light. Consider a light source in *S'* that emits light uniformly in all directions. A beam of that light emitted at an angle θ' with

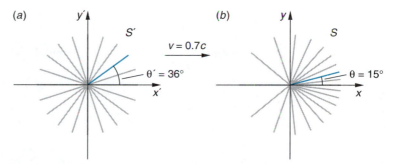

Fig. 1-38 (*a*) The source at rest in *S'* moves with β = 0.7 with respect to *S*. (*b*) Light emitted uniformly in *S'* appears to *S* concentrated into a cone in the forward direction. Rays shown in (*a*) are 18° apart. Rays shown in (*b*) make angles calculated from Equation 1-43. The two colored rays shown are corresponding ones.

respect to the *x'* axis is shown in Figure 1-38*a*. During a time $\Delta t'$ the *x'* displacement of the beam is $\Delta x'$, and these are related to θ' by

$$\frac{\Delta x'}{c\Delta t'} = \frac{\Delta x'}{\Delta(ct')} = \cos\theta' \qquad \textbf{1-41}$$

The direction of the beam relative to the *x* axis in *S* is similarly given by

$$\frac{\Delta x}{\Delta(ct)} = \cos\theta \qquad \textbf{1-42}$$

Applying the inverse Lorentz transformation to Equation 1-42 yields

$$\cos\theta = \frac{\Delta x}{c\Delta t} = \frac{\gamma(\Delta x' + v\Delta t')}{c\gamma(\Delta t' + v\Delta x'/c^2)}$$

Dividing the numerator and denominator by $\Delta t'$ and then by *c*, we obtain

$$\cos\theta = \frac{(\Delta x'/\Delta t' + v)}{c\left(1 + \dfrac{v}{c^2}\Delta x'/\Delta t'\right)} = \frac{\Delta x'/\Delta(ct') + v/c}{1 + \dfrac{v}{c}\cdot\dfrac{\Delta x'}{\Delta(ct')}}$$

and substituting from Equation 1-41 yields

$$\cos\theta = \frac{\cos\theta' + \beta}{1 + \beta\cos\theta'} \qquad \textbf{1-43}$$

Considering the half of the light emitted by the source in *S'* into the forward hemisphere, i.e., rays with θ' between $\pm\pi/2$, note that Equation 1-43 restricts the angles θ measured in *S* for those rays (50 percent of all the light) to lie between $\theta = \pm\cos^{-1}\beta$. For example, for β = 0.5, the observer in *S* would see half of the total

light emitted by the source in S' to lie between $\theta = \pm 60°$, i.e., in a cone of half angle 60° whose axis is along the direction of the velocity of the source. For values of β near unity, θ is very small, e.g., $\beta = .99$ yields $\theta = 8.1°$. This means that the observer in S sees half of all the light emitted by the source to be concentrated into a forward cone with that half angle. (See Figure 1-38b.) Note, too, that the remaining 50 percent of the emitted light is distributed throughout the remaining 344° of the two-dimensional diagram.[23] As a result of the headlight effect, light from a directly approaching source appears far more intense than that from the same source at rest. For the same reason, light from a directly receding source will appear much dimmer than that from the same source at rest. This result has substantial applications in experimental particle physics and astrophysics.

In determining the brightness of stars and galaxies, a critical parameter in understanding them, astronomers must correct for the headlight effect, particularly at high velocities relative to Earth.

QUESTION

12. Notice from Equation 1-43 that some light emitted by the moving source into the rear hemisphere is seen by the observer in S as having been emitted into the forward hemisphere. Explain how that can be, using physical arguments.

Exploring
Superluminal Speeds

We conclude this chapter with a few comments about things that move faster than light. The Lorentz transformations (Equations 1-20 and 1-21) have no meaning in the event that the relative speeds of two inertial frames exceed the speed of light. This is generally taken to be a prohibition on the moving of mass, energy, and information faster than c. However, it is possible for certain processes to proceed at speeds greater than c and for the speeds of moving objects to appear to be greater than c without contradicting relativity theory. A common example of the first of these is the motion of the point where the blades of a giant pair of scissors intersect as the scissors are quickly closed, sometimes called the scissors paradox. Figure 1-39 shows the situation. A long straight rod (one blade) makes an angle θ with the x axis (the second blade) and moves in the $-y$ direction at constant speed $v_y = \Delta y/\Delta t$. During time Δt,

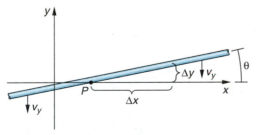

Fig. 1-39 As the long, straight rod moves vertically downward, the intersection of the "blades," point P, moves toward the right at speed $v_p = \Delta x/\Delta t$. In terms of v_y and θ, $v_p = v_y/\tan \theta$.

the intersection of the blades, point *P*, moves to the right a distance Δx. Note from the figure that $\Delta y/\Delta x = \tan\theta$. The speed with which *P* moves to the right is

$$v_p = \Delta x/\Delta t = \frac{\Delta x}{\Delta y/v_y} = \frac{v_y\,\Delta x}{\Delta x\,\tan\theta} \qquad \textbf{1-44}$$

or

$$v_p = v_y/\tan\theta$$

Since $\tan\theta \to 0$ as $\theta \to 0$, it will always be possible to find a value of θ close enough to zero so that $v_p > c$ for any (nonzero) value of v_y. As real scissors are closed, the angle gets progressively smaller, so in principle all that one needs for $v_p > c$ are long blades so that $\theta \to 0$.

QUESTION

13. Use a diagram like Figure 1-32 to explain why the motion of point *P* cannot be used to convey information to observers along the blades.

The point *P* in the scissors paradox is, of course, a geometric point, not a material object, so it is not surprising that it could appear to move at speeds greater than *c*. As an example of an object with mass appearing to do so, consider a tiny meteorite moving through space directly toward you at high speed *v*. As it enters Earth's atmosphere, about 9 km above the surface, frictional heating causes it to glow, and the first light from the glow starts toward your eye. After some time Δt the frictional heating has evaporated all of the meteorite's matter, the glow is extinguished, and its final light starts toward your eye, as illustrated in Figure 1-40. During the time between the first and the final glow, the meteorite traveled a distance $v\Delta t$. During that same time interval light from the first glow has traveled toward your eye a distance $c\Delta t$. Thus, the space interval between the first and final glows is given by

$$\Delta y = c\Delta t - v\Delta t = \Delta t(c - v)$$

and the visual time interval at your eye Δt_{eye} between the arrival of the first and final light is

$$\Delta t_{eye} = \Delta y/c = \frac{\Delta t(c - v)}{c} = \Delta t(1 - \beta)$$

and, finally, the apparent visual speed v_a that you record is

$$v_a = \frac{v\,\Delta t}{\Delta t_{eye}} = \frac{v\,\Delta t}{\Delta t(1 - \beta)} = \frac{\beta c}{1 - \beta} \qquad \textbf{1-45}$$

Clearly, $\beta = 0.5$ yields $v_a = c$ and any larger β yields $v_a > c$. For example, a meteorite approaching you at $v = 0.8c$ is perceived to be moving at $v_a = 4c$. Certain galactic structures may also be observed to move at superluminal speeds, as the sequence of images of galaxy 3C120 in Figure 1-41 illustrates.

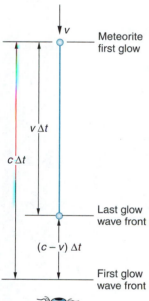

Fig. 1-40 A meteorite moves directly toward the observer's eye at speed *v*. The spatial distance between the wave fronts is $(c - v)\Delta t$ as they move at *c*, so the time interval between their arrival at the observer is not Δt, but Δt_{eye}, which is $(c - v)\Delta t/c = (1 - \beta)\Delta t$; and the apparent speed of approach is $v_a = v\Delta t/\Delta t_{eye} = \beta c/(1 - \beta)$.

As a final example of things that move faster than *c*, it has been proposed that particles with mass might exist whose speeds would always be faster than light speed. One basis for this suggestion is an appealing symmetry: ordinary particles always have $v < c$, and photons and other massless particles have $v = c$, so the existence of particles with $v > c$ would give a sort of satisfying completeness to the classification of particles. Called *tachyons,* their existence would present relativity with serious but not necessarily insurmountable problems of infinite creation energies and causality paradoxes, e.g., alteration of history. (See the next example.) No compelling theoretical arguments preclude their existence and eventual discovery; however, experimental searches to date for tachyons[24] have failed, and the limits set by those experiments indicate that it is highly unlikely that they exist.

EXAMPLE 1-17 Tachyons and Reversing History Use tachyons and an appropriate spacetime diagram to show how the existence of such particles might be used to change history and, hence, alter the future, leading to a paradox.

Solution

In a spacetime diagram of the laboratory frame *S* the worldline of a particle with $v > c$ created at the origin traveling in the $+x$ direction makes an angle less than $45°$ with the *x* axis; i.e., it is below the light worldline, as shown in Figure 1-42. After some time the tachyon reaches a tachyon detector mounted on a spaceship moving rapidly away at $v < c$ in the $+x$ direction. The spaceship frame S' is shown in the figure at *P*. The detector immediately creates a new tachyon, sending it off in the $-x'$ direction and, of course, into the future of S', i.e., with $ct' > 0$. The second tachyon returns to the laboratory at $x = 0$, but at a time *ct before* the first tachyon was emitted, having traveled into the past of *S* to point *M*, where $ct < 0$. Having sent an object into our own past, we would then have the ability to alter events that occur after *M* and produce causal contradictions. For example, the laboratory tachyon detector could be coupled to equipment that created the first tachyon via a computer programmed to cancel emission of the first tachyon if the second tachyon is detected. (Shades of the Terminator!) It is logical contradictions such as this which, together with the experimental results referred to above, lead to the conclusion that faster-than-light particles do not exist.

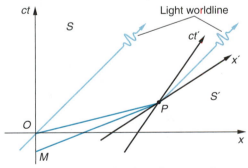

Fig. 1-42 A tachyon emitted at *O* in *S*, the laboratory frame, catches up with a spaceship moving at high speed at *P*. Its detection triggers the emission of a second tachyon at *P* back toward the laboratory at $x = 0$. The second tachyon arrives at the laboratory at $ct < 0$, i.e., before the emission of the first tachyon.

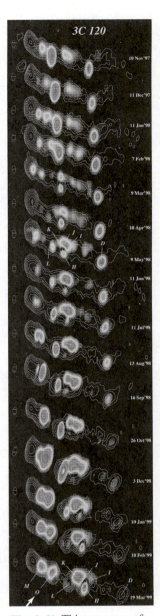

3C 120

10 Nov '97
11 Dec '97
11 Jan '98
7 Feb '98
9 Mar '98
10 Apr '98
9 May '98
11 Jun '98
11 Jul '98
13 Aug '98
16 Sep '98
26 Oct '98
3 Dec '98
10 Jan '99
10 Feb '99
19 Mar '99

Fig. 1-41 This sequence of 16 images of active galaxy 3C120 made by J.-L. Gomez and co-workers between November 1997 and March 1999 reveals a region in the relativistic jet, marked with an arrow in the lowest image, that flashes on and off over a period of a few months and moves in the plane of the sky at about 4.4 times the speed of light. 3C120 is about $450 \times 10^6 \, c \cdot y$ from Earth with a redshift of $z = 0.033$. [*J. L. Gomez et al.,* Science, *September 2000, p. 2317.*]

Summary

TOPIC	RELEVANT EQUATIONS AND REMARKS	
1. Classical relativity		
Galilean transformation	$x' = x - vt \qquad y' = y \qquad z' = z$	**1-3**
Newtonian relativity	Newton's laws are invariant in all systems connected by a Galilean transformation.	
2. Einstein's postulates	The laws of physics are the same in all inertial reference frames. The speed of light is c, independent of the motion of the source.	
3. Relativity of simultaneity	Events simultaneous in one reference frame are not simultaneous in any other inertial frame.	
4. Lorentz transformation	$x' = \gamma(x - vt) \qquad y' = y \qquad z' = z$ $t' = \gamma(t - vx/c^2)$ with $\gamma = (1 - v^2/c^2)^{-1/2}$	**1-20**
5. Time dilation	Proper time is the time interval τ between two events that occur at the same space point. If that interval is $\Delta t' = \tau$, then the time interval in S is $\Delta t = \gamma \Delta t' = \gamma \tau$, where $\gamma = (1 - v^2/c^2)^{-1/2}$	**1-28**
6. Length contraction	The proper length of a rod is the length L_p measured in the rest system of the rod. In S, moving at speed v with respect to the rod, the length measured is $L = L_p/\gamma$	**1-30**
7. Spacetime interval	All observers in inertial frames measure the same interval Δs between pairs of events in spacetime, where $(\Delta s)^2 = (c\,\Delta t)^2 - (\Delta x)^2$	**1-33**
8. Doppler effect		
Source/observer approaching	$f = \sqrt{\dfrac{1 + \beta}{1 - \beta}} f_0$	**1-38**
Source/observer receding	$f = \sqrt{\dfrac{1 - \beta}{1 + \beta}} f_0$	**1-39**

General References

The following general references are written at a level appropriate for readers of this book.

Bohm, D., *The Special Theory of Relativity,* W. A. Benjamin, New York, 1965.

French, A. P., *Special Relativity,* Norton, 1968. Contains an excellent discussion of the historical basis of relativity.

Gamow, G., *Mr. Tompkins in Paperback,* Cambridge University Press, Cambridge, 1965. Contains the delightful Mr. Tompkins stories. In one of these Mr. Tompkins visits a dream world where the speed of light is only about 10 mi/h and relativistic effects are quite noticeable.

Lorentz, H. A., A. Einstein, H. Minkowski, and W. Weyl, *The Principle of Relativity: A Collection of Original Memoirs on the Special and General Theory of Relativity* (trans. W. Perrett and J. B. Jeffery), Dover, New York, 1923. A delightful little book containing Einstein's original paper ["On the Electrodynamics of Moving Bodies," *Annalen der Physik,* **17** (1905)] and several other original papers on special relativity.

Pais, A., *Subtle Is the Lord . . . ,* Oxford University Press, Oxford, 1982.

Resnick, R., *Introduction to Relativity,* Wiley, 1968.

Resnick, R., and D. Halliday, *Basic Concepts in Relativity and Early Quantum Theory,* 2d ed., Macmillan, New York, 1992.

Taylor, E. F., and Wheeler, J. A. *Spacetime Physics,* 2d ed., W. H. Freeman and Co., 1992. This is a good book with many examples, problems, and diagrams.

NOTES

1. Polish astronomer (1473–1543). His book describing heliocentric (i.e., sun-centered) orbits for the planets was published only a few weeks before his death. He had hesitated to release it for many years, fearing that it might be considered heretical. It is not known whether or not he saw the published book.

2. Events are described by measurements made in a coordinate system which defines a frame of reference. The question was, Where is the reference frame in which the law of inertia is valid? Newton knew that no rotating system, e.g., Earth or the sun, would work and suggested the distant "fixed stars" as the fundamental inertial reference frame.

3. The speed of light is exactly 299,792,458 m/s. This value sets the definition of the standard meter as being the distance light travels in 1/299,792,458 s.

4. Over time, an entire continuous spectrum of electromagnetic waves has been discovered, ranging from extremely low-frequency (radio) waves to extremely high-frequency waves (gamma rays), all moving at speed c.

5. Albert A. Michelson (1852–1931), an American experimental physicist whose development of precision optical instruments and their use in precise measurements of the speed of light and the length of the standard meter earned him the Nobel Prize in 1907. Edward W. Morley (1838–1923), American chemist and physicist and professor at Western Reserve College during the period when Michelson was a professor at the nearby Case School of Applied Science.

6. Albert A. Michelson and Edward W. Morley, *American Journal of Science,* **XXXIV**, no. 203 (November 1887).

7. Note that the width depends on the small angle between M'_2 and M_1. A very small angle results in relatively few wide fringes, a larger angle in many narrow fringes.

8. Since the source producing the waves, the sodium lamp, was at rest relative to the interferometer, the frequency would be constant.

9. T. S. Jaseja, A. Javan, J. Murray, and C. H. Townes, *Physical Review,* **133**, A1221 (1964).

10. A. Brillet and J. Hall, *Physical Review Letters,* **42**, 549 (1979).

11. *Annalen der Physik,* **17**, 841 (1905). For a translation from the original German, see the collection of original papers by Lorentz, Einstein, Minkowski, and Weyl (New York: Dover, 1923).

12. Hendrik Antoon Lorentz (1853–1928), Dutch theoretical physicist, discovered the Lorentz transformation empirically while investigating the fact that Maxwell's equations are not invariant under a Galilean transformation, although he did not recognize its importance at the time. An expert on electromagnetic theory, he was one of the first to suggest that atoms of matter might consist of charged particles whose oscillations could account for the emission of light. Lorentz used this hypothesis to explain the splitting of spectral lines in a magnetic field discovered by his student Pieter Zeeman, with whom he shared the 1902 Nobel Prize.

13. One meter of light travel time is the *time* for light to travel 1 m, i.e., $ct = 1$ m, or $t = 1$ m/3.00×10^8 m/s $= 3.3 \times 10^{-9}$ s. Similarly, 1 cm of light travel time is $ct = 1$ cm, or $t = 3.3 \times 10^{-11}$ s, and so on.

14. This example is adapted from a problem in H. Ohanian, *Modern Physics* (Englewood Cliffs, N.J.: Prentice Hall, 1987).

15. Any particle that has mass.

16. Equation 1-33 would lead to imaginary values of Δs for spacelike intervals, an apparent problem. However, the geometry of spacetime is not Euclidean, but Lorentzian. While a consideration of Lorentz geometry is beyond the scope of this chapter, suffice it to say that it enables us to write $(\Delta s)^2$ for spacelike intervals as in Equation 1-35.

17. There are only two such things: photons (including those of visible light), to be introduced in Chapter 3, and gravitons, which are the particles that transmit the gravitational force.

18. Edwin P. Hubble, *Proceedings of the National Academy of Sciences,* **15**, 168 (1929).

19. Walter Kündig, *Physical Review,* **129**, 2371 (1963).

20. C. G. Darwin, *Nature,* **180**, 976 (1957).

21. S. P. Boughn, *American Journal of Physics,* **57**, 791 (1989).

22. E. F. Taylor and J. A. Wheeler, *Spacetime Physics,* 2d ed. (New York: W. H. Freeman & Co., 1992).

23. Seen in three space dimensions by the observer in S, 50 percent of the light is concentrated in 0.06 steradians of 4π-steradian solid angle around the moving source.

24. T. Alväger and M. N. Kreisler, "Quest for Faster-Than-Light Particles," *Physical Review,* **171**, 1357 (1968).

25. Paul Ehrenfest (1880–1933), Austrian physicist and professor at the University of Leiden (the Netherlands), long-time friend and correspondent of Einstein about whom, upon his death, Einstein wrote, "[He was] the best teacher in our profession I have ever known."

26. This experiment is described in J. C. Hafele and R. E. Keating, *Science,* **177**, 166 (1972). Although not as accurate as the experiment described in Section 1-4, its results supported the relativistic prediction.

27. R. Shaw, *American Journal of Physics,* **30**, 72 (1962).

PROBLEMS

Level I

Section 1-1 The Experimental Basis of Relativity

1-1. A small airplane takes off from a field into an 18 m/s west wind. After 10 minutes it has moved 25 km west, 16 km north, and 0.5 km upward with respect to the wind. What are its position coordinates at that time relative to the point where it left the ground?

1-2. In one series of measurements of the speed of light, Michelson used a path length L of 27.4 km (17 mi). (*a*) What is the time needed for light to make the round trip of distance $2L$? (*b*) What is the classical correction term in seconds in Equation 1-7, assuming Earth's speed is $v = 10^{-4}c$? (*c*) From about 1600 measurements, Michelson arrived at a result for the speed of light of 299,796 ± 4 km/s. Is this experimental value accurate enough to be sensitive to the correction term in Equation 1-7?

1-3. A shift of one fringe in the Michelson-Morley experiment would result from a difference of one wavelength or a change of one period of vibration in the round-trip travel of the light when the interferometer is rotated by 90°. What speed would Michelson have computed for Earth's motion through the ether had the experiment seen a shift of one fringe?

1-4. In the "old days" (circa 1935) pilots used to race small, relatively high-powered airplanes around courses marked by a pylon on the ground at each end of the course. Suppose two such evenly matched racers fly at airspeeds of 130 mph. (Remember, this was a long time ago!) Each flies one complete round trip of 25 miles, *but* their courses are perpendicular to one another and there is a 20 mph wind blowing steadily parallel to one course. (*a*) Which pilot wins the race and by how much? (*b*) Relative to the axes of their respective courses, what headings must the two pilots use?

1-5. Paul Ehrenfest[25] suggested the following thought experiment to illustrate the dramatically different observations that might be expected, dependent on whether light moved relative to a stationary ether or according to Einstein's second postulate:

> Suppose that you are seated at the center of a huge dark sphere with a radius of 3×10^8 m and with its inner surface highly reflective. A source at the center emits a very brief flash of light which moves outward through the darkness with uniform intensity as an expanding spherical wave.

What would you see during the first 3 seconds after the emission of the flash if (*a*) the sphere moved through the ether at a constant 30 km/s, and (*b*) if Einstein's second postulate is correct?

1-6. Einstein reported that as a boy he wondered about the following puzzle. If you hold a mirror at arm's length and look at your reflection, what will happen as you begin to run? In particular, suppose you run with speed $v = 0.99c$. Will you still be able to see yourself? If so, what would your image look like, and why?

1-7. Verify by calculation that the result of the Michelson-Morley experiment places an upper limit on Earth's speed relative to the ether of about 5 km/s.

1-8. Consider two inertial reference frames. When an observer in each frame measures the following quantities, which measurements made by the two observers *must* yield the same results? Explain your reason for each answer.

(*a*) The distance between two events
(*b*) The value of the mass of a proton
(*c*) The speed of light
(*d*) The time interval between two events
(*e*) Newton's first law
(*f*) The order of the elements in the periodic table
(*g*) The value of the electron charge

Section 1-2 Einstein's Postulates

1-9. Assume that the train shown in Figure 1-15 is 1.0 km long as measured by the observer at C' and is moving at 150 km/h. What time interval between the arrival of the wave fronts at C' is measured by the observer at C in S?

1-10. Suppose that A', B', and C' are at rest in frame S', which moves with respect to S at speed v in the $+x$ direction. Let B' be located exactly midway between A' and C'. At $t' = 0$ a light flash occurs at B' and expands outward as a spherical wave. (a) According to an observer in S', do the wave fronts arrive at A' and C' simultaneously? (b) According to an observer in S, do the wave fronts arrive at A' and C' simultaneously? (c) If you answered no to either (a) or (b), what is the difference in their arrival times and at which point did the front arrive first?

Section 1-3 The Lorentz Transformation

1-11. Make a graph of the relativistic factor $\gamma = 1/(1 - v^2/c^2)^{1/2}$ as a function of $\beta = v/c$. Use at least 10 values of β ranging from 0 up to 0.995.

1-12. Two events happen at the same point x_0' in frame S' at times t_1' and t_2'. (a) Use Equations 1-21 to show that in frame S the time interval between the events is greater than $t_2' - t_1'$ by a factor γ. (b) Why are Equations 1-20 less convenient than Equations 1-21 for this problem?

1-13. Suppose that an event occurs in inertial frame S with coordinates $x = 75$ m, $y = 18$ m, $z = 4.0$ m at $t = 2.0 \times 10^{-5}$ s. The inertial frame S' moves in the $+x$ direction with $v = 0.85c$. The origins of S and S' coincided at $t = t' = 0$. (a) What are the coordinates of the event in S'? (b) Use the inverse transformation on the results of (a) to obtain the original coordinates.

1-14. Show that the null effect of the Michelson-Morley experiment can be accounted for if the interferometer arm parallel to the motion is shortened by a factor of $(1 - v^2/c^2)^{1/2}$.

1-15. Two spaceships are approaching each other. (a) If the speed of each is $0.9c$ relative to Earth, what is the speed of one relative to the other? (b) If the speed of each relative to Earth is 30,000 m/s (about 100 times the speed of sound), what is the speed of one relative to the other?

1-16. Starting with the Lorentz transformation for the components of the velocity (Equation 1-24), derive the transformation for the components of the acceleration.

1-17. Consider a clock at rest at the origin of the laboratory frame. (a) Draw a spacetime diagram that illustrates that this clock ticks slow when observed from the reference frame of a rocket moving with respect to the laboratory at $v = 0.8c$. (b) When 10 s have elapsed on the rocket clock, how many have ticked by on the lab clock?

1-18. A light beam moves along the y' axis with speed c in frame S', which is moving to the right with speed v relative to frame S. (a) Find u_x and u_y, the x and y components of the velocity of the light beam in frame S. (b) Show that the magnitude of the velocity of the light beam in S is c.

1-19. A particle moves with speed $0.9c$ along the x'' axis of frame S'', which moves with speed $0.9c$ in the positive x' direction relative to frame S'. Frame S' moves with speed $0.9c$ in the positive x direction relative to frame S. (a) Find the speed of the particle relative to frame S'. (b) Find the speed of the particle relative to frame S.

Section 1-4 Time Dilation and Length Contraction

1-20. Use the binomial expansion to derive the following results for values of $v \ll c$ and use when applicable in the problems that follow.

$$(a) \quad \gamma \approx 1 + \frac{1}{2}\frac{v^2}{c^2}$$

$$(b) \quad \frac{1}{\gamma} \approx 1 - \frac{1}{2}\frac{v^2}{c^2}$$

$$(c) \quad \gamma - 1 \approx 1 - \frac{1}{\gamma} \approx \frac{1}{2}\frac{v^2}{c^2}$$

1-21. How great must the relative speed of two observers be for their time-interval measurements to differ by 1 percent (see Problem 1-20)?

1-22. Supersonic jets achieve maximum speeds of about $3 \times 10^{-6}c$. (*a*) By what percentage would you observe such a jet to be contracted in length? (*b*) During a time of 1 y = 3.16×10^7 s on your clock, how much time would elapse on the pilot's clock? How many minutes are lost by the pilot's clock in 1 year of your time?

1-23. A meterstick moves parallel to its length with speed $v = 0.6c$ relative to you. (*a*) Compute the length of the stick measured by you. (*b*) How long does it take for the stick to pass you? (*c*) Draw a spacetime diagram from the viewpoint of your frame with the front of the meterstick at $x = 0$ when $t = 0$. Show how the answers to (*a*) and (*b*) are obtained from the diagram.

1-24. The proper mean lifetime of π mesons (pions) is 2.6×10^{-8}s. If a beam of such particles has speed $0.9c$, (*a*) What would their mean life be as measured in the laboratory? (*b*) How far would they travel (on the average) before they decay? (*c*) What would your answer be to part (*b*) if you neglected time dilation? (*d*) What is the interval in spacetime between creation of a typical pion and its decay?

1-25. You have been posted to a remote region of space to monitor traffic. Near the end of a quiet shift, a spacecraft streaks past. Your laser-based measuring device reports the spacecraft's length to be 85 m. The identification transponder reports it to be the NCXXB-12, a cargo craft of proper length 100 m. In transmitting your report to headquarters, what speed should you give for this spacecraft?

1-26. A spaceship departs from Earth for the star Alpha Centauri, which is 4 light-years away. The spaceship travels at $0.75c$. How long does it take to get there (*a*) as measured on Earth and (*b*) as measured by a passenger on the spaceship?

1-27. Two spaceships pass each other traveling in opposite directions. A passenger on ship *A*, which she knows to be 100 m long, notes that ship *B* is moving with a speed of $0.92c$ relative to *A* and that the length of *B* is 36 m. What are the lengths of the two spaceships measured by a passenger in *B*?

1-28. A meterstick at rest in S' is tilted at an angle of 30° to the x' axis. If S' moves at $\beta = 0.8$, how long is the meterstick as measured in S and what angle does it make with the x axis?

1-29. A rectangular box at rest in S' has sides $a' = 2$ m, $b' = 2$ m, and $c' = 4$ m and is oriented as shown in Figure 1-43. S' moves with $\beta = 0.65$ with respect to the laboratory frame S. (*a*) Compute the volume of the box in S' and in S. (*b*) Draw an accurate diagram of the box as seen by an observer in S.

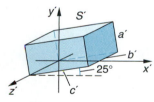

Fig. 1-43 Problem 1-29.

Section 1-5 The Doppler Effect

1-30. How fast must you be moving toward a red light ($\lambda = 650$ nm) for it to appear yellow ($\lambda = 590$ nm)? green ($\lambda = 525$ nm)? blue ($\lambda = 460$ nm)?

1-31. A distant galaxy is moving away from us at speed 1.85×10^7 m/s. Calculate the fractional redshift $(\lambda' - \lambda_0)/\lambda_0$ of the light from this galaxy.

1-32. The light from a nearby star is observed to be shifted toward the blue by 2 percent, i.e., $f_{obs} = 1.02f_0$. Is the star approaching or receding from Earth? How fast is it moving? (Assume motion is directly toward or away from Earth, so as to avoid superluminal speeds.)

1-33. Stars typically emit the red light of atomic hydrogen with wavelength 656.3 nm (called the H_α spectral line). Compute the wavelength of that light observed at Earth from stars receding directly from us with relative speed $v = 10^{-3}c$, $v = 10^{-2}c$, and $v = 10^{-1}c$.

Section 1-6 The Twin Paradox and Other Surprises

1-34. A friend of yours who is the same age as you travels at 0.999c to a star 15 light-years away. She spends 10 years on one of the star's planets and returns at 0.999c. How long has she been away, (a) as measured by you and (b) as measured by her?

1-35. You point a laser flashlight at the moon, producing a spot of light on the moon's surface. At what minimum angular speed must you sweep the laser beam in order for the light spot to streak across the moon's surface with speed $v > c$? Why can't you transmit information between research bases on the moon with the flying spot?

1-36. A clock is placed in a satellite that orbits Earth with a period of 108 min. (a) By what time interval will this clock differ from an identical clock on Earth after 1 y? (b) How much time will have passed on Earth when the two clocks differ by 1.0 s? (Assume special relativity applies and neglect general relativity.)

1-37. Einstein used trains for a number of relativity thought experiments, since they were the fastest objects commonly recognized in those days. Let's consider a train moving at 0.65c along a straight track at night. Its headlight produces a beam with an angular spread of 60° according to the engineer. If you are standing alongside the track (rails are 1.5 m apart), how far from you is the train when its approaching headlight suddenly disappears?

Level II

1-38. In 1971 four portable atomic clocks were flown around the world in jet aircraft, two eastbound and two westbound, to test the time dilation predictions of relativity.[26] (a) If the westbound plane flew at an average speed of 1500 km/h relative to the surface, how long would it have had to fly for the clock on board to lose 1 s relative to the reference clock on the ground at the U.S. Naval Observatory? (b) In the actual experiment the planes circumflew Earth once and the observed discrepancy of the clocks was 273 ns. What was the plane's average speed?

1-39. Show that the spacetime interval Δs is invariant under the Lorentz transformation, i.e., show that

$$(c\,\Delta t)^2 - (\Delta x)^2 = (c\,\Delta t')^2 - (\Delta x')^2$$

1-40. A friend of yours who is the same age as you travels to the star Alpha Centauri, which is $4\ c \cdot y$ away, and returns immediately. He claims that the entire trip took just 6 years. (a) How fast did he travel? (b) How old are you when he returns? (c) Draw a spacetime diagram that verifies your answer to (a) and (b).

1-41. A clock is placed in a satellite that orbits Earth with a period of 90 min. By what time interval will this clock differ from an identical clock on Earth after 1 year? (Assume that special relativity applies.)

1-42. In frame S, event B occurs 2 μs after event A and at $\Delta x = 1.5$ km from event A. (a) How fast must an observer be moving along the +x axis so that events A and B occur simultaneously? (b) Is it possible for event B to precede event A for some observer? (c) Draw a spacetime diagram that illustrates your answers to (a) and (b). (d) Compute the spacetime interval and proper distance between the events.

1-43. A burst of π^+ mesons travels down an evacuated beam tube at Fermilab moving at $\beta = 0.92$ with respect to the laboratory. (a) Compute γ for this group of pions. (b) The proper mean lifetime of pions is 2.6×10^{-8} s. What mean lifetime is measured in the lab? (c) If the burst contained 50,000 pions, how many remain after the group has traveled 50 m down the beam tube? (d) What would be the answer to (c) ignoring time dilation?

1-44. H. A. Lorentz suggested 15 years before Einstein's 1905 paper that the null effect of the Michelson-Morley experiment could be accounted for by a contraction of that arm of the interferometer lying parallel to Earth's motion through the ether to a length

$L = L_p(1 - v^2/c^2)^{-1/2}$. He thought of this, incorrectly, as an actual shrinking of matter. By about how many atomic diameters would the material in the parallel arm of the interferometer have had to shrink in order to account for the absence of the expected shift of 0.4 of a fringe width? (Assume the diameter of atoms to be about 10^{-10} m.)

1-45. Observers in reference frame S see an explosion located at $x_1 = 480$ m. A second explosion occurs 5 μs later at $x_2 = 1200$ m. In reference frame S', which is moving along the $+x$ axis at speed v, the explosions occur at the same point in space. (*a*) Draw a spacetime diagram describing this situation. (*b*) Determine v from the diagram. (*c*) Calibrate the ct' axis and determine the separation in time in μs between the two explosions as measured in S'. (*d*) Verify your results by calculation.

1-46. Two spaceships, each 100 m long when measured at rest, travel toward each other with speeds of $0.85c$ relative to Earth. (*a*) How long is each ship as measured by someone on Earth? (*b*) How fast is each ship traveling as measured by an observer on the other? (*c*) How long is one ship when measured by an observer on the other? (*d*) At time $t = 0$ on Earth, the fronts of the ships are together as they just begin to pass each other. At what time on Earth are their ends together? (*e*) Sketch accurately scaled diagrams in the frame of one of the ships showing the passing of the other ship.

1-47. If v is much less than c, the Doppler frequency shift is approximately given by $\Delta f/f_0 = \pm\beta$, both classically and relativistically. A radar transmitter-receiver bounces a signal off an aircraft and observes a fractional increase in the frequency of $\Delta f/f_0 = 8 \times 10^{-7}$. What is the speed of the aircraft? (Assume the aircraft to be moving directly toward the transmitter.)

1-48. Derive Equation 1-38 for the frequency received by an observer moving with speed v toward a stationary source of electromagnetic waves.

1-49. Frames S and S' are moving relative to each other along the x and x' axes. They set their clocks to $t = t' = 0$ when their origins coincide. In frame S, event 1 occurs at $x_1 = 1\ c \cdot y$ and $t_1 = 1$ y and event 2 occurs at $x_2 = 2.0\ c \cdot y$ and $t_2 = 0.5$ y. These events occur simultaneously in frame S'. (*a*) Find the magnitude and direction of the velocity of S' relative to S. (*b*) At what time do both of these events occur as measured in S? (*c*) Compute the spacetime interval Δs between the events. (*d*) Is the interval spacelike, timelike, or lightlike? (*e*) What is the proper distance L_p between the events?

1-50. Do Problem 1-49 parts (*a*) and (*b*) using a spacetime diagram.

1-51. An observer in frame S standing at the origin observes two flashes of colored light separated spatially by $\Delta x = 2400$ m. A blue flash occurs first, followed by a red flash 5 μs later. An observer in S' moving along the x axis at speed v relative to S also observes the flashes 5 μs apart and with a separation of 2400 m, but the red flash is observed first. Find the magnitude and direction of v.

1-52. A cosmic ray proton streaks through the lab with velocity $0.85c$ at an angle of $50°$ with the $+x$ direction (in the xy plane of the lab). Compute the magnitude and direction of the proton's velocity when viewed from frame S' moving with $\beta = 0.72$.

Level III

1-53. A meterstick is parallel to the x axis in S and is moving in the $+y$ direction at constant speed v_y. Use a spacetime diagram from the viewpoint of S to show that the meterstick will appear tilted at an angle θ' with respect to the x' axis of S' moving in the $+x$ direction at $\beta = 0.65$. Compute the angle θ' measured in S'.

1-54. The equation for the spherical wave front of a light pulse that begins at the origin at time $t = 0$ is $x^2 + y^2 + z^2 - (ct)^2 = 0$. Using the Lorentz transformation, show that such a light pulse also has a spherical wave front in S' by showing that $x^2 + y^2 + z^2 - (ct)^2 = 0$ in S'.

1-55. An interesting paradox has been suggested by R. Shaw[27] that goes like this. A very thin steel plate with a circular hole 1 m in diameter centered on the y axis lies parallel to

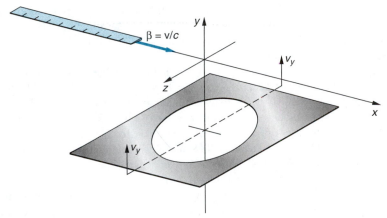

Fig. 1-44 Problem 1-55.

the xz plane in frame S and moves in the $+y$ direction at constant speed v_y as illustrated in Figure 1-44. A meterstick lying on the x axis moves in the $+x$ direction with $\beta = v/c$. The steel plate arrives at the $y = 0$ plane at the same instant that the center of the meterstick reaches the origin of S. Since the meterstick is observed by observers in S to be contracted, it passes through the 1-m hole in the plate with no problem. A paradox appears to arise when one considers that an observer in S', the rest system of the meterstick, measures the diameter of the hole in the plate to be contracted in the x dimension and, hence, becomes too small to pass the meterstick, resulting in a collision. Resolve the paradox. Will there be a collision?

1-56. Two events in S are separated by a distance $D = x_2 - x_1$ and a time $T = t_2 - t_1$. (*a*) Use the Lorentz transformation to show that in frame S', which is moving with speed v relative to S, the time separation is $t_2' - t_1' = \gamma(T - vD/c^2)$. (*b*) Show that the events can be simultaneous in frame S' only if D is greater than cT. (*c*) If one of the events is the *cause* of the other, the separation D must be less than cT since D/c is the smallest time that a signal can take to travel from x_1 to x_2 in frame S. Show that if D is less that cT, t_2' is greater than t_1' in all reference frames. (*d*) Suppose that a signal could be sent with speed $c' > c$ so that in frame S the cause precedes the effect by the time $T = D/c'$. Show that there is then a reference frame moving with speed v less than c in which the effect precedes the cause.

1-57. Two observers agree to test time dilation. They use identical clocks and one observer in frame S' moves with speed $v = 0.6c$ relative to the other observer in frame S. When their origins coincide, they start their clocks. They agree to send a signal when their clocks read 60 min and to send a confirmation signal when each receives the other's signal. (*a*) When does the observer in S receive the first signal from the observer in S'? (*b*) When does he receive the confirmation signal? (*c*) Make a table showing the times in S when the observer sent the first signal, received the first signal, and received the confirmation signal. How does this table compare with one constructed by the observer in S'?

1-58. The compact disc in a CD-ROM drive rotates with angular speed ω. There is a clock at the center of the disc and one at a distance r from the center. In an inertial reference frame, the clock at distance r is moving with speed $u = r\omega$. Show that from time dilation in special relativity, time intervals Δt_0 for the clock at rest and Δt_r for the moving clock are related by

$$\frac{\Delta t_r - \Delta t_0}{\Delta t_0} \approx \frac{r^2\omega^2}{2c^2} \qquad \text{if} \qquad r\omega \ll c$$

1-59. Two rockets A and B leave a space station with velocity vectors $\mathbf{v}_A$ and $\mathbf{v}_B$, relative to the station frame S, perpendicular to one another. (*a*) Determine the velocity of A relative to B, $\mathbf{v}_{BA}$. (*b*) Determine the velocity of B relative to A, $\mathbf{v}_{AB}$. (*c*) Explain why $\mathbf{v}_{AB}$ and $\mathbf{v}_{BA}$ do not point in opposite directions.

1-60. Suppose a system S consisting of a cubic lattice of metersticks and synchronized clocks, e.g., the eight clocks closest to you in Figure 1-14, moves from left to right (the $+x$ direction) at high speed. The metersticks parallel to the x direction are, of course, contracted and the cube would be *measured* by an observer in a system S' to be foreshortened in that direction. However, recalling that your eye constructs images from light waves which reach it simultaneously, not those leaving the source simultaneously, sketch what your eye would *see* in this case. Scale contractions and show any angles accurately. (Assume the moving cube to be farther than 10 m from your eye.)

1-61. Figure 1-12*b* (in the More section about the Michelson-Morley experiment) shows an eclipsing binary. Suppose the period of the motion is T and the binary is a distance L from Earth, where L is sufficiently large so that points A and B in Figure 1-12*b* are a half-orbit apart. Consider the motion of one of the stars and (*a*) show that the star would appear to move from A to B in time $T/2 + 2Lv/(c^2 - v^2)$ and from B to A in time $T/2 - 2Lv/(c^2 - v^2)$, assuming classical velocity addition applies to light, i.e., that emission theories of light were correct. (*b*) What rotational period would cause the star to appear to be at both A and B simultaneously?

1-62. Show that if a particle moves at an angle θ with respect to the x axis with speed u in system S, it moves at an angle θ' with the x' axis in S' given by

$$\tan \theta' = \frac{\sin \theta}{\gamma (\cos \theta - v/u)}$$

Chapter 2

Relativity II

*I*n the opening section of Chapter 1 we discussed the classical observation that, if Newton's second law $\mathbf{F} = m\mathbf{a}$ holds in a particular reference frame, it also holds in any other reference frame that moves with constant velocity relative to it, i.e., in any inertial frame. As shown in Section 1-1, the Galilean transformation (Equations 1-3) leads to the same accelerations $a_x' = a_x$ in both frames, and forces such as those due to stretched springs are also the same in both frames. However, according to the Lorentz transformation, accelerations are not the same in two such reference frames. If a particle has acceleration a_x and velocity u_x in frame S, its acceleration in S', obtained by computing du_x'/dt' from Equation 1-24, is

$$a_x' = \frac{a_x}{\gamma^3(1 - vu_x/c^2)^3}$$

2-1

Thus, F/m must transform in a similar way, or Newton's second law $\mathbf{F} = m\mathbf{a}$ does not hold.

It is reasonable to expect that $\mathbf{F} = m\mathbf{a}$ does *not* hold at high speeds, for this equation implies that a constant force will accelerate a particle to unlimited velocity if it acts for a long time. However, if a particle's velocity was greater than c in some reference frame S, we could not transform from S to the rest frame of the particle because γ becomes imaginary when $v > c$. We can show from the velocity transformation that if a particle's velocity is less than c in some frame S, it is less than c in all frames moving relative to S with $v < c$. This result leads us to expect that particles never have speeds greater than c. Thus, we expect that Newton's second law $\mathbf{F} = m\mathbf{a}$ is not relativistically invariant. We will, therefore, need a new law of motion, but one that reduces to Newton's classical version when $\beta \, (=v/c) \rightarrow 0$, since $\mathbf{F} = m\mathbf{a}$ is consistent with experimental observations when $\beta \ll 1$.

In this chapter we will explore the changes in classical dynamics that are dictated by relativity theory, directing particular attention to the same concepts around which classical mechanics was developed, namely mass, momentum, and energy. We will find these changes to be every bit as dramatic as those we encountered in Chapter 1, including a Lorentz transformation for momentum and energy and a new invariant quantity to stand beside the invariant spacetime interval Δs. Then, in the latter part of the chapter, we will briefly turn our attention to noninertial, or accelerated, reference frames, the realm of the theory of general relativity.

2-1 Relativistic Momentum

Among the most powerful fundamental concepts that you have studied in physics until now have been the ideas of conservation of momentum and conservation of total energy. As we will discuss a bit further in Chapter 13, each of these fundamental laws arises because of a particular symmetry that exists in the laws of physics. For example, the conservation of total energy in classical physics is a consequence of the symmetry, or invariance, of the laws of physics to translations in time. As a consequence, Newton's laws work exactly the same way today as they did when he first wrote them down. The conservation of momentum arises from the invariance of physical laws to translations in space. Indeed, Einstein's first postulate and the resulting Lorentz transformation (Equations 1-20 and 1-21) guarantee this latter invariance in all inertial frames.

The simplicity and universality of these conservation laws leads us to seek equations for relativistic mechanics, replacing Equation 1-1 and others, that are consistent with momentum and energy conservation and are also invariant under a Lorentz transformation. However, it is straightforward to show that the momentum, as formulated in classical mechanics, does not result in relativistic invariance of the law of conservation of momentum. To see that this is so, we will look at an isolated collision between two masses, where we avoid the question of how to transform forces because the net external force is zero. In classical mechanics, the total momentum $\mathbf{p} = \Sigma m_i\mathbf{u}_i$ is conserved. We can see that relativistically, conservation of the quantity $\Sigma m_i\mathbf{u}_i$ is an approximation which holds only at low speeds.

Consider one observer in frame S with a ball A and another in S' with a ball B. The balls each have mass m and are identical when measured at rest. Each observer throws his ball along his y axis with speed u_0 (measured in his own frame) so that the balls collide.[1] Assuming the balls to be perfectly elastic, each observer will see his ball rebound with its original speed u_0. If the total momentum is to be conserved, the y component must be zero because the momentum of each ball is merely reversed by the collision. However, if we consider the relativistic velocity transformations, we can see that the quantity mu_y does not have the same magnitude for each ball as seen by either observer.

Let us consider the collision as seen in frame S (Figure 2-1a). In this frame ball A moves along the y axis with velocity $u_{yA} = u_0$. Ball B has x component of velocity $u_{xB} = v$ and y component

$$u_{yB} = u'_{yB}/\gamma = -u_0\sqrt{1 - v^2/c^2} \qquad \textbf{2-2}$$

Here we have used the velocity transformation equations (1-25) and the facts the u'_{yB} is just $-u_0$ and $u'_{xB} = 0$. We see that the y component of velocity of ball B is smaller in magnitude than that of ball A. The quantity $(1 - v^2/c^2)^{1/2}$ comes from the time dilation factor. The time taken for ball B to travel a given distance along the y axis in S is greater than the time measured in S' for the ball to travel this same distance. Thus in S the total y component of classical momentum is not zero. Since the y components of the velocities are reversed in an elastic collision, momentum as defined by $\mathbf{p} = \Sigma m\mathbf{u}$ is not conserved in S. Analysis of this problem in S' leads to the same conclusion (Figure 2-1b), since the roles of A and B are simply interchanged.[2] In the classical limit $v \ll c$, momentum is conserved, of course, because in that limit $\gamma \approx 1$ and $u_{yB} \approx u_0$.

The reason for defining momentum as $\Sigma m\mathbf{u}$ in classical mechanics is that this quantity is conserved when there is no net external force, as in our collision example.

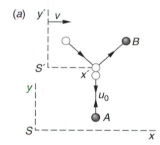

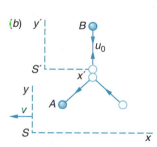

Fig. 2-1 (a) Elastic collision of two identical balls as seen in frame S. The vertical component of the velocity of ball B is u_0/γ in S if it is u_0 in S'. (b) The same collision as seen in S'. In this frame ball A has vertical component of velocity u_0/γ.

We now see that this quantity is conserved only in the approximation $v \ll c$. We shall define *relativistic momentum* **p** of a particle to have the following properties:

1. **p** is conserved in collisions.
2. **p** approaches $m\mathbf{u}$ as u/c approaches zero.

Let's apply the first of these conditions to the collision of the two balls that we just discussed, noting two important points. First, for each observer in Figure 2-1, the speed of each ball is unchanged by the elastic collision. It is either u_0 (for the observer's own ball) or $(u_y^2 + v^2)^{1/2} = u$ (for the other ball). Second, the failure of the conservation of momentum in the collision we described can't be due to the velocities because we used the Lorentz transformation to find the y components. It must have something to do with the mass! Let us write down the conservation of the y component of the momentum *as observed in S*, keeping the masses of the two balls straight by writing $m(u_0)$ for the S observer's own ball and $m(u)$ for the S' observer's ball.

$$m(u_0)u_0 - m(u)u_{yB} = -m(u_0)u_0 + m(u)u_{yB} \qquad \textbf{2-3}$$

(before collision)   **(after collision)**

Equation 2-3 can be readily rewritten as

$$\frac{m(u)}{m(u_0)} = \frac{u_0}{u_{yB}} \qquad \textbf{2-4}$$

If u_0 is small compared to the relative speed v of the reference frames, then it follows from Equation 2-2 that $u_{yB} \ll v$ and, therefore, $u \approx v$.

If we can now imagine the limiting case where $u_0 \rightarrow 0$, i.e., where each ball is at rest in its "home" frame so that the collision becomes a "grazing" one as B moves past A at speed $v = u$, then we conclude from Equations 2-2 and 2-4 that in order for Equation 2-3 to hold, i.e., for the momentum to be conserved,

$$\frac{m(u = v)}{m(u_0 = 0)} = \frac{u_0}{u_0\sqrt{1 - v^2/c^2}}$$

or

$$m(u) = \frac{m}{\sqrt{1 - u^2/c^2}} \qquad \textbf{2-5}$$

Equation 2-5 says that the observer in S *measures* the mass of ball B, moving relative to him at speed u, as equal to $1/(1 - u^2/c^2)^{1/2}$ times the rest mass of the ball, or its mass measured in the frame in which it is at rest. Notice that observers always measure the mass of an object that is in motion with respect to them to be larger than the value measured when the object is at rest.

Thus we see that the law of conservation of momentum will be valid in relativity, provided that we write the momentum **p** of an object with rest mass m moving with velocity **u** relative to an inertial system S to be

$$\mathbf{p} = \frac{m\mathbf{u}}{\sqrt{1 - u^2/c^2}} \qquad \textbf{2-6}$$

The design and construction of the large particle accelerators throughout the world are based directly on the relativistic expressions for momentum and energy.

where u is the speed of the particle. We thus take this equation for the definition of relativistic momentum. It is clear that this definition meets our second criterion, because the denominator approaches 1 when u is much less than c. From this definition, the momenta of the two balls A and B in Figure 2-1 as seen in S are

$$p_{yA} = \frac{mu_0}{\sqrt{1 - u_0^2/c^2}} \qquad p_{yB} = \frac{mu_{yB}}{\sqrt{1 - (u_{xB}^2 + u_{yB}^2)/c^2}}$$

where $u_{yB} = u_0(1 - v^2/c^2)^{1/2}$ and $u_{xB} = v$. It is similarly straightforward to show that $p_{yB} = -p_{yA}$. Because of the similarity of the factor $1/(1 - u^2/c^2)^{1/2}$ and γ in the Lorentz transformation, Equation 2-6 is often written

$$\mathbf{p} = \gamma m\mathbf{u} \qquad \text{with} \qquad \gamma = \frac{1}{\sqrt{1 - u^2/c^2}} \qquad\qquad \textbf{2-7}$$

This use of the symbol γ for two different quantities causes some confusion; the notation is standard, however, and simplifies many of the equations. We shall use this notation except when we are also considering transformations between reference frames. Then, to avoid confusion, we shall write out the factor $(1 - u^2/c^2)^{1/2}$ and reserve γ for $1/(1 - v^2/c^2)^{1/2}$, where v is the relative speed of the frames. Figure 2-2 shows a graph of the magnitude of $\mathbf{p}$ as a function of u/c. The quantity $m(u)$ in Equation 2-5 is sometimes called the *relativistic mass;* however, we shall avoid using the term or a symbol for relativistic mass: in this book, m *always* refers to the mass measured in the rest frame. In this we are following Einstein's view. In a letter to a colleague in 1948 he wrote:[3]

> It is not good to introduce the concept of mass $M = m/(1 - v^2/c^2)^{1/2}$ of a body for which no clear definition can be given. It is better to introduce no other mass than "the rest mass" m. Instead of introducing M, it is better to mention the expression for the momentum and energy of a body in motion.

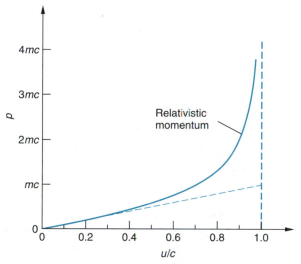

Fig. 2-2 Relativistic momentum as given by Equation 2-6 versus u/c, where u = speed of the object relative to an observer. The magnitude of the momentum p is plotted in units of mc. The fainter dashed line shows the classical momentum mu for comparison.

EXAMPLE 2-1 Measured Values of Moving Mass For what value of u/c will the measured mass of an object γm exceed the rest mass by a given fraction f?

Solution

From Equation 2-5 we see that

$$f = \frac{\gamma m - m}{m} = \gamma - 1 = \frac{1}{\sqrt{1 - u^2/c^2}} - 1$$

Solving for u/c,

$$1 - u^2/c^2 = \frac{1}{(f + 1)^2} \longrightarrow u^2/c^2 = 1 - \frac{1}{(f + 1)^2}$$

or

$$u/c = \frac{\sqrt{f(f + 2)}}{f + 1}$$

from which we can compute the table of values below or the value of u/c for any other f. Note that the value of u/c that results in a given fractional increase f in the measured value of the mass is independent of m. A diesel locomotive moving at a particular u/c will be observed to have the same f as a proton moving with that u/c.

f	u/c	example
10^{-12}	1.4×10^{-6}	jet fighter aircraft
5×10^{-9}	0.0001	Earth's orbital speed
0.0001	0.014	50-eV electron
0.01 (1%)	0.14	quasar 3C 273
1.0 (100%)	0.87	quasar OQ172
10	0.996	muons from cosmic rays
100	0.99995	some cosmic ray protons

EXAMPLE 2-2 Momentum of a Rocket A high-speed interplanetary probe with a mass $m = 50,000$ kg has been sent toward Pluto at a speed $u = 0.8c$. What is its momentum as measured by Mission Control on Earth? If, preparatory to landing on Pluto, the probe's speed is reduced to $0.4c$, by how much does its momentum change?

Solution

1. Assuming that the probe travels in a straight line toward Pluto, its momentum along that direction is given by Equation 2-6:

$$p = \frac{mu}{\sqrt{1 - u^2/c^2}}$$

$$= \frac{(50{,}000 \text{ kg})(0.8c)}{\sqrt{1 - (0.8)^2}}$$

$$= 6.7 \times 10^4 \, c \cdot \text{kg}$$

$$= 2.0 \times 10^{13} \, \text{kg} \cdot \text{m/s}$$

2. When the probe's speed is reduced, the momentum declines along the relativistic momentum curve in Figure 2-2. The new value is computed from the ratio:

$$\frac{p_{0.4c}}{p_{0.8c}} = \frac{m(0.4c)/\sqrt{1 - (0.4)^2}}{m(0.8c)/\sqrt{1 - (0.8)^2}}$$

$$= \frac{1}{2}\frac{\sqrt{1 - (0.8)^2}}{\sqrt{1 - (0.4)^2}}$$

$$= 0.33$$

3. The reduced momentum $p_{0.4c}$ is then given by:

$$p_{0.4c} = 0.33 \, p_{0.8c}$$

$$= (0.33)(6.7 \times 10^4 \, c \cdot \text{kg})$$

$$= 2.2 \times 10^4 \, c \cdot \text{kg}$$

$$= 6.6 \times 10^{12} \, \text{kg} \cdot \text{m/s}$$

Remarks: *Notice from Figure 2-2 that the incorrect classical value of $p_{0.8c}$ would have been $4.0 \times 10^4 \, c \cdot kg$. Also, while the probe's speed was decreased to one-half its initial value, the momentum decreased to one-third of the initial value.*

QUESTION

1. In our discussion of the inelastic collision of balls *A* and *B*, the collision was a "grazing" one in the limiting case. Suppose instead that the collision is a "head-on" one along the *x* axis. If the speed of *S′* (i.e., ball *B*) is low, say, $v = 0.1c$, what would a spacetime diagram of the collision look like?

2-2 Relativistic Energy

As noted in the preceding section, the fundamental character of the principle of conservation of total energy leads us to seek a definition of total energy in relativity that preserves the invariance of that conservation law in transformations between inertial

systems. As with the definition of the relativistic momentum, Equation 2-6, we shall require that the *relativistic total energy E* satisfy two conditions:

1. The total energy E of any isolated system is conserved.
2. E will approach the classical value when u/c approaches zero.

Let's first find a form for E that satisfies the second condition and then see if it also satisfies the first. We have seen that the quantity $m\mathbf{u}$ is not conserved in collisions but that $\gamma m\mathbf{u}$ is, with $\gamma = 1/(1 - u^2/c^2)^{1/2}$. We have also noted that Newton's second law in the form $\mathbf{F} = m\mathbf{a}$ cannot be correct relativistically, one reason being that it leads to the conservation of $m\mathbf{u}$. We can get a hint of the relativistically correct form of the second law by writing it $\mathbf{F} = d\mathbf{p}/dt$. This equation is relativistically correct *if* relativistic momentum $\mathbf{p}$ is used. We thus define the force in relativity to be

$$F = \frac{d\mathbf{p}}{dt} = \frac{d(\gamma m\mathbf{u})}{dt} \qquad\qquad \textbf{2-8}$$

Now then, as in classical mechanics, we shall define kinetic energy E_k as the work done by a net force in accelerating a particle from rest to some velocity u. Considering motion in one dimension only, we have

$$E_k = \int_{u=0}^{u} F\,dx = \int_{0}^{u} \frac{d(\gamma mu)}{dt}\,dx = \int_{0}^{u} u\,d(\gamma mu)$$

Aerial view of the Stanford Linear Accelerator Center (SLAC). Electrons begin their 3-km acceleration to relativistic energies in the upper right, cross under Interstate 280 at nearly the speed of light, and fan out to several experiment stations in the foreground, where their collisions in the underground storage ring create short-lived mesons. [*Stanford Linear Accelerator Center, U.S. Department of Energy.*]

using $u = dx/dt$. The computation of the integral in this equation is not difficult but requires a bit of algebra. It is left as an exercise (Problem 2-2) to show that

$$d(\gamma m u) = m\left(1 - \frac{u^2}{c^2}\right)^{-3/2} du$$

Substituting this into the integrand in Equation 2-8, we obtain

$$E_k = \int_0^u u\, d(\gamma m u) = \int_0^u m\left(1 - \frac{u^2}{c^2}\right)^{-3/2} u\, du$$

$$= mc^2\left(\frac{1}{\sqrt{1 - u^2/c^2}} - 1\right)$$

or

$$E_k = \gamma mc^2 - mc^2 \qquad\qquad \textbf{2-9}$$

Equation 2-9 defines the *relativistic kinetic energy*. Notice that, as we warned earlier, E_k is *not* $mu^2/2$ or even $\gamma mu^2/2$. This is strikingly evident in Figure 2-3. However, consistent with our second condition on the relativistic total energy E, Equation 2-9 does approach $mu^2/2$ when $u \ll c$. We can check this assertion by noting that for $u/c \ll 1$, expanding γ by the binomial theorem yields

$$\gamma = \left(1 - \frac{u^2}{c^2}\right)^{-1/2} \approx 1 + \frac{1}{2}\frac{u^2}{c^2} + \cdots$$

and thus

$$E_k = mc^2\left(1 + \frac{1}{2}\frac{u^2}{c^2} + \cdots - 1\right) \approx \frac{1}{2}mu^2$$

The expression for kinetic energy in Equation 2-9 consists of two terms. One term, γmc^2, depends on the speed of the particle (through the factor γ), and the other term, mc^2, is independent of the speed. The quantity mc^2 is called the *rest energy* of the particle, i.e., the energy associated with the rest mass m. The relativistic total energy E is then defined as the sum of the kinetic energy and the rest energy:

$$E = E_k + mc^2 = \gamma mc^2 = \frac{mc^2}{\sqrt{1 - u^2/c^2}} \qquad\qquad \textbf{2-10}$$

Thus, the work done by a net force increases the energy of the system from the rest energy mc^2 to γmc^2 (or increases the measured mass from m to γm).

For a particle at rest relative to an observer, $E_k = 0$, and Equation 2-10 becomes perhaps the most widely recognized equation in all of physics, Einstein's famous $E = mc^2$. When $u \ll c$ Equation 2-10 can be written as

$$E \approx \frac{1}{2}mu^2 + mc^2$$

Before the development of relativity theory, it was thought that mass was a conserved quantity;[4] consequently, m would always be the same before and after an interaction

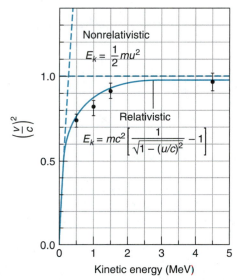

Fig. 2-3 Experimental confirmation of the relativistic relation for kinetic energy. Electrons were accelerated to energies up to several MeV in large electric fields and their velocities were determined by measuring their time of flight over 8.4 m. Note that when the velocity $u \ll c$, the relativistic and nonrelativistic (i.e., classical) relations are indistinguishable. [*W. Bertozzi, American Journal of Physics, 32, 551 (1964).*]

or event and mc^2 would therefore be constant. Since the zero of energy is arbitrary, we are always free to include an additive constant; therefore, our definition of the relativistic total energy reduces to the classical kinetic energy for $u \ll c$ and our second condition on E is thus satisfied.[5]

Be very careful to understand Equation 2-10 correctly. It defines the total energy E, and E is what we are seeking to conserve for isolated systems in all inertial frames, *not* E_k and *not* mc^2. Remember, too, the distinction between *conserved* quantities and *invariant* quantities. The former have the same value before and after an interaction in a particular reference frame. The latter have the same value when measured by observers in different reference frames. Thus, we are not requiring observers in relatively moving inertial frames to measure the same values for E, but rather that E be unchanged in interactions as measured in each frame. To assist us in showing that E as defined by Equation 2-10 is conserved in relativity, we will first see how E and **p** transform between inertial reference frames.

Lorentz Transformation of E and **p**

Consider a particle of rest mass m that has an arbitrary velocity **u** with respect to frame S as shown in Figure 2-4. System S' is a second inertial frame moving in the $+x$ direction. The particle's momentum and energy are given in the S and S' systems, respectively, by:

In S:

$$E = \gamma mc^2$$
$$p_x = \gamma m u_x$$
$$p_y = \gamma m u_y$$
$$p_z = \gamma m u_z$$

2-11

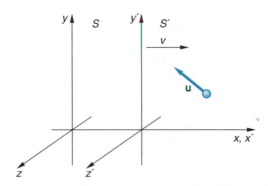

Fig. 2-4 Particle of mass m moves with velocity $\mathbf{u}$ measured in S. System S' moves in the $+x$ direction at speed v. The Lorentz velocity transformation enables determination of the relations connecting measurements of the total energy and the components of the momentum in the two frames of reference.

where

$$\gamma = 1/\sqrt{1 - u^2/c^2}$$

In S':

$$\begin{aligned}
E' &= \gamma' mc^2 \\
p'_x &= \gamma' mu'_x \\
p'_y &= \gamma' mu'_y \\
p'_z &= \gamma' mu'_z
\end{aligned} \qquad \textbf{2-12}$$

where

$$\gamma' = 1/\sqrt{1 - u'^2/c^2}$$

Developing the Lorentz transformations for E and $\mathbf{p}$ requires that we first express γ' in terms of quantities measured in S. (We could just as well express γ in terms of primed quantities. Since this is relativity, it makes no difference which we choose.) The result is

$$\frac{1}{\sqrt{1 - u'^2/c^2}} = \gamma \frac{(1 - vu_x/c^2)}{\sqrt{1 - u^2/c^2}} \qquad \text{where now} \qquad \gamma = \frac{1}{\sqrt{1 - v^2/c^2}} \qquad \textbf{2-13}$$

Substituting Equation 2-13 into the expression for E' in Equations 2-12 yields

$$E' = \frac{mc^2}{\sqrt{1 - u'^2/c^2}} = \gamma\left[\frac{mc^2}{\sqrt{1 - u^2/c^2}} - \frac{mc^2 vu_x/c^2}{\sqrt{1 - u^2/c^2}}\right]$$

The first term in the brackets you will recognize as E, and the second term, canceling the c^2 factors, as vp_x from Equations 2-11. Thus, we have

$$E' = \gamma(E - vp_x) \qquad \textbf{2-14}$$

Similarly, substituting Equation 2-13 and the velocity transformation for u'_x into the expression for p'_x in Equations 2-12 yields

$$p'_x = \frac{mu'_x}{\sqrt{1 - u'^2/c^2}} = \gamma\left[\frac{mu_x}{\sqrt{1 - u^2/c^2}} - \frac{mv}{\sqrt{1 - u^2/c^2}}\right]$$

The first term in the brackets is p_x from Equations 2-11 and, noting that $m(1 - u^2/c^2)^{-1/2} = E/c^2$, the second term is vE/c^2. Thus we have

$$p'_x = \gamma(p_x - vE/c^2) \qquad \textbf{2-15}$$

Using the same approach, it can be shown (Problem 2-45) that

$$p'_y = p_y \qquad \text{and} \qquad p'_z = p_z$$

Together these relations are the *Lorentz transformation for momentum and energy:*

$$\begin{array}{ll} p'_x = \gamma(p_x - vE/c^2) & p'_y = p_y \\ E' = \gamma(E - vp_x) & p'_z = p_z \end{array} \qquad \textbf{2-16}$$

The inverse transformation is

$$\begin{array}{ll} p_x = \gamma(p'_x + vE'/c^2) & p_y = p'_y \\ E = \gamma(E' + vp'_x) & p_z = p'_z \end{array}$$

with

$$\gamma = \frac{1}{\sqrt{1 - v^2/c^2}} = \frac{1}{\sqrt{1 - \beta^2}} \qquad \textbf{2-17}$$

Note the striking similarity between Equations 2-16 and 2-17 and the Lorentz transformation of the space and time coordinates, Equations 1-20 and 1-21. The momentum $\mathbf{p}(p_x, p_y, p_z)$ transforms in relativity exactly like $\mathbf{r}(x, y, z)$, and the total energy E transforms like the time t. We will return to this remarkable result and related matters shortly, but first let's do some examples and then, as promised, show that the energy defined by Equation 2-10 is conserved in relativity.

EXAMPLE 2-3 Transforming Energy and Momentum Suppose a micrometeorite of mass 10^{-9} kg moves past Earth at a speed of $0.01c$. What values will be measured for the energy and momentum of the particle by an observer in a system S' moving relative to Earth at $0.5c$ in the same direction as the micrometeorite?

Solution
Taking the direction of the micrometeorite's travel as the x axis, its energy and momentum as measured by the Earth observer are, using the $u \ll c$ approximation of Equation 2-10:

$$E \approx \tfrac{1}{2}mu^2 + mc^2 = 10^{-9} \text{ kg}[(0.01c)^2/2 + c^2]$$
$$E \approx 1.00005 \times 10^{-9} c^2 \text{ J}$$

and

$$p_x = mu_x = (10^{-9} \text{ kg})(0.01c) = 10^{-11} \, c \text{ kg} \cdot \text{m/s}$$

For this situation $\gamma = 1.1547$, so in S' the measured values of the energy and momentum will be:

$$E' = \gamma(E - vp_x) = (1.1547)[1.00005 \times 10^{-9}c^2 - (0.5c)(10^{-11}c)]$$
$$E' = (1.1547)(1.00005 \times 10^{-9} - 0.5 \times 10^{-11})c^2$$
$$E' = 1.14898 \times 10^{-9} \, c^2 \text{ J}$$

and

$$p_x' = \gamma(p_x - vE/c^2) = (1.1547)[10^{-11}c - (0.05c)(1.00005 \times 10^{-9} \, c^2)/c^2]$$
$$p_x' = (1.1547)(10^{-11} - 5.00025 \times 10^{-10})c$$
$$p_x' = -0.566 \times 10^{-11} \, c \text{ kg} \cdot \text{m/s}$$

Thus, the observer in S' measures a total energy nearly 15 percent larger and a momentum about 40 percent smaller and in the $-x$ direction.

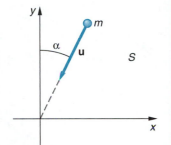

Fig. 2-5 The system discussed in Example 2-4.

EXAMPLE 2-4 A More Difficult Lorentz Transformation of Energy Suppose that a particle with mass m and energy E is moving toward the origin of a system S such that its velocity $\mathbf{u}$ makes an angle α with the y axis as shown in Figure 2-5. Using the Lorentz transformation for energy and momentum, determine the energy E' of the particle measured by an observer in S', which moves relative to S so that the particle moves along the y' axis.

Solution
System S' moves in the $-x$ direction at speed $u \sin \alpha$, as determined from the Lorentz velocity transformation for $u_x' = 0$. Thus, $v = -u \sin \alpha$. Also,

$$E = mc^2/\sqrt{1 - u^2/c^2} \qquad p = mu/\sqrt{1 - u^2/c^2}$$

and from the latter,

$$p_x = -\left(mu/\sqrt{1 - u^2/c^2}\right)\sin \alpha$$

In S' the energy will be

$$E' = \gamma(E - vp_x)$$
$$= \frac{1}{\sqrt{1 - v^2/c^2}} [E - (-u \sin \alpha)(-mu/\sqrt{1 - u^2/c^2})\sin \alpha]$$
$$= \frac{1}{\sqrt{1 - u^2\sin^2\alpha/c^2}} [E - (m/\sqrt{1 - u^2/c^2})u^2\sin^2 \alpha]$$

Multiplying the second term in the brackets by c^2/c^2 and factoring an E from both terms yield

$$E' = E\sqrt{1 - (u^2/c^2)\sin^2 \alpha}$$

Since $u < c$ and $\sin^2 \alpha \leq 1$, we see that $E' < E$, except for $\alpha = 0$ when $E' = E$, in which case S and S' are the same system. Note, too, that for $\alpha > 0$, if $u \to c$, $E' \to E \cos \alpha$. As we will see later, this is the case for light.

QUESTION

2. Recalling the results of the measurements of time and space intervals by observers in motion relative to clocks and measuring rods, discuss the results of corresponding measurements of energy and momentum changes.

Conservation of Energy

As with our discussion of momentum conservation in relativity, let us consider a collision of two identical particles, each with rest mass m. This time, for a little variety, we will let the collision be completely inelastic—i.e., when the particles collide, they stick together. There is a system S', called the *zero-momentum frame*, in which the particles approach each other along the x' axis with equal speeds u—hence equal and opposite momenta—as illustrated in Figure 2-6a. In this frame the collision results in the formation of a composite particle of mass M at rest in S'. If S' moves with respect to a second frame S at speed $v = u$ in the x direction, then the particle on the right before the collision will be at rest in S and the composite particle will move to the right at speed u in that frame. This situation is illustrated in Figure 2-6b.

Using the total energy as defined by Equation 2-10, we have in S'.

Before collision:

$$E'_{before} = \frac{mc^2}{\sqrt{1 - u^2/c^2}} + \frac{mc^2}{\sqrt{1 - u^2/c^2}} \qquad \text{2-18}$$
$$= \frac{2mc^2}{\sqrt{1 - u^2/c^2}}$$

After collision:

$$E'_{after} = Mc^2 \qquad \text{2-19}$$

Energy will be conserved in S' if $E'_{before} = E'_{after}$, i.e., if

$$\frac{2mc^2}{\sqrt{1 - u^2/c^2}} = Mc^2 \qquad \text{2-20}$$

This is ensured by the validity of conservation of momentum, in particular by Equation 2-5, and so energy is conserved in S'. (The validity of Equation 2-20 is important and not trivial. We will consider it in more detail in Example 2-7.) To see if energy as

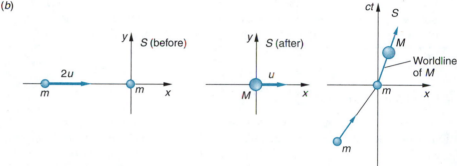

Fig. 2-6 Inelastic collision of two particles of equal rest mass *m*. (*a*) In the zero momentum frame *S'* the particles have equal and opposite velocities and, hence, momenta. After the collision, the composite particle of mass *M* is at rest in *S'*. The diagram on the far right is the spacetime diagram of the collision from the viewpoint of *S'*. (*b*) In system *S* the frame *S'* is moving to the right at speed *u* so that the particle on the right is at rest in *S*, while the left one moves at 2*u*. After collision, the composite particle moves to the right at speed *u*. Again, the spacetime diagram of the interaction is shown on the far right. All diagrams are drawn with the collision occurring at the origin.

we have defined it is also conserved in *S*, we transform to *S* using the inverse energy transform, Equation 2-17. We then have in *S*:

Before collision:

$$E_{\text{before}} = \gamma(E'_{\text{before}} + vp'_x)$$

$$E_{\text{before}} = \gamma\left(\frac{2mc^2}{\sqrt{1 - u^2/c^2}} + up'_x\right)$$

$$= \gamma\left(\frac{2mc^2}{\sqrt{1 - u^2/c^2}}\right) \quad \text{since} \quad p'_x = 0 \qquad \textbf{2-21}$$

After collision:

$$E_{\text{after}} = \gamma(Mc^2 + up'_x) = \gamma Mc^2 \quad \text{since again} \quad p'_x = 0 \qquad \textbf{2-22}$$

The energy will be conserved in *S* and, therefore, the law of conservation of energy will hold in all inertial frames if $E_{\text{before}} = E_{\text{after}}$, i.e., if

$$\gamma\left(\frac{2mc^2}{\sqrt{1 - u^2/c^2}}\right) = \gamma Mc^2 \qquad\qquad \textbf{2-23}$$

which, like Equation 2-20, is ensured by Equation 2-5. Thus, we conclude that the energy as defined by Equation 2-10 is consistent with a relativistically invariant law of conservation of energy, satisfying the first of the conditions set forth at the beginning of this section. While this demonstration has not been a general one, that being beyond the scope of our discussions, you may be assured that our conclusion is quite generally valid.

QUESTION

3. Explain why the result of Example 2-4 does not mean that energy conservation is violated.

EXAMPLE 2-5 **Mass of Cosmic Ray Muons** In Chapter 1, muons produced as secondary particles by cosmic rays were used to illustrate both the relativistic length contraction and time dilation resulting from their high speed relative to observers on Earth. That speed is about $0.998c$. If the rest energy of a muon is 105.7 MeV, what will observers on Earth measure for the total energy of a cosmic ray–produced muon? What will they measure for its mass?

Solution

The electron volt (eV), the amount of energy acquired by a particle with electric charge equal in magnitude to that on an electron (e) accelerated through a potential difference of 1 volt, is a convenient unit in physics, as you may have learned. It is defined as

$$1.0 \text{ eV} = 1.602 \times 10^{-19} \text{ C} \times 1.0 \text{ V} = 1.602 \times 10^{-19} \text{ J} \qquad \textbf{2-24}$$

Commonly used multiples of the eV are the keV (10^3 eV), the MeV (10^6 eV), the GeV (10^9 eV), and the TeV (10^{12} eV). Many experiments in physics involve the measurement and analysis of the energy and/or momentum of particles and systems of particles, and Equation 2-10 allows us to express the masses of particles in energy units, rather than the SI unit of mass, the kilogram. That and the convenient size of the eV facilitate[6] numerous calculations. For example, the mass of an electron is 9.11×10^{-31} kg. Its rest energy is given by

$$E = mc^2 = 9.11 \times 10^{-31} \text{ kg} \cdot c^2 = 8.19 \times 10^{-14} \text{ J}$$

or

$$E = 8.19 \times 10^{-14} \text{ J} \times \frac{1}{1.602 \times 10^{-19} \text{ J/eV}} = 5.11 \times 10^5 \text{ eV}$$

or

$$E = 0.511 \text{ MeV} \qquad \textbf{rest energy} \text{ for the electron}$$

The mass of the particle is often expressed with the same number thus:

$$m = \frac{E}{c^2} = 0.511 \text{ MeV}/c^2 \qquad \textbf{mass for the electron}$$

Now, applying the above to the muons produced by the cosmic rays, each has a total energy E given by

$$E = \gamma mc^2 = \frac{1}{\sqrt{1 - (0.998c)^2/c^2}} \times 105.7 \frac{\text{MeV}}{c^2} \times c^2$$

$$E = 1670 \text{ MeV}$$

and a measured mass (see Equation 2-5) of

$$\gamma m = E/c^2 = 1670 \text{ MeV}/c^2$$

This dependence of the measured mass on the speed of the particle has been verified by numerous experiments. Figure 2-7 illustrates a few of those results.

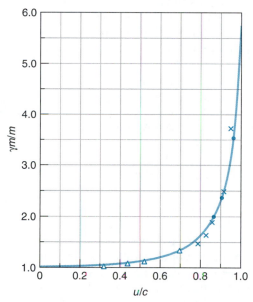

Fig. 2-7 A few of the many experimental measurements of the mass of electrons as a function of their speed u/c. The data points are plotted onto Equation 2-5, the solid line. The data points represent the work of Kaufmann (×, 1901), Bucherer (Δ, 1908), and Bertozzi (●, 1964). Note that Kaufmann's work preceded the appearance of Einstein's 1905 paper on special relativity. [*Adapted from Figure 3-4 in R. Resnick and D. Halliday,* Basic Concepts in Relativity and Early Quantum Theory, *2d ed. (New York: Macmillan, 1992).*]

EXAMPLE 2-6 Change in the Solar Mass Compute the rate at which the sun is losing mass, given that the mean radius R of Earth's orbit is 1.50×10^8 km and the intensity of solar radiation at Earth (called the *solar constant*) is 1.36×10^3 W/m².

Solution

1. The conversion of mass into energy, a consequence of conservation of energy in relativity, is implied by Equation 2-10. With $u = 0$ that equation becomes:

$$E = mc^2$$

2. Assuming that the sun radiates uniformly over a sphere of radius R, the total power P radiated by the sun is given by:

$$P = \text{(area of the sphere)(solar constant)}$$
$$= (4\pi R^2)(1.36 \times 10^3 \text{ W/m}^2)$$
$$= 4\pi(1.50 \times 10^{11} \text{ m})^2(1.36 \times 10^3 \text{ W/m}^2)$$
$$= 3.85 \times 10^{26} \text{ J/s}$$

3. Thus, every second the sun emits 3.85×10^{26} J, which, from Equation 2-10, is the result of converting an amount of mass m given by:

$$m = E/c^2$$
$$= \frac{3.85 \times 10^{26} \text{ J}}{(3.00 \times 10^8 \text{ m/s})^2}$$
$$= 4.3 \times 10^9 \text{ kg}$$

Remarks: *Thus, the sun is losing 4.3×10^9 kg of mass (about 4 million metric tons) every second! If this rate of mass loss were to remain constant (which it will for the next few billion years), the sun's present mass of about 2.0×10^{30} kg would last "only" for about 10^{13} more years!*

Exploring

Another Surprise!

One consequence of the fact that Newton's second law $\mathbf{F} = m\mathbf{a}$ is not relativistically invariant is yet another surprise—the lever paradox. Consider a lever of mass m at rest in S (see Figure 2-8). Since the lever is at rest, the net torque τ_{net} due to the forces $\mathbf{F}_x$ and $\mathbf{F}_y$ is zero, i.e. (using magnitudes):

$$\tau_{net} = \tau_x + \tau_y = -F_x b + F_y a = 0$$

and, therefore,

$$F_x b = F_y a$$

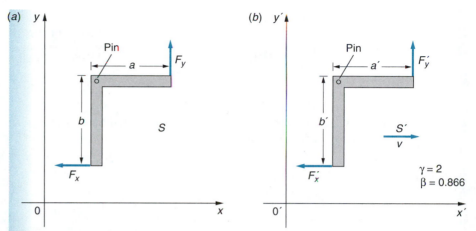

Fig. 2-8 (*a*) A lever in the *xy* plane of system *S* is free to rotate about the pin *P*, but is held at rest by the two forces F_x and F_y. (*b*) The same lever as seen by an observer in a *S'* which is moving with instantaeous speed *v* in the +*x* direction. For the *S'* observer, the lever is moving in the −*x'* direction.

An observer in system *S'* moving with $\beta = 0.866$ ($\gamma = 2$) with respect to *S* sees the lever moving in the −*x'* direction and measures the torque to be

$$\tau'_{net} = \tau'_x + \tau'_y = -F'_x b' + F'_y a' = -F_x b + (F_y/2)(a/2)$$
$$= -F_x b + F_x b/4 = -(3/4)F_x b \neq 0$$

where $F'_x = F_x$ and $F'_y = F_y/2$ (see Problem 2-52) and the lever is rotating!

The resolution of the paradox was first given by the German physicist Max von Laue (1879–1960). Recall that the net torque is the rate of change of the angular momentum **L**. The *S'* observer measures the work done per unit time by the two forces as

For F'_x: $-F'_x v = -F_x v$

For F'_y: zero, since F'_y is perpendicular to the motion

and the change in mass Δm per unit time of the moving lever as

$$\frac{\Delta m}{\Delta t'} = \frac{\Delta E/c^2}{\Delta t'} = \frac{1}{c^2}\frac{\Delta E}{\Delta t'} = -\frac{1}{c^2}F_x v$$

The *S'* observer measures a change in the magnitude of the angular momentum per unit time given by

$$\tau_{net} = \frac{\Delta L'}{\Delta t'} = \frac{b\Delta p'}{\Delta t'} = \frac{bv\Delta m}{\Delta t'}$$

Substituting for $\Delta m/\Delta t'$ from above yields

$$\tau_{net} = \frac{\Delta L'}{\Delta t'} = bv\frac{-F_x v}{c^2} = -bF_x\frac{v^2}{c^2} = -bF_x\beta^2 = -\frac{3}{4}F_x b$$

As a result of the motion of the lever relative to S', an observer in that system sees the force F'_x doing net work on the lever, thus changing its angular momentum over time and the paradox vanishes.

The authors thank Costas Efthimiou for bringing this paradox to our attention.

2-3 Mass/Energy Conversion and Binding Energy

The identification of the term mc^2 as rest energy is not merely a convenience. Whenever additional energy ΔE in any form is stored in an object, the mass of the object is increased by $\Delta E/c^2$. This is of particular importance whenever we want to compare the mass of an object that can be broken into constituent parts with the mass of the parts (for example, an atom containing a nucleus and electrons, or a nucleus containing protons and neutrons). In the case of the atom, the mass changes are usually negligibly small (see Example 2-8). However, the difference between the mass of a *nucleus* and that of its constituent parts (protons and neutrons) is often of great importance.

As an example, consider Figure 2-9a, in which two particles, each with mass m, are moving toward each other, with speeds u. They collide with a spring that compresses and locks shut. (The spring is merely a device for visualizing energy storage.) In the Newtonian mechanics description, the original kinetic energy $E_k = 2(\frac{1}{2} mu^2)$ is converted into potential energy of the spring U. When the spring is unlocked, the potential energy reappears as kinetic energy of the particles. In relativity theory, the internal energy of the system, $E_k = U$, appears as an increase in rest mass of the system. That is, the mass of the system M is now greater than $2m$ by E_k/c^2. (We shall derive this result in the next example.) This change in mass is too small to be observed for ordinary-sized masses and springs, but it is easily observed in transformations that involve nuclei. For example, in the fission of a ^{235}U nucleus, the energy released as kinetic energy of the fission fragments is an appreciable fraction of the rest energy of the original nucleus. (See Example 12-4.) This energy can be calculated by measuring the difference between the mass of

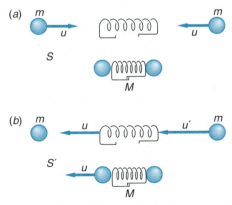

Fig. 2-9 Two objects colliding with a massless spring that locks shut. The total rest mass of the system M is greater than that of the parts $2m$ by the amount E_k/c^2, where E_k is the internal energy, which in this case is the original kinetic energy. (*a*) The event as seen in a reference frame S in which the final mass M is at rest. (*b*) The same event as seen in a frame S' moving to the right at speed u relative to S, so that one of the initial masses is at rest.

the original system and the total mass of the fragments. Einstein was the first to point out this possibility in 1905, even before the discovery of the atomic nucleus, at the end of a very short paper that followed his famous article on relativity.[7] After deriving the theoretical equivalence of energy and mass, he wrote:

> It is not impossible that with bodies whose energy content is variable to a high degree (e.g., with radium salts) the theory may be successfully put to the test.

The relativistic conversion of mass into energy is the fundamental energy source in the nuclear-reactor-based systems that produce electricity in 30 nations and in large naval vessels and nuclear submarines.

EXAMPLE 2-7 Change in Rest Mass of the Two-Particle and Spring System of Figure 2-9 Derive the increase in the rest mass of a system of two particles in a totally inelastic collision. Let m be the mass of each particle so that the total mass of the system is $2m$ when the particles are at rest and far apart, and let M be the rest mass of the system when it has internal energy E_k. The original kinetic energy in the reference frame S (Figure 2-9a) is

$$E_k = 2mc^2(\gamma - 1) \qquad \textbf{2-25}$$

Solution

In a perfectly inelastic collision, momentum conservation implies that both particles are at rest after the collision in this frame, which is the center-of-mass frame. The total kinetic energy is therefore lost. We wish to show that if momentum is to be conserved in any reference frame moving with a constant velocity relative to S, the total mass of the system must increase by Δm, given by

$$\Delta m = \frac{E_k}{c^2} = 2m(\gamma - 1) \qquad \textbf{2-26}$$

We therefore wish to show that the total mass of the system with internal energy is M, given by

$$M = 2m + \Delta m = 2\gamma m \qquad \textbf{2-27}$$

To simplify the mathematics, we choose a second reference frame S' moving to the right with speed $v = u$ relative to frame S so that one of the particles is initially at rest, as shown in Figure 2-9b. The initial speed of the other particle in this frame is

$$u' = \frac{u - v}{1 - uv/c^2} = \frac{-2u}{1 + u^2/c^2} \qquad \textbf{2-28}$$

After collision, the particles move together with speed u toward the left (since they are at rest in S). The initial momentum in S' is

$$p_i' = \frac{mu'}{\sqrt{1 - u'^2/c^2}} \qquad \text{to the left}$$

The final momentum is

$$p_f' = \frac{Mu}{\sqrt{1 - u^2/c^2}} \qquad \text{to the left}$$

Using Equation 2-28 for u', squaring, dividing by c^2, and adding -1 to both sides give

$$1 - \frac{u'^2}{c^2} = 1 - \frac{4u^2/c^2}{(1 + u^2/c^2)^2} = \frac{(1 - u^2/c^2)^2}{(1 + u^2/c^2)^2}$$

Then

$$p_i' = \frac{m[2u/(1 + u^2/c^2)]}{(1 - u^2/c^2)/(1 + u^2/c^2)} = \frac{2mu}{1 - u^2/c^2}$$

Conservation of momentum in frame S' requires that $p_f' = p_i'$, or

$$\frac{Mu}{\sqrt{1 - u^2/c^2}} = \frac{2mu}{1 - u^2/c^2}$$

Solving for M we obtain

$$M = \frac{2m}{\sqrt{1 - u^2/c^2}} = 2\gamma m$$

which is Equation 2-27. Thus, the measured value of M would be $2\gamma m$.

If the latch in Figure 2-9*b* were to come unhooked suddenly, the two particles would fly apart with equal momenta, converting the rest mass Δm back into kinetic energy. The derivation is similar to that in Example 2-7.

Mass and Binding Energy

When a system of particles is held together by attractive forces, energy is required to break up the system and separate the particles. The magnitude of this energy E_b is called the *binding energy* of the system. An important result of the theory of special relativity which we shall illustrate by example in this section is:

The mass of a bound system is less than that of the separated particles by E_b/c^2, where E_b is the binding energy.

In atomic and nuclear physics, masses and energies are typically given in atomic mass units (u) and electron volts (eV) rather than in the standard SI units of kilograms and joules. The u is related to the corresponding SI units by

$$1u = 1.66054 \times 10^{-27} \text{ kg} = 931.5 \text{ MeV}/c^2 \qquad \textbf{2-29}$$

(The eV was defined in terms of the joule in Equation 2-24.) The rest energies of some elementary particles and a few light nuclei are given in Table 2-1, from which you can see by comparing the sums of the masses of the constituent particles with the nuclei listed that the mass of a nucleus is not the same as the sum of the masses of its parts.

The simplest example of nuclear binding energy is that of the deuteron ^{2}H, which consists of a neutron and a proton bound together. Its rest energy is 1875.61 MeV. The sum of the rest energies of the proton and neutron is $938.27 + 939.57 = 1877.84$ MeV.

TABLE 2-1 Rest energies of some elementary particles and light nuclei		
Particle	**Symbol**	**Rest energy (MeV)**
Photon	γ	0
Neutrino (antineutrino)[†]	$\nu(\bar{\nu})$	$< 2.8 \times 10^{-6}$
Electron (positron)	e or e^- (e^+)	0.5110
Muon	$\mu^{\pm}$	105.7
Pi meson	π^0	135
	$\pi^{\pm}$	139.6
Proton	p	938.272
Neutron	n	939.565
Deuteron	^{2}H or d	1875.613
Helion	^{3}He or h	2808.391
Alpha	^{4}He or α	3727.379

† *As we will discuss in Chapter 13, there are theoretical reasons and increasingly strong experimental evidence for the electron neutrinos to have a nonzero mass. There are other types of neutrinos whose masses may be as large as several MeV/c^2.*

Since this is greater than the rest energy of the deuteron, the deuteron cannot *spontaneously* break up into a neutron and a proton without violating conservation of energy. The binding energy of the deuteron is $1877.837 - 1875.613 = 2.224$ MeV. In order to break up the deuteron into a proton and a neutron, at least 2.224 MeV must be added. This can be done by bombarding deuterons with energetic particles or electromagnetic radiation. If a deuteron is formed by combination of a neutron and a proton, the same amount of energy must be released.

EXAMPLE 2-8 **Binding Energy of the Hydrogen Atom** The binding energies of the atomic electrons to the nuclei of atoms are typically of the order of 10^{-6} times those characteristic of particles in nuclei; consequently, the mass differences are correspondingly smaller. The binding energy of the hydrogen atom (the energy needed to remove the electron from the atom) is 13.6 eV. How much mass is lost when an electron and a proton form a hydrogen atom?

Solution
The mass of a proton plus that of an electron must be greater than that of the hydrogen atom by

$$\frac{13.6 \text{ eV}}{931.5 \text{ MeV/u}} = 1.46 \times 10^{-8} \text{ u}$$

The mass difference is so small that it is usually neglected.

2-4 Invariant Mass

In Chapter 1 we discovered that, as a consequence of Einstein's relativity postulates, the coordinates for space and time are linearly dependent on one another in the Lorentz transformation that connects measurements made in different inertial reference frames. Thus, the time t became a coordinate, in addition to the space coordinates x, y, and z, in the four-dimensional relativistic "world" that we call spacetime. We noted in passing that the geometry of spacetime was not the familiar Euclidean geometry of our three-dimensional world, but the four-dimensional Lorentzian geometry. The difference became apparent when one compared the computation of the distance r between two points in space with that of the interval between two events in spacetime. The former is, of course, a vector $\mathbf{r}$ whose magnitude is given by $r^2 = x^2 + y^2 + z^2$. The mathematical form of the vector $\mathbf{r}$ is unchanged (invariant) under a Galilean transformation in space, and quantities that transform like $\mathbf{r}$ are also vectors. The latter we called the spacetime interval Δs, and its magnitude, as we have seen, is given by

$$(\Delta s)^2 = (c\Delta t)^2 - [(\Delta x)^2 + (\Delta y)^2 + (\Delta z)^2] \qquad \textbf{2-30}$$

The interval Δs is the four-dimensional analog of $\mathbf{r}$ and, therefore, is called a *four-vector*. Just as x, y, and z are the components of the three-vector $\mathbf{r}$, the components of the four-vector Δs are Δx, Δy, Δz, and $c\Delta t$. We have seen that Δs is also invariant under a Lorentz transformation in spacetime. Correspondingly, any quantity that transforms like Δs—i.e., is invariant under a Lorentz transformation—will also be a four-vector. The physical significance of the invariant interval Δs is quite profound: for timelike intervals, $\Delta s/c = \tau$ (the proper time interval); for spacelike intervals, $\Delta s = L_p$ (the proper length); and the intervals could be found from measurements made in *any* inertial frame.[8]

In the relativistic energy and momentum we have components of another four-vector. In the preceding sections we saw that momentum and energy, defined by Equations 2-6 and 2-10, respectively, were not only both conserved in relativity, but also together satisfied the Lorentz transformation, Equations 2-16 and 2-17, with the components of the momentum $\mathbf{p}(p_x, p_y, p_z)$ transforming like the space components of $\mathbf{r}(x, y, z)$ and the energy transforming like the time t. The questions then, are, What invariant four-vector are they components of? and, What is its physical significance? The answers to both turn out to be easy to find and yield for us yet another relativistic surprise. By squaring Equations 2-6 and 2-10, you can readily verify that

$$E^2 = (pc)^2 + (mc^2)^2 \qquad \textbf{2-31}$$

This very useful relation we will rearrange slightly to

$$(mc^2)^2 = E^2 - (pc)^2 \qquad \textbf{2-32}$$

Comparing the form of Equation 2-32 with that of Equation 2-30 and knowing that E and $\mathbf{p}$ transform according to the Lorentz transformation, we see that the magnitude of the invariant energy/momentum four-vector is the rest energy of the mass m! Thus, observers in all inertial frames will measure the same value for the rest energy of isolated systems and, since c is constant, the same value for the mass. Note that only in the rest frame of the mass m, i.e., the frame where $\mathbf{p} = 0$, are the rest energy and the total energy equal. Even though we have written Equation 2-31 for a single particle, we could as well have written the equations for momentum and energy in terms of

the total momentum and total energy of an entire ensemble of noninteracting parti-cles with arbitrary velocities. We would only need to write down Equations 2-6 and 2-10 for each particle and add them together. Thus, the Lorentz transformation for momentum and energy, Equations 2-16 and 2-17, holds for any system of particles, and so, therefore, does the invariance of the rest energy expressed by Equation 2-32.

We may state all of this more formally by saying that the *kinematic* state of the system is described by the four-vector Δs where

$$(\Delta s)^2 = (c\Delta t)^2 - [(\Delta x)^2 + (\Delta y)^2 + (\Delta z)^2]$$

and its *dynamic* state is described by the energy/momentum four-vector mc^2, given by

$$(mc^2)^2 = E^2 - (pc)^2$$

The next example illustrates how this works.

EXAMPLE 2-9 **Rest Mass of a Moving Object** A particular object is observed to move through the laboratory at high speed. Its total energy and the components of its momentum are measured by lab workers to be (in SI units) $E = 4.5 \times 10^{17}$ J, $p_x = 3.8 \times 10^8$ kg $\cdot$ m/s, $p_y = 3.0 \times 10^8$ kg $\cdot$ m/s, and $p_z = 3.0 \times 10^8$ kg $\cdot$ m/s. What is the object's rest mass?

Solution A
From Equation 2-32 we can write

$$
\begin{aligned}
(mc^2)^2 &= (4.5 \times 10^{17})^2 - [(3.8 \times 10^8 c)^2 + (3.0 \times 10^8 c)^2 + (3.0 \times 10^8 c)^2] \\
&= (4.5 \times 10^{17})^2 - [1.4 \times 10^{17} + 9.0 \times 10^{16} + 9.0 \times 10^{16}]c^2 \\
&= 2.0 \times 10^{35} - 2.9 \times 10^{34} \\
&= 1.74 \times 10^{35} \\
m &= (1.74 \times 10^{35})^{1/2}/c^2 = 4.6 \text{ kg}
\end{aligned}
$$

Solution B
A slightly different but sometimes more convenient calculation that doesn't involve carrying along large exponents makes use of Equation 2-32 divided by c^4:

$$m^2 = \left(\frac{E}{c^2}\right)^2 - \left(\frac{p}{c}\right)^2 \qquad \textbf{2-33}$$

Notice that this is simply a unit conversion, expressing each term in (mass)^2 units—e.g., kg^2 when E and p are in SI units:

$$
\begin{aligned}
m^2 &= \left(\frac{4.5 \times 10^{17}}{c^2}\right)^2 - \left[\left(\frac{3.8 \times 10^8}{c}\right)^2 + \left(\frac{3.0 \times 10^8}{c}\right)^2 + \left(\frac{3.0 \times 10^8}{c}\right)^2\right] \\
&= (5.0)^2 - [(1.25)^2 + (1.0)^2 + (1.0)^2] \\
&= 25 - 3.56 \\
m &= (21.4)^{1/2} = 4.6 \text{ kg}
\end{aligned}
$$

In the example, we determined the rest energy and mass of a rapidly moving object using measurements made in the laboratory without the need to be in the system in which the object is at rest. This ability is of enormous benefit to nuclear, particle, and astrophysicists whose work regularly involves particles moving at speeds close to that of light. For particles or objects whose rest mass is known, we can use the invariant magnitude of the energy/momentum four-vector to determine the values of other dynamic variables, as illustrated in the next example.

EXAMPLE 2-10 Speed of a Fast Electron The total energy of an electron produced in a particular nuclear reaction is measured to be 2.40 MeV. Find the electron's momentum and speed in the laboratory frame. (The rest mass of the electron is 9.11×10^{-31} kg and its rest energy is 0.511 MeV.)

Solution

The magnitude of the momentum follows immediately from Equation 2-31:

$$pc = \sqrt{E^2 - (mc^2)^2} = \sqrt{(2.40\ \text{MeV})^2 - (0.511\ \text{MeV})^2}$$

$$= 2.34\ \text{MeV}$$

$$p = 2.34\ \text{MeV}/c$$

where we have again made use of the convenience of the eV as an energy unit. The resulting momentum unit MeV/c can be readily converted to SI units by converting the MeV to joules and dividing by c, i.e.,

$$1\ \text{MeV}/c = \frac{1.60 \times 10^{-13}\ \text{J}}{2.998 \times 10^8\ \text{m/s}} = 5.34 \times 10^{-22}\ \text{kg} \cdot \text{m/s}$$

Therefore, the conversion to SI units is easily done, if desired, and yields

$$p = 2.34\ \text{MeV}/c \times \frac{5.34 \times 10^{-22}\ \text{kg} \cdot \text{m/s}}{1\ \text{MeV}/c}$$

$$p = 1.25 \times 10^{-21}\ \text{kg} \cdot \text{m/s}$$

The speed of the particle is obtained by noting from Equation 2-32 or from Equations 2-6 and 2-10 that

$$\frac{u}{c} = \frac{pc}{E} = \frac{2.34\ \text{MeV}}{2.40\ \text{MeV}} = 0.975 \qquad\qquad \textbf{2-34}$$

or

$$u = 0.975c$$

It is extremely important to recognize that the invariant rest energy in Equation 2-32 is that of the *system* and that its value is *not* the sum of the rest energies of the particles of which the system is formed, if the particles move relative to one another. Earlier we used numerical examples of the binding energy of atoms and nuclei that illustrated this

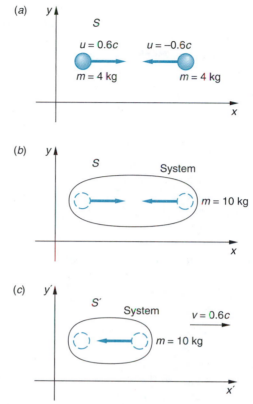

Fig. 2-10 (*a*) Two identical particles with rest mass 4 kg approach each other with equal but oppositely directed momenta. The rest mass of the system made up of the two particles is not 4 kg + 4 kg, because the system's rest mass includes the mass equivalent of its internal motions. That value, 10 kg (*b*), would be the result of a measurement of the system's mass made by an observer in *S*, for whom the system is at rest, or by observers in any other inertial frames. (*c*) Transforming to *S'* moving at *v* = 0.6*c* with respect to *S*, as described in Example 2-11, also yields *m* = 10 kg.

fact by showing that the masses of atoms and nuclei were less than the sum of the masses of their constituents by an amount Δmc^2 that equaled the observed binding energy, but those were systems of interacting particles—i.e., there were forces acting between the constituents. A difference exists, even when the particles do not interact. To see this, let us focus our attention on specifically *what* mass is invariant.

Consider two identical noninteracting particles, each of rest mass $m = 4$ kg, moving toward each other along the x axis of S with momentum of magnitude $p_x = 3\ c \cdot$ kg, as illustrated in Figure 2-10*a*. The energy of each particle, using Equation 2-33, is

$$E/c^2 = \sqrt{m^2 + (p/c)^2} = \sqrt{(4)^2 + (3)^2} = 5 \text{ kg}$$

Thus, the total energy of the system is $5c^2 + 5c^2 = 10\ c^2 \cdot$ kg, since the energy is a scalar. Similarly, the total momentum of the system is $3c - 3c = 0$, since the momentum is a vector and the momenta are equal and opposite. The rest mass of the system is then

$$m = \sqrt{(E/c^2)^2 - (p/c)^2} = \sqrt{(10)^2 - (0)^2} = 10 \text{ kg}$$

Thus, the system mass of 10 kg is *greater* than the sum of the masses of the two particles, 8 kg. (This is in contrast to bound systems, such as atoms, where the system mass is *smaller* than the total of the constituents.) This difference is not binding energy, since the particles are noninteracting. Neither does the 2-kg "mass difference" reside equally with the two particles. In fact it doesn't reside in any particular place, but is a property of the entire system. The correct interpretation is that the mass *of the system* is 10 kg.

While the invariance of the energy/momentum four-vector guarantees that observers in other inertial frames will also measure 10 kg as the mass of this system, let us allow for a skeptic or two and transform to another system S', e.g., the one shown in Figure 2-10c, just to be sure. This transformation is examined in the next example.

EXAMPLE 2-11 **Lorentz Transformation of System Mass** For the system illustrated in Figure 2-10, show that an observer in S', which moves relative to S at $\beta = 0.6$, also measures the mass of the system to be 10 kg.

Solution

1. The mass m measured in S' is given by Equation 2-33, which in this case is:

$$m = [(E'/c^2)^2 - (p_x'/c)^2]^{1/2}$$

2. E' is given by Equation 2-16:

$$E' = \gamma(E - vp_x)$$
$$= \frac{1}{\sqrt{1 - (0.6)^2}}(10c^2 - 0.6c \times 0)$$
$$= (1.25)(10c^2)$$
$$= 12.5\ c^2 \cdot \text{kg}$$

3. p_x' is also given by Equation 2-16:

$$p_x' = \gamma(p_x - vE/c^2)$$
$$= (1.25)[0 - (0.6c)(10c^2)/c^2]$$
$$= -7.5\ c \cdot \text{kg}$$

4. Substituting E' and p_x' into Equation 2-33 yields:

$$m = [(12.5c^2/c^2)^2 - (-7.5c/c)^2]^{1/2}$$
$$= [(12.5)^2 - (-7.5)^2]^{1/2}$$
$$= 10\ \text{kg}$$

Remarks: This result agrees with the value measured in S. The speed of S' chosen for this calculation, v = 0.6c, is convenient in that one of the particles making up the system is at rest in S'; however, that has no effect on the generality of the solution.

Thus, we see that it is the rest energy of any isolated system that is invariant, whether that system be a single atom or the entire universe. And, based on our brief

discussions thus far, we note that the system's rest energy may be greater than, equal to, or less than the sum of the rest energies of the constituents depending on their relative velocities and the detailed character of any interactions between them.

QUESTIONS

4. Suppose two loaded boxcars, each of mass $m = 50$ metric tons, roll toward each other on level track at identical speeds u, collide, and couple together. Discuss the mass of this system before and after the collision. What is the effect of the magnitude of u on your discussion?

5. In 1787 Count Rumford (1753–1814) tried unsuccessfully to measure an increase in the weight of a barrel of water when he increased its temperature from 29°F to 61°F. Explain why, relativistically, you would expect such an increase to occur, and outline an experiment that might, in principle, detect the change. Since Count Rumford preceded Einstein by about 100 years, why might he have been led to such a measurement?

Massless Particles

Equation 2-32 formally allows positive, negative, and zero values for $(mc^2)^2$, just as was the case for the spacetime interval $(\Delta s)^2$. We have been tacitly discussing positive cases thus far in this section; a discussion of possible negative cases we will defer until Chapter 13. Here we need to say something about the $mc^2 = 0$ possibility. Note first of all that the idea of zero rest mass has no analog in classical physics, since classically $E_k = mu^2/2$ and $\mathbf{p} = m\mathbf{u}$. If $m = 0$, then the momentum and kinetic energy are always zero, too, and the "particle" would seem to be nothing at all, experiencing no second-law forces, doing no work, and so forth. However, for $mc^2 = 0$ Equation 2-32 states that, in relativity

$$E = pc \qquad \text{(for } m = 0\text{)} \qquad \textbf{2-35}$$

and, together with Equation 2-34, that $u = c$; i.e., <u>a particle whose mass is zero moves at the speed of light.</u> Similarly, a particle whose speed is measured to be c will have $m = 0$ and satisfy $E = pc$.

We must be careful, however, because Equation 2-32 was obtained from the relativistic definitions of E and $\mathbf{p}$,

$$E = \gamma mc^2 = \frac{mc^2}{\sqrt{1 - u^2/c^2}} \qquad \mathbf{p} = \gamma m\mathbf{u} = \frac{m\mathbf{u}}{\sqrt{1 - u^2/c^2}}$$

As $u \rightarrow c$, $1/(1 - u^2/c^2)^{1/2} \rightarrow \infty$; however, since m is also approaching 0, the quantity γm, which is tending toward 0/0, can (and does) remain defined. Indeed, there is ample experimental evidence for the existence of particles with $mc^2 = 0$.

Current theories suggest the existence of three such particles. Perhaps the most important of these and the one thoroughly verified by experiments is the *photon*, or a particle of electromagnetic radiation (i.e., light). Classically, electromagnetic radiation was interpreted via Maxwell's equations as a wave phenomenon, its energy and momentum being distributed continuously throughout the space occupied by the wave. It was discovered around 1900 that the classical view of light required modification in

certain situations, the change being a confinement of the energy and momentum of the radiation into many tiny packets or bundles, which were referred to as photons. Photons move at light speed, of course, and, as we have noted, are required by relativity to have $mc^2 = 0$. Recall that the spacetime interval Δs for light is also zero. Strictly speaking, of course, the second of Einstein's relativity postulates prevents a Lorentz transformation to the rest system of light, since light moves at c relative to all inertial frames. Consequently, the term *rest mass* has no operational meaning for light.

EXAMPLE 2-12 Rest Energy of a System of Photons Remember that the rest energy of a system of particles is not the sum of the rest energies of the individual particles, if they move relative to one another. This applies to photons, too! Suppose two photons, one with energy 5 MeV and the second with energy 2 MeV, approach each other along the x axis. What is the rest energy of this system?

Solution

The momentum of the 5-MeV photon is (from Equation 2-35) $p_x = 5$ MeV/c and that of the 2-MeV photon is $p_x = -2$ MeV/c. Thus, the energy of the system is $E = 5$ MeV $+ 2$ MeV $= 7$ MeV and its momentum is $p = 5$ MeV/$c - 2$ MeV/$c = 3$ MeV/c. From Equation 2-32 the system's rest energy is

$$mc^2 = \sqrt{(7\ \text{MeV})^2 - (3\ \text{MeV})^2} = 6.3\ \text{MeV}!!$$

A second particle whose rest energy is zero is the *gluon*. This massless particle transmits, or carries, the strong interaction between *quarks*, which are the "building blocks" of all fundamental particles, including protons and neutrons. The existence of gluons is well established experimentally. We will discuss quarks and gluons further in Chapter 13. Finally, there are strong theoretical reasons to expect that gravity is transmitted by a massless particle called the *graviton*, which is related to gravity in much the same way that the photon is related to the electromagnetic field. Gravitons, too, move at speed c. While direct detection of the graviton is beyond our current and foreseeable experimental capabilities, major international cooperative experiments are currently under way to detect gravity waves. (See Section 2-5.)

Until recently a fourth particle, the *neutrino*, was also thought to have zero rest mass. However, accumulating experimental evidence collected by the Super-Kamiokande and SNO imaging neutrino detectors, among others, makes it nearly certain that neutrinos are not massless. We discuss neutrino mass and its implications further in Chapters 11 and 13.

Creation and Annihilation of Particles

The relativistic equivalence of mass and energy implies still another remarkable prediction which has no classical counterpart. As long as momentum and energy are conserved in the process,[9] elementary particles with mass can combine with their *antiparticles*, the masses of both being completely converted to energy in a process called *annihilation*. An example is that of an ordinary electron. An electron can orbit briefly with its antiparticle, called a *positron*,[10] but then the two unite, mutually annihilating and producing two or three photons. The two-photon version of this process is shown schematically in Figure 2-11. Positrons are produced naturally by cosmic

Fig. 2-11 (*a*) A positron orbits with an electron about their common center of mass, shown by the dot between them. (*b*) After a short time, typically of the order of 10^{-10} s for the case shown here, the two annihilate, producing two photons. The orbiting electron-positron pair, suggestive of a miniature hydrogen atom, is called *positronium*.

rays in the upper atmosphere and as the result of the decay of certain radioactive nuclei. P. A. M. Dirac had predicted their existence in 1928 while investigating the invariance of the energy/momentum four-vector.

If the speeds of both the electron and the positron $u \ll c$ (not a requirement for the process, but it makes the following calculation clearer), then the total energy of each particle $E \approx mc^2 = 0.511$ MeV. Therefore, the total energy of the system in Figure 2-11*a* before annihilation is $2mc^2 = 1.022$ MeV. Noting also from the diagram that the momenta of the particles are always opposite and equal, the total momentum of the system is zero. Conservation of momentum then requires that the total momentum of the two photons produced also be zero, i.e., that they move in opposite directions relative to the original center of mass and have equal momenta. Since $E = pc$ for photons, then they must also have equal energy. Conservation of energy then requires that the energy of each photon be 0.511 MeV. (Photons are usually called *gamma rays* when their energies are a few hundred keV or higher.) Notice from Example 2-12 that the magnitude of the energy/momentum four-vector (the rest energy) is not zero, even though both of the final particles are photons. In this case it equals the rest energy of the initial system. Analysis of the three-photon annihilation, although the calculation is a bit more involved, is similar.

By now it will not be a surprise to learn that the reverse process, the creation of mass from energy, can also occur under the proper circumstances. The conversion of mass and energy works both ways. The energy needed to create the new mass can be provided by the kinetic energy of another massive particle or by the "pure" energy of a photon. In either case, in determining what particles might be produced with a given amount of energy, it is important to be sure, as was the case with annihilation, that the appropriate conservation laws are satisfied. As we will discuss in detail in

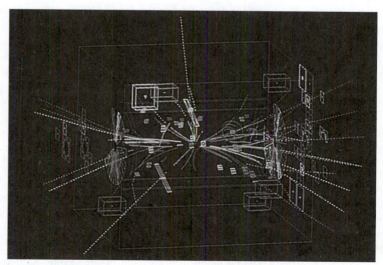

Decay of a *Z* into an electron-positron pair in the UA1 detectors at CERN. This is the computer image of the first *Z* event recorded (30 April 1983). The newly created pair leave the central detector in opposite directions at nearly the speed of light. [*CERN.*]

Fig. 2-12 (*a*) A photon of energy E and momentum $p = E/c$ encounters an electron at rest. The photon produces an electron-positron pair (*b*), and the group move off together at speed $u = 0.8c$.

Chapter 13, this restricts the creation process for certain kinds of particles (including electrons, protons, and neutrons) to producing only particle-antiparticle pairs. This means, for example, that the energy in a photon cannot be used to create a single electron, but must produce an electron-positron pair.

To see how the relativistic creation of mass goes, let us consider a particular situation, the creation of an electron-positron pair from the energy of a photon. The photon moving through space encounters, or "hits," an electron at rest in frame S as illustrated in Figure 2-12a.[11] Usually the photon simply scatters, but occasionally a pair is created. Encountering the existing electron is important, since it is not possible for the photon to produce spontaneously the two rest masses of the pair and also conserve momentum. (See Problem 2-44.) Some other particle must be nearby, not to provide energy to the creation process, but to acquire some of the photon's initial momentum. In this case we have selected an electron for this purpose, because it provides a neat example, but almost any particle would do. (See Example 2-13.)

While near the electron, the photon suddenly disappears, and an electron-positron pair appears. The process must occur very fast, since the photon, moving at speed c, will travel across a region as large as an atom in about 10^{-19} s. Let's suppose that the details of the interaction that produced this pair are such that the three particles all move off together toward the right in Figure 2-12b with the same speed u—i.e., they are all at rest in S', which moves to the right with speed u relative to S.[12] What must the energy E_γ of the photon be in order that this particular electron-positron pair be created? To answer this question, we first write the conservation of energy and momentum:

Before pair creation   **After pair creation**

$$E_i = E_\gamma + mc^2 \qquad\qquad E_f = E_i = E_\gamma + mc^2$$

$$p_i = \frac{E_\gamma}{c} \qquad\qquad p_f = p_i = \frac{E_\gamma}{c}$$

where mc^2 = rest energy of an electron. In the final system after pair creation, the total rest energy is $3mc^2$ in this case. We know this because the invariant rest energy equals the sum of the rest energies of the *constituent* particles (the original electron and the pair) in the system where they do not move relative to one another, i.e., in S'. So in S we have for the system after pair creation:

$$(3mc^2)^2 = E^2 - (pc)^2$$

$$9(mc^2)^2 = (E_\gamma + mc^2)^2 - \left(\frac{E_\gamma c}{c}\right)^2$$

$$9(mc^2)^2 = E_\gamma^2 + 2E_\gamma mc^2 + (mc^2)^2 - E_\gamma^2$$

Noting that the E_γ^2 terms cancel, and dividing the remaining terms by mc^2, we see that

$$E_\gamma = 4mc^2$$

Thus, the initial photon needs energy equal to 4 electron rest energies in order to create 2 new electron rest masses in this case. Why is the "extra" energy needed? Because the three electrons in the final system share momentum E_γ/c, they must *also* have kinetic energy E_k given by

$$E_k = E - 3mc^2 = (E_\gamma + mc^2) - 3mc^2$$
$$= 4mc^2 + mc^2 - 3mc^2 = 2mc^2$$

or the initial photon must provide the $2mc^2$ necessary to create the electron and positron masses and the additional $2mc^2$ of kinetic energy that they and the existing electron will share as a result of momentum conservation. The speed u at which the group of particles moves in S can be found from $u/c = pc/E$ (Equation 2-34):

$$u/c = \frac{\left(\dfrac{E_\gamma}{c} \times c\right)}{(E_\gamma + mc^2)} = \frac{4mc^2}{5mc^2} = 0.8$$

The portion of the incident photon's energy that is needed to provide kinetic energy in the final system is reduced if the mass of the existing particle is larger than that of an electron and, indeed, can be made negligibly small, as illustrated in the following example.

EXAMPLE 2-13 **Threshold for Pair Production** What is the minimum or threshold energy that a photon must have in order to produce an electron-positron pair?

Solution
The energy E_γ of the initial photon must be

$$E_\gamma = mc^2 + E_{k-} + mc^2 + E_{k+} + E_{kM}$$

where mc^2 = electron rest energy, E_{k-} and E_{k+} are the kinetic energies of the electron and positron, respectively, and E_{kM} = kinetic energy of the existing particle of mass M. Since we are looking for the threshold energy, consider the limiting case where the pair are created at rest in S, i.e., $E_{k-} = E_{k+} = 0$ and correspondingly $p_- = p_+ = 0$. Therefore, momentum conservation requires that

$$p_{\text{initial}} = E_\gamma/c = p_{\text{final}} = \frac{Mu}{\sqrt{1 - u^2/c^2}}$$

where u = speed of recoil of the mass M. Since the masses of single atoms are in the range of 10^3 to 10^5 MeV/c^2 and the value of E_γ at the threshold is clearly less than about 2 MeV (i.e., it must be less than the value $E_\gamma = 4mc^2 = 2.044$ MeV), the speed with which M recoils from the creation event is quite small compared with c, even for the smallest M available, a single proton! (See Table 2-1.) Thus, the kinetic energy $E_{kM} \approx \frac{1}{2} Mu^2$ becomes negligible, and we conclude that the minimum energy E_γ of the initial photon that can produce an electron-positron pair is $2mc^2$, i.e., that needed just to create the two rest masses.

Some Useful Equations and Approximations

As we have seen, in relativistic dynamics it is most often the momentum or energy of a particle that is known rather than speed. We saw that Equation 2-6 for the relativistic momentum and Equation 2-10 for the relativistic energy could be combined to eliminate the speed u and yield the very useful relation

$$E^2 = (pc)^2 + (mc^2)^2 \qquad\qquad \textbf{2-31}$$

Extremely Relativistic Case   The triangle shown in Figure 2-13 is sometimes useful in remembering this result. If the energy of a particle is much greater than its rest energy mc^2, the second term on the right of Equation 2-31 can be neglected, giving the useful approximation

$$E \approx pc \qquad \text{for } E \gg mc^2 \qquad\qquad \textbf{2-36}$$

This approximation is accurate to about 1 percent or better if E is greater than about $8mc^2$. Equation 2-36 is the exact relation between energy and momentum for particles with zero rest mass.

From Equation 2-36 we see that the momentum of a high-energy particle is simply its total energy divided by c. A convenient unit of momentum is MeV/c. The momentum of a charged particle is usually determined by measuring the radius of curvature of the path of the particle moving in a magnetic field. If the particle has charge q and a velocity $\mathbf{u}$, it experiences a force in a magnetic field $\mathbf{B}$ given by

$$\mathbf{F} = q\mathbf{u} \times \mathbf{B}$$

where $\mathbf{F}$ is perpendicular to the plane formed by $\mathbf{u}$ and $\mathbf{B}$ and, hence, is always perpendicular to $\mathbf{u}$. Since the magnetic force is always perpendicular to the velocity, it does no work on the particle (the work-energy theorem also holds in relativity), so the energy of the particle is constant. From Equation 2-10 we see that if the energy is constant, γ must be a constant, and therefore the speed u is also constant. Therefore,

$$\mathbf{F} = q\mathbf{u} \times \mathbf{B} = \frac{d\mathbf{p}}{dt} = \frac{d(\gamma m\mathbf{u})}{dt} = \gamma m \frac{d\mathbf{u}}{dt}$$

For the case $\mathbf{u} \perp \mathbf{B}$, the particle moves in a circle with centripetal acceleration u^2/R. (If $\mathbf{u}$ is not perpendicular to $\mathbf{B}$, the path is a helix. Since the component of $\mathbf{u}$ parallel to $\mathbf{B}$ is unaffected, we shall consider only motion in a plane.) We then have

$$quB = m\,\gamma \left| \frac{d\mathbf{u}}{dt} \right| = m\,\gamma \left(\frac{u^2}{R} \right)$$

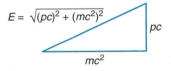

$$E = \sqrt{(pc)^2 + (mc^2)^2}$$

pc

mc^2

Fig. 2-13 Triangle showing the relation between energy, momentum, and rest mass in special relativity. *Caution:* Remember that E and pc are not relativistically invariant. The invariant is mc^2.

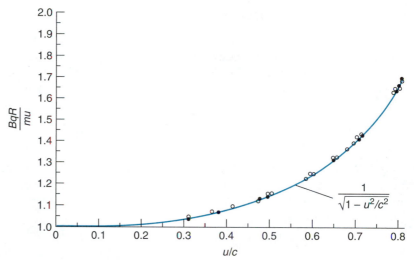

Fig. 2-14 *BqR/mu* versus *u/c* for particle of charge *q* and mass *m* moving in a circular orbit of radius *R* in a magnetic field *B*. The agreement of the data with the curve predicted by relativity theory supports the assumption that the force equals the time rate of change of relativistic momentum. [*Adapted from I. Kaplan,* Nuclear Physics, *2d ed. (Reading, Mass.: Addison-Wesley, 1962), by permission.*]

or

$$BqR = m\,\gamma u = p \qquad\qquad \textbf{2-37}$$

This is the same as the nonrelativistic expression except for the factor of γ. Figure 2–14 shows a plot of *BqR/mu* versus *u/c*. It is useful to rewrite Equation 2–37 in terms of practical but mixed units; the result is

$$p = 300\,BR\left(\frac{q}{e}\right) \qquad\qquad \textbf{2-38}$$

where *p* is in MeV/*c*, *B* is in tesla, and *R* is in meters.

EXAMPLE 2-14 **Electron in a Magnetic Field** What is the approximate radius of the path of a 30-MeV electron moving in a magnetic field of 0.05 tesla (= 500 gauss)?

Solution

1. The radius of the path is given by rearranging Equation 2-38 and substituting $q = e$:

$$R = \frac{p}{300\,B}$$

2. In this situation the total energy *E* is much greater than the rest energy mc^2:

$$E = 30\,\text{MeV} \gg mc^2 = 0.511\,\text{MeV}$$

3. Equation 2-36 may then be used to determine p:

$$p \approx E/c$$
$$= 30 \text{ MeV}/c$$

4. Substituting this approximation for p into Equation 2-38 yields:

$$R = \frac{30 \text{ MeV}/c}{(300)(0.05)}$$
$$= 2 \text{ m}$$

Remarks: In this case the error made by using the approximation, Equation 2-36, rather than the exact solution, Equation 2-31, is only about 0.01 percent.

Nonrelativistic Case   Nonrelativistic expressions for energy, momentum, and other quantities are often easier to use than the relativistic ones, so it is important to know when these expressions are accurate enough. As $\gamma \to 1$, all the relativistic expressions approach the classical ones. In most situations, the kinetic energy or total energy is given, so that the most convenient expression for calculating γ is, from Equation 2-10,

$$\gamma = \frac{E}{mc^2} = 1 + \frac{E_k}{mc^2} \qquad\qquad \textbf{2-39}$$

When the kinetic energy is much less than the rest energy, γ is approximately 1 and nonrelativistic equations can be used. For example, the classical approximation $E_k \approx \left(\frac{1}{2}\right)mu^2 = p^2/2m$ can be used instead of the relativistic expression $E_k = (\gamma - 1)mc^2$ if E_k is much less than mc^2. We can get an idea of the accuracy of these expressions by expanding γ, using the binomial expansion as was done in Section 2-2, and examining the first term that is *neglected* in the classical approximation. We have

$$\gamma = \left(1 - \frac{u^2}{c^2}\right)^{-1/2} \approx 1 + \frac{1}{2}\frac{u^2}{c^2} + \frac{3}{8}\frac{u^4}{c^4} + \ \cdot \ \cdot \ \cdot$$

and

$$E_k = (\gamma - 1)mc^2 \approx \frac{1}{2}mu^2 + \frac{3}{2}\frac{\left(\frac{1}{2}mu^2\right)^2}{mc^2}$$

Then

$$\frac{E_k - \frac{1}{2}mu^2}{E_k} \approx \frac{3}{2}\frac{E_k}{mc^2}$$

For example, if $E_k/mc^2 \approx 1$ percent, the error in using the approximation $E_k \approx \left(\frac{1}{2}\right)mu^2$ is about 1.5 percent.

At very low energies, the velocity of a particle can be obtained from its kinetic energy $E_k \approx \left(\frac{1}{2}\right)mu^2$ just as in classical mechanics. At very high energies, the velocity of a particle is very near c. The following approximation is sometimes useful (see Problem 2-27):

$$\frac{u}{c} \approx 1 - \frac{1}{2\gamma^2} \qquad \text{for} \qquad \gamma \gg 1 \qquad \qquad \textbf{2-40}$$

An exact expression for the velocity of a particle in terms of its energy and momentum was obtained in Example 2-10:

$$\frac{u}{c} = \frac{pc}{E} \qquad \qquad \textbf{2-41}$$

This expression is, of course, not useful if the approximation $E \approx pc$ has already been made.

EXAMPLE 2-15 **Different Particles, Same Energy** An electron and a proton are each accelerated through 10×10^6 V. Find γ, the momentum, and the speed for each.

Solution

Since each particle has a charge of magnitude e, each acquires a kinetic energy of 10 MeV. This is much greater than the 0.511 MeV rest energy of the electron and much less than the 938.3 MeV rest energy of the proton. We shall calculate the momentum and speed of each particle exactly, and then by means of the nonrelativistic (proton) or the extreme relativistic (electron) approximations.

1.   We first consider the electron. From Equation 2-39 we have

$$\gamma = 1 + \frac{E_k}{mc^2} = 1 + \frac{10 \text{ MeV}}{0.511 \text{ MeV}} = 20.57$$

Since the total energy is $E_k + mc^2 = 10.511$ MeV, we have, from the magnitude of the energy/momentum four-vector (Equation 2-31),

$$pc = \sqrt{E^2 - (mc^2)^2} = \sqrt{(10.51)^2 - (0.511)^2}$$
$$= 10.50 \text{ MeV}$$

The exact calculation then gives $p = 10.50$ MeV/c. The high-energy or extreme relativistic approximation $p \approx E/c = 10.51$ MeV/c is in good agreement with the exact result. If we use Equation 2-34, we obtain for the speed $u/c = pc/E = 10.50$ MeV/10.51 MeV $= 0.999$. For comparison, the approximation of Equation 2-40 gives

$$\frac{u}{c} \approx 1 - \frac{1}{2}\left(\frac{1}{\gamma}\right)^2 = 1 - \frac{1}{2}\left(\frac{1}{20.57}\right)^2 = 0.999$$

2.   For the proton, the total energy is $E_k + mc^2 = 10$ MeV $+ 938.3$ MeV $= 948.3$ MeV. From Equation 2-39 we obtain $\gamma = 1 + E_k/mc^2 = 1 + 10/938.3 = 1.01$. Equation 2-31 gives for the momentum

$$pc = \sqrt{E^2 - (mc^2)^2} = \sqrt{(948.3)^2 - (938.3)^2}$$
$$= 137.4 \text{ MeV}$$

The nonrelativistic approximation gives

$$E_k \approx \frac{1}{2} mu^2 = \frac{(mu)^2}{2m} \approx \frac{p^2}{2m} = \frac{p^2 c^2}{2mc^2}$$

or

$$pc \approx \sqrt{2mc^2 E_k} = \sqrt{(2)(938.3)(10)}$$
$$= 137.0 \text{ MeV}$$

The speed can be determined from Equation 2-34 exactly or from $p = mu$ approximately. From Equation 2-34 we obtain

$$\frac{u}{c} = \frac{pc}{E} = \frac{137.4}{948.3} = 0.1449$$

From $p \approx mu$, the nonrelativistic expression for p, we obtain

$$\frac{u}{c} \approx \frac{pc}{mc^2} = \frac{137.0}{938.3} = 0.1460$$

2-5 General Relativity

The generalization of relativity theory to noninertial reference frames by Einstein in 1916 is known as the *general theory of relativity*. This theory is much more difficult mathematically than the special theory of relativity, and there are fewer situations in which it can be tested. Nevertheless, its importance in the areas of astrophysics and cosmology, and the need to take account of its predictions in the design of such things as global navigation systems,[13] call for its inclusion here. A full description of the general theory uses tensor analysis at a quite sophisticated level, well beyond the scope of this book, so we will be limited to qualitative or, in some instances, semi-quantitative discussions. An additional purpose to the discussion that follows is to give you something that few people will ever have, namely, an acquaintance with one of the most remarkable of all scientific accomplishments and a bit of a feel for the man who did it.

    Einstein's development of the general theory of relativity was not motivated by any experimental enigma. Instead, it grew out of his desire to include the descriptions of *all* natural phenomena within the framework of the special theory. By 1907 he realized that he could accomplish that goal with the single exception of the law of gravitation. About that exception he said,[14]

I felt a deep desire to understand the reason behind this [exception].

The exceptional sensitivity of modern electronic systems is such that general relativistic effects are included in the design of the Global Positioning System (GPS).

The "reason" came to him, as he said later, while he was sitting in a chair in the patent office in Bern. He described it like this:[15]

> Then there occurred to me the happiest thought of my life, in the following form. The gravitational field has only a relative existence in a way similar to the electric field generated by magnetoelectric induction. *Because for an observer falling freely from the roof of a house there exists*—at least in his immediate surroundings—*no gravitational field.* [Einstein's italics] . . . The observer then has the right to interpret his state as "at rest."

Out of this "happy thought" grew the *principle of equivalence* that became Einstein's fundamental postulate for general relativity.

Principle of Equivalence

The basis of the general theory of relativity is what we may call Einstein's third postulate, the principle of equivalence, which states:

A homogeneous gravitational field is completely equivalent to a uniformly accelerated reference frame.

This principle arises in a somewhat different form in Newtonian mechanics because of the apparent identity of gravitational and inertial mass. In a uniform gravitational field, all objects fall with the same acceleration g independent of their mass because the gravitational force is proportional to the (gravitational) mass while the acceleration varies inversely with the (inertial) mass. That is, the mass m in

$$\mathbf{F} = m\mathbf{a} \qquad \text{(inertial } m\text{)}$$

and that in

$$\mathbf{F}_G = \frac{GMm}{r^2}\,\hat{\mathbf{r}} \qquad \text{(gravitational } m\text{)}$$

appear to be identical in classical mechanics, although classical theory provides no explanation for this equality. For example, near Earth's surface, $F_G = GMm/r^2 = m_{\text{grav}}\, g = m_{\text{inertial}}\, a = F$. Recent modern experiments have shown $m_{\text{inertial}} = m_{\text{grav}}$ to better than one part in 10^{12}.

To understand what the equivalence principle means, consider a compartment in space far away from any matter and undergoing uniform acceleration $\mathbf{a}$ as shown in Figure 2-15*a*. If people in the compartment drop objects, they fall to the "floor" with acceleration $\mathbf{g} = -\mathbf{a}$. If they stand on a spring scale, it will read their "weight" of magnitude ma. No mechanics experiment can be performed *within* the compartment that will distinguish whether the compartment is actually accelerating in space or is at rest (or moving with uniform velocity) in the presence of a uniform gravitational field $\mathbf{g} = -\mathbf{a}$.

Einstein broadened the principle of equivalence to apply to *all* physical experiments, not just to mechanics. In effect, he assumed that there is no experiment of any kind that can distinguish uniformly accelerated motion from the presence of a gravitational field. A direct consequence of the principle is that $m_{\text{grav}} = m_{\text{inertial}}$ is a requirement, not a coincidence. The principle of equivalence extends Einstein's first

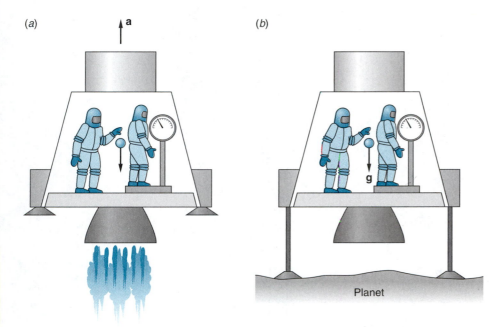

Fig. 2-15 Results from experiments in a uniformly accelerated reference frame (*a*) cannot be distinguished from those in a uniform gravitational field (*b*) if the acceleration **a** and gravitational field **g** have the same magnitude.

postulate, the principle of relativity, to *all* reference frames, noninertial (i.e., accelerated) as well as inertial. It follows that there is no absolute acceleration of a reference frame. Acceleration, like velocity, is only relative.

QUESTION

6. For his 76th (and last) birthday Einstein received a present designed to demonstrate the principle of equivalence. It is shown in Figure 2-16. The object is, starting with the ball hanging down as shown, to put the ball into the cup with a method that works every time (as opposed to random shaking). How would you do it? (*Note*: When it was given to Einstein, he was delighted and did the experiment correctly immediately.)

Some Predictions of General Relativity

In his first paper on general relativity, in 1916, Einstein was able to explain quantitatively a discrepancy of long standing between the measured and (classically) computed values of the advance of the perihelion of Mercury's orbit, about 43 arc seconds/century. It was the first success of the new theory. A second prediction, the bending to light in a gravitational field, would seem to be more difficult to measure owing to the very small effect. However, it was accurately confirmed less than five years later when Arthur Eddington measured the deflection of starlight passing near the limb of the sun during a total solar eclipse. The theory also predicts the slowing of light itself and the slowing of clocks—i.e., frequencies—in gravitational fields, both of considerable importance to the determination of astronomical distances and stellar recession rates. The predicted slowing of clocks, called gravitational redshift, was demonstrated by

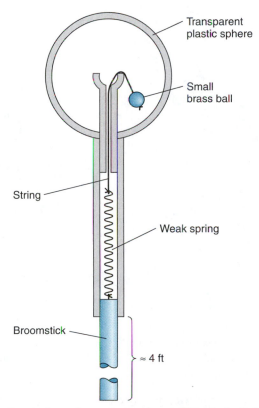

Transparent
plastic sphere

Small
brass ball

String

Weak spring

Broomstick

≈ 4 ft

Fig. 2-16 Principle of equivalence demonstrator given to Einstein by E. M. Rogers. The object is to put the hanging brass ball into the cup by a technique that always works. The spring is weak, too weak to pull the ball in as it stands, and is stretched even when the ball is in the cup. The transparent sphere, about 10 cm in diameter, does not open. [*From A. P. French,* Albert Einstein: A Centenary Volume *(Cambridge, Mass.: Harvard University Press, 1979).*]

Pound and co-workers in 1960 in Earth's gravitational field using the ultrasensitive frequency measuring technique of the Mössbauer effect (see Chapter 11). The slowing of light was conclusively measured in 1971 by Shapiro and co-workers using radar signals reflected from several planets. Two of these experimental tests of relativity's predictions, bending of light and gravitational redshift, are discussed in the Exploring sections that follow. The perihelion of Mercury's orbit and the delay of light are discussed in More sections on the Web page. Many other predictions of general relativity are subjects of active current research. Two of these, black holes and gravity waves, are discussed briefly in the concluding paragraphs of this chapter.

This relativistic effect results in gravitational lenses in the cosmos that focus light from extremely distant galaxies, greatly improving their visibility in telescopes, both on Earth and in orbit.

Exploring

Deflection of Light in a Gravitational Field

With the advent of special relativity, several features of the Newtonian law of gravitation $F_G = GMm/r^2$ became conceptually troublesome. One of these was the implication from the relativistic concept of mass-energy equivalence that even

particles with zero rest mass should exhibit properties like weight and inertia, thought of classically as masslike; classical theory does not include such particles. According to the equivalence principle, however, light, too, would experience the gravitational force. Indeed, the deflection of a light beam passing through the gravitational field near a large mass was one of the first consequences of the equivalence principle to be tested experimentally.

To see why a deflection of light would be expected, consider Figure 2-17, which shows a beam of light entering an accelerating compartment. Successive positions of the compartment are shown at equal time intervals. Because the compartment is accelerating, the distance it moves in each time interval increases with time. The path of the beam of light, as observed from within the compartment, is therefore a parabola. But according to the equivalence principle, there is no way to distinguish between an accelerating compartment and one with uniform velocity in a uniform gravitational field. We conclude, therefore, that a beam of light will accelerate in a gravitational field as do objects with rest mass. For example, near the surface of Earth, light will fall with acceleration 9.8 m/s². This is difficult to observe because of the enormous speed of light. For example, in a distance of 3000 km, which takes about 0.01 s to cover, a beam of light should fall about 0.5 mm. Einstein pointed out that the deflection of a light beam in a gravitational field might be observed when light from a distant star passes close to the sun.[16] The deflection, or bending, is computed as follows. Rewriting the spacetime interval Δs (Equation 1-32) in differential form and converting the space Cartesian coordinates to polar coordinates (in two space dimensions, since the deflection occurs in a plane) yields

$$ds^2 = c^2dt^2 - (dr^2 + r^2d\theta^2) \qquad \textbf{2-42}$$

Einstein showed that this expression is slightly modified in the presence of a (spherical, nonrotating) mass M to become

$$ds^2 = \gamma(r)^2c^2dt^2 - dr^2/\gamma(r)^2 - r^2d\theta^2 \qquad \textbf{2-43}$$

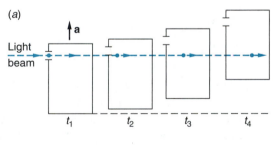

Fig. 2-17 (*a*) Light beam moving in a straight line through a compartment that is undergoing uniform acceleration. The position of the light beam is shown at equally spaced times t_1, t_2, t_3, t_4. (*b*) In the reference frame of the compartment, the light travels in a parabolic path, as would a ball were it projected horizontally. Note that in both (*a*) and (*b*) the vertical displacements are greatly exaggerated for emphasis.

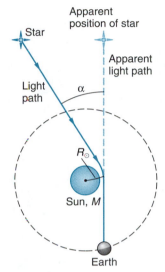

Apparent
position of star

Star

Apparent
light path

Light
path   α

$R_\odot$

Sun, *M*

Earth

Fig. 2-18 Deflection (greatly
exaggerated) of a beam of
starlight due to the gravitational attraction of the sun.

where $\gamma(r) = (1 - 2GM/c^2r)^{1/2}$, with G = universal gravitational constant and r = distance from the center of mass M. The factor $\gamma(r)$ is roughly analogous to the γ of special relativity. In the following Exploring section on gravitational redshift, we describe how $\gamma(r)$ arises. For now, $\gamma(r)$ can be thought of as correcting for *gravitational time dilation* (the first term on the right of Equation 2-43) and *gravitational length contraction* (the second term).

This situation is illustrated in Figure 2-18, which shows the light from a distant star just grazing the edge of the sun. The gravitational deflection of the light (with mass $\gamma m = E/c^2$) can be treated as a refraction of the light. The speed of light is reduced to $\gamma(r)c$ in the vicinity of the mass M, since $\gamma(r) < 1$ (see Equation 2-43), thus bending the wave fronts, and hence the beam, toward M. This is analogous to the deflection of starlight toward Earth's surface as a result of the changing density — hence index of refraction — of the atmosphere. By integrating Equation 2-43 over the entire trajectory of the light beam (recall that $ds = 0$ for light) as it passes by M, the total deflection α is found to be[17]

$$\alpha = 4\,G\,M/c^2\,R_\odot \qquad\qquad \textbf{2-44}$$

where $R_\odot$ = distance of closest approach of the beam to the center of M. For a beam just grazing the sun, $R_\odot$ = solar radius = 6.96×10^8 m. Substituting the values for G and the solar mass ($M = 1.99 \times 10^{30}$ kg) yields $\alpha = 1.75$ arc second.[18]

Ordinarily, of course, the brightness of the sun prevents astronomers (or anyone else) from seeing stars close to the limbs (edges) of the sun, except during a total eclipse. Einstein completed the calculation of α in 1915, and in 1919 expeditions were organized by Eddington[19] at two points along the line of totality of a solar eclipse, both of which were successful in making measurements of α for several stars and in testing the predicted $1/R_\odot$ dependence of α. The measured values of α for grazing beams at the two sites were:

At Sobral (South America):

$$\alpha = 1.98 \pm 0.12 \text{ arc seconds}$$

At Principe Island (Africa):

$$\alpha = 1.61 \pm 0.30 \text{ arc seconds}$$

their average agreeing with the general relativistic prediction to within about 2 percent. Figure 2-19 illustrates the agreement of the $1/R_\odot$ dependence with Equation 2-44. (Einstein learned of the successful measurements via a telegram from H. A. Lorentz.) Since 1919, many measurements of α have been made during eclipses. Since the development of radio telescopes, which are not blinded by sunlight and hence don't require a total eclipse, many more measurements have been made. The latest data agree with the deflection predicted by general relativity to within about 0.1 percent.

The gravitational deflection of light is being put to use by modern astronomers via the phenomenon of *gravitational lenses* to help in the study of galaxies and other large masses in space. Light from very distant stars and galaxies passing near or through other galaxies or clusters of galaxies between the source and Earth can be bent, or refracted, so as to reach Earth in much the same way that light from an object on a bench in the laboratory can be refracted by a glass lens and thus reach the eye of an observer. The intervening galaxy cluster can thus produce images of

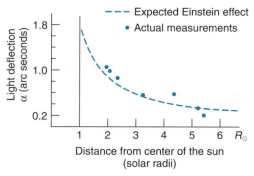

Fig. 2-19 The deflection angle α depends on the distance of closest approach $R_\odot$ according to Equation 2-44. Shown here is a sample of the data for 7 of the 13 stars measured by the Eddington expeditions. The agreement with the relativistic prediction is apparent.

the distant source, even magnified and distorted ones, just as the glass lens can. Figure 2-20a will serve as a reminder of a refracting lens in the laboratory, while Figure 2-20b illustrates the corresponding action of a gravitational lens. The accompanying photograph shows the images of several distant galaxies drawn out into arcs by the lens effect of the cluster of galaxies in the center. The first confirmed discovery of images formed by a gravitational lens was made in 1979 by D. Walsh and his co-workers. It was the double image of the quasar QSO 0957. Since then astronomers have found many such images. Their discovery and interpretation is currently an active area of research.

Exploring

Gravitational Redshift

A second prediction of general relativity concerns the rates of clocks and the frequencies of light in a gravitational field. As a specific case which illustrates the gravitational redshift as a direct consequence of the equivalence principle, suppose we consider two identical light sources (A and A') and detectors (B and B') located in identical spaceships (S and S') as illustrated in Figure 2-21 (page 113). The spaceship S' in Figure 2-21b is located far from any mass. At time $t = 0$, S' begins to accelerate, and simultaneously an atom in the source A' emits a light pulse of its characteristic frequency f_0. During the time t ($= h/c$) for the light to travel from A' to B', B' acquires a speed $v = at = gh/c$, and the detector at B', receding from the original location of A', measures the frequency of the incoming light to be f *redshifted* by a fractional amount $(f_0 - f)/f_0 \approx \beta$ for $v \ll c$. (See Section 1-5.) Thus,

$$(f_0 - f)/f_0 = \Delta f/f_0 \approx \beta = v/c = gh/c^2 \qquad \textbf{2-45}$$

Notice that the right side of Equation 2-45 is equal to the gravitational potential (i.e., the gravitational potential energy per unit mass) $\Delta\phi = gh$ between A and B,

Fig. 2-20 (*a*) Ordinary refracting lens bends light, causing many rays that would not otherwise have reached the observer's eye to do so. Their apparent origin is the image formed by the lens. Notice that the image is not the same size as the object (magnification) and, although not shown here, the shape of the lens can cause the image shape to be different from that of the object. (*b*) Gravitational lens has the same effects on the light from distant galaxies seen at Earth.

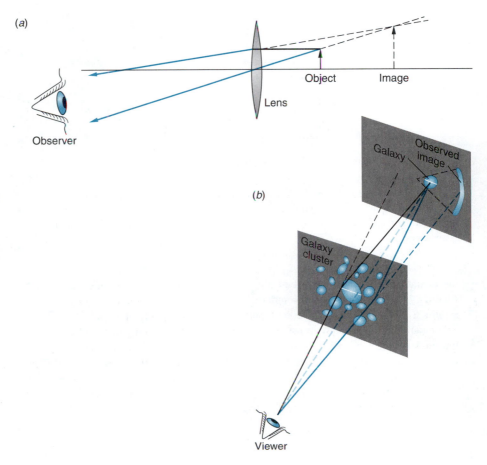

Images of distant galaxies are drawn out into arcs by the massive cluster of galaxies Abell 2218, whose enormous gravitational field acts as a lens to magnify, brighten, and distort the images. Abell 2218 is about 2 billion $c \cdot y$ from Earth. The arcs in this January 2000 Hubble Space Telescope photograph are images of galaxies 10 to 20 billion $c \cdot y$ away. [*NASA/ Science VU/Visuals Unlimited.*]

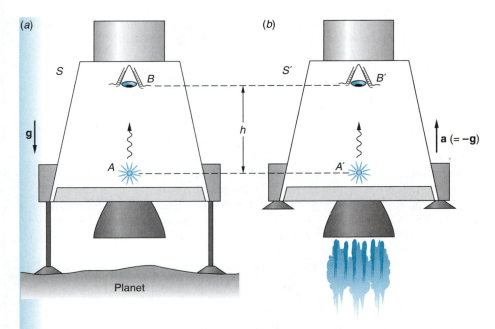

Fig. 2-21 (*a*) System *S* is at rest in the gravitational field of the planet. (*b*) Spaceship *S'*, far from any mass, accelerates with **a** = −**g**.

divided by c^2. According to the equivalence principle, the detector at *B* in *S* must also measure the frequency of the arriving light to be *f*, even though *S* is at rest on the planet and, therefore, the shift cannot be due to the Doppler effect! Since the vibrating atom that produced the light pulse at *A* can be considered to be a clock, and since no "cycles" of the vibration are lost on the pulse's trip from *A* to *B*, the observer at *B* must conclude that the clock at *A* runs slow, compared with an identical clock (or an identical atom) located at *B*. Since *A* is at the lower potential, the observer concludes that clocks run more slowly the lower the gravitational potential. This shift of clock rates to lower frequencies, and hence longer wavelengths, in lower gravitational potentials is the *gravitational redshift*.

In the more general case of a spherical, nonrotating mass *M*, the change in gravitational potential between the surface at some distance *R* from the center and a point at infinity is given by

$$\Delta\phi = \int_R^\infty \frac{GM}{r^2}dr = GM\,(-1/r)\,\Big|_R^\infty = \frac{GM}{R} \qquad \textbf{2-46}$$

and the factor by which gravity shifts the light frequency is found from

$$\Delta f/f_0 = (f_0 - f)/f_0 = GM/c^2R$$

or

$$f/f_0 = 1 - GM/c^2R \qquad \text{(gravitational redshift)} \qquad \textbf{2-47}$$

Notice that if the light is moving the other way, i.e., from high to low gravitational potential, the limits of integration in Equation 2-46 are reversed and Equation 2-47 becomes

$$f/f_0 = 1 + GM/c^2R \qquad \text{(gravitational blueshift)} \qquad \textbf{2-48}$$

Analyzing the frequency of starlight for gravitational effects is exceptionally difficult because several shifts are present. For example, the light is gravitationally redshifted as it leaves the star and blueshifted as it arrives at Earth. The blueshift near Earth is negligibly small with current measuring technology; however, the Doppler redshift due to the receding of nearby stars and distant galaxies from us as a part of the general expansion of the universe is typically much larger than gravitational effects and, together with thermal frequency broadening in the stellar atmospheres, results in large uncertainties in measurements. Thus, it is quite remarkable that the relativistic prediction of Equation 2-48 has been tested in the relatively small gravitational field of Earth. R. V. Pound and his co-workers,[20] first in 1960 and then again in 1964 with improved precision, measured the shift in the frequency of 14.4-keV gamma rays emitted by ^{57}Fe falling through a height h of only 22.5 m. Using the Mössbauer effect, an extremely sensitive frequency shift measuring technique developed in 1958, their measurements agreed with the predicted fractional blueshift $gh/c^2 = 2.45 \times 10^{-15}$ to within 1 percent. A number of tests of Equations 2-47 and 2-48 have been conducted—using atomic clocks carried in aircraft, as described in Section 1-4; and, in 1980, by R. F. C. Vessot and his co-workers, using a precision microwave transmitter carried to 10,000 km from Earth in a space probe. These, too, agree with the relativistically predicted frequency shift, the latter to one part in 14,000.

QUESTION

7. The frequency f in Equation 2-47 can be shifted to zero by an appropriate value of M/R. What would be the corresponding value of R for a star with the mass of the sun? Speculate on the significance of this result.

More

The inability of Newtonian gravitational theory to account correctly for the observed rate at which the major axis of Mercury's orbit precessed about the sun was a troubling problem, pointing as it did to some subtle failure of the theory. Einstein's first paper on general relativity quantitatively explained the advance of the *Perihelion of Mercury's Orbit*, setting the stage for general relativity to supplant the old Newtonian theory. A clear description of the relativistic explanation is on the home page: www.whfreeman.com/modphysics4e   See also Equations 2-49 through 2-51 here, as well as Figure 2-22 and Table 2-2.

More

General relativity includes a gravitational interaction for particles with zero rest mass, such as photons, which are excluded in Newtonian theory. One consequence is the prediction of a *Delay of Light in a Gravitational Field*. This phenomenon and its subsequent observation are described qualitatively on the home page: www.whfreeman.com/modphysics4e   See also Equation 2-52 here, as well as Figures 2-23 and 2-24.

Black Holes   Black holes were first predicted by Oppenheimer and Snyder in 1939. According to the general theory of relativity, if the density of an object such as a star is great enough, the gravitational attraction will be so large that nothing can escape, not even light or other electromagnetic radiation. It is as if space itself were being drawn inward faster than light could move outward through it. A remarkable property of such an object is that nothing that happens inside it can be communicated to the outside world. This occurs when the gravitational potential at the surface of the mass M becomes so large that the frequency of radiation emitted at the surface is gravitationally redshifted to zero. From Equation 2-47 we see that the frequency will be zero when the radius of the mass has the critical value $R_G = GM/c^2$. This result is a consequence of the principle of equivalence, but Equation 2-47 is a $v \ll c$ approximation. A precise derivation of the critical value of R_G, called the *Schwarzschild radius*, yields

$$R_G = \frac{2GM}{c^2} \qquad \textbf{2-53}$$

For an object of mass equal to that of our sun to be a black hole, its radius would be about 3 km. A large number of possible black holes have been identified by astronomers in recent years, one of them at the center of the Milky Way. (See Chapter 14.)

An interesting historical note is that Equation 2-53 was first derived by the nineteenth-century French physicist Pierre Laplace using Newtonian mechanics to compute the escape velocity v_e from a planet of mass M before anyone had ever heard of Einstein or black holes. The result, derived in first-year physics courses by setting the kinetic energy of the escaping object equal to the gravitational potential at the surface of the planet (or star), is

$$v_e = \sqrt{\frac{2GM}{r}}$$

Setting $v_e = c$ gives Equation 2-53. Laplace obtained the correct result by making two fundamental errors that just happened to cancel one another!

Gravitational Waves   Einstein's formulation of general relativity in 1916 explicitly predicted the existence of gravitational radiation. He showed that, just as accelerated electric charges generate time-dependent electromagnetic fields in

Fig. 2-25 Gravitational waves, intense ripples in the fabric of spacetime, are expected to be generated by a merging binary system of neutron stars or black holes. The amplitude decreases with distance due to the $1/R$ fall-off and because waves farther from the source were emitted at an earlier time, when the emission was weaker. [*Image courtesy of Caltech/LIGO.*]

space—i.e., electromagnetic waves—accelerated masses would create time-dependent gravitational fields in space—i.e., *gravitational waves* that propagate from their source at the speed of light. The gravitational waves are propagating warpages, or distortions of spacetime. Figure 2-25 illustrates gravitational radiation emitted by two merging black holes distorting the otherwise flat "fabric" of spacetime.

The best experimental evidence that exists thus far in support of the gravitational wave prediction is indirect. In 1974 Hulse and Taylor[24] discovered the first binary pulsar, i.e., a pair of neutron stars orbiting each other, one of which was emitting periodic flashes of electromagnetic radiation (pulses). In an exquisitely precise experiment they showed that the gradual decrease in the orbital period of the pair was in good agreement with the general relativistic prediction for the rate of loss of gravitational energy via the emission of gravitational waves.

Experiments are currently under way in several countries to detect gravitational waves arriving at Earth *directly*. One of the most promising is LIGO (*L*aser *I*nterferometer *G*ravitational-*W*ave *O*bservatory), a pair of large Michelson interferometers, one in Louisiana and the other 3030 km away in Washington, operating in coincidence. Figure 2-26 illustrates one of the LIGO interferometers. Each arm is 4 km long. The laser beams are reflected back and forth by the mirrors dozens of times before recombining at the photodetector, making the effective lengths of the arms about 400 km. The arrival of a gravitational wave would stretch one arm of the

This application of Michelson's interferometer may well lead to the first direct detection of "ripples," or waves in spacetime.

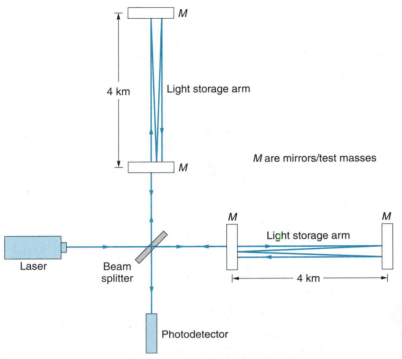

Fig. 2-26 The LIGO detectors are equal-arm Michelson interferometers. The mirrors, each 25 cm in diameter by 10 cm thick and isolated from Earth's motions, are also the test masses of the gravitational wave detector. Arrival of a gravitational wave would change the length of each arm by about the diameter of an atomic nucleus and result in interference fringes at the photodetector.

interferometer by about 1/1000th of the diameter of an atom and squeeze the other arm by the same minuscule amount! Nonetheless, that tiny change in the lengths is sufficient to put the recombining laser beams slightly out of phase and produce interference fringes. The two LIGO interferometers must record the event within 10 ms of each other for the signal to be interpreted as a gravitational wave. LIGO completed its two-year, low-sensitivity initial operational phase and went online in mid-2002. None of the half-dozen experiments under way around the world has yet confirmed detection of a gravitational wave.[25]

There is still an enormous amount to be learned about the predictions and implications of general relativity—not just about such things as black holes and gravity waves, but also, for example, about gravity and spacetime in the very early universe, when forces were unified and the constituents were closely packed. These and other fascinating matters are investigated more specifically in the areas of astrophysics and cosmology (Chapter 14) and particle physics (Chapter 13), fields linked together by general relativity, perhaps the grandest of Einstein's great scientific achievements.

QUESTION

8. Speculate on what the two errors made by Laplace in deriving Equation 2-53 might have been.

Summary

TOPIC	RELEVANT EQUATIONS AND REMARKS	
1. Relativistic momentum	$\mathbf{p} = \gamma m\mathbf{u}$	**2-7**
	The relativistic momentum is conserved and approaches $m\mathbf{u}$ for $v \ll c$. $\gamma = (1 - u^2/c^2)^{-1/2}$ in Equation 2-7, where u = particle speed in S.	
2. Relativistic energy	$E = \gamma mc^2$	**2-10**
Total energy	The relativistic total energy is conserved.	
Kinetic energy	$E_k = \gamma mc^2 - mc^2$	**2-9**
	The rest energy is mc^2. $\gamma = (1 - u^2/c^2)^{-1/2}$ in Equations 2-9 and 2-10.	
3. Lorentz transformation for E and $\mathbf{p}$	$p'_x = \gamma(p_x - vE/c^2) \qquad p'_y = p_y$ $E' = \gamma(E - vp_x) \qquad\quad p'_z = p_z$	**2-16**
	where v = relative speed of the systems and $\gamma = (1 - v^2/c^2)^{-1/2}$	
4. Mass/energy conversion	Whenever additional energy ΔE in any form is stored in an object, the rest mass of the object is increased by $\Delta m = \Delta E/c^2$.	
5. Invariant mass	$(mc^2)^2 = E^2 - (pc)^2$	**2-32**
	The energy and momentum of any system combine to form an invariant four-vector whose magnitude is the rest energy of the mass m.	
6. Force in relativity	The force $\mathbf{F} = m\mathbf{a}$ is not invariant in relativity. Relativistic force is defined as $\mathbf{F} = \dfrac{d\mathbf{p}}{dt} = \dfrac{d(\gamma m\mathbf{u})}{dt}$	**2-8**
7. General relativity principle of equivalence	A homogeneous gravitational field is completely equivalent to a uniformly accelerated frame.	

GENERAL REFERENCES

The following general references are written at a level appropriate for the readers of this book.

Bohm, D., *The Special Theory of Relativity,* W. A. Benjamin, New York, 1965.

French, A. P., *Albert Einstein: A Centenary Volume,* Harvard University Press, Cambridge, Mass., 1979. This is an excellent collection of contributions from many people about Einstein's life and work.

French, A. P., *Special Relativity,* Norton, New York, 1968.

Lorentz, H. A., A. Einstein, H. Minkowski, and W. Weyl, *The Principle of Relativity: A Collection of Original Memoirs on the Special and General Theory of Relativity* (trans. W. Perrett and J. B. Jeffery), Dover, New York, 1923.

Two of Einstein's papers reprinted here are of interest in connection with this chapter: "On the Electrodynamics of Moving Bodies," [*Annalen der Physik,* **17** (1905)], and "Does the Inertia of a Body Depend upon Its Energy Content?" [*Annalen der Physik,* **17** (1905)].

Pais, A., *Subtle Is the Lord . . . ,* Oxford University Press, Oxford, 1982.

Resnick, R., *Introduction to Relativity,* Wiley, New York, 1968.

Resnick, R., and D. Halliday, *Basic Concepts in Relativity and Early Quantum Theory,* 2d ed., Macmillan, New York, 1992.

"Resource Letter SRT-1 on Special Relativity Theory," *American Journal of Physics,* **30**, 462 (1962). This is a list of references.

Rosser, W. G. V., *The Theory of Relativity,* Butterworth, London, 1964.

Special Relativity Theory: Selected Reprints, American Association of Physics Teachers, New York, 1963. Booklet containing some of the papers listed in "Resource Letter SRT-1."

Taylor, E. F., and J. A. Wheeler, *Spacetime Physics,* 2d ed., W. H. Freeman & Co., 1992. A good book with many examples, problems, and diagrams.

NOTES

1. This *gedankenexperiment* ("thought experiment") is based on one first suggested by G. N. Lewis and R. C. Tolman, *Philosophical Magazine,* **18**, 510 (1909).

2. You can see that this is so by rotating Figure 2-1*a* through 180° on its own plane; it then matches Figure 2-1*b* exactly.

3. C. G. Adler, *American Journal of Physics,* **55**, 739 (1987).

4. This idea grew out of the results of the measurements of masses in chemical reactions in the nineteenth century, which, within the limits of experimental uncertainties of the time, were always observed to conserve mass. The conservation of energy had a similar origin in the experiments of James Joule (1818–1889) as interpreted by Hermann von Helmholtz (1821–1894). This is not an unusual way for conservation laws to originate; they still do it this way.

5. The approximation of Equation 2-10 used in this discussion was, of course, not developed from Newton's equations. The rest energy mc^2 has no classical counterpart.

6. "Facilitates" means that we don't have to make frequent unit conversions or carry along large powers of 10 with nearly every factor in many calculations. However, a word of caution is in order: Always remember that the eV is *not* a basic SI unit. When making calculations whose results are to be in SI units, don't forget to convert the eV!

7. A. Einstein, *Annalen der Physik,* **17**, 1905.

8. Strictly speaking, the time component should be written $ic \, \Delta t$, where $i = (-1)^{1/2}$. The i is the origin of the minus sign in the spacetime interval, as well as in Equation 2-32 for the energy/momentum four-vector and other four-vectors in both special and general relativity. Its inclusion was a contribution of Hermann Minkowski (1864–1909), a Russian-German mathematician, who developed the geometric interpretation of relativity and who was one of Einstein's professors in Zurich. Consideration of the four-dimensional geometry is beyond the scope of our discussions, so we will not be concerned with the i.

9. Other conservation laws of physics must also be satisfied, e.g., electric charge, angular momentum.

10. The positron is a particle with the same mass as an ordinary electron, but with a positive electric charge of the same magnitude as that carried by the electron. It and other antiparticles will be discussed in Chapters 11 and 13.

11. Since electrons are thought to be point particles, i.e., they have no space dimensions, it isn't clear what it means to "hit" an electron. Think of it as the photon coming close to the electron's location, hence, in its strong local electric field.

12. Such a system is called a *polyelectron.* It is analogous to an ionized hydrogen molecule, much as positronium is analogous to a hydrogen atom. (See caption for Figure 2-12.)

13. Satellite navigation systems, e.g., the U.S. Air Force Global Positioning System, are now so precise that the minute corrections arising primarily from the general relativistic time dilation must be taken into account by the systems' programs.

14. From Einstein's lecture in Kyoto in late 1922. See A. Pais, *Subtle Is the Lord* . . . (Oxford: Oxford University Press, 1982).

15. From an unpublished paper now in the collection of the Pierpont Morgan Library in New York. See Pais, *Subtle Is the Lord* . . . (Oxford: Oxford University Press, 1982).

16. Einstein inquired of the astronomer George Hale (after whom the 5-m telescope on Palomar is named) in 1913 whether such minute deflections could be measured near the sun. The answer was no, but a corrected calculation two years later doubled the predicted deflection and brought detection to within the realm of possibility.

17. This is not a simple integration. See, e.g., Adler et al., *Introduction to General Relativity* (New York: McGraw-Hill, 1965).

18. Both Newtonian mechanics and special relativity predict half of this value. The particle-scattering formula used in Chapter 4 to obtain Equation 4-3 applied to the gravitational deflection of a photon of mass $h\nu/c^2$ by the solar mass $M_\odot$ at impact parameter b equal to the solar radius $R_\odot$ shows how this value arises.

19. A copy of Einstein's work (he was then in Berlin) was smuggled out of Germany to Eddington in England so that he could plan the project. Germany and England were then at war. Arthur S. Eddington (1882–1944) was then director of the prestigious Cambridge Observatory. British authorities approved the eclipse expeditions in order to avoid the embarrassment of putting such a distinguished scientist as Eddington, a conscientious objector, into a wartime internment camp.

20. See, for example, R. V. Pound and G. A. Rebka, Jr., *Physical Review Letters,* **4**, 337 (1960).

21. These values are relative to the fixed stars.

22. A. Einstein, "The Foundation of the General Theory of Relativity," *Annalen der Physik,* **49**, 769 (1916).

23. I. I. Shapiro et al., *Physical Review Letters,* **26**, 1132 (1971).
24. R. A. Hulse and J. H. Taylor, *Astrophysical Journal,* **195**, L51 (1975).
25. Gravity wave detectors outside the United States are the TAMA 300 (Japan), GEO 600 (Germany), and Virgo (Italy).

NASA and the European Space Agency are designing a space-based gravity wave detector, LISA, that will have arms 5 million kilometers long. The three satellites that LISA will comprise are scheduled for launch in 2011.

PROBLEMS

Level I

Section 2-1 Relativistic Momentum and Section 2-2 Relativistic Energy

2-1. Show that $p_{yA} = -p_{yB}$, where p_{yA} and p_{yB} are the relativistic momenta of the balls on Figure 2-1, given by

$$p_{yA} = \frac{mu_0}{\sqrt{1 - u_0^2/c^2}} \qquad p_{yB} = \frac{mu_{yB}}{\sqrt{1 - (u_{xB}^2 + u_{yB}^2)/c^2}}$$

$$u_{yB} = -u_0\sqrt{1 - \frac{v^2}{c^2}} \qquad u_{xB} = v$$

2-2. Show that $d(\gamma mu) = m(1 - u^2/c^2)^{-3/2}\, du$.

2-3. An electron of rest energy $mc^2 = 0.511$ MeV moves with respect to the laboratory at speed $u = 0.6\,c$. Find (*a*) γ, (*b*) p in units of MeV/c, (*c*) E, and (*d*) E_k.

2-4. How much energy would be required to accelerate a particle of mass m from rest to a speed of (*a*) 0.5 *c*, (*b*) 0.9 *c*, and (*c*) 0.99 *c*? Express your answers as multiples of the rest energy.

2-5. Two 1-kg masses are separated by a spring of negligible mass. They are pushed together, compressing the spring. If the work done in compressing the spring is 10 J, find the change in mass of the system in kilograms. Does the mass increase or decrease?

2-6. At what value of u/c does the measured mass of a particle exceed its rest mass by (*a*) 10%, (*b*) a factor of 5, and (*c*) a factor of 20?

2-7. A cosmic ray proton is moving at such a speed that it can travel from the moon to Earth in 1.5 s. (*a*) At what fraction of the speed of light is the proton moving? (*b*) What is its kinetic energy? (*c*) What value would be measured for its mass by an observer in the Earth reference frame? (*d*) What percent error is made in the kinetic energy by using the classical relation? (The Earth-moon distance is 3.8×10^5 km. Ignore Earth's rotation.)

2-8. How much work must be done on a proton to increase its speed from (*a*) 0.15*c* to 0.16*c*? (*b*) 0.85*c* to 0.86*c*? (*c*) 0.95*c* to 0.96*c*? Notice that the change in the speed is the same in each case.

2-9. The Relativistic Heavy Ion Collider (RHIC) at Brookhaven is colliding fully ionized gold (Au) nuclei accelerated to an energy of 200 GeV per nucleon. Each Au nucleus contains 197 nucleons. (*a*) What is the speed of each Au nucleus just before collision? (*b*) What is the momentum of each at that instant? (*c*) What energy and momentum would be measured for one of the Au nuclei by an observer in the rest system of the other Au nucleus?

2-10. (*a*) Compute the rest energy of 1 g of dirt. (*b*) If you could convert this energy entirely into electrical energy and sell it for 10 cents per kilowatt-hour, how much money would you get? (*c*) If you could power a 100-W light bulb with the energy, for how long could you keep the bulb lit?

2-11. An electron with rest energy of 0.511 MeV moves with speed $u = 0.2c$. Find its total energy, kinetic energy, and momentum.

2-12. A proton with rest energy of 938 MeV has a total energy of 1400 MeV. (*a*) What is its speed? (*b*) What is its momentum?

2-13. The total energy of a particle is twice its rest energy. (*a*) Find u/c for the particle. (*b*) Show that its momentum is given by $p = (3)^{1/2} mc$.

2-14. An electron in a hydrogen atom has a speed about the proton of 2.2×10^6 m/s. (*a*) By what percent do the relativistic and Newtonian values of E_k differ? (*b*) By what percent do the momentum values differ?

2-15. Suppose that you seal an ordinary 60-W light bulb and a suitable battery inside a transparent enclosure and suspend the system from a very sensitive balance. (*a*) Compute the change in the mass of the system if the lamp is on continuously for one year at full power. (*b*) What difference, if any, would it make if the inner surface of the container were a perfect reflector?

Section 2-3 Mass/Energy Conversion and Binding Energy

2-16. Use Appendix A and Table 2-1 to find how much energy is needed to remove one proton from a ^{4}He atom, leaving a ^{3}H atom plus a proton and an electron.

2-17. Use Appendix A and Table 2-1 to find how much energy is required to remove one of the neutrons from a ^{3}H atom to yield a ^{2}H atom plus a neutron?

2-18. The energy released when sodium and chlorine combine to form NaCl is 4.2 eV. (*a*) What is the increase in mass (in unified mass units) when a molecule of NaCl is dissociated into an atom of Na and an atom of Cl? (*b*) What percentage error is made in neglecting this mass difference? (The mass of Na is about 23 u, and that of Cl is about 35.5 u.)

2-19. In a nuclear fusion reaction two ^{2}H atoms are combined to produce ^{4}He. (*a*) Calculate the decrease in rest mass in unified mass units. (*b*) How much energy is released in this reaction? (*c*) How many such reactions must take place per second to produce 1 W of power?

2-20. Calculate the rate of conversion of rest mass to energy (in kg/h) needed to produce 100 MW.

2-21. When a beam of high-energy protons collides with protons at rest in the laboratory (e.g., in a container of water or liquid hydrogen), neutral pions (π^0) are produced by the reaction $p + p \rightarrow p + p + \pi^0$. Compute the threshold energy of the protons in the beam for this reaction to occur. (See Table 2-1 and Example 2-11.)

2-22. The energy released in the fission of a ^{235}U nucleus is about 200 MeV. How much rest mass (in kg) is converted to energy in this fission?

Section 2-4 Invariant Mass

2-23. The K^0 particle decays according to the equation $K^0 \rightarrow \pi^+ + \pi^-$. If a particular K^0 decays while it is at rest in the laboratory, what are the kinetic energies of each of the two pions? (The rest mass of the K^0 is 497.7 MeV/c^2.)

2-24. Compute the force exerted on the palm of your hand by the beam from a 1.0-W flashlight (*a*) if your hand absorbs the light, and (*b*) if the light reflects from your hand. What would be the mass of a particle that exerts that same force in each case if you hold it at Earth's surface?

2-25. An electron-positron pair combined as positronium is at rest in the laboratory. The pair annihilate, producing a pair of photons (gamma rays) moving in opposite directions in the lab. Show that the invariant rest energy of the gamma rays is equal to that of the electron pair.

2-26. Show that Equation 2-31 can be written $E = mc^2(1 + p^2/m^2c^2)^{1/2}$ and use the binomial expansion to show that, when pc is much less than mc^2, $E \approx mc^2 + p^2/2m$.

2-27. An electron of rest energy 0.511 MeV has a total energy of 5 MeV. (*a*) Find its momentum in units of MeV/c. (*b*) Find u/c.

2-28. Make a sketch of the total energy of an electron E as a function of its momentum p. (See Equations 2-36 and 2-41 for the behavior of E at large and small values of p.)

2-29. What is the speed of a particle that is observed to have momentum 500 MeV/*c* and energy 1746 MeV. What is the particle's mass (in MeV/c^2)?

2-30. An electron of total energy 4.0 MeV moves perpendicular to a uniform magnetic field along a circular path whose radius is 4.2 cm. (*a*) What is the strength of the magnetic field B? (*b*) By what factor does γm exceed *m*?

2-31. A proton is bent into a circular path of radius 2 m by a magnetic field of 0.5 T. (*a*) What is the momentum of the proton? (*b*) What is its kinetic energy?

Section 2-5 General Relativity

2-32. Compute the deflection angle α for light from a distant star that would, according to general relativity, be measured by an observer on the moon as the light grazes the edge of Earth.

2-33. A set of twins work in the Sears Tower, a very tall office building in Chicago. One works on the top floor and the other works in the basement. Considering general relativity, which twin will age more slowly? (*a*) They will age at the same rate. (*b*) The twin who works on the top floor will age more slowly. (*c*) The twin who works in the basement will age more slowly. (*d*) It depends on the building's speed. (*e*) None of the previous choices is correct.

2-34. Jupiter makes 8.43 orbits/century and exhibits an orbital eccentricity $\epsilon = 0.048$. Jupiter is 5.2 AU from the sun and has a mass 318 times the Earth's 5.98×10^{24} kg. What does general relativity predict for the rate of precession of Jupiter's perihelion? (It has not yet been measured.) (The astronomical unit AU = the mean Earth-sun distance = 1.50×10^{11} m.)

2-35. A synchronous satellite "parked" in orbit over the equator is used to relay microwave transmissions between stations on the ground. To what frequency must the satellite's receiver be tuned if the frequency of the transmission from Earth is exactly 9.375 GHz? (Ignore all Doppler effects.)

2-36. A particular distant star is found to be 92 $c \cdot$ y from Earth. On a direct line between us and the star and 35 $c \cdot$ y from the distant star is a dense white dwarf star with a mass equal to 3 times the sun's mass $M_\odot$ and a radius of 10^4 km. Deflection of the light beam from the distant star by the white dwarf causes us to see it as a pair of circular arcs like those shown in Figure 2-20(*b*). Find the angle 2α formed by the lines of sight to the two arcs.

Level II

2-37. A clock is placed on a satellite that orbits Earth with a period of 90 min at an altitude of 300 km. By what time interval will this clock differ from an identical clock on Earth after 1 year? (Include both special and general relativistic effects.)

2-38. Referring to Example 2-11, find the total energy E' as measured in S' where $\mathbf{p'} = 0$.

2-39. In the Stanford linear collider, small bundles of electrons and positrons are fired at each other. In the laboratory's frame of reference, each bundle is about 1 cm long and 10 μm in diameter. In the collision region, each particle has an energy of 50 GeV, and the electrons and positrons are moving in opposite directions. (*a*) How long and how wide is each bundle in its own reference frame? (*b*) What must be the minimum proper length of the accelerator for a bundle to have both its ends simultaneously in the accelerator in its own reference frame? (The actual length of the accelerator is less than 1000 m.) (*c*) What is the length of a positron bundle in the reference frame of the electron bundle? (*d*) What are the momentum and energy of the electrons in the rest frame of the positrons?

2-40. The rest energy of a proton is about 938 MeV. If its kinetic energy is also 938 MeV, find (*a*) its momentum and (*b*) its speed.

2-41. A spaceship of mass 10^6 kg is coasting through space when suddenly it becomes necessary to accelerate. The ship ejects 10^3 kg of fuel in a very short time at a speed of

$c/2$ relative to the ship. (*a*) Neglecting any change in the rest mass of the system, calculate the speed of the ship in the frame in which it was initially at rest. (*b*) Calculate the speed of the ship using classical Newtonian mechanics. (*c*) Use your results from (*a*) to estimate the change in the rest mass of the system.

2-42. Professor Spenditt, oblivious to economics and politics, proposes the construction of a circular proton accelerator around Earth's circumference using bending magnets that provide a magnetic field of 1.5 T. (*a*) What would be the kinetic energy of protons orbiting in this field in a circle of radius R_E? (*b*) What would be the period of rotation of these protons?

2-43. In ancient Egypt the annual flood of the Nile was predicted by the rise of Sirius (the Dog Star). Sirius is one of a binary pair whose companion is a white dwarf. Orbital analysis of the pair indicates that the dwarf's mass is 2×10^{30} kg (i.e., about one solar mass). Comparison of spectral lines emitted by the white dwarf with those emitted by the same element on Earth shows a fractional frequency shift of 7×10^{-4}. Assuming this to be due to a gravitational redshift, compute the density of the white dwarf. (For comparison, the sun's density is 1409 kg/m³.)

2-44. Show that the creation of an electron-position pair (or any particle-antiparticle pair, for that matter) by a single photon is not possible in isolation, i.e., that additional mass (or radiation) must be present. (*Hint*: Use the conservation laws.)

2-45. With inertial systems S and S' arranged with their corresponding axes parallel and S' moving in the $+x$ direction, it was apparent that the Lorentz transformation for y and z would be $y' = y$ and $z' = z$. The transformation for the y and z components of the momentum are not so apparent, however. Show that, as stated in Equations 2-16 and 2-17, $p'_y = p_y$ and $p'_z = p_z$.

Level III

2-46. Two identical particles of rest mass m are each moving toward the other with speed u in frame S. The particles collide inelastically with a spring that locks shut (Figure 2-9) and come to rest in S, and their initial kinetic energy is transformed into potential energy. In this problem you are going to show that the conservation of momentum in reference frame S', in which one of the particles is initially at rest, requires that the total rest mass of the system after the collision be $2m/(1 - u^2/c^2)^{1/2}$. (*a*) Show that the speed of the particle not at rest in frame S' is

$$u' = \frac{2u}{1 + u^2/c^2}$$

and use this result to show that

$$\sqrt{1 - \frac{u'^2}{c^2}} = \frac{1 - u^2/c^2}{1 + u^2/c^2}$$

(*b*) Show that the initial momentum in frame S' is $p' = 2mu/(1 - u^2/c^2)$. (*c*) After the collision, the composite particle moves with speed u in S' (since it is at rest in S). Write the total momentum after the collision in terms of the final rest mass M, and show that the conservation of momentum implies that $M = 2m/(1 - u^2/c^2)^{1/2}$. (*d*) Show that the total energy is conserved in each reference frame.

2-47. An antiproton $\bar{p}$ has the same rest energy as a proton. It is created in the reaction $p + p \rightarrow p + p + p + \bar{p}$. In an experiment, protons at rest in the laboratory are bombarded with protons of kinetic energy E_k, which must be great enough so that kinetic energy equal to $2mc^2$ can be converted into the rest energy of the two particles. In the frame of the laboratory,

the total kinetic energy cannot be converted into rest energy because of conservation of momentum. However, in the zero-momentum reference frame in which the two initial protons are moving toward each other with equal speed u, the total kinetic energy can be converted into rest energy. (*a*) Find the speed of each proton u such that the total kinetic energy in the zero-momentum frame is $2mc^2$. (*b*) Transform to the laboratory's frame in which one proton is at rest, and find the speed u' of the other proton. (*c*) Show that the kinetic energy of the moving proton in the laboratory's frame is $E_k = 6mc^2$.

2-48. In a simple thought experiment, Einstein showed that there is mass associated with electromagnetic radiation. Consider a box of length L and mass M resting on a frictionless surface. At the left wall of the box is a light source that emits radiation of energy E, which is absorbed at the right wall of the box. According to classical electromagnetic theory, this radiation carries momentum of magnitude $p = E/c$. (*a*) Find the recoil velocity of the box such that momentum is conserved when the light is emitted. (Since p is small and M is large, you may use classical mechanics.) (*b*) When the light is absorbed at the right wall of the box, the box stops, so the total momentum remains zero. If we neglect the very small velocity of the box, the time it takes for the radiation to travel across the box is $\Delta t = L/c$. Find the distance moved by the box in this time. (*c*) Show that if the center of mass of the system is to remain at the same place, the radiation must carry mass $m = E/c^2$.

2-49. A pion spontaneously decays into a muon and an antineutrino according to (among other processes) $\pi^- \longrightarrow \mu^- + \bar{\nu}_\mu$. Current experimental evidence indicates that the mass m of the $\bar{\nu}_\mu$ is no greater that about 190 keV and may, in fact, be zero. Assuming that the pion decays at rest in the laboratory, compute the energies and momenta of the muon and muon antineutrino (*a*) if the mass of the antineutrino is zero and (*b*) if its mass is 190 keV. The mass of the pion is 139.56755 MeV/c^2 and the mass of the muon is 105.65839 MeV/c^2.

2-50. Use Equation 2-47 to obtain the gravitational redshift in terms of the wavelength λ. Use that result to determine the shift in wavelength of light emitted by a white dwarf star at 720.00 nm. Assume the white dwarf has the same mass as the sun (1.99×10^{30} kg), but a radius equal to only 1 percent of the solar radius $R_\odot$. ($R_\odot = 6.96 \times 10^8$ m.)

2-51. For a particle moving in the xy plane of S, show that the y' component of the acceleration is given by

$$a_y' = \frac{a_y}{\gamma^2(1 - u_x v/c^2)} + \frac{a_x u_y v/c^2}{\gamma^2(1 - u_x v/c^2)^3}$$

2-52. Consider an object of mass m at rest in S acted upon by a force $\mathbf{F}$ with components F_x and F_y. System S' moves with instantaneous velocity $\mathbf{v}$ in the $+x$ direction. Defining the force with Equation 2-8 and using the Lorentz velocity transformation, show that (*a*) $F_x' = F_x$ and (*b*) $F_y' = F_y/\gamma$. (*Hint*: See Problem 2-51.)

2-53. An unstable particle of mass M decays into two identical particles, each of mass m. Obtain an expression for the velocities of the two decay particles in the lab frame (*a*) if M is at rest in the lab and (*b*) if M has total energy $4mc^2$ when it decays and the decay particles move along the direction of M.

Chapter 3

Quantization of Charge, Light, and Energy

The idea that all matter is composed of tiny particles, or atoms, dates back to the speculations of the Greek philosopher Democritus[1] and his teacher Leucippus about 450 B.C. However, there was little attempt to correlate such speculations with observations of the physical world until the seventeenth century. Pierre Gassendi, in the middle of the seventeenth century, and Robert Hooke, somewhat later, attempted to explain states of matter and the transitions between them with a model of tiny, indestructible solid objects flying in all directions. But it was Avogadro's hypothesis, advanced in 1811, that all gases at a given temperature contain the same number of molecules per unit volume, which led to great success in the interpretation of chemical reactions and to development of the kinetic theory, around 1900. It enabled quantitative understanding of many bulk properties of matter and led to general (though not unanimous) acceptance of the molecular theory of matter. Thus, matter is not continuous, as it appears, but is *quantized* (i.e., discrete) on the microscopic scale. It was understood that the small size of the atom prevented the discreteness of matter from being readily observable.

In this chapter, we shall study how three additional great quantization discoveries were made: (1) electric charge, (2) light energy, and (3) energy of oscillating mechanical systems. The quantization of electric charge was not particularly surprising to scientists in 1900; it was quite analogous to the quantization of mass. However, the quantizations of light energy and mechanical energy, which are of central importance in modern physics, were revolutionary ideas.

3-1 Quantization of Electric Charge

Early Measurements of e and e/m

The first estimates of the order of magnitude of the electric charges found in atoms were obtained from Faraday's law. The work of Michael Faraday (1791–1867) in the early to mid-1800s stands out even today for its vision, experimental ingenuity, and thoroughness. The story of this self-educated blacksmith's son who rose from errand boy and bookbinder's apprentice to become the director of the distinguished Royal Institution of London and the foremost experimental investigator of his time is a fascinating one. One aspect of his work concerned the study of the conduction of electricity in liquids. His results and his subsequent statement of the law of electrolysis

(1833) were of great importance for the evidence they gave of the electrical nature of atomic forces. The phenomenon still has interest in that it provides the basis for the study of the field of electrochemistry.

In his experiments, Faraday passed a direct current (dc) through weakly conducting solutions and observed the subsequent liberation of the components of the solution at the electrodes. Quantitatively, Faraday discovered that the same quantity of electricity, *F,* called the faraday and equal to about 96,500 C, always decomposes 1 gram-ionic weight of monovalent ions. For example, if 96,500 C pass through a solution of NaCl, 23 g of Na appear at the cathode and 35.5 g of Cl at the anode. For ions of valence 2, such as Cu or SO_4, it takes 2 faradays to decompose 1 gram-ionic weight. Since a gram-ionic weight is just Avogadro's number of ions N_A, it is reasonable to assume that each monovalent ion contains the same charge, *e,* and

$$F = N_A e$$
3-1

Equation 3-1 is called Faraday's law of electrolysis. Since the faraday could be measured quite accurately, N_A or *e* could be determined if the other were known. Faraday was aware of this but could not determine either quantity. Even so, it seemed logical to expect that electric charge, like matter, was not continuous but consisted of particles of some discrete minimum charge. In 1874, G. J. Stoney[2] suggested that the apparent minimum amount of charge be called an *electron e* and used an estimate of N_A from kinetic theory to compute the value of *e* to be about 10^{-20} C. Based on accumulating experimental evidence, Helmholtz[3] pointed out in 1880 that it is apparently impossible to obtain a subunit of this charge. The first discrete measurement of this smallest unit of charge was made by Townsend in 1897, by an ingenious method that was the forerunner of the famous Millikan oil-drop experiment.

Pieter Zeeman, in 1896, obtained the first evidence for the existence of atomic particles with a specific charge-to-mass ratio by looking at the light emitted by atoms placed in a strong magnetic field. When viewed through a spectroscope without the magnetic field, this light appears as a discrete set of lines called *spectral lines.* According to classical electromagnetic theory, a charge oscillating in simple harmonic motion will emit electromagnetic radiation at the frequency of oscillation. If the moving charge is placed in a magnetic field, there will be an additional force on the charge which, to a first approximation, merely changes the frequency of oscillation. The frequency is either slightly increased, slightly decreased, or unchanged from its original value, depending on the orientation of the line of oscillation relative to the direction of the magnetic field. Then, according to classical theory, if a spectral line from atoms is due to the oscillation of charged particles in the atoms, that line will be split into three very closely spaced lines of slightly different frequencies when the atom is placed in a magnetic field. (This phenomenon is called the *Zeeman effect* and will be discussed further in Chapter 7.) The magnitude of the frequency difference depends on the charge-to-mass ratio *q/m* of the oscillating particle. Zeeman measured such a splitting and calculated *q/m* to be about 1.6×10^{11} C/kg, which compares favorably with the presently accepted value for the electron of 1.759×10^{11} C/kg. From the polarization of the spectral lines, Zeeman concluded that the oscillating particles were negatively charged.

Discovery of the Electron: J. J. Thomson's Experiment

Many studies of electrical discharges in gases were done in the late nineteenth century. It was found that the ions responsible for gaseous conduction carried the same charge as did those in electrolysis. The year following Zeeman's work, J. J. Thomson[4]

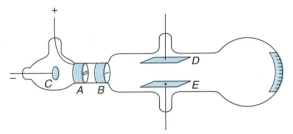

Fig. 3-1 J. J. Thomson's tube for measuring *e/m*. Electrons from the cathode *C* pass through the slits at *A* and *B* and strike a phosphorescent screen. The beam can be deflected by an electric field between the plates *D* and *E* or by a magnetic field (not shown) whose direction is perpendicular to the electric field between *D* and *E*. From measurements of the deflections measured on a scale on the tube at the screen, *e/m* can be determined. [*From J. J. Thomson, "Cathode Rays,"* Philosophical Magazine *(5), 44, 293 (1897).*]

measured the *q/m* value for the so-called cathode rays and pointed out that if their charge was Faraday's minimum charge *e* as determined by Stoney, then their mass was only a small fraction of the mass of a hydrogen atom. He had, in fact, discovered the *electron*. The cathode-ray tube used by J. J. Thomson (the apparatus is shown in Figure 3-1) is typical of those used by his contemporaries. It was the forerunner of the television picture tube, the oscilloscope, and a host of video display terminals on everything from word processors and personal computers to video games and radar screens. At sufficiently low pressure, the space near the cathode becomes dark, and as the pressure is lowered, this dark space extends across the tube until it finally reaches the glass, which then glows as a result of the energy absorbed from the cathode rays. When apertures are placed at *A* and *B,* the glow is limited to a well-defined spot on the glass. This spot can then be deflected by electrostatic or magnetic fields.[5] In 1895, J. Perrin had collected these "cathode rays" on an electrometer and found them to carry a negative electric charge. That direct measurement of the charge-to-mass ratio *e/m* of electrons by J. J. Thomson in 1897 can be justly considered the beginning of our understanding of atomic structure.

Measurement of e/m   When a uniform magnetic field of strength *B* is established perpendicular to the direction of motion of charged particles, the particles move in a circular path. The radius *R* of the path can be obtained from Newton's second law, by setting the magnetic force *quB* equal to the mass *m* times the centripetal acceleration u^2/R.

$$quB = \frac{mu^2}{R} \quad \text{or} \quad R = \frac{mu}{qB} \qquad \textbf{3-2}$$

Present-day particle physicists routinely use the modern equivalent of Thomson's experiment to measure the momenta of elementary particles. Equation 3-2 is the nonrelativistic version of Equation 2-37, i.e., with $\gamma = 1$; Thomson, who didn't know about relativity at the time, of course, was fortunate in that the speeds of his "cathode rays" (electrons) were decidedly nonrelativistic; that is, the electron speeds *u* were much smaller that the speed of light *c*, with $u/c \ll 0.2$. (See Figure 2-2.) In his first measurement, Thomson determined the velocity from measurements of the total charge and the temperature change occurring when the beam struck an insulated collector. For *N* particles, the total charge is $Q = Ne$, while the temperature rise is

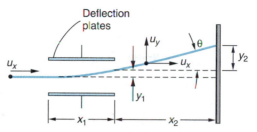

Fig. 3-2 Deflection of the electron beam in Thomson's apparatus. The deflection plates are *D* and *E* in Figure 3-1. Deflection of the beam is shown with the magnetic field off and the top plate positive. Thomson used up to about 200 V between *D* and *E*. A magnetic field was applied perpendicular to the plane of the diagram directed into the page to bend the beam back down to its undeflected position.

proportional to the energy loss $W = N(\frac{1}{2}mu^2)$. Eliminating N and u from these equations, we obtain

$$\frac{e}{m} = \frac{2W}{B^2R^2Q} \qquad\qquad \textbf{3-3}$$

In his second measurement, which came to be known as the *J. J. Thomson experiment,* he adjusted perpendicular B and $\mathscr{E}$ fields so that the particles were *undeflected.* This allowed him to determine the speed by equating the magnitudes of the magnetic and electric forces:

$$quB = q\mathscr{E} \qquad \text{or} \qquad u = \frac{\mathscr{E}}{B} \qquad\qquad \textbf{3-4}$$

He then turned off the B field and measured the deflection of the particles on the screen. This deflection is made up of two parts (see Figure 3-2). While the particles are between the plates they undergo a vertical deflection y_1, given by

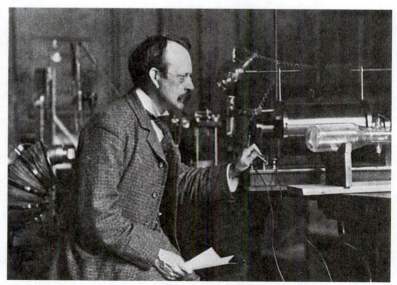

J. J. Thomson in his laboratory. He is facing the screen end of an *e/m* tube; an older cathode-ray tube is visible in front of his left shoulder. [*Courtesy of Cavendish Laboratory.*]

$$y_1 = \frac{1}{2}at_1^2 = \frac{1}{2}\frac{e\mathcal{E}}{m}\left(\frac{x_1}{u_x}\right)^2 \qquad\qquad \textbf{3-5}$$

where x_1 is the horizontal distance traveled. After they leave the plates they undergo additional deflection y_2, given by

$$y_2 = u_y t_2 = at_1\left(\frac{x_2}{u_x}\right) = \frac{e\mathcal{E}}{m}\left(\frac{x_1}{u_x}\right)\left(\frac{x_2}{u_x}\right) = \frac{e\mathcal{E}}{m}\frac{x_1 x_2}{u_x^2} \qquad\qquad \textbf{3-6}$$

where x_2 is the horizontal distance traveled beyond the deflection plates. The total deflection $(y_1 + y_2)$ is proportional to e/m. Combining Equations 3-4, 3-5, and 3-6 and noting that $u = u_x$ for the undeflected beam, we have

$$y_1 + y_2 = \frac{e}{m}\left(\frac{B^2}{\mathcal{E}}\right)\left(\frac{x_1^2}{2} + x_1 x_2\right) \qquad\qquad \textbf{3-7}$$

Note the "direct" character of the measurement. Thomson needed only a voltmeter, an ammeter, and a measuring rod to determine e/m. It is also interesting to note that his original values of e/m from his first method, about 2×10^{11} C/kg, were closer to the present value of 1.76×10^{11} C/kg than those from his second method, 0.7×10^{11} C/kg. The inaccuracy of the results obtained from the second method was due to his having neglected the magnetic field outside the region of the deflecting plates. Despite this inaccuracy, however, the second method had the advantage of reproducibility and is considered the superior experiment.

Thomson's technique of controlling the direction of the electron beam with "crossed" electric and magnetic fields was subsequently applied in the development of cathode-ray tubes used in oscilloscopes and the picture tubes of television receivers.

Thomson repeated the experiment with different gases in the tube and different metals for cathodes and always obtained the same value of e/m within his experimental accuracy, thus showing that these particles were common to all metals. The agreement of these results with Zeeman's led to the unmistakable conclusion that these particles—called *corpuscles* by Thomson and later called *electrons* by Lorentz—having one unit of negative charge e and about 2000 times less mass than the lightest known atom, were constituent in all atoms.

QUESTIONS

1. One advantage of Thomson's evidence over others' (such as Faraday's or Zeeman's) was its directness. Another was that it was not just a statistical inference. How is it shown in the Thomson experiment that e/m is the same for a large number of particles?

2. Thomson noted that his values for e/m were about 2000 times larger than those for the lightest known ion, that of hydrogen. Could he distinguish from his data between the possibility that this was a result of the electron having either a greater charge or smaller mass than the hydrogen ion?

The Mass Spectrometer   One of several devices currently used to measure the charge-to-mass ratio q/m of charged atoms and molecules is the mass spectrometer. The mass spectrometer is used to find the charge-to-mass ratio of ions of known charge by measuring the radius of their circular orbits in a uniform magnetic field.

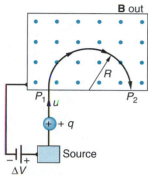

B out

P_1 u

R

P_2

$+ q$

Source

ΔV

Fig. 3-3 Schematic drawing of a mass spectrometer. Ions from an ion source are accelerated through a potential difference ΔV and enter a uniform magnetic field. The magnetic field is directed out of the plane of the page as indicated by the dots. The ions are bent into circular arcs and strike a photographic plate or exit through an aperture to an ion detector at P_2. The radius of the circle is proportional to the mass of the ion.

Equation 3-2 gives the radius of R for the circular orbit of a particle of mass m and charge q moving with speed u in a magnetic field B that is perpendicular to the velocity of the particle. Figure 3-3 shows a simple schematic drawing of a mass spectrometer. Ions from an ion source are accelerated by an electric field and enter a uniform magnetic field produced by an electromagnet. If the ions start from rest and move through a potential drop ΔV, their kinetic energy when they enter the magnetic field equals their loss in potential energy, $q\Delta V$:

$$\tfrac{1}{2} mu^2 = q\Delta V \qquad\qquad \textbf{3-8}$$

The ions move in a semicircle of radius R given by Equation 3-2 and strike a photographic plate or exit through a narrow aperture to an ion detector at point P_2, a distance $2R$ from the point where they enter the magnet. The speed u can be eliminated from Equations 3-2 and 3-8 to find q/m in terms of ΔV, B, and R. The result is

$$\frac{q}{m} = \frac{2\Delta V}{B^2 R^2} \qquad\qquad \textbf{3-9}$$

In the original mass spectrometer, invented by F. W. Aston (who was a student of Thomson's) in 1919, mass differences could be measured to a precision of about 1 part in 10,000. The precision has been improved by introducing a velocity selector between the ion source and the magnet, which makes it possible to limit the range of velocities of the incoming ions and to determine the velocities of the ions more accurately. Today, values of atomic and molecular masses are typically measured with mass spectrometers to precisions of better than 1 part in 10^9. The method normally used is to measure the differences in R between standard masses and the ions of interest, as illustrated in the following example.

EXAMPLE 3-1 Mass Spectrometer Measurements A ^{58}Ni ion of charge $+e$ and mass 9.62×10^{-26} kg is accelerated through a potential difference of 3 kV and deflected in a magnetic field of 0.12 T. (*a*) Find the radius of curvature of the orbit of the ion. (*b*) Find the difference in the radii for curvature of ^{58}Ni ions and ^{60}Ni ions. (Assume that the mass ratio is 58/60.)

Solution

1. For question (*a*), the radius of the ion's orbit is given by rearranging Equation 3-9:

$$R^2 = \frac{2m\Delta V}{qB^2}$$

2. Noting that in this case $q = +e$ and substituting the values yield:

$$R^2 = \frac{(2)(9.62 \times 10^{-26}\,\text{kg})(3000\,\text{V})}{(1.60 \times 10^{-19}\,\text{C})(0.12\,\text{T})^2}$$

$$= 0.251\,\text{m}^2$$
$$R = \sqrt{0.251\,\text{m}^2} = 0.501\,\text{m}$$

3. For question (b), note that according to Equation 3-9 an ion's orbit radius is proportional to the square root of its mass. For identical values of q, V, and B, if R_1 is the radius for the ^{58}Ni ion and R_2 is the radius for the ^{60}Ni ion, their ratio is:

$$\frac{R_2}{R_1} = \sqrt{\frac{M_2}{M_1}}$$
$$= \sqrt{\frac{60}{58}}$$
$$= 1.017$$

4. Substituting the value for the ^{58}Ni radius computed above gives:

$$R_2 = 1.017\, R_1$$
$$= (1.017)(0.501 \text{ m})$$
$$= 0.510 \text{ m}$$

5. The difference ΔR in the radii is then:

$$\Delta R = R_2 - R_1$$
$$= 0.510 \text{ m} - 0.501 \text{ m}$$
$$= 0.009 \text{ m} = 9 \text{ mm}$$

Measuring the Electric Charge: Millikan's Experiment

The fact that Thomson's e/m measurements always yielded the same results regardless of the materials used for the cathodes or the kind of gas in the tube was a persuasive argument that the electrons all carried one unit e of negative electric charge. Thomson initiated a series of experiments to determine the value of e. The first of these experiments, which turned out to be very difficult to do with high precision, was carried out by his student J. S. E. Townsend. The idea was simple: a small (but visible) cloud of identical water droplets, each carrying a single charge e, was observed to drift downward in response to the gravitational force. The total charge on the cloud $Q = Ne$ was measured, as was the mass of the cloud and the radius of a single drop. Finding the radius allowed calculation of N, the total number of drops in the cloud, and, hence, the value of e.

The accuracy of Thomson's method was limited by the uncertain rate of evaporation of the cloud, and the assumption that each droplet contained a single charge could not be verified. R. A. Millikan tried to eliminate the evaporation problem by using a field strong enough to hold the top surface of the cloud stationary so that he could observe the rate of evaporation, and correct for it. That, too, turned out to be very difficult, but then he made a discovery of enormous importance, one that allowed him to measure directly the charge of a single electron! Millikan described his discovery in the following words:

> It was not found possible to balance the cloud as had been originally planned, but it was found possible to do something much better: namely, to hold individual charged drops suspended by the field for periods varying from 30 to 60 seconds. I have never actually timed drops which lasted more than 45 seconds,

although I have several times observed drops which in my judgement lasted considerably longer than this. The drops which it was found possible to balance by an electric field always carried multiple charges, and the difficulty experienced in balancing such drops was less than had been anticipated.[6]

The discovery that he could see individual droplets and that droplets suspended in a vertical electric field sometimes suddenly moved upward or downward, evidently because they had picked up a positive or negative ion, led to the possibility of observing the charge of a single ion. In 1909, Millikan began a series of experiments which not only showed that charges occurred in integer multiples of an elementary unit e, but measured the value of e to about 1 part in 1000. To eliminate evaporation, he used oil drops sprayed into dry air between the plates of a capacitor. These drops were already charged by the spraying process, i.e., friction in the spray nozzle, and during the course of observation they picked up or lost additional charges. By switching the field between the plates, a drop could be moved up or down and observed for several hours. When the charge on a drop changed, the velocity of the drop with the field "on" changed. Assuming only that the terminal velocity of the drop was proportional to the force acting on it (this assumption was carefully checked experimentally), Millikan's experiment gave conclusive evidence that charges always occur in multiples of a fundamental unit e, whose value he determined to be 1.601×10^{-19} C. The currently accepted value is, to three decimal places, 1.602×10^{-19} C. The expanded discussion of Millikan's experiment on the home page includes the value to eight places.

More

Millikan's Oil-Drop Experiment,[7] one of the few truly crucial experiments in physics, is also remarkable for its simple directness and its excellent precision. The discussion of Millikan's experiment on our home page includes a portion of the data on drop number 6, one of several thousand oil drops he used in determining the value of the electron's charge.   See also Equations 3-10 through 3-18 and Figures 3-4 and 3-5 on the home page: www.whfreeman.com/modphysics4e

3-2 Blackbody Radiation

The first clue to the quantum nature of radiation came from the study of thermal radiation emitted by opaque bodies. When radiation falls on an opaque body, part of it is reflected and the rest absorbed. Light-colored bodies reflect most of the visible radiation incident on them, whereas dark bodies absorb most of it. The absorption part of the process can be described briefly as follows. The radiation absorbed by the body increases the kinetic energy of the constituent atoms which oscillate about their equilibrium positions. Recalling that the average translational kinetic energy of the atoms determines the temperature of the body, the absorbed energy causes the temperature to rise. However, the atoms contain charges (the electrons) and they are accelerated by the oscillations. Consequently, as required by electromagnetic theory, the atoms emit electromagnetic radiation which reduces the kinetic energy of the oscillations and tends to reduce the temperature. When the rate of absorption equals that of emission, the temperature is constant and we say that the body is in thermal equilibrium with its surroundings. A good absorber of radiation is therefore also a good emitter.

The electromagnetic radiation emitted under these circumstances is called *thermal radiation*. At ordinary temperatures (below about 600°C) the thermal radiation emitted by a body is not visible; most of the energy is concentrated in wavelengths much longer than those of visible light. As a body is heated, the quantity of thermal radiation emitted increases, and the energy radiated extends to shorter and shorter wavelengths. At about 600–700°C there is enough energy in the visible spectrum so that the body glows and becomes a dull red, and at higher temperatures it becomes bright-red or even "white-hot."

A body that absorbs *all* radiation incident on it is called an *ideal blackbody*. In 1879 Josef Stefan found an empirical relation between the power per unit area radiated by a blackbody and the temperature:

$$R = \sigma T^4 \qquad\qquad\qquad \textbf{3-19}$$

where R is the power radiated per unit area, T is the absolute temperature, and $\sigma = 5.6703 \times 10^{-8}$ W/m²K⁴ is a constant called Stefan's constant. This result was also derived on the basis of classical thermodynamics by Ludwig Boltzmann about five years later, and Equation 3-19 is now called the Stefan-Boltzmann law. Note that the power per unit area radiated by a blackbody depends only on the temperature, and not on any other characteristic of the object, such as its color or the material of which it is composed. Note, too, that R tells us the *rate* at which energy is emitted by the object. For example, doubling the absolute temperature of an object increases the energy flow out of the object by a factor of $2^4 = 16$. An object at room temperature (300 K) will double the rate at which it radiates energy as a result of a temperature increase of only 57°C. Thus, the Stefan-Boltzmann law has an enormous effect on the establishment of thermal equilibrium in physical systems.

Objects that are not blackbodies radiate energy per unit area at a rate less than that of a blackbody at the same temperature. The rate does depend on properties in addition to the temperature, such as color and composition of the surface. The effects of those dependencies are combined into a factor called the *emissivity* ϵ which multiplies the right side of Equation 3-19. The values of ϵ, which is itself temperature dependent, are always less than unity.

Like the total radiated power *R*, the *spectral distribution* of the radiation emitted by a blackbody is found empirically to depend *only* on the absolute temperature *T*. The spectral distribution is determined experimentally as illustrated schematically in Figure 3-6. Let $R(\lambda)d\lambda$ be the power emitted per unit area with wavelength between

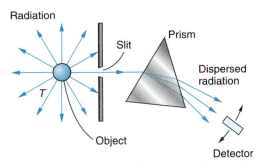

Fig. 3-6 Radiation emitted by the object at temperature *T* that passes through the slit is dispersed according to its wavelength. The prism shown would be an appropriate device for that part of the emitted radiation in the visible region. In other spectral regions other types of devices or wavelength-sensitive detectors would be used.

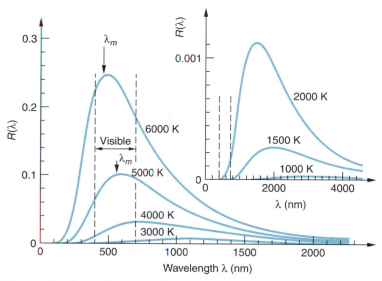

Fig. 3-7 Spectral distribution function $R(\lambda)$ measured at different temperatures. The $R(\lambda)$ axis is in arbitrary units for comparison only. Notice the range in λ of the visible spectrum. The sun emits radiation very close to that of a blackbody at 5800 K. λ_m is indicated for the 5000-K and 6000-K curves.

λ and $\lambda + d\lambda$. Figure 3-7 shows the measured spectral distribution function $R(\lambda)$ versus λ for several values of T ranging from 1000 K to 6000 K.

The $R(\lambda)$ versus λ curves in Figure 3-7 are quite remarkable in several respects. One is that the wavelength at which the distribution is maximum varies inversely with the temperature:

$$\lambda_m \propto \frac{1}{T}$$

or

$$\lambda_m T = \text{constant} = 2.898 \times 10^{-3} \text{ mK} \qquad \textbf{3-20}$$

This result is known as Wien's displacement law. It was obtained by Wilhelm Wien in 1893. Examples 3-2 and 3-3 illustrate its application.

EXAMPLE 3-2 **How Big Is a Star?** Measurement of the wavelength at which the spectral distribution $R(\lambda)$ from a certain star is maximum indicates that the star's surface temperature is 3000 K. If that star is also found to radiate 100 times the power radiated by the sun $P_\odot$, how big is the star? (The symbol $\odot$ = sun.) The sun's surface temperature is found to be 5800 K.

Solution

Assuming the sun and the star both radiate as blackbodies (astronomers nearly always make this assumption, based on, among other things, the fact that the solar spectrum is nearly that of a perfect blackbody), their surface temperatures have been determined from Equation 3-20 to be 5800 K and 3000 K, respectively. Measurement also indicates that $P_{\text{star}} = 100\,P_\odot$. Thus, from Equation 3-19 we have that

$$R_{star} = \frac{P_{star}}{(area)_{star}} = \frac{100 P_\odot}{4\pi r_{star}^2} = \sigma T_{star}^4$$

and

$$R_\odot = \frac{P_\odot}{(area)_\odot} = \frac{P_\odot}{4\pi r_\odot^2} = \sigma T_\odot^4$$

Thus, we have

$$r_{star}^2 = 100 r_\odot^2 \left(\frac{T_\odot}{T_{star}}\right)^4$$

$$r_{star} = 10 r_\odot \left(\frac{T_\odot}{T_{star}}\right)^2 = 10 \left(\frac{5800}{3000}\right)^2 r_\odot$$

$$r_{star} = 37.4 r_\odot$$

Since $r_\odot = 6.96 \times 10^8$ m, this star has a radius of about 2.6×10^{10} m, or about half of the radius of the orbit of Mercury.

Rayleigh-Jeans Equation

The calculation of the distribution function $R(\lambda)$ involves the calculation of the energy density of electromagnetic waves in a cavity. Materials such as black velvet or lampblack come close to being ideal blackbodies, but the best practical realization of an ideal blackbody is a small hole leading into a cavity (such as a keyhole in a closet door; see Figure 3-8). Radiation incident on the hole has little chance of being reflected back out of the hole before it is absorbed by the walls of the cavity. The power radiated *out* of the hole is proportional to the total energy density U (energy per unit volume) of the radiation in the cavity. The proportionality constant can be shown to be $c/4$, where c is the speed of light:[9]

$$R = \tfrac{1}{4} cU \qquad\qquad \textbf{3-21}$$

Similarly, the spectral distribution of the power emitted from the hole is proportional to the spectral distribution of the energy density in the cavity. If $u(\lambda)d\lambda$ is the fraction

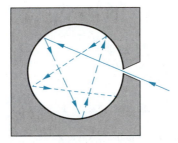

Fig. 3-8 A small hole in the wall of a cavity approximating an ideal blackbody. Radiation entering the hole has little chance of leaving before it is completely absorbed within the cavity.

of the energy per unit volume in the cavity in the range $d\lambda$, then $u(\lambda)$ and $R(\lambda)$ are related by

$$R(\lambda) = \tfrac{1}{4}cu(\lambda) \qquad\qquad \textbf{3-22}$$

The energy density distribution function $u(\lambda)$ can be calculated from classical physics in a straightforward way. The method involves finding the number of modes of oscillation of the electromagnetic field in the cavity with wavelengths in the interval $d\lambda$ and multiplying by the average energy per mode. We shall not go into the details of the calculation here. The result is that the number of modes of oscillation per unit volume, $n(\lambda)$, is independent of the shape of the cavity and is given by

$$n(\lambda) = 8\pi\lambda^{-4} \qquad\qquad \textbf{3-23}$$

According to classical kinetic theory, the average energy per mode of oscillation is kT, the same as for a one-dimensional harmonic oscillator, where k is the Boltzmann constant. Classical theory thus predicts for the energy density spectral distribution function

$$u(\lambda) = kTn(\lambda) = 8\pi kT\lambda^{-4} \qquad\qquad \textbf{3-24}$$

This prediction, initially derived by Lord Rayleigh,[10] is called the *Rayleigh-Jeans law,* and is illustrated in Figure 3-9.

At very long wavelengths the Rayleigh-Jeans law agrees with the experimentally determined spectral distribution, but at short wavelengths this law predicts that $u(\lambda)$ becomes large, approaching infinity as $\lambda \rightarrow 0$, whereas experiment shows (see Figures 3-7 and 3-9) that the distribution actually approaches zero as $\lambda \rightarrow 0$. This enormous disagreement between the experimental measurement of $u(\lambda)$ and the prediction of the fundamental laws of classical physics at short wavelengths was called the *ultraviolet catastrophe.* The word *catastrophe* was not used lightly: Equation 3-24 implies that

$$\int_0^\infty u(\lambda)d\lambda \longrightarrow \infty \qquad\qquad \textbf{3-25}$$

i.e., every object would have an infinite energy density.

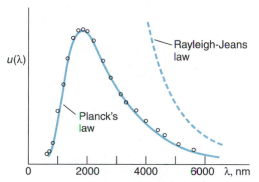

Fig. 3-9 Comparison of Planck's law and the Rayleigh-Jeans law with experimental data at $T = 1600$ K obtained by W. W. Coblentz in about 1915. The $u(\lambda)$ axis is linear. [*Adapted from F. K. Richtmyer, E. H. Kennnard, and J. N. Cooper,* Introduction to Modern Physics, *6th ed. (New York: McGraw-Hill Book Company, 1969), by permission.*]

Planck's Law

In 1900 the German physicist Max Planck[11] announced that by making somewhat strange assumptions, he could derive a function $u(\lambda)$ that agreed with the experimental data. He first found an empirical function that fit the data, and then searched for a way to modify the usual calculation so as to predict his empirical formula. We can see the type of modification needed if we note that, for any cavity, the shorter the wavelength, the more standing waves (modes) will be possible. As $\lambda \to 0$ the number of modes of oscillation approaches infinity, as evidenced in Equation 3-23. In order for the energy density distribution function $u(\lambda)$ to approach zero, we expect the average energy per mode to depend on the wavelength λ and approach zero as λ approaches zero, rather than be equal to the value kT predicted by classical theory.

Parenthetically, we should observe that those working on the ultraviolet catastrophe at the time—and there were many besides Planck—had no a priori way of knowing whether the number of modes $n(\lambda)$ or the average energy per mode kT (or both) was the source of the problem. Both were correct classically. Many attempts were made to rederive each so as to solve the problem. It was the average energy per mode (that is, kinetic theory) that turned out to be at fault.

Classically, the electromagnetic waves in the cavity are produced by accelerated electric charges in the walls of the cavity vibrating like simple harmonic oscillators. Recall that the radiation emitted by such an oscillator has the same frequency as the oscillator itself. The average energy for a one-dimensional simple harmonic oscillator is calculated classically from the energy distribution function, which in turn is found from the Maxwell-Boltzmann distribution function. The energy distribution function has the form (see Chapter 8)

$$f(E) = Ae^{-E/kT} \qquad \textbf{3-26}$$

where A is a constant and $f(E)$ is the fraction of the oscillators with energy equal to E. The average energy is then found, as is any weighted average, from

$$\overline{E} = \int_0^\infty Ef(E)dE = \int_0^\infty EAe^{-E/kT}dE \qquad \textbf{3-27}$$

with the result $\overline{E} = kT$, as was used by Rayleigh and others.

Planck found that he could derive his empirical function by calculating the average energy $\overline{E}$ assuming the energy of the oscillating charges, and hence the radiation that they emitted, was a discrete variable, i.e., that it could take on only the values 0, ϵ, 2ϵ, . . . , $n\epsilon$ where n is an integer; and further, that ϵ was proportional to the frequency of the oscillators and, thus, the radiation. Planck therefore wrote the energy as

$$E_n = n\epsilon = nhf \qquad n = 0, 1, 2, \ldots \qquad \textbf{3-28}$$

where h is a constant now called *Planck's constant*. The Maxwell-Boltzmann distribution law (Equation 3-26) then becomes

$$f_n = Ae^{-E_n/kT} = Ae^{-n\epsilon/kT} \qquad \textbf{3-29}$$

where A is determined by the normalization condition that the sum of all fractions f_n must, of course, be 1, i.e.,

$$\sum_{n=0}^{\infty} f_n = A \sum_{n=0}^{\infty} e^{-n\epsilon/kT} = 1 \qquad \textbf{3-30}$$

The average energy of an oscillator is then given by the discrete-sum equivalent of Equation 3-27,

$$\overline{E} = \sum_{n=0}^{\infty} E_n f_n = \sum_{n=0}^{\infty} E_n A e^{-E_n/kT} \qquad \textbf{3-31}$$

Calculating the sums in Equations 3-30 and 3-31 (see Problem 3-58) yields the result:

$$\overline{E} = \frac{\epsilon}{e^{\epsilon/kT} - 1} = \frac{hf}{e^{hf/kT} - 1} = \frac{hc/\lambda}{e^{hc/\lambda kT} - 1} \qquad \textbf{3-32}$$

Multiplying this result by the number of oscillators per unit volume in the interval $d\lambda$ given by Equation 3-23, we obtain for the energy density distribution function of the radiation in the cavity:

$$u(\lambda) = \frac{8\pi hc\lambda^{-5}}{e^{hc/\lambda kT} - 1} \qquad \textbf{3-33}$$

This function, called *Planck's law,* is sketched in Figure 3-9. It is clear from the figure that the result fits the data quite well.

For very large λ, the exponential in Equation 3-33 can be expanded using $e^x \approx 1 + x + \ldots$ for $x \ll 1$ (see Appendix B4), where $x = hc/\lambda kT$. Then

$$e^{hc/\lambda kT} - 1 \approx \frac{hc}{\lambda kT}$$

and

$$u(\lambda) \longrightarrow 8\pi\lambda^{-4} kT$$

which is the Rayleigh-Jeans formula. For short wavelengths, we can neglect the 1 in the denominator of Equation 3-33, and we have

$$u(\lambda) \longrightarrow 8\pi hc\lambda^{-5} e^{-hc/\lambda kT} \longrightarrow 0$$

as $\lambda \to 0$. The value of the constant in Wien's displacement law also follows from Planck's law, as you will show in Problem 3-23.

The value of Planck's constant, h, can be determined by fitting the function given by Equation 3-33 to the experimental data, although direct measurement (see Section 3-3) is better, but more difficult. The presently accepted value is

$$\begin{aligned} h &= 6.626 \times 10^{-34}\,\text{J}\cdot\text{s} \\ &= 4.136 \times 10^{-15}\,\text{eV}\cdot\text{s} \end{aligned} \qquad \textbf{3-34}$$

Planck tried at length to reconcile his treatment with classical physics but was unable to do so. The fundamental importance of the quantization assumption implied by Equation 3-28 was suspected by Planck and others but was not generally appreciated

until 1905. In that year Einstein applied the same ideas to explain the photoelectric effect and suggested that, rather than being merely a mysterious property of oscillators in the cavity walls and blackbody radiation, quantization is a fundamental characteristic of light energy.

EXAMPLE 3-3 Peak of the Solar Spectrum The surface temperature of the sun is about 5800 K, and measurements of the sun's spectral distribution show that it radiates very nearly like a blackbody, deviating mainly at very short wavelengths. Assuming that the sun radiates like a perfect blackbody, at what wavelength does the peak of the solar spectrum occur?

Solution

1. The wavelength at the peak, or maximum intensity, of a perfect blackbody spectrum is given by Equation 3-20:

$$\lambda_m T = 2.898 \times 10^{-3} \text{ m} \cdot \text{K}$$

2. Rearranging and substituting the sun's surface temperature yields:

$$\lambda_m = (2.898 \times 10^{-3} \text{ m} \cdot \text{K})/T = \frac{2.898 \times 10^{-3} \text{ m} \cdot \text{K}}{5800 \text{ K}}$$

$$= \frac{2.898 \times 10^{6} \text{ nm} \cdot \text{K}}{5800 \text{ K}} = 499.7 \text{ nm}$$

where

$$1 \text{ nm} = 10^{-9} \text{ m}$$

Remarks: This value is near the middle of the visible spectrum.

The electromagnetic spectrum emitted by incandescent bulbs is a common example of blackbody radiation, the amount of visible light being dependent on the temperature of the filament. Another application is the pyrometer, a device that measures the temperature of a glowing object, such as molten metal in a steel mill.

EXAMPLE 3-4 Average Energy of an Oscillator What is the average energy $\overline{E}$ for an oscillator that has a frequency given by $hf = kT$ according to Planck's calculation?

Solution
From Equation 3-32 with $\epsilon = hf = kT$, we have

$$\overline{E} = \frac{\epsilon}{e^{\epsilon/kT} - 1} = \frac{kT}{e^1 - 1} = 0.582 \, kT$$

Recall that, according to classical theory, $\overline{E} = kT$ regardless of the frequency.

EXAMPLE 3-5 Stefan-Boltzmann from Planck Show that the total energy density in a blackbody cavity is proportional to T^4 in accordance with the Stefan-Boltzmann law.

Solution

The total energy density is obtained from the distribution function (Equation 3-33) by integrating over all wavelengths:

$$U = \int_0^\infty u(\lambda)d\lambda = \int_0^\infty \frac{8\pi hc\lambda^{-5}}{e^{hc/\lambda kT} - 1} d\lambda$$

Define the dimensionless variable $x = hc/\lambda kT$. Then $dx = -hc\, d\lambda/\lambda^2 kT$ or $d\lambda = -\lambda^2(kT/hc)dx$. Then

$$U = -\int_0^\infty \frac{8\pi hc\lambda^{-3}}{e^x - 1}\left(\frac{kT}{hc}\right) dx$$

$$= 8\pi hc\left(\frac{kT}{hc}\right)^4 \int_0^\infty \frac{x^3}{e^x - 1} dx$$

Since the integral is now dimensionless, this shows that U is proportional to T^4. The value of the integral can be obtained from tables; it is $\pi^4/15$. Then $U = (8\pi^5 k^4/15\, h^3 c^3) T^4$. This result can be combined with Equations 3-19 and 3-21 to express Stefan's constant σ in terms of π, k, h, and c (see Problem 3-13).

A dramatic example of an application of Planck's law on the current frontier of physics is in tests of the predictions of the so-called Big Bang theory of the formation and present expansion of the universe. Current cosmological theory suggests that the universe originated in an extremely high-temperature explosion, one consequence of which was to fill the infant universe with radiation whose spectral distribution must surely have been that of a blackbody. Since that time, the universe has expanded to its present size and cooled to its present temperature T_{now}. However, it

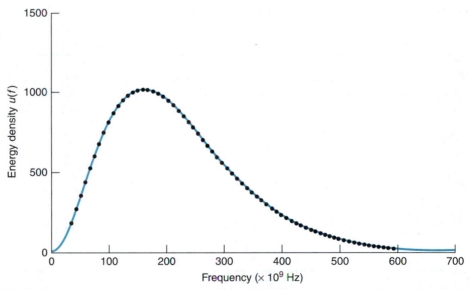

Fig. 3-10 The energy density spectral distribution of the cosmic microwave background radiation. The solid line is Planck's law with $T = 2.735$ K. The measurements were made by the COBE satellite.

should still be filled with radiation whose spectral distribution should be that characteristic of a blackbody at T_{now}.

In 1965, Arno Penzias and Robert Wilson discovered radiation of wavelength 7.35 cm reaching Earth with the same intensity from all directions in space. It was soon recognized that this radiation could be a remnant of the Big Bang fireball, and measurements were subsequently made at other wavelengths in order to construct an experimental energy density $u(\lambda)$ versus λ graph. The most recent data, collected by the Cosmic Background Explorer (COBE) satellite and shown in Figure 3-10, fit the Planck law for a blackbody at 2.735 K. The excellent agreement of the data with Planck's equation, indeed, the best fit that has ever been measured, is considered to be very strong support for the Big Bang theory (see Chapter 14).

3-3 The Photoelectric Effect

It is one of the ironies in the history of science that in the famous experiment of Heinrich Hertz[12] in 1887 in which he produced and detected electromagnetic waves, thus confirming James Clerk Maxwell's wave theory of light, he also discovered the photoelectric effect that led directly to the particle description of light.

Hertz was using a spark gap in a tuned circuit to generate the waves and another similar circuit to detect them. He noticed accidentally that when the light from the generating gap was shielded from the receiving gap, the receiving gap had to be made shorter to allow the sparks to pass. Light from any spark that fell on the terminals of the gap facilitated the passage of the sparks. He described the discovery with these words:

> In a series of experiments on the effects of resonance between very rapid electric oscillations that I carried out and recently published, two electric sparks were produced by the same discharge of an induction coil, and therefore simultaneously. One of these sparks, spark *A,* was the discharge spark of the induction coil, and served to excite the primary oscillation. The second, spark *B,* belonged to the induced or secondary oscillation. I occasionally enclosed spark *B* in a dark case so as to make observations more easily, and in so doing I observed that the maximum spark length became decidedly smaller inside the case than it was before.[13]

Albert A. Michelson, Albert Einstein, and Robert A. Millikan at a meeting in Pasadena, California, in 1931. [*AP/Wide World Photos.*]

The unexpected discovery of the photoelectric effect annoyed Hertz because it interfered with his primary research, but he recognized its importance immediately and interrupted his other work for six months in order to study it in detail. His results, published later that year, were then extended by others. It was found that negative particles were emitted from a clean surface when exposed to light. P. Lenard in 1900 deflected them in a magnetic field and found that they had a charge-to-mass ratio of the same magnitude as that measured by Thomson for cathode rays: the particles being emitted were electrons.

Figure 3-11 shows a schematic diagram of the basic apparatus used by Lenard. When light is incident on a clean metal surface (cathode C), electrons are emitted. If some of these electrons that reach the anode A pass through the small hole, a current results in the external electrometer circuit connected to α. The number of the emitted electrons reaching the anode can be increased or decreased by making the anode positive or negative with respect to the cathode. Letting V be the potential difference between cathode and anode, Figure 3-12a shows the current versus V for two values of the intensity of light incident on the cathode. If cathode C and anode A in Fig. 3-11 are different metals, V must be corrected for the contact potential (see Chap. 10). When V is positive, the electrons are attracted to the anode. At sufficiently large V all the emitted electrons reach the anode and the current reaches its maximum value. Lenard observed that the maximum current is proportional to the light intensity, an expected result since doubling the energy per unit time incident on the cathode should double the number of electrons emitted. Intensities too low to provide electrons with the energy necessary to escape from the metal should result in no emission of electrons. However, in contrast with the classical expectation, there was no minimum intensity below which the current was absent. When V is negative, the electrons are repelled from the anode. Then, only electrons with initial kinetic energy $\frac{1}{2}mv^2$ greater than $e|V|$ can reach the anode. From Figure 3-12a we see that if V is less than $-V_0$ no electrons reach the anode. The potential V_0 is called the *stopping potential*. It is related to the maximum kinetic energy of the emitted electrons by

$$(\tfrac{1}{2}mv^2)_{max} = eV_0 \qquad\qquad \textbf{3-35}$$

The experimental result, illustrated by Figure 3-12a, that V_0 is independent of the incident light intensity was surprising. Apparently, increasing the rate of energy

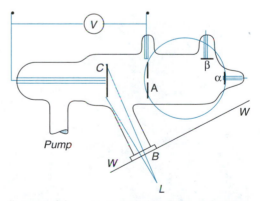

Fig. 3-11 Schematic diagram of the apparatus used by P. Lenard to demonstrate the photoelectric effect and to show that the particles emitted in the process were electrons. Light from the source L strikes the cathode C. Photoelectrons going through the hole in anode A are recorded by the electrometer connected to α. A magnetic field, indicated by the circular pole piece, could deflect the particles to an electrometer connected to β, enabling the establishment of the sign of their charge and their q/m ratio. [*P. Lenard*, Annalen der Physik, *2, 359 (1900)*.]

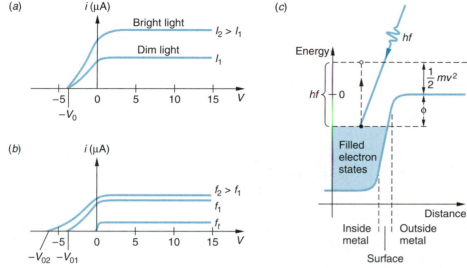

Fig. 3-12 (*a*) Photocurrent *i* versus anode voltage *V* for light of frequency *f* with two intensities I_1 and I_2, where $I_2 > I_1$. The stopping voltage V_0 is the same for both. (*b*) For constant *I*, Einstein's explanation of the photoelectric effect indicates that the magnitude of the stopping voltage should be greater for f_2 than f_1, as observed, and that there should be a threshold frequency f_t below which no photoelectrons were seen, also in agreement with experiment. (*c*) Electron potential energy curve across the metal surface. An electron with the highest energy in the metal absorbs a photon of energy *hf*. Conservation of energy requires that its kinetic energy after leaving the surface will be $hf - \phi$.

falling on the cathode does not increase the maximum kinetic energy of the emitted electrons, contrary to classical expectations. In 1905, Einstein offered an explanation of this result in a remarkable paper in the same volume of *Annalen der Physik* that contained his papers on special relativity and Brownian motion.

Einstein assumed that <u>energy quantization used by Planck in the blackbody problem was a universal characteristic of light</u>. Rather than being distributed evenly in the space through which it is propagated, light energy consists of discrete quanta of energy *hf*. When one of these quanta, called a *photon*, penetrates the surface of the cathode, all of its energy may be given completely to an electron. If ϕ is the energy necessary to remove an electron from the surface (ϕ is called the *work function* and is a characteristic of the metal), the maximum kinetic energy of the electrons leaving the surface will be $hf - \phi$ as a consequence of energy conservation; see Figure 3-12*c*. (Some electrons will have less than this amount because of energy lost in traversing the metal.) Thus the stopping potential V_0 should be given by

$$eV_0 = (\tfrac{1}{2}mv^2)_{\text{max}} = hf - \phi \qquad \textbf{3-36}$$

Equation 3-36 is referred to as the photoelectric-effect equation. As Einstein noted,

> If the derived formula is correct, then V_0, when represented in cartesian coordinates as a function of the frequency of the incident light, must be a straight line whose slope is independent of the nature of the emitting substance.[14]

As can be seen from Equation 3-36, the slope of V_0 versus *f* should equal *h/e*. At the time of this prediction, there was no evidence that Planck's constant had anything to do with the photoelectric effect. There was also no evidence for the dependence of

Among the many applications of the photoelectric effect is the photomultiplier, a device for enabling the accurate measurement of the energy of the light absorbed by the photosensitive surface. The SNO neutrino detector (see Figure 13-7) uses nearly 10,000 photomultipliers.

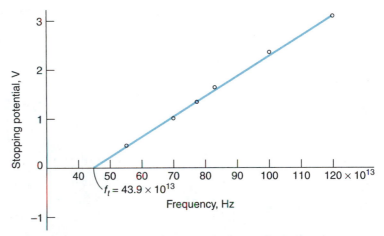

Fig. 3-13 Millikan's data for stopping potential versus frequency for the photoelectric effect. The data fall on a straight line of slope h/e, as predicted by Einstein a decade before the experiment. The intercept on the stopping potential axis is $-\phi/e$. [*R. A. Millikan, Physical Review, 7, 362 (1915).*]

the stopping potential V_0 on frequency. Careful experiments by Millikan, reported in 1914 and in more detail in 1916, showed that Equation 3-36 was correct, and measurements of h from it agreed with the value obtained by Planck. A plot taken from this work is shown in Figure 3-13.

The minimum, or threshold, frequency for photoelectric effect, labeled f_t in this plot and in Figure 3-12*b*, and the corresponding threshold wavelength λ_t are related to the work function ϕ by setting $V_0 = 0$ in Equation 3-36:

$$\phi = hf_t = \frac{hc}{\lambda_t} \qquad \textbf{3-37}$$

Photons of frequency lower than f_t (and therefore having wavelengths greater than λ_t) do not have enough energy to eject an electron from the metal. Work functions for metals are typically on the order of a few electron volts. The work functions for several elements are given in Table 3-1.

EXAMPLE 3-6 Photoelectric Effect in Potassium The threshold wavelength of potassium is 558 nm. What is the work function for potassium? What is the stopping potential when light of wavelength 400 nm is used?

Solution

1. Both questions can be answered with the aid of Equation 3-36:

$$eV_0 = (\tfrac{1}{2}mv^2)_{\text{max}} = hf - \phi$$

$$V_0 = \frac{hf}{e} - \frac{\phi}{e}$$

2. At the threshold wavelength the photoelectrons have just enough energy to overcome the work function barrier, so $(\tfrac{1}{2}mv^2)_{\text{max}} = 0$, hence $V_0 = 0$, and:

$$\frac{\phi}{e} = \frac{hf_t}{e} = \frac{hc}{e\lambda_t}$$

$$= \frac{1240 \text{ eV} \cdot \text{nm}}{558 \text{ nm}}$$

$$= 2.22 \text{ eV}$$

3. When 400-nm light is used, V_0 is given by Equation 3-36:

$$V_0 = \frac{hc}{e\lambda} - \frac{\phi}{e}$$

$$= \frac{1240 \text{ eV} \cdot \text{nm}}{400 \text{ nm}} - 2.22 \text{ eV}$$

$$= 3.10 \text{ eV} - 2.22 \text{ eV}$$

$$= 0.88 \text{ V}$$

Another interesting feature of the photoelectric effect, which is contrary to classical physics but easily explained by the photon hypothesis, is the lack of any time lag between the turning on of the light source and the appearance of electrons. Classically, the incident energy is distributed uniformly over the illuminated surface; the time required for an area the size of an atom to acquire enough energy to allow the emission of an electron can be calculated from the intensity (power per unit area) of the incident radiation. Experimentally, the incident intensity can be adjusted so that this calculated time lag should be several minutes or even hours. But no time lag is ever observed. The photon explanation of this result is that although the rate at which

TABLE 3-1 Photoelectric work functions	
Element	ϕ (eV)
Na	2.28
C	4.81
Cd	4.07
Al	4.08
Ag	4.73
Pt	6.35
Mg	3.68
Ni	5.01
Se	5.11
Pb	4.14

photons are incident upon the metal is very small when the intensity is low, *each photon has enough energy to eject an electron*, and there is some chance that a photon will be absorbed immediately. The classical calculation gives the correct *average* number of photons absorbed per unit time.

EXAMPLE 3-7 Classical Time Lag Light of wavelength 400 nm and intensity 10^{-2} W/m² is incident on potassium. Estimate the time lag for emission of photoelectrons that would be expected classically.

Solution
According to the previous example, the work function for potassium is 2.22 eV. If we take $r = 10^{-10}$ m as a typical radius of an atom, the total energy falling on the atom in time t is

$$E = (10^{-2} \text{ W/m}^2)(\pi r^2)t = (10^{-2} \text{ W/m}^2)(\pi 10^{-20} \text{ m}^2)t$$
$$= (3.14 \times 10^{-22} \text{ J/s})t$$

Setting this energy equal to 2.22 eV ($= 2.22 \times 1.6 \times 10^{-19}$ J) gives

$$(3.14 \times 10^{-22} \text{ J/s})t = (2.22)(1.6 \times 10^{-19} \text{ J})$$
$$t = 1.13 \times 10^3 \text{ s} = 18.8 \text{ min}$$

According to the classical prediction, no atom would be expected to emit an electron until 18.8 min after the light source was turned on. According to the photon model of light, each photon has enough energy to eject an electron immediately. Because of the low intensity, there are few photons incident per second, so that the chance of any particular atom absorbing a photon and emitting an electron in any given time interval is small. However, there are so many atoms in the cathode that some emit electrons immediately.

EXAMPLE 3-8 Incident Photon Intensity In the previous example, how many photons are incident per second per square meter?

Solution
The energy of each photon is $E = hf = hc/\lambda = (1240 \text{ eV} \cdot \text{nm})/400 \text{ nm} = 3.1$ eV $= (3.1 \text{ eV})(1.6 \times 10^{-19} \text{ J/eV}) = 4.96 \times 10^{-19}$ J. Since the incident intensity is 10^{-2} W/m² $= 10^{-2}$ J/s · m², the number of photons per second per square meter is

$$N = \frac{10^2 \text{ J/s} \cdot \text{m}^2}{4.96 \times 10^{-19} \text{ J/photon}}$$
$$= 2.02 \times 10^{16} \text{ photons/s} \cdot \text{m}^2$$

This is, of course, a lot of photons, not a few; however, the number n per atom at the surface is quite small. $n = 2.02 \times 10^{16}$ photons/s · m² $\times \pi(10^{-10})^2$ m²/atom $= 6.3 \times 10^{-4}$ photons/s · atom, or about 1 photon for every 1000 atoms.

3. How is the result that the maximum photoelectric current is proportional to the intensity explained in the photon model of light?

4. What experimental features of the photoelectric effect can be explained by classical physics? What features cannot?

The photoemission of electrons has developed into a significant technique for investigating the detailed structure of molecules and solids, making possible discoveries far beyond anything that Hertz may have imagined. The use of x-ray sources (see Section 3-4) and precision detectors has made possible precise determination of valence electron configurations in chemical compounds, leading to detailed understanding of chemical bonding and the differences between the bulk and surface atoms of solids. Photoelectric-effect microscopes now in advanced development will show the chemical situation of each element in a specimen, a prospect of intriguing and crucial importance in molecular biology and microelectronics. And they are all based on a discovery that annoyed Hertz—at first.

3-4 X Rays and the Compton Effect

Further evidence of the correctness of the photon concept was furnished by Arthur H. Compton, who measured the scattering of x rays by free electrons and, by his analysis of the data, resolved the last lingering doubts regarding special relativity (see Chapter 1). Before we examine Compton scattering in detail, we shall briefly describe some of the early work with x rays.

X Rays

The German physicist Wilhelm K. Roentgen discovered x rays in 1895 when he was working with a cathode-ray tube. His discovery turned out to be the first significant development in quantum physics. He found that "rays" originating from the point where the cathode rays (electrons) hit the glass tube, or a target within the tube, could pass through materials opaque to light and activate a fluorescent screen or photographic film. He investigated this phenomenon extensively and found that all materials were transparent to these rays to some degree and that the transparency decreased with increasing density. This fact led to the medical use of x rays within months after Roentgen's first paper.[15]

Roentgen was unable to deflect these rays in a magnetic field, nor was he able to observe refraction or the interference phenomena associated with waves. He thus gave the rays the somewhat mysterious name of x rays. Since classical electromagnetic theory predicts that charges will radiate electromagnetic waves when accelerated, it is natural to expect that x rays are electromagnetic waves produced by the acceleration of electrons when they are deflected and stopped by a target. Such radiation is called *bremsstrahlung*, the German for "braking radiation." The slight diffraction broadening of an x-ray beam after passing through slits a few thousandths of a millimeter wide indicated their wavelengths to be of the order of 10^{-10} m $= 0.1$ nm. In 1912, Laue suggested that since the wavelengths of x rays were of the same order of magnitude as the spacing of atoms in a crystal, the regular array of atoms in a crystal might act as a

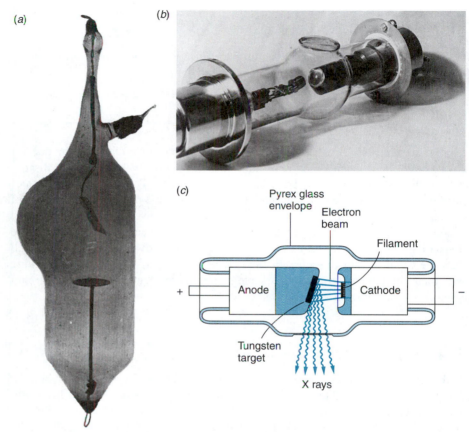

(a) Early x-ray tube. [*Courtesy of Cavendish Laboratory.*] (b) X-ray tubes became more compact over time. This tube was a design typical of the mid-twentieth century. [*Courtesy of Schenectady Museum, Hall of Electrical History, Schenectady, NY.*] (c) Diagram of the components of a modern x-ray tube. Design technology has advanced enormously, enabling very high operating voltages, beam currents, and x-ray intensities, but the essential elements of the tubes remain unchanged.

three-dimensional grating for the diffraction of x rays. Experiment (see Figure 3-14) soon confirmed that x rays are a form of electromagnetic radiation with wavelengths of about 0.01 to 0.10 nm, and that atoms in crystals are arranged in regular arrays.

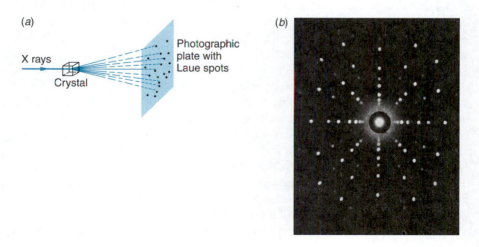

Fig. 3-14 (*a*) Schematic sketch of a Laue experiment. The crystal acts as a three-dimensional grating, which diffracts the x-ray beam and produces a regular array of spots, called a *Laue pattern,* on a photographic plate. (*b*) Modern Laue-type x-ray diffraction pattern using a niobium diboride crystal and 20-kV molybdenum x rays. [*General Electric Company.*]

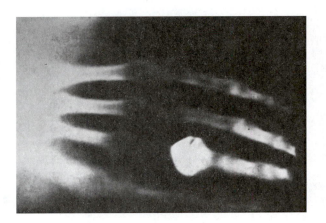

An x ray of Mrs. Roentgen's hand taken by Roentgen shortly after his discovery.

W. L. Bragg, in 1912, proposed a simple and convenient way of analyzing the diffraction of x rays by crystals.[16] He examined the interference of x rays due to scattering from various sets of parallel planes of atoms, now called *Bragg planes*. Two sets of Bragg planes are illustrated in Figure 3-15 for NaCl, which has a simple crystal structure called *face-centered cubic*. Consider Figure 3-16. Waves scattered from the two successive atoms within a plane will be in phase and thus interfere constructively, independent of the wavelength, if the scattering angle equals the incident angle. (This condition is the same as for reflection.) Waves scattered at equal angles from atoms in two different planes will be in phase (constructive interference) if the difference in path length is an integral number of wavelengths. From Figure 3-16 we see that this condition is satisfied if

$$2\,d\sin\theta = m\,\lambda \qquad \text{where} \qquad m = \text{an integer} \qquad \textbf{3-38}$$

Equation 3-38 is called the *Bragg condition*.

Measurements of the spectral distribution of the intensity of x rays as a function of the wavelength using an experimental arrangement such as shown in Figure 3-17 produce the x-ray spectrum and, for classical physics, some surprises. Figure 3-18*a* (page 151) shows two typical x-ray spectra produced by accelerating electrons through two voltages V and bombarding a tungsten target mounted on the anode of the tube. In this figure $I(\lambda)$ is the intensity emitted with the wavelength interval $d\lambda$ at

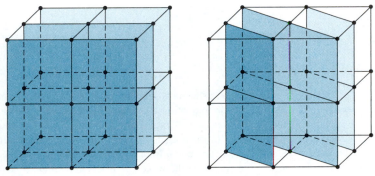

Fig. 3-15 A crystal of NaCl showing two sets of Bragg planes.

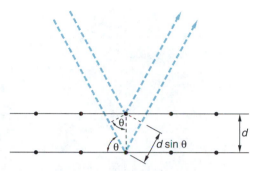

Fig. 3-16 Bragg scattering from two successive planes. The waves from the two atoms shown have a path difference of $2d \sin \theta$. They will be in phase if the Bragg condition $2d \sin \theta = m\lambda$ is met.

each value of λ. Figure 3-18*b* shows the short-wavelength lines produced with a molybdenum target and 35-keV electrons. Three features of the spectra are of immediate interest, only one of which could be explained by classical physics. (1) The spectrum consists of a series of sharp lines, called the *characteristic spectrum,* superimposed on (2) the continuous bremsstrahlung spectrum. The line spectrum is characteristic of the target material and varies from element to element. (3) The continuous spectrum has a sharp cutoff wavelength, λ_m, which is independent of the target material but depends on the energy of the bombarding electrons. If the voltage of the x-ray tube is V in volts, the cutoff wavelength was found to be given empirically by

$$\lambda_m = \frac{1.24 \times 10^3}{V} \text{ nm} \qquad \textbf{3-39}$$

Equation 3-39 is called the *Duane-Hunt rule,* after its discoverers. It was pointed out rather quickly by Einstein that x-ray production by electron bombardment was an inverse photoelectric effect and that Equation 3-36 should apply. The Duane-Hunt λ_m

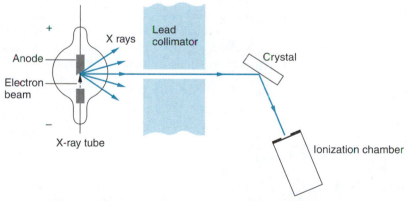

Fig. 3-17 Schematic diagram of Bragg crystal spectrometer. A collimated x-ray beam is incident on a crystal and scattered into an ionization chamber. The crystal and ionization chamber can be rotated to keep the angles of incidence and scattering equal as both are varied. By measuring the ionization in the chamber as a function of angle, the spectrum of the x rays can be determined using the Bragg condition $2d \sin \theta = m\lambda$, where d is the separation of the Bragg planes in the crystal. If the wavelength λ is known, the spacing d can be determined.

(a)

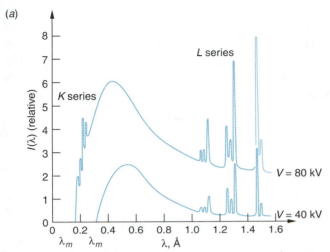

(b)

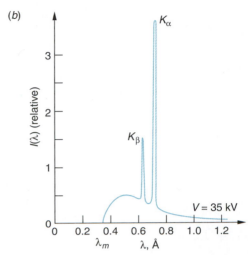

Fig. 3-18 X-ray spectra from tungsten at two accelerating voltages (a) and from molybdenum at one (b). The names of the line series (K and L) are historical and explained in Chapter 4. The L-series lines (not shown) for Mo are at about 0.5 nm. The cutoff wavelength λ_m is independent of the target element and is related to the voltage of the x-ray tube V by $\lambda_m = hc/eV$. The wavelengths of the lines are characteristic of the target element.

simply corresponds to a photon with the maximum energy of the electrons, that is, the photon emitted when the electron loses all of its kinetic energy in a single collision. Since the kinetic energy of the electrons in the x-ray tube is 20,000 eV or larger, the work function ϕ is negligible by comparison. That is, Equation 3-36 becomes $eV \approx hf = hc/\lambda$ or $\lambda = hc/eV = 1.2407 \times 10^{-6}$ V^{-1} m $= 1.24 \times 10^3$ V^{-1} nm. Thus, the Duane-Hunt rule is explained by Planck's quantum hypothesis. (Notice that λ_m can be used to determine h/e.)

The continuous spectrum was understood as the result of the acceleration (i.e., "braking") of the bombarding electrons in the strong electric fields of the target atoms. Maxwell's equations predicted the continuous radiation. The real problem for classical physics was the sharp lines. The wavelengths of the sharp lines were a function of the target element, the set for each element being always the same, but the sharp lines never appeared if V was such that λ_m was larger than the particular line, as can be seen in Figure 3-18a, where the shortest-wavelength group disappears when V is reduced from 80 kV to 40 kV, so that λ_m becomes larger. The origin of the sharp lines was a mystery that had to await the discovery of the nuclear atom. We will explain them in Chapter 4.

Well-known applications of x rays are medical and dental x rays (both diagnostic and treatment) and industrial x-ray inspection of welds and castings. Perhaps not so well known are their use in determining the structure of crystals, identifying black holes in space, and "seeing" the folded shape of proteins in biological materials.

Compton Effect

It had been observed that scattered x rays were "softer" than those in the incident beam, that is, were absorbed more readily. Compton[17] pointed out that if the scattering process were considered a "collision" between a photon of energy hf_1 (and momentum hf_1/c) and an electron, the recoiling electron would absorb part of the total energy, and the energy hf_2 of the scattered photon would therefore be less than the incident one and thus of lower frequency f_2 and momentum hf_2/c. (The fact that electromagnetic radiation of energy E carried momentum E/c was known from classical theory and from experiments of E. F. Nichols and G. F. Hull in 1903. This

relation is also consistent with the relativistic expression $E^2 = p^2c^2 + (mc^2)^2$ for a particle with zero rest mass.) Compton applied the laws of conservation of momentum and energy in their relativistic form (see Chapter 2) to the collision of a photon with an isolated electron to obtain the change in the wavelength $\lambda_2 - \lambda_1$ of the photon as a function of the scattering angle θ. The result, called *Compton's equation* and derived on the home page, is

$$\lambda_2 - \lambda_1 = \frac{h}{mc}(1 - \cos\theta)$$

3-40

The change in wavelength is thus predicted to be independent of the original wavelength. The quantity h/mc has dimensions of length and is called the *Compton wavelength of the electron.* Its value is

$$\lambda_c = \frac{h}{mc} = \frac{hc}{mc^2} = \frac{1.24 \times 10^3\,\text{eV}\cdot\text{nm}}{5.11 \times 10^5\,\text{eV}} = 0.00243\,\text{nm}$$

Because $\lambda_2 - \lambda_1$ is small, it is difficult to observe unless λ_1 is very small so that the fractional change $(\lambda_2 - \lambda_1)/\lambda_1$ is appreciable. For this reason the Compton effect is generally observed only for x rays and gamma radiation.

Compton verified his result experimentally using the characteristic x-ray line of wavelength 0.0711 nm from molybdenum for the incident monochromatic photons, and scattering these photons from electrons in graphite. The wavelength of the scattered photons was measured using a Bragg crystal spectrometer. His experimental arrangement is shown in Figure 3-19; Figure 3-20 shows his results. The first peak at each scattering angle corresponds to scattering with no shift in the wavelength due to scattering by the inner electrons of carbon. Since these are tightly bound to the atom, it is the whole atom that recoils rather than the individual electron. The expected shift for this case is given by Equation 3-40, with m being the mass of the atom, which is

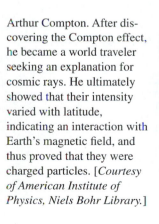

Arthur Compton. After discovering the Compton effect, he became a world traveler seeking an explanation for cosmic rays. He ultimately showed that their intensity varied with latitude, indicating an interaction with Earth's magnetic field, and thus proved that they were charged particles. [*Courtesy of American Institute of Physics, Niels Bohr Library.*]

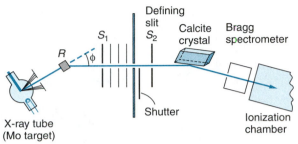

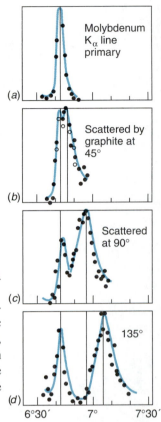

Fig. 3-19 Schematic sketch of Compton apparatus. X rays from the tube strike the carbon block *R* and are scattered into a Bragg-type crystal spectrometer. In this diagram, the scattering angle is 30°. The beam was defined by slits S_1 and S_2. Although the entire spectrum is being scattered by *R*, the spectrometer scanned the region around the K_α line of molybdenum.

about 10^4 times that of the electron; thus this shift is negligible. The variation of $\Delta\lambda$ with θ was found to be that predicted by Equation 3-40.

We have seen in this and the preceding two sections that the interaction of electromagnetic radiation with matter is a discrete interaction which occurs at the atomic level. It is perhaps curious that after so many years of debate about the nature of light, we now find that we must have both a particle (i.e., quantum) theory to describe in detail the energy exchange between electromagnetic radiation and matter, and a wave theory to describe the interference and diffraction of electromagnetic radiation. We shall discuss this so-called particle-wave duality in more detail in Chapter 5.

Fig. 3-20 Intensity versus wavelength for Compton scattering at several angles. The left peak in each case results from photons of the original wavelength that are scattered by tightly bound electrons, which have an effective mass equal to that of the atom. The separation in wavelength of the peaks is given by Equation 3-40. The horizontal scale used by Compton "angle from calcite" refers to the calcite analyzing crystal in Figure 3-19.

More

Derivation of Compton's Equation, applying conservation of energy and momentum to the relativistic collision of a photon and an electron, is included on the home page: www.whfreeman.com/modphysics4e   See also Equations 3-41 and 3-42 and Figure 3-21 here.

QUESTIONS

5. Why is it extremely difficult to observe the Compton effect using visible light?

6. Why is the Compton effect unimportant in the transmission of television and radio waves? How many Compton scatterings could a typical FM signal have before its wavelengths were shifted by 0.01 percent?

EXAMPLE 3-9 X Rays from TV The accelerating voltage of the electrons in a typical color television picture tube is 25 kV. What is the minimum-wavelength x ray produced when these electrons strike surfaces within the tube?

Solution

From Equation 3-41, we have

$$\lambda_m = \frac{1.24 \times 10^3}{V} \text{ nm} = \frac{1.24 \times 10^3}{25{,}000} = 0.050 \text{ nm}$$

These x rays penetrate matter very effectively. Manufacturers provide essential shields to protect against the hazard.

EXAMPLE 3-10 **Compton Effect** In a particular Compton scattering experiment it is found that the incident wavelength λ_1 is shifted by 1.5% when the scattering angle $\theta = 120°$. (a) What is the value of λ_1? (b) What will be the wavelength λ_2 of the shifted photon when the scattering angle is 75°?

Solution

1. Considering question (a), the value of λ_1 is contained in Equation 3-40:

$$\lambda_2 - \lambda_1 = \Delta\lambda = \frac{h}{mc}(1 - \cos\theta)$$
$$= 0.00243\,(1 - \cos 120°) \text{ nm}$$

2. That the scattered wavelength λ_2 is shifted by 1.5 percent from λ_1 means that:

$$\frac{\Delta\lambda}{\lambda_1} = 0.015$$

3. Combining these yields:

$$\lambda_1 = \frac{\Delta\lambda}{0.015} = \frac{0.00243(1 - \cos 120°)}{0.015}$$
$$= 0.243 \text{ nm}$$

4. Question (b) is also solved using Equation 3-40, rearranged as:

$$\lambda_2 = \lambda_1 + 0.00243\,(1 - \cos\theta)$$

5. Substituting $\theta = 75°$ and λ_1 from above yields:

$$\lambda_2 = 0.243 + 0.00243(1 - \cos 75°)$$
$$= 0.243 + 0.002$$
$$= 0.245 \text{ nm}$$

Summary

TOPIC	RELEVANT EQUATIONS AND REMARKS	
1. J. J. Thomson's experiment	Thomson's measurements with cathode rays showed that the same particle (the electron), with e/m about 2000 times that of ionized hydrogen, exists in all elements.	
2. Quantization of electric charge	$e = 1.60217733 \times 10^{-19}$ C	
3. Blackbody radiation		
Stefan-Boltzmann law	$R = \sigma T^4$	**3-19**
Wien's displacement law	$\lambda_m T = 2.898 \times 10^{-3}$ m $\cdot$ K	**3-20**
Planck's radiation law	$u(\lambda) = \dfrac{8\pi hc\lambda^{-5}}{e^{hc/\lambda kT} - 1}$	**3-33**
Planck's constant	$h = 6.626 \times 10^{-34}$ J $\cdot$ s	**3-34**
4. Photoelectric effect	$eV_0 = hf - \phi$	**3-36**
5. Compton effect	$\lambda_2 - \lambda_1 = \dfrac{h}{mc}(1 - \cos\theta)$	**3-40**

GENERAL REFERENCES

The following references are written at a level appropriate for the readers of this book.

Millikan, R. A., *Electrons (+ and −), Protons, Photons, Neutrons, Mesotrons, and Cosmic Rays,* 2d ed., University of Chicago Press, Chicago, 1947. This book on modern physics by one of the great experimentalists of his time contains fascinating, detailed descriptions of Millikan's oil-drop experiment and his verification of the Einstein photoelectric-effect equation.

Mohr, P. J., and B. N. Taylor, "The Fundamental Physical Constants," *Physics Today* (August 2000).

Richtmyer, F. K., E. H. Kennard, and J. N. Cooper, *Introduction to Modern Physics,* 6th ed., McGraw-Hill, New York, 1969. This excellent text was originally published in 1928, intended as a survey course for graduate students.

Shamos, M. H. (ed.), *Great Experiments in Physics,* Holt, Rinehart & Winston, New York, 1962. This book contains 25 original papers and extensive editorial comment. Of particular interest for this chapter are papers by Faraday, Hertz, Roentgen, J. J. Thomson, Einstein (photoelectric effect), Millikan, Planck, and Compton.

Thomson, G. P., *J. J. Thomson, Discoverer of the Electron,* Doubleday/Anchor, Garden City, N.Y., 1964. An interesting study of J. J. Thomson by his son, G. P. Thomson, also a physicist.

Virtual Laboratory (PEARL), Physics Academic Software, North Carolina State University, Raleigh, 1996. Computer simulation software allows the user to analyze blackbody radiation emitted over a wide range of temperatures and investigate the Compton effect in detail.

Weart, S. R. (ed.), *Selected Papers of Great American Physicists,* American Institute of Physics, New York, 1976. The bicentennial commemorative volume of the American Physical Society.

NOTES

1. Democritus (about 470 B.C. to about 380 B.C.). Among his other modern-sounding ideas were the suggestions that the Milky Way was a vast conglomeration of stars and that the moon, like Earth, had mountains and valleys.

2. 1826–1911, Irish physicist who first called the fundamental unit of charge the electron. After Thomson discovered the particle that carried the charge, the name was transferred from the quantity of charge to the particle itself by Lorentz.

3. Hermann von Helmholtz (1821–1894). German physician and physicist who first proposed the law of conservation of energy in 1847 on the basis of his analysis of a meticulous set of experiments conducted some years earlier by James Joule.

4. Joseph J. Thomson (1856–1940). English physicist and director, for more than 30 years, of the Cavendish Laboratory, the first laboratory in the world established expressly for research in physics. He was awarded the Nobel Prize in 1906 for his work on the electron. Seven of his research assistants also won Nobel Prizes.

5. There had been much early confusion about the nature of cathode rays due to the failure of Heinrich Hertz in 1883 to observe any deflection of the rays in an electric field. This failure was later found to be the result of ionization of the gas in the tube; the ions quickly neutralized the charges on the deflecting plates so that there was actually no electric field between the plates. With better vacuum technology in 1897, Thomson was able to work at lower pressure and observe electrostatic deflection.

6. R. A. Millikan, *Philosophical Magazine (6)*, **19**, 209 (1910). Millikan, who held the first physics Ph.D. awarded by Columbia University, was one of the most accomplished experimentalists of his time. He received the Nobel Prize in 1923 for the measurement of the electron's charge. Also among his many contributions, he coined the term *cosmic rays* to describe radiation produced in outer space.

7. R. A. Millikan, *Physical Review*, **32**, 349 (1911).

8. P. J. Mohr and B. N. Taylor, "The Fundamental Physical Constants," *Physics Today* (August 2000).

9. See pp. 135–137 of F. K. Richtmyer, E. H. Kennard, and J. N. Cooper (1969).

10. John W. S. Rayleigh (1842–1919), English physicist, almost invariably referred to by the title that he inherited from his father. He was Maxwell's successor and Thomson's predecessor as director of the Cavendish Laboratory.

11. Max K. E. L. Planck (1858–1947). Most of his career was spent at the University of Berlin. In his later years his renown in the world of science was probably second only to that of Einstein.

12. Heinrich R. Hertz (1857–1894), German physicist, student of Helmholtz. He was the discoverer of electromagnetic "radio" waves, later developed for practical communication by Marconi.

13. H. Hertz, *Annalen der Physik,* **31**, 983 (1887).

14. A. Einstein, *Annalen der Physik,* **17**, 144 (1905).

15. A translation of this paper can be found in E. C. Watson, *American Journal of Physics*, **13**, 284 (1945), and in M. H. Shamos, ed., *Great Experiments in Physics* (New York: Holt, Rinehart & Winston, 1962). Roentgen (1845–1923) was honored in 1901 with the first Nobel Prize in physics for his discovery of x rays.

16. William Lawrence Bragg (1890–1971), Australian-English physicist, an infant prodigy. His work on x-ray diffraction performed with his father, William Henry Bragg (1862–1942), earned for them both the Nobel Prize in physics for 1915, the only father-son team to be so honored thus far. In 1938 W. L. Bragg became director of the Cavendish Laboratory, succeeding Rutherford.

17. Arthur H. Compton (1892–1962), American physicist. It was Compton who suggested the name *photon* for the light quantum. His discovery and explanation of the Compton effect earned him a share of the Nobel Prize in physics in 1927.

Problems

Level I

Section 3-1 Quantization of Electric Charge

3-1. A beam of charged particles consisting of protons, electrons, deuterons, and singly ionized helium atoms and H_2 molecules all pass through a velocity selector, all emerging with speeds of 2.5×10^6 m/s. The beam then enters a region of uniform magnetic field $B = 0.40$ T directed perpendicular to their velocity. Compute the radius of curvature of the path of each type of particle.

3-2. We wish to use a mass spectrometer to separate ^{197}Au from ^{198}Hg in a sample of material. Using the isotopic masses listed in Appendix A and assuming that each singly ionized atom enters the spectrometer at a speed of 1.5×10^5 m/s, answer the following: (*a*) What uniform magnetic field perpendicular to the ion's velocity is needed in order for the orbits to have a radius of 1 m (approximately)? (*b*) What will be the separation ΔR of the two impact points after the ions have covered half a complete circle? (See Figure 3-3.) (*c*) What would your answers to (*a*) and (*b*) change to if the atoms were all doubly ionized?

3-3. Equation 3-4 suggests how a velocity selector for particles or mixtures of different particles all having the same charge can be made. Suppose you wish to make a velocity

selector that allows undeflected passage for electrons whose kinetic energy is 5.0×10^4 eV. The electric field available to you is 2.0×10^5 V/m. What magnetic field will be needed?

3-4. A cosmic-ray proton approaches Earth vertically at the equator, where the horizontal component of Earth's magnetic field is 3.5×10^{-5} T. If the proton is moving at 3.0×10^6 m/s, what is the ratio of the magnetic force to the gravitational force on the proton?

3-5. An electron of kinetic energy 45 keV moves in a circular orbit perpendicular to a magnetic field of 0.325 T. (*a*) Compute the radius of the orbit. (*b*) Find the frequency and period of the motion.

3-6. If electrons have kinetic energy of 2000 eV, find (*a*) their speed, (*b*) the time needed to traverse a distance of 5 cm between plates *D* and *E* in Figure 3-1, and (*c*) the vertical component of their velocity after passing between the plates if the electric field is 3.33×10^3 V/m.

3-7. In J. J. Thomson's first method, the heat capacity of the beam stopper was about 5×10^{-3} cal/°C and the temperature increase was about 2°C. How many 2000-eV electrons struck the beam stopper?

3-8. On drop #16, Millikan measured the following total charges, among others, at different times:

$$25.41 \times 10^{-19} \text{ C} \qquad 17.47 \times 10^{-19} \text{ C} \qquad 12.70 \times 10^{-19} \text{ C}$$
$$20.64 \times 10^{-19} \text{ C} \qquad 19.06 \times 10^{-19} \text{ C} \qquad 14.29 \times 10^{-19} \text{ C}$$

What value of the fundamental quantized charge *e* do these numbers imply?

3-9. Show that the electric field needed to make the rise time of the oil drop equal to its field-free fall time is $\mathcal{E} = 2\ mg/q$.

3-10. One variation of the Millikan oil-drop apparatus arranges the electric field horizontally, rather than vertically, giving the charged droplets an acceleration in the horizontal direction. The result is that the droplet falls in a straight line which makes an angle θ with the vertical. Show that

$$\sin \theta = q\mathcal{E}/bv_t'$$

where v_t' is the terminal speed along the angled path.

3-11. A charged oil droplet falls 5.0 mm in 20.0 s at terminal speed in the absence of an electric field. The specific gravity of air is 1.35×10^{-3}, and that of the oil is 0.75. The viscosity of air is 1.80×10^{-5} N·s/m². (*a*) What are the mass and radius of the drop? (*b*) If the droplet carries 2 units of electric charge and is in an electric field of 2.5×10^5 V/m, what is the ratio of the electric force to the gravitational force on the droplet?

Section 3-2 Blackbody Radiation

3-12. Find λ_m for blackbody radiation at (*a*) $T = 3$ K, (*b*) $T = 300$ K, and (*c*) $T = 3000$ K.

3-13. Use the result of Example 3-5 and Equations 3-19 and 3-21 to express Stefan's constant in terms of *h*, *c*, and *k*. Using the known values of these constants, calculate Stefan's constant.

3-14. Show that Planck's law, Equation 3-33, expressed in terms of the frequency *f*, is

$$u(f) = \frac{8\pi f^2}{c^3} \frac{hf}{e^{hf/kT} - 1}$$

3-15. As noted in the chapter, the cosmic microwave background radiation fits the Planck equations for a blackbody at 2.7 K. (*a*) What is the wavelength at the maximum intensity of the spectrum of the background radiation? (*b*) What is the frequency of the radiation at the maximum? (*c*) What is the total power incident on Earth from the back-

ground radiation?

3-16. Find the temperature of a blackbody if its spectrum has its peak at (*a*) $\lambda_m = 700$ nm, (*b*) $\lambda_m = 3$ cm (microwave region), and (*c*) $\lambda_m = 3$ m (FM radio waves).

3-17. If the absolute temperature of a blackbody is doubled, by what factor is the total emitted power increased?

3-18. Calculate the average energy $\bar{E}$ per mode of oscillation for (*a*) a long wavelength $\lambda = 10\ hc/kT$, (*b*) a short wavelength $\lambda = 0.1\ hc/kT$, and compare your results with the classical prediction kT (see Equation 3-24). (The classical value comes from the equipartition theorem discussed in Chapter 8.)

3-19. A particular radiating cavity has the maximum of its spectral distribution of radiated power at a wavelength of 27.0 μm (in the infrared region of the spectrum). The temperature is then changed so that the total power radiated by the cavity doubles. (*a*) Compute the new temperature. (*b*) At what wavelength does the new spectral distribution have its maximum value?

3-20. A certain very bright star has an effective surface temperature of 20,000 K. Assuming that it radiates as a blackbody, what is the wavelength at which $u(\lambda)$ is maximum?

3-21. The energy reaching Earth from the sun at the top of the atmosphere is 1.36×10^3 W/m^2, called the *solar constant*. Assuming that Earth radiates like a blackbody at uniform temperature, what do you conclude is the equilibrium temperature of Earth?

3-22. A 40-W incandescent bulb radiates from a tungsten filament operating at 3300 K. Assuming that the bulb radiates like a blackbody, (*a*) what are the frequency f_m and the wavelength λ_m at the maximum of the spectral distribution? (*b*) If f_m is a good approximation of the average frequency of the photons emitted by the bulb, about how many photons is the bulb radiating per second? (*c*) If you are looking at the bulb from 5 m away, how many photons enter your eye per second? (The diameter of your pupil is about 5.0 mm.)

3-23. Use Planck's law, Equation 3-33, to derive the constant in Wien's law, Equation 3-20.

Section 3-3 The Photoelectric Effect

3-24. Black-and-white photographic film is exposed by light that has sufficient energy to dissociate the AgBr molecules contained in the photosensitive emulsion. The minimum energy necessary is 0.68 eV. What is the maximum wavelength beyond which this film will not record light? In what region of the spectrum does this light fall?

3-25. The orbiting space shuttle moves around Earth well above 99 percent of the atmosphere, yet it still accumulates an electric charge on its skin due, in part, to the loss of electrons caused by the photoelectric effect with sunlight. Suppose the skin of the shuttle is coated with Ni, which has a relatively large work function $\phi = 4.87$ eV at the temperatures encountered in orbit. (*a*) What is the maximum wavelength in the solar spectrum that can result in the emission of photoelectrons from the shuttle's skin? (*b*) What is the maximum fraction of the total power falling on the shuttle that could potentially produce photoelectrons?

3-26. The work function for cesium is 1.9 eV. (*a*) Find the threshold frequency and wavelength for the photoelectric effect. Find the stopping potential if the wavelength of the incident light is (*b*) 300 nm, and (*c*) 400 nm.

3-27. (*a*) If 5 percent of the power of a 100-W bulb is radiated in the visible spectrum, how many visible photons are radiated per second? (*b*) If the bulb is a point source radiating equally in all directions, what is the flux of photons (number per unit time per unit area) at a distance of 2 m?

3-28. The work function of molybdenum is 4.22 eV. (*a*) What is the threshold frequency for the photoelectric effect in molybdenum? (*b*) Will yellow light of wavelength 560 nm cause ejection of photoelectrons from molybdenum? Prove your answer.

3-29. Find the photon energy corresponding to (*a*) a wavelength of 0.1 nm (about 1 atomic diameter), (*b*) a wavelength of 1 fm (= 10^{-15} m, about 1 nuclear diameter), and (*c*) a frequency of 90.7 MHz in the FM radio band.

3-30. A photoelectric-effect experiment with cesium yields stopping potentials for $\lambda = 435.8$ nm and $\lambda = 546.1$ nm to be 0.95 V and 0.38 V, respectively. Using these data only, find the threshold frequency and work function for cesium and the value of *h*.

3-31. Under optimum conditions, the eye will perceive a flash if about 60 photons arrive at the cornea. How much energy is this in joules if the wavelength is 550 nm?

3-32. The longest wavelength of light that will cause the emission of electrons from cesium is 653 nm. (*a*) What is the work function for cesium? (*b*) If light of 300 nm (ultraviolet) were to shine on cesium, what would be the energy of the ejected electrons?

Section 3-4 X Rays and the Compton Effect

3-33. Use Compton's equation (Equation 3-40) to compute the value of $\Delta\lambda$ in Figure 3-20*d*. To what percent shift in the wavelength does this correspond?

3-34. X-ray tubes currently used by dentists often have accelerating voltages of 80 kV. What is the minimum wavelength of the x rays that they produce?

3-35. Find the momentum of a photon in eV/*c* and in kg · m/s if the wavelength is (*a*) 400 nm, (*b*) 1 Å = 0.1 nm, (*c*) 3 cm, and (*d*)2 nm.

3-36. Gamma rays emitted by radioactive nuclei also exhibit measurable Compton scattering. Suppose a 0.511-MeV photon from a positron-electron annihilation scatters at 110° from a free electron. What are the energies of the scattered photon and the recoiling electron? Relative to the initial direction of the 0.511-MeV photon, what is the direction of the recoiling electron?

3-37. The wavelength of Compton-scattered photons is measured at $\theta = 90°$. If $\Delta\lambda/\lambda$ is to be 1 percent, what should the wavelength of the incident photon be?

3-38. Compton used photons of wavelength 0.0711 nm. (*a*) What is the energy of these photons? (*b*) What is the wavelength of the photons scattered at $\theta = 180°$? (*c*) What is the energy of the photons scattered at $\theta = 180°$? (*d*) What is the recoil energy of the electrons if $\theta = 180°$?

3-39. When photons are scattered by electrons in carbon, the shift in wavelength is 0.29 pm. Compute the scattering angle.

3-40. Compton's equation (Equation 3-40) indicates that a graph of λ_2 versus $(1 - \cos\theta)$ should be a straight line whose slope h/mc allows a determination of *h*. Given that the wavelength of λ in Figure 3-20 is 0.0711 nm, compute λ_2 for each scattering angle in the figure, and graph the results versus $(1 - \cos\theta)$. What is the slope of the line?

3-41. (*a*) Compute the Compton wavelength of an electron and a proton. (*b*) What is the energy of a photon whose wavelength is equal to the Compton wavelength of (1) the electron and (2) the proton?

Level II

3-42. When light of wavelength 450 nm is shone on potassium, photoelectrons with stopping potential of 0.52 V are emitted. If the wavelength of the incident light is changed to 300 nm, the stopping potential is 1.90 V. Using *only* these numbers together with the values of the speed of light and the electron charge, (*a*) find the work function of potassium and (*b*) compute a value for Planck's constant.

3-43. Referring to Figure 3-2, show that the angle of deflection θ is given by

$$\theta = \frac{e}{m}\frac{\mathscr{E}x_1}{u_x^2}$$

3-44. Assuming that the difference between Thomson's calculated e/m in his second experiment and the currently accepted value was due entirely to his neglecting the horizontal component of Earth's magnetic field outside the deflection plates, what value for that component does the difference imply?

3-45. Data for stopping potential versus wavelength for the photoelectric effect using sodium are

λ(nm) 200	300	400	500	600
V_0(V) 4.20	2.06	1.05	0.41	0.03

Plot these data in such a way as to be able to obtain (*a*) the work function, (*b*) the threshold frequency, and (*c*) the ratio h/e.

3-46. Prove that the photoelectric effect cannot occur with a completely free electron, i.e., one not bound to an atom. (*Hint:* Consider the reference frame in which the total momentum of the electron and incident photon is zero.)

3-47. When a beam of monochromatic x rays is incident on a particular NaCl crystal, Bragg reflection in the first order (i.e., with $m = 1$) occurs at $\theta = 20°$. The value of $d = 0.28$ nm. What is the minimum voltage at which the x-ray tube can be operating?

3-48. A 100-W beam of light is shone onto a blackbody of mass 2×10^{-3} kg for 10^4 s. The blackbody is initially at rest in a frictionless space. (*a*) Compute the total energy and momentum absorbed by the blackbody from the light beam, (*b*) calculate the blackbody's velocity at the end of the period of illumination, and (*c*) compute the final kinetic energy of the blackbody. Why is the latter less than the total energy of the absorbed photons?

3-49. Show that the maximum kinetic energy E_k that a recoiling electron can carry away from a Compton scattering event is given by

$$E_k = \frac{hf}{1 + mc^2/2hf}$$

3-50. The x-ray spectrometer on board a satellite measures the wavelength at the maximum intensity emitted by a particular star to be $\lambda_m = 82.8$ nm. Assuming that the star radiates like a blackbody, (*a*) compute its surface temperature. (*b*) What is the ratio of the intensity radiated at $\lambda = 70$ nm and at $\lambda = 100$ nm to λ_m.

3-51. Determine the fraction of the energy radiated by the sun in the visible region of the spectrum (350 nm to 700 nm). (Assume the sun's surface temperature is 5800 K.)

3-52. Millikan's data for the photoelectric effect in lithium are shown in the table:

Incident λ (nm)	253.5	312.5	365.0	404.7	433.9
Stopping voltage V_0 (V)	2.57	1.67	1.09	0.73	0.55

(*a*) Graph these data and determine the work function for lithium. (*b*) Find a value of Planck's constant from the graph in (*a*). (*c*) The work function for lead is 4.14 eV. Which of the wavelengths in the table would not cause emission of photoelectrons from lead?

Level III

3-53. This problem is to derive the Wien displacement law, Equation 3-20. (*a*) Show that the energy density distribution function can be written $u = C\lambda^{-5} (e^{a/\lambda} - 1)^{-1}$, where C is a constant and $a = hc/kT$. (*b*) Show that the value of λ for which $du/d\lambda = 0$ satisfies the equation $5\lambda (1 - e^{-a/\lambda}) = a$. (*c*) This equation can be solved with a calculator by the trial-and-error method. Try $\lambda = \alpha a$ for various values of α until λ/a is determined to four significant figures. (*d*) Show that your solution in (*c*) implies $\lambda_m T = $ constant and calculate the value of the constant.

3-54. This problem is one of *estimating* the time lag (expected classically but not observed) for the photoelectric effect. Assume that a point light source gives 1 W = 1 J/s of light energy. (*a*) Assuming uniform radiation in all directions, find the light intensity in $eV/m^2 \cdot s$ at a distance of 1 m from the light source. (*b*) Assuming some reasonable size for an atom, find the energy per unit time incident on the atom for this intensity. (*c*) If the work function is 2 eV, how long does it take for this much energy to be absorbed, assuming that all the energy hitting the atom is absorbed?

3-55. A photon can be absorbed by a system that can have internal energy. Assume that a 15-MeV photon is absorbed by a carbon nucleus initially at rest. The momentum of the carbon nucleus must be 15 MeV/*c*. (*a*) Calculate the kinetic energy of the carbon nucleus. What is the internal energy of this nucleus? (*b*) The carbon nucleus comes to rest and then loses its internal energy by emitting a photon. What is the energy of the photon?

3-56. The maximum kinetic energy given to the electron in a Compton scattering event plays a role in the measurement of gamma-ray spectra using scintillation detectors. The maximum is referred to as the *Compton edge*. Suppose the Compton edge in a particular experiment is found to be 520 keV. What were the wavelength and energy of the incident gamma rays?

3-57. An electron accelerated to 50 keV in an x-ray tube has two successive collisions in being brought to rest in the target, emitting two bremsstrahlung photons in the process. The second photon emitted has a wavelength 0.095 nm longer than the first. (*a*) What are the wavelengths of the two photons? (*b*) What was the energy of the electron after emission of the first photon?

3-58. Derive Equation 3-32 from Equations 3-30 and 3-31.

Chapter 4

The Nuclear Atom

*A*mong his many experiments, Newton found that sunlight passing through a small opening in a window shutter could be refracted by a glass prism so that it would fall on a screen. The white sunlight thus refracted was spread into a rainbow-colored band—a spectrum. He had discovered *dispersion,* and his experimental arrangement was the prototype of the modern *spectroscope* (Figure 4-1a). When, 150 years later, Fraunhofer[1] dispersed sunlight using an experimental setup similar to that shown in Figure 4-1b to test prisms made of glasses that he had developed, he found that the solar spectrum was crossed by more than 600 narrow, or sharp, dark lines.[2] Soon after, a number of scientists observed sharp *bright* lines in the spectra of light emitted by flames, arcs, and sparks. *Spectroscopy* quickly became an important area of research.

It soon became clear that chemical elements and compounds emit three general types of spectra. *Continuous* spectra, emitted mainly by incandescent solids, show no lines at all, bright or dark, in spectroscopes of the highest possible resolving power. *Band* spectra consist of very closely packed groups of lines that appear to be continuous in instruments of low resolving power. These are emitted when small pieces of solid materials are placed in the source flame or electrodes. The *line* spectra mentioned already arise when the source contains unbound chemical elements. The lines and bands turned out to be characteristic of individual elements and chemical compounds when excited under specific conditions. Indeed, the spectra could be used as a highly sensitive test for the presence of elements and compounds. Line spectra raised an enormous theoretical problem: although classical physics could account for the existence of a continuous spectrum (if not its detailed shape, as we saw with blackbodies), it could in no way explain *why* sharp lines and bands should exist. Explaining the origin of the sharp lines and accounting for the primary features of the spectrum of hydrogen, the simplest element, was a major success of the so-called "old" quantum theory begun by Planck and Einstein and will be the main topic in

Voltaire's depiction of Newton's discovery of dispersion. [Elémens de la Philosophie de Newton, *Amsterdam, 1738.*]

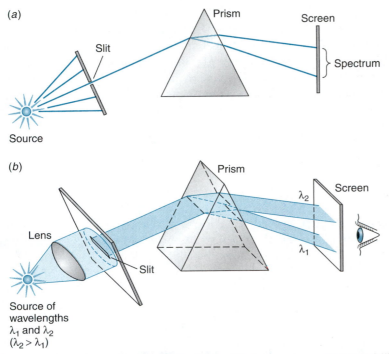

Fig. 4-1 (a) Light from the source passes through a small hole or a narrow slit before falling on the prism. The purpose of the slit is to ensure that all the incident light strikes the prism face at the same angle so that the dispersion by the prism causes the various frequencies that may be present to strike the screen at different places with minimum overlap. (b) The source emits only two wavelengths, $\lambda_2 > \lambda_1$. The source is located at the focal point of the lens so that parallel light passes through the narrow slit, projecting a narrow line onto the face of the prism. Ordinary dispersion in the prism bends the shorter wavelength through the larger total angle, separating the two wavelengths at the screen. In this arrangement each wavelength appears on the screen (or on film replacing the screen) as a narrow line, which is an image of the slit. Such a spectrum was dubbed a "line spectrum" for that reason. Prisms have been almost entirely replaced in modern spectroscopes by diffraction gratings, which have much higher resolving power.

this chapter. Full explanation of the lines and bands requires the later, more sophisticated quantum theory, which we will begin studying in Chapter 5.

4-1 Atomic Spectra

The characteristic radiation emitted by atoms of individual elements in a flame or in a gas excited by an electrical discharge was a subject of vigorous study during the late nineteenth century. When viewed through a spectroscope, this radiation appears as a set of discrete lines, each of a particular color or wavelength; the positions and intensities of the lines are characteristic of the element. The wavelengths of these lines could be determined with great precision, and much effort went into finding and interpreting regularities in the spectra. A major breakthrough was made in 1885 by a Swiss schoolteacher, Johann Balmer, who found that the lines in the visible and near ultraviolet spectrum of hydrogen could be represented by the empirical formula

$$\lambda_n = 364.6 \frac{n^2}{n^2 - 4} \, \text{nm} \qquad \textbf{4-1}$$

The uniqueness of the line spectra of the elements has enabled astronomers to determine the composition of stars, chemists to identify unknown compounds, and theme parks to have laser shows.

where n is a variable integer which takes on the values $n = 3, 4, 5, \ldots$. Figure 4-2a shows the set of spectral lines of hydrogen (now known as the *Balmer series*) whose wavelengths are given by Balmer's formula. For example, the wavelength of the H$_\alpha$ line could be found by letting $n = 3$ in Equation 4-1 (try it!), and other integers each predicted a line that was found in the spectrum. Balmer suggested that his formula might be a special case of a more general expression applicable to the spectra of other elements when ionized to a single electron, i.e., hydrogen-like elements. Such an expression, found independently by J. R. Rydberg and W. Ritz and thus called the *Rydberg-Ritz formula*, gives the reciprocal wavelength[3] as

$$\frac{1}{\lambda_{mn}} = R\left(\frac{1}{m^2} - \frac{1}{n^2}\right) \qquad \text{for} \qquad n > m \qquad\qquad \textbf{4-2}$$

where m and n are integers and R, the *Rydberg constant,* is the same for all series of spectral lines of the same element and varies only slightly, and in a regular way, from element to element. For hydrogen, the value of R is $R_H = 1.096776 \times 10^7 \text{ m}^{-1}$. For

Fig. 4-2 (*a*) Emission line spectrum of hydrogen in the visible and near ultraviolet. The lines appear dark because the spectrum was photographed; hence, the bright lines are exposed (dark) areas on the film. The names of the first five lines are shown, as is the point beyond which no lines appear, H$_\infty$, called the *limit of the series*. (*b*) A portion of the emission spectrum of sodium. The two very close bright lines at 589 nm are the D_1 and D_2 lines. They are the principal radiation from sodium street lighting. (*c*) A portion of the emission spectrum of mercury. (*d*) Part of the dark line (absorption) spectrum of sodium. White light shining through sodium vapor is absorbed at certain wavelengths, resulting in no exposure of the film at those points. Notice that the line at 259.4 nm is visible here in both the bright and dark line spectra. Note that frequency increases toward the right, wavelength toward the left in the four spectra shown.

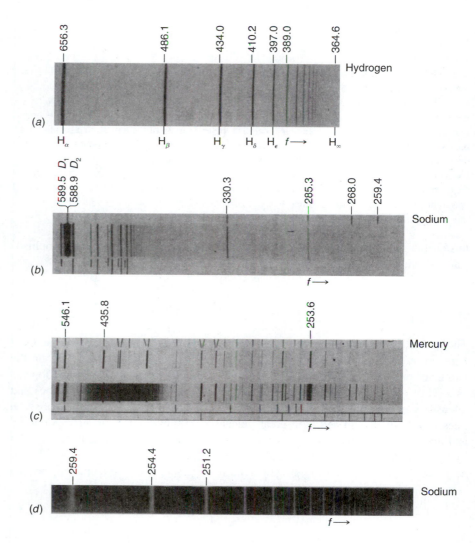

very heavy elements, R approaches the value of $R_\infty = 1.097373 \times 10^7 \text{ m}^{-1}$. Such empirical expressions were successful in predicting other spectra, such as other hydrogen lines outside the visible spectrum.

EXAMPLE 4-1 **Hydrogen Spectral Series** The hydrogen Balmer series reciprocal wavelengths are those given by Equation 4-2 with $m = 2$ and $n = 3, 4, 5, \ldots$. For example, the first line of the series, H_α, would be for $m = 2, n = 3$:

$$\frac{1}{\lambda_{23}} = R\left(\frac{1}{2^2} - \frac{1}{3^2}\right) = \frac{5}{36}R = 1.523 \times 10^6 \text{ m}^{-1}$$

or

$$\lambda_{23} = 656.5 \text{ nm}$$

Other series of hydrogen spectral lines were found for $m = 1$ (by Lyman) and $m = 3$ (by Paschen). Compute the wavelengths of the first lines of the Lyman and Paschen series.

Solution
For the Lyman series ($m = 1$), the first line is for $m = 1, n = 2$.

$$\frac{1}{\lambda_{12}} = R\left(\frac{1}{1^2} - \frac{1}{2^2}\right) = \frac{3}{4}R = 8.22 \times 10^6 \text{ m}^{-1}$$

$$\lambda_{12} = 121.6 \text{ nm} \qquad \text{(in the ultraviolet)}$$

For the Paschen series ($m = 3$), the first line is for $m = 3, n = 4$:

$$\frac{1}{\lambda_{34}} = R\left(\frac{1}{3^2} - \frac{1}{4^2}\right) = \frac{7}{144}R = 5.332 \times 10^5 \text{ m}^{-1}$$

$$\lambda_{34} = 1876 \text{ nm} \qquad \text{(in the infrared)}$$

All of the lines predicted by the Rydberg-Ritz formula for the Lyman and Paschen series are found experimentally. Note that no lines are predicted to lie beyond $\lambda_\infty = 1/R = 91.2 \text{ nm}$ for the Lyman series and $\lambda_\infty = 9/R = 820.6 \text{ nm}$ for the Paschen series and none are found experimentally.

4-2 Rutherford's Nuclear Model

Many attempts were made to construct a model of the atom that yielded the Balmer and Rydberg-Ritz formulas. It was known that an atom was about 10^{-10} m in diameter, that it contained electrons much lighter than the atom, and that it was electrically neutral. The most popular model was that of J. J. Thomson, already quite successful in explaining chemical reactions. Thomson attempted various models consisting of electrons embedded in a fluid that contained most of the mass of the atom and had enough

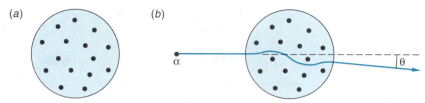

Fig. 4-3 Thomson's model of the atom: (*a*) A sphere of positive charge with electrons embedded in it so that the net charge would normally be zero. The atom shown would have been aluminum. (*b*) An α particle scattered by such an atom would have a scattering angle θ much smaller than 1°.

positive charge to make the atom electrically neutral. (See Figure 4-3*a*.) He then searched for configurations that were stable and had normal modes of vibration corresponding to the known frequency spectrum. One difficulty with all such models was that electrostatic forces alone cannot produce stable equilibrium. Thus, the charges were required to move and, if they stayed within the atom, to accelerate; however, the acceleration would result in continuous radiation, which is not observed. Despite elaborate mathematical calculations, Thomson was unable to obtain from his model a set of frequencies of vibration that corresponded with the frequencies of observed spectra.

The Thomson model of the atom was replaced by one based on the results of a set of experiments conducted by Ernest Rutherford[4] and his students H. W. Geiger and E. Marsden. Rutherford was investigating radioactivity and had shown that the radiations from uranium consisted of at least two types, which he labeled α and β. He showed, by an experiment similar to that of J. J. Thomson, that q/m for the α was half that of the proton. Suspecting that the α particles were doubly ionized helium, Rutherford and his co-workers in a classic experiment let a radioactive substance decay in a previously evacuated chamber; then, by spectroscopy, they detected the spectral lines of ordinary helium gas in the chamber. Realizing that this energetic, massive α particle would make an excellent probe for "feeling about" within the interiors of other atoms, Rutherford began a series of experiments with this purpose.

In these latter experiments, a narrow beam of α particles fell on a zinc sulfide screen, which emitted visible light scintillations when struck (Figure 4-4). The distri-

Hans Geiger and Ernest Rutherford in their Manchester laboratory. [*Courtesy of University of Manchester.*]

bution of scintillations on the screen was observed when various thin metal foils were placed between it and the source. Most of the α particles were either undeflected, or deflected through very small angles of the order of 1°. Quite unexpectedly, however, a few α particles were deflected through angles as large as 90° or more. If the atom consisted of a positively charged sphere of radius 10^{-10} m, containing electrons as in the Thomson model, only a very small deflection could result from a single encounter between an α particle and an atom, even if the α particle penetrated into the atom.

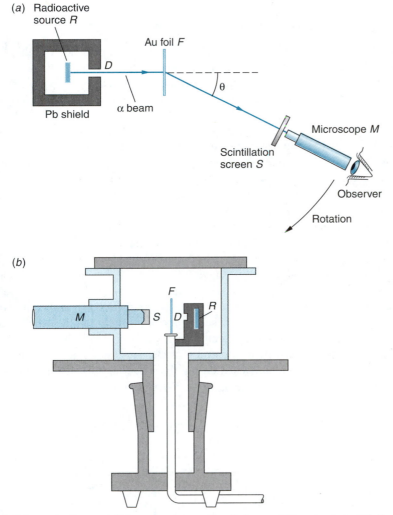

Fig. 4-4 Schematic diagram of the apparatus used by Geiger and Marsden to test Rutherford's atomic model. (*a*) The beam of α particles is defined by the small hole *D* in the shield surrounding the radioactive source *R* of ^{214}Bi (called RaC in Rutherford's day). The α beam strikes an ultrathin gold foil *F* (about 2000 atoms thick), and the α particles are individually scattered through various angles. Those scattering at the angle θ shown strike a small screen *S* coated with a scintillator, i.e., a material that emits tiny flashes of light (scintillations) when struck by an α particle. The scintillations were viewed by the observer through a small microscope *M*. The scintillation screen–microscope combination could be rotated about the center of the foil. The region traversed by the α beam is evacuated. The experiment consisted of counting the number of scintillations as a function of θ. (*b*) A diagram of the actual apparatus as it appeared in Geiger and Marsden's paper describing the results. The letter key is the same as in (*a*). [*Part (b) from H. Geiger and E. Marsden,* Philosophical Review, *25, 507 (1913).*]

Indeed, calculations showed that the Thomson atomic model could not possibly account for the number of large-angle scatterings that Rutherford saw. The unexpected scatterings at large angles were described by Rutherford with these words:

> It was quite the most incredible event that ever happened to me in my life. It was as incredible as if you fired a 15-inch shell at a piece of tissue paper and it came back and hit you.

Rutherford's Scattering Theory and the Nuclear Atom

The question is, then, Why would one obtain the large-angle scattering that Rutherford saw? The trouble with the Thomson atom is that it is too "soft"—the maximum force experienced by the α is too weak to give a large deflection. If the positive charge of the atom is concentrated in a more compact region, however, a much larger force will occur at near impacts. Rutherford concluded that the large-angle scattering obtained experimentally could result only from a single encounter of the α particle with a massive charge confined to a volume much smaller than that of the whole atom. Assuming this "nucleus" to be a point charge, he calculated the expected angular distribution for the scattered α particles. His predictions of the dependence of scattering probability on angle, nuclear charge, and kinetic energy were completely verified in a series of experiments carried out in his laboratory by Geiger and Marsden.

We shall not go through Rutherford's derivation in detail, but merely outline the assumptions and conclusions. Figure 4-5 shows the geometry of an α particle being scattered by a nucleus, which we take to be a point charge Q at the origin. Initially, the α particle approaches with speed v along a line a distance b from a parallel line COA through the origin. The force on the α particle is $F = kq_\alpha Q/r^2$, given by Coulomb's law (see Figure 4-6). After scattering, when the α particle is again far from the nucleus, it is moving with the same speed v parallel to the line OB, which makes an angle θ with line COA. (Since the potential energy is again zero, the final speed must be equal to the initial speed by conservation of energy, assuming, as Rutherford did, that the massive nucleus remains fixed during the scattering.) The distance b is called the *impact parameter*, and the angle θ, the *scattering angle*. The path of the α particle

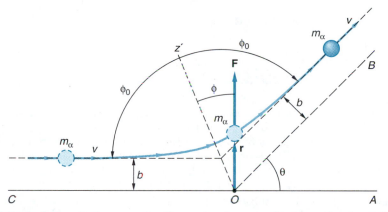

Fig. 4-5 Rutherford scattering geometry. The nucleus is assumed to be a point charge Q at the origin O. At any distance r the α particle experiences a repulsive force $kq_\alpha Q/r^2$. The α particle travels along a hyperbolic path that is initially parallel to line OA a distance b from it and finally parallel to line OB, which makes an angle θ with OA. The scattering angle θ can be related to the impact parameter b by classical mechanics.

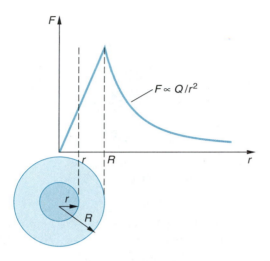

Fig. 4-6 Force on a point charge versus distance r from the center of a uniformly charged sphere of radius R. Outside the sphere the force is proportional to Q/r^2, where Q is the total charge. Inside the sphere, the force is proportional to $q'/r^2 = Qr/R^3$, where $q' = Q(r/R)^3$ is the charge within a sphere of radius r. The maximum force occurs at $r = R$.

can be shown to be a hyperbola, and the scattering angle θ can be related to the impact parameter b from the laws of classical mechanics. The result is

$$b = \frac{kq_\alpha Q}{m_\alpha v^2} \cot \frac{\theta}{2} \qquad \textbf{4-3}$$

Of course, it is not possible to choose or know the impact parameter for any α particle; but, recalling the values of the cotangent between 0° and 90°, all such particles with impact parameters less than or equal to a particular b will be scattered through an angle θ greater than or equal to that given by Equation 4-3; i.e., the smaller the impact parameter, the larger the scattering angle (Figure 4-7). Let the intensity of the incident α particle beam be I_0 particles per second per unit area. The number per second scattered by one nucleus through angles greater than θ equals the number per second that have impact parameters less than $b(\theta)$. This number is $\pi b^2 I_0$.

The quantity πb^2, which has the dimensions of an area, is called the *cross section* σ for scattering through angles greater than θ. The cross section σ is thus

The particle-scattering technique devised by Rutherford to "look" at atoms now has wide application throughout physics. Scattering of high-energy electrons from protons and neutrons provided our first experimental hint of the existence of quarks.

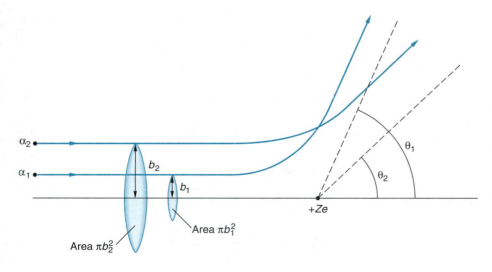

Fig. 4-7 Two α particles with equal kinetic energies approach the positive charge $Q = +Ze$ with impact parameters b_1 and b_2, where $b_1 < b_2$. According to Equation 4-3, the angle θ_1 through which α_1 is scattered will be larger than θ_2. In general, all α particles with impact parameters smaller than a particular value of b will have scattering angles larger than the corresponding value of θ from Equation 4-3. The area πb^2 is called the cross section for scattering with angles greater than θ.

Fig. 4-8 The total number of nuclei of foil atoms in the area covered by the beam is nAt, where n is the number of foil atoms per unit volume, A is the area of the beam, and t is the thickness of the foil.

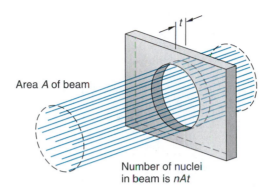

Area A of beam

Number of nuclei
in beam is nAt

defined as the number scattered per nucleus per unit time divided by the incident intensity. The total number of particles scattered per second is obtained by multiplying $\pi b^2 I_0$ by the number of nuclei in the scattering foil (this assumes the foil to be thin enough to make the chance of overlap negligible). Let n be the number of nuclei per unit volume:

$$n = \frac{\rho(\text{g/cm}^3) \, N_A(\text{atoms/mol})}{M(\text{g/mol})} = \frac{\rho N_A}{M} \frac{\text{atoms}}{\text{cm}^3} \qquad \textbf{4-4}$$

For a foil of thickness t, the total number of nuclei "seen" by the beam is nAt, where A is the area of the beam (Figure 4-8). The total number scattered per second through angles greater than θ is thus $\pi b^2 I_0 ntA$. If we divide this by the number of α particles incident per second $I_0 A$, we get the fraction f scattered through angles greater than θ:

$$f = \pi b^2 \, nt \qquad \textbf{4-5}$$

EXAMPLE 4-2 Scattered Fraction f Calculate the fraction of an incident beam of α particles of kinetic energy 5 MeV that Geiger and Marsden expected to see for $\theta \geq 90°$ from a gold foil ($Z = 79$) 10^{-6} m thick.

Solution

1. The fraction f is related to the impact parameter b, the number density of nuclei n, and the thickness t by Equation 4-5:

$$f = \pi b^2 nt$$

2. The particle density n is given by Equation 4-4:

$$n = \frac{\rho N_A}{M} = \frac{(19.3 \text{ g/cm}^3)(6.02 \times 10^{23} \text{ atoms/mol})}{197 \text{ g/mol}}$$

$$= 5.90 \times 10^{22} \text{ atoms/cm}^3 = 5.90 \times 10^{28} \text{ atoms/m}^3$$

3. The impact parameter b is related to θ by Equation 4-3:

$$b = \frac{kq_\alpha Q}{m_\alpha v^2} \cot \frac{\theta}{2} = \frac{(2)(79) \, ke^2}{2K_\alpha} \cot \frac{90°}{2}$$

$$= \frac{(2)(79)(1.44 \text{ eV} \cdot \text{nm})}{(2)(5 \times 10^6 \text{ eV})} = 2.28 \times 10^{-5} \text{ nm}$$

$$= 2.28 \times 10^{-14} \text{ m}$$

4.   Substituting these into Equation 4-5 yields f:

$$f = \pi(2.28 \times 10^{-14}\text{m})^2\left(5.9 \times 10^{28} \frac{\text{atoms}}{\text{m}^3}\right)(10^{-6} \text{ m})$$

$$= 9.6 \times 10^{-5} \approx 10^{-4}$$

Remarks: *This is in good agreement with Geiger and Marsden's measurement of about 1 in 8000 in their first trial. Thus, the nuclear model is in good agreement with their results.*

On the strength of the good agreement between the nuclear atomic model and the measured fraction of the incident α particles scattered at angles $\theta \geq 90°$, Rutherford derived an expression, based on the nuclear model, for the number of α particles ΔN that would be scattered at any angle θ. That number, which also depends on the atomic number Z and thickness t of the scattering foil, on the intensity I_0 of the incident α particles and their kinetic energy E_k, and on the geometry of the detector (A_{sc} is the detector area and r is the foil-detector distance), is given by

$$\Delta N = \left(\frac{I_0 A_{sc} nt}{r^2}\right)\left(\frac{kZe^2}{2E_k}\right)^2 \frac{1}{\sin^4(\theta/2)} \qquad \textbf{4-6}$$

Within the uncertainties of their experiments, which involved visually observing several hundred thousand α particles, Geiger and Marsden verified every one of the predictions of Rutherford's formula over four orders of magnitude of ΔN. The excellent agreement of their data with Equation 4-6 firmly established the nuclear atomic model as the correct basis for further studies of atomic and nuclear phenomena. (See Figure 4-12.)

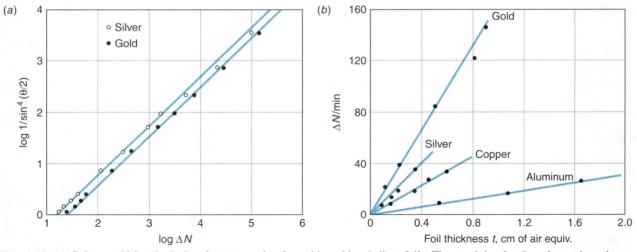

Fig. 4-12 (*a*) Geiger and Marsden's data for α scattering from thin gold and silver foils. The graph is a log-log plot to show the data over several orders of magnitude. Note that scattering angle increases downward along the vertical axis. (*b*) Geiger and Marsden also measured the dependence of ΔN on t predicted by Equation 4-6 for foils made from a wide range of elements, this being an equally critical test. Results for four of the elements used are shown.

More

Rutherford's derivation of Equation 4-6 was based on his atomic model and the well-known Coulomb scattering process of charged particles. *Rutherford's Prediction and Geiger and Marsden's Results* are described on the home page: www.whfreeman.com/modphysics4e See also Equations 4-7 through 4-10 here, as well as Figures 4-9 through 4-12.

The Size of the Nucleus

The fact that the force law is shown to be correct, confirming Rutherford's model, does not imply that the nucleus is a mathematical point charge, however. The force law would be the same even if the nucleus were a ball of charge of some radius R_0, as long as the α particle did not penetrate the ball. (See Figures 4-5 and 4-13.) For a given scattering angle, the distance of closest approach of the α particle to the nucleus can be calculated from the geometry of the collision. For the largest angle, near 180°, the collision is nearly "head-on." The corresponding distance of closest approach r_d is thus an experimental upper limit on the size of the target nucleus. We can calculate the distance of closest approach for a head-on collision r_d by noting that conservation of energy requires the potential energy at this distance to equal the original kinetic energy:

$$(V + E_k)_{\text{large } r} = (V + E_k)_{r_d}$$

$$(0 + \tfrac{1}{2}m_\alpha v^2)_{\text{large } r} = \left(\frac{kq_\alpha Q}{r_d} + 0\right)_{r_d}$$

$$\frac{1}{2}m_\alpha v^2 = \frac{kq_\alpha Q}{r_d}$$

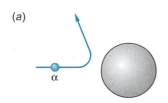

(a)

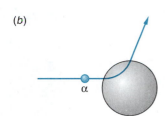

(b)

Fig. 4-13 (*a*) If the α particle does not penetrate the nuclear charge, the nucleus can be considered a point charge located at the center. (*b*) If the particle has enough energy to penetrate the nucleus, the Rutherford scattering law does not hold, but would require modification to account for that portion of the nuclear charge "behind" the penetrating α particle.

or

$$r_d = \frac{kq_\alpha Q}{\tfrac{1}{2}m_\alpha v^2} \qquad \textbf{4-11}$$

For the case of 7.7-MeV α particles, the distance of closest approach for a head-on collision is

$$r_d = \frac{(2)(79)(1.44 \text{ eV} \cdot \text{nm})}{7.7 \times 10^6 \text{ eV}} \approx 3 \times 10^{-5}\,\text{nm} = 3 \times 10^{-14}\,\text{m}$$

For other collisions, the distance of closest approach is somewhat greater, but for α particles scattered at large angles it is of the same order of magnitude. The excellent agreement of Geiger and Marsden's data at large angles with the prediction of Equation 4-6 thus indicates that the radius of the gold nucleus is no larger than about 3×10^{-14} m. If higher-energy particles could be used, the distance of closest approach would be smaller; and as the energy of the α particles increased, we might expect that eventually the particles would penetrate the nucleus. Since, in that event, the force law is no longer $F = kq_\alpha Q/r^2$, the data would not agree with the point-nucleus calculation. Rutherford

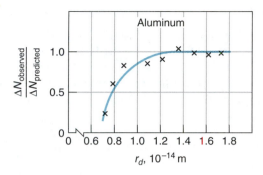

Fig. 4-14 Data from Rutherford's group showing observed α scattering at a large fixed angle versus values of r_d computed from Equation 4-11 for various kinetic energies.

did not have higher-energy α particles available, but he could reduce the distance of closest approach by using targets of lower atomic numbers.[9] For the case of aluminum, with $Z = 13$, the most energetic α particles that he had available (7.7 MeV from ^{214}Bi), scattered at large angles did not follow the predictions of Equation 4-6. However, when their kinetic energy was reduced by passing the beam through thin mica sheets of various thicknesses, the data again followed the prediction of Equation 4-6. Rutherford's data are shown in Figure 4-14. The value of r_d (calculated from Equation 4-11) at which the data begin to deviate from the prediction can be thought of as the surface of the nucleus. From these data, Rutherford estimated the radius of the aluminum nucleus to be about 1.0×10^{-14} m. (The radius of the Al nucleus is actually about 3.6×10^{-15} m. See Chap. 11.)

A unit of length convenient for describing nuclear sizes is the fermi, or femtometer (fm), defined by 1 fm $= 10^{-15}$ m. As we shall see in Chapter 11, the nuclear radius varies from about 1 to 10 fm from the lightest to the heaviest atoms.

EXAMPLE 4-3 Rutherford Scattering at Angle θ In a particular experiment, α particles from ^{226}Ra are scattered at $\theta = 45°$ from a silver foil and 450 particles are counted each minute at the scintillation detector. If everything is kept the same except that the detector is moved to observe particles scattered at 90°, how many will be counted per minute?

Solution
Using Equation 4-6, we have that $\Delta N = 450$ when $\theta = 45°$, but we don't have any of the other parameters available. Letting all of the quantities in the parentheses equal a constant C, we have

$$\Delta N = 450 = C \sin^{-4}\left(\frac{45°}{2}\right)$$

or

$$C = 450 \sin^4\left(\frac{45°}{2}\right)$$

When the detector is moved to $\theta = 90°$, the value of C is unchanged, so

$$\Delta N = C \sin^{-4}\left(\frac{90°}{2}\right) = 450 \sin^4\left(\frac{45°}{2}\right) \sin^{-4}\left(\frac{90°}{2}\right)$$

$$= 38.6 \approx 39 \text{ particles/min}$$

EXAMPLE 4-4 **Alpha Scattering** A beam of α particles with $E_k = 6.0$ MeV impinges on a silver foil 1.0 μm thick. The beam current is 1.0 nA. How many α particles will be counted by a small scintillation detector of area equal to 5 mm² located 2.0 cm from the foil at an angle of 75°? (For silver $Z = 47$, $\rho = 10.5$ gm/cm³, and $M = 108$.)

Solution

1. The number counted ΔN is given by Equation 4-6:

$$\Delta N = \left(\frac{I_0 A_{sc} nt}{r^2}\right)\left(\frac{kZe^2}{2E_k}\right)^2 \frac{1}{\sin^4(\theta/2)}$$

2. Since each α particle has $q_\alpha = 2e$, I_0 is:

$$I_0 = (1.0 \times 10^{-9}\,\text{A})(2 \times 1.60 \times 10^{-19}\,C/\alpha)^{-1}$$
$$= 3.12 \times 10^9\,\alpha/s$$

3. The kinetic energy of each α is:

$$E_k = (6.0\,\text{MeV})(1.60 \times 10^{-13}\,\text{J/MeV})$$
$$= 9.60 \times 10^{-13}\,\text{J}$$

4. For silver, n is given by:

$$n = \rho N_A/M$$
$$= \frac{(110.5\,\text{g/cm}^3)(6.02 \times 10^{23}\,\text{atoms/mol})}{108\,\text{g/mol}}$$
$$= 5.85 \times 10^{22}\,\text{atoms/cm}^3 = 5.85 \times 10^{28}\,\text{atoms/m}^3$$

5. Substituting the given values and computed results into Equation 4-6 gives ΔN:

$$\Delta N = \frac{(3.12 \times 10^9\,\alpha/s)(5 \times 10^{-6}\,\text{m}^2)(5.85 \times 10^{28}\,\text{atoms/m}^3)(10^{-6}\,\text{m})}{(2 \times 10^{-2})^2 \sin^4(75°/2)}$$
$$\times \left[\frac{(9 \times 10^9)(47)(1.60 \times 10^{-19})^2}{(2)(9.60 \times 10^{-13})}\right]$$
$$= 528\,\alpha/s$$

EXAMPLE 4-5 **Radius of the Au Nucleus** The radius of the gold (Au) nucleus has been measured by high-energy electron scattering as 6.6 fm. What kinetic energy α particles would Rutherford have needed so that for 180° scattering, the α particle would just reach the nuclear surface before reversing direction?

Solution

From Equation 4-11, we have

$$\frac{1}{2}m_\alpha v^2 = \frac{kq_\alpha Q}{r_d} = \frac{(9 \times 10^9)(2)(79)(1.6 \times 10^{-19})^2}{6.6 \times 10^{-15}}$$

$$= 5.52 \times 10^{-12}\,\text{J} = 34.5\,\text{MeV}$$

Alpha particles of such energy are not emitted by naturally radioactive materials and hence were not accessible to Rutherford. Thus, he could not have performed an experiment for Au equivalent to that for Al illustrated by Figure 4-14.

QUESTIONS

1. Why can't the impact parameter for a particular α particle be chosen?

2. Why is it necessary to use a very thin target foil?

3. Why could Rutherford place a lower limit on the radius of the Al nucleus but not on the Au nucleus?

4. How could you use the data in Figure 4-12*a* to determine the charge on a silver nucleus relative to that on a gold nucleus?

5. How would you expect the data (not the curve) to change in Figure 4-12 if the foil were so thick that an appreciable number of gold nuclei were hidden from the beam by being in the "shadow" of the other gold nuclei?

4-3 The Bohr Model of the Hydrogen Atom

In 1913, the Danish physicist Niels H. D. Bohr[10] proposed a model of the hydrogen atom which combined the work of Planck, Einstein, and Rutherford and was remarkably successful in predicting the observed spectrum of hydrogen. The Rutherford

Niels Bohr explains a point in front of the blackboard (1956). [*American Institute of Physics, Niels Bohr Library, Margrethe Bohr Collection.*]

model assigned charge and mass to the nucleus but was silent regarding the distribution of the charge and mass of the electrons. Bohr, who had been working in Rutherford's laboratory during the experiments of Geiger and Marsden, made the assumption that the electron in the hydrogen atom moved in an orbit about the positive nucleus, bound by the electrostatic attraction of the nucleus. Classical mechanics allows circular or elliptical orbits in this system, just as in the case of the planets orbiting the sun. For simplicity, Bohr chose to consider circular orbits.

Such a model is mechanically stable, because the Coulomb potential $V = -kZe^2/r$ provides the centripetal force

$$F = \frac{kZe^2}{r^2} = \frac{mv^2}{r} \qquad \textbf{4-12}$$

necessary for the electron to move in a circle of radius r at speed v; but it is electrically unstable because the electron is always accelerating toward the center of the circle. The laws of electrodynamics predict that such an accelerating charge will radiate light of frequency f equal to that of the periodic motion, which in this case is the frequency of revolution. Thus, classically,

$$f = \frac{v}{2\pi r} = \left(\frac{kZe^2}{rm}\right)^{1/2}\frac{1}{2\pi r} = \left(\frac{kZe^2}{4\pi^2 m}\right)^{1/2}\cdot\frac{1}{r^{3/2}} \sim \frac{1}{r^{3/2}} \qquad \textbf{4-13}$$

The total energy of the electron is the sum of the kinetic and the potential energies:

$$E = \frac{1}{2}mv^2 + \left(-\frac{kZe^2}{r}\right)$$

From Equation 4-12, we see that $\frac{1}{2}mv^2 = kZe^2/2r$ (a result that holds for circular motion in any inverse-square force field), so the total energy can be written as

$$E = \frac{kZe^2}{2r} - \frac{kZe^2}{r} = -\frac{kZe^2}{2r} \sim -\frac{1}{r} \qquad \textbf{4-14}$$

Thus, classical physics predicts that, as energy is lost to radiation, the electron's orbit will become smaller and smaller while the frequency of the emitted radiation will become higher and higher, further increasing the rate at which energy is lost and ending when the electron reaches the nucleus. (See Figure 4-15a.) The time required for the electron to spiral into the nucleus can be calculated from classical mechanics and

Fig. 4-15 (*a*) In the classical orbital model, the electron orbits about the nucleus and spirals into the center because of the energy radiated. (*b*) In the Bohr model, the electron orbits without radiating until it jumps to another allowed radius of lower energy, at which time radiation is emitted.

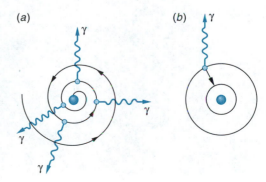

electrodynamics; it turns out to be less than a microsecond. Thus, at first sight, this model predicts that the atom will radiate a continuous spectrum (since the frequency of revolution changes continuously as the electron spirals in) and will collapse after a very short time, a result that fortunately does not occur. Unless excited by some external means, atoms do not radiate at all; and when excited atoms do radiate, a line spectrum is emitted, not a continuous one.

Bohr "solved" these formidable difficulties with two decidedly nonclassical postulates. His first postulate was that <u>electrons could move in certain orbits without radiating</u>. He called these orbits *stationary states*. His second postulate was to assume that <u>the atom radiates when the electron makes a transition from one stationary state to another</u> (Figure 4-15b) <u>and that the frequency f of the emitted radiation is not the frequency of motion in either stable orbit but is related to the energies of the orbits by Planck's theory</u>

$$hf = E_i - E_f \qquad\qquad \textbf{4-15}$$

where h is Planck's constant and E_i and E_f are the energies of the initial and final states. The second assumption, which is equivalent to that of energy conservation with the emission of a photon, is crucial because it deviated from classical theory, which requires the frequency of radiation to be that of the motion of the charged particle. Equation 4-15 is referred to as the Bohr *frequency condition*.

In order to determine the energies of the allowed, nonradiating orbits, Bohr made a third assumption, now known as the *correspondence principle,* which had profound implications:

In the limit of large orbits and large energies, quantum calculations must agree with classical calculations.

Thus the correspondence principle says that, whatever modifications of classical physics are made to describe matter at the submicroscopic level, when the results are extended to the macroscopic world they must agree with those from the classical laws of physics that have been so abundantly verified in the everyday world. While Bohr's detailed model of the hydrogen atom has been supplanted by modern quantum theory, which we shall discuss in later chapters, his frequency condition (Equation 4-15) and the correspondence principle remain as essential features of the new theory.

In his first paper,[11] in 1913, Bohr pointed out that his results implied that the angular momentum of the electron in the hydrogen atom can take on only values that are integral multiples of Planck's constant divided by 2π, in agreement with a discovery made a year earlier by J. W. Nicholson. That is, <u>angular momentum is quantized; it can assume only the values $nh/2\pi$, where n is an integer</u>. Rather than follow the intricacies of Bohr's derivation, we shall use the fundamental conclusion of angular momentum quantization to find his expression for the observed spectra. The development that follows applies not only to hydrogen, but to any atom of nuclear charge $+Ze$ with a single orbital electron—e.g., singly ionized helium He^+, or doubly ionized lithium Li^{++}.

If the nuclear charge is $+Ze$ and the electron charge $-e$, we have noted (Equation 4-12) that the centripetal force necessary to move the electron in a circular orbit is provided by the Coulomb force kZe^2/r^2. Solving Equation 4-12 for the speed of the orbiting electron yields

$$v = \left(\frac{kZe^2}{mr}\right)^{1/2} \qquad \text{4-16}$$

Bohr's quantization of the angular momentum L is

$$L = mvr = \frac{nh}{2\pi} = n\hbar \qquad n = 1, 2, 3, \cdots \qquad \text{4-17}$$

where the integer n is called a *quantum number* and $\hbar = h/2\pi$. (The constant $\hbar$, read "h-bar," is often more convenient to use than h itself, just as the angular frequency $\omega = 2\pi f$ is often more convenient than the frequency f.) Combining Equations 4-16 and 4–17 allows us to write for the circular orbits:

$$r = \frac{n\hbar}{mv} = \frac{n\hbar}{m}\left(\frac{rm}{kZe^2}\right)^{1/2}$$

Squaring this relation gives

$$r^2 = \frac{n^2\hbar^2}{m^2}\left(\frac{rm}{kZe^2}\right)$$

and canceling common quantities yields

$$r_n = \frac{n^2\hbar^2}{mkZe^2} = \frac{n^2 a_0}{Z} \qquad \text{4-18}$$

where

$$a_0 = \frac{\hbar^2}{mke^2} = 0.529\text{Å} = 0.0529 \text{ nm} \qquad \text{4-19}$$

is called the *Bohr radius*. Thus, we find that the stationary orbits of Bohr's first postulate have quantized radii, denoted in Equation 4-18 by the subscript on r_n. Notice that the Bohr radius a_0 for hydrogen ($Z = 1$) corresponds to the orbit radius with $n = 1$, the smallest Bohr orbit possible for the electron in a hydrogen atom. Since $r_n \sim Z^{-1}$, the Bohr orbits for single-electron atoms with $Z > 1$ are closer to the nucleus than the corresponding ones for hydrogen.

The total energy of the electron (Equation 4-14) then becomes, upon substitution of r_n from Equation 4-18,

$$E_n = -\frac{kZe^2}{2r_n} = -\frac{kZe^2}{2}\left(\frac{mkZe^2}{n^2\hbar^2}\right)$$

$$E_n = -\frac{mk^2Z^2e^4}{2\hbar^2 n^2} = -E_0\frac{Z^2}{n^2} \qquad n = 1, 2, 3, \cdots \qquad \text{4-20}$$

where $E_0 = mk^2e^4/2\hbar^2$. Thus, the energy of the electron is also quantized, i.e., the stationary states correspond to specific values of the total energy. This means that energies E_i and E_f that appear in the frequency condition of Bohr's second postulate must be from the allowed set E_n and Equation 4-15 becomes

$$hf = E_{n_i} - E_{n_f} = -E_0 \frac{Z^2}{n_i^2} - \left(-E_0 \frac{Z^2}{n_f^2} \right)$$

or

$$f = \frac{E_0 Z^2}{h} \left(\frac{1}{n_f^2} - \frac{1}{n_i^2} \right)$$ **4-21**

which can be written in the form of the Rydberg-Ritz equation (Equation 4-2) by substituting $f = c/\lambda$ and dividing by c to obtain

$$\frac{1}{\lambda} = \frac{E_0 Z^2}{hc} \left(\frac{1}{n_f^2} - \frac{1}{n_i^2} \right)$$

or

$$\frac{1}{\lambda} = Z^2 R \left(\frac{1}{n_f^2} - \frac{1}{n_i^2} \right)$$ **4-22**

where

$$R = \frac{E_0}{hc} = \frac{mk^2 e^4}{4\pi c \hbar^3}$$ **4-23**

is Bohr's prediction for the value of the Rydberg constant.

Using the values of m, e, c, and $\hbar$ known in 1913, Bohr calculated R and found his result to agree (within the limits of uncertainties of the constants) with the value obtained from spectroscopy, 1.097×10^7 m^{-1}. Bohr noted in his original paper that this equation might be valuable in determining the best values for the constants e, m, and $\hbar$ because of the extreme precision possible in measuring R. This has indeed turned out to be the case.

The possible values of the energy of the hydrogen atom predicted by Bohr's model are given by Equation 4-20 with $Z = 1$:

$$E_n = -\frac{mk^2 e^4}{2\hbar^2 n^2} = -\frac{E_0}{n^2}$$ **4-24**

where

$$E_0 = \frac{mk^2 e^4}{2\hbar^2} = 2.18 \times 10^{-18}\,\text{J} = 13.6\,\text{eV}$$

is the magnitude of E_n with $n = 1$. $E_1 \, (= -E_0)$ is called the *ground state*. It is convenient to plot these allowed energies of the stationary states as in Figure 4-16. Such a plot is called an *energy-level diagram*. Various series of transitions between the stationary states are indicated in this diagram by vertical arrows drawn between the levels. The frequency of light emitted in one of these transitions is the energy difference divided by h according to Bohr's frequency condition, Equation 4-15. The energy required to remove the electron from the atom, 13.6 eV, is called the *ionization energy*, or *binding energy*, of the electron.

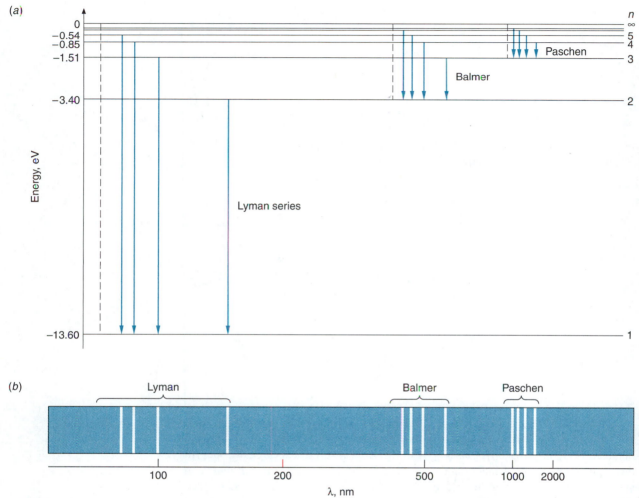

Fig. 4-16 (*a*) Energy-level diagram for hydrogen showing the seven lowest stationary states and the four lowest energy transitions each for the Lyman, Balmer, and Paschen series. There are an infinite number of levels. Their energies are given by $E_n = -13.6/n^2$ eV, where n is an integer. The dashed line shown for each series is the *series limit,* corresponding to the energy that would be radiated by an electron at rest far from the nucleus ($n \rightarrow \infty$) in a transition to the state with $n = n_f$ for that series. The horizontal spacing between the transitions shown for each series is proportional to the wavelength spacing between the lines of the spectrum. (*b*) The spectral lines corresponding to the transitions shown for the three series. Notice the regularities within each series, particularly the short-wavelength limit and the successively smaller separation between adjacent lines as the limit is approached. The wavelength scale in the diagram is not linear.

A bit different sort of application, the Bohr-Rutherford model of the nuclear atom and electron orbits is the picture that, for millions of people, provides their link to the world of the atom and subatomic phenomena.

At the time Bohr's paper was published there were two spectral series known for hydrogen: the Balmer series, corresponding to $n_f = 2$, $n_i = 3, 4, 5, \ldots$ and a series named after its discoverer, Paschen (1908), corresponding to $n_f = 3$, $n_i = 4, 5, 6, \ldots$. Equation 4-22 indicated that other series should exist for different values of n_f. In 1916 Lyman found the series corresponding to $n_f = 1$, and in 1922 and 1924 Brackett and Pfund, respectively, found series corresponding to $n_f = 4$ and $n_f = 5$. As can be easily determined by computing the wavelengths for these series, only the Balmer series lies primarily in the visible portion of the electromagnetic spectrum. The Lyman series is in the ultraviolet, the others in the infrared.

EXAMPLE 4-6 **Wavelength of the H_β Line** Compute the wavelength of the H_β spectral line, i.e., the second line of the Balmer series predicted by Bohr's model. The H_β line is emitted in the transition from $n_i = 4$ to $n_f = 2$.

Solution

1. *Method 1:* The wavelength is given by Equation 4-22 with $Z = 1$:

$$\frac{1}{\lambda} = R\left(\frac{1}{n_f^2} - \frac{1}{n_i^2}\right)$$

2. Substituting $R = 1.097 \times 10^7$ m^{-1} and the values of n_i and n_f:

$$\frac{1}{\lambda} = (1.097 \times 10^7)\left(\frac{1}{2^2} - \frac{1}{4^2}\right)$$

or

$$\lambda = 4.86 \times 10^{-7} = 486 \text{ nm}$$

3. *Method 2:* The wavelength may also be computed from Equation 4-15:

$$hf = hc/\lambda = E_i - E_f$$

or

$$\frac{1}{\lambda} = \frac{1}{hc}(E_i - E_f)$$

4. The values of E_i and E_f are given by Equation 4-24:

$$E_i = -\frac{13.6 \text{ eV}}{n_i^2} = -\frac{13.6 \text{ eV}}{4^2} = -0.85 \text{ eV}$$

$$E_f = -\frac{13.6 \text{ eV}}{n_f^2} = -\frac{13.6 \text{ eV}}{2^2} = -3.4 \text{ eV}$$

5. Substituting these into Equation 4-15 yields:

$$\frac{1}{\lambda} = \frac{[-0.85 \text{ eV} - (-3.4 \text{ eV})](1.60 \times 10^{-19} \text{ J/eV})}{(6.63 \times 10^{-34} \text{ J·s})(3.00 \times 10^8 \text{ m/s})}$$
$$= 2.051 \times 10^6 \text{ m}^{-1}$$

or

$$\lambda = 4.87 \times 10^{-7} \text{ m} = 487 \text{ nm}$$

Remarks: *The difference in the two results is due to rounding of the Rydberg constant to three decimal places.*

Reduced Mass Correction

The assumption by Bohr that the nucleus is fixed is equivalent to the assumption that it has infinite mass. In fact, the Rydberg constant in Equation 4-23 is normally written as R_∞, as we will do henceforth. If the nucleus has mass M its kinetic energy will be $\frac{1}{2}Mv^2 = p^2/2M$, where $p = Mv$ is the momentum. If we assume that the total momentum of the atom is zero, conservation of momentum requires that the momenta of the nucleus and electron be equal in magnitude. The total kinetic energy is then

$$E_k = \frac{p^2}{2M} + \frac{p^2}{2m} = \frac{M + m}{2mM}p^2 = \frac{p^2}{2\mu}$$

where

$$\mu = \frac{mM}{m + M} = \frac{m}{1 + m/M} \qquad \text{4-25}$$

This is slightly different from the kinetic energy of the electron because μ, called the *reduced mass,* is slightly different from the electron mass. The results derived above for a nucleus of infinite mass can be applied directly for the case of a nucleus of mass M if we replace the electron mass in the equations by reduced mass μ, defined by Equation 4-25. (The validity of this procedure is proven in most intermediate and advanced mechanics books.) The Rydberg constant (Equation 4-23) is then written

$$R = \frac{\mu k^2 e^4}{4\pi c\hbar^3} = \frac{mk^2 e^4}{4\pi c\hbar^3}\left(\frac{1}{1 + m/M}\right) = R_\infty\left(\frac{1}{1 + m/M}\right) \qquad \text{4-26}$$

This correction amounts to only 1 part in 2000 for the case of hydrogen and to even less for other nuclei; however, the predicted variation in the Rydberg constant from atom to atom is precisely that which is observed. For example, the spectrum of a singly ionized helium atom, which has one remaining electron, is just that predicted by Equations 4-22 and 4-26 with $Z = 2$ and the proper helium mass. The current value for the Rydberg constant R_∞ from precision spectroscopic measurements[12] is

$$R_\infty = 1.0973731 \times 10^7 \text{ m}^{-1} \qquad \text{4-27}$$

Urey[13] used the reduced mass correction to the spectral lines of the Balmer series to discover (in 1931) a second form of hydrogen whose atoms had twice the mass of ordinary hydrogen. The heavy form was called *deuterium.* The two forms, atoms with the same Z but different masses, are called *isotopes.*

EXAMPLE 4-7 Rydberg Constants for H and He⁺ Compute the Rydberg constants for H and He⁺ applying the reduced mass correction ($m = 9.1094 \times 10^{-31}$ kg, $m_p = 1.6726 \times 10^{-27}$ kg, $m_\alpha = 6.6447 \times 10^{-27}$ kg).

Solution

For hydrogen:

$$R_H = R_\infty \left(\frac{1}{1 + m/M_H} \right) = R_\infty \left(\frac{1}{1 + 9.1094 \times 10^{-31}/1.6726 \times 10^{-27}} \right)$$

$$= 1.09677 \times 10^7 \, \text{m}^{-1}$$

For helium: Since M in the reduced mass correction is the mass of the nucleus, for this calculation we use M equal to the α particle mass.

$$R_{He} = R_\infty \left(\frac{1}{1 + 9.1094 \times 10^{-31}/6.6447 \times 10^{-27}} \right) = 1.09752 \times 10^7 \, \text{m}^{-1}$$

Thus the two Rydberg constants differ by about 0.07 percent.

Correspondence Principle

According to the correspondence principle, which applies also to modern quantum mechanics, when the energy levels are closely spaced, quantization should have little effect; classical and quantum calculations should give the same results. From the energy-level diagram of Figure 4-16, we see that the energy levels are close together when the quantum number n is large. This leads us to a slightly different statement of Bohr's correspondence principle: in the region of very large quantum numbers (n in this case) classical calculation and quantum calculation must yield the same results. To see that the Bohr model of the hydrogen atom does indeed obey the correspondence principle, let us compare the frequency of a transition between level $n_i = n$ and level $n_f = n - 1$ for large n with the classical frequency, which is the frequency of revolution of the electron. From Equation 4-22 we have

$$f = \frac{c}{\lambda} = \frac{Z^2 m k^2 e^4}{4\pi\hbar^3} \left[\frac{1}{(n-1)^2} - \frac{1}{n^2} \right] = \frac{Z^2 m k^2 e^4}{4\pi\hbar^3} \frac{2n-1}{n^2(n-1)^2}$$

For large n we can neglect the 1s subtracted from n and $2n$ to obtain

$$f \approx \frac{Z^2 m k^2 e^4}{4\pi\hbar^3} \frac{2}{n^3} = \frac{Z^2 m k^2 e^4}{2\pi\hbar^3 n^3} \qquad \textbf{4-28}$$

The classical frequency of revolution of the electron is (see Equation 4-13)

$$f_{rev} = \frac{v}{2\pi r}$$

Using $v = n\hbar/mr$ from Equation 4-17 and $r = n^2\hbar^2/mkZe^2$ from Equation 4-18, we obtain

$$f_{rev} = \frac{(n\hbar/mr)}{2\pi r} = \frac{n\hbar}{2\pi mr^2} = \frac{n\hbar}{2\pi m(n^2\hbar^2/mkZe^2)^2}$$

$$f_{rev} = \frac{m^2 k^2 Z^2 e^4 n\hbar}{2\pi m n^4 \hbar^4} = \frac{m k^2 Z^2 e^4}{2\pi\hbar^3 n^3} \qquad \textbf{4-29}$$

which is the same as Equation 4-28.

Fine-Structure Constant

The demonstration of the correspondence principle for large n in the preceding paragraph was for $\Delta n = n_i - n_f = 1$; however, we have seen (see Figure 4-16) that transitions occur in the hydrogen atom for $\Delta n \geq 1$ when n is small, and such transitions should occur for large n, too. If we allow $\Delta n = 2, 3, \ldots$ for large values of n, then the frequencies of the emitted radiation would be, according to Bohr's model, integer multiples of the frequency given in Equation 4-28. In that event, Equations 4-28 and 4-29 would not agree. This disagreement can be avoided by allowing elliptical orbits.[14] A result of Newtonian mechanics, familiar from planetary motion, is that in an inverse-square force field, the energy of an orbiting particle depends only on the major axis of the ellipse and not on its eccentricity. There is consequently no change in the energy at all unless the force differs from inverse square or unless Newtonian mechanics is modified. A. Sommerfeld considered the effect of special relativity on the mass of the electron in the Bohr model in an effort to explain the observed *fine structure* of the hydrogen spectral lines.[15] Since the relativistic corrections should be of the order of v^2/c^2 (see Chapter 2), it is likely that a highly eccentric orbit would have a larger correction, because v becomes greater as the electron moves nearer the nucleus. The Sommerfeld calculations are quite complicated, but we can estimate the order of magnitude of the effect of special relativity by calculating v/c for the first Bohr orbit in hydrogen. For $n = 1$, we have from Equation 4-17 that $mvr_1 = \hbar$. Then, using $r_1 = a_0 = \hbar^2/mke^2$, we have

$$v = \frac{\hbar}{mr_1} = \frac{\hbar}{m(\hbar^2/mke^2)} = \frac{ke^2}{\hbar}$$

and

$$\frac{v}{c} = \frac{ke^2}{\hbar c} = \frac{1.44 \text{ eV} \cdot \text{nm}}{197.3 \text{ eV} \cdot \text{nm}} \approx \frac{1}{137} = \alpha \qquad \textbf{4-30}$$

where we have used another convenient combination

$$\hbar c = \frac{1.24 \times 10^3 \text{ eV} \cdot \text{nm}}{2\pi} = 197.3 \text{ eV} \cdot \text{nm} \qquad \textbf{4-31}$$

The dimensionless quantity $ke^2/\hbar c = \alpha$ is called the *fine-structure constant* because of its first appearance in Sommerfeld's theory, but, as we shall see, it has much more fundamental importance.

Though v^2/c^2 is very small, an effect of this magnitude is observable. In Sommerfeld's theory, the fine structure of the hydrogen spectrum is explained in the following way. For each allowed circular orbit of radius r_n and energy E_n, a set of n elliptical orbits is possible of equal major axes but different eccentricities. Since the velocity of a particle in an elliptical orbit depends on the eccentricity, so then will the mass and momentum, and therefore the different ellipses for a given n will have slightly different energies. Thus, the energy radiated when the electron changes orbit depends slightly on the eccentricities of the initial and final orbits as well as on their major axes. The splitting of the energy levels for a given n is called *fine-structure splitting*, and its value turns out to be of the order of $v^2/c^2 = \alpha^2$, just as Sommerfeld predicted. However, the agreement of Sommerfeld's prediction with the observed fine-structure splitting was quite accidental and led to considerable confusion in the

early days of quantum theory. Although he had used the relativistic mass and momentum, he computed the energy using classical mechanics, leading to a correction much larger than that actually due only to relativistic effects. As we shall see in Chapter 7, fine structure is associated with a completely nonclassical property of the electron called *spin*.

A lasting contribution of Sommerfeld's effort was the introduction of the fine-structure constant $\alpha = ke^2/\hbar c \approx 1/137$. With it we can write the Bohr radius a_0 and the quantized energies of the Bohr model in a particularly elegant form. Equations 4-24 and 4-19 for hydrogen become

$$E_n = -\frac{mk^2e^4}{2\hbar^2n^2} \cdot \frac{c^2}{c^2} = -\frac{mc^2}{2}\alpha^2\frac{1}{n^2} \qquad \text{4-32}$$

$$a_0 = \frac{\hbar^2}{mke^2} \cdot \frac{c}{c} = \frac{\hbar}{mc}\frac{1}{\alpha} \qquad \text{4-33}$$

Since α is a dimensionless number formed of universal constants, *all* observers will measure the same value for it and find that energies and dimensions of atomic systems are proportional to α^2 and $1/\alpha$, respectively. We will return to the implications of this intriguing fact later in the book.

Exploring

Giant Atoms

Giant atoms called *Rydberg atoms,* long understood to be a theoretical possibility and first detected in interstellar space in 1965, are now being produced and studied in the laboratory. Notice in Equation 4-18 that the radius of the electron orbit $r_n \propto n^2$ and n can be any positive integer, so the diameter of a hydrogen atom (or any other atom, for that matter) could be very large, a millimeter or even a meter! What keeps such giant atoms from being common is that the energy difference between adjacent allowed energy states is extremely small when n is large and the allowed states are very near the $E_\infty = 0$ level where ionization occurs, because $E_n \propto 1/n^2$. For example, if $n = 1000$ the diameter of a hydrogen atom would be $r_{1000} \approx 0.1$ *mm*, but both E_{1000} and the difference in energy $\Delta E = E_{1001} - E_{1000}$ are about 10^{-5} eV! This energy is far below the average energy of thermal motion at ordinary temperatures (about 0.025 eV), so random collisions would quickly ionize an atom whose electron happened to get excited to a level with n equal to 20 or so with r still only about 10^{-8} m.

The advent of precisely tunable dye lasers in the 1970s made it possible to nudge electrons carefully into orbits with larger and larger n values. The largest Rydberg atoms made so far, typically using sodium or potassium, are 10,000 times the diameter of ordinary atoms, about 20 μm across or the size of a fine grain of sand, and exist for several milliseconds inside vacuum chambers. For hydrogen, this corresponds to quantum number $n \approx 600$. An electron moving so far from the nucleus is bound by a minuscule force. This provides several intriguing possibilities. For example, very small electric fields might be studied, enabling the tracking of chemical reactions that proceed too quickly to be followed otherwise. More dramatic is the possibility of directly testing Bohr's correspondence principle by directly observing the slow (since $v \propto 1/n$) movement of the electron around the

large *n* orbits—the transition from quantum mechanics to classical mechanics. Computer simulations of the classical motion of a Rydberg electron "wave" (see Chapter 5) in orbit around a nucleus are aiding in the design of experiments to observe the correspondence principle.

QUESTIONS

6. If the electron moves in an orbit of greater radius, does its total energy increase or decrease? Does its kinetic energy increase or decrease?

7. What is the energy of the shortest-wavelength photon that can be emitted by the hydrogen atom?

8. How would you characterize the motion and location of an electron with $E = 0$ and $n \to \infty$ in Figure 4-16?

4-4 X-Ray Spectra

Henry G.-J. Moseley.
[*Courtesy of University of Manchester.*]

The extension of the Bohr theory to atoms more complicated than hydrogen proved difficult. Quantitative calculations of the energy levels of atoms of more than one electron could not be made from the model, even for helium, the next element in the periodic table. However, experiments by H. Moseley in 1913 and J. Franck and G. Hertz in 1914 strongly supported the general Bohr-Rutherford picture of the atom as a positively charged core surrounded by electrons that moved in quantized energy states relatively far from the core. Moseley's analysis of x-ray spectra will be discussed in this section, and the Franck-Hertz measurement of the transmission of electrons through gases will be discussed in the next section.

Using the methods of crystal spectrometry that had just been developed by W. H. Bragg and W. L. Bragg, Moseley[16] measured the wavelengths of the characteristic x-ray line spectra for about 40 different target elements. (Typical x-ray spectra were shown in Figure 3-18.) He noted that the x-ray line spectra varied in a regular way from element to element, unlike the irregular variations of optical spectra. He surmised that this regular variation occurred because characteristic x-ray spectra were due to transitions involving the innermost electrons of the atoms. (see Figure 4-17.) Because the inner electrons are shielded from the outermost electrons by those in intermediate orbits, their energies do not depend on the complex interactions of the outer electrons, which are responsible for the complicated optical spectra. Furthermore, the inner electrons are well shielded from the interatomic forces which are responsible for the binding of atoms in solids.

According to the Bohr theory (published earlier the same year, 1913), the energy of an electron in the first Bohr orbit is proportional to the square of the nuclear charge (see Equation 4-20). Moseley reasoned that the energy, and therefore the frequency, of a characteristic x-ray photon should vary as the square of the atomic number of the target element. He therefore plotted the square root of the frequency of a particular characteristic line in the x-ray spectrum of various target elements versus the atomic number *Z* of the element. Such a plot, now called a *Moseley plot,* is shown in Figure 4-18 (page 188). These curves can be fitted by the empirical equation

$$f^{1/2} = A_n(Z - b) \qquad \textbf{4-34}$$

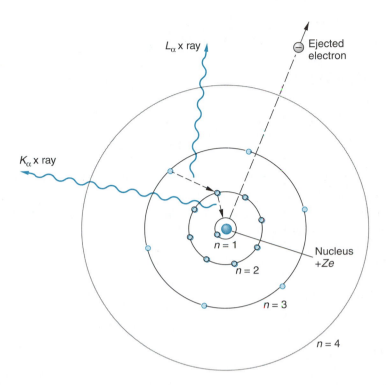

L_α x ray

Ejected electron

K_α x ray

n = 1

n = 2

n = 3

n = 4

Nucleus +Ze

Fig. 4-17 A stylized picture of the Bohr circular orbits for $n = 1, 2, 3,$ and 4. The radii $r_n \sim n^2$. In a high-Z element (elements with $Z \geq 12$ emit x rays), electrons are distributed over all the orbits shown. Should an electron in the $n = 1$ orbit be knocked from the atom, e.g., by being hit by a fast electron accelerated by the voltage across an x-ray tube, the vacancy thus produced is filled by an electron of higher energy (i.e., $n = 2$ or higher). The difference in energy between the two orbits is emitted as a photon, according to the frequency condition, whose wavelength will be in the x-ray region of the spectrum, if Z is large enough.

where A_n and b are constants for each characteristic x-ray line. One family of lines, called the *K series*, has $b = 1$ and slightly different values of A_n for each line in the graph. The other family shown in Figure 4-18, called the *L series,*[17] could be fitted by Equation 4-34 with $b = 7.4$.

If the bombarding electron in the x-ray tube knocks an electron from the inner orbit ($n = 1$) in a target atom completely out of the atom, photons will be emitted corresponding to transitions of electrons in other orbits ($n = 2, 3, \ldots$) to fill the vacancy in the $n = 1$ orbit. (See Figure 4-17.) (Since these lines are called the *K series,* the $n = 1$ orbit came to be called the *K shell.*) The lowest-frequency line corresponds to the lowest energy transition ($n = 2$ to $n = 1$). This line is called the K_α line. The transition $n = 3$ to $n = 1$ is called the K_β line. It is of higher energy, and hence higher frequency, than the K_α line. A vacancy created in the $n = 2$ orbit by emission of a K_α x ray may then be filled by an electron of higher energy, e.g., one in the $n = 3$ orbit, resulting in the emission of a line in the L series, and so on. The multiple L lines in the Moseley plot (Figure 4-18) are due in part to the fact that there turn out to be small differences in the energies of electrons with a given n that are not predicated by the Bohr model. Moseley's work gave the first indication of these differences, but the explanation will have to await our discussion of more advanced quantum theory in Chapter 7.

Using the Bohr relation for a one-electron atom (Equation 4-21) with $n_f = 1$, and using $(Z - 1)$ in place of Z, we obtain for the frequencies of the K series

$$f = \frac{mk^2e^4}{4\pi\hbar^3}(Z - 1)^2\left(\frac{1}{1^2} - \frac{1}{n^2}\right) = cR_\infty(Z - 1)^2\left(1 - \frac{1}{n^2}\right) \qquad \textbf{4-35}$$

where R_∞ is the Rydberg constant. Comparing this with Equation 4-34, we see that A_n is given by

$$A_n^2 = cR_\infty\left(1 - \frac{1}{n^2}\right) \qquad \textbf{4-36}$$

The wavelengths of the lines in the K series are then given by

$$\lambda = \frac{c}{f} = \frac{c}{A_n^2(Z-1)^2} = \frac{1}{R_\infty(Z-1)^2\left(1 - \frac{1}{n^2}\right)} \qquad \textbf{4-37}$$

EXAMPLE 4-8 K_α **for Molybdenum** Calculate the wavelength of the K_α line of molybdenum ($Z = 42$), and compare the result with the value $\lambda = 0.0721$ nm measured by Moseley and with the spectrum in Figure 3-18b.

Solution

Using $n = 2$, $R_\infty = 1.097 \times 10^7$ m^{-1}, and $Z = 42$ we obtain

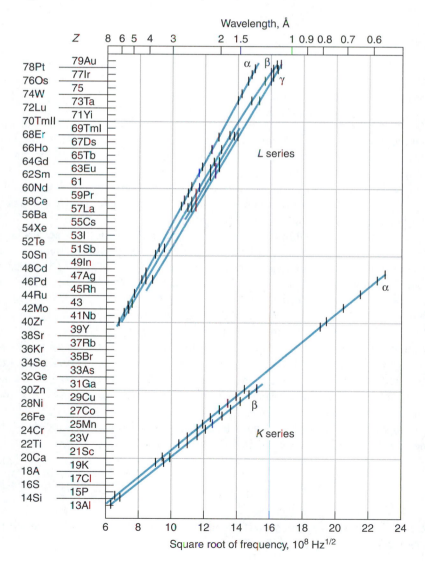

Fig. 4-18 Moseley's plots of the square root of frequency versus Z for characteristic x rays. When an atom is bombarded by high-energy electrons, an inner atomic electron is sometimes knocked out, leaving a vacancy in the inner shell. The K-series x rays are produced by atomic transitions to vacancies in the $n = 1$ (K) shell, whereas the L series is produced by transitions to the vacancies in the $n = 2$ (L) shell. [*From H. Moseley, Philosophical Magazine (6), 27, 713 (1914).*]

$$\lambda = \left[(1.097 \times 10^7\,\text{m}^{-1})(41)^2\left(1 - \frac{1}{4}\right)\right]^{-1} = 7.23 \times 10^{-11}\,\text{m} = 0.0723\,\text{nm}$$

This value is within 0.3 percent of Moseley's measurement and agrees well with that in Figure 3-18b.

The fact that f is proportional to $(Z - 1)^2$ rather than to Z^2 is explained by the partial shielding of the nuclear charge by the other electron remaining in the K shell as "seen" by electrons in the $n = 2$ (L) shell.[18] Using this reasoning, Moseley concluded that, since $b = 7.4$ for the L series, these lines involved electrons farther from the nucleus, which "saw" the nuclear charge shielded by more inner electrons. Assuming that the L series was due to transitions to the $n = 2$ shell, the frequencies for this series are given by

$$f = cR_\infty\left(\frac{1}{2^2} - \frac{1}{n^2}\right)(Z - 7.4)^2 \qquad \textbf{4-38}$$

where $n = 3, 4, 5, \ldots$.

Before Moseley's work, the atomic number was merely the place number of the element in Mendeleev's periodic table of the element arranged by weight. The experiments of Geiger and Marsden showed that the nuclear charge was approximately $A/2$, while x-ray scattering experiments by Barkla showed that the number of electrons in an atom was approximately $A/2$. These two experiments are consistent, since the atom as a whole must be electrically neutral. However, several discrepancies were found in the periodic table as arranged by weight. For example, the 18th element in order of weight is potassium (39.102), and the 19th is argon (39.948). Arrangement by weight, however, puts potassium in the column with the inert gases and argon with the active metals, the reverse of their known chemical properties.

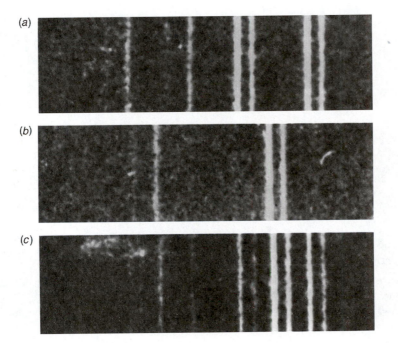

Fig. 4-19 Characteristic x-ray spectra. (*a*) Part of the spectra of neodymium ($Z = 60$) and samarium ($Z = 62$). The two pairs of bright lines are the K_α and K_β lines. (*b*) Part of the spectrum of the artificially produced element promethium ($Z = 61$). This element was first positively identified in 1945 at the Clinton Laboratory (now Oak Ridge). Its K_α and K_β lines fall between those of neodymium and samarium, just as Moseley predicted. (*c*) Part of the spectra of all three of the elements neodymium, promethium, and samarium. [*Courtesy of J. A. Swartout, Oak Ridge National Laboratory.*]

Moseley showed that for these elements to fall on the line $f^{1/2}$ versus Z, argon had to have $Z = 18$ and potassium $Z = 19$. Arranging the elements by the Z number obtained from the Moseley plot, rather than by weight, gave a periodic chart in complete agreement with the chemical properties. Moseley also pointed out that there were gaps in the periodic table at $Z = 43$, 61, and 75, indicating the presence of undiscovered elements. All have subsequently been found. Figure 4-19 illustrates the discovery of promethium ($Z = 61$).

Auger Electrons

The process of producing x rays necessarily results in the ionization of the atom, since an inner electron is ejected. The vacancy created is filled by an outer electron, producing the x rays studied by Moseley. In 1923 Pierre Auger discovered that, as an alternative to x-ray emission, the atom may eject a third electron from a higher-energy outer shell via a radiationless process called the *Auger effect*. In the Auger (pronounced "oh-zhay") process, the energy difference $\Delta E = E_2 - E_1$ that could have resulted in the emission of a K_α x ray is removed from the atom by the third

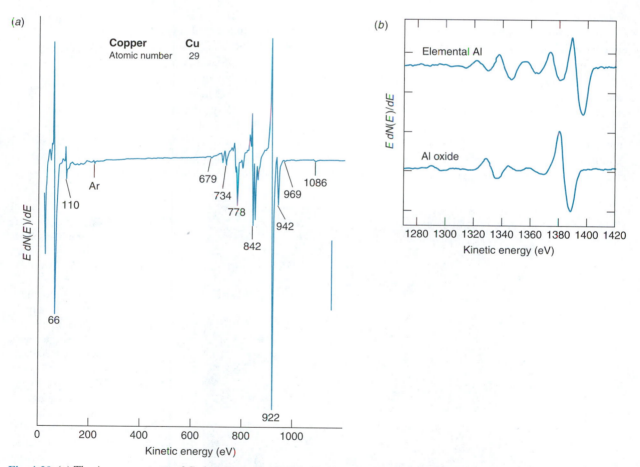

Fig. 4-20 (*a*) The Auger spectrum of Cu bombarded with 10-keV electrons. The energy of the Auger electrons is more precisely determined by plotting the weighted derivative $E \, dN(E)/dE$ of the electron intensity rather than the intensity $N(E)$. (*b*) A portion of the Auger spectrum of Al from elemental Al and Al oxide. Note the energy shift in the largest peaks resulting from adjustments in the Al electron shell energies in the Al_2O_3 molecule.

electron, e.g., one in the $n = 3$ shell. Since the magnitude of $E_3 < \Delta E$, the $n = 3$ electron would leave the atom with a characteristic kinetic energy $\Delta E - |E_3|$, which is determined by the stationary-state energies of the particular atom.[19] Thus, each element has a characteristic Auger electron spectrum. (See Figure 4-20a.) Measurement of the Auger electrons provides a simple and highly sensitive tool for identifying impurities on clean surfaces in electron microscope systems and investigating electron energy shifts associated with molecular bonding. (See Figure 4-20b.)

QUESTION

9. Why did Moseley plot $f^{1/2}$ versus Z rather than f versus Z?

4-5 The Franck-Hertz Experiment

While investigating the inelastic scattering of electrons, J. Franck and G. Hertz[20] performed an important experiment that confirmed by direct measurement Bohr's hypothesis of energy quantization in atoms. First done in 1914, it is now a standard undergraduate laboratory experiment. Figure 4-21a is a schematic diagram of the apparatus. A small heater heats the cathode. Electrons are ejected from the heated cathode and accelerated toward a grid, which is at a positive potential V_0 relative to the cathode. Some electrons pass through the grid and reach the plate P, which is at a slightly lower potential $V_p = V_0 - \Delta V$. The tube is filled with a low-pressure gas of the element

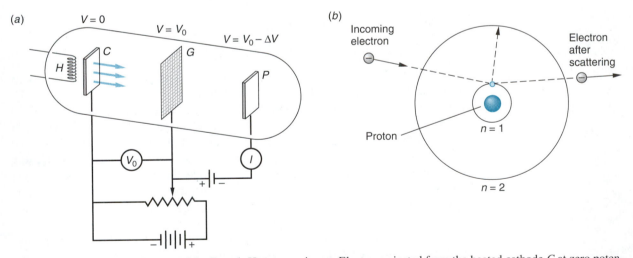

Fig. 4-21 (a) Schematic diagram of the Franck-Hertz experiment. Electrons ejected from the heated cathode C at zero potential are drawn to the positive grid G. Those passing through the holes in the grid can reach the plate P and thereby contribute to the current I, if they have sufficient kinetic energy to overcome the small back potential ΔV. The tube contains a low-pressure gas of the element being studied. (b) Results for hydrogen. If the incoming electron does not have sufficient energy to transfer $\Delta E = E_2 - E_1$ to the hydrogen electron in the $n = 1$ orbit (ground state), then the scattering will be elastic. If the incoming electron does have at least ΔE kinetic energy, then an inelastic collision can occur in which ΔE is transferred to the $n = 1$ electron, moving it to the $n = 2$ orbit. The excited electron will typically return to the ground state very quickly, emitting a photon of energy ΔE.

being investigated (mercury vapor, in Franck and Hertz's experiment). The experiment involves measuring the plate current as a function of V_0. As V_0 is increased from 0, the current increases until a critical value (about 4.9 V for Hg) is reached, at which point the current suddenly decreases. As V_0 is increased further, the current rises again.

The explanation of this result is a bit easier to visualize if we think for the moment of a tube filled with hydrogen atoms instead of mercury. (See Figure 4-21b.) Electrons accelerated by V_0 that collide with hydrogen electrons cannot transfer energy to the latter unless they have acquired kinetic energy $eV_0 = E_2 - E_1 = 10.2$ eV, since the hydrogen electron according to Bohr's model cannot occupy states with energies intermediate between E_1 and E_2. Such a collision will thus be elastic; i.e., the incident electron's kinetic energy will be unchanged by the collision, and thus it can overcome the small retarding potential ΔV and contribute to the current I. However, if $eV_0 \geq 10.2$ eV, then the incoming electron can transfer 10.2 eV to the hydrogen electron in the *ground state* ($n = 1$ orbit), putting it into the $n = 2$ orbit (the *first excited state*). The incoming electron's energy is thus reduced by 10.2 eV; it has been inelastically scattered. With insufficient energy to overcome the small retarding potential ΔV, the incoming electrons can no longer contribute to the plate current I, and I drops sharply.

The situation with Hg in the tube is more complicated, since Hg has 80 electrons. Although Bohr's theory is not capable of predicting their individual energies, we still expect the energy to be quantized with a ground state, first excited state, and so on, for the atom. Thus, the explanation of the observed 4.9-V critical potential for Hg is that the first excited state is about 4.9 eV above the lowest level (ground state). Electrons with energy less than this cannot lose energy to the Hg atoms, but electrons with energy greater than 4.9 eV can make inelastic collisions and lose 4.9 eV. If this happens near the grid, these electrons cannot gain enough energy to overcome the small back voltage ΔV and reach the plate; the current therefore decreases. If this explanation is correct, the Hg atoms that are excited to an energy level of 4.9 eV above the ground state should return to the ground state by emitting light of wavelength

$$\lambda = \frac{c}{f} = \frac{hc}{hf} = \frac{hc}{eV_0} = 253 \text{ nm}$$

There is indeed a line of this wavelength in the mercury spectrum. When the tube is viewed with a spectroscope, this line is seen when V_0 is greater than 4.9 eV, while no lines are seen when V_0 is less than this amount. For further increases in V_0, additional sharp decreases in the current are observed, corresponding either to excitation of other levels in Hg (e.g., the second excited state of Hg is at 6.7 eV above the ground state) or to multiple excitation of the first excited state, i.e., due to an electron losing 4.9 eV more than once. In the usual setup, multiple excitations of the first level are observed and decreases in the current are seen at integer multiples of 4.9 eV.[21] The probability of observing such multiple first-level excitations, or excitations of other levels, depends on the detailed variation of the potential of the tube. For example, a second decrease in the current at $V_0 = 2 \times 4.9 = 9.8$ V results when electrons have inelastic collisions with Hg atoms about halfway between the cathode and grid (see Figure 4-21a). They are reaccelerated, reaching 4.9 eV again in the vicinity of the grid. A plot of the data of Franck and Hertz is shown in Figure 4-22.

The Franck-Hertz experiment was an important confirmation of the idea that discrete optical spectra were due to the existence in atoms of discrete energy levels which could be excited by nonoptical methods. It is particularly gratifying to be able to detect the existence of discrete energy levels directly by measurements using only voltmeters and ammeters.

Electron Energy Loss Spectroscopy

The Franck-Hertz experiment was the precursor of a highly sensitive technique for measuring the quantized energy states of atoms in both gases and solids. The technique, called *electron energy loss spectroscopy* (*EELS*), is particularly useful in solids, where it makes possible measurement of the energy of certain types of lattice vibrations and other processes. It works like this. Suppose that the electrons in an incident beam all have energy E_{inc}. They collide with the atoms of a material, causing them to undergo some process (e.g., vibration, lattice rearrangement, electron excitation) that requires energy E_1. Then, if a beam electron initiates a single such process, it will exit the material with energy $E_{inc} - E_1$—i.e., it has been inelastically scattered. The exit energy can be measured very accurately with, e.g., a magnetic spectrometer similar to that described in Section 3-1, but designed for electrons.[22] Figure 4-23a illustrates a typical experimental arrangement for measuring an energy-loss spectrum.

As an example of its application, if an incident beam of electrons with $E_{inc} = 2$ keV is reflected from a thin Al film, the scattered electron energies measured in the magnetic spectrometer result in the energy-loss spectrum shown in Figure 4-23b, which directly represents the quantized energy levels of the target material. The loss peaks in this particular spectrum are due to the excitation of harmonic vibrations in the film, as well as some surface vibrations. The technique is also used to measure the vibrational energies of impurity atoms that may be absorbed on the surface and, with higher incident electron energies, to measure energy losses at the atomic inner levels, thus yielding information about bonding and other characteristics of absorbed atoms. Inelastic scattering techniques, including those using particles in addition to electrons, provide very powerful means for probing the energy structure of atomic, molecular, and nuclear systems. We will have occasion to refer to them many times throughout the rest of the book.

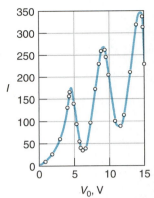

Fig. 4-22 Current versus accelerating voltage in the Franck-Hertz experiment. The current decreases because many electrons lose energy due to inelastic collisions with mercury atoms in the tube and therefore cannot overcome the small back potential indicated in Figure 4-21a. The regular spacing of the peaks in this curve indicates that only a certain quantity of energy, 4.9 eV, can be lost to the mercury atoms. This interpretation is confirmed by the observation of radiation of photon energy 4.9 eV emitted by the mercury atoms, when V_0 is greater than 4.9 V. [*From J. Franck and G. Hertz*, Verband Deutscher Physiklischer Gesellschaften, *16, 457 (1914).*]

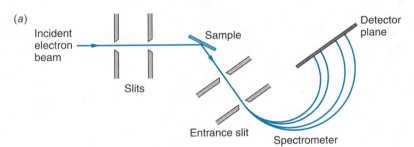

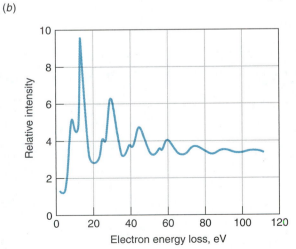

Fig. 4-23 Energy-loss spectrum measurement. (*a*) A well-defined electron beam impinges upon the sample. Electrons inelastically scattered at a convenient angle enter the slit of the magnetic spectrometer, whose B field is directed out of the paper, and turn through radii R determined by their energy $(E_{inc} - E_1)$ via Equation 3-2 written in the form $R = [2m(E_{inc} - E_1)]^{1/2}/eB$. (*b*) An energy-loss spectrum for a thin Al film. [*From C. J. Powell and J. B. Swan*, Physical Review, *115, 869 (1954).*]

4-6 Critique of Bohr Theory and of the "Old" Quantum Mechanics

We have seen in this and the preceding chapters that many phenomena—blackbody radiation, the photoelectric effect, Compton scattering, optical spectra of hydrogen, and the x-ray spectra of many elements—could be "explained" by various ad hoc quantum assumptions. These "theories," a strange mixture of classical physics and quantum assumptions, are now usually referred to as "old" quantum mechanics. Applying this quantum mechanics in the early years of the twentieth century was as much an art as a science, for no one knew exactly what the rules were. The successes of the Bohr theory, however, were substantial and spectacular. The existence of unknown spectral lines was predicted and later observed. Not only was the Rydberg constant given in terms of known constants, but its slight variation from atom to atom was accurately predicted by the slight variation in the reduced mass. The radius of the first Bohr orbit in hydrogen, 0.053 nm, corresponded well with the known diameter of the hydrogen molecule, about 0.22 nm. The wavelengths of the characteristic x-ray spectra could be calculated from the Bohr theory.

The failures of the Bohr theory and the old quantum mechanics were mainly matters of omission. While the correct H atom transitions were predicted, the theory was silent on the *rate* at which they occurred; i.e., there was no way of predicting the relative intensities of spectral lines. There was little success in applying the theory to the optical spectra of more complex atoms. Finally, there was the considerable philosophical problem that its assumptions lacked foundation. There were no a priori reasons to expect that Coulomb's law would work but that the laws of radiation would not, or that Newton's laws could be used even though only certain values of angular momentum were allowed. In the 1920s scientists struggled with these difficulties, and a systematic theory, now known as *quantum mechanics* or *wave mechanics,* was formulated by de Broglie, Schrödinger, Heisenberg, Pauli, Dirac, and others. We shall study some aspects of this theory in the next two chapters and apply it to the study of atoms, nuclei, and solids in the remaining chapters of this book. We shall see that, though this theory is much more satisfying from a philosophical point of view, it is somewhat abstract and difficult to apply in detail to problems. In spite of its shortcomings, the Bohr theory provides a model that is easy to visualize, gives the correct energy levels in hydrogen, and is often useful in describing a quantum-mechanical calculation.

Summary

TOPIC	RELEVANT EQUATIONS AND REMARKS	
1. Atomic spectra	$$\frac{1}{\lambda_{mn}} = R\left(\frac{1}{m^2} - \frac{1}{n^2}\right) \qquad n > m$$	4-2
	This empirical equation computes the correct wavelengths of observed spectral lines. The Rydberg constant R varies in a regular way from element to element.	
2. Rutherford scattering		
Impact parameter	$$b = \frac{kq_\alpha Q}{m_\alpha v^2} \cot \frac{\theta}{2}$$	4-3

TOPIC	RELEVANT EQUATIONS AND REMARKS	
Scattered fraction f	$f = \pi b^2 n t$ for a scattering foil with n nuclei/unit volume and thickness t	4-5
Number of scattered alphas observed	$\Delta N = \left(\dfrac{I_0 A_{sc}\, nt}{r^2}\right)\left(\dfrac{kZe^2}{2E_k}\right)^2 \dfrac{1}{\sin^4(\theta/2)}$	4-6
Size of nucleus	$r_d = \dfrac{kq_\alpha Q}{\frac{1}{2}m_\alpha v^2}$	4-11

3. Bohr model

    Bohr's postulates

1. Electrons occupy only certain nonradiating, stable, circular orbits selected by quantization of the angular momentum L.

$$L = mvr = \frac{nh}{2\pi} = n\hbar \qquad \text{for integer} \qquad n \qquad \text{4-17}$$

2. Radiation of frequency f occurs when the electron jumps from an allowed orbit of energy E_i to one of lower energy E_f. f is given by the frequency condition:

$$hf = E_i - E_f \qquad \text{4-15}$$

    Correspondence principle

In the region of very large quantum numbers classical and quantum calculations must yield the same results.

    Bohr radius

$$a_0 = \frac{\hbar^2}{mke^2} = \frac{\hbar}{mc\alpha} = 0.0529 \text{ nm} \qquad \text{4-19}$$

    Allowed energies

$$E_n = -\frac{Z^2 E_0}{n^2} \qquad \text{for} \qquad n = 1, 2, 3, \ldots \qquad \text{4-20}$$

where $E_0 = mk^2 e^4/2\hbar^2 = 13.6$ eV

    Reduced mass

$$\mu = \frac{mM}{m + M} \qquad \text{4-25}$$

    Fine-structure constant

$$\alpha = \frac{ke^2}{\hbar c} \approx 1/137 \qquad \text{4-30}$$

4. X-ray spectra

    Moseley equation

$$f^{1/2} = A_n(Z - b) \qquad \text{4-34}$$

5. Franck-Hertz experiment

Supported Bohr's theory by verifying the quantization of atomic energies in absorption.

GENERAL REFERENCES

The following general references are written at a level appropriate for the readers of this book.

Boorse, H., and L. Motz (eds.), *The World of the Atom*, Basic Books, New York, 1966. This two-volume, 1873-page work is a collection of original papers, translated and edited. Much of the work referred to in this chapter and throughout this book can be found in these volumes.

Cline, B., *The Questioners: Physicists and the Quantum Theory*, Thomas Y. Crowell, New York, 1965.

Gamow, G., *Thirty Years That Shook Physics: The Story of the Quantum Theory*, Doubleday, Garden City, N.Y., 1965.

Herzberg, G., *Atomic Spectra and Atomic Structure,* Dover, New York, 1944. This is without doubt one of the all-time classics of atomic physics.

Melissinos, A., *Experiments in Modern Physics,* Academic Press, New York, 1966. Many of the classic experiments that are now undergraduate laboratory experiments are described in detail in this text.

Mohr, P. J., and B. N. Taylor, "The Fundamental Physical Constants," *Physics Today* (August 2002).

Shamos, M. H. (ed.), *Great Experiments in Physics,* Holt, Rinehart & Winston, New York, 1962.

Virtual Laboratory (PEARL), Physics Academic Software, North Carolina State University, Raleigh, 1996. Includes an interactive model of the Bohr atom.

Visual Quantum Mechanics, Kansas State University, Manhattan, 1996. The atomic spectra component of this software provides an interactive construction of the energy levels for several elements, including hydrogen and helium.

NOTES

1. Joseph von Fraunhofer (1787–1826), German physicist. Although he was not the first to see the dark lines in the solar spectrum that bear his name (Wollaston had seen seven, 12 years earlier), he systematically measured their wavelengths, named the prominent ones, and showed that they always occurred at the same wavelength, even if the sunlight were reflected from the moon or a planet.

2. To date more than 10,000 Fraunhofer lines have been found in the solar spectrum.

3. Although experimentalists preferred to express their measurements in terms of wavelengths, it had been shown that the many empirical formulas being constructed to explain the observed regularities in the line spectra could be expressed in simpler form if the reciprocal wavelength, called the *wave number* and equal to the number of waves per unit length, were used instead. Since $c = f\lambda$, this was equivalent to expressing the formulas in terms of the frequency.

4. Ernest Rutherford (1871–1937), English physicist, an exceptional experimentalist and a student of J. J. Thomson. He was an early researcher in the field of radioactivity and received the Nobel Prize in 1908 for his work in the transmutation of elements. He bemoaned the fact that his prize was awarded in chemistry, not in physics, as work with the elements was considered chemistry in those days. He was Thomson's successor as director of the Cavendish Laboratory.

5. Alpha particles, like all charged particles, lose energy by exciting and ionizing the molecules of the materials through which they are moving. The energy lost per unit path length $(-dE/dx)$ is a function of the ionization potential of the molecules, the atomic number of the atoms, and the energy of the α particles. It can be computed (with some effort) and is relatively simple to measure experimentally.

6. Notice that $2\pi \sin\theta \, d\theta = d\Omega$, the differential solid angle subtended at the scattering nucleus by the surface in Figure 4-11. Since the cross section $\sigma = \pi b^2$, then $d\sigma = 2\pi b \, db$ and Equation 4-9 can be rewritten as

$$\frac{d\sigma}{d\Omega} = \left(\frac{kZe^2}{m_\alpha v^2}\right)\frac{1}{\sin^4(\theta/2)}$$

$d\sigma/d\Omega$ is called the *differential cross section.*

7. H. Geiger and E. Marsden, *Philosophical Magazine* (6), **25**, 605 (1913).

8. The value of Z could not be measured directly in this experiment; however, relative values for different foil materials could be found and all materials heavier than aluminum had Z approximately equal to half the atomic weight.

9. This also introduces a deviation from the predicted ΔN associated with Rutherford's assumption that the nuclear mass was much larger than the α particle mass. For lighter-atomic-weight elements that assumption is not valid. Correction for the nuclear mass effect can be made, however, and the data in Figure 4-12*b* reflect the correction.

10. Niels H. D. Bohr (1885–1962), Danish physicist and first-rate soccer player. He went to the Cavendish Laboratory to work with J. J. Thomson after receiving his Ph.D.; however, Thomson is reported to have been impatient with Bohr's soft, accented English. Happily, the occasion of Thomson's annual birthday banquet brought Bohr in contact with Rutherford, whom he promptly followed to the latter's laboratory at Manchester, where he learned of the nuclear atom. A giant of twentieth-century physics, Bohr was awarded the Nobel Prize in 1922 for his explanation of the hydrogen spectrum. On a visit to the United States in 1939, he brought the news that the fission of uranium atoms had been observed. The story of his life makes absolutely fascinating reading.

11. N. Bohr, *Philosophical Magazine* (6), **26**, 1 (1913).

12. P. J. Mohr and B. N. Taylor, "The Fundamental Physical Constants," *Physics Today* (August 2002). Only 8 of the 14 current significant figures are given in Equation 4-27. The relative uncertainty in the value is about 1 part in 10^{12}!

13. Harold C. Urey (1893–1981), American chemist. His work opened the way for the use of isotopic tracers in biological systems. He was recognized with the Nobel Prize in 1934.

14. The basic reason that elliptical orbits solve this problem is that the frequency of the radiation emitted classically depends on the acceleration of the charge. The acceleration is constant for a circular orbit, but varies for elliptical orbits, being dependent on the instantaneous distance from the focus. The energy of a particle in a circular orbit of radius r is the same as that of a particle in an elliptical orbit with a semimajor axis of r; so one would expect the only allowed elliptical orbits to be those whose semimajor axis was equal to an allowed Bohr circular orbit radius.

15. Viewed with spectrographs of high resolution, the spectral lines of hydrogen in Figure 4-2a—and, indeed, most spectral lines of all elements—are found to consist of very closely spaced sets of lines, i.e., fine structure. We will discuss this topic in detail in Chapter 7.

16. Henry G.-J. Moseley (1887–1915), English physicist, considered by some the most brilliant of Rutherford's students. He would surely have been awarded the Nobel Prize had he not been killed in action in World War I. His father was a naturalist on the expedition of HMS *Challenger,* the first vessel ever devoted to the exploration of the oceans.

17. The identifiers *L* and *K* were assigned by the English physicist C. G. Barkla, the discoverer of the characteristic x-ray lines, for which he received the Nobel Prize in 1917. He discovered two sets of x-ray lines for each of several elements, the *longer* wavelength of which he called the *L* series, the other the *K* series. The identifiers stuck and were subsequently used to label the atomic electron shells.

18. That the remaining *K* electron should result in *b* = 1, i.e., shielding of exactly 1*e,* is perhaps a surprise. Actually it was a happy accident. It is the combined effect of the remaining *K* electron and the penetration of the electron waves of the outer *L* electrons that resulted in making *b* = 1, as we will see in Chapter 7.

19. Since in multielectron atoms the energies of the stationary states depend in part on the number of electrons in the atom (see Chapter 7), the energies E_n for a given atom change slightly when it is singly ionized, as in the production of characteristic x-ray lines, or doubly ionized, as in the Auger effect.

20. James Franck (1882–1964), German-American physicist; Gustav L. Hertz (1887–1975), German physicist. Franck won an Iron Cross as a soldier in World War I and later worked on the Manhattan Project. Hertz was a nephew of Heinrich Hertz, discoverer of the photoelectric effect. For their work on the inelastic scattering of electrons, Franck and Hertz shared the 1925 Nobel Prize in physics.

21. We should note at this point that there is an energy state in the Hg atom at about 4.6 eV, slightly lower than the one found by Franck and Hertz. However, transitions from the ground state to the 4.6-eV level are not observed, and their absence is in accord with the prediction of more advanced quantum mechanics, as we shall see in Chapter 7.

22. Since *q/m* for electrons is much larger than for ionized atoms, the radius for an electron magnetic spectrometer need not be as large as for a mass spectrometer, even for electron energies of several keV. (See Equation 3-2.)

PROBLEMS

Level I

Section 4-1 Atomic Spectra

4-1. Compute the wavelength and frequency of the series limit for the Lyman, Balmer, and Paschen spectral series of hydrogen.

4-2. The wavelength of a particular line in the Balmer series is measured to be 379.1 nm. What transition does it correspond to?

4-3. An astronomer finds a new absorption line with λ = 164.1 nm in the ultraviolet region of the sun's continuous spectrum. He attributes the line to hydrogen's Lyman series. Is he right? Justify your answer.

4-4. The series of hydrogen spectral lines with *m* = 4 is called Brackett's series. Compute the wavelengths of the first four lines of Brackett's series.

4-5. In a sample that contains hydrogen, among other things, four spectral lines are found in the infrared with wavelengths 7460 nm, 4654 nm, 4103 nm, and 3741 nm. Which one does not belong to a hydrogen spectral series?

Section 4-2 Rutherford's Nuclear Model

4-6. A gold foil of thickness 2.0 μm is used in a Rutherford experiment to scatter α particles with energy 7.0 MeV. (*a*) What fraction of the particles will be scattered at angles greater than 90°? (*b*) What fraction will be scattered at angles between 45° and 75°? (For gold, ρ = 19.3 g/cm³ and *M* = 197 g/mol.)

4-7. (*a*) What is the ratio of the number of particles per unit area on the screen scattered at 10° to those at 1°? (*b*) What is the ratio of those scattered at 30° to those at 1°?

4-8. For α particles of 7.7 MeV (those used by Geiger and Marsden), what impact parameter will result in a deflection of 2° for a thin gold foil?

4-9. What will be the distance of closest approach r_d to a gold nucleus for an α particle of 5.0 MeV? 7.7 MeV? 12 MeV?

4-10. What energy α particle would be needed to just reach the surface of an Al nucleus if its radius is 4 fm?

4-11. If a particle is deflected by 0.01° in each collision, about how many collisions would be necessary to produce an rms deflection of 10°? (Use the result from the one-dimensional random walk problem in statistics stating that the rms deflection equals the magnitude of the individual deflections times the square root of the number of deflections.) Compare this result with the number of atomic layers in a gold foil of thickness 10^{-6} m, assuming that the thickness of each atom is 0.1 nm $= 10^{-10}$ m.

4-12. Consider the foil and α particle energy in Problem 4-6. Suppose that 1000 of those particles suffer a deflection of more than 25°. (*a*) How many of these are deflected by more than 45°? (*b*) How many are deflected between 25° and 45°? (*c*) How many are deflected between 75° and 90°?

Section 4-3 The Bohr Model of the Hydrogen Atom

4-13. The radius of the $n = 1$ orbit in the hydrogen atom is $a_0 = 0.053$ nm. (*a*) Compute the radius of the $n = 6$ orbit. (*b*) Compute the radius of the $n = 6$ orbit in singly ionized helium (He$^+$), which is hydrogenlike.

4-14. Show that Equation 4-19 for the radius of the first Bohr orbit and Equation 4-20 for the magnitude of the lowest energy for the hydrogen atom can be written as

$$a_0 = \frac{hc}{\alpha mc^2} = \frac{\lambda_c}{2\pi\alpha}$$
$$E_1 = \tfrac{1}{2}\alpha^2 mc^2$$

where $\lambda_c = h/mc$ is the Compton wavelength of the electron and $\alpha = ke^2/\hbar c$ is the fine-structure constant. Use these expressions to check the numerical values of the constants a_0 and E_1.

4-15. Calculate the three longest wavelengths in the Lyman series ($n_f = 1$) in nm, and indicate their position on a horizontal linear scale. Indicate the series limit (shortest wavelength) on this scale. Are any of these lines in the visible spectrum?

4-16. If the angular momentum of Earth in its motion around the sun were quantized like a hydrogen electron according to Equation 4-17, what would Earth's quantum number be? How much energy would be released in a transition to the next lowest level? Would that energy release (presumably as a gravity wave) be detectable? What would be the radius of that orbit? (The radius of Earth's orbit is 1.50×10^{11} m.)

4-17. Light of wavelength 410.7 nm is observed in emission from a hydrogen source. (*a*) What transition between hydrogen Bohr orbits is responsible for this radiation? (*b*) To what series does this transition belong?

4-18. An atom in an excited state will on the average undergo a transition to a state of lower energy in about 10^{-8} s. If the electron in a doubly ionized lithium atom (Li^{2+}, which is hydrogenlike) is placed in the $n = 4$ state, about how many revolutions around the nucleus does it make before undergoing a transition to a lower energy state?

4-19. It is possible for a muon to be captured by a proton to form a muonic atom. A muon is identical to an electron except for its mass, which is 105.7 MeV/c^2. (*a*) Calculate the radius of the first Bohr orbit of a muonic atom. (*b*) Calculate the magnitude of the lowest energy. (*c*) What is the shortest wavelength in the Lyman series for this atom?

4-20. In the lithium atom ($Z = 3$) two electrons are in the $n = 1$ orbit and the third is in the $n = 2$ orbit. (Only two are allowed in the $n = 1$ orbit because of the exclusion principle, which will be discussed in Chapter 7.) The interaction of the inner electrons with the outer one can be approximated by writing the energy of the outer electron as

$$E = -Z'^2 \frac{E_1}{n^2}$$

where $E_1 = 13.6$ eV, $n = 2$, and Z' is the effective nuclear charge, which is less than 3 because of the screening effect of the two inner electrons. Using the measured ionization energy of 5.39 eV, calculate Z'.

4-21. Draw to careful scale an energy-level diagram for hydrogen for levels with $n = 1$, 2, 3, 4, ∞. Show the following on the diagram: (*a*) the limit of the Lyman series, (*b*) the H_β line, (*c*) the transition between the state whose binding energy (= energy needed to remove the electron from the atom) is 1.51 eV and the state whose excitation energy is 10.2 eV, and (*d*) the longest wavelength line of the Paschen series.

4-22. A hydrogen atom at rest in the laboratory emits the Lyman α radiation. (*a*) Compute the recoil kinetic energy of the atom. (*b*) What fraction of the excitation energy of the $n = 2$ state is carried by the recoiling atom? (*Hint:* Use conservation of momentum.)

4-23. What is the radius of the $n = 1$ orbit in C^{5+}? What is the energy of the electron in that orbit? What is the wavelength of the radiation emitted by C^{5+} in the Lyman α transition?

4-24. The electron-positron pair that was discussed in Chapter 2 can form a hydrogenlike system called *positronium*. Calculate (*a*) the energies of the three lowest states and (*b*) the wavelength of the Lyman α and β lines. (Detection of those lines is a "signature" of positronium formation.)

4-25. With the aid of tunable lasers, Rydberg atoms of sodium have been produced with $n \approx 100$. The resulting atomic diameter would correspond in hydrogen to $n \approx 600$. (*a*) What would be the diameter of a hydrogen atom whose electron is in the $n \approx 600$ orbit? (*b*) What would be the speed of the electron in that orbit? (*c*) How does the result in (*b*) compare with the speed in the $n \approx 1$ orbit?

Section 4-4 X-Ray Spectra

4-26. (*a*) Calculate the next two longest wavelengths in the K series (after the K_α line) of molybdenum. (*b*) What is the wavelength of the shortest wavelength in this series?

4-27. The wavelength of the K_α x-ray line for an element is measured to be 0.0794 nm. What is the element?

4-28. The L_α line for a certain element has a wavelength of 0.3617 nm. What is the element?

4-29. What is the approximate radius of the $n = 1$ orbit of gold ($Z = 79$)? Compare this with the radius of the gold nucleus, about 7.1 fm.

4-30. What is the minimum potential that must be applied across an x-ray tube in order to observe the (*a*) K_α line of tungsten, (*b*) the K_α line of copper, and (*c*) the L_α line of copper? What is the λ_{min} of the continuous spectrum in each case?

4-31. In a particular x-ray tube, an electron approaches the target moving at 2.25×10^8 m/s. It slows down on being deflected by a nucleus of the target, emitting a photon of energy 32.5 keV. Ignoring the nuclear recoil, but not relativity, compute the final speed of the electron.

4-32. (*a*) Compute the energy of an electron in the $n = 1$ (K shell) of tungsten, using $Z - 1$ for the effective nuclear charge. (*b*) The experimental result for this energy is 69.5 keV. Assume that the effective nuclear charge is $(Z - \sigma)$, where σ is called the screening constant, and calculate σ from the experimental result.

4-33. Construct a Moseley plot similar to Figure 4-18 for the K_β x rays of the elements listed (the x-ray energies are given in keV):

Al 1.56	Ar 3.19	Sc 4.46	Fe 7.06
Ge 10.98	Kr 14.10	Zr 17.66	Ba 36.35

Determine the slope of your plot, and compare it with the K_β line in Figure 4-18.

4-34. Suppose that, in a Franck-Hertz experiment, electrons of energy up to 13.0 eV can be produced in the tube. If the tube contained atomic hydrogen, (*a*) what is the shortest-wavelength spectral line that could be emitted from the tube? (*b*) List all of the hydrogen lines that can be emitted by this tube.

4-35. Using the data in Figure 4-23*b* and a good ruler, draw a carefully scaled energy-level diagram covering the range from 0 eV to 60 eV for the vibrational states of this solid. What approximate energy is typical of the transitions between adjacent levels corresponding to the larger of each pair of peaks?

4-36. The transition from the first excited state to the ground state in potassium results in the emission of a photon with $\lambda = 770$ nm. If potassium vapor is used in a Franck-Hertz experiment, at what voltage would you expect to see the first decrease in current?

4-37. If we could somehow fill a Franck-Hertz tube with positronium, what cathode-grid voltage would be needed to reach the second current decrease in the positronium equivalent of Figure 4-22? (See Problem 4-24.)

4-38. Electrons in the Franck-Hertz tube can also have elastic collisions with the Hg atoms. If such a collision is head on, what fraction of its initial kinetic energy will an electron lose, assuming the Hg atom to be at rest? If the collision is not head on, will the fractional loss be greater or less than this?

Section 4-6 Critique of Bohr Theory and of the "Old" Quantum Mechanics

There are no problems for this section.

Level II

4-39. Derive Equation 4-8 along the lines indicated in the paragraph that precedes it.

4-40. Geiger and Marsden used α particles with 7.7-MeV kinetic energy and found that when they were scattered from thin gold foil, the number observed to be scattered at all angles agreed with Rutherford's formula. Use this fact to compute an upper limit on the radius of the gold nucleus.

4-41. (*a*) The current i due to a charge q moving in a circle with frequency f_{rev} is qf_{rev}. Find the current due to the electron in the first Bohr orbit. (*b*) The magnetic moment of a current loop is iA, where A is the area of the loop. Find the magnetic moment of the electron in the first Bohr orbit in units $A \cdot m^2$. This magnetic moment is called a *Bohr magneton*.

4-42. Use a spreadsheet to calculate the wavelengths (in nm) of the first five spectral lines of the Lyman, Balmer, Paschen, and Brackett series of hydrogen. Show the positions of these lines on a linear scale and indicate which ones lie in the visible.

4-43. Show that a small change in the reduced mass of the electron produces a small change in the wavelength of a spectral line given by $\Delta\lambda/\lambda = -\Delta\mu/\mu$. Use this to calculate the difference $\Delta\lambda$ in the Balmer red line $\lambda = 656.3$ nm between hydrogen and deuterium, which has a nucleus with twice the mass of hydrogen.

4-44. A beam of 10-MeV protons is incident on a thin aluminum foil of thickness 10^{-6} m. Find the fraction of the particles that are scattered through angles greater than (*a*) 10° and (*b*) 90°.

4-45. The Li^{2+} ion is essentially identical to the H atom in Bohr's theory, aside from the effect of the different nuclear charges and masses. (*a*) What transitions in Li^{2+} will yield emission lines whose wavelengths are very nearly equal to the first two lines of the Lyman series in hydrogen? (*b*) Calculate the difference between the wavelength of the Lyman α line of hydrogen and the emission line from Li^{2+} that has very nearly the same wavelength.

4-46. In an α scattering experiment, the area of the α particle detector is 0.50 cm². The detector is located 10 cm from a 1.0-μm-thick silver foil. The incident beam carries a current of 1.0 nA, and the energy of each α particle is 6.0 MeV. How many α particles will be counted per second by the detector at (*a*) $\theta = 60°$? (*b*) $\theta = 120°$?

4-47. The K_α, L_α, and M_α x rays are emitted in the $n = 2 \rightarrow n = 1$, $n = 3 \rightarrow n = 2$, and $n = 4 \rightarrow n = 3$ transitions, respectively. For calcium ($Z = 20$) the energies of these transitions are 3.69 keV, 0.341 keV, and 0.024 keV, respectively. Suppose that energetic photons impinging on a calcium surface cause ejection of an electron from the K shell of the surface atoms. Compute the energies of the Auger electrons that may be emitted from the L, M, and N shells ($n = 2$, 3, and 4) of the sample atoms, in addition to the characteristic x rays.

4-48. Figure 3-18b shows the K_α and K_β characteristic x rays emitted by a molybdenum (Mo) target in an x-ray tube whose accelerating potential is 35 kV. The wavelengths are $K_\alpha = 0.071$ nm and $K_\beta = 0.063$ nm. (a) Compute the corresponding energies of these photons. (b) Suppose we wish to prepare a beam consisting primarily of K_α x rays by passing the molybdenum x rays through a material that absorbs K_β x rays more strongly than K_α x rays by photoelectric effect on K-shell electrons of the material. Which of the materials listed in the accompanying table with their K-shell binding energies would you choose? Explain your answer.

Element	Zr	Nb	Mo	Tc	Ru
Z	40	41	42	43	44
E_K (keV)	18.00	18.99	20.00	21.04	22.12

Level III

4-49. A small shot of negligible radius hits a stationary smooth, hard sphere of radius R, making an angle β with the normal to the sphere, as shown in Figure 4-24. It is reflected at an equal angle to the normal. The scattering angle is $\theta = 180° - 2\beta$, as shown. (a) Show by the geometry of the figure that the impact parameter b is related to θ by $b = R \cos \frac{1}{2} \theta$. (b) If the incoming intensity of the shot is I_0 particles/s · area, how many are scattered through angles greater than θ? (c) Show that the cross section for scattering through angles greater than $0°$ is πR^2. (d) Discuss the implication of the fact that the Rutherford cross section for scattering through angles greater than $0°$ is infinite.

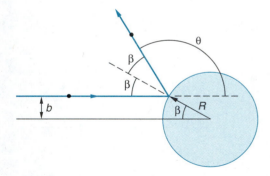

Fig. 4-24 Small particle scattered by a hard sphere of radius R.

4-50. Singly ionized helium He^+ is hydrogenlike. (a) Construct a carefully scaled energy-level diagram for He^+ similar to that in Figure 4-16, showing the levels for $n = 1$, 2, 3, 4, 5, and ∞. (b) What is the ionization energy of He^+? (c) Compute the difference in wavelength between each of the first two lines of the Lyman series of hydrogen and the first two lines of the He^+ Balmer series. Be sure to include the reduced mass correction for both atoms. (d) Show that for every spectral line of hydrogen, He^+ has a spectral line of very nearly the same wavelength. (Mass of $He^+ = 6.65 \times 10^{-27}$ kg.)

4-51. Listed in the table are the L_α x-ray wavelengths for several elements. Construct a Moseley plot from these data. Compare the slope with the appropriate one in Figure 4-18. Determine and interpret the intercept on your graph, using a suitably modified version of Equation 4-35.

Element	P	Ca	Co	Kr	Mo	I
Z	15	20	27	36	42	53
Wavelength (nm)	10.41	4.05	1.79	0.73	0.51	0.33

4-52. In this problem you are to obtain the Bohr results for the energy levels in hydrogen without using the quantization condition of Equation 4-17. In order to relate Equation 4-14 to the Balmer-Ritz formula, assume that the radii of allowed orbits are given by $r_n = n^2 r_0$, where n is an integer and r_0 is a constant to be determined. (*a*) Show that the frequency of radiation for a transition to $n_f = n - 1$ is given by $f \approx kZe^2/hr_0 n^3$ for large n. (*b*) Show that the frequency of revolution is given by

$$f_{rev}^2 = \frac{kZe^2}{4\pi^2 m \, r_0^3 n^6}$$

(*c*) Use the correspondence principle to determine r_0 and compare with Equation 4-19.

4-53. Calculate the energies and speeds of electrons in circular Bohr orbits in a hydrogenlike atom using the relativistic expressions for kinetic energy and momentum.

4-54. (*a*) Write a computer program for your personal computer or programmable calculator that will provide you with the spectral series of H-like atoms. Inputs to be included are n_i, n_f, Z, and the nuclear mass M. Outputs are to be the wavelengths and frequencies of the first six lines and the series limit for the specified n_f, Z, and M. Include the reduced mass correction. (*b*) Use the program to compute the wavelengths and frequencies of the Balmer series. (*c*) Pick an $n_f > 100$, name the series the [your name] series, and use your program to compute the wavelengths and frequencies of the first three lines and the limit.

4-55. Figure 4-25 shows an energy-loss spectrum for He measured in an apparatus such as that shown in Figure 4-23*a*. Use the spectrum to construct and draw carefully to scale an energy-level diagram for He.

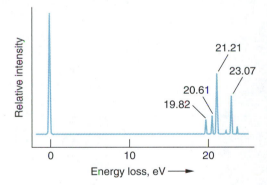

Fig. 4-25 Energy-loss spectrum of helium. Incident electron energy was 34 eV. The elastically scattered electrons cause the peak at 0 eV.

4-56. If electric charge did not exist and electrons were bound to protons by the gravitational force to form hydrogen, derive the corresponding expressions for a_0 and E_n and compute the energy and frequency of the H_α line and the limit of the Balmer series. Compare these with the corresponding quantities for "real" hydrogen.

4-57. A sample of hydrogen atoms are all in the $n = 5$ state. If all the atoms return to the ground state, how many different photon energies will be emitted, assuming all possible transitions occur? If there are 500 atoms in the sample and assuming that from any state all possible downward transitions are equally probable, what is the total number of photons that will be emitted when all of the atoms have returned to the ground state?

Chapter 5

The Wavelike Properties of Particles

*I*n 1924, a French graduate student, Louis de Broglie,[1] proposed in his doctoral dissertation that the dual—i.e., wave-particle—behavior that was by then known to exist for radiation was also a characteristic of matter, in particular, electrons. This suggestion was highly speculative, since there was yet no experimental evidence whatsoever for any wave aspects of electrons or any other particles. What had led him to this seemingly strange idea? It was a "bolt out of the blue," like Einstein's "happy thought," that led to the principle of equivalence (see Chapter 2). De Broglie described it with these words:

> After the end of World War I, I gave a great deal of thought to the theory of quanta and to the wave-particle dualism. . . . It was then that I had a sudden inspiration. Einstein's wave-particle dualism was an absolutely general phenomenon extending to all physical nature.[2]

Since the visible universe consists entirely of matter and radiation, de Broglie's hypothesis is a fundamental statement about the grand symmetry of nature. (There is currently strong observational evidence that approximately 70 percent of the universe consists of some sort of invisible "dark energy." See Chapter 14.)

5-1 The de Broglie Hypothesis

De Broglie stated his proposal mathematically with the following equations for the frequency and wavelength of the electron waves, which are referred to as the *de Broglie relations*:

$$f = \frac{E}{h} \qquad \textbf{5-1}$$

$$\lambda = \frac{h}{p} \qquad \textbf{5-2}$$

where E is the total energy, p is the momentum, and λ is called the *de Broglie wavelength* of the particle. For photons, these same equations result directly from

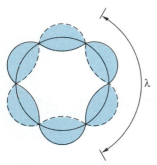

Fig. 5-1 Standing waves around the circumference of a circle. In this case the circle is 3λ in circumference. If the vibrator were, for example, a steel ring that had been suitably tapped with a hammer, the shape of the ring would oscillate between the extreme positions represented by the solid and broken lines.

Einstein's quantization of radiation $E = hf$ and Equation 2-31 for a particle of zero rest energy $E = pc$ as follows:

$$E = pc = hf = \frac{hc}{\lambda}$$

By a more indirect approach using relativistic mechanics, de Broglie was able to demonstrate that Equations 5-1 and 5-2 also apply to particles with mass. He then pointed out that these equations lead to a physical interpretation of Bohr's quantization of the angular momentum of the electron in hydrogenlike atoms, namely, that the quantization is equivalent to a standing-wave condition (see Figure 5-1). We have

$$mvr = n\hbar = \frac{nh}{2\pi} \qquad \text{for} \qquad n = \text{integer}$$

$$2\pi r = \frac{nh}{mv} = \frac{nh}{p} = n\lambda = \text{circumference of orbit} \qquad \textbf{5-3}$$

The idea of explaining discrete energy states in matter by standing waves thus seemed quite promising.

De Broglie's ideas were expanded and developed into a complete theory by Erwin Schrödinger late in 1925. In 1927, C. J. Davisson and L. H. Germer verified the de Broglie hypothesis directly by observing interference patterns, a characteristic of waves, with electron beams. We will discuss both Schrödinger's theory and the Davisson-Germer experiment in later sections, but first we have to ask ourselves why wavelike behavior of matter had not been observed before de Broglie's work. We can see why if we first recall that the wave properties of light were not noticed, either, until apertures or slits with dimensions of the order of the wavelength of light could be obtained. This is because the wave nature of light is not evident in experiments where the primary dimensions of the apparatus are large compared with the wavelength of the light used. For example, if A represents the diameter of a lens or the width of a slit, then diffraction effects[3] (a manifestation of wave properties) are limited to angles θ around the forward direction ($\theta = 0°$) where $\sin \theta = \lambda/A$. In geometric (ray) optics $\lambda/A \rightarrow 0$, so $\theta \approx \sin \theta \rightarrow 0$, too. However, if a characteristic dimension of the apparatus becomes of the order of (or smaller than) λ, the wavelength of light passing through the system, then $\lambda/A \rightarrow 1$. In that event $\theta \approx \lambda/A$ is readily observable, and the wavelike properties of light become apparent. Because Planck's constant is so small, the wavelength given by Equation 5-2 is extremely small for any macroscopic object. This point is among those illustrated in the following section.

5-2 Measurements of Particle Wavelengths

Although we now have diffraction systems of nuclear dimensions, the smallest-scale systems to which de Broglie's contemporaries had access were the spacings between the planes of atoms in crystalline solids, about 0.1 nm. This means that even for an extremely small macroscopic particle, such as a grain of dust ($m \approx 0.1$ mg) moving through air with the average kinetic energy of the atmospheric gas molecules, the smallest diffraction systems available would have resulted in diffraction angles θ

Louis V. de Broglie, who first suggested that electrons might have wave properties. [*Courtesy of Culver Pictures.*]

only of the order of 10^{-10} radians, far below the limit of experimental detectability. The small magnitude of Planck's constant ensures that λ will be smaller than any readily accessible aperture, placing diffraction beyond the limits of experimental observation. For objects whose momenta are larger than that of the dust particle, the possibility of observing *particle* or *matter waves* is even less, as the following example illustrates.

EXAMPLE 5-1 De Broglie Wavelength of a Ping-Pong Ball What is the de Broglie wavelength of a Ping-Pong ball of mass 2.0 g after it is slammed across the table with a speed of 5 m/s?

Solution

$$\lambda = \frac{h}{mv} = \frac{6.63 \times 10^{-34}\,\text{J}\cdot\text{s}}{(2.0 \times 10^{-3}\,\text{kg})(5\,\text{m/s})}$$

$$= 6.6 \times 10^{-32}\,\text{m} = 6.6 \times 10^{-23}\,\text{nm}$$

This is 17 orders of magnitude smaller than typical nuclear dimensions, far below the dimensions of any possible aperture.

The case is different for low-energy electrons, as de Broglie himself realized. At his *soutenance de thèse* (defense of the thesis), de Broglie was asked by Perrin[4] how his hypothesis could be verified, to which he replied that perhaps passing particles, such as electrons, through very small slits would reveal the waves. Consider an electron that has been accelerated through V_0 volts. Its kinetic energy (nonrelativistic) is then

$$E = \frac{p^2}{2m} = eV_0$$

Solving for p and substituting into Equation 5-2,

$$\lambda = \frac{h}{p} = \frac{hc}{pc} = \frac{hc}{(2mc^2 eV_0)^{1/2}}$$

Using $hc = 1.24 \times 10^3$ eV·nm and $mc^2 = 0.511 \times 10^6$ eV, we obtain

$$\lambda = \frac{1.226}{V_0^{1/2}} \text{ nm} \qquad \text{for} \qquad eV_0 \ll mc^2 \qquad\qquad \textbf{5-4}$$

The following example computes an electron de Broglie wavelength, giving a measure of just how small the slit must be.

EXAMPLE 5-2 De Broglie Wavelength of a Slow Electron Compute the de Broglie wavelength of an electron whose kinetic energy is 10 eV.

Solution

1. The de Broglie wavelength is given by Equation 5-1:

$$\lambda = \frac{h}{p}$$

2. *Method 1:* Since a 10-eV electron is nonrelativistic, we can use the classical relation connecting the momentum and the kinetic energy:

$$E_k = \frac{p^2}{2m}$$

or

$$p = \sqrt{2mE_k}$$
$$= \sqrt{(2)(9.11 \times 10^{-31}\,\text{kg})(10\text{ eV})(1.60 \times 10^{-19}\,\text{J/eV})}$$
$$= 1.71 \times 10^{-24}\,\text{kg}\cdot\text{m/s}$$

3. Substituting this result into Equation 5-1:

$$\lambda = \frac{6.63 \times 10^{-24}\,\text{J}\cdot\text{s}}{1.71 \times 10^{-24}\,\text{kg}\cdot\text{m/s}}$$
$$= 3.88 \times 10^{-10}\,\text{m} = 0.39\text{ nm}$$

4. *Method 2:* The electron's wavelength can also be computed from Equation 5-4 with $V_0 = 10$ V:

$$\lambda = \frac{1.226}{V^{1/2}} = \frac{1.226}{\sqrt{10}}$$
$$= 0.39\text{ nm}$$

Remarks: Though this wavelength is small, it is just the order of magnitude of the size of an atom and of the spacing of atoms in a crystal.

The Davisson-Germer Experiment

In a brief note in the August 14, 1925, issue of the journal *Naturwissenschaften,* Walter Elsasser, at the time a student of Franck's (of the Franck-Hertz experiment), proposed that the wave effects of low-velocity electrons might be detected by scattering them from single crystals. The first such measurements of the wavelengths of electrons were made in 1927 by Davisson[5] and Germer, who were studying electron reflection from a nickel target at Bell Telephone Laboratories, unaware of either Elsasser's suggestion or de Broglie's work. After heating their target to remove an oxide coating that had accumulated during an accidental break in their vacuum system, they found that the scattered electron intensity as a function of the scattering angle showed maxima and minima. Their target had crystallized in the process of cooling, and they were observing electron diffraction. Recognizing the importance of their accidental discovery, they then prepared a target consisting of a single crystal of nickel and extensively investigated the scattering of electrons from it. Figure 5-2 illustrates their experimental arrangement. Their data for 54-eV electrons, shown in Figure 5-3, indicate a strong maximum of scattering at $\phi = 50°$. Consider the scattering from a set of Bragg planes, as shown in Figure 5-4. The Bragg condition for constructive interference is $n\lambda = 2d \sin \theta = 2d \cos \alpha$. The spacing of the Bragg planes d is related to the spacing of the atoms D by $d = D \sin \alpha$; thus

$$n\lambda = 2D \sin \alpha \cos \alpha = D \sin 2\alpha$$

or

$$n\lambda = D \sin \phi \qquad \textbf{5-5}$$

where $\phi = 2\alpha$ is the scattering angle.

The spacing D for Ni is known from x-ray diffraction to be 0.215 nm. The wavelength calculated from Equation 5-5 for the peak observed at $\phi = 50°$ by Davisson and Germer is, for $n = 1$,

$$\lambda = 0.215 \sin 50° = 0.165 \text{ nm}$$

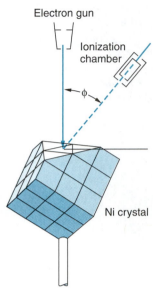

Fig. 5-2 The Davisson-Germer experiment. Low-energy electrons scattered at angle ϕ from a nickel crystal are detected in an ionization chamber. The kinetic energy of the electrons could be varied by changing the accelerating voltage on the electron gun.

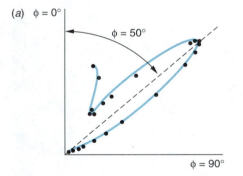

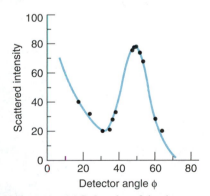

Fig. 5-3 Scattered intensity vs. detector angle for 54-eV electrons. (*a*) Polar plot of the data. The intensity at each angle is indicated by the distance of the point from the origin. Scattering angle ϕ is plotted clockwise starting at the vertical axes. (*b*) The same data plotted on a Cartesian graph. The intensity scales are arbitrary, but the same on both graphs. In each plot there is maximum intensity at $\phi = 50°$, as predicted for Bragg scattering of waves having wavelength $\lambda = h/p$. [*From* Nobel Prize Lectures: Physics *(Amsterdam and New York: Elsevier, © Nobel Foundation, 1964).*]

Fig. 5-4 Scattering of electrons by a crystal. Electron waves are strongly scattered if the Bragg condition $n\lambda = 2d \sin \theta$ is met. This is equivalent to the condition $n\lambda = D \sin \phi$.

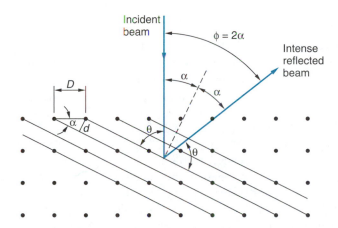

The value calculated from the de Broglie relation for 54-eV electrons is

$$\lambda = \frac{1.226}{(54)^{1/2}} = 0.167 \text{ nm}$$

The agreement with the experimental observation is excellent! With this spectacular result Davisson and Germer then conducted a systematic study to test the de Broglie relation using electrons up to about 400 eV and various experimental arrangements. Figure 5-5 shows a plot of measured wavelengths versus $V_0^{-1/2}$. The wavelengths measured by diffraction are slightly lower than the theoretical predictions because the refraction of the electron waves at the crystal surface has been neglected. We have seen from the photoelectric effect that it takes work of the order of several eV to remove an electron from a metal. Electrons entering a metal thus gain kinetic energy; therefore, their de Broglie wavelength is slightly less inside the crystal.[6]

A subtle point must be made here. Notice that the wavelength in Equation 5-5 depends only on D, the interatomic spacing of the crystal, whereas our derivation of

Clinton J. Davisson (left) and Lester H. Germer at Bell Laboratories, where electron diffraction was first observed. [*Bell Telephone Laboratories, Inc.*]

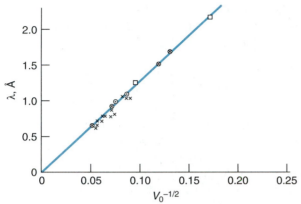

Fig. 5-5 Test of the de Broglie formula $\lambda = h/p$. The wavelength is computed from a plot of the diffraction data plotted against $V_0^{-1/2}$, where V_0 is the accelerating voltage. The straight line is $1.226 V_0^{-1/2}$ nm as predicted from $\lambda = h(2mE)^{-1/2}$. These are the data referred to in the quotation from Davisson's Nobel lecture. ($\times$ From observations with diffraction apparatus; $\otimes$ same, particularly reliable; $\square$ same, grazing beams. $\odot$ From observations with reflection apparatus.) [*From* Nobel Prize Lectures: Physics *(Amsterdam and New York: Elsevier,* © *Nobel Foundation, 1964).*]

that equation included the interplane spacing as well. The fact that the structure of the crystal really is essential shows up when the energy is varied, as was done in collecting the data for Figure 5-5. Equation 5-5 suggests that a change in λ, resulting from a change in the energy, would mean only that the diffraction maximum would occur at some other value of ϕ such that the equation remains satisfied. However, as can be seen from examination of Figure 5-4, the value of ϕ is determined by α, the angle of the planes determined by the crystal structure. Thus, if there are no crystal planes making an angle $\alpha = \phi/2$ with the surface, then setting the detector at $\phi = \sin^{-1}(\lambda/D)$ will not result in constructive interference and strong reflection for that value of λ, even though Equation 5-5 is satisfied. This is neatly illustrated by Figure 5-6, which shows a series of polar graphs (like Figure 5-3a) for electrons of energies from 36 eV through 68 eV. The building to a strong reflection at $\phi = 50°$ is evident for $V_0 = 54$ V, as we have already seen. But Equation 5-5 by itself would also lead us to expect, for example, a strong reflection at $\phi = 64°$ when $V_0 = 40$ V, which obviously does not occur.

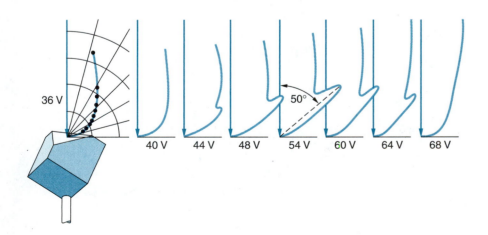

Fig. 5-6 A series of polar graphs of Davisson and Germer's data at electron accelerating potentials from 36 V to 68 V. Note the development of the peak at $\phi = 50°$ to a maximum when $V_0 = 54$ V.

In order to show the dependence of the diffraction on the inner atomic layers, Davisson and Germer kept the detector angle ϕ fixed and varied the accelerating voltage, rather than search for the correct angle for a given λ. Writing Equation 5-5 as

$$\lambda = \frac{D \sin \phi}{n} = \frac{D \sin (2\alpha)}{n} \qquad \textbf{5-6}$$

and noting that $\lambda \propto V_0^{-1/2}$, a graph of intensity versus $V_0^{-1/2}$ for a given angle ϕ should yield (1) a series of equally spaced peaks corresponding to successive values of the integer n, if $\alpha = \phi/2$ is an existing angle for atomic planes; or (2) no diffraction peaks if $\phi/2$ is not such an angle. Their measurements verified the dependence upon the interplane spacing, the agreement with the prediction being about ± 1 percent. Figure 5-7 illustrates the results for $\phi = 50°$. Thus, Davisson and Germer showed conclusively that particles with mass moving at speeds $v \ll c$ do indeed have wavelike properties, as de Broglie had proposed.

Here is Davisson's account of the connection between de Broglie's predictions and their experimental verification:

> Perhaps no idea in physics has received so rapid or so intensive development as this one. De Broglie himself was in the van of this development, but the chief contributions were made by the older and more experienced Schrödinger. It would be pleasant to tell you that no sooner had Elsasser's suggestion appeared than the experiments were begun in New York which resulted in a demonstration of electron diffraction—pleasanter still to say that the work was begun the day after copies of de Broglie's thesis reached America. The true story contains less of perspicacity and more of chance. . . . It was discovered, purely by accident, that the intensity of elastic scattering [of electrons] varies with the orientations of the scattering crystals. Out of this grew, quite naturally, an investigation of elastic scattering by a single crystal of predetermined orientation. . . . Thus the New York experiment was not, at its inception, a test of wave theory. Only in the summer of 1926, after I had discussed the investigation in England with Richardson, Born, Franck and others, did it take on this character.[7]

The diffraction pattern formed by high-energy electron waves scattered from nuclei provides a means by which nuclear radii and the internal distribution of the nuclear charge (the protons) are measured. See Chapter 11.

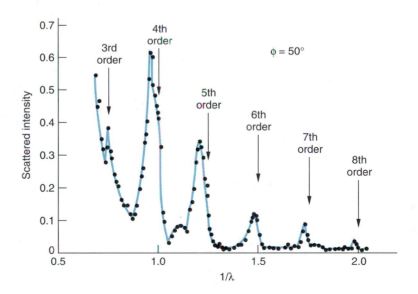

Fig. 5-7 Variation of the scattered electron intensity with wavelength for constant ϕ. The incident beam in this case was 10° from the normal, the resulting refraction causing the measured peaks to be slightly shifted from the positions computed from Equation 5-5, as explained in note 6. [*After C. J. Davisson and L. H. Germer,* Proceedings of the National Academy of Sciences, *14, 619 (1928).*]

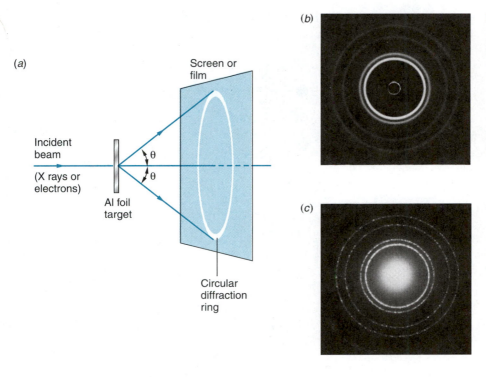

(a)

Fig. 5-8 *(a)* Schematic arrangement used for producing a diffraction pattern from a polycrystalline aluminum target. *(b)* Diffraction pattern produced by x rays of wavelength 0.071 nm and an aluminum foil target. *(c)* Diffraction pattern produced by 600-eV electrons (de Broglie wavelength of about 0.05 nm) and an aluminum foil target. The pattern has been enlarged by 1.6 times to facilitate comparison with *(b)*. [*Courtesy of Film Studio, Education Development Center.*]

A demonstration of the wave nature of relativistic electrons was provided in the same year by G. P. Thomson, who observed the transmission of electrons with energies in the range of 10 to 40 keV through thin metallic foils (G. P. Thomson, the son of J. J. Thomson, shared the Nobel Prize in 1937 with Davisson). The experimental arrangement (Figure 5-8*a*) was similar to that used to obtain Laue patterns with x rays (see Figure 3-14). Because the metal foil consists of many tiny crystals randomly oriented, the diffraction pattern consists of concentric rings. If a crystal is oriented at an angle θ with the incident beam, where θ satisfies the Bragg condition, this crystal will strongly scatter at an equal angle θ; thus there will be a scattered beam making an angle 2θ with the incident beam. Figures 5-8*b* and *c* show the similarities in patterns produced by x rays and electron waves.

Diffraction of Other Particles   The wave properties of neutral atoms and molecules were first demonstrated by Stern and Estermann in 1930 with beams of helium atoms and hydrogen molecules diffracted from a lithium fluoride crystal. Since the particles are neutral, there is no possibility of accelerating them with electrostatic potentials. The energy of the molecules was that of their average thermal motion, about 0.03 eV, which implies a de Broglie wavelength of about 0.10 nm for these molecules, according to Equation 5-2. Because of their low energy, the scattering occurs just from the array of atoms on the surface of the crystal, in contrast to Davisson and Germer's experiment. Figure 5-9 illustrates the geometry of the surface scattering, the experimental arrangement, and the results. Figure 5-9*c* indicates clearly the diffraction of He atom waves.

Since then, diffraction of other atoms, of protons, and of neutrons has been observed (Figures 5-10, 5-11, and 5-12). In all cases the measured wavelengths agree with de Broglie's prediction. There is thus no doubt that all matter has wavelike, as well as particlelike, properties, in symmetry with electromagnetic radiation.

The diffraction patterns formed by helium atom waves are used to study impurities and defects on the surfaces of crystals. Being a noble gas, helium does not react chemically with molecules on the surface or "stick" to the surface.

Fig. 5-9 (*a*) He atoms impinge upon the surface of the LiF crystal at angle θ ($\theta = 18.5°$ in Estermann and Stern's experiment). The reflected beam also makes the same angle θ with the surface, but is also scattered at azimuthal angles ϕ relative to an axis perpendicular to the surface. (*b*) The detector views the surface at angle θ but can scan through the angle ϕ. (*c*) At angle ϕ where the path difference ($d \sin \phi$) between adjacent "rays" is $n\lambda$, constructive interference, i.e., a diffraction peak, occurs. The $n = 1$ peaks occur on either side of the $n = 0$ maximum.

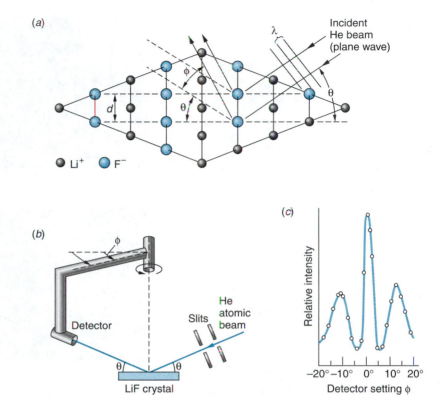

Fig. 5-10 Diffraction pattern produced by 0.0568-eV neutrons (de Broglie wavelength of 0.120 nm) and a target of polycrystalline copper. Note the similarity in the patterns produced by x rays, electrons, and neutrons. [*Courtesy of C. G. Shull.*]

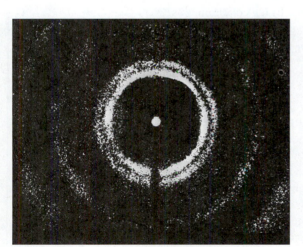

Fig. 5-11 Neutron Laue pattern of NaCl. Compare this with the x-ray Laue pattern in Figure 3-14. [*Courtesy of E. O. Wollan and C. G. Shull.*]

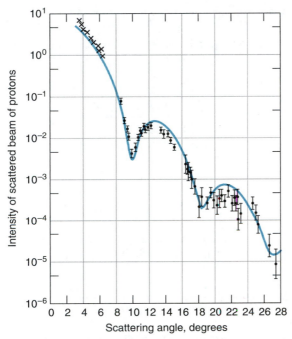

Fig. 5-12 Nuclei provide scatterers whose dimensions are of the order of 10^{-15} m. Here the diffraction of 1-GeV protons from oxygen nuclei results in a pattern similar to that of a single slit.

An Easy Way to Determine de Broglie Wavelengths

It is frequently helpful to know the de Broglie wavelength for particles with a specific kinetic energy. For low energies where relativistic effects can be ignored, the equation leading to Equation 5-4 can be rewritten in terms of the kinetic energy $E_k = \frac{1}{2}mv^2 = p^2/2m$ as follows:

$$\lambda = \frac{h}{p} = \frac{h}{\sqrt{2mE_k}} \qquad\qquad \textbf{5-7}$$

To find the equivalent expression that covers both relativistic and nonrelativistic speeds, we begin with the relativistic equation relating the total energy to the momentum:

$$E^2 = (pc)^2 + (mc^2)^2 \qquad\qquad \textbf{2-31}$$

Writing E_0 for the rest energy mc^2 of the particle for convenience, this expression becomes

$$E^2 = (pc)^2 + E_0^2 \qquad\qquad \textbf{5-8}$$

Since the total energy $E = E_0 + E_k$, Equation 5-8 becomes

$$(E_0 + E_k)^2 = (pc)^2 + E_0^2$$

which, when solved for p, yields

$$p = \frac{(2E_0 E_k + E_k^2)^{1/2}}{c}$$

from which Equation 5-2 gives

$$\lambda = \frac{hc}{(2E_0 E_k + E_k^2)^{1/2}} \qquad \textbf{5-9}$$

This can be written in a particularly useful way applicable to any particle of any energy by dividing the numerator and denominator by the rest energy $E_0 = mc^2$ as follows:

$$\lambda = \frac{hc/mc^2}{(2E_0 E_k + E_k^2)^{1/2}/E_0} = \frac{h/mc}{[2(E_k/E_0) + (E_k/E_0)^2]^{1/2}}$$

Recognizing h/mc as the Compton wavelength λ_c of the particle of mass m (see Section 3-4 and Equation 3-31), we have that, for any particle,

$$\lambda/\lambda_c = \frac{1}{[2(E_k/E_0) + (E_k/E_0)^2]^{1/2}} \qquad \textbf{5-10}$$

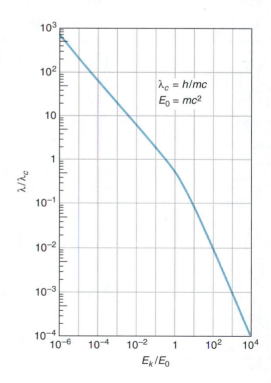

Fig. 5-13 The de Broglie wavelength λ expressed in units of the Compton wavelength λ_c for a particle of mass m versus the kinetic energy of the particle E_k expressed in units of its rest energy $E_0 = mc^2$. For protons and neutrons $E_0 = 0.938$ GeV and $\lambda_c = 1.32$ fm. For electrons $E_0 = 0.511$ MeV and $\lambda_c = 0.00234$ nm.

A log-log graph of λ/λ_c versus E_k/E_0 is shown in Figure 5-13. It has two sections of nearly constant slope, one for $E_k \ll mc^2$ and the other for $E_k \gg mc^2$, connected by a curved portion lying roughly between $0.1 < E_k/E_0 < 10$. The following example illustrates the use of Figure 5-13.

EXAMPLE 5-3 **The de Broglie Wavelength of a Cosmic Ray Proton** Detectors on board a satellite measure the kinetic energy of a cosmic ray proton to be 150 GeV. What is the proton's de Broglie wavelength, as read from Figure 5-13?

Solution
The rest energy of the proton is $mc^2 = 0.938$ GeV and the proton's mass is 1.67×10^{-27} kg. Thus, the ratio E_k/E_0 is

$$\frac{E_k}{E_0} = \frac{150 \text{ GeV}}{0.938 \text{ GeV}} = 160$$

This value on the curve corresponds to about 2×10^{-3} on the λ/λ_c axis. The Compton wavelength of the proton is

$$\lambda_c = \frac{h}{mc} = \frac{6.63 \times 10^{-34} \text{ J} \cdot \text{s}}{(1.67 \times 10^{-27} \text{ kg})(3 \times 10^8 \text{ m/s})} = 1.32 \times 10^{-15} \text{ m}$$

and we have then for the particle's de Broglie wavelength

$$\lambda = (2 \times 10^{-3})(1.32 \times 10^{-15} \text{ m}) = 2.6 \times 10^{-18} \text{ m} = 2.6 \times 10^{-3} \text{ fm}$$

QUESTIONS

1. Since the electrons used by Davisson and Germer were low energy, they penetrated only a few atomic layers into the crystal so it is rather surprising that the effects of the inner layers show so clearly. What feature of the diffraction is most affected by the relatively shallow penetration?

2. How might the frequency of de Broglie waves be measured?

3. Why is it not reasonable to do crystallographic studies with protons?

5-3 Wave Packets

In any discussion of waves the question arises, What's waving? For some waves the answer is clear: for waves on the ocean, it is the water that "waves"; for sound waves in air, it is the molecules that comprise the air; for light, it is the $\mathscr{E}$ and the **B**. So what is waving for matter waves? As will be developed in this section and the next, for matter it is the *probability of finding the particle* that waves.

Classical waves are solutions of the classical *wave equation*

$$\frac{\partial^2 y}{\partial x^2} = \frac{1}{v^2} \frac{\partial^2 y}{\partial t^2} \qquad\qquad \textbf{5-11}$$

Important among classical waves is the *harmonic wave* of amplitude y_0, frequency f, and period T:

$$y = y_0 \cos(kx - \omega t) = y_0 \cos 2\pi\left(\frac{x}{\lambda} - \frac{t}{T}\right) = y_0 \cos \frac{2\pi}{\lambda}(x - vt) \qquad \textbf{5-12}$$

where the *angular frequency* ω and the *wave number*[8] k are defined by

$$\omega = 2\pi f = \frac{2\pi}{T} \qquad \textbf{5-13}a$$

and

$$k = \frac{2\pi}{\lambda} \qquad \textbf{5-13}b$$

and the *wave* or *phase velocity* v_p is given by

$$v_p = f\lambda \qquad \textbf{5-14}$$

Fig. 5-14 Wave pulse moving along a string. A pulse has a beginning and an end; i.e., it is localized, unlike a pure harmonic wave, which goes on forever in space and time.

A familiar wave phenomenon which cannot be described by a single harmonic wave is a pulse, such as the flip of one end of a long string (Figure 5-14), a sudden noise, or the brief opening of a shutter in front of a light source. The main characteristic of a pulse is localization in time and space. A single harmonic wave is not localized in either time or space. The description of a pulse can be obtained by the superposition of a group of harmonic waves of different frequencies and wavelengths. Such a group is called a *wave packet*. The mathematics of representing arbitrarily shaped pulses by sums of sine or cosine functions involves Fourier series and Fourier integrals. We shall illustrate the phenomenon of wave packets by considering some simple and somewhat artificial examples and discussing the general properties qualitatively. Wave groups are particularly important because a wave description of a particle must include the important property of localization.

Consider a simple group consisting of only two waves of equal amplitude and nearly equal frequencies and wavelengths. Such a group occurs in the phenomenon of beats and is described in most introductory textbooks. Let the wave numbers be k_1 and k_2, the angular frequencies ω_1 and ω_2, and the speeds v_1 and v_2. The sum of the two waves is

$$y(x, t) = y_0 \cos(k_1 x - \omega_1 t) + y_0 \cos(k_2 x - \omega_2 t)$$

which, with the use of a bit of trigonometry, becomes

$$y(x, t) = 2y_0 \cos\left(\frac{\Delta k}{2}x - \frac{\Delta w}{2}t\right) \cos\left(\frac{k_1 + k_2}{2}x - \frac{\omega_1 + \omega_2}{2}t\right)$$

where $\Delta k = k_2 - k_1$ and $\Delta \omega = \omega_2 - \omega_1$. Since the two waves have nearly equal values of k and ω, we will write $\bar{k} = (k_1 + k_2)/2$ and $\bar{\omega} = (\omega_1 + \omega_2)/2$ for the mean values. The sum is then

$$y(x, t) = 2y_0 \cos\left(\tfrac{1}{2}\Delta kx - \tfrac{1}{2}\Delta\omega t\right) \cos(\bar{k}x - \bar{\omega}t) \qquad \textbf{5-15}$$

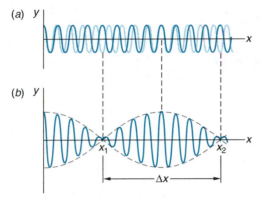

Fig. 5-15 Two waves of slightly different wavelength and frequency produce beats. (*a*) Shows $y(x)$ at a given instant for each of the two waves. The waves are in phase at the origin but because of the difference in wavelength, they become out of phase and then in phase again. (*b*) The sum of these waves. The spatial extent of the group Δx is inversely proportional to the difference in wave numbers Δk, where k is related to the wavelength by $k = 2\pi/\lambda$. Identical figures are obtained if y is plotted versus time t at a fixed point x. In that case the extent in time Δt is inversely proportional to the frequency difference $\Delta\omega$.

Figure 5-15 shows a sketch of $y(x, t_0)$ versus x at some time t_0. The dashed curve is the envelope of the group of two waves, given by the first cosine term in Equation 5-15. The wave within the envelope moves with the speed $\overline{\omega}/\overline{k}$, the phase velocity v_p due to the second cosine term. If we write the first (amplitude modulating) term as $\cos\{\frac{1}{2}\Delta k[x - (\Delta\omega/\Delta k)t]\}$, we see that the envelope moves with speed $\Delta\omega/\Delta k$. The speed of the envelope is called the *group velocity* v_g.

Classical Uncertainty Relations

The range of wavelengths or frequencies of the harmonic waves needed to form a wave packet depends on the extent in space and duration in time of the pulse. In general, if the extent in space Δx is small, the range Δk of wave numbers must be large. Similarly, if the duration in time t is small, the range of frequencies $\Delta\omega$ must be large. It can be shown that for a general wave packet, Δx and Δk are related by

$$\Delta k\, \Delta x \sim 1 \qquad\qquad \textbf{5-16}$$

Similarly,

$$\Delta\omega\, \Delta t \sim 1 \qquad\qquad \textbf{5-17}$$

We have written these as order-of-magnitude equations because the exact value of the products $\Delta x\, \Delta k$ and $\Delta t\, \Delta\omega$ depends on how these ranges are defined, as well as on the particular shape of the packets. Equation 5-17 is sometimes known as the *response time–bandwidth* relation, expressing the result that a circuit component such as an amplifier must have a large bandwidth ($\Delta\omega$) if it is to be able to respond to signals of short duration.

There is a slight variation of Equation 5-16 that is also helpful in interpreting the relation between Δx and Δk. Differentiating the wave number in Equation 5-13*b* yields

The classical uncertainty relations define the range of signal frequencies to which all kinds of communications equipment and computer systems must respond, from cell phones to super-computers.

$$dk = \frac{-2\pi d\lambda}{\lambda^2}$$

5-18

Replacing the differentials by small intervals and concerning ourselves only with magnitudes, Equation 5-18 becomes

$$\Delta k = \frac{2\pi\Delta\lambda}{\lambda^2}$$

which when substituted into Equation 5-16 gives

$$\Delta x \, \Delta\lambda \approx \frac{\lambda^2}{2\pi}$$

5-19

Equation 5-19 says that the product of the spatial extent of a classical wave Δx and the uncertainty (or "error") in the determination of its wavelength $\Delta\lambda$ will always be of the order of $\lambda^2/2\pi$. The following brief examples will illustrate the meaning of Equations 5-16 and 5-17, often referred to as the *classical uncertainty relations,* and Equation 5-19.

EXAMPLE 5-4 $\Delta\lambda$ **for Ocean Waves** Standing in the middle of a 20-m-long pier, you notice that at any given instant there are 15 wave crests between the two ends of the pier. Estimate the minimum uncertainty in the wavelength that could be computed from this information.

Solution

1. The minimum uncertainty $\Delta\lambda$ in the wavelength is given by Equation 5-19:

$$\Delta x \, \Delta\lambda \approx \frac{\lambda^2}{2\pi}$$

2. The wavelength λ of the waves is:

$$\lambda = \frac{20 \text{ m}}{15 \text{ waves}}$$
$$= 1.3 \text{ m}$$

3. The spatial extent of the waves used for this calculation is:

$$\Delta x = 20 \text{ m}$$

4. Solving Equation 5-19 for $\Delta\lambda$ and substituting these values gives:

$$\Delta\lambda \approx \frac{\lambda^2}{2\pi\Delta x} = \frac{(1.3)^2}{2\pi \times 20}$$
$$= 0.013\text{m}$$
$$\Delta\lambda \approx 0.01\text{m} = 1 \text{ cm}$$

> **Remarks:** *This is the minimum uncertainty. Any error that may exist in the measurement of the number of wave crests would add further uncertainty to the determination of* λ.

EXAMPLE 5-5 Frequency Control The frequency of the alternating voltage produced at electric generating stations is carefully maintained at 60.00 Hz. The frequency is monitored on a digital frequency meter in the control room. For how long must the frequency be measured and how often can the display be updated, if the reading is to be accurate to within 0.01 Hz?

Solution
Since $\omega = 2\pi f$, then $\Delta\omega = 2\pi\Delta f = 2\pi(0.01)$ rad/s and

$$\Delta t \sim 1/\Delta\omega = 1/2\pi(0.01)$$
$$\Delta t \sim 16 \text{ s}$$

Thus, the frequency must be measured for about 16 s if the reading is to be accurate to 0.01 Hz and the display cannot be updated more often than once every 16 s.

General Wave Packet

We can construct a more general wave packet than Equation 5-15 if we allow the amplitudes of the various harmonic waves to be different. Such a packet can be represented by an equation of the form

$$y(x, t) \; = \; \sum_i A_i \cos(k_i x - \omega_i t) \qquad\qquad \textbf{5-20}$$

where A_i is the amplitude of the wave with wave number k_i and angular frequency ω_i. The calculation of the amplitudes A_i needed to construct a wave packet of some given shape $y(x, t_0)$ at some particular time is a problem in Fourier series.

If we are restricted to a finite number of waves, it is not possible to obtain a wave packet that is small everywhere outside a well-defined range. The larger the number of waves, the larger the region in which destructive interference makes the envelope small, but eventually all the waves will again be in phase, the envelope will be large, and the pattern will repeat. To represent a pulse that is zero everywhere outside some range, such as that shown in Figure 5-14, we must construct a wave packet from a continuous distribution of waves. We can do this by replacing A_i in Equation 5-20 by $A(k)\, dk$ and changing the sum to an integral. The quantity $A(k)$ is called the distribution function for the wave number k. Either the shape of the wave packet at some fixed time $y(x)$ or the distribution of wave numbers $A(k)$ can be found from the other by methods of Fourier analysis.[9]

Figure 5-16 shows a Gaussian-shaped wave packet and the corresponding wave-number distribution function for a narrow packet (Figure 5-16a) and a wide packet (Figure 5-16b). For this special case, $A(k)$ is also a Gaussian function. The standard deviations of these Gaussian functions are related by

$$\sigma_x \sigma_k = \frac{1}{2} \qquad\qquad \textbf{5-21}$$

Fig. 5-16 Gaussian-shaped wave packets $y(x)$ and the corresponding Gaussian distributions of wave numbers $A(k)$. (*a*) A narrow packet. (*b*) A wide packet. The standard deviations in each case are related by $\sigma_x\sigma_k = 1/2$.

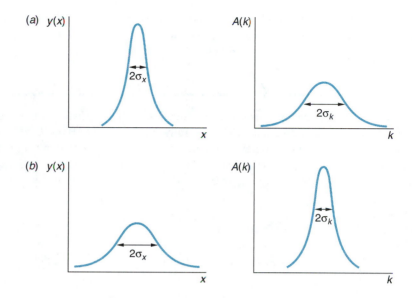

It can be shown that the product of the standard deviations is greater than $1/2$ for a wave packet of any shape other than Gaussian.

For our simple group of only two waves, we found that the envelope moved with the velocity $v_g = \Delta\omega/\Delta k$. For a general wave packet, the group velocity is given by

$$v_g = \frac{d\omega}{dk} \qquad\qquad \textbf{5-22}$$

where the derivative is evaluated at the central wave number. The group velocity of a pulse can be related to the phase velocities of the individual harmonic waves making up the packet. The phase velocity of a harmonic wave is

$$v_p = f\lambda = \left(\frac{\omega}{2\pi}\right)\left(\frac{2\pi}{k}\right) = \frac{\omega}{k}$$

so that

$$\omega = kv_p$$

Differentiating and substituting $d\omega/dk$ from Equation 5-22, we obtain

$$v_g = v_p + k\frac{dv_p}{dk} \qquad\qquad \textbf{5-23}$$

If the phase velocity is the same for all frequencies and wavelengths, then $dv_p/dk = 0$, and the group velocity is the same as the phase velocity. A medium for which the phase velocity is the same for all frequencies is said to be *nondispersive*. Examples are waves on a perfectly flexible string, sound waves in air, and electromagnetic waves in a vacuum. An important characteristic of a nondispersive medium is that, since all the harmonic waves making up a packet move with the same speed, the packet maintains its shape as it moves; thus it does not change its shape in time.

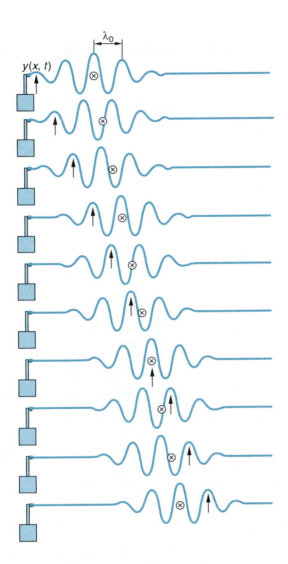

$y(x, t)$

λ_0

Fig. 5-17 Wave packet for which the group velocity is half the phase velocity. Water waves whose wavelengths are a few centimeters, but much less than the water depth, have this property. The arrow travels at the phase velocity, following a point of constant phase for the dominant wavelength. The cross at the center of the group travels at the group velocity. [*Adapted from F. S. Crawford, Jr.,* Berkeley Physics Course *(New York: McGraw-Hill, 1965), vol. 3, p. 294. Courtesy of Education Development Center, Inc., Newton, Mass.*]

Conversely, if the phase velocity is different for different frequencies, the shape of the pulse will change as it travels. In that case, the group velocity and phase velocity are not the same. Such a medium is called a *dispersive* medium; examples are water waves, waves on a wire that is not perfectly flexible, light waves in a medium such as glass or water, in which the index of refraction has a slight dependence on frequency, and electron waves. Figure 5-17 shows a wave packet for which the group velocity is half the phase velocity. The following example also illustrates such a case.

EXAMPLE 5-6 Velocity of Deep Ocean Waves The phase velocity v of waves deep in the ocean is given by $v_p = gT/2\pi$, where g is the acceleration of gravity and T is the period of the wave. What would be the group velocity of a wave packet formed by a group of such waves, expressed in terms of the phase velocity?

Solution

Note that $v_p = gT/2\pi = g/2\pi f = g/\omega$ from the definitions of the period and the angular velocity. Thus,

$$v_p = \frac{\omega}{k} = \frac{g}{\omega}$$

or

$$gk = \omega^2$$

Since the group velocity $v_g = d\omega/dk$ (Equation 5-22), we differentiate the above expression, obtaining

$$g \, dk = 2\omega \, d\omega$$

or

$$v_g = \frac{d\omega}{dk} = \frac{g}{2\omega} = \frac{1}{2} v_p$$

QUESTIONS

4. Which is more important for communication, the group velocity or the phase velocity?

5. What are Δx and Δk for a purely harmonic wave of a single frequency and wavelength?

Particle Wave Packets

The quantity analogous to the displacement $y(x, t)$ for waves on a string, to the pressure $P(x, t)$ for a sound wave, or to the electric field $\mathcal{E}(x, t)$ for electromagnetic waves, is called the *wave function* for particles and is usually designated $\Psi(x, t)$. It is $\Psi(x, t)$ that we will relate to the probability of finding the particle and, as we alerted you earlier, it is the probability that waves. Consider, for example, an electron wave consisting of a single frequency and wavelength; we could represent such a wave by any of the following, exactly as we did the classical wave: $\Psi(x, t) = A \cos (kx - \omega t)$, $\Psi(x, t) = A \sin (kx - \omega t)$, or $\Psi(x, t) = A e^{i (kx - \omega t)}$.

The phase velocity is given by

$$v_p = f\lambda = \left(\frac{E}{h}\right)\left(\frac{h}{p}\right) = \frac{E}{p}$$

where we have used the de Broglie relations for the wavelength and frequency. Using the nonrelativistic expression for the energy of a particle moving at speed v in free space (i.e., no potential energy) with no forces acting upon it,

$$E = \frac{1}{2}mv^2 = \frac{p^2}{2m}$$

we see that the phase velocity is

$$v_p = \frac{E}{p} = \frac{p^2/2m}{p} = \frac{p}{2m} = \frac{v}{2}$$

i.e., the phase velocity of the wave is half the velocity v of an electron with momentum p. The phase velocity does *not* equal the particle velocity. Moreover, a wave of a single frequency and wavelength is not localized but is spread throughout space, which makes it difficult to see how the particle and wave properties of the electron could be related. Thus, for the electron to have the particle property of being localized, the matter waves of the electron must also be limited in spatial extent—i.e., realistically, $\Psi(x, t)$ must be a wave packet containing many more than one wave number k and frequency ω. It is the wave packet $\Psi(x, t)$ that we expect to move at a velocity equal to the particle velocity, which we will show below is indeed the case. The particle, if observed, we will expect to find somewhere within the spatial extent of the wave packet $\Psi(x, t)$, precisely where within that space being the subject of the next section.

To illustrate the equality of the group velocity v_g and the particle velocity v it is convenient to express de Broglie's relations in a slightly different form. Writing Equation 5-1 as follows,

$$E = hf = \frac{h\omega}{2\pi} \quad \text{or} \quad E = \hbar\omega \qquad \textbf{5-24}$$

and Equation 5-2 as

$$p = \frac{h}{\lambda} = \frac{h}{2\pi/k} = \frac{hk}{2\pi} \quad \text{or} \quad p = \hbar k \qquad \textbf{5-25}$$

The group velocity is then given by

$$v_g = \frac{d\omega}{dk} = \frac{dE/\hbar}{dp/\hbar} = \frac{dE}{dp}$$

Again using the nonrelativistic expression $E = p^2/2m$, we have that

$$v_g = \frac{dE}{dp} = \frac{p}{m} = v$$

and the wave packet $\Psi(x, t)$ moves with the velocity of the electron. This was, in fact, one of de Broglie's reasons for choosing Equations 5-1 and 5-2. (De Broglie used the relativistic expression relating energy and momentum, which also leads to the equality of the group velocity and particle velocity.)

An application of phase and particle speeds by nature: produce a wave on a still pond (or in a bathtub) and watch the wavelets that make up the wave appear to "climb over" the wave crest at twice the speed of the wave.

5-4 The Probabilistic Interpretation of the Wave Function

Let us consider in more detail the relation between the wave function $\Psi(x, t)$ and the location of the electron. We can get a hint about this relation from the case of light. The wave equation that governs light is Equation 5-11, with $y = \mathscr{E}$, the electric field,

as the wave function. The energy per unit volume in a light wave is proportional to $\mathscr{E}^2$, but the energy in a light wave is quantized in units of hf for each photon. We expect, therefore, that the number of photons in a unit volume is proportional to $\mathscr{E}^2$, a connection first pointed out by Einstein.

Consider the famous double-slit interference experiment (Figure 5-18). The pattern observed on the screen is determined by the interference of the waves from the slits. At a point on the screen where the wave from one slit is 180° out of phase with that from the other, the resultant electric field is zero; there is no light energy at this point, and the point is dark. If we reduce the intensity to a very low value, we can still observe the interference pattern if we replace the ordinary screen by a scintillation screen or a two-dimensional array of tiny photon detectors and wait a sufficient length of time.

The interaction of light with the detector or scintillator is a quantum phenomenon. If we illuminate the scintillators or detectors for only a very short time with a low-intensity source, we do not see merely a weaker version of the high-intensity pattern; we see, instead, "dots" caused by the interactions of individual photons (see Figure 5-19). At points where the waves from the slits interfere destructively there are no dots, and at points where the waves interfere constructively there are many dots. However, when the exposure is short and the source weak, random fluctuations from the average predictions of the wave theory are clearly evident. If the exposure is long enough that many photons reach the detector, the fluctuations average out and the quantum nature of light is not noticed. The interference pattern depends only on the total number of photons interacting with the detector and not on the rate. Even when the intensity is so low that only one photon at a time reaches the detector, the wave theory predicts the correct average pattern. For low intensities, we therefore interpret $\mathscr{E}^2$ as proportional to the *probability* of detecting a photon in a unit volume of space. At points on the detector where $\mathscr{E}^2$ is zero, photons are never observed, whereas they are most likely to be observed at points where $\mathscr{E}^2$ is large.

It is not necessary to use light waves to produce an interference pattern. Such patterns can be produced with electrons and other particles as well. In the wave theory of electrons, the de Broglie wave of a *single* electron is described by a wave function Ψ. The amplitude of Ψ at any point is related to the probability of finding the particle at that point. In analogy with the foregoing interpretation of $\mathscr{E}^2$, the quantity $|\Psi|^2$ is proportional to the probability of detecting an electron in a unit volume, where $|\Psi|^2 \equiv \Psi^*\Psi$,

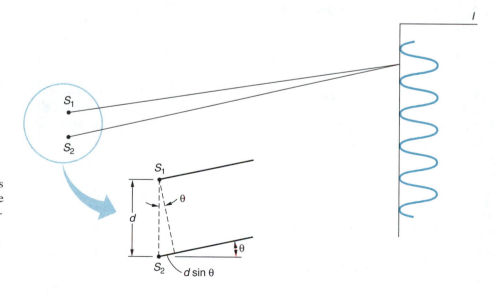

Fig. 5-18 Two-source interference pattern. If the sources are coherent and in phase, the waves from the sources interfere constructively at points for which the path difference ($d \sin \theta$) is an integral number of wavelengths.

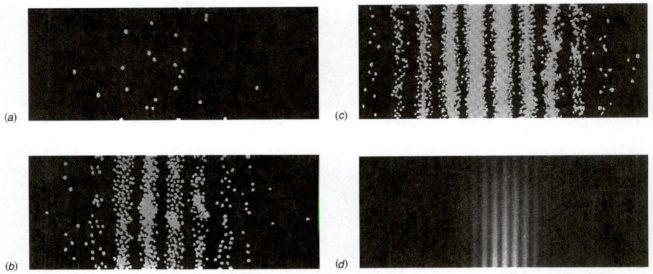

Fig. 5-19 Growth of two-slit interference pattern. The photo (*d*) is an actual two-slit electron interference pattern in which the film was exposed to millions of electrons. The pattern is identical to that usually obtained with photons. If the film were to be observed at various stages, such as after being struck by 28 electrons, then after about 1000 electrons, and again after about 10,000 electrons, the patterns of individually exposed grains would be similar to those shown in (*a*), (*b*), and (*c*), except that the exposed dots would be smaller than the dots drawn here. Note that there are no dots in the region of the interference minima. The probability of any point of the film being exposed is determined by wave theory, whether the film is exposed by electrons or photons. [*Parts (a), (b), and (c) from E. R. Huggins,* Physics 1, © *by W. A. Benjamin, Inc., Menlo Park, California. Photo (d) courtesy of C. Jonsson.*]

the function Ψ^* being the complex conjugate of Ψ. In one dimension, $|\Psi|^2 \, dx$ is the probability of an electron being in the interval dx.[10] (See Figure 5-20.) If we call this probability $P(x)dx$, where $P(x)$ is the probability distribution function, we have

$$P(x) \, dx = |\Psi|^2 \, dx \qquad\qquad \textbf{5-26}$$

In the next chapter we will discuss more thoroughly the amplitudes of matter waves associated with particles, in particular developing the mathematical system for computing the amplitudes and probabilities in various situations. The uneasiness that you may feel at this point regarding the fact that we have not given a precise physical interpretation to the amplitude of the de Broglie matter wave can be attributed in part to the complex nature of the wave amplitude, i.e., it is in general a complex quantity with a real part and an imaginary part, the latter proportional to $i = (-1)^{1/2}$. We cannot directly measure or physically interpret complex numbers in our world of real numbers. However, as we will see, defining the probability in terms of $|\Psi|^2$, which is always real, presents no difficulty in its physical interpretation. Thus, even though the amplitudes of the wave functions Ψ have no simple meaning, the waves themselves behave just as do classical waves, exhibiting the wave characteristics of reflection, refraction, interference, and diffraction and obeying the principles of superposition.

5-5 The Uncertainty Principle

Consider a wave packet $\Psi(x, t)$ representing an electron. The most probable position of the electron is the value of x for which $|\Psi(x, t)|^2$ is a maximum. Since $|\Psi(x, t)|^2$ is proportional to the probability that the electron is at x, and $|\Psi(x, t)|^2$

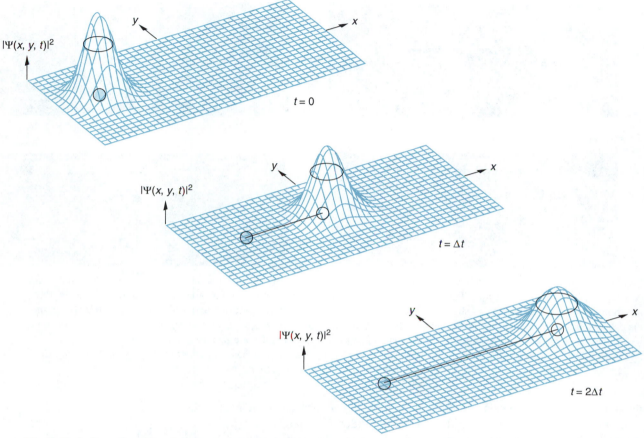

Fig. 5-20 A three-dimensional wave packet representing a particle moving along the *x* axis. The dot indicates the position of a classical particle. Note that the packet spreads out in the *x* and *y* directions. This spreading is due to dispersion, resulting from the fact that the phase velocity of the individual waves making up the packet depends on the wavelength of the waves.

is nonzero for a range of values of *x*, there is an *uncertainty* in the value of the position of the electron. (See Figure 5-20.) This means that if we make a number of position measurements on identical electrons—electrons with the same wave function—we shall not always obtain the same result. In fact, the distribution function for the results of such measurements will be given by $|\Psi(x, t)|^2$. If the wave packet is very narrow, the uncertainty in position will be small. However, a narrow wave packet must contain a wide range of wave numbers *k*. Since the momentum is related to the wave number by $p = \hbar k$, a wide range of *k* values means a wide range of momentum values. We have seen that for all wave packets the ranges Δx and Δk are related by

$$\Delta x \, \Delta k \sim 1 \qquad\qquad \textbf{5-16}$$

Similarly, a packet that is localized in time Δt must contain a range of frequencies $\Delta \omega$, where the ranges are related by

$$\Delta \omega \, \Delta t \sim 1 \qquad\qquad \textbf{5-17}$$

Equations 5-16 and 5-17 are inherent properties of waves. If we multiply these equations by $\hbar$ and use $p = \hbar k$ and $E = \hbar\omega$, we obtain

$$\Delta x \, \Delta p \sim \hbar \qquad\qquad \textbf{5-27}$$

and

$$\Delta E \, \Delta t \sim \hbar \qquad\qquad \textbf{5-28}$$

Equations 5-27 and 5-28 provide a statement of the *uncertainty principle* first enunciated in 1927 by Werner K. Heisenberg.[11] Equation 5-27 expresses the fact that the distribution functions for position and momentum cannot both be made arbitrarily narrow simultaneously (see Figure 5-16); thus measurements of position and momentum will have similar uncertainties which are related by Equation 5-27. Of course, because of inaccurate measurements, the product of Δx and Δp can be, and usually is, much larger than $\hbar$. The lower limit is not due to any technical problem in the design of measuring equipment that might be solved at some later time; it is instead due to the wave and particle nature of both matter and light.

If we define precisely what we mean by the uncertainty in the measurements of position and momentum, we can give a precise statement of the uncertainty principle. We saw in Section 5-3 that, if σ_x is the standard deviation for measurements of position and σ_k is the standard deviation for measurements of the wave number k, the product $\sigma_x\sigma_k$ has its minimum value of $1/2$ when the distribution functions are Gaussian. If we define Δx and Δp to be the standard deviations, the minimum value of their product is $\frac{1}{2}\hbar$. Thus

$$\Delta x \, \Delta p \geq \tfrac{1}{2}\hbar \qquad\qquad \textbf{5-29}$$

Similarly,

$$\Delta E \, \Delta t \geq \tfrac{1}{2}\hbar \qquad\qquad \textbf{5-30}$$

Heisenberg's uncertainty principle is the key to the existence of *virtual particles* that hold the nuclei together (see Chapter 11) and is the root of quantum fluctuations that may have been the origin of the Big Bang (see Chapter 14).

QUESTION

6. Does the uncertainty principle say that the momentum of a particle can never be precisely known?

Exploring

The Gamma-Ray Microscope

Let us see how one might attempt to make a measurement so accurate as to violate the uncertainty principle. A common way to measure the position of an object such as an electron is to look at it with light, i.e., scatter light from it and observe the diffraction pattern. The momentum can be obtained by looking at it again, a short

time later, and computing what velocity it must have had the instant before the light scattered from it. Because of diffraction effects, we cannot hope to make measurements of length (position) that are smaller than the wavelength of the light used, so we will use the shortest-wavelength light that can be obtained, gamma rays. (There is, in principle, no limit to how short the wavelength of electromagnetic radiation can be.) We also know that light carries momentum and energy, so that when it scatters off the electron, the motion of the electron will be disturbed, affecting the momentum. We must, therefore, use the minimum intensity possible, so as to disturb the electron as little as possible. Reducing the intensity decreases the number of photons, but we must scatter at least one photon to observe the electron. The minimum possible intensity, then, is that corresponding to one photon. The scattering of a photon by a free electron is, of course, a Compton scattering, which was discussed in Section 3-4. The momentum of the photon is $hf/c = h/\lambda$. The smaller the λ that is used to measure the position, the more the photon will disturb the electron, but we can correct for that with a Compton-effect analysis, provided only that we know the photon's momentum and the scattering angles of the event.

Figure 5-21 illustrates the problem. (This illustration was first given as a gedankenexperiment, or thought experiment, by Heisenberg. Since a single photon doesn't form a diffraction pattern, think of the diffraction pattern as being built up by photons from many identical scattering experiments.) The position of the electron is to be determined by viewing it through a microscope. We shall assume that only one photon is used. We can take for the uncertainty in position the minimum separation distance for which two objects can be resolved; this is[12]

$$\Delta x = \frac{\lambda}{2\sin\theta}$$

where θ is the half angle subtended by the lens aperture, as shown in Figures 5-21*a* and *b*. Let us assume that the x component of momentum of the incoming photon is known precisely from a previous measurement. To reach the screen and contribute to the diffraction pattern in Figure 5-21*c*, the scattered photon need only go through the lens aperture. Thus, the scattered photon can have any x component of momentum from 0 to $p_x = p\sin\theta$, where p is the total momentum of the scattered photon. By conservation of momentum, the uncertainty in the momentum of the electron after the scattering must be greater than or equal to that of the scattered photon (it would be equal, of course, if the electron's initial momentum were known precisely); thus we write

$$\Delta p_x \geq p\sin\theta = \frac{h}{\lambda}\sin\theta$$

and

$$\Delta x\,\Delta p_x \geq \frac{\lambda}{2\sin\theta}\frac{h\sin\theta}{\lambda} = \frac{1}{2}h$$

Thus, even though the electron prior to our observation may have had a definite position and momentum, our observation has unavoidably introduced an uncertainty in the measured values of those quantities. This illustrates the essential point of the uncertainty principle—that this product of uncertainties cannot be less than about $\hbar$ *in principle,* that is, even in an ideal situation. If electrons rather than photons were used to locate the object, the analysis would not change, since the relation $\lambda = h/p$ is the same for both.

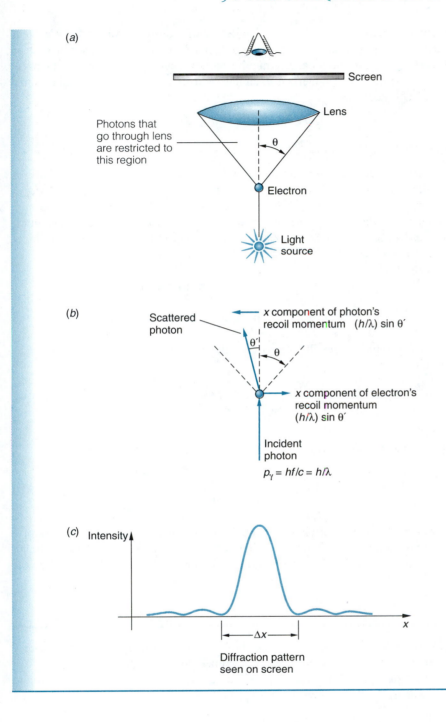

(a)

Screen

Lens

Photons that
go through lens
are restricted to
this region

θ

Electron

Light
source

(b)

Scattered
photon

θ'   θ

x component of photon's
recoil momentum $(h/\lambda) \sin \theta'$

x component of electron's
recoil momentum
$(h/\lambda) \sin \theta'$

Incident
photon

$p_\gamma = hf/c = h/\lambda$

(c) Intensity

Δx

x

Diffraction pattern
seen on screen

Fig. 5-21 (a) "Seeing an electron" with a gamma-ray microscope. (b) Because of the size of the lens, the momentum of the scattered photon is uncertain by $\Delta p_x \approx p \sin \theta = h \sin \theta/\lambda$. Thus the recoil momentum of the electron is also uncertain by at least this amount. (c) The position of the electron cannot be resolved better than the width of the central maximum of the diffraction pattern $\Delta x \approx \lambda/\sin \theta$. The product of the uncertainties $\Delta p_x \Delta x$ is therefore of the order of Planck's constant h.

5-6 Some Consequences of the Uncertainty Principle

In the next chapter we shall see that the Schrödinger wave equation provides a straightforward method of solving problems in atomic physics. However, the solution of the Schrödinger equation is often laborious and difficult. Much semiquantitative information about the behavior of atomic systems can be obtained from the

uncertainty principle alone without a detailed solution of the problem. The general approach used in applying the uncertainty principle to such systems will first be illustrated by considering a particle moving in a box with rigid walls. We then use that analysis in several numerical examples and as a basis for discussing some additional consequences.

Minimum Energy of a Particle in a Box

An important consequence of the uncertainty principle is that a particle confined to a finite space cannot have zero kinetic energy. Let us consider the case of a one-dimensional "box" of length L. If we know that the particle is in the box, Δx is not larger than L. This implies that Δp is at least $\hbar/L$. (Since we are interested in orders of magnitude, we shall ignore the 1/2 in the minimum uncertainty product. In general, distributions are not Gaussian anyway, so $\Delta p \, \Delta x$ will be larger than $\frac{1}{2}\hbar$.)

Let us take the standard deviation as a measure of Δp,

$$(\Delta p)^2 = (p - \bar{p})^2_{av} = (p^2 - 2p\bar{p} + \bar{p}^2)_{av} = \overline{p^2} - \bar{p}^2$$

If the box is symmetric, $\bar{p}$ will be zero since the particle moves to the left as often as to the right. Then

$$(\Delta p)^2 = \overline{p^2} \geq \left(\frac{\hbar}{L}\right)^2$$

and the average kinetic energy is

$$\bar{E} = \frac{\overline{p^2}}{2m} \geq \frac{\hbar^2}{2mL^2} \qquad\qquad \textbf{5-31}$$

Thus, we see that the uncertainty principle indicates that the minimum energy of a particle (*any* particle) in a "box" (*any* kind of "box") cannot be zero. This minimum energy given by Equation 5-31 for a particle in a one-dimensional box is called the *zero-point energy.*

EXAMPLE 5-7 A Macroscopic Particle in a Box Consider a small but macroscopic particle of mass $m = 10^{-6}$ g confined to a one-dimensional box with $L = 10^{-6}$ m, e.g., a tiny bead on a very short wire. Compute the bead's minimum kinetic energy and the corresponding speed.

Solution

1. The minimum kinetic energy is given by Equation 5-31:

$$\bar{E} = \frac{\hbar^2}{2mL^2} = \frac{(1.055 \times 10^{-34}\,\text{J}\cdot\text{s})^2}{(2)(10^{-9}\,\text{kg})(10^{-6}\,\text{m})^2}$$

$$= 5.57 \times 10^{-48}\,\text{J}$$

$$= 3.47 \times 10^{-29}\,\text{eV}$$

2.   The speed corresponding to this kinetic energy is:

$$v = \sqrt{\frac{2E}{m}} = \sqrt{\frac{2(5.57 \times 10^{-48} \text{ J})}{10^{-9} \text{ kg}}}$$

$$= 1.06 \times 10^{-19} \text{ m/s}$$

Remarks: *We can see from this calculation that the minimum kinetic energy implied by the uncertainty principle is certainly not observable for macroscopic objects even as small as 10^{-6} g.*

EXAMPLE 5-8 **An Electron in an Atomic Box** If the particle in a one-dimensional box of length $L = 0.1$ nm (about the diameter of an atom) is an electron, what will be its zero-point energy?

Solution
Again using Equation 5-31, we find that

$$E \approx \frac{(\hbar c)^2}{2mc^2L^2} = \frac{(197.3 \text{ eV} \cdot \text{nm})^2}{2(0.511 \times 10^6 \text{ eV})(0.1 \text{ nm})^2} = 3.81 \text{ eV}$$

This is the correct order of magnitude for the kinetic energy of an electron in an atom.

Size of the Hydrogen Atom

The energy of an electron of momentum p a distance r from a proton is

$$E = \frac{p^2}{2m} - \frac{ke^2}{r}$$

If we take for the order of magnitude of the position uncertainty $\Delta x = r$, we have

$$(\Delta p)^2 = \overline{p^2} \geq \frac{\hbar^2}{r^2}$$

The energy is then

$$E = \frac{\hbar^2}{2mr^2} - \frac{ke^2}{r}$$

There is a radius r_m at which E is minimum. Setting $dE/dr = 0$ yields r_m and E_m:

$$r_m = \frac{\hbar^2}{ke^2m} = a_0 = 0.0529 \text{ nm}$$

and

$$E_m = -\frac{k^2e^4m}{2\hbar^2} = -13.6 \text{ eV}$$

The fact that r_m came out to be exactly the radius of the first Bohr orbit is due to the judicious choice of $\Delta x = r$ rather than $2r$ or $r/2$, which are just as reasonable. It should be clear, however, that any reasonable choice for Δx gives the correct order of magnitude of the size of an atom.

Widths of Spectral Lines

Equation 5-30 implies that the energy of a system cannot be measured exactly unless an infinite amount of time is available for the measurement. If an atom is in an excited state, it does not remain in that state indefinitely but makes transitions to lower energy states until it reaches the ground state. The decay of an excited state is a statistical process.

We can take the mean time for decay τ, called the *lifetime*, to be a measure of the time available to determine the energy of the state. For atomic transitions, τ is of the order of 10^{-8} s. The uncertainty in the energy corresponding to this time is

$$\Delta E \geq \frac{\hbar}{\tau} = \frac{6.58 \times 10^{-16} \text{eV} \cdot \text{s}}{10^{-8} \text{ s}} \approx 10^{-7} \text{ eV}$$

This uncertainty in energy causes a spread $\Delta\lambda$ in the wavelength of the light emitted. For transitions to the ground state, which has a perfectly certain energy E_0 because of its infinite lifetime, the percentage spread in wavelength can be calculated from

$$E - E_0 = \frac{hc}{\lambda}$$

$$dE = -hc\frac{d\lambda}{\lambda^2}$$

$$|\Delta E| \approx hc\frac{|\Delta\lambda|}{\lambda^2}$$

thus

$$\frac{\Delta\lambda}{\lambda} \approx \frac{\Delta E}{E - E_0}$$

The energy width $\Gamma_0 = \hbar/\tau$ is called the *natural line width*. Other effects that cause broadening of spectral lines are the Doppler effect, the recoil effect, and atomic collisions. For optical spectra in the eV energy range, the Doppler width D is about 10^{-6} eV at room temperature, i.e., roughly 10 times the natural width, and the recoil width is negligible. For nuclear transitions in the MeV range, both the Doppler width and the recoil width are of the order of eV, much larger than the natural line width. We shall see in Chapter 11 that in some special cases of atoms in solids at low temperatures, the Doppler and recoil widths are essentially zero and the width of the spectral line is just the natural width. This effect, called the *Mössbauer effect* after its discoverer, is extremely important, for it provides photons of well-defined energy, which are useful in experiments demanding extreme precision. For example, the 14.4-keV photon from ^{57}Fe has a natural width of the order of 10^{-11} of its energy.

QUESTIONS

7. What happens to the zero-point energy of a particle in a one-dimensional box as the length of the box $L \rightarrow \infty$?

8. Why is the uncertainty principle not apparent for macroscopic objects?

EXAMPLE 5-9 Emission of a Photon Most excited atomic states decay, i.e., emit a photon, within about $\tau = 10^{-8}$ s following excitation. What is the minimum uncertainty in the (1) energy and (2) frequency of the emitted photon?

Solution

1. The minimum energy uncertainty is the natural line width $\Gamma_0 = \hbar/\tau$; therefore,

$$\Gamma_0 = \frac{6.63 \times 10^{-34}\,\text{J}\cdot\text{s}}{2\pi \times 10^{-8}\,\text{s}} = \frac{4.14 \times 10^{-15}\,\text{eV}\cdot\text{s}}{2\pi \times 10^{-8}\,\text{s}} = 6.6 \times 10^{-8}\,\text{eV}$$

2. From de Broglie's relation $E = \hbar\omega$ we have

$$\Delta E = \hbar\Delta\omega = \hbar(2\pi\Delta f) = h\Delta f$$

so that Equation 5-30 can be written as

$$\Delta E\,\Delta t = h\Delta f\,\Delta t \geq \hbar$$

or

$$\Delta f\,\Delta t \geq \frac{1}{2\pi}$$

and the minimum uncertainty in the frequency becomes

$$\Delta f \geq \frac{1}{2\pi\Delta t} = \frac{1}{2\pi \times 10^{-8}}$$
$$\Delta f \geq 1.6 \times 10^{7}\,\text{Hz}$$

5-7 Wave-Particle Duality

We have seen that electrons, which were once thought of as simply particles, exhibit the wave properties of diffraction and interference. In earlier chapters we saw that light, which we previously had thought of as a wave, also has particle properties in its interaction with matter, as in the photoelectric effect or the Compton effect. All phenomena—electrons, atoms, light, sound—have both particle and wave characteristics. It is sometimes said that an electron, for example, behaves as both a wave and a particle. This may seem confusing since, in classical physics, the concepts of waves and particles are mutually exclusive. A *classical particle* behaves like a BB shot. It can be localized and

scattered, it exchanges energy suddenly in a lump, and it obeys the laws of conservation of energy and momentum in collisions; but it does *not* exhibit interference and diffraction. A *classical wave* behaves like a water wave. It exhibits diffraction and interference patterns and has its energy spread out continuously in space and time, not quantized in lumps. Nothing, it was thought, could be both a classical particle and a classical wave.

We now see that the classical concepts do not adequately describe either waves or particles. Both matter and radiation have both particle and wave aspects. When emission or absorption is being studied, it is the particle aspects that are dominant. When matter or radiation propagates though space, wave aspects dominate. Notice that emission and absorption are events characterized by exchange of energy and discrete locations. For example, light strikes the retina of your eye and a photon is absorbed, transferring its energy to a particular rod or cone: an observation has occurred. This illustrates the point that *observations* of matter and radiation are described in terms of the particle aspects. On the other hand, predicting the intensity distribution of the light on your retina involves consideration of the amplitudes of waves that have propagated through space and been diffracted at the pupil. Thus, *predictions,* i.e., a priori statements about what may be observed, are described in terms of the wave aspects. Let's elaborate on this just a bit.

Every phenomenon is describable by a wave function that is the solution of a wave equation. The wave function for light is the electric field $\mathcal{E}(x, t)$ (in one dimension), which is the solution of a wave equation like Equation 5-11. We have called the wave function for an electron $\Psi(x, t)$. We shall study the wave equation of which Ψ is the solution, called the *Schrödinger equation,* in the next chapter. The magnitude squared of the wave function gives the probability (per unit volume) that the electron, if looked for, will be found in a given region. The wave function exhibits the classical wave properties of interference and diffraction. In order to predict where an electron, or other particle, is likely to be, we must find the wave function by methods similar to those of classical wave theory. When the electron (or light) interacts and exchanges energy and momentum, the wave function is changed by the interaction. The interaction can be described by classical particle theory, as is done in the Compton effect. There are times when classical particle theory and classical wave theory give the same results. <u>If the wavelength is much smaller than any object or aperture, particle theory can be used as well as wave theory to describe wave propagation, because diffraction and interference effects are too small to be observed.</u> Common examples are geometric optics, which is really a particle theory, and the motion of baseballs and jet aircraft. If one is interested only in time averages of energy and momentum exchange, the wave theory works as well as the particle theory. For example, the wave theory of light correctly predicts that the total electron current in the photoelectric effect is proportional to the intensity of the light.

More

That matter can exhibit wavelike characteristics as well as particlelike behavior can be a difficult concept to understand. A wonderfully clear discussion of wave-particle duality was given by R. P. Feynman and we have used it as the basis of our explanation on the home page of the *Two-Slit Interference Pattern* for electrons: www.whfreeman.com/modphysics4e See also Figures 5-22 and 5-23 and Equation 5-32 here.

Summary

TOPIC	RELEVANT EQUATIONS AND REMARKS
1. De Broglie relations	$f = E/h$ 5-1
	$\lambda = h/p$ 5-2
	Electrons and all other particles exhibit the wave properties of interference and diffraction.
2. Detecting electron waves	
Davisson and Germer	Showed that electron waves diffracted from a single Ni crystal according to Bragg's equation
	$n\lambda = D \sin \phi$ 5-5
3. Wave packets	
Wave equation	$\dfrac{\partial^2 y}{\partial x^2} = \dfrac{1}{v^2}\dfrac{\partial^2 y}{\partial t^2}$ 5-11
Uncertainty relations	$\Delta k\, \Delta x \approx 1$ 5-16
	$\Delta\omega\, \Delta t \approx 1$ 5-17
Wave speed	$v = \omega/k$
Group (packet) speed	$v_g = d\omega/dk$ 5-22
	$v_g = v_p + k\dfrac{dv_p}{dk}$ 5-23
Matter waves	The wave packet moves with the particle speed, i.e., the particle speed is the group speed v_g.
4. Probabilistic interpretation	The magnitude square of the wave function is proportional to the probability of observing a particle in the region dx at x and t.
	$P(x)dx = |\Psi|^2 dx$ 5-26
5. Heisenberg uncertainty principle	$\Delta x\, \Delta p \geq \tfrac{1}{2}\hbar$ 5-29
	$\Delta E\, \Delta t \geq \tfrac{1}{2}\hbar$ 5-30
	where each of the uncertainties is defined to be the standard deviation.
Particle in a box	$\overline{E} \geq \dfrac{\hbar^2}{2mL^2}$ 5-31
	The minimum energy of any particle in any "box" cannot be zero.
Energy of H atom	The Heisenberg principle predicts $E_{min} = -13.6$ eV in agreement with the Bohr model.

GENERAL REFERENCES

The following general references are written at a level appropriate for the readers of this book.

De Broglie, L., *Matter and Light: The New Physics,* Dover, New York, 1939. In this collection of studies is de Broglie's lecture on the occasion of receiving the Nobel Prize, in which he describes his reasoning leading to the prediction of the wave nature of matter.

Feynman, R., "Probability and Uncertainty—The Quantum-Mechanical View of Nature," filmed lecture, available from Educational Services, Inc., Film Library, Newton, Mass.

Feynman, R. P., R. B. Leighton, and M. Sands, *Lectures on Physics,* Addison-Wesley, Reading, Mass., 1965.

Fowles, G. R., *Introduction to Modern Optics,* Holt, Rinehart & Winston, New York, 1968.

Hecht, E., *Optics,* 2d ed., Addison-Wesley, Reading, Mass., 1987.

Jenkins, F. A., and H. E. White, *Fundamentals of Optics,* 4th ed., McGraw-Hill, New York, 1976.

Mehra, J., and H. Rechenberg, *The Historical Development of Quantum Theory,* Vol. 1, Springer-Verlag, New York, 1982.

Resnick, R., and D. Halliday, *Basic Concepts in Relativity and Early Quantum Theory,* 2d ed., Wiley, New York, 1992.

Tipler, P., *Physics for Scientists and Engineers,* 4th ed., W. H. Freeman, New York, 1999. Chapters 15 and 16 include a complete discussion of classical waves.

NOTES

1. Louis V. P. R. de Broglie (1892–1987), French physicist. Originally trained in history, he became interested in science after serving as a radio engineer in the French army (assigned to the Eiffel Tower) and through the work of his physicist brother Maurice. The subject of his doctoral dissertation received unusual attention because his professor, Paul Langevin (who discovered the principle on which sonar is based), brought it to the attention of Einstein, who described de Broglie's hypothesis to Lorentz as ". . . the first feeble ray of light to illuminate . . . the worst of our physical riddles." He received the Nobel Prize in physics in 1929, the first person so honored for work done for a doctoral thesis.

2. L. de Broglie, *New Perspectives in Physics* (New York: Basic Books, 1962).

3. See, e.g., P. Tipler, *Physics for Scientists and Engineers,* 4th ed. (New York: W. H. Freeman, 1999), Section 35-5.

4. Jean-Baptiste Perrin (1870–1942), French physicist. He was the first to show that cathode rays were actually charged particles, setting the stage for J. J. Thomson's measurement of their q/m ratio. He was also the first to measure the approximate size of atoms and molecules and determined Avogadro's number. He received the Nobel Prize in physics for that work in 1926.

5. Clinton J. Davisson (1881–1958), American physicist. He shared the 1937 Nobel Prize in physics with G. P. Thomson for demonstrating the diffraction of particles. Davisson's was the first ever awarded for work done somewhere other than at an academic institution. Germer was one of Davisson's assistants at Bell Telephone Laboratory.

6. Matter (electron) waves, like other waves, change their direction in passing from one medium (e.g., Ni crystal) into another (e.g., vacuum) in the manner described by Snell's law and the indices of refraction of the two media. For normal incidence Equation 5-5 is not affected, but for other incident angles it is altered a bit and that change has not been taken into account in either Figure 5-6 or 5-7.

7. *Nobel Prize Lectures: Physics* (Amsterdam and New York: Elsevier, 1964).

8. In spectroscopy, the quantity $k = \lambda^{-1}$ is called the *wave number.* In the theory of waves, the term *wave number* is used for $k = 2\pi/\lambda$.

9. If you are familiar with Fourier analysis, you will recognize that $y(x)$ and $A(k)$ are essentially Fourier transforms of each other.

10. This interpretation of $|\Psi|^2$ was first developed by the German physicist Max Born (1882–1970). One of his positions early in his career was at the University of Berlin, where he was to relieve Planck of his teaching duties. Born received the Nobel Prize in physics in 1954, in part for his interpretation of $|\Psi|^2$.

11. Werner K. Heisenberg (1901–1976), German physicist. After obtaining his Ph.D. under Sommerfeld, he served as an assistant to Born and to Bohr. He was the director of research for Germany's atomic bomb project during World War II. His work on quantum theory earned him the physics Nobel Prize in 1932.

12. The resolving power of a microscope is discussed in some detail in F. A. Jenkins and H. E. White, *Fundamentals of Optics,* 4th ed. (New York: McGraw-Hill, 1976), pp. 332–334. The expression for Δx used here is determined by Rayleigh's criterion that two points are just resolved if the central maximum of the diffraction pattern from one falls at the first minimum of the diffraction pattern of the other.

13. Richard P. Feynman (1918–1988), American physicist. This discussion is based on one in his classic text, *Lectures on Physics* (Reading, Mass.: Addison-Wesley, 1965). He shared the 1965 Nobel Prize in physics for his development of quantum electrodynamics (QED). It was Feynman who, while a member of the commission on the *Challenger* disaster, pointed out that the booster-stage O-rings were at fault. A genuine legend in American physics, he was also an accomplished bongo drummer and safecracker.

PROBLEMS

Level I

Section 5-1 The de Broglie Hypothesis

5-1. (*a*) What is the de Broglie wavelength of a 1-g mass moving at a speed of 1 m per year? (*b*) What should be the speed of such a mass if its de Broglie wavelength is to be 1 cm?

5-2. If the kinetic energy of a particle is much greater than its rest energy, the relativistic approximation $E \approx pc$ holds. Use this approximation to find the de Broglie wavelength of an electron of energy 100 MeV.

5-3. Electrons in an electron microscope are accelerated from rest through a potential difference V_0 so that their de Broglie wavelength is 0.04 nm. What is V_0?

5-4. Compute the de Broglie wavelengths of (*a*) an electron, (*b*) a proton, and (*c*) an alpha particle of 4.5 keV kinetic energy.

5-5. According to statistical mechanics, the average kinetic energy of a particle at temperature T is $3kT/2$, where k is the Boltzmann constant. What is the average de Broglie wavelength of nitrogen molecules at room temperature?

5-6. Find the de Broglie wavelength of a neutron of kinetic energy 0.02 eV (this is of the order of magnitude of kT at room temperature).

5-7. A free proton moves back and forth between rigid walls separated by a distance $L = 0.01$ nm. (*a*) If the proton is represented by a one-dimensional standing de Broglie wave with a node at each wall, show that the allowed values of the de Broglie wavelength are given by $\lambda = 2L/n$ where n is a positive integer. (*b*) Derive a general expression for the allowed kinetic energy of the proton and compute the values for $n = 1$ and 2.

5-8. What must be the kinetic energy of an electron if the ratio of its de Broglie wavelength to its Compton wavelength is (*a*) 10^2, (*b*) 0.2, and (*c*) 10^{-3}?

5-9. Compute the wavelength of a cosmic ray proton whose kinetic energy is (*a*) 2 GeV and (*b*) 200 GeV.

Section 5-2 Measurements of Particle Wavelengths

5-10. What is the Bragg scattering angle ϕ for electrons scattered from a nickel crystal if their energy is (*a*) 75 eV, (*b*) 100 eV?

5-11. Compute the kinetic energy of a proton whose de Broglie wavelength is 0.25 nm. If a beam of such protons is reflected from a calcite crystal with crystal plane spacing of 0.304 nm, at what angle will the first-order Bragg maximum occur?

5-12. (*a*) The scattering angle for 50-eV electrons from MgO is 55.6°. What is the crystal spacing D? (*b*) What would be the scattering angle for 100-eV electrons?

5-13. A certain crystal has a set of planes spaced 0.30 nm apart. A beam of neutrons strikes the crystal at normal incidence and the first maximum of the diffraction pattern occurs at $\phi = 42°$. What are the de Broglie wavelength and kinetic energy of the neutrons?

5-14. Show that in Davisson and Germer's experiment with 54-eV electrons using the $D = 0.215$ nm planes, diffraction peaks with $n = 2$ and higher are not possible.

5-15. A beam of electrons with kinetic energy 350 eV is incident normal to the surface of a KCl crystal which has been cut so that the spacing D between adjacent atoms in the planes parallel to the surface is 0.315 nm. Calculate the angle ϕ at which diffraction peaks will occur for all orders possible.

Section 5-3 Wave Packets

5-16. Information is transmitted along a cable in the form of short electric pulses at 100,000 pulses/s. (*a*) What is the longest duration of the pulses such that they do not overlap? (*b*)What is the range of frequencies to which the receiving equipment must respond for this duration?

5-17. Two harmonic waves travel simultaneously along a long wire. Their wave functions are $y_1 = 0.002 \cos (8.0x - 400t)$ and $y_2 = 0.002 \cos (7.6x - 380t)$, where y and x are in meters and t in seconds. (*a*) Write the wave function for the resultant wave in the form of Equation 5-15. (*b*) What is the phase velocity of the resultant wave? (*c*) What is the group velocity? (*d*) Calculate the range Δx between successive zeros of the group and relate it to Δk.

5-18. (*a*) Starting from Equation 5-23, show that the group velocity can also be expressed as $v_g = v_p - \lambda(dv_p/d\lambda)$. (*b*) The phase velocity of each wavelength of white light moving through ordinary glass is a function of the wavelength, i.e., glass is a dispersive medium. What is the general dependance of v_p on λ in glass? Is $dv_p/d\lambda$ positive or negative?

5-19. A radar transmitter used to measure the speed of pitched baseballs emits pulses of 2.0-cm wavelength that are 0.25 μs in duration. (*a*) What is the length of the wave packet produced? (*b*) To what frequency should the receiver be tuned? (*c*) What must be the minimum bandwidth of the receiver?

5-20. A certain standard tuning fork vibrates at 880 Hz. If the tuning fork is tapped, causing it to vibrate, then stopped a quarter of a second later, what is the approximate range of frequencies contained in the sound pulse that reached your ear?

5-21. If a phone line is capable of transmitting a range of frequencies $\Delta f = 5000$ Hz, what is the approximate duration of the shortest pulse that can be transmitted over the line?

5-22. (*a*) You are given the task of constructing a double-slit experiment for 5-eV electrons. If you wish the first minimum of the diffraction pattern to occur at 5°, what must be the separation of the slits? (*b*) How far from the slits must the detector plane be located if the first minima on each side of the central maximum are to be separated by 1 cm?

Section 5-4 The Probabilistic Interpretation of the Wave Function

5-23. A 100-g rigid sphere of radius 1 cm has a kinetic energy of 2 J and is confined to move in a force-free region between two rigid walls separated by 50 cm. (*a*) What is the probability of finding the center of the sphere exactly midway between the two walls? (*b*) What is the probability of finding the center of the sphere between the 24.9- and 25.1-cm marks?

5-24. A particle moving in one dimension between rigid walls separated by a distance L has the wave function $\Psi(x) = A \sin(\pi x/L)$. Since the particle must remain between the walls, what must be the value of A?

5-25. The wave function describing a state of an electron confined to move along the x axis is given at time zero by

$$\Psi(x, 0) = Ae^{-x^2/4\sigma^2}$$

Find the probability of finding the electron in a region dx centered at (*a*) $x = 0$, (*b*) $x = \sigma$, and (*c*) $x = 2\sigma$. (*d*) Where is the electron most likely to be found?

Section 5-5 The Uncertainty Principle

5-26. A tuning fork of frequency f_0 vibrates for a time Δt and sends out a waveform that looks like that in Figure 5-24. This wave function is similar to a harmonic wave except that it is confined to a time Δt and space $\Delta x = v \Delta t$, where v is the phase velocity. Let N be the approximate number of cycles of vibration. We can measure the frequency by counting the cycles and dividing by Δt. (*a*) The number of cycles is uncertain by approximately ±1 cycle. Explain why (see the figure). What uncertainty does this introduce in the determination of the frequency f? (*b*) Write an expression for the wave number k in terms of Δx and N. Show that the uncertainty in N of ±1 leads to an uncertainty in k of $\Delta k = 2\pi/\Delta x$.

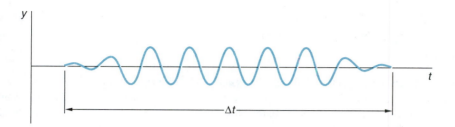

Fig. 5-24 Problem 5-26.

5-27. If an excited state of an atom is known to have a lifetime of 10^{-7} s, what is the uncertainty in the energy of photons emitted by such atoms in the spontaneous decay to the ground state?

5-28. A mass of 1 μg has a speed of 1 cm/s. If its speed is uncertain by 1 percent, what is the order of magnitude of the minimum uncertainty in its position?

5-29. ^{222}Rn decays by the emission of an α particle with a lifetime of 3.823 days. The kinetic energy of the α particle is measured to be 5.490 MeV. What is the uncertainty in this energy? Describe in one sentence how the finite lifetime of the excited state of the radon nucleus translates into an energy uncertainty for the emitted α particle.

5-30. If the uncertainty in the position of a wave packet representing the state of a quantum-system particle is equal to its de Broglie wavelength, how does the uncertainty in momentum compare with the value of the momentum of the particle?

5-31. In one of G. Gamow's Mr. Tompkins tales, the hero visits a "quantum jungle" where $\hbar$ is very large. Suppose that you are in such a place where $\hbar = 50$ J · s. A cheetah runs past you a few meters away. The cheetah is 2 m long from nose to tail tip and its mass is 30 kg. It is moving at 30 m/s. What is the uncertainty in the location of the "midpoint" of the cheetah? Describe in one sentence how the cheetah would look different to you than when $\hbar$ has its actual value.

5-32. In order to locate a particle, e.g., an electron, to within 5×10^{-12} m using electromagnetic waves ("light"), the wavelength must be at least this small. Calculate the momentum and energy of a photon with $\lambda = 5 \times 10^{-12}$ m. If the particle is an electron with $\Delta x = 5 \times 10^{-12}$ m, what is the corresponding uncertainty in its momentum?

5-33. The decay of excited states in atoms and nuclei often leaves the system in another, albeit lower-energy, excited state. (*a*) One example is the decay between two excited states of the nucleus of ^{48}Ti. The upper state has a lifetime of 1.4 ps, the lower state 3.0 ps. What is the fractional uncertainty $\Delta E/E$ in the energy of 1.3117-MeV gamma rays connecting the two states? (*b*) Another example is the H$_\alpha$ line of the hydrogen Balmer series. In this case the lifetime of both states is about the same, 10^{-8} s. What is the uncertainty in the energy of the H$_\alpha$ photon?

Section 5-6 Some Consequences of the Uncertainty Principle

5-34. A neutron has a kinetic energy of 10 MeV. What size object is necessary to observe neutron diffraction effects? Is there anything in nature of this size that could serve as a target to demonstrate the wave nature of 10-MeV neutrons?

5-35. The energy of a certain nuclear state can be measured with an uncertainty of 1 eV. What is the minimum lifetime of this state?

5-36. Show that the relation $\Delta p_s \, \Delta s > \hbar$ can be written $\Delta L \, \Delta\phi > \hbar$ for a particle moving in a circle about the z axis, where p_s is the linear momentum tangential to the circle, s is the arc length, and L is the angular momentum. How well can the angular position of the electron be specified in the Bohr atom?

5-37. An excited state of a certain nucleus has a half-life of 0.85 ns. Taking this to be the uncertainty Δt for emission of a photon, calculate the uncertainty in the frequency Δf, using Equation 5-28. If $\lambda = 0.01$ nm, find $\Delta f/f$.

Section 5-7 Wave-Particle Duality

There are no problems for this section.

Level II

5-38. A neutron in an atomic nucleus is bound to other neutrons and protons in the nucleus by the strong nuclear force when it comes within about 1 fm of another particle. What is the approximate kinetic energy of a neutron that is localized to within such a region? What would be the corresponding energy of an electron localized to within such a region?

5-39. Using the relativistic expression $E^2 = p^2c^2 + m^2c^4$, (a) show that the phase velocity of an electron wave is greater than c. (b) Show that the group velocity of an electron wave equals the particle velocity of the electron.

5-40. Show that if y_1 and y_2 are solutions of Equation 5-11, the function $y_3 = C_1y_1 + C_2y_2$ is also a solution for any values of the constants C_1 and C_2.

5-41. Show that if $\Delta x \, \Delta p = \frac{1}{2}\hbar$, the minimum energy of a simple harmonic oscillator is $\frac{1}{2}\hbar\omega = \frac{1}{2}hf$. What is the minimum energy in joules for a mass of 10^{-2} kg oscillating on a spring of force constant $K = 1$ N/m?

5-42. A particle of mass m moves in a one-dimensional box of length L. (Take the potential energy of the particle in the box to be zero so that its total energy is its kinetic energy $p^2/2m$.) Its energy is quantized by the standing-wave condition $n(\lambda/2) = L$, where λ is the de Broglie wavelength of the particle and n is an integer. (a) Show that the allowed energies are given by $E_n = n^2E_1$ where $E_1 = h^2/8mL^2$. (b) Evaluate E_n for an electron in a box of size $L = 0.1$ nm and make an energy-level diagram for the state from $n = 1$ to $n = 5$. Use Bohr's second postulate $f = \Delta E/h$ to calculate the wavelength of electromagnetic radiation emitted when the electron makes a transition from (c) $n = 2$ to $n = 1$, (d) $n = 3$ to $n = 2$, and (e) $n = 5$ to $n = 1$.

5-43. (a) Use the results of Problem 5-42 to find the energy of the ground state ($n = 1$) and the first two excited states of a proton in a one-dimensional box of length $L = 10^{-15}$ m = 1 fm. (These are of the order of magnitude of nuclear energies.) Calculate the wavelength of electromagnetic radiation emitted when the proton makes a transition from (b) $n = 2$ to $n = 1$, (c) $n = 3$ to $n = 2$, and (d) $n = 3$ to $n = 1$.

5-44. (a) Suppose that a particle of mass m is constrained to move in a one-dimensional space between two infinitely high barriers located A apart. Using the uncertainty principle, find an expression for the zero-point (minimum) energy of the particle. (b) Using your result from (a), compute the minimum energy of an electron in such a space if $A = 10^{-10}$ m and if $A = 1$ cm. (c) Calculate the minimum energy for a 100-mg bead moving on a thin wire between two stops located 2 cm apart.

5-45. A proton and a bullet each move with a speed of 500 m/s, measured with an uncertainty of 0.01 percent. If measurements of their respective positions are made simultaneous with the speed measurements, what is the minimum uncertainty possible in the position measurements?

Level III

5-46. Show that Equation 5-11 is satisfied by $y = f(\phi)$, where $\phi = x - vt$, for any function f.

5-47. An electron and a positron are moving toward each other with equal speeds of 3×10^6 m/s. The two particles annihilate each other and produce two photons of equal energy. (a) What were the de Broglie wavelengths of the electron and positron? Find the (b) energy, (c) momentum, and (d) wavelength of each photon.

5-48. It is possible for some fundamental particles to "violate" conservation of energy by creating and quickly reabsorbing another particle. For example, a proton can emit a π^+ according to $p \rightarrow n + \pi^+$ where the n represents a neutron. The π^+ has a mass of 140 MeV/c^2. The reabsorption must occur within a time Δt consistent with the

uncertainty principle. (*a*) Considering that example by how much ΔE is energy conservation violated? (Ignore kinetic energy.) (*b*) For how long Δt can the π^+ exist? (*c*) Assuming that the π^+ is moving at nearly the speed of light, how far from the nucleus could it get in the time Δt? (As we will discuss in Chapter 11, this is the approximate range of the strong nuclear force.)

5-49. De Broglie developed Equation 5-2 initially for photons, assuming that they had a small but finite mass. His assumption was that RF waves with $\lambda = 30$ m traveled at a speed of at least 99 percent of that of visible light with $\lambda = 500$ nm. Beginning with the relativistic expression $hf = \gamma mc^2$, verify de Broglie's calculation that the upper limit of the rest mass of a photon is 10^{-44} g. (*Hint:* Find an expression for v/c in terms of hf and mc^2, and then let $mc^2 \ll hf$.) ($\gamma = 1/(1 - v^2/c^2)^{1/2}$.)

5-50. Suppose that you drop BBs onto a bull's-eye marked on the floor. According to the uncertainty principle, the BBs do not necessarily fall straight down from the release point to the center of the bull's-eye, but are affected by the initial conditions. (*a*) If the location of the release point is uncertain by an amount Δx perpendicular to the vertical direction and the horizontal component of the speed is uncertain by Δv_x, derive an expression for the minimum spread ΔX of impacts at the bull's-eye, if its is located a distance y_0 below the release point. (*b*) Modify your result in (*a*) to include the effect on ΔX of uncertainties Δy and Δv_y at the release point.

5-51. Using the first-order Doppler-shift formula $f' = f_0(1 + v/c)$, calculate the energy shift of a 1-eV photon emitted from an iron atom moving toward you with energy $3/2\ kT$ at $T = 300$ K. Compare this Doppler line broadening with the natural line width calculated in Example 5-9. Repeat the calculation for a 1-MeV photon from a nuclear transition.

5-52. Calculate the order of magnitude of the shift in energy of a (*a*) 1-eV photon and (*b*) 1-MeV photon resulting from the recoil of an iron nucleus. Do this by first calculating the momentum of the photon, and then by calculating $p^2/2m$ for the nucleus using that value of momentum. Compare with the natural line width calculated in Example 5-9.

Chapter 6

The Schrödinger Equation

*T*he success of the de Broglie relations in predicting the diffraction of electrons and other particles, and the realization that classical standing waves lead to a discrete set of frequencies, prompted a search for a wave theory of electrons analogous to the wave theory of light. In this electron wave theory, classical mechanics should appear as the short-wavelength limit, just as geometric optics is the short-wavelength limit of the wave theory of light. The genesis of the correct theory went something like this, according to Felix Bloch,[1] who was present at the time:

> . . . in one of the next colloquia, Schrödinger gave a beautifully clear account of how de Broglie associated a wave with a particle and how he [i.e., de Broglie] could obtain the quantization rules . . . by demanding that an integer number of waves should be fitted along a stationary orbit. When he had finished Debye[2] casually remarked that he thought this way of talking was rather childish . . . [that to] deal properly with waves, one had to have a wave equation.

In 1926, Erwin Schrödinger[3] published his now-famous wave equation which governs the propagation of matter waves, including those of electrons. A few months earlier, Werner Heisenberg had published a seemingly different theory to explain atomic phenomena. In the Heisenberg theory, only measurable quantities appear. Dynamical quantities such as energy, position, and momentum are represented by matrices, the diagonal elements of which are the possible results of measurement. Though the Schrödinger and Heisenberg theories appear to be different, it was eventually shown by Schrödinger himself that they were equivalent, in that each could be derived from the other. The resulting theory, now called *wave mechanics* or *quantum mechanics,* has been amazingly successful. Though its principles may seem strange to us whose experiences are limited to the macroscopic world, and though the mathematics required to solve even the simplest problem is quite involved, there seems to be no alternative to describe correctly the experimental results in atomic and nuclear physics. In this book we shall confine our study to the Schrödinger theory because it is easier to learn and is a little less abstract than the Heisenberg theory. We shall begin by restricting our discussion to problems in one space dimension.

6-1 The Schrödinger Equation in One Dimension

The wave equation governing the motion of electrons and other particles with mass, which is analogous to the classical wave equation (Equation 5-11), was found by Schrödinger late in 1925 and is now known as the *Schrödinger equation*. Like the classical wave equation, the Schrödinger equation relates the time and space derivatives of the wave function. The reasoning followed by Schrödinger is somewhat difficult and not important for our purposes. In any case, it must be emphasized that we can't derive the Schrödinger equation just as we can't derive Newton's laws of motion. Its validity, like that of any fundamental equation, lies in its agreement with experiment. Just as Newton's second law is not relativistically correct, neither is Schrödinger's equation, which must ultimately yield to a relativistic wave equation. But, as you know, Newton's laws of motion are perfectly satisfactory for solving a vast array of nonrelativistic problems. So, too, will be Schrödinger's equation when applied to the equally extensive range of nonrelativistic problems in atomic, molecular, and solid-state physics. Schrödinger tried without success to develop a relativistic wave equation, a task accomplished in 1928 by Dirac.

Although it would be logical merely to postulate the Schrödinger equation, we can get some idea of what to expect by first considering the wave equation for photons, which is Equation 5-11 with speed $v = c$ and with $y(x, t)$ replaced by the electric field $\mathcal{E}(x, t)$.

$$\frac{\partial^2 \mathcal{E}}{\partial x^2} = \frac{1}{c^2} \frac{\partial^2 \mathcal{E}}{\partial t^2} \qquad \textbf{6-1}$$

As discussed in Chapter 5, a particularly important solution of this equation is the harmonic wave function $\mathcal{E}(x, t) = \mathcal{E}_0 \cos(kx - \omega t)$. Differentiating this function twice, we obtain

$$\frac{\partial^2 \mathcal{E}}{\partial t^2} = -\omega^2 \mathcal{E}_0 \cos(kx - \omega t) = -\omega^2 \mathcal{E}(x, t)$$

and

$$\frac{\partial^2 \mathcal{E}}{\partial x^2} = -k^2 \mathcal{E}(x, t)$$

Substitution into Equation 6-1 then gives

$$-k^2 = -\frac{\omega^2}{c^2}$$

or

$$\omega = kc \qquad \textbf{6-2}$$

Using $\omega = E/\hbar$ and $p = \hbar k$ for electromagnetic radiation, we have

$$E = pc \qquad \textbf{6-3}$$

which, as we saw earlier, is the relation between the energy and momentum of a photon.

Erwin Schrödinger. [*Courtesy of the Niels Bohr Library, American Institute of Physics.*]

Now let us use the de Broglie relations for a particle such as an electron to find the relation between ω and k which is analogous to Equation 6-2 for photons. We can then use this relation to work backward and see how the wave equation for electrons must differ from Equation 6-1. The total energy (nonrelativistic) of a particle of mass m is

$$E = \frac{p^2}{2m} + V \qquad \qquad \textbf{6-4}$$

where V is the potential energy. Using the de Broglie relations, we obtain

$$\hbar\omega = \frac{\hbar^2 k^2}{2m} + V \qquad \qquad \textbf{6-5}$$

This differs from Equation 6-2 for a photon because it contains the potential energy V and because the angular frequency ω does not vary linearly with k. Note that we get a factor of ω when we differentiate a harmonic wave function with respect to time and a factor of k when we differentiate with respect to position. We expect, therefore, that the wave equation that applies to electrons will relate the *first* time derivative to the *second* space derivative, and will also involve the potential energy of the electron.

Finally, we require that the wave equation for electrons will be a differential equation that is linear in the wave function $\Psi(x, t)$. This ensures that, if $\Psi_1(x, t)$ and $\Psi_2(x, t)$ are both solutions of the wave equation for the same potential energy, then any arbitrary linear combination of these solutions is also a solution—i.e., $\Psi(x, t) = a_1\Psi_1(x, t) + a_2\Psi_2(x, t)$ is a solution, with a_1 and a_2 being arbitrary constants. Such a combination is called *linear* because both $\Psi_1(x, t)$ and $\Psi_2(x, t)$ appear only to the first power. Linearity guarantees that the wave functions will add together to produce constructive and destructive interference, which we have seen to be a characteristic

of matter waves, as well as all other wave phenomena. Note, in particular, that (1) the linearity requirement means that *every* term in the wave equation must be linear in $\Psi(x, t)$ and (2) that *any* derivative of $\Psi(x, t)$ is linear in $\Psi(x, t)$.[4]

The Schrödinger Equation

We are now ready to postulate the Schrödinger equation for a particle of mass m. In one dimension, it has the form

$$-\frac{\hbar^2}{2m}\frac{\partial^2 \Psi(x, t)}{\partial x^2} + V(x, t)\Psi(x, t) = i\hbar\frac{\partial \Psi(x, t)}{\partial t} \qquad \textbf{6-6}$$

We will now show that this equation is satisfied by a harmonic wave function in the special case of a free particle, one on which no net force acts, so that the potential energy is constant, $V(x, t) = V_0$. First note that a function of the form $\cos(kx - \omega t)$ does not satisfy this equation because differentiation with respect to time changes the cosine to a sine, but the second derivative with respect to x gives back a cosine. Similar reasoning rules out the form $\sin(kx - \omega t)$. However, the exponential form of the harmonic wave function does satisfy the equation. Let

$$\Psi(x, t) = Ae^{i(kx-\omega t)} \qquad \textbf{6-7}$$
$$= A[\cos(kx - \omega t) + i\sin(kx - \omega t)]$$

where A is a constant. Then

$$\frac{\partial \Psi}{\partial t} = -i\omega Ae^{i(kx-\omega t)} = -i\omega\Psi$$

and

$$\frac{\partial^2 \Psi}{\partial x^2} = (ik^2)Ae^{i(kx-\omega t)} = -k^2\Psi$$

Substituting these derivatives into the Schrödinger equation with $V(x, t) = V_0$ gives

$$\frac{-\hbar^2}{2m}(-k^2\Psi) + V_0\Psi = i\hbar(-i\omega)\Psi$$

or

$$\frac{\hbar^2 k^2}{2m} + V_0 = \hbar\omega$$

which is Equation 6-5.

An important difference between the Schrödinger equation and the classical wave equation is the explicit appearance[5] of the imaginary number $i = (-1)^{1/2}$. The wave functions that satisfy the Schrödinger equation are not necessarily real, as we see from the case of the free-particle wave function of Equation 6-7. Evidently the wave function $\Psi(x, t)$ which solves the Schrödinger equation is not a directly

measurable function like the classical wave function $y(x, t)$, since measurements always yield real numbers. However, as we discussed in Section 5-4, the probability of finding the electron in dx is certainly measurable, just as is the probability that a flipped coin will turn up heads. The probability $P(x)\, dx$ that the electron will be found in the volume dx was defined by Equation 5-26 to be equal to $\Psi^2\, dx$. This probabilistic interpretation of Ψ was developed by Max Born and was recognized, over the early and formidable objections of both Schrödinger and Einstein, as the appropriate way of relating solutions of the Schrödinger equation to the results of physical measurements. The probability that an electron is in the region dx, a real number, can be measured by counting the fraction of time it is found there in a very large number of identical trials. In recognition of the complex nature of $\Psi(x, t)$, we must modify slightly the interpretation of the wave function discussed in Chapter 5 to accommodate Born's interpretation so that the probability of finding the electron in dx is real. We take for the probability

$$P(x, t)\, dx = \Psi^*(x, t)\, \Psi(x, t)\, dx = |\Psi(x, t)|^2\, dx \qquad \textbf{6-8}$$

where Ψ^*, the complex conjugate of Ψ, is obtained from Ψ by replacing i with $-i$ wherever it appears.[6] The complex nature of Ψ serves to emphasize the fact that we should not ask or try to answer the question, "What is waving in a matter wave?" or inquire as to what medium supports the motion of a matter wave. The wave function is a computational device with utility in Schrödinger's theory of wave mechanics. Physical significance is associated not with Ψ itself, but with the product $\Psi^*\Psi = |\Psi|^2$, which is the probability distribution $P(x, t)$ or, as it is often called, the *probability density*. In keeping with the analogy with classical waves and wave functions, $\Psi(x, t)$ is also sometimes referred to as the *probability density amplitude*, or just the *probability amplitude*.

The probability of finding the electron in dx at x_1 or in dx at x_2 is the sum of separate probabilities, $P(x_1)\, dx + P(x_2)\, dx$. Since the electron must certainly be somewhere in space, the sum of the probabilities over all possible values of x must equal 1. That is,[7]

$$\int_{-\infty}^{+\infty} \Psi^*\Psi\, dx = 1 \qquad \textbf{6-9}$$

Equation 6-9 is called the *normalization condition*. This condition plays an important role in quantum mechanics, for it places a restriction on the possible solutions of the Schrödinger equation. In particular, the wave function $\Psi(x, t)$ must approach zero sufficiently fast as $x \to \pm\infty$ so that the integral in Equation 6-9 remains finite. If it does not, then the probability becomes unbounded. As we will see in Section 6-3, it is this restriction together with boundary conditions imposed at finite values of x that leads to energy quantization for bound particles.

In the chapters that follow we are going to be concerned with solutions to the Schrödinger equation for a wide range of real physical systems, but in what follows in this chapter our intent is to illustrate a few of the techniques of solving the equation and to discover the various, often surprising properties of the solutions. To this end we will focus our attention on one-dimensional problems, as noted earlier, and use some potential energy functions with unrealistic physical characteristics, e.g., infinitely rigid walls, which will enable us to illustrate various properties of the solutions without obscuring the discussion with overly complex mathematics.

Separation of the Time and Space Dependencies of $\Psi(x, t)$

Schrödinger's first application of his wave equation was to problems such as the hydrogen atom (Bohr's work) and the simple harmonic oscillator (Planck's work), in which he showed that the energy quantization in those systems can be explained naturally in terms of standing waves. We referred to these in Chapter 4 as stationary states, meaning they did not change with time. Such states are also called *eigenstates*. For such problems that also have potential energy functions that are independent of time, the space and time dependence of the wave function can be separated, leading to a greatly simplified form of the Schrödinger equation.[8] The separation is accomplished by first assuming that $\Psi(x, t)$ can be written as a product of two functions, one of x and one of t, as

$$\Psi(x, t) = \psi(x)\,\phi(t) \qquad\qquad \textbf{6-10}$$

If Equation 6-10 turns out to be incorrect, we will find that out soon enough, but if the potential function is *not* an explicit function of time, i.e., if the potential is given by $V(x)$, our assumption turns out to be valid. That this is true can be seen as follows:

Substituting $\Psi(x, t)$ from Equation 6-10 into the general, time-dependent Schrödinger equation (Equation 6-6) yields

$$\frac{-\hbar^2}{2m}\frac{\partial^2\psi(x)\phi(t)}{\partial x^2} + V(x)\psi(x)\phi(t) = i\hbar\frac{\partial\psi(x)\phi(t)}{\partial t} \qquad\qquad \textbf{6-11}$$

which is

$$\frac{-\hbar^2}{2m}\phi(t)\frac{d^2\psi(x)}{dx^2} + V(x)\psi(x)\phi(t) = i\hbar\psi(x)\frac{d\phi(t)}{dt} \qquad\qquad \textbf{6-12}$$

where the derivatives are now ordinary rather than partial ones. Dividing Equation 6-12 by Ψ in the assumed product form $\psi\phi$ gives

$$\frac{-\hbar^2}{2m}\frac{1}{\psi(x)}\frac{d^2\psi(x)}{dx^2} + V(x) = i\hbar\frac{1}{\phi(t)}\frac{d\phi(t)}{dt} \qquad\qquad \textbf{6-13}$$

Notice that each side of Equation 6-13 is a function of only one of the independent variables x and t. This means that, for example, changes in t cannot affect the value of the left side of Equation 6-13, and changes in x cannot affect the right side. Thus, both sides of the equation must be equal to the same constant C, called the *separation constant,* and we see that the assumption of Equation 6-10 is valid—the variables have been separated. We have thus replaced a partial differential equation containing two independent variables, Equation 6-6, with two ordinary differential equations, each a function of only one of the independent variables:

$$\frac{-\hbar^2}{2m}\frac{1}{\psi(x)}\frac{d^2\psi(x)}{dx^2} + V(x) = C \qquad\qquad \textbf{6-14}$$

$$i\hbar\frac{1}{\phi(t)}\frac{d\phi(t)}{dt} = C \qquad\qquad \textbf{6-15}$$

Let us solve Equation 6-15 first. The reason for doing so is twofold: (1) Equation 6-15 does not contain the potential $V(x)$; consequently, the time-dependent part $\phi(t)$

of *all* solutions $\Psi(x, t)$ to the Schrödinger equation will have the same form when the potential is not an explicit function of time, so we only have to do this once. (2) The separation constant C has particular significance that we want to discover before we tackle Equation 6-14. Writing Equation 6-15 as

$$\frac{d\phi(t)}{\phi(t)} = \frac{C}{i\hbar}\,dt = -\frac{iC}{\hbar}\,dt \qquad \textbf{6-16}$$

The general solution of Equation 6-16 is

$$\phi(t) = e^{-iCt/\hbar} \qquad \textbf{6-17a}$$

which can also be written as

$$\phi(t) = e^{-iCt/\hbar} = \cos\left(\frac{Ct}{\hbar}\right) - i\sin\left(\frac{Ct}{\hbar}\right) = \cos\left(2\pi\frac{Ct}{h}\right) - i\sin\left(2\pi\frac{Ct}{h}\right) \quad \textbf{6-17b}$$

Thus we see that $\phi(t)$, which describes the time variation of $\Psi(x, t)$, is an oscillatory function with frequency $f = C/h$. However, according to the de Broglie relation (Equation 5-1), the frequency of the wave represented by $\Psi(x, t)$ is $f = E/h$; therefore, we conclude that the separation constant $C = E$, the total energy of the particle, and we have

$$\boxed{\phi(t) = e^{-iEt/\hbar}} \qquad \textbf{6-17c}$$

for all solutions to Equation 6-6 involving time-independent potentials. Equation 6-14 then becomes, on multiplication by $\psi(x)$,

$$\boxed{\frac{-\hbar^2}{2m}\frac{d^2\psi(x)}{dx^2} + V(x)\psi(x) = E\psi(x)} \qquad \textbf{6-18}$$

Equation 6-18 is referred to as the *time-independent Schrödinger equation.*

The time-independent Schrödinger equation in one dimension is an ordinary differential equation in one variable x and is therefore much easier to handle than the general form of Equation 6-6. The normalization condition of Equation 6-9 can be expressed in terms of $\psi(x)$, since the time dependence of the absolute square of the wave function cancels. We have

$$\Psi^*(x, t)\Psi(x, t) = \psi^*(x)e^{+iEt/\hbar}\psi(x)e^{-iEt/\hbar} = \psi^*(x)\psi(x) \qquad \textbf{6-19}$$

and Equation 6-9 then becomes

$$\int_{-\infty}^{+\infty} \psi^*(x)\psi(x)dx = 1 \qquad \textbf{6-20}$$

Conditions for Acceptable Wave Functions

The form of the wave function $\psi(x)$ that satisfies Equation 6-18 depends on the form of the potential energy function $V(x)$. In the next few sections we shall study some

simple but important problems in which $V(x)$ is specified. Our example potentials will be approximations to real physical potentials, simplified to make calculations easier. In some cases, the slope of the potential energy may be discontinuous, e.g., $V(x)$ may have one form in one region of space and another form in an adjacent region. (This is a useful mathematical approximation to real situations in which $V(x)$ varies rapidly over a small region of space, such as at the surface boundary of a metal.) The procedure in such cases is to solve the Schrödinger equation separately in each region of space, and then require that the solutions join smoothly at the point of discontinuity.

Since the probability of finding a particle cannot vary discontinuously from point to point, the wave function $\psi(x)$ must be continuous.[9] Since the Schrödinger equation involves the second derivative $d^2\psi/d^2x = \psi''(x)$, the first derivative ψ' (which is the slope) must also be continuous. That is, the graph of $\psi(x)$ versus x must be smooth. (In a special case in which the potential energy becomes infinite, this restriction is relaxed. Since no particle can have infinite potential energy, $\psi(x)$ must be zero in regions where $V(x)$ is infinite. Then, at the boundary of such a region, ψ' may be discontinuous.)

If either $\psi(x)$ or $d\psi/dx$ were not finite or not single-valued, the same would be true of $\Psi(x, t)$ and $d\Psi/dx$. As we will shortly see, the predictions of wave mechanics regarding the results of measurements involve both of those quantities and would thus not necessarily predict finite or definite values for real physical quantities. Such results would not be acceptable, since measurable quantities, such as angular momentum and position, are never infinite or multiple-valued. A final restriction on the form of the wave function $\psi(x)$ is that in order to obey the normalization condition, $\psi(x)$ must approach zero sufficiently fast as $x \rightarrow \pm\infty$ so that normalization is preserved. For future reference, we may summarize the conditions that the wave function $\psi(x)$ must meet in order to be acceptable as follows:

1. $\psi(x)$ must exist and satisfy the Schrödinger equation.

2. $\psi(x)$ and $d\psi/dx$ must be continuous.

3. $\psi(x)$ and $d\psi/dx$ must be finite.

4. $\psi(x)$ and $d\psi/dx$ must be single-valued.

5. $\psi(x) \rightarrow 0$ fast enough as $x \rightarrow \pm\infty$ so that the normalization integral, Equation 6-20, remains bounded.

QUESTIONS

1. Like the classical wave equation, the Schrödinger equation is linear. Why is this important?

2. There is no factor $i = (-1)^{1/2}$ in Equation 6-18. Does this mean that $\psi(x)$ must be real?

3. Why must the electric field $\mathcal{E}(x, t)$ be real? Is it possible to find a nonreal wave function that satisfies the classical wave equation?

4. Describe how the de Broglie hypothesis enters into the Schrödinger wave equation.

5. What would be the effect on the Schrödinger equation of adding a constant rest energy for a particle with mass to the total energy E in the de Broglie relation $f = E/\hbar$?

6. Describe in words what is meant by normalization of the wave function.

EXAMPLE 6-1 A Solution to the Schrödinger Equation Show that for a free particle of mass m moving in one dimension the function $\psi(x) = A \sin kx + B \cos kx$ is a solution to the time-independent Schrödinger equation for any values of the constants A and B.

Solution

A free particle has no net force acting upon it, e.g., $V(x) = 0$, in which case the kinetic energy equals the total energy. Thus, $p = \hbar k = (2mE)^{1/2}$. Differentiating $\psi(x)$ gives

$$\frac{d\psi}{dx} = kA \cos kx - kB \sin kx$$

and differentiating again,

$$\frac{d^2\psi}{dx^2} = -k^2 A \sin kx - k^2 B \cos kx$$

$$= -k^2(A \sin kx + B \cos kx) = -k^2 \psi(x)$$

Substituting into Equation 6-18,

$$\frac{-\hbar^2}{2m}[(-k^2)(A \sin kx + B \cos kx)] = E[A \sin kx + B \cos kx]$$

$$\frac{\hbar^2 k^2}{2m}\psi(x) = E\psi(x)$$

and, since $\hbar^2 k^2 = 2mE$, we have

$$E\psi(x) = E\psi(x)$$

and the given $\psi(x)$ is a solution of Equation 6-18.

6-2 The Infinite Square Well

A problem that provides several illustrations of the properties of wave functions and is also one of the easiest problems to solve using the time-independent, one-dimensional Schrödinger equation is that of the infinite square well, sometimes called the particle in a box. A macroscopic example is a bead moving on a frictionless wire between two massive stops clamped to the wire. We could also build such a "box" for an electron using electrodes and grids in an evacuated tube as illustrated in Figure 6-1a. The walls of the box are provided by the increasing potential between the grids G and the electrode C as shown in Figures 6-1b and c. The walls can be made arbitrarily high and steep by increasing the potential V and reducing the separation between each grid-electrode pair. In the limit such a potential energy function looks like that shown in

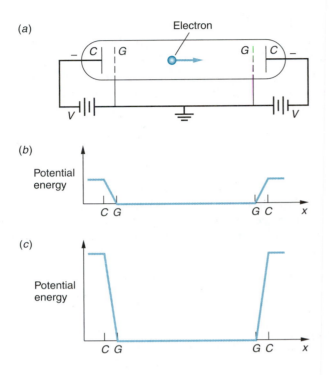

(a)

Electron

(b)

Potential energy

C G   G C   x

(c)

Potential energy

C G   G C   x

Fig. 6-1 (*a*) The electron placed between the two sets of electrodes *C* and grids *G* experiences no force in the region between the grids, which are at ground potential. However, in the regions between each *C* and *G* is a repelling electric field whose strength depends upon the magnitude of *V*. (*b*) If *V* is small, then the electron's potential energy vs. *x* has low, sloping "walls." (*c*) If *V* is large, the "walls" become very high and steep, becoming infinitely high for *V* → ∞.

Figure 6-2, which is a graph of the potential energy of an infinite square well. For this problem the potential energy is of the form

$$V(x) = 0 \qquad 0 < x < L$$
$$V(x) = \infty \qquad x < 0 \quad \text{and} \quad x > L$$

6-21

Although such a potential is clearly artificial, the problem is worth careful study for several reasons: (1) exact solutions to the Schrödinger equation can be obtained without the difficult mathematics which usually accompanies its solution for more realistic potential functions; (2) the problem is closely related to the vibrating-string problem familiar in classical physics; (3) it illustrates many of the important features of all quantum-mechanical problems; and finally (4) this potential is a relatively good approximation to some real situations; e.g., the motion of a free electron inside a metal.

Since the potential energy is infinite outside the well, the wave function is required to be zero there; that is, the particle must be inside the well. (As we proceed through this and other problems, keep in mind Born's interpretation: the probability density of the particle's position is proportional to $|\psi|^2$.) We then need only to solve Equation 6-18 for the region inside the well $0 < x < L$, subject to the condition that since the wave function must be continuous, $\psi(x)$ must be zero at $x = 0$ and $x = L$. Such a condition on the wave function at a boundary (here, the discontinuity of the potential energy function) is called a *boundary condition*. We shall see that, mathematically, it is the boundary conditions together with the requirement that $\psi(x) \to 0$ as $x \to \pm\infty$ that lead to the quantization of energy. A classic example is the case of a vibrating string fixed at both ends. In that case the wave function $y(x, t)$ is the displacement of the string. If the string is fixed at $x = 0$ and $x = L$, we have the same boundary condition on the vibrating-string wave function: namely, that $y(x, t)$ be zero at $x = 0$ and $x = L$. These boundary conditions lead to discrete allowed frequencies

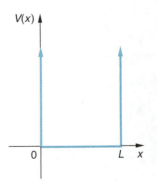

$V(x)$

0   L   x

Fig. 6-2 Infinite square well potential energy. For $0 < x < L$ the potential energy $V(x)$ is zero. Outside this region, $V(x)$ is infinite. The particle is confined to the region in the well $0 < x < L$.

of vibration of the string. It was this quantization of frequencies (which always occurs for standing waves in classical physics), along with de Broglie's hypothesis, which motivated Schrödinger to look for a wave equation for electrons.

The standing-wave condition for waves on a string of length L fixed at both ends is that *an integral number of half wavelengths fit into the length L.*

$$n \frac{\lambda}{2} = L \qquad n = 1, 2, 3, \ldots \qquad \textbf{6-22}$$

We shall show below that the same condition follows from the solution of the Schrödinger equation for a particle in an infinite square well. Since the wavelength is related to the momentum of the particle by the de Broglie relation $p = h/\lambda$ and the total energy of the particle in the well is just the kinetic energy $p^2/2m$ (see Figure 6-1), this quantum condition on the wavelength implies that the energy is quantized and the allowed values are given by

$$E = \frac{p^2}{2m} = \frac{h^2}{2m\lambda^2} = \frac{h^2}{2m(2L/n)^2} = n^2 \frac{h^2}{8mL^2} \qquad \textbf{6-23}$$

Since the energy depends on the integer n, it is customary to label it E_n. In terms of $\hbar = h/2\pi$ the energy is given by

$$E_n = n^2 \frac{\pi^2 \hbar^2}{2mL^2} = n^2 E_1 \qquad n = 1, 2, 3, \ldots \qquad \textbf{6-24}$$

where E_1 is the lowest allowed energy[10] and is given by

$$E_1 = \frac{\pi^2 \hbar^2}{2mL^2} \qquad \textbf{6-25}$$

We now derive this result from the time-independent Schrödinger equation (Equation 6-18), which for $V(x) = 0$ is

$$-\frac{\hbar^2}{2m} \frac{d^2\psi(x)}{dx^2} = E\psi(x)$$

or

$$\psi''(x) = -\frac{2mE}{\hbar^2} \psi(x) = -k^2\psi(x) \qquad \textbf{6-26}$$

where we have substituted the square of the wave number k, since

$$k^2 = \left(\frac{p}{\hbar}\right)^2 = \frac{2mE}{\hbar^2} \qquad \textbf{6-27}$$

and have written $\psi''(x)$ for the second derivative $d^2\psi(x)/dx^2$. Equation 6-26 has solutions of the form

$$\psi(x) = A \sin kx \qquad \textbf{6-28}a$$

and

$$\psi(x) = B \cos kx \qquad \textbf{6-28}b$$

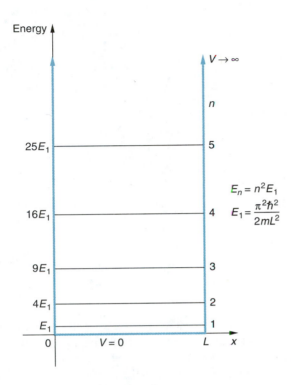

Energy

$V \to \infty$

n

$25E_1$ ———————— 5

$E_n = n^2 E_1$

$16E_1$ ———————— 4 $E_1 = \dfrac{\pi^2\hbar^2}{2mL^2}$

$9E_1$ ———————— 3

$4E_1$ ———————— 2

E_1 ———————— 1

0        $V = 0$ L x

Fig. 6-3 Graph of energy vs. x for a particle in an infinitely deep well. The potential energy $V(x)$ is shown with the colored lines. The set of allowed values for the particle's total energy E_n as given by Equation 6-24 form the energy-level diagram for the infinite square well potential. Classically, a particle can have any value of energy. Quantum mechanically, only the values given by $E_n = n^2(\hbar^2\pi^2/2mL^2)$ yield well-behaved solutions of the Schrödinger equation. As we become more familiar with energy-level diagrams, the x axis will be omitted.

where A and B are constants. The boundary condition $\psi(x) = 0$ at $x = 0$ rules out the cosine solution (Equation 6-28b) because $\cos 0 = 1$, so B must equal zero. The boundary condition $\psi(x) = 0$ at $x = L$ gives

$$\psi(L) = A \sin kL = 0 \qquad\qquad \textbf{6-29}$$

This condition is satisfied if kL is any integer times π, i.e., if k is restricted to the values k_n given by

$$k_n = n\frac{\pi}{L} \qquad n = 1, 2, 3, \ldots \qquad\qquad \textbf{6-30}$$

If we write the wave number k in terms of the wavelength $\lambda = 2\pi/k$, we see that Equation 6-30 is the same as Equation 6-22 for standing waves on a string. The quantized energy values, or *energy eigenvalues,* are found from Equation 6-27, replacing k by k_n as given by Equation 6-30. We thus have

$$E_n = \frac{\hbar^2 k_n^2}{2m} = n^2\frac{\hbar^2\pi^2}{2mL^2} = n^2 E_1$$

which is the same as Equation 6-24. Figure 6-3 shows the energy-level diagram and the potential energy function for the infinite square well potential.

The constant A in the wave function of Equation 6-28a is determined by the normalization condition

$$\int_{-\infty}^{+\infty} \psi_n^* \psi_n\, dx = \int_0^L A_n^2 \sin^2\left(\frac{n\pi x}{L}\right) dx = 1 \qquad\qquad \textbf{6-31}$$

Fig. 6-4 Wave functions $\psi_n(x)$ and probability densities $P_n(x) = \psi_n^2(x)$ for $n = 1$, 2, and 3 for the infinite square well potential.

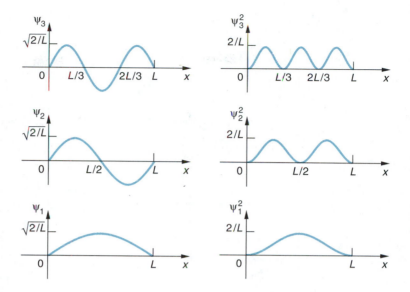

Since the wave function is zero in regions of space where the potential energy is infinite, the contributions to the integral from $-\infty$ to 0 and from L to $+\infty$ will both be zero. Thus, only the integral from 0 to L needs to be evaluated. Integrating, we obtain $A_n = (2/L)^{1/2}$ independent of n, a result first encountered in the solution to Problem 5-24. The normalized wave function solutions for this problem, also called *eigenfunctions,* are then

$$\psi_n(x) = \sqrt{\frac{2}{L}} \sin \frac{n\pi x}{L} \qquad n = 1, 2, 3, \ldots \qquad \textbf{6-32}$$

These wave functions are exactly the same as the standing-wave functions $y_n(x)$ for the vibrating-string problem. The wave functions and the probability distribution functions $P_n(x)$ are sketched in Figure 6-4 for the lowest energy state $n = 1$, called the *ground state,* and for the first two *excited states,* $n = 2$ and $n = 3$. (Since these wave functions are real, $P_n(x) = \psi_n^* \psi_n = \psi_n^2$.) Notice in Figure 6-4 that the maximum amplitudes of each of the $\psi_n(x)$ are the same, $(2/L)^{1/2}$, as are those of $P_n(x)$, $2/L$. Note, too, that both $\psi_n(x)$ and $P_n(x)$ extend to $\pm\infty$. They just happen to be zero for $x < 0$ and $x > L$ in this case.

The number n in the equations above is called a *quantum number.* It specifies both the energy and the wave function. Given any value of n we can immediately write down the wave function and the energy of the system. The quantum number n occurs because of the boundary conditions $\psi(x) = 0$ at $x = 0$ and $x = L$. We shall see in Section 7-1 that for problems in three dimensions, three quantum numbers arise, one associated with boundary conditions on each coordinate.

Comparison with Classical Results

Let us compare our quantum-mechanical solution of this problem with the classical solution. In classical mechanics, if we know the potential energy function $V(x)$, we can find the force from $F_x = -dV/dx$, and thereby obtain the acceleration $a_x = d^2x/dt^2$ from Newton's second law. We can then find the position x as a function of time t if we know the initial position and velocity. In this problem there is no force

when the particle is between the walls of the well because $V = 0$ there. The particle therefore moves with constant speed in the well. Near the edge of the well the potential energy rises discontinuously to infinity—we may describe this as a very large force that acts over a very short distance and turns the particle around at the wall so that it moves away with its initial speed. Any speed, and therefore any energy, is permitted classically. The classical description breaks down because, according to the uncertainty principle, we can never precisely specify both the position and momentum (and therefore velocity) at the same time. We can therefore never specify the initial conditions precisely, and cannot assign a definite position and momentum to the particle. Of course, for a macroscopic particle moving in a macroscopic box, the energy is much larger than E_1 of Equation 6-25, and the minimum uncertainty of momentum, which is of the order of $\hbar/L$, is much less than the momentum and less than experimental uncertainties. Then the difference in energy between adjacent states will be a small fraction of the total energy, quantization will be unnoticed, and the classical description will be adequate.[11]

Let us also compare the classical prediction for the distribution of measurements of position with those from our quantum-mechanical solution. Classically, the probability of finding the particle in some region dx is proportional to the time spent in dx, which is dx/v, where v is the speed. Since the speed is constant, the classical distribution function is just a constant inside the well. The normalized classical distribution function is

$$P_C(x) = \frac{1}{L}$$

In Figure 6-4 we see that for the lowest energy states the quantum distribution function is very different from this. According to Bohr's correspondence principle, the quantum distributions should approach the classical distribution when n is large, that is, at large energies. For any state n, the quantum distribution has n peaks. The distribution for $n = 10$ is shown in Figure 6-5. For very large n, the peaks are close together, and if there are many peaks in a small distance Δx only the average value will be observed. But the average value of $\sin^2 k_n x$ over one or more cycles is 1/2. Thus

$$[\psi_n^2(x)]_{av} = \left[\frac{2}{L}\sin^2 k_n x\right]_{av} = \frac{2}{L}\frac{1}{2} = \frac{1}{L}$$

which is the same as the classical distribution.

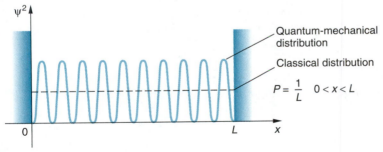

Fig. 6-5 Probability distribution for $n = 10$ for the infinite square well potential. The dashed line is the classical probability density $P = 1/L$, which is equal to the quantum-mechanical distribution averaged over a region Δx containing several oscillations. A physical measurement with resolution Δx will yield the classical result if n is so large that $\psi^2(x)$ has many oscillations in Δx.

The Complete Wave Function

The complete wave function, including its time dependence, is found by multiplying the space part by

$$e^{-i\omega t} = e^{-i(E_n/\hbar)t}$$

according to Equation 6-17. As mentioned previously, a wave function corresponding to a single energy oscillates with angular frequency, $\omega_n = E_n/\hbar$, but the probability distribution $|\Psi_n(x, t)|^2$ is independent of time. This is the wave-mechanical justification for calling such a state a stationary state or eigenstate, as we have done earlier. It is instructive to look at the complete wave function for a particular state n:

$$\Psi_n(x, t) = \sqrt{\frac{2}{L}} \sin k_n x \, e^{-i\omega_n t}$$

If we use the identity

$$\sin k_n x = \frac{(e^{ik_n x} - e^{-ik_n x})}{2i}$$

we can write this wave function as

$$\Psi_n(x, t) = \frac{1}{2i} \sqrt{\frac{2}{L}} \left[e^{i(k_n x - \omega_n t)} - e^{-i(k_n x + \omega_n t)} \right]$$

Just as in the case of the standing-wave function for the vibrating string, we can consider this stationary-state wave function to be the superimposition of a wave traveling to the right and a wave of the same frequency and amplitude traveling to the left.

EXAMPLE 6-2 An Electron in a Wire An electron moving in a thin metal wire is a reasonable approximation of a particle in a one-dimensional infinite well. The potential inside the wire is constant on the average, but rises sharply at each end. Suppose the electron is in a wire 1.0 cm long. (*a*) Compute the ground-state energy for the electron. (*b*) If the electron's energy is equal to the average kinetic energy of the molecules in a gas at $T = 300$ K, about 0.03 eV, what is the electron's quantum number n?

Solution

1.   For question (*a*), the ground-state energy is given by Equation 6-25:

$$E_1 = \frac{\pi^2 \hbar^2}{2mL^2}$$

$$= \frac{\pi^2 (1.055 \times 10^{-34}\,\text{J} \cdot \text{s})^2}{(2)(9.11 \times 10^{-31}\,\text{kg})(10^{-2}\,\text{m})^2}$$

$$= 6.03 \times 10^{-34}\,\text{J} = 3.80 \times 10^{-15}\,\text{eV}$$

2. For question (*b*), the electron's quantum number is given by Equation 6-24:

$$E_n = n^2 E_1$$

3. Solving Equation 6-24 for *n* and substituting $E_n = 0.03$ eV and E_1 from above yield:

$$n^2 = \frac{E_n}{E_1}$$

or

$$n = \sqrt{\frac{E_n}{E_1}}$$
$$= \sqrt{\frac{0.03 \text{ eV}}{3.80 \times 10^{-15} \text{ eV}}}$$
$$= 2.81 \times 10^6$$

Remarks: *The value of E_1 computed above is not only far below the limit of measurability, but also smaller than the uncertainty in the energy of an electron confined into 1 cm.*

EXAMPLE 6-3 **Calculating Probabilities** Suppose that the electron in Example 6-2 could be measured while in its ground state. (*a*) What would be the probability of finding it somewhere in the region $0 < x < L/4$? (*b*) What would be the probability of finding it in a very narrow region $\Delta x = 0.01L$ wide centered at $x = 5L/8$?

Solution
(*a*) The wave function for the $n = 1$ level, the ground state, is given by Equation 6-32 as

$$\psi_1(x) = \sqrt{\frac{2}{L}} \sin \frac{\pi x}{L}$$

The probability that the electron would be found in the region specified is

$$\int_0^{L/4} P_1(x) \, dx = \int_0^{L/4} \frac{2}{L} \sin^2 \left(\frac{\pi x}{L} \right) dx$$

Letting $u = \pi x/L$, hence $dx = L \, du/\pi$, and noting the appropriate change in the limits on the integral, we have that

$$\int_0^{\pi/4} \frac{2}{\pi} \sin^2 u \, du = \frac{2}{\pi} \left(\frac{u}{2} - \frac{\sin 2u}{4} \right) \Bigg|_0^{\pi/4} = \frac{2}{\pi} \left(\frac{\pi}{8} - \frac{1}{4} \right) = 0.091$$

Thus, if one looked for the particle in a large number of identical searches, the electron would be found in the region $0 < x < 0.25$ cm about 9 percent of

Fig. 6-6 The probability density $\psi^2(x)$ vs. x for a particle in the ground state of an infinite square well potential. The probability of finding the particle in the region $0 < x < L/4$ is represented by the larger shaded area. The narrow shaded band illustrates the probability of finding the particle within $\Delta x = 0.01L$ around the point where $x = 5L/8$.

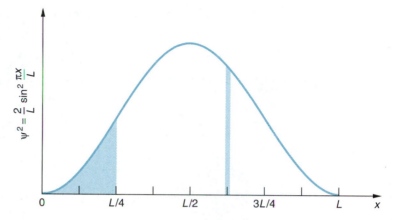

the time. This probability is illustrated by the shaded area on the left side in Figure 6-6.

(*b*) Since the region $\Delta x = 0.01L$ is very small compared with L, we do not need to integrate, but can calculate the approximate probability as follows:

$$P = P(x)\Delta x = \frac{2}{L}\sin^2\frac{\pi x}{L}\Delta x$$

Substituting $\Delta x = 0.01L$ and $x = 5L/8$, we obtain

$$P = \frac{2}{L}\sin^2\frac{\pi(5L/8)}{L}(0.01\ L)$$

$$= \frac{2}{L}(0.854)(0.01L) = 0.017$$

This means that the probability of finding the electron within $0.01L$ around $x = 5L/8$ is about 1.7 percent. This is illustrated in Figure 6-6, where the area of the shaded narrow band at $x = 5L/8$ is 1.7 percent of the total area under the curve.

EXAMPLE 6-4 An Electron in an Atomic-Size Box (*a*) Find the energy in the ground state of an electron confined to a one-dimensional box of length $L = 0.1$ nm. (This box is roughly the size of an atom.) (*b*) Make an energy-level diagram and find the wavelengths of the photons emitted for all transitions beginning at state $n = 3$ or less and ending at a lower energy state.

Solution

(*a*) The energy in the ground state is given by Equation 6-25. Multiplying the numerator and denominator by $c^2/4\pi^2$, we obtain an expression in terms of hc and mc^2, the energy equivalent of the electron mass (see Chapter 2):

$$E_1 = \frac{(hc)^2}{8mc^2L^2}$$

Substituting $hc = 1240$ eV $\cdot$ nm and $mc^2 = 0.511$ MeV, we obtain

$$E_1 = \frac{(1240 \text{ eV} \cdot \text{nm})^2}{8(5.11 \times 10^5 \text{ eV})(0.1 \text{ nm})^2} = 37.6 \text{ eV}$$

This is of the same order of magnitude as the kinetic energy of the electron in the ground state of the hydrogen atom, which is 13.6 eV. In that case, the wavelength of the electron equals the circumference of a circle of radius 0.0529 nm, or about 0.33 nm, whereas for the electron in a one-dimensional box of length 0.1 nm, the wavelength in the ground state is $2L = 0.2$ nm.

(b) The energies of this system are given by

$$E_n = n^2 E_1 = n^2 (37.6 \text{ eV})$$

Figure 6-7 shows these energies in an energy-level diagram. The energy of the first excited state is $E_2 = 4(37.6 \text{ eV}) = 150.4$ eV, and that of the second excited state is $E_3 = 9(37.6 \text{ eV}) = 338.4$ eV. The possible transitions from level 3 to level 2, from level 3 to level 1, and from level 2 to level 1 are indicated by the vertical arrows on the diagram. The energies of these transitions are

$$\Delta E_{3 \to 2} = 338.4 \text{ eV} - 150.4 \text{ eV} = 188 \text{ eV}$$
$$\Delta E_{3 \to 1} = 338.4 \text{ eV} - 37.6 \text{ eV} = 300.8 \text{ eV}$$
$$\Delta E_{2 \to 1} = 150.4 \text{ eV} - 37.6 \text{ eV} = 112.8 \text{ eV}$$

The photon wavelengths for these transitions are

$$\lambda_{3 \to 2} = \frac{hc}{\Delta E_{3 \to 2}} = \frac{1240 \text{ eV} \cdot \text{nm}}{188 \text{ eV}} = 6.60 \text{ nm}$$

$$\lambda_{3 \to 1} = \frac{hc}{\Delta E_{3 \to 1}} = \frac{1240 \text{ eV} \cdot \text{nm}}{300.8 \text{ eV}} = 4.12 \text{ nm}$$

$$\lambda_{2 \to 1} = \frac{hc}{\Delta E_{2 \to 1}} = \frac{1240 \text{ eV} \cdot \text{nm}}{112.8 \text{ eV}} = 11.0 \text{ nm}$$

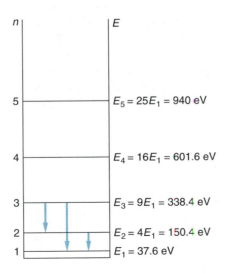

Fig. 6-7 Energy-level diagram for Example 6-4. Transitions from the state $n = 3$ to the states $n = 2$ and $n = 1$, and from the state $n = 2$ to $n = 1$, are indicated by the vertical arrows.

n E

5      $E_5 = 25E_1 = 940$ eV

4      $E_4 = 16E_1 = 601.6$ eV

3      $E_3 = 9E_1 = 338.4$ eV

2      $E_2 = 4E_1 = 150.4$ eV

1      $E_1 = 37.6$ eV

6-3 The Finite Square Well

The quantization of energy that we found for a particle in an infinite square well is a general result that follows from the solution of the Schrödinger equation for any particle confined in some region of space. We shall illustrate this by considering the qualitative behavior of the wave function for a slightly more general potential energy function, the finite square well shown in Figure 6-8. The solutions of the Schrödinger equation for this type of potential energy are quite different, depending on whether the total energy E is greater or less than V_0. We shall defer discussion of the case $E > V_0$ to Section 6-5 except to remark that in that case the particle is not confined and any value of the energy is allowed, i.e., there is no energy quantization. Here we shall assume that $E < V_0$.

Inside the well, $V(x) = 0$ and the time-independent Schrödinger equation (Equation 6-18) becomes Equation 6-26, the same as for the infinite well:

$$\psi''(x) = -k^2\psi(x) \qquad k^2 = \frac{2mE}{\hbar^2}$$

The solutions are sines and cosines (Equation 6-28) except that now we do not require $\psi(x)$ to be zero at the well boundaries, but rather we require that $\psi(x)$ and $\psi'(x)$ be continuous at these points. Outside the well, i.e., for $0 > x > L$, Equation 6-18 becomes

$$\psi''(x) = \frac{2m}{\hbar^2}(V_0 - E)\psi(x) = \alpha^2\psi(x) \qquad \textbf{6-33}$$

where

$$\alpha^2 = \frac{2m}{\hbar^2}(V_0 - E) > 0 \qquad \textbf{6-34}$$

The straightforward method of finding the wave functions and allowed energies for this problem is to solve Equation 6-33 for $\psi(x)$ outside the well and then require that $\psi(x)$ and $\psi'(x)$ be continuous at the boundaries. The solution of Equation 6-33 is not difficult (it is of the form $\psi(x) = Ce^{-\alpha x}$ for positive x), but applying the boundary conditions involves a method that may be new to you; we describe it in the More section on the Graphical Solution of the Finite Square Well.

First, we will explain in words unencumbered by the mathematics how the conditions of continuity of ψ and ψ' at the boundaries and the need for $\psi \to 0$ as $x \to \pm\infty$ lead to the selection of only certain wave functions and quantized energies for values of E within the well, i.e., $0 < E < V_0$. The important feature of Equation 6-33 is that the second derivative ψ'', which is the curvature of the wave function, has the same sign as

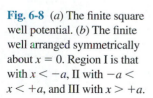

Fig. 6-8 (*a*) The finite square well potential. (*b*) The finite well arranged symmetrically about $x = 0$. Region I is that with $x < -a$, II with $-a < x < +a$, and III with $x > +a$.

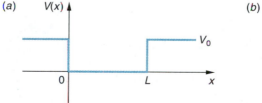

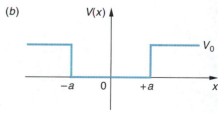

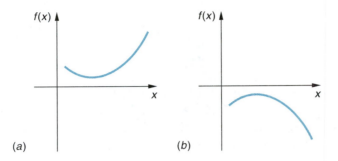

(a)   (b)

Fig. 6-9 (*a*) Positive function with positive curvature; (*b*) negative function with negative curvature.

the wave function ψ. If ψ is positive, ψ'' is also positive and the wave function curves away from the axis, as shown in Figure 6-9*a*. Similarly, if ψ is negative, ψ'' is negative and again, ψ curves away from the axis. This behavior is different from that inside the well, where $0 < x < L$. There, ψ and ψ'' have opposite signs so that ψ always curves toward the axis like a sine or cosine function. Because of this behavior outside the well, for most values of the energy the wave function becomes infinite as $x \rightarrow \pm\infty$, i.e., $\psi(x)$ is not well behaved. Such functions, though satisfying the Schrödinger equation, are not proper wave functions because they cannot be normalized.

Figure 6-10 shows the wave function for the energy $E = p^2/2m = h^2/2m\lambda^2$ for $\lambda = 4L$. Figure 6-11 shows a well-behaved wave function corresponding to wavelength $\lambda = \lambda_1$, which is the ground-state wave function for the finite well, and the behavior of the wave functions for two nearby energies and wavelengths. The exact determination of the allowed energy levels in a finite square well can be obtained from a detailed solution of the problem. Figure 6-12 shows the wave functions and the probability distributions for the ground state and for the first two excited states. From this figure we see that the wavelengths inside the well are slightly longer than the corresponding wavelengths for the infinite well of the same width, so the corresponding energies are slightly less than those of the infinite well. Another feature of the finite well problem is that there are only a finite number of allowed energies, that number depending of the size of V_0. For very small V_0 there is only one allowed energy level, i.e., only one bound state can exist. This will be quite apparent in the detailed solution in the More section.

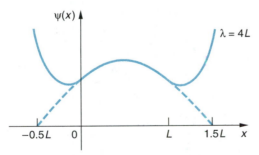

Fig. 6-10 The function that satisfies the Schrödinger equation with $\lambda = 4L$ inside the well is not an acceptable wave function because it becomes infinite at large x. Although at $x = L$ the function is heading toward zero (slope is negative), the rate of increase of the slope ψ'' is so great that the slope becomes positive before the function becomes zero, and the function then increases. Since ψ'' has the same sign as ψ, the slope always increases and the function increases without bound. [*This computer-generated plot courtesy of Paul Doherty, The Exploratorium.*]

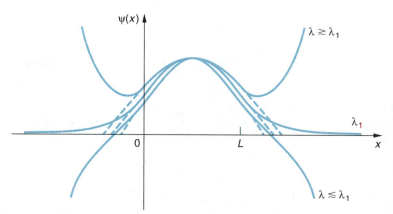

$\psi(x)$

$\lambda \gtrsim \lambda_1$

λ_1

0   L   x

$\lambda \lesssim \lambda_1$

Fig. 6-11 Functions satisfying the Schrödinger equation with wavelengths near the critical wavelength λ_1. If λ is slightly greater than λ_1, the function approaches infinity like that in Figure 6-10. At the wavelength λ_1, the function and its slope approach zero together. This is an acceptable wave function corresponding to the energy $E_1 = h^2/2m\lambda_1^2$. If λ is slightly less than λ_1, the function crosses the $+x$ axis while the slope is still negative. The slope becomes more negative because its rate of change ψ'' is now negative. This function approaches negative infinity at large x. [*This computer-generated plot courtesy of Paul Doherty, The Exploratorium.*]

Note that, in contrast to the classical case, there is some probability of finding the particle outside the well, in the regions $x > L$ or $x < 0$. In these regions, the total energy is less than the potential energy, so it would seem that the kinetic energy must be negative. Since negative kinetic energy has no meaning in classical physics, it is interesting to speculate about the meaning of this penetration of wave function beyond the well boundary. Does quantum mechanics predict that we could measure a negative kinetic energy? If so, this would be a serious defect in the theory. Fortunately, we are saved by the uncertainty principle. We can understand this qualitatively as follows (we shall consider the region $x > L$ only). Since the wave function decreases as $e^{-\alpha x}$, with α given by Equation 6-34, the probability density $\psi^2 = e^{-2\alpha x}$ becomes very small in a distance of the order of $\Delta x \approx \alpha^{-1}$. If we consider $\psi(x)$ to be

Fig. 6-12 Wave functions $\psi_n(x)$ and probability distributions $\psi_n^2(x)$ for $n = 1$, 2, and 3 for the finite square well. Compare these with Figure 6-4 for the infinite square well, where the wave functions are zero at $x = 0$ and $x = L$. The wavelengths are slightly longer than the corresponding ones for the infinite well, so the allowed energies are somewhat smaller.

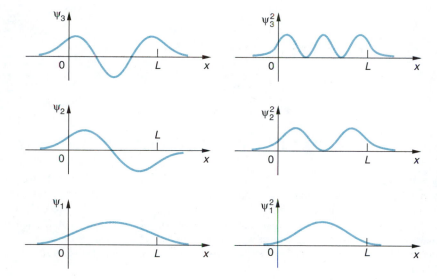

negligible beyond $x = L + \alpha^{-1}$, we can say that finding the particle in the region $x > L$ is roughly equivalent to localizing it in a region $\Delta x \approx \alpha^{-1}$. Such a measurement introduces an uncertainty in momentum of the order of $\Delta p \approx \hbar/\Delta x = \hbar\alpha$ and a minimum kinetic energy of the order of $(\Delta p)^2/2m = \hbar^2\alpha^2/2m = V_0 - E$. This kinetic energy is just enough to prevent us from measuring a negative kinetic energy! The penetration of the wave function into a classically forbidden region does have important consequences in tunneling or barrier penetration, which we shall discuss in Section 6-6.

Much of our discussion of the finite well problem applies to any problem in which $E > V(x)$ in some region and $E < V(x)$ outside that region. Consider, for example, the potential energy $V(x)$ shown in Figure 6-13. Inside the well, the Schrödinger equation is of the form

$$\psi''(x) = -k^2\psi(x) \qquad\qquad \textbf{6-35}$$

where $k^2 = 2m[E - V(x)]/\hbar^2$ now depends on x. The solutions of this equation are no longer simple sine or cosine functions because the wave number $k = 2\pi/\lambda$ varies with x, but since ψ'' and ψ have opposite signs, ψ will always curve toward the axis and the solutions will oscillate. Outside the well, ψ will curve away from the axis so there will be only certain values of E for which solutions exist that approach zero as x approaches infinity.

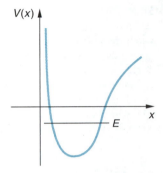

Fig. 6-13 Arbitrary well-type potential with possible energy E. Inside the well $[E > V(x)]$, $\psi(x)$ and $\psi''(x)$ have opposite signs, and the wave function will oscillate. Outside the well, $\psi(x)$ and $\psi''(x)$ have the same sign and, except for certain values of E, the wave function will not be well behaved.

More

In most cases the solution of finite well problems involves transcendental equations and is very difficult. For some finite potentials, however, graphical solutions are relatively simple and provide both insights and numerical results. As an example, we have included the *Graphical Solution of the Finite Square Well* on the home page: www.whfreeman.com/modphysics4e See also Equations 6-36 through 6-43 and Figure 6-14 here.

Quantum Wells

Development of techniques for fabricating devices whose dimensions are of the order of nanometers, called *nanostructures,* has enabled the construction of *quantum wells.* These are finite potential wells of one, two, and three dimensions that can channel electron movement in selected directions or, in the case of three-dimensional wells, called *quantum dots,* restrict electrons to quantized energy states within the well. The latter have potential applications in data storage and *quantum computers,* devices that may greatly enhance computing power and speed.

One-dimensional quantum wells, called *quantum wires,* offer the possibility of dramatically increasing the speed at which electrons move through a device in selected directions. This in turn would increase the speed with which signals move between circuit elements in computer systems. Figure 6-15 is an outline of how such a well might be formed.

Fig. 6-15 (*a*) Two infinite square wells of different widths L_1 and L_2, each containing the same number of electrons, are put together. An electron from well 1 moves to the lowest empty level of well 2. (*b*) The energies of the two highest electrons are equalized, but the unequal charge in the two wells distorts the energy-level structure. The distortion of the lowest empty levels in each well results in a potential well at the junction between the wells. The orientation of the newly formed well is perpendicular to the plane of the figure.

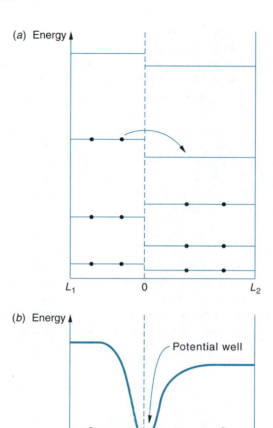

6-4 Expectation Values and Operators

Expectation Values

The objective of theory is to explain experimental observations. In classical mechanics the solution of a problem is typically specified by giving the position of a particle or particles as a function of time. As we have discussed, the wave nature of matter prevents us from doing this for microscopic systems. Instead, we find the wave function $\Psi(x, t)$ and the probability distribution function $|\Psi(x, t)|^2$. The most that we can know about a particle's position is the probability that a measurement will yield various values of x. The *expectation value* of x is defined as

$$\langle x \rangle = \int_{-\infty}^{+\infty} \Psi^*(x, t)\, x\, \Psi(x, t)\, dx \qquad \textbf{6-44}$$

The expectation value of x is the average value of x that we would expect to obtain from a measurement of the positions of a large number of particles with the same wave function $\Psi(x, t)$. As we have seen, for a particle in a state of definite energy the probability distribution is independent of time. The expectation value of x is then given by

$$\langle x \rangle = \int_{-\infty}^{+\infty} \psi^*(x) x \, \psi(x) \, dx \qquad \textbf{6-45}$$

For example, for the infinite square well, we can see by symmetry (or by direct calculation) that $\langle x \rangle$ is $L/2$, the midpoint of the well.

In general, the expectation value of any function $f(x)$ is given by

$$\langle f(x) \rangle = \int_{-\infty}^{+\infty} \psi^* f(x) \, \psi \, dx \qquad \textbf{6-46}$$

For example, $\langle x^2 \rangle$ can be calculated as above, for the infinite square well of width L. It is left as an exercise to show that

$$\langle x^2 \rangle = \frac{L^2}{3} - \frac{L^2}{2n^2\pi^2} \qquad \textbf{6-47}$$

We should note that we don't necessarily expect to make a measurement whose result equals the expectation value. For example, for even n, the probability of measuring $x = L/2$ in some range dx around the midpoint of the well is zero because the wave function $\sin(n\pi x/L)$ is zero there. We get $\langle x \rangle = L/2$ because the probability function $\psi^*\psi$ is symmetrical about that point.

Operators

If we knew the momentum p of a particle as a function of x, we could calculate the expectation value $\langle p \rangle$ from Equation 6-46. However, it is impossible in principle to find p as a function of x since, according to the uncertainty principle, both p and x cannot be determined at the same time. To find $\langle p \rangle$ we need to know the distribution function for momentum. If we know $\psi(x)$, it can be found by Fourier analysis. It can be shown that $\langle p \rangle$ can be found from

$$\langle p \rangle = \int_{-\infty}^{+\infty} \Psi^* \left(\frac{\hbar}{i} \frac{\partial}{\partial x} \right) \Psi \, dx \qquad \textbf{6-48}$$

Similarly, $\langle p^2 \rangle$ can be found from

$$\langle p^2 \rangle = \int_{-\infty}^{+\infty} \Psi^* \left(\frac{\hbar}{i} \frac{\partial}{\partial x} \right) \left(\frac{\hbar}{i} \frac{\partial}{\partial x} \right) \Psi \, dx$$

Notice that in computing the expectation value the operator representing the physical quantity operates on $\Psi(x, t)$, *not* on $\Psi^*(x, t)$; i.e., its correct position is between Ψ^* and Ψ. This is not important to the outcome when the operator is simply some $f(x)$, but it is critical when the operator includes a differentiation, as in the case of the momentum operator.

EXAMPLE 6-5 Expectation Values for p and p^2 Find $\langle p \rangle$ and $\langle p^2 \rangle$ for the ground-state wave function of the infinite square well. (Before we calculate them, what do you think the results will be?)

Solution

We can ignore the time dependence of Ψ, in which case we have

$$\langle p \rangle = \int_0^L \left(\sqrt{\frac{2}{L}} \sin \frac{\pi x}{L} \right) \left(\frac{\hbar}{i} \frac{\partial}{\partial x} \right) \left(\sqrt{\frac{2}{L}} \sin \frac{\pi x}{L} \right) dx$$

$$= \frac{\hbar}{i} \frac{2}{L} \frac{\pi}{L} \int_0^L \sin \frac{\pi x}{L} \cos \frac{\pi x}{L} dx = 0$$

The particle is equally as likely to be moving in the $-x$ as in the $+x$ direction, so its *average* momentum is zero.

Similarly, since

$$\frac{\hbar}{i} \frac{\partial}{\partial x} \left(\frac{\hbar}{i} \frac{\partial}{\partial x} \right) \psi = -\hbar^2 \frac{\partial^2 \psi}{\partial x^2} = -\hbar^2 \left(-\frac{\pi^2}{L^2} \sqrt{\frac{2}{L}} \sin \frac{\pi x}{L} \right)$$

$$= +\frac{\hbar^2 \pi^2}{L^2} \psi$$

we have

$$\langle p^2 \rangle = \frac{\hbar^2 \pi^2}{L^2} \int_0^L \psi^* \psi \, dx = \frac{\hbar^2 \pi^2}{L^2} \int_0^L \psi^* \psi \, dx = \frac{\hbar^2 \pi^2}{L^2}$$

Note that $\langle p^2 \rangle$ is simply $2mE$ since, for the infinite square well, $E = p^2/2m$. The quantity $(\hbar/i)\partial/\partial x$, which operates on the wave function in Equation 6-48, is called the *momentum operator* p_{op}:

$$\boxed{p_{op} = \frac{\hbar}{i} \frac{\partial}{\partial x}} \qquad \textbf{6-49}$$

The time-independent Schrödinger equation (Equation 6-18) can be written conveniently in terms of p_{op}:

$$\left(\frac{1}{2m} \right) p_{op}^2 \psi(x) + V(x) \psi(x) = E\psi(x) \qquad \textbf{6-50}$$

where

$$p_{op}^2 \psi(x) = \frac{\hbar}{i} \frac{\partial}{\partial x} \left[\frac{\hbar}{i} \frac{\partial}{\partial x} \psi(x) \right] = -\hbar^2 \frac{\partial^2 \psi}{\partial x^2}$$

In classical mechanics, the total energy written in terms of the position and momentum variables is called the Hamiltonian function $H = p^2/2m + V$. If we replace the momentum by the momentum operator p_{op} and note that $V = V(x)$, we obtain the Hamiltonian operator H_{op}:

$$H_{op} = \frac{p_{op}^2}{2m} + V(x)$$ **6-51**

The time-independent Schrödinger equation can then be written

$$H_{op}\psi = E\psi$$ **6-52**

The advantage of writing the Schrödinger equation in this formal way is that it allows for easy generalization to more complicated problems such as those with several particles moving in three dimensions. We simply write the total energy of the system in terms of position and momentum and replace the momentum variables by the appropriate operators to obtain the Hamiltonian operator for the system.

Table 6-1 summarizes the several operators representing physical quantities that we have discussed thus far and includes a few more that we will encounter later on.

TABLE 6-1 Some quantum-mechanical operators

Symbol	Physical quantity	Operator
$f(x)$	Any function of x—e.g., the position x, the potential energy $V(x)$, etc.	$f(x)$
p_x	x component of momentum	$\dfrac{\hbar}{i}\dfrac{\partial}{\partial x}$
p_y	y component of momentum	$\dfrac{\hbar}{i}\dfrac{\partial}{\partial y}$
p_z	z component of momentum	$\dfrac{\hbar}{i}\dfrac{\partial}{\partial z}$
E	Hamiltonian (time-independent)	$\dfrac{p_{op}^2}{2m} + V(x)$
E	Hamiltonian (time-dependent)	$i\hbar\dfrac{\partial}{\partial t}$
E_k	kinetic energy	$-\dfrac{\hbar^2}{2m}\dfrac{\partial^2}{\partial x^2}$
L_z	z component of angular momentum	$-i\hbar\dfrac{\partial}{\partial \phi}$

QUESTIONS

7. Explain (in words) why $\langle p \rangle$ and $\langle p^2 \rangle$ in Example 6-5 are not both zero.

8. Can $\langle x \rangle$ ever have a value that has zero probability of being measured?

More

In order for interesting things to happen in systems with quantized energies, the probability density must change in time. Only in this way can energy be emitted or absorbed by the system. *Transitions Between Energy States* on the home page (www.whfreeman.com/modphysics4e) describes the process and applies it to the emission of light from an atom.   See also Equations 6-52*a*−*e* and Figure 6-16 here.

6-5 The Simple Harmonic Oscillator

One of the problems solved by Schrödinger in the second of his six famous papers was that of the simple harmonic oscillator potential, given by

$$V(x) = \tfrac{1}{2}Kx^2 = \tfrac{1}{2}m\omega^2x^2$$

where K is the force constant and ω the angular frequency of vibration defined by $\omega = (K/m)^{1/2} = 2\pi f$. The solution of the Schrödinger equation for this potential is particularly important, as it can be applied to such problems as the vibration of molecules in gases and solids. This potential energy function is shown in Figure 6-17, with a possible total energy E indicated.

In classical mechanics, a particle in such a potential is in equilibrium at the origin $x = 0$, where $V(x)$ is minimum and the force $F_x = -dV/dx$ is zero. If disturbed, the particle with energy E will oscillate back and forth between $x = -A$ and $x = +A$, the points at which the kinetic energy is zero and the total energy is just equal to the potential energy. These points are called the classical turning points. The distance A is related to the total energy E by

$$E = \tfrac{1}{2}m\omega^2A^2 \qquad\qquad \textbf{6-53}$$

Classically, the probability of finding the particle in dx is proportional to the time spent in dx, which is dx/v. The speed of the particle can be obtained from the conservation of energy:

$$\tfrac{1}{2}mv^2 + \tfrac{1}{2}m\omega^2x^2 = E$$

The classical probability is thus

$$P_c(x)\,dx \propto \frac{dx}{v} = \frac{dx}{\sqrt{(2/m)(E - \tfrac{1}{2}m\omega^2x^2)}} \qquad\qquad \textbf{6-54}$$

Any value of the energy E is possible. The lowest energy is $E = 0$, in which case the particle is at rest at the origin.

The Schrödinger equation for this problem is

$$-\frac{\hbar^2}{2m}\frac{d^2\psi(x)}{dx^2} + \frac{1}{2}m\omega^2x^2\,\psi(x) = E\psi(x) \qquad\qquad \textbf{6-55}$$

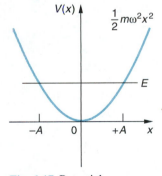

Fig. 6-17 Potential energy function for a simple harmonic oscillator. Classically, the particle with energy E is confined between the "turning points" $-A$ and $+A$.

The mathematical techniques involved in solving this type of differential equation are standard in mathematical physics, but unfamiliar to most students at this level. We will, therefore, discuss the problem qualitatively. We first note that since the potential is symmetric about the origin $x = 0$, we expect the probability distribution function $|\psi(x)|^2$ also to be symmetric about the origin, i.e., to have the same value at $-x$ as at $+x$.

$$|\psi(-x)|^2 = |\psi(x)|^2$$

The wave function $\psi(x)$ must then be either symmetric $\psi(-x) = + \psi(x)$, or antisymmetric $\psi(-x) = -\psi(x)$. We can therefore simplify our discussion by considering positive x only, and find the solutions for negative x by symmetry. (The symmetry of ψ is discussed further in the Exploring section on "Parity"; see page 272.)

Consider some value of total energy E. For x less than the classical turning point A defined by Equation 6-53, the potential energy $V(x)$ is less than the total energy E, whereas for $x > A$, $V(x)$ is greater than E. Our discussion in Section 6-3 applies directly to this problem. For $x < A$, the Schrödinger equation can be written

$$\psi''(x) = -k^2\psi(x)$$

where

$$k^2 = \frac{2m}{\hbar^2}[E - V(x)]$$

and $\psi(x)$ curves toward the axis and oscillates. For $x > A$, the Schrödinger equation becomes

$$\psi''(x) = +\alpha^2\psi(x)$$

with

$$\alpha^2 = \frac{2m}{\hbar^2}[V(x) - E]$$

and $\psi(x)$ curves away from the axis. Only certain values of E will lead to solutions that are well behaved, i.e., which approach zero as x approaches infinity. The allowed values of E for the simple harmonic oscillator must be determined by solving the Schrödinger equation; in this case they are given by

$$E_n = (n + \tfrac{1}{2})\hbar\omega \qquad n = 0, 1, 2, \ldots \qquad \textbf{6-56}$$

Thus, the ground-state energy is $\frac{1}{2}\hbar\omega$ and the energy levels are equally spaced, each excited state being separated from the levels immediately adjacent by $\hbar\omega$.

The wave functions of the simple harmonic oscillator in the ground state and in the first two excited states ($n = 0$, $n = 1$, and $n = 2$) are sketched in Figure 6-18. The ground-state wave function has the shape of a Gaussian curve, and the lowest energy $E_0 = \frac{1}{2}\hbar\omega$ is the minimum energy consistent with the uncertainty principle. The allowed solutions to the Schrödinger equation, the wave functions for the simple harmonic oscillator, can be written

$$\psi_n(x) = C_n e^{-m\omega x^2/2\hbar}H_n(x) \qquad \textbf{6-57}$$

Fig. 6-18 Wave functions for the ground state and the first two excited states of the simple harmonic oscillator potential, the states with $n = 0$, 1, and 2.

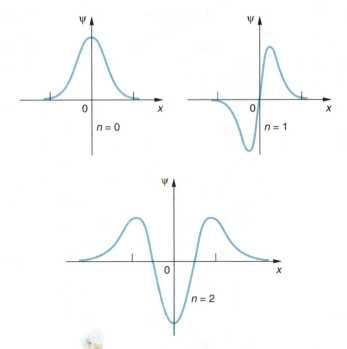

where the constants C_n are determined by normalization and the functions $H_n(x)$ are polynomials of order n called the Hermite polynomials.[13] The solutions for $n = 0$, 1, and 2 (see Figure 6-18) are

$$\psi_0(x) = A_0 e^{-m\omega x^2/2\hbar}$$

$$\psi_1(x) = A_1 \sqrt{\frac{m\omega}{\hbar}}\, x e^{-m\omega x^2/2\hbar} \qquad \textbf{6-58}$$

$$\psi_2(x) = A_2\left(1 - \frac{2m\omega x^2}{\hbar}\right) e^{-m\omega x^2/2\hbar}$$

Molecules vibrate as harmonic oscillators. Measuring vibration frequencies (see Chapter 9) enables determination of force constants, bond strengths, and properties of solids.

Notice that for even values of n the wave functions are symmetric about the origin; for odd values of n, they are antisymmetric. In Figure 6-19 the probability distributions $\psi_n^2(x)$ are sketched for $n = 0$, 1, 2, 3, and 10 for comparison with the classical distribution.

A property of these wave functions that we shall state without proof is that

$$\int_{-\infty}^{+\infty} \psi_n^* x\, \psi_m\, dx = 0 \quad \text{unless} \quad n = m \pm 1 \qquad \textbf{6-59}$$

This property places a condition on transitions that may occur between allowed states. This condition, called a *selection rule*, limits the amount by which n can change for (electric dipole) radiation emitted or absorbed by a simple harmonic oscillator:

The quantum number of the final state must be 1 less than or 1 greater than that of the initial state.

This selection rule is usually written

$$\Delta n = \pm 1 \qquad \textbf{6-60}$$

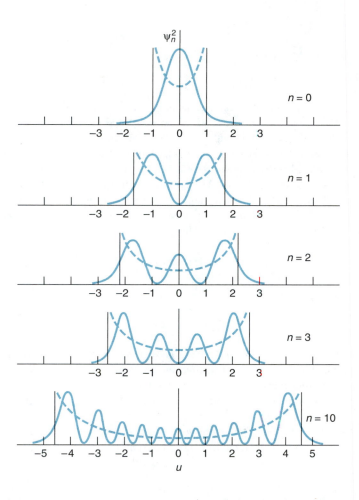

Fig. 6-19 Probability density ψ_n^2 for the simple harmonic oscillator plotted against the dimensionless variable $u = (m\omega/\hbar)^{1/2}x$, for $n = 0, 1,$ 2, 3, and 10. The dashed curves are the classical probability densities for the same energy, and the vertical lines indicate the classical turning points $x = \pm A$.

Since the difference in energy between two successive states is $\hbar\omega$, this is the energy of the photon emitted or absorbed in an electric dipole transition. The frequency of the photon is therefore equal to the classical frequency of the oscillator, as was assumed by Planck in his derivation of the blackbody radiation formula. Figure 6-20 shows an energy-level diagram for the simple harmonic oscillator, with the allowed energy transitions indicated by vertical arrows.

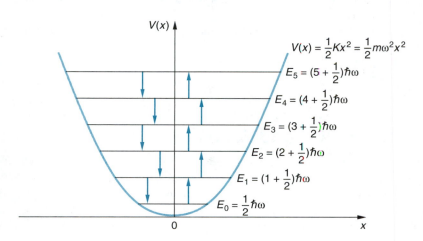

Fig. 6-20 Energy levels in the simple harmonic oscillator potential. Transitions obeying the selection rule $\Delta n = \pm 1$ are indicated by the arrows (those pointing up indicate absorption). Since the levels have equal spacing, the same energy $\hbar\omega$ is emitted or absorbed in all allowed transitions. For this special potential, the frequency of the emitted or absorbed photon equals the frequency of oscillation, as predicted by classical theory.

Exploring

Parity

We made a special point of arranging the simple harmonic oscillator potential symmetrically about $x = 0$ (see Figure 6-17), just as we had done with the finite square well in Figure 6-8*b* and will do with various other potentials in later discussions. The usual purpose in each case is to emphasize the symmetry of the physical situation and to simplify the mathematics. Notice that arranging the potential $V(x)$ symmetrically about the origin means that $V(x) = V(-x)$. This means that the Hamiltonian operator H_{op}, defined in Equation 6-51, is unchanged by a transformation that changes $x \rightarrow -x$. Such a transformation is called a *parity operation* and is usually denoted by the operator P. Thus, if $\psi(x)$ is a solution of the Schrödinger equation

$$H_{op}\psi(x) = E\psi(x) \qquad \textbf{6-52}$$

then a parity operation P leads to

$$H_{op}\psi(-x) = E\psi(-x)$$

and $\psi(-x)$ is also a solution to the Schrödinger equation and corresponds to the same energy. When two (or more) wave functions are solutions corresponding to the same value of the energy E, that level is referred to as *degenerate*. In this case, where two wave functions, $\psi(x)$ and $\psi(-x)$, are both solutions with energy E, we call the energy level doubly degenerate.

It should be apparent from examining the two equations above that $\psi(x)$ and $\psi(-x)$ can differ at most by a multiplicative constant C, i.e.,

$$\psi(x) = C\psi(-x) \qquad \psi(-x) = C\psi(x)$$

or

$$\psi(x) = C\psi(-x) = C^2\psi(x)$$

from which it follows that $C = \pm 1$. If $C = 1$, $\psi(x)$ is an even function, i.e., $\psi(-x) = \psi(x)$. If $C = -1$, then $\psi(x)$ is an odd function, i.e., $\psi(-x) = -\psi(x)$. Parity is used in quantum mechanics to describe the symmetry properties of wave functions under a reflection of the *space* coordinates in the origin, i.e., under a parity operation. The terms even and odd parity describe the symmetry of the wave functions, not whether the quantum numbers are even or odd.

6-6 Reflection and Transmission of Waves

Up to this point, we have been concerned with bound-state problems in which the potential energy is larger than the total energy for large values of x. In this section, we shall consider some simple examples of unbound states for which E is greater than $V(x)$ as x gets larger in one or both directions. For these problems $d^2\psi(x)/dx^2$ and $\psi(x)$ have opposite signs for those regions of x where $E > V(x)$, so $\psi(x)$ in

those regions curves toward the axis and does not become infinite at large values of |x|. Any value of E is allowed. Such wave functions are not normalizable, since $\psi(x)$ does not approach zero as x goes to infinity in at least one direction and, as a consequence,

$$\int_{-\infty}^{+\infty} |\psi(x)|^2 \, dx \longrightarrow \infty$$

A complete solution involves combining infinite plane waves into a wave packet of finite width. The finite packet is normalizable. However, for our purposes it is sufficient to note that the integral above is bounded between the limits a and b, provided only that $|b - a| < \infty$. Such wave functions are most frequently encountered, as we are about to do, in the scattering of beams of particles from potentials, so it is usual to normalize such wave functions in terms of the density of particles ρ in the beam. Thus,

$$\int_a^b |\psi(x)|^2 \, dx = \int_a^b \rho \, dx = \int_a^b dN = N$$

where dN is the number of particles in the interval dx and N is the number of particles in the interval $(b - a)$.[14] The wave nature of the Schrödinger equation leads, even so, to some very interesting consequences.

Step Potential

Consider a region in which the potential energy is the step function

$$V(x) = 0 \qquad \text{for} \qquad x < 0$$
$$V(x) = V_0 \qquad \text{for} \qquad x > 0$$

as shown in Figure 6-21. We are interested in what happens when a beam of particles, each with the same total energy E, moving from left to right encounters the step.

The classical answer is simple. For $x < 0$, each particle moves with speed $v = (2E/m)^{1/2}$. At $x = 0$, an impulsive force acts on it. If the total energy E is less than V_0, the particle will be turned around and will move to the left at its original speed; that is, it will be reflected by the step. If E is greater than V_0, the particle will continue moving to the right but with reduced speed, given by $v = (2(E - V_0)/m)^{1/2}$. We might picture this classical problem as a ball rolling along a level surface and coming to a steep hill of height y_0, given by $mgy_0 = V_0$. If its original kinetic energy is less than V_0, the ball will roll partway up the hill and then back down and to the left along the level surface at its original speed. If E is greater than V_0, the ball will roll up the hill and proceed to the right at a smaller speed.

The quantum-mechanical result is similar to the classical one for $E < V_0$ but quite different when $E > V_0$, as in Figure 6-22a. The Schrödinger equation in each of the two space regions shown in the diagram is given by

Region I

$$(x < 0) \qquad \frac{d^2\psi(x)}{dx^2} = -k_1^2 \psi(x) \qquad \textbf{6-61}$$

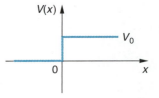

Fig. 6-21 Step potential. A classical particle incident from the left, with total energy E greater than V_0, is always transmitted. The potential change at $x = 0$ merely provides an impulsive force which reduces the speed of the particle. A wave incident from the left is partially transmitted and partially reflected because the wavelength changes abruptly at $x = 0$.

Fig. 6-22 (*a*) A potential step. Particles are incident on the step from the left toward the right, each with total energy $E > V_0$. (*b*) The wavelength of the incident wave (Region I) is shorter than that of the transmitted wave (Region II). Since $k_2 < k_1$, $|C|^2 > |A|^2$; however, the transmission coefficient $T < 1$.

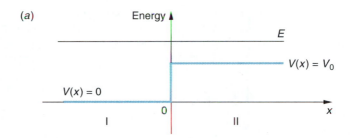

(*a*)

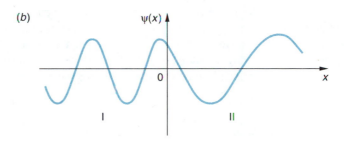

(*b*)

Region II

$$(x > 0) \qquad \frac{d^2\psi(x)}{dx^2} = -k_2^2\psi(x) \qquad \text{6-62}$$

where

$$k_1 = \frac{\sqrt{2mE}}{\hbar} \qquad \text{and} \qquad k_2 = \frac{\sqrt{2m(E - V_0)}}{\hbar}$$

The general solutions are

Region I

$$(x < 0) \qquad \psi_I(x) = Ae^{ik_1x} + Be^{-ik_1x} \qquad \text{6-63}$$

Region II

$$(x > 0) \qquad \psi_{II}(x) = Ce^{ik_2x} + De^{-ik_2x} \qquad \text{6-64}$$

Specializing these solutions to our situation where we are assuming the incident beam of particles to be moving from left to right, we see that the first term in Equation 6-63 represents that beam, since multiplying Ae^{ik_1x} by the time part of $\Psi(x, t)$, $e^{-i\omega t}$, yields a plane wave (i.e., a beam of free particles) moving to the right. The second term, Be^{ik_1x}, represents particles moving to the left in Region I. In Equation 6-64, $D = 0$, since that term represents particles incident on the potential step from the right and there are none. Thus, we have that the constant A is known or at least obtainable (determined by normalization of Ae^{ik_1x} in terms of the density of particles in the beam as explained above) and the constants B and C are yet to be found. We find them by applying the continuity condition on $\psi(x)$ and $d\psi/dx$ at $x = 0$, i.e., by

requiring that $\psi_I(0) = \psi_{II}(0)$ and $d\psi(0)/dx = d\psi_{II}(0)/dx$. Continuity of ψ at $x = 0$ yields

$$\psi_I(0) = A + B = \psi_{II}(0) = C$$

or

$$A + B = C \qquad \qquad \textbf{6-65a}$$

Continuity of $d\psi/dx$ at $x = 0$ gives

$$k_1 A - k_1 B = k_2 C \qquad \qquad \textbf{6-65b}$$

Solving Equations 6-65a and b for B and C in terms of A (see Problem 6-45), we have

$$B = \frac{k_1 - k_2}{k_1 + k_2} A = \frac{E^{1/2} - (E - V_0)^{1/2}}{E^{1/2} + (E - V_0)^{1/2}} A \qquad \qquad \textbf{6-66}$$

$$C = \frac{2k_1}{k_1 + k_2} A = \frac{2E^{1/2}}{E^{1/2} + (E - V_0)^{1/2}} A \qquad \qquad \textbf{6-67}$$

where Equations 6-66 and 6-67 give the relative amplitude of the reflected and transmitted waves, respectively. It is usual to define the coefficients of reflection R and transmission T, the relative *rates* at which particles are reflected and transmitted, in terms of A, B, and C as[15]

$$R = \frac{|B|^2}{|A|^2} = \left(\frac{k_1 - k_2}{k_1 + k_2}\right)^2 \qquad \qquad \textbf{6-68}$$

$$T = \frac{k_2}{k_1} \frac{|C|^2}{|A|^2} = \frac{4k_1 k_2}{(k_1 + k_2)^2} \qquad \qquad \textbf{6-69}$$

from which it can be readily verified (see Problem 6-43) that

$$T + R = 1 \qquad \qquad \textbf{6-70}$$

Among the interesting consequences of the wave nature of the solutions to Schrödinger's equation, notice the following:

1. Even though $E > V_0$, R is *not* 0; i.e., in contrast to classical expectations, some of the particles are reflected from the step. (This is analogous to the internal reflection of electromagnetic waves at the interface of two media.)

2. The value of R depends on the difference between k_1 and k_2, but *not* on which is larger; i.e., a step down in the potential produces the same reflection as a step up of the same size.

Since $k = p/\hbar = 2\pi/\lambda$, the wavelength changes as the beam passes the step. We might also expect that the amplitude of ψ_{II} will be less than that of the incident wave; however, recall that the $|\psi|^2$ is proportional to the particle density. Since particles move more slowly in Region II ($k_2 < k_1$), $|\psi_{II}|^2$ may be larger than $|\psi_I|^2$. Figure 6-22b

Fig. 6-23 Time development
of a one-dimensional wave
packet representing a particle
incident on a step potential
for $E > V_0$. The position of a
classical particle is indicated
by the dot. Note that part of
the packet is transmitted and
part is reflected. The sharp
spikes that appear are artifacts of the discontinuity in
the slope of $V(x)$ at $x = 0$.

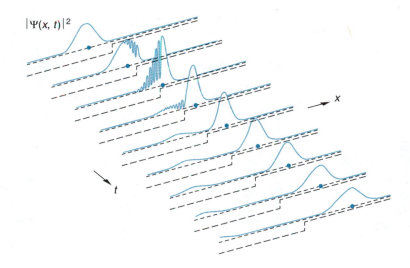

illustrates these points. Figure 6-23 shows the time development of a wave packet
incident on a potential step for $E > V_0$.

Now let us consider the case shown in Figure 6-24a, where $E < V_0$. Classically,
we expect all particles to be reflected at $x = 0$; however, we note that k_2 in Equation
6-64 is now an imaginary number, since $E < V_0$. Thus,

$$\Psi_{II}(x) = Ce^{ik_2x} = Ce^{-\alpha x} \qquad \textbf{6-71}$$

is a *real* exponential function where $\alpha = \sqrt{2m(V_0 - E)}/\hbar$. (We choose the positive
root so that $\psi_{II} \to 0$ as $x \to \infty$.) This means that the numerator and denominator of
the right side of Equation 6-66 are complex conjugates of one another, hence $|B|^2 =
|A|^2$ and $R = 1$ and $T = 0$. Figure 6-25 is a graph of both R and T versus energy for a
potential step. In agreement with the classical prediction, all of the particles (waves)
are reflected back into Region I. However, another interesting result of our solution
of Schrödinger's equation is that the particle waves do not all reflect at $x = 0$. Since

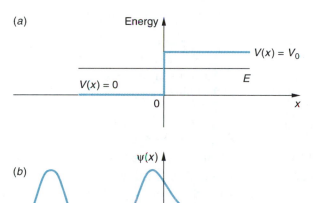

Fig. 6-24 (*a*) A potential
step. Particles are incident on
the step from the left moving
toward the right, each with
total energy $E < V_0$. (*b*) The
wave transmitted into Region
II is a decreasing exponential.
However, the value of R in
this case is 1 and no net
energy is transmitted.

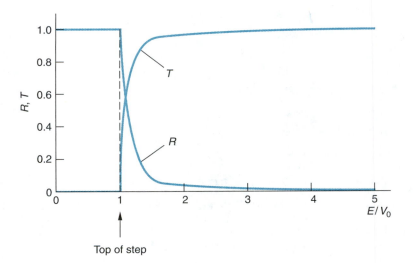

Fig. 6-25 Reflection coefficient R and transmission
coefficient T for a potential
step V_0 high versus energy E
(in units of V_0).

ψ_{II} is an exponential decreasing toward the right, the particle density in Region II is proportional to

$$|\psi_{II}|^2 = |C|^2 e^{-2\alpha x} \qquad\qquad \textbf{6-72}$$

Figure 6-24*b* shows the wave function for the case $E < V_0$. The wave function does not go to zero at $x = 0$ but decays exponentially, as does the wave function for the bound state in a finite square well problem. The wave penetrates slightly into the classically forbidden region $x > 0$ but eventually is completely reflected. (As discussed in Section 6-3, there is no prediction that a negative kinetic energy will be *measured* in such a region, because to locate the particle in such a region introduces an uncertainty in the momentum corresponding to a minimum kinetic energy greater than $V_0 - E$.) This situation is similar to that of total internal reflection in optics.

EXAMPLE 6-6 **Reflection from a Step with $E < V_0$** A beam of electrons, each with energy $E = 0.1\ V_0$, are incident on a potential step with $V_0 = 1$ eV. This is of the order of magnitude of the work function for electrons at the surface of metals. Graph the relative probability $|\psi|^2$ of particles penetrating the step up to a distance $x = 10^{-9}$ m, or roughly five atomic diameters.

Solution
For $x > 0$ the wave function is given by Equation 6-71. The value of $|C|^2$ is, from Equation 6-67,

$$|C|^2 = \left| \frac{2(0.1V_0)^{1/2}}{(0.1\ V_0)^{1/2} + (-0.9\ V_0)^{1/2}} \right|^2 = 0.4$$

where we have taken $|A^2| = 1$. Computing $e^{-2\alpha x}$ for several values of x from 0 to 10^{-9} m gives, with $2\alpha = 2[2m(0.9V_0)]^{1/2}/\hbar$, the first two columns of Table 6-2. Taking $e^{-2\alpha x}$ and then multiplying by $|C|^2 = 0.4$ yield $|\psi|^2$, which is graphed in Figure 6-26.

x (m)	2αx	$|\psi|^2$
TABLE 6-2 $\|\psi\|^2$		
0	0	0.40
0.1×10^{-10}	0.137	0.349
1.0×10^{-10}	1.374	0.101
2.0×10^{-10}	2.748	0.026
5.0×10^{-10}	6.869	0.001
10.0×10^{-10}	13.74	≈ 0

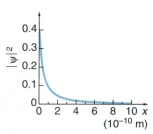

Fig. 6-26

Barrier Potential

Now let us consider one of the more interesting quantum-mechanical potentials, the barrier, illustrated by the example in Figure 6-27. The potential is

$$V(x) = \begin{cases} V_0 & \text{for} \quad 0 < x < a \\ 0 & \text{for} \quad 0 > x \quad \text{and} \quad x > a \end{cases} \qquad \textbf{6-73}$$

Classical particles incident on the barrier from the left in Region I with $E > V_0$ will all be transmitted, slowing down while passing through Region II, but moving at their original speed again in Region III. For classical particles with $E < V_0$ incident from the left, all are reflected back into Region I. The quantum-mechanical behavior of particles incident on the barrier in both energy ranges is *much* different!

(a)

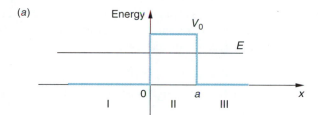

Fig. 6-27 (a) Square barrier potential. (b) Penetration of the barrier by a wave with energy less than the barrier energy. Part of the wave is transmitted by the barrier even though, classically, the particle cannot enter the region $0 < x < a$ in which the potential energy is greater than the total energy.

(b)

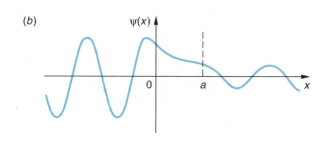

First, let us see what happens when a beam of particles, all with the same energy $E < V_0$, as illustrated in Figure 6-27, is incident from the left. The general solutions to the wave equation are, following the example of the potential step,

$$\psi_I(x) = Ae^{ik_1x} + Be^{-ik_1x} \qquad x < 0$$
$$\psi_{II}(x) = Ce^{-\alpha x} + De^{\alpha x} \qquad 0 < x < a \qquad\qquad \textbf{6-74}$$
$$\psi_{III}(x) = Fe^{ik_1x} + Ge^{-ik_1x} \qquad x > a$$

where, as before, $k_1 = \sqrt{2mE}/\hbar$ and $\alpha = \sqrt{2m(V_0 - E)}/\hbar$. Note that ψ_{II} involves real exponentials, whereas ψ_I and ψ_{III} contain complex exponentials. Since the particle beam is incident on the barrier from the left, we can set $G = 0$. Once again, the value of A is determined by the particle density in the beam and the four constants B, C, D, and F are found in terms of A by applying the continuity condition on ψ and $d\psi/dx$ at $x = 0$ and at $x = a$. The details of the calculation are not of concern to us here, but several of the more interesting results are.

As we discovered for the potential step with $E < V_0$, the wave function incident from the left does not decrease immediately to zero at the barrier but instead will decay exponentially in the region of the barrier. Upon reaching the far wall of the barrier, the wave function must join smoothly to a sinusoidal wave function to the right of the barrier, as shown in Figure 6-27b. This implies that there will be some probability of the particles represented by the wave function being found on the far right outside of the barrier, although classically they should never be able to get through, i.e., there is a probability that the particles approaching the barrier can penetrate it. This phenomenon is called *barrier penetration* or *tunneling* (see Figure 6-28). The relative probability of its occurrence in any given situation is given by the transmission coefficient.

The coefficient of transmission T from Region I into Region III is found to be (see Problem 6-61)

$$T = \frac{|F|^2}{|A|^2} = \left[1 + \frac{\sinh^2 \alpha a}{4\dfrac{E}{V_0}\left(1 - \dfrac{E}{V_0}\right)}\right]^{-1} \qquad\qquad \textbf{6-75}$$

If $\alpha a \gg 1$, Equation 6-75 takes on the somewhat simpler form to evaluate

$$T \approx 16\frac{E}{V_0}\left(1 - \frac{E}{V_0}\right)e^{-2\alpha a} \qquad\qquad \textbf{6-76}$$

Scanning Tunneling Microscope   In the *scanning tunneling microscope* (STM), developed in the 1980s by Gerd Binnig and Heinrich Rohrer, a narrow gap between a conducting specimen and the tip of a tiny probe acts as a potential barrier to electrons bound in the specimen as illustrated in Figure 6-29. A small bias voltage applied between the probe and the specimen causes the electrons to tunnel through the barrier separating the two surfaces if the surfaces are close enough together. The tunneling current is extremely sensitive to the size of the gap, i.e., the width of the barrier, between the probe and specimen. A change of only 0.5 nm (about the diameter of one atom) in the width of the barrier can cause the tunneling current to change by as much as a factor of 10^4. As the probe scans the specimen, a constant tunneling current is maintained by a piezoelectric feedback system that keeps the gap constant. Thus, the surface of the specimen can be mapped out by the vertical motions of the probe. In this way, the

An important application of tunneling is the tunnel diode, a common component of electronic circuits. Another is *field emission*, tunneling of electrons facilitated by an electric field, now being used in wide-angle, flat-screen displays on some laptop computers.

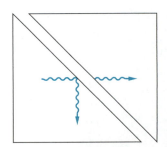

Fig. 6-28 Optical barrier penetration, sometimes called frustrated total internal reflection. Because of the presence of the second prism, part of the wave penetrates the air barrier even though the angle of incidence in the first prism is greater than the critical angle. This effect can be demonstrated with two 45° prisms and a laser or a microwave beam and 45° prisms made of paraffin.

Fig. 6-29 Schematic illustration of the path of the probe of an STM (dashed line) scanned across the surface of a sample while maintaining constant tunneling current. The probe has an extremely sharp micro-tip of atomic dimensions. Tunneling occurs over a small area across the narrow gap, allowing very small features (even individual atoms) to be imaged as indicated by the dashed line.

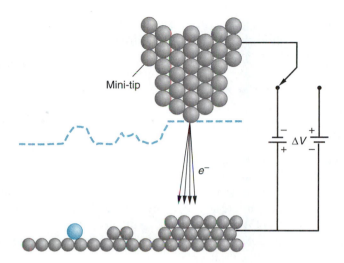

surface features of a specimen can be measured by STMs with a resolution of the order of the size of a single atom.

Scanning tunneling microscopes (STMs) have the disadvantage of requiring a conducting surface for their operation. This problem is avoided in atomic force microscopes (AFMs) that track the sample surface by maintaining a constant interatomic force between the atoms on the scanner tip and the sample's surface atoms. In this AFM image of actin filaments from contractile myofibrils in skeletal muscle the 8-nm width of the filaments is clearly resolved. [*Taken from www.di.com, of Digital Instruments, Veeco Metrology Group, Santa Barbara, CA.*]

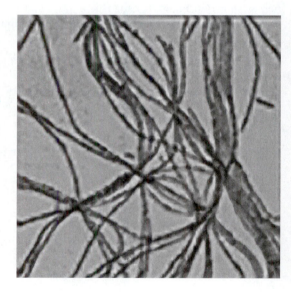

Exploring

Alpha Decay

Barrier penetration was used by Gamow, Condon, and Gurney in 1928 to explain the enormous variation in the mean life for α decay of radioactive nuclei and the seemingly paradoxical very existence of α decay.[16] While radioactive α decay will be discussed more throughly in Chapter 11, in general the smaller the energy of the emitted α particle, the larger the mean life. The energies of α particles from natural radioactive sources range from about 4 to 9 MeV, whereas the mean lifetimes range from

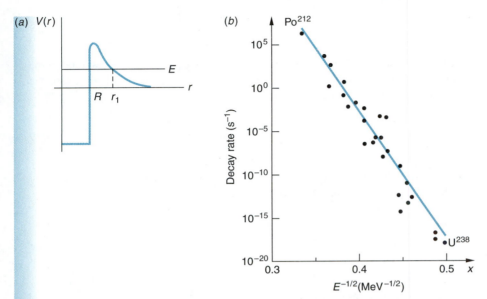

Fig. 6-30 (*a*) Model of potential energy function for an α particle and a nucleus. The strong attractive nuclear force for *r* less than the nuclear radius *R* can be approximately described by the potential well shown. Outside the nucleus the nuclear force is negligible, and the potential is given by Coulomb's law, $V(r) = +kZ2e^2/r$, where *Ze* is the nuclear charge and *2e* is the charge of the α particle. An α particle inside the nucleus oscillates back and forth, being reflected at the barrier at *R*. Because of its wave properties, when the α particle hits the barrier there is a small chance that it will penetrate and appear outside the well at $r = r_1$. The wave function is similar to that shown in Figure 6-27b. (*b*) The decay rate for the emission of α particles from radioactive nuclei. The solid curve is the prediction of Equation 6-79; the points are experimental results.

about 10^{10} years to 10^{-6} s. Gamow represented the radioactive nucleus by a potential well containing an α particle, as shown in Figure 6-30a. For *r* less than the nuclear radius *R,* the α particle is attracted by the nuclear force. Without knowing much about this force, Gamow and his co-workers represented it by a square well. Outside the nucleus, the α particle is repelled by the Coulomb force. This is represented by the Coulomb potential energy $+kZze^2/r$, where $z = 2$ for the α particle and *Ze* is the remaining nuclear charge. The energy *E* is the measured kinetic energy of the emitted α particle, since when it is far from the nucleus its potential energy is zero. We see from the figure that a small increase in *E* reduces the relative height of the barrier $V - E$ and also reduces the thickness. Because the probability of transmission varies exponentially with the relative height and barrier thickness, as indicated by Equation 6-76, a small increase in *E* leads to a large increase in the probability of transmission, and in turn to a shorter lifetime. Gamow and his co-workers were able to derive an expression for the α decay rate and the mean lifetime as a function of energy *E* that was in good agreement with experimental results as follows:

The probability that an α particle will tunnel through the barrier in any one approach is given by *T* from Equation 6-76. In fact, in this case α*a* is so large that the exponential dominates the expression and

$$T \approx e^{-2\sqrt{2m(V_0 - E)}\, a/\hbar} \qquad\qquad \textbf{6-77}$$

which is a very small number, i.e., the α particle is usually reflected. The number of times per second *N* that the α particle approaches the barrier is given approximately by

In the event that $E/V_0 > 1$, there is no reflected wave for $\alpha a = \pi, 2\pi, \ldots$ as a result of destructive interference. For electrons incident on noble gas atoms, the resulting 100 percent transmission is called the Ramsauer-Townsend effect and is a way of measuring atomic diameters for those elements.

$$N \approx \frac{v}{2R} \qquad \textbf{6-78}$$

where v equals the particle's speed inside the nucleus. Thus, the decay rate, or the probability per second that the nucleus will emit an α particle, which is also the reciprocal of the mean life τ, is given by

$$\text{decay rate} = \frac{1}{\tau} \approx \frac{v}{2R} e^{-2\sqrt{2m(V_0 - E)}\, a/\hbar} \qquad \textbf{6-79}$$

Figure 6-30*b* illustrates the good agreement between the barrier penetration calculation and experimental measurements.

Exploring

NH₃ Atomic Clock

Barrier penetration also takes place in the case of the periodic *inversion* of the ammonia molecule. The NH_3 molecule has two equilibrium configurations as illustrated in Figure 6-31*a*. The three hydrogen atoms are arranged in a plane. The nitrogen atom oscillates between two equilibrium positions equidistant from each of the H atoms above and below the plane. The potential energy function $V(x)$ acting on the N atom has two minima located symmetrically about the center of the plane as shown in Figure 6-31*b*. The N atom is bound to the molecule, so the energy is quantized and the lower states lie well below the central maximum of the potential. The central maximum presents a barrier to the N atoms in the lower states through which they slowly tunnel back and forth.[17] The oscillation frequency $f = 2.3786 \times 10^{10}$ Hz when the atom in the state characterized by the energy E_1 in Figure 6-31*b*. This frequency is quite low compared with those of most molecular vibrations, a fact that allowed the N atom tunneling frequency in NH_3 to be used as the standard in the first *atomic clocks*, devices that now provide the world's standard for precision timekeeping.

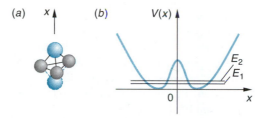

Fig. 6-31 (*a*) The NH_3 molecule oscillates between the two equilibrium positions shown. The H atoms form a plane; the N atom is colored. (*b*) The potential energy of the N atom, where x is the distance above and below the plane of the H atoms. Several of the allowed energies, including the two lowest shown, lie below the top of the central barrier through which the N atom tunnels.

More

Quantum-mechanical tunneling involving two barriers is the basis for a number of devices such as the tunnel diode and the Josephson junction, both of which have a wide variety of useful applications. As an example of such systems, the *Tunnel Diode* is described on the home page: www.whfreeman.com/modphysics4e   See also Equation 6-80 and Figure 6-32 here.

Summary

TOPIC	RELEVANT EQUATIONS AND REMARKS	
1. Schrödinger equation		
Time dependent, one space dimension	$\dfrac{-\hbar^2}{2m}\dfrac{\partial^2\psi(x,\,t)}{\partial x^2} + V(x,\,t)\psi(x,\,t) = i\hbar\,\dfrac{\partial\psi(x,\,t)}{\partial t}$	6-6
Time independent, one space dimension	$\dfrac{-\hbar^2}{2m}\dfrac{d^2\psi(x)}{dx^2} + V(x)\psi(x) = E\psi(x)$	6-18
Normalization condition	$\displaystyle\int_{-\infty}^{+\infty}\Psi^*(x,\,t)\Psi(x,\,t)\,dx = 1$	6-9
	and	
	$\displaystyle\int_{-\infty}^{+\infty}\psi^*(x)\psi(x)\,dx = 1$	6-20
Acceptability conditions	1. $\psi(x)$ and $d\psi/dx$ must be continuous. 2. $\psi(x)$ and $d\psi/dx$ must be finite. 3. $\psi(x)$ and $d\psi/dx$ must be single-valued. 4. $\psi(x) \rightarrow 0$ as $x \rightarrow \infty$.	
2. Infinite square well		
Allowed energies	$E_n = n^2\,\dfrac{\pi^2\hbar^2}{2mL^2}\qquad n = 1, 2, 3, \ldots$	6-24
Wave functions	$\psi_n(x) = \sqrt{\dfrac{2}{L}}\sin\dfrac{n\pi x}{L}\qquad n = 1, 2, 3, \ldots$	6-32
3. Finite square well	For a finite well of width L the allowed energies E_n in the well are lower than the corresponding levels for an infinite well. There is always at least one allowed energy (bound state) in a finite well.	
4. Expectation values and operators	The expectation or average value of a physical quantity represented by an operator, such as the momentum operator p_{op}, is given by	
	$\langle p \rangle = \displaystyle\int_{-\infty}^{+\infty}\psi^* p_{op}\,\psi\,dx = \int_{-\infty}^{+\infty}\psi^*\left(\dfrac{\hbar}{i}\dfrac{\partial}{\partial x}\right)\psi\,dx$	6-48

Continued

TOPIC	RELEVANT EQUATIONS AND REMARKS
5. Simple harmonic oscillator	
Allowed energies	$E_n = (n + \frac{1}{2})\hbar\omega$ $n = 0, 1, 2, \ldots$ **6-56**
6. Reflection and transmission	When the potential changes abruptly in a distance small compared to the de Broglie wavelength, a particle may be reflected even though $E > V(x)$. A particle may also penetrate into a region where $E < V(x)$.

General References

The following general references are written at a level appropriate for the readers of this book.

Brandt, S., and H. D. Dahmen, *The Picture Book of Quantum Mechanics*, Wiley, New York, 1985.

Eisberg, R., and R. Resnick, *Quantum Physics*, 2d ed., Wiley, New York, 1985.

Feynman, R. P., R. B. Leighton, and M. Sands, *Lectures on Physics*, Addison-Wesley, Reading, Mass., 1965

French, A. P., and E. F. Taylor, *An Introduction to Quantum Physics*, Norton, New York, 1978.

Mehra, J., and H. Rechenberg, *The Historical Development of Quantum Theory*, Vol. 1, Springer-Verlag, New York, 1982.

Park, D., *Introduction to the Quantum Theory*, 3d ed., McGraw-Hill, New York, 1992.

Sherwin, C., *Introduction to Quantum Mechanics*, Holt, Rinehart & Winston, New York, 1960.

Visual Quantum Mechanics, Kansas State University, Manhattan, 1996. Computer simulation software allows the user to analyze a variety of one-dimensional potentials, including the square wells and harmonic oscillator discussed in this chapter.

Notes

1. Felix Bloch (1905–1983), Swiss-American physicist. He was a student at the University of Zürich and attended the colloquium referred to. The quote is from an address before the American Physical Society in 1976. Bloch shared the 1952 Nobel Prize in physics for measuring the magnetic moment of the neutron, using a method that he invented that led to the development of the analytical technique of nuclear magnetic resonance (NMR) spectroscopy.

2. Peter J. W. Debye (1884–1966), Dutch-American physical chemist. He succeeded Einstein in the chair of theoretical physics at the University of Zürich and received the Nobel Prize in chemistry in 1936.

3. Erwin R. J. A. Schrödinger (1887–1961), Austrian physicist. He succeeded Planck in the chair of theoretical physics at the University of Berlin in 1928 following the latter's retirement and two years after publishing in rapid succession six papers that set forth the theory of wave mechanics. For that work he shared the physics Nobel Prize with P. A. M. Dirac in 1933. He left Nazi-controlled Europe in 1940, moving his household to Ireland.

4. To see that this is indeed the case, consider the effect on $\partial^2\Psi(x, t)/\partial x^2$ of multiplying $\Psi(x, t)$ by a factor C. Then $\partial^2 C\Psi(x, t)/\partial x^2 = C\partial^2\Psi(x, t)/\partial x^2$, and the derivative is increased by the same factor. Thus, the derivative is proportional to the first power of the function, i.e., it is linear in $\Psi(x, t)$.

5. The imaginary i appears because the Schrödinger equation relates a *first* time derivative to a *second* space derivative as a consequence of the fact that the total energy is related to the *square* of the momentum. This is unlike the classical wave equation (Equation 5-11), which relates two second derivatives. The implication of this is that, in general, the $\Psi(x, t)$ will be complex functions, whereas the $y(x, t)$ are real.

6. The fact that Ψ is in general complex does not mean that its imaginary part doesn't contribute to the values of measurements, which are real. Every complex number can be written in the form $z = a + bi$, where a and b are real numbers and $i = (-1)^{1/2}$. The magnitude or absolute value of z is defined as $(a^2 + b^2)^{1/2}$. The complex conjugate of z is $z^* = a - bi$, so $z^*z = (a - bi)(a + bi) = a^2 + b^2 = |z|^2$; thus the value of $|\Psi|^2$ will contain a contribution from its imaginary part.

7. Here we are using the convention of probability and statistics that certainty is represented by a probability of 1.

8. This method for solving partial differential equations is called *separation of variables*, for obvious reasons. Since most potentials in quantum mechanics, as in classical mechanics, are time-independent, the method may be applied to the Schrödinger equation in numerous situations.

9. We should note that there is an exception to this in the quantum theory of measurement.

10. $E = 0$ corresponding to $n = 0$ is not a possible energy for a particle in a box. As discussed in Section 5-6, the uncertainty principle limits the minimum energy for such a particle to values $> \hbar^2/2mL^2$.

11. Recalling that linear combinations of solutions to Schrödinger's equation will also be solutions, we should note here that simulation of the classical behavior of a macroscopic particle in a macroscopic box requires wave functions that are the superpositions of many stationary states. Thus, the classical particle never has definite energy in the quantum-mechanical sense.

12. To simplify the notation in this section we shall sometimes omit the functional dependence and merely write ψ_n for $\psi_n(x)$ and Ψ_n for $\Psi_n(x, t)$.

13. The Hermite polynomials are known functions which are tabulated in most books on quantum mechanics.

14. It is straightforward to show that the only difference between a $\psi(x)$ normalized in terms of the particle density and one for which $|\psi(x)|^2$ is the probability density is a multiplicative constant.

15. T and R are derived in terms of the particle currents, i.e., particles/unit time, in most introductory quantum mechanics books.

16. Rutherford had shown that the scattering of 8.8-MeV α particles from the decay of ^{212}Po obeyed the Coulomb force law down to distances of the order of 3×10^{-14} m, i.e., down to about nuclear dimensions. Thus, the Coulomb barrier at that distance was at least 8.8 MeV high; however, the energy of α particles emitted by ^{238}U is only 4.2 MeV, less than half the barrier height. How that could be possible presented classical physics with a paradox.

17. Since the molecule's center of mass is fixed in an inertial reference frame, the plane of H atoms also oscillates back and forth in the opposite direction to the N atom; however, their mass being smaller than that of the N atom, the amplitude of the plane's motion is actually larger than that of the N atom. It is the relative motion that is important.

18. See, for example, F. Capasso and S. Datta, "Quantum Electron Devices," *Physics Today,* **43**, 74 (1990). Leo Esaki was awarded the Nobel Prize in physics in 1973 for inventing the resonant tunnel diode.

PROBLEMS

Level 1

Section 6-1 The Schrödinger Equation in One Dimension

6-1. Show that the wave function $\Psi(x, t) = Ae^{kx-\omega t}$ does not satisfy the time-dependent Schrödinger equation.

6-2. Show that $\Psi(x, t) = Ae^{i(kx-\omega t)}$ satisfies both the time-dependent Schrödinger equation and the classical wave equation (Equation 6-1).

6-3. In a region of space, a particle has a wave function given by $\psi(x) = Ae^{-x^2/2L^2}$ and energy $\hbar^2/2mL^2$, where L is some length. (*a*) Find the potential energy as a function of x, and sketch V versus x. (*b*) What is the classical potential that has this dependence?

6-4. (*a*) For Problem 6-3, find the kinetic energy as a function of x. (*b*) Show that $x = L$ is the classical turning point. (*c*) The potential energy of a simple harmonic oscillator in terms of its angular frequency ω is given by $V(x) = \frac{1}{2}m\omega^2x^2$. Compare this with your answer to part (*a*) of Problem 6-3, and show that the total energy for this wave function can be written $E = \frac{1}{2}\hbar\omega$.

6-5. (*a*) Show that the wave function $\Psi(x, t) = A \sin (kx - \omega t)$ does *not* satisfy the time-dependent Schrödinger equation. (*b*) Show that $\Psi(x, t) = A \cos (kx - \omega t) + iA \sin (kx - \omega t)$ does satisfy this equation.

6-6. The wave function for a free electron, i.e., one on which no net force acts, is given by $\psi(x) = A \sin (2.5 \times 10^{10} x)$ where x is in meters. Compute the electron's (*a*) momentum, (*b*) total energy, and (*c*) de Broglie wavelength.

6-7. A particle with mass m and total energy zero is in a particular region of space where its wave function is $\psi(x) = Ce^{-x^2/L^2}$. (*a*) Find the potential energy $V(x)$ versus x and (*b*) make a sketch of $V(x)$ versus x.

6-8. Normalize the wave function in Problem 6-2 between $-a$ and $+a$. Why can't that wave function be normalized between $-\infty$ and $+\infty$?

Section 6-2 The Infinite Square Well

6-9. A particle is in an infinite square well of size L. Calculate the ground-state energy if (*a*) the particle is a proton and $L = 0.1$ nm, a typical size for a molecule; and (*b*) the particle is a proton and $L = 1$ fm, a typical size for a nucleus.

6-10. A particle is in the ground state of an infinite square well potential given by Equation 6-21. Find the probability of finding the particle in the interval $\Delta x = 0.002\ L$ at (a) $x = L/2$, (b) $x = 2L/3$, and (c) $x = L$. (Since Δx is very small, you need not do any integration.)

6-11. Do Problem 6-10 for particle in the second excited state ($n = 3$) of an infinite square well potential.

6-12. A mass of 10^{-6} g is moving with a speed of about 10^{-1} cm/s in a box 1 cm in length. Treating this as a one-dimensional infinite square well, calculate the approximate value of the quantum number n.

6-13. (a) For the classical particle of Problem 6-12, find Δx and Δp, assuming that $\Delta x/L = 0.01$ percent and $\Delta p/p = 0.01$ percent. (b) What is $(\Delta x \Delta p)/\hbar$?

6-14. A particle of mass m is confined to a tube of length L. (a) Use the uncertainty relationship to estimate the smallest possible energy. (b) Assume that the inside of the tube is a force-free region and that the particle makes elastic reflections at the tube ends. Use Schrödinger's equation to find the ground-state energy for the particle in the tube. Compare the answer to that of part (a).

6-15. (a) What is the wavelength associated with the particle of Problem 6-14 if the particle is in its ground state? (b) What is the wavelength if the particle is in its second excited state (quantum number $n = 3$)? (c) Use de Broglie's relationship to find the magnitude for the momentum of the particle in its ground state. (d) Show that $p^2/2m$ gives the correct energy for the ground state of this particle in the box.

6-16. The wavelength of light emitted by a ruby laser is 694.3 nm. Assuming that the emission of a photon of this wavelength accompanies the transition of an electron from the $n = 2$ level to the $n = 1$ level of an infinite square well, compute L for the well.

6-17. Suppose a macroscopic bead with a mass of 2.0 g is constrained to move on a straight frictionless wire between two heavy stops clamped firmly to the wire 10 cm apart. If the bead is moving at a speed of 20 nm/yr (i.e., to all appearances it is at rest), what is the value of its quantum number n?

6-18. An electron moving in a one-dimensional infinite square well is trapped in the $n = 5$ state. (a) Show that the probability of finding the electron between $x = 0.2\ L$ and $x = 0.4\ L$ is 1/5. (b) Compute the probability of finding the electron within the "volume" $\Delta x = 0.01\ L$ at $x = L/2$.

6-19. In the early days of nuclear physics before the neutron was discovered, it was thought that the nucleus contained only electrons and protons. If we consider the nucleus to be a one-dimensional infinite well with $L = 10$ fm and ignore relativity, compute the ground-state energy for (a) an electron and (b) a proton in the nucleus. (c) Compute the energy difference between the ground state and the first excited state for each particle. (Differences between energy levels in nuclei are found to be typically of the order of 1 MeV.)

6-20. An electron is in the ground state with energy E_n of a one-dimensional infinite well with $L = 10^{-10}$ m. Compute the force that the electron exerts on the wall during an impact on either wall. (*Hint:* $F = -dE_n/dL$. Why?) How does this result compare with the weight of an electron at the surface of Earth?

6-21. The wave functions of a particle in a one-dimensional infinite square well are given by Equation 6-32. Show that for these functions $\int \psi_n(x)\psi_m(x)\ dx = 0$, i.e., that $\psi_n(x)$ and $\psi_m(x)$ are orthogonal.

Section 6-3 The Finite Square Well

6-22. Sketch (a) the wave function and (b) the probability distribution for the $n = 4$ state for the finite square well potential.

6-23. Repeat Problem 6-22 for the $n = 5$ state of the well.

6-24. An electron is confined to a finite square well whose "walls" are 8.0 eV high. If the ground-state energy is 0.5 eV, estimate the width of the well.

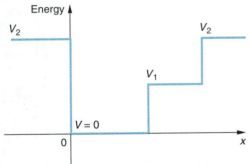

Fig. 6-33 Problem 6-25.

6-25. Using arguments concerning curvature, wavelength, and amplitude, sketch very carefully the wave function corresponding to a particle with energy E in the finite potential well shown in Figure 6-33.

6-26. For a finite square well potential that has six quantized levels, if $a = 10$ nm (*a*) sketch the finite well, (*b*) sketch the wave function from $x = -2a$ to $x = +2a$ for $n = 3$, and (*c*) sketch the probability density for the same range of x.

6-27. The mass of the deuteron (the nucleus of the hydrogen isotope ^{2}H) is 1.88 GeV/c^2. How deep must a finite potential well be whose width is 2×10^{-15} m if there are two energy levels in the well?

Section 6-4 Expectation Values and Operators

6-28. Find (*a*) $\langle x \rangle$ and (*b*) $\langle x^2 \rangle$ for the second excited state ($n = 3$) in an infinite square well potential.

6-29. (*a*) Show that the classical probability distribution function for a particle in a one-dimensional infinite square well potential of length L is given by $P(x) = 1/L$. (*b*) Use your result in (*a*) to find $\langle x \rangle$ and $\langle x^2 \rangle$ for a classical particle in such a well.

6-30. Show directly from the time-independent Schrödinger equation that $\langle p^2 \rangle = \langle 2m[E - V(x)] \rangle$ in general and that $\langle p^2 \rangle = \langle 2mE \rangle$ for the infinite square well. Use this result to compute $\langle p^2 \rangle$ for the ground state of the infinite square well.

6-31. Find $\sigma_x = \sqrt{\langle x^2 \rangle - \langle x \rangle^2}$, $\sigma_p = \sqrt{\langle p^2 \rangle - \langle p \rangle^2}$, and $\sigma_x \sigma_p$ for the ground-state wave function of an infinite square well. (Use the fact that $\langle p \rangle = 0$ by symmetry and $\langle p^2 \rangle = \langle 2mE \rangle$ from Problem 6-30.)

6-32. Compute $\langle x \rangle$ and $\langle x^2 \rangle$ for the ground state of a harmonic oscillator (Equation 6-58). Use $A_0 = (m\omega/\hbar\pi)^{1/4}$.

6-33. Use conservation of energy to obtain an expression connecting x^2 and p^2 for a harmonic oscillator, then use it along with the result from Problem 6-32 to compute $\langle p^2 \rangle$ for the harmonic oscillator ground state.

6-34. (*a*) Using A_0 from Problem 6-32, write down the total wave function $\Psi_0(x, t)$ for the ground state of a harmonic oscillator. (*b*) Use the operator for p_x from Table 6-1 to compute $\langle p^2 \rangle$.

Section 6-5 The Simple Harmonic Oscillator

6-35. For the harmonic oscillator ground state $n = 0$ the Hermite polynomial $H_n(x)$ in Equation 6-57 is given by $H_0 = 1$. Find (*a*) the normalization constant C_0, (*b*) $\langle x^2 \rangle$, and (*c*) $\langle V(x) \rangle$ for this state. (*Hint:* Use Table B1 to compute the needed integrals.)

6-36. For the first excited state, $H_1(x) = x$. Find (*a*) the normalization constant C_1, (*b*) $\langle x \rangle$, (*c*) $\langle x^2 \rangle$, (*d*) $\langle V(x) \rangle$ for this state (see Problem 6-35).

6-37. A quantum harmonic oscillator of mass m is in the ground state with classical turning points at $\pm A$. (*a*) With the mass confined to the region $\Delta x \approx 2A$, compute Δp for this

state. (*b*) Compare the kinetic energy implied by Δp with (1) the ground-state total energy and (2) the expectation value of the kinetic energy.

6-38. Compute the spacing between adjacent energy levels per unit energy, i.e., $\Delta E_n / E_n$, for the quantum harmonic oscillator and show that the result agrees with Bohr's correspondence principle (see Section 4-3) by letting $n \to \infty$.

6-39. The period of a macroscopic pendulum made with a mass of 10 g suspended from a massless cord 50 cm long is 1.42 s. (*a*) Compute the ground-state (zero-point) energy. (*b*) If the pendulum is set into motion so that the mass raises 0.1 mm above its equilibrium position, what will be the quantum number of the state? (*c*) What is the frequency of the motion in (*b*)?

6-40. Show that the wave functions for the ground state and the first excited state of the simple harmonic oscillator, given in Equation 6-58, are orthogonal, that is, show that $\int \psi_0(x) \psi_1(x)\, dx = 0$.

Section 6-6 Reflection and Transmission of Waves

6-41. A free particle of mass m with wave number k_1 is traveling to the right. At $x = 0$, the potential jumps from zero to V_0 and remains at this value for positive x. (*a*) If the total energy is $E = \hbar^2 k_1^2 / 2m = 2V_0$, what is the wave number k_2 in the region $x > 0$? Express your answer in terms of k_1 and V_0. (*b*) Calculate the reflection coefficient R at the potential step. (*c*) What is the transmission coefficient T? (*d*) If one million particles with wave number k_1 are incident upon the potential step, how many particles are expected to continue along in the positive x direction? How does this compare with the classical prediction?

6-42. In Problem 6-41, suppose that the potential jumps from zero to $-V_0$ at $x = 0$ so that the free particle speeds up instead of slowing down. The wave number for the incident particle is again k_1, and the total energy is $2V_0$. (*a*) What is the wave number for the particle in the region of positive x? (*b*) Calculate the reflection coefficient R at the potential step. (*c*) What is the transmission coefficient T? (*d*) If one million particles with wave number k_1 are incident upon the potential step, how many particles are expected to continue along in the positive x direction? How does this compare with the classical prediction?

6-43. Use Equations 6-68 and 6-69 to derive Equation 6-70.

6-44. For particles incident on a step potential with $E < V_0$, show that $T = 0$ using Equation 6-70.

6-45. Derive Equations 6-66 and 6-67 from those that immediately precede them.

6-46. A beam of electrons, each with kinetic energy $E = 2.0$ eV, is incident on a potential barrier with $V_0 = 6.5$ eV and width 5.0×10^{-10} m. (See Figure 6-26.) What fraction of the electrons in the beam will be transmitted through the barrier?

6-47. A beam of protons, each with kinetic energy 40 MeV, approaches a step potential of 30 MeV. (*a*) What fraction of the beam is reflected and transmitted? (*b*) How does your answer change if the particles are electrons?

Level II

6-48. A proton is in an infinite square well potential given by Equation 6-21 with $L = 1$ fm. (*a*) Find the ground-state energy in MeV. (*b*) Make an energy-level diagram for this system. Calculate the wavelength of the photon emitted for the transitions (*c*) $n = 2$ to $n = 1$, (*d*) $n = 3$ to $n = 2$, and (*e*) $n = 3$ to $n = 1$.

6-49. A particle is in the ground state of an infinite square well potential given by Equation 6-21. Calculate the probability that the particle will be found in the region (*a*) $0 < x < \frac{1}{2}L$, (*b*) $0 < x < \frac{1}{3}L$, and (*c*) $0 < x < \frac{3}{4}L$.

6-50. (*a*) Show that for large n, the fractional difference in energy between state n and state $n + 1$ for a particle in an infinite square well is given approximately by

$$\frac{E_{n+1} - E_n}{E_n} \approx \frac{2}{n}$$

(b) What is the approximate percentage energy difference between the states $n_1 = 1000$ and $n_2 = 1001$? (c) Comment on how this result is related to Bohr's correspondence principle.

6-51. In this problem you will obtain the time-independent Schrödinger equation from the time-dependent equation by the method of separation of variables. (a) Substitute the trial function $\Psi(x, t) = \psi(x)f(t)$ into Equation 6-6, and divide each term by $\psi(x)f(t)$ to obtain the equation

$$i\hbar \frac{f'(t)}{f(t)} = -\frac{\hbar^2}{2m} \frac{\psi''(x)}{\psi(x)} + V(x)$$

(b) Since the left side of the equation in (a) does not vary with x, the right side cannot vary with x. Similarly, neither side can vary with t; thus they both must equal some constant C. Show that this implies that $f(t)$ is given by $f(t) = e^{-i(C/\hbar)t}$. Use the de Broglie relation to argue that C must be the total energy E. (c) Use the result of (b) to obtain Equation 6-14.

6-52. Quantum mechanics predicts that any particle localized in space has a nonzero velocity and consequently can never be at rest. Consider a Ping-Pong ball of diameter 2 cm and mass 2 g that can move back and forth in a box of length 2.001 cm. Hence, the space in which the ball moves is only 0.001 cm in length. (a) What is the minimum speed of the Ping-Pong ball according to Schrödinger's equation? (b) What is the period of one oscillation?

6-53. A particle of mass m is in an infinite square well potential given by

$$V = \infty \qquad x < -\tfrac{1}{2}L$$
$$V = 0 \qquad -\tfrac{1}{2}L < x < +\tfrac{1}{2}L$$
$$V = \infty \qquad +\tfrac{1}{2}L < x$$

Since this potential is symmetric about the origin, the probability density $|\psi(x)|^2$ must also be symmetric. (a) Show that this implies that either $\psi(-x) = \psi(x)$ or $\psi(-x) = -\psi(x)$. (b) Show that the proper solutions of the time-independent Schrödinger equation can be written

$$\psi(x) = \sqrt{\frac{2}{L}} \cos \frac{n\pi x}{L} \qquad n = 1, 3, 5, 7, \ldots$$

and

$$\psi(x) = \sqrt{\frac{2}{L}} \sin \frac{n\pi x}{L} \qquad n = 2, 4, 6, 8, \ldots$$

(c) Show that the allowed energies are the same as those for the infinite square well given by Equation 6-24.

6-54. The wave function $\Psi_0(x) = Ae^{-x^2/2L^2}$ represents the ground-state energy of a harmonic oscillator. (a) Show that $\psi_1 = L\, d\psi_0(x)/dx$ is also a solution of Schrödinger's equation. (b) What is the energy of this new state? (c) From a look at the nodes of this wave function, how would you classify this excited state?

6-55. For the wave functions

$$\psi(x) = \sqrt{\frac{2}{L}} \sin \frac{n\pi x}{L} \qquad n = 1, 2, 3, \ldots$$

corresponding to an infinite square well of length L, show that

$$\langle x^2 \rangle = \frac{L^2}{3} - \frac{L^2}{2n^2\pi^2}$$

6-56. A 10-eV electron is incident on a potential barrier of height 25 eV and width 1 nm. (*a*) Use Equation 6-76 to calculate the order of magnitude of the probability that the electron will tunnel through the barrier. (*b*) Repeat your calculation for a width of 0.1 nm.

6-57. A particle of mass m moves in a region in which the potential energy is constant $V = V_0$. (*a*) Show that neither $\Psi(x, t) = A \sin(kx - \omega t)$ nor $\Psi(x, t) = A \cos(kx - \omega t)$ satisfies the time-dependent Schrödinger equation. (*Hint*: If $C_1 \sin \phi + C_2 \cos \phi = 0$ for all values of ϕ, then C_1 and C_2 must be zero.) (*b*) Show that $\Psi(x, t) = A[\cos(kx - \omega t) + i \sin(kx - \omega t)] = Ae^{i(kx - \omega t)}$ does satisfy the time-independent Schrödinger equation providing that k, V_0, and ω are related by Equation 6-5.

6-58. A particle of mass m on a table at $z = 0$ can be described by the potential energy

$$V = mgz \quad \text{for} \quad z > 0$$
$$V = \infty \quad \text{for} \quad z < 0$$

For some positive value of total energy E, indicate the classically allowed region on a sketch of $V(z)$ versus z. Sketch also the kinetic energy versus z. The Schrödinger equation for this problem is quite difficult to solve. Using arguments similar to those in Section 6-3 about the curvature of a wave function as given by the Schrödinger equation, sketch your "guesses" for the shape of the wave function for the ground state and the first two excited states.

Level III

6-59. Use the Schrödinger equation to show that the expectation value of the kinetic energy of a particle is given by

$$\langle E_k \rangle = \int_{-\infty}^{+\infty} \psi(x)\left(-\frac{\hbar^2}{2m}\frac{d^2\psi(x)}{dx^2}\right) dx$$

6-60. An electron in an infinite square well with $L = 10^{-12}$ m is moving at relativistic speed; hence, the momentum is *not* given by $p = (2mE)^{1/2}$. (*a*) Use the uncertainty principle to verify that the speed is relativistic. (*b*) Derive an expression for the electron's allowed energy levels and (*c*) compute E_1. (*d*) By what fraction does E_1 computed in (*c*) differ from the nonrelativistic E_1?

6-61. (*a*) Derive Equation 6-75. (*b*) Show that, if $\alpha a \gg 1$, Equation 6-76 follows from Equation 6-75 as an approximation.

6-62. A beam of protons, each with energy $E = 20$ MeV, is incident on a potential step 40 MeV high. Graph the relative probability of finding protons at values of $x > 0$ from $x = 0$ to $x = 5$ fm. (*Hint*: Take $|A|^2 = 1$ and refer to Example 6-6.)

Chapter 7 — Atomic Physics

In this chapter we shall apply quantum theory to atomic systems. For all neutral atoms except hydrogen the Schrödinger equation cannot be solved exactly. Despite this, it is in the realm of atomic physics that the Schrödinger equation has had its greatest success because the electromagnetic interaction of the electrons with each other and with the atomic nucleus is well understood. With powerful approximation methods and high-speed computers, many features of complex atoms such as their energy levels and the wavelengths and intensities of their spectra can be calculated, often to whatever accuracy is desired. The Schrödinger equation for the hydrogen atom was first solved in Schrödinger's first paper, published in 1926. This problem is of considerable importance not only because the Schrödinger equation can be solved exactly in this case, but also because the solutions obtained form the basis for the approximate solutions for other atoms. We shall therefore discuss this problem in some detail. Although the mathematics that arises in solving the Schrödinger equation is a bit difficult in a few places, we shall be as quantitative as possible, presenting results without proof and discussing important features of these results qualitatively only when necessary. Whenever possible, we shall give simple physical arguments to make important results plausible.

7-1 The Schrödinger Equation in Three Dimensions

In Chapter 6 we considered motion in just one dimension, but of course the real world is three-dimensional. While there are many cases in which the one-dimensional form brings out the essential physical features, there are some important aspects introduced in three-dimensional problems which we also want to examine. In rectangular coordinates, the time-independent Schrödinger equation is

$$-\frac{\hbar^2}{2m}\left(\frac{\partial^2\psi}{\partial x^2} + \frac{\partial^2\psi}{\partial y^2} + \frac{\partial^2\psi}{\partial z^2}\right) + V\psi = E\psi \qquad \textbf{7-1}$$

The wave function and the potential energy are generally functions of all three coordinates x, y, and z.

Infinite Square Well in Three Dimensions

Let us consider the three-dimensional version of the particle in a box. The potential energy function $V(x, y, z) = 0$ for $0 < x < L$, $0 < y < L$, and $0 < z < L$. V is infinite outside this cubical region. For this problem, the wave function must be zero at the walls of the box and will be a sine function inside the box. In fact, if we consider just one coordinate such as x, the solution will be the same as in the one-dimensional box discussed in Section 6-2. That is, the x dependence of the wave function will be of the form $\sin k_1 x$ with the restriction $k_1 L = n_1 \pi$, where n_1 is an integer. The complete wave function $\psi(x, y, z)$ can be written as a product of a function of x only, a function of y only, and a function of z only:

$$\psi(x, y, z) = \psi_1(x)\,\psi_2(y)\,\psi_3(z) \qquad \text{7-2}$$

where each of the functions ψ_n is a sine function as in the one-dimensional problem. For example, if we try the solution

$$\psi(x, y, z) = A \sin k_1 x \sin k_2 y \sin k_3 z \qquad \text{7-3}$$

we find by inserting this function into Equation 7-1 that the energy is given by

$$E = \frac{\hbar^2}{2m}(k_1^2 + k_2^2 + k_3^2)$$

which is equivalent to

$$E = \frac{(p_x^2 + p_y^2 + p_z^2)}{2m}$$

with $p_x = \hbar k_1$, and so forth. Using the restrictions on the wave numbers $k_i = n_i\pi/L$ from the boundary condition that the wave function be zero at the walls, we obtain for the total energy

$$E_{n_1 n_2 n_3} = \frac{\hbar^2 \pi^2}{2mL^2}(n_1^2 + n_2^2 + n_3^2) \qquad \text{7-4}$$

where n_1, n_2, and n_3 are integers.

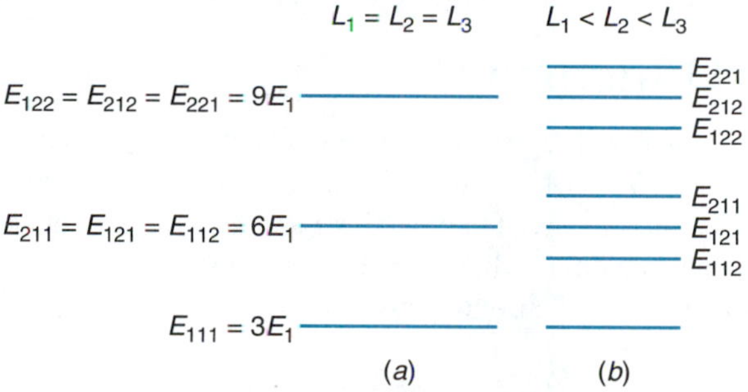

Fig. 7-1 Energy-level diagram for (*a*) cubic infinite square well potential and (*b*) noncubic infinite square well. In the cubic well, the energy levels above the ground state are threefold degenerate, i.e., there are three wave functions having the same energy. The degeneracy is removed when the symmetry of the potential is removed, as in (*b*). The diagram is only schematic and none of the levels in (*b*) necessarily has the same value of the energy as any level in (*a*).

Notice that the energy and wave function are characterized by three quantum numbers, each arising from a boundary condition on one of the coordinates. In this case the quantum numbers are independent of one another, but in more general problems the value of one quantum number may affect the possible values of the others. For example, as we shall see in a moment, in problems such as the hydrogen atom that have a spherical symmetry, the Schrödinger equation is most readily solved in spherical coordinates r, θ, and ϕ. The quantum numbers associated with the boundary conditions on these coordinates are interdependent.

The lowest energy state, the ground state for the cubical box, is given by Equation 7-4 with $n_1 = n_2 = n_3 = 1$. The first excited energy level can be obtained in three different ways: either $n_1 = 2$, $n_2 = n_3 = 1$ or $n_2 = 2$, $n_1 = n_3 = 1$ or $n_3 = 2$, $n_1 = n_2 = 1$, since we see from Equation 7-4 that $E_{211} = E_{121} = E_{112}$. Each has a different wave function. For example, the wave function for $n_1 = 2$ and $n_2 = n_3 = 1$ is of the form

$$\psi_{211} = A \sin \frac{2\pi x}{L} \sin \frac{\pi y}{L} \sin \frac{\pi z}{L}$$

An energy level that has more than one wave function associated with it is said to be *degenerate*. In this case there is threefold degeneracy, because there are three wave functions $\psi(x, y, z)$ corresponding to the same energy. The degeneracy is related to the symmetry of the problem, and anything that destroys or breaks the symmetry will also destroy or remove the degeneracy.[1] If, for example, we considered a noncubical box $V = 0$ for $0 < x < L_1$, $0 < y < L_2$, and $0 < z < L_3$, the boundary condition at the walls would lead to the quantum conditions $k_1 L_1 = n_1 \pi$, $k_2 L_2 = n_2 \pi$, and $k_3 L_3 = n_3 \pi$, and the total energy would be

$$E_{n_1 n_2 n_3} = \frac{\hbar^2 \pi^2}{2m} \left(\frac{n_1^2}{L_1^2} + \frac{n_2^2}{L_2^2} + \frac{n_3^2}{L_3^2} \right) \qquad \textbf{7-5}$$

Figure 7-1 shows the energy levels for the ground state and first two excited states when $L_1 = L_2 = L_3$, for which the excited states are degenerate, and when L_1, L_2, and L_3 are slightly different, in which case the excited levels are slightly split apart and the degeneracy is removed.

The Schrödinger Equation in Spherical Coordinates

We can treat the hydrogen atom as a single particle, an electron moving with kinetic energy $p^2/2m_e$ and a potential energy $V(r)$ due to the electrostatic attraction of the proton:

$$V(r) = -\frac{Zke^2}{r} \qquad \textbf{7-6}$$

As in the Bohr theory, we include the atomic number Z, which is 1 for hydrogen, so we can apply our results to other similar systems, such as ionized helium He^+, where $Z = 2$. We also note that we can account for the motion of the nucleus by replacing the electron mass m_e by the reduced mass $\mu = m_e/(1 + m_e/M_N)$, where M_N is the

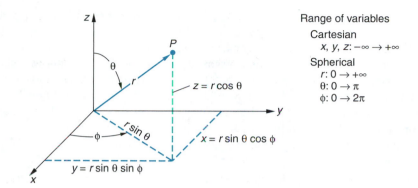

Fig. 7-2 Geometric relations between spherical and rectangular coordinates.

Range of variables

Cartesian
$x, y, z: -\infty \rightarrow +\infty$

Spherical
$r: 0 \rightarrow +\infty$
$\theta: 0 \rightarrow \pi$
$\phi: 0 \rightarrow 2\pi$

$z = r \cos \theta$

$x = r \sin \theta \cos \phi$

$y = r \sin \theta \sin \phi$

mass of the nucleus. The time-independent Schrödinger equation for a particle of mass μ moving in three dimensions is Equation 7-1, with m replaced by μ:

$$-\frac{\hbar^2}{2\mu}\left(\frac{\partial^2 \psi}{\partial x^2} + \frac{\partial^2 \psi}{\partial y^2} + \frac{\partial^2 \psi}{\partial z^2}\right) + V\psi = E\psi \qquad \textbf{7-7}$$

Since the potential energy $V(r)$ depends only on the radial distance $r = (x^2 + y^2 + z^2)^{1/2}$, the problem is most conveniently treated in spherical coordinates r, θ, and ϕ. These are related to x, y, and z by

$$z = r \cos \theta$$
$$x = r \sin \theta \cos \phi \qquad \textbf{7-8}$$
$$y = r \sin \theta \sin \phi$$

These relations are shown in Figure 7-2. The transformation of the three-dimensional Schrödinger equation into spherical coordinates is straightforward but involves much tedious calculation which we shall omit. The result is

$$-\frac{\hbar^2}{2\mu}\frac{1}{r^2}\frac{\partial}{\partial r}\left(r^2 \frac{\partial \psi}{\partial r}\right) - \frac{\hbar^2}{2\mu r^2}\left[\frac{1}{\sin \theta}\frac{\partial}{\partial \theta}\left(\sin \theta \frac{\partial \psi}{\partial \theta}\right)\right.$$
$$\left. + \frac{1}{\sin^2 \theta}\frac{\partial^2 \psi}{\partial \phi^2}\right] + V(r)\psi = E\psi \qquad \textbf{7-9}$$

Despite the formidable appearance of this equation, it was not difficult for Schrödinger to solve because it is similar to other partial differential equations that arise in classical physics, and such equations had been thoroughly studied. We shall present the solution of this equation in detail, taking care to point out the origin of the quantum number associated with each dimension.

7-2 Quantization of Angular Momentum and Energy in the Hydrogen Atom

In this section we shall solve the time-independent Schrödinger equation for hydrogen and hydrogenlike atoms. We shall see how the quantization of both the energy and the angular momentum arise as natural consequences of the acceptability

conditions on the wave function (see Section 6-1) and discover the origin and physical meaning of the quantum numbers n, l, and m.

The first step in the solution of a partial differential equation such as Equation 7-9 is to search for separable solutions by writing the wave function $\psi(r, \theta, \phi)$ as a product of functions of each single variable. We write

$$\psi(r, \theta, \phi) = R(r)\, f(\theta)\, g(\phi) \qquad \textbf{7-10}$$

where R depends only on the radial coordinate r, f depends only on θ, and g depends only on ϕ. When this form of $\psi(r, \theta, \phi)$ is substituted into Equation 7-9, the partial differential equation can be transformed into three ordinary differential equations, one for $R(r)$, one for $f(\theta)$, and one for $g(\phi)$. Most of the solutions of Equation 7-9 are, of course, not of this separable product form; however, if enough product solutions of the form of Equation 7-10 can be found,[2] all solutions can be expressed as superpositions of them. Even so, the separable solutions given by Equation 7-10 turn out to be the most important ones physically, because they correspond to definite values (*eigenvalues*) of energy and angular momentum. When Equation 7-10 is substituted into Equation 7-9 and the indicated differentiations are performed, we obtain

$$-\frac{\hbar^2}{2\mu} fg\, \frac{1}{r^2} \frac{d}{dr}\left(r^2 \frac{dR}{dr}\right) - \frac{\hbar^2}{2\mu r^2} Rg\, \frac{1}{\sin\theta} \frac{d}{d\theta}\left(\sin\theta\, \frac{df}{d\theta}\right)$$
$$-\frac{\hbar^2}{2\mu r^2} \frac{Rf}{\sin^2\theta} \frac{d^2 g}{d\phi^2} + VRfg = ERfg \qquad \textbf{7-11}$$

since derivatives with respect to r do not affect $f(\theta)$ and $g(\phi)$, derivatives with respect to θ do not affect $R(r)$ and $g(\phi)$, and those with respect to ϕ do not affect $R(r)$ and $f(\theta)$. Separation of the r-dependent functions from the θ- and ϕ-dependent ones is accomplished by multiplying Equation 7-11 by $-2\mu r^2/(\hbar^2 Rfg)$ and rearranging slightly to obtain

$$\frac{1}{R(r)} \frac{d}{dr}\left(r^2 \frac{dR(r)}{dr}\right) + \frac{2\mu r^2}{\hbar^2}[E - V(r)] =$$
$$-\left[\frac{1}{f(\theta)\sin\theta} \frac{d}{d\theta}\left(\sin\theta\, \frac{df(\theta)}{d\theta}\right) + \frac{1}{g(\phi)\sin^2\theta} \frac{d^2 g(\phi)}{d\phi^2}\right] \qquad \textbf{7-12}$$

Note two points about Equation 7-12: (1) The left side contains only terms that are functions of r, while the right side has only terms depending on θ and ϕ. Since the variables are independent, changes in r cannot change the value of the right side of the equation, nor can changes in θ and ϕ have any effect on the left side. Thus, the two sides of the equation must be equal to the same constant, which we will call, with foresight, $l(l + 1)$. (2) The potential is a function only of r, so the solution of the right side, the angular part, of Equation 7-12 will be the same for *all* potentials that are only functions[3] of r.

In view of the second point above, we will first solve the angular equation, so that its results will be available to us as we consider solutions to the r-dependent equation, referred to usually as the *radial equation*, for various $V(r)$. Setting the right side of Equation 7-12 equal to $l(l + 1)$, multiplying by $\sin^2\theta$, and rearranging slightly, we obtain

Hydrogenlike atoms, those with a single electron, have been produced from elements up to and including U^{91+}. Highly ionized atomic beams are used to further our understanding of relativistic effects and atomic structure. Collision of two completely ionized Au atoms moving at nearly the speed of light produced the "star" of thousands of particles reproduced on the cover of this book.

$$\frac{1}{g(\phi)}\frac{d^2 g(\phi)}{d\phi^2} = -l(l+1)\sin^2\theta - \frac{\sin\theta}{f(\theta)}\frac{d}{d\theta}\left[\sin\theta\,\frac{df(\theta)}{d\theta}\right] \qquad \textbf{7-13}$$

Once again we see that the two sides of the relation, Equation 7-13, are each a function of only one of the independent variables; hence both sides must be equal to the same constant, which we will, again with foresight, call $-m^2$. Setting the left side of Equation 7-13 equal to $-m^2$ and solving for $g(\phi)$ yield

$$g_m(\phi) = e^{im\phi} \qquad \textbf{7-14}$$

The single-valued condition on ψ implies that $g(\phi + 2\pi) = g(\phi)$, which in turn requires that m be a positive or negative integer or zero.

Now letting the right side of Equation 7-13 equal $-m^2$ and solving for $f(\theta)$, we obtain (not intended to be obvious)

$$f_{lm}(\theta) = \frac{(\sin\theta)^{|m|}}{2^l l!}\left[\frac{d}{d(\cos\theta)}\right]^{l+|m|}(\cos^2\theta - 1)^l \qquad \textbf{7-15}$$

TABLE 7-1 Spherical harmonics

$l = 0$	$m = 0$	$Y_{00} = \sqrt{\dfrac{1}{4\pi}}$
$l = 1$	$m = 1$	$Y_{11} = -\sqrt{\dfrac{3}{8\pi}}\sin\theta\,e^{i\phi}$
	$m = 0$	$Y_{10} = \sqrt{\dfrac{3}{4\pi}}\cos\theta$
	$m = -1$	$Y_{1-1} = \sqrt{\dfrac{3}{8\pi}}\sin\theta\,e^{-i\phi}$
$l = 2$	$m = 2$	$Y_{22} = \sqrt{\dfrac{15}{32\pi}}\sin^2\theta\,e^{2i\phi}$
	$m = 1$	$Y_{21} = -\sqrt{\dfrac{15}{8\pi}}\sin\theta\cos\theta\,e^{i\phi}$
	$m = 0$	$Y_{20} = \sqrt{\dfrac{5}{16\pi}}(3\cos^2\theta - 1)$
	$m = -1$	$Y_{2-1} = \sqrt{\dfrac{15}{8\pi}}\sin\theta\cos\theta\,e^{-i\phi}$
	$m = -2$	$Y_{2-2} = \sqrt{\dfrac{15}{32\pi}}\sin^2\theta\,e^{-2i\phi}$

Note: A 3-D color representation of the spherical harmonics is on the Internet at http://ww3.uniovi.es/~quimica.fisica/qeg/harmonics/charmonics.html

where
$$l = 0, 1, 2, 3, \ldots$$
$$m = 0, \pm1, \pm2, \ldots, \pm l$$

The condition that $f(\theta)$ be finite at $\theta = 0$ and $\theta = \pi$ restricts the values of l to zero and positive integers and limits $m \leq l$. The notation reflects the link between l and m, namely, that each value of l has associated values of m ranging up to $\pm l$. The functions $f_{lm}(\theta)$, given by Equation 7-15, are called the *associated Legendre functions*. The subset of those with $m = 0$ is referred to as the *Legendre polynomials*.

The product of $f_{lm}(\theta)$ and $g_m(\phi)$, which describes the angular dependence of $\psi(r, \theta, \phi)$ for *all* spherically symmetric potentials, forms an often encountered family of functions $Y_{lm}(\theta, \phi)$,

$$Y_{lm}(\theta, \phi) = f_{lm}(\theta)g_m(\phi) \qquad \textbf{7-16}$$

called the *spherical harmonics*. The first few of these functions, which give the combined angular dependence of the motion of the electron in the hydrogen atom, are given in Table 7-1. The associated Legendre functions and the Legendre polynomials ($m = 0$) can, if needed, be easily taken from the same table.

Quantization of the Angular Momentum

The definition of the angular momentum **L** of a mass m moving with velocity **v**, hence momentum **p**, at some location **r** relative to the origin, given in most introductory physics textbooks, is

$$\mathbf{L} = \mathbf{r} \times \mathbf{p}$$

where the momentum $\mathbf{p} = m(d\mathbf{r}/dt)$. In cases where $V = V(r)$, such as the electron in the hydrogen atom, **L** is conserved (see Problem 7-15) and the classical motion of the mass m lies in a fixed plane perpendicular to **L**, which contains the coordinate origin. The momentum **p** has components (in that plane) $\mathbf{p}_r$ along **r** and $\mathbf{p}_t$ perpendicular to **r**, as illustrated in Figure 7-3, whose magnitudes are given by

$$p_r = \mu\left(\frac{dr}{dt}\right) \qquad \text{and} \qquad p_t = \mu r\left(\frac{dA}{dt}\right)$$

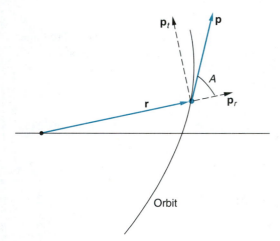

Fig. 7-3 The orbit of a classical particle with $V = V(r)$ lies in a plane perpendicular to **L**. The components of the momentum **p** parallel and perpendicular to **r** are $\mathbf{p}_r$ and $\mathbf{p}_t$, respectively. The momentum **p** makes an angle A with the displacement **r**.

and the magnitude of the conserved (i.e., constant) vector $\mathbf{L}$ is

$$L = rp \sin A = rp_t$$

The kinetic energy can be written in terms of these components as

$$\frac{p^2}{2\mu} = \frac{p_r^2 + p_t^2}{2\mu} = \frac{p_r^2}{2\mu} + \frac{L^2}{2\mu r^2}$$

from which the classical total energy E is given by

$$\frac{p_r^2}{2\mu} + \frac{L^2}{2\mu r^2} + V(r) = E \qquad \textbf{7-17}$$

Rewriting Equation 7-17 in terms of the "effective" potential $V_{\text{eff}}(r) = L^2/2\mu r^2 + V(r)$, as is often done, we obtain

$$\frac{p_r^2}{2\mu} + V_{\text{eff}}(r) = E \qquad \textbf{7-18}$$

which is identical in form to Equation 6-4, which we used as a basis for our introduction to the Schrödinger equation.

Equation 7-17 can be used to write the Schrödinger equation, just as we did in Chapter 6 by inserting de Broglie's relation and the appropriate differential operators in spherical coordinates for p_r^2 and L^2. Doing so is a lengthy though not particularly difficult exercise whose details we will omit here. For p_r^2 the operator turns out to be

$$(p_r^2)_{\text{op}} = -\hbar^2 \frac{1}{r^2} \frac{\partial}{\partial r}\left(r^2 \frac{\partial}{\partial r}\right) \qquad \textbf{7-19}$$

which, divided by 2μ and operating on ψ, you recognize as the first term of the Schrödinger equation in spherical coordinates (Equation 7-9). Similarly, the operator for L^2 turns out to be

$$(L^2)_{\text{op}} = -\hbar^2 \left[\frac{1}{\sin\theta} \frac{\partial}{\partial\theta}\left(\sin\theta \frac{\partial}{\partial\theta}\right) + \frac{1}{\sin^2\theta} \frac{\partial^2}{\partial\phi^2}\right] \qquad \textbf{7-20}$$

which, divided by $2\mu r^2$ and operating on ψ, is the second term of the Schrödinger equation in spherical coordinates (Equation 7-9). The right side of Equation 7-12, which equals $l(l + 1)$, can now be written as follows when multiplied by $\hbar^2 f(\theta)g(\phi)$, remembering that $f_{lm}(\theta)g_m(\phi) = Y_{lm}(\theta, \phi)$:

$$-\hbar^2\left[\frac{1}{\sin\theta} \frac{\partial}{\partial\theta}\left(\sin\theta \frac{\partial}{\partial\theta}\right) + \frac{1}{\sin^2\theta} \frac{\partial^2}{\partial\phi^2}\right]Y_{lm}(\theta, \phi) = l(l + 1)\hbar^2 Y_{lm}(\theta, \phi) \qquad \textbf{7-21}a$$

or

$$(L^2)_{\text{op}}Y_{lm}(\theta, \phi) = l(l + 1)\hbar^2 Y_{lm}(\theta, \phi) \qquad \textbf{7-21}b$$

or, since $\psi(r, \theta, \phi) = R(r) Y(\theta, \phi)$,

$$(L^2)_{op}\psi(r, \theta, \phi) = l(l + 1)\hbar^2\psi(r, \theta, \phi) \qquad \textbf{7-21c}$$

Thus, we have the very important result that, for all potentials where $V = V(r)$, the angular momentum is quantized and its allowed magnitudes (eigenvalues) are given by

$$|\mathbf{L}| = \sqrt{l(l + 1)}\hbar \qquad \text{for} \qquad l = 0, 1, 2, 3, \ldots \qquad \textbf{7-22}$$

where l is referred to as the *angular momentum quantum number* or the *orbital quantum number.*

In addition, if we use the same substitution method on L_z, the z component of $\mathbf{L}$, it can be shown that the z component of the angular momentum is also quantized and its allowed values are given by

$$L_z = m\hbar \qquad \text{for} \qquad m = 0, \pm 1, \pm 2, \ldots, \pm l \qquad \textbf{7-23}$$

The physical significance of Equation 7-23 is that the angular momentum $\mathbf{L}$, whose magnitude is quantized with values $\sqrt{l(l + 1)}\hbar$, can only point in those directions *in space* such that the projection of $\mathbf{L}$ on the z axis is one or another of the values given by $m\hbar$. Thus $\mathbf{L}$ is also *space-quantized.* The quantum number m is referred to as the *magnetic quantum number.*

Figure 7-4 shows a diagram, called the *vector model* of the atom, illustrating the possible orientations of the angular momentum vector. Note the perhaps unexpected result that the angular momentum vector never points in the z direction, since the maximum z component $m\hbar$ is always less than the magnitude $\sqrt{l(l + 1)}\hbar$. This is a consequence of the uncertainty principle for angular momentum (which we shall not derive) that implies that no two components of angular momentum can be precisely known simultaneously,[4] except in the case of zero angular momentum. It is worth noting that for a given value of l there are $2l + 1$ possible values of m, ranging from $-l$ to $+l$ in integral steps. Operators for L_x and L_y can also be obtained by the substitution method; however, operating with them on ψ does not produce eigenvalues. This is mainly because specifying rotation about the x and y axes requires measurement of both θ and ϕ.

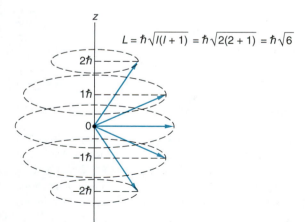

$$L = \hbar\sqrt{l(l + 1)} = \hbar\sqrt{2(2 + 1)} = \hbar\sqrt{6}$$

Fig. 7-4 Vector model illustrating the possible orientations of $\mathbf{L}$ in space and the possible values of L_z for the case where $l = 2$.

EXAMPLE 7-1 Quantized Values of L If a system has angular momentum characterized by the quantum number $l = 2$, what are the possible values of L_z, what is the magnitude L, and what is the smallest possible angle between **L** and the z axis?

Solution

1. The possible values of L_z are given by Equation 7-23:

$$L_z = m\hbar$$

2. The values of m for $l = 2$ are:

$$m = 0, \pm 1, \pm 2$$

3. Thus, allowed values of L_z are:

$$L_z = -2\hbar, -1\hbar, 0, \hbar, 2\hbar$$

4. The magnitude of **L** is given by Equation 7-22. For $l = 2$:

$$|\mathbf{L}| = \sqrt{l(l + 1)}\,\hbar$$
$$= \sqrt{6}\hbar = 2.45\hbar$$

5. From Figure 7-4 the angle θ between **L** and the z axis is given by:

$$\cos\theta = \frac{L_z}{L} = \frac{m\hbar}{\sqrt{l(l + 1)}\,\hbar}$$

$$= \frac{m}{\sqrt{l(l + 1)}}$$

6. The smallest possible angle θ between **L** and the z axis is that for $m = \pm l$, which for $l = 2$ gives:

$$\cos\theta = \frac{2}{\sqrt{6}} = 0.816$$

or

$$\theta = 35.3°$$

Quantization of the Energy

The results discussed so far apply to any system that is spherically symmetric, that is, one for which the potential energy depends on r only. The solution of the radial equation for $R(r)$, on the other hand, depends on the detailed form of $V(r)$. The new quantum number associated with the coordinate r is called the *principal quantum number n*. This quantum number, as we shall see, is related to the energy in the hydrogen atom. Figure 7-5 shows a sketch of the potential energy function of

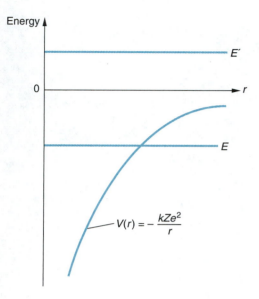

Energy

0

E'

r

E

$V(r) = -\dfrac{kZe^2}{r}$

Fig. 7-5 Potential energy of an electron in a hydrogen atom. If the total energy is greater than zero, as E', the electron is not bound and the energy is not quantized. If the total energy is less than zero, as E, the electron is bound. Then, as in one-dimensional problems, only certain discrete values of the total energy lead to well-behaved wave functions.

Equation 7-6. If the total energy is positive, the electron is not bound to the atom. We are interested here only in bound-state solutions, for which E is negative. For this case, the potential energy function becomes greater than E for large r, as shown in the figure. As we have discussed previously, for bound systems only certain values of the energy E lead to well-behaved solutions. These values are found by solving the radial equation, which is formed by equating the left side of Equation 7-12 to the constant $l(l + 1)$. For $V(r)$ of the hydrogen atom, given by Equation 7-6, the radial equation is

$$\frac{-\hbar^2}{2\mu r^2} \frac{d}{dr}\left(r^2 \frac{dR(r)}{dr}\right) + \left[-\frac{kZe^2}{r} + \frac{\hbar^2 l(l + 1)}{2\mu r^2}\right]R(r) = ER(r) \qquad \textbf{7-24}$$

The radial equation can be solved using standard methods of differential equations whose details we will omit here, except to note that (1) we expect a link to appear between the principal quantum number n and the angular momentum quantum number l (since the latter already appears in Equation 7-24) and (2) in order that the solutions of Equation 7-24 be well behaved, only certain values of the energy are allowed, just as we discovered for the square well and the harmonic oscillator. The allowed values of E are given by

$$E_n = -\left(\frac{kZe^2}{\hbar}\right)^2 \frac{\mu}{2n^2} = -\frac{Z^2 E_1}{n^2} \qquad \textbf{7-25}$$

where $E_1 = \frac{1}{2}(ke^2/\hbar)^2\mu \approx 13.6$ eV and the principal quantum number n can take on the values $n = 1, 2, 3, \ldots$, with the further restriction that n must be greater than l. These energy values are identical with those found from the Bohr model. The radial functions resulting from the solution of Equation 7-24 for hydrogen are given by Equation 7-26 where the $\mathcal{L}_{nl}(r/a_0)$ are standard functions called Laguerre polynomials:

$$R_{nl}(r) = A_{nl0}e^{-r/a_0 n}r^l \mathcal{L}_{nl}\left(\frac{r}{a_0}\right) \qquad \textbf{7-26}$$

TABLE 7-2 Radial functions for hydrogen

$n = 1$ $l = 0$ $R_{10} = \dfrac{2}{\sqrt{a_0^3}} e^{-r/a_0}$

$n = 2$ $l = 0$ $R_{20} = \dfrac{1}{\sqrt{2a_0^3}}\left(1 - \dfrac{r}{2a_0}\right)e^{-r/2a_0}$

$l = 1$ $R_{21} = \dfrac{1}{2\sqrt{6a_0^3}}\dfrac{r}{a_0}e^{-r/2a_0}$

$n = 3$ $l = 0$ $R_{30} = \dfrac{2}{3\sqrt{3a_0^3}}\left(1 - \dfrac{2r}{3a_0} + \dfrac{2r^2}{27a_0^2}\right)e^{-r/3a_0}$

$l = 1$ $R_{31} = \dfrac{8}{27\sqrt{6a_0^3}}\dfrac{r}{a_0}\left(1 - \dfrac{r}{6a_0}\right)e^{-r/3a_0}$

$l = 2$ $R_{32} = \dfrac{4}{8\sqrt{30a_0^3}}\dfrac{r^2}{a_0^2}e^{-r/3a_0}$

and the Bohr radius $a_0 = \hbar^2/(ke^2\mu)$. The radial functions $R_{nl}(r)$ for $n = 1, 2,$ and 3 are given in Table 7-2.

Summary of the Quantum Numbers

The allowed values of and restrictions on the quantum numbers n, l, and m associated with the variables r, θ, and ϕ are summarized as follows:

$$n = 1, 2, 3, \ldots$$
$$l = 0, 1, 2, \ldots, (n - 1)$$
$$m = -l, (-l + 1), \ldots, 0, 1, 2, \ldots, +l$$

7-27

The fact that the energy of the hydrogen atom depends only on the principal quantum number n and not on l is a peculiarity of the inverse-square force. It is related to the result in classical mechanics that the energy of a mass moving in an elliptical orbit in an inverse-square force field depends only on the major axis of the orbit and not on the eccentricity. The largest value of angular momentum ($l = n - 1$) corresponds most nearly to a circular orbit, whereas a small value of l corresponds to a highly eccentric orbit. (Zero angular momentum corresponds to oscillation along a line through the force center.) For central forces that do not obey an inverse-square law, the energy does depend on the angular momentum (both classically and quantum mechanically), so it depends on both n and l.

The quantum number m is related to the z component of angular momentum. Since there is no preferred direction for the z axis for any central force, the energy cannot depend on m. We shall see later that if we place an atom in an external magnetic field, there is a preferred direction in space and the energy then does depend on the value of m. (This effect, called the Zeeman effect, is discussed in a More section on the Web site. See page 327.)

Figure 7-6 shows an energy-level diagram for hydrogen. This diagram is similar to Figure 4-16*a* except that states with the same n but different l are shown separately.

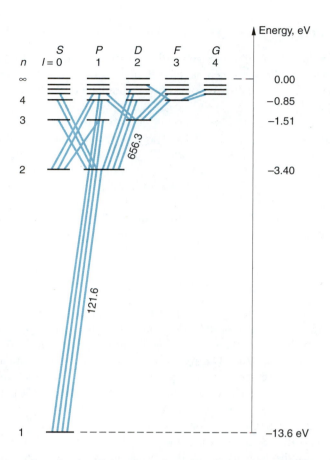

Fig. 7-6 Energy-level diagram for the hydrogen atom, showing transitions obeying the selection rule $\Delta l = \pm 1$. States with the same n value but different l value have the same energy, $-E_1/n^2$, where $E_1 = 13.6$ eV, as in the Bohr theory. The wavelengths of the Lyman α ($n = 2 \rightarrow n = 1$) and Balmer α ($n = 3 \rightarrow n = 2$) lines are shown in nm. Note that the latter has two possible transitions due to the l degeneracy.

These states are referred to by giving the value of n, along with a code letter: S standing for $l = 0$, P for $l = 1$, D for $l = 2$, and F for $l = 3$. These code letters are remnants of the spectroscopist's descriptions of various series of spectral lines as *S*harp, *P*rincipal, *D*iffuse, and *F*undamental. (For values of l greater than 3 the letters follow alphabetically; thus G for $l = 4$, etc.) The allowed electric dipole transitions between energy levels obey the selection rules

$$\Delta m = 0 \quad \text{or} \quad \pm 1$$
$$\Delta l = \pm 1$$

7-28

The fact that the quantum number l of the atom must change by ± 1 when the atom emits or absorbs a photon is related to conservation of angular momentum and the fact that the photon itself has an intrinsic angular momentum which has a maximum component along any axis of $1\hbar$. For the principal quantum number, Δn is unrestricted.

QUESTIONS

1. Why wasn't quantization of angular momentum noticed in classical physics?

2. What are the similarities and differences between the quantization of angular momentum in the Schrödinger theory and in the Bohr model?

3. Why doesn't the energy of the hydrogen atom depend on l? Why doesn't it depend on m?

7-3 Hydrogen Atom Wave Functions

The wave functions $\psi_{nlm}(r, \theta, \phi)$ satisfying the Schrödinger equation for the hydrogen atom are rather complicated functions of r, θ, and ϕ. In this section we shall write some of these functions and display some of their more important features graphically.

As we have seen, the ϕ dependence of the wave function, given by Equation 7-14, is simply $e^{im\phi}$. The θ dependence is described by the associated Legendre functions $f_{lm}(\theta)$ given by Equation 7-15. The complete angular dependence is then given by the spherical harmonic functions $Y_{lm}(\theta, \phi)$, the product of $g_m(\phi)$ and $f_{lm}(\theta)$ as indicated by Equation 7-16 and, for the first few, tabulated in Table 7-1. The solutions to the radial equation $R_{nl}(r)$ are of the form indicated by Equation 7-26 and are listed in Table 7-2 for the three lowest values of the principal quantum number n. Referring to Equation 7-10, our assumed product solutions of the time-independent Schrödinger equation, we have that the complete wave function of the hydrogen atom is

$$\psi_{nlm}(r, \theta, \phi) = C_{nlm}R_{nl}(r)f_{lm}(\theta)g_m(\phi) \qquad \textbf{7-29}$$

where C_{nlm} is a constant determined by the normalization condition.

We see from the form of this expression that the complete wave function depends on the quantum numbers n, l, and m that arose because of the boundary conditions on $R(r)$, $f(\theta)$, and $g(\phi)$. The energy, however, depends only on the value of n. From Equation 7-27 we see that for any value of n there are n possible values of l ($l = 0, 1, 2, \ldots, n - 1$); and for each value of l there are $2l + 1$ possible values of m ($m = -l, -l + 1, \ldots, +l$). Except for the lowest energy level (for which $n = 1$, and therefore l and m can only be zero) there are generally many different wave functions corresponding to the same energy. As discussed in the previous section, the origins of this degeneracy are the $1/r$ dependence of the potential energy and the fact that there is no preferred direction in space.

The Ground State

Let us examine the wave functions for several particular states beginning with the lowest-energy level, the ground state, which has $n = 1$. Then l and m must both be zero. The Laguerre polynomial $\mathscr{L}_{10}$ in Equation 7-26 is equal to 1, and the wave function is

$$\psi_{100} = C_{100}e^{-Zr/a_0} \qquad \textbf{7-30}$$

The constant C_{100} is determined by normalization:

$$\int \psi^*\psi \, d\tau = \int_0^\infty \int_0^\pi \int_0^{2\pi} \psi^*\psi r^2 \sin\theta \, d\phi \, d\theta \, dr = 1$$

using for the volume element in spherical coordinates (see Figure 7-7)

$$d\tau = (r \sin\theta \, d\phi)(r \, d\theta)(dr)$$

Because $\psi^*\psi$ is spherically symmetric for this state, the integration over angles gives 4π. Carrying out the integration over r gives[5]

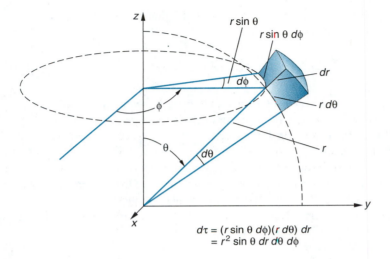

Fig. 7-7 Volume element $d\tau$ in spherical coordinates.

$$d\tau = (r\sin\theta\, d\phi)(r\, d\theta)\, dr$$
$$= r^2 \sin\theta\, dr\, d\theta\, d\phi$$

$$C_{100} = \frac{1}{\sqrt{\pi}}\left(\frac{Z}{a_0}\right)^{3/2} = \frac{1}{\sqrt{\pi}}\left(\frac{1}{a_0}\right)^{3/2} \qquad \text{for} \qquad Z = 1 \qquad \textbf{7-31}$$

The probability of finding the electron in the volume $d\tau$ is $\psi^*\psi\, d\tau$.

The probability density $\psi^*\psi$ is illustrated in Figure 7-8. The probability density for the ground state is maximum at the origin. It is often more interesting to determine the probability of finding the electron in a spherical shell between r and $r + dr$.

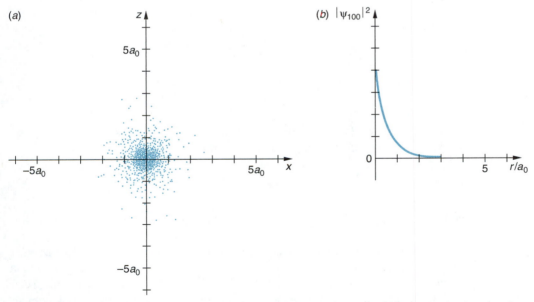

Fig. 7-8 Probability density $\psi^*\psi$ for the ground state in hydrogen. The quantity $e\psi^*\psi$ can be thought of as the electron charge density in the atom. (*a*) The density is spherically symmetric, is greatest at the origin, and decreases exponentially with r. This computer-generated plot was made by making hundreds of "searches" for the hydrogen electron in the *x-z* plane (i.e., for $\phi = 0$), recording each finding with a dot. (*b*) The more conventional graph of the probability density $|\psi_{100}|^2$ vs. r/a_0. Compare the two graphs carefully. [*This computer-generated plot courtesy of Paul Doherty, The Exploratorium.*]

This probability, $P(r) \, dr$, is just the probability density $\psi^*\psi$ times the volume of the spherical shell of thickness dr:

$$P(r) \, dr = \psi^*\psi 4\pi r^2 \, dr = 4\pi r^2 C_{100}^2 e^{-2Zr/a_0} \, dr \qquad \textbf{7-32}$$

The angular dependence of the electron probability distributions is critical to our understanding of the bonding of atoms into molecules and solids (see Chapters 9 and 10).

Figure 7-9 shows a sketch of $P(r)$ versus r/a_0. It is left as a problem (see Problem 7-21) to show that $P(r)$ has its maximum value at $r = a_0/Z$. In contrast to the Bohr model for hydrogen, in which the electron stays in a well-defined orbit at $r = a_0$, we see that it is *possible* for the electron to be found at any distance from the nucleus. However, the most probable distance is a_0, and the chance of finding the electron at a much different distance is small. It is useful to think of the electron as a charged cloud of charge density $\rho = e\psi^*\psi$. (We must remember, though, that the electron is always *observed* as one charge.) Note that the angular momentum in the ground state is zero, contrary to the Bohr model assumption of $1\hbar$.

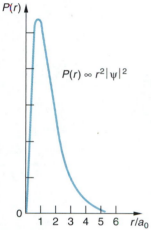

$P(r) \propto r^2|\psi|^2$

Fig. 7-9 Radial probability density $P(r)$ vs. r/a_0 for the ground state of the hydrogen atom. $P(r)$ is proportional to $r^2|\psi_{100}|^2$. The most probable distance r is the Bohr radius a_0.

The Excited States

In the first excited state, $n = 2$ and l can be either 0 or 1. For $l = 0$, $m = 0$; and again we have a spherically symmetric wave function, given by

$$\psi_{200} = C_{200}\left(2 - \frac{Zr}{a_0}\right)e^{-Zr/2a_0} \qquad \textbf{7-33}$$

For $l = 1$, m can be $+1$, 0, or -1. The corresponding wave functions are (see Tables 7-1 and 7-2)

$$\psi_{210} = C_{210}\frac{Zr}{a_0}e^{-Zr/2a_0}\cos\theta \qquad \textbf{7-34}$$

$$\psi_{21\pm1} = C_{21\pm1}\frac{Zr}{a_0}e^{-Zr/2a_0}\sin\theta \, e^{\pm i\phi} \qquad \textbf{7-35}$$

Figure 7-10a shows $P(r)$ for these wave functions. The distribution for $n = 2$, $l = 1$ is maximum at the radius of the second Bohr orbit,

$$r_{max} = 2^2 a_0$$

while for $n = 2$ and $l = 0$, $P(r)$ has two maxima, the larger of which is near this radius.

Radial probability distributions can be obtained in the same way for the other excited states of hydrogen. For example, those for the second excited state $n = 3$ are shown in Figure 7-10b. The main radial dependence of $P(r)$ is contained in the factor e^{-Zr/na_0}, except near the origin. A detailed examination of the Laguerre polynomials shows that $\psi \to r^l$ as $r \to 0$. Thus, for a given n, ψ_{nlm} is greatest near the origin when l is small.

An important feature of these wave functions is that for $l = 0$, the probability densities are spherically symmetric, whereas for $l \neq 0$ they depend on the angle θ. The probability density plots of Figure 7-11 illustrate this result for the first excited state $n = 2$. These angular distributions of the electron charge density depend only on the

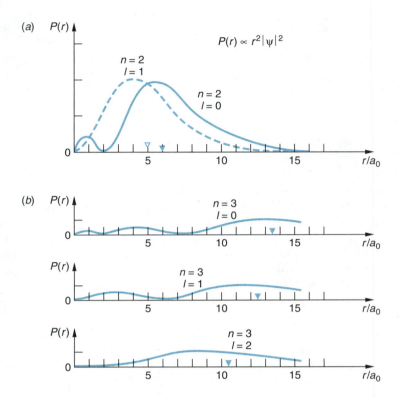

Fig. 7-10 (*a*) Radial probability density $P(r)$ vs. r/a_0 for the $n = 2$ states in hydrogen. $P(r)$ for $l = 1$ has a maximum at the Bohr value $2^2 a_0$. For $l = 0$ there is a maximum near this value and a smaller submaximum near the origin. The markers on the r/a_0 axis denote the values of $\langle r/a_0 \rangle$. (*b*) $P(r)$ vs. r/a_0 for the $n = 3$ states in hydrogen.

value of l and not on the radial part of the wave function. Similar charge distributions for the valence electrons in more complicated atoms play an important role in the chemistry of molecular bonding.

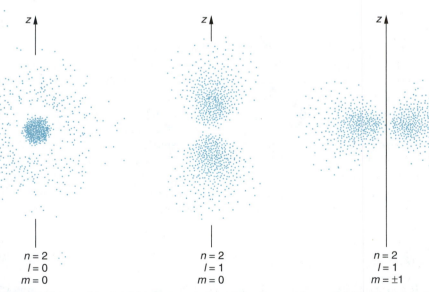

Fig. 7-11 Probability densities $\psi^*\psi$ for the $n = 2$ states in hydrogen. The probability is spherically symmetric for $l = 0$. It is proportional to $\cos^2\theta$ for $l = 1$, $m = 0$, and to $\sin^2$ for $l = 1$, $m = \pm1$. The probability densities have rotational symmetry about the z axis. Thus, the three-dimensional charge density for the $l = 1$, $m = 0$ state is shaped roughly like a dumbbell, while that for the $l = 1$, $m = \pm1$ states resembles a doughnut, or toroid. The shapes of these distributions are typical for all atoms in S states ($l = 0$) and P states ($l = 1$) and play an important role in molecular bonding. [*This computer-generated plot courtesy of Paul Doherty, The Exploratorium.*]

4. At what value of r is $\psi^{*}\psi$ maximum for the ground state of hydrogen? Why is $P(r)$ maximum at a different value of r?

7-4 Electron Spin

As was mentioned in Chapter 4, when a spectral line of hydrogen or other atoms is viewed with high resolution it shows a *fine structure;* that is, it is seen to consist of two or more closely spaced lines. As we noted then, Sommerfeld's relativistic calculation based on the Bohr model agrees with the experimental measurements of this fine structure for hydrogen, but the agreement turned out to be accidental, since his calculation predicts fewer lines than are seen for other atoms. In order to explain fine structure and to clear up a major difficulty with the quantum-mechanical explanation of the periodic table (Section 7-6), W. Pauli[6] in 1925 suggested that in addition to the quantum numbers n, l, and m the electron has a fourth quantum number, which could take on just two values.

As we have seen, quantum numbers arise from boundary conditions on some coordinate. Pauli originally expected that the fourth quantum number would be associated with the time coordinate in a relativistic theory, but this idea was not pursued. In the same year, S. Goudsmit and G. Uhlenbeck,[7] graduate students at Leiden, suggested that this fourth quantum number was the z component, m_s, of an intrinsic angular momentum of the electron, called *spin.* They represented the spin vector $\mathbf{S}$ with the same form that Schrödinger's wave mechanics gave for $\mathbf{L}$:

$$|\mathbf{S}| = \sqrt{s(s + 1)}\hbar \qquad\qquad 7\text{-}36$$

Since this intrinsic spin angular momentum is described by a quantum number s like the orbital angular momentum quantum number l, we expect $2s + 1$ possible values of the z component just as there are $2l + 1$ possible z components of the orbital angular momentum. If m_s is to have only two values as Pauli had suggested, then s could only be $\frac{1}{2}$ and m_s only $\pm\frac{1}{2}$. In addition to explaining fine structure and the periodic table, this proposal of electron spin explained the unexpected results of an interesting experiment that had been performed by O. Stern and W. Gerlach in 1922 which is described briefly in an Exploring section later on (see pages 311–313). To understand why the electron spin results in the splitting of the energy levels needed to account for the fine structure, we must consider the connection between the angular momentum and the magnetic moment of any charged particle system.

Magnetic Moment

If a system of charged particles is rotating, it has a *magnetic moment* proportional to its angular momentum. This result is sometimes known as the *Larmor theorem.* Consider a particle of mass M and charge q moving in a circle of radius r with speed v and frequency $f = v/2\pi r$. The angular momentum of the particle is $L = Mvr$. The magnetic moment of a current loop is the product of the current and the area of the loop. For a circulating charge, the current is the charge times the frequency,

$$i = qf = \frac{qv}{2\pi r} \qquad \textbf{7-37}$$

and the magnetic moment μ is[8]

$$\mu = iA = q\left(\frac{v}{2\pi r}\right)(\pi r^2) = \frac{1}{2}qvr = \frac{1}{2}q\left(\frac{L}{M}\right) \qquad \textbf{7-38}$$

From Figure 7-12 we see that, if q is positive, the magnetic moment is in the same direction as the angular momentum. If q is negative, μ and $\mathbf{L}$ point in opposite directions, i.e., are antiparallel. This enables us to write Equation 7-38 as a vector equation:

$$\mu = \frac{q}{2M}\mathbf{L} \qquad \textbf{7-39}$$

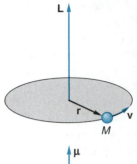

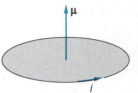

Fig. 7-12 A particle moving in a circle has angular momentum $\mathbf{L}$. If the particle has a positive charge, the magnetic moment due to the current is parallel to $\mathbf{L}$.

Equation 7-39, which we have derived for a single particle moving in a circle, also holds for a system of particles in any type of motion if the charge-to-mass ratio q/M is the same for each particle in the system.

Applying this result to the *orbital* motion of the electron in the hydrogen atom and substituting the magnitude of $\mathbf{L}$ from Equation 7-22, we have for the magnitude of μ

$$\mu = \frac{e}{2m_e}L = \frac{e\hbar}{2m_e}\sqrt{l(l+1)} = \sqrt{l(l+1)}\mu_B \qquad \textbf{7-40}$$

and, from Equation 7-23, a z component of

$$\mu_z = -\frac{e\hbar}{2m_e}m = -m\mu_B \qquad \textbf{7-41}$$

where m_e is the mass of the electron, $m\hbar$ is the z component of the angular momentum, and μ_B is a natural unit of magnetic moment called a *Bohr magneton*, which has the value

$$\mu_B = \frac{e\hbar}{2m_e} = 9.27 \times 10^{-24} \text{ joule/tesla}$$
$$= 5.79 \times 10^{-9} \text{ eV/gauss} = 5.79 \times 10^{-5} \text{ eV/tesla} \qquad \textbf{7-42}$$

The proportionality between μ and $\mathbf{L}$ is a general property of rotating charge distributions; however, the particular relation expressed by Equation 7-39 is for a single charge q rotating in a circle. To allow the same mathematical form to be used for other, more complicated situations, it is customary to express the magnetic moment in terms of μ_B and a dimensionless quantity g called the *gyromagnetic ratio*, or simply the *g factor*, where the value of g is determined by the details of the charge distribution. In the case of the orbital angular momentum $\mathbf{L}$ of the electron, $g_L = 1$ and Equation 7-39 would be written

$$\mu = \frac{-g_L\mu_B\mathbf{L}}{\hbar} \qquad \textbf{7-43}$$

The orbital motion and spin of the electrons are the origin of magnetism in metals, such as iron, cobalt, and nickel (see Chapter 10). Devices ranging from giant electricity transformers to decorative refrigerator magnets rely on these quantum properties of electrons.

and Equations 7-40 and 7-41 as

$$\mu = \sqrt{l(l+1)}\, g_L\mu_B \qquad \text{7-44}$$

$$\mu_z = -mg_L\mu_B \qquad \text{7-45}$$

There are minus signs in Equations 7-43 and 7-45 because the electron has a negative charge. The magnetic moment and the angular momentum vectors associated with the orbital motion are therefore oppositely directed, and we see that <u>quantization of angular momentum implies quantization of magnetic moments.</u> Other magnetic moments and *g* factors that we will encounter will have the same form.

Finally, the behavior of a system with a magnetic moment in a magnetic field can be visualized by considering a small bar magnet (Figure 7-13). When placed in an external magnetic field **B** there is a torque $\boldsymbol{\tau} = \boldsymbol{\mu} \times \mathbf{B}$ that tends to align the magnet with the field **B**. If the magnet is spinning about its axis, the effect of the torque is to make the spin axis precess about the direction of the external field, just as a spinning top or gyroscope precesses about the direction of the gravitational field.

To change the orientation of the magnet relative to the applied field direction (whether or not it is spinning), work must be done on it. If it moves through angle $d\theta$, the work required is

$$dW = \tau\, d\theta = \mu B \sin\theta\, d\theta = d(-\mu B \cos\theta) = d(-\boldsymbol{\mu} \cdot \mathbf{B})$$

The potential energy of the magnetic moment **μ** in the magnetic field **B** can thus be written

$$U = -\boldsymbol{\mu} \cdot \mathbf{B} \qquad \text{7-46}$$

If **B** is in the *z* direction, the potential energy is

$$U = -\mu_z B \qquad \text{7-47}$$

Applying these arguments to the *intrinsic spin* of the electron results in the predictions

$$\mu = \sqrt{s(s+1)}\,\mu_B = \sqrt{\tfrac{3}{4}}\,\mu_B \qquad \text{and} \qquad \mu_z = m_s\mu_B = \pm\tfrac{1}{2}\mu_B \qquad \text{7-48}$$

Since the atomic electron is in a magnetic field arising from the apparent motion of the nuclear charge around the electron, the two values of m_s correspond to two different energies, according to Equation 7-47. <u>It is this splitting of the energy levels that results in the fine structure of the spectral lines.</u>

The restriction of the spin, and hence the intrinsic magnetic moment, to two orientations in space with $m_s = \pm\tfrac{1}{2}$ is another example of space quantization. The magnitude of the magnetic moment due to the spin angular momentum can be determined from quantitative measurement of the deflection of the beam in a Stern-Gerlach experiment. The result is *not* $\tfrac{1}{2}$ Bohr magneton, as predicted by Equation 7-41 with $m = m_s = \tfrac{1}{2}$, but twice this value. (This type of experiment is not an accurate way to measure magnetic moments, although the measurement of angular momentum is accurate because it involves simply counting the number of lines.) The *g* factor for the electron, g_s in Equation 7-49, has been precisely measured to be $g_s = 2.002319$.

(a)

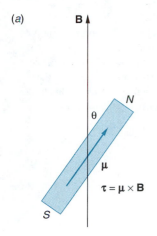

(b)

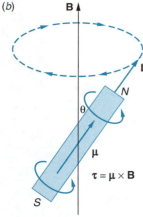

Fig. 7-13 Bar-magnet model of magnetic moment. (*a*) In an external magnetic field, the moment experiences a torque which tends to align it with the field. If the magnet is spinning (*b*), the torque causes the system to precess around the external field.

$$\mu_z = -m_s g_s \mu_B \qquad\qquad \textbf{7-49}$$

This result, and the fact that s is a half integer rather than an integer like the orbital quantum number l, make it clear that the classical model of the electron as a spinning ball is not to be taken literally. Like the Bohr model of the atom, the classical picture is useful in describing results of quantum-mechanical calculations, and it often gives useful guidelines as to what to expect from an experiment. The phenomenon of spin, while not a part of Schrödinger's wave mechanics, is included in the relativistic wave mechanics formulated by Dirac. In its nonrelativistic limit, Dirac's wave equation predicts $g_s = 2$, which is approximately correct. The exact value of g_s is correctly predicted by *quantum electrodynamics (QED)*, the relativistic quantum theory that describes the interaction of electrons with electromagnetic fields. Although beyond the scope of our discussions, QED is arguably the most precisely tested theory in physics.

Exploring

Stern-Gerlach Experiment

If a magnetic moment $\boldsymbol{\mu}$ is placed in an *inhomogeneous* external magnetic field $\mathbf{B}$, the $\boldsymbol{\mu}$ will feel an external force that depends on μ_z and the divergence of $\mathbf{B}$. This is because the force $\mathbf{F}$ is the negative gradient of the potential, so

$$\boldsymbol{F} = -\nabla U = -\nabla(-\boldsymbol{\mu} \cdot \mathbf{B}) \qquad\qquad \textbf{7-50}$$

from Equation 7-46. If we arrange the inhomogeneous $\mathbf{B}$ field so that it is homogeneous in the x and y directions, then the gradient has only $\partial B/\partial z \neq 0$ and $\mathbf{F}$ has only a z component, i.e.,

$$F_z = \mu_z(dB/dz) = -mg_L\mu_B(dB/dz) \qquad\qquad \textbf{7-51}$$

This effect was used by Stern and Gerlach[9] in 1922 (before spin) to measure the possible orientations in space, i.e., the space quantization, of the magnetic moments of silver atoms. The experiment was repeated in 1927 (after spin) by Phipps and Taylor using hydrogen atoms.

The experimental setup is shown in Figure 7-14. Atoms from an oven are collimated and sent through a magnet whose poles are shaped so that the magnetic field B_z increases slightly with z, while B_x and B_y are constant in the x and y directions, respectively. The atoms then strike a collector plate. Figure 7-15 illustrates the effect of the dB/dz on several magnetic moments of different orientations. In addition to the torque, which merely causes the magnetic moment to precess about the field direction, there is the force F_z in the positive or negative z direction, depending on whether μ_z is positive or negative, since dB/dz is always positive. This force deflects the magnetic moment up or down by an amount that depends on the magnitudes of both dB/dz and the z component of the magnetic moment μ_z. Classically, one would expect a continuum of possible orientations of the magnetic moments. However, since the magnetic moment is proportional to $\mathbf{L}$,

Fig. 7-14 In the Stern-
Gerlach experiment, atoms
from an oven are collimated,
passed through an inhomogeneous magnetic field, and
detected on a collector plate.

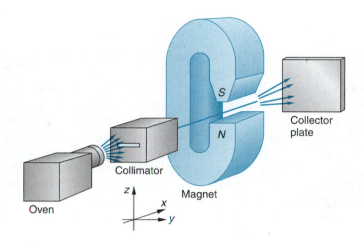

which is quantized, quantum mechanics predicts that μ_z also can have only the
$2l + 1$ values corresponding to the $2l + 1$ possible values of m. We therefore
expect $2l + 1$ deflections (counting 0 as a deflection). For example, for $l = 0$ there
should be one line on the collector plate corresponding to no deflection, and for
$l = 1$ there should be three lines corresponding to the three values $m = -1$, $m = 0$,
and $m = +1$. The $l = 1$ case is illustrated in Figure 7-15.

Using neutral silver atoms Stern and Gerlach expected to see only a single
line, the middle line in Figure 7-15b, because the ground state of silver was known
to be an $l = 0$ state; therefore, $m = 0$ and $\mu = 0$. The force F_z would then be zero
and no deflection of the atomic beam should occur. However, when the experiment
was done with either silver or hydrogen atoms, there were *two* lines, as shown in
Figure 7-15c. Since the ground state of hydrogen also has $l = 0$ we should again
expect only one line, were it not for the electron spin. If the electron has spin angu-
lar momentum of magnitude $|\mathbf{S}| = \sqrt{s(s + 1)}\hbar$, where $s = \frac{1}{2}$, the z component can
be either $+\hbar/2$ or $-\hbar/2$. Since the orbital angular momentum is zero, the total

Fig. 7-15 (*a*) In an inhomogeneous magnetic field
the magnetic moment **μ**
experiences a force F_z whose
direction depends on the
direction of the z component
μ_z of **μ** and whose magnitude
depends on those of μ_z and
dB_z/dz. The beam from an
oven (not shown) is collimated into a horizontal line.
(*b*) The pattern for the $l = 1$
case illustrated in (*a*). The
three images join at the edges
and have different detailed
shapes due to differences
in the field inhomogeneity.
(*c*) The pattern observed for
silver and hydrogen.

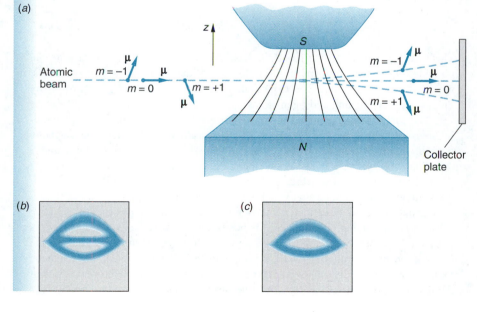

internal angular momentum of the atom is simply the spin[10] and two lines would be expected. Stern and Gerlach had made the first direct observation of electron spin and space quantization.

The Complete Hydrogen Atom Wave Functions

Our description of the hydrogen atom wave functions in Section 7-3 is not complete because we did not include the spin of the electron. The hydrogen atom wave functions are also characterized by the spin quantum number m_s, which can be $+\frac{1}{2}$ or $-\frac{1}{2}$. (We need not include the quantum number s because it always has the value $s = \frac{1}{2}$.) A general wave function is then written $\psi_{nlm_lm_s}$ where we have included the subscript l on m_l to distinguish it from m_s. There are now two wave functions for the ground state of the hydrogen atom, $\psi_{100+\frac{1}{2}}$ and $\psi_{100-\frac{1}{2}}$, corresponding to an atom with its electron spin "parallel" or "antiparallel" to the z axis (as defined, for example, by an external magnetic field). In general, the ground state of a hydrogen atom is a linear combination of these wave functions:

$$\psi = C_1\psi_{100+\frac{1}{2}} + C_2\psi_{100-\frac{1}{2}}$$

The probability of measuring $m_s = +\frac{1}{2}$ (for example, by observing to which spot the atom goes in the Stern-Gerlach experiment) is $|C_1|^2$. Unless atoms have been preselected in some way (such as by passing them through a previous inhomogeneous magnetic field or by their having recently emitted a photon), $|C_1|^2$ and $|C_2|^2$ will each be $\frac{1}{2}$, so that measuring the spin "up" ($m_s = +\frac{1}{2}$) and measuring the spin "down" ($m_s = -\frac{1}{2}$) are equally likely.

QUESTIONS

5. Does a system have to have a net charge to have a magnetic moment?

6. Consider the two beams of hydrogen atoms emerging from the magnetic field in the Stern-Gerlach experiment. How does the wave function for an atom in one beam differ from that of an atom in the other beam? How does it differ from the wave function for an atom in the incoming beam before passing through the magnetic field?

(a)
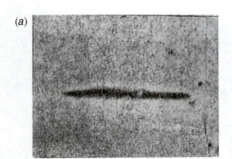

(b)
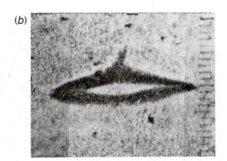

Photographs made by Stern and Gerlach with an atomic beam of silver atoms. (a) When the magnetic field is zero, all atoms strike in a single, undeviated line. (b) When the magnetic field is nonzero, the atoms strike in upper and lower lines, curved due to differing inhomogeneities. [From O. Stern and W. Gerlach, Zeitschr. f. Physik, **9**, 349 (1922).]

7-5 Total Angular Momentum and the Spin-Orbit Effect

In general an electron in an atom has both orbital angular momentum characterized by the quantum number l and spin angular momentum characterized by the quantum number s. Analogous classical systems that have two kinds of angular momentum are Earth, which is spinning about its axis of rotation in addition to revolving about the sun, or a precessing gyroscope, which has angular momentum of precession in addition to its spin. Classically the total angular momentum

$$\mathbf{J} = \mathbf{L} + \mathbf{S} \qquad \text{7-52}$$

is an important quantity because the resultant torque on a system equals the rate of change of the total angular momentum, and in the case of central forces, the total angular momentum is conserved. For a classical system, the magnitude of the total angular momentum J can have any value between $L + S$ and $|L - S|$. We have already seen that in quantum mechanics, angular momentum is more complicated; both $\mathbf{L}$ and $\mathbf{S}$ are quantized and their relative directions are restricted. The quantum-mechanical rules for combining orbital and spin angular momenta or any two angular momenta (such as for two particles) are somewhat difficult to derive, but they are not difficult to understand. For the case of orbital and spin angular momenta, the magnitude of the total angular momentum $\mathbf{J}$ is given by

$$|\mathbf{J}| = \sqrt{j(j + 1)}\,\hbar \qquad \text{7-53}$$

where the *total angular momentum quantum number j* can be either

$$j = l + s \qquad \text{or} \qquad j = |l - s| \qquad \text{7-54}$$

Fig. 7-16 (*a*) Simplified vector model illustrating the addition of orbital and spin angular momenta. Case shown is for $l = 1$ and $s = \frac{1}{2}$. There are two possible values of the quantum number for the total angular momentum: $j = l + s = \frac{3}{2}$ and $j = l - s = \frac{1}{2}$. (*b*) Vector addition of the orbital and spin angular momenta, also for the case $l = 1$ and $s = \frac{1}{2}$. According to the uncertainty principle the vectors can lie anywhere on the cones, corresponding to the definite values of their z components. Note that there are two ways of forming the states with $j = \frac{3}{2}$, $m_j = \frac{1}{2}$ and $j = \frac{1}{2}$, $m_j = \frac{1}{2}$.

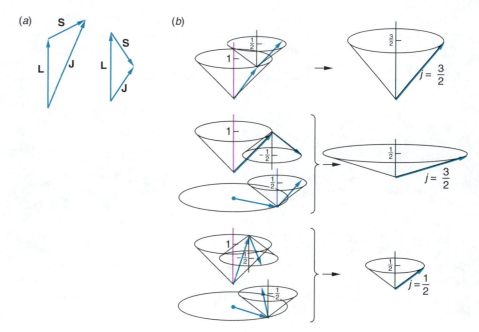

and the z component of $\mathbf{J}$ is given by

$$J_z = m_j \hbar \qquad \text{where} \qquad m_j = -j, -j + 1, \ldots, j - 1, j \qquad \textbf{7-55}$$

(If $l = 0$, the total angular momentum is simply the spin, and $j = s$.) Figure 7-16a is a simplified vector model illustrating the two possible combinations $j = l + \frac{1}{2} = \frac{3}{2}$ and $j = l - \frac{1}{2} = \frac{1}{2}$ for the case of an electron with $l = 1$. The lengths of the vectors are proportional to $[l(l + 1)]^{1/2}$, $[s(s + 1)]^{1/2}$, and $[j(j + 1)]^{1/2}$. The spin and orbital angular momentum vectors are said to be "parallel" when $j = l + s$ and "antiparallel" when $j = |l - s|$. A quantum-mechanically more accurate vector addition is shown in Figure 7-16b. The quantum number m_j can take on $2j + 1$ possible values in integer steps between $-j$ and $+j$, as indicated by Equation 7-55. Equation 7-55 also implies that $m_j = m_l + m_s$, since $J_z = L_z + S_z$.

Equation 7-54 is a special case of a more general rule for combining two angular momenta which is useful when dealing with more than one particle. For example, there are two electrons in the helium atom, each with spin, orbital, and total angular momentum. The general rule is:

If $\mathbf{J}_1$ is one angular momentum (orbital, spin, or a combination) and $\mathbf{J}_2$ is another, the resulting total angular momentum $\mathbf{J} = \mathbf{J}_1 + \mathbf{J}_2$ has the value $[j(j + 1)]^{1/2} \hbar$ for its magnitude, where j can be any of the values

$$j_1 + j_2, j_1 + j_2 - 1, \ldots, |j_1 - j_2|$$

EXAMPLE 7-2 **Addition of Angular Momenta I** Two electrons each have zero orbital angular momentum. What are the possible quantum numbers for the total angular momentum of the two-electron system?

Solution
In this case $j_1 = j_2 = \frac{1}{2}$. The general rule then gives two possible results, $j = 1$ and $j = 0$. These combinations are commonly called parallel and antiparallel, respectively.

EXAMPLE 7-3 **Addition of Angular Momenta II** An electron in an atom has orbital angular momentum $\mathbf{L}_1$ with quantum number $l_1 = 2$ and a second electron has orbital angular momentum $\mathbf{L}_2$ with quantum number $l_2 = 3$. What are the possible quantum numbers for the total orbital angular momentum $\mathbf{L} = \mathbf{L}_1 + \mathbf{L}_2$?

Solution
Since $l_1 + l_2 = 5$ and $|l_1 - l_2| = 1$, the possible values of l are 5, 4, 3, 2, and 1.

Spectroscopic Notation

Spectroscopic notation, a kind of shorthand developed in the early days of spectroscopy to condense information and simplify the description of transitions between states, has since been adopted for general use in atomic, molecular, nuclear, and

particle physics. The notation code appears to be arbitrary,[11] but it is easy to learn and, as you will discover, convenient to use. For single electrons we have:

1. For single-electron states the letter code *s p d f g h* . . . is used in one-to-one correspondence with the values of the orbital angular momentum quantum number *l*: 0 1 2 3 4 5 . . . . For example, an electron with $l = 2$ is said to be in a *d* state.

2. The single-electron (Bohr) energy levels are called *shells*, labeled *K L M N O* . . . in one-to-one correspondence with the values of the principal quantum number *n*: 1 2 3 4 5 . . . . For example, an electron with $n = 3$ in an atom is said to be in the *M* shell. (This notation is less commonly used.)

For atomic states that may contain one or more particles the notation includes the principal quantum number and the angular momenta quantum numbers. The total orbital angular momentum quantum number is denoted by a capital letter in the same sequence as in rule 1 above, i.e., *S P D F* . . . correspond to *l* values 0 1 2 3 . . . . The value of *n* is written as a prefix and the value of the total angular momentum quantum number *j* by a subscript. The magnitude of the total spin quantum number *s* appears as a left superscript in the form 2s + 1.[12] Thus, a state with $l = 1$, a *P* state, would be written as

$$n^{2s+1}P_j$$

For example, the ground state of hydrogen is written $1^2S_{1/2}$, read "one doublet *S* one-half." The $n = 2$ state can have $l = 0$ or $l = 1$, so the spectroscopic notation for these states is $2^2S_{1/2}$, $2^2P_{3/2}$, and $2^2P_{1/2}$. (The principal quantum number and spin superscript are sometimes not included if they are not needed in specific situations.)

(*a*)

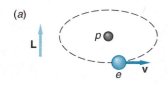

(*b*)

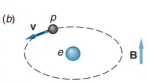

Fig. 7-17 (*a*) An electron moving about a proton with angular momentum **L** up. (*b*) The magnetic field **B** seen by the electron due to the apparent (relative) motion of the proton is also up. When the electron spin is parallel to **L**, the magnetic moment is antiparallel to **L** and **B**, so the spin-orbit energy has its largest value.

Spin-Orbit Coupling

Atomic states with the same *n* and *l* values but different *j* values have slightly different energies because of the interaction of the spin of the electron with its orbital motion. This effect is called the *spin-orbit effect*. The resulting splitting of the spectral lines such as the one that results from the splitting of the 2*P* level in the transition $2P \rightarrow 1S$ in hydrogen is called *fine-structure splitting*. We can understand the spin-orbit effect qualitatively from a simple Bohr model picture, as shown in Figure 7-17. In this picture, the electron moves in a circular orbit with speed *v* around a fixed proton. In the figure, the orbital angular momentum **L** is up. In the frame of reference of the electron, the proton moves in a circle around it, thus constituting a circular loop current which produces a magnetic field **B** at the position of the electron. The direction of **B** is also up, parallel to **L**. The potential energy of a magnetic moment in a magnetic field depends on its orientation and is given by:

$$U = -\boldsymbol{\mu} \cdot \mathbf{B} = -\mu_z B \qquad \text{7-56}$$

The potential energy is lowest when the magnetic moment is parallel to **B** and highest when it is antiparallel. Since the magnetic moment of the electron is directed opposite to its spin (because the electron has a negative charge), the spin-orbit energy is highest

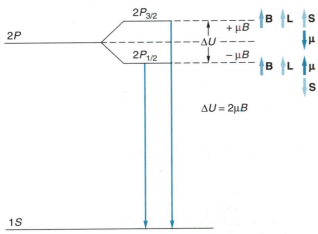

Fig. 7-18 Fine-structure energy-level diagram. On the left, the levels in the absence of a magnetic field are shown. The effect of the magnetic field due to the relative motion of the nucleus is shown on the right. Because of the spin-orbit interaction, the magnetic field splits the $2P$ level into two energy levels, with the $j = \frac{3}{2}$ level having slightly greater energy than the $j = \frac{1}{2}$ level. The spectral line due to the transition $2P \rightarrow 1S$ is therefore split into two lines of slightly different wavelengths.

when the spin is parallel to **B** and thus to **L**. The energy of the $2P_{3/2}$ state in hydrogen, in which **L** and **S** are parallel, is therefore slightly higher than the $2P_{1/2}$ state, in which **L** and **S** are antiparallel (Figure 7-18).[13] The measured splitting is about 4.5×10^{-5} eV for the $2P_{1/2}$ and $2P_{3/2}$ levels in hydrogen. For other atoms, the fine-structure splitting is larger than this. For example, for sodium it is about 2×10^{-3} eV, as will be discussed in Section 7-7.

EXAMPLE 7-4 Fine-Structure Splitting The fine-structure splitting of the $2P_{3/2}$ and $2P_{1/2}$ levels in hydrogen is 4.5×10^{-5} eV. From this, estimate the magnetic field that the $2p$ electron in hydrogen experiences. Assume **B** is parallel to the z axis.

Solution

1. The energy of the $2p$ electrons is shifted in the presence of a magnetic field by an amount given by Equation 7-56:

$$U = -\boldsymbol{\mu} \cdot \mathbf{B} = -\mu_z B$$

2. U is positive or negative depending on the relative orientation of $\boldsymbol{\mu}$ and **B**, so the total energy difference ΔE between the two levels is:

$$\Delta E = 2U = 2\mu_z B$$

3. Since the magnetic moment of the electron is μ_B, $\mu_z \approx \mu_B$ and:

$$\Delta E \approx 2\mu_B B$$

4.   Solving this for B and substituting for u_B and the energy splitting ΔE give:

$$B \approx \frac{\Delta E}{2\mu_B}$$

$$\approx \frac{4.5 \times 10^{-5}\,\text{eV}}{(2)(5.79 \times 10^{-5}\,\text{eV/T})}$$

$$\approx 0.39\,\text{T}$$

Remarks: *This is a substantial magnetic field.*

When an atom is placed in an *external* magnetic field **B**, the total angular momentum **J** is quantized in space relative to the direction of **B** and the energy of the atomic state characterized by the angular momentum quantum number j is split into $2j + 1$ energy levels corresponding to the $2j + 1$ possible values of the z component of **J** and therefore to the $2j + 1$ possible values of the z component of the total magnetic moment. This splitting of the energy levels in the atom gives rise to a splitting of the spectral lines emitted by the atom. The splitting of the spectral lines of an atom placed in an external magnetic field was discovered by P. Zeeman and is known as the *Zeeman effect*. (See the More section on page 327.)

7-6 The Schrödinger Equation for Two (or More) Particles

Our discussion of quantum mechanics so far has been limited to situations in which a single particle moves in some force field characterized by a potential energy function *V*. The most important physical problem of this type is the hydrogen atom, in which a single electron moves in the Coulomb potential of the proton nucleus. This problem is actually a two-body problem, as the proton also moves in the Coulomb potential of the electron. However, as in classical mechanics, we can treat this as a one-body problem by considering the proton to be at rest and replacing the electron mass with the reduced mass. When we consider more complicated atoms we must face the problem of applying quantum mechanics to two or more electrons moving in an external field. Such problems are complicated by the interaction of the electrons with each other, and also by the fact that the electrons are identical.

The interaction of the electrons with each other is electromagnetic, and essentially the same as that expected classically for two charged particles. The Schrödinger equation for an atom with two or more electrons cannot be solved exactly, and approximation methods must be used. This is not very different from the situation in classical problems with three or more particles. The complication arising from the identity of electrons is purely quantum-mechanical and has no classical counterpart.

The indistinguishability of identical particles has important consequences related to the *Pauli exclusion principle*. We shall illustrate the origin of this important principle in this section by considering the simple case of two noninteracting identical particles in a one-dimensional infinite square well.

The time-independent Schrödinger equation for two particles of mass m is

$$-\frac{\hbar^2}{2m}\frac{\partial^2\psi(x_1, x_2)}{\partial x_1^2} - \frac{\hbar^2}{2m}\frac{\partial^2\psi(x_1, x_2)}{\partial x_2^2} + V\psi(x_1, x_2) = E\psi(x_1, x_2) \qquad \textbf{7-57}$$

where x_1 and x_2 are the coordinates of the two particles. If the particles are interacting, the potential energy V contains terms with both x_1 and x_2, which cannot usually be separated. For example, if the particles are charged, their mutual electrostatic potential energy (in one dimension) is $+ke^2/|x_2 - x_1|$. If they do not interact, however, we can write V as $V_1(x_1) + V_2(x_2)$. For the case of an infinite square well potential, we need solve the Schrödinger equation only inside the well where $V = 0$ and require the wave function to be zero at the walls of the well. Solutions of Equation 7-57 can be written as products of single-particle solutions and linear combinations of such solutions. The single-particle product solutions are

$$\psi_{nm}(x_1, x_2) = \psi_n(x_1)\psi_m(x_2) \qquad \textbf{7-58}$$

where $\psi_n(x_1)$ and $\psi_m(x_2)$ are the single-particle wave functions for an infinite square well given by Equation 6-32. Thus for $n = 1$, and $m = 2$,

$$\psi_{12} = C \sin \frac{\pi x_1}{L} \sin \frac{2\pi x_2}{L} \qquad \textbf{7-59}$$

The probability of finding particle 1 in dx_1 and particle 2 in dx_2 is $|\psi(x_1, x_2)|^2 \, dx_1 \, dx_2$, which is just the product of the separate probabilities $|\psi(x_1)|^2 \, dx_1$ and $|\psi(x_2)|^2 \, dx_2$. However, even though we have labeled the particles 1 and 2, if they are identical we cannot distinguish which is in dx_1 and which is in dx_2. For identical particles, therefore, we must construct the wave function so that the probability density is the same if we interchange the labels:

$$|\psi(x_1, x_2)|^2 = |\psi(x_2, x_1)|^2 \qquad \textbf{7-60}$$

Equation 7-60 holds if $\psi(x_1, x_2)$ is either symmetric or antisymmetric on exchange of particles—that is,

$$\psi(x_2, x_1) = +\psi(x_1, x_2) \qquad \text{symmetric}$$
$$\psi(x_2, x_1) = -\psi(x_1, x_2) \qquad \text{antisymmetric}$$

We note that the general wave function of the form of Equation 7-58 and the example (Equation 7-59) are neither symmetric nor antisymmetric. If we interchange x_1 and x_2 we get a different wave function, implying that the particles can be distinguished. These forms are thus *not* consistent with the indistinguishability of identical particles. However, from among all of the possible linear combination solutions of the single-product functions, we see that, if ψ_{nm} and ψ_{mn} are added or subtracted, we form symmetric or antisymmetric wave functions necessary to preserve the indistinguishability of the two particles:

$$\psi_S = C[\psi_n(x_1)\psi_m(x_2) + \psi_n(x_2)\psi_m(x_1)] \qquad \text{symmetric}$$
$$\psi_A = C[\psi_n(x_1)\psi_m(x_2) - \psi_n(x_2)\psi_m(x_1)] \qquad \text{antisymmetric}$$

Pauli Exclusion Principle

There is an important difference between the antisymmetric and symmetric combinations. If $n = m$, the antisymmetric wave function is identically zero for all x_1 and x_2, whereas the symmetric function is not. More generally, it is found that electrons (and

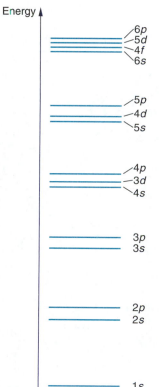

Energy

6p
5d
4f
6s

5p
4d
5s

4p
3d
4s

3p
3s

2p
2s

1s

Fig. 7-19 Relative energies of the atomic shells and subshells.

George Gamow and Wolfgang Pauli in Switzerland in 1930. [*Courtesy of George Gamow.*]

many other particles, including protons and neutrons) can only have antisymmetric *total* wave functions, that is

$$\Psi_{nlm_l m_s} = R_{nl} Y_{lm_l} X_{m_s} \qquad \textbf{7-61}$$

where R_{nl} is the radial wave function, Y_{lm_l} is the spherical harmonic, and X_{m_s} is the spin wave function. Thus, single-particle wave functions such as $\psi_n(x_1)$ and $\psi_m(x_1)$ for two such particles cannot have exactly the same set of values for the quantum numbers. This is an example of the *Pauli exclusion principle*. For the case of electrons in atoms and molecules, four quantum numbers describe the state of each electron, one for each space coordinate and one associated with spin. The Pauli exclusion principle for electrons states that:

> No more than one electron may occupy a given quantum state specified by a particular set of single-particle quantum numbers n, l, m_l, m_s.

The effect of the exclusion principle is to exclude certain states in the many-electron system. It is an additional quantum condition imposed on solutions of the Schrödinger equation. It will be applied to the development of the periodic table in the following section. Particles such as α particles, deuterons, photons, and mesons have symmetric wave functions and do not obey the exclusion principle.

7-7 Ground States of Atoms: The Periodic Table

We now consider qualitatively the wave functions and energy levels for atoms more complicated than hydrogen. As we have mentioned, the Schrödinger equations for atoms other than hydrogen cannot be solved exactly because of the interaction of the electrons with each other, so approximation methods must be used. We shall discuss the energies and wave functions for the ground states of atoms in this section, and consider the excited states and spectra for some of the less complicated cases in the next section. We can describe the wave function for a complex atom in terms of single-particle wave functions. By neglecting the interaction energy of the electrons that description can be simplified to products of the single-particle wave functions. These wave functions are similar to those of the hydrogen atom and are characterized by the quantum numbers n, l, m_l, m_s. The energy of an electron is determined mainly by the quantum numbers n (which is related to the radial part of the wave function) and l (which characterizes the orbital angular momentum). Generally, the lower the value of n and l, the lower the energy of the state. (See Figure 7-19.) The specification of n and l for each electron in an atom is called the *electron configuration*. Customarily, the value of l and the various electron shells are specified with the same code defined in the subsection "Spectroscopic Notation" in Section 7-5. The electron configuration of the atomic ground states is given in Appendix C.

The Ground States of the Atoms

Helium (Z = 2)   The energy of the two electrons in the helium atom consists of the kinetic energy of each electron, a potential energy of the form $-kZe^2/r_i$ for each electron corresponding to its attraction to the nucleus, and a potential energy of inter-

action V_{int} corresponding to the mutual repulsion of the two electrons. If $\mathbf{r}_1$ and $\mathbf{r}_2$ are the position vectors for the two electrons, V_{int} is given by

$$V_{int} = +\frac{ke^2}{|\mathbf{r}_2 - \mathbf{r}_1|} \qquad \textbf{7-62}$$

Because this interaction term contains the position variables of the two electrons, its presence in the Schrödinger equation prevents the separation of the equation into separate equations for each electron. If we neglect the interaction term, however, the Schrödinger equation can be separated and solved exactly. We then obtain separate equations for each electron, with each equation identical to that for the hydrogenlike atom with $Z = 2$. The allowed energies are then given by

$$E = -\frac{Z^2 E_0}{n_1^2} - \frac{Z^2 E_0}{n_2^2} \qquad \text{where} \qquad E_0 = 13.6 \text{ eV} \qquad \textbf{7-63}$$

The lowest energy, $E_1 = -2(2)^2 E_0 \approx -108.8$ eV, occurs for $n_1 = n_2 = 1$. For this case, $l_1 = l_2 = 0$. The total wave function, neglecting the spin of the electrons, is of the form

$$\psi = \psi_{100}(r_1, \theta_1, \phi_1)\psi_{100}(r_2, \theta_2, \phi_2) \qquad \textbf{7-64}$$

The quantum numbers n, l, and m_l can be the same for the two electrons only if the fourth quantum number m_s is different, i.e., if one has $m_s = +\frac{1}{2}$ and the other has $m_s = -\frac{1}{2}$. The resultant spin of the two electrons must therefore be zero.

We can obtain a first-order correction to the ground-state energy by using the approximate wave function of Equation 7-64 to calculate the average value of the interaction energy V_{int}, which is simply the expectation value $\langle V_{int} \rangle$. The result of this calculation is

$$\langle V_{int} \rangle = +34 \text{ eV} \qquad \textbf{7-65}$$

With this correction, the ground-state energy is

$$E \approx -108.8 + 34 = -74.8 \text{ eV} \qquad \textbf{7-66}$$

This approximation method, in which we neglect the interaction of the electrons to find an approximate wave function and then use this wave function to calculate the interaction energy, is called *first-order perturbation theory*. The approximation can be continued to higher orders: for example, the next step is to use the new ground-state energy to find a correction to the ground-state wave function. This approximation method is similar to that used in classical mechanics to calculate the orbits of the planets about the sun. In the first approximation the interaction of the planets is neglected and the elliptical orbits are found for each planet. Then using this result for the position of each planet, the perturbing effects of the nearby planets can be calculated.

The experimental value of the energy needed to remove both electrons from the helium atom is about 79 eV. The discrepancy between this result and the value 74.8 eV is due to the inaccuracy of the approximation used to calculate $\langle V_{int} \rangle$, as indicated by the rather large value of the correction (about 30 percent). (It should be pointed out that there are better methods of calculating the interaction energy

for helium that give much closer agreement with experiment.) The helium *ion* He$^+$, formed by removing one electron, is identical to the hydrogen atom except that $Z = 2$; so the ground-state energy is

$$-Z^2(13.6) = -54.4 \text{ eV}$$

The energy needed to remove the first electron from the helium atom is 24.6 eV. The corresponding potential, 24.6 V, is called the *first ionization potential* of the atom. The ionization energies are given in Appendix C.

The configuration of the ground state of the helium atom is written $1s^2$. The 1 signifies $n = 1$, the s signifies $l = 0$, and the 2 signifies that there are two electrons in this state. Since l can only be zero for $n = 1$, the two electrons fill the K shell ($n = 1$).

Lithium (Z = 3)   Lithium has three electrons. Two are in the K shell ($n = 1$), but the third cannot have $n = 1$ because of the exclusion principle. The next-lowest energy state for this electron has $n = 2$. The possible l values are $l = 1$ or $l = 0$.

In the hydrogen atom, these l values have the same energy because of the degeneracy associated with the inverse-square nature of the force. This is not true in lithium and other atoms because the charge "seen" by the outer electron is not a point charge.[14] The positive charge of the nucleus $+Ze$ can be considered to be approximately a point charge, but the negative charge of the K-shell electrons $-2e$ is spread out in space over a volume whose radius is of the order of a_0/Z. We can in fact take for the charge density of each inner electron $\rho = -e|\psi|^2$, where ψ is a hydrogenlike $1s$ wave function (neglecting the interaction of the two electrons in the K shell). The probability distribution for the outer electron in the $2s$ or $2p$ state is similar to that shown in Figure 7-10. We see that the probability distribution in both cases has a large maximum well outside the inner K-shell electrons, but that the $2s$ distribution also has a small bump near the origin. We could describe this by saying that the electron in the $2p$ state is nearly always outside the shielding of the two $1s$ electrons in the K shell so that it sees an effective central charge of $Z_{\text{eff}} \approx 1$; whereas in the $2s$ state the electron penetrates this "shielding" more often and therefore sees a slightly larger effective positive central charge. The energy of the outer electron is therefore lower in the $2s$ state than in the $2p$ state, and the lowest energy configuration of the lithium atom is $1s^2 2s$.

The total angular momentum of the electrons in this atom is $\frac{1}{2}\hbar$ due to the spin of the outer electron, since each of the electrons has zero orbital angular momentum, and the inner K-shell electrons are paired to give zero spin. The first ionization potential for lithium is only 5.39 V. We can use this result to calculate the effective positive charge seen by the $2s$ electron. For $Z = Z_{\text{eff}}$ and $n = 2$ we have

$$E = \frac{Z^2 E_0}{n^2} = \frac{Z_{\text{eff}}^2 (13.6 \text{ eV})}{2^2} = 5.39 \text{ eV}$$

which gives $Z_{\text{eff}} \approx 1.3$. It is generally true that the smaller the value of l, the greater the penetration of the wave function into the inner shielding cloud of electrons: the result is that for given n, the energy of the electron increases with increasing l. (See Figure 7-19.)

Beryllium (Z = 4)   The fourth electron has the least energy in the $2s$ state. The exclusion principle requires that its spin be antiparallel to the other electron in this state, so that the angular momentum of the four electrons in this atom is 0. The

electron configuration of beryllium is $1s^2 2s^2$. The first ionization potential is 9.32 V. This is greater than that for lithium because of the greater value of Z.

Boron to Neon (Z = 5 to Z = 10)   Since the 2s subshell is filled, the fifth electron must go into the 2p subshell, that is, $n = 2$ and $l = 1$. Since there are three possible values of m_l ($+1$, 0, and -1) and two values of m_s for each, there can be six electrons in this subshell. The electron configuration for boron is $1s^2 2s^2 2p$. Although it might be expected that boron would have a greater ionization potential than beryllium because of the greater Z, the 2p wave function penetrates the shielding of the core electrons to a lesser extent and the ionization potential of boron is actually about 8.3 V, slightly less than that of beryllium. The electron configuration of the elements carbon (Z = 6) to neon (Z = 10) differs from boron only by the number of electrons in the 2p subshell. The ionization potential increases slightly with Z for these elements, reaching the value of 21.6 V for the last element in the group, neon. Neon has the maximum number of electrons allowed in the $n = 2$ shell. The electron configuration of neon is $1s^2 2s^2 2p^6$. Because of its very high ionization potential, neon, like helium, is chemically inert. The element just before this, fluorine, has a "hole" in this shell, that is, it has room for one more electron. It readily combines with elements such as lithium, which has one outer electron that is donated to the fluorine atom to make a F^- ion and a Li^+ ion, which bond together. This is an example of ionic bonding, to be discussed in Chapter 9.

Sodium to Argon (Z = 11 to Z = 18)   The 11th electron must go into the $n = 3$ shell. Since this electron is weakly bound in the Na atom, Na combines readily with atoms such as F. The ionization potential for sodium is only 5.14 V. Because of the lowering of the energy due to penetration of the electronic shield formed by the other 10 electrons — similar to that discussed for Li — the 3s state is lower than the 3p or 3d state. (With $n = 3$, l can have the values 0, 1, or 2.) This energy difference between subshells of the same n value becomes greater as the number of electrons increases. The configuration of Na is thus $1s^2 2s^2 2p^6 3s^1$. As we move to higher-Z elements, the 3s subshell and then the 3p subshell begin to fill up. These two subshells can accommodate $2 + 6 = 8$ electrons. The configuration of argon (Z = 18) is $1s^2 2s^2 2p^6 3s^2 3p^6$. There is another large energy difference between the 18th and 19th electrons, and argon, with its full 3p subshell, is stable and inert.

Atoms with Z > 18   One might expect that the 19th electron would go into the 3d subshell, but the shielding or penetration effect is now so strong that the energy is lower in the 4s shell than in the 3d shell. The 19th electron in potassium (Z = 19) and the 20th electron in calcium (Z = 20) go into the 4s rather than the 3d subshell. The electron configurations of the next 10 elements, scandium (Z = 21) through zinc (Z = 30), differ only in the number of electrons in the 3d subshell except for chromium (Z = 24) and copper (Z = 29), each of which has only one 4s electron. These elements are called *transition elements*. Since their chemical properties are mainly due to their 4s electrons, they are quite similar chemically.

Figure 7-20 shows a plot of the first ionization potential of an atom versus Z up to Z = 90. The sudden decrease in ionization potential after the Z numbers 2, 10, 18, 36, and 54 mark the closing of a shell or subshell. A corresponding sudden increase occurs in the atomic radii, as illustrated in Figure 7-21. The ground-state electron configurations of the elements are tabulated in Appendix C.

Fig. 7-20 First ionization energy vs. *Z* up to *Z* = 90. The energy is the binding energy of the last electron in the atom. This energy increases with *Z* until a shell is closed at *Z* values of 2, 10, 18, 36, 54, and 86. The next electron must go into the next higher shell and hence is farther from the center of core charge and thus less tightly bound. The ionization potential (in volts) is numerically equal to the ionization energy (in eV).

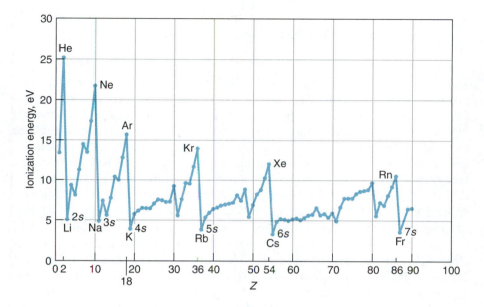

Fig. 7-21 The atomic radii vs. *Z* shows a sharp rise following the completion of a shell as the next electron must have the next larger *n*. The radii then decline with increasing *Z*, reflecting the penetration of wave functions of the electrons in the developing shell. The recurring patterns here and in Figure 7-20 are examples of the behavior of many atomic properties that give the periodic table its name.

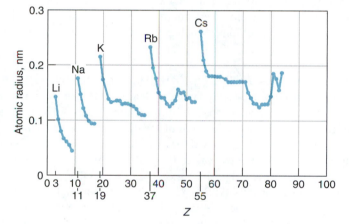

QUESTIONS

7. Why is the energy of the 3*s* state considerably lower than that of the 3*p* state for sodium, whereas in hydrogen these states have essentially the same energy?

8. Discuss the evidence from the periodic table of the need for a fourth quantum number. How would the properties of He differ if there were only three quantum numbers, *n, l,* and *m*?

7-8 Excited States and Spectra of Atoms

Alkali Atoms

In order to understand atomic spectra we need to understand the excited states of atoms. The situation for an atom with many electrons is, in general, much more complicated than that of hydrogen. An excited state of the atom usually involves a change

in the state of one of the electrons, or more rarely two or even more electrons. Even in the case of the excitation of only one electron, the change in state of this electron changes the energies of the others. Fortunately, there are many cases in which this effect is negligible, and the energy levels can be calculated accurately from a relatively simple model of one electron plus a stable core. This model works particularly well for the alkali metals: Li, Na, K, Rb, and Cs. These elements are in the first column of the periodic table. The optical spectra of these elements are similar in many ways to that of hydrogen.

Another simplification is possible because of the wide difference between excitation energy of a core electron and the excitation energy of an outer electron. Consider the case of sodium, which has a neon core (except $Z = 11$ rather than $Z = 10$) and an outer $3s$ electron. If this electron did not penetrate the core, it would see an effective nuclear charge of $Z_{eff} = 1$ resulting from the $+11e$ nuclear charge and the $-10e$ of the completed electron shells. The ionization energy would be the same as the energy of the $n = 3$ electron in hydrogen, about 1.5 eV. Penetration into the core increases Z_{eff} and so lowers the energy of the outer electron, i.e., binds it more tightly, thereby increasing the ionization energy. The measured ionization energy of sodium is about 5 eV. The energy needed to remove one of the outermost core electrons, a $2p$ electron, is about 31 eV, whereas that needed to remove one of the $1s$ electrons is about 1041 eV. An electron in the inner core cannot be excited to any of the filled $n = 2$ states because of the exclusion principle. Thus the minimum excitation of an $n = 1$ electron is to the $n = 3$ shell, which requires an energy only slightly less than that needed to remove this electron completely from the atom. Since the energies of photons in the visible range (about 400 to 800 nm) vary only from about 1.5 to 3 eV, the optical (i.e., visible) spectrum of sodium must be due to transitions involving only the outer electron. Transitions involving the core electrons produce line spectra in the x-ray region of the electromagnetic spectrum.

Figure 7-22 shows an energy-level diagram for the optical transitions in sodium. Since the spin angular momentum of the neon core adds up to zero, the spin of each state in sodium is $\frac{1}{2}$. Because of the spin-orbit effect, the states with $j = l - \frac{1}{2}$ have a slightly lower energy than those with $j = l + \frac{1}{2}$. Each state is therefore a doublet (except for the S states). The doublet splitting is very small and is not evident on the energy scale of Figure 7-22 but is shown in Figure 7-18. The states are labeled by the usual spectroscopic notation, with the superscript 2 before the letter indicating that the state is a doublet. Thus $^2P_{3/2}$, read as "doublet P three-halves," denotes a state in which $l = 1$ and $j = 3/2$. (The S states are customarily labeled as if they were doublets even though they are not. This is done because they belong to the set of levels with $S = \frac{1}{2}$ but, unlike the others, have $l = 0$ and are thus not split. The number indicating the n value of the electron is often omitted.) In the first excited state, the outer electron is excited from the $3s$ level to the $3p$ level, which is about 2.1 eV above the ground state. The spin-orbit energy difference between the $P_{3/2}$ and $P_{1/2}$ states due to the spin-orbit effect is about 0.002 eV. Transitions from these states to the ground state give the familiar sodium yellow doublet

$$3p(^2P_{1/2}) \longrightarrow 3s(^2S_{1/2}) \qquad \lambda = 589.6 \text{ nm}$$
$$3p(^2P_{3/2}) \longrightarrow 3s(^2S_{1/2}) \qquad \lambda = 589.0 \text{ nm}$$

The energy levels and spectra of other alkali atoms are similar to those for sodium.

It is important to distinguish between doublet energy states and doublet spectral lines. All transitions beginning or ending on an S state give double lines because they

Among the many applications of atomic spectra is their use in answering questions about the composition of stars and the evolution of the universe. (See Chapter 14.)

Fig. 7-22 Energy-level diagram for sodium (Na) with some transitions indicated. Wavelengths shown are in nanometers. The spectral lines labeled D_1 and D_2 are very intense and are responsible for the yellow color of lamps containing sodium. The energy splittings of the D and F levels, also doublets, are not shown.

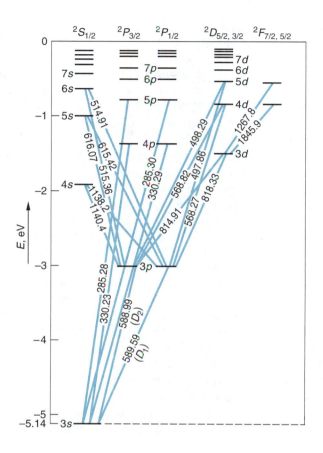

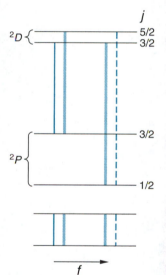

Fig. 7-23 The transitions between a pair of doublet energy states in singly ionized calcium. The transition represented by the dotted line is forbidden by the $\Delta j = \pm 1, 0$ selection rule. The darkness of the lines indicates relative intensity. Under low resolution the faint line on the left of the spectrum at the bottom merges with its neighbor and the compound doublet (or triplet) looks like a doublet.

involve one doublet state and one singlet state (the selection rule $\Delta l = \pm 1$ rules out transitions between two S states). There are four possible energy differences between two doublet states. One of these is ruled out by a selection rule on j, which is[15]

$$\Delta j = \pm 1 \text{ or } 0 \qquad \text{(but no } j = 0 \text{ to } j = 0\text{)} \qquad \textbf{7-67}$$

Transitions between pairs of doublet energy states therefore result in three spectral lines, i.e., a triplet. Under relatively low resolution the three lines look like two as illustrated in Figure 7-23, because two of them are very close together. For this reason they are often referred to as a *compound doublet* to preserve the verbal hint that they involve doublet energy states.

More

Atoms with more than one electron in the outer shell have more complicated energy-level structures. Additional total spin possibilities exist for the atom, resulting in multiple sets of nearly independent energy states and multiple sets of spectral lines. *Multielectron Atoms* and their spectra are described on the home page: www.whfreeman.com/modphysics4e   See also Equations 7-68 and 7-69 and Figures 7-24 through 7-27 here.

More

Our tradition tells us that Mrs. Bohr encountered an obviously sad young Wolfgang Pauli sitting in the garden of Bohr's Institute for Theoretical Physics in Copenhagen, and asked considerately if he was unhappy. His reply was, "Of course I'm unhappy! I don't understand the anomalous Zeeman Effect!" On the home page we explain *The Zeeman Effect* so you, too, won't be unhappy: www.whfreeman.com/modphysics4e   See also Equations 7-70 through 7-74 and Figures 7-28 through 7-31 here.

Exploring

Frozen Light

Using the quantum properties of atomic energy states, tunable lasers, and a Bose-Einstein condensate (BEC) of sodium atoms (see Chapter 8), physicists have been able to slow a light pulse to a dead stop, then regenerate it some time later and send it on its way. Here is how its done.

Consider the $3s$ and $3p$ energy levels of sodium in Figure 7-22. L-S coupling does not cause splitting of the $3s$ state because the orbital angular momentum of that state is zero; however, we will discover in Chapter 11 (see also Problem 7-72) that protons and neutrons also have intrinsic spins and magnetic moments, resulting in a *nuclear* spin and magnetic moment. Although the latter is smaller than the electron's magnetic moment by a factor of about 1000, it causes a very small splitting of the $3s$ level exactly analogous to that due to L-S coupling in states with nonzero orbital angular momenta. Called *hyperfine structure* (because it's smaller than the fine-structure splitting discussed earlier), the $3s$ level is split into two levels spaced about 3.5×10^{-6} eV above and below the original $3s$ state.

Producing the BEC results in a cigar-shaped "cloud" about 1 centimeter long suspended by a magnetic field in a vacuum chamber. The cloud contains several million sodium atoms all with their spins aligned and all in the lower of the two $3s$ hyperfine levels, the new ground state. (See Figure 7-32a.) The light pulse that we wish to slow (the probe beam) is provided by a laser precisely tuned to the energy difference between the lower of the $3s$ hyperfine levels (the new ground state) and the $3p$ state. A second laser (the coupling beam) is precisely tuned to the energy difference between the higher of the $3s$ hyperfine levels and the $3p$ state and illuminates the BEC perpendicular to the probe beam.

If the probe beam alone were to enter the sample, all of the atoms would be excited to the $3p$ level, absorbing the beam completely. As the atoms relaxed back to the ground state, sodium yellow light would be emitted randomly in all directions. If the coupling beam alone entered the sample, no excitation of the $3p$ level would result because the coupling beam doesn't have enough energy to excite electrons from the ground state to the $3p$ state. However, if the coupling beam is illuminating the sample with all atoms in the ground state and the probe beam is turned on, as the leading edge of the probe pulse enters the sample (Figure 7-32b),

Fig. 7-32 (*a*) The coupling beam illuminates the sodium Bose-Einstein condensate, whose atoms are in the ground state with spins aligned. (*b*) The leading edge of the probe beam pulse enters the sample. (*c*) Quantum superposition shifts the spins and the rapidly changing refractive index dramatically slows and shortens the probe beam inside the condensate. (*d*) Now completely contained inside the sample, the speed of the probe pulse is about 15 m/s. (*e*) The coupling beam is turned off and the probe pulse stops, its information stored in the shifted spins of the atoms. (*f*) Coupling beam is turned back on, the probe pulse regenerates, moves slowly to the edge of the sample, then leaves at 3×10^8 m/s. [*Courtesy of Samuel Velasco.*]

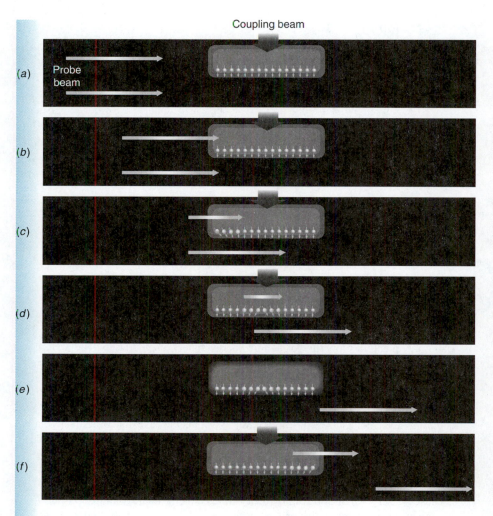

the two beams together shift the sodium atoms into a quantum superposition of both states, meaning that in that region of the sample *each* atom is in *both* hyperfine states (Figure 7-32*c*). Instead of both beams now being able to excite those atoms to the 3*p* level, the two processes cancel, a phenomenon called *quantum interference,* and the BEC becomes transparent to the probe beam, as in Figure 7-32*c*. A similar cancellation causes the index of refraction of the sample to change very steeply over the narrow frequency range of the probe pulse, slowing the leading edge from 3×10^8 m/s to about 15 m/s. As the rest of the probe pulse (still moving at 3×10^8 m/s) enters the sample and slows, it piles up behind the leading edge, dramatically compressing the pulse to about 0.05 mm in length, which fits easily within the sample. Over the region occupied by the compressed pulse the quantum superposition shifts the atomic spins in synchrony with the superposition as illustrated in Figure 7-32*d*.

At this point the coupling beam is turned off. The BEC immediately becomes opaque to the probe beam, the pulse comes to a stop and turns off! The light has "frozen"! The information imprinted on the pulse is now imprinted like a hologram on the spins of the atoms in the superposition states. (See Figure 7-32*e*.) When the coupling pulse is again turned on, the sample again becomes transparent to the probe pulse. The "frozen" probe pulse is regenerated carrying the original information,

moves slowly to the edge of the sample, then zooms away at 3×10^8 m/s. (See Figure 7-32f.)

The ability to slow and stop light raises new opportunities in many areas. For example, it may enable the development of quantum communications that cannot be eavesdropped upon. Building large-scale quantum computers may depend upon the ultrahigh-speed switching potential of quantum superpositions in slow light systems. Astrophysicists may be able to use BEC in vortex states, already achieved experimentally, with slow light to simulate in the laboratory the dragging of light into black holes. Stay tuned!

Summary

TOPIC	RELEVANT EQUATIONS AND REMARKS	
1. Schrödinger equation in three dimensions	The equation is solved for the hydrogen atom by separating it into three ordinary differential equations, one for each coordinate r, θ, ϕ. The quantum numbers n, l, and m arise from the boundary conditions to the solutions of these equations.	
2. Quantization		
Angular momentum	$\lvert \mathbf{L} \rvert = \sqrt{l(l+1)}\,\hbar \qquad l = 0, 1, \ldots, (n-1)$	7-22
z component of L	$L_z = m\hbar \qquad m = 0, \pm 1, \pm 2, \ldots, \pm l$	7-23
Energy	$E_n = -\left(\dfrac{kZe^2}{\hbar}\right)^2 \dfrac{\mu}{2n^2} = -13.6\,\dfrac{Z^2}{n^2}\,\text{eV}$	7-25
3. Hydrogen wave functions	$\Psi_{nlm} = C_{nlm} R_{nl}(r) Y_{lm}(\theta, \phi)$ where C_{nlm} are normalization constants, R_{nl} are the radial functions, and Y_{lm} are the spherical harmonics.	
4. Electron spin	The electron spin is not included in Schrödinger's wave equation.	
Magnitude of S	$\lvert \mathbf{S} \rvert = \sqrt{s(s+1)}\,\hbar \qquad s = \tfrac{1}{2}$	7-36
z component of S	$s_z = m_s \hbar \qquad m_s = \pm\tfrac{1}{2}$	
Stern-Gerlach experiment	This was the first direct observation of the electron spin.	
5. Spin-orbit coupling	L and S add to give the total angular momentum $\mathbf{J} = \mathbf{L} + \mathbf{S}$ whose magnitude is given by	
	$\lvert \mathbf{J} \rvert = \sqrt{j(j+1)}\,\hbar$	7-53
	where $j = l + s$ or $\lvert l - s \rvert$. This interaction leads to the fine-structure splitting of the energy levels.	
6. Exclusion principle	No more than one electron may occupy a given quantum state specified by a particular set of the single-particle quantum numbers n, l, m_l, and m_s.	

GENERAL REFERENCES

The following general references are written at a level appropriate for the readers of this book.

Brehm, J. J., and W. J. Mullin, *Introduction to the Structure of Matter,* Wiley, New York, 1989.

Eisberg, R., and R. Resnick, *Quantum Physics,* 2d ed., Wiley, New York, 1985.

Herzberg, G., *Atomic Spectra and Atomic Structure,* Dover, New York, 1944.

Kuhn, H. G., *Atomic Spectra,* Academic Press, New York, 1962.

Mehra, J., and H. Rechenberg, *The Historical Development of Quantum Theory,* Vol. 1, Springer-Verlag, New York, 1982.

Pauling, L., and S. Goudsmit, *The Structure of Line Spectra,* McGraw-Hill, New York, 1930.

NOTES

1. Degeneracy may arise because of a particular symmetry of the physical system, such as the symmetry of the potential energy described here. Degeneracy may also arise for completely different reasons and can certainly occur for nonproduct wave functions. The latter are sometimes called accidental degeneracies and both types can exist in the same system.

2. "Enough" means a complete set in the mathematical sense.

3. Such potentials are called central field or, sometimes, conservative potentials. The Coulomb potential and the gravitational potential are the most frequently encountered examples.

4. $L_z = |\mathbf{L}|$ would mean that $L_x = L_y = 0$.

5. The functions Y_{lm} and R_{nl} listed in Tables 7-1 and 7-2 are normalized. The C_{nlm} are simply the products of those corresponding normalization constants.

6. Wolfgang Pauli (1900–1958), Austrian physicist. A bona fide child prodigy, while a graduate student at Münich he wrote a paper on general relativity that earned Einstein's interest and admiration. Pauli was eighteen at the time. A brilliant theoretician, he became the conscience of the quantum physicists, assaulting "bad physics" with an often devastatingly sharp tongue. He belatedly won the Nobel Prize in physics in 1945 for his discovery of the exclusion principle.

7. Samuel A. Goudsmit (1902–1978) and George E. Uhlenbeck (1900–1988), Dutch-American physicists. While graduate students at Leiden, they proposed the idea of electron spin to their thesis adviser Paul Ehrenfest, who suggested that they ask H. A. Lorentz his opinion. After some delay, Lorentz pointed out that an electron spin of the magnitude necessary to explain the fine structure was inconsistent with special relativity. Returning to Ehrenfest with this disturbing news, they found that Ehrenfest had already sent their paper to a journal for publication.

8. Since the same symbol μ is used for both the reduced mass and the magnetic moment, some care is needed to keep these unrelated concepts clear. The symbol m is sometimes used to designate the magnetic moment, but there is confusion enough between the symbol m of the quantum number for the z component of angular momentum and m_e as the electron mass.

9. Otto Stern (1888–1969), German-American physicist, and Walther Gerlach (1899–1979), German physicist. After working as Einstein's assistant for two years, Stern developed the atomic/molecular beam techniques that enabled him and Gerlach, an excellent experimentalist, to show the existence of space quantization in silver. Stern received the 1943 Nobel Prize in physics for his pioneering molecular beam work.

10. The nucleus of an atom also has angular momentum and therefore a magnetic moment; but the mass of the nucleus is about 2000 times that of the electron for hydrogen, and greater still for other atoms. From Equation 7-39 we expect the magnetic moment of the nucleus to be on the order of 1/2000 of a Bohr magneton since M is now m_p rather than m_e. This small effect does not show up in the Stern-Gerlach experiment.

11. The letters first used, *s, p, d, f,* weren't really arbitrary. They described the visual appearance of certain groups of spectral lines: *s*harp, *p*rincipal, *d*iffuse, and *f*undamental. After improved instrumentation vastly increased the number of measurable lines, the letters went on alphabetically. As we noted in Chapter 4, the *K, L,* etc., notation was assigned by Barkla.

12. This particular form for writing the total spin was chosen because it also corresponded to the number of lines in the fine structure of the spectrum; e.g., hydrogen lines were doublets and $s = \frac{1}{2}$.

13. A more precise interpretation is that the electron, possessing an intrinsic magnetic moment due to its spin, carries with it a dipole magnetic field. This field varies in time due to the orbital motion of the electron, thus generating a time-varying electric field at the (stationary) proton which produces the energy shift.

14. Actually, it's not quite true for hydrogen either. W. Lamb showed that the $2S$ and $2P$ levels of hydrogen differ slightly in energy. That difference together with the spin-orbit splitting of the $2P$ state puts the $2^2P_{1/2}$ level 4.4×10^{-6} eV below the $2^2S_{1/2}$ level, an energy difference called the Lamb shift. It enables the $2^2S_{1/2}$ state, which would otherwise have been metastable due to the $\Delta l = \pm 1$ selection rule, to deactivate to the $1^2S_{1/2}$ ground state via a transition to the $2^2P_{1/2}$ level. The Lamb shift is accounted for by relativistic quantum theory.

15. We can think of this rule in terms of the conservation of angular momentum. The intrinsic spin angular momentum of a photon has the quantum number $s = 1$. For electric dipole radiation, the photon spin is its total angular momentum relative to the center of mass of the atom. If the initial angular momentum quantum number of the atom is j_1 and the final is j_2, the rules for combining angular momenta imply that $j_2 = j_1 + 1, j_1$, or $j_1 - 1$, if $j_1 \neq 0$. If $j_1 = 0$, j_2 must be 1.

16. This is true for nearly all two-electron atoms, such as He, Be, Mg, and Ca, except for the triplet P states in the very heavy atom mercury, where fine-structure splitting is of about the same order of magnitude as the single-triplet splitting.

17. Pieter Zeeman (1865–1943), Dutch physicist. His discovery of the Zeeman effect, which so enlightened our understanding of atomic structure, was largely ignored until its importance was pointed out by Lord Kelvin. Zeeman shared the 1902 Nobel Prize in physics with his professor H. A. Lorentz for its discovery.

18. The terminology is historical, arising from the fact that the effect in transitions between singlet states could be explained by Lorentz's classical electron theory and hence was "normal," while the effects in other transitions could not, and were thus mysterious or "anomalous."

19. This calculation can be found in G. Herzberg, *Atomic Spectra and Atomic Structure* (Dover: New York, 1944).

20. After Alfred Landé (1888–1975), German physicist. His collaborations with Born and Heisenberg led to the correct interpretation of the anomalous Zeeman effect.

PROBLEMS

Level I

Section 7-1 The Schrödinger Equation in Three Dimensions

7-1. Find the energies E_{311}, E_{222}, and E_{321} and construct an energy-level diagram for the three-dimensional cubic well which includes the third, fourth, and fifth excited states. Which of the states on your diagram are degenerate?

7-2. A particle is confined to a three-dimensional box that has sides L_1, $L_2 = 2L_1$, and $L_3 = 3L_1$. Give the sets of quantum numbers n_1, n_2, and n_3 that correspond to the lowest 10 energy levels of this box.

7-3. A particle moves in a potential well given by $V(x, y, z) = 0$ for $-L/2 < x < L/2$, $0 < y < L$, and $0 < z < L$ and $V = \infty$ outside these ranges. (a) Write an expression for the ground-state wave function for this particle. (b) How do the allowed energies compare with those for a box having $V = 0$ for $0 < x < L$, rather than for $-L/2 < x < L/2$?

7-4. Write down the wave functions for the 5 lowest energy levels of the particle in Problem 7-2.

7-5. (a) Repeat Problem 7-2 for the case $L_2 = 2L_1$ and $L_3 = 4L_1$. (b) What sets of quantum numbers correspond to degenerate energy levels?

7-6. Write down the wave functions for the lowest 10 quantized energy states for the particle in Problem 7-5.

7-7. Suppose the particle in Problem 7-1 is an electron and $L = 0.10$ nm. Compute the energy of the transitions from each of the third, fourth, and fifth excited states to the ground state.

7-8. Consider a particle moving in a two-dimensional space defined by $V = 0$ for $0 < x < L$ and $0 < y < L$ and $V = \infty$ elsewhere. (a) Write down the wave functions for the particle in this well. (b) Find the expression for the corresponding energies. (c) What are the sets of quantum numbers for the lowest-energy degenerate state?

Section 7-2 Quantization of the Angular Momentum and Energy in the Hydrogen Atom

7-9. If $n = 3$, (a) what are the possible values of l? (b) For each value of l in (a), list the possible values of m. (c) Using the fact that there are two quantum states for each value of l and m because of electron spin, find the total number of electron states with $n = 3$.

7-10. Find the total number of electron states with (a) $n = 2$ and (b) $n = 4$. (See Problem 7-9.) (c) Compute the energy of each state in eV.

7-11. The moment of inertia of a compact disc is about 10^{-5} kg · m². (a) Find the angular momentum $L = I\omega$ when it rotates at $\omega/2\pi = 735$ rev/min and (b) find the approximate value of the quantum number l.

7-12. Draw an accurately scaled vector model diagram illustrating the possible orientations of the angular momentum vector **L** for (*a*) $l = 1$, (*b*) $l = 2$, (*c*) $l = 4$. (*d*) Compute the magnitude of **L** in each case.

7-13. For $l = 2$, (*a*) what is the minimum value of $L_x^2 + L_y^2$? (*b*) What is the maximum value of $L_x^2 + L_y^2$? (*c*) What is $L_x^2 + L_y^2$ for $l = 2$ and $m = 1$? Can either L_x or L_y be determined from this? (*d*) What is the minimum value of n that this state can have?

7-14. For $l = 1$, find (*a*) the magnitude of the angular momentum L and (*b*) the possible values of m. (*c*) Draw to scale a vector diagram showing the possible orientations of **L** with the z axis. (*d*) Repeat the above for $l = 3$.

7-15. Show that, if V is a function only of r, then $d\mathbf{L}/dt = 0$, i.e., that **L** is conserved.

7-16. What are the possible values of n and m if (*a*) $l = 3$, and (*b*) $l = 4$, and (*c*) $l = 0$? (*d*) Compute the minimum possible energy for each case.

7-17. A hydrogen atom electron is in the $6f$ state. (*a*) What are the values of n and l? (*b*) Compute the energy of the electron. (*c*) Compute the magnitude of **L**. (*d*) Compute the possible values of L_z in this situation.

7-18. At what values of r/a_0 is the radial function R_{30} equal to zero? (See Table 7-2.)

Section 7-3 Hydrogen Atom Wave Functions

7-19. For the ground state of the hydrogen atom, find the values of (*a*) ψ, (*b*) ψ^2, and (*c*) the radial probability density $P(r)$ at $r = a_0$. Give your answers in terms of a_0.

7-20. For the ground state of the hydrogen atom, find the probability of finding the electron in the range $\Delta r = 0.03a_0$ at (*a*) $r = a_0$ and at (*b*) $r = 2a_0$.

7-21. The radial probability distribution function for hydrogen in its ground state can be written $P(r) = Cr^2 e^{-2Zr/a_0}$, where C is a constant. Show that $P(r)$ has its maximum value at $r = a_0/Z$.

7-22. Compute the normalization constant C_{210} in Equation 7-34.

7-23. Find the probability of finding the electron in the range $\Delta r = 0.02a_0$ at (*a*) $r = a_0$ and (*b*) $r = 2a_0$ for the state $n = 2$, $l = 0$, $m = 0$ in hydrogen. (See Problem 7-25 for the value of C_{200}.)

7-24. Show that the radial probability density for the $n = 2$, $l = 1$, $m = 0$ state of a one-electron atom can be written as

$$P(r) = A \cos^2 \theta r^4 e^{-Zr/a_0}$$

where A is a constant.

7-25. The value of the constant C_{200} in Equation 7-33 is

$$C_{200} = \frac{1}{\sqrt{2\pi}} \left(\frac{Z}{a_0} \right)^{3/2}$$

Find the values of (*a*) ψ, (*b*) ψ^2, and (*c*) the radial probability density $P(r)$ at $r = a_0$ for the state $n = 2$, $l = 0$, $m = 0$ in hydrogen. Give your answers in terms of a_0.

7-26. Show that an electron in the $n = 2$, $l = 1$ state of hydrogen is most likely to be found at $r = 4a_0$.

7-27. Neglecting the electron spin, show that the number of degenerate states of the nth level of hydrogen is given by n^2.

7-28. Show that the hydrogen wave function ψ_{100} is a solution of the Schrödinger equation.

Section 7-4 Electron Spin

7-29. If a classical system does not have a constant charge-to-mass ratio throughout the system, the magnetic moment can be written

$$\mu = g\frac{Q}{2M}L$$

where Q is the total charge, M is the total mass, and $g \neq 1$. (a) Show that $g = 2$ for a solid cylinder ($I = \frac{1}{2}MR^2$) that spins about its axis and has a uniform charge on its cylindrical surface. (b) Show that $g = 2.5$ for a solid sphere ($I = \frac{2}{5}MR^2$) that has a ring of charge on the surface at the equator, as shown in Figure 7-33.

7-30. Assuming the electron to be a classical particle, a sphere of radius 10^{-15} m and a uniform mass density, use the magnitude of the spin angular momentum $|\mathbf{S}| = [s(s + 1)]^{1/2}\hbar = (3/4)^{1/2}\hbar$ to compute the speed of rotation at the electron's equator. How does your result compare with the speed of light?

7-31. How many lines would be expected on the detector plate of a Stern-Gerlach experiment (see Figure 7-15) if we use a beam of (a) potassium atoms, (b) calcium atoms, (c) oxygen atoms, and (d) tin atoms?

7-32. The force on a magnetic moment with z component μ_z moving in an inhomogeneous magnetic field is given by Equation 7-51. If the silver atoms in the Stern-Gerlach experiment traveled horizontally 1 m through the magnet and 1 m in a field-free region at a speed of 250 m/s, what must have been the gradient of B_z, dB_z/dz, in order that the beams each be deflected a maximum of 0.5 mm from the central, or no-field, position?

7-33. (a) The angular momentum of the yttrium atom in the ground state is characterized by the quantum number $j = 3/2$. How many lines would you expect to see if you could do a Stern-Gerlach experiment with yttrium atoms? (b) How many lines would you expect to see if the beam consisted of atoms with zero spin, but $l = 1$?

Section 7-5 Total Angular Momentum and the Spin-Orbit Effect

7-34. List in spectroscopic notation all of the states in atomic hydrogen for $n = 2$ and $n = 4$, including the subscript for total angular momentum.

7-35. Suppose the outer electron in a potassium atom is in a state with $l = 2$. Compute the magnitude of $\mathbf{L}$. What are the possible values of j and the possible magnitudes of $\mathbf{J}$?

7-36. A hydrogen atom is in the $3D$ state ($n = 3$, $l = 2$). (a) What are the possible values of j? (b) What are the possible values of the magnitude of the total angular momentum? (c) What are the possible z components of the total angular momentum?

7-37. The total angular momentum of a hydrogen atom in a certain excited state has the quantum number $j = 3/2$. What can be the values of the orbital angular momentum quantum number l?

7-38. For a particular single-electron state j can be 5/2 or 7/2. What is l? Is this an s, p, d, f, or g state?

7-39. Consider a system of two electrons, each with $l = 1$ and $s = 1/2$. (a) What are the possible values of the quantum number for the total orbital angular momentum $\mathbf{L} = \mathbf{L}_1 + \mathbf{L}_2$? (b) What are the possible values of the quantum number S for the total spin $\mathbf{S} = \mathbf{S}_1 + \mathbf{S}_2$? (c) Using the results of parts (a) and (b), find the possible quantum numbers j for the combination $\mathbf{J} = \mathbf{L} + \mathbf{S}$. (d) What are the possible quantum numbers j_1 and j_2 for the total angular momentum of each particle? (e) Use the results of part (d) to calculate the possible values of j from the combinations of j_1 and j_2. Are these the same as in part (c)?

7-40. The prominent yellow doublet lines in the spectrum of sodium result from transitions from the $3P_{3/2}$ and $3P_{1/2}$ states to the ground state. The wavelengths of these two lines are 589.6 nm and 589.0 nm. (a) Calculate the energies in eV of the photons corresponding to these wavelengths. (b) The difference in energy of these photons equals the difference in energy ΔE of the $3P_{3/2}$ and $3P_{1/2}$ states. This energy difference is due to the spin-orbit effect. Calculate ΔE. (c) If the $3p$ electron in sodium sees an internal magnetic field B, the spin-orbit energy splitting will be of the order of $\Delta E = 2\mu_B B$, where μ_B is the Bohr magneton. Estimate B from the energy difference ΔE found in part (b).

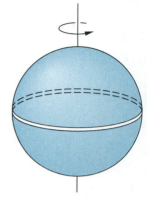

Fig. 7-33 Solid sphere with charge Q uniformly distributed on ring.

Section 7-6 The Schrödinger Equation for Two (or More) Particles

7-41. Show that the wave function of Equation 7-59 satisfies the Schrödinger equation (Equation 7-57) with $V = 0$ and find the energy of this state.

7-42. Two neutrons are in an infinite square well with $L = 2.0$ fm. What is the minimum total energy that the system can have? (Neutrons, like electrons, have antisymmetric wave functions. Ignore spin.)

7-43. Five identical noninteracting particles are placed in an infinite square well with $L = 1.0$ nm. Compute the lowest total energy for the system if the particles are (*a*) electrons and (*b*) pions. Pions have symmetric wave functions and their mass is 264 m_e.

Section 7-7 Ground States of Atoms: The Periodic Table

7-44. Write the electron configuration of (*a*) carbon, (*b*) oxygen, and (*c*) argon.

7-45. Write the electron configuration of (*a*) chlorine, (*b*) calcium, and (*c*) germanium.

7-46. In Figure 7-20 there are small dips in the ionization potential curve at $Z = 31$ (gallium), $Z = 49$ (indium), and $Z = 81$ (thallium) that are not labeled in the figure. Explain these dips, using the electron configuration of these atoms given in Appendix C.

7-47. Which of the following atoms would you expect to have its ground state split by the spin-orbit interaction: Li, B, Na, Al, K, Ag, Cu, Ga? (*Hint:* Use Appendix C to see which elements have $l = 0$ in their ground state and which do not.)

7-48. If the $3s$ electron in sodium did not penetrate the inner core its energy would be $-13.6 \text{ eV}/3^2 = -1.51$ eV. Because it does penetrate it sees a higher effective Z and its energy is lower. Use the measured ionization potential of 5.14 V to calculate Z_{eff} for the $3s$ electron in sodium.

7-49. What elements have these ground-state electron configurations? (*a*) $1s^2 2s^2 2p^6 3s^2 3p^2$ and (*b*) $1s^2 2s^2 2p^6 3s^2 3p^6 4s^2$?

7-50. Give the possible values of the z component of the orbital angular momentum of (*a*) a d electron, (*b*) an f electron, and (*c*) an s electron.

Section 7-8 Excited States and Spectra of Atoms

7-51. Which of the following elements should have an energy-level diagram similar to that of sodium and which should be similar to mercury: Li, He, Ca, Ti, Rb, Ag, Cd, Mg, Cs, Ba, Fr, Ra?

7-52. The optical spectra of atoms with two electrons in the same outer shell are similar, but they are quite different from the spectra of atoms with just one outer electron because of the interaction of the two electrons. Separate the following elements into two groups such that those in each group have similar spectra: lithium, beryllium, sodium, magnesium, potassium, calcium, chromium, nickel, cesium, and barium.

7-53. Which of the following elements should have optical spectra similar to that of hydrogen and which should have optical spectra similar to that of helium: Li, Ca, Ti, Rb, Ag, Cd, Ba, Hg, Fr, Ra?

7-54. The quantum numbers n, l, and j for the outer electron in potassium have the values 4, 0, and $\frac{1}{2}$ respectively in the ground state; 4, 1, and $\frac{1}{2}$ in the first excited state; and 4, 1, and $\frac{3}{2}$ in the second excited state. Make a table giving the n, l, and j values for the 12 lowest energy states in potassium.

7-55. Which of the following transitions in sodium do not occur as electric dipole transitions? (Give the selection rule that is violated.)

$$4S_{1/2} \longrightarrow 3S_{1/2} \qquad 4S_{1/2} \longrightarrow 3P_{3/2} \qquad 4P_{3/2} \longrightarrow 3S_{1/2} \qquad 4D_{5/2} \longrightarrow 3P_{1/2}$$

$$4D_{3/2} \longrightarrow 3P_{1/2} \qquad 4D_{3/2} \longrightarrow 3S_{1/2} \qquad 5D_{3/2} \longrightarrow 4S_{1/2} \qquad 5P_{1/2} \longrightarrow 3S_{1/2}$$

7-56. Transitions between the inner electron levels of heavier atoms result in the emission of characteristic x rays, as was discussed in Section 4-4. (*a*) Calculate the energy of the electron in the *K* shell for tungsten using $Z - 1$ for the effective nuclear charge. (*b*) The experimental result for this energy is 69.5 keV. Assume that the effective nuclear charge is $(Z - \sigma)$, where σ is called the screening constant, and calculate σ from the experimental result for the energy.

7-57. Since the *P* states and the *D* states of sodium are all doublets, there are four possible energies for transitions between these states. Indicate which three transitions are allowed and which one is not allowed by the selection rule of Equation 7-67.

7-58. The relative penetration of the inner-core electrons by the outer electron in sodium can be described by the calculation of Z_{eff} from $E = \dfrac{-[Z_{\text{eff}}^2(13.6 \text{ eV})]}{n^2}$ and comparing with $E = -13.6 \text{ eV}/n^2$ for no penetration (see Problem 7-48). (*a*) Find the energies of the outer electron in the 3*s*, 3*p*, and 3*d* states from Figure 7-22. (*Hint:* An accurate method is to use -5.14 eV for the ground state as given and find the energy of the 3*p* and 3*d* states from the photon energies of the indicated transitions.) (*b*) Find Z_{eff} for the 3*p* and 3*d* states. (*c*) Is the approximation $-13.6 \text{ eV}/n^2$ good for any of these states?

7-59. A hydrogen atom in the ground state is placed in a magnetic field of strength $B_z = 0.55$ T. (*a*) Compute the energy splitting of the spin states. (*b*) Which state has the higher energy? (*c*) If you wish to excite the atom from the lower to the higher energy state with a photon, what frequency must the photon have? In what part of the electromagnetic spectrum does this lie?

7-60. Show that the change in wavelength $\Delta\lambda$ of a transition due to a small change in energy is

$$\Delta\lambda \approx -\frac{\lambda^2}{hc}\Delta E$$

(*Hint:* Differentiate $E = hc/\lambda$.)

7-61. (*a*) Find the normal Zeeman energy shift $\Delta E = e\hbar B/2m_e$ for a magnetic field of strength $B = 0.05$ T. (*b*) Use the result of Problem 7-60 to calculate the wavelength changes for the singlet transition in mercury of wavelength $\lambda = 579.07$ nm. (*c*) If the smallest wavelength change that can be measured in a spectrometer is 0.01 nm, what is the strength of the magnetic field needed to observe the Zeeman effect in this transition?

Level II

7-62. If the outer electron in lithium moves in the $n = 2$ Bohr orbit, the effective nuclear charge would be $Z_{\text{eff}}e = 1e$, and the energy of the electron would be $-13.6 \text{ eV}/2^2 = -3.4$ eV. However, the ionization energy of lithium is 5.39 eV, not 3.4 eV. Use this fact to calculate the effective nuclear charge Z_{eff} seen by the outer electron in lithium. Assume that $r = 4a_0$ for the outer electron.

7-63. Show that the expectation value of r for the electron in the ground state of a one-electron atom is $\langle r \rangle = (3/2)a_0/Z$.

7-64. If a rigid body has moment of inertia I and angular velocity ω, its kinetic energy is

$$E = \tfrac{1}{2}I\omega^2 = \frac{(I\omega)^2}{2I} = \frac{L^2}{2I}$$

where L is the angular momentum. The solution of the Schrödinger equation for this problem leads to quantized energy values given by

$$E_l = \frac{l(l+1)\hbar^2}{2I}$$

(*a*) Make an energy-level diagram of these energies, and indicate the transitions that obey the selection rule $\Delta l = \pm 1$. (*b*) Show that the allowed transition energies are E_1, $2E_1$, $3E_1$, $4E_1$, etc., where $E_1 = \hbar^2/I$. (*c*) The moment of inertia of the H_2 molecule is $I = \frac{1}{2}m_p r^2$, where m_p is the mass of the proton and $r \approx 0.074$ nm is the distance between the protons. Find the energy of the first excited state $l = 1$ for H_2, assuming it is a rigid rotor. (*d*) What is the wavelength of the radiation emitted in the transition $l = 1$ to $l = 0$ for the H_2 molecule?

7-65. In a Stern-Gerlach experiment hydrogen atoms in their ground state move with speed $v_x = 14.5$ km/s. The magnetic field is in the z direction and its maximum gradient is given by $dB_z/dz = 600$ T/m. (*a*) Find the maximum acceleration of the hydrogen atoms. (*b*) If the region of the magnetic field extends over a distance $\Delta x = 75$ cm and there is an additional 1.25 m from the edge of the field to the detector, find the maximum distance between the two lines on the detector.

7-66. Find the minimum value of the angle between the angular momentum **L** and the z axis for a general value of l, and show that for large values of l, $\theta_{\min} \approx 1/l^{1/2}$.

7-67. The wavelengths of the photons emitted by potassium corresponding to transitions from the $4P_{3/2}$ and $4P_{1/2}$ states to the ground state are 766.41 nm and 769.90 nm. (*a*) Calculate the energies of these photons in electron volts. (*b*) The difference in energies of these photons equals the difference in energy ΔE between the $4P_{3/2}$ and $4P_{1/2}$ states in potassium. Calculate ΔE. (*c*) Estimate the magnetic field that the $4p$ electron in potassium experiences.

7-68. The radius of the proton is about $R_0 = 10^{-15}$ m. The probability that the electron is inside the volume occupied by the proton is given by

$$P = \int_0^{R_0} P(r)\, dr$$

where $P(r)$ is the radial probability density. Compute P for the hydrogen ground state. (*Hint:* Show that $e^{-2r/a_0} \approx 1$ for $r \ll a_0$ is valid for this calculation.)

7-69. (*a*) Calculate the Landé g factor (Equation 7-73) for the $^2P_{1/2}$ and $^2S_{1/2}$ levels in a one-electron atom and show that there are four different energies for the transition between these levels in a magnetic field. (*b*) Calculate the Landé g factor for the $^2P_{3/2}$ level and show that there are six different energies for the transition $^2P_{3/2} \to {}^2S_{1/2}$ in a magnetic field.

7-70. (*a*) Show that the function

$$\psi = A\frac{r}{a_0}e^{-r/2a_0}\cos\theta$$

is a solution of Equation 7-9, where A is a constant and a_0 is the Bohr radius. (*b*) Find the constant A.

Level III

7-71. Consider a hypothetical hydrogen atom in which the electron is replaced by a K^- particle. The K^- is a meson with spin 0, hence, no intrinsic magnetic moment. The only magnetic moment for this atom is that given by Equation 7-43. If this atom is placed in a magnetic field with $B_z = 1.0$ T, (*a*) what is the effect on the $1s$ and $2p$ states? (*b*) Into how many lines does the $2p \to 1s$ spectral line split? (*c*) What is the fractional separation $\Delta\lambda/\lambda$ between adjacent lines? (See Problem 7-60.) The mass of the K^- is 493.7 MeV/c^2.

7-72. If relativistic effects are ignored, the $n = 3$ level for one-electron atoms consists of the $3^2S_{1/2}$, $3^2P_{1/2}$, $3^2P_{3/2}$, $3^2D_{3/2}$, and $3^2D_{5/2}$ states. Compute the spin-orbit effect splittings of $3P$ and $3D$ states for hydrogen.

7-73. In the anomalous Zeeman effect, the external magnetic field is much weaker than the internal field seen by the electron as a result of its orbital motion. In the vector model (Figure 7-29) the vectors **L** and **S** precess rapidly around **J** because of the internal field and **J** precesses slowly around the external field. The energy splitting is found by first calculating the component of the magnetic moment μ_J in the direction of **J** and then finding the component of μ_z in the direction of **B**. (a) Show that $\mu_J = \dfrac{\boldsymbol{\mu} \cdot \mathbf{J}}{J}$ can be written

$$\mu_J = -\frac{\mu_B}{\hbar J}(L^2 + 2S^2 + 3\mathbf{S} \cdot \mathbf{L})$$

(b) From $J^2 = (\mathbf{L} + \mathbf{S}) \cdot (\mathbf{L} + \mathbf{S})$ show that $\mathbf{S} \cdot \mathbf{L} = \frac{1}{2}(J^2 - L^2 - S^2)$. (c) Substitute your result in part (b) into that of part (a) to obtain

$$\mu_J = -\frac{\mu_B}{2\hbar J}(3J^2 + S^2 - L^2)$$

(d) Multiply your result by J_z/J to obtain

$$\mu_z = -\mu_B\left(1 + \frac{J^2 + S^2 - L^2}{2J^2}\right)\frac{J_z}{\hbar}$$

7-74. If the angular momentum of the nucleus is **I** and that of the atomic electrons is **J**, the total angular momentum of the atom is $\mathbf{F} = \mathbf{I} + \mathbf{J}$, and the total angular momentum quantum number f ranges from $I + J$ to $|I - J|$. Show that the number of possible f values is $2I + 1$ if $I < J$ or $2J + 1$ if $J < I$. (If you can't find a general proof, show it for enough special cases to convince yourself of its validity.) (Because of the very small interaction of the nuclear magnetic moment with that of the electrons, a hyperfine splitting of the spectral lines is observed. When $I < J$, the value of I can be determined by counting the number of lines.)

7-75. Because of the spin and magnetic moment of the proton, there is a very small splitting of the ground state of the hydrogen atom called *hyperfine splitting*. The splitting can be thought of as caused by the interaction of the electron magnetic moment with the magnetic field due to the magnetic moment of the proton, or vice versa. The magnetic moment of the proton is parallel to its spin and is about $2.8\mu_N$, where $\mu_N = e\hbar/2m_p$ is called the *nuclear magneton*. (a) The magnetic field at a distance r from a magnetic moment varies with angle, but it is of the order of $B \sim 2k_m\mu/r^3$, where $k_m = 10^{-7}$ in SI units. Find B at $r = a_0$ if $\mu = 2.8\mu_N$. (b) Calculate the order of magnitude of the hyperfine splitting energy $\Delta E \approx 2\mu_B B$, where μ_B is the Bohr magneton and B is your result from part (a). (c) Calculate the order of magnitude of the wavelength of radiation emitted if a hydrogen atom makes a "spin flip" transition between the hyperfine levels of the ground state. (Your result is greater than the actual wavelength of this transition, 21.22 cm, because $\langle r^{-3}\rangle$ is appreciably smaller than a_0^{-3}, making the energy ΔE found in part (b) greater. The detection of this radiation from hydrogen atoms in interstellar space is an important part of radio astronomy.)

Chapter 8

Statistical Physics

The physical world that we experience with our senses consists entirely of *macroscopic* objects, i.e., systems that are large compared with atomic dimensions and, thus, are assembled from very large numbers of atoms. As we proceed to the description of such systems from our starting point of studying single-electron atoms, then multielectron atoms, we expect to encounter increasing complexity and difficulty in correctly explaining their observed properties. Classically, the behavior of any macroscopic system could, in principle, be predicted in detail from the solution of the equation of motion for each constituent particle, given its state of motion at some particular time; however, the obvious problems with such an approach soon become intractable. For example, consider the difficulties that would accompany the task of accounting for the measured properties of a standard liter of any gas by simultaneously solving the equations of motion for all of the 10^{22} molecules of which the system is composed. Fortunately, we can predict the values of the measurable properties of macroscopic systems without the need to track the motions of each individual particle. This remarkable shortcut is made possible by the fact that we can apply general principles of physics, such as conservation of energy and momentum, to large ensembles of particles, ignoring their individual motions, and determine the *probable* behavior of the system from *statistical* considerations. We then use the fact that there is a relation between the calculated probable behavior and the observed properties of the system. This successful, so-called microscopic approach to explaining the behavior of large systems is called *statistical mechanics*. It depends critically on the system's containing a sufficiently large number of particles that ordinary statistical theory is valid.[1]

In this chapter we will investigate how this statistical approach can be applied to predict the way in which a given amount of energy will most likely be distributed among the particles of a system. You have already encountered kinetic theory, the first successful such microscopic approach, in introductory physics. We shall see how, in an isolated system of particles in thermal equilibrium, the particles must be able to exchange energy, one result of which is that the energy of any individual particle may sometimes be larger and sometimes smaller than the average value for a particle in the system. Classically, statistical theory requires that the values of the energy taken on by an individual particle over time, or the values of the energy assumed by all of the particles in the system at any particular time, be determined by a specific probability distribution, the *Boltzmann distribution*. We shall then see how quantum considerations require modification of the procedures used for classical particles, obtaining in the process the quantum-mechanical *Fermi-Dirac distribution* for particles with antisymmetric wave functions, such as electrons, and the *Bose-Einstein*

distribution for particles with symmetric wave functions, such as helium atoms. Finally, we shall apply the distributions to several physical systems, comparing our predictions with experimental observations and gaining an understanding of such important phenomena as superfluidity, Bose-Einstein condensation, and the specific heat of solids.

8-1 Classical Statistics

More

Some introductory physics courses include a discussion of the kinetic theory of gases, but many do not. Since the assumptions, definitions, and basic results of kinetic theory form the foundation of classical statistics, we have included *Kinetic Theory: A Brief Review* on the home page: www.whfreeman.com/modphysics4e   See also Equations 8-1 through 8-12, Example 8-1, and Figure 8-1 here.

Boltzmann Distribution

Statistical physics is concerned with the distribution of a fixed amount of energy among a large number of particles, from which the observable properties of the system may be deduced. Boltzmann[2] derived a distribution relation that predicts the probable numbers of particles that will occupy each of the available energy states in a classical system consisting of a large number of identical particles in thermal equilibrium, and is therefore the fundamental distribution function of classical statistical physics. *Boltzmann's distribution* $f_B(E)$ is given by

$$f_B(E) = Ae^{-E/kT} \qquad\qquad \textbf{8-13}$$

where *A* is a normalization constant whose value depends on the particular system being considered and *k* is the *Boltzmann constant:*

$$k = 1.381 \times 10^{-23}\,\text{J/K} = 8.617 \times 10^{-5}\,\text{eV/K}$$

Boltzmann's derivation was done to establish the fundamental properties of a distribution function for the velocities of molecules in a gas in thermal equilibrium that had been obtained by Maxwell a few years before and to show that the velocity distribution for a gas that was not in thermal equilibrium would evolve toward Maxwell's distribution over time. Boltzmann's derivation is more complex than is appropriate for our discussions, but in Appendix B3 we present a straightforward numerical derivation that results in an approximation of the correct distribution and then show by a simple mathematical argument that the form obtained is exact and is the only one possible.

The quantity $e^{-E/kT}$ is called the *Boltzmann factor.* Equation 8-13 can be combined with Equation B3-1a to find the number of particles with energy E, yielding

$$n(E) = g(E)f_B(E) = Ag(E)e^{-E/kT} \qquad\qquad \textbf{8-14}$$

Fig. 8-2 $n(E)$ versus E for
data from Table B3-1. Solid
curve is the exponential
$n(E) = Be^{-E/E_c}$, where the
constants B and E_c have been
adjusted to give the best fit to
the data points.

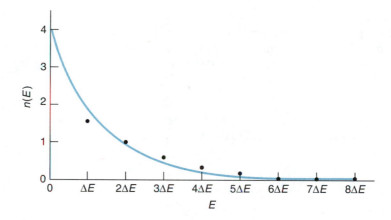

Classically, the energy E is a continuous function and so is $n(E)$. (See Figure 8-2.) Consequently, $g(E)$ and $f_B(E)$ are also continuous functions. The statistical weight (degeneracy) $g(E)$ of Equation 8-14 is then referred to as the *density of states*, meaning that $g(E)\,dE$ equals the number of states with energy between E and $E + dE$. To see how the Boltzmann distribution works and the utility of the Boltzmann factor, let us consider two examples.

EXAMPLE 8-2 **The Law of Atmospheres** Consider an ideal gas in a uniform gravitational field. (*a*) Find how the density of the gas depends upon the height above ground. (*b*) Assuming that air is an ideal gas with molecular weight 28.6, compute the density of air 1 km above the ground when $T = 300$ K. (The density at the ground is 1.292 kg/m³ at 300 K.)

Solution
(*a*) Let the force of gravity be in the negative z direction and consider a column of gas of cross-sectional area A. The energy of a gas molecule is then

$$E = \frac{p_x^2}{2m} + \frac{p_y^2}{2m} + \frac{p_z^2}{2m} + mgz = \frac{p^2}{2m} + mgz$$

where $p^2 = p_x^2 + p_y^2 + p_z^2$ and mgz is the potential energy of a molecule at height z above the ground. The density ρ is proportional to f_B, since ρ is proportional to N, the number of molecules in a unit volume at height z, and N is proportional to f_B.
   From Equation 8-13 we have

$$f_B = Ae^{-p^2/2mkT}e^{-mgz/kT}$$

Since we are interested only in the dependence on z, we can integrate over the other variables p_x, p_y, and p_z. The integration merely gives a new normalization constant A', i.e., the result is equivalent to ignoring these variables. The fraction of the molecules between z and $z + dz$ is then

$$f_B(z)\,dz = A'e^{-mgz/kT}\,dz \qquad\qquad \textbf{8-15}$$

The constant A' is obtained from the normalization condition $\int_0^\infty f_B(z)dz = 1$. The result is $A' = mg/kT$. The density, therefore, also decreases exponentially with the distance above the ground. This is known as the *law of atmospheres*.

(b) The ratio of the density at $z = 1000$ m to that at $z = 0$ m is the same as $f_B(1000)/f_B(0)$, where $f_B(z)$ is given by Equation 8-15. Thus,

$$\frac{\rho(1000)}{\rho(0)} = \frac{f_B(1000)}{f_B(0)} = \frac{e^{-mg(1000)/k(300)}}{e^{-mg(0)/k(300)}} = e^{-mg(1000)/k(300)}$$

Substituting $m = 28.6 \times 1.67 \times 10^{-27}$ kg and $g = 9.8$ m/s^2 yields

$$\rho(1000) = \rho(0)e^{-0.113} = 1.292 \times 0.893 = 1.154 \text{ kg/m}^3$$

EXAMPLE 8-3 **H Atoms in First Excited State** The first excited state E_2 of the hydrogen atom is 10.2 eV above the ground state E_1. What is the ratio of the number of atoms in the first excited state to the number in the ground state at (a) $T = 300$ K and (b) $T = 5800$ K?

Solution

1. The number of atoms in a state with energy E is given by Equation 8-14:

$$n(E) = Ag(E)e^{-E/kT}$$

2. The ratio of the number in the first excited state to the number in the ground state is then:

$$\frac{n_2}{n_1} = \frac{Ag_2e^{-E_2/kT}}{Ag_1e^{-E_1/kT}} = \frac{g_2}{g_1}e^{-(E_2-E_1)/kT}$$

3. The statistical weight (= degeneracy) of the ground state g_1, including spin, is 2; the degeneracy of the first excited state g_2 is 8 (one $l = 0$ and three $l = 1$ states, each with two spin states). Therefore:

$$\frac{g_2}{g_1} = \frac{8}{2} = 4$$

and

$$\frac{n_2}{n_1} = 4e^{-(E_2-E_1)/kT}$$

4. For question (a), at $T = 300$ K, $kT \approx 0.026$ eV. Substituting this and $E_2 - E_1 = 10.2$ eV from above gives:

$$\frac{n_2}{n_1} = 4e^{-(10.2)/(0.026)}$$

$$= 4e^{-392} \approx 10^{-171}$$

$$\approx 0$$

5. For question (*b*), at the surface of the sun where $T = 5800$ K, $kT \approx 0.500$. Substituting this and $E_2 - E_1 = 10.2$ eV gives:

$$\frac{n_2}{n_1} = 4e^{-(10.2)/(0.500)} = 4e^{-20.4}$$

$$\approx e^{-19} \approx 10^{-8}$$

Remarks: *The result in step 4 illustrates that, because of the large energy difference between the two states compared with kT, very few atoms are in the first excited state. Even fewer would be in the higher excited states, which explains why a container of hydrogen sitting undisturbed at room temperature does not spontaneously emit the visible Balmer series. At the surface of the sun (step 5 above) about 10^{15} atoms of every mole of atomic hydrogen are in the first excited state.*

More

In learning about systems containing large numbers of particles, the meaning of the *temperature* needs to be more carefully defined. It is closely related to another descriptor of such systems, the *entropy*. To help you understand both concepts better we have included *Temperature and Entropy* on the home page: www.whfreeman.com/modphysics4e

Maxwell Distribution of Molecular Speeds

The Boltzmann distribution is a very fundamental relation from which many properties of classical systems, both gases and condensed matter, can be derived. We will limit ourselves to discussing two of the most important, beginning with Maxwell's distribution of the speeds of molecules in a gas. Maxwell derived both the velocity and speed distributions of gases in 1859, some five years before Boltzmann derived Equation 8-13. Maxwell obtained the velocity distribution, which can also be used to obtain the speed distribution, by assuming that the components v_x, v_y, and v_z of the velocity were independent and that, therefore, the probabilities of a molecule having a certain v_x, v_y, v_z could be factored into the product of the separate probabilities of its having v_x, v_y, and v_z. He also assumed that the distribution could depend only on the speed, i.e., the velocity components could occur only in the combination $v_x^2 + v_y^2 + v_z^2$. He thus wrote for the velocity distribution function $F(v_x, v_y, v_z)$

$$F(v_x, v_y, v_z) = f(v_x)f(v_y)f(v_z) \qquad \textbf{8-16}$$

where $f(v_x)$ is the distribution function for v_x only, i.e., $f(v_x)dv_x$ is the fraction of the total number of molecules which have their x component of velocity between v_x and $v_x + dv_x$.[3] From these assumptions Maxwell was able to derive the probability distributions of the velocity components. The form for $f(v_x)$ is

$$f(v_x) = Ce^{-mv_x^2/2kT} \qquad\qquad \textbf{8-17}$$

with similar expressions for $f(v_y)$ and $f(v_z)$, and the constant C is determined by the normalization condition

$$\int_{-\infty}^{+\infty} f(v_x)\, dv_x = \int_{-\infty}^{+\infty} Ce^{-mv_x^2/2kT}\, dv_x = 1 \qquad\qquad \textbf{8-18}$$

We shall need to evaluate integrals of the form that appears in Equation 8-18 several times in this chapter. Table B1-1 in Appendix B1 lists those that we will encounter. Using the table to evaluate Equation 8-18 with $\lambda = m/2kT$, we find

$$C = (\lambda/\pi)^{1/2} = \left(\frac{m}{2\pi kT}\right)^{1/2} \qquad\qquad \textbf{8-19}$$

Substituting this result for C into Equation 8-18, we have

$$f(v_x) = \left(\frac{m}{2\pi kT}\right)^{1/2} e^{-mv_x^2/2kT} \qquad\qquad \textbf{8-20}$$

Figure 8-3 shows a sketch of $f(v_x)$ versus v_x. Of course, $f(v_x)$ is symmetric about the origin, $f(v_x) = f(-v_x)$, so the average of v_x is zero. As can be seen from the figure, the most probable v_x is also zero. The complete velocity distribution is

$$F(v_x, v_y, v_z) = \left(\frac{m}{2\pi kT}\right)^{3/2} e^{-m(v_x^2 + v_y^2 + v_z^2)/2kT} \qquad\qquad \textbf{8-21}$$

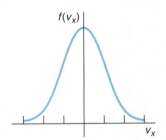

Fig. 8-3 The distribution function $f(v_x)$ for the x component of velocity. This is a Gaussian curve symmetric about the origin.

The utility of distribution functions is that they enable the calculation of average or expectation values of physical quantities, i.e., they allow us to make predictions regarding the physical properties of systems. The determination of the average value of a quantity whose distribution is known is discussed for classical systems in Appendix B2. The observation from Figure 8-3 that the average value of v_x is zero can be verified by computing $\langle v_x \rangle$ from Equation B2-6 using the distribution of v_x given by Equation 8-20 and Table B1-1:

$$\langle v_x \rangle = \int_{-\infty}^{+\infty} v_x f(v_x)\, dv_x = \int_{-\infty}^{+\infty} v_x \left(\frac{m}{2\pi kT}\right)^{1/2} e^{-mv_x^2/2kT}\, dv_x$$

Writing $\lambda = m/2kT$ we have

$$\langle v_x \rangle = (\lambda/\pi) \int_{-\infty}^{+\infty} v_x e^{-\lambda v_x^2}\, dv_x$$

From Table B1-1 we see that the value of the integral is zero, so $\langle v_x \rangle = 0$, as expected.

We shall now derive the probability distribution function for the speeds of the molecules in an ideal gas from the Boltzmann distribution. Consider the system to consist of N classical particles per unit volume, each of whose energy is entirely translational kinetic energy. (If the particles had other forms of energy, we could integrate over those variables, as was illustrated in Example 8-2.) So we have for each molecule

$$E = \tfrac{1}{2}mv^2 = \tfrac{1}{2}m(v_x^2 + v_y^2 + v_z^2)$$

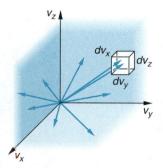

Fig. 8-4 Velocity vectors in velocity space. The velocity distribution function gives the fraction of molecular velocities whose vectors end in a cell of volume $dv_x\,dv_y\,dv_z$.

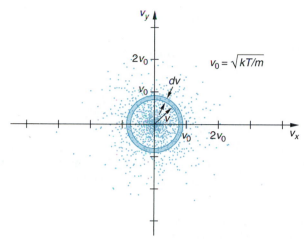

Fig. 8-5 Two-dimensional representation of velocity distribution in velocity space. Each molecular velocity with components v_x, v_y, and v_z is represented by a point in velocity space. The velocity distribution function is the density of points in this space. The density is maximum at the origin. The speed distribution is found by multiplying the density times the volume of the spherical shell $4\pi v^2\,dv$. [*This computer-generated plot courtesy of Paul Doherty, The Exploratorium.*]

The velocities of the molecules vary continuously from 0 to ∞; hence the energy is also continuous. We then have that the number of molecules in the interval dE at E is given by Equation 8-14 as

$$n(E)\,dE = Ag(E)e^{-E/kT}\,dE = Ag(E)e^{-mv^2/2kT}\,dE \qquad \textbf{8-22}$$

To find the density of states $g(E)$, we need to introduce the concept of *velocity space*, which can be thought of as the pictorial representation of the velocity distribution F given by Equation 8-21. Imagine the velocity vector of each molecule placed with its tail at the origin of a coordinate system v_x, v_y, v_z as in Figure 8-4. The tip of each velocity vector ends at a point whose coordinates in this three-dimensional space are (v_x, v_y, v_z) and the length of each is $v = (v_x^2 + v_y^2 + v_z^2)^{1/2}$, which is that molecule's speed. Of our N molecules, the number whose vectors end in the velocity "volume" element $dv_x\,dv_y\,dv_z$ is $NF(v_x, v_y, v_z)dv_x\,dv_y\,dv_z$.[4] (See Figure 8-4.) A simpler representation is shown in Figure 8-5, where each molecular velocity with components v_x, v_y, v_z is represented by a point, i.e., just the tip of its velocity vector. From Figure 8-5 we note that the number of possible states $f(v)\,dv$ with speeds between v and $v + dv$ is proportional to the volume of the spherical shell between v and $v + dv$. Since the volume of the sphere is $(4/3)\pi v^3$, the differential volume of the shell is $4\pi v^2 dv$. Thus, we have

$$f(v)\,dv = C4\pi v^2\,dv \qquad \textbf{8-23}$$

where C is the proportionality constant. Each value of v corresponds to a single value of the energy, since $E = \frac{1}{2}mv^2$, so the density of energy states $g(E)dE$ equals $f(v)dv$, and we have that

$$g(E)\,dE = 4\pi Cv^2\,dv \qquad \textbf{8-24}$$

and substituting Equation 8-24 into Equation 8-22 yields

$$n(E)\,dE = 4\pi A'v^2 e^{-mv^2/2kT}\,dv \qquad \textbf{8-25}$$

where A' is another constant. Again, since each value of v corresponds to a single value of E, we may write

$$n(v)\,dv = n(E)\,dE = 4\pi A' v^2 e^{-mv^2/2kT}\,dv \qquad \textbf{8-26}$$

We then find A' from the condition that

$$N = \int_0^\infty n(v)\,dv = 4\pi A' \int_0^\infty v^2 e^{-mv^2/2kT}\,dv \qquad \textbf{8-27}$$

Evaluating the integral, we have

$$A' = N\left(\frac{m}{2\pi kT}\right)^{3/2}$$

and inserting this A' into Equation 8-26 yields the famous *Maxwell distribution of molecular speeds:*

$$n(v)\,dv = 4\pi N\left(\frac{m}{2\pi kT}\right)^{3/2} v^2 e^{-mv^2/2kT}\,dv \qquad \textbf{8-28}$$

The distribution of speeds is shown graphically in Figure 8-6. The most probable speed v_m, the average speed $\langle v \rangle$, and the rms speed v_{rms} are indicated in the figure. Although the velocity distribution function F is a maximum at the origin ($v = 0$), the speed distribution function $n(v)$ approaches zero as $v \to 0$ because the latter is proportional to the volume of the spherical shell, $4\pi v^2\,dv$, which approaches zero. At very high speeds, the speed distribution function again approaches zero because of the exponential factor $e^{-mv^2/2kT}$.

The most probable speed v_m is that where $n(v)$ has its maximum value. It is left as an exercise (see Problem 8-9) to show that its value is

$$v_m = \left(\frac{2kT}{m}\right)^{1/2} \qquad \textbf{8-29}$$

The average speed $\langle v \rangle$ is obtained in general and for a specific situation in the next example.

One of the ways used to separate ^{235}U from the far more abundant ^{238}U isotope is to react the uranium metal with fluorine, forming UF_6, a gas. ^{235}UF diffuses through a membrane just a bit faster than ^{238}UF, since both molecules have the same average kinetic energy. After several stages of diffusion, the concentration of ^{235}U is high enough for making nuclear reactor fuel (see Chapter 12).

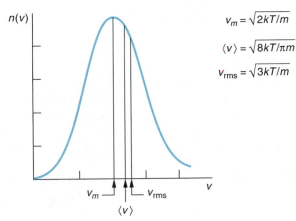

$$v_m = \sqrt{2kT/m}$$

$$\langle v \rangle = \sqrt{8kT/\pi m}$$

$$v_{rms} = \sqrt{3kT/m}$$

Fig. 8-6 Maxwell speed distribution function $n(v)$. The most probable speed v_m, the average speed $\langle v \rangle$, and the rms speed v_{rms} are indicated.

EXAMPLE 8-4 **Average Speed of N_2 Molecules** Obtain the average speed $\langle v \rangle$ of the Maxwell distribution and use it to compute the average speed of nitrogen molecules at 300 K.

Solution

1. The average speed $\langle v \rangle$ is found by multiplying the distribution of speeds (Equation 8-28) by v, integrating over all possible speeds, and dividing by the total number of molecules N:

$$\langle v \rangle = \frac{1}{N}\int_0^\infty vn(v)\,dv = \int_0^\infty Av^3 e^{-\lambda v^2}\,dv$$

where $\lambda = m/2kT$ and $A = 4\pi(m/2kT)^{3/2}$.

2. Writing this as

$$\langle v \rangle = AI_3$$

where

$$I_3 = \int_0^\infty v^3 e^{-\lambda v^2}\,dv$$

3. Using Table B1-1 for evaluating I_3, we have:

$$\langle v \rangle = A\lambda^{-2}/2$$
$$= \frac{4\pi}{2}\left(\frac{m}{2\pi kT}\right)^{3/2}\left(\frac{2kT}{m}\right)^2$$
$$= \left(\frac{8kT}{\pi m}\right)^{1/2}$$

8-30

4. The $\langle v \rangle$ found in step 3 can now be used to find the average speed of nitrogen molecules at $T = 300$ K. Substituting the mass of a nitrogen molecule into Equation 8-30 yields:

$$\langle v \rangle = \left[\frac{8 \times 1.38 \times 10^{-23} \times 300}{\pi \times 4.68 \times 10^{-26}}\right]^{1/2}$$
$$= 475 \text{ m/s}$$
$$\approx 1700 \text{ km/h}$$

The average speed is about 8 percent less than $v_{rms} = (3kT/m)^{1/2}$, as indicated in Figure 8-6. The rms speed was calculated from Equation 8-12 and can also be computed from the speed distribution following the same procedure as in Example 8-4 or, as we will see below, from the equipartition theorem. Figure 8-7, a plot of Equation 8-28 for H_2 and O_2 molecules at 300 K, illustrates the effect of mass on the speed distribution.

The first direct measurement of the speed distribution of molecules was made by O. Stern in 1926. Since then, measurements have been made by Zartman and Ko (1930); I. Estermann, O. C. Simpson, and O. Stern (1946); and Miller and Kusch

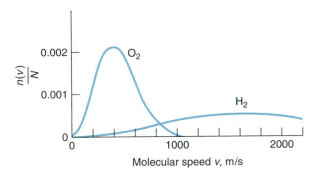

Fig. 8-7 Graph of $n(v)/N$ versus v from Equation 8-28 for O_2 and H_2 molecules, both at $T = 300$ K.

(1955). These experiments employed various methods of selecting a range of speeds of molecules escaping from a small hole in an oven and determining the number of molecules in this range. Zartman and Ko, for example, allowed the beam to pass through a slit in a rotating cylinder and measured the intensity versus position on the collecting plate. In the more recent experiment of Miller and Kusch, illustrated in Figure 8-8, a collimated beam from the oven is aimed at a fixed detector. Most of the beam is stopped by a rotating cylinder. Small helical slits in the cylinder allow passage of those molecules in a narrow speed range determined by the angular velocity of the cylinder. The Miller and Kusch results are shown in Figure 8-9.

Maxwell's speed distribution has been precisely verified, so there is little incentive to perform additional measurements. However, the technique of Miller and Kusch is applicable to the measurement of any sort of molecular speed distribution, and variations of it are used to measure the speeds in jet or nozzle molecular beams.

Evaporation is a cooling process, even at very low temperatures! The sample from which a BE condensate will form, confined at about 1 mK, is cooled further by allowing the atoms in the high-speed "tail" of the Maxwell distri-bution to "leak" from the sample, taking kinetic energy with them and thus reducing the temperature (see Section 8-3).

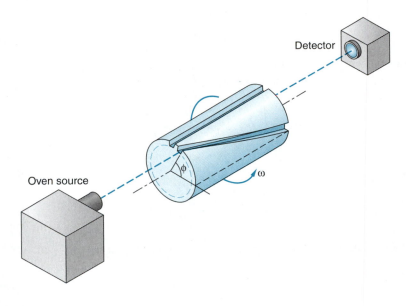

Detector

Oven source

Fig. 8-8 Schematic sketch of apparatus of Miller and Kusch for measuring the speed distribution of molecules. Only one of the 720 helical slits in the cylinder is shown. For a given angular velocity ω, only molecules of a certain speed from the oven pass through the helical slits to the detector. The straight slit is used to align the apparatus. [*From R. C. Miller and P. Kusch*, Physical Review, **99**, 1314 (1955).]

Maxwell Distribution of Kinetic Energy

As a bonus, the distribution of the molecular translational kinetic energy and the average kinetic energy of a molecule can also be determined from Equation 8-22. Since $E = \frac{1}{2}mv^2$, $v^2 = 2E/m$, and $dv = (2mE)^{-1/2}dE$, Equation 8-24 can be written as

$$g(E)\,dE = 4\pi C(2E/m)(2mE)^{1/2}\,dE \qquad \textbf{8-31}$$

Fig. 8-9 Data of Miller and Kusch showing the distribution of speed of thallium atoms from an oven at 870 K. The data have been corrected to give the distribution inside the oven, since the faster molecules approach the exit slit more frequently and skew the external distribution slightly. The measured value for v_m at 870 K is 376 m/s. The solid curve is that predicted by the Maxwell speed distribution. [*From R. C. Miller and P. Kusch,* Physical Review, **99**, *1314 (1955).*]

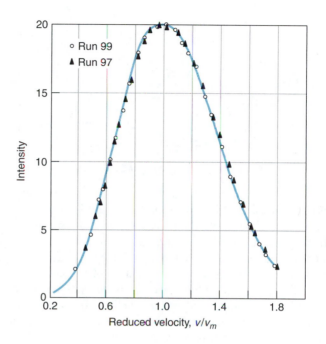

Substituting Equation 8-31 into Equation 8-22, we have

$$n(E)\,dE = 4\pi A'(2/m^3)^{1/2}E^{1/2}e^{-E/kT}\,dE \tag{8-32}$$

where A' is again evaluated from the condition that

$$N = \int_0^\infty n(E)\,dE = 4\pi A'(2/m^3)^{1/2}\int_0^\infty E^{1/2}e^{-E/kT}\,dE \tag{8-33}$$

The integral in Equation 8-33 is not included in Table B1-1. It is of the form $\int_0^\infty x^n e^{-ax}dx$, the value of which is given in terms of the gamma function by

$$\int_0^\infty x^n e^{-ax}\,dx = \frac{\Gamma(n+1)}{a^{n+1}} \tag{8-34}$$

where $\Gamma(n+1) = n\Gamma(n)$ and $\Gamma(\tfrac{1}{2}) = (\pi)^{1/2}$. With the aid of Equation 8-34, we find that A' is again equal to

$$A' = N\left(\frac{m}{2\pi kT}\right)^{3/2}$$

which allows us to write *Maxwell's distribution of kinetic energy* as

$$n(E)\,dE = \frac{2\pi N}{(\pi kT)^{3/2}}\,E^{1/2}e^{-E/kT}\,dE \tag{8-35}$$

The kinetic energy distribution is sketched in Figure 8-10. The average kinetic energy is computed in the same manner as the average speed; i.e., the distribution is multiplied by E (the quantity being averaged), and the result is integrated over all values of E (from $0 \rightarrow \infty$) and divided by the number of molecules N.

$$\langle E\rangle = \frac{1}{N}\int_0^\infty E n(E)\,dE = \frac{2\pi}{(\pi kT)^{3/2}}\int_0^\infty E^{3/2}e^{-E/kT}\,dE \tag{8-36}$$

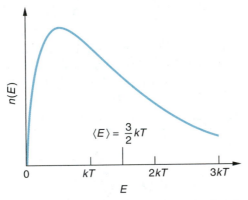

Fig. 8-10 Maxwell distribution of kinetic energies for the molecules of an ideal gas. The average energy $\langle E \rangle = 3kT/2$ is shown.

Evaluating the integral with the aid of Equation 8-34,[5] we find that

$$\langle E \rangle = \tfrac{3}{2} kT \qquad\qquad \textbf{8-37}$$

EXAMPLE 8-5 Escape of H$_2$ from Earth's Atmosphere A rule of thumb used by astrophysicists is that a gas will escape from a planet's atmosphere in 10^8 years if the average speed of its molecules is one-sixth of the escape velocity. Compute the average speed from the average kinetic energy and show that the absence of hydrogen in Earth's atmosphere suggests that Earth must be older than 10^8 years. (Mass of H$_2$ molecules = 3.34×10^{-27} kg.)

Solution

The escape speed at the bottom of the atmosphere, i.e., Earth's surface, is 11.2 km/s and one-sixth of that value is 1.86 km/s. Assuming $T = 300$ K, the average energy of a hydrogen molecule (or any other molecule, since $\langle E \rangle$ is independent of mass) is

$$\langle E \rangle = \frac{3}{2} kT = \frac{3 \times 1.38 \times 10^{-23} \times 300}{2} = 6.21 \times 10^{-21} \, \text{J}$$

Thus,

$$\tfrac{1}{2}mv^2 = 6.21 \times 10^{-21} \, \text{J}$$

or, for hydrogen molecules,

$$v^2 = \frac{2 \times 6.21 \times 10^{-21}}{3.34 \times 10^{-27}} = 3.72 \times 10^6$$

Therefore,

$$v = 1.93 \, \text{km/s}$$

Since $v > (1/6)v_{\text{esc}} = 1.86$ km/s, the absence of hydrogen in the atmosphere can be interpreted as indicating the age of Earth to be greater than 10^8 years.

5. H_2 molecules can escape so freely from Earth's gravitational field that H_2 is not found in Earth's atmosphere. (See Example 8-5.) Yet the average speed of H_2 molecules at ordinary atmospheric temperatures is much less than the escape speed. How then can all of the H_2 molecules escape?

6. Why wouldn't you expect all molecules in a gas to have the same speed?

Heat Capacities of Gases and Solids

The second important property of classical systems derivable from the Boltzmann distribution is one that applies to both gases and solids. Called the *equipartition theorem*, it states that:

> In equilibrium, each degree of freedom contributes $\frac{1}{2}kT$ to the average energy per molecule.

A *degree of freedom* is a coordinate or a velocity component that appears squared in the expression for the total energy of a molecule. For example, the one-dimensional harmonic oscillator has two degrees of freedom, x and v_x; a monatomic gas molecule has three degrees of freedom, v_x, v_y, and v_z.

More

That each degree of freedom in a classical material should have the same average energy per molecule is not at all obvious. On the home page we have included *A Derivation of the Equipartition Theorem* for a special case, the harmonic oscillator, to illustrate how the more general result arises: www.whfreeman.com/modphysics4e See also Equations 8-38 through 8-46 here.

C_V for Gases   The power of the equipartition theorem is its ability to predict accurately the heat capacities of gases and solids, but therein is also found its most dramatic failures. As an example, consider a rigid-dumbbell model of a diatomic molecule (Figure 8-11a) that can translate in the x, y, and z directions and can rotate about axes x' and y' through the center of mass and perpendicular to the z' axis along the line joining the two atoms.[6] The energy for this rigid-dumbbell model molecule is then

$$E = \tfrac{1}{2}mv_x^2 + \tfrac{1}{2}mv_y^2 + \tfrac{1}{2}mv_z^2 + \tfrac{1}{2}I_{x'}\omega_{x'}^2 + \tfrac{1}{2}I_{y'}\omega_{y'}^2$$

where $I_{x'}$ and $I_{y'}$ are the moments of inertia about the x' and y' axes. Since this molecule has 5 degrees of freedom, 3 translational and 2 rotational, the equipartition theorem predicts the average energy to be $(5/2)kT$ per molecule. The energy per mole U is then $(5/2)N_A kT = (5/2)RT$ and the molar heat capacity at constant volume $C_V = (\partial U/\partial T)_V$ is $(5/2)R$. The observation that C_V for both nitrogen and oxygen is about

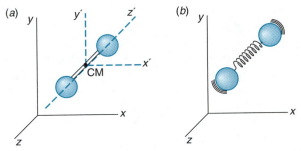

Fig. 8-11 (a) Rigid-dumbbell model of a diatomic gas molecule that can translate along the x, y, or z axis, and rotate about the x' or y' axis fixed to the center of mass. If the spheres are smooth or are points, rotation about the z' axis can be neglected. (b) Nonrigid-dumbbell model of a diatomic gas molecule that can translate, rotate, and vibrate.

$(5/2)R$ enabled Clausius to speculate (about 1880) that these gases must be diatomic gases which can rotate about two axes as well as translate. (See Table 8-1.)

If a diatomic molecule is not rigid, the atoms can also vibrate along the line joining them (Figure 8-11b). Then, in addition to the translational energy of the center of mass and rotational energy, there can be vibrational energy. The vibration, a simple

TABLE 8-1 C_V for some gases at 15°C and 1 atm

Gas	C_V (cal/mol·deg)	C_V/R
Ar	2.98	1.50
He	2.98	1.50
CO	4.94	2.49
H_2	4.87	2.45
HCl	5.11	2.57
N_2	4.93	2.49
NO	5.00	2.51
O_2	5.04	2.54
Cl_2	5.93	2.98
CO_2	6.75	3.40
CS_2	9.77	4.92
H_2S	6.08	3.06
N_2O	6.81	3.42
SO_2	7.49	3.76

$R = 1.987$ cal/mol·deg

From J. R. Partington and W. G. Shilling, The Specific Heats of Gases (London: Ernest Benn, Ltd., 1924).

harmonic motion, adds two more squared terms to the energy, one for the potential energy and one for kinetic energy. For a diatomic molecule that is translating, rotating, and vibrating, the equipartition theorem thus predicts a molar heat capacity of $(3 + 2 + 2)\frac{1}{2}R$, or $(7/2)R$. However, measured values of C_V for diatomic molecules (see Table 8-1) show no contribution from the vibrational degrees of freedom. The equipartition theorem provides no explanation for their absence.

Experimental values of C_V for several diatomic gases are included in Table 8-1. For all of these except Cl_2, the data are consistent with the equipartition theorem prediction assuming a rigid nonvibrating molecule. The value for Cl_2 is about halfway between that predicted for a rigid molecule and that predicted for a vibrating molecule. The situation for molecules with three or more atoms, several of which are also listed in Table 8-1, is more complicated and will not be examined in detail here.

The equipartition theorem in conjunction with the point-atom, rigid-dumbbell model was so successful in predicting the molar heat capacity for most diatomic molecules, it was difficult to understand why it did not do so for all of them. Why should some diatomic molecules vibrate and not others? Since the atoms are not points, the moment of inertia about the line joining the atoms, while small, is not zero, and there are three terms for rotational energy rather than two. Assuming no vibration, C_V should then be $(6/2)R$. This agrees with the measured value for Cl_2 but not for the other diatomic gases. Furthermore, monatomic molecules would have three terms for rotational energy if the atoms were not points, and C_V should also be $(6/2)R$ for these atoms rather than the $(3/2)R$ that is observed. Since the average energy is calculated by *counting* terms, it should not matter how small the atoms are as long as they are not merely points. In addition to these difficulties, it is found experimentally that the molar heat capacity depends on temperature, contrary to the predictions from the equipartition theorem. The most spectacular case is that of H_2, shown in Figure 8-12. It seems as if at very low temperatures, below about 60 K, H_2 behaves like a monatomic molecule and does not rotate. It seems to undergo a transition, and between about 250 K and 1000 K it has $C_V = (5/2)R$, thus behaving like a rotating rigid dumbbell. At very high temperatures H_2 begins to vibrate, but the molecule dissociates before C_V reaches $(7/2)R$. Other diatomic gases show similar behavior except that at low temperatures they liquefy before C_V reaches $(3/2)R$. The failure of the equipartition theorem to account for these observations occurs because classical mechanics itself fails when applied to atoms and molecules. It must be replaced by quantum mechanics.

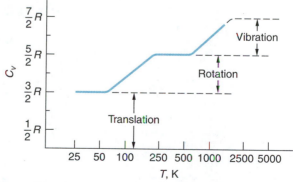

Fig. 8-12 Temperature dependence of molar heat capacity of H_2. Between about 250 and 1000 K, C_V is $\frac{5}{2}R$, as predicted by the rigid-dumbbell model. At low temperatures, C_V is only $\frac{3}{2}R$, as predicted for a nonrotating molecule. At high temperatures C_V seems to be approaching $\frac{7}{2}R$, as predicted for a dumbbell model that rotates and vibrates, but the molecule dissociates before this plateau is reached.

C_V for Solids   The equipartition theorem is also useful in understanding the heat capacity of solids. In 1819, Dulong and Petit pointed out that the molar heat capacity of most solids was very nearly equal to 6 cal/K · mol ≈ 3R. This result was used by them to obtain unknown molecular weights from the experimentally determined heat capacities. The *Dulong-Petit law* is easily derived from the equipartition theorem by assuming that the internal energy of a solid consists entirely of the vibrational energy of the molecules (see Figure 8-13). If the force constants in the *x*, *y*, and *z* directions are κ_1, κ_2, and κ_3, the vibrational energy of each molecule is

$$E = \tfrac{1}{2}mv_x^2 + \tfrac{1}{2}mv_y^2 + \tfrac{1}{2}mv_z^2 + \tfrac{1}{2}\kappa_1 x^2 + \tfrac{1}{2}\kappa_2 y^2 + \tfrac{1}{2}\kappa_3 z^2$$

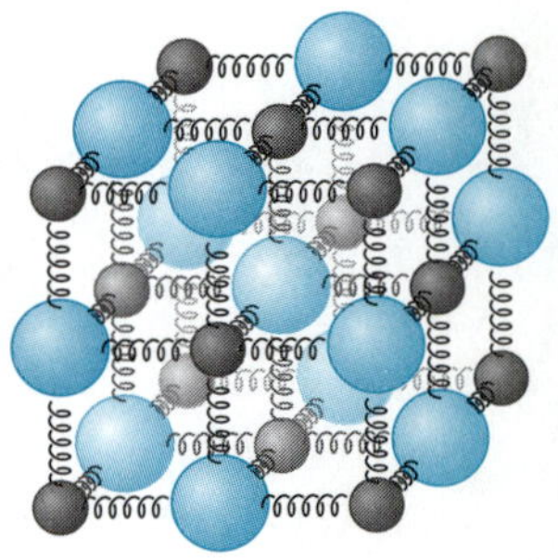

Since there are six squared terms, the average energy per molecule is $6(\tfrac{1}{2}kT)$, and the total energy of 1 mole is $3N_A kT = 3RT$, giving $C_V = 3R$.

At high temperatures, all solids obey the Dulong-Petit law. For temperatures below some critical value, C_V drops appreciably below the value of 3R and approaches zero as *T* approaches zero. The critical temperature is a characteristic of the solid. It is lower for soft solids such as lead than for hard solids such as diamond. The temperature dependence of C_V for several solids is shown in Figure 8-14.

The fact that C_V for metals is not appreciably different from that for insulators is puzzling. The classical model of a metal is moderately successful in describing electrical and heat conduction. It assumes that approximately one electron per atom is free to move about the metal, colliding with the atoms much as the molecules do in a gas. According to the equipartition theorem, this "electron gas" should have an average kinetic energy of (3/2)*kT* per electron; thus the molar heat capacity should be about (3/2)*R* greater for a conductor than for an insulator. Although the molar heat capacity for metals is slightly greater than 3R at very high temperatures, the difference is much less than the (3/2)*R* predicted for the contribution of the electron gas.

The Boltzmann distribution and statistical mechanics were enormously successful in predicting the observed thermal properties of physical systems; however, the failure of the theory to account correctly for the heat capacities of gases and solids was a serious problem for classical physics, constituting, as it did, a failure of classical mechanics itself. The search for an understanding of specific heats was instrumental in the discovery of energy quantization at the beginning of the twentieth century. The following sections show how quantum mechanics provides a basis for the complete understanding of the problem.

Fig. 8-13 Simple model of a solid consisting of atoms connected to one another by springs. The internal energy of the solid then consists of kinetic and potential vibrational energy.

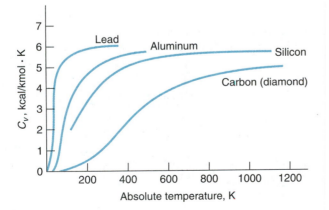

Fig. 8-14 Temperature dependence of molar heat capacity of several solids. At high temperatures C_V is 3R, as predicted by the equipartition theorem. However, at low temperatures C_V approaches zero. The critical temperature at which C_V becomes nearly 3R is different for different solids.

EXAMPLE 8-6 Broadening of Spectral Lines In Chapter 5 we saw that spectral lines emitted by atoms had a certain natural width due to the uncertainty principle. However, in luminous gases, such as sodium and mercury vapor lamps and the visible surface of the sun, the atoms are moving with the Maxwell velocity distribution. The velocity distribution results in a Doppler effect that Rayleigh showed was proportional to the Boltzmann factor and led to a broadening Δ of spectral lines equal to

$$\Delta = 0.72 \times 10^{-6} \lambda \sqrt{T/M} \qquad\qquad \textbf{8-47}$$

where λ is the wavelength of the line, T is the absolute temperature, and M is the molecular weight. From this, compute the velocity (Doppler) broadening of the hydrogen H_α line emitted by H atoms at the surface of the sun where $T = 5800$ K.

Solution
The wavelength of the H_α line is 656.3 nm and the atomic weight of H is 1, so

$$\Delta = 0.72 \times 10^{-6} \times 656.3\sqrt{5800/1} = 0.036 \text{ nm}$$

For comparison, the natural width of the H_α line is about 0.0005 nm. Note that the effect of the pressure of the gas in causing spectral line broadening via collisions is also an important factor and, in fact, at high pressures, is the dominant cause. Collisions reduce the level lifetime, hence broaden the energy (uncertainty principle). This is the reason that the sun's visible spectrum is a continuous one.

8-2 Quantum Statistics

Bose-Einstein and Fermi-Dirac Distributions

The classical systems that were the subject of Section 8-1 consisted of identical but distinguishable particles. They were treated like billiard balls: exactly the same as one another, but with numbers painted on their sides. Indeed, that was the point of the first assumption on the first page of the kinetic theory review on the home page. However, the wave nature of particles in quantum mechanics prevents identical particles from being distinguished from one another. The finite extent and the overlap of wave functions make identical particles indistinguishable. Thus, if two identical particles 1 and 2 pass within a de Broglie wavelength of one another in some event, we cannot tell which of the emerging particles is 1 and which is 2—i.e., we cannot distinguish between the several possible depictions of the event in Figure 8-15. The

Fig. 8-15 The wave nature of quantum-mechanical particles prevents us from determining which of the four possibilities shown actually occurred when the two identical, indistinguishable particles passed within a de Broglie wavelength of each other.

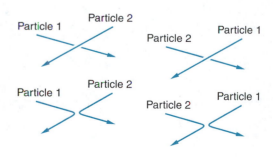

treatment of classical particles that led to the Boltzmann distribution can be extended to systems containing large numbers of identical indistinguishable particles. (See Appendix B3.) The first such theoretical treatment for particles with zero or integer spins—i.e., those that do not obey the exclusion principle, such as helium atoms (spin 0) and photons (spin 1)—was done by Bose[7] in 1924 when he realized that the Boltzmann distribution did not account adequately for the behavior of photons. Bose's new statistical distribution for photons was generalized to massive particles by Einstein shortly thereafter. The resulting distribution function, called the *Bose-Einstein distribution* $f_{BE}(E)$, is given by

$$f_{BE}(E) = \frac{1}{e^{\alpha}e^{E/kT} - 1} \qquad \textbf{8-48}$$

where e^{α} is a system-dependent normalization constant. Particles whose statistical distributions are given by Equation 8-48 are called *bosons*.

Following the discovery of electron spin and Dirac's development of relativistic wave mechanics for spin $\frac{1}{2}$ particles, Fermi[8] and Dirac[9] completed the statistical mechanics for quantum-mechanical particles by deriving the probability distribution for large ensembles of identical indistinguishable particles that obey the exclusion principle. The result is called the *Fermi-Dirac distribution* $f_{FD}(E)$ and is given by

$$f_{FD}(E) = \frac{1}{e^{\alpha}e^{E/kT} + 1} \qquad \textbf{8-49}$$

where, again, e^{α} is a system-dependent normalization constant. Particles whose behavior is described by Equation 8-49 are called *fermions* or Fermi-Dirac particles.

Comparison of the Distribution Functions

We can write the Boltzmann distribution (Equation 8-13) in the form

$$f_B(E) = \frac{1}{e^{\alpha}e^{E/kT}} \qquad \textbf{8-50}$$

where the normalization constant A in Equation 8-13 is replaced by $e^{-\alpha}$. After doing so, one is immediately struck by the very close resemblance between the three distributions (Equations 8-48, 8-49, and 8-50), the Fermi-Dirac and Bose-Einstein probability functions differing from that of Boltzmann only by the ± 1 in the denominator. The question immediately arises as to the significance of this seemingly small difference. In particular, since integrals of the form $\int_0^{\infty} F(E) f_{BE}(E)\, dE$ and $\int_0^{\infty} F(E) f_{FD}(E)\, dE$ require the use of numerical methods for their solutions, it would be helpful to know if and under what conditions the Boltzmann distribution can be used for indistinguishable quantum-mechanical particles.

Let us first examine the physical meaning of the difference between the distributions. Consider a system of two identical particles, 1 and 2, one of which is in state n and the other in state m. As we discussed in Section 6-7, there are two possible single-particle product solutions to the Schrödinger equation. They are

$$\psi_{nm}(1, 2) = \psi_n(1)\psi_m(2) \qquad \textbf{8-51}a$$
$$\psi_{nm}(2, 1) = \psi_n(2)\psi_m(1) \qquad \textbf{8-51}b$$

Enrico Fermi on a picnic in Michigan in July of 1935. The bandage covers a cut on his forehead received when he accidentally hit himself with his racquet while playing tennis.

where the numbers 1 and 2 represent the space coordinates of the two particles. If the two identical particles are distinguishable from one another, i.e., if they are classical particles, then we can tell the difference between the two states represented by Equations 8-51a and 8-51b. However, for indistinguishable particles the solutions must be the symmetric or antisymmetric combinations given in Section 6-7:

$$\psi_S = \frac{1}{\sqrt{2}} \left[\psi_n(1)\psi_m(2) + \psi_n(2)\psi_m(1) \right] \qquad \textbf{8-52}a$$

$$\psi_A = \frac{1}{\sqrt{2}} \left[\psi_n(1)\psi_m(2) - \psi_n(2)\psi_m(1) \right] \qquad \textbf{8-52}b$$

The factor $1/\sqrt{2}$ is the normalization constant. As we have discussed earlier, the antisymmetric function ψ_A describes particles that obey the exclusion principle, i.e., fermions. The symmetric function ψ_S describes indistinguishable particles that do not obey the exclusion principle, i.e., bosons.

Writing $\psi_A \equiv \psi_{FD}$ and $\psi_S \equiv \psi_{BE}$ to remind us of the probability distributions followed by the fermions and bosons, respectively, let us now consider the probability that, if we look for the two particles, we will find them *both* in the same state, say, state n. For two distinguishable particles Equations 8-51a and 8-51b both become

$$\psi_{nn}(1, 2) = \psi_{nn}(2, 1) = \psi_n(1)\psi_n(2) = \psi_n(2)\psi_n(1) = \psi_B \qquad \textbf{8-53}$$

where we have written $\psi_{nn}(1, 2) \equiv \psi_B$ to remind us that distinguishable particles follow the Boltzmann distribution. Thus, the probability density of finding both distinguishable particles in state n is

$$\psi_B^* \psi_B = \psi_n^*(1)\psi_n^*(2)\psi_n(1)\psi_n(2) \qquad \textbf{8-54}$$

Turning to indistinguishable particles, the wave function for two bosons both occupying state n is, from Equation 8-52a,

$$\psi_{BE} = \frac{1}{\sqrt{2}} \left[\psi_n(1)\psi_n(2) + \psi_n(2)\psi_n(1) \right] = \frac{2}{\sqrt{2}} \psi_n(1)\psi_n(2) \qquad \textbf{8-55}$$

and the probability density of finding both bosons in state n is then

$$\psi_{BE}^{*}\psi_{BE} = 2\psi_{n}^{*}(1)\psi_{n}^{*}(2)\psi_{n}(1)\psi_{n}(2) = 2\psi_{B}^{*}\psi_{B} \qquad \textbf{8-56}$$

Thus, the probability that both bosons would be found by an experiment to be occupying the same state is *twice* as large as for a pair of classical particles. This surprising discovery can be generalized to large ensembles of bosons as follows:

> The presence of a boson in a particular quantum state *enhances* the probability that other identical bosons will be found in the same state.

It is as if the presence of the boson attracts other identical bosons. Thus, the -1 that appears in the denominator of Equation 8-48 results physically in an increased probability that multiple bosons will occupy a given state, compared with the probability for classical particles in the same circumstances. The laser is the most common example of this phenomenon (see Chapter 9). We will consider another result of this intriguing behavior in Section 8-3.

If the two indistinguishable particles are fermions, the wave function for both occupying the same state is, as we have previously discussed in Section 7-6,

$$\psi_{FD} = \frac{1}{\sqrt{2}}\left[\psi_{n}(1)\psi_{n}(2) - \psi_{n}(2)\psi_{n}(1)\right] = 0 \qquad \textbf{8-57}$$

And, of course, the probability density $\psi_{FD}^{*}\psi_{FD} = 0$, also. This result, too, can be generalized to large ensembles of fermions as follows:

> The presence of a fermion in a particular quantum state *prevents* any other identical fermions from occupying the same state.

It is as if identical fermions actually repel one another. The $+1$ in the denominator of Equation 8-49 is thus due to the exclusion principle. We will consider consequences of this peculiar property of fermions further in Chapter 10. Figure 8-16 compares the distributions of bosons and fermions.

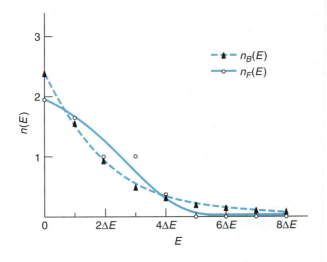

Fig. 8-16 $n(E)$ versus E for a system of six identical, indistinguishable particles. $n_B(E)$ is for particles with zero or integer spin (bosons). $n_F(E)$ is for particles with $\frac{1}{2}$-integer spin (fermions). Compare with Figure 8-2.

Fig. 8-17 Graph of the distributions f_B, f_{BE}, and f_{FD} versus energy for the value $\alpha = 0$. f_{BE} always lies above f_B, which in turn is always above f_{FD}. All three distributions are approximately equal for energies larger than about $5\,kT$.

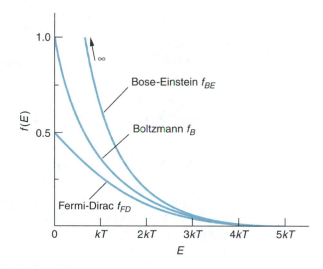

With the physical discussion above in mind, let us now compare the three functions. Figure 8-17 shows a comparison of the three distributions for $\alpha = 0$ over the energy range from zero up to $5kT$. Notice that for any given energy the f_{BE} curve for bosons lies above f_B for classical particles, reflecting the enhanced probability pointed out by Equation 8-56. Similarly, the f_{FD} curve for fermions lies below those for both f_{BE} and f_B, a consequence of the exclusion of identical fermions from states that are already occupied. Notice that Equations 8-49 and 8-50 both approach the Boltzmann distribution when $e^{\alpha} \gg e^{E/kT}$. For this situation $f_{BE}(E) \approx f_B(E) \ll 1$ and $f_{FD}(E) \approx f_B(E) \ll 1$. Thus, $f_{BE}(E)$ and $f_{FD}(E)$ both approach the classical Boltzmann distribution when the probability that a particle occupies the state with energy E is much less than 1. The same is also clearly the case when, for a given α, $E \gg kT$, as Figure 8-17 illustrates.

At the beginning of this section we noted that identical quantum particles were rendered indistinguishable from one another by the overlap of their de Broglie waves. This provides another means of determining for a given system when the Boltzmann distribution may be used that can be shown to be equivalent to the $f_B(E) \ll 1$ condition above, but which is sometimes easier to apply. If the de Broglie wavelength λ is much smaller than the average separation $\langle d \rangle$ of the particles, then we can neglect the overlap of the de Broglie waves, in which case the particles can be treated as if they were distinguishable.

$$\lambda \ll \langle d \rangle \qquad \textbf{8-58}$$

where

$$\lambda = \frac{h}{p} = \frac{h}{\sqrt{2mE_k}} = \frac{h}{\sqrt{2m(3kT/2)}} = \frac{h}{\sqrt{3mkT}} \qquad \textbf{8-59}$$

The average separation of the particles is $\langle d \rangle = (V/N)^{1/3}$, where N/V is the number of particles per unit volume in the system. Thus, the condition stated by Equation 8-58 becomes

$$\frac{h}{\sqrt{3mkT}} \ll (V/N)^{1/3}$$

which when cubed and rearranged becomes

$$\left(\frac{N}{V}\right)\frac{h^3}{(3mkT)^{3/2}} \ll 1 \qquad\qquad \textbf{8-60}$$

Equation 8-60 gives the condition under which the Boltzmann distribution can be used. Note that, in general, the condition requires low particle densities and high temperatures for particles of a given mass. The next example illustrates the application of the condition.

EXAMPLE 8-7 Statistical Distribution of He in the Atmosphere He atoms have spin 0 and, hence, are bosons. He makes up 5.24×10^{-6} of the molecules in the atmosphere. (a) Can the Boltzmann distribution be used to predict the thermal properties of atmospheric helium at $T = 273$ K? (b) Can it be used for liquid helium at $T = 4.2$ K?

Solution

(a) N_A atoms of air occupy 2.24×10^{-2} m³ at standard conditions. The number of He atoms per unit volume is then

$$\frac{N}{V} = \frac{6.02 \times 10^{23} \times 5.24 \times 10^{-6}}{2.24 \times 10^{-2}\,\text{m}^3} = 1.41 \times 10^{20} \text{ molecules He/m}^3$$

The left side of Equation 8-60 is then

$$\frac{(1.41 \times 10^{20}) \times (6.63 \times 10^{-34})^3}{(3 \times 1.66 \times 10^{-27} \times 4 \times 1.38 \times 10^{-23} \times 273)^{3/2}} = 6.3 \times 10^{-11} \ll 1$$

The behavior of the helium in the atmosphere can therefore be described by the Boltzmann distribution.

(b) The density of liquid helium at its boiling point $T = 4.2$ K is 0.124 g/cm³. The particle density N/V is then

$$\frac{N}{V} = \frac{N_A \text{ molecules}}{4 \text{ g}} \times (0.124 \text{ g/cm}^3) \times (10^2 \text{ cm/m})^3 = 1.87 \times 10^{28} \text{ He atoms/m}^3$$

The left side of Equation 8-60 is then

$$\frac{(1.87 \times 10^{28})(6.63 \times 10^{-34})^3}{(3 \times 1.66 \times 10^{-27} \times 4 \times 1.38 \times 10^{-23} \times 4.7)^{3/2}} = 3.71$$

which is *not* $\ll 1$. Therefore, the Boltzmann distribution does not adequately describe the behavior of liquid helium, so the Bose-Einstein distribution must be used.

Using the Distribution: Finding n(E)

In order to find the actual number of particles $n(E)$ with energy E, each of the three distribution functions given by Equations 8-48, 8-49, and 8-50 must be multiplied by the density of states as indicated by Equation 8-14.

$$n_B(E) = g_B(E)f_B(E)$$ **8-61a**

$$n_{BE}(E) = g_{BE}(E)f_{BE}(E)$$ **8-61b**

$$n_{FD}(E) = g_{FD}(E)f_{FD}(E)$$ **8-61c**

Finding $g(E)$ enables the constant e^α to be determined for particular systems from the normalization condition that we have used several times, namely, the total number of particles $N = \int_0^\infty n(E)\,dE$.

Density of States   As an example of determining $g(E)$, consider an equilibrium system of N classical particles confined in a cubical volume of side L. Treating the cube as a three-dimensional infinite square well, in Chapter 7 we found the energy of a particle in such a well to be

$$E_{n_1 n_2 n_3} = \frac{\hbar^2 \pi^2}{2mL^2}(n_1^2 + n_2^2 + n_3^2)$$ **7-4**

which we will for the convenience of our present discussion write as

$$E_n = E_0(n_x^2 + n_y^2 + n_z^2)$$ **8-62**

where x, y, and z replace 1, 2, and 3 and $E_0 = \hbar^2\pi^2/2mL^2$. The three quantum numbers n_x, n_y, and n_z specify the particular quantum state of the system. Recalling that $g(E)$ is the number of states with energy between E and $(E + dE)$, our task is to find an expression for the total number of states from zero energy up to E, then differentiate that result to find the number within the shell dE. This is made quite straightforward by (1) observing that Equation 8-62 is the equation of a sphere of radius $R = (E/E_0)^{1/2}$ in $n_x n_y n_z$-"space" and (2) recalling that the quantum numbers must be integers, each combination of which represents a particular energy and corresponds to a point in the "space." (See Figure 8-18.) Since the quantum numbers must all be positive, the "space" is confined to that octant of the sphere, as Figure 8-18 shows. The number of states N within radius R (equal to the number of different combinations of the quantum numbers) is the volume given by

$$N = \left(\frac{1}{8}\right)\left(\frac{4\pi R^3}{3}\right) = \frac{\pi}{6}\left(\frac{E}{E_0}\right)^{3/2}$$ **8-63**

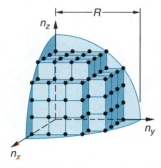

Fig. 8-18 A representation of the allowed quantum states for a system of particles confined in a three-dimensional infinite square well. The radius $R \propto E^{1/2}$.

The density of states in $n_x n_y n_z$-"space" is

$$g(E) = \frac{dN}{dE} = \frac{\pi}{4}E_0^{-3/2}E^{1/2} = \frac{(2m)^{3/2}L^3}{4\pi^2\hbar^3}E^{1/2}$$ **8-64**

or

$$g(E) = \frac{(2m)^{3/2}V}{4\pi^2\hbar^3}E^{1/2} = \frac{2\pi(2m)^{3/2}V}{h^3}E^{1/2} \qquad \textbf{8-65}$$

where the volume $V = L^3$. If the particles were electrons, then each state could accommodate two (one with spin up and one with spin down) and the density of states $g_e(E)$ would be twice that given by Equation 8-65, or

$$g_e(E) = \frac{4\pi(2m_e)^{3/2}}{h^3}VE^{1/2} \qquad \textbf{8-66}$$

We can compute the constant e^α in the Boltzmann distribution for these two cases from the normalization condition

$$N = \int_0^\infty n_B(E)\,dE = \int_0^\infty g_B(E)f_B(E)\,dE = \int_0^\infty g_B(E)e^{-\alpha}e^{-E/kT}\,dE \qquad \textbf{8-67}$$

If the distinguishable particles are electrons, $g_B(E) = g_e(E)$, and we have that

$$N = e^{-\alpha}\frac{4\pi(2m_e)^{3/2}V}{h^3}\int_0^\infty E^{1/2}e^{-E/kT}\,dE$$

which, with the aid of Equation 8-34, yields

$$N = \frac{2(2\pi m_e kT)^{3/2}V}{h^3}e^{-\alpha}$$

or

$$e^{-\alpha} = \frac{Nh^3}{2(2\pi m_e kT)^{3/2}V} \qquad \text{or} \qquad e^\alpha = \frac{2(2\pi m_e kT)^{3/2}V}{Nh^3} \qquad \textbf{8-68}$$

For particles that do not obey the exclusion principle, the 2 multiplying the parentheses in Equation 8-68 is not present. Note that $e^{-\alpha}$ depends upon the number density of particles N/V. Note, too, that $e^{-\alpha}$ is essentially the quantity on the left side of Equation 8-60, which was obtained from de Broglie's relation for classical particles. Thus, the test for when the Boltzmann distribution may be used given by Equation 8-60 is equivalent to the condition that $e^{-\alpha} \ll 1$.

Questions

7. How can identical particles also be distinguishable classically?

8. What are the physical conditions under which the Boltzmann distribution holds for a system of particles?

9. Do the opposite spins of two electrons in the same state make them distinguishable from one another?

10. What is a boson? a fermion?

8-3 The Bose-Einstein Condensation

We saw in Section 8-2 that, for ordinary gases, the Bose-Einstein distribution differs very little from the classical Boltzmann distribution, basically because there are many quantum states per particle due to the low density of gases and the large mass of the particles. However, for liquid helium, there is approximately one particle per quantum state at very low temperatures, and the classical distribution is invalid, as was illustrated in Example 8-7. The somewhat daring idea that liquid helium can be treated as an ideal gas obeying the Bose-Einstein distribution was suggested in 1938 by F. London in an attempt to understand the amazing properties of helium at low temperatures. When liquid helium is cooled, several remarkable changes take place in its properties at a temperature of 2.17 K. In 1924, Kamerlingh Onnes and J. Boks measured the density of liquid helium as a function of temperature and discovered a cusp in the curve at that temperature, as illustrated in Figure 8-19. In 1928, W. H. Keesom and M. Wolfke suggested that this discontinuity in the slope of the curve was an indication of a phase transition. They used the terms "helium I" for the liquid above 2.17 K, called the *lambda point* (see Figure 8-20), and "helium II" for the liquid below that temperature. In London's theory, called the two-fluid model, helium II is imagined to consist of two parts, a normal fluid with properties similar to helium I and a superfluid (i.e., a fluid with viscosity ≈ 0) with quite different properties. The density of liquid helium II is the sum of the densities of the normal fluid and the superfluid:

$$\rho = \rho_s + \rho_n \qquad\qquad \textbf{8-69}$$

As the temperature is lowered from the lambda point, the fraction consisting of the superfluid increases and that of the normal fluid decreases until, at absolute zero, only the superfluid remains. The superfluid corresponds to the helium atoms being in the lowest possible quantum state, the ground state. These atoms are not excited to higher states, so the superfluid cannot contribute to viscosity. When the viscosity of

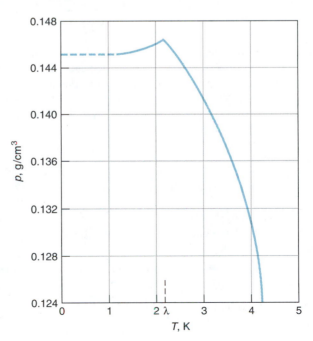

Fig. 8-19 Plot of density of liquid helium versus tempera-ture, by Kamerlingh Onnes and Boks. Note the disconti-nuity at 2.17 K. [*From F. London,* Superfluids *(New York: Dover Publications, Inc., 1964). Reprinted by permission of the publisher.*]

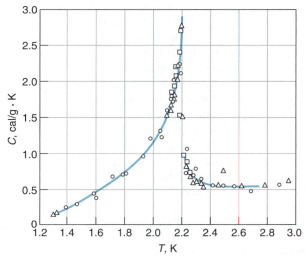

Fig. 8-20 Specific heat of liquid helium versus temperature. Because of the resemblance of this curve to the Greek letter λ, the transition point is called the lambda point. [*From F. London*, Superfluids *(New York: Dover Publications, Inc., 1964). Reprinted by permission of the publisher.*]

helium II is measured by the rotating disk method, only the normal-fluid component exerts a viscous force on the disk. As the temperature is lowered, the fraction of helium in the normal component decreases from 100 percent at the lambda point to 0 percent at $T = 0$ K; thus the viscosity decreases rapidly with temperature in agreement with experiment.

It is not at all obvious that liquid helium should behave like an ideal gas, because the atoms do exert forces on each other. However, these are weak van der Waals forces (to be discussed in Chapter 9), and the fairly low density of liquid helium (0.145 g/cm^3 near the lambda point) indicates that the atoms are relatively far apart. The ideal-gas model is therefore a reasonable first approximation. It is used mainly because it is relatively simple and because it yields qualitative insight into the behavior of this interesting fluid.

Exploring
Liquid Helium

In a classic experiment conducted in 1908 H. Kamerlingh Onnes[10] succeeded in liquefying helium, condensing the last element that had steadfastly remained in gaseous form and culminating a determined effort that had consumed nearly a quarter of a century of his life. Even then, he nearly missed seeing it. After several hours of cooling, the temperature of the helium sample, being measured by a constant-volume helium gas thermometer, refused to fall any further. The liquid hydrogen being used to precool the system was gone and it appeared that the experiment had failed, when one of the several interested visitors gathered in Kamerlingh Onne's lab suggested that perhaps the temperature was steady because the thermometer was immersed in boiling liquid that was so completely transparent as to be very hard to

H. Kamerlingh Onnes and J. D. Van der Waals by the helium liquefier in the Kamerlingh Onnes Laboratory in Leiden in 1911. [*Courtesy of the Kamerlingh Onnes Laboratory.*]

see. At the visitor's suggestion, a light was shone from below onto the glass sample vessel and the gas-liquid interface became clearly visible! Condensation to the very low density, transparent liquid had occurred at 4.2 K.

The liquid helium must have been boiling vigorously. Soon afterward Kamerlingh Onnes was able to reduce the temperature further, passing below 2.17 K, at which point the vigorous boiling abruptly ceased. He must have observed the sudden cessation of the violent boiling, yet he made no mention of it then or in the reports of any of his many later experiments. Indeed, it was another quarter century before any mention of this behavior would appear in the literature,[11] even though many investigators must have surely seen it. The abrupt halt in boiling at 2.17 K signaled a phase transition in which helium changed from a normal fluid to a *superfluid*, that is, bulk matter that flows essentially without resistance (viscosity ≈ 0). Of all the elements, only the two naturally occurring isotopes of helium exhibit this property. The transition to the superfluid phase in ^{4}He occurs at 2.17 K. In ^{3}He, which accounts for only 1.3×10^{-4} percent of natural helium, the transition occurs at about 2 mK. This should not be interpreted as due in some way to a peculiarity in the structure of helium. Liquid phases of other bosons do not become superfluids because all other such systems solidify at temperatures well above the critical temperature for Bose-Einstein condensation. Only helium remains liquid under its vapor pressure at temperatures approaching absolute zero.[12] The fundamental reason that it does not solidify is that the interaction potential energy (see Secton 9-3) between helium molecules is quite weak. Since helium atoms have small mass, their zero-point motion (i.e., their motion in the lowest allowed energy level—see Section 5-6) is large, in fact so large that its kinetic energy exceeds the interaction potential energy, thus melting the solid at low pressure. It is the superfluid phase of ^{4}He that we will be referring to throughout the remainder of this section. It turns out that ^{3}He becomes a superfluid for a different reason. (*Hint:* ^{4}He has spin 0, hence is a boson; ^{3}He has spin $\frac{1}{2}$ and is thus a fermion.)

Experimental Characteristics of Superfluid ^{4}He

In 1932 W. Keesom and K. Clusius measured the specific heat as a function of temperature and made a dramatic discovery of an enormous discontinuity, obtaining the curve shown in Figure 8-20. Because of the similarity of this curve to the Greek letter λ, the transition temperature 2.17 K is called the *lambda point*. Figure 8-21 shows this same curve measured with much greater resolution. Just above the lambda point, He boils vigorously as it evaporates. The bubbling immediately ceases at the lambda point, although evaporation continues. This effect is due to the sudden large increase in the thermal conductivity at the lambda point. In normal liquid helium, like other liquids, the development of local hot spots causes local vaporization resulting in the formation of bubbles. Below the lambda point the thermal conductivity becomes so large, dissipating heat so rapidly, that local hot spots cannot form. Measurements of thermal conductivity show that helium II conducts heat better than helium I by a factor of more than a million; in fact, helium II is a better heat conductor than any metal, exceeding that of copper at room temperature by a factor of 2000. This conduction process is different from ordinary heat conduction, for the rate of conduction is not proportional to the temperature difference. Bubble formation ceases (even though evaporation continues) because all parts of the fluid are at exactly the same temperature.

This lambda point transition is clearly visible on the surface of the liquid shown in Figures 8-22*a* and *b*, which also illustrate the phenomenon largely responsible for applying the name *superfluid* to helium II. The small container of liquid helium suspended above the surface has a bottom made of tightly packed, ultrafine powder (fine emery powder or jeweler's rouge). The microscopic channels through the powder are too small for the ordinary liquid to pass through, but when the temperature

Liquid helium, because of its extemely low boiling temperature, is the standard coolant for superconducting magnets throughout the world. Medical diagnostic MRI systems use such magnets. The large particle accelerators at, e.g., CERN and Fermilab, use hundreds of them.

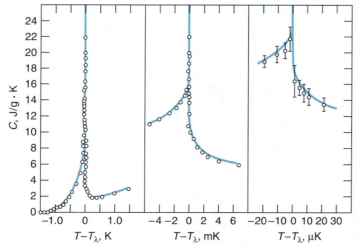

(a)

(b)

Fig. 8-21 The lambda point with high resolution. The specific heat curve maintains its shape as the scale is expanded. [*From M. J. Buckingham and W. M. Fairbank, "The Nature of the* λ-*Transition*," Progress in Low Temperature Physics, *edited by C. J. Gorter, Vol. III* (*Amsterdam: North-Holland Publishing Company, 1961*).]

drops below the lambda point, the superfluid flows through essentially unimpeded, the viscosity suddenly dropping at that point by a factor of about 1 million.[13]

Figures 8-23a and b illustrate the *creeping film* effect. A container containing liquid helium has a thin film (several atomic layers thick) of helium vapor coating the walls, just as is the case with any other enclosed liquid. However, if the level of liquid helium in the container is raised above the general level in the reservoir, such as the cup in the photo of Figure 8-23a, the superfluid film on the walls creeps up the inner walls, over the top, and down the outside and returns to the reservoir until both surfaces are level or the cup is empty! In the *thermomechanical effect*, which involves two containers of liquid helium II connected by a superleak, if heat is added to one side, e.g., by a small heater as illustrated in Figure 8-24a, the superfluid on the other side migrates *toward* the heated side where the level of liquid (still superfluid) rises. If the system is suitably arranged as in Figure 8-24b, the rising liquid can jet out a fine capillary in the so-called *fountain effect*.[14]

Fig. 8-22 (*a*) Liquid helium being cooled by evaporation just above the lambda point boils vigorously. (*b*) Below the lambda point the boiling ceases and the superfluid runs out through the fine pores in the bottom of the vessel suspended above the helium bath. [*Courtesy of Clarendon Laboratory. From K. Mendelssohn,* The Quest for Absolute Zero: The Meaning of Low Temperature Physics, *World University Library (New York: McGraw-Hill Book Company, 1966).*]

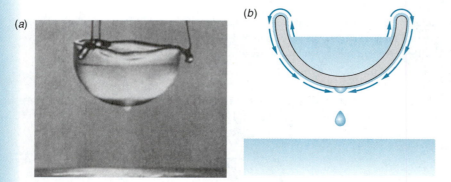

Fig. 8-23 (*a*) The creeping film. The liquid helium in the dish is at a temperature of about 1.6 K. A thin film creeps up the sides of the dish, over the edge, and down the outside to form the drop shown, which then falls into the reservoir below. [*Courtesy of A. Leitner, Rensselaer Polytechnic Institute.*] (*b*) Diagram of creeping film. If the dish is lowered until partially submerged in the reservoir, the superfluid creeps out until the levels in the dish and reservoir are the same. If the level in the cup is initially lower than that of the reservoir, superfluid creeps into the dish.

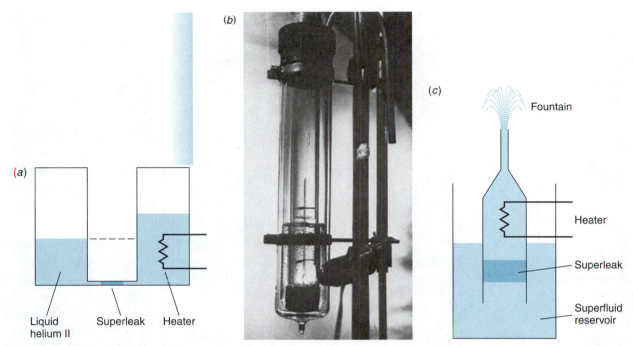

Fig. 8-24 (*a*) Diagram of the thermomechanical effect. The level of the fluid rises in the container where the heat is being added. (*b*) A bulb containing liquid helium is in a cold bath of liquid helium II at 1.6 K. When light containing infrared radiation is focused on the bulb, liquid helium rises above the ambient level. The height of the level depends on the narrowness of the tube. If the tube is packed with powder and the top drawn out into a fine capillary, the superfluid spurts out in a jet as shown, hence the name "fountain effect." [*Photo courtesy of Helix Technology Corporation.*] (*c*) Diagram showing the components in the photograph in (*b*).

Superfluid ^{3}He

Physicists thought for a long time that ^{3}He could not form a superfluid, since its nucleus consists of two protons and a neutron. It thus has 1/2-integer spin and obeys Fermi-Dirac statistics, which prohibits such particles from sharing the same energy state. However, early in the 1970s Lee, Osheroff, and Richardson showed that when cooled to 2.7 mK the spins of *pairs* of ^{3}He atoms can align parallel, creating, in effect, a boson of spin 1 and enabling the liquid to condense to a superfluid state. Two additional superfluid states were subsequently discovered, a spin 0 state (antiparallel spins) at 1.8 mK and a second spin 1 state that is created when an external magnetic field aligns the spins of the ^{3}He pairs. The three scientists received the 1996 Nobel Prize for their discovery.

In the Bose-Einstein distribution the number of particles in the energy range dE is given by $n(E)\,dE$, where we have from Equation 8-61*b*

$$n(E) = \frac{g(E)}{e^{\alpha}e^{E/kT} - 1} \qquad\qquad \textbf{8-70}$$

where $g(E)$ is given by Equation 8-65. The constant α, which is determined by normalization, cannot be negative, for if it were, $n(E)$ would be negative for low values of E. This situation would make no sense physically, since, if α were negative for small energies (i.e., $|\alpha| > E/kT$), then $f_{BE}(E)$ would be negative. But $f_{BE}(E)$ is the number of particles in the state with energy E and a negative value would be meaningless. The normalization condition is

$$N = \int_0^\infty n(E)\,dE = \frac{2\pi V}{h^3}(2m)^{3/2}\int_0^\infty \frac{E^{1/2}\,dE}{e^\alpha e^{E/kT} - 1} = \frac{2\pi V}{h^3}(2mkT)^{3/2}\int_0^\infty \frac{x^{1/2}\,dx}{e^{\alpha+x} - 1} \qquad \textbf{8-71}$$

where $x = E/kT$ and the integral in this equation is a function of α.

The usual justification for using a continuous energy distribution to describe a quantum system with discrete energies is that the energy levels are numerous and closely spaced. In this case, as we have already seen, for a gas of N particles in a macroscopic box of volume V (the container), this condition holds, as you can demonstrate for yourself by computing the spacing using Equation 7-4 for a three-dimensional box. However, in replacing the discrete distribution of energy states by a continuous distribution we ignore the ground state. This is apparent from Equation 8-65, where we see that $g(E) \propto E^{1/2}$; therefore, if $E = 0$, $g(E) = 0$, also. This has little effect for a gas consisting of Fermi-Dirac particles, since there can be only two particles in any single state, and ignoring two particles out of 10^{22} causes no difficulty. In a Bose-Einstein gas, however, there can be any number of particles in a single state. If we ignore the ground state as we have up to now, the normalization condition expressed by Equation 8-71 cannot be satisfied below some minimum critical temperature T_c corresponding to the minimum possible value of α, $\alpha = 0$. This implies that at very low temperatures there are a significant number of particles in the ground state.

The critical temperature T_c can be found by evaluating Equation 8-71 numerically. The integral has a maximum value of 2.315 when α has its minimum value of 0. This implies a maximum value of N/V given by

$$\frac{N}{V} \leq \frac{2\pi}{h^3}(2mkT)^{3/2}(2.315)$$

Since N/V is determined by the density of liquid helium, this implies a value for the critical temperature, given by

$$T \geq \frac{h^2}{2mk}\left[\frac{N}{2\pi(2.315)V}\right]^{2/3} = T_c \qquad \textbf{8-72}$$

Inserting the known constants and the density of helium, we find for the critical temperature

$$T_c = 3.1\text{K} \qquad \textbf{8-73}$$

For temperatures below 3.1 K the normalization Equation 8-71 cannot be satisfied for any value of α. Evidently at these temperatures there are a significant number of particles in the ground state, which we have not included.

We can specifically include the ground state by replacing Equation 8-71 with

$$N = N_0 + \frac{2\pi V}{h^3}(2mkT)^{3/2}\int_0^\infty \frac{x^{1/2}\,dx}{e^{\alpha+x} - 1} \qquad \textbf{8-74}$$

where N_0 is the number in the ground state. If we choose $E_0 = 0$ for the energy of the ground state, this number is

$$N_0 = \frac{g_0}{e^\alpha e^{E_0/kT} - 1} = \frac{1}{e^\alpha - 1} \qquad \textbf{8-75}$$

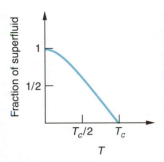

Fig. 8-25 Graph of the fraction of superfluid in a sample of liquid helium as a function of temperature.

where g_0, the density of states or statistical weight, is 1 for a single state. We see that N_0 becomes large as α becomes small. With the inclusion of N_0, which depends on α, the normalization condition (Equation 8-74) can be met and α can be computed numerically for any temperature and density. For temperatures below the critical temperature T_c we see from Equation 8-75 that $e^{\alpha} = 1 + 1/N_0$. Expanding e^{α} for small α yields $e^{\alpha} = 1 + \alpha + \ldots$, (see Appendix B4) and we thus conclude that α is of the order of N_0^{-1}, and that the fraction of molecules in the ground state is given approximately by

$$\frac{N_0}{N} \approx 1 - \left(\frac{T}{T_c}\right)^{3/2} \qquad \textbf{8-76}$$

In the London two-fluid model the N_0 atoms that we added in Equation 8-79 have condensed to the ground state. These particles in the ground state constitute the superfluid. The remaining $(N - N_0)$ atoms are the normal fluid. That fraction of the fluid which is superfluid for $T \leq T_c$ is shown in Figure 8-25.

The value $T_c = 3.1$ K is not very different from the observed lambda point temperature $T = 2.17$ K, especially considering that our calculation is based on the assumption that the liquid helium is an ideal gas. The process of atoms dropping into the ground state as the temperature is lowered below T_c is called *Bose-Einstein condensation*. Such an occurrence was predicted by Einstein in 1924, before there was any evidence that such a process could occur in nature.

The Bose-Einstein Condensate

Like all atoms, the constituents of ^{4}He (protons, neutrons, and electrons) are fermions; however, they are assembled in such a way that the total spin of the ground state is

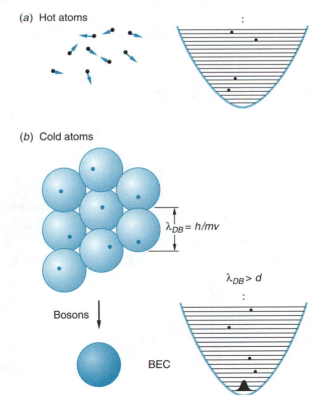

Fig. 8-26 (*a*) The atoms in a sample of dilute gas in any macroscopic container are distributed over a very large number of levels, making the probability of any one level being occupied quite small. (*b*) Cooled to the point where the de Broglie wavelength becomes larger than the interatomic spacing, atoms fall into the ground state, all occupying the same region of space.

integer (zero), so that the ^{4}He *atom* is a boson. Indeed, a review of the periodic table shows that, although atoms can be either fermions or bosons, the ground-state spins are mostly integer, so in their lowest energy state most atoms are bosons. This fact is of no great consequence in determining the properties of a gas in a macroscopic container because the spacing between the quantized energies is extremely small, so the probability that any particular level is occupied by an atom is also small. For example, the spacing between adjacent levels in a cubical box with a volume of 1 cm^3 containing sodium gas is about 10^{-20} eV (see Equation 8-62), so even at relatively low temperatures the atoms in a sample of a few billion would be widely spread among the allowed levels, as in Figure 8-26a. In addition, the average distance between atoms in the box would be about $(10^{-6}$ m$^3/10^9$ atoms$)^{1/3} = 10^{-5}$ m, or tens of thousands of atomic diameters, so the interactions between the atoms are minuscule.

If our goal is to form a Bose-Einstein condensate (BEC) from the widely separated atomic bosons of the gas sample in the box, the obvious approach is that used to condense any gas; that is, the sample is cooled and the density is increased until the gas liquefies. However, this approach presents us with a formidable problem: as the gas liquefies, the atoms get very close together, the density approximating that of the solid. The atoms now interact strongly, mainly via their outer electrons, and thus all begin to act like fermions! (This is essentially what happens in liquid helium II, where even at very low temperatures the fraction of the atoms in the ground state [superfluid phase] is only about 10 percent or so.)

This problem was solved by C. E. Wieman and E. Cornell in 1995, more than 70 years after Einstein's prediction. They did it by forming the BEC directly from a supersaturated vapor, cooling the sample but never allowing it to reach ordinary thermal equilibrium.[15] This was done with standard cooling methods and a very neat "trick." First, a sample of rubidium vapor at room temperature was illuminated by the beams from six small diode lasers of appropriate frequency. Collisions of the laser photons with atoms in the low-speed tail of the Maxwell distribution (see Figure 8-6) slowed those atoms and within a second or two a sample of about 10^7 atoms collected in the volume defined by the intersecting laser beams, about 1.5 cm in diameter. The temperature of this laser-cooled sample was about 1 mK. Then a special magnetic trap (i.e., a magnetic field shaped so as to confine the atoms) was used to "squeeze" the cooled sample, whose atomic spins $(=2\hbar)$ had been polarized in the $m = 2\hbar$ direction. (Polarizing the spins was the "trick" referred to above. Equilibrium is reached in the spin-polarized vapor very rapidly, long before the true thermal equilibrium state—the solid—can form, thus maintaining the sample as a supersaturated vapor.) The warmer atoms on the high-speed tail of the Maxwell distribution of the trapped atoms are allowed to escape through a "leak" in the magnetic trap, taking with them a substantial amount of the kinetic energy and evaporatively cooling the remaining few thousand atoms to less than 100 nK, just as water molecules evaporating from the surface of a cup of hot coffee cool that which remains in the cup. These remaining cold atoms fall into the ground state of the confining potential and have, within the experimental uncertainties, reached absolute zero. They are the condensate. The BEC is illustrated in Figure 8-26b. The condensate, if left undisturbed in the dark, lives for 15 to 20 seconds, its destruction eventually resulting from collisions with impurity atoms in the vacuum that are also colliding with the hot (room temperature) walls of the experimental cell. The peak in Figure 8-27 is a *macroscopic quantum wave function* of the condensate.

Since the discovery of Wieman and Cornell, several other physicists have produced Bose-Einstein condensates. One of the largest produced (by Ketterle and co-workers) contained 9×10^7 sodium atoms, was about a millimeter long, and lived

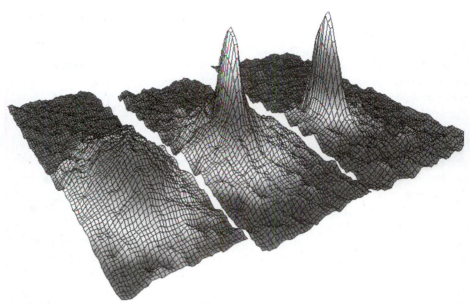

Fig. 8-27 Two-dimensional velocity distributions of the trapped cloud for three experimental runs with different amounts of cooling (different final *rf*). The axes are the *x* and *z* velocities, and the third axis is the number density of atoms per unit velocity-space volume. This density is extracted from the measured optical thickness of the shadow. The distribution on the left shows a gentle hill and corresponds to a temperature of about 200 nK. The middle picture is about 100 nK and shows the central condensate spire on the top of the noncondensed background hill. In the picture on the right, only condensed atoms are visible, indicating that the sample is at absolute zero, to within experimental uncertainty. The gray bands around the peaks are an artifact left over from the conversion of false-color contour lines into the present black and white. [*From C. E. Wieman, American Journal of Physics, **64** (7), 853 (1996).*]

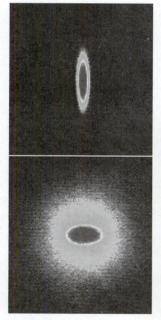

Fig. 8-28 Successive images show shadow of a millimeter-long cloud of atoms containing Bose-Einstein condensate as it expands from its initial cigar shape (top). [*From D. S. Durfee, Science, **272,** 1587 (1996).*]

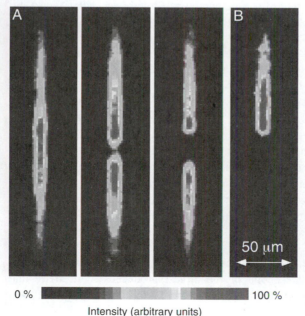

Fig. 8-29 Two identical condensates of sodium atoms, each containing about 5×10^6 atoms, were produced in a double potential well. [*From D. S. Durfee, Science, **275,** 639 (1997).*]

(a)

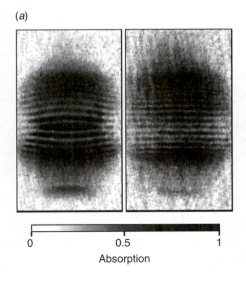

0   0.5   1

Absorption

(b)

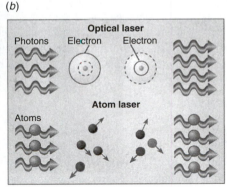

Fig. 8-30 (*a*) When the two condensates shown in Figure 8-29 were allowed to expand freely and overlapped, phase contrast imagery revealed interference fringes, the "signature" of coherent waves—the first atomic laser. [*From D. S. Durfee,* Science, *275, 639 (1997).*] (*b*) Optical lasers amplify light by stimulating atoms to emit photons. Atom lasers amplify by stimulating more atoms to join the "beam." [*From* Science, *279, 986 (1998). Courtesy of L. Carroll.*]

for half a minute. Its direct photograph is shown in Figure 8-28. As of this writing, the largest condensates are made of hydrogen and contain about 10^9 atoms.

Does this new discovery have any potential use? The answer is probably many that we can't even imagine yet, but here is one possibiltiy. The BEC can form the basis of an *atomic laser*. This was demonstrated in late 1996, also by Ketterle and his colleagues, and is illustrated in Figures 8-29 and 8-30. The condensate is coherent matter, just as the laser beam is coherent light. It could place atoms on substrates with extraordinary precision, conceivably replacing microlithography in the production of microcircuitry. Here is another: it could form the basis for atomic interferometers, enabling measurements far more precise than those made with visible lasers, since the de Broglie wavelengths are much shorter than those of light. Ketterle, Cornell, and Wieman shared the 2001 Nobel Prize in physics for their work.

QUESTIONS

11. Explain how the escaping "hot" rubidium atoms cool those remaining in the sample.

12. What is Bose-Einstein condensation?

13. Would you expect a gas or liquid of ^{3}He atoms to be much different from one of ^{4}He atoms? Why or why not?

8-4 The Photon Gas: An Application of Bose-Einstein Statistics

Photon Gas

Planck's empirical expression for the energy spectrum of the blackbody radiation in a cavity (Equation 3-33) can now be derived by treating the photons in the cavity as a gas consisting of bosons. The distribution is then given by

$$f_{BE}(E) = \frac{1}{e^{\alpha} e^{E/kT} - 1} \qquad \textbf{8-48}$$

As we saw in Section 8-2 and in particular in the discussion of Equation 8-68, the value of α is determined by the total number of particles that the system contains. However, in the case of photons contained in a cavity that we are discussing, that seems to present a problem, since the total number of photons is not constant. Photons are continually being created (emitted by the oscillators in the cavity walls) and destroyed (absorbed by the oscillators). Even so, this does indeed specify the value of α: it tells us that Equation 8-48 *for photons* cannot be a function of e^{α}, i.e.,

$$f_{\mathrm{ph}}(E) = \frac{1}{e^{E/kT} - 1} \qquad \textbf{8-77}$$

The fact that the total number of photons is not constant makes it necessary that $\alpha = 0$ so that $e^{\alpha} = 1$. We will see in a moment that this must be true.

The number of photons with energy E is found by substituting Equation 8-77 into Equation 8-61*b*, which yields

$$n_{\mathrm{ph}}(E) = g_{\mathrm{ph}}(E) f_{\mathrm{ph}}(E)$$

or

$$n_{\mathrm{ph}}(E) = \frac{g_{\mathrm{ph}}(E)}{e^{E/kT} - 1} \qquad \textbf{8-78}$$

The density of states $g_{\mathrm{ph}}(E)$ is derived in the same manner as it was for massive particles in Section 8-3. The result, which we first encountered as $n(\lambda) = 8\pi\lambda^{-4}$ in our discussion of Planck's derivation of the blackbody spectrum, is given in terms of the photon frequency f as

$$g_{\mathrm{ph}}(E)\,dE = \frac{8\pi V f^2\,df}{c^3} = \frac{8\pi V E^2\,dE}{c^3 h^3} \qquad \textbf{8-79}$$

where V is the volume of the cavity. The energy density $U(E)\,dE$ in the energy interval between E and $E + dE$ is then given by

$$U(E)\,dE = \frac{E g_{\mathrm{ph}}(E) f_{\mathrm{ph}}(E)\,dE}{V} = \frac{8\pi E^3\,dE}{c^3 h^3 (e^{E/kT} - 1)} \qquad \textbf{8-80}$$

or, in terms of the photon frequency f, using $E = hf$ for the conversion, we have

$$U(f)\,df = \frac{8\pi f^2}{c^3} \frac{hf\,df}{e^{hf/kT} - 1} \qquad \textbf{8-81}$$

Equation 8-81 is identical to Equation 3-33 when the latter is converted from wavelength λ to frequency f as the variable using $c = f\lambda$. We saw in Chapter 3 that Equation 3-33 is in precise agreement with experimental observations. This agreement serves as justification for the Bose-Einstein distribution function for photons given by Equation 8-77 that resulted from our argument that $\alpha = 0$ for photons. Notice that

Planck's derivation presented in Chapter 3, in which the radiation in the blackbody cavity was treated as a set of distinguishable standing electromagnetic waves to which he (correctly) applied the Boltzmann distribution, agrees exactly with the derivation presented here, in which the radiation is treated as indistinguishable particles to which the Bose-Einstein distribution must be applied. This is an example of the wave-particle duality of photons.

EXAMPLE 8-8 Photon Density of the Universe   The high temperature of the early universe implied a thermal (i.e., blackbody) electromagnetic radiation field which has, over eons, cooled to the present 2.7 K. This cosmic background radiation was discovered in 1965. Compute the number of these photons per unit volume in the universe.

Solution

1.   The number of photons with energy E is given by Equation 8-78:

$$n_{ph}(E) = \frac{g_{ph}(E)}{e^{E/kT} - 1}$$

2.   The total number per unit volume N/V is then given by:

$$\frac{N}{V} = \frac{1}{V}\int_0^\infty n_{ph}(E)\,dE = \frac{1}{V}\int_0^\infty \frac{g_{ph}(E)\,dE}{e^{E/kT} - 1}$$

3.   Substituting the density of states $g_{ph}(E)$ from Equation 8-79 yields:

$$\frac{N}{V} = \int_0^\infty \frac{8\pi E^2\,dE}{(ch)^3(e^{E/kT} - 1)}$$

$$= \frac{8\pi(kT)^3}{(ch)^3}\int_0^\infty \frac{(E/kT)^2(dE/kT)}{e^{E/kT} - 1}$$

4.   Letting $x = E/kT$, this can be written:

$$\frac{N}{V} = 8\pi\left(\frac{kT}{ch}\right)^2\int_0^\infty \frac{x^2\,dx}{e^x - 1}$$

5.   Evaluating the integral from standard tables:

$$\int_0^\infty \frac{x^2\,dx}{e^x - 1} \approx 2.40$$

6.   Substituting values into the expression for N/V in step 4 yields:

$$\frac{N}{V} = 8\pi\left(\frac{1.38 \times 10^{-23}\,\text{J/K} \times 2.7\,\text{K}}{3.00 \times 10^8\,\text{m/s} \times 6.63 \times 10^{-34}\,\text{J}\cdot\text{s}}\right)^3 (2.40)$$

$$= 3.97 \times 10^8\ \text{photons/m}^3$$

Quantization of the Energy States of Matter

It was pointed out earlier that the molar heat capacity C_V for solids falls appreciably below the classical Dulong-Petit value of $3R$ when the temperature falls below some critical value. In 1908 Einstein showed that the failure of the equipartition theorem in predicting the specific heats of solids at low temperatures could be understood if it were assumed that the atoms of the solid could have only certain discrete energy values. Einstein's calculation is closely related to Planck's calculation of the average energy of a harmonic oscillator, assuming the oscillator can take on only a discrete set of energies. The calculation itself presents no real problem, as we have seen in Chapter 3. Einstein's most important contribution in this area was the extension of the idea of quantization to any oscillating system, including matter. We shall see in this subsection how the idea of quantized energy states for matter also explains the puzzling behavior of the heat capacities of diatomic gases that was pointed out in Section 8-1. In particular we shall be able to understand why the H_2 molecule seems to have only 3 degrees of freedom (corresponding to translation) at low temperatures, 5 degrees of freedom at intermediate temperatures (corresponding to translation and rotation), and 7 degrees of freedom at high temperatures (corresponding to translation, rotation, and vibration).

Consider 1 mole of a solid consisting of N_A molecules, each free to vibrate in three dimensions about a fixed center. For simplicity, Einstein assumed that all the molecules oscillate at the same frequency f in each direction. The problem is then equivalent to $3N_A$ distinguishable one-dimensional oscillators, each with frequency f. The classical distribution function for the energy of a set of one-dimensional oscillators is the Boltzmann distribution given by Equation 8-13. Following Planck, Einstein assumed that the energy of each oscillator could take on only the values given by

$$E_n = nhf \qquad \textbf{8-82}$$

where $n = 0, 1, 2, \ldots$, rather than kT as predicted by the equipartition theorem. He then used the Boltzmann distribution[16] to compute the average energy $\langle E \rangle$ for the distinguishable oscillators, just as we have done previously, from

$$\langle E \rangle = \int_0^\infty E n_B(E) \, dE \qquad \textbf{8-83}$$

obtaining

$$\langle E \rangle = \frac{hf}{e^{hf/kT} - 1} \qquad \textbf{8-84}$$

which is, of course, the same as Equation 3-32. At high temperatures the quantity hf/kT is small and we can expand the exponential, using $e^x \approx 1 + x + \cdots$ for $x \ll 1$ (see Appendix B4), where $x = hf/kT$. Then

$$e^{hf/kT} - 1 \approx \left(1 + \frac{hf}{kT} + \cdots \right) - 1 \approx \frac{hf}{kT}$$

and $\langle E \rangle$ approaches kT, in agreement with the equipartition theorem from classical statistics (see Section 8-1).

The total energy for $3N_A$ oscillators is now

$$U = 3N_A\langle E\rangle = \frac{3N_A hf}{e^{hf/kT} - 1}$$ **8-85**

and the heat capacity is

$$C_V = \frac{dU}{dT} = 3N_A k\left(\frac{hf}{kT}\right)^2 \frac{e^{hf/kT}}{(e^{hf/kT} - 1)^2}$$ **8-86**

It is left as an exercise (see Problem 8-28) to show directly from Equation 8-86 that $C_V \to 0$ as $T \to 0$ and $C_V \to 3N_A k = 3R$ as $T \to \infty$.

By comparing the Einstein calculation of the average energy per molecule, Equation 8-84, with the classical one, we can gain some insight into the problem of when the classical theory will work and when it will fail. Let us define the critical temperature,

$$T_E = \frac{hf}{k}$$ **8-87**

called the *Einstein temperature.* The energy distribution in terms of this temperature is

$$f_B(E_n) = Ae^{-E_n/kT} = Ae^{-nhf/kT} = Ae^{-nT_E/T}$$

For temperatures T much higher than T_E, small changes in n have little effect on the exponential in the distribution, that is, $f_B(E_n) \approx f_B(E_{n+1})$. Then E can be treated as a continuous variable. However, for temperatures much lower than T_E, even the smallest possible change in n, $\Delta n = 1$, results in a significant change in $e^{-nT_E/T}$, and we would expect that the discontinuity of possible energy values becomes significant. Since hard solids have stronger binding forces than soft ones, their frequencies of molecular oscillation and therefore their Einstein temperatures are higher. For lead and gold, T_E is of the order of 50 to 100 K; ordinary temperatures of around 300 K are "high" for these metals, and they obey the classical Dulong-Petit law at these temperatures. For diamond, T_E is well over 1000 K; in this case 300 K is a "low" temperature, and C_V is much less than the Dulong-Petit value of $3R$ at this temperature.

The agreement between Equation 8-86 and experimental measurements justifies Einstein's approach to understanding the molar heat capacity of solids. Figure 8-31 shows a comparison of this equation with experiments. The curve fits the experimental points well except at very low temperatures, where the data fall slightly above the curve.

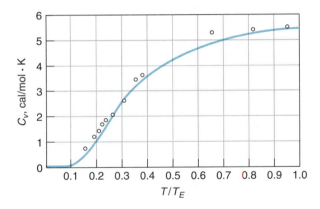

Fig. 8-31 Molar heat capacity of diamond versus reduced temperature T/T_E. The solid curve is that predicted by Einstein. [*From Einstein's original paper,* Annalen der Physik, *22 (4), 180 (1907).*]

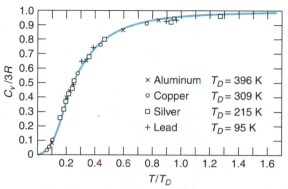

Fig. 8-32 Molar heat capacity of several solids vs. reduced temperature T/T_D, where T_D is the Debye temperature defined as $T_D = hf_D/k$. The solid curve is that predicted by Debye. The data are taken from Debye's original paper. $C_V/3R = 1$ is the Dulong-Petit value. [*From* Annalen der Physik, **39** *(4), 789 (1912), as adapted by David MacDonald,* Introductory Statistical Mechanics for Physicists *(New York: John Wiley & Sons, Inc., 1963); by permission.*]

The lack of detailed agreement of the curve with the data at low *T* is due to the oversimplification of the model. A refinement of this model was made by P. Debye, who gave up the assumption that all molecules vibrate at the same frequency. He allowed for the possibility that the motion of one molecule could be affected by that of the others and treated the solid as a system of coupled oscillators. The effect was to allow a range of vibrational frequencies from $f = 0$ up to a maximum f_D called the *Debye frequency*, used to define the *Debye temperature* $T_D = hf_D/k$. This contrasts with the infinite range of oscillation modes in the blackbody cavity. Debye's argument was that the number of vibrational modes or frequencies cannot exceed the number of degrees of freedom of the atoms that constitute the solid. Calculations with the Debye model are somewhat more involved and will not be considered here. The improvement of the Debye model over the Einstein model is shown by Figure 8-32. Note that *all* solids fall on the same curve.

Understanding Specific Heats of Gases

Let us now see if we can understand the specific heats of diatomic gases on the basis of discrete, or quantized, energies. In Section 8-1 we wrote the energy of a diatomic molecule as the sum of translational, rotational, and vibrational energies. If *f* is the frequency of vibration, and the vibrational energy is quantized by $E_{vib} = nhf$, as we assumed for solids, we know from the previous calculation (see Equation 8-86) that for low temperatures the average energy of vibration approaches zero and vibration will not contribute to C_V. We can define a critical temperature for vibration of a diatomic gas molecule by

$$T_v = \frac{hf}{k} \qquad\qquad \textbf{8-88}$$

where *f* is the frequency of vibration. Apparently $T_v > 15°C$ for all the diatomic gases listed in Table 8-1 except for Cl_2. From Figure 8-12 we can see that T_v is of the order of 1000 to 5000 K for H_2.

The rotational energy of a diatomic molecule is

$$E_R = \tfrac{1}{2}I\omega^2$$

where I is the moment of inertia and ω is the angular velocity of rotation. It is not obvious how the rotational energy is quantized, or even if it is; however, let us make use of a result from Section 7-2, where we learned that the angular momentum is quantized. If L is the angular momentum of a diatomic molecule, $L = I\omega$, and we can write the energy as

$$E_R = \frac{L^2}{2I}$$

Equation 7-22 tells us that $L^2 = l(l + 1)\hbar^2$, where $l = 0, 1, 2, \ldots$. Thus, the rotational energy becomes

$$E_R = l(l + 1)\frac{h^2}{8\pi^2 I} \qquad\qquad \textbf{8-89}$$

The energy distribution function will contain the factor

$$e^{-E_R/kT} = e^{-l(l+1)(h^2/8\pi^2 IkT)}$$

and we can define a critical temperature for rotation similar to that for vibration as

$$T_R = \frac{E_R}{k} = \frac{h^2}{8\pi^2 Ik} \qquad\qquad \textbf{8-90}$$

If this procedure is correct, we expect that for temperatures $T \gg T_R$, i.e., $E_R \gg kT$, the equipartition theorem will hold for rotation and the average energy of rotation will approach $\frac{1}{2}kT$ for each axis of rotation, while for low temperatures, $T \ll T_R$, the average energy of rotation will approach 0. Let us examine T_R for some cases of interest:

1. H_2 for rotation about the x or y axis as in Figure 8-11a, taking the z axis as the line joining the atoms. The moments of inertia I_x and I_y through the center of mass are

$$I_x = I_y = \tfrac{1}{2}MR^2$$

The separation of the atoms is about $R \approx 0.08$ nm. The mass of the H atom is about $M \approx 940 \times 10^6$ eV/c^2. We first calculate kT_R:

$$kT_R = \frac{h^2}{8\pi^2 I} = \frac{(hc)^2}{4\pi^2 Mc^2 R^2} = \frac{(1.24 \times 10^3 \text{ eV} \cdot \text{nm})^2}{4\pi^2 (940 \times 10^6 \text{ eV})(0.08 \text{ nm})^2} \approx 6.4 \times 10^{-3} \text{ eV}$$

Using $k \approx 2.6 \times 10^{-2}$ eV/300 K, we obtain

$$T_R = \frac{6.4 \times 10^{-3}}{2.6 \times 10^{-2}} 300 \text{ K} \approx 74 \text{ K}$$

As can be seen from Figure 8-12, this is indeed the temperature region below which the rotational energy does not contribute to the heat capacity.

2. O_2. Since the mass of the oxygen atom is 16 times that of the hydrogen atom and the separation is roughly the same, the critical temperature for rotation

will be $T_R \approx (74/16) \approx 4.6$ K. For all temperatures at which O_2 exists as a gas, $T \gg T_R$.

3. A monatomic gas, or rotation of diatomic gas about the z axis. We shall take the H atom for calculation. The moment of inertia of the atom is mainly due to the electron since the radius of the nucleus is extremely small (about 10^{-15} m). The distance from the nucleus to the electron is about the same as the separation of atoms in the H_2 molecule. Since the mass of the electron is about 2000 times smaller than that of the atom, we have

$$I_H \approx \frac{1}{2000} I_{H_2}$$

and

$$T_R \approx 2000 \times 74 \text{ K} \approx 1.5 \times 10^5 \text{ K}$$

This is much higher than the dissociation temperature for any gas. Thus $\langle E_R \rangle \approx 0$ for monatomic gases and for rotation of diatomic gases about the line joining the atoms for all attainable temperatures.

We see that energy quantization explains, at least qualitatively, the temperature dependence of the specific heats of gases and solids.

EXAMPLE 8-9   Average Vibrational Energy What is the average energy of vibration of the molecules in a solid if the temperature is (a) $T = hf/2k$, (b) $T = 4hf/k$?

Solution

(a) This is lower than the critical temperature for vibration hf/k given by Equation 8-88, so we expect a result considerably lower than the high temperature limit of kT given by the equipartition theorem. From Equation 8-84 we have

$$\langle E \rangle = \frac{hf}{e^{hf/kT} - 1} = \frac{2kT}{e^2 - 1} = 0.31 \, kT$$

(b) This temperature is four times the critical temperature, so we expect a result near the high temperature limit of kT. Using $hf/kT = \frac{1}{4}$ in Equation 8-84 we have

$$\langle E \rangle = \frac{0.25 \, kT}{e^{0.25} - 1} = 0.880 \, kT$$

EXAMPLE 8-10   Number of Oscillators At the "low" and "high" temperatures of Example 8-9, find the ratio of the number of oscillators with energy $E_1 = hf$ to the number with $E_0 = 0$.

Solution

At any temperature T, the Boltzmann distribution for the fraction of oscillators with energy $E_n = nhf$ is $f_B(E_n) = Ae^{-E_n/kT} = Ae^{-nhf/kT}$. For $n = 0$ this gives $f_0 = Ae^0 = A$. The ratio f_n/f_0 is then $f_n/f_0 = e^{-nhf/kT}$.

(a) For $n = 1$ and $kT = \frac{1}{2}hf$ we have $f_1/f_0 = e^{-hf/kT} = e^{-2} = 0.135$. Most of the oscillators are in the lowest energy state $E_0 = 0$.

(b) For the higher temperature $kT = 4hf$ we get $f_1/f_0 = e^{-hf/kT} = e^{-0.25} = 0.779$. At the higher temperature the states are more nearly equally populated and the average energy is larger.

EXAMPLE 8-11 **Debye Frequency** Note from Figure 8-32 that the Debye temperature of silver is 215 K. Compute the Debye frequency for silver and predict the Debye temperature for gold. Silver and gold have identical crystal structures and similar physical properties.

Solution

1. From the definition of the Debye temperature T_D, the Debye frequency f_D for silver can be computed:

$$T_D = \frac{hf_D}{k}$$

or

$$f_D = \frac{kT_D}{h} = \frac{1.38 \times 10^{-23}\ \text{J/K} \times 215\ \text{K}}{6.63 \times 10^{-34}\ \text{J} \cdot \text{s}}$$

$$= 4.48 \times 10^{12}\ \text{Hz}$$

2. We would expect the interatomic forces of silver and gold to be roughly the same, hence their vibrational frequencies to be in inverse ratio to the square root of their atomic masses:

$$\frac{f_D(\text{Ag})}{f_D(\text{Au})} = \sqrt{\frac{M(\text{Au})}{M(\text{Ag})}}$$

$$= \frac{kT_D(\text{Ag})/h}{kT_D(\text{Au})/h} = \frac{T_D(\text{Ag})}{T_D(\text{Au})}$$

3. Solving this for $T_D(\text{Au})$ yields:

$$T_D(\text{Au}) = T_D(\text{Ag})\sqrt{\frac{M(\text{Au})}{M(\text{Ag})}} = 215\sqrt{\frac{108}{197}}$$

$$= 159\ \text{K}$$

Remarks: This estimate is in reasonable agreement with the measured value of 164 K.

8-5 Properties of a Fermion Gas

The fact that metals conduct electricity so well led to the conclusion that they must contain electrons free to move about through a lattice of more or less fixed positive metal ions. Indeed, this conclusion had led to the development of a free-electron theory

to explain the properties of metals within three years after the electron's discovery by Thomson and long before wave mechanics was even a glimmer in Schrödinger's eye. The free-electron theory of metals was quite successful in explaining a number of metallic properties, as we shall discuss further in Chapter 10; however, it also suffered a few dramatic failures. For example, in a conductor at temperature T the lattice ions have average energy $3kT$ consisting, as we have seen, of $3kT/2$ of kinetic energy and $3kT/2$ of potential energy, leading to a molar heat capacity $C_V = 3R$ (rule of Dulong-Petit). Interactions (i.e., collisions) between the free electrons and lattice ions would be expected to provide the electrons with an average translational kinetic energy of $3kT/2$ at thermal equilibrium, resulting in a total internal energy U for metals of $3kT + 3kT/2 = 9kT/2$. Thus, metals should have $C_V = 4.5R$. In fact, they do not. The heat capacity of conductors is essentially the same as that of other solids, except for a slight temperature-dependent increase that is much smaller than $3R/2$. The problems with the classical free-electron theory are due mainly to the fact that electrons are indistinguishable particles that obey the exclusion principle, and as a consequence they have the Fermi-Dirac distribution of energies, rather than the Boltzmann distribution. In this section we will investigate the general characteristics of systems comprising fermions. In Chapter 10 we will see how the absence of a significant electron contribution to the heat capacity of conductors is explained.

In the Fermi-Dirac distribution given by

$$f_{FD}(E) = \frac{1}{e^\alpha e^{E/kT} + 1}$$ **8-49**

it is convenient to write α as

$$\alpha = \frac{-E_F}{kT}$$ **8-91**

where E_F is called the *Fermi energy*. Doing so allows Equation 8-49 to be written as

$$f_{FD}(E) = \frac{1}{e^{(E-E_F)/kT} + 1}$$ **8-92**

The Fermi energy is an important quantity in systems of fermions, such as the electron gas in metals (discussed in Chapter 10) and the neutron gas in a neutron star. Notice in particular that for $E = E_F$ the quantity $e^{(E-E_F)/kT} = 1$ for all values of the temperature greater than zero and, hence, $f_{FD}(E_F) = 1/2$. If we consider a system of fermions at $T = 0$ K, we find that

For $E < E_F$:

$$f_{FD}(E) = \frac{1}{e^{(E-E_F)/kT} + 1} = 1$$

and

For $E < E_F$:

$$f_{FD}(E) = \frac{1}{e^\infty + 1} = 0$$

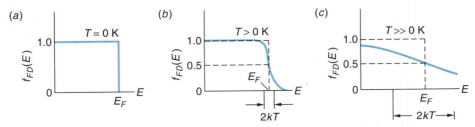

Fig. 8-33 Fermi-Dirac distribution function $f_{FD}(E)$ for three different temperatures. (*a*) At $T = 0$ K all levels above E_F are unoccupied. (*b*) For $T > 0$ K with $kT < E_F$, some particles near the Fermi energy can move to levels within about kT above E_F. (*c*) For high temperatures where $kT > E_F$, even particles in the lower energy states may move to higher levels, so that $f_{FD}(0) < 1$.

In other words, at absolute zero all energy states from the ground state up to the Fermi energy are occupied and all energy states above the Fermi energy are empty. This is in sharp contrast with a system of bosons, such as the rubidium BEC, where all particles condense to the ground state at $T = 0$ K. This situation is illustrated in Figure 8-33*a*. If the system contains N fermions, we can find its Fermi energy by filling the energy states in increasing order starting with the ground state. The energy state occupied by the Nth particle will be the Fermi energy. We can find the total energy of the system simply by adding up the energies of all N particles and their average energy by dividing that total by N. Each of these calculations will be done for electrons in Section 10-3.

If the temperature of the system is increased to some temperature $T > 0$ K, but with kT remaining smaller than E_F, fermions within about kT of the Fermi energy could now move to previously unoccupied levels lying within about kT above the Fermi energy in response to collisions with the lattice ions. However, fermions occupying levels much lower than kT below E_F would not be able to move, since the additional kT of energy that they might acquire in a collision would not be enough to move them past levels occupied by other fermions in order to reach the unoccupied levels near or above E_F. Figure 8-33*b* illustrates this situation. At temperatures so high that $kT > E_F$, fermions in even the very low lying energy states will be able to move to higher states. Only then can $f_{FD}(0)$ drop below 1, as shown in Figure 8-33*c*. This latter situation also corresponds to the lowest curve in Figure 8-17.

The number $n_{FD}(E)$ of fermions with energy E is given by Equation 8-61*c*. The density of states was computed for fermions in Section 8-3 and is given by Equation 8-66, so we have for fermions that

$$n_{FD}(E) = \frac{\pi}{2}\left(\frac{8m}{h^2}\right)^{3/2} \frac{VE^{1/2}}{e^{(E-E_F)/kT} + 1} \qquad \textbf{8-93}$$

Figure 8-34 is a graph of Equation 8-93 for three different temperatures. The $T = 0$ K curve is the result of multiplying $f_{FD}(E)$ in Figure 8-33*a* by the $g_{FD}(E)$ function, which increases as $E^{1/2}$. The curves for $T = 300$ K and $T = 1200$ K result from multiplying $g_{FD}(E)$ by appropriate versions of Figure 8-33*b*. The shaded areas for $T > 0$ K represent those electrons near the Fermi energy, a very small number, that are able to move into the empty states above E_F at each temperature.

Quantum Degenerate Fermion Gas

Since fermions have half-integer spins, the Pauli exclusion principle prohibits two identical fermions from occupying the same quantum state. Thus a system of half-integer spin atoms cannot all occupy the ground state to form a fermion version of the

Fig. 8-34 The distribution of fermion energies at three different temperatures for a material whose Fermi energy is 4.8 eV. Curves are plots of Equation 8-93 for the indicated values of temperature. (See text for explanation of shaded area.)

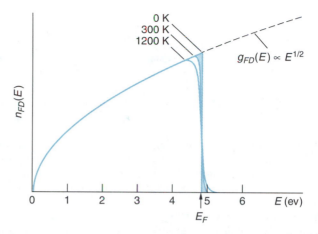

Bose-Einstein condensate as is possible for integer spin bosons. The fermion analogue of the BEC occurs when the atoms fill all of the energy states from the ground state up to the Fermi energy. The transition to this quantum degenerate state for a gas of fermions is a gradual one, quite unlike the sudden phase transition to the BEC. This makes it harder to detect, in addition to which the exclusion principle makes evaporative cooling that is so important in producing the BEC much less effective as the temperature of the fermion gas decreases. In 1999 these problems were solved by Deborah Jin and Brian DeMarco, four years after the first BEC was produced. They loaded a magnetic trap with ^{40}K (total atomic spin = 9/2), dividing the atoms between two magnetic substates to solve the evaporative cooling problem. One of several ways used to detect the quantum degenerate state of the ^{40}K atoms was to determine the total energy (from the momentum distribution) of the approximately 8×10^5 atoms in the sample (see Figure 8-35). Classically, the total energy $(3/2)N_A kT \rightarrow 0$ as $T \rightarrow 0$. Quantum mechanically, however, the total energy should be higher than expected classically as T decreases and remain finite as $T \rightarrow 0$. This is exactly what Jin and DeMarco observed. High on the

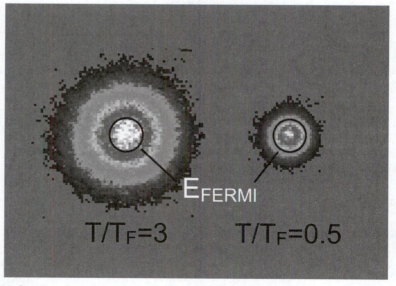

Fig. 8-35 Quantum degenerate state of a Fermi gas. The images show that more of the atoms of the ultracold gas lie below the Fermi energy (black circles) than above it in the right sample than in the left one. The colder cloud on the right contains 0.78 million ^{40}K atoms at $T = 0.29$ μK. The cloud on the left contains 2.5 million atoms at $T = 2.4$ μK. [*Brian DeMarco.*]

list of new things their discovery may make possible is the study of Cooper pairs (see Section 10-8) as they condense into a superconductor.

QUESTIONS

14. Why does the exclusion principle make evaporative cooling less effective as T decreases for fermions in a single-spin state?

15. Why does the total energy of the fermion gas not approach zero as $T \rightarrow 0$?

Summary

TOPIC	RELEVANT EQUATIONS AND REMARKS	
1. Boltzmann distribution	$f_B(E) = Ae^{-E/kT} = \dfrac{1}{e^{\alpha}e^{E/kT}}$	8-13
	where the distribution $f_B(E)$ is the probability that the state with energy E will be occupied.	
Boltzmann's constant	$k = 1.381 \times 10^{-23}$ J/K $= 8.617 \times 10^{-5}$ eV/K	
Maxwell distribution	$n(v)\,dv = 4\pi N \left(\dfrac{m}{2\pi kT}\right)^{3/2} v^2 e^{-mv^2/2kT}\,dv$	8-28
Equipartition theorem	In equilibrium, each degree of freedom contributes $\frac{1}{2}kT$ to the average energy per molecule.	
Average kinetic energy	$\langle E_k \rangle = \frac{3}{2}kT$	8-37
	where $\langle E_k \rangle$ is the average *translational* kinetic energy per molecule.	
Dulong-Petit law	$C_V = 3R$	
2. Quantum statistics		
Bose-Einstein distribution	$f_{BE}(E) = \dfrac{1}{e^{\alpha}e^{E/kT} - 1}$	8-48
Fermi-Dirac distribution	$f_{FD}(E) = \dfrac{1}{e^{\alpha}e^{E/kT} + 1}$	8-49
	In all three distributions f_B, f_{BE}, and f_{FD}, e^{α} is a normalization constant that depends on the particle density. The FD distribution applies to particles with $\frac{1}{2}$-integral spin, the BE distribution to particles with zero or integral spin. At high energies both f_{BE} and f_{FD} approach f_B.	
	The Boltzmann distribution will be a good approximation of either f_{BE} or f_{FD} if $e^{\alpha} \ll 1$.	
3. Applications		
Liquid helium	^{4}He becomes a superfluid at 2.17 K, called the lambda point. ^{3}He, the only other naturally occurring isotope that has this property, becomes superfluid at about 2 mK.	
Bose-Einstein condensate	Bosons undergo a phase transition, condensing to the lowest quantum state.	
Degenerate Fermi gas	Fermions condensed to states from the ground state to the Fermi energy.	

GENERAL REFERENCES

The following general references are written at a level appropriate for the readers of this book.

Blatt, F. J., *Modern Physics,* McGraw-Hill, New York, 1992.

Brehm, J. J., and W. J. Mullin, *Introduction to the Structure of Matter,* Wiley, New York, 1989.

Eisberg, R., and R. Resnick, *Quantum Physics of Atoms, Molecules, Solids, Nuclei, and Particles,* 2d ed., Wiley, New York, 1985. An excellent but somewhat more advanced discussion of quantum statistics can be found in Chapter 11 of this book.

Kittel, C., and H. Kroemer, *Thermal Physics,* W. H. Freeman, New York, 1995.

Leitner, A., *Liquid Helium II: The Superfluid,* Michigan State University, East Lansing, 1963. This 39-minute film is an excellent introduction to the subject of liquid helium II.

London, F., *Superfluids,* Vol. II: *Macroscopic Theory of Superfluid Helium,* 2d rev. ed., Dover, New York, 1954.

Mandel, F., *Statistical Physics,* Wiley, New York, 1988.

Mendelssohn, K., *The Quest for Absolute Zero: The Meaning of Low Temperature Physics,* World University Library, McGraw-Hill, New York, 1966.

NOTES

1. The statistical approach may also be used as an approximation in systems where the number of particles is not particularly large. For example, in Chapter 11 we will discuss briefly a statistical model of the atomic nucleus, a system containing only on the order of 100 particles.

2. Ludwig E. Boltzmann (1844–1906), Austrian physicist. His pioneering statistical interpretation of the second law of thermodynamics earned for him recognition as the founder of statistical mechanics. He explained theoretically the experimental observations of Stefan, whom he served as an assistant while in college, that the quantity of radiation increased with the fourth power of the temperature. He eventually succeeded Stefan in the chair of physics at Vienna. Boltzmann was a strong proponent of the atomic theory of matter, and his suicide was apparently motivated in part by opposition to his views by others.

3. To avoid having to repeat this rather long phrase frequently, which will occur for E as well as v, we shall hereafter use the expression "the number in dv_x at v_x" or simply "the number in dv_x."

4. An alternate derivation of the distribution of molecular speeds can be done at this point by noting that NF equals the density of states in velocity space.

5. Or refer to a table of integrals.

6. Historically, rotation about the z' axis of the dumbbell was ruled out by assuming either that the atoms are points and the moment of inertia about this axis is therefore zero (not true), or that the atoms are hard smooth spheres, in which case rotation about this axis cannot be changed by collisions and therefore does not participate in the exchange of energy (also not true). Either of these assumptions also rules out the possibility of rotation of a monatomic molecule.

7. Satyendra Nath Bose (1894–1974), Indian physicist. Following publication of his paper on the statistics of indistinguishable particles, which was translated into German for publication by Einstein himself, Bose spent two years in Europe, then returned to India to devote himself to teaching. Lacking a Ph.D., he was denied a professorship until a one-sentence postcard from Einstein was received at Dacca University in his support.

8. Enrico Fermi (1901–1954), Italian-American physicist. An exceedingly prolific scientist and intrepid amateur tennis player whose work encompassed solid-state, nuclear, and particle physics, he is perhaps best known as the father of the nuclear reactor. He was awarded the Nobel Prize in physics in 1938 for his work in nuclear physics.

9. Paul A. M. Dirac (1902–1984), English physicist. His development of relativistic wave mechanics for spin $\frac{1}{2}$ particles led to his prediction in 1930 of the existence of the positron. Its discovery by Anderson two years later resulted in Dirac's being awarded (along with Schrödinger) the 1933 Nobel Prize in physics. From 1932 until his retirement he occupied the Lucasian Chair of Mathematics, which had been held 250 years earlier by Newton.

10. Heike Kamerlingh Onnes (1853–1926), Dutch physicist. His success in liquefying helium enabled him to investigate the properties of other materials at liquid helium temperatures. This, in turn, led to his discovery of superconductivity in 1911. His work on the behavior of materials at low temperatures earned him the physics Nobel Prize in 1913.

11. J. C. McLennan, H. D. Smith, and J. O. Wilhelm, *Philosophical Magazine,* **14**, 161 (1932).

12. At very low temperatures liquid ^{4}He does solidify at a pressure of about 25 atm, liquid ^{3}He at about 30 atm.

13. Narrow channels that permit only the superfluid to pass are, of course, called *superleaks.*

14. These and many other properties are elegantly displayed in the film *Liquid Helium II: The Superfluid,* available from the Instructional Media Center, Michigan State University, East Lansing, Michigan 48824.

15. In the thermodynamic equilibrium state their sample, rubidium, is a solid metal at room temperature.

16. Einstein used the Boltzmann distribution in its discrete form $f_B(E) = \sum_{n=0}^{\infty} A e^{-E_n/kT}$.

PROBLEMS

Level I

Section 8-1 Classical Statistics

8-1. (a) Calculate v_{rms} for H_2 at $T = 300$ K. (b) Calculate the temperature T for which v_{rms} for H_2 equals the escape speed of 11.2 km/s.

8-2. (a) The ionization energy for hydrogen atoms is 13.6 eV. At what temperature is the average kinetic energy of translation equal to 13.6 eV? (b) What is the average kinetic energy of translation of hydrogen atoms at $T = 10^7$ K, a typical temperature in the interior of the sun?

8-3. The molar mass of oxygen gas (O_2) is about 32 g/mol and that of hydrogen gas (H_2) about 2 g/mol. Compute (a) the rms speed of O_2 and (b) the rms speed of H_2 when the temperature is 0°C.

8-4. Show that the SI units of $(3RT/M)^{1/2}$ are m/s.

8-5. (a) Find the total kinetic energy of translation of 1 mole of N_2 molecules at $T = 273$ K. (b) Would your answer be the same, greater, or less for 1 mole of He atoms at the same temperature?

8-6. Use the Maxwell distribution of molecular speeds to calculate the average value of v^2 for the molecules of a gas.

8-7. Neutrons in a reactor have a Maxwell speed distribution when they are in thermal equilibrium. Find $\langle v \rangle$ and v_m for neutrons in thermal equilibrium at 300 K. Show that $n(v)$ (Equation 8-28) has its maximum value at $v = v_m = (2kT/m)^{1/2}$.

8-8. (a) Show that Equation 8-20 can be written

$$f(v_x) = (2\pi)^{-1/2} v_0^{-1} e^{-v_x^2/2v_0^2}$$

where $v_0 = v_{x,\,rms} = (kT/m)^{1/2}$. Consider 1 mole of gas and approximate dv_x by $\Delta v_x = 0.01v_0$. Find the number of molecules in Δv_x at (b) $v_x = 0$, (c) $v_x = v_0$, (d) $v_x = 2v_0$, and (e) $v_x = 8v_0$.

8-9. Show that the most probable speed v_m of the Maxwell distribution of speeds is given by Equation 8-29.

8-10. Compute the total translational kinetic energy of one liter of oxygen held at a pressure of one atmosphere.

8-11. From the absorption spectrum it is determined that about one out of 10^6 hydrogen atoms in a certain star is in the first excited state, 10.2 eV above the ground state (other excited states can be neglected). What is the temperature of the star? (Take the ratio of statistical weights to be 4, as in Example 8-3.)

8-12. The first excited rotational energy state of the H_2 molecule ($g_2 = 3$) is about 4×10^{-3} eV above the lowest energy state ($g_1 = 1$). What is the ratio of the numbers of molecules in these two states at room temperature (300 K)?

8-13. A monatomic gas is confined to move in two dimensions so that the energy of an atom is $E_k = \frac{1}{2}mv_x^2 + \frac{1}{2}mv_y^2$. What are C_V, C_P, and γ for this gas? (C_P, the heat capacity at constant pressure, is equal to $C_V + nR$ and $\gamma = C_P/C_V$.)

8-14. Use the Dulong-Petit law that $C_V = 3R$ for solids to calculate the specific heat $c_V = C_V/M$ in cal/g for (a) aluminum, $M = 27.0$ g/mol, (b) copper, $M = 63.5$ g/mol, and (c) lead, $M = 207$ g/mol, and compare your results with the values given in a handbook.

8-15. Calculate the most probable kinetic energy E_m from the Maxwell distribution of kinetic energies (Equation 8-35).

8-16. (a) Show that the speed distribution function can be written $n(v) = 4\pi^{-1/2}(v/v_m)^2 v_m^{-1} e^{-(v/v_m)^2}$, where v_m is the most probable speed. Consider 1 mole of molecules and approximate dv by $\Delta v = 0.01\,v_m$. Find the number of molecules with speeds in dv at (b) $v = 0$, (c) $v = v_m$, (d) $v = 2v_m$, and (e) $v = 8v_m$.

8-17. The temperature of the sun's surface is 5800 K. Compute the relative number of hydrogen atoms in this region that are in the $n = 1, 2, 3,$ and 4 energy levels. See Example 8-3 and don't forget the degeneracies of the states.

Section 8-2 Quantum Statistics

8-18. Find the number density N/V for electrons such that (a) $e^{-\alpha} = 1$ and (b) $e^{-\alpha} = 10^{-6}$.

8-19. (a) Compute $e^{-\alpha}$ from Equation 8-68 for O_2 gas at standard conditions. (b) At what temperature is $e^{-\alpha} = 1$ for O_2?

8-20. Given three containers all at the same temperature, one filled with a gas of classical molecules, one with a fermion gas, and one with a boson gas, which will have the highest pressure? Which will have the lowest pressure? Support your answer.

8-21. (a) For $T = 5800$ K, at what energy will the Bose-Einstein distribution function $f_{BE}(E)$ equal 1 (for $\alpha = 0$)? (b) Still with $\alpha = 0$, to what value must the temperature change if $f_{BE}(E) = 0.5$ for the energy in part (a)?

8-22. A container at 300 K contains H_2 gas at a pressure of 1 atmosphere. At this temperature H_2 obeys the Boltzmann distribution. To what temperature must the H_2 gas be cooled before quantum effects become important and the use of the Boltzmann distribution no longer appropriate? (*Hint:* Equate the de Broglie wavelength at the average energy to the average spacing between molecules, using the ideal gas law to compute the density.)

Section 8-3 The Bose-Einstein Condensation

8-23. Compute N_0/N from Equation 8-76 for (a) $T = 3T_c/4$, (b) $T = \frac{1}{2}T_c$, (c) $T = T_c/4$, and (d) $T = T_c/8$.

8-24. Show that $N_0 \approx 1/\alpha$ for small values of α as asserted in the paragraph above Equation 8-76.

8-25. Like ^{4}He, the most common form of neon, ^{20}Ne, is a rare gas and the ^{20}Ne atoms have zero spin and hence are bosons. But unlike helium, neon does not become superfluid at low temperatures. Show that this is to be expected by computing neon's critical temperature and comparing it with the element's freezing point of 24.5 K.

Section 8-4 The Photon Gas: An Application of Bose-Einstein Statistics

8-26. If the sun were to become cooler (without changing its radius), the energy density at the surface would decrease according to Equation 8-80. Suppose the sun's temperature were to decrease by 5 percent. Compute the fractional change in the rate at which solar energy arrives at Earth. (Assume that the sun's surface is in equilibrium and radiates as a blackbody.)

8-27. Find the average energy of an oscillator at (a) $T = 10 \; hf/k$, (b) $T = hf/k$, (c) $T = 0.1 \; hf/k$, and compare your results with that from the equipartition theorem.

8-28. (a) Show that the rule of Dulong-Petit follows directly from Einstein's specific heat formula (Equation 8-86) as $T \rightarrow \infty$. (b) Show that $C_V \rightarrow 0$ as $T \rightarrow 0$.

8-29. Using Figure 8-14, compute the (approximate) frequency of atomic oscillations in silicon and in aluminum at 200 K.

8-30. Use Equation 8-86 to calculate the value of C_V for a solid at the Einstein temperature $T_E = hf/k$.

Section 8-5 Properties of a Fermion Gas

8-31. Use Equation 8-93 to plot an accurate graph of $n_{FD}(E)/V$ for electrons whose Fermi energy is 4.8 eV from $E = 4.5$ eV to $E = 5.1$ eV at $T = 300$ K. Determine from the graph the number of electrons per unit volume just below the Fermi energy that can move to states just above the Fermi energy.

Level II

8-32. The molar heat capacity data given in Table 8-2 are taken from *AIP Handbook,* 2d ed. (McGraw-Hill, New York, 1963). Plot the data for these solids all on one graph and sketch in the curves C_V versus T. Estimate the Einstein temperature for each of the solids using the result of Problem 8-30.

8-33. Recalling that the Fermi-Dirac distribution function applies to all fermions, including protons and neutrons, each of which have spin $\frac{1}{2}$, consider a nucleus of ^{22}Ne consisting of 10 protons and 12 neutrons. Protons are distinguishable from neutrons, so two of each particle (spin up, spin down) can be put into each energy state. Assuming that the radius of the ^{22}Ne nucleus is 3.1×10^{-15} m, estimate the Fermi energy and the average energy of the nucleus in ^{22}Ne. Express your results in MeV. Do the results seem reasonable?

8-34. What is the ground-state energy of ten noninteracting bosons in a one-dimensional box of length L?

8-35. Make a plot of $f_{FD}(E)$ versus E for (a) $T = 0.1\,T_F$, and (b) $T = 0.5\,T_F$, where $T_F = E_F/k$.

8-36. Compute the fraction of helium atoms in the superfluid state at (a) $T = T_c/2$ and (b) $T = T_c/4$.

8-37. The depth of the potential well for free electrons in a metal can be accurately determined by observing that the photoelectric work function is the energy necessary to remove an electron at the top of the occupied states from the metal; an electron in such a state has the Fermi energy. Assuming each atom provides one free electron to the gas, compute the depth of the well for the free electrons in gold. The work function for gold is 4.8 eV.

8-38. The speed distribution of molecules in a container is the Maxwell distribution $f(v) \propto v^2 e^{-mv^2/2kT}$. The number with speed v that hit the wall in a given time is proportional to the speed v and to $f(v)$. Thus, if there is a very small hole in the wall (too small

TABLE 8-2 Heat capacities in cal/mol·K for Au, diamond, Al, and Be

T, K	Au	Diamond	Al	Be
20	0.77	0.00	0.05	0.003
50	3.41	0.005	0.91	0.04
70	4.39	0.016	1.85	0.12
100	5.12	0.059	3.12	0.43
150	5.62	0.24	4.43	1.36
200	5.84	0.56	5.16	2.41
250	5.96	0.99	5.56	3.30
300	6.07	1.46	5.82	3.93
400	6.18	2.45	6.13	4.77
500	6.28	3.24	6.42	5.26
600	6.40	3.85	6.72	5.59
800	6.65	4.66	7.31	6.07
1000	6.90	5.16	7.00	6.51

to have much effect on the distribution inside), the speed distribution of those that escape is $F(v) \propto v f(v) \propto v^3 e^{-mv^2/2kT}$. Show that the mean energy of those that escape is $2kT$.

8-39. At what temperature are the amounts of superfluid helium and normal liquid helium equal?

8-40. Estimate the frequency and energy of vibration of the H_2 molecule from the graph of C_V versus T in Figure 8-12.

Level III

8-41. This problem is related to the equipartition theorem. Consider a system in which the energy of a particle is given by $E = Au^2$, where A is a constant and u is any coordinate or momentum which can vary from $-\infty$ to $+\infty$. (*a*) Write the probability of the particle having u in the range du and calculate the normalization constant C in terms of A. (*b*) Calculate the average energy $\langle E \rangle = \langle Au^2 \rangle$ and show that $\langle E \rangle = \frac{1}{2} kT$.

8-42. Calculate the average value of the magnitude of v_x from the Maxwell distribution.

8-43. Show that $f_{FD}(E) \rightarrow f_B(E)$ for $E \gg E_F$.

8-44. Carry out the integration indicated in Equation 8-67 to show that α is given by Equation 8-68.

8-45. Consider a system of N particles which has only two possible energy states, $E_1 = 0$ and $E_2 = \epsilon$. The distribution function is $f_i = Ce^{-E_i/kT}$. (*a*) What is C for this case? (*b*) Compute the average energy $\langle E \rangle$ and show that $\langle E \rangle \rightarrow 0$ as $T \rightarrow 0$ and $\langle E \rangle \rightarrow \epsilon/2$ as $T \rightarrow \infty$. (*c*) Show that the heat capacity is

$$C_V = Nk \left(\frac{\epsilon}{kT} \right)^2 \frac{e^{-\epsilon/kT}}{(1 + e^{-\epsilon/kT})^2}$$

(*d*) Sketch C_V versus T.

8-46. If the assumptions leading to the Bose-Einstein distribution are modified so that the number of particles is not assumed constant, the resulting distribution has $e^{\alpha} = 1$. This distribution can be applied to a "gas" of photons. Consider the photons to be in a cubic box of side L. The momentum components of a photon are quantized by the standing-wave conditions $k_x = n_1 \pi/L$, $k_y = n_2 \pi/L$, and $k_z = n_3 \pi/L$, where $p = \hbar(k_x^2 + k_y^2 + k_z^2)^{1/2}$ is the magnitude of the momentum. (*a*) Show that the energy of a photon can be written $E = N(\hbar c\pi/L)$, where $N^2 = n_1^2 + n_2^2 + n_3^2$. (*b*) Assuming two photons per space state because of the two possible polarizations, show that the number of states between N and $N + dN$ is $\pi N^2 dN$. (*c*) Find the density of states and show that the number of photons in the energy interval dE is

$$n(E) \, dE = \frac{8\pi (L/hc)^3 E^2 \, dE}{e^{E/kT} - 1}$$

(*d*) The energy density in dE is given by $u(E) \, dE = En(E) \, dE/L^3$. Use this to obtain the Planck blackbody radiation formula for the energy density in $d\lambda$, where λ is the wavelength:

$$u(\lambda) = \frac{8\pi hc\lambda^{-5}}{e^{hc/\lambda kT} - 1}$$

Part 2

Applications

Part 1 introduced the principles of the special and general relativity theories and illustrated how they led to profound alteration of the classical views of space and time. We then saw how the ideas and methods of quantum mechanics developed and how their application to atomic physics yields an understanding of atomic structure and spectra. In Part 2 we shall extend the applications of mainly quantum theory, but also occasionally relativity, to a wide variety of systems of particular interest to engineers, chemists, and physicists.

These applications form the foundation for a wide range of inquiry and research in physics and chemistry and provide the basic understanding of the principles underlying many practical devices. They include molecular bonding and spectra (Chapter 9); the structure of solids and their thermal and electrical properties (Chapter 10); superconductors (Chapter 10); nuclear structure, radioactivity, and nuclear reactions (Chapters 11 and 12); and elementary particles (Chapter 13). Practical applications include the study of lasers (Chapter 9); semiconductors, semiconductor junctions, and transistors (Chapter 10); and radioisotope dating and elemental analysis, nuclear fission, nuclear fusion, and reactors (Chapter 12). Many of these applications have revolutionized contemporary society. Part 2 concludes with a review of astrophysics and cosmology, topics that stimulate the imagination of everyone. They are found in Chapter 14 on the home page: www.whfreeman.com/modphysics4e

These chapters are independent of one another and can be studied in any order, although Chapter 12 should follow Chapter 11 unless the reader is familiar with elementary nuclear physics.

Chapter **9**

Molecular Structure and Spectra

*I*n this chapter we shall study the bonding of molecules—systems of two or more atoms. Properly, a molecule is the smallest constituent of a substance which retains its chemical properties. The study of the properties of molecules forms the basis for theoretical chemistry. The application of quantum mechanics to molecular physics has been spectacularly successful in explaining the structure of molecules and the complexity of their spectra, and in answering such puzzling questions as why two H atoms join together to form a molecule but three H atoms do not. As in atomic physics, the detailed quantum-mechanical calculations are often difficult. When the difficulty would tend to obscure understanding of the physics, we will, as before, make our discussions semiquantitative or qualitative. In the final sections we will discuss the interaction of electromagnetic radiation with molecules, concluding with a discussion of the common general types of lasers.

There are essentially two extreme views we can take of a molecule. Consider, for example, H_2. We can think of it either as two H atoms somehow joined together, or as a quantum-mechanical system of two protons and two electrons. The latter picture is more fruitful in this case because neither of the electrons in the H_2 molecule can be considered as belonging to either proton. Instead, the wave function for each electron is spread out in space about the whole molecule. For more complicated molecules, however, an intermediate picture is useful. Consider the N_2 molecule as an example. We need not consider the complicated problem of 2 nuclei and 14 electrons. The electron configuration of an N atom in the ground state is $1s^2 2s^2 2p^3$. Of the three electrons in the $2p$ state, two are in an $m_l = -1$ state with their spins paired (that is, with spins antiparallel so that the resultant spin for those two is zero). The third one is in an $m_l = 0$ level and its spin is, of course, unpaired. Only the electron with the unpaired spin is free to take part in the bonding of the N_2 molecule. We therefore can consider this molecule as two N^+ ions and two electrons that belong to the molecule as a whole. The molecular wave functions for these bonding electrons are called *molecular orbitals*. In many cases these molecular wave functions can be constructed from linear combinations of the atomic wave functions with which we are familiar.

Another type of bonding involves the transfer of one or more electrons between atoms, the bond resulting from Coulomb attraction between the ions, an example being NaCl. Again in this case, as in all four types of molecular bonding, it is the wave properties of the spin $\frac{1}{2}$ electrons that are the key to understanding.

9-1 The Ionic Bond

The two principal types of bonds that join two or more atoms together to form a molecule are called *ionic* and *covalent* bonds. Other types of bonds that are important in the bonding of liquids and solids are *dipole-dipole* bonds and *metallic* bonds. In many cases the bonding is a mixture of these mechanisms. We shall discuss all of these in this chapter and the next, but it is important to recognize that all types of molecular bonding arise for the same fundamental reasons: the total energy of the stable bound molecule is lower than the total energy of the constituent atoms when they are widely separated, and there is a net attractive force between constituent atoms when their separation becomes larger than some equilibrium value. The bonding mechanisms are primarily due to electrostatic forces between the atoms or ions of the system together with the wave properties of electrons and the fact that they obey the exclusion principle. The complete description of molecular bonding is in most cases quite complex, involving as it does the mutual interactions of many electrons and nuclei; consequently, we will discuss each type using simplified models consisting of two or a few atoms, then illustrate qualitatively the extension of the results to more complex molecules.

The easiest type of bond to understand is the ionic bond, typically the strongest of the bonds and the one found in most salts. Consider KCl as an example. For the molecule to be stable, we must be able to show that $E(KCl) < E(K) + E(Cl)$ when the K and Cl atoms are far apart and at rest. Let us define the energy of the system to be zero when the neutral atoms are widely separated. (See Figure 9-1.) The potassium atom has one $4s$ electron outside an argon core, $1s^2 2s^2 2p^6 3s^2 3p^6$. The ionization energy for K is low, as it is for all the alkali metals; for K only 4.34 eV is required to remove the outer electron from the atom. (See Table 9-1.) The removal of one electron from K leaves a positive ion with a spherically symmetric, closed-shell core. Chlorine, on the other hand, is only one electron short of having a closed argon core. The energy released by the acquisition of one electron is called the *electron affinity*, which in the case of Cl is 3.62 eV. Energy is released because the wave function of the "extra" electron penetrates the outer shell to a degree (see Figure 7-10*b*) and thus

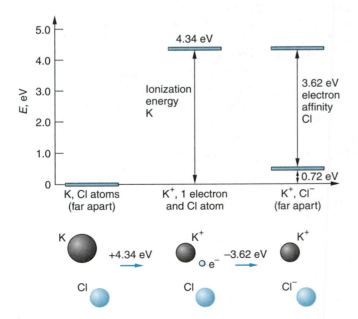

Fig. 9-1 Net energy required to ionize a K and a Cl atom. An addition of 4.34 eV is required to remove the $4s$ electron from the neutral K atom, forming K^+ and a free electron. That electron (or some electron) can then occupy the vacancy in the $3p$ shell of the Cl atom, forming a Cl^- ion. The electron is positively bound, with the release of 3.62 eV. Formation of the widely separated K^+ and Cl^- ions thus requires a net addition of 0.72 eV.

TABLE 9-1	Ionization energies of alkali metal atoms and electron affinities of halogen atoms		
Alkali metal	**Ionization energy (eV)**	**Halogen**	**Electron affinity (eV)**
Li	5.39	F	3.40
Na	5.14	Cl	3.62
K	4.34	Br	3.36
Rb	4.18	I	3.06
Cs	3.89	At	2.8
Fr	4.0		

Source: Data from Handbook of Chemistry and Physics, *75th ed. (New York: Chemical Rubber Co., 1994).*

sees a net positive charge. The acquisition of one electron by chlorine leaves a negative ion with a spherically symmetric, closed-shell electron core. Thus the formation of a K^+ ion and a Cl^- ion by the donation of one electron of K to Cl requires just $4.34 - 3.62 = 0.72$ eV. If this were the whole story, the KCl molecule would not form; however, the electrostatic potential energy of the two ions separated by a distance r is $-ke^2/r$. When the separation of the ions is less than about 2.8 nm, the negative potential energy of attraction is of greater magnitude than the energy needed to create the ions, and the ions move toward each other.

Since the electrostatic attraction increases as the ions get closer, it would seem that equilibrium could not exist. For very small separation of the ions, however, the wave functions of the $3p$ electrons in the K^+ ion and the $3p$ electrons in the Cl^- ion begin to overlap. Since the $3p$ shells in each ion contain electrons with sets of quantum numbers identical to those in the other, a strong repulsion develops due to the exclusion principle. This "exclusion-principle repulsion" is primarily responsible for the repulsion of the atoms in all molecules (except H_2), no matter which type of bonding occurs. When the ions are very far apart, the wave function for a core electron of one ion does not overlap that of the other ion. We can distinguish the electrons by the ion to which they belong, and the electrons of one ion can have the same quantum numbers as in the other ion. However, when the ions are close, the wave functions of their core electrons begin to overlap, and some of the electrons must go into higher-energy quantum states because of the exclusion principle, thus increasing the total energy of the system. This is not a sudden process; the energy states of the electrons are gradually changed as the ions move closer together. The total potential energy U of the KCl system can be expressed in terms of the separation r of the ion centers as the sum of the electrostatic potential, the net ionization energy, and the exclusion-principle repulsion:

$$U(r) = -\frac{ke^2}{r} + E_{ex} + E_{ion} \qquad \textbf{9-1}$$

where $E_{ion} = 0.72$ eV for K^+ and Cl^-, as was found above. The exclusion-principle repulsion E_{ex} can be written as

$$E_{\text{ex}} = \frac{A}{r^n} \qquad\qquad \textbf{9-2}$$

where A and n are constants for each ionic molecule. Figure 9-2a is a sketch of the potential energy of the K^+ and Cl^- ions versus their separation. The energy is lowest at an equilibrium separation r_0 of about 0.27 nm. At smaller separations, the energy rises steeply as a result of the exclusion principle. The energy E_d required to separate the ions and form K and Cl *atoms,* called the *dissociation energy,* is about 4.40 eV. Figure 9-2b shows the total potential energy of another ionically bonded molecule, NaCl. Note the differences between the two total potential energy curves that are due to the higher ionization potential and smaller closed-shell core of Na compared to K. Example 9-1 illustrates calculations used to construct curves like those in the diagram. Example 9-2 describes how the constants A and n in Equation 9-2 are found.

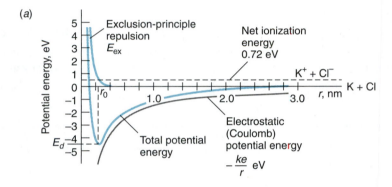

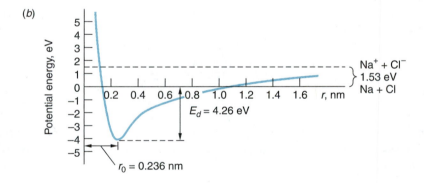

Fig. 9-2 (*a*) Potential energy for K^+ and Cl^- ions as a function of separation distance r. The energy at infinite separation was chosen to be 0.72 eV, corresponding to the energy needed to form the ions from neutral atoms. The minimum energy for this curve is at the equilibrium separation $r_0 = 0.27$ nm for the ions in the molecule. (*b*) Potential energy for Na^+ and Cl^- ions as a function of r. Differences between the two similar molecules are due to the higher ionization potential and smaller core of Na.

EXAMPLE 9-1 Ionic Bonding in NaF The ionization potential of sodium is 5.14 eV, the electron affinity of fluorine is 3.40 eV, and the equilibrium separation of sodium fluoride (NaF) is 0.193 nm. (*a*) How much energy is needed to form Na^+ and F^- ions from neutral sodium and fluorine atoms? (*b*) What is the electrostatic potential energy of the Na^+ and F^- ions at their equilibrium separation? (*c*) The dissociation energy of NaF is 4.99 eV. What is the energy due to repulsion of the ions at the equilibrium separation?

Solution

(*a*) Since the energy needed to ionize sodium is 5.14 eV and the electron affinity of F is 3.40 eV, the energy needed to form Na^+ and F^- ions from neutral sodium and fluorine atoms is 5.14 eV − 3.40 eV = 1.74 eV = E_{ion}.

(*b*) The electrostatic potential energy of the Na^+ and F^- ions at their equilibrium separation (with $-ke^2/r = 0$ at infinite separation) is

$$-\frac{ke^2}{r_0} = -\frac{(8.99 \times 10^9 \text{ N} \cdot \text{m}^2/\text{C}^2)(1.60 \times 10^{-19} \text{ C})}{1.93 \times 10^{-10} \text{ m}}$$

$$= -1.19 \times 10^{-18} \text{ J} = -7.45 \text{ eV}$$

(*c*) Choosing the total potential energy at infinity to be 1.74 eV (the net ionization energy needed to form Na^+ and F^- from the neutral atoms), the net electrostatic (Coulomb) potential U_C is

$$U_C = -\frac{ke^2}{r} + 1.74 \text{ eV}$$

At the equilibrium separation r_0, this energy is $U_C = -7.45 \text{ eV} + 1.74 \text{ eV} = -5.71$ eV. Since the measured dissociation energy is 4.99 eV, the potential energy due to exclusion-principle repulsion E_{ex} of the Na^+ and F^- at equilibrium separation, from Equation 9-1, must be 5.71 eV − 4.99 eV = 0.72 eV.

EXAMPLE 9-2 Contribution from Exclusion-Principle Repulsion Find the values of *A* and *n* in Equation 9-2 for NaF.

Solution
From Example 9-1 we have that the potential energy due to exclusion-principle repulsion at equilibrium separation of the ions is

$$E_{ex}(r_0) = \frac{A}{r_0^n} = \frac{A}{(0.193 \text{ nm})^n} = 0.72 \text{ eV}$$

At $r = r_0$ the net force on each ion must be zero, because the potential energy has its minimum value at that point. This means that at $r = r_0$ the net Coulomb force F_C is equal in magnitude and opposite in sign to the exclusion-principle repulsive force, i.e.,

$$F_C = -\left(\frac{dU_C}{dr}\right)_{r=r_0} = \left(\frac{nA}{r^{n+1}}\right)_{r=r_0}$$

At $r = r_0$,

$$F_C = \frac{U_C(r_0)}{r_0} = \frac{ke^2}{r_0^2} = 38.7 \text{ eV} = \frac{nA}{r_0^{n+1}}$$

Thus, we have that

$$\frac{nA}{r_0^{n+1}} = \frac{n}{r_0}\frac{A}{r_0^n} = \frac{n}{r_0}(0.72 \text{ eV}) = 38.7 \text{ eV/nm}$$

or

$$n = \frac{38.7 \text{ eV/nm}}{0.72 \text{ eV}} \times 0.193 \text{ nm} = 10.4 \approx 10$$

and, therefore, $A = 5.4 \times 10^{-8} \text{ eV} \cdot \text{nm}^{10}$. Finally, for NaF, E_{ex} is given by

$$E_{ex} = \frac{(5.4 \times 10^{-8} \text{ eV} \cdot \text{nm}^{10})}{r^{10}}$$

It should be emphasized that our discussion of ionic bonding and, in particular, the graphs of potential energy in Figure 9-2 apply to the *ground states* of the molecules. The outer (valence) electrons of molecules may occupy excited states, just as they do in atoms. Since the electron wave functions of the excited states tend to extend farther from the ions than do those of the ground state, the potential energy curve is broader and more shallow than for the ground state, resulting in a slightly weaker bond and a larger equilibrium separation of the ions. In our discussion we have ignored two additional contributions to the total energy of the molecule: (1) the zero-point energy (see Section 5-6), which decreases the magnitude of E_d, and (2) the van der Waals attraction, which increases the magnitude of E_d. Both are small and tend to partially offset one another. The latter, which arises from induced dipole moments, is the only form of bonding available for certain molecules and will be discussed later in this chapter.

The equilibrium separation of 0.27 nm is for gaseous diatomic KCl (which can be obtained by evaporation of solid KCl). Normally, KCl exists in a cubic crystal structure, with K^+ and Cl^- at alternate corners of a cube. The separation of the ions in a crystal is somewhat larger—about 0.32 nm. Because of the presence of neighboring ions of opposite charge, the Coulomb energy per ion pair is lower when the ions are in a crystal. This energy is usually expressed as $\alpha k e^2 / r_0$, where r_0 is the equilibrium separation distance or *bond length* and α, called the *Madelung constant,* depends on the crystal structure, as will be discussed further in Chapter 10. For KCl, α is about 1.75. The values of E_d and r_0 listed in Table 9-2 are for several ionically bonded (gaseous) molecules.

One final comment concerning ionic bonding: few of the molecules in Table 9-2 are bonded exclusively by the ionic mechanism. As we shall see in the next section, they may also be covalently bonded.

9-2 The Covalent Bond

A completely different mechanism is responsible for the bonding of such molecules as H_2, N_2, H_2O, and CO and also leads to bonding of many of the molecules in Table 9-2. If we calculate the energy needed to form the ions H^+ and H^- by the transfer of an electron from one atom to the other, we find the net ionization energy to be more than 12 eV. Adding this energy to the electrostatic energy (including the repulsion of the protons), we find that there is no separation distance for which the total energy is negative. The bond of H_2 thus cannot be ionic. The attraction of two hydrogen atoms is instead an entirely quantum-mechanical effect. The decrease in energy when two hydrogen atoms approach each other is due to the sharing of the two electrons by both atoms and is intimately connected with the symmetry properties of the electron wave functions. We can gain some insight into this phenomenon by first studying a simple one-dimensional quantum mechanics problem—that of two finite square wells each of width L.

TABLE 9-2 Dissociation energies E_d and equilibrium separations r_0 for several ionic molecules* in the gaseous state		
Molecule	Dissociation energy (eV)	Equilibrium separation (nm)
NaCl	4.27	0.236
NaF	4.95	0.193
NaH	2.08	0.189
NaBr	3.76	0.253
LiCl	4.85	0.202
LiH	2.47	0.239
LiI	3.67	0.238
KCl	4.40	0.267
KBr	3.94	0.282
RbF	5.12	0.227
RbCl	4.37	0.279
CsI	3.57	0.337

*The two entries of molecules formed by an alkali atom and a hydrogen atom may seem odd, but hydrogen atoms, like those of a number of other elements, may form molecules as either positive or negative ions. The ionization energy of H is, of course, 13.6 eV; its electron affinity is 0.75 eV.

Source: Data from Handbook of Chemistry and Physics, 75th ed. (New York: Chemical Rubber Co., 1994).

Consider first a single electron that is equally likely to be in either well. Since the wells are identical, symmetry requires that $|\Psi|^2$ be symmetric about the midpoint of the wells. Then Ψ must be either symmetric or antisymmetric about that point. These two possibilities for the ground state are shown in Figure 9-3. Previously, we did not distinguish between these two possibilities when superimposing (i.e., adding)

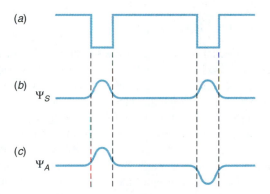

Fig. 9-3 (*a*) Two square wells far apart. The electron wave function can be either (*b*) symmetric or (*c*) antisymmetric. The probability distributions and energies are the same for the two wave functions when the wells are far apart.

wave functions, because the energies $\pi^2\hbar^2/2mL^2$ and the probability densities Ψ^2 for both of these wave functions are the same when the wells are far apart. Figure 9-4 shows the symmetric and antisymmetric wave functions when the wells are very close together. Now the parts of the wave function describing the electron in one well or the other overlap, and the symmetric and antisymmetric resultant wave functions are quite different. Notice that for the symmetric wave functions the probability of the electron being found in the region between the wells is much larger than for the antisymmetric wave function. In the limiting case of no separation, the symmetric wave function Ψ_S approaches the ground-state wave function for a particle in a well of size $2L$ and the antisymmetric wave function Ψ_A approaches that for the first excited state in such a well; thus Ψ_S is a lower energy state than Ψ_A. There are two important results from this discussion:

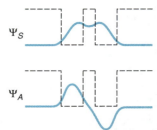

Fig. 9-4 Symmetric and anti-symmetric space wave functions for two square wells close together. The probability distributions and energies are not the same for the two wave functions in this case. The symmetric space wave function (and, therefore, the probability density) is larger between the wells than the antisymmetric space wave function.

1. The originally equal energies for Ψ_A and Ψ_S are split into two different energies as the wells become close.

2. The wave function for the symmetric state is large in the region between the wells, whereas that for the antisymmetric state is small.

Now consider adding a second electron to the two wells. The *total* wave function for the two electrons must be antisymmetric on exchange of the electrons, since they obey the Pauli exclusion principle. Note that exchanging the electrons in the wells is the same as exchanging the wells, i.e., for a two-particle system, exchange symmetry is the same as space symmetry. The two electrons can therefore be in the space-symmetric state if the spins are antiparallel ($S = 0$) or in the space-antisymmetric state if their spins are parallel ($S = 1$).

H_2^+ Molecule

Now let us consider a real physical system with one electron, the hydrogen molecule ion H_2^+. For a one-dimensional model, the double potential well formed by the two protons is illustrated in Figure 9-5. The Hamiltonian (total energy) operator for this system is (see Equation 6-51)

$$H_{op} = \frac{P_{op}^2}{2m} + ke^2\left(-\frac{1}{r_1} - \frac{1}{r_2} + \frac{1}{r_0}\right)$$

In the ground state, the hydrogen atom wave function is proportional to e^{-r/a_0}. For our one-dimensional model, we shall write this as $e^{-|x|/a_0}$. The symmetric and

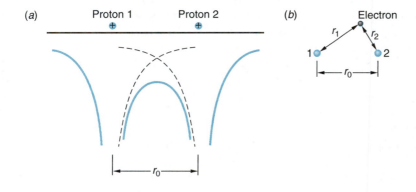

(a) Proton 1   Proton 2

(b) Electron

Fig. 9-5 Coulomb potential for an electron resulting from two protons separated by a distance r. The solid line is the total potential for a one-dimensional model. The circled plus signs mark the locations of the protons.

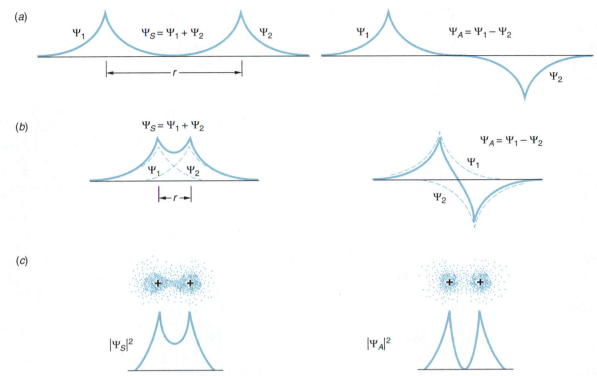

Fig. 9-6 One-dimensional symmetric and antisymmetric electron space wave functions for (*a*) two protons far apart and (*b*) two protons close together. (*c*) Probability distributions for wave functions in (*b*). Computer-drawn electron density about the protons is shown above the probability densities.

antisymmetric combinations for two values of the distance between the protons are shown in Figure 9-6. In general,

$$\Psi_S = \left(\frac{1}{\sqrt{2}}\right)(\Psi_{100}(r_1) + \Psi_{100}(r_2))$$

and

$$\Psi_A = \left(\frac{1}{\sqrt{2}}\right)(\Psi_{100}(r_1) - \Psi_{100}(r_2))$$

The results are similar to the square-well case: Ψ_S is large in the region between the protons, while Ψ_A is small in that region. Only in the case where the electron wave function and, hence, the probability density is large near the center of the molecule do we expect a stable molecular bond to form. This concentration of negative charge between the protons for Ψ_S holds the protons together. Similarly, we would not expect Ψ_A to result in a stable molecule. The justification of this conclusion would be the solution of the Schrödinger equation and calculation of $|\Psi|^2$ for H_2^+.

The solution and calculation are quite difficult, so we will simply state the results for the energy of the molecule as a function of the separation r of the protons, describing in the process how, in general, the potential energy function arises. Referring first to Figure 9-6*a*, when the protons are far apart, the electron's energy is -13.6 eV. The potential energy U_p (repulsion) of the protons is negligibly small for large r and, since there is only a single electron in the system, there is no exclusion-principle repulsion.

As the two protons are brought closer together as in Figure 9-6b, U_p increases and the energy of the electron decreases, since the electron experiences a greater Coulomb force and becomes more tightly bound. Consider what is happening to the energy of the electron as the separation r of the protons is reduced. As $r \rightarrow 0$, the electron's wave function is approaching that of an atom with $Z = 2$. The symmetric wave function Ψ_S has a maximum at $r = 0$ and thus corresponds to the $1s$ (ground) state of the $Z = 2$ atom. As we have already seen (Equation 7-25), its energy is $E_1 = -13.6\, Z^2/n^2 = -54.4$ eV. For our discussion here, let us call the electron's energy E_S for the wave function Ψ_S. Thus, $E_S = -13.6$ eV for $r \rightarrow \infty$ and $E_S = -54.4$ eV for $r \rightarrow 0$. The anti-symmetric wave function Ψ_A is zero at $r = 0$ and thus corresponds to the $2p$ (first excited) state of the $Z = 2$ atom, this state being the lowest energy state with a wave function that vanishes at $r = 0$. (See Equation 7-26 and Table 7-2.) The energy of this state is $E_2 = -13.6\, Z^2/n^2 = -13.6$ eV. As above, if we call E_A the energy of the electron for the wave function Ψ_A, then $E_A = -13.6$ eV for $r \rightarrow \infty$ (where $|\Psi_S|^2$ and $|\Psi_A|^2$ are the same) and $E_A = -13.6$ eV for $r \rightarrow 0$. Recall that the smaller average slope of Ψ_S compared to Ψ_A as $r \rightarrow 0$ implies a smaller energy for the symmetric state. The variations of both E_S and E_A are shown in Figure 9-7.

The potential energy U_p of the protons as a function of their separation is, of course, $U_p = ke^2/r$ and the total energy of the H_2^+ molecule is then $U_p + E_S$ or $U_p + E_A$, depending on which of the electronic wave functions happens to exist. As can be seen in Figure 9-7, only one of the total energy functions has a minimum and can, therefore, result in bonding of the H_2^+ molecule. The potential energy function $E_{total} = U_p + E_S$ has a minimum at $r = 0.106$ nm. This tells us that the H_2^+ molecule is stable, with

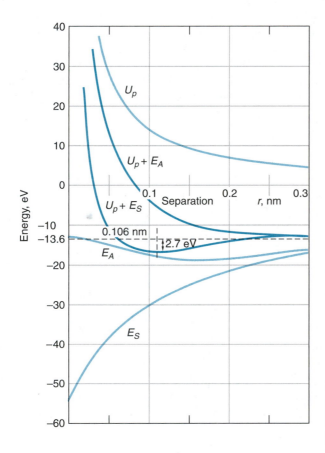

Fig. 9-7 Dependence of the molecular potential energy on the separation of the protons and on the symmetry of the electron wave function for the H_2^+ system.

equilibrium separation $r_0 = 0.106$ nm and binding energy $= E_{\text{total}}\,(r \rightarrow \infty) - E_{\text{total}}(r_0) = -13.6 - (-16.3) = 2.7$ eV. In contrast, the potential energy function $E_{\text{total}} = U_p + E_A$ has no minimum; therefore, the antisymmetric wave function does not result in a stable molecule, as we expected at the outset of this discussion. Note that the H_2^+-type bond will tend to be unstable unless the nuclei have the same Z.

H_2 Molecule

Formation of the H_2 molecule is very similar to that of H_2^+. We can think of it as two H atoms in their ground states, initially far apart. Each has a $1s$ electronic *orbital*,[1] i.e., an electron the space part of whose wave function is Ψ_{100}, with an energy of -13.6 eV. Thus, the total energy of the H_2 system for large r (i.e., $r \rightarrow \infty$) is -27.2 eV. As the two atoms approach one another, the wave functions begin to overlap, again as illustrated by Figures 9-6a and b, so that the two atoms (protons) share both electrons. Just as was discussed above, the two wave functions may add to produce a symmetric total wave function Ψ_S that results in a stable bound H_2 molecule or an antisymmetric one Ψ_A, which does not lead to a stable molecule. Since the *total* wave function Ψ must always be antisymmetric to an exchange of the electrons, the *space* wave function Ψ_S ($= R_{nl}Y_{lm}$) must be associated with an antisymmetric *spin* function χ_A (see Section 7-6). Thus, Ψ_S is a singlet state ($S = 0$) and Ψ_A is a triplet state ($S = 1$).

There is a difference between the H_2 molecule and the H_2^+ molecule that needs explanation. Just as H_2^+, the H_2 molecule has two *molecular* states whose total energy at large r is, as we have seen, -27.2 eV. As r gets smaller, the molecule still has two states, but their energies separate, as sketched in Figure 9-8a. The lower energy E_S is, as before, associated with Ψ_S, the electronic wave function of the stable molecule, known also as the *bonding orbital*. The wave function Ψ_A associated with the energy E_A that does not result in bonding is also called the *antibonding orbital*. The difference is that there are now two electrons whose probability density is large in the region between the protons, both in the Ψ_S molecular orbital. Since electrons obey the exclusion principle, their spins must be antiparallel ($S = 0$). Thus, a molecular

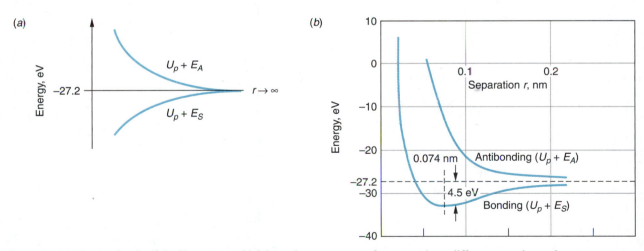

Fig. 9-8 (*a*) The two levels of the H_2 system, which have the same energy for $r \rightarrow \infty$, have different energies as the atoms approach one another. (*b*) Potential energy versus separation for two hydrogen atoms. $U_p + E_S$ is for the symmetric (bonding) space wave function, and $U_p + E_A$ is for the antisymmetric (antibonding) space wave function. As the separation approaches zero, both curves approach $+\infty$.

orbital, just like an atomic orbital, can be occupied by no more than two electrons. For H_2 both electrons can thus occupy the bonding orbital. Both electrons being in s states, H_2 is referred to as being *s-bonded*.

Figure 9-8*b* illustrates the potential energy functions for H_2. The energy corresponding to Ψ_S, the bonding orbital, has a minimum of $E = -31.7$ eV at $r = 0.074$ nm—i.e., the equilibrium separation $r_0 = 0.074$ nm—and the binding energy is $E(r \rightarrow \infty) - E(r_0) = -27.2 - (-31.7) = 4.5$ eV. The effect of adding the second electron to H_2^+ to form H_2 is evident from a comparison of Figures 9-7 and 9-8*b*. The increased charge concentration between the protons binds them more tightly, the binding energy increasing from 2.7 eV to 4.5 eV and the equilibrium separation decreasing by 30 percent. The sharing of the outer, or valence, electrons in a molecule, as in our H_2 example, is the mechanism of the *covalent* molecular bond. The basic requirement for covalent bonding is that the wave functions of the valence electrons of the participating atoms overlap as much as possible. Unlike the H_2^+ case, the covalent bond is just as strong for nonidentical nuclei as it is for identical nuclei.[2]

We can now see why three H atoms do not bond to form H_3. If a third H atom is brought near an H_2 molecule, the third electron cannot be in a $1s$ state and have its spin antiparallel to both the other electrons. It must, therefore, occupy the higher-energy, antibonding orbital. If it is in an antisymmetric state with respect to exchange with one of the electrons, the repulsion of this atom is greater than the attraction of the other. Thus, as the three atoms are pushed together, the third electron is, in effect, forced into a higher quantum state by the exclusion principle. The bond between two H atoms is called a *saturated bond* because there is no room for another electron. The two electrons being shared essentially fill the $1s$ states of both atoms. This is basically the reason why covalent bonds involving three (or more) electrons are typically unstable. However, be aware that the H_3^+ ion *is* stable. Discovered by J. J. Thomson in 1911, this simplest of all polyatomic molecules provides important cosmic spectral lines for astrophysicists and a calculation benchmark for quantum chemists.

It should be clear now why He atoms do not bond together to form He_2. There are no valence electrons that can be shared. As two He atoms approach one another, the bonding and antibonding molecular orbitals form, just as they do for H_2; however, each orbital can accommodate only two electrons (with spins antiparallel), so two of the four electrons in the He_2 system cannot remain in the $1s$ atomic states, but must be in the antibonding orbital. The net effect is that He_2 does not form a stable bond. At low temperatures or high pressures, He atoms do bond together; but the bonds are very weak and are due to van der Waals forces, which we shall discuss in Section 9-3. The bonding is so weak that at atmospheric pressure He boils at 4.2 K, and it does not form a solid at any temperature unless the pressure is greater than about 20 atm.

Although the H_3 molecule is not bound, the H_3^+ ion is! Discovered by J. J. Thomson in 1911 and lacking a stable excited state, H_3^+ is used as a probe in Jupiter's atmosphere and serves as the benchmark for quantum chemistry calculations for polyatomic molecules.

Covalently bonded fullerene molecules have been assembled into nanotubes, i.e., tubes with diameters in the nanometer range. Adding a few impurity atoms per molecule turns it into a superconductor. (See Section 10-8.)

Covalent or Ionic?

When two identical atoms bond, as in homonuclear diatomic molecules such as O_2 or N_2, the bonding is purely covalent. Since the wave functions of the two atoms are exactly alike, neither atom dominates and the electrons are completely shared between them. However, the bonding of two dissimilar atoms is often a mixture of covalent and ionic bonding. Even in NaCl, the electron donated by sodium to chlorine has some probability of being at the sodium atom because its wave function does not suddenly fall to zero. Thus, this electron is partially shared in a covalent bond, although this bonding is only a small part of the total bond, which is mainly ionic.

A measure of the degree to which a bond is ionic or covalent can be obtained from the electric dipole moment of the molecule. For example, if the bonding in NaCl were purely ionic, the center of positive charge would be at the Na^+ ion and the center of negative charge would be at the Cl^- ion. The electric dipole moment would have the magnitude

$$p_{ionic} = er_0 \qquad\qquad \textbf{9-3}$$

where r_0 is the equilibrium separation of the ions. Thus, the dipole moment of NaCl would be

$$
\begin{aligned}
p_{ionic} &= er_0 \\
&= (1.60 \times 10^{-19}\,\text{C})(2.36 \times 10^{-10}\,\text{m}) = 3.78 \times 10^{-29}\,\text{C}\cdot\text{m}
\end{aligned}
$$

The actual measured electric dipole moment of NaCl is

$$p_{measured} = 3.00 \times 10^{-29}\,\text{C}\cdot\text{m}$$

A purely covalent molecule would be expected to have an electric dipole moment of zero. We can define the ratio of $p_{measured}$ to p_{ionic} as the fractional amount of ionic bonding. For NaCl, this ratio is $3.00/3.78 = 0.79$. Thus, the bonding in NaCl is about 79 percent ionic and 21 percent covalent.

EXAMPLE 9-3 Bonding in LiH The measured electric dipole moment of LiH is $1.96 \times 10^{-29}\,\text{C}\cdot\text{m}$. This molecule is among those listed in Table 9-3 (on the home page) as being covalent *s*-bonded. What portion of the LiH bond is covalent?

Solution
The equilibrium separation of LiH from the table is 0.160 nm. If it were a purely ionically bonded molecule, its dipole moment p_{ionic} would be

$$p_{ionic} = (1.60 \times 10^{-19}\,\text{C})(0.160 \times 10^{-9}\,\text{m}) = 2.56 \times 10^{-29}\,\text{C}\cdot\text{m}$$

The fractional amount of the bond that is ionic is $1.96/2.56 = 0.77$. Thus, LiH is only about 23 percent covalently *s*-bonded.

More

In addition to the *s*-bonded H_2 molecule, there are many other covalently bonded molecules involving shared pairs of *s* electrons, *s* and *p* electrons, and *p* electrons. Important among these are the *sp* bonds involving carbon that are the basis for the vast array of hydrocarbon molecules and compounds. Several examples, including the remarkable fullerenes, are discussed in *Other Covalent Bonds* on the home page: www.whfreeman.com/modphysics4e   See also Equations 9-4 and 9-5 here, as well as Tables 9-3 through 9-6 and Figures 9-9 through 9-17.

Exploring

9-3 Other Bonding Mechanisms

The two bonding mechanisms that we have discussed thus far, ionic and covalent, account for a large fraction of the cases in which atoms combine to form molecules. As is described in Chapter 10, when atoms combine on a larger scale to form solids, these exact same mechanisms are responsible for the bonding in many solids. In addition to these, two other types of bonding occur in solids. One of these, *molecular bonding,* or *dipole-dipole bonding,* also occurs in the formation of many large molecules from smaller molecules and will be discussed in this section. The second type, *metallic bonding,* is responsible for the structure of metals in the solid state and has no single-molecule version or counterpart. For that reason, our discussion of metallic bonding will be deferred to Chapter 10.

Dipole-Dipole Bonding

It was first suggested by J. D. van der Waals[5] in 1873 that any two separated molecules will be attracted toward one another by electrostatic forces. Similarly, atoms that do not otherwise form ionic or covalent bonds will be attracted to one another by the same sort of weak electrostatic bonds. The practical result of this is that at temperatures low enough so that the disruptive effects of thermal agitation are negligible, all substances will condense into a liquid and then a solid form. (Recall that helium is the only element that does not solidify at any temperature under its own vapor pressure.) The relatively weak electrostatic forces responsible for this sort of intermolecular attraction arise because of the electrostatic attraction of electric dipoles.

The electric field due to an electric dipole is illustrated in Figure 9-18a. The electric field $\mathbf{E}_d$ at point A due to the dipole is given by

$$\mathbf{E}_d = k\left[\frac{\mathbf{p}}{r^3} - \frac{3(\mathbf{p}\cdot\mathbf{r})}{r^5}\mathbf{r}\right] \qquad \text{9-6}$$

whose magnitude for $r \gg a$ is

$$\mathbf{E}_d = \frac{kqa}{r^3} = \frac{kp_1}{r^3} \qquad \text{9-7}$$

where $|\mathbf{p}_1| = qa$ is the dipole moment.[6] Thus, the electric field of the dipole, and hence the electric force on a charge, falls off as $1/r^3$. This result, which is correct even if the point A is not on the perpendicular, is to be compared with the $1/r^2$

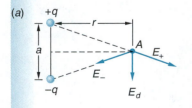

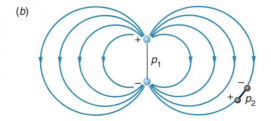

Fig. 9-18 (*a*) The electric field $\mathbf{E}_d$ at a point A on a line perpendicular to the axis of an electric dipole $p_1 = qa$. (*b*) The field of $\mathbf{E}_d$ acts on a second dipole p_2 to orient it along the field lines. The force on a charge due to p_1 is $\propto 1/r^3$.

dependence of the Coulomb force that occurs in the covalent and ionic bonds: the force on a test charge due to the dipole qa is weaker at a distance r than that due to a charge q. A second dipole $\mathbf{p}_2$ that happens into the vicinity of $\mathbf{p}_1$ will then orient itself along the $\mathbf{E}_d$ field lines as illustrated in Figure 9-18b as a result of the electric force on its charges. The potential energy of the second dipole $\mathbf{p}_2$ in the field of $\mathbf{p}_1$ is given by

$$U = -\mathbf{p}_2 \cdot \mathbf{E}_d \qquad\qquad \textbf{9-8}$$

and, since $\mathbf{E}_d$ falls off like $1/r^3$, the electric force $\mathbf{F}\ (=-\partial U/\partial r)$ between two *permanent* dipoles falls off as $1/r^4$. Thus, it is attractive ($\mathbf{F}$ is negative), relatively weak, and of short range.

Polar Molecules

It is then not hard to see physically why molecules with permanent electric dipole moments—so-called *polar molecules* such as H_2O and NaCl—will attract other polar molecules. Consider the H_2O molecule as an example. Although the molecule is electrically neutral, its bonding is partially ionic, so the electrons tend to be concentrated nearer the oxygen atom, making it look like the negative end of a dipole. The two protons then look like the positive end of the dipole. There will then be a mutual attraction between the molecule and other nearby molecules with potential energy given by Equation 9-8. (See Figure 9-19.) Pairs of polar molecules will thus move closer to each other, decreasing their potential energy, until the combined effects of the increasing nuclear repulsion and the exclusion principle produce a minimum in the total potential energy similar to those of Figures 9-2 and 9-8b. For H_2O the resulting bonding energy is about 0.5 eV per molecule. Although this is only about 10 percent of the strength of the H — OH bond in the water molecule, it is this dipole-dipole force that bonds H_2O molecules to one another to form ice and is responsible in part for the beautiful hexagonal patterns that we see in snowflakes (Figure 9-19c).

When dipole-dipole bonds between molecules with permanent dipole moments involve hydrogen, as is the case for water, the bond is referred to as a *hydrogen bond*. The hydrogen bond is of enormous importance, since it is the bonding mechanism responsible for the cross-linking that allows giant biological molecules and polymers to hold their fixed shape. For example, it is the hydrogen bond that forms the linkage between the two strands of the double helix DNA molecule. It is the weakness of the hydrogen bonds relative to the covalent/ionic bonds along each strand that allows the two strands to unwind from one another in the DNA molecular replication process. Notice that the hydrogen bond can be viewed as the sharing of a proton by two negatively charged atoms, oxygen atoms in the case of water. (See Figure 9-19.) In this way it is similar to the sharing of electrons that is responsible for the covalent bond. Hydrogen bonding is facilitated by the small mass of the proton and the absence of inner-core electrons.

Fig. 9-19 (a) Schematic of four H_2O molecules. The water molecules' permanent dipole moments are shown by the vectors **p**. (b) The four polar water molecules represented as electric dipoles. Notice that the attractive dipole-dipole force tends to align the dipoles so that the nearest neighbors of each charge are charges of the opposite sign. (c) A snowflake—one result of dipole-dipole bonding.

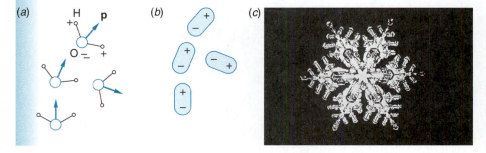

Nonpolar Molecules

A nonpolar molecule will be polarized by the field of a polar molecule and thus have an induced dipole moment and be attracted to the polar molecule. If $\mathbf{p}_2$ in Figure 9-18b is an induced dipole, then

$$\mathbf{p}_2 = \alpha \mathbf{E}_d \qquad \textbf{9-9}$$

where α is a constant characteristic of the nonpolar molecule called the *polarizability*. In this case we expect the potential energy of the interaction to fall off like $1/r^6$, since we have from Equations 9-8 and 9-9 that

$$U = -\mathbf{p}_2 \cdot \mathbf{E}_d = -\alpha E_d^2 = -\alpha k^2 p_1^2/r^6 \qquad \textbf{9-10}$$

Once again, the energy is negative, signifying that the force between the dipoles is attractive. The force $F = -\partial U/\partial r$ is thus proportional to $1/r^7$, i.e., the force is very short range, dropping rapidly with increasing r. Indeed, increasing the separation of the molecules by a factor of 2 reduces the attractive force between them to only 0.008 of its original value.

Perhaps surprisingly, two molecules, neither of which has a permanent dipole moment, can also attract one another via the mechanism just described. It is somewhat harder to see why an attractive force exists between two nonpolar molecules. Though the *average* dipole moment $\overline{\mathbf{p}}$ of a nonpolar molecule is zero, the *average square* dipole moment $\overline{p^2}$ is not, because the electrons are in constant motion and at any given instant there will be an excess or deficiency of them in one part or another of the molecule. A measurement that we might do in the laboratory reveals the average value (zero), not the instantaneous value. The instantaneous dipole moment of a nonpolar molecule is, in general, not zero. When two nonpolar molecules are nearby, the fluctuations in the instantaneous dipole moments tend to be correlated so as to produce attraction, as illustrated in Figure 9-20. The potential energy is again given approximately by Equation 9-10, so that the potential energy is proportional to $1/r^6$ and the attractive force is proportional to $1/r^7$. This attractive force between nonpolar molecules is called the *van der Waals force*[7] or, occasionally, the *London dispersion force* after Fritz London, the German physicist who in 1930 first explained the physical origin of the interaction.

Fig. 9-20 Nonpolar molecules have, on the average, symmetric distribution, as illustrated by the pair of molecules at the top of the figure. However, instantaneous fluctuations in the electron distribution are asymmetric and tend to be correlated with those of nearby molecules as shown in the other three examples. The correlated distributions lead to an attractive force proportional to $1/r^7$ that draws the molecules closer to one another as shown.

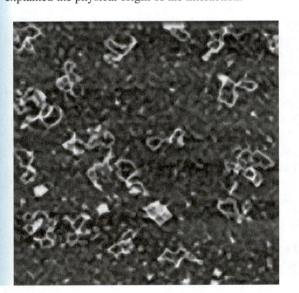

The 2-nm height of DNA molecules is readily imaged by an atomic force microscope (AFM). [*Taken from www.di.com, Digital Instruments, Veeco Metrology Group, Santa Barbara, CA.*]

Scientists have recently succeeded in trapping a sample of *molecules* in a single quantum level at a temperature in the millikelvin range. This ability raises the possibilities for, among other things, high-precision molecular spectroscopy and producing a molecular Bose-Einstein condensate.

As van der Waals first suggested, dipole-dipole forces act between all molecules and, in addition, between all atoms. They are the only forces that occur between rare gas atoms, without which the atoms of these elements would not condense into liquids or form solids. (The single exception to the latter is He, whose quantum-mechanical zero-point energy exceeds the minimum of the potential energy resulting from Equation 9-10 and core repulsion.) The dipole-dipole forces between molecules, although relatively weak, are also responsible for the physical phenomena of surface tension and friction.

QUESTIONS

1. Why would you expect the separation distance between the two protons to be larger in the H_2^+ ion than in the H_2 molecule?

2. Would you expect the NaCl molecule to be polar or nonpolar?

3. Would you expect the N_2 molecule to be polar or nonpolar?

4. Does neon occur naturally as Ne or Ne_2? Why?

9-4 Energy Levels and Spectra of Diatomic Molecules

As is the case with an atom, a molecule often emits electromagnetic radiation when it makes a transition from an excited energy state to a state of lower energy. Conversely, a molecule can absorb radiation and make a transition from a lower energy state to a higher energy state. The study of molecular emission and absorption spectra thus provides us with information about the energy states of molecules. For simplicity, we will consider only diatomic molecules here.

As might be expected, the energy levels of molecular systems are even more complex than those of atoms. The energy of a molecule can be conveniently separated into three parts: electronic, due to the excitation of its electrons; vibrational, due to the oscillations of the atoms of the molecule; and rotational, due to the rotation of the molecule about an axis through its center of mass. Fortunately, the magnitudes of these energies are sufficiently different that they can be treated separately. Electrons in molecules can be excited to higher states, just as those in atoms. For example, a $1s$ electron in the H_2 molecule can be excited to a $2p$ level, emitting a photon as it returns to the ground state. The energies due to the electronic excitations of a molecule are of the order of magnitude of 1 eV, the same as for the excitation of atoms. We have already discussed such transitions and will not consider them further in this section. The energies of vibration and rotation are about 100 to 1000 times smaller and will be the focus of our attention.

Rotational Energy Levels

Classically, the kinetic energy of rotation is

$$E = \frac{1}{2} I \omega^2 = \frac{(I\omega)^2}{2I} = \frac{L^2}{2I} \qquad \textbf{9-11}$$

where I is the moment of inertia, ω the angular velocity of rotation, and $L = I\omega$ the angular momentum. The solution of the Schrödinger equation for the rotation of a rigid body leads to the quantization of the angular momentum, with values given by

$$L^2 = l(l + 1)\hbar^2 \qquad l = 0, 1, 2, \ldots \qquad \textbf{9-12}$$

where l is the *rotational quantum number*. This is the same quantum condition on angular momentum that holds for the orbital angular momentum of an electron in an atom. Note, however, that L in Equation 9-11 refers to the angular momentum of the entire molecule rotating about an axis through its center of mass. The energy levels of a rotating molecule are therefore given by

$$E = \frac{l(l + 1)\hbar^2}{2I} = l(l + 1)E_{0r} \qquad l = 0, 1, 2, \ldots \qquad \textbf{9-13}$$

where E_{0r} is the *characteristic rotational energy* of a particular molecule, which is inversely proportional to its moment of inertia:

$$E_{0r} = \frac{\hbar^2}{2I} \qquad \textbf{9-14}$$

The rotational energy-level scheme is shown in Figure 9-21. Transitions between these levels produce the *pure rotational spectrum* of a molecule. While all diatomic molecules have rotational energy levels, those without permanent dipole moments (symmetric molecules such as H_2, Cl_2, or CO_2) cannot emit or absorb electric dipole radiation by only changing the rotational quantum state and thus do not have a pure rotational spectrum. For molecules that do have dipole moments and emit pure rotational spectra the quantum number l is subject to the selection rule $\Delta l = \pm 1$, just as it was for the atomic electrons. Thus, the energy separation between adjacent rotation states is given by

$$\Delta E_{l, l+1} = \frac{[(l + 1)(l + 2) - l(l + 1)]\hbar^2}{2I} = \frac{(l + 1)\hbar^2}{I} \qquad \textbf{9-15}$$

A measurement of the rotational energy of a molecule from its rotational spectrum can be used to determine the moment of inertia of the molecule, which can then be used to find the equilibrium separation of the atoms in the molecule, i.e., the bond length. The moment of inertia about an axis through the center of mass of a diatomic molecule (see Figure 9-22) is

$$I = m_1 r_1^2 + m_2 r_2^2$$

Using $m_1 r_1 = m_2 r_2$, which relates the distances r_1 and r_2 from the atoms to the center of mass, and $r_0 = r_1 + r_2$ for the separation of the atoms, we can write the moment of inertia as

$$I = \mu r_0^2 \qquad \textbf{9-16}$$

where μ, the reduced mass, is

$$\mu = \frac{m_1 m_2}{m_1 + m_2} \qquad \textbf{9-17}$$

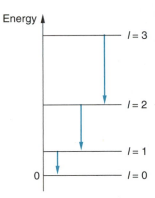

Fig. 9-21 Energy levels and allowed transitions for a rotating rigid body as given by Equation 9-13.

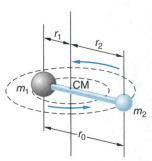

Fig. 9-22 Diatomic molecule rotating about an axis through its center of mass.

If the masses are equal ($m_1 = m_2$), as in H_2 and O_2, the reduced mass $\mu = m/2$ and

$$I = \frac{1}{2} m r_0^2 \qquad \textbf{9-18}$$

A unit of mass convenient for discussing atomic and molecular masses is the *unified mass unit* u, which is defined as one-twelfth of the mass of neutral carbon-12 (^{12}C) atom. The mass of one ^{12}C atom is thus 12 u. The mass of an atom in unified mass units is therefore numerically equal to the molar mass of the atom in grams. The unified mass unit is related to the gram and kilogram by

$$1\ u = \frac{1\ g}{N_A} = \frac{10^{-3}\ kg}{6.0221 \times 10^{23}} = 1.6605 \times 10^{-27}\ kg = 931.5 \times 10^6\ eV \qquad \textbf{9-19}$$

where N_A is Avogadro's number.

EXAMPLE 9-4 **The Reduced Mass of HCl** Compute the reduced mass of the HCl molecule.

Solution

1. The reduced mass μ is given by Equation 9-17:

$$\mu = \frac{m_1 m_2}{m_1 + m_2}$$

2. From the periodic table on the inside back cover of this book, the mass of the hydrogen atom is 1.01 u, and that of the chlorine atom is 35.5 u. Substituting these gives:

$$\mu = \frac{(1.01\ u)(35.5\ u)}{1.01\ u + 35.5\ u}$$

$$= 0.982\ u$$

Remarks: *Note that the reduced mass of the HCl molecule is less than that of a single hydrogen atom.*

EXAMPLE 9-5 **Equilibrium Separation in CO** The energy difference ΔE between the $l = 0$ and $l = 1$ rotational levels in the CO molecule is found experimentally from measurement of the wavelength $\lambda = 2.6$ mm of the corresponding transition. For CO, ΔE is equal to 4.77×10^{-4} eV. Find the equilibrium separation, or bond length r_0, of the CO molecule.

Solution

1. The bond length r_0 is given in terms of the moment of inertia I of the molecule by Equation 9-16:

$$I = \mu r_0^2 \quad \text{or} \quad r_0 = \sqrt{\frac{I}{\mu}}$$

2. I in terms of ΔE is given by Equation 9-15:

$$\Delta E_{l, l+1} = \frac{(l + 1)\hbar^2}{I} \quad \text{or} \quad I = \frac{(l + 1)\hbar^2}{\Delta E_{l, l+1}}$$

3. Substituting $l = 0$ and $\Delta E = 4.77 \times 10^{-4}$ eV into step 2 gives:

$$I = \frac{\hbar^2}{4.77 \times 10^{-4} \text{ eV}}$$

4. The reduced mass of the CO molecule is computed from Equation 9-17 using atomic mass values from the periodic table:

$$\mu = \frac{m_1 m_2}{m_1 + m_2} = \frac{(12 \text{ u})(16 \text{ u})}{12 \text{ u} + 16 \text{ u}}$$
$$= 6.86 \text{ u}$$

5. Substituting these results into step 1 gives:

$$r_0 = \left(\frac{\hbar^2}{4.77 \times 10^{-4} \text{ eV} \times 6.86 \text{ u}}\right)^{1/2}$$
$$= \frac{1.055 \times 10^{-34} \text{ J} \cdot \text{s}}{[(4.77 \times 10^{-4} \text{ eV})(1.60 \times 10^{-19} \text{ J/eV})(6.86 \text{ u})(1.66 \times 10^{-27} \text{ kg/u})]^{1/2}}$$
$$= 0.133 \text{ nm}$$

The rotational energy levels are several orders of magnitude smaller than those due to electron excitation, which have energies of the order of 1 eV or higher. For example, the characteristic rotational energy of the O_2 molecule, whose eqilibrium separation is about 0.1 nm, is 2.59×10^{-4} eV calculated from Equation 9-14. Transitions within a given set of rotational energy levels yield photons in the far infrared region of the electromagnetic spectrum. Notice that the rotational energies are also small compared with the typical thermal energy kT at normal temperatures. For $T = 300$ K, for example, kT is about 2.6×10^{-2} eV. Thus, at ordinary temperatures, a molecule can easily be excited to the lower rotational energy levels by collisions with other molecules. But such collisions cannot excite the molecule to electronic energy levels above the ground state.

Vibrational Energy Levels

The molecular vibrational energies are a bit harder to estimate than were the rotational energies. Our discussion is aided by the fact that the molecular potential energy functions of Figures 9-2, 9-7, and 9-8b can be closely approximated by parabolas in the vicinity of the equilibrium point. (See Figure 9-23b.) Thus, we can

use the results of our study of the simple harmonic oscillator in Chapter 6. The energy levels are given by

$$E_v = (v + \tfrac{1}{2})hf \qquad v = 0, 1, 2, 3, \ldots \qquad \textbf{9-20}$$

where f is the frequency of the vibration and v is the *vibrational quantum number.*[8] An interesting feature of this result is that the energy levels are equally spaced with intervals $\Delta E_{v,v+1} = hf$ as shown in Figure 9-23a. The frequency of vibration of a diatomic molecule can be related to the force exerted by one atom on the other. Consider two objects of mass m_1 and m_2 connected by a spring of force constant K. The frequency of oscillation of this system can be shown to be (see Problem 9-23)

$$f = \frac{1}{2\pi} \sqrt{\frac{K}{\mu}} \qquad \textbf{9-21}$$

where μ is the reduced mass given by Equation 9-17. The effective force constant of a diatomic molecule can thus be determined from a measurement of the frequency of oscillation of the molecule.

We could get a good estimate of f by fitting the one-dimensional parabolic harmonic oscillator potential energy function for the molecule as illustrated in Figure 9-23b, but for simplicity we can get a rough idea of the order of magnitude of the vibrational energies by observing that the energy of an atom of mass m in a square well of width r_0 is (Figure 9-24)

$$E_n = n^2 \frac{h^2}{8mr_0^2} = n^2 \frac{4\pi^2 \hbar^2}{8mr_0^2} = n^2 \frac{\pi^2}{2} \frac{\hbar^2}{mr_0^2}$$

Except for the factor $\pi^2/2 \approx 5$ (and the n^2), this expression is the same as the characteristic rotational energy E_{0r}; thus we expect the vibrational energies to be somewhat larger than the rotational energies.

The selection rule for transitions between vibrational states (of the same electronic state) requires that v change only by ± 1, so the energy of a photon emitted by

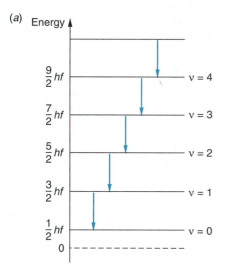

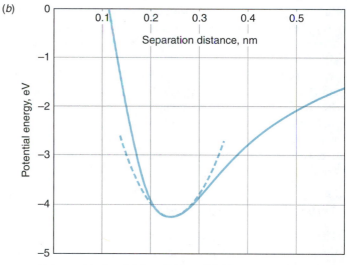

Fig. 9-23 (a) The energy levels of the molecular vibrations are equally spaced in the vicinity of the equilibrium spacing of the atoms. (b) A harmonic oscillator potential fitted to the actual potential energy function of the NaCl molecule shown in Figure 9-2b.

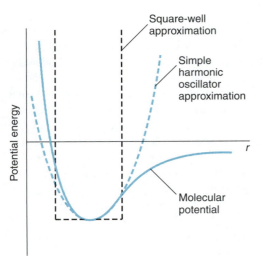

Fig. 9-24 Molecular potential. The simple harmonic oscillator approximation, used to calculate the energy levels, and a square-well approximation, used to estimate the order of magnitude of the energy levels, are each indicated by dashed curves.

such a transition is hf and the frequency is the same as the frequency of vibration. A typical measured frequency of a transition between vibrational states is 5×10^{13} Hz, which gives for the order of magnitude of vibrational energies

$$E \sim hf = (4.14 \times 10^{-15}\,\text{eV}\cdot\text{s})(5 \times 10^{13}\,\text{s}^{-1}) = 0.2\,\text{eV}$$

Thus, a typical vibrational energy is actually about 1000 times greater than the typical rotational energy E_{0r} of the O_2 molecule we noted above and about 8 times greater than the typical thermal energy $kT = 0.026$ eV at $T = 300$ K. In contrast with the rotational levels, the molecular vibrational states are not readily excited by collisions at ordinary temperatures.

EXAMPLE 9-6 Force Constant of CO The observed vibrational frequency of the CO molecule is 6.42×10^{13} Hz. What is the effective force constant for this molecule?

Solution

1. The force constant K is given in terms of the vibrational frequency f by Equation 9-21:

$$f = \frac{1}{2\pi}\sqrt{\frac{K}{\mu}}$$

2. The reduced mass μ of the CO molecule was computed in step 4 of Example 9-5:

$$\mu = 6.86\,\text{u}$$

3. Solving Equation 9-21 for K and substituting the values of f and μ give:

$$
\begin{aligned}
K &= (2\pi f)^2 \mu \\
&= (2\pi \times 6.42 \times 10^{13}\,\text{Hz})^2(6.86\,\text{u})(1.66 \times 10^{-27}\,\text{kg/u}) \\
&= 1.86 \times 10^3\,\text{N/m}
\end{aligned}
$$

Emission Spectra

Figure 9-25 shows schematically some electronic, vibrational, and rotational energy levels of a diatomic molecule. The vibrational levels are labeled with the quantum number v and the rotational levels with the label l. The lower vibrational levels are evenly spaced, with $\Delta E = hf$. For higher vibrational levels, the approximation that the vibration is simple harmonic is not valid and the levels are not quite evenly spaced. The actual potential spreads somewhat more rapidly, as can be seen in Figure 9-24, and the spacing of the vibrational levels becomes closer for large values of the quantum number v. Notice in Figure 9-25 that the potential energy curves representing the force between the two atoms in the molecule do not have exactly the same shape for the electronic ground and excited states. This implies that the fundamental frequency of vibration f is different for different electronic states. For transitions between vibrational states of different electronic states, the selection rule $\Delta v = \pm 1$ does not hold. Such transitions result in the emission of photons of wavelength in or near the visible spectrum.

The spacing of the rotational levels increases with increasing values of l. Since the energies of rotation are so much smaller than those of vibrational or electronic excitations of a molecule, molecular rotation shows up in molecular spectra as a fine splitting of the spectral lines. When the fine structure is not resolved, the spectrum appears as bands as shown in Figure 9-26a. Close inspection of these bands reveals that they have a fine structure due to the rotational energy levels, as shown in the enlargement in Figure 9-26b.

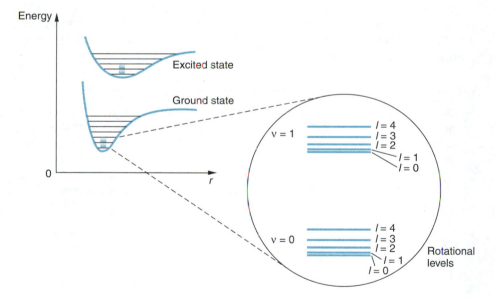

Fig. 9-25 Electronic, vibrational, and rotational energy levels of a diatomic molecule. The rotational levels are shown in an enlargement of the $v = 0$ and $v = 1$ vibrational levels of the electronic ground state.

Absorption Spectra

Much molecular spectroscopy is done using infrared absorption techniques in which only the vibrational and rotational energy levels of the ground-state electronic level are excited. We shall therefore now direct our attention to what is called the *vibration-rotation spectrum*. For ordinary temperatures, the vibrational energies are sufficiently large in comparison with the thermal energy kT that most of the molecules are in the lowest vibrational state $v = 0$, for which the energy is $E_0 = \frac{1}{2}hf$. The transition from

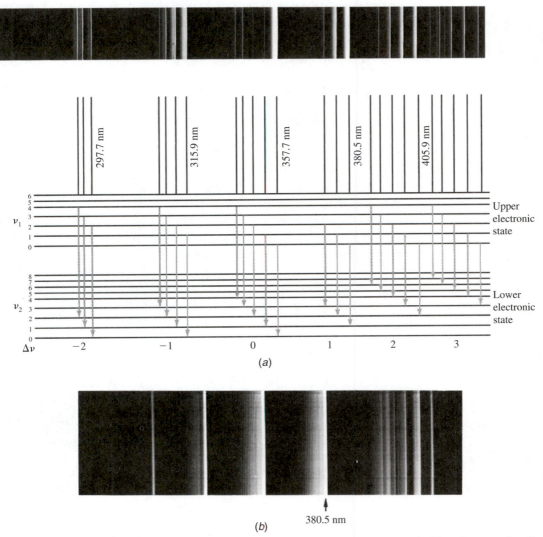

Fig. 9-26 Part of the emission spectrum of N_2. (*a*) These components of the band are due to transitions between the vibrational levels of two electronic states, as indicated in the diagram. (*b*) An enlargement of part of (*a*) shows that the apparent lines in (*a*) are in fact band heads with structure caused by rotational levels. [*Courtesy of J. A. Marquisee.*]

$v = 0$ to $v = 1$ is the predominant transition in absorption. The rotational energies, however, are sufficiently smaller than kT that the molecules are distributed among several rotational energy states, the relative number in each state being determined by the Boltzmann factor. If the molecule is originally in a rotational state characterized by the quantum number l, its initial energy, in addition to that of the electronic state, is

$$E_l = \tfrac{1}{2}hf + l(l + 1)E_{0r} \qquad\qquad \textbf{9-22}$$

where E_{0r} is given by Equation 9-14. From this state, two transitions are permitted by the selection rules. For a transition to the next highest vibrational state $v = 1$ and a rotational state characterized by $l + 1$, the final energy is

$$E_{l+1} = \tfrac{3}{2}hf + (l + 1)(l + 2)E_{0r} \qquad\qquad \textbf{9-23}$$

For a transition to the next highest vibrational state and to a rotational state characterized by $l - 1$, the final energy is

$$E_{l-1} = \tfrac{3}{2}hf + (l - 1)lE_{0r} \qquad \textbf{9-24}$$

The energy differences are

$$\Delta E_{l \to l+1} = E_{l+1} - E_l = hf + 2(l + 1)E_{0r} \qquad \textbf{9-25}$$

where $l = 0, 1, 2, \ldots$, and

$$\Delta E_{l \to l-1} = E_{l-1} - E_l = hf - 2lE_{0r} \qquad \textbf{9-26}$$

where $l = 1, 2, 3, \ldots$. (In Equation 9-26, l begins at $l = 1$ because from $l = 0$ only the transition $l \to l + 1$ is possible.) Figure 9-27 illustrates these transitions. The frequencies of these transitions are given by

$$f_{l \to l+1} = \frac{\Delta E_{l \to l+1}}{h} = f + \frac{2(l + 1)E_{0r}}{h} \qquad l = 0, 1, 2, \ldots \qquad \textbf{9-27}$$

and

$$f_{l \to l-1} = \frac{\Delta E_{l \to l-1}}{h} = f - \frac{2lE_{0r}}{h} \qquad l = 1, 2, 3, \ldots \qquad \textbf{9-28}$$

The frequencies for the transitions $l \to l + 1$ are thus $f + 2(E_{0r}/h)$, $f + 4(E_{0r}/h)$, $f + 6(E_{0r}/h)$, and so forth; those corresponding to the transition $l \to l - 1$ are

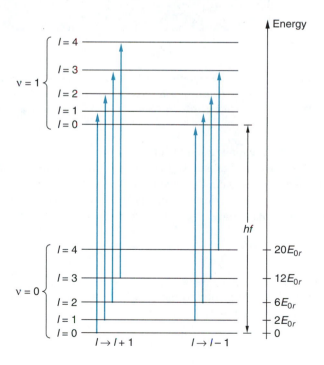

Fig. 9-27 Absorptive transitions between the lowest vibrational states $v = 0$ and $v = 1$ in a diatomic molecule. These transitions obey the selection rule $\Delta l = \pm 1$ and fall into two bands. The energies of the $l \to l + 1$ band are $hf + 2E_{0r}$, $hf + 4E_{0r}$, $hf + 6E_{0r}$, and so forth, whereas the energies of the $l \to l - 1$ band are $hf - 2E_{0r}$, $hf - 4E_{0r}$, $hf - 6E_{0r}$, and so forth.

$f - 2(E_{0r}/h), f - 4(E_{0r}/h), f - 6(E_{0r}/h)$, and so forth. We thus expect the absorption spectrum to contain frequencies equally spaced by $2E_{0r}/h$ except for a gap of $4E_{0r}/h$ at the vibrational frequency f as shown in Figure 9-28. A measurement of the position of the gap gives f and a measurement of the spacing of the absorption peaks gives E_{0r}, which is inversely proportional to the moment of inertia of the molecule.

Figure 9-29 shows the absorption spectrum of HCl. The double-peak structure results from the fact that chlorine occurs naturally in two isotopes, ^{35}Cl and ^{37}Cl, which result in slightly different moments of inertia. If all of the rotational levels were equally populated initially, we would expect the intensities of the absorption lines to be equal. However, the population $n(E_l)$ of a rotational level l is proportional to the density of states $g(E_l)$, which equals the degeneracy of the level in this case, that is, the number of states with the same value of l, which is $2l + 1$, and to the Boltzmann factor $e^{-E_l/kT}$, where E_l is the energy of the state.

$$n(E_l) = g(E_l)e^{-E_l/kT} \qquad \textbf{9-29}$$

or

$$n(E_l) = (2l + 1)e^{-[\frac{1}{2}hf + l(l+1)E_{0r}]/kT} \qquad \textbf{9-30}$$

The $(2l + 1)$-fold degeneracy of the rotational state with angular momentum $l\hbar$ makes the thermal equilibrium population proportional to $(2l + 1)\exp[-l(l + 1)\hbar^2/2IkT]$. Therefore, the $l = 0$ state is usually not the most densely populated state at room temperature. For low values of l, the population increases slightly because of the degeneracy factor, whereas for higher values of l, the population decreases because of the Boltzmann factor. The intensities of the absorption lines therefore increase with l for low values of l and then decrease with l for high values of l, as can be seen from the figure. We can find out where the maximum population of the rotational states is located and, hence, which lines will be the most intense by differentiating Equation 9-30 with respect to l and setting dn/dl equal to zero. The result is

$$l_{max} = \frac{1}{2}\left[\sqrt{\frac{4kT}{h^2/mr^2}} - 1\right] \qquad \textbf{9-31}$$

For a measurement made at room temperature, $kT = 0.026$ eV and thus $l_{max} \approx 3$. This, too, can be seen in Figure 9-29.

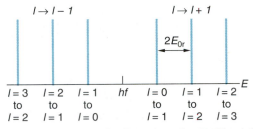

Fig. 9-28 Expected absorption spectrum of a diatomic molecule. The right branch corresponds to the transitions $l \rightarrow l + 1$ and the left branch to the transitions $l \rightarrow l - 1$. The lines are equally spaced by $2E_{0r}$. The energy midway between the branches is hf, where f is the frequency of vibration of the molecule.

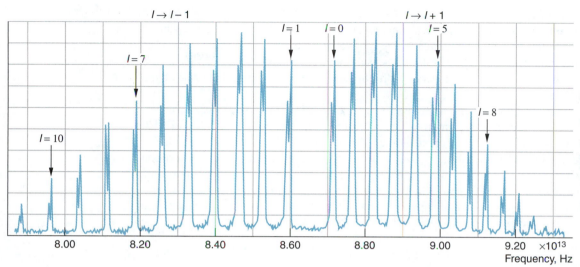

Fig. 9-29 Absorption spectrum of the diatomic molecule HCl. The double-peak structure results from the two isotopes of chlorine, ^{35}Cl (abundance 75.5 percent) and ^{37}Cl (abundance 24.5 percent). The intensities of the peaks vary because the population of the initial state depends on l.

Notice also in Figure 9-29 that the spacing between adjacent peaks, which we expected to be constant and equal to $2E_{0r}$ on the basis of our calculation above, is in fact not constant. The reason for this is our assumption that the moment of inertia of the molecule is constant. The rotation of the molecule tends to increase the separation of the atoms, and hence increase the moment of inertia and decrease the rotational energy. As might then be expected and the figure also shows, this effect becomes larger as l increases.

As mentioned above, the gap in the spectrum in Figure 9-29 is due to the absence of a transition beginning on the $l = 0$ level in the $l \rightarrow l - 1$ group of peaks. The center of the gap is at the characteristic oscillation frequency f of the molecule given by Equation 9-21. From the figure we see that f for HCl is about 8.65×10^{13} Hz, or about 0.36 eV, corresponding to a force constant K of about 476 N/m. Table 9-7 lists the rotational and vibrational constants for several diatomic molecules. All diatomic molecules[9] have a gap at f in their vibration-rotation spectra; however, many polyatomic molecules have more complex vibrations and rotations, one result of which is that $\Delta l = 0$ may be allowed, i.e., vibrational energy may change without an accompanying rotational transition. In that event, a line will occur in the vibration-rotation spectrum at the frequency f. Such lines are given the rather enigmatic name of *Q branch*.[10]

9-5 Absorption, Stimulated Emission, and Scattering

Absorption

Information about the energy levels of an atom or molecule is usually obtained from the radiation emitted when the atom or molecule makes a transition from an excited state to a state of lower energy. As mentioned in the previous section, we can also obtain information about such energy levels from the absorption spectrum. When atoms and molecules are irradiated with a continuous spectrum of radiation, the transmitted radiation

TABLE 9-7 Rotational and vibrational constants for selected diatomic molecules

Molecule	Equilibrium separation r_0 (nm)	Frequency f (Hz)	E_{0r} (eV)
H_2	0.074	1.32×10^{14}	7.56×10^{-3}
Li_2	0.267	1.05×10^{13}	8.39×10^{-5}
O_2	0.121	4.74×10^{13}	1.78×10^{-4}
LiH	0.160	4.22×10^{13}	9.27×10^{-4}
HCl^{35}	0.127	8.97×10^{13}	1.32×10^{-3}
$NaCl^{35}$	0.251	1.14×10^{13}	2.36×10^{-5}
KCl^{35}	0.279	8.40×10^{12}	1.43×10^{-5}
KBr^{79}	0.294	6.93×10^{12}	9.1×10^{-6}

Symmetric molecules such as H_2 or O_2 have no electric dipole moment. The vibration or rotation of these molecules does not involve a changing dipole moment and there is no vibrational-rotational electric dipole absorption or radiation for these molecules.

shows dark lines corresponding to absorption of light at discrete wavelengths. Absorption spectra of atoms were the first line spectra observed. Fraunhofer in 1817 labeled the most prominent absorption lines in the spectrum of sunlight; it is for this reason that the two intense yellow lines in the spectrum of sodium are called the *Fraunhofer D lines*. Since at normal temperatures atoms and molecules are in their ground states or in low-lying excited states, the absorption spectra are usually simpler than the emission spectra. For example, only those lines corresponding to the Lyman emission series are seen in the absorption spectrum of atomic hydrogen because nearly all the atoms are originally in their ground states. In a section on the home page in Chapter 6 on "Transitions Between Energy States," we described how transitions between quantum states in an atomic system occur as a result of interaction with oscillating electromagnetic fields. In particular, if the frequency greater than f_{12} is present in radiation incident on an atom whose ground-state and an excited-state energies are respectively E_1 and E_2, then there is a probability that the atom will undergo a transition from the lower energy state E_1, absorbing the energy $hf_{12} = E_2 - E_1$ from the radiation. This absorption of energy resulting from the interaction between the electric field of the radiation oscillating at f_{12} and the charge on the atomic electrons was first described quantum-mechanically by Einstein, who expressed the probability of absorption per atom per unit time as $B_{12}u(f)$, where $u(f)$ is the energy density of the radiation per unit frequency and B_{12} is Einstein's coefficient of absorption. In addition to absorption, several other interesting phenomena occur when electromagnetic radiation—i.e., photons—is incident on atoms or molecules. These are illustrated in Figure 9-30. In Figure 9-30a a photon of energy hf is absorbed and the system makes a transition to the excited state. Later, the system makes a transition to a lower state and/or back to the ground state with the *spontaneous emission* of one or more photons via the mechanism described on the home page in the section "Transitions Between Energy States" in Chapter 6. This process is called *fluorescence*. If state 2 happens to be the first excited state, then this two-step process is called

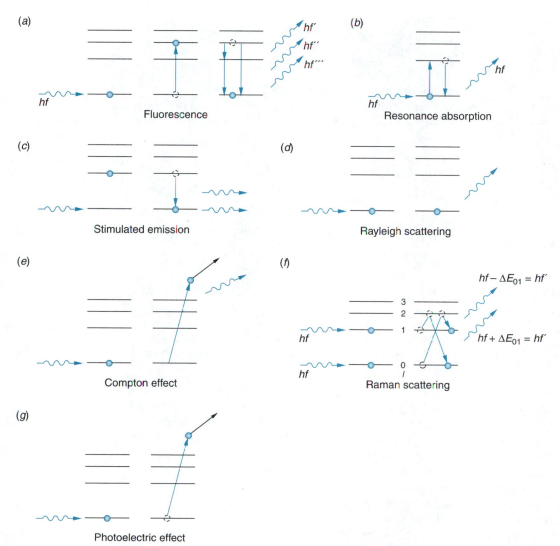

Fig. 9-30 Description of photon interactions with an atom. (*a*) The photon is absorbed and the atom, in an excited state, later emits one or more photons as it decays to a state of lower energy. This is a two-step process called *fluorescence,* and the emitted photons are uncorrelated with the incident photon. (*b*) If the energy of the incident photon matches one of the excitation energies of the atom, resonance radiation results. (*c*) The atom, in an excited state, is stimulated to make a transition to a lower state by an incident photon of just the right energy. The emitted and incident photons have the same energy and are coherent. The Rayleigh scattering process (*d*) and Raman scattering (*f*) differ from (*a*) and (*b*) in that they are single-step processes and there is a correlation between the incident and emitted photons. Parts (*e*) and (*g*) illustrate Compton scattering and the photoelectric effect, discussed in Chapter 3.

resonance absorption and the photon emitted is called resonance radiation as shown in Figure 9-30*b*. As a result of motions that occur while the system is in state 2, there is no correlation in direction or phase between the incident and emitted photons. While in state 2 the system has definite probabilities of making spontaneous transitions to each of the lower states as determined by the probability density given by Equation 6-52*d*. For example, the probability per atom per unit time of returning to state 1 with the spontaneous emission of a photon can be expressed by the quantity A_{21} (transitions per unit time). Notice that the reciprocal $1/A_{21}$ has the units of time per transition, i.e., it is a

measure of how long the system stays in state 2 before returning to state 1. This is t_s, the lifetime of the state where $t_s = 1/A_{21}$. For most atomic (electric dipole) transitions this characteristic time is of the order of 10^{-8} s. A_{21} is called Einstein's coefficient of spontaneous emission.

Stimulated Emission

In addition to the spontaneous emission of fluorescent and resonant radiation with probability A_{21}, which is independent of the energy density $u(f)$ of the incident radiation, emission can also be induced to occur by the oscillating electromagnetic field of the incident radiation. Called *stimulated emission,* its probability does depend upon $u(f)$. This phenomenon, like absorption and spontaneous emission, was first analyzed by Einstein (in 1917). The probability of stimulated emission per atom per unit time (transition rate) can be written as $B_{21}u(f)$, where B_{21} is called Einstein's coefficient of stimulated emission. In this process the electric field of an incident photon with energy hf equal to the energy difference $E_2 - E_1$ in Figure 9-30c stimulates the atom or molecule in state 2 to emit a photon with energy $E_2 - E_1 = hf$ which is propagated in the same direction and with the same phase as the incident photon. Such photons (or radiation) are said to be *coherent.*

The relation between the three Einstein coefficients can be found as follows. Consider a system of atoms and radiation in thermal equilibrium at temperature T. Let N_1 and N_2 be the number of atoms occupying the states with energies E_1 and E_2. The ratio N_2/N_1 is determined by the Boltzmann factor, given by Equation 8-14 assuming the two states have the same degeneracy.

$$\frac{N_2}{N_1} = e^{-(E_2-E_1)/kT} = e^{-hf/kT} \qquad \text{9-32}$$

This ratio represents a dynamic equilibrium in which the number of absorption transitions $(E_1 \rightarrow E_2)$ per unit time equals the sum of the number of spontaneous and stimulated emissions $(E_2 \rightarrow E_1)$ per unit time. Since the number of atoms making a transition (of any type) is proportional to the population of the state on which the transition begins and to the probability, we can express the dynamic equilibrium as

$$N_1 B_{12} u(f) = N_2(A_{21} + B_{21}u(f)) \qquad \text{9-33}$$

Solving Equation 9-33 for the energy density $u(f)$ of the radiation yields

$$u(f) = \frac{\dfrac{A_{21}}{B_{21}}}{\dfrac{N_1}{N_2}\dfrac{B_{12}}{B_{21}} - 1} \qquad \text{9-34}$$

Inserting N_1/N_2 from Equation 9-32, we have that

$$u(f) = \frac{\dfrac{A_{21}}{B_{21}}}{\dfrac{B_{12}}{B_{21}} e^{hf/kT} - 1} \qquad \text{9-35}$$

This expression for the energy density of radiation of frequency f in thermal equilibrium at temperature T with atoms of energies E_1 and E_2 must be consistent with Planck's law for a blackbody spectrum at temperature T given by Equation 8-81:

$$u(f) = \frac{8\pi h f^3}{c^3}\left(\frac{1}{e^{hf/kT} - 1}\right) \qquad \text{9-36}$$

Comparing Equation 9-35 and 9-36, we conclude that

$$\frac{B_{12}}{B_{21}} = 1 \qquad \text{9-37}$$

and that

$$\frac{A_{21}}{B_{21}} = \frac{8\pi h f^3}{c^3} \qquad \text{9-38}$$

Although this analysis gives us only the ratios of the coefficients, A_{21} can be computed from quantum mechanics, as was discussed in the home-page section for Chapter 6 referred to previously, and the other coefficients may then be computed from the result.

There are several points of interest in these equations. For instance, Equation 9-37 tells us that the coefficients for absorption and stimulated emission are the same for the same pair of states. Notice, too, that Equation 9-38 says that the ratio of the spontaneous emission coefficient to that for stimulated emission is proportional to f^3. This means that the larger $\Delta E = E_2 - E_1$, the more likely spontaneous emission will be comparable to stimulated emission. Rewriting Equation 9-36 as

$$\frac{A_{21}}{B_{21}u(f)} = e^{hf/kT} - 1 \qquad \text{9-39}$$

yields the result that, in equilibrium situations, spontaneous emission is far more probable than stimulated emission for $hf \gg kT$. Since this is usually the case for electronic transitions in both atoms and molecules, de-excitation of excited electronic states by stimulated emission is normally ignored in these transitions. Stimulated emission does become important when $hf \approx kT$ and may dominate de-excitation of excited states when $hf \ll kT$. This latter condition exists for ordinary temperatures in the microwave region of the spectrum. We will return to these matters in Section 9-6 in connection with the discussion of lasers and masers.

EXAMPLE 9-7 Spontaneous versus Stimulated Emission Compare the relative probabilities of spontaneous and stimulated emission in an equilibrium system at room temperature ($T = 300$ K) for transitions that occur in (*a*) the visible and (*b*) the microwave regions of the spectrum.

Solution

Equation 9-39 gives the ratio of the probability for spontaneous emission A_{21} to that for stimulated emission $B_{21}u(f)$. At $T = 300$ K, $kT = 0.026$ eV.

(a) In the visible region of the spectrum $hf \approx 2$ eV, so $hf/kT = 2/0.026 = 77$. Therefore,

$$\frac{A_{21}}{B_{21}u(f)} = e^{77} - 1 \approx 10^{33}$$

Clearly, under these conditions spontaneous emission is favored over stimulated emission by an enormous factor.

(b) In the microwave region of the spectrum $hf \approx 10^{-4}$ eV, so $hf/kT = 10^{-4}/0.026 = 0.0038 \approx 1/260$ and stimulated emission is rather heavily favored.

Scattering

In addition to the interactions between incident radiation and atomic or molecular systems described above, photons may also be scattered both elastically and inelastically. The process by which photons scatter elastically, i.e., without a change in their frequency, is called *elastic* or *Rayleigh scattering,* since it was first described adequately by a classical scattering theory derived by Rayleigh in about 1900. Rayleigh scattering is illustrated in Figure 9-30d. In the classical theory, the oscillating electric field of the incident radiation produces an oscillating acceleration of the atomic electrons, causing them to radiate electromagnetic waves of the same frequency as and in phase with the incident wave. Thus, the electrons of the target atoms and molecules absorb energy from the incident wave and re-emit or scatter it in all directions without changing its frequency. The intensity of the scattered radiation is proportional to f^4. Rayleigh scattering is the origin of the unmodified line in our discussion of the Compton scattering of x rays in Section 3-4. (See Figure 3-21.) We saw there that if the incident wavelength λ_1 was large compared with the Compton shift $\lambda_2 - \lambda_1$, i.e., visible wavelengths or larger, then the scattered wave always had a wavelength equal to the incident wavelength to within experimental accuracy regardless of whether the electron or atomic mass is used in Equation 3-40. So as $\lambda \rightarrow \infty$, the quantum explanation of Chapter 3 and Rayleigh's classical explanation of elastic scattering agree. However, for incident wavelengths in the x-ray and gamma-ray regions of the spectrum, Compton scattering, shown in Figure 9-30e, becomes increasingly important for low-Z atoms whose electron binding energies are not large. In the gamma-ray region as $\lambda \rightarrow 0$ the photon energy becomes so large that even the most tightly bound electrons are freed in the process and the Compton effect becomes the dominant process.

The incident and scattered photons are also correlated in the *inelastic* scattering process illustrated in Figure 9-30f. Such scattering of light from molecules was first observed by the Indian physicist C. V. Raman[11] and is known as *Raman scattering,* or sometimes as the *Raman effect.* The scattered photon may have less energy than the incident photon or it may have greater energy if the molecule is initially in an excited vibrational or rotational energy state. Both possibilities are illustrated in Figure 9-30f. Thus, the scattered frequency is not the same as the incident frequency, nor is it related to a characteristic frequency of the molecule. It is found that for incident monochromatic radiation of frequency f the scattered radiation contains not only the frequency f (Rayleigh scattering; see Figure 9-31), but also much weaker lines on either side of the Rayleigh line with frequencies given by

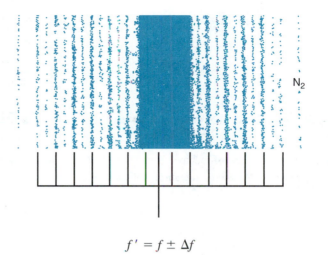

N_2

$$f' = f \pm \Delta f \qquad \textbf{9-40}$$

These are the Raman lines illustrated in Figure 9-31. If the incident frequency is varied, the Raman lines are observed to move along the frequency axis at the same rate so that the *difference* Δf between f and f' remains constant. It is this difference Δf that corresponds to characteristic transitions of the scattering molecule.

Although the measurements of Δf for each line in the Raman spectrum enables construction of the rotational levels for a given molecule,[12] its quantum-mechanical explanation is different from that of the rotational spectrum. In particular, the selection rule for the rotational quantum number in the Raman effect is $\Delta l = 0, \pm 2$. The $\Delta l = 0$ value yields Rayleigh scattering, while $\Delta l = \pm 2$ yields the Raman lines. One can see how this comes about physically by studying the transitions shown in Figure 9-30*f*. An electron initially in the $l = 0$ state absorbs energy $\Delta E_{01} + \Delta E_{12}$ from the incident photon of frequency f and emits energy ΔE_{12}. Thus, the energy of the scattered photon is

$$hf' = hf - (\Delta E_{01} + \Delta E_{12}) + \Delta E_{12} = hf - \Delta E_{01} \qquad \textbf{9-41}$$

or

$$f' = f - \Delta f$$

where $\Delta f = \Delta E_{01}/h$. If the electron is initially in the $l = 1$ state, then it absorbs ΔE_{12} from the incident photon and emits $\Delta E_{12} + \Delta E_{01}$. Thus, the scattered photon has energy

$$hf' = hf - \Delta E_{12} + (\Delta E_{12} + \Delta E_{01}) = hf + \Delta E_{01} \qquad \textbf{9-42}$$

or

$$f' = f + \Delta f$$

Many Raman spectra have been studied. They provide a valuable source of information regarding molecular quantum states including, as was pointed out earlier, the structure of the rotational levels for homonuclear diatomic molecules. For example, the detailed understanding of the complex vibrations and rotations of the ammonia molecule referred to in Section 6-6 that enabled the development of the first atomic clocks was made possible by studies of the Raman rotational-vibrational spectrum of the NH_3 molecule, the so-called *ammonia inversion spectrum.*

Finally, Figure 9-30*g* illustrates the photoelectric effect, the final example of the interaction of radiation with matter, in which the absorption of the photon ionizes the atom or molecule. Like Compton scattering, this effect was discussed in Chapter 3 and will not be considered further here.

QUESTIONS

5. How does Rayleigh scattering differ from resonance absorption?

6. How does the photoelectric effect differ from all the other processes illustrated in Figure 9-30?

7. Why is stimulated emission usually not observed?

9-6 Lasers and Masers

The *laser* (*l*ight *a*mplification by *s*timulated *e*mission of *r*adiation) is a device that produces a strong beam of coherent photons by stimulated emission. The *maser*, where *m*icrowave replaces *l*ight in the definition from which the acronym is formed, was the laser's predecessor. Both devices depend on stimulated emission for their operation. We shall discuss it more fully here because of its application to these important devices. Stimulated emission occurs if the atom is initially in an excited state and if the energy of the photon incident on the atom is just $E_2 - E_1$, where E_2 is the excited energy of the atom and E_1 is the energy of a lower state or the ground state. In this case, the oscillating electromagnetic field of the incident photon accelerates the electron(s) at a rate that matches the photon's frequency and thus, we say, stimulates the excited atom, which may then emit a photon in the same direction as the incident photon and with the same phase. We have seen that the relative probabilities of stimulated emission and absorption B_{21} and B_{12} are equal (Equation 9-37). Ordinarily, at normal temperatures, nearly all atoms will initially be in the ground state, so absorption will be the main effect. That is, $N_1 \gg N_2$, so

$$N_1 u(f) B_{12} \gg N_2 u(f) B_{21}$$

where N_1 and N_2 are the populations of the two states. To produce more stimulated emission transitions than absorption transitions, we must arrange to have more atoms in the excited state than in the ground state ($N_2 > N_1$). This condition is called *population inversion*. It can be achieved if the excited state E_2 is a metastable state. Once population inversion is achieved, any light emitted by a spontaneous $E_2 \rightarrow E_1$ transition is amplified by stimulated emission from the excited atoms that it encounters. Population inversion is often obtained by a method called *optical pumping* in which atoms are "pumped" up to energy levels greater than E_2 by the absorption of an intense auxiliary radiation. The atoms then decay down to the metastable state E_2 by either spontaneous emission or by nonradiative transitions such as those due to collisions.

The Ruby Laser

Figure 9-32*a* shows a schematic diagram of the first laser, a ruby laser built by Theodore Maiman in 1960.[13] It consists of a small rod of ruby (a few centimeters long) surrounded by a helical gaseous flashtube. The ends of the ruby rod are flat and

(a)

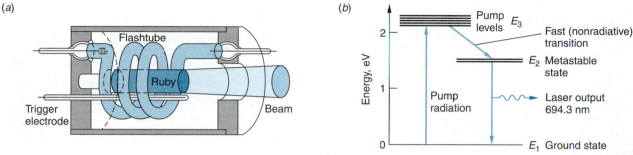

(b)

Fig. 9-32 (a) Schematic diagram of the first ruby laser. (b) Energy levels of chromium in ruby, Al_2O_3.

perpendicular to the axis of the rod. Ruby is a transparent crystal of Al_2O_3 containing a small amount (about 0.05 percent) of chromium. It appears red because the chromium ions (Cr^{3+}) have strong absorption bands in the blue and green regions of the visible spectrum. The energy levels of chromium that are important for the operation of a ruby laser are shown in Figure 9-32b.

When the mercury- or xenon-filled flashtube is fired, there is an intense burst of light lasting a few milliseconds. Absorption excites many of the chromium ions to the bands of energy levels called *pump levels* in Figure 9-32b. The excited chromium ions give up their energy to the crystal in nonradiative transitions and drop down to a pair of metastable states labeled E_2 in the figure. These metastable states are about 1.79 eV above the ground state. If the flash is intense enough, more atoms will make the transition to the states E_2 than remain in the ground state. As a result, the populations of the ground state and the metastable states become inverted. When some of the atoms in the states E_2 decay to the ground state by spontaneous emission, they emit photons of energy 1.79 eV and wavelength 694.3 nm. Some of these photons then stimulate other excited atoms to emit photons of the same energy and wavelength, moving in the same direction with the same phase.

The ruby laser, like other conventional lasers, acts as a resonating optical cavity. In the ruby laser, both ends of the crystal are silvered such that one end is almost totally reflecting (about 99.9 percent) and the other end is only partially reflecting (about 99 percent) so that some of the beam is transmitted through that slightly transparent end. If the ends are parallel, standing waves are set up, as shown in Figure 9-33, and an intense beam of coherent light emerges through the partially silvered

Fig. 9-33 Laser as a resonating optical cavity. If mirror 1 is the partially reflecting end, then (a) illustrates the longitudinal standing-wave modes, for which $L = m\lambda/2$, where λ is the laser wavelength and m is integral. If the sides of the cavity are also reflective, as in (b), then standing-wave modes transverse to the long axis are also possible. Notice that the exit beam for these modes is not parallel to the long axis of the laser.

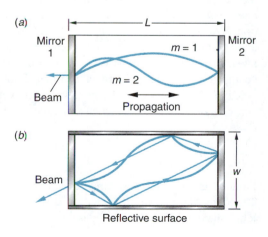

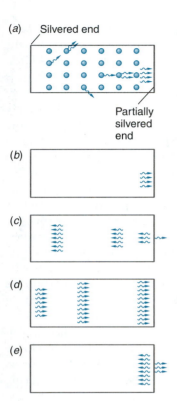

(a) Silvered end

Partially
silvered
end

(b)

(c)

(d)

(e)

Fig. 9-34 Buildup of photon beam in a laser. (a) Some of the atoms spontaneously emit photons, some of which travel to the right and stimulate other atoms to emit photons parallel to the axis of the crystal. The others are absorbed, transmitted through the walls, or otherwise lost to the lasing process. (b) Four photons strike the partially silvered right face of the laser. (c) One photon has been transmitted and the others have been reflected. As these photons traverse the laser crystal, they stimulate other excited atoms to emit photons and the beam intensity increases. By the time the beam reaches the right face again (d), it comprises many photons. (e) Some of these photons are transmitted to become part of the external laser beam and the rest are reflected to sustain the process.

end. Figure 9-34 illustrates the buildup of the beam inside the laser. When photons traveling parallel to the axis of the crystal strike the silvered ends, all are reflected from the back face and most are reflected from the front face, with a few escaping through the partially silvered front face. During each pass through the crystal, the photons stimulate more and more atoms so that an intense photon beam is developed.

Modern ruby lasers generate intense light beams with energies ranging from 50 J to 100 J in pulses lasting a few milliseconds. This pulse length is approximately equal to that of the flashtube, whose output excites atoms into the pump levels shown in Figure 9-32b. The output of the laser during that time is actually a series of very short pulses, each of the order of a microsecond long, as illustrated in Figure 9-35. This is because the pump levels depopulate quickly compared to the pump rate. Therefore, the flash requires some time to reestablish the population inversion which generates the next short pulse.

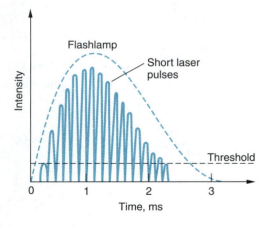

Fig. 9-35 A single output pulse from a ruby laser. The pulse actually consists of a series of very short pulses each about 1 μs long. Flashlamp intensities below the threshold do not produce a sufficient population inversion to initiate lasing. Not shown is a weak background of incoherent spontaneous emission that accompanies the coherent laser light.

Notice in Figure 9-35 that the first of the very brief laser pulses, or "spikes," begins very soon after the population inversion $N_2 > N_1$ occurs and ends when N_2 falls back to N_1 due to stimulated emissions. Extremely intense spikes can be generated via a technique called *Q-switching*, whereby the resonating property of the cavity is temporarily destroyed in order to reduce sharply the stimulated emissions so as to allow the pumping radiation to make $N_2 >>> N_1$. The resonant status is then suddenly restored and an extremely intense laser pulse results. This is how the very-high-energy pulses mentioned above are typically produced. The "Q" refers to the cavity's *quality factor*, or its ability to maintain the intensity of the reverberating wave. If the end mirrors are low-loss and the medium very transparent to the laser frequency, then the wave will die out slowly and the cavity is of high quality, or high Q. If Q is low, then substantial light is lost in each pass and the wave will die out quickly. If Q is too low, lasing will not occur at all. Q can be made very low, for example, by replacing the totally-reflecting-end mirror with an external one of equal reflectivity which rotates. When the rotating mirror is not parallel to the one on the other end of the cavity, Q is very low and little stimulated emission occurs as the pumping flash builds the population of state E_2 so that $N_2 >>> N_1$. When the rotating mirror becomes parallel to the other, Q suddenly becomes very high (hence the name Q-switch) and the extremely intense laser pulse is generated as E_2 depopulates.

Sustaining laser action requires that the increase in the number of coherent photons produced by stimulated emission per round trip through the resonating cavity be greater than or equal to the decrease resulting from all losses, such as transmission through the partially-reflecting-end mirror and scattering. Though it's a bit difficult, we have information to calculate the population inversion density necessary for lasing with the aid of the Einstein coefficients from Section 9-5, so let's try it. To begin, let us combine all of the various ways by which photons may be lost into a single characteristic time t_p. That is, the intensity of radiation I of a particular frequency f in the resonant cavity will decay due to the losses according to

$$I = I_0 e^{-t/t_p} \qquad \textbf{9-43}$$

where I_0 is the intensity at $t = 0$. Thus, the rate at which intensity is lost is given by

$$\left(\frac{dI}{dt}\right)_{loss} = -\frac{I_0}{t_p} e^{-t/t_p} = -\frac{I}{t_p} \qquad \textbf{9-44}$$

The net rate at which the intensity of the frequency f gains due to the difference between the gain from stimulated emissions $E_2 \rightarrow E_1$ and offsetting loss from absorptions $E_1 \rightarrow E_2$ is equal to the difference in the populations $(N_2 - N_1)$ times the intensity per photon times the transition probability $u(f)B_{21}$. The transition probability $u(f)B_{21}$ must be corrected for the width Δf of the spectral line emitted in the $E_2 \rightarrow E_1$ transition arising from the finite width of the level E_2 as described in Chapter 5.[14] The correction is a multiplicative factor approximately equal to $2/\pi\Delta f$. Taking these together, we obtain

$$\left(\frac{dI}{dt}\right)_{gain} = (N_2 - N_1)\frac{hfc}{V}\frac{2}{\pi\Delta f}u(f)B_{21} \qquad \textbf{9-45}$$

where V is the volume of the resonant cavity and hfc/V is the intensity per photon. Using Equation 9-38 and the fact that A_{21} is the reciprocal of the lifetime for spontaneous emission t_s, Equation 9-45 can be written as

$$\left(\frac{dI}{dt}\right)_{gain} = \frac{(N_2 - N_1)}{V}(hfc)\left[\frac{u(f)c^3}{4\pi^2 hf^3 \Delta f t_s}\right] \qquad \text{9-46}$$

or

$$\left(\frac{dI}{dt}\right)_{gain} = (n_2 - n_1)\frac{c^3 I}{4\pi^2 f^2 \Delta f t_s} \qquad \text{9-47}$$

where $n_2 = N_2/V$ and $n_1 = N_1/V$ are the *population densities* of the states and $cu(f) = I$, the intensity.[15] If the density of states (degeneracies) $g(E)$ of E_2 and E_1 are not equal, then Equation 9-47 must be modified to

$$\left(\frac{dI}{dt}\right)_{gain} = \left[n_2 - n_1\left(\frac{g(E_2)}{g(E_1)}\right)\right]\frac{c^3 I}{4\pi^2 f^2 \Delta f t_s} \qquad \text{9-48}$$

Thus, the condition for laser action becomes

$$\left(\frac{dI}{dt}\right)_{gain} \geq \left(\frac{dI}{dt}\right)_{loss} \qquad \text{9-49}$$

or

$$\left[n_2 - n_1\left(\frac{g(E_2)}{g(E_1)}\right)\right]\frac{c^3 I}{4\pi^2 f^2 \Delta f t_s} \geq \frac{I}{t_p} \qquad \text{9-50}$$

The equal sign provides the threshold condition for the initiation of lasing. The greater-than sign represents sustained laser action. Solving the threshold condition yields the *critical population inversion density* Δn_c.

$$\Delta n_c = \frac{4\pi^2 f^2 \Delta f t_s}{c^3 t_p} \qquad \text{9-51}$$

where

$$n_2 - n_1\left(\frac{g(E_2)}{g(E_1)}\right) = \Delta n_c$$

Equation 9-51 describes the population inversion that must be established if laser action is to be achieved for a given frequency and spontaneous emission lifetime. It also points out that the only property of the cavity that affects Δn_c is its characteristic decay lifetime t_p.

The ruby laser is an example of a three-level laser, referring to the energy levels in Figure 9-32b. Such lasers have a practical disadvantage for many applications in that more than half of the atoms must be pumped from $E_1 \rightarrow E_3$ in order to obtain the necessary population inversion between levels E_2 and E_1. In addition, the source of the excitation energy, the flashlamp, produces light over a broad range of frequencies, most of which do not contribute to exciting the level E_3 and are thus wasted. The large pumping requirement and relatively low excitation efficiency mean that substantial energy must be dissipated as heat, so three-level solid-state lasers like the ruby laser must be pulsed in order to allow the system time to cool periodically. A more advantageous system is

one that does not require that such a large fraction of the atoms be excited at any one time and avoids the excess heat produced by optical pumping. Such lasers provide continuous output and are called *continuous-wave* or *cw* lasers.

Helium-Neon Lasers

In 1961, the first successful operation of a cw laser, a continuous helium-neon gas laser, was announced by Ali Javan, W. R. Bennet, Jr., and D. R. Herriott.[16] Figure 9-36 shows a schematic diagram of the type of helium-neon laser commonly used for physics demonstrations, survey instruments, and laser pointers. It consists of a gas tube containing 15 percent helium gas and 85 percent neon gas. A totally reflecting flat mirror is mounted on one end of the gas tube and a partially reflecting concave mirror is placed at the other end. The concave mirror focuses parallel light at the flat mirror and also acts as a lens that transmits part of the light so that it emerges as a parallel beam.

Population inversion is achieved somewhat differently in the helium-neon laser than in the ruby laser. Figure 9-37 shows the energy levels of helium and neon that are important for operation of the laser. (The complete energy-level diagrams for helium and neon are considerably more complicated.) Helium has excited states, the 2^3S and 2^1S levels, that lie 19.72 eV and 20.61 eV, respectively, above the 1^1S ground state. Both are metastable because of the $\Delta l = \pm 1$ selection rule, the 2^3S level being more strongly forbidden due to the $\Delta S = 0$ selection rule, discussed in home-page section "Multielectron Atoms" for Chapter 7, that prohibits intercombination lines. Helium atoms are excited to these states by an electric discharge. Neon has closely spaced groups of excited states at 19.83 eV and 20.66 eV above its ground state. The energies of these neon states almost exactly match the excited states of helium. The neon atoms are excited to these levels by collisions with excited helium atoms. The kinetic energy of the helium atoms provides the extra energy, about 0.05 eV, needed to excite the neon atoms. There is another excited state of neon that is 18.70 eV above its ground state and 1.96 eV below the 20.66-eV state. Since this state is normally unoccupied, population inversion between these states is obtained immediately. The stimulated emission that occurs between these states results in photons of energy 1.96 eV and wavelength 632.8 nm, which produces a bright red light. After stimulated emission, the atoms in the 18.70-eV state decay to the ground state by spontaneous emission of a photon with a wavelength of about 600 nm followed by a nonradiative de-excitation, typically collision with the cavity wall. The collisions are an important part of the laser process, since if the diameter of the tube (see Figure 9-36) is too large, the probability of collision with the wall decreases and the

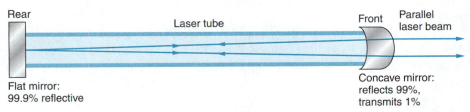

Rear · Laser tube · Front · Parallel laser beam

Flat mirror: 99.9% reflective

Concave mirror: reflects 99%, transmits 1%

Fig. 9-36 Schematic drawing of a helium-neon laser. The use of a concave mirror rather than a second plane mirror makes the alignment of the mirrors less critical than it is for the ruby laser. The concave mirror on the right also serves as a lens that focuses the emitted light into a parallel beam.

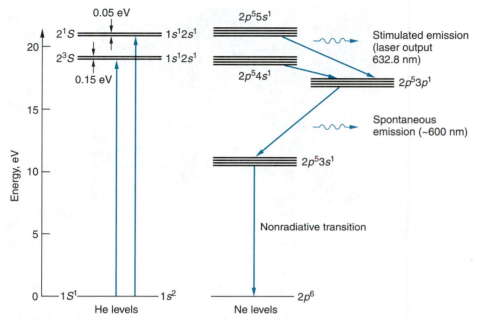

Fig. 9-37 Energy levels of helium and neon that are important for the helium-neon laser. The helium atoms are excited by electrical discharge to energy states 19.72 eV and 20.61 eV above the ground state. They collide with neon atoms, exciting some neon atoms to energy states 19.83 eV and 20.66 eV above the ground state. Population inversion is thus achieved between these levels and one at 18.70 eV above the ground state. The spontaneous emission of photons of energy 1.96 eV from the upper state stimulates other atoms in the upper state to emit photons of energy 1.96 eV, producing the characteristic He-Ne red laser light. Emission from the 19.83-eV neon state to the 18.70-eV level also produces laser output at about 1100 nm.

600-nm radiation may re-excite the 18.70-eV level. This reduces the population inversion and decreases the laser gain. Stimulated emission also occurs from the state at 19.83 eV to the 18.70-eV level, producing laser light with wavelength of 1100 nm (infrared). Helium-neon lasers have recently been developed that lase at a number of other visible and infrared wavelengths. The several possible laser wavelengths are not present simultaneously, since each device is designed to operate at a particular wavelength.

Note that there are four energy levels involved in producing the 632.8-nm helium-neon laser line, whereas the ruby laser involved only three levels. In a three-level laser, population inversion is difficult to achieve because more than half the atoms in the ground state must be excited, i.e., $N_2 > N_1/2$ in Equation 9-46. In a four-level laser, population inversion is easily achieved because the state after stimulated emission is not the ground state but an excited state that is normally unpopulated, so that $N_1 \approx 0$.

New Lasers and Applications

A laser beam is coherent, very narrow, and intense. Its coherence makes the laser beam useful in the production of holograms, such as those used on credit cards and in "heads up" displays. The precise direction and small angular spread of the beam

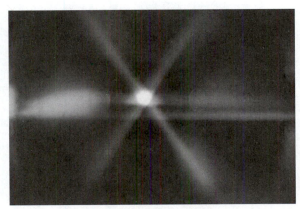

Three counterpropagating pairs of orthogonal laser beams illuminate about 100 million sodium atoms at their intersection. The pressure of the laser light cools the atoms, slowing them to rms velocities comparable to those resulting from recoil due to emission or absorption of a single photon. Cesium atoms have been cooled by this method to 2.5 μK. [*National Institute of Science and Technology.*]

Long-range fiber optic communication lines will be enhanced by the recent development of the erbium-doped fiber optic amplifier. Light from a diode laser "pumps up" a segment of erbium-doped optical fiber in the line. A signal moving down the line stimulates emission from the erbium atoms, resulting in amplification of the signal.

make it useful as a surgical tool for destroying cancer cells or reattaching a detached retina. Lasers are also used by surveyors for precise alignment over large distances. Distances can be accurately measured by reflecting a laser pulse from a mirror and measuring the time the pulse takes to travel to the mirror and back. The distance to the moon has been measured to within a few centimeters using a mirror placed on the moon by *Apollo* astronauts for that purpose. Laser beams are also used in fusion research. An intense laser pulse is focused on tiny pellets of deuterium-tritium in a combustion chamber. The beam heats the pellets to temperatures of the order of 10^8 K in a very short time, causing the deuterium and tritium to fuse and release energy. (See Section 12-2.) At the other end of the temperature scale, in 1989 physicists at the National Institute of Science and Technology, focusing three orthogonal pairs of lasers on a sample containing only a few cesium atoms, succeeded in slowing the rms velocity of the atoms to just a few times that corresponding to the recoil from absorption or emission of a single photon, achieving a low temperature of 2.5 μK.[17] (See the photo above.) Orthogonal pairs of laser beams, called *optical traps,* capable of cooling samples containing millions of atoms down to the microkelvin range are used in creating Bose-Einstein condensates and the degenerate Fermi gas, discussed in Chapter 8.

Laser technology is advancing so fast that it is possible to mention only a few of the recent developments. In addition to the ruby laser, there are many other solid-state lasers with output wavelengths ranging from about 18 nm (soft x rays) to about 3900 nm (infrared). Lasers that generate more than 1 kW of continuous power have been constructed. Pulsed lasers can now deliver nanosecond pulses of power exceeding 10^9 W. Various gas lasers produce wavelengths ranging from the far infrared to the ultraviolet. Semiconductor lasers (also known as diode lasers or junction lasers; these will be discussed further in Chapter 10) the size of a pinhead can develop 200 mW of power. In addition to their ubiquitous use in supermarket checkout counters, compact disc players, copiers, and computer printers, very recent developments in materials physics have enabled scientists to construct reliable diode lasers that emit in the blue to ultraviolet region of the spectrum. They should enable significantly increased high-density optical storage on digital versatile discs (DVDs). Liquid lasers using chemical dyes can be tuned over a range of wavelengths (about 70 nm for continuous lasers and

more than 170 nm for pulsed lasers). A relatively new laser, the free-electron laser, extracts light energy from a beam of free electrons moving through a spatially varying magnetic field. The free-electron laser has the potential for very high power and high efficiency and can be tuned over a large range of wavelengths. There appears to be no limit to the variety and uses of modern lasers.

QUESTIONS

8. What are the advantages of a four-level laser over a three-level laser?
9. What is the function of helium in a helium-neon laser? Why not just use neon?

EXAMPLE 9-8 Critical Population Inversion Comparison Compare the critical population inversion necessary for laser action in the ruby and He-Ne lasers. Compute the corresponding power requirements.

Solution

The critical population density Δn_c is given by Equation 9-51. The typical parameters of these systems are as follows:

Parameter	Ruby laser	He-Ne laser
λ	694.3 nm	632.8 nm
f	4.32×10^{14} s^{-1}	4.74×10^{14} s^{-1}
n (refractive index)	1.76	1.00
t_s	3×10^{-3} s	10^{-7} s
t_p	2.9×10^{-8} s	3.3×10^{-4} s
Δf	3.3×10^{11} s^{-1}	9×10^8 s^{-1}
N(Cr^{3+} concentration)	2×10^{19}/cm^3	—

For ruby laser:

$$\Delta n_c = \frac{4\pi^2 f^2 \Delta f\, t_s}{c^3 p} = \frac{4\pi^2 (4.32 \times 10^{14})^2 (3.3 \times 10^{11})(3 \times 10^{-3})}{(3 \times 10^8/1.76)^3\, 2.9 \times 10^{-8}}$$

$$\Delta n_c = 5.08 \times 10^{22}\,\text{atoms/m}^3 = 5.08 \times 10^{16}\,\text{atoms/cm}^3$$

For He-Ne laser:

$$\Delta n_c = \frac{4\pi^2 (4.74 \times 10^{14})^2 (9 \times 10^8)(10^{-7})}{(3 \times 10^8)^3 (3.3 \times 10^{-7})}$$

$$\Delta n_c = 8.96 \times 10^{13}\,\text{atoms/m}^3 = 8.96 \times 10^7\,\text{atoms/cm}^3$$

Thus, the critical population density is far smaller for the He-Ne laser.

The minimum power input P needed to maintain the laser action in the helium-neon system is approximately equal to $\Delta n_c(hf/t_s)$, since $N_1 \approx 0$, or

$$P(\text{He-Ne}) \approx \Delta n_c(hf/t_s)$$

$$= \frac{(8.96 \times 10^7)(6.63 \times 10^{-34})(4.74 \times 10^{14})}{10^{-7}} \approx 2.8 \times 10^{-4}\,\text{W/cm}^3$$

For the ruby laser, about one-half of the Cr^{3+} ions must be in the pumped level E_3 in Figure 9-33b and the power per unit volume necessary to maintain that population is approximately

$$P(\text{ruby}) \approx \frac{N}{2}\left(\frac{hf}{t_s}\right) \approx \frac{(2 \times 10^{19})(6.63 \times 10^{-34})(4.32 \times 10^{14})}{2 \times 3 \times 10^{-3}} \approx 955\,\text{W/cm}^3$$

Summary

TOPIC	RELEVANT EQUATIONS AND REMARKS
1. The ionic bond	The bonding mechanism typical of most salts, it involves the transfer of one or more electrons to form ions that are attracted by the Coulomb force. The exclusion principle limits the close approach of the ions, resulting in a minimum in the potential energy $U(r)$. For a diatomic molecule, $$U(r) = -k\frac{e^2}{r} + E_{ex} + E_{ion} \qquad \text{9-1}$$ where E_{ion} is the net ionization energy and E_{ex} is the exclusion-principle energy. The latter is given by $$E_{ex} = \frac{A}{r^n} \qquad \text{9-2}$$ where A and n are constants.
2. The covalent bond	This bond is a quantum-mechanical effect arising from the sharing of one or more electrons by identical or similar atoms. The symmetry of the molecular wave functions resulting from their superposition of electron orbitals determines whether bonding will occur. The wave function for the symmetric state Ψ_S is large between the atomic potential wells, resulting in minimum potential energy and bonding. The antisymmetric wave function Ψ_A is small in that region. Bonding of two nonidentical atoms is often a mixture of ionic and covalent bonding.
Other covalent bonds	Covalent bonds differ in detail, depending upon which electrons are shared. For example, H_2, with only s electrons, is s-bonded. O_2 is pp-bonded. There are also sp bonds, as in, for example, H_2O.
3. Dipole-dipole bonds	Bonding between atoms and molecules may arise due to interactions between dipole moments. The interaction may involve molecules with either permanent electric dipole moments (polar molecules) or induced dipole moments (nonpolar molecules). The potential energy U of a dipole $\mathbf{p}_2$ in the electric field $\mathbf{E}_d$ of dipole $\mathbf{p}_1$ is given by $$U = -\mathbf{p}_2 \cdot \mathbf{E}_d \qquad \text{9-8}$$

TOPIC	RELEVANT EQUATIONS AND REMARKS
	The force between permanent dipoles decreases as $1/r^4$. If one or both of the dipoles is an induced dipole, the force between them decrease as $1/r^7$.
4. Molecular spectra	The energy states of diatomic molecules consist of rotational bands superimposed on more widely spaced vibrational levels, which are in turn superimposed on the much more widely spaced atomic electron levels.
Rotational energies	The rotational energies of a diatomic molecule are

$$E = \frac{l(l+1)\hbar^2}{2I} = l(l+1)E_{0r} \quad l = 0, 1, 2, \ldots \qquad \textbf{9-13}$$

where I is the moment of inertia, $E_{0r} = \hbar^2/2I$ is the characteristic rotational energy, and l is the rotational quantum number, which obeys the selection rule $\Delta l = \pm 1$.

| Vibrational energies | The vibrational energies of a diatomic molecule are |

$$E_v = (v + 1/2)hf \qquad v = 0, 1, 2, \ldots \qquad \textbf{9-20}$$

where f is the vibrational frequency and v is the vibrational quantum number, which obeys the selection rules $\Delta v = \pm 1$.

| 5. Absorption, stimulated emission, and scattering | A photon incident on an atom can be absorbed, producing fluorescence or resonance radiation, or scattered elastically (Rayleigh scattering) or inelastically (Raman scattering). If the photon energy is greater than the ionization energy of the atom, Compton scattering or the photoelectric effect can occur. If the atom is initially in an excited state, an incident photon of the proper energy can stimulate emission of another photon of the same energy. The incident and emitted photons are in phase and travel parallel to each other. In an equilibrium system the probabilities (Einstein coefficients) for absorption and for stimulated emission between two states are equal. |
| 6. Lasers and masers | Lasers and masers are important applications of stimulated emission, differing only in the wavelengths of their outputs. Amplification by stimulated emission depends on the possibility of obtaining population inversion, in which there are more atoms in an excited state than in the ground state or in other excited states of lower energy. Population inversion is usually obtained by optical pumping and is produced more readily in four-level systems than in three-level systems. |

GENERAL REFERENCES

The following general references are written at a level appropriate for the readers of this book.

Brehm, J. J., and W. J. Mullin, *Introduction to the Structure of Matter,* Wiley, New York, 1989.

Eisberg, R., and R. Resnick, *Quantum Physics of Atoms, Molecules, Solids, Nuclei, and Particles,* 2d ed., Wiley, New York, 1985.

Herzberg, G., *Atomic Spectra & Atomic Structure,* Dover, New York, 1944.

Pauling, L., *The Chemical Bond,* Cornell University Press, Ithaca, N.Y., 1967.

Schawlow, A. L., "Laser Light," *Scientific American,* September 1968. This article and several other excellent articles on lasers and masers are reprinted in *Lasers and Light,* W. H. Freeman, New York, 1969.

Serway, R. A., C. J. Moses, and Curt A. Moyer, *Modern Physics,* Saunders, Philadelphia, 1997.

NOTES

1. The term *orbital* is frequently used in molecular physics and in chemistry to refer to the space part of the electron wave functions, i.e., the quantum numbers n, l, and m_l. In molecular physics the electrons of interest are usually the outermost (valence) ones of the constituent atoms which become associated with the entire molecule, rather than their original atoms, so we speak of "molecular orbitals" as well as "atomic orbitals."

2. Molecules whose atoms are identical, such as H_2, are sometimes called *homopolar* or *homonuclear.* Those whose atoms are not identical are called *heteropolar* or *heteronuclear.*

3. Both C_{60} and the other fullerenes are named after the philosopher and engineer R. Buckminster Fuller, who invented the architectural geodesic dome structure. Such domes, as Fuller pointed out, can be considered as networks of pentagons and hexagons.

4. Leonhard Euler (1707–1783), Swiss mathematician. Arguably the most prolific mathematician of all time, he published 866 papers during his lifetime and, despite having lost his sight in 1766 (in part due to his earlier observations of the sun), he left so many manuscripts at his death that it took another 35 years to get them all published. He introduced the symbol e as the base of the natural logarithms and i as the square root of -1.

5. Johannes D. van der Waals (1837–1923), Dutch physicist. Largely self-taught, he became interested in the fact that the ideal-gas law derived from kinetic theory does not hold exactly for real gases. This led him to question the assumption that no forces act between individual gas molecules except during collisions, which resulted in his development of an equation, the van der Waals equation, which more accurately describes real gases. He was awarded the 1910 Nobel Prize in physics for his work.

6. This result is derived in most introductory physics books. See, e.g., P. Tipler, *Physics for Scientists and Engineers,* 4th ed. (New York: W. H. Freeman, 1992), p. 671.

7. Terminology concerning the dipole-dipole forces is a bit confused. Some textbooks use *van der Waals* to describe all three types of dipole-dipole forces. We will follow the more common (and traditional) use, reserving *van der Waals* for the attractive force between induced dipoles only.

8. We use v (the Greek letter nu) here rather than n so as not to confuse the vibrational quantum number with the principal quantum number n for electronic energy levels.

9. The nitric oxide (NO) molecule is an exception due to its odd electron.

10. Also, the $l \rightarrow l - 1$ group of lines are called the *P branch* and the $l \rightarrow l + 1$ group the *R branch.*

11. Chandrasekhara V. Raman (1888–1970), Indian physicist. Graduating from college at the age of 16, like Einstein he became a civil servant and worked at science in his spare time. He had predicted that visible light should be inelastically scattered even before Heisenberg had predicted and Compton had found the effect for x rays. He was awarded the 1930 Nobel Prize in physics for his work, becoming the first Asian to be so recognized in the sciences.

12. There is also a Raman effect for the vibrational and electronic levels of molecules.

13. T. H. Maiman, "Stimulated Optical Radiation in Ruby," *Nature,* **187**, 493 (1960).

14. The correction essentially accounts for the fact that, due to the finite line width, the energy density $u(f)$ in the transition probability must include a narrow range of frequencies Δf, rather than just the single frequency f.

15. Recall that the energy per unit volume $u(f)$ times c is the intensity, e.g., W/m^2 in SI units.

16. A. Javan, W. B. Bennet, Jr., and D. R. Herriott, *Physical Review Letters,* **6**, 106 (1961).

17. Since then, other cooling techniques, such as adiabatic nuclear demagnetization, have achieved low temperatures in the nanokelvin range.

PROBLEMS

Level I

Section 9-1 The Ionic Bond

9-1. The dissociation energy is sometimes expressed in kilocalories per mole. (*a*) Find the relation between electron volts per molecule and kilocalories per mole. (*b*) Find the dissociation energy of molecular NaCl in kilocalories per mole. (*c*) The dissociation energy of the Li_2 molecule is 106 kJ/mole. Find the value in eV per molecule.

9-2. The dissociation energy of Cl_2 is 2.48 eV. Consider the formation of an NaCl molecule by the reaction

$$Na + \tfrac{1}{2}Cl_2 \longrightarrow NaCl$$

Is this reaction endothermic (requiring energy) or exothermic (releasing energy)? How much energy per molecule is required or given off?

9-3. Using the data in Table 9-1, compute the net energy required to transfer an electron between the following pairs of atoms: Cs to F, Li to I, and Rb to Br.

9-4. Using the data in Tables 9-1 and 9-2, estimate the dissociation energy of the three ionically bonded molecules CsI, NaF, and LiI. Your results are probably all higher than those in Table 9-2. Explain why.

9-5. The equilibrium separation of the Rb^+ and Cl^- ions in RbCl is about 0.267 nm. (a) Calculate the potential energy of attraction of the ions, assuming them to be point charges. (b) The ionization energy of rubidium is 4.18 eV, and the electron affinity of Cl is 3.62 eV. Find the dissociation energy, neglecting the energy of repulsion. (c) The measured dissociation energy is 4.37 eV. What is the energy due to repulsion of the ions?

9-6. Compute the Coulomb energy of the KBr molecule at the equilibrium separation. Use that result to compute the exclusion-principle repulsion at r_0.

9-7. If the exclusion-principle repulsion in Problem 9-6 is given by Equation 9-2, compute the coefficient A and the exponent n.

9-8. Compute the dissociation energy of molecular NaBr in kilocalories per mole.

9-9. Note in Table 9-2 that the equilibrium separations of the KBr and RbCl molecules are very nearly equal. Compute the exclusion-principle repulsion for these molecules.

Section 9-2 The Covalent Bond

9-10. Hydrogen can bond covalently with many atoms besides those listed in Tables 9-3 and 9-5, including sulfur, tellurium, phosphorus, and antimony. What would you expect to be the chemical formula of the resulting molecules? (*Hint:* Use the table of electron configurations in Appendix C.)

9-11. What kind of bonding mechanism would you expect for (a) the KCl molecule, (b) the O_2 molecule, and (c) the CH_4 molecule?

9-12. The equilibrium separation of the atoms in the HF molecule is 0.0917 nm, and its measured electric dipole moment is 6.40×10^{-30} C·m. What percentage of the bonding is ionic?

9-13. The equilibrium separation of CsF is 0.2345 nm. If its bonding is 70 percent ionic, what should its measured electric dipole moment be?

9-14. Ionic bonding in the BaO molecule involves the transfer of two electrons from the Ba atom. If the equilibrium separation is 0.193 nm and the measured electric dipole moment is 26.7×10^{-30} C·m, to what extent is the bond actually ionic?

Section 9-3 Other Bonding Mechanisms

9-15. Find three other elements with the same subshell electron configuration in the two outermost orbitals as carbon. Would you expect the same kind of hybrid bonding for these elements as for carbon? Support your answer.

9-16. The dipole moment **p** of the water molecule, illustrated in Figure 9-19, is actually the vector sum of two equal dipoles p_1 and p_2 directed from the oxygen atom to each of the hydrogen atoms. The measured value of the angle between the two hydrogen atoms is 104.5°, the O—H bond length is 0.0956 nm, and the magnitude of **p** is 6.46×10^{-30} C·m. Compute the fraction of the electron charge that is transferred from each hydrogen to the oxygen.

9-17. The polarizability of Ne is 1.1×10^{-37} m·C²/N. (a) At what separation would the dipole-dipole energy between a molecule of H_2O and an atom of Ne in the atmosphere be sufficient to withstand collision with an N_2 molecule moving with the average kinetic energy for $T = 300$ K. (b) At what separation does this energy occur for a typically bonded molecule? (c) On the basis of these results, do you expect H_2O—Ne bonds to be very likely? Explain your answer.

9-18. The hydrogen bonds linking the two helical strands of the DNA molecule have bond strengths of about 0.3 eV, or approximately 15 percent of the strengths of the

ionic/covalent bonds along the strands. (*a*) What is the wavelength of a photon with sufficient energy to break this bond? (*b*) In what part of the spectrum does this wavelength lie? (*c*) Since there exists a significant intensity at this wavelength in the environment, why haven't all the DNA hydrogen bonds long since broken?

9-19. Would you expect the following molecules to be polar or nonpolar? Explain your answer in each case. (*a*) NaCl; (*b*) O_2.

Section 9-4 Energy Levels and Spectra of Diatomic Molecules

9-20. The characteristic rotational energy E_{0r} for the N_2 molecules is 2.48×10^{-4} eV. From this, find the separation distance of the nitrogen atoms in N_2.

9-21. For the O_2 molecule, the separation of the atoms is 0.121 nm. Calculate the characteristic rotational energy $E_{0r} = \hbar^2/2I$ in eV.

9-22. Compute the reduced masses of the $H^{35}Cl$ and $H^{37}Cl$ molecules.

9-23. Derive Equation 9-21.

9-24. Calculate the reduced mass in unified mass units for (*a*) H_2, (*b*) N_2, (*c*) CO, and (*d*) HCl.

9-25. The characteristic rotational energy $E_{0r} = \hbar^2/2I$ for KCl is 1.43×10^{-5} eV. (*a*) Find the reduced mass for the KCl molecule. (*b*) Find the separation distance of the K^+ and Cl^- ions.

9-26. Use the data from Table 9-7 to find the force constant for (*a*) the $H^{35}Cl$ and (*b*) the $K^{79}Br$ molecules.

9-27. The equilibrium separation of HBr is 0.141 nm. Treating the Br atom as fixed, compute the four lowest rotational energies of the HBr molecule and show them in a carefully sketched energy-level diagram.

9-28. The vibrational spectrum of Li_2 consists of a series of equally spaced lines in the microwave region 1.05×10^{13} Hz apart. Compute the equilibrium separation for Li_2.

9-29. Compute the difference in the rotational energy E_{0r} for $K^{35}Cl$ and $K^{37}Cl$.

9-30. What type of bonding mechanism would you expect for (*a*) NaF, (*b*) KBr, (*c*) N_2, and (*d*) Ne?

Section 9-5 Absorption, Stimulated Emission, and Scattering

9-31. The five lowest levels of a certain monatomic gas have the values $E_1 = 0$, $E_2 = 3.80$ eV, $E_3 = 4.30$ eV, $E_4 = 7.2$ eV, and $E_5 = 7.5$ eV. (*a*) If the temperature is high enough that all levels are occupied and the gas is illuminated with light of wavelength 2400 nm, what transitions can occur? (*b*) Which of those found in part (*a*) will still occur if the temperature is so low that only the state E_1 is occupied? (*c*) Repeat (*a*) and (*b*) for light of 250-nm wavelength. (*d*) What wavelength of the incident light would stimulate emission from state E_4?

9-32. A hydrogen discharge tube is operated at about 300 K in the laboratory in order to produce the Balmer series. Compute the ratio of the probability for spontaneous emission of the H_α line to that for stimulated emission.

9-33. Determine the ratio of the number of molecules in the $v = 1$ state to the number in the $v = 0$ state for a sample of O_2 molecules at 273 K. Repeat the calculation for 77 K. (Ignore rotational motion.)

9-34. The nuclei in the F_2 molecule are separated by 0.14 nm. (*a*) Compute the energy separations and sketch an energy-level diagram for the lowest four rotational levels with $v = 0$. (*b*) What are the wavelengths of possible transitions between these levels?

Section 9-6 Lasers and Masers

9-35. A pulse from a ruby laser has an average power of 10 MW and lasts 1.5 ns. (*a*) What is the total energy of the pulse? (*b*) How many photons are emitted in this pulse?

9-36. A helium-neon laser emits light of wavelength 632.8 nm and has a power output of 4 mW. How many photons are emitted per second by this laser?

9-37. A laser beam is aimed at the moon a distance 3.84×10^8 m away. The angular spread of the beam is given by the diffraction formula, $\sin \theta = 1.22\, \lambda/D$, where D is the diameter of the laser tube. Calculate the size of the beam on the moon for $D = 10$ cm and $\lambda = 600$ nm.

9-38. A particular atom has two energy levels with a transition wavelength of 420 nm. At 297 K there are 2.5×10^{21} atoms in the lower state. (*a*) How many atoms are in the upper state? (*b*) Suppose that 1.8×10^{21} of the atoms in the lower state are pumped to the upper state. How much energy could this system release in a single laser pulse?

Level II

9-39. (*a*) Calculate the electrostatic potential energy of Na^+ and Cl^- ions at their equilibrium separation distance of 0.24 nm, assuming the ions to be point charges. (*b*) What is the energy of repulsion at this separation? (*c*) Assume that the energy of repulsion is given by Equation 9-2. From Figure 9-2*b*, this energy equals ke^2/r at about $r = 0.14$ nm. Use this and your answer to part (*b*) to calculate n and A. (Though this calculation is not very accurate, the energy of repulsion does vary much more rapidly with r than does the energy of attraction.)

9-40. (*a*) Show that the reduced mass μ is smaller than either atomic mass in a diatomic molecule. (*b*) Compute μ for $H^{35}Cl$ and for $H^{37}Cl$.

9-41. The equilibrium separation of the K^+ and Cl^- ions in KCl is about 0.267 nm. (*a*) Calculate the potential energy of attraction of the ions assuming them to be point charges at this separation. (*b*) The ionization energy of potassium is 4.34 eV and the electron affinity of chlorine is 3.61 eV. Find the dissociation energy for KCl, neglecting any energy of repulsion (see Figure 9-2*a*). (*c*) The measured dissociation energy is 4.40 eV. What is the energy due to repulsion of the ions at the equilibrium separation?

9-42. Use the equilibrium separation for the K^+ and Cl^- ions given in Problem 9-41 and the reduced mass of KCl to calculate the characteristic rotational energy E_{0r} of KCl.

9-43. In this problem, you are to find how the van der Waals force between a polar and a nonpolar molecule depends on the distance between the molecules. Let the dipole moment of the polar molecule be in the x direction and the nonpolar molecule be a distance x away. (*a*) How does the electric field due to an electric dipole depend on the distance x? (*b*) Use the facts that the potential energy of an electric dipole of moment **p** in an electric field **E** is $U = -\mathbf{p} \cdot \mathbf{E}$ and that the induced dipole moment of the nonpolar molecule is proportional to **E** to find how the potential energy of interaction of the two molecules depends on separation distance. (*c*) Using $F_x = -dU/dx$, find the x dependence of the force between the two molecules.

9-44. The microwave spectrum of CO has lines at 0.86 mm, 1.29 mm, and 2.59 mm. (*a*) Compute the photon energies and carefully sketch the energy-level diagram that corresponds. What molecular motion produces these lines? (*b*) Compute the equilibrium separation (bond length) of CO.

9-45. Carefully draw a potential energy curve for a diatomic molecule (like Figure 9-2*b*) and indicate the mean values of r for two vibrational levels. Show that because of the asymmetry of the curve, r_{av} increases with increasing vibrational energy and, therefore, solids expand when heated.

9-46. A sample of HCl is illuminated with light of wavelength 435.8 nm. (*a*) Compute the wavelengths of the four lines in the rotational Raman spectrum that are closest to that of the incident light. (*b*) Compare the difference in their frequencies with the corresponding lines in Figure 9-29.

9-47. Use data from Table 9-7 to compute the first excited vibrational and the first excited rotational states of (*a*) the Li_2 and (*b*) the $K^{79}Br$ molecules.

9-48. Calculate the effective force constant for HCl from its reduced mass and the fundamental vibrational frequency obtained from Figure 9-29.

9-49. Notice in Figure 9-32*b* that the level E_2 in Cr^{3+} is a doublet, the pair of states being separated by only 0.0036 eV. (*a*) Assume that all of the Cr^{3+} ions in a certain laser are in the three states E_1 and E_2 (doublet) and compute the relative populations of these levels. (*b*) If only the lower state of the E_2 doublet can produce laser light but both levels must be pumped together, determine the pumping power necessary for laser action to occur. The density of states (degeneracy) of level E_1 is 4 and for *each* of the E_2 levels is 2.

9-50. The central frequency for the absorption band of HCl shown in Figure 9-29 is at $f = 8.66 \times 10^{13}$ Hz, and the absorption peaks are separated by about $\Delta f = 6 \times 10^6$ Hz. Using this information, find (*a*) the lowest (zero-point) vibrational energy for HCl, (*b*) the moment of inertia of HCl, and (*c*) the equilbrium separation of the atoms.

Level III

9-51. The potential energy between two atoms in a molecule can often be described rather well by the Lenard-Jones potential, which can be written

$$U(r) = U_0\left[\left(\frac{a}{r}\right)^{12} - 2\left(\frac{a}{r}\right)^6\right]$$

where U_0 and a are constants. (*a*) Find the interatomic separation r_0 in terms of a for which the potential energy is minimum. (*b*) Find the corresponding value of U_{min}. (*c*) Use Figure 9-8*b* to obtain numerical values for r_0 and U_0 for the H_2 molecule. Express your answer in nanometers and electron volts. (*d*) Make a plot of the potential energy $U(r)$ versus the internuclear separation r for the H_2 molecule. Plot each term separately, together with the total $U(r)$.

9-52. (*a*) Find the exclusion-principle repulsion for NaCl. (*b*) Use Equation 9-2 to find A and n.

9-53. Show that the H^+-H^- system cannot be ionically bonded. [*Hint:* Show that $U(r)$ has no negative minimum.]

9-54. (*a*) Calculate the fractional difference $\Delta\mu/\mu$ for the reduced masses of the $H^{35}Cl$ and $H^{37}Cl$ molecules. (*b*) Show that the mixture of isotopes in HCl leads to a fractional difference in the frequency of a transition from one rotational state to another given by $\Delta f/f = -\Delta\mu/\mu$. (*c*) Compute $\Delta f/f$ and compare your result with Figure 9-29.

9-55. For a molecule such as CO, which has a permanent electric dipole moment, radiative transitions obeying the selection rule $\Delta l = \pm 1$ between two rotational energy levels of the same vibrational energy state are allowed. (That is, the selection rule $\Delta v = \pm 1$ does not hold.) (*a*) Find the moment of inertia of CO for which $r_0 = 0.113$ nm, and calculate the characteristic rotational energy E_{0r} in electron volts. (*b*) Make an energy-level diagram for the rotational levels for $l = 0$ to $l = 5$ for some vibrational level. Label the energies in electron volts, starting with $E = 0$ for $l = 0$. (*c*) Indicate on your diagram transitions that obey $\Delta l = -1$ and calculate the energy of the photons emitted. (*d*) Find the wavelength of the photon emitted for each transition in (*c*). In what region of the electromagnetic spectrum are these photons?

Chapter 10 Solid-State Physics

The many and varied properties of solids have intrigued us for centuries. Technological developments involving metals and alloys have shaped the courses of civilizations, and the symmetry and beauty of naturally occurring, large single crystals have consistently captured our imaginations. However, the origins of the physical properties of solids were not understood even in rudimentary form until the development of quantum mechanics. The application of quantum mechanics to solids has provided the basis for much of the technological progress of modern times. We will study briefly some aspects of the structure of solids in Section 10-1 and then concentrate on their electrical properties.

10-1 The Structure of Solids

In our everyday world we see matter in three phases: gases, liquids, and solids. In a gas the average distance between two atoms or molecules is large compared with the size of an atom or molecule. The molecules have little influence on one another, except during their frequent but brief collisions. In a liquid or solid the atoms or molecules are close together and exert forces on one another comparable to the forces that bind atoms into molecules. (There is a fourth phase of matter, plasma, which occurs when the matter consists largely—or entirely—of ions and free electrons. Usually this condition exists only at very high temperatures, such as inside stars, in intense electrical discharges—e.g., lightning—and in the laboratory. The properties of a plasma are very different from those of an ordinary gas because of the long-range electrical and magnetic effects arising from the charges of the particles. The recently discovered low-temperature gas phase of matter, the Bose-Einstein condensate, was discussed in Chapter 8.) In a liquid, the molecules form temporary short-range bonds which are continually broken and re-formed as the result of the thermal kinetic energy of the molecules. The strength of the bonds depends on the type of molecule. For example, as we discussed in Section 9-3, the bonds between helium atoms are very weak van der Waals bonds, and He does not liquefy at atmospheric pressure until the very low temperature of 4.2 K is reached.

If a liquid is slowly cooled, the kinetic energy of its molecules is reduced and the molecules will arrange themselves in a regular crystalline array, producing the maximum number of bonds and leading to a minimum potential energy. However, if the liquid is cooled rapidly so that its internal energy is removed before the molecules have time to arrange themselves, a solid is often formed that is not crystalline but resembles a "snapshot" of a liquid. Such a solid is called *amorphous;* it displays

short-range order but not the long-range order (over many atomic diameters) characteristic of a crystal. Glass is a common amorphous solid. A characteristic of the long-range ordering of a crystal is that it has a well-defined melting point, whereas an amorphous solid merely softens as its temperature is increased. Many materials may solidify in either an amorphous or a crystalline state, depending on how they are prepared. Others exist only in one form or the other. Most common solids are polycrystalline—i.e., they are collections of single crystals. The size of such single crystals is typically a fraction of a millimeter; however, large single crystals occur naturally and can be produced artificially (Figure 10-1). We shall discuss only simple crystalline solids in this chapter.

The most important property of a single crystal is its symmetry and regularity of structure: it can be thought of as a single unit structure repeated throughout the solid. The smallest unit of a crystal is called the *unit cell*. The structure of the unit cell depends on the type of bonding between the atoms, ions, or molecules in the crystal. If more than one kind of atom is present, the structure will also depend on their relative size. The structure may also change in response to changes in pressure and/or temperature. The bonding mechanisms are those discussed in Chapter 9: ionic, cova-

(b)

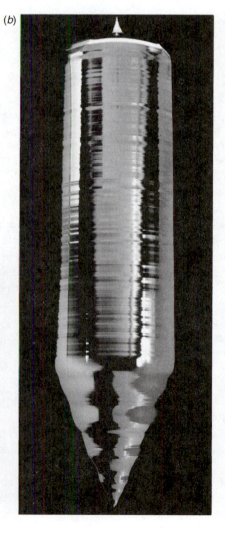

(a)

Fig. 10-1 (*a*) A single crystal of quartz, one of several naturally occurring crystalline forms of SiO_2. [*Courtesy of Sawyer Research Products, Inc.*] (*b*) A synthetic silicon crystal is created beginning with a raw material containing silicon (for instance, common beach sand), purifying out the silicon, and melting it. From a seed crystal, the molten silicon grows into a cylindrical crystal, such as the one shown here. The crystals (typically about 1.3 m long) are formed under highly controlled conditions to ensure that they are flawless, and sliced into thousands of thin wafers, onto which the layers of an integrated circuit are etched. [*Courtesy of the Museum of Modern Art, New York City.*]

lent, and dipole-dipole, the latter including the hydrogen and van der Waals bonds. In addition, a quantum-mechanical mechanism responsible for bonding metals in the solid state, *metallic bonding,* will be described later in this section.

Ionic and Covalent Solids

Figure 10-2 shows the structure of the ionic crystal NaCl. The Na^+ and Cl^- ions are spherically symmetric (see Section 9-1) with the Cl^- ions approximately twice as large as the Na^+ ions. The minimum potential energy of this crystal occurs when an ion of either kind has six nearest neighbors of the other kind. This structure is called *face-centered-cubic (fcc)* because the unit cell is a cube and an ion, in this case Cl^-, occupies the center of each face. Note that the Na^+ and Cl^- ions are *not* paired into NaCl molecules in solid NaCl.

The net attractive part of the potential energy of an ion in a crystal can be written

$$U_{att} = -\alpha \frac{ke^2}{r}$$ **10-1**

where r is the separation distance between neighboring ions (which is 0.282 nm for the Na^+ and Cl^- ions in crystalline NaCl); and α, called the *Madelung constant,* depends on the geometry of the crystal. If only the six nearest neighbors of each ion were important, α would be 6. However, in addition to the 6 neighbors of the opposite charge at a distance r there are 12 ions of the same charge at a distance $2^{1/2}r$, 8 ions of opposite charge at distance $3^{1/2}r$, and so on. The Madelung constant is thus an infinite sum:

$$\alpha = 6 - \frac{12}{\sqrt{2}} + \frac{8}{\sqrt{3}} - \frac{6}{2} + \frac{20}{\sqrt{5}} - \cdots$$ **10-2**

Unfortunately, the sum in Equation 10-2 does not converge! We are saved by the fact that NaCl crystals are not spherical, as the analysis above implies. A better physical approach is to use cubic shells, rather than spherical ones; then the cubic-shell equivalent of Equation 10-2 does converge, albeit slowly. The result for face-centered-cubic structures like NaCl is $\alpha = 1.7476$. The geometric details of other ionic arrangements result in slightly different values for α. (See Table 10-1.)

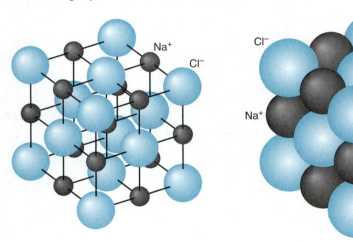

Fig. 10-2 Structure of the face-centered-cubic (fcc) NaCl crystal.

TABLE 10-1 Properties of selected crystalline solids

Solid	Bonding	Equilibrium separation (nm)	Crystal symmetry	Madelung constant	Cohesive energy (eV/atom)	Melting point (K)
NaCl	ionic	0.282	fcc	1.7476	3.19	1074
LiBr	ionic	0.275	fcc	1.7476	3.10	823
KCl	ionic	0.315	fcc	1.7476	3.24	1043
RbF	ionic	0.282	fcc	1.7476	3.55	1068
CsCl	ionic	0.348	sc	1.7627	3.27	918
ZnO	ionic	0.222	hcp	1.4985	7.22	2248
Li	metallic	0.302	bcc	—	1.63	454
Fe	metallic	0.248	bcc	—	4.28	1811
Au	metallic	0.288	fcc	—	3.81	1338
Zn	metallic	0.266	hcp	—	1.35	693
C	covalent	0.154	fcc	—	7.37	†
Si	covalent	0.235	fcc	—	4.63	1687
Ge	covalent	0.245	fcc	—	3.85	1211
H_2O	dipole-dipole	0.367	hcp	—	0.52*	273
C_{60}	dipole-dipole	1.00	fcc	—	1.5*	?
Ne	dipole-dipole	0.313	fcc	—	0.020	24

*eV/molecule.
† *Diamond transforms to graphite at high temperature. The latter then sublimes at about 3800 K.*

When Na^+ and Cl^- ions are very close together, they repel each other because of the overlap of the wave functions of their electrons and the exclusion-principle repulsion discussed in Section 9-1. A simple empirical expression for the potential energy associated with this repulsion that works fairly well is

$$U_{rep} = \frac{A}{r^n}$$

where A and n are constants.[1] The total potential energy of an ion is then

$$U = -\alpha \frac{ke^2}{r} + \frac{A}{r^n} \qquad \text{10-3}$$

The equilibrium separation $r = r_0$ is that at which the force $F = -dU/dr$ is zero. Differentiating and setting $dU/dr = 0$ at $r = r_0$, we obtain

$$A = \frac{\alpha k e^2 r_0^{n-1}}{n} \qquad\qquad \textbf{10-4}$$

The total potential energy of an ion in the crystal can thus be written

$$U = -\alpha \frac{ke^2}{r_0}\left[\frac{r_0}{r} - \frac{1}{n}\left(\frac{r_0}{r}\right)^n\right] \qquad\qquad \textbf{10-5}$$

At $r = r_0$, we have

$$U(r_0) = -\alpha \frac{ke^2}{r_0}\left(1 - \frac{1}{n}\right) \qquad\qquad \textbf{10-6}$$

If we know the equilibrium separation r_0, which can be found from x-ray diffraction experiments or computed from the crystal density, the value of n can be found approximately from the *dissociation energy* or *lattice energy* of the ionic crystal, which is the energy needed to break up the crystal into its constituent ions. In the case of NaCl the measured dissociation energy is 770 kJ/mol. Using 1 eV $= 1.602 \times 10^{-19}$ J and the fact that 1 mol of NaCl contains N_A pairs of ions, we can express the dissociation energy in electron volts per ion pair. The conversion between electron volts per ion pair and kilojoules per mole is

$$1\frac{eV}{\text{ion pair}} \times \frac{6.022 \times 10^{23} \text{ ion pairs}}{\text{mol}} \times \frac{1.602 \times 10^{-19} \text{ J}}{1 \text{ eV}}$$

The result is

$$1\frac{eV}{\text{ion pair}} = 96.47 \frac{kJ}{\text{mol}} \qquad\qquad \textbf{10-7}$$

Thus 770 kJ/mol = 7.98 eV per ion pair. Substituting -7.98 eV for $U(r_0)$, 0.282 nm for r_0 (see Example 10-1), and 1.75 for α in Equation 10-6, we can solve for n. The result is $n = 9.35 \approx 9$.

The dissociation energy is also used to compute the *cohesive energy* of a crystal, which is the potential energy per atom or per atomic pair, rather than per ion pair, and is the term used for all crystalline bonding mechanisms. For the NaCl illustration above, 7.98 eV is the energy needed to remove a Na^+ and Cl^- pair from the crystal. Forming Cl from Cl^- requires the input of 3.62 eV, and forming Na from Na^+ releases 5.15 eV. Therefore, the energy necessary to remove the neutral Na and Cl pair from the crystal is 7.98 eV + 3.62 eV $-$ 5.14 eV = 6.46 eV, and the cohesive energy of NaCl is 6.46 eV per Na and Cl pair. This result is in good agreement with the observed value of 3.19 eV/atom in Table 10-1. A large cohesive energy implies a high melting point and vice versa.

EXAMPLE 10-1 Equilibrium Spacing r_0 in a NaCl Crystal Calculate the equilibrium spacing r_0 for NaCl from the measured density of NaCl, which is $\rho = 2.16$ g/cm^3.

Solution

We consider each ion to occupy a cubic volume of side r_0. The mass of 1 mol of NaCl is 58.4 g, which is the sum of the atomic masses of sodium and chlorine. The ions occupy a volume of $2N_A r_0^3$, where $N_A = 6.02 \times 10^{23}$ is Avogadro's number. The density is thus related to r_0 by

$$\rho = \frac{m}{V} = \frac{m}{2N_A r_0^3}$$

Then

$$r_0^3 = \frac{m}{2N_A \rho} = \frac{58.4 \text{ g}}{2(6.02 \times 10^{23})(2.16 \text{ g/cm}^3)} = 2.24 \times 10^{-23} \text{ cm}^3$$

$$r_0 = 2.82 \times 10^{-8} \text{ cm} = 0.282 \text{ nm}$$

EXAMPLE 10-2 Measuring r_0 from X-Ray Diffraction Molybdenum K_α x rays ($\lambda = 0.071$ nm) strike the diagonal Bragg planes of the NaCl crystal shown on the right in Figure 3-15 such that a diffraction maximum (a bright Laue spot) is observed for $\theta = 10.25°$. Determine the value of r_0.

Solution

1. Since NaCl is a cubic crystal, the distance d between the diagonal Bragg planes is related to the equilibrium separation r_0 by:

$$d = \frac{r_0}{\sqrt{2}}$$

2. The x-ray diffraction maxima satisfy the Bragg condition, Equation 3-38:

$$2d \sin \theta = m\lambda$$

3. For $m = 1$ and substituting d from above:

$$2\left(\frac{r_0}{\sqrt{2}}\right) \sin \theta = \lambda$$

4. Solving this for r_0 and substituting values from above give:

$$r_0 = \frac{\sqrt{2}\lambda}{2 \sin \theta}$$

$$= \frac{(\sqrt{2})(0.071 \text{ nm})}{(2)(\sin 10.25°)}$$

$$= 0.282 \text{ nm}$$

Remarks: *This result agrees with the value calculated from the density of NaCl in Example 10-1.*

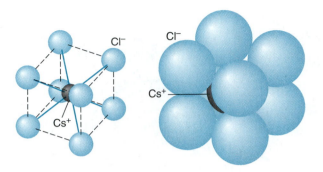

Fig. 10-3 Structure of the simple-cubic (sc) crystal CsCl.

Most ionic crystals, such as LiF, KF, KCl, KI, AgCl, and others formed by molecules in Table 9-2, have a face-centered-cubic structure. Some elemental solids that also have this structure are Ag, Al, Au, Ca, Cu, Ni, and Pb.

Figure 10-3 illustrates the structure of another ionic crystal, CsCl, which is called *simple cubic (sc)*, because it can be considered as two interpenetrating cubic structures, one of Cs^+ ions and the other of Cl^- ions. In this structure, each ion has eight nearest-neighbor ions of the opposite charge. The Madelung constant for ionic crystals with simple cubic structure is 1.7627. Other crystals with this structure include CsI, TlI, TlBr, LiHg, and NH_4Cl. Some elemental solids, such as Ba, Cs, Fe, K, Li, Mo, and Na also crystallize with the structure shown in Figure 10-3; when the atoms are the same at the vertices and in the center of the cube, the structure is called *body-centered-cubic (bcc)*.

Figure 10-4 illustrates another important crystal structure called *hexagonal close-packed (hcp)*. This is the structure obtained by stacking identical spheres such as Ping-Pong balls. In one layer, each ball touches six others; hence the name hexagonal. In the next layer, each ball fits into the triangular depressions of the first layer. In the third layer, each ball fits into a triangular depression of the second layer such that it lies directly over a ball in the first layer. Elements with hexagonal close-packed crystal structure include Be, Cd, Ce, Mg, Os, Zn, Zr, and others. There are a total of 14 different types of three-dimensional crystal lattice structures of which we have discussed only a few of the most common ones.

Fig. 10-4 Hexagonal close-packed (hcp) crystal structure.

EXAMPLE 10-3 Madelung Constant for a Two-Dimensional Crystal Calculate out to four terms in the series the Madelung constant for the hypothetical univalent, two-dimensional ionic crystal shown in Figure 10-5.

Solution

The net attractive potential is given by Equation 10-1. Considering the negative ion at the origin of Figure 10-5, there are four positive ions located a distance r away, as indicated by circle A in the diagram. There are four negative ions lying on circle B, whose radius is $2^{1/2}r$. Four negative ions are located on circle C, whose distance from the ion at the origin is $2r$, and, finally, eight positive ions lie on circle D at $5^{1/2}r$ from the origin. Therefore, to four terms the net attractive potential is

$$U_{att} = -ke^2\left(\frac{4}{r} - \frac{4}{2^{1/2}r} - \frac{4}{2r} + \frac{8}{5^{1/2}r}\right)$$

Fig. 10-5 A hypothetical
univalent two-dimensional
ionic crystal (Example 10-3).

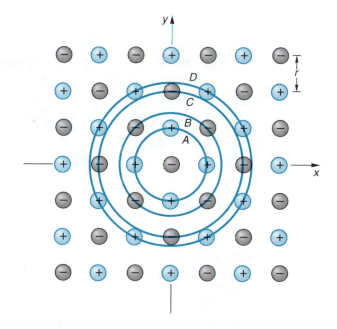

or

$$U_{att} = -\frac{ke^2}{r}\left(4 - \frac{4}{2^{1/2}} - 2 + \frac{8}{5^{1/2}}\right)$$

The quantity in parentheses is the Madelung constant α correct to four terms in the infinite expansion; thus we have $\alpha \approx 2.749$.

In covalently bonded crystals the nature of the individual bonds is just like that in covalently bonded molecules, as was described in Section 9-2. The electron-sharing character of the bond enhances its effectiveness in crystals, for example, enabling tetravalent carbon atoms to form bonds with as many as four other carbon atoms. The crystal structure is determined by the directional nature of the bonds. Figure 10-6 illustrates the diamond structure of carbon (which is also the structure of Ge and Si),

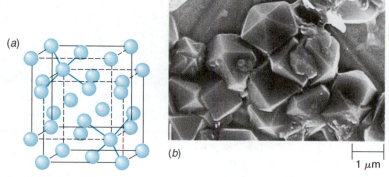

Fig. 10-6 (*a*) Diamond crystal structure showing how this structure can be considered to be a combination of two interpenetrating face-centered-cubic structures. (*b*) Synthetic diamonds magnified about 50,000 times. In diamond, each carbon atom is at the center of a tetrahedron formed by four other carbon atoms. [*Courtesy of Chris Kovach/Discover Publications.*]

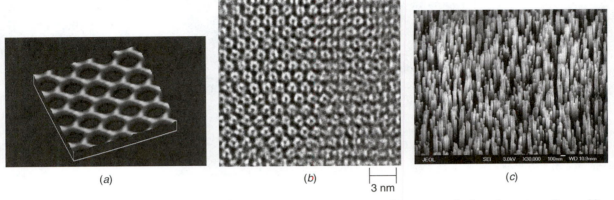

Fig. 10-7 (*a*) An atomic-force micrograph of graphite. The brighter spots at each vertex are single carbon atoms. In graphite, carbon atoms are arranged in sheets, each sheet made up of atoms in hexagonal rings. The sheets slide easily across one another, a property that allows graphite to function as a lubricant. [*Courtesy of Srinivas Manne, University of California at Santa Barbara.*] (*b*) This high-resolution transmission electron micrograph shows clearly the close-packed fcc arrangement of the C_{60} molecules in the solid fullerene. [*Courtesy of P. R. Buseck, Science, **257**, 215 (1992).*] (*c*) Carbon nanotubes grown on a titanium substrate. The nanotubes are perpendicular to the substrate and range between 40 nm and 100 nm in diameter. [*Courtesy of Z. F. Ren et al., Boston College.*]

in which each atom is bonded to four others located at the vertices of a regular tetrahedron as a result of the sp^3 hybridization discussed in the Chapter 9 More section "Other Covalent Bonds" on the home page. The diamond structure can be considered to be two interpenetrating face-centered-cubic structures. This arrangement with equal bond angles is particularly tightly bound and results in the carbon diamond structure having one of the largest atomic cohesive energies of all solids, about 7.37 eV per carbon atom. Carbon has two other well-defined crystalline structures, graphite and solid fullerenes,[2] both the result of carbon orbitals hybridized in the sp^2 configuration. In graphite, illustrated in Figure 10-7*a*, three of the valence electrons link each atom to three near neighbors via directed bonds forming a planar hexagonal structure. The planes thus formed are connected by much weaker dipole-dipole forces. This results in a structure consisting of strong sheets that can be readily separated from one another. The structure of the fullerenes, using solid C_{60} as an example, is quite different from both diamond and graphite. As described in Section 9-2, the C_{60} molecule achieves its spheroid shape by incorporating 12 pentagons into the hexagonal structure, thus distorting the graphite planes into the soccer-ball configuration. The C_{60} molecules are then bonded to each other by dipole-dipole forces, just as the sheets of graphite are. As a result, the cohesive energy per atom is quite high, about 7.4 eV or nearly equal to that of diamond, but the cohesive energy per molecule is low, only 1.5 eV. The C_{60} crystal, shown in Figure 10-7*b*, is face-centered-cubic. The equilibrium separation between the molecules is 1.00 nm. The nanotubes shown in Figure 10.7*c* are a remarkable example of carbon's possible bonding configurations.

Racing bicycles and Formula 1 race cars are constructed from woven carbon fibers. They absorb shock extremely well and are both lighter and stronger than older bikes and race cars made of steel or aluminum.

Metallic Bonding in Solids

All solid metals, formed from the metal elements that make up more that half of the periodic table, are bonded by the *metallic bond,* which, as was noted earlier, has no single-molecule counterpart. It is somewhat analogous to the covalent bond in which the atoms of the molecule share one or more electrons. In the metallic bond one or

two of the valence electrons of each atom are free to move throughout the solid, and *all* of the atoms share all of those electrons. Thus, the metallic crystal can be pictured as a lattice of fixed, positive ions immersed in an electron gas. It is the attraction between the positively charged lattice and the negatively charged electron gas that results in bonding of the solid.[3]

To see how metallic bonding occurs, let us consider a specific simple example, bonding in solid lithium. The electron structure of the lithium atom is $1s^2 2s$ and the radial wave function of the $2s$ electron, which "sees" a hydrogenlike core consisting of the nucleus and the completed $1s$ shell, is

$$\psi_{20} = C_{20}\left(2 - \frac{r}{a_0}\right)e^{-r/2a_0} \qquad \textbf{10-8}$$

where C_{20} is a normalization constant and a_0 is the Bohr radius. The probability density corresponding to this wave function for a single lithium atom located at $r = 0$ is shown in one dimension in Figure 10-8a. The probability density decays exponentially to zero as r approaches $\pm\infty$. Figure 10-8b illustrates the probability density of the electrons in the metal, which must be the same around each Li ion core. The peaks of the probability density are now closer to the positive Li ion core than was the case for the isolated atom. Thus, the potential energy of the electrons has been reduced. However, the effect of assembling the atoms into a lattice has also been to effectively

Even hydrogen becomes a metal under ultrahigh pressure. The pressure reduces the conduction-valence band gap (see Section 10-6) from about 15 eV to 0.3 eV. Understanding metallic hydrogen will be of significant benefit in fusion energy research (see Section 12-2).

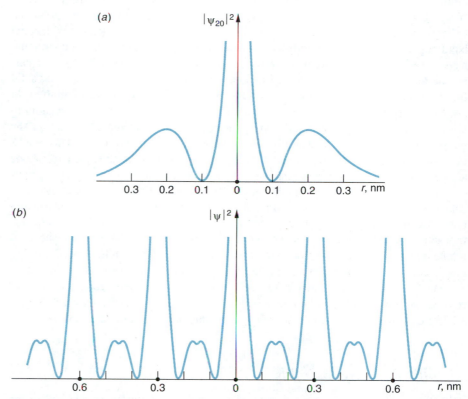

Fig. 10-8 (*a*) Probability density for the $2s$ electron in an isolated Li atom. (*b*) Probability density for the $2s$ electrons in a (one-dimensional) Li crystal. The large dots on the r axis represent Li nuclei. Note that $|\psi|^2$ is compressed relative to that of the single atom and that an electron is, on the average, confined to within about ± 0.3 nm of a Li nucleus, rather than between $\pm\infty$.

confine the electrons to within about ± 0.3 nm of the ion core, rather than the larger volume of the isolated atom. The uncertainty principle implies an increase in the momentum, hence kinetic energy, of the electrons. The metallic bond is stable because the rise in kinetic energy is more than offset by the decrease in the potential energy, thus lowering the total energy of the system of atoms. The net effect is greatest when the difference in size between the atom and the core is large (so that the magnitude of the potential energy reduction is large) and when the number of valence electrons is small (so that the increase in kinetic energy is as small as possible). These conditions are increasingly satisfied as one moves toward the left across the periodic table.

QUESTIONS

1. Why is r_0 different for solid NaCl than for the diatomic molecule?
2. Why would you not expect NaCl to have an hcp structure?
3. How can you account for the difference in the Madelung constants of NaCl and CsCl?
4. Although it is in the same column of the periodic table as Li, why is it that solid hydrogen is not metallically bonded?

10-2 Classical Theory of Conduction

Because metals conduct electricity so readily, there must be charges in metals that are relatively free to move. The idea that metals contain electrons free to move about through a lattice of relatively fixed positive ions was proposed by the German physicist Paul Drude around 1900, just three years after Thomson's discovery of the electron, and was developed by H. A. Lorentz about 1909. This microscopic model, now called the *classical model of electrical conduction,* successfully predicts Ohm's law and relates electrical conduction and heat conduction to the motion of free electrons in conductors. However, the model gives the wrong temperature dependence for electrical conductivity, and it predicts that the heat capacity of metals should be greater than that of insulators by $(3/2)R$ per mole, which is not observed. Despite these failures, the classical free-electron theory is a good starting point for a more sophisticated treatment of metals based on quantum mechanics. The main defects in the classical theory are the use of the classical Maxwell-Boltzmann distribution function for electrons in a metal and the treatment of the scattering of electrons by the lattice as a classical particle scattering.

In the Drude model, a metal is pictured as a regular three-dimensional array of atoms or ions with a large number of electrons free to move about the whole metal. In copper, for example, there is approximately one free electron per copper atom. The density of free electrons can be measured using the Hall effect (see Section 10-7). In the absence of an electric field, the free electrons move about the metal much like gas molecules in a container. Unlike an ordinary gas, however, thermal equilibrium is maintained by collisions of electrons with the lattice ions rather than by collisions of electrons with each other. Since the velocity vectors of the electrons are randomly oriented, the average velocity due to this thermal energy is zero. On the other hand, the speed of electrons is quite high and can be calculated from the equipartition theorem. The result is the same as that for ideal-gas molecules, with

the electron mass m_e instead of the molecular mass in Equation 8-30. For example, at temperature $T = 300$ K the mean speed is

$$\langle v \rangle = \sqrt{\frac{8kT}{\pi m_e}} = \sqrt{\frac{8(1.38 \times 10^{-23} \text{ J/K})(300 \text{ K})}{\pi (9.11 \times 10^{-31} \text{ kg})}} = 1.08 \times 10^5 \text{ m/s} \qquad \textbf{10-9}$$

Electrical Conduction

When an electric field is applied, for example, by connecting a wire to a battery which establishes a potential difference along the wire, the free electrons experience a momentary acceleration due to the force $-e\mathcal{E}$. The electrons acquire a small velocity in the direction opposite the field, but the kinetic energy acquired is quickly dissipated by collisions with the fixed ions in the wire. The electrons are then again accelerated by the field. The net result of this repeated acceleration and dissipation of energy is that the electrons have a small *drift velocity* $\mathbf{v}_d$ opposite to the electric field superimposed on their large random thermal velocity. The motion of the free electrons in a metal is analogous to that of the molecules of a gas such as air. In still air, the molecules move with large instantaneous velocities between collisions, but the average velocity is zero. When there is a breeze, the air molecules have a small drift velocity in the direction of the breeze superimposed on the much larger instantaneous velocity. This drift of negative charge opposite to the electric field constitutes an electric current along the field direction.

The current in a wire is the amount of charge passing through a cross-sectional area A per unit time. We can relate the current I to the number of electrons per unit volume n, the drift velocity $\mathbf{v}_d$, the charge on the electrons e, and the cross-sectional area A. We will assume that each electron moves with a drift velocity $\mathbf{v}_d$. In a time Δt all the particles in the volume $Av_d\Delta t$, shaded in Figure 10-9, pass through the area element. If the number of electrons per unit volume is n, the number in this volume is $nAv_d\Delta t$, and the total charge is

$$\Delta Q = enAv_d\Delta t$$

The current is thus

$$I = \frac{\Delta Q}{\Delta t} = neAv_d \qquad \textbf{10-10}$$

We can get an idea of the order of magnitude of the drift velocity for electrons in a conducting wire by putting typical magnitudes into Equation 10-10.

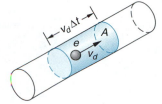

Fig. 10-9 In time Δt, all the charges in the shaded volume pass through A. If there are n charge carriers per unit volume, each with charge e, the total charge in this volume is $\Delta Q = nev_d A \, \Delta t$, where v_d is the drift velocity of the charge carriers. The total current is then $I = \Delta Q/\Delta t = nev_d A$.

EXAMPLE 10-4 Drift Velocity of Electrons in Copper What is the magnitude of the drift velocity of electrons in a typical copper wire of radius 0.815 mm carrying a current of 1 A?

Solution

If we assume one free electron per copper atom, the density of free electrons is the same as the density of atoms n_a, which is related to the mass density ρ, Avogadro's number N_A, and the molar mass M by

$$n_a = \frac{\rho N_A}{M}$$

For copper $\rho = 8.92$ g/cm^3 and $M = 63.5$ g/mol. Then

$$n_a = \frac{(8.93 \text{ g/cm}^3)(6.02 \times 10^{23} \text{ atoms/mol})}{63.5 \text{ g/mol}} = 8.47 \times 10^{22} \text{ atoms/cm}^3$$

The density of electrons is then

$$n = 8.47 \times 10^{22} \text{ electrons/cm}^3 = 8.47 \times 10^{28} \text{ electrons/m}^3$$

The magnitude of the drift velocity is therefore

$$\mathbf{v}_d = \frac{I}{Ane}$$

$$= \frac{1 \text{ C/s}}{\pi(0.000815 \text{ m})^2(8.47 \times 10^{28} \text{ m}^{-3})(1.6 \times 10^{-19} \text{ C})} \approx 3.54 \times 10^{-5} \text{ m/s}$$

We see that typical drift velocities are of the order of 0.01 mm/s, which is quite small. Notice in particular that the magnitude of the drift velocity is very small compared with the average speed of the electrons due to their thermal energy as given by Equation 10-9.

According to Ohm's law, the current in a conducting wire segment is proportional to the voltage drop across the segment.

$$I = \frac{V}{R}$$

where the resistance R does not depend on the current I or the voltage drop V. It is proportional to the length of the wire segment L and inversely proportional to the cross-sectional area A:

$$R = \rho \frac{L}{A}$$

where ρ is the resistivity. For a uniform electric field $\mathcal{E}$, the voltage drop across a segment of length L is $V = \mathcal{E}L$. Substituting $\rho L/A$ for R, and $\mathcal{E}L$ for V, we can write Ohm's law

$$I = \frac{V}{R} = \frac{\mathcal{E}L}{\rho \dfrac{L}{A}} = \frac{1}{\rho}\mathcal{E}A \qquad \textbf{10-11}$$

Recalling from introductory physics that the conductivity σ is the reciprocal of ρ and that the current density $j = I/A$, Equation 10-11 for Ohm's law can also be written

$$j = \sigma\mathcal{E} \qquad \textbf{10-12}$$

in terms of which the magnitude of the drift velocity can be written with the aid of Equation 10-10 as

$$v_d = \frac{j}{ne}$$

10-13

For materials that obey Ohm's law, the resistivity ρ and the conductivity σ must be independent of $\mathscr{E}$.

At first glance it is surprising that any material obeys Ohm's law since, in the presence of an electric field a free electron experiences a force of magnitude $e\mathscr{E}$. If this were the only force acting on the electron, it would have an acceleration $e\mathscr{E}/m_e$ and its velocity would steadily increase. However, Ohm's law implies that there is a steady-state situation in which the drift velocity of the electron is proportional to the field $\mathscr{E}$ because the current I is proportional to $\mathscr{E}$ (Equation 10-11) and also to v_d (Equation 10-10), i.e., $v_d = j/ne = \sigma\mathscr{E}/ne$. In the classical model, it is assumed that a free electron is accelerated for a short time and then collides with a lattice ion. After the collision, the velocity of the electron is assumed to be completely unrelated to that before the collision. The justification for this assumption is that, as we have seen, the drift velocity is very small compared to the average thermal velocity. The objective of the classical theory of conduction is to find an expression for ρ in terms of the properties of metals. Doing so is aided by the following consideration of the mean free path.

Mean Free Path λ

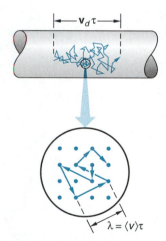

Let τ be the average time before an electron, picked at random, makes its next collision. Because the collisions are random, this time does not depend on the time elapsed since the electron's last collision. If we look at an electron immediately after it makes a collision, the average time before its next collision will be τ. Thus τ, called the *collision time* or the *relaxation time*, is the average time between collisions. It is also the average time since the *last* collision of an electron picked at random.[4] The drift velocity $\mathbf{v}_d$ is the average velocity of an electron picked at random since the average thermal velocity is zero. Since the acceleration is $e\mathscr{E}/m_e$, the drift velocity is

$$\mathbf{v}_d = e\,\frac{\mathscr{E}}{m_e}\tau$$

10-14

The average distance the electron travels between collisions is called the *mean free path* λ. It is the product of the average speed $\langle v \rangle$ and the average time between collisions τ (see Figure 10-10):

$$\lambda = \langle v \rangle \tau$$

In terms of the mean free path, the drift velocity is

$$\mathbf{v}_d = \frac{e\mathscr{E}\lambda}{m_e\langle v \rangle}$$

Fig. 10-10 Path of electron in a wire. Superimposed on the random thermal motion is a slow drift at speed $\mathbf{v}_d$ in the direction of the electric force $e\mathscr{E}$. The mean free path λ, the mean time between collisions τ, and the mean speed $\langle v \rangle$ are related by $\lambda = \langle v \rangle \tau$.

Using this result with Equation 10-10, we obtain

$$I = neAv_d = \frac{ne^2\lambda\mathcal{E}A}{m_e\langle v\rangle}$$ **10-15**

or

$$j = \frac{I}{A} = \frac{ne^2\lambda\mathcal{E}}{m_e\langle v\rangle}$$ **10-16**

Comparing these with Ohm's law, Equation 10-11 or 10-12, we have for the resistivity

$$\rho = \frac{m_e\langle v\rangle}{ne^2\lambda}$$ **10-17**

and for the conductivity

$$\sigma = \frac{1}{\rho} = \frac{ne^2\lambda}{m_e\langle v\rangle}$$ **10-18**

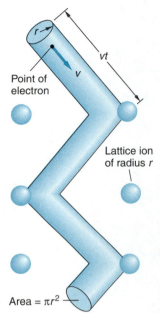

Fig. 10-11 Model of an electron moving through the lattice ions in copper. The electron, which is considered to be a point, collides with a lattice ion if it comes within a distance r of the center of the ion, where r is the radius of the ion. If the electron has speed v, it collides with all the ions in the cylindrical volume $\pi r^2 vt$ in time t.

We can relate the mean free path to the size of the ions in the metal lattice. Consider one electron moving with speed v through a region of stationary ions (Figure 10-11). Since this speed is related to its thermal energy, it is essentially unaffected by collisions. Assuming that the size of the electron is negligible, it will collide with an ion if it comes within a distance r from the center of the ion where r is the radius of the ion. In some time t, the electron moves a distance vt and collides with every ion in the cylindrical tube of volume $\pi r^2 vt$ surrounding the path of the electron. (After each collision, the direction of the electron changes so the path is really a zigzag one, like that shown in Figure 10-10.) The number of ions in this volume and hence the number of collisions in the time t is $n_a\pi r^2 vt$ where n_a is the number of ions per unit volume. The total path length divided by the number of collisions is the mean free path

$$\lambda = \frac{vt}{n_a\pi r^2 vt} = \frac{1}{n_a\pi r^2}$$ **10-19**

EXAMPLE 10-5 Mean Free Path and Relaxation Time of Electrons Estimate the mean free path and the relaxation time of electrons in copper.

Solution

1. The mean free path λ is related to the number of copper ions per unit volume n_a and the radius r of a copper ion by Equation 10-19:

$$\lambda = \frac{1}{n_a\pi r^2}$$

2. The number of copper ions per unit volume was computed in Example 10-4:

$$n_a = 8.47 \times 10^{22} \text{ ions/cm}^3$$

3. Using $r \approx 10^{-10}$ m $= 10^{-8}$ cm as the radius of a copper ion, substituting these into Equation 10-19 gives:

$$\lambda = \frac{1}{\pi(8.47 \times 10^{22} \text{ ions/cm}^3)(10^{-8} \text{ cm})^2}$$

$$= 3.8 \times 10^{-8} \text{cm} = 3.8 \times 10^{-10} \text{m} = 0.38 \text{ nm}$$

4. The relaxation time τ is given by Equation 10-14. In terms of the mean free path λ and the average speed $\langle v \rangle$ of the ions, this is:

$$\lambda = \langle v \rangle \tau \qquad \text{or} \qquad \tau = \frac{\lambda}{\langle v \rangle}$$

5. Substituting λ from above and the value of $\langle v \rangle$ for copper ions computed in Equation 10-9, we have that:

$$\tau = \frac{3.8 \times 10^{-10} \text{ m}}{1.1 \times 10^5 \text{ m/s}} = 3.5 \times 10^{-15} \text{ s}$$

EXAMPLE 10-6 Conductivity and Resistivity of Copper Calculate the values of the resistivity and the conductivity of copper at 300 K.

Solution
Using either Equation 10-17 or 10-18 together with the results of Example 10-5, we have

$$\rho = \frac{m_e \langle v \rangle}{ne^2 \lambda} = \frac{m_e}{ne^2 \tau}$$

$$= \frac{9.11 \times 10^{-31} \text{ kg}}{(8.47 \times 10^{28} \text{ electrons/m}^3)(1.60 \times 10^{-19} \text{ C})^2(3.5 \times 10^{-15} \text{ s})}$$

$$= 1.20 \times 10^{-7} \Omega \cdot \text{m}$$

and $\sigma = 1/\rho = 8.33 \times 10^6 \ (\Omega \cdot \text{m})^{-1}$.

This value for the resistivity is about 7 times greater than the measured value of $1.7 \times 10^{-8} \ \Omega \cdot \text{m}$. We return to this discrepancy in Section 10-4.

Defects in the Classical Theory

With the average speed given by Equation 10-9 and the mean free path by Equation 10-19, the resistivity has been expressed in terms of the properties of metals, which was the objective of the classical theory of conduction. According to Ohm's law, the resistivity is independent of the electric field $\mathcal{E}$. The quantities in Equation 10-17 that might depend on the electric field are the average speed $\langle v \rangle$ and the mean free path λ.

As we have seen, the drift velocity is very much smaller than the average thermal speed of the electrons in equilibrium with the lattice ions. Thus the electric field has essentially no effect on the average speed of the electrons. The mean free path of the electrons depends on the size of the lattice ions and on the density of the ions, neither of which depends on the electric field $\mathscr{E}$. Thus the classical model predicts Ohm's law with the resistivity as given by Equation 10-17.

Although successful in predicting Ohm's law, the classical theory of conduction has several defects. We saw from Example 10-6 that the magnitude of the resistivity of copper calculated from Equation 10-17 is about 7 times the measured value at $T = 300$ K. The temperature dependence of ρ is also not correct. Experimentally, the resistivity varies linearly with temperature over a wide range of temperatures. The temperature dependence of resistivity in Equation 10-17 is given completely by the speed $\langle v \rangle$, which according to Equation 10-9 is proportional to $T^{1/2}$. Thus this calculation does not give a linear dependence on temperature. Finally, the classical model says nothing about why some materials are conductors, others insulators, and still others semiconductors.

In the quantum-mechanical theory of electrical conduction, which is discussed in Section 10-4, the resistivity is again given by Equation 10-17, but the average speed and the mean free path are interpreted in terms of quantum theory. We discovered in Section 8-5 that the average energy of the electrons, hence their average speed, is not proportional to $T^{1/2}$, but is approximately independent of T because electrons do not obey the Boltzmann distribution law, but instead obey the Fermi-Dirac distribution. Also, in the quantum-mechanical calculation of the mean free path the wave nature of the electron is important and must be taken into account.

Heat Capacity

If the electron gas were a classical ensemble of identical distinguishable particles, it would obey Boltzmann statistics (see Chapter 8) and have the Maxwell distribution of speeds. It should then have an average kinetic energy $(3/2)kT$ and we would expect the molar heat capacity of a metal to be $(3/2)R$ greater than that of an insulator—that is, $3R$ from the lattice vibrations (rule of Dulong and Petit—see Section 8-1) and $(3/2)R$ from the electron gas.

$$C_v = (3R)_{\text{lattice vibrations}} + (3/2)R_{\text{electron gas}} = (9/2)R$$

As was noted in Section 8-5, this is not observed. The molar heat capacity of metals is very nearly $3R$. At higher temperatures it is slightly greater, but the increase is nowhere near $(3/2)R$ predicted by the classical theory. The increase is, in fact, proportional to temperature, and at $T = 300$ K it is only about $0.02R$.

More

Good conductors of electricity are also good conductors of heat. Classical physics accounts for this with a theory based on a simple model, as described in *Thermal Conduction—The Classical Model* on the home page: www.whfreeman.com/modphysics4e   See also Equations 10-20 through 10-28 here, as well as Figure 10-12, Table 10-2, and Questions 5 and 6.

10-3 Free-Electron Gas in Metals

Classically, at $T = 0$, all the electrons in a metal would have zero kinetic energy. As a conductor is heated, the lattice ions acquire an average kinetic energy of $(3/2)kT$, which is imparted to the electron gas by interactions of the lattice with the electrons. The electrons classically would be expected to have a mean kinetic energy of $(3/2)kT$ in equilibrium. Quantum mechanically, however, since the electrons are confined to the space occupied by the metal, it is clear from the uncertainty principle that even at $T = 0$ an electron cannot have zero kinetic energy. Furthermore, the exclusion principle prevents more than two electrons (with opposite spins) from being in the lowest energy level. At $T = 0$, we expect the electrons to have the lowest energies consistent with the exclusion principle. It is instructive to consider a one-dimensional model first.

One-Dimensional Model

To simplify visualization, let us first consider N electrons in a one-dimensional infinite square well of width L. The physical analog of such a model could be a long, thin metal wire. As we have seen previously, the allowed energies are given by

$$E_n = \frac{n^2 h^2}{8mL^2} = n^2 E_1 \qquad \textbf{10-29}$$

where m is the electron mass and $E_1 = h^2/8mL^2$ is the energy of the ground state. Since two electrons can be put in the $n = 1$ level, two in the $n = 2$ level, etc., at $T = 0$, the N electrons in the system will fill $N/2$ levels, i.e., from the $n = 1$ to the $n = N/2$ states. (See Figure 10-13a.) The energy of the last filled level (or half-filled level, if N happens to be odd) is the Fermi energy, which for our one-dimensional system is

$$E_F = E_{N/2} = \frac{(N/2)^2 h^2}{8mL^2} = \frac{h^2}{32m}\left(\frac{N}{L}\right)^2 \qquad \textbf{10-30}$$

We see that the Fermi energy is a function of the number of electrons per unit length, which is the *number density* or number per unit volume in one dimension. The number density of electrons in copper, computed in Example 10-4, is $8.47 \times 10^{28}/\text{m}^3$. In one dimension this corresponds to

Fig. 10-13 (*a*) A one-dimensional infinite square well for N electrons at $T = 0$ K. Two electrons, one with spin up and one with spin down, occupy each level. The Fermi energy is the energy of the level with $n = N/2$, the highest occupied level. (*b*) The levels are so closely spaced they can be assumed to be continuous. The density of states $g(E)$ is the number of states between E and $E + dE$ divided by dE.

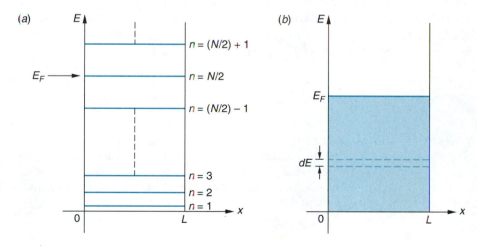

$$\frac{N}{L} = (8.47 \times 10^{28}/\text{m}^3)^{1/3} = 4.40 \times 10^9/\text{m} = 0.440/\text{Å} = 4.40/\text{nm}$$

Using this value, we see that the Fermi energy for a one-dimensional copper system, such as a wire, is

$$E_F = \frac{(hc)^2}{32mc^2}\left(\frac{N}{L}\right)^2 = \frac{(1240 \text{ eV} \cdot \text{nm})^2 (4.40 \text{ nm})^2}{(32)(5.11 \times 10^5 \text{ eV})} = 1.82 \text{ eV}$$

This value is much larger than the room temperature value of kT, which is about 0.026 eV. The average energy of the electrons is the total energy divided by N:

$$\langle E \rangle = \frac{1}{N} \sum_{n=1}^{N/2} 2n^2 E_1$$

where the factor of 2 accounts for the two electrons in each energy state. Since $N/2 \gg 1$, the summation can be replaced by an integral, so we have that

$$\langle E \rangle = \frac{E_1}{N} \int_0^{N/2} 2n^2 \, dn = \frac{E_1}{N}\frac{2}{3}\left(\frac{N}{2}\right)^3 = \frac{h^2}{8mL^2}\frac{2}{3N}\left(\frac{N}{2}\right)^3 = \frac{1}{3}E_F \qquad \textbf{10-31}$$

Our one-dimensional calculation thus gives an average energy for copper's free electrons of about 0.6 eV at $T = 0$. This is 15 times the room-temperature average kinetic energy of molecules in the atmosphere. The temperature at which the average energy would be 0.6 eV for a one-dimensional Boltzmann distribution is about 14,000 K, obtained from $\frac{1}{2}kT = 0.6$ eV.

The expression for the number $n(E)$ of electrons with energy E in the one-dimensional system follows from Equation 8-61c.

$$n(E) \, dE = g(E)f_{FD}(E) \, dE$$

where $f_{FD}(E) = 1$ for $T = 0$ K and $E < E_F$ and $f_{FD}(E) = 0$ for $T = 0$ K and $E > E_F$. The density of states $g(E)$ is the number dn of states between E and $E + dE$ divided by dE and multiplied by 2 to account for the two spin states per space state (see Figure 10-13b):

$$g(E) = 2\frac{dn}{dE}$$

Since $E = n^2 E_1$, then $dE = 2E_1 n \, dn = 2E_1^{1/2}E^{1/2} \, dn$, and we have that

$$g(E) = E_1^{-1/2}E^{-1/2}$$

The number of electrons with energy E at $T = 0$ K in the one-dimensional conductor is then

$$n(E) = \begin{cases} E_1^{-1/2} E^{-1/2} & \text{for} \quad E < E_F \\ 0 & \text{for} \quad E > E_F \end{cases} \qquad \textbf{10-32}$$

Three-Dimensional Electron Gas

Now let us extend the discussion to three-dimensional systems. The Fermi energy can be computed from the general expression for the number of fermions $n_{FD}(E)$ given by Equation 8-61c. The number density N/V of electrons in three dimensions, where V is the volume of the metal, is

$$\frac{N}{V} = \frac{1}{V}\int_0^\infty n_{FD}(E)\,dE = \frac{\pi}{2}\left(\frac{8m}{h^2}\right)^{3/2}\int_0^\infty \frac{E^{1/2}\,dE}{e^{(E-E_F)/kT}+1} \qquad \textbf{10-33}$$

For arbitrary values of T, Equation 10-33 must be evaluated numerically, but for $T = 0$ K the solution is straightforward since, as noted above, $f_{FD}(E) = 0$ or 1 as E is greater than or less than E_F. In that event we have that

$$\frac{N}{V} = \frac{\pi}{2}\left(\frac{8m}{h^2}\right)^{3/2}\int_0^{E_F} E^{1/2}\,dE = \frac{\pi}{2}\left(\frac{8m}{h^2}\right)^{3/2}\frac{2}{3}E_F^{3/2} \qquad \textbf{10-34}$$

Solving for E_F we have for $T = 0$ K that

$$E_F = \frac{h^2}{2m}\left(\frac{3N}{8\pi V}\right)^{2/3} \qquad \textbf{10-35}$$

Table 10-3 lists the number density of free electrons for several elements. Notice that E_F increases slowly with N/V, as would be expected at $T = 0$ K, since all states up to

TABLE 10-3	Free-electron number densities, Fermi energies, and Fermi temperatures for selected elements		
Element	N/V ($\times\,10^{28}$ m^{-3})	Fermi energy (eV)	Fermi temperature ($\times\,10^4$ K)
Al	18.1	11.7	13.6
Ag	5.86	5.53	6.41
Au	5.90	5.55	6.43
Cu	8.47	7.06	8.19
Fe	17.0	11.2	13.0
K	1.40	2.13	2.47
Li	4.70	4.77	5.53
Mg	8.61	7.14	8.28
Mn	16.5	11.0	12.8
Na	2.65	3.26	3.78
Sn	14.8	10.3	11.9
Zn	13.2	9.50	11.0

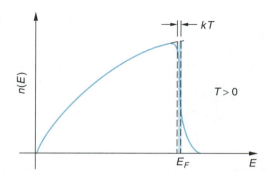

Fig. 10-14 The fraction of the N electrons in the metal that contribute to C_v is the ratio of the shaded rectangle to the total area under the $n(E)$ vs. E curve.

E_F are being filled and an increasing N/V requires more states to be filled, i.e., a larger value of E_F. The number $n(E)$ of electrons with energy E is then given by

$$n(E) = \frac{\pi}{2}\left(\frac{8m}{h^2}\right)^{3/2} VE^{1/2} = \frac{3N}{2}E_F^{-3/2}E^{1/2} \qquad \textbf{10-36}$$

and the average energy of an electron at $T = 0$ K by

$$\langle E \rangle = \frac{1}{N}\int_0^{E_F} En(E)\, dE = \frac{3}{2}E_F^{-3/2}\int_0^{E_F} E^{3/2}\, dE = \frac{3}{5}E_F \qquad \textbf{10-37}$$

At temperatures greater than zero, some electrons will gain energy and occupy higher energy states. However, electrons cannot move to a higher or lower energy state unless the state is unoccupied. Since the kinetic energy of the lattice ions is of the order of kT, electrons cannot gain much more energy than kT in collisions with the lattice; therefore only those electrons with energies within about kT of the Fermi energy can gain energy as the temperature is increased. At $T = 300$ K, kT is only 0.026 eV, so the exclusion principle prevents all but a very few electrons near the top of the energy distribution from gaining energy by random collisions. Figure 10-14 shows the small fraction of the free electrons that move at $T = 300$ K (shaded area between the $T = 0$ K and $T = 300$ K curves). Even for temperatures as high as several thousand degrees, the energy distribution of an electron gas does not differ very much from that at $T = 0$ K.

For values of $T > 0$ we must remember that the Fermi energy is defined by Equation 8-92, since for $T > 0$ there is no state below which all states are full and above which all states are empty. Equation 8-92 defines the Fermi energy as that energy for which $f_{FD}(E) = \frac{1}{2}$. For all but extremely high temperatures, the difference between the Fermi energy at temperature T, $E_F(T)$, and that at $T = 0$ K, $E_F(0)$, is essentially negligible. As is clear from Equation 8-92 and Figure 8-33b, the value of $f_{FD}(E)$ at arbitrary T differs from that at $T = 0$ K only for those energies within about kT of the Fermi energy.

Fermi Temperature

It is convenient to define the *Fermi temperature* T_F by

$$E_F = kT_F \qquad \textbf{10-38}$$

For temperatures much lower than the Fermi temperature, the average energy of the lattice ions will be much less than the Fermi energy; thus the electron energy

distribution will not differ greatly from that at $T = 0$. The Fermi temperature corresponding to $E_F = 7.0$ eV for copper is about 81,000 K. Table 10-3 lists the Fermi temperatures for several elements. At temperatures much larger than the Fermi temperature (i.e., much larger than 81,000 K for copper) $f_{FD}(E)$ can be shown to approach $e^{-E/kT}$ and the Fermi-Dirac distribution approaches the Boltzmann distribution. This result is not very important for the understanding of the behavior of conductors since there are no conductors that remain as solids or even liquids at such extreme temperatures.

EXAMPLE 10-7 Fermi Energy and Temperature of Silver Compute (*a*) the Fermi energy and (*b*) the Fermi temperature for silver at 0 K.

Solution
The density of silver is 10.50 g/cm³ and its molecular weight is 107.9 g/mol. Assuming that each silver atom contributes one electron to the Fermi gas, the number density N/V is computed as follows:

$$\frac{N}{V} = (10.50 \text{ g/cm}^3)(1/107.9 \text{ g/mol})(6.02 \times 10^{23} \text{ electrons/mol})$$

$$= 5.86 \times 10^{22} \text{ electrons/cm}^3 = 5.86 \times 10^{28} \text{ electrons/m}^3$$

Which agrees with the entry in Table 10-3.

(*a*) The Fermi energy is then, from Equation 10-35,

$$E_F = \frac{(6.63 \times 10^{-34} \text{ J·s})^2}{2(9.11 \times 10^{-31} \text{ kg})} \left(\frac{3 \times 5.86 \times 10^{28}}{8\pi}\right)^{2/3}$$

$$= 8.84 \times 10^{-19} \text{ J} = 5.53 \text{ eV}$$

in agreement with the entry for Ag in Table 10-3.

(*b*) The Fermi temperature is then

$$T_F = \frac{E_F}{k} = \frac{8.84 \times 10^{-19} \text{ J}}{1.38 \times 10^{-23} \text{ J/K}} = 6.41 \times 10^4 \text{ K}$$

again, in agreement with Table 10-3.

10-4 Quantum Theory of Conduction

With two relatively simple but important quantum-mechanical modifications of the classical free-electron theory, we can understand the electrical conductivity, heat capacity, and thermal conductivity of metals. First, we must replace the classical Boltzmann distribution with the Fermi distribution of energies in the electron gas, as was discussed in Section 8-5. Second, we must consider the effect of the wave properties of the electrons on their scattering by the lattice ions. We will discuss the latter modification qualitatively.

Electrical Conduction

We might expect that most of the electrons would not participate in the conduction of electricity because of the exclusion principle, but this is not the case, because the electric field accelerates all the electrons together. Figure 10-15 shows the Fermi-Dirac distribution function versus velocity for some temperature T that is small compared with T_F (such as $T = 300$ K). The function is approximately 1 for $-u_F < v_x < +u_F$, where the *Fermi speed* u_F is the speed corresponding to the Fermi energy

$$u_F = \left(\frac{2E_F}{m_e}\right)^{1/2} \qquad \textbf{10-39}$$

EXAMPLE 10-8 Fermi Speed in Al   Compute the Fermi speed of electrons in aluminum.

Solution
From Table 10-3, the Fermi energy E_F of Al is 11.7 eV. Thus,

$$u_F(\text{Al}) = \left(\frac{2 \times 11.7 \text{ eV} \times 1.60 \times 10^{-19} \text{ J/eV}}{9.11 \times 10^{-31} \text{ kg}}\right)^{1/2} = 2.03 \times 10^6 \text{ m/s}$$

The dashed curve in Figure 10-15 shows the Fermi distribution after the electric field has been acting for some time t. Although all of the electrons have been shifted to higher velocities, the net effect is equivalent to shifting only the electrons near the Fermi level; therefore, we can use the classical equations for the resistivity (Equation 10-17) and conductivity (Equation 10-18) if we use the Fermi speed u_F in place of $\langle v \rangle$:

$$\rho = \frac{1}{\sigma} = \frac{m_e u_F}{ne^2 \lambda} \qquad \textbf{10-40}$$

We now have two problems. First, since u_F is independent of temperature (to a very good approximation), the above expression for σ and ρ is independent of temperature, unless the mean free path depends on it. The second problem concerns the magnitudes. We saw in Example 10-6 that the classical expression for σ yielded a result that was too small by a factor of 7, using $\langle v \rangle$ calculated from the Maxwell-Boltzmann distribution. Since u_F is about 19 times the value of $\langle v \rangle$, the magnitude of σ predicted from Equation 10-40 will be even smaller by another factor of 19 and the magnitude of ρ will, correspondingly, be larger than the observed value by the same factor.

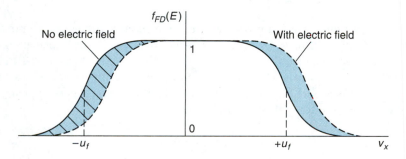

Fig. 10-15 Occupation probability $f_{FD}(E)$ vs. velocity in one dimension, with no electric field and with an electric field in the $+x$ direction. The difference is greatly exaggerated.

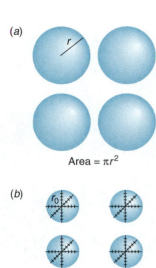

(a)

Area = πr^2

(b)

Area = $\pi \overline{r^2}$

Fig. 10-16 (*a*) Classical picture of the lattice ions as spherical balls of radius *r* that present an area πr^2 to the electrons. (*b*) Quantum-mechanical picture of the lattice ions as points that are vibrating in three dimensions. The area presented to the electrons is πr_0^2, where r_0 is the amplitude of oscillation of the ions.

The resolution of both of these problems lies in the way that the value of the mean free path is calculated. If we use u_F from Equation 10-39 and the experimental value $\rho \approx 1.7 \times 10^{-8} \ \Omega \cdot m$ for copper in Equation 10-40, we obtain for the mean free path $\lambda \approx 39$ nm, about 100 times the value of 0.38 nm that was calculated from Equation 10-19 in Example 10-5 using 0.1 nm as the radius of the Cu ions.

We shouldn't be too surprised that the mean free path of electrons in the copper lattice is not given correctly by classical kinetic theory. The reason for this large discrepancy between the classical calculation of the mean free path and the "experimental" result calculated from Equation 10-40 is that the wave nature of the electron must be taken into account. The collision of an electron with a lattice ion is not similar to the collision of a baseball and a tree. Instead, it involves the scattering of the electron wave by the regularly spaced ions of the lattice. If the wavelength is long compared with the crystal spacing, as is approximately the case here, Bragg scattering cannot occur. Detailed calculations of the scattering of electron waves by a *perfectly* ordered crystal of infinite extent show that there is *no scattering*, and the mean free path is infinite. The scattering of electron waves arises from imperfections in the crystal lattice. The most common imperfections are due to impurities or to thermal vibrations of the lattice ions.

In Equation 10-19 for the classical mean free path, the quantity πr^2 can be thought of as the cross-sectional area of the lattice ions as seen by the electron, where *r* is the ion radius. Figure 10-16*a* depicts the classical picture in which the lattice ions have area πr^2. According to quantum mechanics applied to the scattering of electron waves, however, the "area" of the ion's cross section seen by the electron wave has nothing to do with the size of the ion. Instead, it depends upon the *deviations* of the lattice ions from a perfectly ordered array. We can estimate the magnitude of the deviations and thus compute a more accurate value for the mean free path as follows.

Let us assume that the lattice ions are *points* which are vibrating because of their thermal energy. (See Figure 10-16*b*.) We shall take for the scattering cross section $\pi \overline{r^2}$, where $\overline{r^2} = \overline{x^2} + \overline{y^2}$ is the mean-square displacement of the point atom in a plane perpendicular to the direction of the electron and represents a measure of the deviation of the ion from its equilibrium location. We can calculate $\overline{r^2}$ from the equipartition theorem. We have

$$\frac{1}{2} K \overline{r^2} = \frac{1}{2} M \omega^2 \overline{r^2} = kT \qquad \textbf{10-41}$$

where K is the force constant, *M* the mass of the ion, and $\omega = (K/M)^{1/2}$ is the angular frequency of vibration. The mean free path is then

$$\lambda = \frac{1}{n \pi \overline{r^2}} = \frac{M \omega^2}{2 \pi n k} \frac{1}{T} \qquad \textbf{10-42}$$

We thus see that this argument gives the correct temperature dependence for σ and ρ; that is, $\rho \propto T$ rather than $\rho \propto T^{1/2}$, as was obtained from the classical calculation.

We can then calculate the magnitude of $\overline{r^2}$, and therefore λ, using the Einstein model of a solid, which is fairly accurate except at very low temperatures. In the Einstein model (see Section 8-4) all the atoms vibrate with the same frequency. The Einstein temperature was defined by Equation 8-87 as

$$kT_E = hf = \hbar \omega$$

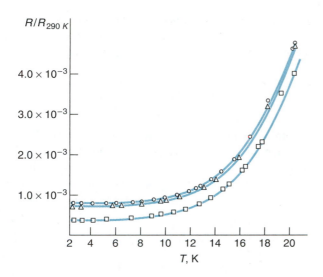

Fig. 10-17 Relative resistance vs. temperature for three samples of sodium. The three curves have the same temperature dependence but have different magnitudes because of differing amounts of impurities in the samples. [*From D. MacDonald and K. Mendelssohn,* Proceedings of the Royal Society, *A202, 103 (1950).*]

Using this for ω, we have

$$\overline{r^2} = \frac{2kT}{M\omega^2} = \frac{2T\hbar^2}{MkT_E^2} = \frac{2(\hbar c)^2}{Mc^2 kT_E}\frac{T}{T_E} \qquad \textbf{10-43}$$

The Einstein temperature for copper is about 200 K, corresponding to an energy of $kT_E = 0.0172$ eV. Using this and $Mc^2 = 63.5 \times 931$ MeV for the mass of a copper ion, the value of $\overline{r^2}$ at $T = 300$ K is

$$\overline{r^2} = \frac{2(197.3\text{ eV} \cdot \text{nm})^2}{(63.5 \times 931 \times 10^6\text{ eV})(0.0172\text{ eV})}\frac{300\text{ K}}{200\text{ K}} = 1.14 \times 10^{-4}\text{ nm}^2$$

Since this is about 100 times smaller than the area presented by a copper ion of radius 0.1 nm, the mean free path is about 100 times larger than that calculated from the classical model, in agreement with that calculated from the measured value of the conductivity. We see, therefore, that the free-electron model of metals gives a good account of electrical conduction if the classical average speed is replaced by the Fermi speed u_F and if collisions are interpreted in terms of the scattering of electron waves for which only deviations from a perfectly ordered lattice are important.

The presence of impurities in a metal also causes deviations from perfect regularity in the crystal. The effects of impurities on resistivity are approximately independent of temperature. The resistivity of a metal containing impurities can be written $\rho = \rho_t + \rho_I$, where ρ_t is due to the thermal motion of the lattice and ρ_I is due to impurities. Figure 10-17 shows a typical resistance versus temperature curve for a metal with impurities. As the temperature approaches zero, ρ_t approaches zero and the resistivity approaches the constant ρ_I.

Heat Capacity

Let us estimate the contribution of the electron gas to the molar heat capacity. At $T = 0$, the average energy of the electrons, given by Equation 10-37, is $(3/5)E_F$, so the total energy for N electrons is $U = (3/5)NE_F$. At a temperature T, only those electrons near the Fermi level can be excited by random collisions with the lattice ions, which have an

average energy of the order of kT. The fraction of the electrons that are excited is of the order kT/E_F, and their energy is increased from that at $T = 0$ by an amount of the order of kT. We can thus write for the energy of the N electrons at temperature T

$$U = \frac{3}{5} NE_F + \alpha N \frac{kT}{E_F} kT \qquad \textbf{10-44}$$

where α is some constant, which we expect to be of the order of 1 if our reasoning is correct. The calculation of α requires the use of the complete Fermi electron distribution at an arbitrary temperature T and is quite difficult. Such a calculation, first carried out by Sommerfeld, shows that this equation is correct with $\alpha = \pi^2/4$. Using this result, the contribution of the electrons to the molar heat capacity is

$$C_v(\text{electrons}) = \frac{dU}{dT} = 2\alpha Nk \frac{kT}{E_F} = \frac{\pi^2}{2} R \frac{T}{T_F} \qquad \textbf{10-45}$$

where $Nk = R$ for 1 mole and $T_F = E_F/k$ is the Fermi temperature. We see that because of the large value of T_F, the contribution of the electron gas is a small fraction of R at ordinary temperatures. Using $T_F = 81,900$ K for copper, the molar heat capacity of the electron gas at $T = 300$ K is

$$C_v = \frac{\pi^2}{2} \left(\frac{300}{81,900} \right) R = 0.018\, R$$

which is in reasonable agreement with the value estimated from Figure 10-14 and in good agreement with experiment.

More

Quantum theory readily accounts for heat conduction, predicting results in good agreement with observations. *Thermal Conduction—The Quantum Model* is outlined briefly on the home page: www.whfreeman.com/modphysics4e See also Equations 10-46 and 10-47 here.

QUESTIONS

7. When the temperature is lowered from 300 K to 4 K, the resistivity of pure copper drops by a much greater factor than that of brass. Why?

8. Explain why, physically, you would expect the mean free path of electrons in a metal to decrease as the temperature increases.

10-5 Magnetism in Solids

Electron spins with their associated magnetic moments are the origin of magnetism in solids. If the atoms of the solid have unpaired spins, the solid itself may have a net magnetic moment. Since the atoms are effectively fixed in one or another of several

crystalline structures, the interactions between them may have a substantial effect on the magnetism exhibited by the solid. Several types of magnetism are observed in solids, *ferromagnetism* being perhaps the most familiar, though hardly the most common among elements and compounds. In this section we will describe each of the several types.

Paramagnetism

Consider a solid consisting of atoms that each have an unpaired electron spin, that is, each atom has a net spin of $1/2$ (actually $\sqrt{3/4}\,\hbar$, of course) and the atoms do not interact magnetically. Examples of such solids are the rare earth elements and many of the transition elements. In that event, the only magnetic energy the system may have results from interaction with an applied external field $\mathbf{B}$. Such a solid, one with no net magnetic moment in the absence of an applied external field, is called *paramagnetic*.

The magnetic moment of each atom is thus that of the unpaired electron $\boldsymbol{\mu} = g_s \mu_s \mathbf{s}/\hbar$. Its z component is given by Equation 7-49:

$$\mu_z = -m_s g_s \mu_B \qquad\qquad \textbf{7-49}$$

where g_s is the g factor for the electron and μ_B is the Bohr magneton. In an applied field $\mathbf{B}$ the possible energies of the magnetic moment are

$$U = -\mu_z B \qquad\qquad \textbf{7-47}$$

or

$$U = m_s g_s \mu_B B \qquad\qquad \textbf{10-48}$$

Since $m_s = \pm 1/2$, the $m_s = -1/2$ orientation of $\mathbf{s}$ (called "spin down," because $\mathbf{s}$ is antiparallel to $\mathbf{B}$) is of lower energy than the $m_s = +1/2$ orientation (called "spin up," of course). Thus, in a thermal distribution the spin-down states will contain more atoms than the spin-up states and the solid will have a net magnetic moment per unit volume $\mathbf{M}$ whose magnitude is given by

$$M = \mu\,(\rho_+ - \rho_-)$$

where ρ_+ and ρ_- are the densities of electrons with spin up and spin down, respectively. Since $\rho_- > \rho_+$ and μ is negative, M is positive. For sufficiently small fields $\mathbf{M}$ is proportional to $\mathbf{B}$.

$$\mu_0 \mathbf{M} = \chi \mathbf{B} \qquad\qquad \textbf{10-49}$$

where χ is called the *magnetic susceptibility*. For high temperatures such that $\mu B \ll kT$, it can be shown that (see Problem 10-57)

$$\chi = \frac{\mu_0 M}{B} = \frac{\rho \mu^2}{kT} \qquad\qquad \textbf{10-50}$$

where $\rho = (\rho_+ + \rho_-)$ is the total electron density. Equation 10-50 is known as *Curie's law*, after Pierre Curie. Thus, as T increases, the ability of the magnetic field to align the spins decreases. Many solids exhibit Curie's law behavior. For low temperatures

where $\mu B \gg kT$, $M \rightarrow \mu\rho$ as $T \rightarrow 0$, corresponding to the alignment of all the magnetic moments with the field.

Equation 10-50 does not apply to the magnetism arising from electrons in metals. The reason is that $T \ll T_F$, since $T_F = 10^4 - 10^5$ K for metals. Thus, the electrons are highly degenerate, each allowed level containing two with paired spins. When an external **B** field is applied, spins cannot just "flip" to align with the field, since doing so would violate the exclusion principle. A spin flip must be accompanied by raising that electron to a higher, unoccupied energy state. Thus, even at $T = 0$ K, metals have a finite susceptibility. This type of magnetic behavior is called *Pauli paramagnetism*.

Diamagnetism

Recall that a free electron moving perpendicular to a magnetic field experiences a magnetic force $\mathbf{F} = -e(\mathbf{v} \times \mathbf{B})$. The resulting circular motion produces a current loop with a magnetic moment *opposite* to the direction of the applied field. (To see this, use the right-hand rule.) Now consider two electrons with paired spins orbiting in opposite directions in an atom. (See Figure 10-18.) If an external **B** field perpendicular to the plane of the orbits is turned on, the net force ($\mathbf{F}_{\text{Coulomb}} - \mathbf{F}_{\text{magnetic}}$) on electron 1 is reduced, reducing its *orbital* magnetic moment, which is parallel to **B**. The net force on electron 2 is increased, increasing its magnetic moment. The result is a net magnetic moment opposite to the direction of the applied field. This magnetic behavior is called *diamagnetism*. The diamagnetic effect is seen only in solids consisting of atoms whose electron spins are all paired. As we will see in Section 10-9, the "test" of superconductivity is that the material exhibit perfect diamagnetism.

Fig. 10-18 Electrons 1 and 2 orbit the atomic core (not shown) in opposite directions. The magnetic field **B** is perpendicular to the plane of the orbits. The magnetic forces $\mathbf{F}_1$ and $\mathbf{F}_2$ increase the orbital magnetic moment of electron 2 and decrease that of electron 1, resulting in a net moment opposite to **B**.

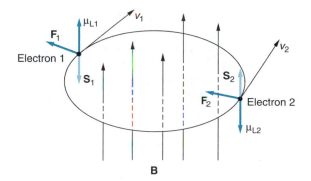

Ferromagnetism

The first magnetic effect discovered, a result of its existence in iron which led to its early use as a compass, *ferromagnetism* is the consequence of a phase transition in certain materials. At high temperatures a piece of iron is unmagnetized, the spin directions of the atoms having rotational symmetry—all spin directions are equally probable. (In an applied **B** field, iron is paramagnetic at high temperatures.) As the temperature decreases, at a certain temperature T_C, called the *Curie temperature,* the magnetic interaction between the atoms exceeds the randomizing effect of thermal agitation, spontaneously breaking the rotational symmetry and causing a phase transition in the solid that tends to align the spins parallel to each other, converting the sample into a permanent magnet. Only four elements besides iron exhibit ferromagnetism:

nickel, cobalt, gadolinium, and dysprosium. There are also several ferromagnetic compounds, including some that contain none of the ferromagnetic elements.

In certain compounds the magnetic interaction between the atoms tends to align the spins on adjacent atoms antiparallel below a certain temperature, analogous to the Curie temperature, called the *Neel temperature, T_N*. Such materials are called *antiferromagnetic*. Examples are FeO, $NiCl_2$, MnO, and MnS. In a few other materials the spins on adjacent sites are antiparallel below T_N, but because they contain two different types of positive ions, the spins do not exactly cancel and the material is left with a small net magnetization. Such materials are called *ferrimagnetic*. The most common example is the iron ore magnetite, $FeO \cdot Fe_2O_3$.

10-6 Band Theory of Solids

We have seen that, if the electron gas is treated as a Fermi gas and the electron-lattice collisions treated as the scattering of electron waves, the free-electron model gives a good account of the electrical and thermal properties of conductors. This simple model, however, gives no indication of why one material is a good conductor and another is an insulator. The conductivity (and its reciprocal, the resistivity) vary enormously from the best insulators to the best conductors. For example, the resistivity of a typical insulator (such as quartz) is of the order of $10^{16} \ \Omega \cdot m$, whereas that of a typical conductor (most metals) is of the order of $10^{-8} \ \Omega \cdot m$ and that of a superconductor is less than $10^{-19} \ \Omega \cdot m$.

To understand why some materials conduct and others do not, we must refine the free-electron model and consider the effect of the lattice on the electron energy levels. There are two standard approaches to this problem of determining the energy levels of electrons in a crystal. One is to consider the problem of an electron moving in a periodic potential, and to determine the possible energies by solving the Schrödinger equation. The other is to determine the energy levels of the electrons in a solid by following the behavior of the energy levels of individual atoms as they are brought together to form the solid, in much the same way that we did in Section 9-2 in the explanation of the covalent bonding in the H_2 molecule. Both approaches lead to the result that the energy levels are grouped into allowed and forbidden bands. The details of the band structure of a particular material determine whether that material is a conductor, an insulator, or a semiconductor. Qualitative discussion of the first of these methods is given in this section. The second is described on the home page in "Energy Bands in Solids—An Alternate Approach."

Kronig-Penney Model

Consider first the problem of an electron moving in a periodic potential. Figure 10-19*a* shows a one-dimensional sketch of the potential energy function for a lattice of positive ions. The most important feature of this potential is not the shape, but the fact that it is periodic. A simpler periodic potential consisting of finite square wells is shown in Figure 10-19*b*. The model based on this potential is called the *Kronig-Penney model*. It has the important feature of periodicity and is easier to treat mathematically; however, even for this model the mathematical solution of the Schrödinger equation is quite involved, and we shall only outline it here. For both potential functions shown in Figure 10-19, for certain ranges of energy there exist traveling-wave-type solutions of the Schrödinger equation. This result is based on an important discovery made by Bloch[6]

Fig. 10-19 (*a*) One-dimensional potential energy of an electron in a crystal. $U(x)$ approaches $-\infty$ at the atom sites. (*b*) Simplified (Kronig-Penney) model of potential energy of an electron in a crystal.

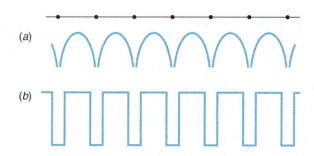

(*a*)

(*b*)

that solutions to the Schrödinger equation for periodic potentials must be of the form (in one dimension)

$$\psi(x) = u_k(x)e^{ikx} \qquad \text{10-51}$$

where $u_k(x) = u_k(x + L) = u_k(x + nL)$, L is the periodic spacing of the potential wells, and n is an integer. The function e^{ikx} is a plane wave, i.e., a free electron (see Section 6-6) with wave number $k = 2\pi/\lambda$. As Bloch himself described it:

> I felt that the main problem was to explain how the electrons could sneak by all the ions in a metal. . . . I found to my delight the wave differed from the plane wave of free electrons only by a periodic modulation.

Thus, we require that the solutions of the Schrödinger equation

$$-\frac{\hbar^2}{2m}\frac{d^2\psi(x)}{dx^2} + U(x)\psi(x) = E\psi(x) \qquad \text{10-52}$$

with $U(x)$ being the Kronig-Penney potential of periodic square wells have the form of the *Bloch function* given by Equation 10-51. The solution for the region $0 < x < a$ in Figure 10-20 is

$$\psi(x) = A_1 e^{ik'x} + A_2 e^{-ik'x} \qquad \text{10-53}$$

where $k' = 2\pi/\lambda = (2mE)^{1/2}/\hbar$. In the region $-b < x < 0$ the solutions are of the form

$$\psi(x) = B_1 e^{\alpha x} + B_2 e^{-\alpha x} \qquad \text{10-54}$$

where $\alpha = [2m(U_0 - E)]^{1/2}/\hbar$. The requirement that $\psi(x)$ have the form of Equation 10-51 means that

$$\psi(x + a + b) = u_k(x + a + b)e^{ik(x+a+b)}$$
$$\psi(x + a + b) = u_k(x)e^{ikx}e^{ik(a+b)}$$
$$\psi(x + a + b) = \psi(x)e^{ik(a+b)} \qquad \text{10-55a}$$

where $a + b$ is the periodic spacing of the wells. In general,

$$\psi(x + n(a + b)) = \psi(x)e^{ikn(a+b)} \qquad \text{10-55b}$$

As was done in Section 6-3 for solving the finite one-dimensional square well, the constants A_1, A_2, B_1, and B_2 are chosen so as to make $\psi(x)$ and $d\psi/dx$ continuous at $x = 0$ and $x = a$. Obtaining the constants is beyond the scope of our discussion here,

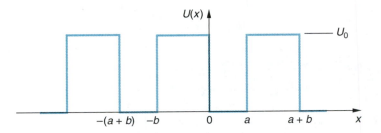

Fig. 10-20 A portion of the Kronig-Penney potential of Figure 10-19b showing the width of the square wells a and their periodic spacing (a + b).

but as in Chapter 6, doing so yields a conditional equation connecting k, k', and α with a and b, the parameters of the lattice. The result is that, in order to satisfy the requirement of Equation 10-55, only certain ranges of electron energies are allowed. These energy ranges, called *bands*, are separated by forbidden energy regions called *energy gaps*, in which no traveling wave can exist. Figure 10-21a shows the energy versus the wave number k for a completely free electron. This is, of course, merely a sketch of $E = \hbar^2 k^2 / 2m$. Figure 10-21b shows E versus k for an electron in the periodic potential of Figure 10-20. The energy gaps occur at

$$ka = \pm n\pi \qquad \textbf{10-56}$$

where n is an integer and a is the lattice spacing.[7] We can understand this result in terms of the Bragg reflection of the electron waves. Consider E to be small (near zero in Figure 10-21b) so that k is small, hence λ is large. As E increases, k eventually becomes large enough so that λ becomes small enough to suffer a Bragg reflection (constructive interference) from the lattice. (See Section 3-4.) Bragg reflection is governed by the Bragg condition (Equation 3-38)

$$n\lambda = 2a \sin \theta$$

In a one-dimensional system such as we are considering here, reflection means $\theta = 90°$. Since $k = 2\pi/\lambda$, Equation 10-56 becomes the condition for Bragg reflection. The reason

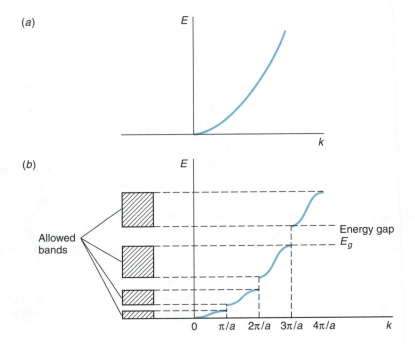

Fig. 10-21 (a) Energy vs. k for a free electron. (b) Energy vs. k for a nearly free electron in the one-dimensional periodic potential of Figure 10-20 with $b = 0$ and $U_0 \rightarrow \infty$. Energy gaps occur at the k values which satisfy the Bragg scattering condition. In each case only the portions with $k > 0$ are shown. The complete curves are symmetric about $k = 0$.

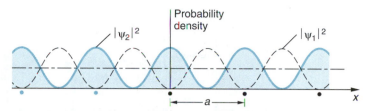

Fig. 10-22 Probability density (proportional to the charge distribution) for standing waves of wave number $k = \pi/a$ in a one-dimensional crystal. The solid curve $|\psi_2|^2$ is a maximum at the lattice ion sites, and has a lower potential energy than the dashed curve $|\psi_1|^2$.

that traveling waves cannot exist for these wave numbers is that the amplitude of the reflection from one atom in the chain becomes equal to and in phase with the forward electron wave from the preceding atom, so that standing waves are set up. Figure 10-22 shows a sketch of the electron probability density $|\psi|^2$ for the two types of standing waves for the lowest energy gap, where the value $k = \pi/a$:

$$\psi_1 = \sin kx = \sin \frac{\pi x}{a} \qquad \psi_2 = \cos kx = \cos \frac{\pi x}{a}$$

Since ψ_2 gives a higher concentration of electron charge density near the ion sites than ψ_1, the potential energy is less for ψ_2 than for ψ_1. The difference in the potential energies corresponds to the magnitude of the energy gap. Within the allowed energy bands, the energy has a continuous range if the number of atoms in the chain is infinite; for N atoms, there are N allowed energy levels in each band. Since the number of atoms is very large in a macroscopic solid, the energy bands can be considered continuous. Calculations in three dimensions are more difficult, of course, but the results are similar. The allowed ranges of the wave vector **k** are called *Brillouin zones*. Referring to Figure 10-21a, the first Brillouin zone has $-\pi/a < k < +\pi/a$, the second has $-2\pi/a < k < -\pi/a$ and $\pi/a < k < 2\pi/a$, and so on.

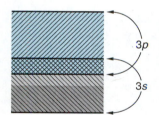

3p

3s

2p

2s

1s

Fig. 10-23 Energy-band structure of sodium. The empty 3p band overlaps the half-filled 3s band. Just above the filled states are many empty states into which electrons can be excited by an electric field, so sodium is a conductor.

Conductors, Insulators, and Semiconductors

Conductors   We can now understand why some solids are conductors and others are insulators. Consider sodium. There is room for two electrons in the 3s state of each atom, but each sodium atom has only one 3s electron. Therefore, when N sodium atoms are bound in a solid, the 3s energy band is only half filled. In addition, the empty 3p band overlaps the 3s band. The allowed energy bands of sodium are shown schematically in Figure 10-23. We can see that many allowed energy states are available immediately above the filled lower half of the 3s band, so the valence electrons can easily be raised to a higher energy state by an electric field. Accordingly, sodium is a good conductor. Magnesium, on the other hand, has two 3s electrons, so the 3s band is filled. However, like sodium, the empty 3p band overlaps the 3s band, so magnesium is also a conductor. The band occupied by the outer, or valence, electrons is called the *valence band*. The next allowed band is called the *conduction band*. Thus, a conductor is a solid whose valence band is only partly filled or whose conduction band overlaps its valence band. There are a few elements, notably antimony, arsenic, and bismuth, in which the conduction band overlaps the

valence band only very slightly, limiting the number of available empty states. These materials are called *semimetals*. (See Figures 10-25a and b, page 472.)

Insulators   A solid that has a completely filled valence band is an insulator if the energy gap between the valence band and the empty conduction band is larger than about 2 eV, as illustrated in Figure 10-25c. For example, ionic crystals are insulators. The band structure of an ionic crystal, such as NaCl, is quite different from that of a metal. The energy bands arise from the energy levels of the Na^+ and Cl^- ions. Both of these ions have a closed-shell configuration, so the highest occupied band in NaCl is completely full. The next allowed band, which is empty, arises from the excited states of Na^+ and Cl^-. There is a large energy gap between the filled band and this empty band. Typical electric fields applied to NaCl will be too weak to excite an electron from the upper energy levels of the filled valence band across the large gap into the lower energy levels of the empty conduction band, so NaCl is an insulator. When an applied electric field is sufficiently strong to cause an electron to be excited to the empty band, the phenomenon called *dielectric breakdown* occurs.

Intrinsic Semiconductors   If the gap between a filled valence band and an empty conduction band is small, the solid is a semiconductor. Consider carbon, which has two $2s$ electrons and two $2p$ electrons. We might expect carbon to be a conductor because of the four unfilled $2p$ states. However, the $2s$ and $2p$ levels mix when carbon forms covalent bonds.[8] Figure 10-24 shows the splitting of the eight $2s$-$2p$ levels when carbon bonds in the diamond structure. This splitting is due to the nature of the covalent bond and is similar to the splitting of the $1s$ levels in hydrogen discussed in Section 9-2. The energy of the levels corresponding to the four space-symmetric wave functions (one for the $2s$ levels and three for the $2p$ levels) is lowered while the energy of the other four levels (one $2s$ and three $2p$) is raised. The valence band therefore contains four levels per atom which are filled, and the conduction band is empty. At the diamond lattice spacing of about 0.154 nm, the energy gap between the filled valence band and the empty conduction band is

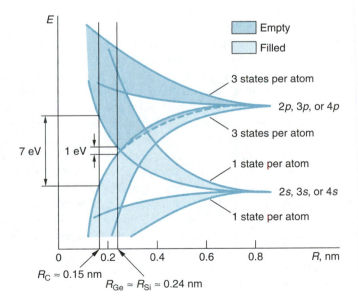

Fig. 10-24 Splitting of the $2s$ and $2p$ states of carbon, the $3s$ and $3p$ states of silicon, or the $4s$ and $4p$ states of germanium vs. separation of the atoms. The energy gap between the four filled states in the valence band and the empty states in the conduction band is 7 eV for the diamond-lattice spacing, $R_C = 0.154$ nm. For the silicon spacing $R_{Si} = 0.235$ nm, the energy gap is 1.09 eV. The splitting is similar for the $4s$ and $4p$ levels in germanium, which has an atom spacing of 0.243 nm, giving an energy gap of only 0.7 eV.

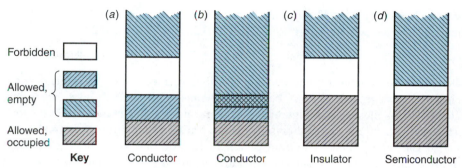

Fig. 10-25 Four possible band structures for a solid. (*a*) The allowed band is only partially full, so electrons can be excited to nearby energy states. At 0 K the Fermi level is at the top of the filled states. (*a*) is a conductor. (*b*) is a conductor because the allowed bands overlap. In (*c*) there is a forbidden band with a large energy gap between the filled band and the next allowed band; this is an insulator. (*d*) The energy gap between the filled band and the next allowed band is very small, so some electrons are excited to the conduction band at normal temperatures, leaving holes in the valence band. The Fermi level is approximately in the middle of the gap. (*d*) is a semiconductor.

about 7 eV. Since this gap is large compared to the energy that an electron might receive by thermal excitation due to scattering from the lattice ions, which on the average is of the order of $kT \approx 0.026$ eV at $T = 300$ K, very few electrons can reach the conduction band. Thus, diamond is an insulator. The band structure is similar for silicon, which has two $3s$ and two $3p$ electrons, and for germanium, which has two $4s$ and two $4p$ electrons. At the silicon lattice spacing of 0.235 nm the energy gap is about 1 eV; at the germanium lattice spacing of 0.243 nm the energy gap is only about 0.7 eV. For these gaps, at ordinary temperatures there are an appreciable number of electrons in the conduction band due to thermal excitation, although the number is still small compared with the number in a typical conductor. Solids such as these are called *intrinsic semiconductors*. Figure 10-25*d* illustrates the band structure of intrinsic semiconductors.

In the presence of an electric field, the electrons in the conduction band of an intrinsic semiconductor can be accelerated because there are empty states nearby. Also, for each electron that has been excited to the conduction band there is a vacancy, or hole, in the nearby filled valence band. In the presence of an electric field, other electrons in this band can be excited to the vacant energy level, thus filling that hole but creating another hole. This contributes to the electric current and is most easily described as the motion of a hole in the direction of the field and opposite to the motion of the electrons. The hole thus acts like a positive charge. An analogy of a two-lane, one-way road with one lane full of parked cars and the other empty may help to visualize the conduction of holes. If a car moves out of the filled lane into the empty lane, it can move ahead freely. As the other cars move up to occupy the space left, the empty space propagates backward in the direction opposite the motion of the cars. Both the forward motion of the car in the nearby empty lane and the backward propagation of the empty space contribute to a net forward propagation of the cars.

An interesting characteristic of semiconductors is that the conductivity increases (and the resistivity decreases) as the temperature increases, which is contrary to the case for normal conductors. The reason is that as the temperature is increased, the number of free electrons is increased because there are more electrons in the conduction band. The number of holes in the valence band is also increased, of course. In semiconductors, the effect of the increase in the number of charge carriers, both elec-

TABLE 10-4 Values of $f_{FD}(E)$ for $T = 293$ K						
$E - E_F$ (eV)	0.05	0.10	0.25	1.0	2.5	7.5
Multiple of kT	2	4	10	40	100	300
$f_{FD}(E)$	0.12	0.019	5.1×10^{-5}	6.5×10^{-18}	1.1×10^{-43}	1.3×10^{-129}

trons and holes, exceeds the effect of the increase in resistivity due to the increased scattering of the electrons by the lattice ions due to thermal vibrations. Semiconductors therefore have negative temperature coefficients of resistivity.

Whether a solid with a filled valence band will be a semiconductor or an insulator depends critically on the width of the energy gap E_g, as Figure 10-24 suggests. A comparison of the relative numbers of electrons with various energies that *could* be above the Fermi level (located at the center of the band gap) at ordinary temperatures illustrates why this is true. Those numbers are given by the Fermi-Dirac distribution $f_{FD}(E)$ given by Equation 8-92:

$$f_{FD}(E) = \frac{1}{e^{(E - E_F)/kT} + 1}$$ **8-92**

At $T = 293$ K, $kT = 0.025$ eV. Recall that for $E = E_F$, $f_{FD}(E) = 1/2$ (see Section 8-5). For $(E - E_F) = 0.10$, or $4(kT)$, we have

$$f_{FD}(E) = \frac{1}{e^{0.10/0.025} + 1} = 0.018$$

Repeating this calculation for several additional values of $(E - E_F)$ yields the relative numbers of electrons in Table 10-4. From the numbers in the table we see that, if a certain material has an energy gap E_g between the valence and conduction bands of 0.25 eV, for example, then approximately 10^{-5} of the electrons within kT of the Fermi level would be excited to the conduction band and thus able to participate in the conduction of electricity. This is a sizable number, given the numbers of electrons near the Fermi level, so we expect this material to have a higher electrical conductivity than materials with larger values of E_g.

For a gap of 1.0 eV, just four times that of the previous example, the relative number of electrons excited to the conduction band decreases by more than 12 orders of magnitude, illustrating the sharp decline of $f_{FD}(E)$ as the energy gap increases. The calculation of $f_{FD}(E)$ above also illustrates the increased conductivity of semiconductors as the temperature increases described earlier. If the temperature of a material with an energy gap of 1.0 eV is increased to 393 K from 293 K, as in Table 10-4, $f_{FD}(E)$ increases to 1.5×10^{-13}, thus increasing the relative number of electrons in the conduction band by nearly four orders of magnitude. Table 10-5 lists the energy gaps for several semiconducting elements and compounds. Notice that the energy gap is slightly temperature-dependent.

A concept that is helpful in understanding a number of characteristics of semiconductors is that of *effective mass*. As pointed out above, Figure 10-21a is a graph of $E = \hbar^2 k^2/2m_e$, the energy of a free electron of wavelength $\lambda = 2\pi/k$. The curvature of the E versus k graph is given by $d^2E/dk^2 = \hbar^2/m_e$, and we may say that the

TABLE 10-5 Energy gap E_g and dielectric constant κ for selected semiconductors

Material	E_g (eV)		κ	Material	E_g (eV)		κ
	0 K	293 K			0 K	293 K	
Si	1.15	1.11	11.8	CdTe	1.56	1.44	10.2
Ge	0.74	0.67	15.9	PbS	0.28	0.37	17.0
Te	—	0.33	—	InP	1.41	1.27	12.4
GaAs	1.53	1.35	13.1	CdSe	1.85	1.74	10.1
InSb	0.23	0.16	17.8	GaP	2.40	2.24	11.1
ZnS	—	3.54	5.2	PbTe	0.19	0.25	30.1

curvature is determined by $1/m_e$, the reciprocal mass. In Figure 10-21a $1/m_e$ is of course constant; however, in regions near the energy gaps in Figure 10-21b the curvature is much higher than that for the free electron. Since the behavior of electrons near the band/gap boundary is of considerable interest, particularly in the discussion of impurity semiconductors and devices in Section 10-7, it is helpful to continue to describe the curvature of the E versus k curve near the boundary in terms of a reciprocal mass. Accordingly, we define the effective mass m^* as

$$\frac{1}{m^*} = \frac{1}{\hbar^2}\frac{d^2E}{dk^2}$$

10-57

Then, as in the case of the free electron, the curvature of E versus k for electrons bound in the crystal energy bands is also described in terms of a reciprocal mass, $1/m^*$. For a free electron $m^* = m_e$, as is also the case for electrons that are not close to the boundaries in Figure 10-21b. Close to the band/gap boundaries, however, is a different matter. Starting from $k = 0$ in the figure, the curvature is initially constant and equal to that of a free electron, thus $m^* = m_e$, but near the boundary where $k = \pi/a$ the curvature becomes large and, very close to the boundary, negative; hence m^* becomes smaller than m_e and also eventually negative! Just above the gap, the curvature is large and positive, so $m^* < m_e$ and positive. For the situation where E_g is small compared to the width of the band, the values of the effective mass are typically of the order of $0.01 - 0.1$ of the mass of a free electron. We will make further use of the effective mass in Section 10-7.

QUESTIONS

9. How does the change in resistivity of copper compare with that of silicon when the temperature increases?

10. Suppose an electron is excited from the valence band of a semiconductor to a state several levels above the lower edge of the conduction band. Devise an explanation for why it will quickly "decay" to a level at the bottom of the conduction band.

More

An alternative to the Kronig-Penney model of a solid is based on the molecular bonding model discussed in Section 9-2 for hydrogen. *Energy Bands in Solids—An Alternate Approach* is described briefly on the home page: www.whfreeman.com/modphysics4e   See also Figures 10-26 and 10-27 here.

10-7 Impurity Semiconductors

Most semiconductor devices, such as the semiconductor diode and the transistor, make use of *impurity semiconductors,* which are created through the controlled addition of certain impurities to intrinsic semiconductors. This process is called *doping.* Figure 10-28 illustrates the lattice structure of pure silicon, and Figure 10-29a is a schematic illustration of silicon doped with a small amount of arsenic such that arsenic atoms replace a few of the silicon atoms in the crystal lattice. Arsenic has five valence electrons in the $n = 4$ shell, whereas silicon has four valence electrons in the $n = 3$ shell. Four of the five arsenic electrons take part in covalent bonds with the four neighboring silicon atoms, and the fifth electron is very loosely bound to the atom. This extra electron occupies an energy level that is just slightly below the conduction band in the solid, and is easily excited into the conduction band, where it can contribute to electrical conduction. The fifth arsenic valence electron and the arsenic ion core form a hydrogenlike system. Thus, Bohr theory (see Section 4-3) can be used to calculate the approximate values of the energies available to it, provided only that we make allowance for the fact that the electron-arsenic ion system is embedded in the semiconductor crystal, rather than being isolated from other atoms. First, the crystal is a medium with a high dielectric constant; thus the potential energy function in the Schrödinger equation for a hydrogenlike atom (Equation 7-6) becomes[9] $V(r) = (-Zke^2/R)(1/\kappa)$, where κ is the dielectric constant of the material and $k = 1/4\pi\epsilon_0$. Secondly, the electron mass in the Schrödinger equation must be replaced by the effective mass m^*, which accounts for the fact that the electron "sees" a three-dimensional version of the periodic potential of Figure 10-19. With these two modifications the solution of the Schrödinger equation is carried out just as in Chapter 7. The results for the allowed energies and average values of the radii of the Bohr orbits for the fifth arsenic electron are given by

$$E_n = -\frac{1}{2}\left(\frac{ke^2}{\hbar}\right)^2 \frac{m_e}{n^2} \times \frac{m^*}{m_e} \times \frac{1}{\kappa^2} = -\frac{1}{2}\left(\frac{ke^2}{\hbar}\right)^2 \frac{m^*}{\kappa^2} \frac{1}{n^2} \qquad \textbf{10-58}$$

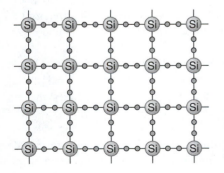

Fig. 10-28 A two-dimensional schematic illustration of solid silicon. Each atom forms a covalent bond with four neighbors, sharing one of its four valence electrons with each neighbor.

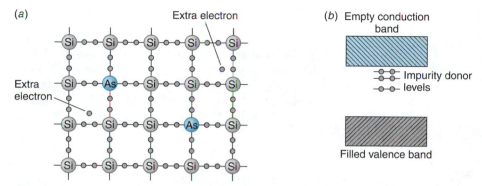

Fig. 10-29 (*a*) A two-dimensional schematic illustration of silicon doped with arsenic. Because arsenic has five valence electrons, there is an extra, weakly bound electron that is easily excited to the conduction band, where it can contribute to electrical conduction. (*b*) Band structure of an *n*-type semiconductor such as silicon doped with arsenic. The impurity atoms provide filled energy levels that are just below the conduction band. These levels donate electrons to the conduction band.

$$\langle r_n \rangle = a_0 n^2 \times \frac{m_e}{m^*} \times \kappa \qquad\qquad \textbf{10-59}$$

where a_0 is the Bohr radius, equal to 0.0529 nm (see Equation 4-19), and n is the principal quantum number.

To understand where these energy levels lie relative to the bands and gap of the silicon, consider that when the arsenic atom is ionized by removing the fifth electron, that electron is then free to participate in electrical conduction, i.e., it is then in the conduction band. Thus, we conclude that $E_\infty = 0$ is at the bottom edge of the conduction band and the other E_n hydrogenlike levels lie below it in the gap. The energy of the ground state E_1 can be calculated from the experimentally determined value of the electron's effective mass in silicon, about 0.2 m_e, and the dielectric constant of silicon given in Table 10-5. Substituting these into Equation 10-58 yields $E_1 = -0.020$ eV below the conduction band, which is substantially smaller than the -13.6-eV ground state for hydrogen. Similarly, substitution into Equation 10-59 yields $\langle r_1 \rangle = 3.1$ nm, or about 60 times the ground-state radius of hydrogen.[10] These energies are quite close to the conduction band, as illustrated in Figure 10-29*b*; thus these electrons can be easily excited to the conduction band since their ionization energy is comparable to kT at room temperature.

These hydrogenlike levels just below the conduction band are called *donor levels* because they donate electrons to the conduction band without leaving holes in the valence band. Such a semiconductor is called an *n-type semiconductor* because the major charge carriers are *negative* electrons. The conductivity of a doped semiconductor can be controlled by controlling the amount of impurity added. The addition of just one part per million can increase the conductivity by several orders of magnitude.

Another type of impurity semiconductor can be made by replacing a silicon atom in the crystal lattice with a gallium atom, which has three electrons in its valence level (see Figure 10-30*a*). The gallium atoms accept electrons from the valence band of the silicon in order to complete their four covalent bonds, thus creating holes in the valence band. The effect on the band structure of silicon achieved by doping it with gallium is shown in Figure 10-30*b*. The empty levels shown just above the valence band are due to the holes from the ionized gallium atoms. These levels are called *acceptor levels* because they accept electrons from the filled valence band when these

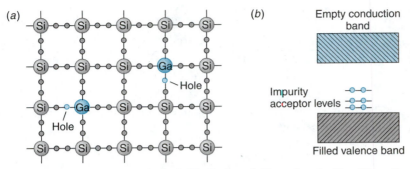

Fig. 10-30 (*a*) Two-dimensional schematic illustration of silicon doped with gallium. Because gallium has only three valence electrons, there is a hole in one of its bonds. As electrons move into the hole, the hole moves about, contributing to the conduction of electrical current. (*b*) Band structure of a *p*-type semiconductor such as silicon doped with gallium. The impurity atoms provide empty energy levels just above the filled valence band that accept electrons from the valence band.

electrons are thermally excited to a higher energy state. They arise because the holes, which act like positive charges, may be bound to the negative gallium core much like the fifth electron was bound to the positive arsenic core. Thus, the hole-gallium ion system also forms a hydrogenlike system and the energy levels of the hole can also be calculated approximately using the Bohr model with results similar to Equation 10-58. Since the energy-band diagrams like Figures 10-29*b* and 10-30*b* are drawn with electron energy increasing upward, hole energy in those diagrams increases downward. Ionizing the hole-gallium system means returning the hole to the valence band; hence these levels are just above the top of the valence band as shown in the figure and their magnitudes are of the same order as those of the donor levels discussed previously. Increasing the energy of holes is equivalent to promoting electrons from the valence band into the acceptor levels. This creates holes in the valence band that are free to propagate in the direction of an electric field. Such a semiconductor is called a *p-type semiconductor* because the charge carriers are *positive* holes. The fact that conduction is due to the motion of holes can be verified by the Hall effect, described in the Exploring section on page 478.

EXAMPLE 10-9 Donor Ionization Energy in Ge If phosphorus is used to dope germanium to form an *n*-type semiconductor, what is the ionization energy of the levels? What is the radius of the electron's orbit? Phosphorus has five valence electrons. (The effective mass for electrons in germanium is about 0.1 m_e.)

Solution

1. The magnitude of the ionization energy is computed from Equation 10-58 with $n = 1$:

$$E_1 = \frac{1}{2}\left(\frac{ke^2}{\hbar}\right)^2 \frac{m^*}{\kappa^2}$$

2. The dielectric constant κ for germanium is given in Table 10-5:

$$\kappa = 15.9$$

3. Substituting values into Equation 10-58 gives:

$$E_1 = \frac{1}{2}\left(\frac{9 \times 10^9 \, \text{N} \cdot \text{m}^2/c^2 \times (1.60 \times 10^{-19} \, \text{C})^2}{1.055 \times 10^{-34} \, \text{J} \cdot \text{s}}\right)^2 \frac{(0.1 \times 9.11 \times 10^{-31} \, \text{kg})}{(15.9)^2}$$

$$= 8.6 \times 10^{-22} \, \text{J} = 5.4 \times 10^{-3} \, \text{eV}$$

4. The orbit radius $\langle r_1 \rangle$ of the fifth phosphorus electron is computed from Equation 10-59 with $n = 1$:

$$\langle r_1 \rangle = a_0 \frac{m_e}{m^*} \kappa$$

5. Substituting values, where the Bohr radius $a_0 = 0.0529$ nm, gives:

$$\langle r_1 \rangle = 0.0529 \times \frac{m_e}{0.1 \, m_e} \times 15.9$$

$$= 8.4 \, \text{nm}$$

Remarks: *The value computed above for E_1 is very close to the experimental value of 12.0×10^{-3} eV, even though our calculation is a Bohr model approximation.*

Exploring

Hall Effect

The number of donated electrons in a doped *n*-type semiconductor, or holes in a doped *p*-type semiconductor, is typically much greater than the intrinsic number of electron-hole pairs created by thermal excitation of electrons from the valence band to the conduction band. In an electric field, the current will therefore consist of both majority carriers (electrons in an *n*-type or holes in a *p*-type semiconductor) and minority carriers. The reality of conduction by motion of positive holes is brought out in the Hall effect, illustrated in Figure 10-31*a*. In this figure a thin strip of a doped semiconductor is connected to a battery (not shown), so that there is a current to the right. A uniform magnetic field *B* is applied perpendicular to the current. For the direction of the current and magnetic field shown, the magnetic

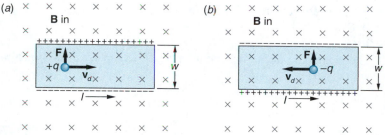

Fig. 10-31 The Hall effect. The force on the charge carriers is up whether the carriers are positive charges moving to the right (*a*) or negative charges moving to the left (*b*). The sign of the charge carriers can be determined by the sign of the potential difference between the top and bottom of the strip, and the drift velocity can be determined by the magnitude of this potential difference. The thickness *t* of the strip is not shown.

force on a moving charged particle $q\mathbf{v}_d \times \mathbf{B}$ is upward (where $\mathbf{v}_d$ is the drift velocity) independent of whether the current is due to a positive charge moving to the right or a negative charge moving to the left. Let us assume for the moment that the charge carriers are electrons, as in Figure 10-31b. The magnetic force will then cause the electrons to drift up to the top of the strip, leaving the bottom of the strip with an excess positive charge. This will continue until the electrostatic field $\mathscr{E}$ caused by the charge separation produces an electric force on the charge carriers just balancing the magnetic force. The condition for balance is $q\mathscr{E} = qv_dB$. If w is the width of the strip, there will be a potential difference called the Hall voltage

$$V_H = \mathscr{E}w = v_dBw \qquad \textbf{10-60}$$

between the top and bottom of the strip. This potential difference can be measured with a high-resistance voltmeter. A measurement of the sign of the potential difference (i.e., whether the top of the strip is at a higher potential due to positive charge or lower potential due to negative charge) determines the sign of the majority carriers. Such measurements reveal that, indeed, the charge carriers are negative in n-type and positive in p-type semiconductors. The value of the Hall voltage provides a measurement of the drift velocity v_d. Since the current density $j = nqv_d$ can be easily measured from the total current and cross-sectional area of the strip, measurement of the drift velocity determines n, the number of charge carriers per unit volume.

Hall-effect probes are frequently used to measure magnetic field strengths. A current is established in a calibrated metal strip. Measuring the Hall voltage then yields the value of B (see Equation 10-61).

EXAMPLE 10-10 Hall Effect in Aluminum A strip of aluminum of width $w = 1.5$ cm and thickness $t = 250$ μm is placed in a uniform magnetic field of 0.55 T oriented perpendicular to the plane of the strip. When a current of 25 A is established in the strip, a voltage of 1.64 μV is measured across the width of the strip. What is the density of charge carriers in aluminum and how many charge carriers are provided, on the average, by each atom?

Solution
Substituting for the drift velocity v_d in terms of the current density in Equation 10-60 yields

$$V_H = v_dBw = \frac{jBw}{nq} = \frac{iB}{qnt} \qquad \textbf{10-61}$$

since $j = i/wt$. The density of the charge carriers in aluminum is then given by

$$n = \frac{iB}{qtV_H} = \frac{(25 \text{ A})(0.55 \text{ T})}{(1.6 \times 10^{-19}\,\text{C})(250 \times 10^{-6}\,\text{m})(1.64 \times 10^{-6}\,\text{V})}$$

$$= 2.10 \times 10^{29} \text{ carriers/m}^3$$

The density of atoms N in aluminum is given by the following, where the density $\rho(\text{Al}) = 2.72 \times 10^3$ kg/m^3 and the molar mass $M = 26.98$ kg/mole:

$$N = \frac{N_A\rho}{M} = \frac{(6.02 \times 10^{26}\,\text{atoms/mole})(2.702 \times 10^3\,\text{kg/m}^3)}{26.98 \text{ kg/mole}}$$

$$= 6.02 \times 10^{28} \text{ atoms/m}^3$$

Thus, each aluminum atom contributes on the average $n/N = 3.5$ charge carriers.

The Quantum Hall Effect

According to Equation 10-61, the Hall voltage should increase linearly with the magnetic field B for a given current. In 1980, while studying the Hall effect in thin semiconductors at very low temperatures and very large magnetic fields, von Klitzing[11] discovered that a plot of V_H versus B was *not* linear, but included a series of plateaus, as shown in Figure 10-32a. That is, the Hall voltage is quantized. More specifically, if we define the Hall resistance $R_H = V_H / i$, it is the Hall resistance that is quantized, taking on only the values

$$R_H = \frac{V_H}{i} = \frac{R_K}{n}$$ **10-62**

where R_K, called the *von Klitzing constant,* is related to the fundamental electron charge e and Planck's constant h by

$$R_K = \frac{h}{e^2} = \frac{6.22 \times 10^{-34} \text{ J} \cdot \text{s}}{(1.602 \times 10^{-19} \text{ C})^2} = 25{,}813 \ \Omega$$ **10-63**

The values of n found by von Klitzing were small positive integers ($n = 1, 2, 3, \ldots$), as indicated in Figure 10-32a. Then in 1982 Tsui and his co-workers,[12] while investigating the quantum Hall effect in ultrapure semiconductors, discovered quantized values of the Hall resistance for values of n that were rational fractions formed from small integers. Values of R_H have been found thus far for $n = \frac{1}{2}, \frac{1}{3}, \frac{1}{5}, \frac{1}{7}, \frac{2}{3}, \frac{4}{3}, \frac{5}{3}, \frac{4}{5}, \frac{6}{7}$, and $\frac{5}{2}$. Several of these are seen in Figure 10-32b.

Von Klitzing's discovery is referred to as the *integral quantized Hall effect* (*IQHE*) and that of Tsui and his colleagues as the *fractional quantized Hall effect* (*FQHE*). The theoretical models that have been developed to explain these phenomena are as yet incomplete and, in any case, beyond the scope of our discussion here; however, we can give a brief qualitative description of the IQHE. In the "normal" Hall effect the material carries a current i due to an applied electric field $\mathscr{E}$. The electric field is perpendicular to the applied magnetic field **B** and, as a result, the charge carriers move in a circular path, or orbit, of radius $r = m^*v/qB$. The fact that electrons obey the Pauli exclusion principle prevents the orbits from

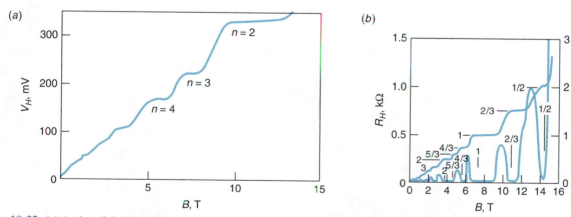

Fig. 10-32 (*a*) A plot of the Hall voltage vs. applied magnetic field shows plateaus, indicating that the Hall voltage is quantized. These data were taken at a temperature of 1.39 K with the current i held fixed at 25.52 μA. (*b*) The fractional quantum Hall effect. The Hall resistance R_H (the curve with the plateaus) is read on the left vertical axis, the normal resistance R_N (the curve with the peaks) on the right vertical axis. [*Data collected by Y. W. Suen and co-workers at Princeton University.*]

overlapping and determines how closely the electrons can group together on the negative side of the sample. Recalling that the orbital motion of electrons is quantized with only certain radii being allowed—namely, those for which the orbit circumference equals an integral number of de Broglie wavelengths—increasing the magnetic field decreases the orbit radius, but such decreases must occur suddenly and result in another, smaller allowed radius. Thus, more electron orbits can fit without overlapping in a given area and the density of charge carriers increases on the edges of the semiconductor sample. This increases the frequency of collisions, and hence the Hall resistance. Since the orbit radii change only in quantized steps, so must the Hall resistance. Surprisingly, when the Hall resistance is on one of the plateaus, the ordinary resistance $R = V/i$ falls to zero, as illustrated by the multiple peaked curve in Figure 10-32b. The additional plateaus that occur in the FQHE are due to electron-electron spin interactions.

Because the von Klitzing constant can be measured with a precision of better than 1 part in 10^{10}, the quantum Hall effect is now used to define the standard of resistance. The ohm is defined so that R_K has the value 25,812.807 Ω exactly.

10-8 Semiconductor Junctions and Devices

Semiconductor devices such as diodes and transistors make use of *n*-type and *p*-type semiconductors joined together as shown in Figure 10-33. In practice, the two types of semiconductors are often a single silicon crystal doped with donor impurities on one side and acceptor impurities on the other. The region in which the semiconductor changes from a *p*-type to an *n*-type is called a *junction*.

When an *n*-type and *p*-type semiconductor are placed in contact, the initially unequal concentrations of electrons and holes result in the diffusion of electrons across the junction from the *n* side to the *p* side until equilibrium is established. The result of this diffusion is a net transport of positive charge from the *p* side to the *n* side. Unlike the case when two different metals are in contact, there are fewer electrons available to participate in this diffusion because the semiconductor is not a particularly good conductor. The diffusion of electrons and holes creates a double layer of charge at the junction similar to that on a parallel-plate capacitor. There is thus a potential difference *V* across the junction, which tends to inhibit further diffusion. In equilibrium, the *n* side with its net positive charge will be at a higher potential than the *p* side with its net negative charge. In the junction region, there will be very few charge carriers of either type, so the junction region has a high resistance. Figure 10-34 shows the energy-level diagram for a *pn* junction. The junction region is also called the *depletion region* because it has been depleted of charge carriers.

Diodes

A semiconductor with a *pn* junction can be used as a simple diode rectifier. In Figure 10-35, an external potential difference has been applied across the junction by connecting a battery and resistor to the semiconductor. When the positive terminal of the battery is connected to the *p* side of the junction as shown in Figure 10-35a, the diode is said to be *forward-biased*. Forward biasing lowers the potential across the junction. The diffusion of electrons and holes is thereby increased as they attempt to reestablish equilibrium, resulting in a current in the circuit. If the positive terminal of the battery is connected to the *n* side of the junction as shown in Figure 10-35b, the diode is said to be

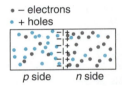

• − electrons
• + holes

p side   *n* side

Fig. 10-33 A *pn* junction. Because of the difference in their concentrations, holes diffuse from the *p* side to the *n* side and electrons diffuse from the *n* side to the *p* side. As a result, there is a double layer of charge at the junction, with the *p* side negative and the *n* side positive.

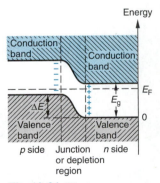

Energy

Conduction band

Conduction band

E_F

ΔE

E_g

0

Valence band

Valence band

p side   Junction   *n* side
or depletion
region

Fig. 10-34 Electron energy levels for an unbiased *pn* junction.

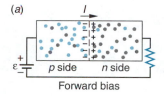

(a)

Forward bias

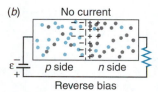

(b)   No current

Reverse bias

Fig. 10-35 A *pn*-junction diode. (*a*) Forward-biased *pn* junction. The applied potential difference enhances the diffusion of holes from the *p* side to the *n* side and electrons from the *n* side to the *p* side, resulting in a current *I*. (*b*) Reverse-biased *pn* junction. The applied potential difference inhibits the further diffusion of holes and electrons, so there is no current.

reverse-biased. Reverse biasing tends to increase the potential difference across the junction, thereby further inhibiting diffusion. Figure 10-36 shows a plot of current versus voltage for a typical semiconductor junction. Essentially, the junction conducts only in one direction, the same as a vacuum-tube diode. Junction diodes have replaced vacuum tube diodes in nearly all applications except when a very high current is required.

We can get an idea of how the current depends upon applied voltage quantitatively if we note that the electrons and holes, being at the high energy end of the distribution, are approximately described by the Maxwell-Boltzmann distribution. Let N_e be the number of conduction electrons in the *n* region. With no external voltage, only a small fraction given by $N_e e^{-eV/kT}$ will have enough energy to diffuse across the contact potential difference. When a forward bias V_b is applied, the number that can cross the barrier becomes

$$N_e e^{-e(V - V_b)/kT} = (N_e e^{-eV/kT})e^{+eV_b/kT}$$

The current due to the majority electron carriers in the *n* region will be

$$I = I_0 e^{+eV_b/kT}$$

where I_0 is the current with no bias. The current due to the minority carriers, the holes from the *n* side, will be merely I_0, the same as with no bias. (The minority carriers are swept across the junction by the contact potential V with or without a bias voltage.) The net current due to carriers from the *n* side will therefore be

$$I_{net} = I_0(e^{+eV_b/kT} - 1) \qquad \textbf{10-64}$$

If we now consider the current due to the majority and minority carriers from the *p* side, we obtain the same results. We can use Equation 10-64 for the total current if we interpret I_0 as the total current due to both kinds of minority carriers, holes in the *n* region and electrons in the *p* region. For positive V_b the exponential quickly dominates. For $V_b = 0$ the current is 0 and for V_b less than zero, the current saturates at $-I_0$ due to the flow of minority carriers. Note that the current in Figure 10-36 suddenly increases in magnitude at extreme values of reverse bias. In such large electric fields, two things can happen: either electrons are stripped from their atomic bonds or the few free electrons that exist in a reversed-biased junction are accelerated across the junction and gain enough energy to cause others to break loose. The first effect is

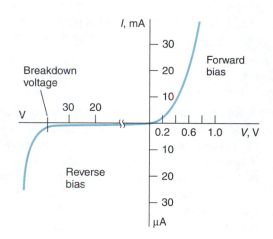

Fig. 10-36 Current vs. applied voltage across a *pn* junction. Note the different scales for the forward- and reverse-bias conditions.

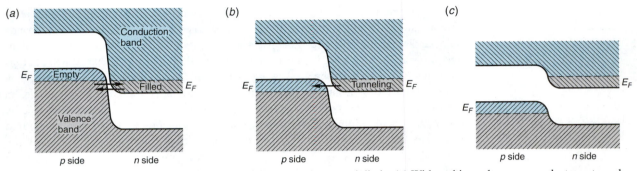

Fig. 10-37 Electron energy levels for a heavily doped *pn*-junction tunnel diode. (*a*) With no bias voltage, some electrons tunnel in each direction. (*b*) With a small bias voltage, the tunneling current is enhanced in one direction, making a sizable contribution to the net current. (*c*) With further increases in the bias voltage, the tunneling current decreases dramatically.

called *Zener breakdown;* the second, *avalanche breakdown.* Although such a break-down can be disastrous in a circuit where it is not intended, the fact that it occurs at a sharp voltage value makes it of use in a special voltage reference standard known as a *Zener diode.*

An interesting effect that we can discuss only qualitatively occurs if both the *n* side and the *p* side of a *pn*-junction diode are so heavily doped that the bottom of the con-duction band lies below the top of the valence band. Figure 10-37*a* shows the energy-level diagram for this situation. Since there are states on the *p* side with the same energy as states on the *n* side and the depletion region is now so narrow, electrons can tunnel across the potential barrier (see Secton 6-6). This flow of electrons is called *tun-neling current,* and such a heavily doped diode is called a *tunnel diode.*

At equilibrium with no bias, there is an equal tunneling current in each direction. When a small bias voltage is applied across the junction, the energy-level diagram is as shown in Figure 10-37*b,* and the tunneling of electrons from the *n* to the *p* side is increased whereas that in the opposite direction is decreased. This tunneling current in addition to the usual current due to diffusion results in a considerable net current. When the bias voltage is increased slightly, the tunneling current decreases because there are fewer states on the *p* side with the same energy as states on the *n* side. Although the diffusion current is increased, the net current is decreased. At large bias voltages the energy-level diagram is as shown in Figure 10-37*c,* the tunneling current is completely negligible, and the total current increases with increasing bias voltage due to diffusion as in an ordinary *pn*-junction diode. Figure 10-38 shows the current versus voltage curve for a tunnel diode. Such diodes are used in electric circuits because of their very fast response time. When operated near the peak in the current versus voltage curve, a small change in bias voltage results in a large change in the current.

Among the many applications of semiconductors with *pn* junctions are particle detectors called *surface-barrier detectors.* These consist of a *pn*-junction semicon-ductor with a large reverse bias so that there is ordinarily no current. When a high-energy particle, such as an electron, passes through the semiconductor, it excites electrons into the conduction band, creating many electron-hole pairs as it loses energy. The intrinsic electric field sweeps the electrons toward the positive (*n*) side of the junction and the holes toward the negative (*p*) side. The resulting current pulse signals the passage of the particles and records the energy lost by the particle in the detector. The pulses are of short duration ($10^{-8} - 10^{-7}$ seconds), making possible high energy-resolution measurements.

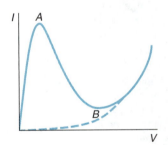

Fig. 10-38 Current vs. applied voltage for a tunnel diode. Up to point *A,* an increase in the bias voltage enhances tunneling. Between points *A* and *B,* an increase in the bias voltage inhibits tun-neling, i.e., the diode acts as if it has negative resistance. After point *B,* the tunneling is negligible, and the diode behaves like an ordinary *pn*-junction diode, shown by the dashed line.

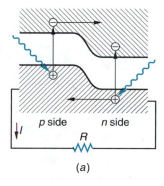

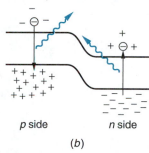

Fig. 10-39 (*a*) A *pn* junction as a solar cell. Radiation striking the junction produces electrons and holes. The electrons are swept from the *p* side and holes from the *n* side by the intrinsic electric field. The accumulated charge results in a potential difference that produces a current through an external load. (*b*) A *pn* junction as an LED. Large forward bias produces current of electrons moving to the left and holes moving to the right. When they recombine, radiation is emitted.

Light-emitting and -absorbing *pn*-junction semiconductors function similarly to gaseous atoms emitting and absorbing light, with the conduction and valence bands being analogous to the atomic energy levels. The light-absorbing *pn* junction semiconductor diode, or *solar cell,* is illustrated schematically in Figure 10-39a. When photons with energy greater than the gap energy (1.1 eV in silicon) strike the *pn* junction, they can excite electrons from the valence band into the conduction band, leaving holes in the valence band. This region is already rich in holes. Some of the electrons created by the photons will recombine with holes, but some will migrate to the junction. From there they are accelerated into the *n*-type region by the intrinsic electric field between the double layer of charge. This creates an excess negative charge in the *n*-type region and excess positive charge in the *p*-type region. The result is a potential difference, a *photovoltage,* between the two regions, which in practice is about 0.6 V. If a load resistance is connected across the two regions, a charge flows through the resistance. Some of the incident light energy is thus converted into electrical energy. The current in the resistor is proportional to the number of incident photons, which is in turn proportional to the intensity of the incident light.

Light-emitting diodes (LEDs) are *pn*-junction semiconductors with a large forward bias that produces a large excess concentration of electrons on the *p* side and holes on the *n* side of the junction. (See Figure 10-39b.) Under these conditions, the diode emits light as the electrons and holes recombine. This is essentially the reverse of the process that occurs in a solar cell. Following the first practical demonstration of an LED (in 1962), the performance of LEDs has steadily improved. (See Figure 10-40.) They can be fabricated in all of the primary colors and show potential for serving as a common source of white light in the future. LEDs already provide a viable alternative to filtered incandescent lighting in applications requiring monochromatic light. They are used, for example, as indicator lamps in appliances, electronic equipment, automobile dashboards, calculators, and digital watches. In traffic signals the red, amber, and green LED arrays use only 10 percent of the power consumed by the standard 140-W incandescent lamps. Rapid development of organic

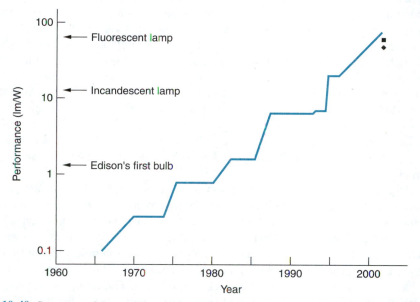

Fig. 10-40 Summary of the performance improvements in LEDs over the span of their existence. The ■ marks the current perfomance of small-molecule OLEDs; the ◆ marks that of the polymer OLEDs. A few performance benchmarks are indicated on the vertical axis.

Fig. 10-41 The resonant cavity is formed by cleaving the ends of the diode crystal parallel to one another and with the proper separation. Gallium arsenide and similar compounds, which have much higher photon-production efficiency than silicon, are typically used as diode laser semiconductors. Their light-energy-out to electrical-energy-in ratios are greater than 50 percent.

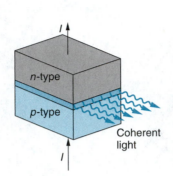

semiconductor light-emitting diodes (OLEDs) in the 1990s was catalyzed by worldwide efforts to construct large, full-color, flat-screen displays. Fabricated from small organic molecules and various polymers, OLEDs have an advantage over LEDs in that they can be produced on a large scale at very low cost. In LEDs high forward currents result in a very large population inversion, i.e., electrons on the *p* side and holes on the *n* side, so that stimulated emission dominates the light-emission process and lasing results. By appropriate construction of the diode, a resonant cavity can be formed, leading to the production of a coherent beam of laser light in a selected direction (see Figure 10-41).

Transistors

The transistor, invented in 1948 by William Shockley, John Bardeen, and Walter Brattain,[13] has revolutionized the electronics industry and our everyday world. A simple junction or bipolar transistor consists of three distinct semiconductor regions called the *emitter,* the *base,* and the *collector.* The base is a very thin region of one type of semiconductor sandwiched between two regions of the opposite type. The emitter semiconductor is much more heavily doped than either the base or the collector. In an *npn* transistor, the emitter and collector are *n*-type semiconductors and the base is a *p*-type semiconductor; in a *pnp* transistor, the base is an *n*-type semiconductor and the emitter and collector are *p*-type semiconductors. In a *pnp* transistor holes are emitted by the emitter; in an *npn* transistor electrons are emitted. Figures 10-42 and 10-43 show, respectively, a *pnp* transistor and an *npn* transistor with the symbols used to represent each transistor in circuit diagrams. Notice that a transistor consists

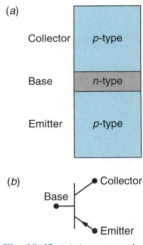

Fig. 10-42 (*a*) A *pnp* transistor. The heavily doped emitter emits holes that pass through the thin base to the collector. (*b*) Symbol for a *pnp* transistor in a circuit. The arrow points in the direction of the conventional current, which is the same as that of the emitted holes.

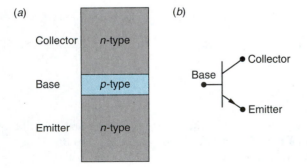

Fig. 10-43 (*a*) An *npn* transistor. The heavily doped emitter emits electrons that pass through the thin base to the collector. (*b*) Symbol for an *npn* transistor. The arrow points in the direction of the conventional current, which is opposite the direction of the emitted electrons.

Many computers use Pentium 4 processors like the one shown here with its cover removed. The Pentium 4 contains 55 million transistors and can process up to 2.53 billion instructions per second. The processor itself is the central area, about 15 mm square; it can handle a wide range of digital video, audio, and 3-D graphics applications. The rows of small circles are connectors. [*Photo courtesy of Intel.*]

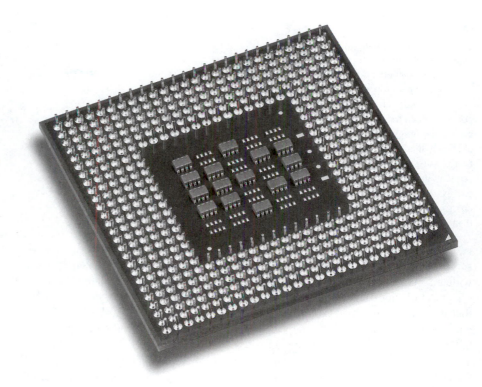

of two *pn* junctions. The operation of a *pnp* transistor is described in the More section "How Transistors Work." The operation of an *npn* transistor is similar.

More

How Transistors Work on the home page at www.whfreeman.com/modphysics4e describes the way transistors function in electrical circuits. Also here are Equations 10-65 through 10-69, Example 10-11, and Figures 10-44 and 10-45.

QUESTIONS

11. Why is a semiconductor diode less effective at high temperatures?

12. Explain why adding impurities to metals decreases their conductivity, but adding impurities to semiconductors increases their conductivity.

13. What would you expect to be the effect on the conductivity when impurities are added to an insulator?

10-9 Superconductivity

In 1911, just a few years after he had succeeded in liquefying helium and while he was investigating the properties of materials at liquid helium temperatures, the Dutch physicist H. Kamerlingh Onnes discovered that for some materials there exists a

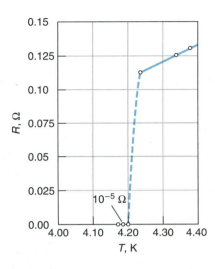

R, Ω

$10^{-5}\ \Omega$

T, K

Fig. 10-46 Plot by Kamerlingh Onnes of the resistance of mercury vs. temperature, showing sudden decrease at the critical temperature $T = 4.2$ K signifying the onset of superconductivity.

certain temperature, called the *critical temperature T_c*, below which the resistivity is zero and the conductivity $\sigma = 1/\rho \rightarrow \infty$. This phenomenon is called *superconductivity*. Figure 10-46 shows the plot Kamerlingh Onnes obtained of the resistance of mercury versus temperature. The critical temperature for mercury is 4.2 K. The critical temperature varies from material to material, but below this temperature the electrical resistance of the material is zero. Critical temperatures for other superconducting elements range from less than 0.1 K for hafnium and iridium to 9.2 K for niobium. The critical temperatures of several superconducting materials are given in Table 10-6. In the presence of a magnetic field B, the critical temperature is lower than it is when there is no field. As the magnetic field increases, the critical temperature decreases as illustrated

TABLE 10-6 T_c and B_c values for some type I and type II superconductors

Type I element	T_c (K)	B_c (at 0 K, T)	Type II compound	T_c (K)	B_{c2} (at 0 K, T)
Al	1.175	0.0105	Nb_3Sn	18.1	24.5
Cd	0.517	0.0028	Nb_3Ge	23.2	34.0
Hg	4.154	0.0411	NbN	16.0	15.3
In	3.408	0.0282	V_3Ga	16.5	35.0
Nb	9.25	0.2060	V_3Si	17.1	15.6
Os	0.66	0.0070	PbMoS	14.4	6.0
Pb	7.196	0.0803	CNb	8.0	1.7
Sn	3.722	0.0305	MgB_2	39.0	16
Tl	2.38	0.0178	Rb_3C_{60}	29.0	?
Zn	0.85	0.0054	Cs_2RbC_{60}	33.0	?

Fig. 10-47 Variation of the critical temperature with magnetic field for lead. Note that B_c approaches zero as T approaches T_c.

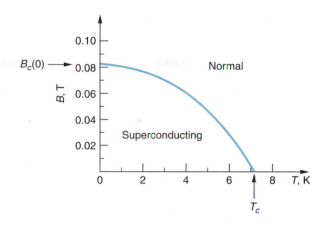

Electromagnets wound with superconducting wire are used in applications ranging from medical diagnostic MRI systems to beam focusing and bending magnets at large-particle accelerators worldwide.

in Figure 10-47. If the magnetic field is greater than some critical field B_c, superconductivity does not exist at any temperature. The values of T_c in the table are for $B = 0$.

Many metallic compounds are also superconductors. For example, the superconducting alloy Nb_3Ge, discovered in 1973, has a critical temperature of 23.2 K, which was the highest known until 1986, when the first of the complex high T_c cuprate ceramic superconductors was discovered. More recently, in 2001, Jun Akimitsu discovered that the metal compound MgB_2, available "off the shelf" for about \$2/g, became superconducting at 39 K, as of this writing the highest T_c yet for a conventional superconductor. (See Table 10-6.) Despite the cost and inconvenience of refrigeration with expensive liquid helium, which boils at 4.2 K, many superconducting magnets have been built using such materials.

The conductivity of a superconductor cannot be defined since its resistance is zero. There can be a current in a superconductor even when the electric field in the superconductor is zero. Such currents are called *supercurrents*. Indeed, steady currents have been observed to persist for years without apparent loss in superconducting rings in which there was no electric field.

Meissner Effect

Consider a superconducting material that is originally at a temperature greater than the critical temperature and is in the presence of a small external magnetic field $B < B_c$. We now cool the material below the critical temperature so that it becomes superconducting. Since the resistance is now zero, there can be no emf in the superconductor. Thus, from Faraday's law, the magnetic field in the superconductor cannot change. We therefore expect from classical physics that the magnetic field in the superconductor will remain constant. However, it is observed experimentally that when a superconductor is cooled below the critical temperature in an external magnetic field, the magnetic field lines are expelled from the superconductor and thus the magnetic field inside the superconductor is zero. (See Figure 10-48.) This effect was discovered by H. W. Meissner and R. Ochsenfeld in 1933 and is now known as the *Meissner effect*. It, not zero resistance, is the criterion that determines if a material is a superconductor. The mechanism by which the magnetic field lines are expelled or, more specifically, canceled within the bulk of the superconductor is a supercurrent (called a screening current) induced on the surface in such a

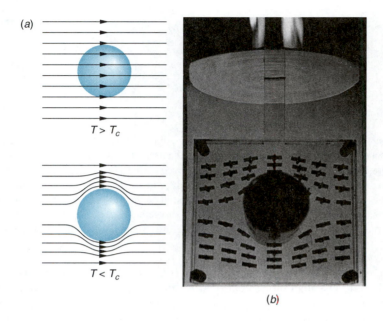

(a)

$T > T_c$

$T < T_c$

(b)

Fig. 10-48 (a) The Meissner effect in a superconducting sphere cooled in a constant applied magnetic field. As the temperature drops below the critical temperature T_c, the magnetic field lines are expelled from the sphere. (b) Demonstration of the Meissner effect. A superconducting tin cylinder is situated with its axis perpendicular to a horizontal magnetic field. The directions of the field lines near the cylinder are indicated by weakly magnetized compass needles mounted in a Lucite sandwich so that they are free to turn. [*Courtesy of A. Leitner, Rensselaer Polytechnic Institute.*]

direction as to exactly cancel the external field within the material.[14] Establishing the supercurrent "costs" the superconductor an amount of energy per unit volume equal to $B^2/2\mu_0$, where μ_0 is the permeability of the vacuum. When the field B becomes larger than B_c, there is insufficient energy available and the material reverts to its "normal" resistive state. The magnetic levitation shown in the photograph below results from the repulsion between the permanent magnet producing the external field and the magnetic field produced by the currents induced in the superconductor. Only certain superconductors called *type I*, or *"soft,"* superconductors exhibit the complete Meissner effect. Type I superconductors are primarily very pure metal elements. Figure 10-49a shows a plot of the magnetization M

A small, cubicle permanent magnet levitates above a disk of the superconductor yttrium-barium-copper oxide, cooled by liquid nitrogen to 77 K. At temperatures below 92 K, the disk becomes superconducting. The magnetic field of the cube sets up circulating electric supercurrents in the superconducting disk, such that the resultant magnetic field in the superconductor is zero. These currents produce a magnetic field opposite to that of the cube, and thus the cube is repelled. [*Courtesy of IBM Research.*]

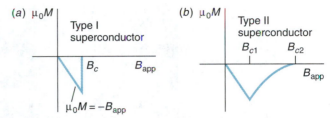

Fig. 10-49 Plots of μ_0 times the magnetization M vs. applied magnetic field for type I and type II superconductors. (*a*) In a type I superconductor, the resultant magnetic field is zero below a critical applied field B_c because the field due to induced currents on the surface of the super-conductor exactly cancels the applied field. Above the critical field, the material is a normal conductor and the magnetization is too small to be seen on this scale. (*b*) In a type II super-conductor, the magnetic field starts to penetrate the superconductor at a field B_{c1}, but the material remains superconducting up to the field B_{c2}, after which it becomes a normal conductor.

times μ_0 versus the applied magnetic field B_{app} for a type I superconductor. For a magnetic field less than the critical field B_c, the magnetic field $\mu_0 M$ induced in the superconductor is equal and opposite to the external magnetic field; that is, the superconductor is a perfect diamagnet. The values of B_c for type I superconductors are all too small for such materials to be useful in the coils of a superconducting magnet. (See Table 10-6.)

Other materials, known as *type II,* or *"hard," superconductors,* have a magnetiza-tion curve similar to that in Figure 10-49*b*. Such materials are usually alloys or metals that have large resistivities in the normal state. Type II superconductors exhibit *two* critical magnetic fields, B_{c1} and B_{c2}, as shown in Figure 10-50 for tantalum. Applied fields less than B_{c1} result in the Meissner effect of total magnetic flux cancellation and the entire sample is superconducting, as in type I superconductors. Applied fields greater than B_{c2} result in complete penetration of the magnetic field throughout the sample and the resistivity of the material returns to normal. However, in the region between B_{c1} and B_{c2} there is partial penetration of the magnetic field, the field lines being confined to *flux tubes,* also called *vortices,* in which the material has normal resistivity. The surrounding material remains field-free and superconducting, as illus-trated schematically in Figure 10-51. Each flux tube contains one quantized unit of magnetic flux, as will be described later in this section. For many type II superconduc-

Fig. 10-50 Critical magnetic fields B_{c1} and B_{c2} for Ta (99.95%) as a function of temperature. Below the B_{c1} curve Ta exhibits the Meiss-ner effect. Between the two curves is a mixed, or vortex, state with filaments of normal Ta penetrating the supercon-ducting state. Above the B_{c2} curve there is complete mag-netic field penetration and the entire sample has normal resistivity.

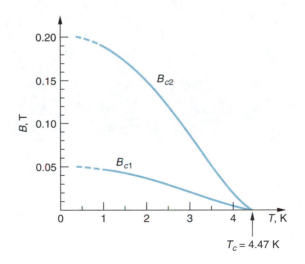

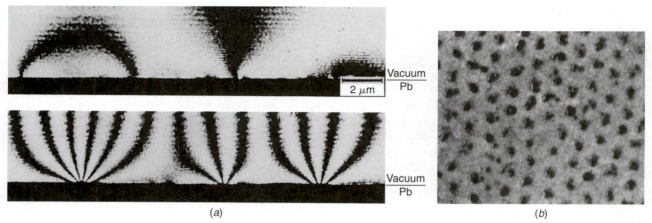

(a)   (b)

(*a*) Fluxoids penetrating a superconducting film. The image has been formed by a new technique—electron holography—in which coherent electron beams are used in place of coherent light beams to create a hologram. Electrons passing by a magnetic field are phase-shifted; i.e., the phase term in their wave function changes. (The shift arises from a phenomenon known as the Aharonov-Bohm effect.) By superposing such a phase-shifted beam with an unshifted reference beam, an interference pattern is created that can be interpreted as an image of the magnetic field. For the upper image, a magnetic field was applied perpendicular to a thin superconducting lead film. When the field was weak it was expelled by the Meissner effect. A stronger field, however, penetrated the film. The fluxoids shown arose from vortices of current set up in the superconductor—not from the applied field directly. In the upper right is an isolated fluxoid; in the upper left is an antiparallel pair of fluxoids. The lower micrograph, in which the lead film is thicker, shows penetration by bundles of fluxoids. [*Courtesy of Akira Tonomura, Hitachi Ltd., Saitama, Japan.*] (*b*) A lattice of fluxoid vortices penetrating the surface of a superconductor. They were made visible for the photograph by a dusting of fine ferromagnetic particles. [*Courtesy of U. Essmann.*]

tors the critical field B_{c2} may be several hundred times larger than the typical values of critical fields for type I superconductors (see Table 10-6). For example, the alloy Nb_3Ge has a critical field $B_{c2} = 34$ T. Such materials can be used to construct high-field superconducting magnets.

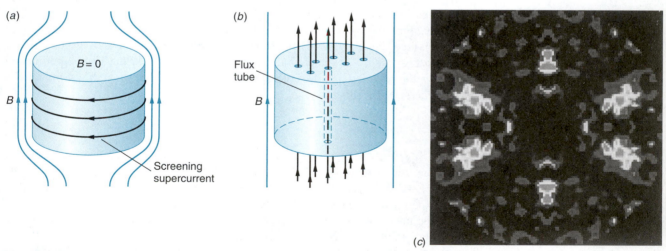

(c)

Fig. 10-51 (*a*) Below B_{c1} the type II material shows the Meissner effect. For temperatures below T_c the material is superconducting and $B = 0$ throughout the volume. (*b*) For $B_{c1} < B < B_{c2}$ magnetic field lines penetrate the material, but are confined to flux tubes of normally resistive material that form the so-called vortex lattice. For a given $T < T_c$, as the applied field B approaches B_{c2} the size of the superconducting region shrinks as more flux tubes occupy the volume. When $B > B_{c2}$ the entire material has normal resistivity. (*c*) The lattice of magnetic vortices in UPt_3, a strongly type II superconductor, is shown clearly by neutron diffraction.

Exploring

Flux Quantization

Consider a superconducting loop of area A carrying a current. There can be a magnetic flux $\phi_m = B_n A$ through the loop due to the current in the loop. According to Faraday's law of induction, if the flux changes, an emf will be induced in the loop that is proportional to the rate of change of the flux. But there can be no emf in the loop because there is no resistance. Therefore, the flux through the ring is frozen and cannot change. Indeed, the quantum-mechanical treatment of superconductivity reveals that the total flux through the loop is quantized and is given by

$$\phi_m = n\frac{h}{2e} \qquad n = 1, 2, 3, \ldots$$

The quantum of flux, called a *fluxoid,* is

$$\phi_0 = \frac{h}{2e} = 2.0678 \times 10^{-15} \ \text{T} \cdot \text{m}^2$$

Each flux tube in a type II superconductor with $B_{c1} < B < B_{c2}$ contains one quantum of flux.

BCS Theory

Our discussion of the classical free-electron theory in Section 10-2 considered the ions of the crystal lattice to be fixed. Resistivity was due to the interactions of the electrons with the ions of the lattice and both electron-electron interactions and the effects of lattice vibrations, i.e., electron-phonon interactions, were ignored. In the quantum theory of conduction, lattice vibrations were explicitly taken into account (see Equations 10-41 to 10-43). Lattice vibrations are also responsible for the *isotope effect*[15] in superconductivity, discovered in 1950. This experimental observation revealed that the critical temperature depended upon the isotopic mass of the crystal according to

$$M^{\alpha}T_c = \text{constant} \qquad\qquad \textbf{10-70}$$

where M is the average isotopic mass and α varies from material to material. For example, for mercury $\alpha = 0.50$ and $T_c = 4.185$ K for samples of average isotopic mass $M = 199.5$ u, whereas $T_c = 4.146$ K for samples with $M = 203.4$ u. Table 10-7 lists experimental values for α for a few superconductors.

The importance of the discovery represented by Equation 10-70 is to tell us that the lattice vibrations, hence the electron-phonon interactions, cannot be ignored. The assumption of fixed lattice ions is equivalent to assuming that $M \rightarrow \infty$ for electron-lattice ion interactions. But if $M \rightarrow \infty$, then T_c would be zero for all materials. In agreement with experimental observations, BCS theory also predicts the flux quantization described in the Exploring section above and the temperature dependence of B_c.

$$B_c(T)/B_c(0) = 1 - (T/T_c)^2$$

TABLE 10-7 Experimental values of α for a few superconductors			
Material	α	Material	α
Cd	0.32	Nb$_3$Sn	0.08
Hg	0.50	Os	0.15
Pb	0.49	Zn	0.45

Data from C. Kittel, Introduction to Solid State Physics, *7th ed. (New York: Wiley, 1995).*

It had been recognized for some time that superconductivity is due to a collective behavior of the conducting electrons, and discovery of the isotope effect pointed to the crucial interaction as being with the phonons. In 1957, John Bardeen, Leon Cooper, and Bob Schrieffer published a successful theory of superconductivity now known as the *BCS theory*.[16] According to this theory, the electrons in a superconductor are coupled in pairs at low temperatures. The coupling comes about because of the interaction between electrons and the crystal lattice. An electron moving through the lattice of positive ions interacts with and perturbs it as illustrated in Figure 10-52. The electron attracts the positive ions nearby, displacing them slightly, resulting in a region of increased positive charge density. Because the ions are bound to the lattice by elastic forces, this region of increased charge density propagates through the material as a vibrational wave in the lattice, i.e., a *phonon*. The momentum of the phonon has been provided by the electron and we can think of the electron as having emitted a phonon. A second electron that encounters the wave of increased positive charge concentration is attracted toward it by the Coulomb interaction and can absorb the momentum carried by the wave, i.e., it may absorb the phonon. Thus, the two electrons can interact via the phonon and (very important) the interaction is an attractive one, since both electrons experience an attractive force toward the region of increased positive charge density. At low temperatures ($T < T_c$) the attraction between the two electrons can exceed the Coulomb repulsion between them. Thus, the electrons can form a bound state called a *Cooper pair,* provided that the temperature is low enough so that the number and energy of randomly generated thermal phonons will not disrupt its formation. The electrons in a Cooper pair have opposite spins and equal and opposite linear momenta. Thus they form a system with zero spin and zero momentum. Each Cooper pair may be considered as a single particle with zero spin. Such a particle does not obey the Pauli exclusion principle, so any number of Copper pairs may be in the same quantum state with the same energy.[17] In the ground state of a superconductor (at $T = 0$), all the electrons are in Cooper pairs and all the Cooper pairs are in the same energy state. In the superconducting state, the Cooper pairs are correlated so that they all act together. In order for the electrons in a superconducting state to absorb or emit energy, the binding of the Cooper pairs must be broken. The energy needed to break up a Cooper pair is analogous to that needed to break up a molecule into its constituent atoms. This energy is called the *superconducting energy gap E_g*. In the BCS theory, this energy at absolute zero is predicted to be

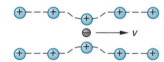

Fig. 10-52 An electron traveling through the lattice of positive ions generates a wave of increased charge density, shown in two dimensions by the dashed lines. The momentum of the wave comes at the expense of the electron's momentum. A second electron may encounter the wave and absorb its momentum. The net effect is an attraction between the two electrons and the production, for $T < T_c$, of a Cooper pair.

$$E_g = 3.5 \, kT_c \qquad\qquad \textbf{10-71}$$

EXAMPLE 10-12 Energy Gap of Cadmium (*a*) Calculate the superconducting energy gap at $T = 0$ K predicted by the BCS theory for cadmium and compare the result with the measured result of 1.50×10^{-4} eV. (*b*) Compute the wavelength of a photon whose energy is just sufficient to break up a Cooper pair in cadmium.

Solution

(*a*) From Table 10-6, we have that $T_c = 0.517$ K for cadmium. The BCS prediction of the energy gap is then

$$E_g = 3.5 \, kT_c = \frac{3.5(1.38 \times 10^{-23} \text{ J/K})(0.517 \text{ K})}{(1.60 \times 10^{-19} \text{ J/eV})} = 1.56 \times 10^{-4} \text{ eV}$$

This differs from the measured values of 1.50×10^{-4} eV by about 4 percent.

(*b*) $E_g = hf = hc/\lambda$, or we have that

$$\lambda = hc/E_g = \frac{(6.63 \times 10^{-34} \text{ J/s})(3.00 \times 10^8 \text{ m/s})}{(1.56 \times 10^{-4} \text{ eV})(1.60 \times 10^{-19} \text{ J/eV})} = 7.97 \times 10^{-3} \text{ m}$$

This wavelength is in the short-wavelength microwave region of the electromagnetic spectrum.

Note that the energy gap for a typical superconductor is much smaller than the energy gap for a typical semiconductor, which is of the order of 1 eV. As the temperature is increased from $T = 0$, some of the Cooper pairs are broken. The resulting individual (unpaired) electrons interact with the Cooper pairs, reducing the energy gap until at $T = T_c$ the energy gap is zero (see Figure 10-53). Notice, too, that the gap energy is typically larger than that available from the thermal energy of the system. For example, for $T = 0.5T_c$, $E_g(T) = (0.95)E_g(0) \approx (3.3)kT_c$, whereas the thermal energy $kT = (0.5)kT_c$.

The Cooper pairs that we have discussed so far have zero momentum, so there are as many electrons traveling in one direction as the other and there is no current. Cooper pairs can also be formed with a net momentum **p** rather than zero momentum, but all the pairs have the same momentum. In this state, current is carried by the

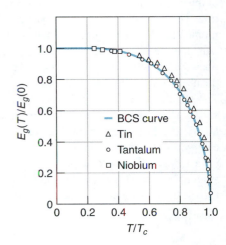

Fig. 10-53 Ratio of the energy gap at temperature T to that at $T = 0$ as a function of the relative temperature T/T_c. The solid curve is that predicted by the BCS theory.

Cooper pairs. In ordinary conductors, resistance is present because the current carriers can be scattered with a change in momentum. As we have discussed, this scattering may be due to impurity atoms or thermal vibrations of the lattice ions. In a superconductor, the Cooper pairs are constantly scattering each other, but since the total momentum remains constant in this process, there is no change in the current. A Cooper pair cannot be scattered by a lattice ion because all the pairs act together. The only way that the current can be decreased by scattering is if a pair is broken up, which requires energy greater than or equal to the energy gap E_g. At reasonably low currents, scattering events in which the total momentum of a Cooper pair is changed are completely prohibited, so there is no resistance.

EXAMPLE 10-13 How Big Is a Cooper Pair? Calculate an estimate of the separation Δx of the electrons forming a Cooper pair, assuming that the binding energy of the pair equals the gap energy E_g and that, like semiconductors, the gap is centered on the Fermi energy E_F.

Solution

The energy of either electron is, with the aid of the de Broglie relation, given by

$$E = \frac{p^2}{2m^*} = \frac{\hbar^2 k^2}{2m^*}$$

and

$$\Delta E = \frac{2k\hbar^2 \Delta k}{2m^*}$$

If we associate E with the Fermi energy and ΔE with the gap, then

$$\frac{\Delta E}{E} \approx \frac{E_g}{E_F} \approx \frac{2k\hbar^2 \Delta k}{2m^*} \times \frac{2m^*}{\hbar^2 k^2} \approx \frac{2\Delta k}{k}$$

Since the Fermi energy is typically of the order of 1 eV and the gap of the order of 10^{-4} eV, as computed in Example 10-12, then $E_g/E_F \approx 10^{-4}$ and

$$\Delta k \approx 0.5 \times 10^{-4}\, k$$

where k refers to the value at the Fermi level. As was discussed in Section 10-6 and illustrated in Figure 10-21, $k = \pi/a$ at the top of the first allowed band, where the energy is approximately E_F. The lattice spacing $a \approx 0.1$ nm, so we have that $k \approx \pi/0.1$, and $\Delta k = 10^{-3}$ nm. From the uncertainty relation (Equation 5-16), we then have that the uncertainty in the location of either electron, i.e., the extent of their wave functions in space, is

$$\Delta x = \frac{1}{\Delta k} \approx 10^3\, \text{nm}$$

or roughly equal to 10,000 atomic diameters or approximately equal to the wavelength of visible light.

TABLE 10-8	Critical temperatures of some high T_c superconductors
Material	T_c, K
LaBaCuO	30
La_2CuO_4	40
$YBa_2Cu_3O_7$	92
$DyBa_2Cu_3O_7$	92.5
$C_{60}(CHBr_3)$	117
BiSrCaCuO	120
TlBaCaCuo	125

High-Temperature Superconductivity

For many years, the highest known critical temperature for a superconductor was 23.2 K for the alloy Nb_3Ge. Then, in 1986, Bednorz and Muller found that an oxide of lanthanum, barium, and copper became superconducting at 30 K. Soon afterward, in 1987, superconductivity with a critical temperature of 92 K was found in a ceramic of copper oxide containing yttrium and barium ($YBa_2Cu_3O_7$). Since then, several copper oxides have been found with critical temperatures as high as 135 K. Table 10-8 lists some of the high-temperature superconductors along with their critical temperatures. These discoveries have revolutionized the study of superconductivity because relatively inexpensive liquid nitrogen, which boils at 77 K, can be used for a coolant. However, there are many problems, such as the brittleness of ceramics, that thus far make these new superconductors difficult to use.

High-temperature superconductors are all type II superconductors with very high upper critical fields. For some, B_{c2} is estimated to be as high as 100 T. Although the BCS theory appears to be the correct starting place for understanding these new superconductors, they have many features that are not clearly understood. Thus, there is much work, both experimental and theoretical, to be done.

Exploring

Josephson Junctions

In Section 6-6, we discussed barrier penetration—the tunneling of a single particle through a potential barrier. The tunneling of electrons from one metal to another can be observed by separating the two metals with a thin layer only a few nanometers thick of an insulating material such as aluminum oxide. When both metals are normal metals (not superconductors), the current resulting from the tunneling of electrons through the insulating layer obeys Ohm's law for low applied voltages (see Figure 10-54a).

When one of the metals is a normal metal and the other is a superconductor, there is no current (at absolute zero) unless the applied voltage V is greater than a critical voltage $V_c = E_g/2e$, where E_g is the superconductor energy gap. Figure 10-54b shows the plot of current versus voltage for this situation. The current jumps abruptly when V is great enough to break up a Cooper pair. (At temperatures above absolute zero, there is a small current because some of the electrons in the superconductor are thermally excited above the energy gap and therefore are not paired.) The superconducting energy gap can thus be accurately measured by measuring the critical voltage V_c.

In 1962, Brian Josephson[18] proposed that when two superconductors form a junction, now called a *Josephson junction*, Cooper pairs could tunnel from one superconductor to the other with no resistance. The current is observed with no voltage applied across the junction and is given by

$$I = I_{max} \sin(\phi_2 - \phi_1) \qquad \textbf{10-72}$$

where I_{max} is the maximum current, which depends on the thickness of the barrier, ϕ_1 is the phase of the wave function for the Cooper pairs in one of the superconductors, and ϕ_2 is the phase of the corresponding wave function in the other superconductor. (The phase of a wave function is the exponent $Et/\hbar = \omega t$ of the time part of the total wave function. See Section 6-1.) This result has been observed experimentally and is known as the *dc Josephson effect*.

Josephson also predicted that if a dc voltage were applied across a Josephson junction, there would be a current that alternates with frequency f given by

$$f = \frac{2eV}{h} \qquad \textbf{10-73}$$

This result, known as the *ac Josephson effect*, has also been observed experimentally, and careful measurement of the frequency allows a precise determination of the ratio e/h. Because frequency can be measured so accurately, the ac Josephson effect is also used to establish precise voltage standards. The inverse effect, in which the application of an alternating voltage across a Josephson junction results in a dc current, has also been observed.

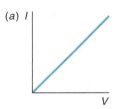

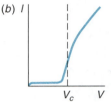

Fig. 10-54 Tunneling current vs. voltage for a junction of two metals separated by a thin oxide layer. (*a*) When both metals are normal metals, the current is proportional to the voltage as predicted by Ohm's law. (*b*) When one metal is a normal metal and one is a superconductor, the current is approximately zero until the applied voltage exceeds the critical voltage $V_c = E_g/2e$.

EXAMPLE 10-14 **AC Josephson Effect** Using $e = 1.602 \times 10^{-19}$ C and $h = 6.626 \times 10^{-34}$ J·s, calculate the frequency of the Josephson current if the applied voltage is 1 μV.

Solution
From Equation 10-73, we obtain

$$f = \frac{2eV}{h} = \frac{2(1.602 \times 10^{-19}\,\text{C})(10^{-6}\,\text{V})}{6.626 \times 10^{-34}\,\text{J·s}} = 4.836 \times 10^8\,\text{Hz}$$

$$= 483.6\,\text{MHz}$$

There is a third effect observed with Josephson junctions. When a dc magnetic field is applied through a superconducting ring containing two Josephson junctions, the total supercurrent shows interference effects that depend on the intensity of the

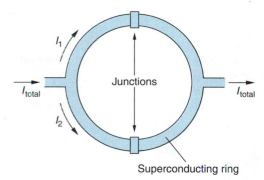

Fig. 10-55 A superconducting ring with two Josephson junctions. When there is no applied magnetic field through the ring, the currents I_1 and I_2 are in phase. A very small applied magnetic field produces a phase difference in the two currents that produces interference in the total current exiting the ring.

magnetic field (Figure 10-55). This effect can be used to measure very weak magnetic fields. It is the basis for a device called a *SQUID* (for *S*uperconducting *Qu*antum *Inter*ference *D*evice) that can detect magnetic fields as low as 10^{-14} T. Such a device can detect the magnetic fields produced by the tiny currents flowing in the heart and brain.

Summary

TOPIC	RELEVANT EQUATIONS AND REMARKS
1. Structure of solids	Solids are often found in crystalline form in which a small structure called the *unit cell* is repeated over and over. The structure of the unit cell depends on the type of bonding between the atoms, ions, or molecules forming the crystal.
Ionic and covalent solids	The attractive part of the potential energy of an ion in an ionic crystal is

$$U_{\text{att}} = -\alpha\,\frac{ke^2}{r} \qquad \text{10-1}$$

where r is the separation between neighboring ions and α is the Madelung constant, which depends on the crystal geometry. The constant α is 1.7476 for face-centered-cubic crystals.

In covalently bonded crystals the individual bonds are just like those in covalently bonded molecules.

The metallic bond has no single-molecule counterpart. One or more valence electrons are free to move throughout the solid and *all* of the atoms share all of the free electrons, making this bond roughly analogous to the covalent bond.

2. Classical free-electron theory	Electrical resistivity ρ is given by

$$\rho = \frac{m_e\langle v\rangle}{ne^2\lambda} \qquad \text{10-17}$$

where $\langle v\rangle$ is the mean speed of the electrons and λ is the mean free path between collisions. The latter is given by

$$\lambda = \frac{1}{n_a\pi r^2} \qquad \text{10-19}$$

where n_a is the ion density. These yield Ohm's law correctly, but result in the wrong temperature dependence of the resistivity.

TOPIC	RELEVANT EQUATIONS AND REMARKS
3. Electron gas in metals	The average energy of the electrons at ordinary temperatures is much larger than kT; $$\langle E \rangle = \frac{3}{5} E_F \qquad \text{10-37}$$ where typical values of the Fermi energy E_F are 1 to 2 eV.
4. Quantum theory of conduction	This theory results from making two important corrections to the classical free-electron theory. First, the Fermi-Dirac distribution of electron energies is used, rather than the Maxwell-Boltzmann distribution. Second, the effect of the wave characteristics of the electrons is considered in their scattering from the lattice ions. The resulting theory is in good agreement with observations.
5. Magnetism in solids	The origin of magnetism in solids is the electron spins and their associated magnetic moments.
6. Band theory of solids	When many atoms are brought together to form a solid, the individual energy levels are split into bands of allowed energies. The splitting depends on the type of bonding and the lattice separation. In a conductor, the upper-most band containing electrons is only partially full, so there are many available states for excited electrons. In an insulator, the uppermost band containing electrons, the valence band, is completely full and there is a large energy gap between it and the next allowed band, the conduction band. In a semiconductor, the energy gap between the filled valence band and the empty conduction band is small, so at ordinary temperatures an appreciable number of electrons are thermally excited into the conduction band.
Kronig-Penney model	The solid is modeled as a periodic potential. The wave functions are then $$\psi(x) = u_k(x)e^{ikx} \qquad \text{10-51}$$ where the function $u_k(x)$ is periodic with a period equal to that of the spacing of the potential wells and e^{ikx} is a free electron, i.e., a plane wave. The energy gaps occur at $$ka = \pm n\pi \qquad \text{10-56}$$ for integer n and a equal to the lattice spacing.
7. Impurity semiconductors	The conductivity of a semiconductor can be greatly increased by doping. In an n-type semiconductor, the doping adds electrons just below the conduction band. In a p-type semiconductor, holes are added just above the valence band. A junction between an n-type and p-type semiconductor has applications in many devices, such as diodes, solar cells, and light-emitting diodes. A transistor consists of a very thin semiconductor of one type sandwiched between two semiconductors of the opposite type. Transistors are used in amplifiers because a small variation in the base current results in a large variation in the collector current.
8. Superconductivity	In a superconductor the resistance drops suddenly to zero below a critical temperature T_c. Magnetic field lines are expelled and $B = 0$ inside a type I semiconductor, a phenomenon called the Meissner effect. Superconductivity at low temperatures is described by BCS theory, in which free electrons form Cooper pairs. Recently discovered high-temperature semiconductors are only partially understood in terms of BCS theory.

General References

The following general references are written at a level appropriate for the readers of this book.

Blatt, F., *Modern Physics,* McGraw-Hill, New York, 1992.

Burns, G., *Solid State Physics,* Academic Press, Orlando, Fla., 1985.

Eisberg, R., and R. Resnick, *Quantum Physics of Atoms, Molecules, Solids, Nuclei, and Particles,* 2d ed., Wiley, New York, 1985.

Fermi, E., *Molecules, Crystals, and Quantum Statistics* (trans. M. Ferro-Luzzi), W. A. Benjamin, New York, 1966.

Holden, A., *The Nature of Solids,* Columbia University Press, New York, 1968. An excellent nonmathematical treatment of the properties of solids.

Kittel, C., *Introduction to Solid State Physics,* 7th ed., Wiley, New York, 1995.

Leitner, A., *Introduction to Superconductivity,* Michigan State University, East Lansing, 1965. This excellent film, running 48 minutes, is probably the best available introduction to superconductivity.

Shockley, W., *Electrons and Holes in Semiconductors,* Van Nostrand, Princeton, N. J., 1950.

Thorton, S., and A. Rex, *Modern Physics for Scientists and Engineers,* 2d ed., Saunders College Publishing, Fort Worth, Tex., 2000.

Notes

1. The constant n is often called the Born exponent.

2. Carbon also has a fourth solid form, charcoal, which has no well-defined crystalline structure.

3. Notice that this view of the metal fits the definition of a plasma set forth in the opening paragraph of the chapter. Though not usually thought of in that way, metals are indeed low-temperature plasmas.

4. It is tempting but incorrect to think that if τ is the average time between collisions, the average time since its last collision is $(\frac{1}{2})\tau$ rather than τ. If you find this confusing, you may take comfort in the fact that Drude used the incorrect value $(\frac{1}{2})\tau$ in his original work.

5. Drude's mistake of using $v_d = \frac{1}{2}eE\,\tau/m_e$ led him to a prediction of the Lorentz number twice as large as this and, in fact, in much better agreement with experiment.

6. Felix Bloch (1905–1983), Swiss-American physicist. He devised a method for measuring atomic magnetic fields in liquids and solids which led to the development of nuclear magnetic resonance (NMR) spectroscopy and earned for him a share (with E. M. Purcell) of the 1952 Nobel Prize in physics. He was the first director-general of CERN, the European Center for Nuclear Research.

7. The graph of the energy bands and gaps of Figure 10-20*b* results from a simplified version of the conditional equation connecting k, k', and α in which $b \rightarrow 0$ and $U_0 \rightarrow \infty$. In that limit the lattice spacing is a, rather than $a + b$, as in Figure 10-19.

8. This mixing, called hybridization, was discussed in Section 9-2.

9. See, e.g., Section 25-5 in P. Tipler, *Physics for Scientists and Engineers,* 4th ed. (New York: W. H. Freeman, 1999).

10. The fact that the radius of the bound electron is several times the equilibrium spacing of the atoms helps justify our tacit assumption that the fifth electron sees a uniform dielectric constant in the crystal.

11. Klaus von Klitzing (b. 1943), German physicist. He received the 1985 Nobel Prize in physics for this discovery.

12. Daniel C. Tsui (b. 1939), Chinese-American physicist. He received the 1998 Nobel Prize in physics (with H. L. Stormer and R. B. Laughlin) for his discovery.

13. William B. Shockley (1910–1989), John Bardeen (1908–1991), and Walter H. Brattain (1902–1987), American physicists. Shockley discovered that doped germanium crystals were excellent rectifiers and, subsequently, the three Bell Laboratories colleagues discovered that two such "solid-state rectifiers" combined would amplify current. The discovery of this device, the transistor, earned them the 1956 Nobel Prize in physics.

14. Actually, the field decreases exponentially across the surface, reaching zero at a depth of about 10 nm.

15. Isotopes are atoms with the same atomic number Z, but different atomic mass numbers A. Isotopes will be discussed in Chapter 11.

16. John Bardeen (1908–1991), Leon N. Cooper (b. 1930), and J. Robert Schrieffer (b. 1931), American physicists. Developed at the University of Illinois, the BCS theory earned the collaborators the 1972 Nobel Prize in physics and Bardeen became the only person thus far to win two physics Nobel Prizes (see note 13).

17. This may make it seem like the Cooper pair is a boson and superconductivity another example of Bose-Einstein condensation (see Section 8-3); however, the large size of the Cooper pair (see Example 10-13) means many pairs overlap and that the symmetry of the pair with respect to an exchange of electrons must also take into account exchanges involving electrons in different pairs. The result is that the Cooper pair is neither a pure boson nor a pure fermion.

18. Brian D. Josephson (b. 1940), Welsh physicist. For this discovery, made while he was still a graduate student, he shared the 1973 physics Nobel Prize with L. Esaki and I. Giaever. Bardeen had strongly opposed Josephson's tunneling prediction until experiments, led by those of Giaever (also done while he was a graduate student), confirmed tunneling by Cooper pairs.

PROBLEMS

Level I

Section 10-1 The Structure of Solids

10-1. Calculate the distance r_0 between the K$^+$ and Cl$^-$ ions in KCl, assuming that each ion occupies a cubic volume of side r_0. The molar mass of KCl is 74.55 g/mol and its density is 1.984 g/cm^3.

10-2. The distance between the Li$^+$ and Cl$^-$ ions in LiCl is 0.257 nm. Use this and the molecular mass of LiCl (42.4 g/mol) to compute the density of LiCl.

10-3. Find the value of n in Equation 10-6 that gives the measured dissociation energy of 741 kJ/mol for LiCl, which has the same structure as NaCl and for which $r_0 = 0.257$ nm.

10-4. The crystal structure of KCl is the same as that of NaCl. (*a*) Calculate the electrostatic potential energy of attraction of KCl, assuming that r_0 is 0.314 nm. (*b*) Assuming that $n = 9$ in Equation 10-6, calculate the dissociation energy in eV per ion pair and in kcal/mole. (*c*) The measured dissociation energy is 165.5 kcal/mole. Use this to determine n in Equation 10-6.

10-5. The observed dissociation energy of solid LiBr is 788 kJ/mol. Compute the cohesive energy of LiBr and compare the result with the value in Table 10-1. (Ionization energies for Li and Br are in Table 9-1.)

10-6. Suppose hard spheres of radius R are located at the corners of a unit cell with a simple cubic structure. (*a*) If the hard spheres touch so as to take up minimum volume, what is the size of the unit cell? (*b*) What fraction of the volume of the unit cell is occupied by hard spheres?

10-7. Using the data for ionic and metallic crystals from Table 10-1, (*a*) graph cohesive energy versus melting point and put the best straight line through the points. (*b*) Determine the cohesive energies of cobalt, silver, and sodium, whose melting temperatures are 1495°C, 962°C, and 98°C, respectively. (The measured values are: cobalt 4.43 eV, silver 2.97 eV, and sodium 1.13 eV.)

10-8. Figure 10-56 shows a one-dimensional ionic lattice consisting of doubly charged positive ions and twice as many singly charged negative ions. Compute the Madelung constant for this "crystal" to within 1 percent.

Fig. 10-56 Problem 10-8.

Section 10-2 Classical Theory of Conduction

10-9. (*a*) Given a mean free path $\lambda = 0.4$ nm and a mean speed $\langle v \rangle = 1.17 \times 10^5$ m/s for the current flow in copper at a temperature of 300 K, calculate the classical value for the resistivity ρ of copper. (*b*) The classical model suggests that the mean free path is temperature-independent and that $\langle v \rangle$ depends on temperature. From this model, what would ρ be at 100 K?

10-10. Find (*a*) the current density and (*b*) the drift velocity if there is a current of 1 mA in a No. 14 copper wire. (The diameter of No. 14 wire, which is often used in household wiring, is 0.064 in = 0.163 cm.)

10-11. A measure of the density of the free-electron gas in a metal is the distance r_s, which is defined as the radius of the sphere whose volume equals the volume per conduction electron. (*a*) Show that $r_s = (3/4\pi n_a)^{1/3}$, where n_a is the free-electron number density. (*b*) Calculate r_s for copper in nanometers.

10-12. Calculate the number density of free electrons in (*a*) Ag ($\rho = 10.5$ g/cm^3) and (*b*) Au ($\rho = 19.3$ g/cm^3), assuming one free electron per atom, and compare your results with the values listed in Table 10-3.

10-13. Calculate the number density of free electrons for (*a*) Mg ($\rho = 1.74$ g/cm^3) and (*b*) Zn ($\rho = 7.1$ g/cm^3), assuming two free electrons per atom, and compare your results with the values listed in Table 10-3.

10-14. (*a*) Using $\lambda = 0.37$ nm and $\langle v \rangle = 1.08 \times 10^5$ m/s at $T = 300$ K, calculate σ and ρ for copper from Equations 10-17 and 10-18. Using the same value of λ, find σ and ρ at (*b*) $T = 200$ K and (*c*) $T = 100$ K.

Section 10-3 Free-Electron Gas in Metals

10-15. Find the average energy of the electrons at $T = 0$ K in (*a*) copper ($E_F = 7.06$ eV) and (*b*) Li ($E_F = 4.77$ eV).

10-16. Calculate the Fermi energy for magnesium in a long, very thin wire.

10-17. Compute (*a*) the Fermi energy and (*b*) the Fermi temperature for silver and for iron and compare your results with the corresponding values in Table 10-3.

10-18. Show that for $T = 300$ K about 0.1 percent of the free electrons in metallic silver have an energy greater than E_F.

Section 10-4 Quantum Theory of Conduction

10-19. What is the Fermi speed, i.e., the speed of a conduction electron whose energy is equal to the Fermi energy E_F, for (*a*) Na, (*b*) Au, and (*c*) Sn? (See Table 10-3.)

10-20. The resistivities of Na, Au, and Sn at $T = 273$ K are 4.2 $\mu\Omega \cdot$ cm, 2.04 $\mu\Omega \cdot$ cm, and 10.6 $\mu\Omega \cdot$ cm, respectively. Use these values and the Fermi speeds calculated in Problem 10-19 to find the mean free paths λ for the conduction electrons in these elements.

10-21. At what temperature is the heat capacity due to the electron gas in copper equal to 10 percent of that due to lattice vibrations?

10-22. Use Equation 10-44 with $\alpha = \pi^2/4$ to calculate the average energy of an electron in copper at $T = 300$ K. Compare your result with the average energy at $T = 0$ and the classical result of $(3/2)kT$.

10-23. Compute the maximum fractional contribution to the heat capacity of solid iron that can be made by the electrons.

Section 10-5 Magnetism in Solids

10-24. The magnetic polarization P of any material is defined as $P = (\rho_+ - \rho_-)/\rho$. Compute the high-temperature polarization of a paramagnetic solid at $T = 200$ K in a magnetic field of 2.0 T.

10-25. Show that the magnetic susceptibility χ is a dimensionless quantity.

Section 10-6 Band Theory of Solids

10-26. The energy gap between the valence band and the conduction band in silicon is 1.14 eV at room temperature. What is the wavelength of a photon that will excite an electron from the top of the valence band to the bottom of the conduction band?

10-27. Work Problem 10-26 for (*a*) germanium, for which the energy gap is 0.74 eV, and (*b*) for diamond, for which the energy gap is 7.0 eV.

10-28. A photon of wavelength 3.35 μm has just enough energy to raise an electron from the valence band to the conduction band in a lead sulfide crystal. (*a*) Find the energy gap between these bands in lead sulfide. (*b*) Find the temperature T for which kT equals this energy gap.

10-29. Consider a small silicon crystal measuring 100 nm on each side. (*a*) Compute the total number N of silicon atoms in the crystal. (The density of silicon is 2.33 g/cm^3.) (*b*) If the conduction band in silicon is 13 eV wide and recalling that there are 4N states in this

band, compute an approximate value for the energy spacing between adjacent conduction band states for the crystal.

Section 10-7 Impurity Semiconductors

10-30. Arsenic has five valence electrons. If arsenic is used as a dopant in silicon, compute (a) the ionization energy and (b) the orbit radius of the fifth arsenic electron. The effective mass for electrons in silicon is $0.2\ m_e$. (c) What is the ratio of the ionization energy of the fifth electron to the energy gap in silicon?

10-31. Gallium has three valence electrons. If gallium is used to dope germanium, compute (a) the ionization energy of the hole and (b) the orbit radius of the hole. The effective mass of holes in germanium is $0.34\ m_e$.

10-32. What type of semiconductor is obtained if silicon is doped with (a) aluminum and (b) phosphorus? (See Appendix C for the electron configurations of these elements.)

10-33. The donor energy levels in an n-type semiconductor are 0.01 eV below the conduction band. Find the temperature for which $kT = 0.01$ eV.

10-34. A strip of tin is 10 mm wide and 0.2 mm thick. When a current of 20 A is established in the strip and a uniform magnetic field of 0.25 T is oriented perpendicular to the plane of the strip, a Hall voltage of 2.20 μV is measured across the width of the strip. Compute (a) the density of charge carriers in tin and (b) the average number of charge carriers contributed by each tin atom. The density of tin is 5.75×10^3 kg/m^3 and its molecular mass is 118.7.

Section 10-8 Semiconductor Junctions and Devices

10-35. For a temperature of 300 K, use Equation 10-64 to find the bias voltage V_b for which the exponential term has the value (a) 10 and (b) 0.1.

10-36. For what value of bias voltage V_b does the exponential in Equation 10-64 have the value (a) 5 and (b) 0.5 for $T = 200$ K?

10-37. Compute the fractional change in the current through a pn-junction diode when the forward bias is changed from +0.1 V to +0.2 V.

10-38. For $T = 77$ K, use Equation 10-64 to find the bias voltage V_b for which the exponential term had the value (a) 10 and (b) 1. (c) Compute I_{net} for $I_0 = 1$ ma.

Section 10-9 Superconductivity

10-39. Three naturally occurring isotopes of lead are ^{206}Pb, ^{207}Pb, and ^{208}Pb. Using the value of α from Table 10-7 and the isotopic masses from Appendix A, compute the critical temperatures of these isotopes.

10-40. Compute (a) the superconducting energy gap for indium and (b) the wavelength of a photon that could just break up a Cooper pair in indium at $T = 0$ K.

10-41. (a) Use Equation 10-71 to calculate the superconducting energy gap for tin and compare your result with the measured value of 6×10^{-4} eV. (b) Use the measured value to calculate the wavelength of a photon having sufficient energy to break up a Cooper pair in tin at $T = 0$ K.

10-42. Use the BCS curve in Figure 10-53 to estimate the energy gaps in (a) tin, (b) niobium, (c) aluminum, and (d) zinc, all at $T = 0.5T_c$.

10-43. Expressing the temperature T as a fraction of the critical temperature T_c, according to BCS theory at what temperature is (a) $B_c = 0.1B_c(0)$, (b) $B_c = 0.5B_c(0)$, (c) $B_c = 0.9B_c(0)$?

Level II

10-44. Estimate the fraction of free electrons in copper that are in excited states above the Fermi energy at (a) room temperature of 300 K and (b) 1000 K.

10-45. A one-dimensional model of an ionic crystal consists of a line of alternating positive and negative ions with distance r_0 between adjacent ions. (*a*) Show that the potential energy of attraction of one ion in the line is

$$V = -\frac{2ke^2}{r_0}\left(1 - \frac{1}{2} + \frac{1}{3} - \frac{1}{4} + \frac{1}{5} - \cdots\right)$$

(*b*) Using the result that

$$\ln(1 + x) = x - \frac{x^2}{2} + \frac{x^2}{3} - \frac{x^4}{4} + \cdots$$

show that the Madelung constant for this one-dimensional model is $\alpha = 2\ln 2 = 1.386$.

10-46. Estimate the Fermi energy of zinc from its electronic molar heat capacity of $(3.74 \times 10^{-4}\ \text{J/mol}\cdot\text{K})T$.

10-47. The density of the electron states in a metal can be written $g(E) = AE^{1/2}$, where A is a constant and E is measured from the bottom of the conduction band. (*a*) Show that the total number of states is $(2/3)A(E_F)^{3/2}$. (*b*) About what fraction of the conduction electrons are within kT of the Fermi energy? (*c*) Evaluate this fraction for copper at $T = 300$ K.

10-48. Germanium can be used to measure the energy of incident particles. Consider a 660-keV gamma ray emitted from ^{137}Cs. (*a*) Given that the band gap in germanium is 0.72 eV, how many electron-hole pairs can be generated by this incident gamma ray? (*b*) The number of pairs N in part (*a*) will have statistical fluctuations given by $\pm N^{1/2}$. What then is the energy resolution of this detector in this photon energy region?

10-49. A doped *n*-type silicon sample with 10^{16} electrons per cubic centimeter in the conduction band has a resistivity of $5 \times 10^{-3}\ \Omega\cdot\text{m}$ at 300 K. Find the mean free path of the electrons. Use $0.2\ m_e$ for the effective mass of the electron. Compare your result with the mean free path of electrons in copper at 300 K.

10-50. A "good" silicon diode has a current-voltage characteristic given by

$$I = I_0(e^{eV_b/kT} - 1)$$

Let $kT = 0.025$ eV (room temperature) and the saturation current $I_0 = 1$ nA. (*a*) Show that for small reverse-bias voltages, the resistance is 25 MΩ. (*Hint:* Do a Taylor expansion of the exponential function, or use your calculator and enter small values for V_b.) (*b*) Find the dc resistance for a reverse bias of 0.5 V. (*c*) Find the dc resistance for a 0.5-V forward bias. What is the current in this case? (*d*) Calculate the ac resistance dV/dI for a 0.5-V forward bias.

10-51. The relative binding of the extra electron in the arsenic atom that replaces an atom in silicon or germanium can be understood from a calculation of the first Bohr orbit of this electron in these materials. Four of arsenic's outer electrons form covalent bonds, so the fifth electron sees a singularly charged center of attraction. This model is a modified hydrogen atom. In the Bohr model of the hydrogen atom, the electron moves in free space at a radius a_0 given by

$$a_0 = \frac{\epsilon_0 h^2}{\pi m_e e^2}$$

When an electron moves in a crystal, we can approximate the effect of the other atoms by replacing ϵ_0 with $\kappa\epsilon_0$ and m_e with an effective mass for the electron. For silicon κ is 12 and the effective mass is about $0.2 m_e$, and for germanium κ is 16 and the effective mass is about $0.1 m_e$. Estimate the Bohr radii for the outer electron as it orbits the impurity arsenic atom in silicon and germanium.

10-52. The mean free path of an electron in a metal depends on both the lattice oscillations of the metal ions and those of any impurity ions according to $1/\lambda = 1/\lambda_m + 1/\lambda_i$. The resistivity of pure copper is increased by about $1.2 \times 10^{-8}\ \Omega \cdot m$ by the addition of 1 percent (by number of atoms) of a certain impurity dispersed evenly throughout the metal. (a) Estimate λ_i from this information. (b) The impuity atoms are "seen" by the electrons to have an effective diameter d. Estimate the scattering cross section d^2 from Equation 10-19, where $d = 2r$.

Level III

10-53. When arsenic is used to dope silicon, the fifth arsenic electron and the As^+ ion act like a hydrogen atom system, except that the potential function $V(r)$ and the electron mass must be modified as described in Section 10-7 to account for the crystal lattice. With these modifications, (a) solve the Schrödinger equation, using the solution in Chapter 7 as a guide. (b) Obtain Equation 10-58, and (c) sketch a properly scaled energy-level diagram for the fifth electron for $n = 1$ through 5.

10-54. The quantity K is the force constant for a "spring" consisting of a line of alternating positive and negative ions. If these ions are displaced slightly from their equilibrium separation r_0, they will vibrate with a frequency

$$f = \frac{1}{2\pi}\sqrt{\frac{K}{m}}$$

(a) Use the values of α, n, and r_0 for NaCl and the reduced mass for the NaCl molecule to calculate this frequency. (b) Calculate the wavelength of electromagnetic radiation corresponding to this frequency, and compare your result with the characteristic strong infrared absorption bands in the region of about $\lambda = 61\ \mu m$ that are observed for NaCl.

10-55. Consider a model for a metal in which the lattice of positive ions forms a container for a classical electron gas with n electrons per unit volume. In equilibrium, the average electron velocity is zero, but the application of an electric field produces an acceleration of the electrons. If we use a relaxation time τ to account for the electron-lattice collisions, then we have the equation

$$m\frac{dv}{dt} + \frac{m}{\tau}v = -eE$$

(a) Solve the equation for the drift velocity in the direction of the applied electric field. (b) Verify that Ohm's law is valid, and find the resistivity as a function of n, e, m, and the relaxation time τ.

10-56. Imagine a cubical crystal like NaCl, with a negative charge at the center of a Cartesian coordinate system with scale units equal to the interatomic distance. (a) Show that an ion at a position r units along the x axis, s units along the y axis, and t units along the z axis has a charge of $e(-1)^r \cdot (-1)^s \cdot (-1)^t = e(-1)^{r+s+t}$, where e is the electron charge. (b) Using Equation 10-2 as a guide, calculate the Madelung constant for a cube 2 units on a side. Do the same for cubes of sides 4, 6, 8, 10, 12, 16, and 20 units. (You will probably want to use a computer spreadsheet to write a program to do the calculations for the larger cubes.) Are your answers approaching the value $\alpha = 1.7476$?

10-57. (a) Show that for a paramagnetic solid with electron energies given by Equation 10-48 the magnetization per unit volume M is given by

$$M = \mu\rho \tan h(\mu B/kT)$$

(b) For $\mu B \ll kT$ show that the susceptibility is given by Equation 10-50.

Chapter 11 — Nuclear Physics

The first information about the atomic nucleus came from the discovery of radioactivity by A. H. Becquerel[1] in 1896. Intrigued by Roentgen's discovery of x rays the previous year, Becquerel was investigating the possibility that minerals that exhibit fluorescence after exposure to sunlight might also be emitting x rays. He was using the simple technique of placing a sample of such a mineral, potassium uranyl sulfate, on top of a photographic plate wrapped in black paper lying in the sunlight on a window ledge. Sure enough, an image of the sample appeared on the developed plate and he concluded that x rays had indeed been emitted. But when a similar sample lying on a wrapped photographic plate in a drawer without exposure to sunlight during a period of cloudy weather produced an image just as dark, he investigated further and found that the sample was spontaneously emitting a previously unknown penetrating radiation. He had discovered radioactivity.[2]

The rays emitted by radioactive nuclei were studied by many physicists in the early decades of the twentieth century. They were first classified by Rutherford as α, β, and γ, according to their ability to penetrate matter and to ionize air: α radiation penetrates the least and produces the most ionization, γ radiation penetrates the most with the least ionization, and β radiation is intermediate between them. It was soon found in a classic experiment performed by Rutherford that α rays are ^{4}He nuclei. It was also quickly discovered that β rays are electrons and γ rays are very short-wavelength electromagnetic radiation. Geiger and Marsden's α-particle scattering experiments in 1911 (see Section 4-2) and the successes of the Bohr model of the atom led to the modern view of an atom as consisting of a tiny, massive nucleus with a radius of 1 to 10 femtometer (fm; 1 fm $= 10^{-15}$ m) surrounded by a cloud of electrons at a relatively great distance, of the order of 0.1 nm = 100,000 fm, from the nucleus.

In 1928, the correct explanation of α radioactivity as a quantum-mechanical, barrier-penetration phenomenon was given by G. Gamow, R. W. Gurney, and E. U. Condon. Then, in rapid succession in 1932, the *neutron* was discovered by J. Chadwick and the *positron* by C. D. Anderson, and the first nuclear reaction using artificially accelerated particles (protons) was observed by J. D. Cockcroft and E. T. S. Walton.[3] Thus, it is quite reasonable to mark that year as the beginning of modern nuclear physics. With the discovery of the neutron, it became possible to understand some of the properties of nuclear structure; the advent of particle accelerators made many experimental studies possible without the severe limitations on particle type and energy imposed by naturally radioactive sources.

In this chapter we will discuss some of the general properties of atomic nuclei and the important features of radioactivity. While our discussions will of necessity be only semiquantitative, we will consider the nature of the nuclear force as it is currently understood and describe one of the most useful models in terms of which many nuclear properties may be understood.

11-1 Composition of the Nucleus

The experiments of Moseley (see Section 4-4) showed that the nuclear charge is Z times the proton charge, where Z is the *atomic number,* which is about half the *atomic mass number A* (except for hydrogen, for which $Z = A$). Thus the nucleus has a mass about equal to that of A protons, but a charge of only $Z \approx \frac{1}{2}A$ protons. Before the discovery of the neutron, it was difficult to understand this unless there were $A - Z$ electrons in the nucleus to balance the charge without changing the mass very much. The idea that the nucleus contained electrons was supported by the observation of β decay, in which electrons are ejected by certain radioactive nuclei. However, there were serious difficulties with this model. A relatively simple calculation from the uncertainty principle (see Problem 11-2) shows that an electron has a minimum kinetic energy of about 100 MeV if it is confined in the region of $r < 10^{-14}$ m; however, the energies of the electrons emitted in β decay are only of the order of 1 or 2 MeV. There is, in addition, no evidence for such a strong attractive force between nuclei and electrons as would be implied by a negative potential energy of 50 to 100 MeV inside the nucleus. Furthermore, since the electrostatic potential energy of the electron and nucleus is negative, there is no barrier to be overcome, as there is in α decay (see Figure 11-1). If the electron's total energy were positive, as required for β decay, the electron should escape from the nucleus immediately and most naturally occurring β emitters should have long since disappeared. A further difficulty is the observation that the magnetic moments of nuclei are of the order of nuclear magnetons, $\mu_N = e\hbar/2m_p$, about 2000 times smaller than a Bohr magneton $\mu_B = e\hbar/2m_e$, which would be expected if there were electrons inside the nucleus.

A further convincing argument against electrons existing in the nucleus concerns angular momentum. Protons and neutrons are fermions with spins of 1/2 and, as such, both obey the exclusion principle. The angular momentum of the nitrogen nucleus has a quantum number of 1, which can be inferred from a very small splitting of atomic spectral lines called *hyperfine structure* (see Section 11-2). It is also known (from molecular spectra—see Section 9-4) that the nitrogen nucleus obeys Bose-Einstein rather than Fermi-Dirac statistics. If ^{14}N contained 14 protons and 7 electrons, each with spin 1/2, the resultant angular momentum would have to be 1/2, 3/2, 5/2, etc., and the nucleus would obey Fermi-Dirac statistics.

In 1920 Rutherford suggested that there might be a neutral particle, possibly a proton and an electron tightly bound together, which he called a *neutron.* When such a particle was found by Chadwick in 1932, the idea that electrons were permanent

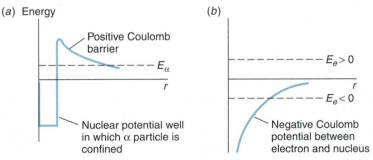

(*a*) Energy   (*b*)

Positive Coulomb barrier

E_α

r

Nuclear potential well in which α particle is confined

$E_e > 0$

r

$E_e < 0$

Negative Coulomb potential between electron and nucleus

Fig. 11-1 (*a*) Potential barrier for an α particle compared with (*b*), potential for a negative electron. Because there is no barrier for the electron, it will not be bound at all unless the total energy is negative, in which case it can never escape. The very narrow steep rise to the potential in (*a*) as $r \rightarrow 0$ represents the "hard core" of the nucleus.

TABLE 11-1 Fundamental properties of atomic constituents					
Particle	Charge	Mass (u)	Mass (kg)	Spin	Magnetic moment
Proton	$+e$	1.007276	1.6726×10^{-27}	1/2	$2.79285 \; \mu_N$
Neutron	0	1.008665	1.6749×10^{-27}	1/2	$-1.91304 \; \mu_N$
Deuteron	$+e$	2.013553	3.3436×10^{-27}	1	$0.85744 \; \mu_N$
Electron	$-e$	5.4858×10^{-4}	9.1094×10^{-31}	1/2	$1.00116 \; \mu_B$

constituents of nuclei was abandoned. Instead, the nucleus was assumed to contain N neutrons and Z protons, a total of $A = N + Z$ particles. The notion of the neutron being a proton and electron bound together has also been abandoned, since the spin of the neutron is 1/2. N is referred to as the *neutron number.* Thus, the nucleus is composed of protons and neutrons, the *nucleons,* which collectively occupy a volume whose radius is of the order of 1 to 10 fm. All of the large variety of nuclei with their broad diversity of properties are assembled from various numbers of these two particles. The fundamental properties of the individual nucleons are given in Table 11-1. We should note at this point that the nucleons are not fundamental particles. Each of the two types of nucleons is composed of a set of three *quarks,* fundamental particles that interact with each other via the strong force, which accounts for the fact that the nucleons also feel that force. Quarks and their interactions will be discussed in Chapter 13.

11-2 Ground-State Properties of Nuclei

Understanding nuclei, like atoms, requires the application of quantum theory. It was the study of nuclear spectra, the energy and particles emitted spontaneously by radioactive nuclei, that provided the first indication of the existence of quantized energy levels, angular momenta, and magnetic moments in nuclei, just as the regularities in atomic spectra had earlier pointed the way to Bohr's theory and, ultimately, to wave mechanics. Interpreting the nuclear studies presents more complex problems due to the existence of two nucleons, the possible emission of several different particles in addition to photons from excited energy states, and our incomplete knowledge of the nuclear potential function.

In this section we shall discuss some of the properties of nuclei in the ground state and mention a few methods of determining these properties. In Section 11-3 we will study radioactivity, which provides information about the excited states of nuclei. Several of the general references at the end of this chapter contain good discussions of the experimental methods used in measuring nuclear properties. We will use the following standard terminology: the letter N stands for the number of neutrons in a nucleus, and Z for the number of protons (the atomic number); $A = N + Z$ is the total number of nucleons, the mass number. The mass number is an integer approximately equal to the atomic weight. A particular nuclear species is called a *nuclide.* Nuclides are denoted by the chemical symbol with a presuperscript giving

the value of A, such as ^{16}O or ^{15}O. Sometimes Z is given as a presubscript, such as $^{15}_8$O, though this is not necessary because each element (Z number) has a unique chemical symbol. Occasionally, N is also given as a subscript, such as $^{15}_8$O$_7$, although this, too, is unnecessary, since $N = A - Z$. Nuclides with the same Z, such as ^{15}O and ^{16}O, are called *isotopes*. Nuclides with the same N, such as $^{13}_6$C$_7$ and $^{14}_7$N$_7$, are called *isotones*, while nuclides with the same A, such as ^{14}C and ^{14}N, are called *isobars*.

Size and Shape of Nuclei

Nuclear Radii   All of the methods for measuring nuclear radii agree that the radii are proportional to the cube root of the mass number. The nuclear radius can be determined by scattering experiments similar to the first ones of Rutherford, or in some cases from measurements of radioactivity. Indeed, as we discussed in Section 4-2 and as illustrated in Figure 11-2, Rutherford's original α-particle scattering experiment furnished the first measurement of the nuclear radius. An interesting, nearly classical method of determining the nuclear radius involves the measurement of the energy of β decay between *mirror nuclides*, which are nuclides whose Z and N numbers are interchanged (see Figure 11-3). For example, ^{15}O, with eight protons and seven neutrons, and ^{15}N, with eight neutrons and seven protons, are mirror nuclides. Assuming that the nuclear force between nucleons is independent of the kind of nucleons, the only difference in energy between ^{15}O and ^{15}N is electrostatic. The electrostatic energy of a ball of uniform charge can be shown to be given by

$$U = \frac{3}{5}\frac{1}{4\pi\epsilon_0}\frac{q^2}{R} \qquad \textbf{11-1}$$

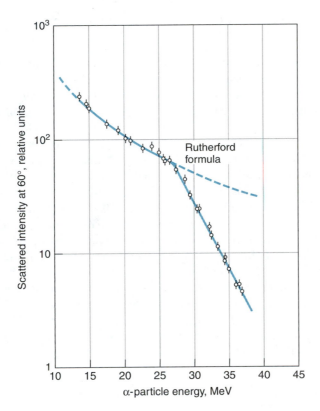

Fig. 11-2 Rutherford's α scattering formula (Equation 4-6) is shown by the dashed line. α particles of increasing energy incident on the nuclei of a Pb target scatter as would be expected by the Rutherford formula until their energy reaches about 27 MeV. At greater energies the α particles approach the Pb nuclei closely enough so that the nucleons of the α and the Pb interact via the attractive nuclear force and the scattered intensity falls below that predicted by the Rutherford equation. [*Data from R. M. Eisberg and C. E. Porter,* Rev. Mod. Phys., *33, 190 (1961).*]

Fig. 11-3 Mirror nuclides. If all the neutrons are changed to protons and all the protons are changed to neutrons, ^{15}N becomes its mirror, ^{15}O. The ground-state energy of mirror pairs differs only in the electrostatic energy.

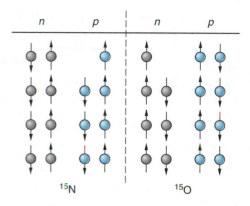

where q is the charge and R is the radius. ^{15}O is radioactive and, as we will discuss further in a later section, decays to ^{15}N by emitting a positron and a neutrino. The energy difference between ^{15}O and ^{15}N, the beta decay energy, is then

$$\Delta U = \frac{3}{5} \frac{1}{4\pi\epsilon_0} \frac{e^2}{R} \left[Z^2 - (Z - 1)^2 \right] \qquad \textbf{11-2}$$

with $Z = 8$. A measurement of the energy of decay, equal to ΔU, thus gives a measurement of R. Assuming a uniform charge distribution, measurements of the positron decay energies (see Section 11-4) for 18 pairs of mirror nuclides give for the nuclear radius

$$R = R_0 A^{1/3} \qquad \text{with} \qquad R_0 = 1.2 \pm 0.2 \text{ fm} \qquad \textbf{11-3}$$

where A is the atomic mass number. The value of R_0 in Equation 11-3 includes the effect of a quantum-mechanical correction using a charge distribution calculated from the nuclear shell model discussed in Section 11-6. The consistency of these results with other methods of determining R is a strong indication that the nuclear part of the potential energy is the same for each pair of mirror nuclei.

The most extensive measurements of nuclear radii have been carried out by Robert Hofstadter and co-workers in a series of experiments begun in 1953.[4] In these experiments, nuclei were bombarded with electrons having energies of about 200 to 500 MeV. The wavelength of a 500-MeV electron is about 2.5 fm, which is smaller than the radius of heavy nuclei. It is thus possible to learn something about the detailed structure of the charge distribution of nuclei by analyzing the diffraction pattern that results from the scattering of these electrons. The analysis is fairly complicated because the electrons are relativistic. Figure 11-4 shows the diffraction pattern of high-energy electrons scattered by ^{16}O and ^{12}C nuclei. If we consider the incoming electron beam to be a plane wave of wavelength λ, the scattering process is similar to the diffraction of light from a circular hole of radius R, discussed in most introductory physics textbooks, where R in this case is the nuclear radius. The first minimum of the diffraction pattern is then given approximately by

$$\sin \theta = 0.61 \lambda/R \qquad \textbf{11-4}$$

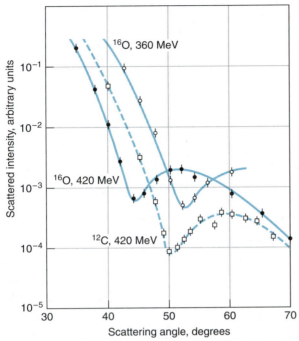

Fig. 11-4 Diffraction pattern of high-energy electrons scattered by ^{16}O and ^{12}C. The angle at which the minimum occurs in each pattern is given by Equation 11-4.

Example 11-2 below shows how the nuclear radius can be calculated from Equation 11-4 with the aid of Figure 11-4. Figure 11-5a shows some charge distributions obtained from detailed analysis of these experiments. The mean electromagnetic radius R and the surface thickness t, indicated in Figure 11-5b, are given by

$$R = (1.07 \pm 0.02)A^{1/3}\,\text{fm}$$
$$t = 2.4 \pm 0.3\,\text{fm}$$

11-5

These results are consistent with those obtained from the β-decay studies of mirror nuclides.

EXAMPLE 11-1 **Nuclear Radii of ^{4}He and ^{238}U** Use Equation 11-3 to compute the radii of ^{4}He and ^{238}U.

Solution

For ^{4}He: $R_{\text{He}} = 1.2(4)^{1/3} = 1.90\,\text{fm}$

For ^{238}U: $R_{\text{U}} = 1.2(238)^{1/3} = 7.42\,\text{fm}$

Thus, the nuclear radius varies only by a factor of about 4 from the lightest nuclides to the heaviest.

Fig. 11-5 (*a*) Charge density versus distance for several nuclei as determined by high-energy electron scattering experiments. (*b*) Definitions of parameters R_0 and t used to describe nuclear charge density. The skin thickness t is measured from 10 percent to 90 percent of the central core density. [*From R. Hofstadter, Annual Review of Nuclear Science, 7, 231 (1957).*]

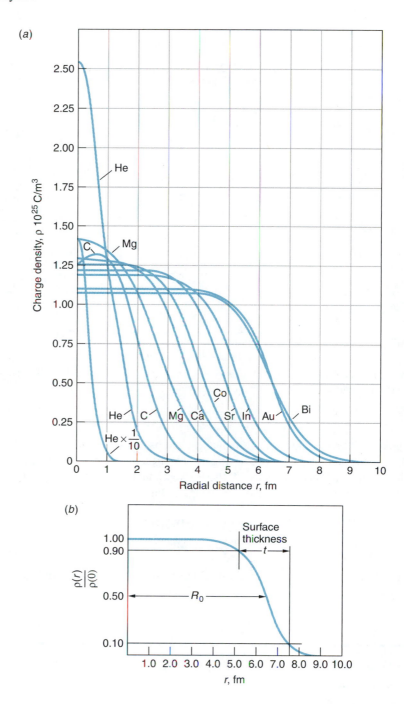

(*a*)

(*b*)

EXAMPLE 11-2 Nuclear Radius of ^{16}O Using the data for 420-MeV electrons scattered from ^{16}O in Figure 11-4, compute a value for the radius of the ^{16}O nucleus.

Solution

1.   The radius R of the ^{16}O nucleus is computed from Equation 11-4:

$$\sin \theta = \frac{0.61\, \lambda}{R} \qquad \text{or} \qquad R = \frac{0.61\, \lambda}{\sin \theta}$$

2. The angle θ in Equation 11-4 is the first minimum of the diffraction pattern. From Figure 11-4 we see that the first minimum occurs at about:

$$\theta = 44°$$

3. The de Broglie wavelength λ of the electrons is:

$$\lambda = \frac{h}{p}$$

4. The momentum p of the 420-MeV electrons is computed from the relativistic expression, Equation 2-32:

$$p^2 c^2 = E^2 - (mc^2)^2$$
$$= (420)^2 - (0.511)^2$$
$$\approx (420\ \text{MeV})^2$$

or

$$p = 420\ \text{MeV}/c = 2.2 \times 10^{-19}\ \text{kg} \cdot \text{m/s}$$

5. Substituting this value in λ from step 3 gives:

$$\lambda = \frac{6.63 \times 10^{-34}\ \text{J} \cdot \text{s}}{2.24 \times 10^{-19}\ \text{kg} \cdot \text{m/s}}$$
$$= 2.96 \times 10^{-15}\ \text{m} = 2.96\ \text{fm}$$

6. The radius R is computed by substituting the values for θ and λ into Equation 11-4:

$$R = \frac{(0.61)(2.96\ \text{fm})}{\sin 44°}$$
$$= 2.60\ \text{fm}$$

Remarks: This result agrees well with the values of R_0 for the low-Z nuclei in Figure 11-5a.

A different kind of measurement of the nuclear radius can be made using the attenuation of a beam of fast neutrons as it moves through a sample. The total cross section for attenuation can be shown to be

$$\sigma = 2\pi \left(R + \frac{\lambda}{2\pi} \right)^2 \qquad\qquad \textbf{11-6}$$

where R is the nuclear radius and λ is the de Broglie wavelength of the neutron. The neutrons must be fast enough so that $\lambda/2\pi < R$ in order to gain information about

R from measurement of σ. These experiments do not measure the charge distribution but, instead, measure the "radius" of the nuclear force between a neutron and the nucleus. The results of these measurements are

$$R = R_0 A^{1/3} \qquad \text{with} \qquad R_0 = 1.4 \text{ fm} \qquad \textbf{11-7}$$

These different types of experiments thus give comparable but not identical results, depending on whether the particular experiment measures the nuclear force radius (neutrons) or the nuclear charge radius (electrons). The fact that the radius is proportional to $A^{1/3}$ implies that the volume of the nucleus is proportional to *A*. Since the mass of the nucleus is also approximately proportional to *A*, the densities of all nuclei are approximately the same. A drop of liquid also has a constant density independent of its size, and this fact has led to a model in which the nucleus is viewed as analogous to a liquid drop. This model has been helpful in computing nuclear masses and in understanding certain types of nuclear behavior, particularly the fission of heavy elements. The numerical value of the nuclear density is about 10^{17} kg/m³. This fantastically high density, compared with 10^3 kg/m³ for atoms, is a consequence of the fact that nearly all the mass of the atom is concentrated in a region whose radius is only about 10^{-5} that of the atom. A cubic millimeter of nuclear matter has a mass of about 200,000 metric tonnes, or about the same mass as a supertanker filled with petroleum!

EXAMPLE 11-3 Radius of a Neutron Star In certain supernova events, the envelope of the star is blown away, leaving a core consisting entirely of neutrons. This stellar remnant is called a *neutron star* and its density is approximately the same as that of atomic nuclei. Compute the radius of a neutron star whose mass is equal to that of the sun, 1.99×10^{30} kg.

Solution

The mass of the neutron star is $M = \rho V$, where *V* is the volume and the density ρ is approximately 10^{17} kg/m³. Assuming the neutron star to be a sphere, we have that

$$M = 1.99 \times 10^{30} \text{ kg} = \rho V = (10^{17} \text{ kg/m}^3)(4\pi R^3/3)$$

where *R* is the radius of the star in meters. Solving for R^3 yields

$$R^3 = \frac{(1.99 \times 10^{30} \text{ kg})(3)}{(4\pi)(10^{17} \text{ kg/m}^3)} = 4.75 \times 10^{12} \text{ m}^3$$

and taking the cube root

$$R = 1.68 \times 10^4 \text{ m} = 16.8 \text{ km}$$

By way of comparison, the mean diameter of the sun is 1.39×10^6 km.

Nuclear Shape   With a few exceptions, nuclei are nearly spherical. Most of the exceptions occur in the rare earth elements (the transition region in the periodic table, $Z = 57$ to $Z = 71$), in which the shape is ellipsoidal, with the major

axis differing from the minor axis by about 20 percent or less. In these heavy nuclides, the inner atomic electron wave functions penetrate the nucleus, and deviations from spherical shape, which correspond to deviations in the nuclear charge distributions, show up as small changes in the atomic energy levels. In direct analogy with the fact that the potential at points outside a static distribution of charges is determined by the dimensions of the distribution[5] and, conversely, that measuring the potential yields information about the distribution, measuring these small changes in the atomic energy levels yields information about the nuclear charge distribution, even though it can't be measured directly. If the nucleus is shaped like a watermelon (see Figure 11-6a), with the extent of the distribution larger along the z axis than along the x and y axes, the average value of z^2 is larger than the average value of x^2 and y^2. In this case the *electric quadrupole moment Q*, which is proportional to $3(z^2)_{av} - (x^2 + y^2 + z^2)_{av}$, is positive. This is the most common case for nonspherical nuclei. Nuclei with negative quadrupole moments are shaped more like flattened pumpkins, with the two equal axes longer than the third axis, as in Figure 11-6b. The average value of the electric quadrupole moment is given by

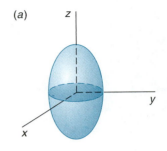

(a)

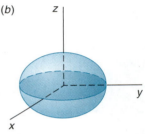

(b)

Fig. 11-6 Nonspherical nuclear shapes. Nuclei with positive quadrupole moments have $(z^2)_{av}$ greater than $(x^2)_{av}$ or $(y^2)_{av}$ and are of watermelon shape, as in (a). Nuclei with negative quadrupole moments have $(z^2)_{av}$ less than $(x^2)_{av}$ or $(y^2)_{av}$ and are shaped like flattened pumpkins, as in (b).

$$\langle Q \rangle = Z\int \psi^*[3z^2 - (x^2 + y^2 + z^2)]\psi\, dV$$

$$> 0 \quad \text{for } z^2 > x^2, y^2 \quad \text{(Figure 11-6a)}$$
$$= 0 \quad \text{for } z^2 = x^2 = y^2 \quad \text{(spherical)} \qquad \textbf{11-8}$$
$$< 0 \quad \text{for } z^2 < x^2, y^2 \quad \text{(Figure 11-6b)}$$

Figure 11-7 shows the measured values of the electric quadrupole moment for the odd A nuclei, i.e., those for which either Z or N is odd. Equation 11-8 is evaluated for wave functions corresponding to the nuclear charge distributions of various theoretical models of the nucleus and compared with the values in Figure 11-7. As you might imagine, the calculations are formidable!

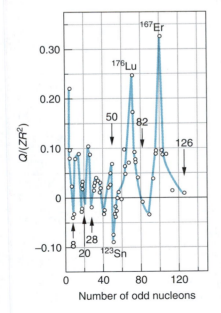

Fig. 11-7 The electric quadrupole moment Q divided by Z and R^2, where R is the average nuclear radius, is plotted versus the number of nucleons of the odd type (Z or N). The arrows indicate the points where $Q/ZR^2 = 0$, corresponding to spherical shape.

Nuclear Stability

Among the more than 3000 known nuclides, there are only 266 whose ground states are stable. All of the rest have unstable ground states which eventually undergo radioactive decay, that is, transition to some state of a different element. Figure 11-8 shows a plot of the neutron number N versus the proton number Z for the stable

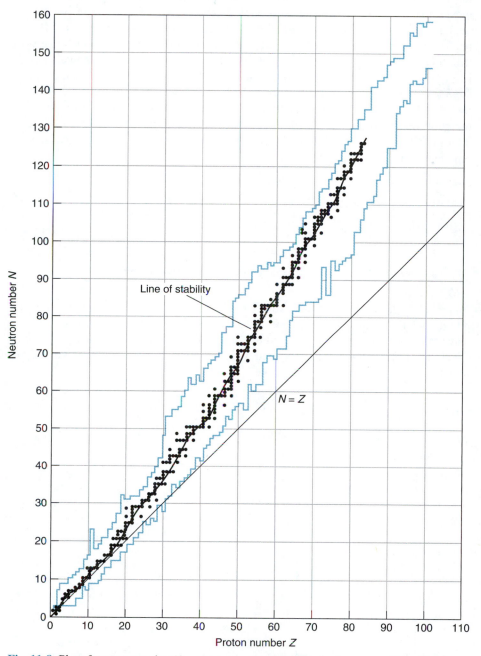

Fig. 11-8 Plot of neutron number N versus proton number Z for the known nuclides. The 266 stable nuclides are indicated by the black dots. The area between the irregular colored lines represents the known unstable, or radioactive, nuclides whose lifetimes are longer than about a millisecond. The curved line through the stable nuclides is called the *line of stability*.

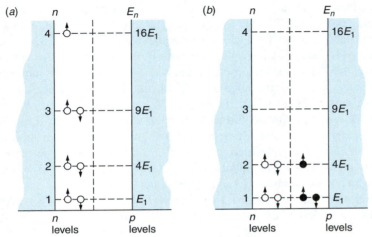

Fig. 11-9 (a) Seven neutrons in an infinite square well. In accordance with the exclusion principle, only two neutrons can be in a given space state. The total energy is $16E_1 + (2 \times 9E_1) + (2 \times 4E_1) + (2 \times 1E_1) = 44E_1$. (b) Four neutrons and three protons in the same infinite square well. Because protons and neutrons are not identical, four particles (two neutrons and two protons) can be in the state $n = 1$. The total energy is $(3 \times 4E_1) + (4 \times 1E_1) = 16E_1$. This is much less than in (a). The integers on the left of each well are infinite square well principal quantum numbers.

nuclides and the known unstable ones whose lifetimes are longer than about a millisecond. The straight line is $N = Z$. The general shape of the *line of stability,* shown by the light curve tracing through the stable nuclides in Figure 11-8, can be understood in terms of the exclusion principle and the electrostatic energy of the protons. Consider the kinetic energy of A particles in a one-dimensional square well, which is an adequate model for demonstrating this point. The energy is least if $\frac{1}{2}A$ are neutrons and $\frac{1}{2}A$ are protons and greatest if all the particles are of one type (see Figure 11-9). There is therefore a tendency, due to the exclusion principle, for N and Z to be equal. If we include the electrostatic energy of repulsion of the protons, the result is changed somewhat. This potential energy is proportional to Z^2. At large A, the energy is increased less by adding two neutrons than by adding one neutron and one proton; so the difference $N - Z$ increases with increasing Z.

There is also a tendency for nucleons to pair with other identical nucleons. Of the 266 nuclides that are stable, 159 have even Z and even N, 50 have odd Z and even N, 53 have even Z and odd N, and only 4 have both odd N and Z. (See Table 11-2.)

TABLE 11-2	N versus Z for stable isotopes	
	Z	
N	**Even**	**Odd**
Even	159	50
Odd	53	4

Since there are about 100 different elements and about 270 stable nuclides, there is an average of about 2.7 stable isotopes per element. There is a larger than average number of stable isotopes for nuclei with Z equal to 20, 28, 50, and 82. For example, tin, with $Z = 50$, has 10 stable isotopes. Similarly, nuclides with these same numbers of neutrons have a larger than average number of isotones. These numbers, called *magic numbers*, are a manifestation of shell structure in very much the same way that the atomic "magic numbers" 2, 10, 18, and 36 correspond to closed-electron-shell structure. As we shall discuss further in Section 11-6, the nuclear magic numbers, which also include 2, 8, and 126, represent configurations of particular stability. An *island of stability* is hypothesized to exist around $Z = 126$. In the search for it thus far, a few atoms with atomic numbers up to 116 have been created in that region. (Atoms with atomic numbers 113 and 115 have not yet been found.)

Nuclides that fall between the irregular colored lines in Figure 11-8, except those marked by the black dots, are radioactive. We shall discuss radioactivity in Section 11-3.

Masses and Binding Energies

The mass of an atom can be accurately measured in a mass spectrometer, which measures q/M for ions by bending them in a magnetic field.[6] The mass of an atom is slightly smaller than the mass of the nucleus plus the mass of the electrons because of the binding energy of the electrons. The binding energy of the electrons is defined by

$$B_{\text{atomic}} = M_N c^2 + Z m_e c^2 - M_A c^2 = \Delta m c^2 \qquad \textbf{11-9}$$

where M_N is the mass of the nucleus, M_A is the mass of the atom, m_e is the mass of an electron, and Δm is the mass equivalent of B_{atomic}. (See Section 2-3.) Because the binding energies of atoms are only of the order of keV, compared with nuclear binding energies of many MeV, atomic binding energies are usually neglected in nuclear physics. The binding energy of a nucleus with Z protons and N neutrons is defined as

$$B_{\text{nuclear}} = Z m_p c^2 + N m_n c^2 - M_A c^2 \qquad \textbf{11-10}$$

where m_p is the mass of a proton, and m_n the mass of a neutron, and M_A the mass of the nucleus of mass number A. Since the mass of an atom is very nearly equal to the mass of the nucleus plus the mass of the electrons (neglecting the atomic binding energy), the nuclear binding energy can be accurately computed from

$$B_{\text{nuclear}} = Z M_H c^2 + N m_n c^2 - M_A c^2 \qquad \textbf{11-11}$$

where M_A is the atomic mass and M_H is the mass of a hydrogen atom. Note that the masses of the Z electrons cancel out. This expression is more convenient to use than Equation 11-10 because it is the mass of the atom that is usually measured in mass spectrometers. The atomic masses of all stable nuclides and of many unstable ones are listed in Appendix A.

Once the mass of a nucleus or atom is determined, the binding energy can be computed from Equation 11-10 or 11-11. The binding energy per nucleon B/A is plotted against A for the most stable isotope of each element in Figure 11-10. The mean value is about 8.3 MeV/nucleon. The fact that this curve is approximately constant (for $A > 16$) indicates that the nuclear force is a *saturated* force. This is partially explained by the short range of the nuclear force (see Section 11-5). If each nucleon interacted with every other nucleon, there would be $A - 1$ interactions for each nucleon, and the

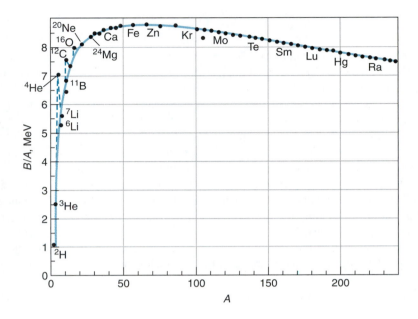

Fig. 11-10 The binding energy per nucleon versus atomic mass number A. The solid curve represents the Weizsäcker semiempirical binding-energy formula, Equation 11-12.

binding energy per nucleon would be proportional to $A - 1$ rather than constant. Figure 11-10 indicates that, instead, there is a fixed number of interactions per nucleon, as would be the case if each nucleon were attracted only to its nearest neighbors. Such a situation also leads to a constant nuclear density, consistent with the radius measurements. If the binding energy per nucleon were instead proportional to the number of nucleons, then the radius would be approximately constant, as is the case for atoms.

More

Of the several models of the nucleus physicists have developed, the liquid-drop model has been one of the most useful. It has been successful in describing the fission process and nuclear reactions and, in particular, predicting the binding energies (i.e., masses) of isotopes and individual nucleons within the nucleus. These topics are discussed in *Liquid-Drop Model and the Semiempirical Mass Formula* on the home page: www.whfreeman.com/modphysics4e   See also Equations 11-12 through 11-14 and Table 11-3 here, as well as Examples 11-4 through 11-6 and Figure 11-10.

Nuclear Angular Momenta and Magnetic Moments

The spin quantum number of both the neutron and the proton is 1/2, which means that the nucleons are fermions. The angular momentum of the nucleus is a combination of the spin angular momenta of the nucleons plus any orbital angular momentum due to the motion of the nucleons. This resultant angular momentum is usually called *nuclear spin* and designated by the symbol **I**. The nucleons individually have magnetic moments which also combine to produce the *nuclear magnetic moment*. Evidence for nuclear spin and magnetic moment was first found in atomic spectra. The nuclear spin adds to the angular momentum $\mathbf{J} = \mathbf{L} + \mathbf{S}$ of the electrons to form a total angular momentum $\mathbf{F}$:

$$\mathbf{F} = \mathbf{I} + \mathbf{J} \qquad\qquad \textbf{11-15}$$

The possible quantum numbers for F are $(I + J)$, $(I + J - 1)$, . . . , $|I - J|$, according to the usual rule for combining angular momenta. F obeys the selection rule $\Delta F = \pm 1, 0$, but no $F = 0 \rightarrow F = 0$. The number of possible values of F is $(2J + 1)$ or $(2I + 1)$, whichever is the smaller. Because of the energy of the interaction between the electronic magnetic moment and the nuclear magnetic moment associated with I, each atomic spectral line is split into $(2J + 1)$ or $(2I + 1)$ components. This splitting is one of several effects that are the result of interactions of the nuclear spins and moments with the environment of the nucleus, including its own atomic electrons, collectively called *hyperfine structure*.[8] The hyperfine splitting of the spectral lines associated with the nuclear magnetic moment occurs for a reason that is exactly analogous to the spin-orbit coupling discussed in Section 7-5 that is the origin of the fine structure of the spectral lines. The coupling between I and J expressed by Equation 11-15 results in a splitting of the *atomic* energy levels by an amount ΔE, in addition to the spin-orbit splitting of Equation 7-68, given by the analogous relation

$$\Delta E = g_N m_I \mu_N B_e \qquad\qquad \textbf{11-16}$$

where g_N is the nuclear Landé factor, m_I is the magnetic quantum number of the z component of I, $\mu_N = e\hbar/2m_p$ is the nuclear magneton, and B_e is the magnetic field at the nucleus produced by the electrons (see Table 11-4). The product $g_N m_I \mu_N$ is the nuclear magnetic moment. Except for μ_N, the quantities on the right side of Equation 11-16 are all of the same order of magnitude as the corresponding ones in Equation 7-68; however, the ratio $\mu_N/\mu_B \approx 10^{-3}$. Thus, the hyperfine splitting for a given atom is very small, about 10^{-3} times the fine-structure splitting. Using as an example the sodium doublet levels $^2P_{1/2}$, $^2P_{3/2}$, and $^2S_{1/2}$ shown in Figure 7-31 that produce the yellow D lines, Figure 11-11 illustrates the hyperfine splitting of these levels resulting from *I-J* coupling. It can be observed only with extremely high resolution. The use of tunable dye lasers and atomic beam fluorescence spectroscopy has made high-precision measurements of these extremely small energy splittings possible in recent years.

TABLE 11-4 Magnetic field B_e at the nucleus due to electron for selected alkali elements

Element	n	B_e, $^2S_{1/2}$ (T)	B_e, $^2P_{1/2}$ (T)	B_e, $^2P_{3/2}$ (T)
H	1	17	—	—
Li	2	13	—	—
Na	3	44	4.2	2.5
K	4	63	7.9	4.6
Rb	5	130	16	8.6
Cs	6	210	28	13

Source: Data from E. Segrè, Nuclei and Particles, 2d ed. (Menlo Park, CA: Benjamin Cummings, 1977), p. 259.

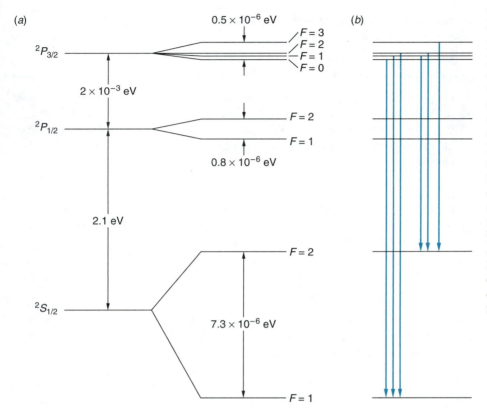

Fig. 11-11 (*a*) Transitions between the sodium doublet levels produce the yellow *D* lines, $^2P_{1/2} \rightarrow {}^2S_{1/2}$ being D_1 and $^2P_{3/2} \rightarrow {}^2S_{1/2}$ being D_2. Coupling between the atomic angular momentum *J* and the nuclear spin $I = 3/2$ results in the hyperfine splitting, each level having total angular momentum $\mathbf{F} = \mathbf{I} + \mathbf{J}$. Note that the hyperfine splitting of each of the doublet levels is about 10^{-3} times that of the fine-structure splitting of the ^2P level. (*b*) The selection rule $\Delta F = \pm 1, 0$ leads to the D_2 line being split into six components. The D_1 line is correspondingly split into four components (not shown).

For the case $I \leq J$ there are $(2I + 1)$ different *F* states; thus the nuclear spin can be determined by counting the number of lines in the hyperfine splitting. The spin of all even-even nuclides (those with even *Z* and even *N*) is zero in the ground state. Evidently the nucleons couple together in such a way that their angular momenta add to zero in pairs, as is often the case for electrons in atoms. There is no such simple rule for other nuclides with either odd *N* or odd *Z* or both. Some of the successes of the shell model to be discussed in Section 11-6 are the correct prediction of nuclear spins for many nuclei.

The magnetic moment of the nucleus $g_N m_I \mu_N$ is of the order of the nuclear magneton, $\mu_N = e\hbar/2m_p$, since the magnitude of g_N is typically between 1 and 5 and the maximum value of $|m_I| = I$. The exact value is difficult to predict because it depends on the detailed motion of the nucleons. If the proton and neutron obeyed the Dirac relativistic wave equation, as does the electron, the magnetic moment due to spin would be 1 nuclear magneton for the proton and 0 for the neutron because it had no charge.[9] The experimentally determined moments of the nucleons are

$$(\mu_p)_z = +2.79285 \ \mu_N$$
$$(\mu_n)_z = -1.91304 \ \mu_N$$

As we shall see in Chapter 13, the proton and neutron are more complex particles than the electron. It is interesting that the deviations of these moments from those predicted by the Dirac equation are about the same magnitude, 1.91 for the neutron and 1.79 for the proton. The reason that the magnetic moments of the nucleons have these particular values is not yet completely understood, the current theoretical

The degeneracy of the hyerfine levels in nuclei with nonzero spins, e.g., the proton in ^{1}H, is removed by an external **B** field, a nuclear analog of the Zeeman effect. Transitions between these levels, separated (in ^{1}H) by $2\mu_p B$, oscillate at the spin precession rate. Detection of the resulting absoption or emission of radiation enables "mapping" of the hydrogen-containing soft tissue, the basis for medical *magnetic resonance imaging (MRI)*.

predictions of μ_p and μ_n agreeing with high-precision, experimentally measured values only to within about 1 percent.

EXAMPLE 11-7 Nuclear Spin of Thallium-205 High-resolution spectroscopic study of the spectrum of ^{205}Tl reveals that each component of the doublet $^2P_{1/2} \rightarrow$ $^2S_{1/2}$ (377.7 nm), $^2P_{3/2} \rightarrow {}^2S_{1/2}$ (535.2 nm) consists of three hyperfine components. This requires that there be two hyperfine levels for each J. Determine the spin of the ^{205}Tl nucleus.

Solution
If $I \leq J$, then there are $(2I + 1)$ different F levels and, if $I > J$, there are $(2J + 1)$ different F levels. Since the hyperfine spectrum indicates that there are two levels for each J, then for the $^2P_{3/2}$ level either

$$2I + 1 = 2 \qquad \text{or} \qquad 2J + 1 = 2$$

But we already know that $J = (3/2)$, so $(2J + 1)$ cannot equal 2; therefore $(2I + 1) = 2$ and the spin of the ^{205}Tl nucleus (in its ground state) must be 1/2. Note that for the $^2P_{1/2}$ and $^2S_{1/2}$ levels both of the equations above are satisfied, since in these two cases $I = J$.

QUESTIONS

1. Why is N approximately equal to Z for stable nuclei? Why is N greater than Z for heavy nuclei?

2. Why are there no stable isotopes with $Z > 83$?

3. The mass of ^{12}C, which contains 6 protons and 6 neutrons, is exactly 12.000 u by the definition of the unified mass unit. Why isn't the mass of ^{16}O, which contains 8 protons and 8 neutrons, exactly 16.000 u?

11-3 Radioactivity

Of the more than 3000 nuclides known, only 266 are stable. All of the rest are radioactive; that is, they decay into other nuclides by emitting radiation. The term *radiation* here refers to particles as well as electromagnetic radiation. In 1900 Rutherford discovered that the rate of emission of radiation from a substance was not constant but decreased exponentially with time. This exponential time dependence is characteristic of all radioactivity and indicates that it is a statistical process. Because each nucleus is well shielded from others by the atomic electrons, pressure and temperature changes have no effect on nuclear properties.[10]

For a statistical decay (in which the decay of any individual nucleus is a random event), the number of nuclei decaying in a time interval dt is proportional to dt and to the number of nuclei present. If $N(t)$ is the number of radioactive nuclei at time t and $-dN$ is the number that decay in dt (the minus sign is necessary because N decreases), we have

$$-dN = \lambda N \, dt \qquad \qquad \textbf{11-17}$$

where the constant of proportionality, λ, is called the *decay constant*. λ is the probability per unit time of the decay of any given nucleus. The solution of this equation is

$$N(t) = N_0 e^{-\lambda t} \qquad \textbf{11-18}$$

where N_0 is the number of nuclei at time $t = 0$. The decay rate is

$$R = -\frac{dN}{dt} = \lambda N_0 e^{-\lambda t} = R_0 e^{-\lambda t} \qquad \textbf{11-19}$$

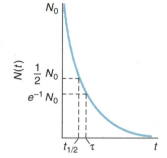

Fig. 11-12 Exponential radioactive decay law. The number of nuclei remaining at time t decreases exponentially with time t. The half-life $t_{1/2}$ and the mean life $\tau = 1/\lambda$ are indicated. The decay rate $R(t) = \lambda N(t)$ has the same time dependence.

Note that *both the number of nuclei and the rate of decay decrease exponentially with time*. It is the decrease in the rate of decay that is determined experimentally. Figure 11-12 shows N versus t. If we multiply the numbers on the N axis by λ, this becomes a graph of R versus t.

We can calculate the *mean lifetime* from Equation 11-18. The number of nuclei with lifetimes between t and $t + dt$ is the number that decay in dt, which is $\lambda N\, dt$; thus the fraction with lifetimes in dt is

$$f(t)\, dt = \frac{\lambda N\, dt}{N_0} = \lambda e^{-\lambda t}\, dt \qquad \textbf{11-20}$$

Using this distribution function, the mean lifetime is

$$\tau = \int_0^\infty t f(t)\, dt = \int_0^\infty t \lambda e^{-\lambda t}\, dt = \frac{1}{\lambda} \qquad \textbf{11-21}$$

which is the reciprocal of the decay constant λ. The *half-life* $t_{1/2}$ is defined as the time after which the number of radioactive nuclei has decreased to half its original value. From Equation 11-18,

$$\tfrac{1}{2}N_0 = N_0 e^{-\lambda t_{1/2}}$$

or

$$e^{\lambda t_{1/2}} = 2$$

$$t_{1/2} = \frac{\ln 2}{\lambda} = (\ln 2)\tau = \frac{0.693}{\lambda} = 0.693\,\tau \qquad \textbf{11-22}$$

After each time interval of one half-life, the number of nuclei left in a given sample and the decay rate have both decreased to half of their previous values. For example, if the decay rate is R_0 initially, it will be $(1/2)R_0$ after one half-life, $(1/2)(1/2)R_0$ after two half-lives, and so forth. During one mean lifetime, the number of nuclei remaining in the sample and the decay rate have decreased to $1/e$ of their previous values. Thus, if the initial decay rate is R_0, it will be $(1/e)R_0$ after time τ has elapsed, $(1/e)(1/e)R_0$ after time 2τ, and so on. The SI unit of radioactivity is the *becquerel* (Bq), which is defined as one decay per second:

$$1\ \mathrm{Bq} = 1\ \mathrm{decay/s} \qquad \textbf{11-23}$$

A historical unit of activity, the *curie* (Ci), is also frequently used. The curie is defined as

$$1 \text{ Ci} = 3.7 \times 10^{10} \text{ decay/s} = 3.7 \times 10^{10} \text{ Bq} \qquad \textbf{11-24}$$

The curie is the disintegration rate of 1 g of radium. Since this is a very large unit, the millicurie (mCi), microcurie (μCi), and picocurie (pCi) are also often used.

EXAMPLE 11-8 **Counting Rate of a Radioactive Sample** A radioactive source has a half-life of 1 minute. At time $t = 0$ it is placed near a detector and the counting rate (the number of decay particles detected per unit time) is observed to be 2000 counts/s. (*a*) Find the mean life and the decay constant. (*b*) Find the counting rate at times $t = 1$ min, 2 min, 3 min, and 10 min.

Solution

1. For question (*a*), the mean life τ is related to the half-life $t_{1/2}$ by Equation 11-22:

$$t_{1/2} = (\ln 2) \, \tau$$

or

$$\tau = \frac{t_{1/2}}{\ln 2} = \frac{1 \text{ min}}{0.693} = 1.44 \text{ min} = 86.6 \text{ s}$$

2. From Equation 11-21, the decay constant is given by:

$$\lambda = \frac{1}{\tau}$$

$$= \frac{1}{86.6 \text{ s}} = 1.16 \times 10^{-2} \, \text{s}^{-1}$$

3. *Method 1.* For question (*b*), the counting rate is proportional to the decay rate R in Equation 11-19. The counting rate at $t = 0$ has the same proportionality to R_0, so we can write the counting rate as R, substituting values for λ and for $t_{1/2}$:

$$R = 2000e^{-\lambda t} = 2000e^{-(1.16 \times 10^{-2})t}$$

$$= 2000e^{-(\ln 2)t/t_{1/2}}$$

$$= 2000e^{-(0.693)t}$$

where t is now in minutes.

4. The counting rate R can now be computed for each of the times $t = 1$ min, 2 min, 3 min, and 10 min as follows:

$$R(1 \text{ min}) = 2000e^{-(0.693)(1)}$$

$$= 2000 \times 0.50 = 1000 \text{ counts/s}$$

$$R(2 \text{ min}) = 2000e^{-(0.693)(2)} = 500 \text{ counts/s}$$

and similarly

$$R(3 \text{ min}) = 250 \text{ counts/s}$$
$$R(10 \text{ min}) = 1.95 \text{ counts/s}$$

5. *Method 2.* Since the half-life is 1 min, the counting rate at $t = 1$ min will be half that at $t = 0$; at $t = 2$ min it will be half of that at $t = 1$ min, and so on. In general, at $t = n$ min the count rate will be:

$$R = (1/2)^n R_0$$

and again

$$R(1 \text{ min}) = (1/2)^1 \, 2000 = 1000 \text{ counts/s}$$

and

$$R(10 \text{ min}) = (1/2)^{10}(2000)$$
$$= (0.0010)(2000) = 1.95 \text{ counts/s}$$

More

Very often the decay of a radioactive nucleus results in a new nucleus that is also radioactive and that, in general, has a different decay constant. In some cases such sequential decays may result in a dozen or more different radioactive isotopes. *Production and Sequential Decays* on the home page describes the way to calculate the total activity and the net rate at which new isotopes are produced. Home page: www.whfreeman.com/modphysics4e   See Equations 11-25 through 11-29 and Figures 11-13 and 11-14 here, as well as Examples 11-9 and 11-10 and Questions 4 and 5.

11-4 Alpha, Beta, and Gamma Decay

From the time when Becquerel's discovery of radioactivity gave the first hint of the existence of the nucleus, much of what physicists have learned about nuclear structure has resulted from studies of radioactive nuclides, that is, by studying the transitions of nuclei from one quantum state to another of lower energy. Only 266 of the 3000 isotopes that have either been discovered in nature or created in the laboratory are stable. All of the rest, plus nearly all of a theoretically estimated 2000 more possible isotopes that have yet to be discovered, are radioactive. The radioisotopes decay by one or another of at least nine different modes; however, most decays occur via one or, sometimes, two of the most common modes: alpha, beta, and gamma. Others occur by more unusual routes, such as emission of a proton or neutron or spontaneous fission. A few may decay by modes that are exceedingly rare, such as a double beta decay, the confirmation of whose very existence is a matter of considerable current theoretical

and experimental interest. The fundamental purpose of these studies is to obtain information about nuclear structure and the nature of the strong nuclear force.

In the subsections that follow we will discuss the three most common types of decay in some detail, touching on certain of the others when pertinent. In these discussions it will be helpful to keep two points in mind. The first of these is that the line of stability in Figure 11-8 is the floor of an energy valley formed by plotting the binding energy for each isotope on an energy scale perpendicular to the N and Z axes as illustrated in Figure 11-15*a*. In Figure 11-15*a* the energy is artificially truncated; however, there are theoretical limitations placed on the numbers of protons and neutrons that can be assembled into a nucleus, even a highly unstable one. These limits, given the whimsical name *driplines,* are shown in Figure 11-15*b* and define the *N-Z* boundaries within which lie the 5000 or so isotopes that may, in principle, exist. The limits are set by the energies at which the nuclei will spontaneously emit a proton or neutron.

The second point to bear in mind is that radioactive decay processes conform to the same conservation laws that are obeyed by all physical processes. In particular, (1) relativistic mass-energy, (2) electric charge, (3) linear momentum, (4) angular momentum, (5) nucleon number, and (6) lepton number[11] are all conserved quantities. The first four of these are already familiar to you from your previous study of physics. The last two relate specifically to the interactions and decays of fundamental particles and will be discussed in Chapter 13. As we discuss the three most common modes of radioactive decay, consequences of each of the conservation laws will be illustrated.

Fig. 11-15 (*a*) The graph of Z vs. N with the nuclear binding energy B (in MeV) plotted upward. The surface thus formed is truncated at 100 MeV to make the energy valley more clearly visible. (*b*) More than 5000 theoretically predicted nuclei lie between the proton and neutron driplines. Only about 3000 (those between the inner irregular colored lines) are found in nature or have been created in the laboratory, and only about 270 of those are stable (black dots). The edges of the truncation in (*a*) are analogous to artificial driplines.

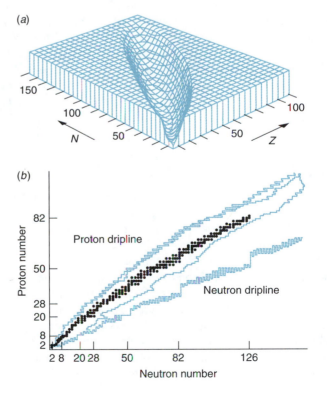

Alpha Decay

In order for a radioactive substance to be found in nature, either it must have a half-life that is not much shorter than the age of Earth (about 4.5×10^9 years) or it must be continually produced by the decay of another radioactive substance or by a nuclear reaction. For a nucleus to be radioactive at all, its mass must be greater than the sum of the masses of the decay products. Many heavy nuclei are unstable to α decay. Because the Coulomb barrier inhibits the decay process (the α particle must "tunnel" through a region in which its energy is less than the potential energy, as shown in Figure 11-1a), the half-life for α decay can be very long if the decay energy is small, that is, if the width of the barrier to be tunneled through is large. Indeed, the relation between the half-life of an α emitter and the energy of the α particle is so striking that it was first noticed by two research assistants in Rutherford's laboratory, Geiger and Nuttall, in 1911, the same year that Rutherford discovered the nucleus. The general relation, called the Geiger-Nuttall rule, is illustrated in Figure 11-16 and given by Equation 11-30.

$$\log t_{1/2} = A E_\alpha^{-1/2} + B \qquad \textbf{11-30}$$

where E_α is the kinetic energy of the emitted α particle and A and B are experimentally determined constants.

The α particles emitted by a tiny amount of ^{241}Am are used to ionize the air inside smoke detectors. When smoke is present, the ionized air molecules stick to the smoke particles, reducing a trickle current maintained in the ionized air, thereby triggering an alarm. Ionization-type smoke detectors are considerably more sensitive than those using photoelectric sensors.

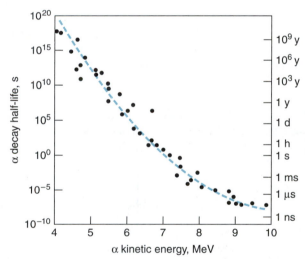

Fig. 11-16 The Geiger-Nuttall relation is illustrated by the semilogarithmic graph of the α decay half-life versus the kinetic energy of the emitted α particle for the naturally occurring α emitters. The broken line represents the empirical Geiger-Nuttall rule given by Equation 11-30.

Subsequently, an expression for the half-life of an α emitter was derived from the Schrödinger equation treating α decay as a barrier-penetration phenomenon. Its good agreement with experimental results was one of the earliest successful applications of wave mechanics. Briefly, the derivation considered an α particle confined within the nucleus with energy E_α as was shown in Figure 11-1. The wave functions for two such particles are illustrated in Figure 11-17. The potential for $r > R$ is taken to be the Coulomb function $V(r) = zZe^2/4\pi\epsilon_0 r$ where $z = 2$ for the α particle, with a smooth transition to the nuclear potential. The probability that the α particle will penetrate the barrier on any one approach is the transmission coefficient T that was derived in Section 6-6, Equations 6-75 and 6-76. The decay constant $\lambda = 1/\tau = 0.693/t_{1/2}$ is then given by the product of the transmission coefficient and the frequency with which the nuclear α particle approaches the barrier. The latter, given by Equation 6-78, depends

Fig. 11-17 Schematic representations of the wave functions of two α particles with energies $E_{\alpha 1}$ and $E_{\alpha 2}$ within the nuclear potential well. The probability of α1 penetrating the barrier is larger than that for α2, since the barrier is narrower at $E_{\alpha 1}$. Thus, the amplitude of $\psi(\alpha 1)$ is larger outside the nucleus than that of $\psi(\alpha 2)$. Hence, $\lambda(\alpha 1) > \lambda(\alpha 2)$ and, therefore, $t_{1/2}(\alpha 1) < t_{1/2}(\alpha 2)$.

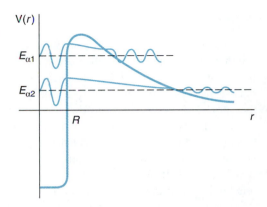

on the α particle's speed v, determined by its kinetic energy for $r < R$ in Figure 11-17, and the value of the nuclear radius. Thus,

$$\lambda = \frac{Tv}{2R} \qquad\qquad \textbf{11-31}$$

The result of the wave-mechanical derivation, done by Taagepera and Nurmia, is

$$\log t_{1/2} = 1.61(ZE_\alpha^{-1/2} - Z^{2/3}) - 28.9 \qquad\qquad \textbf{11-32}$$

where $t_{1/2}$ is in years, E_α is in MeV, and Z refers to the daughter nucleus. Notice that the dependence of $t_{1/2}$ upon the nuclear radius provides a method of measuring nuclear radii that is independent of the methods mentioned in Section 11-2.

Alpha Decay Chains   All very heavy nuclei ($Z > 83$) are theoretically unstable to α decay because the mass of the parent radioactive nucleus is greater than the sum

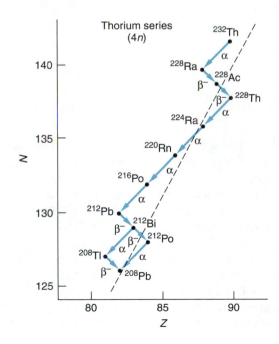

Fig. 11-18 The thorium ($4n$) α-decay series. The broken line is the line of stability (floor of the energy valley) shown in Figures 11-8 and 11-15.

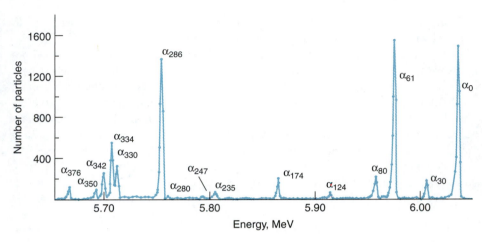

Fig. 11-19 Alpha-particle spectrum from ^{227}Th. The highest-energy α particles correspond to decay to the ground state of ^{223}Ra with a transition energy of $Q = 6.04$ MeV. The next highest energy particles, $α_{30}$, result from transitions to the first excited state of ^{223}Ra, 30 keV above the ground state. The energy levels of the daughter nucleus, ^{223}Ra, can be determined by measurement of the α-particle energies.

of the masses of the decay products—the daughter nucleus and an α particle. When a nucleus emits an α particle, both N and Z decrease by 2, and A decreases by 4. There are four possible α-decay chains or sequences, depending on whether A equals $4n$, $(4n + 1)$, $(4n + 2)$, or $(4n + 3)$, where n is an integer. For the longest-lived nucleus in each sequence, $n = 58$ for the first and fourth and $n = 59$ for the second and third. All but one of these are found in nature. The $(4n + 1)$ series is not, because its longest-lived member (other than the stable end product ^{209}Bi), ^{237}Np, has a half-life

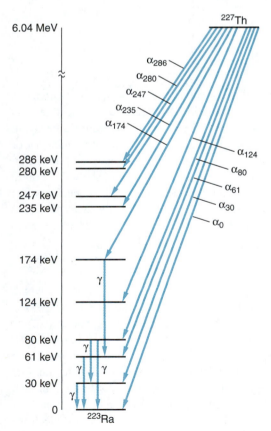

Fig. 11-20 Energy levels of ^{223}Ra determined by measurement of α-particle energies from ^{227}Th, as shown in Figure 11-19. Only the lowest-lying levels and some of the γ-ray transitions are shown.

of only 2×10^6 years, which is much shorter than the age of Earth; hence ^{237}Np present when Earth was formed has long since decayed away.

Figure 11-18 (page 528) illustrates the thorium series, which has $A = 4n$ and begins with an α decay from ^{232}Th to ^{228}Ra. Decreasing n successively by 1 generates A for possible daughter nuclides until a stable one is reached. The daughter nuclide of an α decay is on the left or neutron-rich side of the stability curve (dashed line), so it often decays by β^- decay, in which one neutron changes to a proton by emitting an electron. In Figure 11-18 ^{228}Ra decays by β^- decay to ^{228}Ac, which in turn decays to ^{228}Th. There are then four α decays to ^{212}Pb, which β^- decays to ^{212}Bi. There is a branch point at ^{212}Bi, which decays either by α decay to ^{208}Tl or by β^- decay to ^{212}Po. The branches meet at the stable lead isotope ^{208}Pb. The $(4n + 2)$ series begins with ^{238}U and ends with ^{206}Pb. The $(4n + 3)$ series starts with ^{235}U and ends with ^{209}Pb.

More

The energy spectrum of the alpha particles emitted by a heavy nucleus such as ^{232}Th shows a number of sharp peaks with energies less than the decay energy Q. The highest energy of these corresponds to the transition from the parent's ground state to that of the daughter. The others are the result of alpha transitions to excited states of the daughter. In *Energetics of Alpha Decay* on the home page we describe how they can be used to construct the excited levels of the daughter nucleus. Home page: www.whfreeman.com/modphysics4e   See also Equations 11-33 through 11-36 and Example 11-11 here.

Beta Decay

There are three radioactive decay processes in which the mass number A remains unchanged, while Z and N change by ± 1. These are β^- decay, in which a neutron inside a nucleus changes into a proton with the emission of an electron; β^+ decay, in which a proton inside a nucleus changes into a neutron with the emission of a positron; and electron capture, in which a proton in a nucleus changes to a neutron by capturing an atomic electron, usually a $1s$ electron from the K shell since these have the highest probability density in the vicinity of the nucleus. Those nuclei on the neutron-rich side of the energy valley in Figure 11-15 will tend to decay by β^- emission, while those on the proton-rich side will most probably decay by β^+ emission or electron capture. We shall discuss each of these processes briefly.

β^- *Decay*
The simplest example of β^- decay is that of the free neutron, which decays into a proton plus an electron with a half-life of about 10.8 minutes. The energy of decay is 0.78 MeV, which is the difference between the rest energy of the neutron (939.57 MeV) and that of the proton plus electron (938.28 + 0.511 MeV). More generally, in β^- decay, a nucleus of mass number A, atomic number Z, and neutron number N changes into one with mass number A, atomic number $Z' = Z + 1$, and neutron number $N' = N - 1$, conserving charge with the emission of an electron. The energy of decay Q is c^2 times the difference between the mass of the parent nucleus and that of the decay products. If we add the mass of Z electrons

to both the parent nucleus and the decay products, we can write Q in terms of the *atomic* masses of the parent and daughter atoms:

$$\frac{Q}{c^2} = M_P - M_D \qquad \textbf{11-37}$$

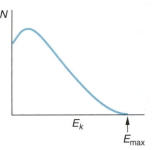

Fig. 11-21 Energy spectrum of electrons emitted in β decay. The number of electrons per unit energy interval N is plotted versus kinetic energy. The fact that all the electrons do not have the same kinetic energy E_{max} suggests that there is another particle emitted which shares the energy available for decay.

Another way of understanding this result is to note that in β^- decay an electron of mass m_e leaves the atom, which is now a daughter *ion* of nuclear charge $(Z + 1)$ and Z atomic electrons. To obtain the mass of the *neutral* daughter atom, we must add the mass of an electron m_e so the total mass change is just the difference in mass between the parent and daughter *atoms*. If the decay energy Q were shared only by the daughter atom and the emitted electron, the energy of the electron would be uniquely determined by conservation of energy and momentum, just as in α decay. Experimentally, however, the energies of the electrons emitted in β decay are observed to vary from zero to the maximum energy available. A typical energy spectrum is shown in Figure 11-21; compare this with the discrete spectrum of α-particle energies of Figure 11-19 (page 529). Thus, in a particular decay event in which the electron carried away less than the energy E_{max}, it would appear that energy was not conserved, since in that decay $Q/c^2 < M_P - M_D$. A moment of reflection will persuade you that linear momentum would not be conserved either and, recalling that the neutron, proton, and electron are all spin 1/2 particles, neither would the angular momentum.

A solution to this apparent multiple failure of conservation laws was first suggested by Pauli in 1930. He proposed that a third particle was emitted in β decay which carried the energy, linear momentum, and angular momentum needed to conserve these quantities in each individual decay. It would carry no electric charge, since charge was already conserved in β decay. Its mass would be much less than that of the electron, since the maximum energy of electrons emitted in β decay is observed to be very nearly equal to the value of Q, the total energy available for the decay. In 1933 Fermi developed a highly successful quantum theory of β decay that incorporated Pauli's proposed particle, which Fermi called the *neutrino* ("little neutral one," in Italian) to distinguish it from the massive neutron which had been discovered by Chadwick earlier that same year. It was not until 1956 in an experiment performed by Clyde Cowan and Frederick Reines that neutrinos were first observed in the laboratory. It is now known that there are six kinds of neutrinos, one (v_e) associated with electrons, one (v_μ) associated with muons, one (v_τ) associated with the τ particle, and the *antiparticles* of each of those, written $\bar{v}_e$, $\bar{v}_\mu$, and $\bar{v}_\tau$. The electrons, muons, and taus together with the neutrinos constitute a family of particles called *leptons,* which will be discussed further in Chapter 13. The decay of the free neutron is then expressed by

$$n \longrightarrow p + \beta^- + \bar{v}_e \qquad \textbf{11-38}$$

and that of ^{198}Au, a more or less typical β^- emitter, by

$$^{198}\text{Au} \longrightarrow {}^{198}\text{Hg} + \beta^- + \bar{v}_e \qquad \textbf{11-39}$$

where the lepton conservation law (see Section 13-3) dictates the emission of an electron antineutrino to accompany a β^- decay. Presently the subject of intense experimental and theoretical research, current results place the upper limit of the electron neutrino's mass at about 2.8 eV/c^2, or no more than about 5×10^{-6} times the mass of the electron.

β^+ *Decay*   In β^+ decay, a proton changes into a neutron with the emission of a positron and a neutrino. A free proton cannot decay by positron emission because of conservation of energy (the rest energy of the neutron is greater than that of the proton), but because of binding energy effects, a proton inside a nucleus may emit a positron. A typical β^+ decay is

$$^{13}_{7}\text{N} \longrightarrow {}^{13}_{6}\text{C} + \beta^+ + \nu_e \qquad \textbf{11-40}$$

The only naturally occurring positron emitter known to exist is ^{40}K, which also may decay by β^- emission or electron capture! The decay equation is

$$^{40}_{19}\text{K} \longrightarrow {}^{40}_{18}\text{Ar} + \beta^+ + \nu_e \qquad \textbf{11-41}$$

As in all nuclear transformations, the decay energy Q is related to the difference in mass between the parent nucleus and the decay products. Note that if we add the mass of Z electrons to the nuclear masses ($Z = 7$ in the case of Equation 11-40 and $Z = 19$ in Equation 11-41), we obtain on the right side of each equation the mass of the daughter atom plus two extra electron masses (the positron and electron have identical mass). The decay energy for β^+ decay is thus related to the atomic mass of the parent and daughter atoms by

$$\frac{Q}{c^2} = M_P - (M_D + 2m_e) \qquad \textbf{11-42}$$

Again, we can understand this by noting that in β^+ decay a positron of mass m_e leaves the system, which is now a negative daughter ion of nuclear charge ($Z - 1$) and Z atomic electrons. To obtain the mass of the neutral daughter atom, we must subtract the mass of another electron, giving a net change of $2m_e$ in addition to the difference in mass of the parent and daughter atoms. Thus, β^+ decay cannot occur unless that energy difference is at least $2m_ec^2 = 1.022$ MeV.

As we have mentioned, neither electrons nor positrons exist inside the nucleus prior to the decay. They are created in the process of decay by the conversion of energy to mass, just as photons are created when an atom makes a transition from a higher to a lower energy state. In this regard β decay differs from α decay. There is, however, a fundamental difference between the emission of electrons (and neutrinos) that de-excite the bound states of nucleons that compose a nucleus and the emission of photons accompanying the de-excitation of the electrons bound to a nucleus. The latter bonding is due to the electromagnetic interaction, whereas the nucleons are bound by the strong nuclear force. However, electrons and neutrinos are not affected by the strong nuclear force and, since the neutron is uncharged, the electromagnetic interaction is not involved in its decay. Thus, in order to explain β decay, we must invoke a new interaction. Since β-decay lifetimes are typically quite long compared to the characteristic nuclear time scale ($\approx 10^{-23}$ s, the time for a particle moving at near the speed of light to cross the nucleus), the new interaction must act for a long (nuclear) time to generate the decay. In other words, it is weaker than the strong attractive force between the nucleons and is, therefore, called the *weak interaction* or the *weak force*. So we now have two nuclear forces, a strong one and a weak one. Like the former, the latter also has a short range.

Electron Capture   In electron capture, a proton inside a nucleus captures an atomic electron and changes into a neutron with the emission of a neutrino; thus the effect on the atomic number is the same as in β^+ decay. The energy available for this process is given by

$$\frac{Q}{c^2} = M_P - M_D \qquad\qquad \textbf{11-43}$$

Whenever the mass of an atom of atomic number Z is greater than that of the adjacent atom with atomic number $(Z - 1)$, electron capture is possible. If the mass difference is greater than $2m_e$, β^+ decay is also possible, and these two processes compete. The probability of electron capture is negligible unless the atomic electron is in the immediate vicinity of the nucleus. This probability is proportional to the square of the electron wave function integrated over the volume of the nucleus. It is significant only for the $1s$ electrons of the K shell or, with much lower probability, the $2s$ electrons of the L shell. A typical example of electron capture is

$$^{51}_{24}\text{Cr} \longrightarrow\ ^{51}_{23}\text{V} + \nu_e \qquad\qquad \textbf{11-44}$$

which has $Q = 0.751$ MeV. Note that the emission of the neutrino conserves leptons since the captured electron has disappeared.

Further understanding of the β-decay processes can be gained by considering their relation to the energy valley of the N versus Z graphs shown in Figure 11-15, with the energy scale computed from the Weizsäcker formula (Equation 11-14). Cuts through Figure 11-15a at constant mass number A yield parabolas, since Equation 11-14 is quadratic in Z, one parabola for $a_5 = 0$ (odd A) and two parabolas for $a_5 = \pm 12$ MeV/c^2 (even A). Figure 11-22 illustrates an example of each case. The β decays always proceed down the sides of the energy valley toward the lowest-energy, stable isotope on the valley floor. Notice in Figure 11-22b the possible double β decay from ^{60}Fe to ^{60}Ni. Since β decay proceeds via the weak interaction the probability of the weak force producing

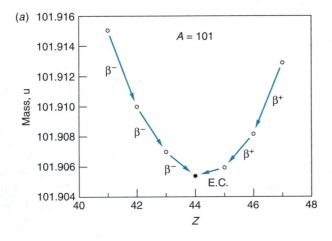

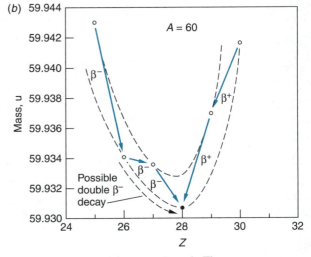

Fig. 11-22 Profiles of constant atomic mass show the cross section of the energy valley of the N vs. Z graph. The energy axes are expressed in mass units as computed from the Weizsäcker mass formula. (*a*) Odd-A nuclei, such as $A = 101$ shown, have Z and N odd-even or even-odd and $a_5 = 0$. (*b*) Even-A nuclei are either even-even with $a_5 = 12$ MeV/c^2 or odd-odd with $a_5 = -12$ MeV/c^2. The even-even parabola lies below the odd-odd one.

two β^- particles simultaneously is indeed small, as you might imagine. Prior to 1985 its existence had been inferred only indirectly by abundance measurements on decay products in geologic materials. In 1985 Steven Elliott and his co-workers made the first direct observation of double beta decay using ^{82}Se as the source. The decay equation is

$$^{82}_{34}\text{Se} \longrightarrow {}^{82}_{36}\text{Kr} + \beta^- + \beta^- + \bar{v}_e + \bar{v}_e \qquad \textbf{11-45}$$

The half-life for the double β decay measured by Elliott is 1.1×10^{20} years! Since recent experiments show that the neutrino has a very small mass, current theory would enable the decay in Equation 11-45 to proceed without the emission of neutrinos, albeit with an even lower probability. The implications of a neutrinoless double beta decay are profound for both particle physics and cosmology. Although active searches are currently underway, no such decays have yet been observed.

EXAMPLE 11-12 **Maximum β^+ Energy from ^{40}K** We noted earlier that one of the decay modes of ^{40}K is positron emission, shown in Equation 11-41. What is the maximum energy of the positrons?

Solution

1. The maximum energy Q of the positrons is given by Equation 11-42, where ^{40}K is the parent and ^{40}Ar is the daughter:

$$\frac{Q}{c^2} = M_P - (M_D + 2m_e)$$

2. The atomic masses are given in Appendix A:

$$M(^{40}\text{K}) = 39.964000 \text{ u}$$
$$M(^{40}\text{Ar}) = 39.962384 \text{ u}$$
$$m_e = 5.4858 \times 10^{-4} \text{ u}$$

3. Substituting these into Equation 11-42 yields:

$$\frac{Q}{c^2} = 39.964000 \text{ u} - [39.962384 + 2 \times 5.4858 \times 10^{-4}] \text{ u}$$

$$= 0.000519 \text{ u} \times 931.5 \text{ MeV}/c^2 \cdot \text{u}$$

$$= 0.483 \text{ MeV}/c^2$$

Remarks: *Neglecting the recoil of the Ar nucleus, the decay energy $Q = 0.483$ MeV is the maximum energy of the emitted positrons.*

EXAMPLE 11-13 **The Decay of $^{233}_{93}$Np** Determine which decay mode or modes among α decay and the three types of β decay are allowed for $^{233}_{93}$Np.

Solution

The four decays whose possibility of occurrence we are to find are:

$$\alpha \text{ decay:} \qquad {}^{233}_{93}\text{Np} \longrightarrow {}^{229}_{91}\text{Pa} + \alpha$$

$$\beta^- \text{ decay:} \qquad {}^{233}_{93}\text{Np} \longrightarrow {}^{233}_{94}\text{Pu} + \beta^- + \bar{v}_e$$

$$\beta^+ \text{ decay:} \qquad {}^{233}_{93}\text{Np} \longrightarrow {}^{233}_{92}\text{U} + \beta^+ + v_e$$

$$\text{electron capture:} \qquad {}^{233}_{93}\text{Np} \longrightarrow {}^{233}_{92}\text{U} + v_e$$

The decay energy Q for each of these is computed as follows:

α decay (Equation 11-34):

$$\frac{Q}{c^2} = 233.040805 - (229.032085 + 4.002603)$$

$$= 0.006117 \text{ u} = 5.70 \text{ MeV}/c^2$$

which is greater than zero; therefore, α decay is allowed.

β^- decay (Equation 11-37):

$$\frac{Q}{c^2} = 233.040805 - 233.042963$$

$$= -0.002158 \text{ u} = -2.01 \text{ MeV}/c^2$$

β^- decay is forbidden.

β^+ decay (Equation 11-42):

$$\frac{Q}{c^2} = 233.040805 - (233.039630 + 2 \times 5.4858 \times 10^{-4})$$

$$= 0.000078 \text{ u} = 0.07 \text{ MeV}/c^2$$

β^+ decay is allowed.

Electron capture (Equation 11-43):

$$\frac{Q}{c^2} = 233.040805 - 233.039630$$

$$= 0.001175 \text{ u} = 1.09 \text{ MeV}/c^2$$

Electron capture is allowed.

Thus, the available decay energy would allow α decay, β^+ decay, and electron capture, although the energy for β^+ decay is very small. β^- decay is forbidden. Experimentally, ^{233}Np decays more than 99 percent of the time by electron capture and about 0.3 percent of the time by α decay. β^+ decay has not been observed.

Gamma Decay

In γ decay, a nucleus in an excited state decays to a lower energy state of the same isotope by the emission of a photon. This decay is the nuclear analogue of the emission of light by atoms. Since the spacing of the nuclear energy levels is of the order

of MeV (as compared with eV in atoms), the wavelengths of the emitted photons are of the order of

$$\lambda = \frac{hc}{E} \approx \frac{1240 \text{ MeV} \cdot \text{nm}}{1 \text{ MeV}} = 1.24 \times 10^{-3} \text{ nm}$$

Gamma-ray emission usually follows beta decay or alpha decay. For example, if a radioactive parent nucleus decays by beta decay to an excited state of the daughter nucleus, the daughter nucleus often decays to its ground state by emission of one or more γ rays. The mean life for γ decay is usually very short. Direct measurements of mean lives as short as 10^{-11} s are possible. Measurements of lifetimes smaller than 10^{-11} s are difficult, but can sometimes be accomplished by determining the natural line width Γ and using the uncertainty relation $\tau = \hbar/\Gamma$. A few γ emitters have very long lifetimes, of the order of hours and even, in a few cases, years. Nuclear energy states with such long lifetimes are called *isomers* or *metastable states*. The differences in γ-ray lifetimes are a consequence of the quantum-mechanical selection rules that govern transitions between the energy levels of nuclei, just as they do between atomic energy levels. For example, large angular momentum (spin) changes are forbidden for γ transitions; that is, they have very low probability. This is the major reason that, for instance, the first excited state of ^{93}Nb, an isomer, decays to the ground state with a half-life of 13.6 years. The spin of the isomeric state is 1/2, while that of the ground state is 9/2. The decay requires the γ ray to carry away $4\hbar$ of angular momentum, a very unlikely occurrence which accounts for the long half-life.

The energy *hf* of a gamma-ray photon is the difference in energy of the states between which the transition occurs. That is,

$$hf = E_{\text{high}} - E_{\text{low}} \qquad \textbf{11-46}$$

where E_{high} is the energy of the upper level and E_{low} is that of the lower level. Several gamma decays are shown in Figure 11-20 (see page 529) between some of the excited states of ^{223}Ra that resulted from the α decay of ^{227}Th. For example, a γ ray is emitted from the 174-keV level of ^{223}Ra, reducing the excitation energy of that nucleus to 61 keV above the ground state. Using Equation 11-46, the energy of that γ ray is equal to 174 keV − 61 keV = 113 keV. To be more precise, conservation of momentum requires that the ^{223}Ra nucleus carry a small part of this energy as it recoils from the emission of the photon. (See Figure 11-23.) The energy of the nuclear recoil E_r is given by

Fig. 11-23 A nucleus of rest energy Mc^2 emits a photon of energy *hf* and momentum $p = hf/c$. Conservation of momentum requires that the nucleus also recoil with momentum *p*.

$$E_r = \frac{p^2}{2M} = \frac{(hf)^2}{2Mc^2} \qquad \textbf{11-47}$$

where *M* is the nuclear mass. All gamma-ray energies are small compared with atomic and nuclear rest energies; that is, $hf \ll Mc^2$ or $hf/Mc^2 \ll 1$; therefore, $E_r \ll hf$. Thus, Equation 11-46 is an excellent approximation of the gamma ray's energy.

Internal Conversion   An important alternative to gamma-ray emission for the de-excitation of an excited nuclear state, particularly low-lying states, is the process of internal conversion. In this process the excitation energy of the state is transferred to an orbital electron, which is ejected from the atom, rather than being emitted as a photon.

Those electrons with the highest probabilities of being close to the nucleus, the K and L electrons, are the ones most likely to be emitted. The ejected electron has kinetic energy equal to the nuclear transition energy minus the electron's binding energy. Since the latter are accurately known for nearly all elements, measuring the kinetic energies of the *conversion electrons* enables determination of many nuclear excited states. While internal conversion is quantum-mechanically a one-step process, it was initially pictured as the emission of a photon followed by a photoelectric-effect interaction with an orbital electron of the same atom; hence the name *internal conversion.*

Exploring
Mössbauer Effect

An interesting feature of γ decay is the Mössbauer effect. The photons emitted by nuclei making a transition from an excited state to the ground state are not mono-energetic, but have a distribution of energies because of the energy width of the excited state. The natural width of the energy distribution of photons Γ is related to the mean lifetime τ of the excited state by $\Gamma = \hbar/\tau$, consistent with the uncertainty principle. The width and thus the lifetime can, in principle, be determined by the technique of *resonance fluorescence,* the absorption and reemission of a photon emitted by an atom or a nucleus of the same type. If the excited state has energy centered at E_0 with width Γ, the cross section for the absorption of photons has a sharp maximum at the excitation energy E_0 and drops to half the maximum value at $E_0 \pm (1/2)\Gamma$. The integral of the cross section over energy is proportional to Γ, so a measurement of absorption cross section versus energy can be used to determine Γ and therefore the lifetime τ. Resonance fluorescence is observed for atomic transitions, but generally not for nuclear transitions because of the difference in the recoil between the two cases. The recoil is negligible compared with Γ for atomic transitions because of their low energy (≈ 1 eV), which can be seen as follows. The typical lifetime of atomic states is about 10^{-8} s; therefore

$$\Gamma = \frac{\hbar}{\tau} \approx 10^{-7} \text{eV}$$

while the recoil energy E_r, also given by Equation 11-47 with M equal to the atomic mass, is

$$E_r = \frac{(1 \text{ eV})^2}{10^{11} \text{ eV}} \approx 10^{-11} \text{ eV}$$

for an atom with $A = 50$. Thus, the natural width of the photon emitted in the atomic transition is of the order of 10^4 larger than the recoil energy. (See Figure 11-24a.) In the nuclear case, however, the photon energy is 10^5 to 10^6 times larger. For a nuclear state with the same lifetime and mass number as above, the recoil energy is

$$E_r = \frac{(10^5 \text{ eV})^2}{10^{11} \text{ eV}} \approx 10^{-1} \text{ eV}$$

The exceptional precision of frequency measurements made possible by the Mössbauer effect has applications in a broad range of areas, such as measurements of gravitational redshift, impurities and imperfections in crystalline solids, and the transverse Doppler effect (see Section 1-5), to name just three.

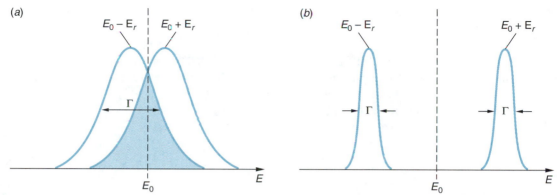

Fig. 11-24 Schematic diagram of the photons emitted (left) and absorbed (right) by (*a*) an atomic state and (*b*) a nuclear state. In the atomic case the large energy overlap (shaded area) between the photon emitted by a state E_0 and that which the atom must absorb to excite the state E_0 enables the phenomenon of resonance absorption. In the corresponding nuclear case shown in (*b*), the magnitude of the recoil energy relative to the natural line width eliminates the overlap and with it the resonance absorption of gamma rays. (The energy axes of the two diagrams are different.)

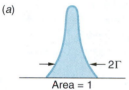

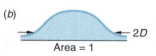

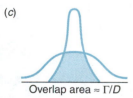

Fig. 11-25 (*a*) Unbroadened line with natural width Γ. (*b*) Doppler-broadened line with the same area as in (*a*). (*c*) Absorption in resonance fluorescence is proportional to the overlap area, which is approximately Γ/D.

Thus, the recoil energy is roughly a million times larger than the line width, and the resonance absorption rendered possible by the overlap of emitted and absorbed photons illustrated in Figure 11-24*a* for atomic transitions does not exist for nuclear gamma transitions, as Figure 11-24*b* illustrates. Thus, in general, if the width of the excited state Γ is less than $2E_r = E_0/Mc^2$, no photons will be emitted by a nucleus with energy great enough to be absorbed by another nucleus of the same kind, and resonance fluorescence of gamma radiation cannot take place, *unless* the lines are greatly broadened by the Doppler effect, so that at least a small overlap of the lines in Figure 11-24*b* occurs.

The thermal motion of atoms gives a Doppler broadening of the lines but does not shift the central energy, because the motion is random and the chances of increase or decrease of energy are equal. At ordinary room temperatures, the Doppler energy width is of the order of $D = 10^{-6} E_0$, which is about 10 times the natural width for atomic transitions and much larger than the natural width for nuclear transitions. Because the Doppler width D is of the order of magnitude of the recoil energy E_r for nuclear transitions, the emission and absorption lines do have some overlap, and some resonance fluorescence is possible (see Figure 11-25).

In 1950, P. Moon successfully observed nuclear resonance fluorescence by placing a source on the rim of an ultracentrifuge rotor that revolved such that the rim had a speed of about 800 m/s, introducing an external Doppler shift compensating for the recoil loss. By varying the speed, he was able to measure the absorption cross section as a function of energy and determine a mean life of the order of 10^{-11} s for his source.

In 1958, Rudolf Mössbauer[12] used an ^{191}Ir source of 129-keV photons, for which the Doppler broadening at room temperature is about twice the recoil shift, so that the lines in Figure 11-24*b* overlapped a bit and resonance fluorescence could be observed. When he cooled the source and absorber, he expected to see the absorption decrease because of the decrease in the Doppler width and thus in the overlap. Instead, however, he observed an increase in the absorption. The absorption, in fact, was as much as would be expected if there had been no recoil at all! The qualitative explanation of this effect is that at sufficiently low temperatures an atom in a solid cannot recoil individually because of the quantization of the vibrational energy states in the lattice. The recoil momentum is absorbed by the crystal as a whole. The effective mass in Equation 11-47 is thus the mass of the crystal,

(a)

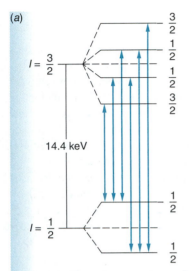

(b)

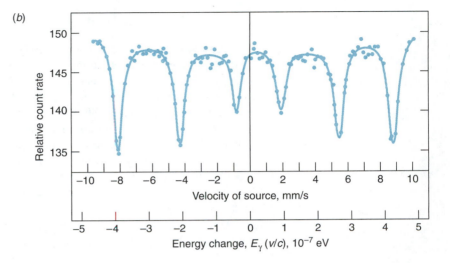

Fig. 11-26 (a) Schematic diagram of the decay of the isomeric state of ^{57}Fe at 14.4 keV for atoms bound in an ordinary iron lattice, showing the hyperfine splitting of the levels due to the magnetic field at the nucleus. (b) The absorption of the 14.4-keV ^{57}Fe gamma ray by ^{57}Fe bound in a lattice of Fe_2O_3 as a function of the relative source-absorber velocity, showing the nuclear Zeeman effect. [*From O. C. Kistner and A. W. Sunyar,* Physical Review Letters, *4, 412 (1960).*]

which is so much larger than that of the atom that the recoil energy is completely negligible. The emitted photon, therefore, has energy E_0 that can be absorbed without recoil by another nucleus which is similarly bound in a lattice. Mössbauer was able to destroy the resonance by moving the source or absorber, thereby introducing an external Doppler shift. However, this shift need be only of the order of Γ, which is 4.6×10^{-6} eV for ^{191}Ir. The velocity needed to obtain a Doppler shift of this energy is only a few centimeters per second. In the event that the excited state is an isomer, then the lines in Figure 11-2b are particularly narrow. As a result, a frequently used source for Mössbauer measurements is ^{57}Fe, which has an isomeric state at 14.4 keV with a lifetime of about 10^{-7} seconds, corresponding to a line width of about 10^{-8} eV, or about $1/10^{12}$ of the transition energy. The ability to "scan" the line from the gamma-emitting source across the line of the gamma-absorbing sample by varying the Doppler velocity of the source or the absorber has enabled scientists to conduct a wide variety of experiments with a precision much higher than had been possible before Mössbauer's discovery. For example, Figure 11-26a shows the Zeeman effect in the ^{57}Fe 14.4-keV gamma ray that arises due to the nuclear magnetic field, thus making possible measurement of the magnetic field at the location of the iron nucleus.

QUESTIONS

6. Why is the decay series $A = (4n + 1)$ not found in nature?

7. A decay by α emission is often followed by a β decay. When this occurs, it is usually a β^- decay. Why?

8. How can the application of very high pressure affect the lifetime of a sample that decays by electron capture? Why are other types of decay not affected?

11-5 The Nuclear Force

The study of nuclear physics is quite different from that of atomic physics. The simplest atom, the hydrogen atom, can be completely understood by solving the Schrödinger equation using the known potential energy of interaction between the electron and proton, $V(r) = -ke^2/r$ (though, as we have seen, the mathematics needed is fairly complicated). The simplest nucleus (other than a single proton) is the deuteron, consisting of a proton and a neutron. We cannot solve the Schrödinger equation for this problem and then compare with the experiment because, although many of its characteristics have been determined, the exact mathematical form of the potential energy of interaction V is not known. There is no macroscopic way to measure the force between a neutron and a proton. It is clear from the fact that many nuclei are stable that there are other forces much stronger than electromagnetic or gravitational forces between nucleons. Considering ^{4}He as an example, the electrostatic potential energy of two protons separated by 1 fm is

$$V = \frac{ke^2}{r} = \frac{1.44 \text{ MeV} \cdot \text{fm}}{1 \text{ fm}} = 1.44 \text{ MeV}$$

and note that it is positive—i.e., the electrostatic force between the protons is, of course, repulsive. However, the energy needed to remove a proton or neutron from ^{4}He is about 20 MeV. The force responsible for such a large binding energy must be attractive and significantly stronger than the electrostatic force. This must certainly be the case, since the neutrons are electrically neutral and, hence, do not feel the Coulomb force and the protons are all positively charged and thus feel a repulsive electrostatic force. Nor can we appeal to the gravitational attractive force between the protons to offset their Coulomb repulsion since, as Example 11-14 illustrates, the gravitational force between pairs of protons in the nucleus is insignificantly small compared to their Coulomb repulsion. Thus, the attractive force that holds the nucleons together must be strong, stronger even than the electromagnetic interaction. It is called the *nuclear* or *hadronic force* or often simply the *strong force*.

The determination of the characteristics of the nuclear force is one of the central problems of nuclear physics. Much information about this force can be and has been obtained from scattering experiments involving protons, neutrons, and other particles. Although the results of a scattering experiment can be predicted unambiguously from a knowledge of the force law, the force law cannot be completely determined from the results of such experiments. The results of scattering experiments do indicate (1) that the nuclear force has the same strength between any two nucleons—that is, *n-n*, *p-p*, or *n-p*; (2) that the force is strong when the particles are close together and drops rapidly to zero when the particles are separated by a few femtometers; and (3) that it is a saturated force. The potential energy of the nucleon-nucleus interaction can be roughly represented by a square well of about 40 MeV depth and a few fm width.

EXAMPLE 11-14 Ratio of F_{grav}/F_{Coul} Between Protons Compare the gravitational attractive force between two protons in an atomic nucleus (or anywhere else, for that matter) with the electrostatic repulsion between them.

Solution

The electrostatic repulsion for two protons separated by a distance r is

$$F_{\text{Coul}} = \frac{1}{4\pi\epsilon_0}\frac{e^2}{r^2} = \frac{(1.60 \times 10^{-19}\,\text{C})^2}{4\pi\epsilon_0 r^2}$$

and the gravitational attraction between them is

$$F_{\text{grav}} = G\frac{m_p^2}{r^2} = \frac{G(1.67 \times 10^{-27}\,\text{kg})^2}{r^2}$$

The ratio is independent of r and equal to

$$\frac{F_{\text{grav}}}{F_{\text{Coul}}} = \frac{Gm_p^2}{(1/4\pi\epsilon_0)e^2} = \frac{(6.67 \times 10^{-11}\,\text{N}\cdot\text{m}^2/\text{kg}^2)(1.67 \times 10^{-27}\,\text{kg})^2}{(8.99 \times 10^9\,\text{N}\cdot\text{m}^2/\text{C}^2)(1.60 \times 10^{-19}\,\text{C})^2}$$

$$\frac{F_{\text{grav}}}{F_{\text{Coul}}} = 8.1 \times 10^{-37} \approx 10^{-36}$$

Solution of the nuclear wave equation presents all of the mathematical complexities of our earlier studies of atomic and molecular systems plus some truly monumental new ones. Like the atomic and molecular systems, the nucleus (except for ^{1}H and ^{2}H) is a many-body system with all of the accompanying calculational difficulties. In addition, the nuclear interaction is far more complex than the electromagnetic interaction and, even worse, it is not yet known how the nuclear interaction can be expressed in closed, analytic form. That is, we do not know the nuclear force law equivalent of Coulomb's law for the electrostatic force. This means that we cannot yet write down the exact form of the nuclear potential function that must be included in the wave equation in order to solve for the nuclear wave functions and allowed energies.

Substantial progress has been made in recent years toward obtaining the analytic expression for the interaction. For instance, an estimate of the depth of the nuclear potential can be made by assuming its shape to be approximated by a square well and computing the ground-state energy of a nucleon, based on a reasonable assumption of the well width. Using 2 fm as a typical width for light nuclei (see Figure 11-5), the potential $-V$ for a nucleon is approximately

$$-V \approx E_1 \approx \frac{h^2}{8\,ma^2} = \frac{(6.63 \times 10^{-34}\,\text{J}\cdot\text{s})}{(8)(1.67 \times 10^{-27}\,\text{kg})(2 \times 10^{-15}\,\text{m})^2(1.60 \times 10^{-13}\,\text{J/MeV})}$$

$$V \approx -50\,\text{MeV}$$

Two protons separated by that same distance experience an electrostatic Coulomb repulsive potential given by

$$V_{\text{Coulomb}} = \frac{1}{4\pi\varepsilon_0}\frac{e^2}{a} = \frac{(9 \times 10^9\,\text{N}\cdot\text{m}^2/\text{C}^2)(1.60 \times 10^{-19}\,\text{C})^2}{(2 \times 10^{-15}\,\text{m})(1.60 \times 10^{-13}\,\text{J/MeV})}$$

$$V_{\text{Coulomb}} = 0.72\,\text{MeV}$$

Thus, our square well approximation suggests that at 2 fm the attractive nuclear potential exceeds the Coulomb repulsion experienced by a proton by nearly two orders of magnitude.[13]

More detailed understanding of the nature of the nuclear force and the shape and depth of the potential is provided by two types of experiments. First, just as atomic

spectroscopy yielded information that enabled the determination of such things as the energies, spins, and magnetic moments of the electronic structure of atoms, nuclear spectroscopy—i.e., the study of the emission and absorption of particles and radiation by the nuclei—yields valuable information concerning the ground and excited states of nuclei including energies, magnetic moments, electric quadrupole moments, and spins. The second source of our detailed information comes from the analysis of scattering experiments. These are experiments in which particles that feel the nuclear force, such as protons or alpha particles, are used as projectiles "fired" at target nuclei. The de Broglie wavelengths of projectile protons with kinetic energies of 20 MeV (or more) are of the order of nuclear dimensions:

$$\lambda = \frac{h}{p} = \frac{h}{\sqrt{2\,mE}} = \frac{6.63 \times 10^{-34}\,\text{J}\cdot\text{s}}{\sqrt{2 \times 1.67 \times 10^{-27}\,\text{kg} \times 20\,\text{MeV} \times 1.60 \times 10^{-13}\,\text{J/MeV}}}$$

$$\lambda = 6 \times 10^{-15}\,\text{m} = 6\,\text{fm}$$

Thus, such protons will experience considerable diffraction in collisions with the target nuclei. Analysis of the resulting diffraction pattern yields detailed information concerning the interaction between the particles. Many such experiments, particularly protons scattered from protons, called *p-p* scattering, and neutrons scattered from protons, or *n-p* scattering, reveal that the nuclear potential for proton-proton pairs and neutron-proton pairs are of the form sketched in Figure 11-27. Although the shape of the potential for neutron-neutron pairs can only be determined indirectly, since free neutrons are radioactive and we do not know how to make targets consisting only of neutrons (such as the matter of neutron stars), it appears to be identical to that of *n-p* pairs. In fact, when the Coulomb repulsion component of the *p-p* pair potential in Figure 11-27*b* is subtracted from the total potential *V(r)*, the remaining nuclear *p-p* potential is also the same as those for *n-p* and *n-n* pairs. This leads to the very important conclusion that <u>the nuclear force is independent of the charge of the nucleons.</u> This suggests that the proton and neutron can be considered as different charge states of the same particle, the nucleon. We will pursue this suggestion further in Chapter 13.

As described in Section 11-2, the charge radius of the proton is about 1 fm. The neutron is approximately the same size. As Figure 11-27 illustrates, two nucleons experience the attractive nuclear force as long as they are within about 2.5 fm of one another, but the force diminishes rapidly over the next 1/2 fm of separation and is

Fig. 11-27 (*a*) The approximate shape of the potential between *n-p* and *n-n* pairs. The hard core suggested by the nearly constant central density of the nucleus has a radius of about 0.5 fm. (*b*) The *p-p* potential differs from those in (*a*) by the added Coulomb repulsion, which dominates beyond about 3 fm. Notice that the *n-p* and *n-n* potential well is slightly deeper than the *p-p* potential due to the absence of the Coulomb repulsion.

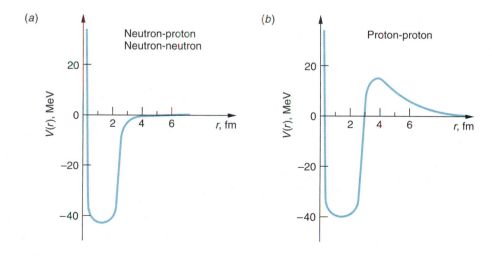

essentially zero beyond 3 fm. Thus, we also conclude that the nuclear force is a short-range force. Nucleon pairs also experience an extremely strong repulsive component of the nuclear force when they approach within about 0.5 fm. This *hard core* is consistent with the observation that the central density is nearly the same for all nuclei (see Figure 11-7). That is, as more and more nucleons are added, the size of the nucleus increases in such a way that the density remains approximately constant, so something must prevent the nucleons from crowding too closely together. The short range of the nuclear force together with the repulsion of the hard core means that, as the size of the nucleus increases beyond the 2.5- to 3-fm range of the force, an individual nucleon will be able to interact with only a limited number of the other particles in the nucleus, namely, its nearby neighbors which are within range of its force. This is analogous to the limited number of bonds associated with each atom in the covalent bonding of solids. For example, each carbon atom in diamond bonds with only four of its nearest neighbors and we could describe the carbon covalent bond as being a saturated bond. Similarly, the nuclear force is a saturated force.

The Nuclear Exchange Force

Without knowing the analytic form of the nuclear potential function, we have been able to conclude that the nuclear force is a short-range, saturated, charge-independent, spin-dependent force with a hard core and a small noncentral component and is about two orders of magnitude stronger than the electrostatic force. What could be the origin or mechanism for such a force was first suggested by H. Yukawa[14] in 1935.

Yukawa proposed that the nuclear force resulted from an exchange of particles between the nucleons. He based his theory on an analogy with the quantum-mechanical explanation of the electrostatic interaction, one of two exchange mechanisms that you have previously studied, though perhaps not by that name. Classically, any distribution of charges produces an electric field $\mathscr{E}$, and the force felt by another charge q located in the field is the product $q\mathscr{E}$. Any change in the charge distribution changes $\mathscr{E}$; however, the information that a change has occurred does not appear instantaneously throughout the field, but is propagated outward at the speed of light. Time-dependent changes in the charge distribution create time-dependent changes in $\mathscr{E}$, that is, electromagnetic radiation, or waves.[15] We have seen that the particle representation of the electromagnetic radiation is the photon. Quantum-mechanically, every charge is continually emitting and absorbing photons, even when it is not moving. They are called *virtual photons,* meaning that they are not directly observable. A charge can emit a virtual photon of energy hf without changing its energy or recoiling, i.e., without violating conservation of energy and momentum, provided that the photon exists for no longer than $\Delta t = \hbar/\Delta E$, where $\Delta E = hf$, as required by the uncertainty principle. The distance that the virtual photon can travel during the time Δt, called the range R, is given by

$$R = c\Delta t = c\hbar/\Delta E \qquad\qquad \textbf{11-48}$$

and substituting for ΔE,

$$R = c\hbar/hf = c/2\pi f = \lambda/2\pi \qquad\qquad \textbf{11-49}$$

A second charge located up to a distance R from the first can absorb the photon, and a similar photon emitted by the second charge may be absorbed by the first, all without

Fig. 11-28 Schematic representation of the exchange of a meson by a pair of nucleons. The meson is emitted by the nucleon on the left, which recoils as a result, and is absorbed after a time Δt by the nucleon on the right, which also recoils. The effect on the nucleons is as if they had interacted with each other. This kind of spacetime diagram of the exchange interaction is called a Feynman diagram. The x and t axes are normally omitted.

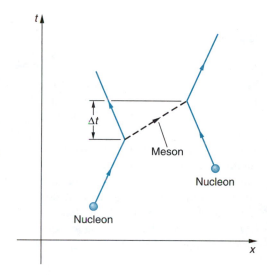

violating energy and momentum conservation. It is this exchange of virtual photons that results in the electrostatic Coulomb force between the two stationary charges in quantum mechanics. Note that there is no limit to the wavelength of the photon in Equation 11-49 since the energy of the photon may be arbitrarily small, the photon having no rest mass. Thus the distance separating the two charges, the range R of the Coulomb force, may also be infinite, as you have already learned.

An exchange mechanism was also used in BCS theory to account for the attractive force between the electrons of the Cooper pairs. (See Section 10-9.) In that case the exchange particles were the phonons and the range of the force was not infinite, but determined by the fact that $\Delta E \approx$ the energy gap.

Yukawa proposed that the nuclear force could also be explained in terms of the exchange of virtual particles by the nucleons. These particles, which he called *mesons,* were pictured as the analogs of the virtual photons in the electromagnetic interaction and established the *meson field* in analogy with the electromagnetic field. The mechanism for the nuclear force was proposed to be an exchange of a meson between a pair of nucleons as illustrated by Figure 11-28. Yukawa accounted for the observed short range of the nuclear force by assigning mass to the meson. Thus, the energy uncertainty ΔE in Equation 11-48 would be

$$\Delta E \geq mc^2$$

where m is the mass of the meson and mc^2 is its rest energy. The range R of the meson and, therefore, the nuclear force that it mediates cannot be larger than

$$R = c\Delta t = c\hbar/\Delta E = \hbar/mc \qquad \textbf{11-50}$$

since the speed of the meson must be less that the speed of light. Recall that h/mc is the Compton wavelength λ_c of the particle whose mass is m, so $R = \lambda_c/2\pi$. The range of the nuclear force was known to be about 1 fm, which enabled an approximation of the meson's expected mass from Equation 11-50:

$$m \approx 3.5 \times 10^{-28} \text{ kg} \approx 380 \, m_e \approx 200 \text{ MeV}/c^2$$

The observed charge independence of the nuclear force was incorporated by Yukawa into the theory by allowing the mesons to carry $+e$, 0, or $-e$ charge. Thus, referring to Figure 11-28, the exchange of a neutral meson would leave both of the nucleons with their original charge, while the exchange of a charged meson would interchange their charges. Note that $m = 0$ for photons in Equation 11-50 implies the infinite range of the electromagnetic force.

If the nucleon that emits the meson happens to interact with another particle (or nucleus) which has sufficient kinetic energy in the emitting nucleon's rest system to supply the meson's rest energy and also provide the recoil momentum to the emitting nucleon, thus conserving both energy and momentum, the virtual meson can become real and be observable in the laboratory. Such a situation is shown schematically in Figure 11-29. Note the analogy to the emission of photons (bremsstrahlung) by accelerated electrons in an x-ray tube (see Section 3-4). It was interactions such as those shown in Figure 11-29 in which Yukawa's mesons, now called π *mesons* or *pions,* were first seen in cosmic rays in 1947, more than a decade after they were proposed.[16] The mass measured for the pions is 140 MeV/c^2, in quite good agreement with Yukawa's predicted approximate value of about 200 MeV/c^2, and all three charge versions were subsequently discovered, providing beautiful confirmation of Yukawa's theory. Since then additional mesons have been discovered and our understanding of the nuclear force has been modified to include the effect of their being exchanged by nucleons as well, but the pions remain as the dominant carrier of the force between nucleons and the cornerstone of our understanding of it. As we shall discuss further in Chapter 13, current particle theory holds that the nucleons and the mesons are both composites of other fundamental particles, called *quarks.* The interaction between quarks to form these particles is also viewed as the exchange of a field particle, the *gluon,* between quark pairs in direct analogy with our discussion above.

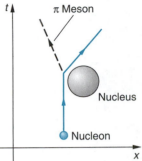

Fig. 11-29 A Feynman diagram of a nucleon emitting a virtual pion in the vicinity of a nucleus. If the nucleus can provide at least the pion's rest energy and participate in the conservation of momentum, the pion may become real, i.e., visible in the laboratory.

EXAMPLE 11-15 Range of the Nuclear Force Using the experimentally measured mass of the pion, 140 MeV/c^2, estimate the range of the nuclear force.

Solution
The range R cannot be larger than $\hbar c/mc^2$ according to Equation 11-50. We then have that

$$R = \hbar c/mc^2 = \frac{(1.06 \times 10^{-34}\, J \cdot s)(3.00 \times 10^8\, m/s)}{(140\, MeV/c^2)(c^2)(1.60 \times 10^{-13}\, J/MeV)}$$

$$R = 1.4 \times 10^{-15}\, m = 1.4\, fm$$

QUESTIONS

9. What property of the nuclear force is indicated by the fact that all nuclei have about the same density?

10. How does the nuclear force differ from the electromagnetic force?

11. Mesons that have been discovered in recent years are all more massive that the pion. What does that mean regarding the range of the force that they mediate?

Exploring

Probability Density of the Exchange Mesons

A nucleon continually emits and absorbs virtual mesons. The time Δt during which a virtual meson exists can be estimated from Equation 11-50.

$$\Delta t = \hbar/mc^2 = \frac{(1.055 \times 10^{-34}\ \text{J} \cdot \text{s})}{(140\ \text{MeV}/c^2)(c^2)(1.60 \times 10^{-13}\ \text{J/MeV})}$$

$$\Delta t = 5 \times 10^{-24}\text{s}$$

This is not a very long time! Thus, a 10^{-20} second time-exposure "snapshot" of a nucleon would show a cloud consisting of more than 10,000 mesons surrounding the nucleon! The probability density of the mesons can be determined using the results that we obtained from relativity and wave mechanics in Chapters 2 and 6, respectively. The relativistic expression connecting the total energy E and momentum p, the magnitude of the energy/momentum four-vector, is

$$(mc^2)^2 = E^2 - (pc)^2 \qquad\qquad \textbf{2-32}$$

Using the appropriate operator substitutions from Table 6-1,

$$E \longrightarrow i\hbar\,\frac{\partial}{\partial t} \qquad p^2 \longrightarrow -\hbar^2\nabla^2 \qquad\qquad \textbf{11-51}$$

Equation 2-32 can be written as

$$\nabla^2\Phi(\mathbf{r},\,t) - \frac{1}{c^2}\frac{\partial^2\Phi(\mathbf{r},\,t)}{\partial t^2} = \left(\frac{mc}{\hbar}\right)^2\Phi(\mathbf{r},\,t) \qquad\qquad \textbf{11-52}$$

where $\Phi(\mathbf{r},\,t)$ is the wave function of the meson. Equation 11-52 is a relativistic wave equation. It was first obtained by Oskar Klein and Walter Gordon in 1926, the same year that Schrödinger developed his nonrelativistic wave equation.

That the extent of the meson field is related to the range of the nuclear force given by Equation 11-50 can be illustrated by computing the probability density of the meson $|\Phi|^2$ for a static, or time-independent distribution. This is roughly analogous to the virtual photon distribution, or the electric field intensity, for a stationary

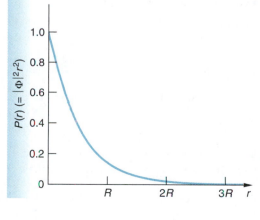

Fig. 11-30 Probability $P(r)$, equal to $|\Phi|^2 r^2$, for the virtual mesons emitted by a nucleon. The range $R = \hbar/mc$, the Compton wavelength of the mesons divided by 2π. There are essentially no mesons beyond about $3R$.

charge. In this case the time derivative of Φ vanishes and Equation 11-52 can be written as

$$\nabla^2\Phi(\mathbf{r}) = \left(\frac{mc}{\hbar}\right)^2\Phi(\mathbf{r}) = \frac{1}{R^2}\Phi(\mathbf{r}) \qquad \textbf{11-53}$$

whose solution is

$$\Phi(\mathbf{r}) = \frac{Ae^{-r/R}}{\mathbf{r}} \qquad \textbf{11-54}$$

where A is a factor determined by the normalization condition. The probability density is then

$$|\Phi(\mathbf{r})|^2 = \frac{|A|^2 e^{-2r/R}}{\mathbf{r}^2} \qquad \textbf{11-55}$$

and we see that the probability density of the mesons falls off exponentially at a rate determined by R. In other words, R determines the range of the exchange mesons as we had interpreted it in Equation 11-50. Figure 11-30 illustrates the probability distribution function $P(r) = |\Phi|^2 r^2$ for the virtual mesons. For values of r greater than about $0.5R$, the curve agrees well with experimental results; however, for small values of r the measured meson density is much lower than Figure 11-30 would suggest. Indeed, if the predicted values at very small r values actually existed, they would lead to some quite unusual nuclear properties that are, in fact, not observed. Nuclear theorists conclude that the number of pions at very small r is somehow suppressed, likely as a result of the quark-gluon interaction mentioned above. This is an area of active current research.

11-6 The Shell Model

Although the general features of the binding energy of nuclei are well accounted for by the semiempirical mass formula which was based on modeling the nucleus as a liquid drop, the binding energy and other properties do not vary with perfect smoothness from nucleus to nucleus. It is not surprising that the smooth curve predicted by Equation 11-12 does not fit the data for very small A, for which the addition of a single proton or a neutron makes a drastic difference. However, even for medium and large A there are some substantial fluctuations of nuclear properties in neighboring nuclei. Consider the binding energy of the last neutron in a nucleus. (Note that this is not the same as the average binding energy per nucleon.) We can calculate this from the semiempirical mass formula by computing the difference in mass $M[(A-1), Z] + m_n - M(A, Z)$. Figure 11-31 shows a plot of the difference between the experimentally measured binding energy and that calculated from Equation 11-12 as a function of the neutron number N. There are large fluctuations near $N = 20, 28, 50, 82,$ and 126. These are also the neutron numbers of the nuclei that have an unusually large number of isotones. Nuclei with these proton numbers (except that no element with $Z = 126$ has been observed) have an unusually large number of isotopes.

These numbers are the "magic numbers" that were referred to in Section 11-2. In the regions between these magic numbers, the binding energy of the last neutron is

Existence of 126 as a magic number has prompted searches for unusually stable (but still radioactive) isotopes with $Z = 126$. Finding them will strengthen our understanding of nuclear structure. Thus far, the highest Z discovered (as yet unconfirmed) is 116.

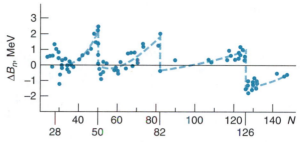

Fig. 11-31 Difference in the measured binding energy of the last neutron and that calculated from mass formula vs. neutron number. Note the similarity of this curve and the ionization energy of atoms vs. Z (Figure 7-20). The neutron numbers 28, 50, 82, and 126 correspond to closed shells. These data show that the neutron with N = magic number $+1$ is much less tightly bound than that with N = magic number.

predicted quite accurately by the semiempirical mass formula. Figure 11-31 should be compared with Figure 7-20, which shows the binding energy of the last electron in an atom as a function of the atomic number Z. The similarity of these two figures suggests a shell structure of the nucleus analogous to the shell structure of atoms. There is considerable additional evidence for these magic numbers, such as the electric quadrupole moments (Figure 11-7), the neutron capture cross sections illustrated in Figure 11-32, and the binding energies of the last neutron for isotopes of a given Z as shown in Figure 11-33. Additional evidence of nuclear shell structure is discussed in Mayer and Jensen (1955).

Although the unusual stability of the nuclei with N or Z equal to one of the magic numbers was noticed in the 1930s, there was no successful explanation in terms of shell structure until 1949. In the discussion of atoms in Chapter 7, we started with a fixed positive charge $+Ze$ and computed the energies of individual electrons, assuming first that each electron was independent of the others as long as the exclusion principle was not violated. The interaction of the outer electrons with the inner core could be taken care of by assuming an effective nuclear charge which is less than Z because of the screening of the inner electrons. This works quite well

Fig. 11-32 The capture cross section measures the probability that a neutron approaching a nucleus will be captured, or bound to the nucleus. The solid line traces the average value. Notice the sharp drop in capture probability of nearly two orders of magnitude at $N = 50, 82,$ and 126.

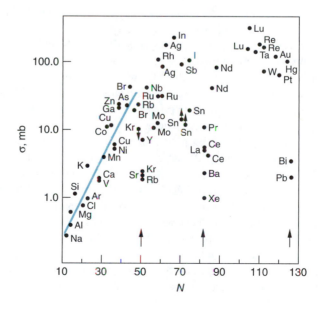

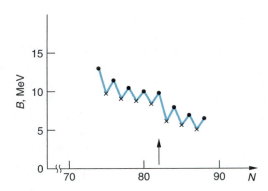

Fig. 11-33 Binding energy B for the last neutron of the isotopes of Ce ($Z = 58$). These data are typical of nuclei with $Z > 20$. B decreases sharply (about 2 MeV) for $N = 82 + 1$. This graph also shows the pairing energy associated with a_5 in the Weizsäcker formula (see Section 11-2), where the last neutron is more tightly bound if N is even than if N is odd.

since the electrons are relatively far from each other in an atom. We could therefore use the individual electron quantum states of the hydrogen atom described by n, l, m_l, and m_s as a first approximation for the electrons in complex atoms. The atomic magic numbers come about naturally due to the large energy difference between one shell or subshell and the next. The actual calculations of atomic wave functions and atomic energies require powerful approximation or numerical techniques, but they can be done reliably because the forces involved are well known.

The situation is not the same for the nuclear shell model. In the first place, there is no central potential analogous to the fixed positive charge of the atom. The interaction of the nucleons with each other is the only interaction present. In addition to being noncentral, the situation is further complicated by the fact that we know little about the strong force between nucleons beyond what we have discussed: that it is saturated, has a short range, is charge-independent, and is spin-dependent. At first sight, it is difficult to imagine a neutron or proton moving almost freely in a well-defined orbit when there are $A - 1$ particles nearby exerting very strong forces on it. Despite these difficulties, the observed properties, such as are illustrated in Figures 11-7, 11-31, 11-32, and 11-33, give strong motivation to try a model in which each nucleon moves about more or less freely in an average potential field produced by the other nucleons. Figure 11-34 shows how such an average potential could be produced. The assumption that the nucleon can move in an orbit without making many collisions can be rationalized by using the exclusion principle. Consider N neutrons in some potential well. In the ground state, the N lowest energy levels will be filled. A collision between two neutrons that does not result in their merely exchanging states is forbidden by the exclusion principle if there are no accessible unfilled states. A collision involving the exchange of identical particles has no effect. Thus, only those nucleons in the highest filled levels, where there are empty states available nearby, can collide with each other. This is analogous to the result that most of the free electrons in a metal cannot absorb energy in random collisions with the lattice

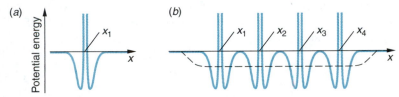

Fig. 11-34 (a) A single nucleon moving in one dimension sees the potential due to a second nucleon located at x_1. (b) The potential seen by the single nucleon due to four other nucleons located along the x axis fluctuates rapidly; however, the average of the four potentials can be reasonably well approximated by the dashed curve, a finite well with sloping sides.

because all the nearby energy levels are full. Like the electrons, the nucleons also have a Fermi level.

The first shell model calculations attempted to use a square well about 40 MeV deep to fit the nuclear energy levels, but they failed to produce the correct magic numbers. In 1949, M. Mayer and J. H. D. Jensen[17] independently showed that, with a modification in these calculations, the magic numbers do follow directly from a relatively simple shell model. In the Exploring section that follows we shall consider some of the qualitative aspects of the nuclear shell model. Detailed calculation of energies and wave functions require many approximations, the understanding of which is a major area of continuing study in nuclear physics.

Exploring

Finding the "Correct" Shell Model

Let us consider one nucleon of mass m moving in a spherically symmetric potential, $V(r)$. The Schrödinger equation for this problem in three dimensions is the same as Equation 7-9. Since we are assuming $V(r)$ to be independent of θ and ϕ, the angular part of the equation can be separated and solved, as discussed in Chapter 7. The result is that the square of the angular momentum is restricted to the values $l(l + 1)\hbar^2$, and the z component to the values $m_l\hbar$. The radial equation is then Equation 7-24 with $V(r)$ replacing the Coulomb potential:

$$-\frac{\hbar^2}{2mr^2}\frac{d}{dr}\left(r^2\frac{dR}{dr}\right) + \left[\frac{l(l+1)\hbar^2}{2mr^2} + V(r)\right]R = ER \qquad \textbf{11-56}$$

The solution of this equation, of course, depends on the form of the potential energy $V(r)$. Though $V(r)$ is not known, we certainly expect it to be quite different from the $1/r$ potential used in Chapter 7 for atoms. Because the nuclear force is so strong and is negligible beyond a few fermis of the nuclear surface, it does not matter too much what the exact form of $V(r)$ is. Various guesses have been made. The simplest is the finite square well (Figure 11-35b),

$$V(r) = -V_0 \qquad \text{for } r < r_N$$
$$V(r) = 0 \qquad \text{for } r > r_N$$

where r_N is the nuclear radius. This corresponds to an infinite attractive force at the nuclear surface and does not produce the correct magic numbers. Figure 11-36a shows the energy levels obtained for an infinite square well and Figure 11-36b shows the levels for a finite well with rounded corners such as that of Figure 11-35a. This latter potential has the mathematical form

$$V(r) = \frac{-V_0}{1 - e^{(r-R_0)/t}} \qquad \textbf{11-57}$$

where the radius R_0 and the skin thickness t are defined in Figure 11-5b. The levels are labeled with the number n and the spectroscopic notation s for $l = 0$, p for $l = 1$, etc. The number n is *not* the principal quantum number, but simply an index

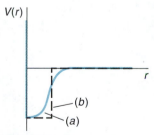

Fig. 11-35 (*a*) Nuclear potential well with rounded corners. (*b*) Finite square well approximation.

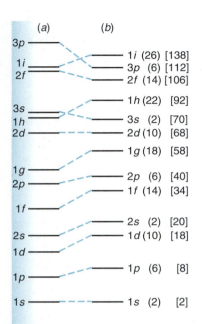

(a) (b)

3p

1i (26) [138]
1i
3p (6) [112]
2f
2f (14) [106]

1h (22) [92]

3s
1h
3s (2) [70]
2d
2d (10) [68]

1g (18) [58]

1g
2p
2p (6) [40]
1f (14) [34]

1f

2s (2) [20]
2s
1d (10) [18]
1d

1p (6) [8]
1p

1s
1s (2) [2]

Fig. 11-36 Energy levels for a single particle in (a) an infinite square well and (b) a finite square well with rounded corners such as shown in Figure 11-35a. The maximum number of particles in each level is given in parentheses, followed by the total number through that level in brackets.

that counts the levels with a particular l-value. For example, 1p is the lowest energy state with $l = 1$, 2p is the next lowest $l = 1$ state, and so on. The first number after the spectroscopic label in Figure 11-36b is the number of identical particles that can exist in that level. This number is $2(2l + 1)$, that is, $(2l + 1)$ different m_l states times 2 for the two possible orientations of the spin. The second number is the total number of particles up to and including that level. From this calculation we should expect the magic numbers to be 2, 8, 20, 40, 70, 92, and 138, since there are relatively large energy differences after these numbers. Though the first three numbers, 2, 8, and 20, do agree with the observed stability of ^{4}He ($N = 2$ and $Z = 2$), ^{16}O ($Z = N = 8$), and ^{40}Ca ($Z = N = 20$), the rest of the numbers are not the magic numbers observed. For example, there is no evidence from this figure for the magic number 50. Calculations using various other potential wells give about the same ordering and spacing of the energy levels.

Mayer and Jensen resolved this problem by proposing that the spin dependence of the nuclear force results in a very strong spin-orbit interaction, coupling the spin of each nucleon to its own orbital angular momentum. Thus, the nuclear spin-orbit effect depends upon j-j coupling,[18] rather than the L-S coupling that characterizes the electron spin-orbit interaction (see Section 7-5). This strong spin-orbit interaction results in a decrease in the energy if the spin and the orbital angular momentum of the nucleon are parallel and an increase if they are antiparallel. We have seen that in the atomic spin-orbit interaction, the energy of the atom depends on whether j is $l + 1/2$ or $l - 1/2$; however, this fine-structure splitting of the atomic energy levels is very small compared with the energy difference between the shells or subshells, and can be neglected in the first approximation to atomic energies. The situation is different for nuclei. The strength of the interaction results in a large splitting of the energy for a given l if l is large. (The shell model does not provide a prediction of the required interaction strength. The strength is an adjustable parameter whose value is chosen to yield the observed energy structure of the nucleus.) Figure 11-37 shows the energy levels with the strong spin-orbit interaction proposed by Mayer and Jensen. As noted earlier, the levels with the spin and orbital angular momentum parallel have a lower energy than those with the spin and orbital angular momentum antiparallel, i.e., the higher j values have lower energies, unlike the situation for atoms. (The fact that the force of attraction

Fig. 11-37 Energy levels for a single particle in a nuclear well, including spin-orbit splitting. The maximum number of particles in each level is given at the right, followed by the total number through that level in brackets. The total numbers just before the large energy gaps are the magic numbers. The spacing shown here is for protons; the spacing for neutrons is slightly different (lower).

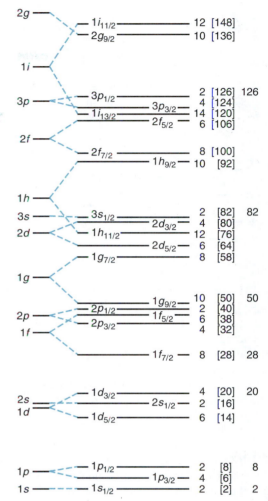

between a nucleon and a nucleus is greater when spin and orbital angular momentum of the nucleon are parallel can also be shown from scattering experiments.) Note, too, that the splitting is large for large l values. Indeed, the splitting of the $1g$ level is so great that the large energy difference that occurs between the $1g_{9/2}$ ($n = 1$, $l = 4$, $j = l + s = 9/2$) and the $1g_{7/2}$ ($n = 1$, $l = 4$, $j = l - s = 7/2$) levels is enough to place those two sublevels in different major shells. Since there are $(2j + 1)$ values of m_j, there can be 10 neutrons or protons in the $1g_{9/2}$ level, making a total of 50 up through this level. The next large energy difference occurs because of the splitting of the $1h$ level, and this accounts for the magic number 82. Being distinct particles, the protons and neutrons occupy different sets of energy states. Figure 11-37 illustrates the energy spacing for protons, which, due to the electrostatic force, is slightly different than that for neutrons.

From qualitative considerations alone it is not possible to decide the exact order of the energy levels, for example, whether the $2s_{1/2}$ level is higher or lower than the $1d_{3/2}$ level. Questions of this nature can usually be answered from empirical evidence. As an example of the predictions of the shell model, we shall consider a nuclide with one neutron or one proton outside a closed shell. These are the simplest nuclides (except for those with closed shells of both neutrons and protons) and are somewhat analogous to the alkali atoms with one outer electron. Many of the energy levels of these nuclides can be understood in terms of the excitation of the one odd

TABLE 11-5 Angular momenta and magnetic moments of selected odd-A nuclei

Isotope	Number of odd particles	Z or N, a magic number	Predicted level	Measured spin	Measured magnetic moment (μ_N)
$^{11}_{5}B_6$	5	—	$p_{3/2}$	3/2	+2.689
$^{13}_{6}C_7$	7	—	$p_{1/2}$	1/2	+0.702
$^{15}_{7}N_8$	7	N	$p_{1/2}$	1/2	−0.283
$^{17}_{8}O_9$	9	Z	$d_{5/2}$	5/2	−1.894
$^{17}_{9}F_8$	9	N	$d_{5/2}$	5/2	+4.722
$^{27}_{13}Al_{14}$	13	—	$d_{5/2}$	5/2	+3.641
$^{39}_{19}K_{20}$	19	N	$d_{3/2}$	3/2	+0.09
$^{41}_{20}Ca_{21}$	21	Z	$f_{7/2}$	7/2	−1.595
$^{41}_{21}Sc_{20}$	21	N	$f_{7/2}$	7/2	—
$^{57}_{28}Ni_{29}$	29	Z	$p_{3/2}$	3/2	—
$^{91}_{40}Zr_{51}$	51	—	$g_{7/2}$	7/2	−1.303
$^{115}_{49}In_{66}$	49	—	$g_{9/2}$	9/2	—
$^{205}_{81}Tl_{124}$	81	—	$s_{1/2}$	1/2	+1.628
$^{209}_{83}Bi_{126}$	83	N	$h_{9/2}$	9/2	+4.080

nucleon. Table 11-5 lists several nuclei with one nucleon added to or removed from a closed shell or subshell along with the predicted state of this nucleon and the measured spin and magnetic moment of the nucleus. In all these cases but one, the spin prediction is correct. This simple shell model is also reasonably successful in predicting the magnetic moments for these nuclei. For example, the magnetic moment of ^{17}O is observed to be −1.89, which is quite close to that of a single neutron. This is predicted by the shell model for this nucleus, since the other eight neutrons and the eight protons form a closed shell. Similarly, the magnetic moment of ^{11}B is +2.69, very close to that of the odd proton, and that of ^{41}Ca is −1.60, close to the odd neutron. In general, however, the measured values of the magnetic moments for odd-A nuclei do not agree with the simple model that attributes them solely to the odd nucleon. For a more complete discussion of the success of this shell model, the reader may enjoy perusing Mayer and Jensen's excellent book.

The most serious deficiency of the simple shell model is in the region of the rare earth nuclei. The quadrupole moments predicted from the orbital motion of the individual protons are much smaller than those observed. Many of the excited states of these nuclei can be more simply understood as being due to the rotation or vibration of the nucleus as a whole, considering it to be a deformed liquid drop. From the shell-model point of view, the rare earth nuclei lie about midway between the neutron magic numbers of 82 and 126. This is just the region for which shell-model

calculations are the most difficult since there are many particles outside a closed shell. There are several extensions of the shell model that have been fairly successful in understanding these nonspherical nuclei. In one of these, called the *collective model,* the closed-shell core nucleons are treated as a liquid drop deformed by the interaction with the outer nucleons that orbit about the core and drag it along with them. In another model, called the *unified model,* the Schrödinger equation is solved for individual particles in a nonspherically symmetric potential corresponding to an ellipsoidal nucleus. Much of the work with these models was done by J. Rainwater, A. Bohr (son of Niels Bohr), and B. Mottleson.[19]

Summary

TOPIC	RELEVANT EQUATIONS AND REMARKS
1. Composition of the nuclei	Nuclei have Z protons, N neutrons, and mass number $A = Z + N$. Nuclei with the same Z but different N (and A) are called isotopes. The nucleons are Fermi-Dirac (spin 1/2) particles and both have intrinsic magnetic moments.
2. Ground-state properties of nuclei	
Size and shape	The mean radius of the nuclear charge distribution is
	$$R = (1.07 \pm 0.02)A^{1/3}\,\text{fm} \qquad \text{11-6}$$
	The radii thus vary from about 1 fm for the proton to about 10 fm for the heaviest nuclei. With few exceptions, nuclei are nearly spherical.
Binding energy and mass	The binding energy of the nucleus is given by
	$$B_{\text{nuclear}} = ZM_{\text{H}}c^2 + Nm_n c^2 - M_A c^2 \qquad \text{11-11}$$
Magnetic moments	The moments of the proton and neutron are
	$$(\mu_p)_z = +2.79285\,\mu_N$$
	$$(\mu_n)_z = -1.91304\,\mu_N$$
	where $\mu_N = e\hbar/2m_p$ is the nuclear magneton.
3. Radioactivity	The decay rate R of radioactive nuclei is
	$$R = -\frac{dN}{dt} = \lambda N_0 e^{-\lambda t} = R_0 e^{-\lambda t} \qquad \text{11-19}$$
	where λ is the decay constant. N_0 and R_0 are the number of nuclei present and the decay rate at $t = 0$.
Half-life	$$t_{1/2} = \frac{\ln 2}{\lambda} = 0.693\,\tau \qquad \text{11-22}$$
	where $\tau = 1/\lambda$ is the mean life.
Units	1 decay/s = 1 becquerel = 1 Bq $\qquad$ 11-23
Alpha, beta, and gamma decay	These are the three most common forms of radioactive decay. Alpha particles are ^{4}He nuclei, beta particles are electrons and positrons, and gamma rays are very short wavelength electromgnetic radiation.

TOPIC	RELEVANT EQUATIONS AND REMARKS
4. The nuclear force	The nuclear force is: (*a*) About 10^2 stronger than the Coulomb force (*b*) Short-range (≈ 0 beyond 3 fm) (*c*) Charge-independent (*d*) Saturated (*e*) Dependent on spin orientation The nuclear force is considered to be an exchange force in which the attraction between a pair of nucleons is due to an exchange of virtual pions. The range R of the force, determined by the uncertainty principle, is $$R = c\Delta t = c\hbar/\Delta E = \hbar/mc \qquad \textbf{11-50}$$ where m is the mass of the virtual pion.
5. The shell model	An independent particle model, similar to that used for assigning energy states to the atomic electrons but one that makes use of a strong spin-orbit coupling for each nucleon, accounts for the shell-like structure of the protons and neutrons. It explains the magic numbers 2, 8, 20, 28, 50, 82, and 126 in terms of the completion of the shells. Shell-model calculations are relatively successful in predicting nuclear spins and magnetic moments, particularly in the vicinity of closed shells.

GENERAL REFERENCES

The following general references are written at a level appropriate for the readers of this book.

American Association of Physics Teachers, *Mössbauer Effect: Selected Reprints,* American Institute of Physics, New York, 1963.

Antony, M., *Nuclide Chart 2002,* Strasbourg, 2002.

Beyer, R. (ed.), *Foundations of Nuclear Physics,* Dover, New York, 1949. This paperback contains 13 original papers, 8 in English—by Anderson, Chadwick, Cockcroft and Walton, Fermi, Lawrence and Livingston, Rutherford (two papers), and Yukawa; the others are in German or French.

Fermi, E., *Nuclear Physics,* rev. ed., University of Chicago Press, Chicago, 1974.

Frauenfelder, H., *The Mössbauer Effect,* W. A. Benjamin, New York, 1962.

Frauenfelder, H., and E. M. Henley, *Subatomic Physics,* 2d ed., Prentice Hall, Englewood Cliffs, N.J., 1991.

Krane, K. S., *Introductory Nuclear Physics,* Wiley, New York, 1987.

Lilley, J., *Nuclear Physics,* Wiley, New York, 2001.

Mayer, M., and J. H. D. Jensen, *Elementary Theory of Nuclear Shell Structure,* Wiley, New York, 1955.

Segrè, E., *Nuclei and Particles,* 2d ed., Benjamin Cummings, Menlo Park, Calif., 1977.

NOTES

1. Antoine Henri Becquerel (1852–1908), French physicist. He held the scientific post at the Museum of Natural History in Paris that had been held by his father and grandfather before him, and his research on the fluorescence of potassium uranyl sulfate was a continuation of work that his father had begun. His discovery of radioactivity, which revolutionized existing theories of atomic structure, earned him a share of the 1903 Nobel Prize in physics, together with Marie and Pierre Curie.

2. The phenomenon was named *radioactivity* by Marie Curie in 1898.

3. These accomplishments were of such importance to the development of nuclear physics that all four men were subsequently awarded Nobel Prizes: James Chadwick in 1935, Carl Anderson in 1936 (shared with Victor Hess, the discoverer of cosmic rays), and John Cockcroft and Ernest Walton in 1951.

4. Robert Hofstadter (1915–1990), American physicist. His electron scattering measurements also revealed that the proton and neutron possessed internal structure, opening the way to a more fundamental understanding of the structure of matter. For his work he shared the 1961 Nobel Prize in physics with Rudolf Mössbauer.

5. See, for example, Section 24-2 in P. Tipler, *Physics for Scientists and Engineers,* 4th ed. (New York: W. H. Freeman, 1999).

6. See, for example, Section 28-2 in P. Tipler, *Physics for Scientists and Engineers,* 4th ed. (New York: W. H. Freeman, 1999).

7. See P. A. Seeger, *Nuclear Physics,* **25**, 1 (1961).

8. The electric quadrupole moment of the nucleus, discussed earlier in this section, also causes hyperfine splitting, as do externally applied magnetic and electric fields. The effect of the reduced mass (isotope effect) mentioned in Chapter 4 is also considered a hyperfine effect.

9. Actually, the electron's magnetic moment deviates slightly from that predicted by the Dirac wave equation, one Bohr magneton. Quantum electrodynamics is able to account for the small deviation observed experimentally with an error of less than 1 part in 10^8, one of the most remarkable agreements between quantum theory and experiment in physics.

10. This statement requires a small qualification. An alternative to β^+ decay, discussed in Section 11-4, is electron capture, in which an orbital electron may be captured by the nucleus. The probability of its occurrence depends upon the probability density of the electrons, which can be affected slightly by very high external pressures.

11. Leptons include the electrons and neutrinos that are emitted in β decay. (See Chapter 13.)

12. Rudolf Ludwig Mössbauer (b. 1929), German physicist. His discovery of the recoilless emission and absorption of gamma rays, made while he was a graduate student in Munich, enabled the verification (by Pound and Rebka in 1960) of the gravitational redshift predicted by general relativity. Mössbauer shared the 1961 Nobel Prize in physics with Robert Hofstadter.

13. Note that this electrostatic potential corresponds to a force of nearly 60 N, or the weight of a 6-kg mass! It is acting not on 6 kg, however, but on only 1.67×10^{-27} kg.

14. Hideki Yukawa (1907–1981), Japanese physicist. His paper presenting the exchange meson theory of the nuclear force was his first publication. He was awarded the 1949 physics Nobel Prize for the discovery.

15. See, for example, Section 32-3 in P. Tipler, *Physics for Scientists and Engineers,* 4th ed. (New York: W. H. Freeman, 1999).

16. Previously unknown particles had been observed in cosmic rays at about the same time that Yukawa proposed the meson exchange theory. He sent an article to the journal *Nature* in 1937 suggesting that they might be the mesons, but the journal rejected the article. Those particles were later found to be muons, a product of the decay of Yukawa's pi mesons.

17. Maria Goeppert-Mayer (1906–1972), German-American physicist, and Johannes Hans Daniel Jensen (1907–1973), German physicist. Goeppert-Mayer's antecedents for many generations had been university professors, while Jensen was the son of a gardener. They coauthored a famous (among physicists, at least) book explaining their nuclear shell model and for that work shared the 1963 Nobel Prize in physics with Eugene Wigner.

18. In *j-j* coupling the spin and orbital angular momentum of each particle add to give a total angular momentum **j** for that particle, and then **J** equals the sum of the individual *j* vectors. In *L-S* coupling the spins of all the particles and the orbital angular momenta of all the particles add to yield total **S** and total **L**, which then add to yield **J**.

19. Leo James Rainwater (1917–1986), American physicist; Aage Niels Bohr (b. 1922), Danish physicist; and Ben Roy Mottelson (b. 1926), Danish-American physicist. Rainwater's work on the collective motions of nucleons was prompted by a remark made by Charles Townes, discoverer of the maser/laser principle. Bohr later directed the theoretical physics institute that had been founded by his father. Rainwater, Mottelson, and Bohr shared the 1975 Nobel Prize in physics for this work.

PROBLEMS

Level I

Section 11-1 Composition of the Nucleus

11-1. What are the number of protons and the number of neutrons in each of the following isotopes? ^{18}F, ^{25}Na, ^{51}V, ^{84}Kr, ^{120}Te, ^{148}Dy, ^{175}W, and ^{222}Rn.

11-2. Electrons emitted in β decay have energies of the order of 1 MeV or smaller. Use this fact and the uncertainty principle to show that electrons cannot exist inside the nucleus.

11-3. The spin of the ground state of ^{6}Li, which comprises 7.5 percent of natural lithium, is zero. Show that this value is not compatible with a model of the nucleus that consists of protons and electrons.

11-4. The magnetic moment of ^{14}N is 0.4035 μ_N. Show that this value is not compatible with a model of the nucleus that consists of protons and electrons.

11-5. Suppose that the deuteron really did consist of two protons and one electron. (It doesn't!) Compute the spin and magnetic moment of such a deuteron's ground state and compare the results with the values in Table 11-1.

Section 11-2 Ground-State Properties of Nuclei

11-6. Give the symbols for at least two isotopes and two isotones of each of the following nuclides: (a) ^{18}F, (b) ^{208}Pb, and (c) ^{120}Sn.

11-7. Give the symbols for at least two isobars and one isotope of each of the following nuclides: (a) ^{14}O, (b) ^{63}Ni, and (c) ^{236}Np.

11-8. Approximating the mass of a nucleus with mass number A as $A \times$ u and using Equation 11-3, compute the nuclear density in SI units.

11-9. Use the masses in the table in Appendix A to compute the total binding energy and the binding energy per nucleon of the following nuclides: (a) ^{9}Be, (b) ^{13}C, and (c) ^{57}Fe.

11-10. Use Equation 11-3 to compute the radii of the following nuclei: (a) ^{16}O, (b) ^{56}Fe, (c) ^{197}Au, and (d) ^{238}U.

11-11. Find the energy needed to remove a neutron from (a) ^{4}He, (b) ^{7}Li, and (c) ^{14}N.

11-12. Use the Weizsäcker formula to compute the mass of ^{23}Na. Compute the percent difference between the result and the value in the table in Appendix A.

11-13. Compute the "charge distribution radius" from Equation 11-5 and the "nuclear force radius" from Equation 11-7 for the following nuclides: (a) ^{16}O, (b) ^{63}Cu, and (c) ^{208}Pb.

11-14. ^{39}Ca and ^{39}K are a mirror pair, ^{39}Ca decaying into ^{39}K. Use Equations 11-1 and 11-2 to compute the radius of ^{40}Ca.

Section 11-3 Radioactivity

11-15. The counting rate from a radioactive source is 4000 counts per second at time $t = 0$. After 10 s, the counting rate is 1000 counts per second. (a) What is the half-life? (b) What is the counting rate after 20 s?

11-16. A certain source gives 2000 counts per second at time $t = 0$. Its half-life is 2 min. (a) What is the counting rate after 4 min? (b) After 6 min? (c) After 8 min?

11-17. A sample of a radioactive isotope is found to have an activity of 115.0 Bq immediately after it is pulled from the reactor that formed it. Its activity 2 h 15 min later is measured to be 85.2 Bq. (a) Calculate the decay constant and the half-life of the sample. (b) How many radioactive nuclei were there in the sample initially?

11-18. The half-life of radium is 1620 years. (a) Calculate the number of disintegrations per second of 1 g of radium and show that the disintegration rate is approximately 1 Ci. (b) Calculate the approximate energy of the α particle in the decay ^{226}Ra $\rightarrow$ ^{222}Rn $+ \alpha$, assuming the energy of recoil of the Rn nucleus is negligible. (Use the mass table of Appendix A.)

11-19. The counting rate from a radioactive source is 8000 counts per second at time $t = 0$. Ten minutes later the rate is 1000 counts per second. (a) What is the half-life? (b) What is the decay constant? (c) What is the counting rate after 1 minute?

11-20. The counting rate from a radioactive source is measured every minute. The resulting number of counts per second are 1000, 820, 673, 552, 453, 371, 305, 250, ... (a) Plot the counting rate versus time and (b) use your graph to estimate the half-life. (c) What would be the approximate result of the next measurement after the 250 counts per second?

11-21. ^{62}Cu is produced at a constant rate (e.g., by the (γ, n) reaction on ^{63}Cu placed in a high-energy x-ray beam) and decays by β^+ decay with a half-life of about 10 min. How long does it take to produce 90 percent of the equilibrium value of ^{62}Cu?

11-22. The decay constant of ^{235}U is $9.8 \times 10^{-10} \, y^{-1}$. (*a*) Compute the half-life. (*b*) How many decays occur each second in a 1.0-μg sample of ^{235}U? (*c*) How many ^{235}U atoms will remain in the 1.0-μg sample after 10^6 years?

11-23. The decay constant of ^{22}Na is $0.266 \, y^{-1}$. (*a*) Compute the half-life. (*b*) What is the activity of a sample containing 1.0 g of ^{22}Na? (*c*) What is the activity of the sample after 3.5 years have passed? (*d*) How many ^{22}Na atoms remain in the sample at the time?

Section 11-4 Alpha, Beta, and Gamma Decay

11-24. The stable isotope of sodium is ^{23}Na. What kind of radioactivity would you expect of (*a*) ^{22}Na and (*b*) ^{24}Na?

11-25. Using Figure 11-16, find the parameters A and B in Equation 11-30.

11-26. Make a diagram like Figure 11-18 for the $(4n + 1)$ decay chain which begins with ^{237}Np, a nuclide which is no longer present in nature. (Use Appendix A.)

11-27. Show that the α particle emitted in the decay of ^{232}Th carries away 4.01 MeV, or 98 percent of the total decay energy.

11-28. ^7Be decays exclusively by electron capture to ^7Li with a half-life of 53.3 d. Would the characteristics of the decay be altered and, if so, how if (*a*) a sample of ^7Be were placed under very high pressure or (*b*) all four electrons were stripped from each ^7Be atom in the sample.

11-29. Compute the energy carried by the neutrino in the electron capture decay of ^{67}Ga to the ground state of ^{67}Zn.

11-30. Compute the maximum energy of the β^- particle emitted in the decay of ^{72}Zn.

11-31. In Example 11-13 we saw that ^{233}Np could decay by emitting an α particle. Show that decay by emission of a nucleon of either type is forbidden for this nuclide.

11-32. With the aid of Figures 11-19 and 11-20, list the energies of all of the possible γ rays that may be emitted by ^{223}Ra following the α decay of ^{227}Th.

11-33. ^8Be is very unusual among low-Z nuclides; it decays by emittng two α particles. Show why ^8Be is unstable toward α decay.

11-34. ^{80}Br can undergo all three types of β decay. (*a*) Write down the decay equation in each case. (*b*) Compute the decay energy for each case.

Section 11-5 The Nuclear Force

11-35. Assuming that the average separation between two protons in ^{12}C is equal to the nuclear diameter, compute the Coulomb force of repulsion and the gravitational force of attraction between the protons. If the nuclear potential seen by the protons is 50 MeV for separations up to 3 fm, compare the nuclear force to the other two forces.

11-36. Suppose the range of the nuclear force was 5 fm. Compute the mass (in MeV/c^2) of an exchange particle that might mediate such a force.

11-37. The repulsive force that results in the "hard core" of the nucleus might be due to the exchange of a particle, just as the strong attractive force is. Compute the mass of such an exchange particle if the range of the repulsive force equals about 0.25 fm, the radius of the core.

Section 11-6 The Shell Model

11-38. The nuclei listed below have filled j shells plus or minus one nucleon. (For example, $^{29}_{14}Si$ has the $1d_{5/2}$ shell filled for both neutrons and protons, plus one neutron in the $2s_{1/2}$ shell.) Use the shell model to predict the orbital and total angular momentum of these nuclei:

$$^{29}_{14}Si \qquad ^{37}_{17}Cl \qquad ^{71}_{31}Ga \qquad ^{59}_{27}Co \qquad ^{73}_{32}Ge \qquad ^{33}_{16}S \qquad ^{87}_{38}Sr$$

11-39. Use the shell model to predict the nuclear magnetic moments of the isotopes listed in Problem 11-38.

11-40. The atomic spectral lines of ^{14}N exhibit a hyperfine structure indicating that the ground state is split into three closely spaced levels. What must be the spin of the ^{14}N ground state?

11-41. Which of the following nuclei have closed neutron shells? ^{36}S, ^{50}V, ^{50}Ca, ^{53}Mn, ^{61}Ni, ^{82}Ge, ^{88}Sr, ^{93}Ru, ^{94}Ru, ^{131}In, and ^{145}Eu?

11-42. Sketch diagrams like Figure 11-9 for the ground states of ^{3}H, ^{3}He, ^{14}N, ^{14}C, ^{15}N, ^{15}O, and ^{16}O.

11-43. Which of the following nuclei have closed proton shells? ^{3}He, ^{19}F, ^{12}C, ^{40}Ca, ^{50}Ti, ^{56}Fe, ^{60}Ni, ^{60}Cu, ^{90}Zr, ^{124}Sn, ^{166}Yb, and ^{204}Pb?

11-44. (a) Use Figure 11-37 to draw a diagram like Figure 11-9 for ^{13}N. (b) What value would you predict for the value of j? (c) What value would you predict for j for the first excited state? (d) Draw a diagram like Figure 11-9 for the first excited state. (Is there only one possible?)

11-45. Use Figure 11-37 to predict the values of j for the ground states of ^{30}Si, ^{37}Cl, ^{55}Co, ^{90}Zr, and ^{107}In.

Level II

11-46. Using Equation 11-14 and the constants in Table 11-3, find the Z for which $dM/dZ = 0$, i.e., the minimum of curves like Figure 11-22a for (a) $A = 27$, (b) $A = 65$, and (c) $A = 139$. Do these calculations give the correct stable isobars ^{27}Al, ^{65}Cu, and ^{139}La?

11-47. An empirical expression for distance that α particles can travel in air, called the *range*, is $R(\text{cm}) = (0.31)E^{3/2}$ for E in MeV and $4 < E < 7$ MeV. (a) What is the range in air of a 5-MeV α particle? (b) Express this range in g/cm^2, using $\rho = 1.29 \times 10^{-3}$ g/cm^3 for air. (c) Assuming the range in g/cm^2 is the same as aluminum ($\rho = 2.70$ g/cm^3), find the range in aluminum in cm for a 5-MeV α particle.

11-48. Show that the average electrostatic energy of a proton-proton pair is about $6ke^2/5R$, where R is the separation of the pair and $k = 1/4\pi\epsilon_0$.

11-49. A sample of ^{114}Nd has a mass of 0.05394 kg and emits an average of 2.36 α particles per second. Determine the decay constant and the half-life.

11-50. A sample of radioactive material is found initially to have an activity of 115.0 decays/minute. After 4d 5h, its activity is measured to be 73.5 decays/minute. (a) Calculate the half-life of this material. (b) How long (after $t = 0$) will it take for the sample to reach an activity of 10.0 decays/minute? (c) How long after the time in (b) will it take for the activity to reach 2.5 decays/minute?

11-51. The half-life of ^{227}Th is 18.72 days. It decays by α emission to ^{223}Ra, an α emitter whose half-life is 11.43 days. A particular sample contains 10^6 atoms of ^{227}Th and no ^{223}Ra at time $t = 0$. (a) How many atoms of each type will be in the sample at $t = 15$ days? (b) At what time will the number of atoms of each type be equal?

11-52. The Mössbauer effect was discovered using the decay of the 0.12939-MeV second excited state of ^{191}Ir. The lifetime of this isomer is 0.13 ns. (a) Compute the width Γ of this level. (b) Compute the recoil energy of a free ^{191}Ir atom that emits the 0.12939-MeV photon. (c) Resonant (recoilless) absorption occurs when ^{191}Ir is bound into a lattice. If a Doppler shift equal to Γ destroys the resonance absorption, show that the Doppler velocity v necessary is given by:

$$v \approx \frac{c\Gamma}{e}$$

11-53. ^{3}He and ^{3}H are a pair of mirror nuclei. Compute the difference in total binding energy between the two nuclides and compare the result to the electrostatic repulsion of the protons in ^{3}He. Let the protons be separated by the radius of the helium nucleus.

11-54. Use the masses in Appendix A to compute the energy necessary to separate a neutron from ^{47}Ca and ^{48}Ca. From those results determine a value for a_5 in the Weizsäcker formula (Equation 11-14) and compare it with the value in Table 11-3.

11-55. The centripetal force of a nucleus with $I \neq 0$ makes it more stable toward α decay. Use Figure 11-1a and a (classical) argument to show why this is the case.

Level III

11-56. (a) Compute the binding-energy differences between the two nuclides of the mirror pairs (^{7}Li, ^{7}Be), (^{11}B, ^{11}C), and (^{15}N, ^{15}O). (b) From each value computed in (a), determine a value of the constant a_3 in Equation 11-14. Compare each value and their average with the value given in Table 11-3.

11-57. (a) Differentiate the Weizäcker empirical mass formula with respect to Z, as in Problem 11-46, and show that the minima of the constant A curves that result, i.e., Z values for the most stable isotopes, are given by

$$Z = \frac{A}{2} \left[\frac{1 + \dfrac{(m_n - m_p)c^2}{4a_4}}{1 + \dfrac{a_3 A^{2/3}}{4a_4}} \right]$$

(a) Determine the atomic number for the most stable nuclides for $A = 29, 59, 78, 119$, and 140. (c) Compare the results in (b) with the data in Appendix A and discuss any differences.

11-58. (a) Use Figure 11-37 to make a diagram like Figure 11-9 for the ground state of ^{11}B. What do you predict for the value of j for this state? (b) The first excited state of ^{11}B involves excitation of a proton. Draw the diagram for this state and predict its j value. (c) The j value for the second excited state is 5/2. Draw a diagram of the nucleons like Figure 11-9 that could account for that value. (d) Repeat parts (a) and (b) for ^{17}O, where the excitation of the first excited state involves a neutron. (e) The j value for the second excited state of ^{17}O is 1/2. Draw a diagram like Figure 11-9 that would explain that value.

11-59. Approximately 2000 nuclides remain to be discovered between the proton and neutron driplines in Figure 11-15b. Consider those which lie on the energy parabola (see Figure 11-22) for $A = 151$, whose only stable isotope is ^{151}Eu. (a) From the data in Appendix A, draw an accurate diagram of the $A = 151$ parabola showing known nuclides *and* those yet to be discovered between $Z = 50$ and $Z = 71$. (b) Determine where the edges of the driplines lie for $A = 151$, i.e., the lowest mass isotopes for which spontaneous proton or neutron emission becomes possible.

11-60. There are theoretical reasons to expect that a cluster of relatively long-lived nuclides will exist in the neighborhood of the doubly magic nucleus with $Z = 126$ and $N = 184$, the latter being the next magic number beyond 126 predicted by the shell model. (a) Compute the mass of this exotic nucleus using Equation 11-14. (b) Computing the necessary masses of the nearby nuclei, predict the decay modes that would be available to the doubly magic nucleus.

11-61. Assume that a neutron decays into a proton plus an electron without the emission of a neutrino. The energy shared by the proton and electron is then 0.782 MeV. In the rest frame of the neutron, the total momentum is zero, so the momentum of the proton must be equal and opposite that of the electron. This determines the relative energies of the two particles, but because the electron is relativistic, the exact calculation of these relatives energies in somewhat difficult. (a) Assume that the kinetic energy of the electron is 0.782 MeV and calculate the momentum p of the electron in units of MeV/c. (*Hint:* Use Equation 2-32.) (b) From your result for (a), calculate the kinetic energy $p^2/2m_p$ of the proton. (c) Since the total energy of the electron plus proton is 0.782 MeV,

the calculation in (b) gives a correction to the assumption that the energy of the electron is 0.782 MeV. What percentage of 0.782 MeV is this correction?

11-62. Radioactive nuclei with a decay constant of λ are produced in an accelerator at a constant rate R_p. The number of radioactive nuclei N then obeys the equation $dN/dt = R_p - \lambda N$. (a) If N is zero at $t = 0$, sketch N versus t for this situation. (b) The isotope ^{62}Cu is produced at a rate of 100 per second by placing ordinary copper (^{63}Cu) in a beam of high-energy photons. The reaction is

$$\gamma + {}^{63}\text{Cu} \longrightarrow {}^{62}\text{Cu} + n$$

^{62}Cu decays by β decay with a half-life of 10 minutes. After a time long enough so that $dN/dt \approx 0$, how many ^{62}Cu nuclei are there?

11-63. The $(4n + 3)$ decay chain begins with ^{235}U and ends on ^{207}Pb. (a) How many α decays are there in the chain? (b) How many β decays are there? (c) Compute the total energy released when one ^{235}U atom decays through the complete chain. (d) Assuming no energy escapes, determine the approximate temperature rise of 1 kg of ^{235}U metal over the period of 1 year.

Chapter *12* Nuclear Reactions and Applications

Much of the information about nuclei is obtained by bombarding them with various particles and observing the results. The results may include a scattering of the incident particle and various kinds of nuclear reactions. Although the first such experiments were limited by the need to use radiation from naturally occurring sources, mainly α particles, they produced many important discoveries. Then, in 1932, Cockcroft and Walton succeeded in producing the reaction

$$p + {}^7\text{Li} \longrightarrow {}^8\text{Be} \longrightarrow {}^4\text{He} + {}^4\text{He}$$

using artificially accelerated protons. At about the same time, the Van de Graaff electrostatic generator was built (by R. Van de Graaff in 1931), as was the first cyclotron (by E. O. Lawrence and M. S. Livingston in 1932). These machines provided a way of studying *any* nuclide and a means of investigating the excited states of nuclei in detail. Since then, an enormous technology has been developed for accelerating and detecting particles, and many nuclear reactions and fundamental particle interactions have been studied.

Among the myriad nuclear reactions that have been investigated are two types of special interest: *fission* and *fusion.* Both are processes by which nuclear mass is converted into other forms of energy, such as thermal and electrical energy, just as some atomic mass is converted in chemical reactions such as oxidation. Fission reactions currently provide a significant, albeit controversial, means of producing electrical energy in several countries, accounting for just over 7.5 percent of the world's total consumption of energy in 2000.[1] The similar potential of fusion reactions has not yet been realized at a practical level; however, of far more intrinsic importance is the role of fusion in the production of energy in stars. The grim reality that both fission and fusion are also the basis for weapons of enormous destructive power means that this application of nuclear reactions influences political debate to a greater degree than has perhaps any other scientific discovery in history.

The applications of radioactivity and nuclear reactions are by no means limited to fission and fusion. The radiations emitted by radioisotopes have long been used in medical diagnosis and treatment. These contributions were measurably enhanced with the development of *computer-assisted tomography*[2] *(CAT)* in the 1970s, which made possible not only x-ray CAT scans but also the more recent development of *positron-emission tomography,* called *PET.* Neutron-induced nuclear reactions provide an extremely sensitive technique, called *neutron activation analysis (NAA),* for measuring trace amounts of certain isotopes for most elements in the periodic table. An

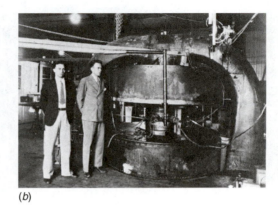

(b)

(a)

(*a*) The Cockcroft-Walton accelerator. Walton is sitting in the shielded enclosure in the foreground. J. D. Cockcroft and E. T. S. Walton produced the first transmutation of nuclei with artificially accelerated particles in 1932, for which they received the Nobel Prize (1951). (*b*) M. S. Livingston and E. O. Lawrence standing in front of their 27-in. cyclotron in 1934. Lawrence won the Nobel Prize (1939) for the invention of the cyclotron. [*(a) Courtesy of Cavendish Laboratory. (b) Courtesy of Lawrence Radiation Laboratory, University of California, Berkeley.*]

ultrasensitive technique for measuring trace amounts of many isotopes, including long-lived radioactive ones, is *accelerator mass spectrometry* (AMS). The uses of NAA and AMS range from helping law enforcement agencies catch criminals and museums detect counterfeit paintings to enabling scientists to identify the origin of environmental pollutants and the ages of anthropological artifacts. High-intensity gamma-ray sources are used in a variety of ways, from assessing the integrity of pipeline welds to preserving fresh fruits and survival rations. Elemental analysis with a sensitivity comparable to NAA is possible with *particle-induced x-ray emission* (PIXE). Several of these as well as additional applications will be discussed in this chapter.

Nuclear radiation is certainly not without its dangers. The high energies carried by particles emitted by nuclei, being a million times larger than those typical of molecular bonds, have the potential for causing massive disruption of molecular systems, including those that form biological tissue. How the energy loss in matter occurs and how it is measured is discussed in the section "Interaction of Particles and Matter" on the home page.

12-1 Nuclear Reactions

When a particle is incident on a nucleus, any of several different things can happen. The particle may be scattered elastically or inelastically (in which case the nucleus is left in an excited state and decays by emitting photons or other particles), or the original particle may be absorbed and another particle or particles emitted.

(*a*) Schematic diagram of a two-stage, or tandem, Van de Graaff accelerator. Negative ions at ground potential (atoms of a large fraction of the elements in the periodic table form stable negative ions) enter the beam tube at the top and are accelerated to the positive high-voltage terminal in the center, acquiring eV of kinetic energy. In the charge exchange canal, electrons are stripped from the negative ions in collisions with gas molecules, producing positive ions with charges up to $+Ze$. The positive ions are accelerated back to ground potential, acquiring an additional kinetic energy as large as Z eV. Large Van de Graaff accelerators have terminal voltages V over 16 million volts. Thus, for example, oxygen atoms stripped of all their electrons may be accelerated to energies of 100 MeV or more. (*b*) A portion of the tandem Van de Graaff laboratory at Purdue University. The high-voltage terminal is in the tank at the right rear, insulated from the surroundings by inert gas under high pressure. The beam travels in the tube and is deflected to experimental areas by the bending magnets. The Purdue accelerator is used extensively in accelerator mass spectrometry. [*Courtesy of David Elmore, Purdue University.*]

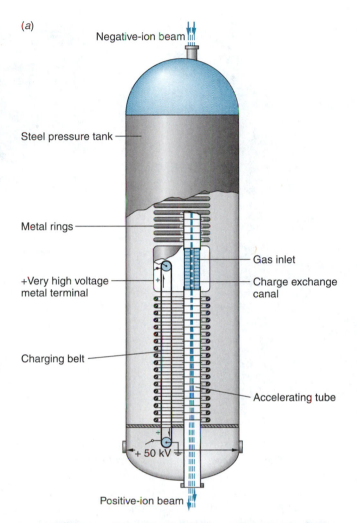

(*a*)

Negative-ion beam

Steel pressure tank

Metal rings

Gas inlet

+Very high voltage metal terminal

Charge exchange canal

Charging belt

Accelerating tube

+ 50 kV

Positive-ion beam

(*b*)

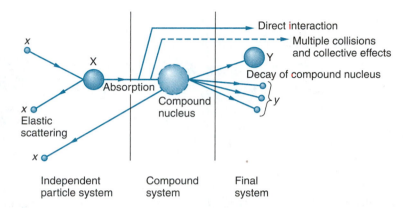

Fig. 12-1 Schematic representation of the several possible stages of the nuclear reaction X (x, y) Y, according to the theory developed by V. Weisskopf and H. Feshbach.

Figure 12-1 illustrates schematically the several possible stages of a nuclear reaction. *Elastic scattering* refers to the reflection of the incident particle's wave at the edge of the nuclear potential well. This is the kind of scattering for α particles that was described by Rutherford's theory in Section 4-2. If the incident particle interacts with a single nucleon in the nucleus so that the nucleon leaves the nucleus, the reaction is called a *direct interaction*. Direct interactions are more probable at high energies, since the incident particle can penetrate deeper into the nucleus. If the nucleon does not leave the nucleus but interacts with several other nucleons, complicated excited states can be formed in the nucleus. In such a case, when the energy carried by the incident particle is shared by many nucleons, the excited nucleus is called a *compound nucleus*. The compound nucleus can decay by emitting a particle identical to the incident particle and with the same kinetic energy (also elastic scattering) or by emission of one or more other particles (including photons). The decay of the compound nucleus can be treated as a statistical process independent of the detailed manner of formations, just as in the case of a radioactive nucleus.

In this section we shall study some of the systematics of nuclear reactions and some typical reactions produced by incident neutrons, protons, or deuterons. We shall limit the discussion to energies of less than 140 MeV. At higher energies, mesons and other particles can be created. The study of higher-energy reactions is generally undertaken to reveal the properties of fundamental particles and of the nuclear force rather than the structure of the nucleus and will be discussed further in Chapter 13.

Energy Conservation

Consider a general reaction of particle x incident on nucleus X resulting in nucleus Y and particle y. The reaction may be written

$$x + X \longrightarrow Y + y + Q$$

or, as we will usually write it, X(x, y)Y. The quantity Q, defined by

$$Q = (m_x + m_X - m_y - m_Y)c^2 \qquad \textbf{12-1}$$

is the energy released in the reaction and is called the *Q value* of the reaction.

When energy is released by a nuclear reaction, the reaction is said to be *exothermic*. In an exothermic reaction, the total mass of the initial particles is greater than that of the final particles and the Q value is positive. If the total mass of the initial particles

Fig. 12-2 Energetics of nuclear reaction in center-of-mass system and laboratory system. The energies are related by $E_{lab} = [(M + m)/M]E_{CM}$.

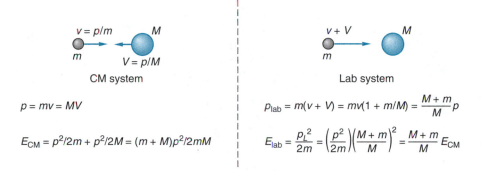

CM system

$p = mv = MV$

$E_{CM} = p^2/2m + p^2/2M = (m + M)p^2/2mM$

Lab system

$p_{lab} = m(v + V) = mv(1 + m/M) = \dfrac{M + m}{M} p$

$E_{lab} = \dfrac{p_L^2}{2m} = \left(\dfrac{p^2}{2m}\right)\left(\dfrac{M + m}{M}\right)^2 = \dfrac{M + m}{M} E_{CM}$

is less than that of the final particles, the Q value is negative and energy is required for the reaction to take place. The reaction is then *endothermic*. Examples are:

$$n + {}^1H \longrightarrow {}^2H + \gamma + 2.22 \text{ MeV (exothermic)}$$
$$\gamma + {}^2H \longrightarrow {}^1H + n - 2.22 \text{ MeV (endothermic)}$$

Thus, an endothermic reaction cannot take place unless a certain threshold energy is supplied to the system. In the reference frame in which the total momentum is zero (the center-of-mass frame), the threshold energy is just $|Q|$. However, many reactions occur with nucleus X at rest relative to the laboratory. In this frame, called the *laboratory frame,* the incident particle x must have energy greater than $|Q|$ because, by conservation of momentum, the kinetic energy of y and Y cannot be zero. Consider the nonrelativistic case of x, of mass m, incident on X, of mass M (see Figure 12-2). In the center-of-mass frame, both particles have momenta of equal magnitude, and the total kinetic energy is

$$E_{CM} = \frac{p^2}{2m} + \frac{p^2}{2M} = \frac{1}{2}p^2\left(\frac{m + M}{mM}\right) \qquad \textbf{12-2}$$

where $p = mv = MV$. We transform to the lab frame by adding V to each velocity so that M is at rest and m has velocity $v + V$. The momentum of m in the lab frame is then

$$p_{lab} = m(v + V) = mv\left(1 + \frac{m}{M}\right) = p\left(\frac{m + M}{M}\right) \qquad$$

and its energy is

$$E_{lab} = \frac{p_{lab}^2}{2m} = \frac{p^2}{2m}\left(\frac{m + M}{M}\right)^2 = \frac{m + M}{M}E_{CM} \qquad \textbf{12-3}$$

The threshold for an endothermic reaction in the lab frame is thus

$$E_{th} = \frac{m + M}{M}|Q| \qquad \textbf{12-4}$$

(If the incident particle is a photon, the Lorentz transformation must be used. For low energies, the momentum of a photon is small and approximate methods can be used. For a photon, $pc = E$, whereas for a proton or neutron, $pc = (2mc^2E)^{1/2} \gg E$ for $E \ll 940$ MeV.)

EXAMPLE 12-1 *Q* **Value of a Nuclear Reaction**   Find the Q value of the reaction

$$p + {}^7Li \longrightarrow {}^4He + {}^4He$$

and state whether the reaction is exothermic or endothermic. The atomic mass of ^{7}Li is 7.016003 u.

Solution

Using 1.007825 u for the mass of ^{1}H and 4.002602 u for the mass of ^{4}He from Appendix A, we have for the total mass of the initial particles

$$m_i = 1.007825 \text{ u} + 7.016003 \text{ u} = 8.023828 \text{ u}$$

and for the total mass of the final particles

$$m_f = 2(4.002602 \text{ u}) = 8.005204 \text{ u}$$

Since the initial mass is greater than the final mass by

$$\Delta m = m_i - m_f = 8.023828 \text{ u} - 8.005204 \text{ u} = 0.018624 \text{ u}$$

mass is converted into energy and the reaction is exothermic. The Q value is positive and given by

$$Q = (\Delta m)c^2 = (0.018624 \text{ u})c^2(931.5 \text{ MeV/u} \cdot c^2) = 17.35 \text{ MeV}$$

Note that we used the mass of atomic hydrogen rather than that of the proton and the atomic masses of the ^{7}Li and ^{4}He atoms rather than the masses of the individual nuclei so that the masses of the four electrons on each side of the reaction cancel.

EXAMPLE 12-2 **Threshold Energy in Lab Frame** Compute the minimum kinetic energy of protons incident on ^{13}C nuclei at rest in the laboratory that will produce the endothermic reaction ^{13}C$(p, n)^{13}$N.

Solution

1. The minimum, or threshold, energy of the incident protons in the lab frame is given by Equation 12-4:

$$E_{\text{th}} = \frac{m + M}{M} |Q|$$

2. The magnitude of the Q value of the reaction is:

$$\frac{|Q|}{c^2} = m_{\text{final}} - m_{\text{initial}}$$

$$= [M(^{13}\text{N}) + m_n] - [M(^{13}\text{C}) + M(^1\text{H})]$$

3. The masses of the particles involved are tabulated in Appendix A:

$$M(^{13}\text{C}) = 13.003355 \text{ u}$$
$$M(^1\text{H}) = 1.007825 \text{ u}$$
$$m_n = 1.008665 \text{ u}$$
$$M(^{13}\text{N}) = 13.005738 \text{ u}$$

4. Substituting these into the expression for $|Q|$ gives:

$$|Q| = (14.014403 - 14.011180) \, \text{u} \cdot c^2$$
$$= 0.003223 \, \text{u} \times 931.5 \, \text{MeV/u} \cdot c^2$$
$$= 3.00 \, \text{MeV}$$

5. Substituting this value, $m = M(^1\text{H})$, and $M = M(^{13}\text{C})$ into Equation 12-4 gives:

$$E_{\text{th}} = \frac{1.007825 + 13.003355}{13.003355} \times 3.00$$
$$= 3.23 \, \text{MeV}$$

Cross Section

The probability that a particle incident on a nucleus will scatter or induce a reaction depends on the particle's energy and what particular particle and nucleus are involved. It is as if different kinds of particles approaching a given nucleus "see" targets of different sizes. Similarly, identical particles with different energies "see" the same target nucleus larger or smaller than actual size. This effect is a consequence of the detailed arrangement of the allowed energy states of the target nucleus. A useful measure of the effective size of a nucleus for a particular scattering or nuclear reaction is the *cross section* σ. If I is the number of particles incident per unit time per unit area (the incident intensity) and R is the number of reactions per unit time per nucleus, the cross section is defined as

$$\sigma = \frac{R}{I} \qquad\qquad \textbf{12-5}$$

Consider, for example, the bombardment of ^{13}C by protons. A number of reactions might occur. Elastic scattering is written $^{13}\text{C}(p, p)^{13}\text{C}$; the first p indicates an incident proton, the second indicates that the particle that leaves is also a proton. If the scattering is inelastic, the outgoing proton is indicated by p' and the nucleus in the resulting excited state by $^{13}\text{C}^*$ and one writes $^{13}\text{C}(p, p)^{13}\text{C}^*$. Some other possible reactions are

$$
\begin{array}{ll}
(p, n) & ^{13}\text{C}(p, n)^{13}\text{N} \\
\text{capture} & ^{13}\text{C}(p, \gamma)^{14}\text{N} \\
(p, \alpha) & ^{13}\text{C}(p, \alpha)^{10}\text{B}
\end{array}
$$

Each possible scattering or reaction has its own cross section, called the *partial cross section*. The partial cross section is also defined by Equation 12-5 with R equal to the number of events of the specific kind per unit time per nucleus. The total cross section is the sum of the partial cross sections:

$$\sigma = \sigma_{p, p} + \sigma_{p, p'} + \sigma_{p, n} + \sigma_{p, \gamma} + \sigma_{p, \alpha} + \cdots$$

Cross sections have the dimensions of area. Since nuclear cross sections are of the order of the square of the nuclear radius, that is, $(10^{-14} \, \text{m})^2$, a convenient unit for them is the *barn,* defined by

$$1 \text{ barn} = 10^{-24} \text{ cm}^2 = 10^{-28} \text{ m}^2 \qquad \textbf{12-6}$$

The cross section for a particular reaction is a function of energy. For an endothermic reaction, it is zero for energies below the threshold.

Compound Nucleus

In 1936, Niels Bohr pointed out that many low-energy reactions could be described as two-stage processes—the formation of a compound nucleus and its subsequent decay. In this description, the incident particle is absorbed by the target nucleus and the energy is shared by all the nucleons of the compound nucleus. After a time that is long compared with the time necessary for the incident particle to cross the nucleus, enough of the excitation energy of the compound nucleus becomes concentrated in one particle for it to escape. The emission of a particle is a statistical process that depends only on the state of the compound nucleus and not on how it was produced. An incident 1-MeV proton has a speed of about 10^7 m/s, so that it takes time $R/v \approx 10^{-14}/10^7 = 10^{-21}$ s to cross a nucleus. The lifetime of a compound nucleus can be inferred to be about 10^{-16} s. This is too short to be measured directly, but it is so long compared with 10^{-21} s that it is reasonable to assume that the decay is independent of how it was formed.

The compound nucleus for the reactions on ^{13}C shown above is ^{14}N*. This nucleus can be formed by many other reactions, such as

$$
\begin{aligned}
^{10}\text{B} + \alpha &\longrightarrow {}^{14}\text{N*} \longrightarrow {}^{12}\text{C} + d \\
^{13}\text{N} + n &\longrightarrow {}^{14}\text{N*} \longrightarrow {}^{10}\text{B} + \alpha \\
^{14}\text{N} + \gamma &\longrightarrow {}^{14}\text{N*} \longrightarrow {}^{14}\text{N} + \gamma \\
^{12}\text{C} + d &\longrightarrow {}^{14}\text{N*} \longrightarrow {}^{13}\text{N} + n
\end{aligned}
\qquad \textbf{12-7}
$$

The reactions on the left are called the *entrance channels* and the decays on the right are called the *exit channels*.

Since the decay of ^{14}N* is independent of the formation, we can write the cross section for a particular reaction such as ^{13}C$(p, n)^{13}$N as the product of the cross section for the formation of the compound nucleus, σ_c, and the relative probability of decay by neutron emission, P_n:

$$\sigma_{p,n} = \sigma_c P_n \qquad \textbf{12-8}$$

An illustration of the statistical decay of the compound nucleus is afforded by the energy distribution of neutrons from reactions such as (see Figure 12-3).

$$\gamma + {}^{209}\text{Bi} \longrightarrow {}^{208}\text{Bi} + n$$

where σ shows a broad peak at 14 to 20 MeV and neutrons "evaporate" as ^{208}Bi decays to the ground state.

Excited States of Nuclei from Nuclear Reactions

The excited states of a nucleus can be determined in two ways from nuclear reactions. A peak in the cross section $\sigma(E)$ as a function of energy indicates an excited state of the compound nucleus, corresponding to the relatively large probability of

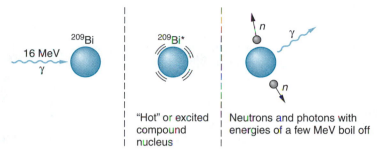

Fig. 12-3 Nuclear reaction via formation of compound nucleus. The 16-MeV photon is absorbed by the ^{209}Bi nucleus, producing an excited nucleus which lives so long that excitation energy is shared by many nucleons. The excited nucleus then decays by emitting neutrons and photons, each with energy of the order of a few MeV.

the incident particle giving up all its energy in the single event of exciting an allowed energy level. (Think of the Franck-Hertz experiment as an analogy.) Information about the lifetimes τ of the excited states of the compound nucleus is obtained by measuring the energy width Γ of these peaks, or *resonances,* and using the uncertainty principle $\tau\Gamma \approx \hbar$. Figure 12-4 shows the cross section for formation of ^{14}N by the reaction ^{10}B $+ \alpha \rightarrow$ ^{14}N* as a function of the α-particle energy. The peaks in this curve indicate energy levels in the ^{14}N nucleus. The Q value for this reaction is $M(^{10}$B$)c^2 + M(\alpha)c^2 - M(^{14}N)c^2 = 11.61$ MeV. The Q value is the binding energy of the incident particle in the compound nucleus, which is always of the order of 6 to 10 MeV; thus levels of energy less than 6 MeV cannot be reached in the compound nucleus.

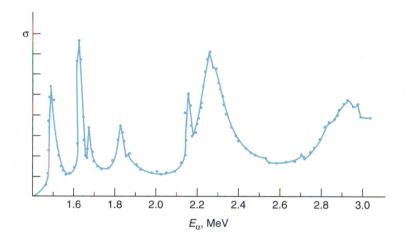

Fig. 12-4 Cross section for the reaction ^{10}B $+ \alpha \rightarrow$ ^{14}N* vs. energy. The resonances indicate energy levels in the compound nucleus ^{14}N*.

The kinetic energy in the center-of-mass frame is related to the lab energy of the α particle by

$$E_{\text{CM}} = \frac{M}{M + m} E_{\text{lab}} = \frac{10}{14} E_{\text{lab}}$$

The peak in Figure 12-4 at $E_{\text{lab}} = 1.63$ MeV corresponds to an excited state in ^{14}N of energy $E = 11.61 + (10/14)(1.63) = 12.77$ MeV. The same level can be excited by the reaction ^{12}C $+ ^2$H $\rightarrow$ ^{14}N*. For this case, the Q value is 10.26 MeV. Thus, the deuteron energy in the lab must be

$$E_d = \left(\frac{14}{12}\right)(12.77 - 10.26) = 2.93 \text{ MeV}$$

A second way to determine the energy levels in a nucleus is to observe the energies of particles scattered inelastically. In this case, the energy levels of the target nucleus are determined. Figure 12-5 shows the energy spectrum of protons from the reaction $p + {}^{14}\text{N} \rightarrow {}^{14}\text{N*} + p$ using 6.92-MeV protons. (The horizontal scale in this figure is proportional to the momentum of the protons, since this is what is measured experimentally.) The two peaks in the curve correspond to energy losses of 2.31 and 3.75 MeV, which indicated energy levels in ${}^{14}\text{N}$ of 2.31 and 3.75 MeV. The excited product nucleus decays from these states by γ emission. The method of inelastic scattering can determine energy levels of the target nucleus lying relatively close to the ground state, whereas the levels excited in the compound nucleus must be much higher because of the Q values for formation of the compound nucleus.

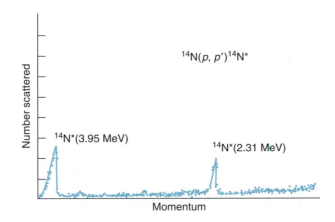

Fig. 12-5 Spectrum of protons scattered from ${}^{14}\text{N}$, indicating the energy levels in ${}^{14}\text{N}$.

Reactions with Neutrons

Nuclear reactions involving neutrons are important for understanding the elemental analytical technique of neutron activation analysis and the operation of nuclear reactors. The most likely reaction with a nucleus for a neutron of more than about 1 MeV is scattering. However, even if the scattering is elastic, the neutron loses some energy to the nucleus because conservation of momentum requires that the nucleus recoil. If a neutron is scattered many times in a material, its energy decreases until it is of the order of the energy of thermal motion kT, where k is the Boltzmann constant and T is the absolute temperature. (At ordinary room temperatures, kT is about 0.025 eV.) The neutron is then equally likely to gain or lose energy from a nucleus when it is elastically scattered. A neutron with energy of the order of kT is called a *thermal neutron*.

At low energies, a neutron is more likely to be captured, with the emission of a γ ray from the excited nucleus:

$$n + {}^{A}_{Z}\text{M} \longrightarrow {}^{A+1}_{Z}\text{M} + \gamma$$

For example,

$$n + {}^{107}\text{Ag} \longrightarrow {}^{108}\text{Ag} + \gamma$$

Neutrons are used to dope silicon with phosphorus more uniformly than the conventional diffusion method. Irradiating Si with neutrons produces the P dopant via the reaction and subsequent decay: $n + {}^{30}\text{Si} \rightarrow {}^{31}\text{Si} \rightarrow {}^{31}\text{P} + \beta^- + \bar{\nu}$. Silicon doped with P this way can operate at higher power levels in rectifier applications than diffusion-doped silicon.

Fig. 12-6 Neutron capture cross section for Ag vs. energy. The dashed-line extension would be expected if there were no resonances and the cross section were merely proportional to the time spent near the nucleus, i.e., proportional to $1/v$. The resonance widths of a few eV indicate states with lifetimes of the order of $h/\Gamma \approx 10^{-16}$ s.

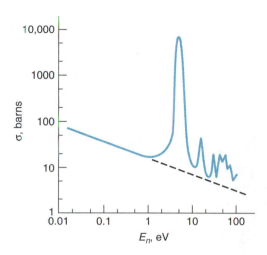

Since the binding energy of a neutron is of the order of 6 to 10 MeV and the kinetic energy of the neutron is negligible by comparison, the excitation energy of the compound nucleus is from 6 to 10 MeV, and γ rays of this energy are emitted. Figure 12-6 shows the neutron capture cross section for silver as a function of the energy of the neutron. Except for the resonances, the cross section $\sigma(n, \gamma)$ varies smoothly with energy, decreasing with increasing energy approximately as $1/v$, where v is the speed of the neutron. This energy dependence can be understood as follows: Consider a neutron moving with speed v near a nucleus of diameter $2R$. The time it takes the neutron to pass the nucleus is $2R/v$. Thus, the neutron capture cross section is proportional to the time spent by the neutron in the vicinity of the nucleus. The dashed line in Figure 12-6 indicates this $1/v$ dependence.[3] At the maximum of the large resonance, the value of the cross section is very large ($\sigma > 5000$ barns) compared with a value of only about 10 barns just past the resonance. Many elements show similar resonances in the neutron capture cross sections. For example, the maximum cross section for ^{113}Cd is about 57,000 barns. Thus, ^{113}Cd is a strong absorber, which makes it very useful as a shield against low-energy neutrons.[4]

QUESTIONS

1. What is meant by the cross section for a nuclear reaction? Why is that term used to describe it?

2. Why is the neutron capture cross section (excluding resonances) proportional to $1/v$?

3. What is meant by the Q value of a reaction? Why is the reaction threshold not equal to Q?

4. Why can't low-lying energy levels (1 to 2 MeV above the ground state) be studied using neutron capture?

EXAMPLE 12-3 Determination of Reaction Rates The cross section for the reaction ^{91}Zr$(n, \gamma)^{92}$Zr is 900 millibarns for thermal neutrons. This reaction is produced in the so-called thermal column of a reactor where the *flux* of thermal neutrons is 6.5×10^{12} neutrons/cm$^2 \cdot$ s. The sample of natural Zr is a circular foil

1.0 cm in diameter and 20.0 μm thick. The density of Zr is 6.506 g/cm³ and ⁹¹Zr makes up 11.27 percent of natural Zr. Compute the rate of this reaction.

Solution

First we need to compute the number of ⁹¹Zr atoms in the sample. This number is given by

$$N(^{91}\text{Zr}) = \frac{N_A V \rho_{\text{Zr}}}{M_{\text{Zr}}} \times 0.1127$$

where the volume of the sample $V = 2.00 \times 10^{-3} \times (\pi/4)$ cm³ and the molecular weight of Zr, $M_{\text{Zr}} = 91.22$ g/mol. Thus,

$$N(^{91}\text{Zr}) = \frac{(6.02 \times 10^{23} \text{ atoms/mol})\left(2.00 \times 10^{-3} \times \frac{\pi}{4} \text{ cm}^3\right) \times 6.506 \text{ g/cm}^3}{91.22 \text{ g/mol}}$$

$$N(^{91}\text{Zr}) = 1.04 \times 10^{19} \text{ atoms}$$

From the definition of the cross section given by Equation 12-5, the number of (n, γ) reactions per unit time per ⁹¹Zr nucleus is

$$R = \sigma I = (900 \times 10^{-3} \text{ barns} \times 10^{-24} \text{ cm}^2/\text{barn}) \times 6.5 \times 10^{12} \text{ neutrons/cm}^2 \cdot \text{s}$$

$$R = 5.85 \times 10^{-12} \text{ s}^{-1} \text{per } ^{91}\text{Zr nucleus}$$

The rate $\Re$ at which the reaction ⁹¹Zr (n, γ)⁹²Zr proceeds is then

$$\Re = N(^{91}\text{Zr}) R = (1.04 \times 10^{19} \text{ }^{91}\text{Zr nuclei})(5.85 \times 10^{-12} \text{ s}^{-1} \text{ per } ^{91}\text{Zr nucleus})$$

$$\Re = 6.08 \times 10^7 \text{ s}^{-1}$$

This is a low reaction rate, given the high neutron flux. It is the result of the low neutron capture cross section of ⁹¹Zr and the other naturally occurring Zr isotopes. This is a principal reason why zirconium is used to enclose nuclear reactor fuel elements.

12-2 Fission, Fusion, and Nuclear Reactors

Two nuclear reactions, fission and fusion, are of particular importance. In the fission of ²³⁵U, for example, the uranium nucleus is excited by the capture of a neutron and splits into two nuclei, each with very roughly half of the original total mass. A typical fission reaction is

$$^{235}\text{U} + n \longrightarrow {}^{92}\text{Kr} + {}^{142}\text{Ba} + 2n + 179.4 \text{ MeV} \qquad \textbf{12-9}$$

The Coulomb force of repulsion drives the fission fragments apart, giving them very large kinetic energies. As a result of collisions with other atoms, this energy eventually shows up as thermal energy. In fusion, two light nuclei such as those of deuterium and tritium (²H and ³H) fuse together to form a heavier nucleus (in this case ⁴He plus a neutron). A typical reaction is

$$^{2}\text{H} + {}^{3}\text{H} \longrightarrow {}^{4}\text{He} + n + 17.6 \text{ MeV} \qquad \textbf{12-10}$$

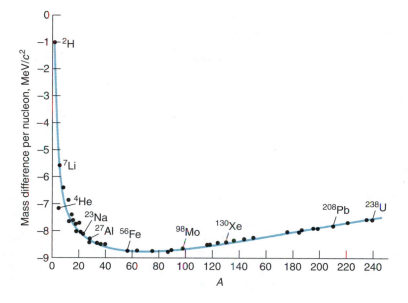

Fig. 12-7 Plot of mass difference per nucleon $(M - Zm_p - Nm_n)/A$ in units of MeV/c^2 vs. A. The rest energy per nucleon is smaller for intermediate-mass nuclei than for either very light or very heavy nuclei.

Figure 12-7 shows a plot of the mass difference per nucleon $(M - Zm_p - Nm_n)/A$ versus A in units of MeV/c^2. This curve is just the negative of the binding-energy curve of Figure 11-10. From Figure 12-7 we see that the rest energy per particle of both very heavy nuclides ($A \approx 200$) and very light nuclides ($A \leq 20$) is more than that for nuclides of intermediate mass. Thus in both fission and fusion the total mass decreases and energy is released. Since for $A = 200$ the rest energy is about 1 MeV per nucleon greater than for $A = 100$, about 200 MeV is released in the fission of a heavy nucleus. The energy release in fusion depends on the particular reaction. For the ^{2}H + ^{3}H reaction in Equation 12-10, 17.6 MeV is released. Although this is less than the energy released in a single fission, it is a greater amount of energy per unit mass, as Example 12-4 illustrates.

The application of both fission and fusion to the development of nuclear weapons has had a profound effect on our lives during the past 60 years. The peaceful application of these reactions to the development of energy resources may well have an even greater effect in the future, provided that satisfactory solutions are found to problems concerning safety, environmental protection, and the spread of nuclear weapons technology. In this section, we will look at some of the features of fission and fusion that are important for their application in reactors to generate power.

EXAMPLE 12-4 Energy Release in Fission and Fusion Compare the energy release per unit mass in the fusion of deuterium and tritium (Equation 12-10) with that of a typical fission reaction, such as that of ^{235}U given by Equation 12-9.

Solution

(*a*) A quick approximate comparison can be made by noting that the energy difference per nucleon between ^{235}U and its fission products is about 1.0 MeV. In the fusion of ^{2}H + ^{3}H it is 17.6 MeV/5 nucleons = 3.5, or about 3.5 times larger. Thus, the energy released per kilogram will also be about 3.5 times larger in the fusion reaction.

(b) The mass differences per nucleon for ^{235}U and the two fission products in Equation 12-9 can be estimated from Figure 12-7. A more accurate calculation of the total binding energy can be made with the aid of Equation 11-12 and used to compute the total mass differences as follows:

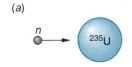
(a)

^{235}U: -7.6 MeV/c^2 per nucleon $\longrightarrow$ -1797.1 MeV/c^2 per nucleus

^{92}Kr: -8.7 MeV/c^2 per nucleon $\longrightarrow$ -800.9 MeV/c^2 per nucleus

^{142}Ba: -8.4 MeV/c^2 per nucleon $\longrightarrow$ -1189.5 MeV/c^2 per nucleus

The difference between the mass of ^{235}U and the sum of masses for the fission products is 193.3 MeV/c^2. Thus, the energy release per fission event (with these particular products) is 193.3 MeV. The mass of ^{235}U (see Appendix A) is 235.043924 u $= 3.9030 \times 10^{-25}$ kg. Therefore, the energy release per kilogram in the fission of ^{235}U is

(b)

$$\frac{\left(\dfrac{193.3 \text{ MeV}}{^{235}\text{U}}\right)}{\left(\dfrac{3.903 \times 10^{-25} \text{ kg}}{^{235}\text{U}}\right)} = 4.95 \times 10^{26} \text{ MeV/kg}$$

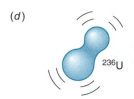
(c)

The energy release in the deuterium/tritium fusion reaction is

$$\frac{17.6 \text{ MeV}}{M_d + M_t} = \frac{17.6 \text{ MeV}}{8.353 \times 10^{-27} \text{ kg}} = 2.11 \times 10^{27} \text{ MeV/kg}$$

(d)

Thus, the fusion reaction releases about 4.3 times the energy/kg released by the fission reaction.

Fission

The fission of uranium was discovered in 1938 by O. Hahn and F. Strassmann,[5] who found, by careful chemical analysis, that medium-mass elements (in particular, barium) were produced in the bombardment of uranium with neutrons. The discovery that several neutrons are emitted in the fission process led to speculation concerning the possibility of using these neutrons to cause further fissions, thereby producing a chain reaction. When ^{235}U captures a thermal neutron, the resulting ^{236}U nucleus undergoes fission about 85 percent of the time and emits gamma rays as it de-excites to the ground state about 15 percent of the time. The fission process is somewhat analogous to the oscillation of a liquid drop, as shown in Figure 12-8. If the oscillations are violent enough, the drop splits in two. Using the liquid-drop model, A. Bohr and J. Wheeler calculated the critical energy E_c needed by the ^{236}U nucleus to undergo fission. (^{236}U is the compound nucleus formed by the capture of a neutron by ^{235}U.) The critical energy is the magnitude of the Coulomb barrier seen by the fragments, as illustrated in Figure 12-9. For this nucleus, the critical energy is about 6.2 MeV, which is less than the 6.5 MeV of excitation energy produced when ^{235}U captures a neutron. The capture of a neutron by ^{235}U therefore produces an excited state of the ^{236}U nucleus that has more than enough energy to break apart. On the other hand, the critical energy for the fission of the ^{239}U nucleus is 5.9 MeV. The capture of a neutron by a

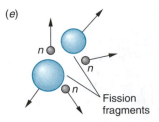
(e)

Fig. 12-8 Schematic illustration of nuclear fission. (a) The absorption of a neutron by ^{235}U leads to (b) ^{236}U in an excited state. (c) Oscillation deforms the excited ^{236}U nucleus. (d) The oscillation of ^{236}U has become unstable. (e) The nucleus splits apart into two nuclei of medium mass and emits several neutrons that can produce fission in other nuclei.

Fig. 12-9 The nucleus may exist instantaneously as two fragments as shown on the left; however, the Coulomb potential barrier prevents their fission. To overcome the barrier, energy equal to the critical energy must be provided.

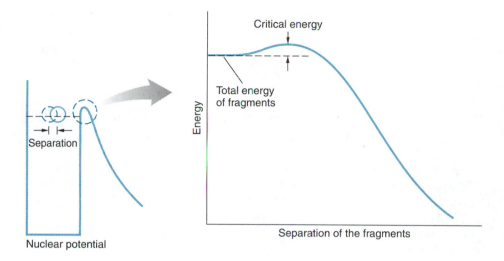

^{238}U nucleus produces an excitation energy of only 5.2 MeV. Therefore, when a thermal neutron is captured by ^{238}U to form ^{239}U, the excitation energy is not great enough for fission to occur. In this case the excited ^{239}U nucleus de-excites by γ or α emission. Nuclides that may fission upon capturing a slow neutron are called *fissile*.

We noted in Chapter 11 that all nuclei with $Z > 83$ are radioactive. Among the possible decay modes of the very heavy nuclei ($Z > 90$) is that of spontaneous fission. These nuclei may break apart into two nuclei even if left to themselves without absorbing a neutron. We can also understand spontaneous fission using the analogy of a liquid drop of positive charges. If the drop is not too large, surface tension can overcome the repulsive forces of the charges and hold the drop together. There is, however, a certain maximum size beyond which the drop will be unstable and will spontaneously break apart, since the repulsive force is proportional to the number of protons which is proportional to the volume, hence to R^3, whereas the surface tension is proportional to the surface area, hence increases only as R^2. (See Section 11-2.) Spontaneous fission puts an upper limit on the size of a nucleus and therefore on the

Fig. 12-10 Distribution of fission fragments from the thermal neutron-induced fission of ^{235}U. Symmetric fission, in which the uranium nucleus splits into two nuclei of nearly equal mass, is much less probable than asymmetric fission, in which the fragments have unequal masses. Note the symmetry of the light and heavy lobes of the distribution, including the small variations in the tops of the peaks and the convex outer edges. [*Data from G. J. Dilorio,* Direct Physical Measurement of Mass Yields in Thermal Fission of Uranium-235 *(New York: Garland, 1979).*]

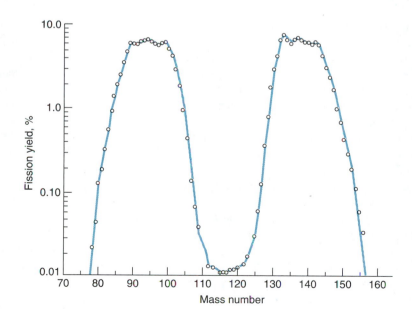

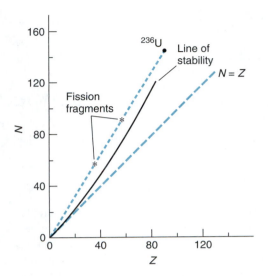

Fig. 12-11 Fission of ^{236}U (^{235}U + n) produces fragments that are neutron-rich and well to the left of the line of stability. As a result, the fission is accompanied by the prompt emission of one or more of the excess neutrons followed by β^- decay of the fission fragments to further reduce their neutron numbers.

number of elements that are possible. It should be noted that the probability for spontaneous fission in naturally occurring nuclides is quite low compared with the other possible decay modes. For example, the half-life of ^{238}U for α decay is 4.5×10^9 years, while that for spontaneous fission is about 10^{16} years. The reason is that fission, like α decay, is inhibited by the Coulomb barrier. Even though the process is energetically possible, the large positively charged fission fragments have a very low probability of tunneling through the Coulomb barrier part of the nuclear potential.

A fissioning nucleus can break into two medium-mass fragments in many different ways, as shown in Figure 12-10. Depending on the particular reaction, one, two, or three neutrons may be emitted. The average number of neutrons emitted in the thermal neutron-induced fission of ^{235}U is about 2.4. Equation 12-9 is a typical fission reaction. The reason that several neutrons are emitted is that the fission fragments are typically neutron-rich and far off the line of stability as shown in Figure 12-11. As a result, neutrons are spontaneously emitted during fission and the fragments β^- decay toward stability. The Coulomb force of repulsion drives the fission fragments apart with very large kinetic energies. This energy is transferred to other nearby atoms via collisions, eventually showing up as thermal energy of the surroundings. We have seen that about 200 MeV per nucleus is released in such a fission. This is a large amount of energy. By contrast, in the chemical combustion reaction, only about 4 eV is released per molecule of oxygen consumed.

The fission fragments and their decay products that build up in reactors are the source of many radioisotopes used in medical diagnosis, treatment, and research. Important among these is ^{99}Mo, the source of ^{99}Tc. the most widely used radioisotope in nuclear medicine.

EXAMPLE 12-5 Kilowatt-Hours from ^{235}U Calculate the total energy in kilowatt-hours released in the fission of 1 g of ^{235}U, assuming that 200 MeV is released per fission.

Solution

Since 1 mol of ^{235}U has a mass of 235 g and contains $N_A = 6.02 \times 10^{23}$ nuclei, the number of ^{235}U nuclei in 1 g is

$$N = \frac{6.02 \times 10^{23} \text{ nuclei/mol}}{235 \text{ g/mol}} = 2.56 \times 10^{21} \text{ nuclei/g}$$

The energy released per gram is then

$$\frac{200 \text{ MeV}}{\text{nucleus}} \times \frac{2.56 \times 10^{21} \text{ nuclei}}{1 \text{ g}} \times \frac{1.6 \times 10^{-19} \text{ J}}{1 \text{ eV}}$$

$$\times \frac{1 \text{ h}}{3600 \text{ s}} \times \frac{1 \text{ kW}}{1000 \text{ J/s}} = 2.28 \times 10^4 \text{ kW} \cdot \text{h/g}$$

This is approximately equal to the amount of electrical energy used by a typical U.S. household in 15 months.

Nuclear Fission Reactors   The discovery that several neutrons were emitted in the fission process led to speculation concerning the possibility of using these neutrons to initiate other fissions, thereby producing a *chain reaction*. On December 2, 1942, less than four years after Hahn and Strassmann's discovery of fission, a group led by Enrico Fermi produced the first self-sustaining chain reaction in a nuclear reactor that they had constructed at the University of Chicago.[6]

To sustain a chain reaction in a fission reactor, one of the neutrons (on the average) emitted in the fission of ^{235}U must be captured by another ^{235}U nucleus and cause it to fission. The *reproduction factor k* of a reactor is defined as the average number of neutrons from each fission that cause a subsequent fission. In the case of ^{235}U the maximum possible value of k is about 2.4, but it is normally less than this for two important reasons: (1) some of the neutrons may escape from the region containing fissionable nuclei, and (2) some of the neutrons may be captured by nonfissioning nuclei in the reactor. If k is exactly 1, the reaction will be self-sustaining. If it is less than 1, the reaction will die out. If k is significantly greater than 1, the reaction rate will increase rapidly and "run away." In the design of nuclear bombs, such a runaway reaction is necessary. In power reactors, the value of k must be kept very nearly equal to 1. (See Figure 12-12.) If k is exactly equal to 1, the reactor is said to be *critical*; for $k < 1$ it is described as being *subcritical* and for $k > 1$ as *supercritical*.

Fig. 12-12 Schematic representation of a fission chain reaction in ^{235}U. The fission fragments are shown only for the first three fissions. The average number of neutrons produced is 2.4 per fission. In this example $k = 1.6$. Notice that, while there are 42 neutrons in the diagram, the judicious placement of absorbers to absorb as few as two of those causing fission would be sufficient to make $k = 1$ and control the reaction.

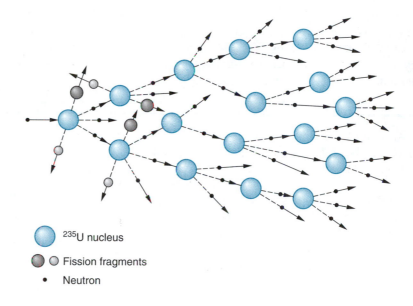

⬤ ^{235}U nucleus

◓ ◯ Fission fragments

•   Neutron

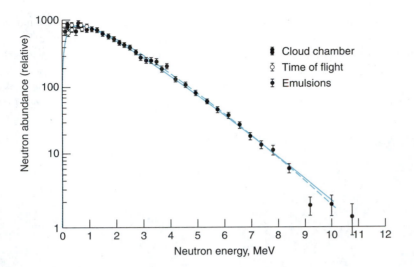

Fig. 12-13 The energy spectrum of the neutrons emitted in the thermal neutron-induced fission of ^{235}U. [*Data from R. B Leachman,* Proceedings of the International Conference on the Peaceful Uses of Atomic Energy, *Vol. 2 (New York: United Nations, 1956).*]

Since the neutrons emitted in fission mostly have energies of the order of 1 MeV or higher (see Figure 12-13), whereas the cross section for neutron capture leading to fission in ^{235}U is largest at small energies, as illustrated in Figure 12-14, the chain reaction can be sustained only if the neutrons are slowed down before they escape from the reactor. At high energies (1 to 2 MeV), neutrons lose energy rapidly by inelastic scattering from ^{238}U, the principal constituent of natural uranium. (Natural uranium contains 99.28 percent ^{238}U and only 0.72 percent fissile ^{235}U.) Once the neutron energy is below the excitation energies of the nuclei in the reactor (about 1 MeV), the main process of energy loss is by elastic scattering, in which a neutron collides with a nucleus at rest and, by conservation of momentum, transfers some of its kinetic energy to the nucleus. Such energy transfers are efficient only if the masses of the two bodies are comparable. A neutron will not transfer much energy in an elastic collision with a heavy ^{238}U nucleus. Such a collision is analogous to one between a marble and a billiard ball. The marble will be deflected by the much more massive billiard ball with essentially no changes in its kinetic energy. Therefore, a *moderator* consisting of

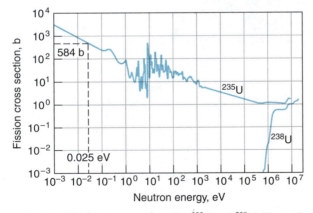

Fig. 12-14 Neutron-induced fission cross sections for ^{235}U and ^{238}U. The region below 0.01 eV for ^{235}U shows the $1/v$ dependence, as does the cross section for the (n, γ) reaction and for the same reason. The radiative absorption reaction competes with fission and has a cross section of 97 b at 0.025 eV. The numerous resonances between 1 eV and 100 eV are associated with excited states of the ^{236}U* nucleus.

material, such as water or graphite, that contains light nuclei is placed around the fissile material in the core of the reactor to slow down the neutrons with relatively few collisions so as to minimize the number lost from the reactor. The neutrons are slowed down by elastic collisions with the nuclei of the moderator until they are in thermal equilibrium with the moderator, at which time they have approximately a Maxwell-Boltzmann energy distribution with average energy of $(3/2)kT$. Table 12-1 lists the

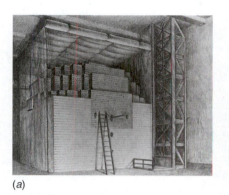

(a)

(b)

(c)

(a) A sketch of the world's first nuclear reactor, the CP-1 (for Chicago Pile number 1). Projecting from the near face next to the top of the ladder is one of the cadmium-plated rods used to control the chain reaction by absorbing neutrons. The cubical balloon surrounding the reactor, open on the near side, was to contain neutron-activated radioactive air. News of the reactor's successful test was transmitted by A. H. Compton, one of those present, to President Roosevelt's adviser (and Harvard University president) J. B. Conant in a phone call thus: "The Italian navigator [i.e., Fermi] has landed in the New World," said Compton. "How were the natives?" asked Conant. "Very friendly," was Compton's reply. (b) The only photograph of CP-1 known to exist, taken during addition of 19th layer of graphite. Alternate layers of graphite, containing uranium metal and/or uranium oxide, were separated by layers of solid-graphite blocks. Layer 18, almost covered, contained uranium oxide. (c) Enrico Fermi, leader of the group of scientists who succeeded in initiating the first man-made nuclear chain reaction, on December 2, 1942. [*(a) and (b) American Institute of Physics, Emilio Segrè Visual Archives; courtesy of Argonne National Laboratory, University of Chicago. (c) Courtesy of Argonne National Laboratory.*]

TABLE 12-1 Properties of selected nuclei as moderators		
Nucleus	σ (n, γ) barns	Number of collisions to thermalize
^{1}H	0.333	18
^{2}H	0.51×10^{-3}	25
^{4}He	0	43
^{12}C	3.5×10^{-3}	110
^{238}U	2.75	2200

approximate number of collisions needed to reduce 1-MeV neutrons to thermal energy for a few nuclei.

Reactors using ordinary water as a moderator cannot easily achieve $k = 1$ using natural uranium as a fuel for a combination of reasons. First, although the number of neutrons emitted per fission is 2.4 (equal to the maximum value of k), we have noted that some of these are lost by escaping from the reactor or being absorbed in nonfission reactions. Recalling from Section 12-1 that the total cross section is the sum of the partial cross sections and recognizing that the ratio of the cross section for a particular reaction (Equation 12-5) and the total cross section is the relative probability of that reaction's occurring, then the relative probability that a thermal neutron will cause a fission reaction is given by $\sigma_f/(\sigma_f + \sigma_a)$, where σ_f is the partial cross section for fission and σ_a is the partial cross section for all other kinds of absorption of thermal neutrons. The latter are mainly (n, γ) reactions. Thus we can write k as

$$k = 2.4 \frac{\sigma_f}{\sigma_f + \sigma_a} \qquad \textbf{12-11}$$

The values of σ_f and σ_a for natural uranium are computed from the isotopic abundances above and the cross sections for each isotope. The fission cross section for ^{235}U is 584 b for thermal neutrons, while that for ^{238}U is zero. The cross sections for the (n, γ) reactions are 97 b for ^{235}U and 2.75 b for ^{238}U. (See Table 12-1 and Figure 12-14.) The values of σ_f and σ_a are then given by

$$\sigma_f = \frac{0.72}{100} \sigma_f(^{235}\text{U}) + \frac{99.28}{100} \sigma_f(^{238}\text{U}) = 4.20 + 0 = 4.20 \text{ b}$$

$$\sigma_a = \frac{0.72}{100} \sigma_a(^{235}\text{U}) + \frac{99.28}{100} \sigma_a(^{238}\text{U}) = 0.70 + 2.73 = 3.43 \text{ b}$$

Therefore, the largest possible value of k that we can expect from natural uranium used as a reactor fuel is, from Equation 12-11,

$$k = 2.4 \frac{\sigma_f}{\sigma_f + \sigma_a} = 2.4 \frac{4.20}{4.20 + 3.43} = 1.32$$

Fig. 12-15 Schematic diagram of the *nuclear fuel cycle* for uranium-fueled light-water reactors. The UF$_6$ conversion plant converts solid U$_3$O$_8$, called *yellowcake* because of its color, into gaseous UF$_6$ for the enrichment facility. ^{235}UF$_6$ is separated from ^{238}UF$_6$ based on the fact that both molecules have the same average kinetic energy, $(3/2)kT$, and hence different diffusion rates due to their slightly different masses. The complete cycle includes the reprocessing facility and the repository for highly radioactive fission products.

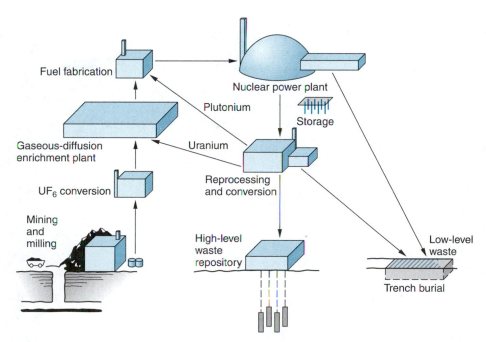

This value is already quite close to 1.0, so if loss of neutrons by leakage from the reactor or by absorption in the moderator is significant, the value of k may easily be less than 1.0. Because of the relatively large neutron capture cross section for the hydrogen nucleus (see Table 12-1), reactors using ordinary water as a moderator and natural uranium as a fuel have difficulty reaching $k = 1$. By enriching the uranium fuel in ^{235}U, that is, by increasing the ^{235}U content from 0.7 percent to, for example, 3 percent, the value of k computed from Equation 12-11 becomes 1.82, sufficient to make $k = 1$ attainable in operation. (Figure 12-15 shows where the enrichment process fits into the uranium fuel cycle.) Natural uranium can be used if heavy water (D$_2$O) is used instead of ordinary (light) water (H$_2$O) as the moderator. This is possible because the cross section of deuterium for the (n, γ) reaction for thermal neutrons is much smaller than that of ^{1}H. Although heavy water is expensive, most Canadian reactors use it for a moderator to avoid the cost of constructing uranium enrichment facilities and to help mitigate the problem of spent-fuel storage.[7] Table 12-2 lists the cross sections for fission by thermal neutrons and the critical energies for several nuclei.

EXAMPLE 12-6 **Thermal Neutron Fission of ^{239}Pu and ^{233}Pa** Determine the excitation energies of ^{239}Pu and ^{233}Pa when each absorbs a thermal neutron. Compare the results with the critical energies for fission and comment on the observed fission cross sections in Table 12-2.

Solution
The excitation energy for ^{239}Pu is given by

$$E = [(M(^{239}\text{Pu}) + m_n) - M(^{240}\text{Pu})]c^2$$
$$= [(239.052157 + 1.008665)\,\text{u} - 240.053808\,\text{u}]c^2$$
$$= (0.007014\,\text{u})c^2 \times 931.5\,\text{MeV/u} \cdot c^2$$
$$= 6.53\,\text{MeV}$$

This is larger than the critical energy for fission in Table 12-2 by 0.53 MeV, so we expect ^{239}Pu to have a significant thermal neutron fission cross section, as it does.

A corresponding calculation for ^{233}Pa yields an excitation energy of 5.22 MeV, well below the critical energy for fission of 7.1 MeV given in Table 12-2. The observed low cross section of ^{233}Pa for fission by thermal neutrons is in agreement with that result.

Figure 12-16 shows some of the features of a pressurized-water reactor commonly used in the United States to generate electricity. Fission in the core heats the water in the primary loop, which is closed, to a high temperature. This water, which also serves as the moderator, is under high pressure to prevent it from boiling. The hot water is pumped to a heat exchanger, where it heats the water in the secondary loop and converts it to steam, which is then used to drive the turbines that produce electrical power. Note that the isolation of the water in the secondary loop from that in the primary loop prevents its contamination by the radioactive nuclei in the reactor core.

The ability to control the reproduction factor k is important if a power reactor is to operate with any degree of safety. There are both natural negative feedback mechanisms and mechanical methods of control. If k is greater than 1 and the reaction rate

TABLE 12-2 Thermal neutron fission cross sections for selected nuclei

Nuclide	Cross section (barns)	Critical energy for $A + 1$ (MeV)
^{229}Th	30	8.3
^{230}Th	$<10^{-3}$	8.3
^{230}Pa	1500	7.6
^{233}Pa	$<10^{-1}$	7.1
^{233}U	531	6.5
^{234}U	$<5 \times 10^{-3}$	6.5
^{235}U	584	6.2
^{238}U	2.7×10^{-6}	5.9
^{236}Np	3000	5.9
^{238}Np	17	6.0
^{239}Pu	742	6.0
^{240}Pu	$<8 \times 10^{-2}$	6.3
^{241}Am	3.2	6.5
^{244}Am	2200	6.0
^{244}Cm	1	6.3
^{245}Cm	2000	5.9

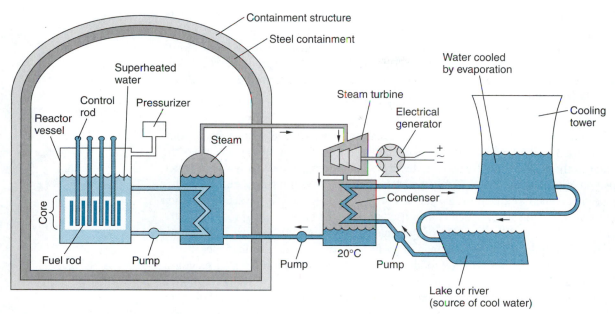

Fig. 12-16 Simplified drawing of a pressurized-water reactor (PWR). The water in contact with the reactor core serves as both the moderator and the heat-transfer material. It is isolated from the water used to produce the steam that drives the turbines. Many features, such as the backup cooling mechanisms, are not shown here. A second type of power reactor, not shown here, is the boiling-water reactor (BWR). In this system steam produced from boiling water in the core is circulated directly to the turbine without using the isolation loop.

increases, the temperature of the reactor increases. If water is used as a moderator its density decreases with increasing temperature, and it becomes a less effective moderator. A second important method is the use of control rods made of a material, such as cadmium, which has a very large neutron capture cross section. When a reactor is started, the control rods are inserted, so that k is less than 1. As they are gradually withdrawn from the reactor, the neutron capture decreases and k increases to 1. If k becomes greater than 1, the rods are again inserted.

Control of the reaction rate of a nuclear reactor with mechanical control rods is possible only because some of the neutrons emitted in the fission process are delayed and because the time needed for a neutron to slow from 1 or 2 MeV to thermal energy and to diffuse through the fuel is of the order of a millisecond. (The number of neutrons available for fission is determined by a time constant consisting of the thermalization time, about a microsecond, and the diffusion time, about a millisecond.) If all the neutrons emitted in fission were prompt neutrons, i.e., emitted immediately in the fission process, mechanical control would not be possible because statistical fluctuations in the number of prompt neutrons would cause the reactor to run out of control before the rods could be inserted. However, about 0.65 percent of the neutrons emitted are delayed by an average time of about 14 seconds, and it is these neutrons that make control of the reactor possible. These neutrons are emitted not in the fission process itself, but in the decay of the fission fragments. A typical decay is

$$^{87}\text{Br} \longrightarrow {}^{87}\text{Kr*} + \beta^- + \bar{\nu}$$
$$\downarrow$$
$$^{87}\text{Kr*} \longrightarrow {}^{86}\text{Kr} + n$$

The pressure vessel containing the fuel core composed of 14 tons of natural uranium and 165 pounds of highly enriched uranium is shown being lowered into the world's first full-scale nuclear power plant at Shippingport, Pennsylvania, on October 5, 1957. The reactor was built by Westinghouse (now Siemans) for the Duquesne Light Company. Small in comparison with reactors currently operating, the 90-MWe unit was shut down in 1982 and subsequently became the first commercial nuclear plant to be dismantled. The pressure vessel, now packed with concrete, is in storage at the federal nuclear waste facility in Hanford, Washington. [*American Institute of Physics, Emilio Segrè Visual Archives; courtesy of Westinghouse.*]

In the decay of ^{87}Br, which has a 56-s half-life, the excitation energy of the ^{87}Kr* nucleus happens to exceed the neutron separation energy and a neutron is emitted. This neutron is thus delayed by 56 seconds on the average. The effect of the delayed neutrons can be seen in the following examples.

EXAMPLE 12-7 **Fission Rate Doubling Time** If the average time between fission generations (the time it takes for a neutron emitted in one fission to cause another) is 1 ms = 0.001 s and the reproduction factor is 1.001, how long will it take for the reaction rate to double?

Solution

1. Since the initial reaction rate $R(0)$ times k is the reaction rate one generation later, then the reaction rate after N generations $R(N)$ is given by:

$$R(N) = R(0) \, k^N$$

2. For the reaction rate to double, $R(N) = 2R(0)$:

$$2R(0) = R(0) \, k^N$$

or

$$2 = (1.001)^N$$

3.   Solving this for the number of generations N:

$$N \ln (1.001) = \ln 2$$

$$N = \frac{\ln 2}{\ln (1.001)} = 693 \approx 700$$

Remarks: *Thus it takes about 700 generations for the reaction rate to double. The time for 700 generations is 700(0.001 s) = 0.70 s. This is not enough time for response by the mechanical control system that inserts the control rods.*

EXAMPLE 12-8 **Average Generation Time** Assuming that 0.65 percent of the neutrons emitted are delayed by 14 s, find the average generation time and the doubling time if $k = 1.001$.

Solution

Since 99.35 percent of the generation times are 0.001 s and 0.65 percent are 14 s, the average generation time is

$$t_{av} = 0.9935(0.001 \text{ s}) + 0.0065(14 \text{ s}) = 0.092 \text{ s}$$

Note that these few delayed neutrons increase the generation time by nearly 100-fold. The time for 700 generations is

$$700(0.092 \text{ s}) = 64.4 \text{ s}$$

This is plenty of time for the mechanical insertion of control rods.

More

Safety Issues of Fission Reactors have been the focus of intense public debate since the first major reactor accident occurred in 1957. The matters in question, which extend well beyond the safe operation of nuclear electric generating stations, are outlined on the home page: www.whfreeman.com/modphysics4e

Breeder Reactors   Because the small fraction of ^{235}U in natural uranium limits the economically recoverable supply of uranium and because of the limited capacity of enrichment facilities, reactors based upon the fission of ^{235}U cannot be expected to meet long-term energy needs. A possible alternative is the *breeder reactor*, a type of reactor that has the potential for producing more fissile fuel than it consumes. When the relatively plentiful but essentially nonfissile ^{238}U captures a neutron, the result is an (n,γ) reaction producing ^{239}U, which β^- decays (with a half-life of 23.5 minutes) to ^{239}Np, which in turn decays by β^- emission (with a half-life of 2.35 days) to the fissile nuclide ^{239}Pu:

$$^{238}U + n \longrightarrow {}^{239}U^* \longrightarrow {}^{239}U + \gamma$$
$$\downarrow$$
$$^{239}U \longrightarrow {}^{239}Np + \beta^- + \bar{\nu} \qquad \textbf{12-12}$$
$$\downarrow$$
$$^{239}Np \longrightarrow {}^{239}Pu + \beta^- + \bar{\nu}$$

Since ^{239}Pu fissions with fast neutrons in addition to slow neutrons, a *fast breeder reactor* needs no moderator. A further advantage is that the average yield of neutrons per absorbed neutron (that is, the maximum value of k) for ^{239}Pu is 2.7 for a neutron energy of 1 MeV. Thus, a reactor initially fueled with a mixture of ^{238}U and ^{239}Pu needs only one of the 2.7 neutrons to sustain the chain reaction and will breed as much fuel as it uses or more if one or more of the neutrons emitted in the fission of ^{239}Pu is captured by ^{238}U. Practical studies indicate that a typical fast breeder reactor can be expected to double its fuel supply in 7 to 10 years.

There are three major safety problems with fast breeder reactors which have limited their commercial use. The fraction of delayed neutrons is only 0.3 percent for the fission of ^{239}Pu, so the time between generations is much less than for ordinary reactors. Mechanical control is therefore much more difficult. Also, since the operating temperature of a breeder reactor is relatively high and a moderator is not desired, a heat-transfer material such as liquid sodium metal is used rather than water (which is the moderator as well as the heat-transfer material in an ordinary ^{235}U-fueled reactor). If the temperature of the reactor increases, the resulting decrease in the density of the heat-transfer material leads to positive feedback since it will absorb fewer neutrons than before, making more available for fission, which further increases the temperature, and so on. As it happens, there is another temperature-dependent process at work, particularly in fast breeder reactors, that helps mitigate this problem. As the temperature increases, the resonances for the (n,γ) reaction broaden due to Doppler effect, increasing the number of neutrons absorbed and decreasing the number available for producing fission reactions. This is a very important intrinsic safety feature. The third problem concerns the loss of the reactor coolant. While this is also a serious problem for the water-moderated, thermal-neutron reactors discussed earlier, as we describe in the section "Safety Issues of Fission Reactors" on the home page, it is particularly so for fast breeder reactors since the coolant is not serving as a moderator and its loss does not shut down the fission reactions. Because of these and other safety considerations and new, lower projections of future electricity demand, commercial breeder reactors are not yet in use in the United States.[8] There are, however, several in operation in France, Great Britain, and Russia.

There is also the potential for constructing a breeder reactor utilizing thermal-neutron fissions. It is based on ^{232}Th, the only isotope of thorium that occurs naturally, and employs ^{233}U as the fissile nuclide. There is somewhat more thorium than uranium in Earth's crust, so the energy ultimately available is essentially doubled if both ^{238}U and ^{232}Th are used in breeder reactors. ^{233}U does not occur in nature. It is produced as follows:

$$^{232}Th + n \longrightarrow {}^{233}Th^* \longrightarrow {}^{233}Th + \gamma$$
$$\downarrow$$
$$^{233}Th \longrightarrow {}^{233}Pa + \beta^- + \bar{\nu} \qquad \textbf{12-13}$$
$$\downarrow$$
$$^{233}U + \beta^- + \bar{\nu}$$

The half-life of ^{233}Th is 22.3 min and that of ^{233}Pa is 27.0 days. The cross section of ^{233}U for fission by thermal neutrons is only slightly smaller than that of ^{235}U, but it produces more neutrons per fission, 2.5 compared with 2.4. The difference may not seem significant, but it is sufficient to allow ^{233}U to sustain a chain reaction and provide a neutron to initiate the breeding reaction of Equation 12-13. Neither ^{235}U nor ^{239}Pu produces enough neutrons on thermal neutron–induced fission to breed replacement or excess fissile nuclei. Thus, ^{233}U is a better thermal reactor fuel than ^{235}U and is much better than ^{239}Pu.

Fusion   The production of power from the fusion of light nuclei has the potential for future use because of the relative abundance of the fuel and the absence of some of the hazards presented by fission reactors. In fusion, two light nuclei such as deuterium (^{2}H) and tritium (^{3}H) fuse together to form a heavier nucleus. A typical fusion reaction is

$$^2\text{H} + {}^3\text{H} \longrightarrow {}^4\text{He} + n + 17.6\,\text{MeV} \qquad \textbf{12-14}$$

As was shown in Example 12-4, the energy released in this fusion reaction is (17.6 MeV)/(5 nucleons) = 3.52 MeV per nucleon, or about 3.5 times as great as the 1 MeV per nucleon released in fission. The technology necessary to make fusion a practical source of energy has not yet been developed. We will consider the fusion reaction of Equation 12-14; other reactions present similar problems.

Because of the Coulomb repulsion between the ^{2}H and ^{3}H nuclei, very large kinetic energies, of the order of 1 MeV, are needed to get the nuclei close enough together for the attractive nuclear forces to become effective and cause fusion. Such energies can be obtained in an accelerator, but since the scattering of one nucleus by the other is much more probable than fusion, the bombardment of one nucleus by the other in an accelerator requires the input of more energy than is recovered. Therefore, to obtain energy from fusion, the particles must be heated to a temperature great enough for the fusion reaction to occur as the result of random thermal collisions. Because a significant number of particles have kinetic energies greater than the mean kinetic energy $(3/2)kT$ and because some particles can tunnel through the Coulomb barrier, a temperature T corresponding to $kT \approx 10$ keV is adequate to ensure that a reasonable number of fusion reactions will occur if the density of particles is sufficiently high. The temperature corresponding to $kT = 10$ keV is of the order of 10^8 K. Such temperatures occur in the interiors of stars, where such reactions are common. At these temperatures, a gas consists of positive ions and negative electrons called a *plasma*. One of the problems arising in attempts to produce controlled fusion reactions is that of confining the plasma long enough for the reactions to take place. In the interior of the sun the plasma in confined by the enormous gravitational field of the sun. In a laboratory on Earth, confinement is a difficult problem.

The energy required to heat a plasma is proportional to the density of its ions n, whereas the fusion rate is proportional to n^2, the square of the density (since the rate is the product of the Maxwell energy distribution and the fusion cross section, both of which are proportional to n). If τ is the confinement time, the output energy is thus proportional to $n^2\tau$. If the output energy is to exceed the input energy, we must have

$$C_1 n^2 \tau > C_2 n$$

where C_1 and C_2 are constants. In 1957, the British physicist J. D. Lawson evaluated these constants from estimates of the efficiencies of various hypothetical fusion reactors and derived the following relation between density and confinement time, known as *Lawson's criterion*:

$$n\tau > 10^{20}\,\text{s} \cdot \text{particles/m}^3 \qquad\qquad \textbf{12-15}$$

If Lawson's criterion is met and the thermal energy of the ions is great enough ($kT \approx$ 10 keV), the energy released by a fusion reactor will just equal the energy input; that is, the reactor will just break even. For the reactor to be practical, much more energy must be released.

Two schemes for achieving Lawson's criterion are currently under investigation. In one scheme, *magnetic confinement,* a magnetic field is used to confine the plasma.[9] In the most common arrangement, first developed in Russia and called the *tokamak,* the plasma is confined in a large toroid. The magnetic field is a combination of the doughnut-shaped magnetic field due to the current in the windings of the

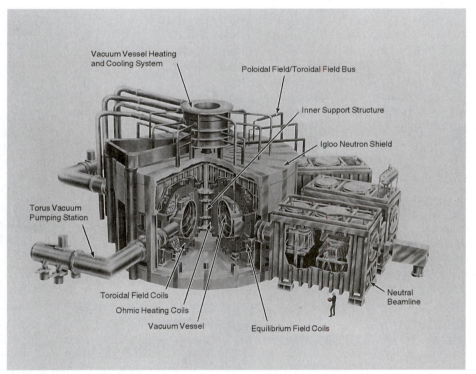

Schematic of the tokamak fusion test reactor (TFTR). The toroidal coils, encircling the 7.7-m-diameter doughnut-shaped vacuum vessel, are designed to conduct current for 3-s pulses, separated by waiting times of 5 min. Pulses peak at 73,000 A, producing a magnetic field of 5.2 T. This field is the principal means of confining the deuterium-tritium plasma that circulates within the vacuum vessel. Current for the pulses is delivered by converting the rotational energy of two 600-ton flywheels. Sets of poloidal coils, perpendicular to the toroidal coils, carry an oscillating current that generates a current through the confined plasma itself, heating it ohmically. Additional poloidal fields help stabilize the confined plasma. Between four and six neutral-beam injection systems (only one of which is shown in the schematic) are used to inject high-energy deuterium atoms into the deuterium-tritium plasma, heating it beyond what could be obtained ohmically—ultimately to the point of fusion. [*Courtesy of Plasma Physics Laboratory, Princeton University.*]

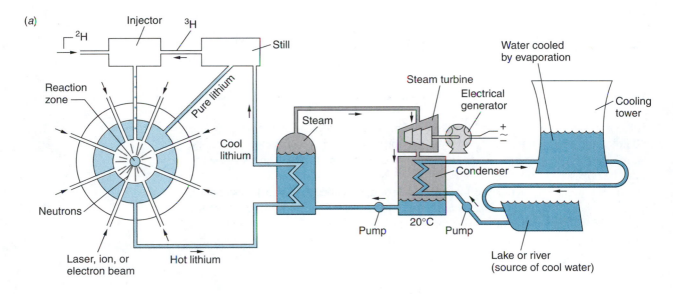

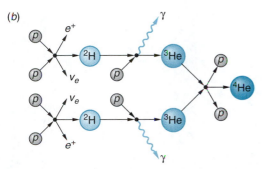

Fig. 12-17 (*a*) Schematic diagram of a possible fusion reactor using inertial confinement and the $^2\text{H} + {}^3\text{H} \rightarrow {}^4\text{He} + n$ reaction. This reaction produces 17.6 MeV per fusion, and the neutron produced reacts with either ^6Li (slow neutron) or ^7Li (fast neutron) to produce the ^3H needed for the reaction. The latter reaction produces an additional slow neutron; thus, every two neutrons produced by fusion have the potential for generating three ^3H nuclei; that is, this system may also be a tritium breeder. (*b*) The proton-proton reaction is the primary source of the sun's energy. The neutrino produced in the initial reaction escapes from the core. The net energy produced per cycle is about 26.7 MeV.

toroid and the self-field due to the current of the circulating plasma. The breakeven point has been achieved recently using magnetic confinement, but we are still a long way from building a practical fusion reactor.

In a second scheme, called *inertial confinement,* a pellet of frozen-solid deuterium and tritium is bombarded from all sides by intense pulsed laser beams of energies of the order of 10^6 J lasting about 10^{-8} s. (Intense ion and electron beams are also used.) Computer simulation studies indicate the momentum absorbed by the hydrogen nuclei from the beams should compress the pellet to about 10^4 times its normal density and heat it to a temperature greater than 10^8 K. This should produce about 10^6 J of fusion energy in 10^{-10} s, which is so brief that confinement is achieved by inertia alone. (See Figure 12-17.) In theory, after this burst of fusion energy is radiated away from the site to be absorbed by a heat-transfer fluid, such as liquid lithium, another pellet is injected at the confluence of the beams and the process repeats.

Because the breakeven point has only recently been just barely achieved in magnetic confinement fusion, and because the building of a fusion reactor involves many practical problems that have not yet been solved, including, for example, activation of the reactor walls, the availability of fusion to meet world energy needs is not

expected for several decades. However, fusion holds great promise as an energy source for the future.

EXAMPLE 12-9 **Fusion Temperature for $^1H + {}^1H \rightarrow {}^2H + e^+ + \nu$** The fusion of two protons requires that two particles be separated by no more than about 10^{-14} m in order for the attractive force of the nuclear potential to overcome the repulsive force of the Coulomb potential. Compute (*a*) the minimum temperature of a hydrogen plasma that will enable a proton with the average energy of those in the plasma to overcome the Coulomb barrier and (*b*) the energy released in the fusion.

Solution

(*a*) The height of the potential energy barrier seen by the protons is given by

$$U = \frac{1}{4\pi\epsilon_0} \frac{e^2}{r} = \frac{(9 \times 10^9 \text{ N} \cdot \text{m}^2/\text{C}^2)(1.60 \times 10^{-19} \text{ C}^2)}{3.0 \times 10^{-15} \text{ m}}$$

$$U = 7.76 \times 10^{-14} \text{ J} = 0.48 \text{ MeV}$$

In order to overcome this barrier the average energy of the protons in the plasma, $(3/2)kT$, must equal at least half this amount; that is, each of the two fusing protons must have 3.84×10^{-14} J.

$$(3/2)kT = 3.84 \times 10^{-14} \text{ J}$$

where k is Boltzmann's constant. Thus,

$$T = \frac{2 \times 3.84 \times 10^{-14} \text{ J}}{3 \times 1.38 \times 10^{-23} \text{ J/K}} = 1.9 \times 10^9 \text{ K}$$

(*b*) The energy released, equal to the Q value of the fusion reaction, is

$$Q = 2m(^1H) - m(^2H) - 2m_ec^2$$
$$= 2 \times 1.007825 \text{ u} - 2.014102 \text{ u} - 0.001097 \text{ u}$$
$$= 0.000451 \text{ u} \times 931.5 \text{ MeV}/c^2 = 0.42 \text{ MeV}$$

where the atomic mass values are given in Appendix A. Thus, the energy release per $^1H + {}^1H$ fusion is 0.42 MeV. That of the $^2H + {}^3H$ fusion illustrated in Figure 12-17a is 17.6 MeV, which explains why the latter reaction is used in controlled fusion experiments.

The Source of the Sun's Energy   The present energy content of the sun as calculated from thermodynamics would be radiated away in about 3×10^7 years. Since life has existed on Earth for approximately 100 times that long, we can conclude that the sun has been radiating at close to its present rate for at least 3×10^9 years. Therefore, the sun must have a supply of energy far larger than that represented by the hot plasma and the observed radiation field. The source of the sun's energy is nuclear fusion. Current theory proposes that, as the young sun contracted, its temperature rose. Eventually the temperature of the core reached about 1.5×10^7 K, which is high enough for the hydrogen nuclei (protons) in the plasma to have sufficient energy

(a)

(b)

(a) The Nova inertial confinement fusion reactor's target chamber, an aluminum sphere approximately 5 m in diameter, inside which 10 beams from the world's most powerful laser converge onto a hydrogen-containing pellet 0.5 mm in diameter. The resulting fusion reaction is visible as a tiny star (b), lasting 10^{-10} s, releasing 10^{13} neutrons. [(*a*) *and* (*b*) *Courtesy of Lawrence Livermore National Laboratory, U.S. Department of Energy.*]

on the average (about 1 keV) to fuse into helium nuclei. This reaction, actually a chain of reactions, was first proposed by H. A. Bethe and is referred to as the *proton-proton cycle*. The first reaction in the chain is:

$$^1\text{H} + {}^1\text{H} \longrightarrow {}^2\text{H} + e^+ + \nu_e + 0.42 \text{ MeV}$$

The probability for this reaction is very low except for those protons in the high-energy tail of the Maxwell-Boltzmann distribution. This sets a limit on the rate at which the sun can produce energy and thus ensures a long lifetime for the sun and similar stars. This limit is sometimes called the "bottleneck" of the solar

fusion cycle. Once ^{2}H (deuterium) is formed, the following reaction becomes very probable:

$$^2\text{H} + {}^1\text{H} \longrightarrow {}^3\text{He} + \gamma + 5.49 \text{ MeV}$$

It is followed by:

$$^3\text{He} + {}^3\text{He} \longrightarrow {}^4\text{He} + 2{}^1\text{H} + \gamma + 12.86 \text{ MeV}$$

This process by which hydrogen nuclei are "burned" to helium nuclei is shown schematically in Figure 12-17b. There are other possible reactions for converting ^{3}He to ^{4}He, all of which have the same net Q value. Their rates, however, differ depending on the composition and temperature of the interior.

The neutrinos produced in the proton-proton cycle escape from the core, providing our only means for direct observation of the sun's interior. The measured value of the total power radiated by the sun and the known total Q value of the proton-proton cycle enable a calculation of the total reaction rate. In addition, the alternative reactions for ^{4}He have different neutrino energy spectra, thus providing a way of determining the relative contributions of each reaction and gaining information about the composition and temperature of the core. However, the measured rate at which solar neutrinos arrive at Earth is less than half that predicted by theoretical calculations based on the standard solar model. This discrepancy is referred to as the *solar neutrino problem*. Solving this problem is the focus of a major international research effort. Recent results from the Sudbury (Canada) and Super-Kamiokande (Japan) neutrino observatories indicate that neutrinos have a small mass and may transform, or oscillate, from one type to another. (See Section 13-5.)

QUESTIONS

5. Why is a moderator needed in an ordinary nuclear fission reactor?

6. Explain why water is more effective than lead in slowing down fast neutrons.

7. What happens to the neutrons produced in fission that do not produce another fission?

8. What is the advantage of a breeder reactor over an ordinary one? What are the disadvantages?

9. Why does fusion occur spontaneously in the sun but not on Earth?

10. Explain why the fission reaction stops if a light-water reactor suffers an accidental loss of coolant.

More

The *Interaction of Particles and Matter* is of central importance in understanding the biological effects of radiation, in the development and use of nuclear radiation detectors, and in protecting the environment from potential radiation hazards. This topic is discussed for charged particles, neutrons, and photons on the home page: www.whfreeman.com/modphysics4e See also Equations 12-16 through 12-26 here, as well as Figures 12-18 through 12-23 and Example 12-10.

12-3 Applications

Certainly among the most important of the applications of nuclear reactions and interactions have been those developed in the field of nuclear medicine, particularly in the area of diagnosis, but also including the treatment of cancer and certain other diseases. State-of-the-art detectors and computer-based data analysis have made critical contributions to these developments. Also important to a broad spectrum of disciplines ranging from art through chemistry and geology to zoology are the precision isotope-specific analytical techniques of *accelerator mass spectrometry* and *neutron activation analysis*. Anthropologists, archeologists, and geologists routinely rely on the decay properties of a number of radioisotopes to determine the age of artifacts and samples. Examples of these applications will be discussed briefly in this concluding section of the chapter.

Potential oil- and gas-bearing regions in exploratory oil wells are identified by lowering an intense source of neutrons (usually a mixture of ^{239}Pu and ^{9}Be or ^{241}Am and ^{9}Be) into the well along with a gamma-ray detector. The neutrons produce gamma rays via $X(n, \gamma)Y$ reactions in the surrounding rock. Analysis of the gamma-ray spectra identifies elements in the rock that are typical indicators of the presence of oil and natural gas.

Neutron Activation Analysis

This isotope-specific analytical method for elements is capable of very high sensitivity and accuracy. While some elements are more readily analyzed by activation analysis than others, it is particularly useful for the many elements that cannot be conveniently assayed by the more standard chemical methods of trace analysis. It has

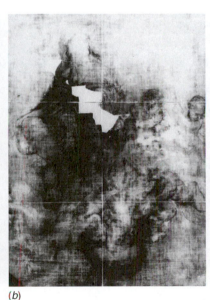
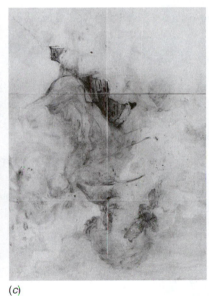

(a)   (b)   (c)

An application of neutron activation analysis. Hidden layers in paintings are analyzed by bombarding the painting with neutrons and observing the radiative emissions from nuclei that have captured a neutron. Different elements used in the painting have different half-lives. (*a*) Van Dyck's painting *Saint Rosalie Interceding for the Plague-Stricken of Palermo.* The black-and-white images in (*b*) and (*c*) were formed using a special film sensitive to electrons emitted by the radioactively decaying elements. Image (*b*), taken a few hours after the neutron irradiation, reveals the presence of manganese, found in umber, a dark earth pigment used for the painting's base layer. (Blank areas show where modern repairs, free of manganese, have been made.) The image in (*c*) was taken four days later, after the umber emissions had died away and when phosphorus, found in charcoal and boneblack, was the main radiating element. Upside down is revealed a sketch of Van Dyck himself. The self-portrait, executed in charcoal, had been overpainted by the artist. (See Problem 12-28.) [(*a*) *Courtesy of Metropolitan Museum of Art, New York City.* (*b*) *and* (*c*) *Courtesy of Paintings Conservation Department, Metropolitan Museum of Art, New York City.*]

a wide range of applications from identifying trace pollutants in the environment through semiconductor processing and materials science to the analysis and authentication of works of art.

The method consists of exposing the sample to be analyzed to a high flux of slow neutrons. Isotope $^A_Z M$ of the element of interest undergoes the reaction $^A_Z M$ (n, γ) $^{A+1}_Z M$, as described in Section 12-1, where $^{A+1}_Z M$ is radioactive. $^{A+1}_Z M$ can be identified by its half-life and the energy of its beta- and gamma-ray emissions. The activity $R(t)$ after the beginning of the neutron irradiation is given by

$$R(t) = \lambda N(t) = R_0(1 - e^{-\lambda t})$$
    12-27

where λ is the decay constant of $^{A+1}_Z M$ and R_0 is the constant production rate of that isotope. $R(t)$ is measured and R_0 is computed from Equation 12-5, since $R_0 = N_0 R$, where N_0 is the number of $^A_Z M$ nuclei in the sample. Thus,

$$R_0 = N_0 R = N_0 \sigma I$$
    12-28

where σ is the cross section for the reaction $^A_Z M$ (n, γ) $^{A+1}_Z M$ in cm^2 and I is the neutron flux in neutrons/s$\cdot cm^2$. Equation 12-27 can then be written

$$R(t) = N_0 \sigma I(1 - e^{-\lambda t})$$
    12-29

When the half-life is short enough, irradiation is usually continued to saturation, that is, until $R(t) = R(\infty) = N_0 \sigma I$. Table 12-3 gives saturation activities per μg for a few isotopes. The number of atoms of $^A_Z M$ in the sample is, at the saturation activity,

$$N_0 = \frac{R(\infty)}{\sigma I}$$

and the mass of $^A_Z M$ in the sample is

$$m(^A_Z M) = \frac{N_0 W}{N_A} = \frac{R(\infty) W}{N_A \sigma I}$$
    12-30

where W is the atomic weight of the element and N_A is Avogadro's number.

TABLE 12-3 Selected saturation activities $(I = 10^{12}$ neutrons/s$\cdot cm^2)$		
$^A_Z M$	$^{A+1}_Z M$	Saturation activity $R(\infty)$ decays/min$\cdot \mu g$
^{55}Mn	^{56}Mn	8.8×10^6
^{63}Cu	^{64}Cu	1.7×10^6
^{127}I	^{128}I	1.6×10^6
^{197}Au	^{198}Au	1.7×10^7

EXAMPLE 12-11 The "Gold" Chain After buying a chain advertised as 10 percent pure gold, the suspicious purchaser irradiates one 25-mg link in a constant neutron flux of 10^{10} neutrons/s·cm² for a time long enough for any gold activity to saturate. She then measures the activity of the link to be 7.5×10^4 decays/s with a detector whose efficiency is 12 percent. What is the percent by weight of gold in the link? (σ for ^{197}Au is 98.8 barns.)

Solution

Since the detector efficiency is 12 percent, the actual value of $R(\infty)$ is

$$R(\infty) = \frac{7.5 \times 10^4 \text{ decays/s}}{0.12} = 6.3 \times 10^5 \text{ decays/s}$$

From Equation 12-30 we can then compute

$$m(^{197}\text{Au}) = \frac{(6.3 \times 10^5 \text{ decays/s})(197 \text{ g/mol})}{(6.02 \times 10^{23} \text{ atoms/mol})(98.8 \times 10^{-24} \text{ cm}^2)(10^{10} \text{ neutrons/s/cm}^2)}$$

$$m(^{197}\text{Au}) = 2.1 \times 10^{-4} \text{ g}$$

The weight percent of gold in the link is then

$$\%\text{Au} = \left(\frac{2.1 \times 10^{-4} \text{ g}}{25 \times 10^{-3} \text{ g}}\right) \times 100 = 0.8\%$$

or less than 1/10 of the advertised amount.

Nuclear Magnetic Resonance

In Section 7-5, we saw that the energy levels of the atom were split in the presence of an external magnetic field (the Zeeman effect) because of the interaction of the atomic magnetic moment and the field. Since nuclei also have magnetic moments, the energy levels of nuclei are also split in the presence of a magnetic field. We can readily understand this by considering the simplest case, the hydrogen atom, for which the nucleus is a single proton.

The potential energy of a magnetic moment $\boldsymbol{\mu}$ in an external magnetic field $\mathbf{B}$ is given by

$$U = -\boldsymbol{\mu} \cdot \mathbf{B} \qquad \text{12-31}$$

The potential energy is lowest when the magnetic moment is aligned with the field and highest when it is in the opposite direction. Since the spin quantum number of the proton is 1/2, the proton's magnetic moment has two possible orientations in an external magnetic field: parallel to the field (spin up) or antiparallel to the field (spin down). The difference in energy of these two orientations (Figure 12-24) is

$$\Delta E = 2(\mu_z)_p B \qquad \text{12-32}$$

When hydrogen atoms are irradiated with photons of energy ΔE, some of the nuclei are induced to make transitions from the lower state to the upper state by resonance

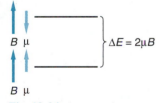

Fig. 12-24 A proton has two energy states in the presence of a magnetic field, corresponding to whether the magnetic moment of the proton is aligned parallel or antiparallel to the field.

absorption. These nuclei then decay back to the lower state, emitting photons of energy ΔE. The frequency of the photons absorbed and emitted is found from

$$hf = \Delta E = 2(\mu_z)_p B$$

In a magnetic field of 1 T, this energy is

$$\Delta E = 2(\mu_z)_p B$$
$$= 2(2.79 \, \mu_N)\left(\frac{3.15 \times 10^{-8} \, \text{eV/T}}{1 \, \mu_N}\right)(1 \, \text{T})$$
$$= 1.76 \times 10^{-7} \, \text{eV}$$

and the frequency of the photons is

$$f = \frac{\Delta E}{h} = \frac{1.76 \times 10^{-7} \, \text{eV}}{4.14 \times 10^{-15} \, \text{eV} \cdot \text{s}}$$
$$= 4.25 \times 10^{7} \, \text{Hz} = 42.5 \, \text{MHz}$$

This frequency is in the radio band of the electromagnetic spectrum, and the radiation is called *RF (radio-frequency) radiation.* The measurement of this resonance frequency for free protons can be used to determine the magnetic moment of the proton.

When a hydrogen atom is in a molecule, the magnetic field at the proton is the sum of the external magnetic field and the local magnetic field due to the electrons and nuclei of the surrounding material. Since the resonance frequency is proportional to the total magnetic field seen by the proton, a measurement of this frequency can give information about the internal magnetic field seen in the molecule. This is called *nuclear magnetic resonance.* It is a sensitive tool for probing the internal magnetic structure of materials.

Nuclear magnetic resonance is also used as an alternative to x rays or ultrasound for medical imaging, in which case it is called *magnetic resonance imaging* (MRI). A patient can be placed in a magnetic field (provided by superconducting magnets) that is constant in time but not in space. When the patient is irradiated by a broadband RF source, the resonance frequency of the absorbed and emitted RF photons is then dependent on the value of the magnetic field, which can be related to specific positions in the body of the patient. Since the energy of the photons is much less than the energy of molecular bonds and the intensity used is low enough so that it produces negligible heating, the RF photons produce little, if any, biological damage. Diagnosis with MRI requires no surgical procedure and is more sensitive than other methods in detecting tumors in soft tissue.

Computer-Assisted Tomography

Wilhelm Roentgen received the first physics Nobel Prize in 1901 for his discovery of x rays in 1895, an event which also marked the beginning of *radiography,* the use of radiation and particle beams to produce images that are otherwise inaccessible. For half a century x rays were the probing beam of medical imaging. Then in the late 1940s the introduction of radioisotopes into a patient's body made it possible for physicians to target particular organs and produce images that recorded their behavior, a technique now a part of the specialty of nuclear medicine. The isotopes used are typically relatively short-lived gamma emitters, since α and β particles have

Fig. 12-25 Schematic drawing of a scintillation crystal with a Pb collimator to define a focus, a gamma camera. As the detector is moved around the patient, the intensity of the gamma radiation yields information about the location and concentration of the source radioisotope in the body, which can be used by a computer to produce an image of the distribution. Actual gamma cameras incorporate collimators with hundreds or even thousands of tiny channels for the gamma rays to reach the crystal.

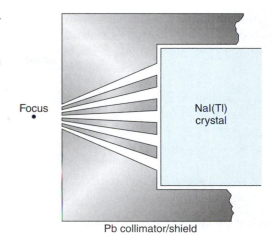

ranges in biological tissue that are too short to be useful. The detector normally employed is a collimated (to provide directional information) scintillation crystal viewed by a photomultiplier. (See Figure 12-25.) The image is then constructed by a computer from the output of the photomultiplier.

Just as with ordinary x-ray radiographs, the images formed by the gamma camera are two-dimensional projections of a three-dimensional distribution. Thus, radiographs provide no depth information, a very serious disadvantage. G. Hounsfield solved this problem in 1972 with the invention of the computer-assisted tomography (CT or CAT) scanner.[10] A fan-shaped x-ray beam collimated to a thickness of a few millimeters is rotated about the patient and the transmitted fan beam is recorded by an arc of detectors opposite the source, as illustrated in Figure 12-26. The measurements are then reconstructed into an image of a two-dimensional image (*not* a projection) of a transverse slice of the body—a tomograph. By simultaneously making a series of two-dimensional projections with a gamma camera and combining the results with the CT scan, the distribution of the trace radioisotopes in two-dimensional transverse sections can be constructed. The combination system is called *single photon emission computer tomography,* or SPECT.

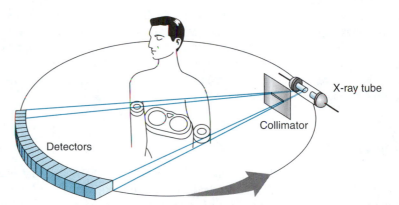

Fig. 12-26 Sections of the patient's body transverse to the long axis are imaged by the CT scanner. The fan-shaped x-ray beam, a few millimeters thick, and the bank of detectors, typically proportional or wire counters, rotate about the long axis to produce each complete image. The patient is moved slowly along the axis, while the scanner produces successive images, their sum constituting a full three-dimensional composite.

It had been recognized early on that the collimators that were essential to the operation of CT scanners and gamma cameras placed a serious restriction on their sensitivity. It was also recognized that the collimators could be eliminated and the sensitivity significantly enhanced if the trace radioisotope employed was a positron emitter. The reason is that the positron is stopped within a few millimeters in the tissue and its subsequent annihilation results in two 0.511-MeV photons emitted in opposite directions. Detection of the photons by counters 180° apart whose outputs are analyzed by a time-of-flight coincidence spectrometer yields a precise location for the decay. (See Figure 12-27.) However, this idea did not find its way into a useful diagnostic scanner until the mid-1980s, because of the absence of detectors with good efficiency for the 0.511-MeV photons and small enough to localize the incident photons to within a millimeter or so. This problem was solved with the invention by C. Thompson and his co-workers of the bismuth germanate (BGO) crystal. Currently, nearly all commercial positron emission tomography (PET) scanners rely on detector rings made of BGO crystals, as illustrated in Figure 12-27a. A PET scan of brain activity made with BGO detectors is shown in Figure 12-27b. The availability of PET scans is limited to locations in the proximity of cyclotron facilities, because most biologically useful positron emitters, those that readily participate in reactions in the body, are ^{11}C, ^{13}N, ^{15}O, and ^{18}F. They have short half-lives of 20 min, 10 min, 2 min, and 110 min, respectively, and supplies must be regularly replenished by nuclear reactions.

Technetium ($Z = 43$) does not occur in nature. Predicted by Moseley in 1914 and first produced by Segrè in 1937, ^{99}Tc is by far the most widely used radioisotope in nuclear medicine research and diagnosis. Its decay produces a 140-keV gamma ray easily detected by scintillation and germanium detectors.

(a)

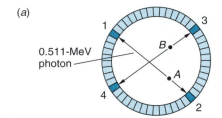

(b)

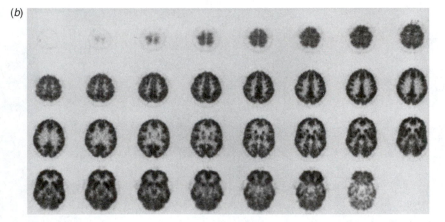

Fig. 12-27 (a) Nuclei emit positrons at *A* and *B*. The oppositely directed 0.511-MeV photons from each annihilation are detected by a pair of BGO crystal detectors in the annular ring around the subject (not shown). Electronic coincidence circuits establish the line along which each pair of photons traveled. (b) The pattern of coincidence measurements is used by a computer to construct an image of the distribution of the radioisotope in the plane of the detector ring. This sequence of PET scans shows the utilization of glucose in the brain, traced by 7 mCi of a positron emitter. The sequence begins in the upper left. [*Courtesy of D. W. Townsend, Division of Nuclear Medicine, University Hospital of Geneva, Geneva, Switzerland.*]

Radioactive Dating

Radioactivity occurs in nature as a result of (1) decays within the three decay chains originating with long-lived α emitters discussed in Section 11-4, (2) the existence of isolated long-lived primordial radioisotopes such as ^{40}K ($t_{1/2} = 1.25 \times 10^9$ y), and (3) the production of isolated radioisotopes due to reactions between cosmic ray protons and neutrons and nuclei in the atmosphere. Each of these provides a means by which the age of materials, such as rocks and archeological artifacts, can be measured. As one might guess, the very long-lived isotopes, such as ^{40}K and ^{232}Th ($t_{1/2} = 1.24 \times 10^{10}$ y), are used in determining the ages of "old" rocks, while shorter-lived isotopes are employed in determining the ages of "younger" rocks, other inorganic materials, and archeological samples containing carbon, such as charcoal.

The general technique used in determining the age of a sample by radioactive dating is to measure the present abundance ratio of two isotopes, at least one of which is either radioactive or the stable end product of a radioactive decay, relative to the abundance ratio that is known (or assumed) to have existed at the time when the material was formed. Table 12-4 lists the present isotopic abundances of a few of the naturally occurring isolated radioisotopes used in dating.

^{14}C Dating   An important example, used in dating archeological materials containing carbon such as bone and charcoal, measures the abundance ratio $^{14}C/^{12}C$. Radioactive ^{14}C is continuously produced in the atmosphere by the reaction $^{14}N(n, p)^{14}C$. The neutrons are produced by cosmic rays. ^{14}C is a β^- emitter that decays back to ^{14}N via the reaction

$$^{14}C \longrightarrow {}^{14}N + \beta^- + \bar{\nu}_e \qquad \textbf{12-33}$$

with $t_{1/2} = 5730$ years.[11]

"Group of Stags" from the Lascaux Caves in France. Prehistoric paintings such as this are ^{14}C-dated, the oldest found so far having been painted 33,000 to 38,000 B.C., depending on the $^{14}C/^{12}C$ ratio used for that period. [*Art Resource.*]

TABLE 12-4 Selected naturally occurring isolated radioactive nuclides

Nuclide	$t_{1/2}$ (y)	Abundance (%)	Daughter
^{14}C	5730	1.35×10^{-10}	^{14}N
^{40}K	1.25×10^9	0.0117	^{40}A
^{87}Rb	4.88×10^{10}	27.83	^{87}Sr
^{147}Sm	1.06×10^{11}	15.0	^{143}Nd
^{176}Lu	3.59×10^{10}	2.59	^{176}Hf
^{187}Re	4.30×10^{10}	62.60	^{187}Os

The chemical behavior of ^{14}C atoms is the same as that of ordinary ^{12}C atoms. For example, atoms with ^{14}C nuclei combine with oxygen to form CO_2 molecules. Since living organisms continually exchange CO_2 with the atmosphere, the ratio of ^{14}C to ^{12}C in a living organism is the same as the equilibrium ratio in the atmosphere, which is presently about 1.35×10^{-12}. When an organism dies, it no longer absorbs ^{14}C from the atmosphere. The ratio ^{14}C/^{12}C in a dead sample continually decreases due to the radioactive decay of ^{14}C. A measurement of the decay rate per gram of carbon thus allows the calculation of the time of death of the organism, as illustrated by Example 12-13.

EXAMPLE 12-12 ^{14}C Decay Rate in Living Organisms Calculate the decay rate of ^{14}C per gram of carbon in a living organism, assuming the ratio ^{14}C/^{12}C $= 1.35 \times 10^{-12}$. The half-life of ^{14}C is 5730 years.

Solution

1. Combining Equation 11-19 with Equation 11-22, the decay rate R can be written in terms of the half-life and the number of radioactive atoms N as:

$$R = -\frac{dN}{dt} = \lambda N = \frac{0.693}{t_{1/2}}N$$

2. N is computed from the ^{14}C/^{12}C ratio by first computing the number of ^{12}C in a unit mass, e.g., in 1 g:

$$N_{12_C} = \frac{N_A}{M} = \frac{6.02 \times 10^{23} \text{ atoms/mol}}{12 \text{ g/mol}}$$
$$= 5.02 \times 10^{22} \text{ nuclei/g}$$

3. The number N of ^{14}C nuclei per gram is then given by:

$$N_{14_C} = 1.35 \times 10^{-12} N_{12_C}$$
$$= (1.35 \times 10^{-12})(5.02 \times 10^{22})$$
$$= 6.78 \times 10^{10} \text{ nuclei/g}$$

4.   The decay rate is then:

$$R = \frac{(0.693)(6.78 \times 10^{10}\,g^{-1})(60\,s/min)}{(5730\,y)(3.16 \times 10^7\,s/y)}$$

$$= 15.6\ \text{decays/min} \cdot g$$

Remarks: Thus, the decay rate for a living organism is 15.6 decays per minute per gram of carbon.

EXAMPLE 12-13 Age of a Bone Fragment A bone fragment found in central Mexico was thought to be associated with the army of Cortez, who conquered the Aztecs in the early 1500s. The fragment contains 200 g of carbon and has a β-decay rate of 400 decays/min. Could the sample have come from a person who died during the sixteenth century?

Solution

First we obtain a rough estimate. If the bone were from a living organism, we would expect the decay rate to be 200 g × 15.6 decays/min · g = 3120 decays/min. Since 400/3120 is roughly 1/8 = 1/2³ (actually 1/7.8), the sample must have decayed for about 3 half-lives, or about 3 × 5730 years. To find the age more accurately, we note that after n half-lives, the decay rate decreases by a factor of $(1/2)^n$. We therefore find n from

$$\left(\frac{1}{2}\right)^n = \frac{400}{3120}$$

or

$$2^n = \frac{3120}{400} = 7.8$$

$$n \ln 2 = \ln 7.8$$

$$n = \frac{\ln 7.8}{\ln 2} = 2.96$$

The age is therefore $t = nt_{1/2} = 2.96(5730\ \text{years}) = 16{,}980$ years. Thus the bone fragment is much older than 500 years and cannot be related to Cortez's conquests. Instead, it places early humans in Mesoamerica at least 17,000 years ago.

Note that the calculation in Example 12-13 assumes that the ^{14}N concentration in the atmosphere and the cosmic ray intensity 17,000 years ago were essentially the same as they are today. Actually, neither has remained unchanged over that period of time. Accurate ^{14}C measurements must include corrections for (1) the variations of Earth's magnetic field, which affects the cosmic ray intensity, and (2) the changing composition of the atmosphere, which depends upon global geological and chemical activity and on the average temperature of the atmosphere. For example, current evidence suggests that just prior to 9000 years ago the ^{14}C/^{12}C ratio was about 1.5 times as large as the current value. The ratio has also been significantly altered over the past century by the burning of fossil fuels, which adds ^{14}C-free carbon to the atmosphere,

and by atmospheric testing of hydrogen weapons, which added ^{14}C during the 1950s. Accelerator mass spectrometry, which was originally developed for just this purpose, enables determination of the $^{14}C/^{12}C$ ratio with sufficient accuracy to extend the applicability of ^{14}C dating back 50,000 years before the present with samples as small as a few milligrams. Calibration of the ratio for earlier periods requires cross-dating with other methods, such as U/Th dating.

Dating Ancient Rocks   Starting with Equation 11-18, a useful relation can be derived for the age of a sample that initially contains N_0 radioactive parent nuclei which decay to a stable daughter with a half-life $t_{1/2}$. Assuming there are no daughter nuclei present initially, after a time t has elapsed there will be N_P parent nuclei and N_D daughter nuclei in the sample. From Equation 11-18,

$$t = \frac{1}{\lambda} \ln\left(\frac{N_0}{N_P}\right) = \frac{t_{1/2}}{\ln 2} \ln\left(\frac{N_0}{N_P}\right) \qquad \text{12-34}$$

Since $N_P + N_D = N_0$ at any time, Equation 12-34 can be written as

$$t = \frac{t_{1/2}}{\ln 2} \ln\left(1 + \frac{N_D}{N_P}\right) \qquad \text{12-35}$$

where N_D/N_P is the isotopic ratio at age t.

Several isotopic abundance ratios are used as "rock clocks" for samples of geologic age. These include $^{238}U/^{206}Pb$, $^{87}Rb/^{87}Sr$, $^{40}K/^{40}Ar$, and the dual ratio $^{238}U/^{234}U/^{230}Th$. These have been used to determine the age of Earth rocks, moon rocks, meteorites, and, by inference, the solar system itself. The oldest rocks on Earth have been dated at about 4.5×10^9 years. At that time the molten surface froze, fixing the isotopic ratios, which thereafter changed only as a result of decay. Surprisingly perhaps, all meteorites turn out to be about the same age, 4.5×10^9 years, regardless of their composition or when they collided with Earth. This suggests that they originated in or are the debris of other bodies within the solar system that formed at the same time as Earth. This value for the age of the Earth is supported by a number of independent ratio measurements, initially the relative abundances of ^{238}U and ^{235}U and the $^{238}U/^{206}Pb$ ratio, and corroborated more recently by measurements of the $^{40}K/^{40}Ar$ and $^{87}Rb/^{87}Sr$ ratios.

EXAMPLE 12-14 $^{87}Rb/^{87}Sr$ Dating   The $^{87}Rb/^{87}Sr$ ratio for a particular rock is found to be 40.0. How old is the rock?

Solution
Note first that in Equation 12-35 the radioactive parent appears in the denominator of the ratio; therefore, in this case $N_D/N_P = 1/(^{87}Rb/^{87}Sr) = 1/40.0 = 0.025$. Substituting this value and the half-life of ^{87}Rb from Table 12-4 into Equation 12-35, we have

$$t = \frac{4.88 \times 10^{10}\,y}{\ln 2} \ln(1 + 0.025) = \frac{4.88 \times 10^{10}\,y}{0.693} \times 0.0247 = 1.74 \times 10^8\,y$$

This is a young rock, considerably younger than the 4.5×10^9 y age of Earth.

Rocks found on Earth's surface range in age from zero up to 3.7×10^9 years. None are older. In contrast, rocks brought back from the surface of the moon by *Apollo* astronauts have ages ranging from 3.1 to 4.5×10^9 years; none are younger. The implications of these results from radioactive dating are: (1) Earth surface rocks older than 3.7×10^9 years have weathered, eroded, and been recycled into other rocks or into the mantle and (2) the moon's internal heat source (gravity and radioactivity) cooled sufficiently to solidify all its material and fix the initial isotopic ratios about 1.5×10^9 years after it was formed. Earth's internal heat source has not yet reached that point.

Accelerator Mass Spectrometry

Originally developed to extend the usable time span and improve the accuracy of ^{14}C dating of archeological materials, *accelerator mass spectrometry (AMS)* is an ultra-sensitive analytical technique in which the atoms of interest in a sample are counted directly rather than irradiating the sample with slow neutrons, then counting the gamma rays emitted by the radioactive daughter produced, or measuring the radiations emitted by long-lived, naturally occurring radionuclides. To understand how AMS works, we will use its application to ^{14}C dating as an illustration. At the present time the $^{14}C/^{12}C$ ratio in living organic material is about 10^{-12}. Thus, a 1-g sample of carbon contains about 5×10^{10} ^{14}C atoms. Since the half life of ^{14}C is 5730 y, a 1.0-g sample of 20,000-year-old charcoal would emit about one β^- per minute. To record 10,000 decays (the number needed for a statistical accuracy of 1 percent) would require counting for one week and involve only 2×10^{-6} of the ^{14}C atoms present in the sample, a very inefficient method.

Mass spectrometry, which records *every* atom in the sample, provides a possible alternative (see Section 3-1). However, conventional mass spectrometers do not have the capability of measuring isotope ratios at the level of $^{14}C/^{12}C$ (or the other radioisotopes listed in Table 12-5) due to the presence of isobars and molecules with nearly the same mass. In the case of ^{14}C these include ^{14}N from residual air within the spectrometer and $^{12}CH_2$ and ^{13}CH, both from the sample itself or contamination. AMS works in part like a conventional mass spectrometer, but it reduces background due to mass ambiguities by taking advantage of the operational characteristics of medium-energy accelerators, particularly cyclotrons and tandem Van de Graaffs. Using the latter as the basis of our discussion and referring to the photograph and diagram on page 564 and to Figure 12-28, the positive high-voltage terminal is in the middle of the accelerator with the two ends of the beam tube essentially at ground potential. The atoms of the sample are converted to negative ions in the ion source. The atoms of most elements can form stable negative ions, a notable exception being

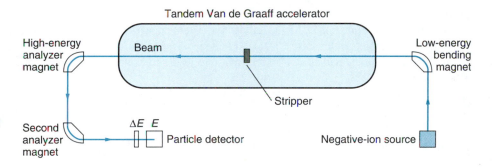

Fig. 12-28 Schematic drawing of a tandem Van de Graaff accelerator configured as an accelerator mass spectrometer.

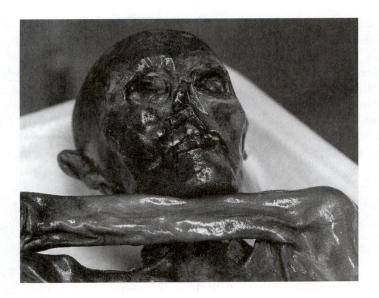

The perfectly preserved mummy of Ötzi the Iceman was found in the Tyrolean Alps in 1991. Accelerator mass spectrometry places his date of death between 3300 and 3200 B.C. Very recent (2003) measurements of oxygen isotopic ratios in his teeth and bones have pinpointed the area where he lived. [©*South Tyrol Museum of Archaeology, Italy, www.iceman.it.*]

nitrogen. Thus, AMS immediately removes background due to ^{14}N. A bending magnet deflects the ions according to their radii of curvature (see Equation 3-9). The negative ions are accelerated to the positive terminal, where a stripper removes several electrons, thus forming positive ions. If more than three electrons are removed, most molecules break apart. The ions are then accelerated further (to 50–100 MeV), emerging from the machine into another bending magnet which effectively removes the moleclar fragments that in general do not have the same radii of curvature as do the atomic ions. After passing through another 90° bending magnet that cleans the beam of any residual molecular fragments, the high-energy beam enters the detector, a so-called E-ΔE counting telescope (see Figure 12-28). The very thin ΔE detector measures the energy loss by the atoms, which for particles with the same energy is approximately proportional to Z^2, thus rejecting atoms with a different atomic number than that of interest. The high-energy ions are then stopped in the E detector, which measures the energy of each one. The product $E \times \Delta E$ for each atom is

TABLE 12-5 Radioisotopes measurable with AMS			
Nuclide	Half-life (y)	Stable isobar	Sensitivity
^{3}H	12.3	^{3}He	10^{-14}
^{10}Be	1.5×10^6	^{10}B	10^{-15}
^{14}C	5.730×10^3	^{14}N	2×10^{-15}
^{26}Al	7.40×10^5	^{26}Mg	10^{-15}
^{36}Cl	3.01×10^5	^{36}S	2×10^{-15}
^{41}Ca	1.0×10^5	^{41}K	10^{-15}
^{129}I	1.6×10^7	^{129}Xe	10^{-14}

approximately proportional to mZ^2. Thus, requiring sample masses of only a few milligrams, AMS measures the mass and atomic number of each atom, and it does so with very high precision and extremely low background.

Table 12-5 lists several long-lived radioisotopes that can be effectively assayed with AMS. For example, the technique has been used to time the migration of surface water into deep aquifers by measuring the concentration of ^{36}Cl, produced by cosmic ray bombardment of argon in the atmosphere. Using only a few strands, the famous Shroud of Turin was ^{14}C-dated by AMS as having been made in the Middle Ages, around 1300. Ötzi the Iceman discovered in the Tyrolean Alps, was found to have lived during the late Neolithic age, about 5200 years ago. Some meteorites have been found to contain ^{26}Al in excess of the concentration attributable to cosmic ray production, raising the intriguing question of its origin in the cosmos.

Particle-Induced X-ray Emission

An elemental analysis technique similar to neutron activation analysis (NAA), *particle-induced x-ray emission (PIXE)* involves bombarding the material of interest with low-energy (a few MeV) ions, such as protons or alpha particles. Coulomb

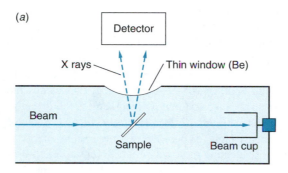

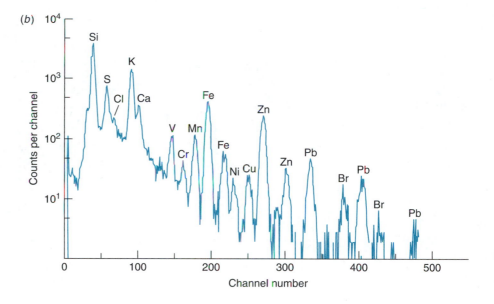

Fig. 12-29 (*a*) Schematic drawing of a typical particle-induced x-ray emission system. (*b*) PIXE spectrum from an aerosol bombarded with 2-MeV protons. [*S. A. E. Johansson and T. B. Johansson, Nuclear Instruments and Methods, 137, 473, 1976.*]

interactions between the ions and the target atoms ionize the latter by ejecting K- or L-shell electrons. Since the interactions occur over atomic dimensions, the cross sections are quite high, as much as 1000 b for low-Z atoms, decreasing smoothly to about 1 b at Z = 82 (Pb). The vacancies produced are quickly filled by electrons from higher energy shells, emitting K and L x rays or Auger electrons in the process, which are characteristic of the elements in the target (see Section 4-4). Since the bombarding particles are relatively low energy, they do not penetrate far into matter, so the interactions occur near the surface. That fact, together with the low energy of the emitted x rays, 10 to 100 keV, dictates the use of thin samples. Figure 12-29a is a schematic of a typical PIXE experimental arrangement. The sensitivity of PIXE is comparable to NAA and has the advantage of being applicable to all elements above Z = 20, whereas NAA is restricted to those nuclides with sufficiently large thermal-neutron absorption cross sections. The main disadvantage of PIXE is x-ray energy ambiguities. For example, the energy of the L_α x ray from Pb is 10.55 keV, while that of the K_α line of As is 10.54 keV. The resolution of the cooled Si(Li) detectors used for x rays is about 100 eV, insufficient to resolve the two lines. Figure 12-29b shows a typical PIXE spectrum.

QUESTIONS

11. If the $^{14}C/^{12}C$ ratio was 1.5 times larger than that used in Example 12-13, is the calculated age too large or too small? Explain.

12. Some meteorites are found to contain measurable amounts of ^{26}Al, whose $t_{1/2}$ is only 7.4×10^5 years. Devise a scenario that would account for its presence.

13. ^{40}Ar is a gas at ordinary temperatures. Explain why solid rocks can be accurately dated using the $^{40}Kr/^{40}Ar$ ratio in spite of that fact.

14. Explain why accelerator mass spectrometry can achieve reliable results using samples of only 1 mg.

More

The biological effects of ionizing radiation were largely unknown in the early days of atomic and nuclear physics. It took such things as the plight of the radium-dial painters, x-ray crystallographers with missing fingertips, and young cyclotron physicists with cataracts to focus scientific attention on the risks that attend exposure to ionizing radiation in the home, the work place, and the environment. Questions of *Radiation Dosage*, its definition, origin, and effects are discussed on the home page: www.whfreeman.com/modphysics4e See also Equations 12-36 through 12-38 here, as well as Tables 12-6 through 12-9.

Summary

TOPIC	RELEVANT EQUATIONS AND REMARKS
1. Nuclear reactions	The Q value of a reaction $X(x, y)Y$ determines if energy is released or must be supplied. Q is given by
	$$Q = (m_x + m_X - m_y - m_Y)c^2 \qquad \text{12-1}$$
Cross section	The cross section σ measures the effective size of a nucleus for a particular nuclear reaction.
	$$\sigma = \frac{R}{I} \qquad \text{12-5}$$
	where R is the number of reactions per unit time per nucleus and I is the incident particle intensity.
2. Fission, fusion, and nuclear reactors	Fission is the process by which heavy elements such as ^{235}U and ^{239}Pu capture a neutron and split into two medium-mass nuclei. Each event releases about 1 MeV/nucleon. Very heavy elements may also fission spontaneously.
	Fusion is the reaction in which two light nuclei, such as ^2H and ^3H, fuse together to produce a heavier nucleus. Each event releases 1 to 4 MeV/nucleon.
Fission reactors	Fission reactors sustain the chain reaction for a neutron reproduction factor k equal to 1 or greater. For uranium
	$$k = 2.4 \frac{\sigma_f}{\sigma_f + \sigma_a} \qquad \text{12-11}$$
Fusion reactors	The technology to make fusion reactors a practical source of energy has not yet been developed. The "breakeven" point is known as Lawson's criterion:
	$$n\tau > 10^{20} \, \text{s} \cdot \text{particles/m}^3 \qquad \text{12-15}$$
	where n is the ion density in the plasma and τ is the confinement time.
3. Applications	The applications of nuclear reactions in medicine include the use of nuclear radiation in the treatment of diseases and the use of nuclear-based imaging techniques in diagnosis and research. Nuclear magnetic resonance imaging (MRI) is an alternative to x-ray imaging with the advantage that the RF photons involved produce little damage to biological tissue. Computer-assisted tomography using short-lived positron emitters (PET) provides rapid, three-dimensional images. Radioactive dating employs a number of naturally occurring radioisotopes to determine the age of rocks and artifacts. Accelerator mass spectrometry and neutron activation analysis are highly sensitive means of measuring the concentration of particular isotopes of nearly every element in the periodic table. Their use ranges from analysis of environmental contaminants to the detection of art fraud.

GENERAL REFERENCES

The following general references are written at a level appropriate for the readers of this book.

Antony, M., *Nuclide Chart 2002,* Strasbourg, 2002.

Biological Effects of Ionizing Radiation (BEIR III), National Academy of Sciences/National Research Council, Washington, D.C., 1988.

Das, A., and T. Ferbil, *Introduction to Nuclear and Particle Physics,* Wiley, New York, 1994.

DiLavore, P., *Energy: Insights from Physics,* Wiley, New York, 1984.

Frauenfelder, H., and E. M. Henley, *Subatomic Physics,* 2d ed., Prentice Hall, Englewood Cliffs, N.J., 1991.

Hogan, W. J., R. Bangertor, and G. L. Kulcinski, "Energy from Inertial Fusion," *Physics Today,* **45**, No. 9, 42 (1992).

Knoll, G. E., *Radiation Detection and Measurement,* Wiley, New York, 1979.

Lapp, R. E., and H. L. Andrews, *Nuclear Radiation Physics,* 4th ed., Prentice Hall, Englewood Cliffs, N.J., 1972.

Lilley, J., *Nuclear Physics: Principles and Applications,* Wiley, Chichester, England, 2001.

Nero, A. V., Jr., *A Guidebook to Nuclear Reactors,* University of California Press, Berkeley, 1979.

Priest, J., *Energy: Principles, Problems, and Alternatives,* 5th ed., Kendall/Hunt, Dubuque, Iowa, 2000.

Segrè, E., *Nuclei and Particles,* 2d ed., Benjamin Cummings, Menlo Park, Calif., 1977.

NOTES

1. The United States produced about 31 percent of the world's nuclear power in 2000.

2. The term *tomography* is from the Greek *tomos,* meaning "slice," and *graphé,* meaning "picture." Thus, a tomograph is the pictorial representation of a slice through the object or body being studied.

3. This dependence, which occurs only for (n, γ) reactions with relatively low-energy neutrons, was first measured by Emilio Segrè in 1935.

4. The first such resonance was observed unexpectedly in the results of a neutron irradiation of silver conducted by Edoardo Amaldi and others on the morning of October 22, 1934. By 3:00 P.M. that day, Enrico Fermi had developed the correct explanation of the strange phenomenon. The paper describing the discovery was written that evening and delivered to the scientific journal *Ricerca Scientifica* the next morning, less than 24 hours after the discovery!

5. Otto Hahn (1879–1968), German physical chemist, and Fritz Strassman (1902–1980), German chemist. Hahn recognized that uranium nuclei bombarded with neutrons were breaking apart, but carefully avoided characterizing the event as fission, since no such thing had been recorded before. He received the 1944 Nobel Prize in chemistry for the discovery.

6. Actually, Fermi's reactor was the first *constructed* fission reactor. About 2 billion years ago several deposits of natural uranium located in what is now Gabon, West Africa, began chain reactions that continued for probably several hundred thousand years before naturally shutting themselves off. The evidence that verified the discovery of the first of these, a fascinating example of scientific detective work, may be found in G. A. Cowan, "A Natural Fission Reactor," *Scientific American,* July 1976. The sites are being mined and efforts to preserve one of the natural reactors as an international historic site are currently underway.

7. There are 104 commercial power reactors currently operating in the United States. All are light-water reactors (LWRs), about 70 percent being pressurized-water reactors (PWRs) and the rest boiling-water reactors (BWRs).

8. There was one earlier exception. The Enrico Fermi reactor, a relatively small (67-MWe) liquid-metal fast breeder reactor (LMFBR) built by the Detroit Edison Company, began operating in 1963. On October 5, 1966, it suffered a partial core meltdown due to a blockage in the liquid sodium coolant lines. It was not restarted and was subsequently decommissioned.

9. An elementary discussion of a magnetic bottle can be found in P. A. Tipler, *Physics for Scientists and Engineers,* 4th ed. (New York: W. H. Freeman, 1999), pp. 862–863.

10. Godfrey Hounsfield (b. 1919), English engineer. He shared the 1979 Nobel prize for medicine for the invention of the CT scanner.

11. The radiocarbon dating technique was developed by Willard F. Libby (1908–1980), an American chemist. He received the 1960 Nobel Prize in chemistry for his work.

12. *Health Risks of Radon and Other Internally Deposited Alpha-Emitters* (Washington, D.C.: National Academy of Sciences/National Research Council, National Academy Press, 1988).

PROBLEMS

Level I

Section 12-1 Nuclear Reactions

12-1. Using data from Appendix A, find the Q values for the following reactions: (a) $^2H + ^2H \rightarrow ^3H + ^1H + Q$, (b) $^3He(d, p)\,^4He$, and (c) $^6Li + n \rightarrow ^3H + ^4He + Q$.

12-2. (a) Find the Q value for the reaction $^3H + ^1H \rightarrow ^3He + n + Q$. (b) Find the threshold for this reaction if stationary ^1H nuclei are bombarded with ^3H nuclei from an accelerator. (c) Find the threshold for this reaction if stationary ^3H nuclei are bombarded with ^1H nuclei from an accelerator.

12-3. What is the compound nucleus for the reaction of deuterons on ^{14}N? What are the possible product nuclei and particles for this reaction?

12-4. Using data from Appendix A, compute the Q value for the reaction (a) $^{12}C(\alpha, p)\,^{15}N$ and (b) $^{16}O(d, p)\,^{17}O$.

12-5. The cross section for the reaction $^{75}As(n, \gamma)\,^{76}As$ is 4.5 b for thermal neutrons. A sample of natural As in the form of a crystal 1 cm $\times$ 2 cm that is 30 μm thick is exposed to a thermal neutron flux of 0.95×10^{13} neutrons/cm$^2 \cdot$ s. Compute the rate at which this reaction proceeds. (Natural arsenic is 100 percent ^{75}As. Its density is 5.73 g/cm^3.)

12-6. Write three different reactions that could produce the products (a) $n + ^{23}Na$, (b) $p + ^{14}C$, and (c) $d + ^{31}P$.

12-7. Write down the correct symbol for the particle or nuclide represented by the x in the following reactions: (a) $^{14}N(n, p)x$, (b) $^{208}Pb(n, x)^{208}Pb$, (c) $x(\alpha, p)^{61}Cu$, (d) $^9Be(x, n)^{12}C$, (e) $^{16}O(d, \alpha)x$, (f) $^{162}Dy(\alpha, 6n)x$, (g) $x(d, n)^4He$, (h) $^{90}Zr(d, x)^{91}Zr$.

Section 12-2 Fission, Fusion, and Nuclear Reactors

12-8. A few minutes after the Big Bang the first fusion reaction occurred in the early universe. It was $n + p \rightarrow d + \gamma$. Compute the Q for this reaction.

12-9. Assuming an average energy release of 200 MeV per fission, calculate the number of fissions per second needed for a 500-MW reactor.

12-10. If the reproduction factor of a reactor is $k = 1.1$, find the number of generations needed for the power level to (a) double, (b) increase by a factor of 10, and (c) increase by a factor of 100. Find the time needed in each case if (d) there are no delayed neutrons, so the time between generations is 1 ms, and (e) there are delayed neutrons that make the average time between generations 100 ms.

12-11. Write down the several reactions possible when ^{235}U captures a thermal neutron and $1n$, $2n$, $3n$, or $4n$ are produced.

12-12. Assuming an average energy release of 17.6 MeV/fusion, calculate the rate at which ^2H must be supplied to a 500-MW fusion reactor.

12-13. From Figure 12-14, the cross section for the capture of 1.0-MeV neutrons by ^{238}U is 0.02 b. A 5-g sample of ^{238}U is exposed to a total flux of 1.0-MeV neutrons of 5.0×10^{11}/m^2. Compute the number of ^{239}U atoms produced.

12-14. Compute the total energy released in the following set of fusion reactions. This is the proton-proton cycle, which is the primary source of the sun's energy.

$$^1H + {}^1H \longrightarrow {}^2H + e^+ + \nu_e$$

$$^2H + {}^1H \longrightarrow {}^3He + \gamma$$

$$^3He + {}^3He \longrightarrow {}^4He + 2{}^1H + \gamma$$

12-15. A particular nuclear power reactor operates at 1000 MWe (megawatts electric) with an overall efficiency in converting fission energy to electrical energy of 30 percent.

What mass of ^{235}U must fission in order for the power plant to operate for (a) one day, (b) one year. (c) If the energy were provided by burning coal instead of ^{235}U, what would be the answers to (a) and (b)? (Burning coal produces approximately 3.15×10^7 J/kg.)

12-16. (a) Assuming that the natural abundance of deuterium given in Appendix A is reflected in the formation of water molecules, compute the energy that would be released if all the deuterons in 1.0 m^3 of water were fused via the reaction $^2H + {}^1H \rightarrow {}^3He + \gamma$. (b) Given that the world's 5.9×10^9 people used 3.58×10^{20} J in 1999, how long (in hours) would the result in part (a) have lasted a "typical" person?

12-17. Consider the possible fission reaction

$$n + {}^{235}_{92}U \longrightarrow {}^{120}_{48}Cd + {}^{112}_{44}Ru + 3n$$

(a) Compute the energy released in the reaction. (b) Is this reaction likely to occur? Explain.

Section 12-3 Applications

12-18. A bone claimed to be 10,000 years old contains 15 g of carbon. What should the decay rate of ^{14}C be for this bone?

12-19. A sample of animal bone unearthed at an archeological site is found to contain 175 g of carbon, and the decay rate of ^{14}C in the sample is measured to be 8.1 Bq. How old is the bone?

12-20. The $^{87}Rb/^{87}Sr$ ratio for a particular rock is measured to be 36.5. How old is the rock?

12-21. In a PIXE experiment, an element with $A = 80$ forms 0.001 percent by weight of a thin foil whose mass is 0.35 mg/cm^2. The foil is bombarded with a 250-nA proton beam for 15 minutes. The cross section for exciting the L shell is 650 b. If the probability that the excited atom will emit an L x ray is 0.60 and the overall efficiency of the x-ray detector is 0.0035, how many counts will the detector record during the 15-minute bombardment?

12-22. The naturally occurring $A = 4n$ decay series begins with ^{232}Th and eventually ends on ^{208}Pb. (See Figure 11-18.) A particular rock is measured to contain 4.11 g of ^{232}Th and 0.88 g of ^{208}Pb. Compute the age of the rock.

12-23. Compute the resonance frequency of free protons in a magnetic field of (a) 0.5×10^{-4} T (approximate strength of Earth's field), (b) 0.25 T, and (c) 0.5 T.

12-24. A small piece of papyrus is to be ^{14}C-dated using AMS. During a 10-minute run with the system set to record ^{14}C, 1500 ions are counted. With the system set to transmit $^{12}C^{+3}$ ions the beam current is 12 μA. (a) Compute the $^{14}C/^{12}C$ ratio, assuming both isotopes are transmitted with the same efficiency. (b) If the entire sample is consumed in 75 minutes, what was the mass of ^{12}C it contained? (Assume a constant consumption rate and an efficiency of 0.015. (c) How old is the sample?

12-25. A wooden spear found in the mountains of southeastern Spain was found to have ^{14}C activity of 2.05 disintegrations per minute per gram. How old is it? (The ^{14}C activity of live wood is 15.6 disintegrations per minute per gram.)

Level II

12-26. (a) Calculate the radii of $^{141}_{56}Ba$ and $^{92}_{36}Kr$ from Equation 11-4. (b) Assume that after the fission of ^{235}U into ^{141}Ba and ^{92}Kr, the two nuclei are momentarily separated by a distance r equal to the sum of the radii found in (a), and calculate the electrostatic potential energy for these two nuclei at this separation. Compare your result with the measured fission energy of 175 MeV.

12-27. Consider a neutron of mass m moving with speed v_L and colliding head on with a nucleus of mass M. (a) Show that the speed of the center of mass in the lab frame is $V = mv_L/(m + M)$. (b) What is the speed of the nucleus in the center-of-mass frame before the

collision? after the collision? (*c*) What is the speed of the nucleus in the original lab frame after the collision? (*d*) Show that the energy of the nucleus after the collision is

$$\frac{1}{2}M(2V)^2 = \left[\frac{4mM}{(m + M)^2}\right]\frac{1}{2}mv_L^2$$

and use this to obtain Equation 12-25.

12-28. Suppose that the Van Dyck painting shown in the photographs on page 594 was irradiated with a thermal neutron flux of 10^{12} neutrons/cm$^2 \cdot$s for 2 h. In terms of the numbers of manganese and phosphorus atoms initially present, determine the activity (*a*) 2 hours and (*b*) 2 days after the irradiation stopped. The (*n*, γ) cross section for ^{31}P is 0.180 b and for ^{55}Mn is 13.3 b. (Both isotopes are 100 percent of the naturally occurring elements.)

12-29. The total energy consumed in the United States in 1 y is about 7.0×10^{19} J. How many kilograms of ^{235}U would be needed to provide this amount of energy if we assume that 200 MeV of energy is released by each fissioning uranium nucleus, that 3 percent of the uranium atoms undergo fission, and that all of the energy-conversion mechanisms used are 25 percent efficient?

12-30. The rubidium isotope ^{87}Rb is a β emitter with a half-life of 4.9×10^{10} y that decays into ^{87}Sr. It is used to determine the age of rocks and fossils. Rocks containing the fossils of early animals contain a ratio of ^{87}Sr to ^{87}Rb of 0.010. Assuming that there was no ^{87}Sr present when the rocks were formed, calculate the age of these fossils.

12-31. In 1989, researchers claimed to have achieved fusion in an electrochemical cell at room temperature. They claimed a power output of 4 W from deuterium fusion reactions in the palladium electrode of their apparatus. (*a*) If the two most likely reactions are

$$^2\text{H} + {}^2\text{H} \longrightarrow {}^3\text{He} + n + 3.27 \text{ MeV}$$

and

$$^2\text{H} + {}^2\text{H} \longrightarrow {}^3\text{H} + {}^1\text{H} + 4.03 \text{ MeV}$$

with 50 percent of the reactions going by each branch, how many neutrons per second would we expect to be emitted in the generation of 4 W of power? (*b*) If one-tenth of these neutrons were absorbed by the body of an 80.0-kg worker near the device, and if each absorbed neutron carries an average energy of 0.5 MeV with an RBE of 4, to what radiation dose rate in rems per hour would this correspond? (*c*) How long would it take for a person to receive a total dose of 500 rems? (This is the dose that is usually lethal to half of those receiving it.)

12-32. Neutron activation analysis is used to study a small sample of automotive enamel found at the scene of a hit-and-run collision. The sample was exposed to a thermal-neutron flux of 3.5×10^{12} neutrons/cm$^2 \cdot$s for 2.0 minutes. Placed immediately in a gamma-ray detector, it was found to have an activity of 35 Bq due to ^{60}Co and 115 Bq due to ^{51}Ti. Compute the total amount of each metal in the original sample. (The cross section for ^{59}Co is 19 b; that for ^{50}Ti is 0.15 b.)

12-33. A fusion reactor using only deuterium for fuel would have the following two reactions taking place in it

$$^2\text{H} + {}^2\text{H} \longrightarrow {}^3\text{He} + n + 3.27 \text{ MeV}$$

and

$$^2\text{H} + {}^2\text{H} \longrightarrow {}^3\text{H} + {}^1\text{H} + 4.03 \text{ MeV}$$

The ^{3}H produced in the second reaction reacts immediately with another ^{2}H to produce

$$^3\text{H} + {}^2\text{H} \longrightarrow {}^4\text{He} + n + 17.7 \text{ MeV}$$

The ratio of ^{2}H to ^{1}H atoms in naturally occurring hydrogen is 1.5×10^{-4}. How much energy would be produced from 4 liters of water if all of the ^{2}H nuclei undergo fusion?

12-34. (*a*) Using the Compton scattering result that the maximum change in wavelength is $\Delta\lambda = 2hc/Mc^2$ and the approximation $\Delta E \approx hc\,\Delta\lambda/\lambda^2$, show that for a photon to transfer an amount of energy E_p to a proton, the energy of the photon must be at least $E = [(1/2)Mc^2E_p]^{1/2}$. (*b*) Calculate the photon energy needed to produce a 5.7-MeV proton by Compton scattering. (*c*) Calculate the energy given a ^{14}N nucleus in a head-on collision with a 5.7-MeV neutron. (*d*) Calculate the photon energy needed to give a ^{14}N nucleus this energy by Compton scattering.

12-35. A photon of energy E is incident on a deuteron at rest. In the center-of-mass reference frame, both the photon and the deuteron have momentum p. Prove that the approximation $p \approx E/c$ is good by showing that the deuteron with this momentum has energy much less than E. If the binding energy of the deuteron is 2.22 MeV, what is the threshold energy in the lab for photodisintegration?

Level III

12-36. Energy is generated in the sun and other stars by fusion. One of the fusion cycles, the proton-proton cycle, consists of the following reactions:

$$^1\text{H} + {}^1\text{H} \longrightarrow {}^2\text{H} + \beta^+ + \nu$$
$$^1\text{H} + {}^2\text{H} \longrightarrow {}^3\text{He} + \gamma$$

followed by either

$$^3\text{He} + {}^3\text{He} \longrightarrow {}^4\text{He} + {}^1\text{H} + {}^1\text{H}$$

or

$$^1\text{H} + {}^3\text{He} \longrightarrow {}^4\text{He} + \beta^+ + \nu$$

(*a*) Show that the net effect of these reactions is

$$4{}^1\text{H} \longrightarrow {}^4\text{He} + 2\beta^+ + 2\nu + \gamma$$

(*b*) Show that the rest mass energy of 24.7 MeV is released in this cycle, not counting the 2×0.511 MeV released when each positron meets an electron and is annihilated according to $e^+ + e^- \rightarrow 2\gamma$. (*c*) The sun radiates energy at the rate of about 4×10^{26} W. Assuming that this is due to the conversion of four protons into helium plus γ rays and neutrinos, which releases 26.7 MeV, what is the rate of proton consumption in the sun? How long will the sun last if it continues to radiate at its present level? (Assume that protons constitute about half the total mass of the sun, which is about 2×10^{30} kg.)

12-37. The fusion reaction between ^{2}H and ^{3}H is

$$^3\text{H} + {}^2\text{H} \longrightarrow {}^4\text{He} + n + 17.7 \text{ MeV}$$

Using the conservation of momentum and the given Q value, find the final energies of both the ^{4}He nucleus and the neutron, assuming that the initial momentum of the system is zero.

12-38. (*a*) A particular light-water ^{235}U-fueled reactor had a reproduction factor of 1.005 and an average neutron lifetime of 0.08 s. By what percentage will the rate of energy production by the reactor increase in 5 s? (*b*) By what fraction must the neutron flux in the reactor be reduced in order to reduce the reproduction factor to 1.000?

12-39. Compute the reproduction factor for uranium enriched to (*a*) 5 percent and (*b*) 95 percent in ^{235}U. Compute corresponding fission rate doubling time in each case. Assuming no loss of neutrons and the release of 200 MeV/fission, at what rate will energy be produced in each case 1.0 s after the first fission occurs.

Chapter *13* Particle Physics

*I*n Dalton's atomic theory of matter (1808), the atom was considered to be the smallest indivisible constituent of matter, that is, an elementary particle.[1] Then, with the discovery of the electron by Thomson (1897), the Rutherford-Bohr theory of the nuclear atom (1913), and the discovery of the neutron by Chadwick (1932), it became clear that atoms and even nuclei have considerable structure. For a brief time, it was thought there were just four "elementary" particles: the proton, neutron, electron, and photon. However, Anderson discovered the positron, or antielectron, later in 1932; and shortly thereafter, the muon, pion, and many other particles were predicted and discovered.

Since the 1950s, several nations have constructed increasingly larger and more sophisticated particle accelerators capable of producing greater and greater energies with the goal of finding additional particles predicted by various theories. An important consideration in such complex experiments, which often involve hundreds of scientists from many nations, is the question of how we can tell if a particle is truly elementary or composed of a combination of other particles. For example, both the proton and neutron were once thought to be elementary, but probing with high-energy (short-wavelength) electron beams revealed that they have excited states, just as do atoms and nuclei. When the wavelength of the electrons became short enough (at electron energies greater than about 10 GeV), internal structure was discovered. We now consider each to be a composite particle composed of three, still more fundamental particles. At present, we know of several hundred particles that at one time or another have been considered to be elementary. Research teams at the giant accelerator laboratories around the world continue to search for and find new particles. Some of these have such short lifetimes (of the order of 10^{-23} s) that they can be detected only indirectly. Many are observed only in reactions produced with high-energy accelerators. However, stability is not a good criterion for elementarity. For example, the deuteron is not considered to be an elementary particle, even though it is stable, whereas the muon is considered to be elementary, even though it decays with a mean lifetime of about 2.2 μs. In addition to the usual particle properties of mass, charge, and spin, the search for elementary particles unveiled new properties which have been given whimsical names such as strangeness, charm, and color.

In this chapter, we will first look at the various ways of classifying the multitude of particles that have been found. We will then consider the fundamental interactions between particles and the conservation laws that apply to them. Finally, we will describe the current theory of elementary particles, called the *standard model,* in which all matter in nature—from the exotic particles produced in the giant accelerator laboratories to ordinary grains of sand—is considered to be constructed from just four groups of elementary particles, two of leptons and two of quarks.

The construction of large particle accelerators in various countries has, over the years, been an impetus for developing bigger and better superconducting electromagnets. These high-field, efficient magnets are used in applications ranging from medical diagnostic magnetic resonance imaging (MRI) systems to magnetically levitated (maglev) trains.

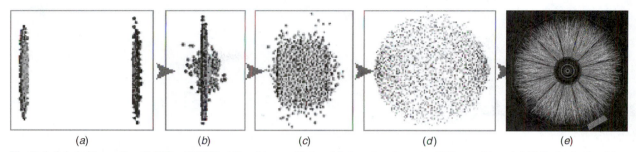

| (a) | (b) | (c) | (d) | (e) |

The Relativistic Heavy Ion Collider (RHIC) at Brookhaven National Laboratory began colliding gold nuclei (fully ionized gold atoms) late in 2000, each of the ions moving at 99.99 percent of the speed of light. (*a*) Two Lorentz-contracted ions approach each other. (*b*) The collision "melts" the protons and neutrons and (*c*) for an instant releases the quarks and gluons from which the nucleons were formed. (*d*) From the enormous energy of the collision thousands more are created, creating in turn thousands of particles. (*e*) Computer construction of the tracks of the thousands of particles created in a single collision of two gold ions. A color version of this photograph is on the cover of this book. [*Courtesy of Brookhaven National Laboratory, STAR experiment.*]

13-1 Particles and Antiparticles

The Positron

In 1932, the same year as the discovery of the neutron, the positron was discovered (and named) by Carl Anderson.[2] This particle has the same mass and intrinsic angular momentum as the electron but has positive charge; therefore, its intrinsic magnetic moment is parallel, rather than antiparallel, to its spin. It is the antiparticle of the electron and is represented by the symbol e^+, or sometimes in radioactive decay equations by β^+. The existence of the positron had been predicted by Dirac from his relativistic wave equation,[3] though there was some difficulty about the interpretation of this prediction. (See Section 2-4.)

The energy of a relativistic particle is given by Equation 2-31:

$$E^2 = (pc)^2 + (mc^2)^2$$

2-31

Air view of the European Laboratory for Particle Physics (CERN), just outside Geneva, Switzerland. The large circle shows the Large Electron-Positron collider (LEP) tunnel; it is 27 kilometers in circumference. The irregular dashed line is the border between France and Switzerland (in the foreground). LEP was retired in 2000. The tunnel (and much of the hardware) is being "recycled" for construction of the new Large Hadron Collider (LHC), currently scheduled for completion in 2007. [*CERN.*]

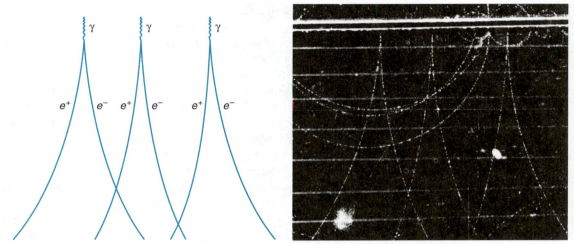

Fig. 13-1 Tracks of electron-positron pairs produced by 300-MeV synchrotron x rays at the Lawrence Livermore Laboratory. The magnetic field in the chamber points out of the page. [*Photo courtesy of Lawrence Radiation Laboratory, University of California, Berkeley.*]

from which we can write

$$E = \pm[(pc)^2 + (mc^2)^2]^{1/2} \qquad \textbf{13-1}$$

Though we can usually choose the plus sign and ignore the negative-energy solution with a "physical argument," the mathematics of the Dirac equation requires the existence of wave functions corresponding to these negative-energy states. Dirac postulated that all the negative-energy states were filled with electrons. They would, therefore, exert no net force on anything and thus would not be observable. Dirac invoked the exclusion principle to suggest that only holes in this "infinite sea" of negative-energy states would be observable. The holes would act as positive charges with positive energy. Anderson's discovery of a particle with mass identical to that of the electron but with positive charge indicated that the interpretation was reasonable. The positron is produced simultaneously with an electron in pair production (see Figure 13-1). The process can be thought of as the interaction (photoelectric effect) of a photon with a negative-energy electron, raising the electron to a positive-energy state (where it appears as a normal electron) and leaving a hole, which appears as a positron, as illustrated schematically in Figure 13-2.

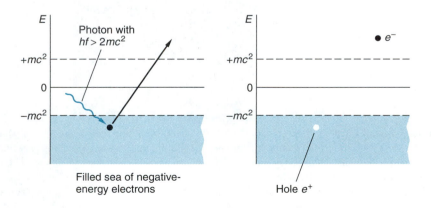

Fig. 13-2 Pair production was initially viewed as resulting from the collision of a photon with a negative-energy electron. The electron is excited to a positive-energy state, leaving a hole that appears as a positron.

This notion that we are immersed in an infinite sea of negative-energy electrons is an unsettling one, however. It was rendered unnecessary with the development of quantum electrodynamics (QED) by Feynman[4] and others in the late 1940s. QED, whose predictions have been verified to the highest precision of any physical theory, requires that *every* particle must have a corresponding antiparticle with the same mass but opposite electric charge. For example, the theory predicts that protons and neutrons, which are both spin 1/2 particles whose wave functions are solutions of the Dirac equation, should have antiparticles. The creation of a proton-antiproton pair requires at least $2m_pc^2 = 1877$ MeV, which was not available except in cosmic rays until the development of high-energy accelerators in the 1950s. The antiproton (designated $\bar{p}$) was discovered by Segrè[5] and Chamberlain at Berkeley in 1955 using a beam of protons of 6.2-GeV kinetic energy from the Bevatron particle accelerator. (See Figure 13-3.) The antineutron ($\bar{n}$) (a particle with the same mass as the neutron but with a positive magnetic moment) was discovered two years later. (The standard notation for an antiparticle is the overbar; however, in many cases it is customary to specify the charge instead, as we did for the positron.)

Particles with integral spin, whose wave functions are not solutions of the Dirac equation, also have antiparticles. For example, those with zero spin, which are described by the Klein-Gordon relativistic wave equation (see Equation 11-52), include the pions, the exchange particle of the nuclear force. In general, an antiparticle has exactly the same mass as the particle, but with electric charge, *baryon number*, and *strangeness* (see Section 13-3) opposite in sign to that of the particle.

Although the positron is stable, it has only a short-term existence in our universe because of the large supply of electrons in matter. The fate of the positron is annihilation according to the reaction

$$e^+ + e^- \longrightarrow \gamma + \gamma \qquad \text{or} \qquad e^+ + e^- \longrightarrow \gamma + \gamma + \gamma \qquad \textbf{13-2}$$

Whether bound (as positronium—see Section 2-4) or unbound, annihilation occurs from S states (zero orbital angular momentum), the antiparallel spins ^1S state producing

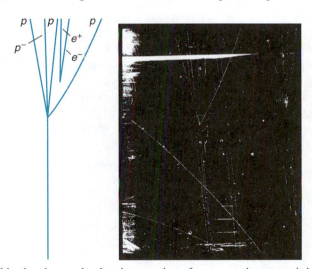

Fig. 13-3 Bubble chamber tracks showing creation of proton-antiproton pair in the collision of an incident 25-GeV proton from the Brookhaven Alternating Gradient Synchrotron with a liquid hydrogen nucleus (stationary proton). The reaction is $p + p \rightarrow p + p + p + \bar{p}$. The energy necessary to create the pair is $2m_pc^2 = 1.877$ GeV in the center-of-mass system. A relativistic calculation in the laboratory frame shows that the beam protons must have at least $6m_pc^2 \approx 5.6$ GeV to reach the reaction threshold. [*Photo courtesy of R. Ehrlich.*]

The tunnel of the proton-antiproton collider at CERN. The same bending and focusing magnets can be used for protons or antiprotons moving in opposite directions. The rectangular box in the foreground is a focusing magnet; the next four boxes are bending magnets. [*CERN.*]

two quanta as on the left in Equation 13-2, the parallel spins ^3S state producing three photons. The fact that we call electrons *particles* and positrons *antiparticles* does not imply that positrons are less fundamental than electrons, but was initially merely an arbitrary choice reflecting the nature of our part of the universe. If our matter were made up of negative protons, positive electrons, and neutrons with positive magnetic moments, then particles such as positive protons, negative electrons, and neutrons with negative magnetic moments would suffer quick annihilation and would probably be called the antiparticles. Antihydrogen atoms (an antiproton and a positron) were first produced at the European Center for Nuclear Research (CERN) in 1995. (See Figure 13-4.)

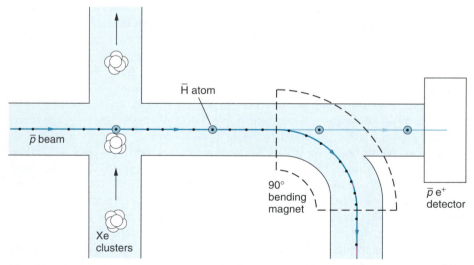

Fig. 13-4 Millions of antiprotons per second (solid circles) circulate in the a storage ring at CERN. Frozen clusters of xenon atoms (open circles) cross the path of the antiproton beam. Occasionally interaction between an antiproton and a xenon cluster produces an $e^- - e^+$ pair and the positron is captured by the antiproton, thus forming an antihydrogen atom. The negative antiprotons are deflected by the 90° bending magnet, but the neutral antihydrogen atoms are not. They continue on to the detector, where they are ionized and the presence of the positron and antiproton is verified.

EXAMPLE 13-1 Proton-Antiproton Annihilation A proton and an antiproton at rest annihilate according to the reaction

$$p^+ + p^- \longrightarrow \gamma + \gamma$$

Find the energies and wavelengths of the photons.

Solution

Since the proton and the antiproton are at rest, conservation of momentum requires that the two photons created in their annihilation have equal and opposite momenta and therefore equal energies. Since the total energy on the left side of the reaction is $2m_p c^2$, the energy of each photon is

$$E_\gamma = m_p c^2 = 938 \text{ MeV}$$

The wavelength is

$$\lambda = \frac{c}{f} = \frac{hc}{hf} = \frac{hc}{E_\gamma} = \frac{1240 \text{ eV} \cdot \text{nm}}{9.38 \times 10^8 \text{ eV}} = 1.32 \times 10^{-15} \text{ m} = 1.32 \text{ fm}$$

Feynman Diagrams

As a part of quantum electrodynamics Feynman developed a wonderfully clear yet powerful technique for describing all electromagnetic phenomena. Like QED itself, the technique of *Feynman diagrams* is so good that it is used as a model by other quantum field theories (notably quantum chromodynamics [QCD], which we will discuss in Section 13-4). The detailed rules for drawing Feynman diagrams are directly related to the equations of QED and are beyond the scope of our discussions here; however, a brief description of a simplified version of the diagrams and a few basic rules will be ample for our use in illustrating the phenomena of interest in this chapter.

Feynman diagrams are spacetime diagrams, that is, *ct* versus *x* graphs, similar to those developed and used in Chapters 1 and 2. As noted in Figure 11-28, where a Feynman diagram was used to illustrate the meson exchange in the nuclear force, the *ct* and *x* axes are normally not drawn. In this chapter, as in the earlier relativity chapters, time (*ct*) is positive upward and space (*x*) is positive to the right. (Particle physicists often reverse these two, making time flow horizontally toward the right and space upward.) Particles are represented by straight lines with an arrow. A particle line whose arrow points backward in time is interpreted as the corresponding antiparticle moving forward in time. The arrows allow us to omit the overbars in the diagrams. The lines are symbolic and do *not* represent the particle trajectories. It is the *interaction* that we are interested in describing. Particles that are their own antiparticles, like the photon, have no arrows and are represented by wiggly or broken lines of various sorts. All electromagnetic phenomena can be represented by the combinations of the process illustrated in Figure 13-5, called the *primitive vertex*. This diagram is read as follows: a moving charged particle enters, emits (or absorbs) a photon, and leaves.

Let's examine the Feynman diagram for some familiar events. In Figure 13-6, two electrons approach each other, exchange a photon, and then move away from each other. That's Coulomb repulsion of like charges![6] It serves to illustrate one more rule: particle lines that both begin and end within the diagram are virtual particles,

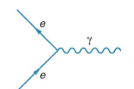

Fig. 13-5 The primitive vertex of the Feynman diagram. The particle, shown as an electron, could be a proton or any other particle that feels the electromagnetic force. Note that the photon line has no arrow. This diagram also represents the photoelectric effect.

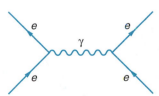

Fig. 13-6 Feynman diagram describing Coulomb repulsion of charges of the same sign.

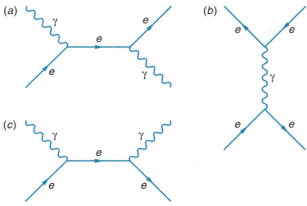

Fig. 13-7 (*a*) The Compton effect. A photon enters, is absorbed by an electron, which then emits a photon and leaves. (*b*) At the lower vertex an electron and a positron enter and annihilate, producing a photon. At the upper vertex the photon creates a particle-antiparticle pair. (*c*) Another possible pair annihilation process.

that is, like Yukawa's exchange pion in Section 11-5, they are not observed in the laboratory. The photon in Figure 13-6 is a *virtual photon.* Only lines that enter or leave the diagram represent observable particles. The diagram makes clear why we say that the electromagnetic force is *mediated* by photons. Figure 13-7*a* illustrates Compton scattering. Figure 13-7*b* describes an electron-positron scattering and includes both pair production (upper part) and pair annihilation (lower part). There can be many diagrams representing any given reaction.[7] For example, Figure 13-7*c* is also a possible pair annihilation process and Figure 13-7*b* would also be the diagram drawn to represent Coulomb attraction between charges of opposite sign. With this introduction we will now use simple Feynman diagrams throughout the remainder of this chapter to visualize reactions that might otherwise be very difficult to understand.

Richard Feynman, who called himself a "curious character," shared the 1965 Nobel Prize in physics for his contributions to the development of quantum electrodynamics. [*American Institute of Physics, Emilio Segrè Visual Archives, Physics Today Collection.*]

EXAMPLE 13-2 Feynman Diagram of Pion Exchange In Section 11-5 the nuclear force was described in terms of the exchange of virtual pions between pairs of nucleons. Draw two possible Feynman diagrams that illustrate this process.

Solution

First consider the case of two identical nucleons, say, two neutrons. Using the rules outlined above and noting that the virtual pions exists for too short a time to be measured, we draw its line horizontally (i.e., with $\Delta(ct) = 0$). The exchange is diagrammed as follows:

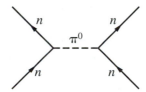

Since both particles are neutral, the exchange pion must be a π^0, since charge is conserved. Also, since either particle could emit and absorb the π^0, we don't show an arrow on its line.

Next consider the interaction between a neutron and a proton. The rules are the same, but we've elected to show exchange of a π^+, so now the pion line has an arrow since that exchange can go only one way.

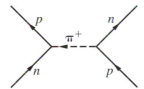

Can you draw diagrams for the *n-p* interaction using a π^0 and a π^-?

QUESTIONS

1. Explain *why* the small neutrino cross section for absorption in matter means that a large flux is needed to see neutrino reactions. Contrast this situation with the detection of positrons.

2. What problem would arise in using Dirac's filled infinite sea of negative-energy states to explain the existence of particle-antiparticle pairs of pions whose spins are zero?

3. Why do electron-positron pairs annihilate mainly from *S* states?

13-2 Fundamental Interactions and the Classification of Particles

All the different forces observed in nature, from ordinary friction to the tremendous forces involved in supernova explosions, can be understood in terms of the four basic interactions that occur among elementary particles. In order of decreasing strength, these are

1. The strong interaction
2. The electromagnetic interaction
3. The weak interaction
4. The gravitational interaction

Molecular forces and most of the everyday forces that we observe between macroscopic objects (for example, friction, contact forces, and forces exerted by springs and strings) are complex manifestations of the electromagnetic interaction, which occurs between all particles that carry electric charge. Although gravity, the interaction between all particles with mass, plays an important role in our lives, it is so weak compared with other forces that its role in the interactions between elementary particles is essentially negligible. The weak interaction describes, among others, the interaction between electrons or positrons and nucleons that results in beta decay, which we discussed in Chapter 11. The strong interaction describes, for example, the force between nucleons that holds nuclei together. The four basic interactions, or forces, provide a convenient structure for the classification of particles. Some particles participate in all four interactions, whereas others participate in only some of them.

In 1979, Glashow, Salam, and Weinberg shared the physics Nobel Prize for development of the *electroweak theory,* successfully unifying theories of the electromagnetic and the weak interactions. This event, which came exactly 100 years after Maxwell had accomplished unification of the theories of electricity and magnetism, was a major advancement in achieving unification of the theoretical descriptions of the four basic interactions. Developing such a unified field theory has been a goal of physics for a long time, one that was vigorously sought without success by Einstein, among many others. As we will discuss in Section 13-4, the electroweak unification occurs only at high particle energies. Current efforts to unify the electroweak, strong, and gravitational interactions will be discussed in Section 13-5.

The term "strength" of the interactions refers specifically to the relative magnitudes of the dimensionless *coupling constants* that multiply the fundamental space-dependent part of the potential energy function whose gradient determines the particular force. The relative strengths stated below are only approximate since there is no unambiguous method of comparison, particularly for the weak interaction. As an example, the electric (Coulomb) potential energy of two charges is $U(r) = -(1/4\pi\epsilon_0)e^2/r$. The multiplier of the space-dependent function $1/r$ is made dimensionless[8] by dividing both sides of the equation by the quantity $\hbar c$:

$$V(r) = U(r)/\hbar c = -\frac{e^2}{4\pi\epsilon_0 \hbar c}\frac{1}{r} \qquad \textbf{13-3}$$

where $V(r)$ is in m^{-1}. The quantity $(e^2/4\pi\epsilon_0\hbar c)$ you will recognize as the fine-structure constant $\alpha \approx 1/137$, first encountered in our discussion of Bohr's model of the hydrogen atom (see Section 4-3). The fine-structure constant is thus the coupling constant of the fundamental electromagnetic interaction. As we found in Chapter 4, energies resulting from this interaction are proportional to α^2 and characteristic dimensions (e.g., the Bohr radius a_0) are proportional to $1/\alpha$. (See Equations 4-32 and 4-33.) Moreover, the probability densities for atomic phenomena discussed in Chapter 7 are all directly dependent on the value of α. (See Equation 7-32.)

Just as Yukawa postulated the pion as the mediator, or carrier, of the force between nucleons (see Section 11-5), the current, highly successful *standard model* of particle theory, to be discussed in Section 13-4, postulates a particle as the mediator of each fundamental interaction. Each of these particles, all of which the theory requires to be bosons, will be introduced briefly in the following paragraphs concerned with each of the interactions.

Strong Interaction

Particles that interact via the strong interaction are called *hadrons* (from the Greek *hadros,* meaning "robust"). There are two subgroups of hadrons: those with 1/2-integral spins (1/2, 3/2, 5/2, etc.) are called *baryons* (Greek *barys,* "heavy"), while those with zero or integral spin are called *mesons.* The term *meson,* derived from the Greek *mesos,* meaning "middle," was chosen because the first mesons discovered had masses intermediate between the electron and the proton; however, many mesons heavier than the proton were subsequently discovered, so the name is no longer an indicator of the masses of these hadrons. The range of the strong force is about 10^{-15} m, or 1 fm. (See Chapter 11.) The coupling constant α_s of the strong interaction is approximately 1, or about 10^2 larger than the fine-structure constant α

A negative kaon (K) enters a bubble chamber from the bottom and decays into a π^-, which moves off to the right, and a π^0, which immediately decays into two photons whose paths are indicated by the dashed lines in the drawing. Each photon interacts in the lead sheet, producing an electron-positron pair. The spiral at the right is an electron that has been knocked out of an atom in the chamber. (Other, extraneous tracks have been removed from the photograph.)

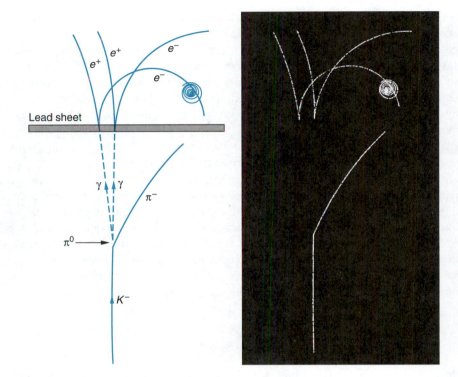

of the electromagnetic force. Within the framework of the standard model, the strong force is due to *color charge,* in analogy to the electromagnetic force being due to electric charge, but more on this later. Its characteristic *interaction time* is extremely short, only about 10^{-23} s, meaning that an event caused by this interaction "happens" in this length of time. Thus, if the probability is to be high that two particles will interact via the strong force by exchanging a virtual particle, the two must remain within the range of the force from each other for at least 10^{-23} s. Similarly, particles that decay due to the strong force do so within about 10^{-23} s. This is about the time it takes light to travel a distance equal to the diameter of a nucleus.

Table 13-1 lists some of the properties of the hadrons that are stable against decay via the strong interaction, that is, those with lifetimes significantly longer than 10^{-23} s. Those that decay via the electromagnetic and weak interactions have much longer lifetimes, typically of the order of 10^{-18} s and 10^{-10} s, respectively. Notice that all baryons ultimately decay to a proton. Note, too, that the baryons cluster into "charge multiplets" of about the same mass: the nucleons (n and p) of mass about 939 MeV, the lambda of mass about 1116 MeV, the Σ particles of mass about 1190 MeV, the Ξ particles of mass about 1315 MeV, and the Ω of mass 1672 MeV. The differences in masses within multiplets (such as between the neutron and proton) are due primarily to differences in the masses of the constituent quarks (see Section 13-4). There are six mesons in Table 13-1: three pions, two kaons, and the eta particle. The mesons also cluster into charge multiplets. As with the baryons, the mass differences within each multiplet are due to their electric charge. Note, however, that the mass of the π^+ is exactly equal to that of the π^-, as it must be since these particles are antiparticles of each other.

Hadrons are rather complicated entities with complex structures. If we use the term *elementary particle* to mean a point particle without structure that is not constructed from some more elementary entities, hadrons do not fit the bill. The standard model considers all hadrons to be composed of more fundamental entities called *quarks,* which are truly elementary particles. The mediating particle of the strong force is the *gluon,* rather

TABLE 13-1 Hadrons that are stable against decay via the strong interaction

Name	Symbol	Mass (MeV/c^2)	Spin $\hbar$	Charge e	Antiparticle	Mean lifetime (s)	Typical decay products[†]
Baryons							
Nucleon	p (proton) or N^+	938.3	$\frac{1}{2}$	$+1$	p^-	$>10^{32}$ y	
	n (neutron) or N^0	939.6	$\frac{1}{2}$	0	$\bar{n}$	930	$p + e^- + \bar{\nu}_e$
Lambda	Λ^0	1116	$\frac{1}{2}$	0	$\overline{\Lambda}^0$	2.5×10^{-10}	$p + \pi^-$
Sigma	Σ^+	1189	$\frac{1}{2}$	$+1$	$\overline{\Sigma}^-$	0.8×10^{-10}	$n + \pi^+$
	Σ^0	1192	$\frac{1}{2}$	0	$\overline{\Sigma}^0$	10^{-20}	$\Lambda^0 + \gamma$
	Σ^-	1197	$\frac{1}{2}$	-1	$\overline{\Sigma}^+$	1.7×10^{-10}	$n + \pi^-$
Xi*	Ξ^0	1315	$\frac{1}{2}$	0	$\overline{\Xi}^0$	3.0×10^{-10}	$\Lambda^0 + \pi^0$
	Ξ^-	1321	$\frac{1}{2}$	-1	$\overline{\Xi}^+$	1.7×10^{-10}	$\Lambda^0 + \pi^-$
Omega	Ω^-	1672	$\frac{3}{2}$	-1	Ω^+	1.3×10^{-10}	$\Xi^0 + \pi^-$
Charmed lambda	Λ_c^+	2285	$\frac{1}{2}$	$+1$	$\overline{\Lambda}_c^-$	1.8×10^{-13}	$p + K^- + \Lambda^+$
Mesons							
Pion	π^+	139.6	0	$+1$	π^-	2.6×10^{-8}	$\mu^+ + \nu_\mu$
	π^0	135	0	0	Self	0.8×10^{-16}	$\gamma + \gamma$
	π^-	139.6	0	-1	π^+	2.6×10^{-8}	$\mu^- + \bar{\nu}_\mu$
Kaon	K^+	493.7	0	$+1$	K^-	1.24×10^{-8}	$\pi^+ + \pi^0$
	K^0	497.7	0	0	$\overline{K}^0$	0.88×10^{-10} and $5.2 \times 10^{-8\ddagger}$	$\pi^+ + \pi^-$ $\pi^+ + e^- + \bar{\nu}_e$
Eta	η^0	549	0	0	Self	2×10^{-19}	$\gamma + \gamma$

†Other decay modes also occur for most particles.
‡The K^0 has two distinct lifetimes, sometimes referred to as K^0_{short} and K^0_{long}. All other particles have a unique lifetime.
*The Ξ particle is sometimes called the cascade.

than the pion as was concluded by Yukawa's analysis that was discussed in Chapter 11. We will explain how the pion appears to mediate the force between nucleons when we discuss quarks and gluons further in Section 13-4. Being complex particles composed of other, more fundamental particles, the hadrons each have a ground state and a set of quantized excited states directly analogous to the allowed energy levels of atoms and nuclei, which are of course also complex particles composed of other, more fundamental particles. These excited hadron states usually decay via the strong interaction and thus have large energy widths, as required by the uncertainty principle and in contrast with the much slower atomic transitions and nuclear decays. Excited hadron states are usually observed as resonances in the cross section for scattering of one hadron on another and are therefore also called *resonance particles*. We describe resonance particles more thoroughly on the home page (see page 642).

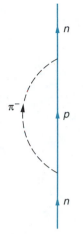

Fig. 13-8 A neutron emits a virtual π^-. During the time Δt that the positive proton and the π^- exist, they can interact with other charged particles. After time Δt the π^- is reabsorbed by the proton.

Electromagnetic Interaction

All particles with electric charge or magnetic moment participate in the electromagnetic interaction. In addition, neutral particles without magnetic moments may also participate in the interaction if the emission of a virtual particle results in charged particles. A neutron emitting and reabsorbing a virtual π^- as shown in Figure 13-8 is an example of a neutral particle involved in an electromagnetic interaction. The range of the electromagnetic force is infinite, and its strength is about 1/137 times that of the strong interaction, as we discussed earlier. Its characteristic interaction time is about 10^{-18} s. According to QED, the mediator of the electromagnetic force is the photon. Decays via the electromagnetic interaction always result in the emission of one or more photons. Notice in Table 13-1 that the Σ^0, π^0, and η^0 decay via the electromagnetic interaction.

Weak Interaction

All hadrons participate in the weak interaction. In addition, there is another group of particles that participate in the weak interaction, but do not feel the strong force. The particles in this group are called *leptons*. Leptons are thought to be point particles with no structure and can be considered to be truly elementary in the sense that they are not composed of other particles. All leptons have spin $\frac{1}{2}\hbar$ and are thus fermions. There are three pairs of leptons: the electron, the muon, and the tau and a distinct neutrino associated with each of these three particles. Interactions involving all six leptons have been observed experimentally. Each of the six leptons has an antiparticle. The masses of these particles are quite different.[9] The mass of the electron is 0.511 MeV/c^2, the mass of the muon is 106 MeV/c^2, and that of the tau is 1777 MeV/c^2.

For a long time following Pauli's prediction of their existence, neutrinos were thought to be massless, but there was considerable debate over the possibility that they might have a very small mass, perhaps of the order of a few eV/c^2. Experiments begun in the early 1970s designed to detect electron neutrinos emitted from the sun found a much smaller number than expected (see Section 14-2). This discrepancy could be explained by neutrino *oscillations*, that is, the transformation of one type of neutrino into another, since the early experiments were sensitive only to electron neutrinos. However, the standard model requires that neutrinos have mass in order to oscillate. In addition, a mass as small as 40 eV/c^2 for the neutrino would have great cosmological significance. The answer to the question of whether the universe will continue to expand indefinitely or will reach a maximum size and begin to contract

Fig. 13-9 Electron antineutrino energy vs. arrival time in the Kamiokande detector in Japan for antineutrinos emitted by the supernova 1987A. The spread in arrival times (about 13 s) permits a calculation of an upper limit to the mass of the $\bar{\nu}_e$.

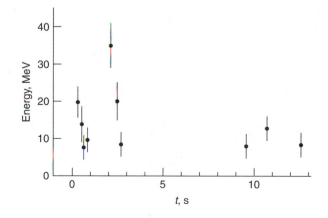

depends on the total mass of the universe. Thus, the answer could depend on whether the rest mass of the neutrino is merely very small rather than zero. Observation of electron neutrinos from the supernova 1987A provided a means of putting an upper limit on the mass of these neutrinos. Since the velocity of a particle with mass depends on its energy (for a given mass, higher-energy particles move faster than lower-energy ones), the arrival time of a burst of neutrinos with mass from a super- nova would be spread out in time. The fact that the electron neutrinos from super- nova 1987A all arrived at Earth within 13 seconds of one another placed an upper limit of about 16 eV/c^2 on their mass, but did not rule out the possibility of the mass being zero. (See Figure 13-9 and Problem 13-11.) Then in 2001 the Sudbury Neutrino Observatory (Canada) reported the first direct observations of oscillation of solar electron neutrinos into other neutrino types, or *flavors*. Combined with preci- sion measurements from the Super-Kamiokande neutrino detector (Japan) and others, the sum of the masses of the three neutrino flavors lies between 0.05 and 8.4 eV/c^2 and the mass of the electron neutrino between 0.07 and 2.8 eV/c^2. It is now certain that the contribution of neutrino mass in the cosmos is insufficient to account for more than a small fraction of the "missing mass" of the universe (see Section 14-2). This is an area of intense current research.

The range of the weak force is about 10^{-18} m or about 10^{-3} fm. Example 13-3 shows how the range of the weak force is determined. Its characteristic interaction time varies from about 10^{-16} s to about 10^{-10} s. No particular name is given to the entity that produces the weak force, although it is occasionally called the *weak charge* or *flavor charge,* in analogy with electric charge. The strength of the weak interaction relative to the strong interaction is about 10^{-5}. The weak force is carried by three particles, the W^+ and W^- (W for "weak") and the Z^0 (Z for "zero"). All three have spin $1\hbar$ and thus are bosons. They were all discovered in 1983 by C. Rubbia and his co-workers at CERN[10] after a long search. (See Figures 13-10 and 13-11.) The Z^0 is the second heaviest elementary particle known, with a mass of 91 GeV/c^2, or nearly 100 times that of the proton. The $W^\pm$, with masses of 81 GeV/c^2, are the next heaviest. Their mediations of two typical weak interactions, the scattering of a muon neutrino by an electron and the scattering of an electron neutrino and an electron, are illustrated in Figure 13-12.

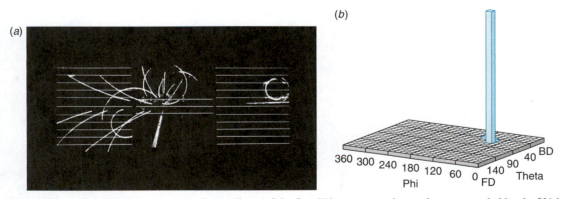

Fig. 13-10 (*a*) The production and subsequent decay of one of the first W bosons ever detected were recorded by the UA1 detector at the CERN Sp$\overline{p}$S proton-antiproton collider. A W^+ is produced which decays by $W^+ \rightarrow \tau^+ + \nu_\tau$. The tau decays into charged particles and is clearly seen as a pencil-jet in the central detector. Conservation of energy and momentum yield results consistent with a missing ν_e from the decay. [*CERN.*] (*b*) The UA1's energy detectors surrounding the beam pipe recorded the energetic e^+ and its angular position relative to the decay event.

(a)

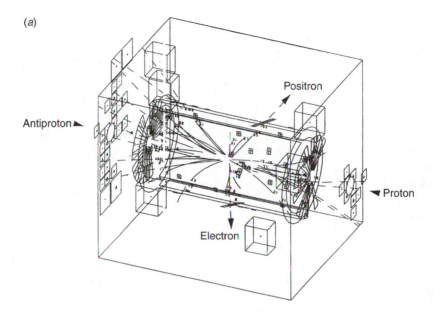

(b)

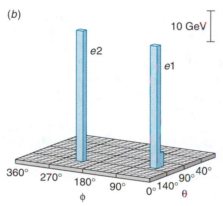

Fig. 13-11 (*a*) This computer reconstruction of the CERN UA1 detector shows the first Z^0 decay ever recorded, obtained by Rubbia's group in 1983. Millions more such events have since been seen. [CERN Courier, *33, 4 (1993)*.] (*b*) The energy plot of the electron-positron pair from the $Z^0 \rightarrow e^+ + e^-$ decay. Energy, plotted vertically, is measured by individual detectors that "wrap around" the central cylinder of the UA1. The angular locations of the recorded electron and positron are measured relative to the position of the Z^0. Graphs like this are called "Lego plots."

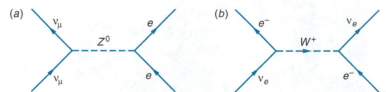

Fig. 13-12 (*a*) The scattering of a muon neutrino from an electron involves the exchange of a Z^0. Such an exchange is called a *neutral current* interaction. The interaction does not convert the electron into a muon neutrino. (*b*) The scattering of an electron neutrino from an electron may also occur via a neutral current interaction as in (*a*), but a *charge current* interaction in which a charged W is exchanged is also possible, and both would contribute to the cross section. Measuring the cross sections thus provides a means of testing the standard model.

EXAMPLE 13-3 Range of the Weak Interaction The mass of the Z^0 has been accurately measured to be 91.16 GeV/c^2. What range does that value imply for the neutral current weak interaction mediated by the Z^0?

Solution

1. The range, the distance R traveled in time $t = \hbar/\Delta E$ by a particle moving at about c, is given by Equation 11-50:

$$R = \frac{\hbar}{mc} = \frac{\hbar c}{mc^2}$$

2. Substituting the mass of the Z^0 into this expression for R gives:

$$R = \frac{(1.055 \times 10^{-34}\,\text{J}\cdot\text{s})(3.00 \times 10^8\,\text{m/s})}{(91.16\,\text{GeV}/c^2)(1.60 \times 10^{-10}\,\text{J/GeV})}$$

$$= 2.18 \times 10^{-18}\,\text{m} = 2.18 \times 10^{-3}\,\text{fm}$$

Gravitational Interaction

All particles participate in the gravitational interaction, but this interaction is so weak as to be unimportant in the discussion of elementary particles. As we have seen previously, its strength relative to the strong interactions is about 10^{-38}. The interaction has infinite range, with the force decreasing as $1/r^2$, as does the electrostatic force. The mediating particle for this force is the *graviton,* which is expected to be uncharged, massless, and have spin $2\hbar$. This particle has not yet been observed, nor does experimental capability to do so yet exist. Experiments with the objective of detecting gravity waves are currently underway. (See Section 2-5.) The gravitational interaction is produced by mass, which is the "gravitational charge" corresponding to the color charge, electric charge, and weak charge of the strong, electromagnetic, and weak interactions, respectively. Table 13-2 summarizes the characteristics of the four fundamental interactions.

TABLE 13-2 Characteristics of the fundamental interactions

Interaction	Exchange boson	Mass (GeV/c^2)	Spin ($\hbar$)	Source	Range (m)	Interaction time (s)	Coupling constant
Strong	Gluon	0	1	Color charge	10^{-15}	10^{-23}	$\alpha_s \approx 1$
Electromagnetic	Photon	0	1	Electric charge	∞	10^{-18}	$\alpha = 1/137$
Weak	$W^{\pm}$, Z^0	81, 91	1, 1	Weak charge	10^{-18}	10^{-16}–10^{-10}	10^{-5}
Gravity	Graviton	0	2	Mass	∞	—	10^{-38}

Exploring

A Further Comment About Interaction Strengths

At the beginning of this section we defined the strengths of the interactions in terms of the coupling constants, relating their approximate values to the most familiar one, which is the fine-structure constant $\alpha = e^2/4\pi\epsilon_0 \hbar c$. In QED the electric charge

$$e = \sqrt{4\pi\epsilon_0 \hbar c \alpha} \propto \sqrt{\alpha}$$

is the amplitude of the coupling of the photon (the exchange boson) to the electron (the particle). Thus the probability of events involving that coupling, such as the photoelectric effect (illustrated in Figure 13-5), is proportional to $e^2 \propto \alpha$.

The time-independent solution to the Klein-Gordon equation (Equation 11-52) can also be interpreted as the static potential $U(r)$ of the field of a point charge represented by the exchange particles. We then have

$$U(r) = \frac{Ae^{-r/R}}{r} \qquad \textbf{13-4}$$

where A is a constant of integration and $R = \hbar/mc$ is both the range of the force and the Compton wavelength $\lambda_c/2\pi$ of the exchange boson. For the electromagnetic interaction the range R is infinite and $U(r)$ becomes

$$U(r) = \frac{A}{r} \qquad \textbf{13-5}$$

Recalling from classical electromagnetism that the electrostatic potential of a point charge q is $U(r) = q/4\pi\epsilon_0 r$, we see that the constant A in Equation 13-5 plays the same role as the charge. In this manner a coupling constant proportional to A^2, just as $\alpha \propto e^2$, can be obtained for each of the interactions, albeit not without some difficulty, involving for the strong and weak interactions mathematics beyond the scope of our discussions. As we will see in Section 13-4, this use of QED as a model is a powerful aid in understanding both the weak and the strong interactions. The coupling constants and other characteristics of the four interactions are given in Table 13-2.

One last comment before we leave this topic: the coupling constants are not actually constants. Again, this can be most clearly illustrated using the electromagnetic interaction. Consider a positive point charge q embedded in a dielectric as shown in Figure 13-13. The charge q polarizes the nearby molecules of the dielectric. As a result, the charge q is partially screened by the negative ends of the polarized molecules and the electric field of q at a distance r away is correspondingly reduced. Thus, the value measured for q is the effective charge q_{eff} which depends on how far from q the measurement is made, where q_{eff} is given by

$$q_{\text{eff}} = \frac{q}{\epsilon} \qquad \textbf{13-6}$$

and ϵ is the dielectric constant of the material, which you remember is a measure of how difficult it is to polarize the material. Only by measuring very close to q, roughly

speaking within the molecular equilibrium separation r_0 (closer than the closest molecule so that there is no screening), will you actually measure the value q. This is shown in Figure 13-13b. Notice, also, that (1) measurements made at large values of r yield q/ϵ, not q, and (2) the value of q_{eff} *increases* for very small values of r.

The production and absorption of virtual particles in QED results in the vacuum behaving like a dielectric. The positive charge q (or any charge) is continually emitting and absorbing virtual photons. Some of the photons occasionally create electron-positron pairs, which then annihilate, as the Feynman diagram in Figure 13-13c illustrates. The virtual electron and positron are attracted and repelled, respectively, by q, resulting in *vacuum polarization* which partially screens q, just as it was screened when embedded in the dielectric. And just as in the dielectric, the full value of the charge q is not seen, or measured, until you get inside the screen. In vacuum polarization the role of the equilibrium separation r_0 is played by the Compton wavelength of the electron $\lambda_c = h/mc = 2.43 \times 10^{-12}$ m. Thus, even in a vacuum the "actual" value of q can only be measured at distances closer than about 2.43×10^{-12} m. What we measure experimentally and refer to as "the charge of the electron" is actually the completely screened effective charge. Thus, the fine-structure constant α, which is proportional to the square of the electric charge, will *increase* at very small distances from q.

A corresponding discussion can be given for the weak and strong interactions, but there are significant differences. The photon, which mediates the electromagnetic interaction, does not carry electric charge. However, the $W^\pm$ and Z^0, which mediate the weak interaction, have mass and do carry weak charge. (The $W^\pm$ do carry electric charge.) The gluons, which mediate the strong force, carry color charge. This latter difference results in an important characteristic of the strong force called *confinement* that we will discuss further in Section 13-4.

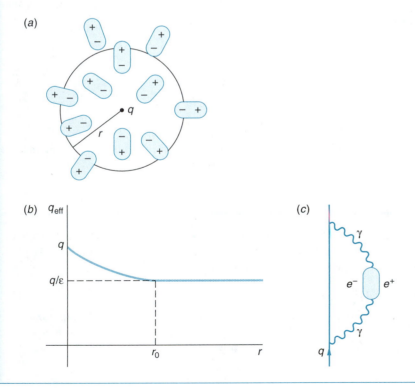

(a)

(b) q_{eff}

(c)

Fig. 13-13 (*a*) A positive charge q placed in a dielectric material polarizes the dielectric by orienting the nearby molecules with their negative ends closest to q. An observer at some distance r from q sees a reduced electric field because of the screen of negative charges. (*b*) The value q_{eff} is measured for the charge. At small distances, those less than the equilibrium separation of the molecules of the dielectric, the value of q_{eff} approaches the value of q. (*c*) The vacuum also polarizes like a dielectric due to production of virtual electron-positron pairs by virtual photons. The effect is to increase the value of the fine-structure constant at very short interaction distances.

QUESTIONS

4. How are baryons and mesons similar? How are they different?

5. What properties do all leptons have in common?

6. The mass of the muon is nearly equal to that of the pion. How do these particles differ?

7. The bonding of the electrons to nuclei to form atoms is an example of the electromagnetic interaction. Use the interaction's properties to explain why the dimensions of atoms are of the order of 10^{-10} m.

8. Describe a way in which the world would be different if electrons felt the strong interaction.

EXAMPLE 13-4 **Neutron Decay** The free neutron decays via the weak interaction with a half-life of 10.4 min according to the reaction

$$n \longrightarrow p + e^- + \bar{\nu}_e$$

Use a Feynman diagram to illustrate the details of this decay.

Solution
Since this decay involves a change in the charge of the hadron, the mediating boson is a W^-. The W^- then decays to the e^- and $\bar{\nu}_e$. The Feynman diagram describing these events is therefore as shown below, recalling that particles shown moving backward in time are to be interpreted as the corresponding antiparticle moving forward in time.

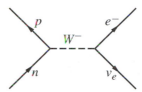

In words, this diagram is read like this: A neutron emits a W^-, changing (decaying) to a proton. The W^- then decays to an e^- and $\bar{\nu}_e$.

EXAMPLE 13-5 **Estimate of Cross Section for Strong Interaction** Obtain a rough estimate for the cross section of a typical strong interaction scattering of two hadrons, such as pions by protons or protons by protons.

Solution
1. The cross section σ for an interaction or reaction is given approximately by the area of a circle whose radius is the range of the interaction. (See Section 12-1.) For the strong interaction we can write, therefore, that:

$$\sigma_S = \pi R_S^2$$

2. From Table 13-2 we find the range of the strong interaction R_S to be 10^{-15} m. Therefore, σ_S is equal to:

$$\sigma_S = \pi(10^{-15} \text{ m})^2$$
$$= 3.1 \times 10^{-30} \text{ m}^2 = 31 \text{ mb}$$

Remarks: *The cross section, as noted in Section 12-1, is actually dependent on the collision energy, but typical values are of the order of tens of millibarns, in agreement with our approximation.*

13-3 Conservation Laws and Symmetries

One of the maxims of nature, sometimes referred to as the *totalitarian principle,* is "anything that can happen, does happen." If a conceivable decay or reaction does *not* occur, then there must be a reason. The reason is usually expressed in terms of a conservation law. You are already familiar with several such laws. The conservation of energy rules out the decay of any particle for which the total mass of the decay products would be greater than the initial mass of the particle before decay. The conservation of linear momentum requires that when an electron and positron annihilate, two photons (at least) must be emitted. Angular momentum must also be conserved in a reaction or decay. A fourth conservation law that restricts the possible particle decays and reactions is that of electric charge. The net electric charge before a decay or reaction must equal the net charge after the decay or reaction.

Baryon Number

In Section 11-4 we mentioned two additional conservation laws in our discussion of radioactive decay, conservation of nucleon number and of lepton number. We now need to state these more explicitly. The first is a special case of the following more general law:

The baryon number is conserved.

All baryons have baryon quantum number $B = +1$, all antibaryons have $B = -1$, and all other particles are assigned $B = 0$. Conservation of baryon number requires that the total B for all particles before a decay or reaction occurs must be equal to that for all particles afterward. As an example of baryon conservation, consider the production of the antiproton in Figure 13-3 again. The reaction is

$$p + p \longrightarrow p + p + p + \bar{p} \qquad \textbf{13-7}$$

The total baryon number before the reaction is $B = +1 + 1 = +2$. That after the reaction is $B = +1 + 1 + 1 - 1 = +2$. Thus, conservation of B requires that three protons appear on the right side of Equation 13-7, that is, the production of an antiproton is always accompanied by the production of a proton. Conservation of baryon number together with the conservation of energy implies that the least massive baryon, the proton, must be stable. Whether that is in fact true is a matter of current debate among particle physicists. We will return to that debate later in this section.

Lepton Number

The leptons are fundamental particles, and conservation of leptons applies independently to each of the three types, or *flavors*.

The lepton number for each flavor of leptons is independently conserved.

The lepton quantum number for the electron and the electron neutrino is $L_e = +1$, and that for the positron and electron antineutrino is $L_e = -1$. All other particles, including the other leptons, have $L_e = 0$. In a similar fashion the lepton quantum numbers L_μ are assigned for the muon generation and L_τ for the tau generation. To see how conservation of lepton number works, consider the following decays:

$$p \longrightarrow \pi^0 + e^+ \qquad \text{13-8}$$

$$\mu^+ \longrightarrow e^+ + \nu_e + \overline{\nu}_\mu \qquad \text{13-9}a$$

$$\mu^+ \longrightarrow e^+ + \gamma \qquad \text{13-9}b$$

$$n \longrightarrow p + e^- + \overline{\nu}_e \qquad \text{13-10}$$

The decay shown in Equation 13-8 would conserve energy, charge, angular momentum, and linear momentum, but it has not been observed. It conserves neither baryon number B or lepton number L_e. The decay of the μ^+, given by Equation 13-9a results in both an electron neutrino and a muon antineutrino. The μ^+ has $L_\mu = -1$ and $L_e = 0$. The decay products also have $L_\mu = -1$ (the $\overline{\nu}_\mu$) and $L_e = -1 + 1 = 0$ (the e^+ and ν_e). The μ^+ decay given in Equation 13-9b has been searched for by many groups without success for many years. Its absence was the first indicator that L_e and L_μ were independently conserved. Equation 13-10, the decay of the neutron, conserves both

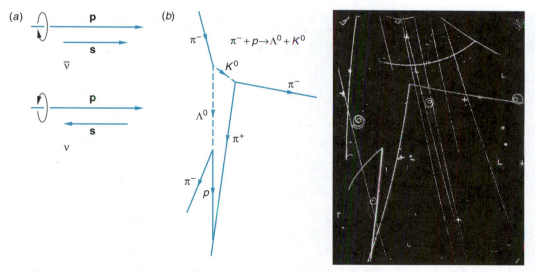

Fig. 13-14 (*a*) The spin of antineutrinos is parallel to the momentum. The spin of neutrinos is antiparallel to the momentum. Described in terms of *helicity* $= m_s/s$ with the z axis in the direction of **p**, antineutrinos have helicity $+1$ and neutrinos have helicity -1. (*b*) An early photograph of bubble chamber tracks at the Lawrence Berkeley Laboratory, showing the production, represented by Equation 13-25, and decay of two strange particles, the K^0 and the Λ^0. These neutral particles are identified by the tracks of their decay particles. The lambda particle was named because of the similarity of the tracks of its decay particles and the Greek letter Λ. The incident π^- meson had energy of 1 GeV. [(*b*) *Lawrence Berkeley Laboratory/Photo Researchers.*]

B and L_e. Conservation of lepton number implies that the neutrino emitted in the beta decay of a free neutron is an electron antineutrino. The fact that neutrinos and anti-neutrinos are indeed different is illustrated by an experiment in which ^{37}Cl is bombarded with the intense antineutrino flux from the decay of neutrons in a large reactor. If neutrinos and antineutrinos were identical, we would expect the following reaction:

$$^{37}_{17}\text{Cl} + \bar{\nu}_e \longrightarrow {}^{37}_{18}\text{Ar} + e^- \qquad \textbf{13-11}$$

This reaction is not observed. However, when the antineutrinos are used to bombard protons, the reaction

$$\bar{\nu}_e + p \longrightarrow n + e^+ \qquad \textbf{13-12}$$

is observed. Note that L_e is -1 on the left side of Equation 13-11 (like $\bar{\nu}_e + n$), but $+1$ on the right (like $p + e^-$). $L_e = -1$ on both sides of Equation 13-12. This is the reaction in which the antineutrino was first observed by Reines and Cowan. (See Section 11-4.) The neutrino and its antiparticle are uncharged particles without structure, hence without magnetic moments, and have identical masses and spins. The difference between them is a subtle but profound one: they are polarized. The neutrino spin is always antiparallel to its momentum; the antineutrino has its spin and momentum always parallel. (See Figure 13-14*a*.) Table 13-3 summarizes the quantum numbers and properties of the leptons.

TABLE 13-3 Properties of the leptons

Lepton	Spin ($\hbar$)	Mass (MeV/c^2)	Lifetime (s)	L_e	L_μ	L_τ
e^-	$\frac{1}{2}$	0.5110	Stable	1	0	0
ν_e	$\frac{1}{2}$	≤ 2.8 eV/c^2	Stable	1	0	0
μ^-	$\frac{1}{2}$	105.659	2.197×10^{-6}	0	1	0
ν_μ	$\frac{1}{2}$	≤ 3.5 eV/c^2	Stable	0	1	0
τ^-	$\frac{1}{2}$	1784	3.3×10^{-13}	0	0	1
ν_τ	$\frac{1}{2}$	≤ 8.4 eV/c^2	Stable	0	0	1

EXAMPLE 13-6 Conservation Laws What conservation laws (if any) are violated by the following reactions?

(*a*) $n \longrightarrow p + \pi^-$

(*b*) $\Lambda^0 \longrightarrow \bar{p} + \pi^+$

(*c*) $\pi^- \longrightarrow \mu^- + \bar{\nu}_\mu$

Solution

(*a*) There are no leptons in this decay, so there is no problem with the conservation of lepton number. The net charge is zero before and after the decay, so charge is conserved. Also, the baryon number is +1 before and after the decay. However, the rest energy of the proton (938.3 MeV) plus that of the pion (139.6 MeV) is greater than the rest energy of the neutron (939.6 MeV). Thus, this decay violates the conservation of energy.

(*b*) Again, there are no leptons involved, and the net charge is zero before and after the decay. Also, the rest energy of the Λ^0 (1116 MeV) is greater than the rest energy of the antiproton (938.3 MeV) plus that of the pion (139.6 MeV), so energy is conserved with the loss in rest energy equaling the gain in kinetic energy of the decay products. However, this decay does not conserve baryon number, which is +1 for the Λ^0, −1 for the antiproton, and 0 for the pion.

(*c*) There are no baryons involved, so conservation of baryon number is not a problem. The net charge is −1 before and after the decay, so charge is conserved. Also, the rest energy of the π^- (139.6 MeV) is greater than that of the μ^- (105.7 MeV) and the $\bar{\nu}_\mu$, so energy is conserved, the difference appearing as kinetic energy of the muon and neutrino. Finally, $L_\mu = 0$ on the left side and $L_\mu = 1 - 1 = 0$ on the right side, so lepton number is also conserved. This is the reaction by which the π^- decays.

More

Each conservation law results from a particular symmetry in the laws that govern the physical universe. Since it is not necessarily obvious under what mathematical operations the laws of physics will be symmetric, on a pragmatic level it is fair to ask, quantum-mechanically, *When Is a Physical Quantity Conserved?* We provide an answer to this question on the home page: www.whfreeman.com/modphysics4e   See also Equations 13-13 through 13-24 here, as well as Example 13-7.

More Conservation Laws

Strangeness   There are some conservation laws that are not universal but apply only to certain kinds of interactions. In particular, there are quantities that are conserved in decays and reactions that occur via the strong interaction but not in decays or reactions that occur via the weak interaction. This is somewhat analogous to the selection rules discussed in atomic transitions. For example, the selection rule $\Delta l = \pm 1$ holds for electric dipole transitions from one atomic state to another. An atom in a state with $l = 2$ cannot decay to a lower energy state with $l = 0$ via electric dipole radiation because of this selection rule, but it can decay via an electric quadrupole transition, which is generally much slower than electric dipole transitions. One of the quantities conserved in strong interactions that is particularly important is *strangeness*. This quantity was introduced by M. Gell-Mann[12] and K. Nishijima in 1952 to explain the seemingly strange behavior of the heavy baryons and mesons. Consider the reaction in which a high-energy π^- interacts with a proton,

The need to transfer rapidly enormous volumes of data collected by detectors at the major particle physics laboratories throughout the world to the thousands of collaborating scientists in many countries led to the development of a high-speed, worldwide computer network. It grew into the *Internet!*

$$p + \pi^- \longrightarrow \Lambda^0 + K^0 \qquad \textbf{13-25}$$

shown in Figure 13-14b. The cross section for this reaction is large, as would be expected since it takes place via the strong interaction (see Example 13-5). However, the decay times for both Λ^0 and K^0 are of the order of 10^{-10} s, which is characteristic of the weak interaction. When first discovered, their unexpectedly long lifetimes were very strange, so these and other particles showing similar behavior were called *strange particles.*

These particles are always produced in pairs and never singly, even when all other conservation laws are met. This behavior is described by assigning a new quantum number, called strangeness, to these particles. The strangeness of the ordinary hadrons—the nucleons and pions—was arbitrarily chosen to be zero. The strangeness of the K^0 was arbitrarily chosen to be +1. Therefore, the strangeness of the Λ^0 particle must be −1 so that strangeness is conserved in the reaction of Equation 13-25. The strangeness of other particles could then be assigned by looking at their various reactions and decays. In reactions and decays that occur via the strong and electromagnetic interactions, strangeness is conserved. In those that occur via the weak interaction, strangeness is not conserved, but can only change by ±1.

Isospin   We mentioned earlier that the hadrons cluster into *charge multiplets,* groups of particles with nearly the same mass, such as the multiplet consisting of the proton and neutron. In addition, we learned in Section 11-5 that the strong (nuclear) force is independent of electric charge. Were it not for the electromagnetic interaction, the masses of the particles in a given charge multiplet would be the same. We are thus led to the view that the members of the multiplet are simply different charge states of the same particle. The "splitting" of particle mass states is analogous to the splitting of atomic energy states due to the spin-orbit interaction. (See Section 7-5.) Because of the analogy with isotopes (atoms with the same *Z,* but slightly different masses) and with the splitting of different spin states, the term *isospin* is used to describe this multiplicity. The isospin **T** is treated as a vector in a three-dimensional "charge space," just as the orbital angular momentum **L** is a vector in real space. The component of **T** in the "z direction" is called T_3 and is quantized, just as the z components of the orbital and intrinsic angular momenta of atomic electrons are quantized. The charge q on a particle is related to its value of T_3 by

$$q = eQ = e\left(T_3 + \frac{B + S}{2}\right) \qquad \textbf{13-26}$$

where Q is the charge quantum number. The value of T of the nucleon is 1/2, with the two possible values $T_3 = +1/2$ for the proton and $T_3 = -1/2$ for the neutron. The isospin T is also 1/2 for the Xi doublet, and 0 for the lambda and omega singlets. It is 1 for the Σ triplet (with $T_3 = +1$ for Σ^+, 0 for Σ^0, and −1 for Σ^-). In the case of the mesons, the pion isospin triplet has $T = 1$, the kaon doublet $T = 1/2$, and the eta singlet $T = 0$. The rules for combining isospin are the same as those for combining real spin or angular momentum. If only the strong interaction is present, then T_{op} and H_{op} commute and **T** is conserved. Decays and reactions in which the total isospin of the system is not conserved do not proceed via the strong interaction.

Hypercharge   Four of the quantum numbers that we have discussed thus far turn out to be related to one another. These are strangeness, charge, isospin, and baryon number. The relation is

$$S = 2(Q - T_3) - B \qquad\qquad \textbf{13-27}$$

Strangeness is now used less frequently than a simpler quantity called *hypercharge*, which is defined as the sum of the strangeness and baryon number. With the aid of Equation 13-27 the hypercharge quantum number Y is then given by

$$Y = S + B = 2(Q - T_3) \qquad\qquad \textbf{13-28}$$

Stated simply, the hypercharge is twice the average charge of a given multiplet. For example, the average charge of the nucleon multiplet is $(1e + 0)/2 = (1/2)e$. Thus, for the nucleon $Y = 1$, as given by Equation 13-28. Since baryon number is strictly conserved and strangeness is conserved only in strong interactions, hypercharge, too, is conserved only in strong interactions. Since $\Delta S = \pm 1$ or 0 in weak interactions, changes in hypercharge are similarly restricted to $\Delta Y = \pm 1$ or 0. Table 13-4 lists the values of these additional quantum numbers for those hadrons that are stable against decay via the strong interaction. Note that, if it were not for the conservation of strangeness or hypercharge in the strong interaction, all the baryons except the nucleons would decay via the strong interaction and live only for about 10^{-23} s.

TABLE 13-4 Some quantum numbers of the hadrons that are stable against decay via the strong interaction

Particle	Spin, $\hbar$	T	T_3	B	S	Y
p	$\frac{1}{2}$	$\frac{1}{2}$	$+\frac{1}{2}$	1	0	1
n	$\frac{1}{2}$	$\frac{1}{2}$	$-\frac{1}{2}$	1	0	1
Λ^0	$\frac{1}{2}$	0	0	1	-1	0
Σ^+	$\frac{1}{2}$	1	$+1$	1	-1	0
Σ^0	$\frac{1}{2}$	1	0	1	-1	0
Σ^-	$\frac{1}{2}$	1	-1	1	-1	0
Ξ^0	$\frac{1}{2}$	$\frac{1}{2}$	$+\frac{1}{2}$	1	-2	-1
Ξ^-	$\frac{1}{2}$	$\frac{1}{2}$	$-\frac{1}{2}$	1	-2	-1
Ω^-	$\frac{3}{2}$	0	0	1	-3	-2
π^+	0	1	$+1$	0	0	0
π^0	0	1	0	0	0	0
π^-	0	1	-1	0	0	0
K^+	0	$\frac{1}{2}$	$+\frac{1}{2}$	0	$+1$	$+1$
K^0	0	$\frac{1}{2}$	$-\frac{1}{2}$	0	$+1$	$+1$
η^0	0	0	0	0	0	0

Note: The isospin T is the same for all the particles in a multiplet and for their antiparticles. The values of T_3, B, S, and Y for the antiparticles are the negatives of those for the particles.

The singlet, doublet, and triplet charge multiplets discussed above are clearly represented in graphs of Y versus T_3. Studies of the regularities apparent in such graphs (see Figure 13-15) were instrumental in the development of the quark model of fundamental particles to be discussed in Section 13-4. The regularities are analogous to those observed in the multiplet structure of atomic energy states that ultimately led to the understanding of atomic structure.

The conservation laws and the properties of charge Q, lepton number L, baryon number B, and strangeness S give us some insight into the relation between particles and their antiparticles. A particle and its antiparticle must have opposite signs for the values of each of these properties. Any particle that has a nonzero value for any of these properties will therefore have a distinct antiparticle. The photon, graviton, and the π^0 have $Q = 0$, $L = 0$, $B = 0$, and $S = 0$ and are therefore in some sense their own antiparticles. The π^+ and π^- mesons are somewhat special because they have charge but have zero values for L, B, and S. They are therefore antiparticles of each other, but since there is no conservation law for mesons, it is impossible to say which is the particle and which is the antiparticle.

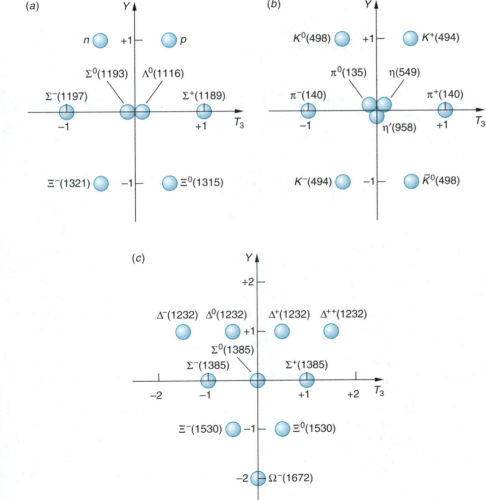

Fig. 13-15 Graphs of hypercharge Y vs. the T_3 component of the isospin. (*a*) Baryons with spin $\frac{1}{2}\hbar$. (*b*) Mesons with spin 0. (*c*) Baryons with spin $\frac{3}{2}\hbar$. Except for the Ω^-, these are resonance particles as discussed in Section 13-2 and on the home page. Masses in parentheses are in MeV/c^2. Notice in each case that particles of like charge lie along downward-sloping diagonals and particles of like hypercharge (and strangeness) lie along horizontal lines.

EXAMPLE 13-8 Applying the Conservation Laws State whether the following decays can occur via the strong interaction, via the electromagnetic interaction, via the weak interaction, or not at all:

$$(a) \ \Sigma^+ \longrightarrow p + \pi^0 \qquad (b) \ \Sigma^0 \longrightarrow \Lambda^0 + \gamma \qquad (c) \ \Xi^0 \longrightarrow n + \pi^0$$

Solution
We first note the mass of each decaying particle is greater than that of the decay products, so there is no problem with energy conservation in any of the decays. In addition, there are no leptons involved in any of the decays, and charge and baryon number are both conserved in all the decays.

(a) From Figure 13-15, we can see that the hypercharge of the Σ^+ is 0 whereas the hypercharge of the proton is $+1$ and that of the pion is zero. This decay is possible via the weak interaction but not the strong interaction. It is, in fact, one of the decay modes of the Σ^+ particle with a lifetime of the order of 10^{-10} s.

(b) Since the hypercharge of both the Σ^0 and Λ^0 is 0, this decay can proceed via the electromagnetic interaction. It is, in fact, the dominant mode of decay of the Σ^0 particle with a lifetime of about 10^{-20} s.

(c) The hypercharge of the Ξ^0 is -1 whereas that of the neutron is $+1$ and that of the pion is zero. Since hypercharge cannot change by 2 in a decay or reaction, this decay cannot occur.

QUESTIONS

9. How can you tell if a decay proceeds via the strong, electromagnetic, or weak interactions?

10. Can the strangeness or hypercharge of a new particle be determined even if the number of particles in the multiplet is unknown? How, or why not?

Parity   As our final example of a conservation law, we consider *parity*. The parity of a nucleus or particle is defined in the same way as for an atom. (See Section 6-5.) If the wave function changes sign upon reflection of the coordinates, the parity is said to be odd, or -1. If the wave function does not change sign, the parity is even, or $+1$. The parity quantum number P is different from the other quantum numbers we have been considering in that it can have only the values $+1$ or -1. If the value of the parity of a system changes, the new value is -1 times the old value. Parity is therefore a multiplicative property rather than an additive property like baryon number, strangeness, or hypercharge. The parity of an atomic wave function is related to the orbital angular momentum by $P = (-1)^l$. The parity is odd or even depending on whether l is odd or even. In our discussion of radiation from atoms, we saw that the parity of an atom can change just as the angular momentum of the atom changes when the atom emits light. For electric dipole transitions, $\Delta l = \pm 1$, so the parity and angular momentum quantum numbers always change. However, if the complete system including the photon is considered, the total angular momentum and the total parity do not change in atomic transitions, that is, parity is conserved in electromagnetic interactions.

Until 1956 it was assumed that parity is conserved in all nuclear reactions and radioactive decays. In that year, T. D. Lee and C. N. Yang suggested that parity might

not be conserved in weak interactions. This suggestion grew out of attempts to understand the peculiar behavior of what were then known as the τ and θ mesons. These particles were identical in every way except that the θ meson decayed into two pions with positive parity, whereas the τ decayed into three pions with negative parity. (Each elementary particle can be assigned an intrinsic parity. That of the pion is negative.) The τ-θ puzzle was this: Are there two different particles with all properties identical except parity, or is it possible that parity is not conserved in some reactions? After careful study Lee and Yang found all the experimental evidence for parity conservation pertained to strong or electromagnetic interactions and not to weak interactions. They suggested that the nonconservation of parity could be observed experimentally by measuring the angular distribution of electrons emitted in β decay of nuclei that have their spins aligned. Such an experiment was performed in December 1956 by a group led by C. S. Wu and E. Ambler. The results confirmed Lee and Yang's predictions. The τ and θ mesons are a single particle, now known as the K^0 meson, which has two distinct modes of decay.

The conservation of parity essentially means that a process described by the coordinates x, y, and z appears the same if described by the coordinates $x' = -x$, $y' = -y$, and $z' = -z$. The system x, y, z is called a *right-handed coordinate system* because $\mathbf{x} \times \mathbf{y}$ is in the $+\mathbf{z}$ direction. Similarly, the system x', y', z' is called a *left-handed coordinate system* because $\mathbf{x}' \times \mathbf{y}'$ is in the negative $\mathbf{z}'$ direction. No rotation can change a right-handed coordinate system into a left-handed one; but reflection in a mirror does, as shown in Figure 13-16a. We can thus state the law of conservation of parity in more physical terms: if parity is conserved, the mirror image of a process cannot be distinguished from the process itself. Figure 13-16b shows a spinning nucleus emitting an electron in the direction of its spin. In the mirror, the nucleus appears to be emitting the electron in the direction opposite to that of its spin. If parity is conserved in β decay, the chance of emission in the direction of the nuclear spin must equal the chance of emission in the opposite direction, i.e., there can be no preferred direction. Whether or not one direction is actually preferred in β decay is usually not observable because the nuclear spins are randomly oriented. Wu and Ambler aligned the nuclei in ^{60}Co by

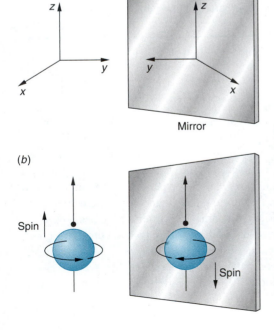

(a)

Mirror

(b)

Spin

Spin

Fig. 13-16 (*a*) The mirror image of a right-handed coordinate system ($\mathbf{x} \times \mathbf{y}$ in the $\mathbf{z}$ direction) is a left-handed coordinate system ($\mathbf{x} \times \mathbf{y}$ in the $-\mathbf{z}$ direction). No combination of translation and rotation can change a right-handed coordinate system into a left-handed system. (*b*) Spinning nucleus emitting an electron in the direction of its spin. In the mirror, the image nucleus is emitting the electron in the direction opposite to its spin because the mirror reverses the direction of the spin vector.

TABLE 13-5 Conserved quantities in fundamental particle interactions

Conserved Quantity	Interaction		
	Strong	Electromagnetic	Weak
Energy Momentum Charge (Q) Baryon Number (B) Lepton Number (L)	Yes	Yes	Yes
Isospin (T)	Yes	No	No ($\Delta T = \pm 1, 0$)
Hypercharge (Y)	Yes	Yes	No ($\Delta Y = \pm 1, 0$)
Strangeness (S)	Yes	Yes	No ($\Delta S = \pm 1, 0$)
Parity (P)	Yes	Yes	No

placing their sample in a magnetic field at a very low temperature (about 0.01 K). They found that more particles were emitted opposite to the spin of the nucleus than in the direction of the spin, indicating that parity is not conserved in weak interactions.

Table 13-5 summarizes the conservation laws discussed in this section.

QUESTIONS

11. Suppose a new uncharged meson is discovered. What condition is necessary for it to have a distinct antiparticle?

12. How might Table 13-1 be different if strangeness were not conserved in hadronic interactions?

More

Particles and excited states of particles that decay via the strong interaction have mean lives of only 10^{-23} s or so, not nearly long enough to be tracked by a particle detector. Such particles are instead detected by measuring resonances in the scattering cross sections in a way analogous to Franck and Hertz's detection of the first excited state of the Hg atom by measuring the resonances in the electron scattering from Hg atoms. Many fundamental particles have been found in this way. See a description on the home page (www.whfreeman.com/modphysics4e) in *Resonances and Excited States,* which also includes a partial list of meson and baryon resonances. See also Figures 13-17 through 13-19 and Examples 13-9 and 13-10 here.

13-4 The Standard Model

The *standard model* is currently (since 1978) the most widely accepted theory of elementary particle physics. It is the combination of the *quark model* of particle structure, the unified theory of electromagnetic and weak interactions called the *electroweak theory,* and the strong interaction analogue of quantum electrodynamics called *quantum chromodynamics* (QCD). It has been remarkably, though not totally, successful in explaining the character of fundamental particles and the interactions between them. In our discussions thus far in this chapter we have had occasion to allude to a number of specific features of the standard model. In this section we will consider each of its three major constituents in some detail. Since the complexity of the standard model's mathematical detail is beyond the level of this book, much of our discussion will be descriptive.

Searches for experimental support for the standard model led to the development of many new types of particle detectors. Several have found applications beyond particle physics, one example being BGO crystal detectors used in medical diagnostic PET scanners (see Figure 12-27).

Quark Model of the Hadrons

The Eightfold Way   The construction of large high-energy particle accelerators beginning in the 1950s enabled the production of a flood of previously unseen hadrons.[13] Among the many attempts at understanding and classifying the jumble of hadrons, the most successful scheme is known as the *eightfold way.*[14] It was suggested independently by Gell-Mann and Y. Ne'eman in 1961. In this scheme, hadrons comprising the charge multiplets were arranged in groups, called *supermultiplets,* in which each member had the same intrinsic spin and parity, J^P, where J is the intrinsic spin and P is the parity. (See Table 13-6.) Three of Gell-Mann's supermultiplets are shown in Figure 13-15: (*a*) the eight lightest baryons, called the *baryon octet;* (*b*) the eight lightest mesons, the *meson octet* (actually a *nonet*); and (*c*) the next ten heavier baryons, the *baryon decuplet.* Figure 13-20 shows the energies of the baryon octet in a diagram analogous to the fine-structure splitting of atomic states. The energy splittings between the isospin multiplets (from 78 to 176 MeV) are about 20 times the splitting within the multiplets. There are no completed baryon supermultiplets beyond the octet and decuplet, although there are several partially completed ones. The known mesons complete six nonets. Note that there is also an *antibaryon* octet,

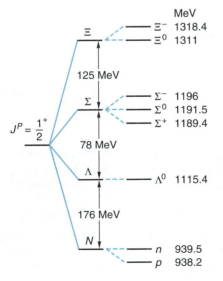

Fig. 13-20 The energy-level diagram of the baryon octet, the supermultiplet of the hadronically stable $J^P = \frac{1}{2}^+$ baryons. In the absence of any interactions, all these particles should have the same mass. The strong nuclear interaction splits the mass states into four states, corresponding to the nucleon (N), lambda (Λ), sigma (Σ), and xi (Ξ) particles. The weaker electromagnetic interaction further splits the particles into the N doublet, Σ triplet, and Ξ doublet.

Murray Gell-Mann, who proposed the existence of strangeness, developed the classification system for hadrons [SU(3)], and postulated the existence of fractionally charged particles, which he called quarks. He won the Nobel Prize in 1969. [*American Institute of Physics, Niels Bohr Library.*]

TABLE 13-6 A partial list of resonance particles

Particle	Mass (MeV/c^2)	Width (MeV)	Primary decay mode	T	B	S	$J^{P\dagger}$
Meson resonances							
$\rho(770)$	770	153	$\pi\pi$	1	0	0	1^-
$\omega(783)$	783	10	$\pi^+\pi^-\pi^0$	1	0	0	1^-
$\omega(1670)$	1666	166	$\rho\pi$	0	0	0	3^-
$J/\psi(3100)$	3097	0.06	Hadrons	0	0	0	1^-
$K^*(890)$	892	51	$K\pi$	$\frac{1}{2}$	0	$+1$	1^-
$K^*(1420)$	1425	100	$K\pi$	$\frac{1}{2}$	0	$+1$	3^-
Baryon resonances							
$\Delta(1232)$	1232	120	$N\pi$	$\frac{3}{2}$	1	0	$\frac{3}{2}^+$
$\Delta(1620)$	1620	140	$N\pi\pi$	$\frac{3}{2}$	1	0	$\frac{1}{2}^-$
$\Delta(1700)$	1685	250	$N\pi\pi$	$\frac{3}{2}$	1	0	$\frac{3}{2}^-$
$N(1470)$	1470	300	$N\pi$	$\frac{1}{2}$	1	0	$\frac{1}{2}^+$
$N(1670)$	1670	160	$N\pi\pi$	$\frac{1}{2}$	1	0	$\frac{5}{2}^-$
$N(1688)$	1688	145	$N\pi$	$\frac{1}{2}$	1	0	$\frac{5}{2}^+$
$\Lambda(1405)$	1405	40	$\Sigma\pi$	0	1	-1	$\frac{1}{2}^-$
$\Lambda(1520)$	1520	16	$N\overline{K}$	0	1	-1	$\frac{3}{2}^-$
$\Lambda(1670)$	1670	30	$N\overline{K}$	0	1	-1	$\frac{1}{2}^-$
$\Sigma(1385)$	1382	35	$\Lambda\pi$	1	1	-1	$\frac{3}{2}^-$
$\Sigma(1670)$	1670	50	$\Sigma\pi$	1	1	-1	$\frac{3}{2}^-$
$\Sigma(2030)$	2030	175	$N\overline{K}$	1	1	-1	$\frac{7}{2}^+$
$\Xi(1530)$	1532	9	$\Xi\pi$	$\frac{1}{2}$	1	-2	$\frac{3}{2}^+$
$\Xi(1820)$	1823	30	$\Lambda\overline{K}$	$\frac{1}{2}$	1	-2	$\frac{3}{2}?$
$\Xi(2030)$	2030	20	$\Sigma\overline{K}$	$\frac{1}{2}$	1	-2	?

†J^P *stands for the spin J and parity P of the particle.*

decuplet, etc., but for the mesons their antiparticles are members of the same nonet. Gell-Mann's accomplishment is the elementary particle analog of Mendeleev's development of the periodic table of the chemical elements which was first published in 1869, nearly one hundred years earlier.

The eightfold way is based on part of a mathematical theory known as the theory of continuous groups that was developed by the Norwegian mathematician S. Lie, among others. The simplest Lie group is known as SU(2), for *s*pecial *u*nitary group of 2 × 2 matrices. A special condition on the 2 × 2 arrays reduces the number of

components from 4 to 3. The three independent components of these arrays correspond to the three components of angular momentum (or isospin). As we have seen previously, the various possible values of angular momentum J have corresponding states which occur in multiplets having 1, 2, 3, 4, . . . , $(2J + 1)$ elements which we describe as having angular momentum of 0, 1/2, 1, 3/2, . . . $\hbar$ units. The next higher Lie group is known as SU(3), for special unitary group of 3×3 arrays. Again, a special condition reduces the number of components from 9 to 8 (hence the name eightfold way). The eight quantities in the application of SU(3) group theory to hadrons consist of the three components of isospin, the hypercharge, and four that are yet to be named. Without going into the details of group theory, we shall merely state that the SU(3) group leads to multiplets of 1, 3, 8, 10, . . . elements. Rather than assigning a single number to these multiplets analogous to the angular momentum quantum number of SU(2), it is more useful to make two-dimensional diagrams called *weight diagrams,* which are the geometric patterns of points, triangles, and hexagons shown in Figure 13-21. In the application of SU(3) to particle theory, the axes are Y and T_3, as in Figure 13-15.

In the plot of Y versus T_3 for the $J^P = 3/2^+$ baryons (the decuplet shown in Figure 13-15c) neither the Ξ nor the Ω^- had been discovered prior to 1961. Note that the difference in rest energy between each line of the decuplet is about 140 MeV. A constant energy difference between successive multiplets in the decuplet is predicted by SU(3) theory. The prediction of the Ω^- particle by Gell-Mann in 1961 and its discovery in 1964 with just the mass and spin Gell-Mann had predicted was one of the spectacular successes of the eightfold way. Note that the Ω^- is the only particle in the decuplet that is not a resonance particle. The mass of the Ω^- is just small enough that energy conservation prevents it from decaying via a strangeness-conserving strong interaction such as $\Omega^- \rightarrow \Xi^0 + K^-$.

Other supermultiplets can be formed from the unstable baryons and mesons, but there are no observed groups of three particles corresponding to the triplet allowed by SU(3) theory illustrated in Figure 13-21. This fact and the absence of a *reason* for the supermultiplets of the eightfold way led Gell-Mann and G. Zweig in 1964 to propose independently that all hadrons are composed of even more fundamental constituents called *quarks.*[15] Their proposal is the basis of the quark model, arguably the most important advance in our understanding of elementary particles.

In the original model, quarks came in three types, called *flavors,* labeled u, d, and s (for *up*, *down*, and *strange*). (Later discoveries, as we will see, added three more quarks, labeled c, b, and t for *charm*, *bottom*, and *top*.) An unusual property of quarks is that they carry fractional electron charges and baryon number. The charge of the u quark is $2e/3$ and that of the d and s quarks is $-e/3$. Each quark has $B = 1/3$. Each quark has spin $\frac{1}{2}\hbar$; thus quarks are fermions. The strangeness of the u and d quarks is 0 and that of the s quark is -1. Each quark has an antiquark with the opposite electric charge, baryon number, and strangeness. The three types form the triangular SU(3)

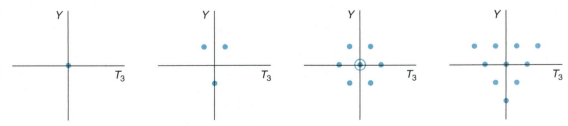

Fig. 13-21 Weight diagrams occurring in SU(3) group theory. The circle and dot at the origin in the hexagon indicate two particles at the origin, making this pattern an octet.

Fig. 13-22 The SU(3) weight diagrams (Y vs. T_3) for the three light quarks and their antiquarks. As in the super-multiplet diagrams of the eightfold way, the downward-sloping lines are constant charge; the horizontal lines are constant strangeness.

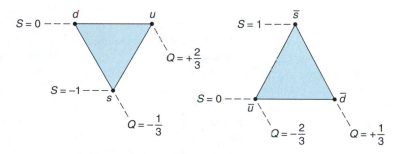

weight diagram of Figure 13-21 as shown in detail in Figure 13-22. The properties of the quarks are listed in Table 13-7. The basic assertion of the quark model is that all baryons consist of three quarks (or three antiquarks for antiparticles), whereas mesons consist of a quark and an antiquark. The mesons thus have baryon number $B = 0$, as required. The proton consists of the combination *uud* and the neutron *udd*. Baryons with a strangeness $S = -1$ contain one *s* quark. All the particles listed in Table 13-1 can be constructed from these three quarks and three antiquarks.[16]

The great strength of the quark model is that all the allowed combinations of three quarks or quark-antiquark pairs result in known hadrons. Strong evidence for the existence of quarks inside a nucleon is provided by high-energy scattering experiments called *deep inelastic scattering*. In these experiments, a nucleon is bombarded with electrons or muons of energies from 15 to 200 GeV. Analyses of particles scattered at large angles indicate the presence within the nucleon of spin 1/2 particles of

TABLE 13-7 Properties of quarks and antiquarks

Flavor	Spin ($\hbar$)	Charge (e)	Mass (MeV/c^2)	Baryon number	U	D	S	C	T	B
Quarks										
u (up)	$\frac{1}{2}$	$+\frac{2}{3}$	336	$+\frac{1}{3}$	+1	0	0	0	0	0
d (down)	$\frac{1}{2}$	$-\frac{1}{3}$	338	$+\frac{1}{3}$	0	−1	0	0	0	0
s (strange)	$\frac{1}{2}$	$-\frac{1}{3}$	540	$+\frac{1}{3}$	0	0	−1	0	0	0
c (charmed)	$\frac{1}{2}$	$+\frac{2}{3}$	1,500	$+\frac{1}{3}$	0	0	0	+1	0	0
t (top)	$\frac{1}{2}$	$+\frac{2}{3}$	174,000	$+\frac{1}{3}$	0	0	0	0	+1	0
b (bottom)	$\frac{1}{2}$	$-\frac{1}{3}$	5,000	$+\frac{1}{3}$	0	0	0	0	0	+1
Antiquarks										
$\bar{u}$	$\frac{1}{2}$	$-\frac{2}{3}$	336	$-\frac{1}{3}$	−1	0	0	0	0	0
$\bar{d}$	$\frac{1}{2}$	$+\frac{1}{3}$	338	$-\frac{1}{3}$	0	+1	0	0	0	0
$\bar{s}$	$\frac{1}{2}$	$+\frac{1}{3}$	540	$-\frac{1}{3}$	0	0	+1	0	0	0
$\bar{c}$	$\frac{1}{2}$	$-\frac{2}{3}$	1,500	$-\frac{1}{3}$	0	0	0	−1	0	0
$\bar{t}$	$\frac{1}{2}$	$-\frac{2}{3}$	174,000	$-\frac{1}{3}$	0	0	0	0	−1	0
$\bar{b}$	$\frac{1}{2}$	$+\frac{1}{3}$	5,000	$-\frac{1}{3}$	0	0	0	0	0	−1

TABLE 13-8 Properties of three-quark combinations

Combination	Spin ($\hbar$)	Charge (e)	Baryon number	Strangeness	Hypercharge	T_3
uuu	$\frac{3}{2}$	+2	1	0	+1	$+\frac{3}{2}$
uud	$\frac{1}{2}, \frac{3}{2}$	+1	1	0	+1	$+\frac{1}{2}$
udd	$\frac{1}{2}, \frac{3}{2}$	0	1	0	+1	$-\frac{1}{2}$
uus	$\frac{1}{2}, \frac{3}{2}$	+1	1	−1	0	+1
uss	$\frac{1}{2}, \frac{3}{2}$	0	1	−2	−1	$+\frac{1}{2}$
uds	$\frac{1}{2}, \frac{3}{2}$	0	1	−1	0	0
ddd	$\frac{3}{2}$	−1	1	0	+1	$-\frac{3}{2}$
dds	$\frac{1}{2}, \frac{3}{2}$	−1	1	−1	0	−1
dss	$\frac{1}{2}, \frac{3}{2}$	−1	1	−2	−1	$-\frac{1}{2}$
sss	$\frac{3}{2}$	−1	1	−3	−2	0

sizes much smaller than that of the nucleon. These experiments are analogous to Rutherford's scattering of α particles by atoms in which the presence of a tiny nucleus in the atom was inferred from the large-angle scattering of the α particles.

Since the conservation laws represented by the several quantum numbers in Table 13-7 are additive, it is simply a matter of arithmetic to determine the properties of the hadrons. For example, a particle formed by the combindation *uds* can have a spin of either 1/2 or 3/2, charge equal to $+2/3 - 1/3 - 1/3 = 0$, and baryon number $B = 1/3 + 1/3 + 1/3 = 1$. Table 13-8 lists the possible three-quark combinations (baryons), and Table 13-9 lists the possible quark-antiquark combinations (mesons).

The eight spin 1/2 baryons comprise the baryon octet of Figure 13-15a. The three quarks of which each member is composed are shown in Figure 13-23a. Notice

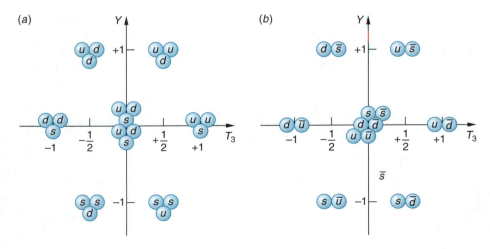

Fig. 13-23 (a) The graph of Y vs. T_3 for the spin $\frac{1}{2}$ three-quark combinations—the baryon octet. (b) The graph of Y vs. T_3 for the quark-antiquark combinations that form the lightest meson nonet.

Combination	Spin ($\hbar$)	Charge (e)	Baryon number	Strangeness	Hypercharge	T_3
$u\bar{u}$	0, 1	0	0	0	0	0
$u\bar{d}$	0, 1	+1	0	0	0	+1
$u\bar{s}$	0, 1	+1	0	+1	+1	$+\frac{1}{2}$
$d\bar{u}$	0, 1	−1	0	0	0	−1
$d\bar{d}$	0, 1	0	0	0	0	0
$d\bar{s}$	0, 1	0	0	+1	+1	$-\frac{1}{2}$
$s\bar{u}$	0, 1	−1	0	−1	−1	$-\frac{1}{2}$
$s\bar{d}$	0, 1	0	0	−1	−1	$+\frac{1}{2}$
$s\bar{s}$	0, 1	0	0	0	0	0

TABLE 13-9 Properties of quark-antiquark combinations for two quarks

that Table 13-9 lists *nine* quark-antiquark combinations, rather than eight, as given by the eightfold way. The ninth meson identified by the quark model as a part of this group, the η′, had already been found, but had been thought to be a singlet in the eightfold way. Figure 13-23b shows the quark-antiquark composition of the first of the several meson nonets, the one illustrated in Figure 13-15b.

EXAMPLE 13-11 Predicting the Properties of Particles What are the properties of the particles made up of the following quarks: (a) $u\bar{d}$, (b) $\bar{u}d$, (c) *dds*, and (d) *uss*?

Solution
(a) Since $u\bar{d}$ is a quark-antiquark combination, it has baryon number 0 and is therefore a meson. There is no strange quark here, so the strangeness of the meson is zero. The charge of the up quark is $+2e/3$ and that of the anti-down quark is $+e/3$, so the charge of the meson is $+1e$. This is the quark combination of the π^+ meson.

(b) The particle $\bar{u}d$ is also a meson with zero strangeness. Its electric charge is $-2e/3 + (-e/3) = -1e$. This is the quark combination of the π^- meson.

(c) The particle *dds* is a baryon with strangeness −1 since it contains one strange quark. Its electric charge is $-e/3 - e/3 - e/3 = -1e$. This is the quark combination for the Σ^- particle.

(d) The particle *uss* is a baryon with strangeness −2. Its electric charge is $+2e/3 - e/3 - e/3 = 0$. This is the quark combination for the Ξ^0 particle.

Exploring

Where Does the Proton Get Its Spin?

In the quark model of the hadrons the proton consists of two up quarks and a down quark, *uud*. The electric charge and quantum numbers of the proton, as with the neutron and other composite particles, are correctly given by summing the corresponding quantities for the constituent quarks. For example, the proton's charge is $+(2/3)e + (2/3)e - (1/3)e = +1e$, and its spin is the $+(1/2)\hbar$ combination of the three spin $(1/2)\hbar$ quarks. However, a series of deep elastic scattering experiments of electrons and muons on protons have yielded a surprising result. Begun in 1987 at CERN and continued up to the present there and at Stanford, the experiments consist of scattering extremely high-energy (= very short wavelength) muons or electrons whose spins are polarized off protons whose spins are also polarized. Measuring the exit angles and energies of the scattered particles is a rich source of information concerning the spin structure of the nucleon. Surprisingly, the experimental results indicate that the spins of the three constituent, or "valence," quarks account for only 20–30 percent of the proton's spin! Aptly called "the spin crisis," the results have underscored that our understanding of nucleon structure and quantum chromodynamics (QCD) is incomplete in some important respect.

Nor does the spin crisis stop there. The results also show that the "sea" of virtual quark-antiquark pairs that surround the valence quarks (just as virtual pions surround the nucleons themselves in the nucleus) is strongly polarized with its collective spin direction *opposite* to the proton's net spin. Even more mysterious, the "sea" turns out to contain an unexpectedly large number of strange (*s*) quarks. As one scientist put it, there is no simple "gee whiz" explanation for the spin crisis. Several theories have been advanced to account for the discovery, but thus far none have been successful. The spin crisis is currently the focus of vigorous experimental and theoretical research.

Color The quark model as described thus far, essentially that developed over the decade following the introduction of the Gell-Mann's quark hypothesis, contained two significant problems: despite numerous experimental searches, no free quarks had been found; and the model's construction of baryons was inconsistent with the Pauli exclusion principle. For example, the $\Delta^{++}(1232)$ has spin $3\hbar/2$ and thus contains three *u* quarks (fermions) with exactly the same set of quantum numbers.

The solution to the exclusion-principle dilemma came from O. W. Greenberg, who postulated that each quark flavor (*u, d,* and *s*) came in three *colors* in addition to their other properties. The color charge of a quark has three possible values: *red, blue,* and *green*. Thus, a blue quark would have blueness $+1$, redness 0, and greenness 0, and its antiquark would have blueness -1, and so on. The terms *color* and *color charge* are, of course, simply labels to describe the new properties and are in no way related to the usual meanings of the words. The use of the three primary colors for this purpose did, however, provide a very simple rule to ensure that the exclusion principle was obeyed:

All particles that occur in nature are colorless.

The term *colorless* means that either

1. The total amount of color (i.e., the sum of the color quantum numbers) is zero, or
2. There are equal amounts of all three colors present (in analogy with the combining of the three primary colors to produce white).

Thus, for example, the three up quarks that compose the $\Delta^{++}(1232)$ are one each u_r, u_b, and u_g.

The J/ψ Puzzle   The solution provided by color seemed an artificial one, as did the explanation for seeing no free quarks described in the next subsection, but strong support for the model came late in 1974 from an unexpected quarter. Two groups independently discovered a new meson. The first, S. Ting and his co-workers at Brookhaven, called it the *J*, while the second group, B. Richter and his co-workers at SLAC,[17] called it the ψ. Now referred to as the *J/ψ*, the new meson had three times the mass of the proton and a lifetime of 10^{-20} s, extraordinarily long for a strongly interacting particle. The exceptionally long lifetime pointed to new physics,[18] and within months after its discovery it was recognized that the *J/ψ* was composed of a fourth quark and its antiquark. The fourth quark, which had been proposed by S. Glashow and others for compelling theoretical reasons some years earlier so as to make equal

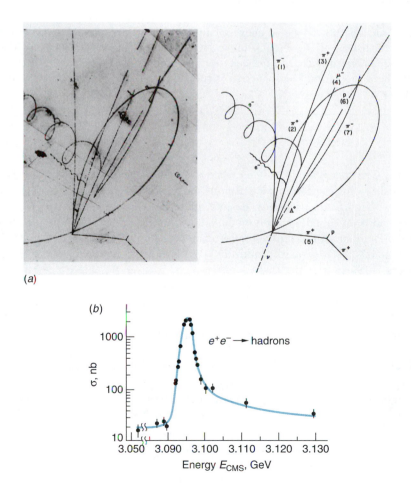

(a)

(b)

Fig. 13-24 (*a*) Discovery of the first charmed baryon, the Λ_c^+. The reaction is $\nu_\mu + p \rightarrow \Lambda_c^+ + \mu^- + \pi^+ + \pi^-$. The charmed baryon decays via $\Lambda_c^+ \rightarrow \Lambda^0 + \pi^+$ too soon to leave a track, but the subsequent decay of the Λ^0 is easily seen. [*Brookhaven National Laboratory.*] (*b*) A portion of the experimental data obtained by B. Richter and his co-workers at SLAC showing the *J/ψ* resonance.

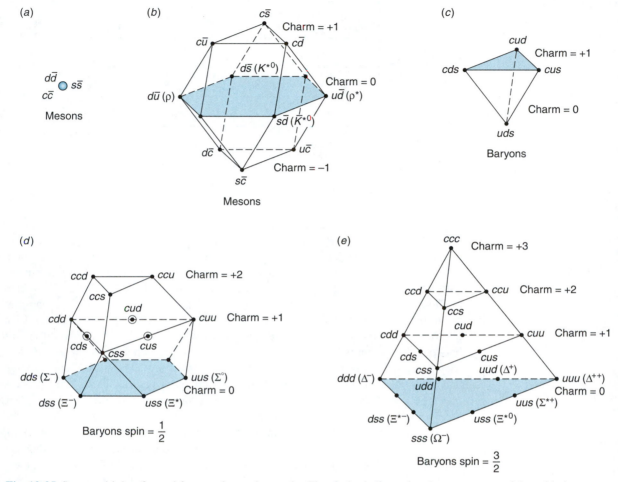

Fig. 13-25 Supermultiplets formed from *u, d, s,* and *c* quarks. The circles indicate that there are two particles with the same quark composition and different energies.

numbers of quarks and leptons (before discovery of the τ and $ν_τ$), is called the *charm* quark and $J/ψ = (c\bar{c})$.[19] Discovery of the first charmed baryon, the $Λ_c^+$, is shown in Figure 13-24. Figure 13-25 shows some supermultiplets formed with four quarks. This discovery made two nicely symmetric sets of four leptons (*e, $ν_e$, μ, $ν_μ$*) and four quarks (*u, d, s, c*) and, of course, their antiparticles. Then in 1975 a new lepton was found! The new lepton, the τ, presumably had an associated neutrino, the $ν_τ$, and the numerical symmetry of the flavors of particles was again upset. But within two years a new heavy meson, the upsilon ϒ, was discovered and quickly recognized as being composed of a fifth quark-antiquark pair. The fifth quark is called the *bottom* (or sometimes *beauty*) quark and $ϒ = (b\bar{b})$. The theory then predicts a sixth quark, called, as you might guess, the *top* (or *truth*) quark. The *t* quark was found in 1995 by two groups at Fermilab, thus restoring Glashow's symmetry of fundamental quarks and leptons and completing the new periodic table of the constituents of fundamental particles. (See Figure 13-26.) At 174 GeV/c^2, the *t* quark is the most massive fundamental particle that has been discovered. There are substantial theoretical and experimental reasons to believe that there are no more quarks or leptons to be found. (See Figure 13-27.) Table 13-7 (page 646) lists the up, down, strangeness, charm, top, and bottom quantum numbers for the six flavors of quarks and their antiquarks.

Fig. 13-26 Periodic table of elementary particle constituents.

Family \ Flavor	1	2	3	Electric charge
1	ν_e	ν_μ	ν_τ	0
2	e^-	μ^-	τ^-	-1
3	u	c	t	$+\frac{2}{3}$
4	d	s	b	$-\frac{1}{3}$

Quantum Chromodynamics

Quantum chromodynamics (QCD) is the modern theory that describes the strong interaction between quarks and gluons. It is directly analogous to quantum electrodynamics (QED), which so successfully accounts for the electromagnetic interaction. Indeed, QCD was modeled on QED. As stated earlier, the particle (boson) that mediates the strong quark-quark interaction is the gluon, and the fundamental process (analogous to $e \rightarrow e + \gamma$ shown in Figure 13-5) is illustrated by the Feynman diagram in Figure 13-28a. The gluons are the QCD analog of the photon in QED. Like photons, they are massless and have spin $1\hbar$; however, there is one crucial difference between the two particles. The gluons carry color charge, whereas the photon is electrically neutral. In fact, the gluons are bicolored, carrying one unit of a color charge and one of an anticolor charge and, hence, are not color neutral. Thus, in the process $q \rightarrow q + g$ the quark may change color (but not flavor), as shown in Figure 13-28b. Since the gluons carry net color charge, they can also interact with each other via the strong interaction *and* also form an octet in the SU(3) group theory representation, just as do the mesons.[20] This means that, in addition to effects analogous to the vacuum polarization in QED discussed in Section 13-2 and shown in Figure 13-13, there are also gluon-gluon loops as shown in Figure 13-29. The effect of such gluon loops is to decrease the value of the strong interaction coupling constant α_s at extremely

Fig. 13-27 Both the shape and height of Z^0 resonance are theoretically related to the number of flavors of the leptons and quarks. As that number increases, the maximum cross section decreases and the energy width (at half the maximum height) becomes larger. Current measurements, shown by the black circles, are fully consistent with three flavors, excluding both two and four.

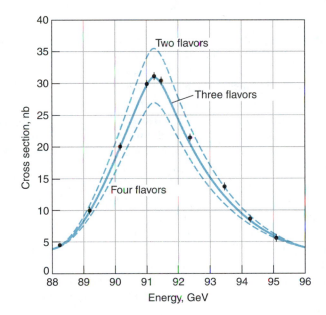

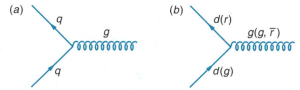

Fig. 13-28 (*a*) The fundamental vertex of QCD in which a quark emits a virtual gluon. (*b*) Since gluons carry a color and an anticolor, the emission of the gluon may also change the color of the quark.

short distances ($\leq 10^{-18}$ m). Thus, as a pair of quarks move extremely close to one another, their coupling decreases, a condition called *asymptotic freedom*. The result is that inside the nucleon the quarks move more or less as free particles, a result that hundreds of experiments have confirmed.

One of the possible potential functions for the strong interaction has the approximate form

$$V_{QCD}(r) = -\frac{4\alpha_s}{3r} + kr \qquad \textbf{13-32}$$

It has been reasonably well tested experimentally at short distances. Notice that V_{QCD} increases indefinitely with r (see Figure 13-30), that is, the strong force at large r, $F_{QCD} = -\nabla V_{QCD} = $ constant, rather than going to zero, as do the Coulomb and gravitational forces. This prevents the quarks from getting too far apart, effectively containing them inside the hadrons, a result called *quark confinement*. This is the QCD explanation for why free quarks have not yet been found. When a large amount of energy is added to a quark system such as a nucleon, a quark-antiquark pair is created and the original quarks remain confined within the original system. This is the

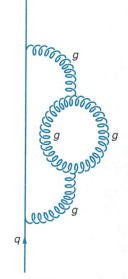

Fig. 13-29 Feynman diagram of a quark emitting a gluon, which then creates two gluons that recombine, the resulting gluon being absorbed by the quark.

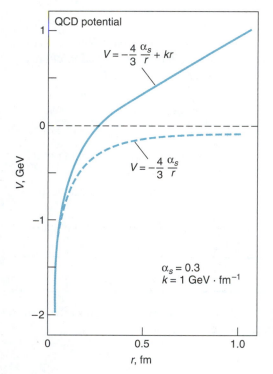

Fig. 13-30 The potential seen by quarks in QCD. In this diagram the strong coupling constant $\alpha_s = 0.3$ and $k = 1$ GeV/fm in Equation 13-32.

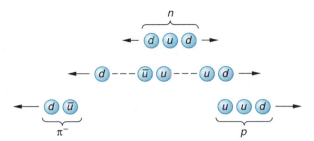

Fig. 13-31 Shown is one possible illustration of quark confinement. If energy is added to remove a d quark from a neutron, a $(\bar{u}, u)$ pair is created. The $\bar{u}$ and one of the d quarks combine to form a π^-, while the u from the pair and the original u and d combine to produce a proton and no free quark appears.

origin of the virtual pions identified by the Yukawa model of the nuclear force as the mediator of that interaction. (See Figure 13-31.)

During particle decays and interactions quarks transform into one another. For example, the β^- decay of the neutron given by Equation 11-38 and illustrated by Example 13-4 proceeds according to the quark model as follows:

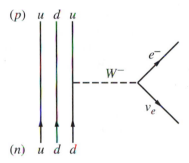

All baryons eventually decay in one or more steps to the lightest (lowest-energy) baryon, the proton. The decay of the proton is prohibited by conservation of energy and baryon number. Example 13-12 illustrates the decay of the Λ^0.

QUESTIONS

13. How can you tell whether a particle is a meson or a baryon by looking at its quark content?

14. Are there any quark-antiquark combinations that result in nonintegral electric charge?

15. What experimental evidence exists to support the assertion that natural particles are colorless?

EXAMPLE 13-12 **Decay of Λ^0** Draw a Feynman diagram that shows the quarks involved in the decay of the Λ^0, which goes according to

$$\Lambda^0 \longrightarrow p + e^- + \bar{\nu}_e$$

Solution

From Table 13-8 we see that the Λ^0 is composed of an up, a down, and a strange quark. The proton consists of two up quarks and a down quark. The decay results from the weak interaction. Thus, the accompanying diagram is a possibility. Note that strangeness is not conserved in the weak interaction that transforms the s quark into the u quark.

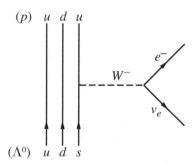

The Electroweak Theory

In the *electroweak theory*, the electromagnetic and weak interactions are considered to be two different manifestations of a more fundamental electroweak interaction. At very high energies ($\gg 100$ GeV), the electroweak interaction is mediated by four bosons. From symmetry considerations, these would be a triplet consisting of W^+, W^0, and W^-, all of equal mass, and a singlet boson B^0 of some other mass. Neither the W^0 nor the B^0 would be observed directly, but one linear combination of the W^0 and the B^0 would be the Z^0 and another would be the photon. At ordinary energies, the symmetry is spontaneously broken.

By "spontaneously broken symmetry" we mean the following: The Hamiltonian H_{op} retains the complete symmetry, but the ground state computed from that H_{op} does not, or, as we say, the symmetry is broken. For example, magnetism in solids arises due to interaction of the spins of the atoms of the crystal lattice. For a ferromagnet, such as iron, the H_{op} describing that interaction is invariant under rotation, but in the ground state magnetic domains are spontaneously formed in the sample. The spin direction changes from domain to domain, but is the same inside each domain. A domain is certainly not invariant to a rotation of the spins. Thus, the ground state spontaneously breaks the rotational symmetry. (To further help you visualize what "spontaneously broken symmetry" means, think of a small plastic strip, like a short ruler, the ends gripped between your thumb and index finger. As you squeeze, the strip will snap into a curve to one side or the other, breaking the original left-right symmetry.)

The broken symmetry in the electroweak interaction leads to the separation of the electromagnetic interaction mediated by the photon and the weak interaction mediated by the W^+, W^-, and Z^0 particles. The fact that the photon is massless and that the W and Z particles have masses of the order of 100 GeV/c^2 shows that the symmetry assumed in the electroweak theory does not exist at lower energies. The symmetry-breaking agent is called a *Higgs field,* which requires a new boson, the *Higgs boson,* whose rest energy is expected to be of the order of 1 TeV (1 TeV = 10^{12} eV). The Higgs boson has not yet been observed. Calculations show that the Higgs bosons (if they exist) should be produced in a head-on collision between

protons of energies of the order of 20 TeV. Such energies are not presently available; however, experiments currently under way at the Relativistic Heavy Ion Collider (RHIC) at Brookhaven National Laboratory may be able to find the first Higgs. In addition, the Large Hadron Collider (LHC) under construction at CERN and scheduled to begin operating in 2007 should also be capable of finding the Higgs. Watch for developments!

The Standard Model—A Summary

The combination of the quark model, electroweak theory, and quantum chromodynamics is called the *standard model*. In this model, the fundamental particles are the leptons and quarks, each of which comes in six flavors as shown in Figure 13-26. The force carriers are the photon, the $W^\pm$ and Z^0 particles, and eight types of gluons. The leptons and quarks are all spin 1/2 fermions, which obey the Pauli exclusion principle. The force carriers are integral-spin bosons, which do not obey the Pauli exclusion principle. Every force in nature is due to one of the four basic interactions: strong, electromagnetic, weak, and gravitational. A particle experiences one of the basic interactions if it carries a charge associated with that interaction. Electric charge is the familiar charge that we have studied previously. It is carried by the quarks and charged leptons. Weak charge, also called flavor charge, is carried by leptons and quarks. The charge associated with the strong interaction is called color charge and is carried by quarks and gluons but not by leptons. The charge associated with the gravitational force is mass. It is important to note that the photon, which mediates the electromagnetic interaction, does not carry electric charge. Similarly, the $W^\pm$ and Z^0 particles, which mediate the weak interaction, do not carry weak charge. However, the gluons, which mediate the strong interaction, do carry color charge. This fact is related to the confinement of quarks.

All matter is made up of leptons and quarks. There are no known composite particles consisting of leptons bound together by the weak force. Leptons exist only as isolated particles. Hadrons (baryons and mesons) are composite particles consisting of quarks bound together by the color charge. A result of the QCD theory is that only color-neutral combinations of quarks are allowed. Three quarks of different colors can combine to form color-neutral baryons, such as the neutron and proton. Mesons contain a quark and an antiquark and are also color-neutral. Excited states of hadrons are considered to be different particles. For example, the Δ^+ particle is an excited state of the proton. Both are made up of the *uud* quarks, but the proton is in the ground state with spin 1/2 and a rest energy of 938 MeV, whereas the Δ^+ particle is in the first excited state with spin 3/2 and a rest energy of 1232 MeV. The two *u* quarks can be in the same spin state in the Δ^+ without violating the exclusion principle because they have different color. All baryons eventually decay to the lightest baryon, the proton. The proton cannot decay because of the conservation of energy and baryon number.

The strong interaction has two parts, the fundamental or color interaction and the *residual strong interaction*. The fundamental interaction is responsible for the force exerted by one quark on another and is mediated by gluons. The residual strong interaction is responsible for the force between color-neutral nucleons, such as the neutron and proton. This force is due to the residual strong interactions between the color-charged quarks that make up the nucleons and can be viewed as being mediated by the exchange of mesons. The residual strong interaction between

color-neutral nucleons is analogous to the residual electromagnetic interaction between neutral atoms that bind them together to form molecules.

For each particle there is an antiparticle. A particle and its antiparticle have identical mass and spin but opposite electric charge. For leptons, the lepton numbers L_e, L_μ, and L_τ of the antiparticles are the negatives of the corresponding numbers for the particles. For example, the lepton number for the electron is $L_e = +1$ and that for the positron is $L_e = -1$. For hadrons, the baryon number, strangeness, charm, topness, and bottomness are the sums of those quantities for the quarks that make up the hadron. The number for each antiparticle is the negative of the number for the corresponding particle. For example, the lambda particle Λ^0, which is made up of the uds quarks, has $B = 1$ and $S = -1$, whereas its antiparticle $\overline{\Lambda}^0$, which is made up of the $\overline{uds}$ quarks, has $B = -1$ and $S = +1$. A particle such as the photon γ or the Z^0 particle that has zero electric charge, $B = 0$, $L = 0$, $S = 0$ and zero charm, top, and bottom, is its own antiparticle. Note that the K^0 meson ($d\overline{s}$) has a zero value for all of these quantities except strangeness, which is $+1$. Its antiparticle, the $\overline{K}^0$ meson ($\overline{d}s$), has strangeness -1, which makes it distinct from the K^0. The π^+ ($u\overline{d}$) and π^- ($\overline{u}d$) have electric charge, but zero values for L, B, and S. They are antiparticles of each other, but since there is no conservation law for mesons, it is impossible to say which is the particle and which is the antiparticle. Similarly, the W^+ and W^- are antiparticles of each other. Table 13-8 (page 647) lists the quark compositions of several particles.

EXAMPLE 13-13 **Decay of the Ω^-** The Ω^- decays according to the equation

$$\Omega^- \longrightarrow \Lambda^0 + K^-$$

and the resulting Λ^0 and K^- usually decay according to

$$\Lambda^0 \longrightarrow p + \pi^- \qquad \text{and} \qquad K^- \longrightarrow \mu^- + \nu_\mu$$

Write each of these reactions in terms of quarks.

Solution
Using Table 13-10, the Ω^- decay is given by

$$sss \longrightarrow uds + s\overline{u}$$

in which an s is changed to a d and a $u\overline{u}$ pair is created. The Λ^0 and K decay according to, for the Λ^0,

$$uds \longrightarrow uud + \overline{u}d$$

where again an s is changed to a d and a $u\overline{u}$ pair is created; and, for the K meson,

$$s\overline{u} \longrightarrow \mu^- + \overline{\nu}_\mu$$

where an s is changed to a u and the $u\overline{u}$ pair annihilate.

TABLE 13-10 Quark composition of selected particles

Baryons	Quarks	Mesons	Quarks
p	uud	π^+	$u\bar{d}$
n	udd	π^-	$\bar{u}d$
Λ^0	uds	K^+	$u\bar{s}$
Δ^{++}	uuu	K^0	$d\bar{s}$
Σ^+	uus	$\bar{K}^0$	$s\bar{d}$
Σ^0	uds	K^-	$s\bar{u}$
Σ^-	dds	J/ψ	$c\bar{c}$
Ξ^0	uss	D^+	$c\bar{d}$
Ξ^-	dss	D^0	$c\bar{u}$
Ω^-	sss	D_s^+	$c\bar{s}$
Λ_c^+	udc	B^+	$u\bar{b}$
Σ_c^{++}	uuc	$\bar{B}^0$	$\bar{d}b$
Σ_c^+	udc	B^0	$d\bar{b}$
Ξ_c^+	usc	B^-	$\bar{u}b$

13-5 Beyond the Standard Model

Grand Unification Theories

At the beginning of Section 13-4 we noted that the standard model of particle physics, while correctly accounting for a wide range of observations, has left a number of fundamental questions unanswered. Of premier importance among these are why nature requires four interactions, rather than one, and why their strengths and properties should be so different. The successful unification of the electromagnetic and weak interactions into the electroweak theory discussed earlier has led to a number of efforts to include the strong interaction and, ultimately, the gravitational interaction into a single, so-called *grand unification theory,* or GUT.[21] As in the electroweak theory, the different strengths at energies well below the rest energies of the mediating bosons would be accounted for by spontaneous symmetry breaking. GUTs also explain the equality of the electron and proton charges.

A central feature of current GUTs is that the coupling constants of all four interactions approach the same value, approximately that of the fine-structure constant α, at some very high energy. It is a remarkable experimental observation that the measured values of the coupling constants do appear to be tending toward a common

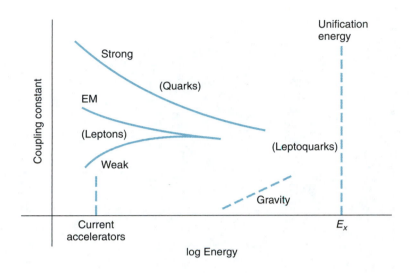

Fig. 13-32 The coupling constants of the four interactions appear to be approaching a common value at some energy in the range of 10^{15} to 10^{17} GeV. Since existing accelerators can reach only about 30 GeV, the extrapolation to the unification energy E_x is highly uncertain.

value. Unfortunately, extrapolation to the common point must be made over an extraordinarily large energy range, that point of common value being at about 10^{15} GeV, compared with about 3×10^3 GeV that can be reached with existing accelerators. (See Figure 13-32.) To assume that nature has no surprises or new physics to await us somewhere in that colossal energy range ignores the lessons of history.

Proton Decay

In GUTs the quarks and leptons are states of one particle, the leptoquark, and occur symmetrically in the same multiplet. This would account for why there are equal numbers of quark and lepton flavors and also lead to the prediction that each type of particle can be changed into the other, just as the proton and neutron can be interchanged now. If that is the case, then baryon number is no longer a conserved quantity and the proton should not be stable. Current versions of GUTs place the lifetime of the proton at about 10^{30} to 10^{33} years, the long lifetime being the result of the large energy at which unification of the interactions occurs. Current experiments have placed the lower limit on the proton lifetime at about 10^{32} years; no proton decays have been detected. The nonconservation of baryon number in the early universe when energies were very high provides an explanation of a major cosmological problem, namely, why the present universe has many more baryons than antibaryons.

Lepton numbers would no longer be conserved at the unification energy and currently forbidden reactions such as $\mu^- \rightarrow e^- + \gamma$ and $\mu^+ \rightarrow e^+ + e^+ + e^-$ would be allowed. Experimental searches have been made, but no lepton-number nonconserving events have been found.

Massive Neutrinos

From the time Pauli first suggested their existence in 1930, neutrinos were thought to have zero rest mass. Then, based on Bahcall's theoretical calculation of the solar neutrino flux and Davis's remarkable measurement of the flux at only about 30 percent of Bahcall's prediction, the solar neutrino problem emerged (see Section 12-2). Its recent solution by the detection of neutrino oscillations by the SNO experiment gives

The neutrino detector at the Sudbury Neutrino Observatory (SNO). The spherical acrylic vessel is 12 m in diameter, contains 1000 tonnes of ultra-pure heavy water (D_2O), and is located 2000 m below ground. Čherenkov light produced by neutrino reactions in the water is viewed by 9456 photomultipliers, each 20 cm in diameter. [*Photo courtesy of Sudbury Neutrino Observatory.*]

support to GUTs since most GUTs require that neutrinos have mass. Their mass is given approximately by

$$m_\nu \approx \frac{M_{eW}^2}{M_x} \qquad\qquad \textbf{13-33}$$

where M_{eW} is a characteristic mass of the electroweak interaction, roughly 10^2 GeV/c^2, and M_x is the unification mass $E_x/c^2 \approx 10^{15}$ GeV/c^2 (see Figure 13-32). Nearly all GUTs project M_x values of this order of magnitude, which in turn means that all neutrinos would have m_ν less than about 1 eV. The theories also predict $m(\nu_e) \ll m(\nu_\mu) \ll m(\nu_\tau)$. The impact of massive neutrinos on both the solar neutrino problem discussed in Chapter 12 and the universe's "missing mass" problem discussed in Chapter 14 is substantial. Mikheyev, Smirnov, and Wolfenstein proposed a solution to the solar neutrino problem

in which a ν_e can oscillate to a ν_μ or ν_τ. For this complex process, called the *MSW effect,* to occur, the neutrino wave functions $\psi(\nu_e)$, $\psi(\nu_\mu)$, and $\psi(\nu_\tau)$ must each consist of super-positions of the three mass states. The relative phases of the mass states may change for two reasons: (1) In passing through the solar matter (electrons and protons), the three mass states scatter differently, hence their relative phases change. (2) The mass states move at different speeds through space, also resulting in a change in the relative phase. The net result is that a neutrino emitted in the sun as a ν_e may oscillate to a ν_μ or ν_τ before reaching Earth, and therefore not be detected by experiments searching for electron neutrinos. Experimental evidence for the existence of oscillations was provided by the SNO measurements, which also indicate that neutrino mass can account for only a small fraction of the universe's "missing mass."

Magnetic Monopoles

Magnetic monopoles, first suggested by Dirac in 1929, are also proposed by GUTs. Dirac showed that relativistic quantum mechanics leads to the quantization of both the electric charge e and the magnetic charge q_m. The magnetic charge of a monopole would be

$$q_m = n\frac{\hbar c}{2e} \qquad \text{for } n = 1, 2, \ldots \qquad \textbf{13-34}$$

It is important to note that $q_m^2/\hbar c \approx \hbar c/e^2 \approx 1/137$. In the unified theories the quantization of electric charge occurs naturally in units of e, and magnetic monopoles of charge q_m and mass M_m are then predicted. The predicted values of M_m are very large, about 10^{16} GeV/c^2, far beyond the energy achievable in any accelerator. Cosmic ray searches for monopoles place an upper limit on their flux at about 10^{-15} cm^{-2} s^{-1} per unit solid angle. Coincidentally, this value corresponds approximately to the maximum flux that could exist in the Milky Way without having long since destroyed the galactic magnetic field. As of this writing, only a single observation of a magnetic monopole has been reported in the literature, by B. Cabrera in 1982.

Quantum Gravity

The addition of quantum gravity to grand unified theories is a formidable task. Called *superstring theories* because of their basic view of fundamental particles as strings, rather than points, perhaps the most promising of the current versions is based on a ten-dimensional universe (nine space dimensions and one time dimension) in which six of the space dimensions have been collapsed or curled up in themselves. The string "lengths" are much shorter than can be measured, about 10^{-35} m. Besides the inclusion of quantum gravity, superstring theories also produce the *gauge theories*[22] with the correct exchange bosons; however, although they are the subject of considerable interest to theoretical physicists, there is as yet no experimental support for these theories and it is not clear to what extent, if any, they represent physical reality. Many questions are still unanswered. For example, do the quarks have internal structure? What is the origin of isospin? There is some indication that hadrons are surrounded by a "sea" of quark-antiquark pairs. What is their role? How is the fractional charge of the quarks related to color? Investigating these problems experimentally will require new, higher-energy accelerators and more advanced detectors than currently exist anywhere in the world. Obviously, there is much to be done.

Summary

TOPIC	RELEVANT EQUATIONS AND REMARKS
1. Particles and antiparticles	Each fundamental particle found in nature has a distinct antiparticle.
Feynman diagrams	These are spacetime diagrams that provide a useful way of visualizing interactions between particles—for example, Coulomb repulsion of like charges:

$$e \quad e$$
$$\gamma$$
$$e \quad e$$

2. Fundamental interactions	1. Strong interaction
	2. Electromagnetic interaction
	3. Weak interaction
	4. Gravitational interaction
Interaction "strengths"	This term refers to the magnitudes of the dimensionless coupling constants that multiply the space-dependent part of the potential energy functions.
Exchange particles	Each interaction is mediated by the exchange of one or more field particles. For example, the strong interaction between a proton and a neutron via exchange of a π^+ is represented by this Feynman diagram:

$$p \quad n$$
$$\pi^+$$
$$n \quad p$$

3. Conservation laws and symmetries	Conservation laws are associated with symmetries of the particle Hamiltonians. In addition to energy, momentum, electric charge, and angular momentum, all interactions obey the following:
	1. The baryon number is conserved.
	2. The lepton number for each flavor is independently conserved.
	Some quantities, such as strangeness, are conserved in strong but not in weak interactions.
4. Standard model	The standard model is a combination of the quark model, electroweak theory, and QCD.
Color	All quarks have color charge with one of three possible values: red, blue, or green. The exclusion principle requires that all particles that occur in nature are colorless.
QCD	The potential function of the strong interaction has the approximate form

$$V_{QCD}(r) = -\frac{4\alpha_s}{3r} + kr \qquad \text{13-32}$$

| Beyond the standard model | Grand unification theories (GUTs) attempt to unify all four basic interactions mathematically. While thus far unsuccessful, some predict, among other things, proton decay, massive neutrinos, and magnetic monopoles. |

GENERAL REFERENCES

The following general references are written at a level appropriate for the readers of this book.

Das, A., and T. Ferbel, *Introduction to Nuclear and Particle Physics,* Wiley, New York, 1994.

Eisberg, R., and R. Resnick, *Quantum Physics,* 2d ed., Wiley, New York, 1985.

Frauenfelder, H., and E. M. Henley, *Subatomic Physics,* 2d ed., Prentice Hall, Englewood Cliffs, N.J., 1991.

Griffiths, D., *Introduction to Elementary Particles,* Prentice Hall, New York, 1991.

Perkins, D. H., *Introduction to High Energy Physics,* 3d ed., Harper & Row, Menlo Park, Calif., 1987.

Rubbia, C., and M. Jacob, "The Z^0," *American Scientist,* **78**, 502 (1990).

NOTES

1. The word *atom* comes from the Greek word *atomos,* meaning "indivisible," that was coined by the philosopher Democritus, a contemporary of Socrates, about 2400 years ago. In addition to suggesting that matter consisted of a variety of tiny atoms, he also suggested that the Milky Way was made of a large number of individual stars and that the moon had mountains and valleys just like Earth.

2. Carl David Anderson (1905–1991), American physicist. His discovery of the positron in cosmic ray cloud chamber tracks was followed three years later by his discovery of the muon in cloud chamber tracks recorded on Pike's Peak in Colorado. These discoveries earned him a share of the 1936 Nobel Prize in physics.

3. The Dirac equation for particles with 1/2-integral spin, like the electron, is the relativistic analogue of the Schrödinger equation; however, it is not obtained by operator substitution into Equation 2-31, since the resulting wave function does not include the effects of spin.

4. Richard Phillips Feynman (1918–1988), American physicist who described himself as a "curious character." An almost legendary figure among U.S. physicists, he was one of many who worked on the Manhattan Project at Los Alamos, where he also became an accomplished safecracker. An excellent bongo drummer and a passable artist, he shared the 1965 Nobel Prize in physics with Julian Schwinger and Sin-itiro Tomonaga, all of whom independently contributed to the development of quantum electrodynamics. His books *Surely You're Joking, Mr. Feynman!* and *What Do You Care What People Think?* provide delightful insights into his life.

5. Emilio Gino Segrè (1905–1989), Italian-American physicist. A lifelong friend and colleague of Fermi, Segrè shared the 1959 Nobel Prize in physics with Owen Chamberlain, a member of his Berkeley research group, for the discovery of the antiproton. Of greater interest to most people might be his discovery of technetium ($Z = 43$), the first chemical element to be artificially created. An isotope of technetium, ^{99m}Tc, is by far the most widely used radioisotope in medical diagnosis, treatment, and research.

6. This process is called Møller scattering in QED.

7. In fact, an infinite number. The contribution that each possible diagram makes to the total process decreases sharply as the number of vertices increases, so complex diagrams may typically be ignored.

8. The reason for making the coupling constant dimensionless is so all observers will measure comparable values, independent of the units they may have used.

9. The name *lepton,* which means "light particle," was originally selected to reflect the small mass of these particles relative to the hadrons; however, the τ (discovered by M. Perl in 1975) has a mass nearly twice that of the proton, so the name is no longer an indicator of the mass of these particles.

10. Carlo Rubbia (b. 1934), Italian physicist. A former director-general of CERN, he shared the 1984 Nobel Prize in physics with Simon van der Meer, also of CERN, for their contributions to the discovery of the $W^{\pm}$ and Z^0.

11. Operators, like H_{op}, that result in real (i.e., observable) values are called *Hermitian* operators. They obey the rule

$$\int a(x)F_{op}b(x)\,dx = \int b(x)F_{op}^*a(x)\,dx$$

12. Murray Gell-Mann (b. 1929), American physicist. He received the 1969 Nobel Prize in physics for this and other work on fundamental particles and their interactions.

13. The rate of discovery became so large that one physicist quipped that " . . . by 1990 all physicists would be famous because there would be a particle named for each physicist ($\approx 30,000$)." Most "discoveries" turned out to be spurious.

14. From a saying attributed to the Buddha: "Now this, O monks, is the noble truth of the way that leads to the cessation of pain: this is the noble *Eightfold Way:* namely, right views, right intention, right speech, right action, right living, right effort, right mindfulness, and right concentration."

15. The name "quark" was suggested to Gell-Mann by a quotation from *Finnegans Wake* by James Joyce: "Three quarks for Master Mark." Joyce did not tell us and the context does not make clear exactly what a quark is.

16. The correct quark combinations of hadrons are not always obvious because of the symmetry requirements on the

total wave function. For example, the π^0 meson is represented by a linear combination of $u\bar{u}$ and $d\bar{d}$.

17. Samuel Chao Chung Ting (b. 1936), American physicist, and Burton Richter (b. 1931), American physicist, shared the 1976 Nobel Prize in physics for this important discovery.

18. One physicist put the long lifetime of the J/ψ in biological terms by comparing it with someone coming upon a remote mountain village where the average age of the inhabitants was 70,000 years. That would be a definite indication of new biology.

19. Particle physicists call the discovery of the J/ψ the "November revolution," referring to the enormous support of the quark model that its November 1974 publication provided.

20. They form nine combinations, just like the mesons, but for the gluons the ninth combination is really a singlet and, hence, is independent.

21. Since no theory of quantum gravity complementing QED and QCD exists, current efforts to develop GUTs include only the strong and electroweak interactions.

22. Theories in which the interaction is determined by the invariance of the theory (i.e., its mathematical equations) under particular transformations are called *gauge theories*. For example, classical electrodynamics is a gauge theory (although not usually referred to as such), as are QED and QCD. Historically, interactions were "figured out" by clever physicists on the basis of experimental evidence. A bit of a surprise, Schrödinger's wave mechanics is not a gauge theory.

PROBLEMS

Level I

Section 13-1 Particles and Antiparticles

13-1. Two pions at rest annihilate according to the reaction $\pi^+ + \pi^- \rightarrow \gamma + \gamma$. (*a*) Why must the energies of the two gamma rays be equal? (*b*) Find the energy of each gamma ray. (*c*) Find the wavelength of each gamma ray.

13-2. Find the minimum energy of the photon needed for the following reactions: (*a*) $\gamma \rightarrow \Lambda^+ + \pi^-$, (*b*) $\gamma \rightarrow p + \bar{p}$, and (*c*) $\gamma \rightarrow \mu^- + \mu^+$.

13-3. Draw a Feynman diagram illustrating each of the following nucleon scattering events: (*a*) *n-p* where a π^0 is exchanged, (*b*) *n-p* where a π^- is exchanged, and (*c*) *p-p* where a π^0 is exchanged.

13-4. Find (*a*) the energy of the electron, (*b*) the energy of the ^{32}S nucleus, and (*c*) the momentum of each, in the decay $^{32}\text{P} \rightarrow {}^{32}\text{S} + e^-$, assuming no neutrino in the final state ($n \rightarrow p + e^-$). (The rest mass of ^{32}P is 31.973908 u.)

13-5. The fate of an antiproton is usually annihilation via the reaction $p + \bar{p} \rightarrow \gamma + \gamma$. Assume that the proton and antiproton annihilate at rest. (*a*) Why must there be two photons rather than just one? (*b*) What is the energy of each photon? (*c*) What is the wavelength of each photon? (*d*) What is the frequency of each photon?

13-6. Figure 13-3 shows the production of the first antiproton. It was produced by the reaction $p + p \rightarrow p + p + p + \bar{p}$ and required a minimum kinetic energy of 5.6 GeV. (The proton beam energy was actually 25 GeV.) Less energy would be required by either of the following reactions: Why is neither of them a possible alternative? Justify your answer.

(*a*) $p + p \rightarrow p + e^- + e^+ + \bar{p}$ (*b*) $p + p \rightarrow p + \bar{p}$

13-7. What is the uncertainty in the rest energies of the following particles? (*a*) $\Lambda(1670)$, (*b*) $\Sigma(2030)$, (*c*) $\Delta(1232)$

Section 13-2 Fundamental Interactions and the Classification of Particles

13-8. Name the interaction responsible for each of the following decays:
(*a*) $n \rightarrow p + e^- + \bar{\nu}_e$
(*b*) $\pi^0 \rightarrow \gamma + \gamma$
(*c*) $\Delta^+ \rightarrow \pi^0 + p$
(*d*) $\pi^+ \rightarrow \mu^+ + \nu_\mu$

13-9. Which of the following decays, $\pi^0 \rightarrow \gamma + \gamma$ or $\pi^- \rightarrow \mu^- + \bar{\nu}_\mu$, would you expect to have the longer lifetime? Why?

13-10. Which of the four fundamental interactions is most likely responsible for the following reactions:

(a) ^{16}O (excited state) $\rightarrow$ ^{16}O (ground state) $+ \gamma$

(b) $v_e + e \rightarrow v_e + e$

(c) $p + \bar{p} \rightarrow \gamma + \gamma$

(d) $p + \bar{v}_e \rightarrow n + e^+$

(e) $\pi^0 + p \rightarrow \pi^0 + p$

(f) ^{3}H $\rightarrow$ ^{3}He $+ e^- + \bar{v}_e$

13-11. Using the information concerning the neutrinos from SN1987A, including Figure 13-9, compute an upper limit to the mass of the electron neutrino.

13-12. The rest energies of the Σ^+ and Σ^- are slightly different, but those of the π^+ and π^- are exactly the same. Explain this difference in behavior.

13-13. Draw Feynman diagrams of the following decays:

(a) $\mu^+ \rightarrow e^+ + v_e + \bar{v}_\mu$

(b) $\pi^- \rightarrow \mu^- + \bar{v}_\mu$

(c) $\tau^- \rightarrow \mu^- + \bar{v}_\mu + v_\tau$

Section 13-3 Conservation Laws and Symmetries

13-14. State which of the decays or reactions that follow violate one or more of the conservation laws, and give the law or laws violated in each case.

(a) $p \rightarrow n + e^+ + \bar{v}_e$

(b) $n \rightarrow p + \pi^-$

(c) $e^+ + e^- \rightarrow \gamma$

(d) $p + \bar{p} \rightarrow \gamma + \gamma$

(e) $v_e + p \rightarrow n + e^+$

(f) $p \rightarrow \pi^+ + e^+ + e^-$

13-15. Determine the change in strangeness in each reaction that follows, and state whether the reaction can proceed via the strong interaction, the electromagnetic interaction, the weak interaction, or not at all:

(a) $\Omega^- \rightarrow \Xi^0 + \pi^-$

(b) $\Xi^0 \rightarrow p + \pi^- + \pi^0$

(c) $\Lambda^0 \rightarrow p + \pi^-$

13-16. Determine the change in strangeness for each decay, and state whether the decay can proceed via the strong interaction, the electromagnetic interaction, the weak interaction, or not at all:

(a) $\Omega^- \rightarrow \Lambda^0 + \bar{v}_e + e^-$

(b) $\Sigma^+ \rightarrow p + \pi^0$

(c) $\Sigma^0 \rightarrow \Lambda^0 + \gamma$

13-17. The rules for determining the isospin of two or more particles are the same as those for combining angular momentum. For example, since $T = 1/2$ for nucleons, the combination of two nucleons can have either $T = 1$ or $T = 0$, or may be a mixture of these isospin states. Since $T_3 = +1/2$ for the proton, the combination $p + p$ has $T_3 = +1$ and therefore must have $T = 1$. Find T_3 and the possible values of T for the following:

(a) $n + n$

(b) $n + p$

(c) $\pi^+ + p$

(d) $\pi^- + n$

(e) $\pi^+ + n$

13-18. Which of the following decays are allowed and which are forbidden? If the decay is allowed, state which interaction is responsible. If it is forbidden, state which conservation law its occurrence would violate.

(a) $\pi^- \rightarrow e^- + \gamma$

(b) $\pi^0 \rightarrow e^- + e^+ + \nu_e + \overline{\nu}_e$

(c) $\pi^+ \rightarrow e^- + e^+ + \mu^+ + \nu_\mu$

(d) $\Lambda^0 \rightarrow \pi^+ + \pi^-$

(e) $n \rightarrow p + e^- + \overline{\nu}_e$

13-19. For each of the following particles, write down two possible decays that satisfy all conservation laws: (a) Ω^-, (b) Σ^+, (c) Λ^0, (d) π^0, and (e) K^+.

13-20. Consider the following reactions:

$$K^- + p \longrightarrow K^0 + K^+ + \Omega^-$$
$$ \hookrightarrow \Xi^0 + \pi^-$$

Given that $B = 1$ for the proton and $B = 0$ for mesons and that baryon number is conserved, determine the baryon number of the Ω^- and the Ξ^0.

13-21. Which of the following decays and reactions conserved strangeness?

(a) $\overline{p} + p \rightarrow \gamma + \gamma$

(b) $\Xi^- \rightarrow \pi^- + \Lambda^0$

(c) $\Sigma^+ \rightarrow \Lambda^0 + \pi^+$

(d) $\pi^- + p \rightarrow \pi^- + \Sigma^+$

(e) $\Omega^- \rightarrow \Xi^- + \pi^0$

Section 13-4 The Standard Model

13-22. Find the baryon number, charge, isospin, and strangeness for the following quark combinations and identify the corresponding hadron: (a) *uud*, (b) *udd*, (c) *uuu*, (d) *uss*, (e) *dss*, (f) *suu*, and (g) *sdd*.

13-23. Find the baryon number, charge, isospin, and strangeness for the following quark combinations and identify the corresponding hadron (the charge and strangeness of the antiquarks are the negatives of those of the corresponding quarks, as with any other particle-antiparticle pair): (a) $u\overline{d}$, (b) $\overline{u}d$, (c) $u\overline{s}$, (d) $s\overline{s}$, and (e) $\overline{d}s$.

13-24. Draw two Feynman diagrams that represent the decay of the antibottom quark.

13-25. Some quark combinations can exist in two or more isospin states, with each state corresponding to a different hadron. One such combination is *uds*. (a) What is the value of T_3 for this combination? (b) What are the possible values of total isospin T for this combination? (c) Find the baryon number, charge, and strangeness of this combination, and identify the hadron corresponding to each isospin state.

13-26. The Δ^{++} particle is a baryon that decays via the strong interaction. Its strangeness, charm, topness, and bottomness are all zero. What combination of quarks gives a particle with these properties?

13-27. Compute the approximate range of a weak interaction mediated by a W^+.

13-28. One mode of weak decay of the $\overline{K}^0$ is

$$\overline{K}^0 \longrightarrow \pi^+ + \mu^- + \overline{\nu}_\mu$$

Showing the quark content of the particles, draw the Feynman diagram of this so-called semileptonic decay.

13-29. The Λ^0 undergoes a weak decay as follows: $\Lambda^0 \rightarrow p + \pi^-$. Showing the quark content of the particles, draw the Feynman diagram of this so-called nonleptonic decay.

13-30. Show that the neutron cannot undergo the weak decay shown for the Λ^0 in Problem 13-29.

13-31. The decay of the Λ^0 shown in Problem 13-29 can also proceed via the strong interaction. Showing the quark content of the particles, draw the Feynman diagram that illustrates the strong decay of the Λ^0.

13-32. Find a possible combination of quarks that gives the correct values for electric charge, baryon number, and strangeness for (a) K^+ and (b) K^0.

13-33. The D^+ meson has strangeness 0, but it has charm of $+1$. (a) What is a possible quark combination that will give the correct properties for this particle? (b) Repeat (a) for the D^- meson, which is the antiparticle of the D^+.

13-34. The lifetime of the Σ^0 is 6×10^{-20} s. The lifetime of the Σ^+ is 0.8×10^{-10} s, and that of the Σ^- is 1.48×10^{-10} s, nearly twice as long. How can these differences in lifetimes between members of the same isospin multiplet be explained?

Section 13-5 Beyond the Standard Model

13-35. Grand unification theories predict that the proton is unstable. If that turns out to be true, why does it mean that baryon number is not conserved? If leptons and quarks are interchangeable at the unification energy, does this mean that there is a new, conserved "leptoquark number"? Justify your answers.

13-36. GUTs predict a lifetime of about 10^{32} y for the proton. If that is the case, how many protons will decay each year in the world's oceans? (Assume the average depth of the oceans to be 1 km and that they cover 75 percent of Earth's surface.)

13-37. Protons might decay via a number of different modes. What conservation laws are violated by the following possibilities?

(a) $p \rightarrow e^+ + \Lambda^0 + \nu_e$
(b) $p \rightarrow \pi^+ + \gamma$
(c) $p \rightarrow \pi^+ + K^0$

Level II

13-38. Find a possible quark combination for the following particles: (a), $\bar{n}$, (b) Ξ^0, (c) Σ^+, (d) Ω^-, and (e) Ξ^-.

13-39. State the properties of the particles made up of the following quarks: (a) ddd, (b) $u\bar{c}$, (c) $u\bar{b}$, and (d) $\overline{sss}$.

13-40. Show that the Z^0 cannot decay into two identical zero-spin particles.

13-41. Consider the following decay chain:

$$\Xi^0 \longrightarrow \Lambda^0 + \pi^0$$
$$\Lambda^0 \longrightarrow p + \pi^-$$
$$\pi^0 \longrightarrow \gamma + \gamma$$
$$\pi^- \longrightarrow \mu^- + \bar{\nu}_\mu$$
$$\mu^- \longrightarrow e^- + \bar{\nu}_e + \nu_\mu$$

(a) Are all the final products shown stable? If not, finish the decay chain. (b) Write the overall decay reaction for Ξ^0 to the final products. (c) Check the overall decay reaction for the conservation of electric charge, baryon number, lepton number, and strangeness. (d) In the first step of the chain, could the Λ^0 have been a Σ^0?

13-42. Show that the following decays conserve all lepton numbers.

(a) $\mu^+ \rightarrow e^+ + \nu_e + \bar{\nu}_\mu$
(b) $\tau^- \rightarrow \mu^- + \bar{\nu}_\mu + \nu_\tau$
(c) $n \rightarrow p + e^- + \bar{\nu}_e$
(d) $\pi^- \rightarrow \mu^- + \bar{\nu}_\mu$

13-43. A π^0 with energy 850 MeV decays in flight via the reaction $\pi^0 \rightarrow \gamma + \gamma$. Compute the angles (in the lab) made by the momenta of the gammas with the original direction of the π^0.

13-44. Test the following decays for violation of the conservation of energy, electric charge, baryon number, and lepton number:
(a) $\Lambda^0 \rightarrow p + \pi^-$
(b) $\Sigma^- \rightarrow n + p^-$
(c) $\mu^- \rightarrow e^- + \bar{\nu}_e + \nu_\mu$
Assume that linear and angular momentum are conserved. State which conservation laws (if any) are violated in each decay.

13-45. Consider the following decay chain:

$$\Omega^- \longrightarrow \Xi^0 + \pi^-$$
$$\Xi^0 \longrightarrow \Sigma^+ + e^- + \bar{\nu}_e$$
$$\pi^- \longrightarrow \mu^- + \bar{\nu}_\mu$$
$$\Sigma^+ \longrightarrow n + \pi^+$$
$$\pi^+ \longrightarrow \mu^+ + \nu_\mu$$
$$\mu^+ \longrightarrow e^+ + \bar{\nu}_\mu + \nu_e$$
$$\mu^- \longrightarrow e^- + \bar{\nu}_e + \nu_\mu$$

(a) Are all the final products shown stable? If not, finish the decay chain. (b) Write the overall decay reaction for Ω^- to the final products. (c) Check the overall decay reaction for the conservation of electric charge, baryon number, lepton number, and strangeness.

Level III

13-46. The mass of the hydrogen atom is smaller than the sum of the masses of the proton and the electron, the difference being the binding energy. The mass of the π^+ is 139.6 MeV/c^2; however, the masses of the quarks of which it is composed are only a few MeV/c^2. How can that be explained?

13-47. (a) Calculate the total kinetic energy of the decay products for the decay: $\Lambda^0 \rightarrow p + \pi^-$. Assume the Λ^0 is initially at rest. (b) Find the ratio of the kinetic energy of the pion to the kinetic energy of the proton. (c) Find the kinetic energies of the proton and the pion for this decay.

13-48. A Σ^0 particle at rest decays into a Λ^0 plus a photon. (a) What is the total energy of the decay products? (b) Assuming that the kinetic energy of the Λ^0 is negligible compared with the energy of the photon, calculate the approximate momentum of the photon. (c) Use your result for (b) to calculate the kinetic energy of the Λ^0. (d) Use your result for (c) to obtain a better estimate of the momentum and the energy of the photon.

13-49. In this problem, you will calculate the difference in the time of arrival of two neutrinos of different energy from a supernova that is 170,000 light-years away. Let the energies of the neutrinos be $E_1 = 20$ MeV and $E_2 = 5$ MeV, and assume that the rest mass of a neutrino is 2.4 eV/c^2. Because their total energy is so much greater than their rest energy, the neutrinos have speeds that are very nearly equal to c and energies that are approximately $E \approx pc$. (a) If t_1 and t_2 are the times it takes for neutrinos of speeds u_1 and u_2 to travel a distance x, show that

$$\Delta t = t_2 - t_1 = x\frac{u_1 - u_2}{u_1 u_2} \approx \frac{x \, \Delta u}{c^2}$$

(b) The speed of a neutrino of rest mass m_0 and total energy E can be found from Equation 2-10. Show that when $E \gg m_0 c^2$, the speed u is given by

$$\frac{u}{c} \approx 1 - \frac{1}{2}\left(\frac{m_0 c^2}{E}\right)^2$$

(c) Use the result for (b) to calculate $u_1 - u_2$ for the energies and rest mass given, and calculate Δt from the result for (a) for $x = 170{,}000 \ c \cdot \text{y}$. (d) Repeat the calculation in (c) using $m_0 c^2 = 40 \ \text{eV}$ for the rest energy of a neutrino.

13-50. There are three possible decay modes for the τ^-. (a) Draw the Feynman diagrams for each mode. (b) Which mode is the most probable? Explain why.

Appendix A

Table of Atomic Masses

Z	Element	Symbol	Chemical atomic weight	Mass number (* indicates radioactive)	Atomic mass	Percent abundance	Half-life and decay mode (if unstable)
0	(Neutron)	n		1*	1.008665		10.4 m β^-
1	Hydrogen	H	1.00798	1	1.007825	99.985	
	Deuterium	D		2	2.014102	0.015	
	Tritium	T		3*	3.016049		12.33 y β^-
2	Helium	He	4.00260	3	3.016029	0.00014	
				4	4.002603	99.99986	
				6*	6.018886		0.81 s β^-
				8*	8.033922		0.12 s β^-
3	Lithium	Li	6.941	6	6.015121	7.5	
				7	7.016003	92.5	
				8*	8.022486		0.84 s β^-
				9*	9.026789		0.18 s β^-
				11*	11.043897		8.7 ms β^-
4	Beryllium	Be	9.0122	7*	7.016928		53.3 d ec
				9	9.012174	100	
				10*	10.013534		1.5×10^6 y β^-
				11*	11.021657		13.8 s β^-
				12*	12.026921		23.6 ms β^-
				14*	14.042866		4.3 ms β^-
5	Boron	B	10.811	8*	8.024605		0.77 s β^+
				10	10.012936	19.9	
				11	11.009305	80.1	
				12*	12.014352		0.0202 s β^-
				13*	13.017780		17.4 ms β^-
				14*	14.025404		13.8 ms β^-
				15*	15.031100		10.3 ms β^-
6	Carbon	C	12.011	9*	9.031030		0.13 s β^+
				10*	10.016854		19.3 s β^+
				11*	11.011433		20.4 m β^+
				12	12.000000	98.90	
				13	13.003355	1.10	
				14*	14.003242		5730 y β^-
				15*	15.010599		2.45 s β^-
				16*	16.014701		0.75 s β^-
				17*	17.022582		0.20 s β^-

(Continued)

Z	Element	Symbol	Chemical atomic weight	Mass number (* indicates radioactive)	Atomic mass	Percent abundance	Half-life and decay mode (if unstable)	
7	Nitrogen	N	14.0067	12*	12.018613		0.0110 s	β^+
				13*	13.005738		9.96 m	β^+
				14	14.003074	99.63		
				15	15.000108	0.37		
				16*	16.006100		7.13 s	β^-
				17*	17.008450		4.17 s	β^-
				18*	18.014082		0.62 s	β^-
				19*	19.017038		0.24 s	β^-
8	Oxygen	O	15.9994	13*	13.024813		8.6 ms	β^+
				14*	14.008595		70.6 s	β^+
				15*	15.003065		122 s	β^+
				16	15.994915	99.71		
				17	16.999132	0.039		
				18	17.999160	0.20		
				19*	19.003577		26.9 s	β^-
				20*	20.004076		13.6 s	β^-
				21*	21.008595		3.4 s	β^-
9	Fluorine	F	18.99840	17*	17.002094		64.5 s	β^+
				18*	18.000937		109.8 m	β^+
				19	18.998404	100		
				20*	19.999982		11.0 s	β^-
				21*	20.999950		4.2 s	β^-
				22*	22.003036		4.2 s	β^-
				23*	23.003564		2.2 s	β^-
10	Neon	Ne	20.180	18*	18.005710		1.67 s	β^+
				19*	19.001880		17.2 s	β^+
				20	19.992435	90.48		
				21	20.993841	0.27		
				22	21.991383	9.25		
				23*	22.994465		37.2 s	β^-
				24*	23.993999		3.38 m	β^-
				25*	24.997789		0.60 s	β^-
11	Sodium	Na	22.98977	21*	20.997650		22.5 s	β^+
				22*	21.994434		2.61 y	β^+
				23	22.989767	100		
				24*	23.990961		14.96 h	β^-
				25*	24.989951		59.1 s	β^-
				26*	25.992588		1.07 s	β^-
12	Magnesium	Mg	24.3051	23*	22.994124		11.3 s	β^+
				24	23.985042	78.99		
				25	24.985838	10.00		
				26	25.982594	11.01		
				27*	26.984341		9.46 m	β^-
				28*	27.983876		20.9 h	β^-
				29*	28.375346		1.30 s	β^-

Z	Element	Symbol	Chemical atomic weight	Mass number (* indicates radioactive)	Atomic mass	Percent abundance	Half-life and decay mode (if unstable)	
13	Aluminum	Al	26.98154	25*	24.990429		7.18 s	β^+
				26*	25.986892		7.4×10^5 y	β^+
				27	26.981538	100		
				28*	27.981910		2.24 m	β^-
				29*	28.980445		6.56 m	β^-
				30*	29.982965		3.60 s	β^-
14	Silicon	Si	28.086	27*	26.986704		4.16 s	β^+
				28	27.976927	92.23		
				29	28.976495	4.67		
				30	28.973770	3.10		
				31*	30.975362		2.62 h	β^-
				32*	31.974148		172 y	β^-
				33*	32.977928		6.13 s	β^-
15	Phosphorus	P	30.97376	30*	29.978307		2.50 m	β^+
				31	30.973762	100		
				32*	31.973908		14.26 d	β^-
				33*	32.971725		25.3 d	β^-
				34*	33.973636		12.43 s	β^-
16	Sulfur	S	32.066	31*	30.979554		2.57 s	β^+
				32	31.972071	95.02		
				33	32.971459	0.75		
				34	33.967867	4.21		
				35*	34.969033		87.5 d	β^-
				36	35.967081	0.02		
17	Chlorine	Cl	35.453	34*	33.973763		32.2 m	β^+
				35	34.968853	75.77		
				36*	35.968307		3.0×10^5 y	β^-
				37	36.965903	24.23		
				38*	37.968010		37.3 m	β^-
18	Argon	Ar	39.948	36	35.967547	0.337		
				37*	36.966776		35.04 d	ec
				38	37.962732	0.063		
				39*	38.964314		269 y	β^-
				40	39.962384	99.600		
				42*	41.963049		33 y	β^-
19	Potassium	K	39.0983	39	38.963708	93.2581		
				40*	39.964000	0.0117	1.28×10^9 y	β^+, ec, β^-
				41	40.961827	6.7302		
				42*	41.962404		12.4 h	β^-
				43*	42.960716		22.3 h	β^-

(Continued)

Z	Element	Symbol	Chemical atomic weight	Mass number (* indicates radioactive)	Atomic mass	Percent abundance	Half-life and decay mode (if unstable)	
20	Calcium	Ca	40.078	40	39.962591	96.941		
				41*	40.962279		1.0×10^5 y	ec
				42	41.958618	0.647		
				43	42.958767	0.135		
				44	43.955481	2.086		
				46	45.953687	0.004		
				48	47.952534	0.187		
21	Scandium	Sc	44.9559	41*	40.969250		0.596 s	β^+
				43*	42.961151		3.89 h	β^+
				45	44.955911	100		
				46*	45.955170		83.8 d	β^-
22	Titanium	Ti	47.88	44*	43.959691		49 y	ec
				46	45.952630	8.0		
				47	46.951765	7.3		
				48	47.947947	73.8		
				49	48.947871	5.5		
				50	49.944792	5.4		
23	Vanadium	V	50.9415	48*	47.952255		15.97 d	β^+
				50*	49.947161	0.25	1.5×10^{17} y	β^+
				51	50.943962	99.75		
24	Chromium	Cr	51.996	48*	47.954033		21.6 h	ec
				50	49.946047	4.345		
				52	51.940511	83.79		
				53	52.940652	9.50		
				54	53.938883	2.365		
25	Manganese	Mn	54.93805	53*	52.941292		3.74×10^6 y	ec
				54*	53.940361		312.1 d	ec
				55	54.938048	100		
				56*	55.938908		2.58 h	β^-
26	Iron	Fe	55.847	54	53.939613	5.9		
				55*	54.938297		2.7 y	ec
				56	55.934940	91.72		
				57	56.935396	2.1		
				58	57.933278	0.28		
				60*	59.934078		1.5×10^6 y	β^-
27	Cobalt	Co	58.93320	57*	56.936294		271.8 d	ec
				58*	57.935755		70.9 h	ec, β^+
				59	58.933198	100		
				60*	59.933820		5.27 y	β^-
				61*	60.932478		1.65 h	β^-

Z	Element	Symbol	Chemical atomic weight	Mass number (* indicates radioactive)	Atomic mass	Percent abundance	Half-life and decay mode (if unstable)
28	Nickel	Ni	58.693	58	57.935346	68.077	
				59*	58.934350		7.5×10^4 y ec, β^+
				60	59.930789	26.223	
				61	60.931058	1.140	
				62	61.928346	3.634	
				63*	62.929670		100 y β^-
				64	63.927967	0.926	
29	Copper	Cu	63.546	63	62.929599	69.17	
				64*	63.929765		12.7 h ec
				65	64.927791	30.83	
				66*	65.928871		5.1 m β^-
30	Zinc	Zn	65.39	64	63.929144	48.6	
				66	65.926035	27.9	
				67	66.927129	4.1	
				68	67.924845	18.8	
				70	69.925323	0.6	
31	Gallium	Ga	69.723	69	68.925580	60.108	
				70*	69.926027		21.1 m β^-
				71	70.924703	39.892	
				72*	71.926367		14.1 h β^-
32	Germanium	Ge	72.61	69*	68.927969		39.1 h ec, β^+
				70	69.924250	21.23	
				72	71.922079	27.66	
				73	72.923462	7.73	
				74	73.921177	35.94	
				76	75.921402	7.44	
				77*	76.923547		11.3 h β^-
33	Arsenic	As	74.9216	73*	72.923827		80.3 d ec
				74*	73.923928		17.8 d ec, β^+
				75	74.921594	100	
				76*	75.922393		1.1 d β^-
				77*	76.920645		38.8 h β^-
34	Selenium	Se	78.96	74	73.922474	0.89	
				76	75.919212	9.36	
				77	76.919913	7.63	
				78	77.917307	23.78	
				79*	78.918497		6.5×10^4 y β^-
				80	79.916519	49.61	
				82*	81.916697	8.73	1.4×10^{20} y $2\beta^-$

(*Continued*)

Z	Element	Symbol	Chemical atomic weight	Mass number (* indicates radioactive)	Atomic mass	Percent abundance	Half-life and decay mode (if unstable)
35	Bromine	Br	79.904	79	78.918336	50.69	
				80*	79.918528		17.7 m β^+
				81	80.916287	49.31	
				82*	81.916802		35.3 h β^-
36	Krypton	Kr	83.80	78	77.920400	0.35	
				80	79.916377	2.25	
				81*	80.916589		2.11×10^5 y ec
				82	81.913481	11.6	
				83	82.914136	11.5	
				84	83.911508	57.0	
				85*	84.912531		10.76 y β^-
				86	85.910615	17.3	
37	Rubidium	Rb	85.468	85	84.911793	72.17	
				86*	85.911171		18.6 d β^-
				87*	86.909186	27.83	4.75×10^{10} y β^-
				88*	87.911325		17.8 m β^-
38	Strontium	Sr	87.62	84	83.913428	0.56	
				86	85.909266	9.86	
				87	86.908883	7.00	
				88	87.905618	82.58	
				90*	89.907737		29.1 y β^-
39	Yttrium	Y	88.9058	88*	87.909507		106.6 d ec, β^+
				89	88.905847	100	
				90*	89.914811		2.67 d β^-
40	Zirconium	Zr	91.224	90	89.904702	51.45	
				91	90.905643	11.22	
				92	91.905038	17.15	
				93*	92.906473		1.5×10^6 y β^-
				94	93.906314	17.38	
				96	95.908274	2.80	
41	Niobium	Nb	92.9064	91*	90.906988		6.8×10^2 y ec
				92*	91.907191		3.5×10^7 y ec
				93	92.906376	100	
				94*	93.907280		2×10^4 y β^-
42	Molybdenum	Mo	95.94	92	91.906807	14.84	
				93*	92.906811		3.5×10^3 y ec
				94	93.905085	9.25	
				95	94.905841	15.92	
				96	95.904678	16.68	
				97	96.906020	9.55	
				98	97.905407	24.13	
				100	99.907476	9.63	

Z	Element	Symbol	Chemical atomic weight	Mass number (* indicates radioactive)	Atomic mass	Percent abundance	Half-life and decay mode (if unstable)
43	Technetium	Tc	$(98)^{\dagger}$	97*	96.906363		2.6×10^6 y ec
				98*	97.907215		4.2×10^6 y β^-
				99*	98.906254		2.1×10^5 y β^-
44	Ruthenium	Ru	101.07	96	95.907597	5.54	
				98	97.905287	1.86	
				99	98.905939	12.7	
				100	99.904219	12.6	
				101	100.905558	17.1	
				102	101.904348	31.6	
				104	103.905428	18.6	
45	Rhodium	Rh	102.9055	102*	101.906794		207 d ec
				103	102.905502	100	
				104*	103.906654		42 s β^-
46	Palladium	Pd	106.42	102	101.905616	1.02	
				104	103.904033	11.14	
				105	104.905082	22.33	
				106	105.903481	27.33	
				107*	106.905126		6.5×10^6 y β^-
				108	107.903893	26.46	
				110	109.905158	11.72	
47	Silver	Ag	107.868	107	106.905091	51.84	
				108*	107.905953		2.39 m ec, β^+ β^-
				109	108.904754	48.16	
				110*	109.906110		24.6 s β^-
48	Cadmium	Cd	112.41	106	105.906457	1.25	
				108	107.904183	0.89	
				109*	108.904984		462 d ec
				110	109.903004	12.49	
				111	110.904182	12.80	
				112	111.902760	24.13	
				113*	112.904401	12.22	9.3×10^{15} y β^-
				114	113.903359	28.73	
				116	115.904755	7.49	
49	Indium	In	114.82	113	112.904060	4.3	
				114*	113.904916		1.2 m β^-
				115*	114.903876	95.7	4.4×10^{14} y β^-
				116*	115.905258		54.4 m β^-

† *Chemical atomic weights within parentheses are approximate.*

(Continued)

Z	Element	Symbol	Chemical atomic weight	Mass number (* indicates radioactive)	Atomic mass	Percent abundance	Half-life and decay mode (if unstable)
50	Tin	Sn	118.71	112	111.904822	0.97	
				114	113.902780	0.65	
				115	114.903345	0.36	
				116	115.901743	14.53	
				117	116.902953	7.68	
				118	117.901605	24.22	
				119	118.903308	8.58	
				120	119.902197	32.59	
				121*	120.904237		55 y β^-
				122	121.903439	4.63	
				124	123.905274	5.79	
51	Antimony	Sb	121.76	121	120.903820	57.36	
				123	122.904215	42.64	
				125*	124.905251		2.7 y β^-
52	Tellurium	Te	127.60	120	119.904040	0.095	
				122	121.903052	2.59	
				123*	122.904271	0.905	1.3×10^{13} y ec
				124	123.902817	4.79	
				125	124.904429	7.12	
				126	125.903309	18.93	
				128*	127.904463	31.70	$> 8 \times 10^{24}$ y $2\beta^-$
				130*	129.906228	33.87	1.2×10^{21} y $2\beta^-$
53	Iodine	I	126.9045	126*	125.905619		13 d ec, β^+, β^-
				127	126.904474	100	
				128*	127.905812		25 m β^-, ec, β^+
				129*	128.904984		1.6×10^7 y β^-
54	Xenon	Xe	131.29	124	123.905894	0.10	
				126	125.904268	0.09	
				128	127.903531	1.91	
				129	128.904779	26.4	
				130	129.903509	4.1	
				131	130.905069	21.2	
				132	131.904141	26.9	
				134	133.905394	10.4	
				136	135.907215	8.9	
55	Cesium	Cs	132.9054	133	132.905436	100	
				134*	133.906703		2.1 y β^-
				135*	134.905891		2×10^6 y β^-
				137*	136.907078		30 y β^-

Z	Element	Symbol	Chemical atomic weight	Mass number (* indicates radioactive)	Atomic mass	Percent abundance	Half-life and decay mode (if unstable)
56	Barium	Ba	137.33	130	129.906289	0.106	
				132	131.905048	0.101	
				133*	132.905990		10.5 y ec
				134	133.904492	2.42	
				135	134.905671	6.593	
				136	135.904559	7.85	
				137	136.905816	11.23	
				138	137.905236	71.70	
57	Lanthanum	La	138.905	137*	136.906462		6×10^4 y ec
				138*	137.907105	0.0902	1.05×10^{11} y ec, β^+
				139	138.906346	99.9098	
58	Cerium	Ce	140.12	136	135.907139	0.19	
				138	137.905986	0.25	
				140	139.905434	88.43	
				142	141.909241	11.13	
59	Praseodymium	Pr	140.9076	140*	139.909071		3.39 m ec, β^+
				141	140.907647	100	
				142*	141.910040		25.0 m β^-
60	Neodymium	Nd	144.24	142	141.907718	27.13	
				143	142.909809	12.18	
				144*	143.910082	23.80	2.3×10^{15} y α
				145	144.912568	8.30	
				146	145.913113	17.19	
				148	147.916888	5.76	
				150	149.920887	5.64	
61	Promethium	Pm	(145)	143*	142.910928		265 d ec
				145*	144.912745		17.7 y ec
				146*	145.914698		5.5 y ec
				147*	146.915134		2.623 y β^-
62	Samarium	Sm	150.36	144	143.911996	3.1	
				146*	145.913043		1.0×10^8 y α
				147*	146.914894	15.0	1.06×10^{11} y α
				148*	147.914819	11.3	7×10^{15} y α
				149	148.917180	13.8	
				150	149.917273	7.4	
				151*	150.919928		90 y β^-
				152	151.919728	26.7	
				154	153.922206	22.7	

(*Continued*)

Z	Element	Symbol	Chemical atomic weight	Mass number (* indicates radioactive)	Atomic mass	Percent abundance	Half-life and decay mode (if unstable)	
63	Europium	Eu	151.96	151	150.919846	47.8		
				152*	151.921740		13.5 y	ec, β^+
				153	152.921226	52.2		
				154*	153.922975		8.59 y	β^-
				155*	154.922888		4.7 y	β^-
64	Gadolinium	Gd	157.25	148*	147.918112		75 y	α
				150*	149.918657		1.8×10^6 y	α
				152*	151.919787	0.02	1.1×10^{14} y	α
				154	153.920862	2.18		
				155	154.922618	14.80		
				156	155.922119	20.47		
				157	156.923957	15.65		
				158	157.924099	24.84		
				160	159.927050	21.86		
65	Terbium	Tb	158.9253	158*	157.925411		180 y	ec, β^+,β^-
				159	158.925345	100		
				160*	159.927551		72.3 d	β^-
66	Dysprosium	Dy	162.50	156	155.924277	0.06		
				158	157.924403	0.10		
				160	159.925193	2.34		
				161	160.926930	18.9		
				162	161.926796	25.5		
				163	162.928729	24.9		
				164	163.929172	28.2		
67	Holmium	Ho	164.9303	165	164.930316	100		
				166*	165.932282		1.2×10^3 y	β^-
68	Erbium	Er	167.26	162	161.928775	0.14		
				164	163.929198	1.61		
				166	165.930292	33.6		
				167	166.932047	22.95		
				168	167.932369	27.8		
				170	169.935462	14.9		
69	Thulium	Tm	168.9342	169	168.934213	100		
				171*	170.936428		1.92 y	β^-
70	Ytterbium	Yb	173.04	168	167.933897	0.13		
				170	169.934761	3.05		
				171	170.936324	14.3		
				172	171.936380	21.9		
				173	172.938209	16.12		
				174	173.938861	31.8		
				176	175.942564	12.7		

Z	Element	Symbol	Chemical atomic weight	Mass number (* indicates radioactive)	Atomic mass	Percent abundance	Half-life and decay mode (if unstable)
71	Lutetium	Lu	174.967	173*	172.938930		1.37 y ec
				175	174.940772	97.41	
				176*	175.942679	2.59	3.8×10^{10} y β^-
72	Hafnium	Hf	178.49	174*	173.940042	0.162	2.0×10^{15} y α
				176	175.941404	5.206	
				177	176.943218	18.606	
				178	177.943697	27.297	
				179	178.945813	13.629	
				180	179.946547	35.100	
73	Tantalum	Ta	180.9479	180	179.947542	0.012	
				181	180.947993	99.988	
74	Tungsten (Wolfram)	W	183.85	180	179.946702	0.12	
				182	181.948202	26.3	
				183	182.950221	14.28	
				184	183.950929	30.7	
				186	185.954358	28.6	
75	Rhenium	Re	186.207	185	184.952951	37.40	
				187*	186.955746	62.60	4.4×10^{10} y β^-
76	Osmium	Os	190.2	184	183.952486	0.02	
				186*	185.953834	1.58	2.0×10^{15} y α
				187	186.955744	1.6	
				188	187.955744	13.3	
				189	188.958139	16.1	
				190	189.958439	26.4	
				192	191.961468	41.0	
				194*	193.965172		6.0 y β^-
77	Iridium	Ir	192.2	191	190.960585	37.3	
				193	192.962916	62.7	
78	Platinum	Pt	195.08	190*	189.959926	0.01	6.5×10^{11} y α
				192	191.961027	0.79	
				194	193.962655	32.9	
				195	194.964765	33.8	
				196	195.964926	25.3	
				198	197.967867	7.2	
79	Gold	Au	196.9665	197	196.966543	100	
				198*	197.968217		2.70 d β^-
				199*	198.968740		3.14 d β^-

(Continued)

Z	Element	Symbol	Chemical atomic weight	Mass number (* indicates radioactive)	Atomic mass	Percent abundance	Half-life and decay mode (if unstable)	
80	Mercury	Hg	200.59	196	195.965806	0.15		
				198	197.966743	9.97		
				199	198.968253	16.87		
				200	199.968299	23.10		
				201	200.970276	13.10		
				202	201.970617	29.86		
				204	203.973466	6.87		
81	Thallium	Tl	204.383	203	202.972320	29.524		
				204*	203.973839		3.78 y	β^-
				205	204.974400	70.476		
		(Ra E″)		206*	205.976084		4.2 m	β^-
		(Ac C″)		207*	206.977403		4.77 m	β^-
		(Th C″)		208*	207.981992		3.053 m	β^-
		(Ra C″)		210*	209.990057		1.30 m	β^-
82	Lead	Pb	207.2	202*	201.972134		5×10^4 y	ec
				204	203.973020	1.4		
				205*	204.974457		1.5×10^7 y	ec
				206	205.974440	24.1		
				207	206.975871	22.1		
				208	207.976627	52.4		
		(Ra D)		210*	209.984163		22.3 y	β^-
		(Ac B)		211*	210.988734		36.1 m	β^-
		(Th B)		212*	211.991872		10.64 h	β^-
		(Ra B)		214*	213.999798		26.8 m	β^-
83	Bismuth	Bi	208.9803	207*	206.978444		32.2 y	ec, β^+
				208*	207.979717		3.7×10^5 y	ec
				209	208.980374	100		
		(Ra E)		210*	209.984096		5.01 d	α, β^-
		(Th C)		211*	210.987254		2.14 m	α
				212*	211.991259		60.6 m	α, β^-
		(Ra C)		214*	213.998692		19.9 m	β^-
				215*	215.001836		7.4 m	β^-
84	Polonium	Po	(209)	209*	208.982405		102 y	α
		(Ra F)		210*	209.982848		138.38 d	α
		(Ac C′)		211*	210.986627		0.52 s	α
		(Th C′)		212*	211.988842		0.30 μs	α
		(Ra C′)		214*	213.995177		164 μs	α
		(Ac A)		215*	214.999418		0.0018 s	α
		(Th A)		216*	216.001889		0.145 s	α
		(Ra A)		218*	218.008965		3.10 m	α
85	Astatine	At	(210)	215*	214.998638		$\approx$ 100 μs	α
				218*	218.008685		1.6 s	α
				219*	219.011297		0.9 m	α

Z	Element	Symbol	Chemical atomic weight	Mass number (* indicates radioactive)	Atomic mass	Percent abundance	Half-life and decay mode (if unstable)	
86	Radon	Rn	(222)					
		(An)		219*	219.009477		3.96 s	α
		(Tn)		220*	220.011369		55.6 s	α
		(Rn)		222*	222.017571		3.823 d	α
87	Francium	Fr	(223)	222*	222.017585		14.2 m	β^-
		(Ac K)		223*	223.019733		22 m	β^-
88	Radium	Ra	226.025					
		(Ac X)		223*	223.018499		11.43 d	α
		(Th X)		224*	224.020187		3.66 d	α
		(Ra)		226*	226.025402		1600 y	α
		(Ms Th$_1$)		228*	228.031064		5.75 y	β^-
89	Actinium	Ac	227.028	227*	227.027749		21.77 y	β^-
		(Ms Th$_2$)		228*	228.031015		6.15 h	β^-
90	Thorium	Th	232.0381					
		(Rd Ac)		227*	227.027701		18.72 d	α
		(Rd Th)		228*	228.028716		1.913 y	α
				229*	229.031757		7300 y	α
		(Io)		230*	230.033127		75,000 y	α, sf
		(UY)		231*	231.036299		25.52 h	β^-
		(Th)		232*	232.038051	100	1.40×10^{10} y	α
		(UX$_1$)		234*	234.043593		24.1 d	β^-
91	Protactinium	Pa	231.0359	231*	231.035880		32,760 y	α
		(UZ)		234*	234.043300		6.7 h	β^-
92	Uranium	U	238.0289	231*	231.036264		4.2 d	β^+
				232*	232.037131		69 y	α
				233*	233.039630		1.59×10^5 y	α
		(UII)		234*	234.040946	0.0055	2.45×10^5 y	α
		(Ac U)		235*	235.043924	0.720	7.04×10^8 y	α
		(UI)		236*	236.045562		2.34×10^7 y	α
				238*	238.050784	99.2745	4.47×10^9 y	α
				239*	239.054290		23.5 m	β^-
93	Neptunium	Np	237.048	235*	235.044057		396 d	α
				236*	236.046559		1.54×10^5 y	ec
				237*	237.048168		2.14×10^6 y	α
94	Plutonium	Pu	(244)	236*	236.046033		2.87 y	α, sf
				238*	238.049555		87.7 y	α, sf
				239*	239.052157		24,120 y	α, sf
				240*	240.053808		6560 y	α, sf
				241*	241.056846		14.4 y	β^-
				242*	242.058737		3.7×10^5 y	α, sf
				244*	244.064200		8.1×10^7 y	α, sf

(Continued)

Z	Element	Symbol	Chemical atomic weight	Mass number (* indicates radioactive)	Atomic mass	Percent abundance	Half-life and decay mode (if unstable)	
95	Americium	Am	(243)	240*	240.055285		2.12 d	ec
				241*	241.056824		432 y	α, sf
96	Curium	Cm	(247)	247*	247.070347		1.56×10^7 y	α
				248*	248.072344		3.4×10^5 y	α, sf
97	Berkelium	Bk	(247)	247*	247.070300		1380 y	α
				249*	249.074979		327 d	β^-
98	Californium	Cm	(251)	250*	250.076400		13.1 y	α, sf
				251*	251.079580		898 y	α
99	Einsteinium	Es	(252)	252*	252.082974		1.29 y	α
				253*	253.084817		2.02 d	α, sf
100	Fermium	Fm	(257)	253*	253.085173		3.00 d	ec
				254*	254.086849		3.24 h	α, sf
101	Mendelevium	Md	(258)	256*	256.093988		75.6 m	ec, β^+
				258*	258.098594		55 d	α
102	Nobelium	No	(259)	257*	257.096855		25 s	α
				259*	259.100932		58 m	α, sf
103	Lawrencium	Lr	(260)	259*	259.102888		6.14 s	α, sf
				260*	260.105346		3.0 m	α, sf
104	Rutherfordium	Rf	(261)	260*	260.160302		24 ms	sf
				261*	261.108588		65 s	α, sf
105	Dubnium	Db	(262)	261*	261.111830		1.8 s	α
				262*	262.113763		35 s	α
106	Seaborgium	Sg	(263)	263*	263.118310		0.78 s	α, sf
107	Bohrium	Bh	(262)	262*	262.123081		0.10 s	α, sf
108	Hassium	Hs	(269)	265*	265.129984		1.8 ms	α
				267*	267.131770		60 ms	α
109	Meitnerium	Mt	(268)	266*	266.137789		3.4 ms	α, sf
				268*	268.138820		70 ms	α
110	not yet named	?	(281)	269*	269.145140		0.17 ms	α
				271*	271.146080		1.1 ms	α
				273*	272.153480		8.6 ms	α

Z	Element	Symbol	Chemical atomic weight	Mass number (* indicates radioactive)	Atomic mass	Percent abundance	Half-life and decay mode (if unstable)
111	not yet named	?	(272)	272*	272.153480		1.5 ms α
112	not yet named	?	(277)	277*	?		0.2 ms α
114	not yet named	?	(289)	285	?		? α

Appendix B1

Probability Integrals

When calculating various average values using the Maxwell-Boltzmann distribution, integrals of the following type occur:

$$I_n = \int_0^\infty x^n e^{-\lambda x^2}\, dx$$

where n is an integer. These can be obtained from I_0 and I_1 by differentiation. Consider I_n to be a function of λ and take the derivative with respect to λ:

$$\frac{dI_n}{d\lambda} = \int_0^\infty -x^2 x^n e^{-\lambda x^2}\, dx = -I_{n+2} \qquad \textbf{B1-1}$$

Thus if I_0 is known, all the I_n for even n can be obtained, and if I_1 is known, all the I_n for odd n can be obtained from Equation B1-1. I_1 can easily be evaluated, using the substitution $u = \lambda x^2$. Then $du = 2\lambda x\, dx$ and

$$I_1 = \int_0^\infty x e^{-\lambda x^2}\, dx = \frac{1}{2}\lambda^{-1} \int_0^\infty e^{-u}\, du = \frac{1}{2}\lambda^{-1}$$

Then I_3 and I_5 are

$$I_3 = -\frac{d\left(\frac{1}{2}\lambda^{-1}\right)}{d\lambda} = \frac{1}{2}\lambda^{-2}$$

and

$$I_5 = -\frac{I_3}{d\lambda} = \lambda^{-3}$$

The evaluation of I_0 is more difficult, but it can be done using a trick. We evaluate I_0^2

$$I_0^2 = \int_0^\infty e^{-\lambda x^2}\, dx \int_0^\infty e^{-\lambda y^2}\, dy = \int_0^\infty \int_0^\infty e^{-\lambda(x^2+y^2)}\, dx\, dy \qquad \textbf{B1-2}$$

where we have used y as the dummy variable of integration in the second integral. If we now consider this to be an integration over the xy plane, we can change to polar coordinates $r^2 = x^2 + y^2$ and $\tan \phi = y/x$. The element of area $dx\, dy$ becomes $r\, dr\, d\phi$ and the integration over positive x and y becomes integration from $r = 0$ to $r = \infty$ and from $\phi = 0$ to $\phi = \pi/2$. Then we have

$$I_0^2 = \int_0^\infty \int_0^{\pi/2} e^{-\lambda r^2} r \, dr \, d\phi = \frac{\pi}{2} I_1 = \frac{\pi}{4} \lambda^{-1}$$

and

$$I_0 = \frac{1}{2} \sqrt{\pi} \lambda^{-1/2}$$

We then obtain $I_2, I_4, \ldots$ by differentiation. For example,

$$I_2 = -\frac{dI_0}{d\lambda} = \frac{1}{4} \sqrt{\pi} \lambda^{-3/2}$$

Table B1−1 lists the values of the integral I_n calculated above for values of n from 0 to 5.

TABLE B1-1 Values of the integral $I_n = \displaystyle\int_0^\infty x^n e^{-\lambda x^2} \, dx$ for $n = 0$ to $n = 5$	
n	I_n
0	$\frac{1}{2} \pi^{1/2} \lambda^{-1/2}$
1	$\frac{1}{2} \lambda^{-1}$
2	$\frac{1}{4} \pi^{1/2} \lambda^{-3/2}$
3	$\frac{1}{2} \lambda^{-2}$
4	$\frac{3}{8} \pi^{1/2} \lambda^{-5/2}$
5	λ^{-3}
If n is even	$\displaystyle\int_{-\infty}^{+\infty} x^n e^{-\lambda x^2} \, dx = 2I_n$
If n is odd	$\displaystyle\int_{-\infty}^{+\infty} x^n e^{-\lambda x^2} \, dx = 0$

Appendix B2

Distribution Functions

The calculation of the pressure of a gas in the More section "Kinetic Theory: A Brief Review" in Chapter 8 gives us interesting information about the average square speed, and therefore the average energies, of the molecules in a gas, but it does not yield any details about the *distribution* of molecular velocities. Distribution functions are encountered frequently in Chapter 8 and in several later chapters. Here we shall discuss distribution functions in general, with some elementary examples from common experience.

Suppose a teacher gave a 25-point quiz to a large number N of students. In order to describe the results of the quiz, they might give the average or median score, but this would not be a complete description. For example, if all N students received 12.5, this is quite a different result than if $N/2$ students received 25 and $N/2$ received 0, though both results have the same average. A complete description would be to give the number n_i who received the score s_i for all scores s_i between 0 and 25. An alternative would be to divide n_i by the total number of students N to give the fraction of students $f_i = n_i/N$ receiving the score s_i. Both n_i and f_i (which depend on the variable s) are called *distribution functions*. The fractional distribution f_i is slightly more convenient to use. The probability that one of the N students selected at random received the score s_i equals the number of students that received that score, $n_i = Nf_i$, divided by the total number N; thus this probability equals the distribution function f_i. Note that

$$\sum_i f_i = \sum_i \frac{n_i}{N} = \frac{1}{N} \sum_i n_i$$

and since

$$\sum_i n_i = N$$

we have

$$\sum_i f_i = 1 \qquad \textbf{B2-1}$$

Equation B2-1 is called the *normalization condition* for fractional distribution functions. A possible distribution function for a 25-point quiz is shown in Figure B2-1.

To find the average score, all the scores are added and the result is divided by N. Since each score s_i was obtained by $n_i = Nf_i$ students, this procedure is equivalent to

$$\bar{s} = \frac{1}{N} \sum_i s_i n_i = \sum_i s_i f_i \qquad \textbf{B2-2}$$

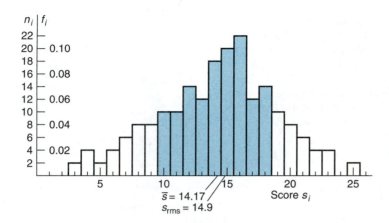

B2–1 Grade distribution for a 25-point quiz given to 200 students; n_i is the number, and $f_i = n_i/N$ is the fraction, of students receiving the score s_i. The average score $\bar{s}$ and the root-mean-square score s_{rms} are indicated. The shaded area indicates the scores within 1 standard deviation of the mean.

We shall take Equation B2-2 as the definition of the *average* (or *mean*) score $\bar{s}$. Similarly, the average of any function $g(s)$ is defined by

$$\overline{g(s)} = \sum_i g(s_i)f_i \qquad \textbf{B2-3}$$

In particular, the mean square score is often useful:

$$\overline{s^2} = \sum_i s_i^2 f_i$$

A useful quantity characterizing a distribution is the *standard deviation* σ, defined by

$$\sigma = \left[\sum_i \left(s_i - \bar{s}\right)^2 f_i \right]^{1/2} \qquad \textbf{B2-4}$$

Note that

$$\sum_i \left(s_i - \bar{s}\right)^2 f_i = \sum_i s_i^2 f_i + \bar{s}^2 \sum_i f_i - 2\bar{s}\sum_i s_i f_i = \overline{s^2} - \bar{s}^2$$

Therefore,

$$\sigma = (\overline{s^2} - \bar{s}^2)^{1/2} \qquad \textbf{B2-5}$$

The standard deviation measures the spread of the values s_i about the mean. For most distributions there will be few values that differ from $\bar{s}$ by more than a few multiples of σ. In the case of the normal Gaussian distribution, common in the theory of errors, about two-thirds of the values lie within $\pm\sigma$ of the mean value. A Gaussian distribution is shown in Figure B2-2.

If a student were selected at random from the class and one had to guess that student's score, the best guess would be the score obtained by the greatest number of students, called the most probable score, s_m. For the distribution in Figure B2-1, s_m is 16 and the average score, $\bar{s}$, is 14.17. The root-mean-square score, $s_{rms} = (\overline{s^2})^{1/2}$, is 14.9, and the standard deviation σ is 4.6. Note that 66 percent of the scores for this distribution lie within $\bar{s} \pm \sigma = 14.17 \pm 4.6$.

B2–2 Gaussian or normal distribution curve. The curve is symmetrical about the mean value $\bar{x}$, which is also the most probable value. Sixty-eight percent of the area under the curve is within 1 standard deviation of the mean. This curve describes the distribution of random errors in many experimental situations.

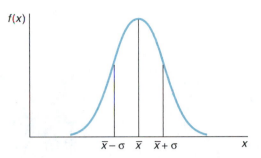

Now consider the case of a continuous distribution. Suppose we wanted to know the distribution of heights of a large number of people. For a finite number N, the number of persons *exactly* 6 ft tall would be zero. If we assume that height can be determined to any desired accuracy, there is an infinite number of possible heights, and the chance that anybody has a particular exact height is zero. We would therefore divide the heights into intervals Δh (for example, Δh could be 0.1 ft) and ask what fraction of people have heights that fall in any particular interval. This number depends on the size of the interval. We define the distribution function $f(h)$ as the fraction of the number of people with heights in a particular interval, divided by the size of the interval. Thus for N people, $Nf(h)\Delta h$ is the number of people whose height is in the interval between h and $h + \Delta h$. A possible height-distribution function is plotted in Figure B2-3. The fraction of people with heights in a particular interval is the area of the rectangle $\Delta h \times f(h)$. The total area represents the sum of all fractions; thus it must equal 1. If N is very large, we can choose Δh very small and still have $f(h)$ vary only slightly between intervals. The histogram $f(h)$ versus h approaches a smooth curve as $N \rightarrow \infty$ and $\Delta h \rightarrow 0$. In many cases of importance, the number of objects N is extremely large and the intervals can be taken as small as measurement allows. The distribution functions $f(h)$ are usually considered to be continuous functions, intervals are written dh, and the sums are replaced by integrals. For example, if $f(h)$ is a continuous function, the average height, which we will write as $\langle h \rangle$ for the continuous function $f(h)$, is[1]

$$\langle h \rangle = \int h f(h)\, dh \qquad \qquad \textbf{B2-6}$$

and the normalization condition expressing the fact that the sum of all fractions is 1 is

$$\int f(h)\, dh = 1 \qquad \qquad \textbf{B2-7}$$

B2–3 A possible height distribution. The fraction of the number of heights between h and $h + \Delta h$ is proportional to the shaded area. The histogram can be approximated by a continuous curve as shown.

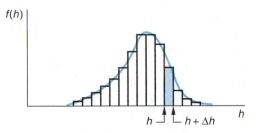

[1]The limits on the integration depend on the range of the variable. For this case, h ranges from 0 to ∞. We shall often omit explicit indication of the limits when the range of the variable is clear.

Appendix B3

Derivation of the Boltzmann Distribution

Appendix B3 is on the home page: whfreeman.com/modphysics4e

Appendix B4

Binomial and Exponential Series

A. Binomial Series

$$(1 + x)^m = 1 + mx + \frac{m(m - 1)}{2!}x^2 + \frac{m(m - 1)(m - 2)}{3!}x^3 +$$

$$\cdots + \frac{m(m - 1)(m - 2)\cdots(m - n + 2)}{(n - 1)!}x^{n-1} + R_n$$

where

$$R_n = \frac{m(m - 1)(m - 2)\cdots(m - n + 1)}{n!}x^n(1 + ax)^{m-n}$$

for all cases, where $0 < a < 1$

$$R_n < \left| \frac{m(m - 1)(m - 2)\cdots(m - n + 1)}{n!}x^n \right| \text{ if } x > 0$$

$$R_n < \left| \frac{m(m - 1)(m - 2)\cdots(m - n + 1)}{n!} \frac{x^n}{(1 + x)^{n-m}} \right| \text{ for } x < 0, n > m$$

$$R_n < |x^n|(1 + x)^m \text{ if } -1 < m < 0$$

If m is a negative integer or a positive or negative fraction, the binomial expansion is valid only when $|x| < 1$. Except when m is a positive integer, a binomial such as $(a + b)^m$ must be written in one of the following forms before expanding it:

$$a^m\left(1 + \frac{b}{a}\right)^m \text{ if } a > b \qquad b^m\left(1 + \frac{a}{b}\right)^m \text{ if } b > a$$

B. Exponential Series

$$e^x = 1 + x + \frac{x^2}{2!} + \frac{x^3}{3!} + \cdots + \frac{x^{n-1}}{(n - 1)!} + \frac{x^n}{n!}e^{\alpha x}$$

$$a^x = 1 + x \log a + \frac{(x \log a)^2}{2!} + \cdots + \frac{(x \log a)^{n-i}}{(n - 1)!} + \frac{(x \log a)^n}{n!}a^{\alpha x}$$

where $0 < \alpha < 1$.

Appendix C

Electron Configurations

Electron configurations of the atoms in their ground states. For a few of the rare earth elements ($Z = 57$ to 71) and the heavy elements ($Z > 89$), the configurations are not firmly established.

Z	Element	Ionization energy (eV)	K n:1 l:s	L 2 $s\ p$	M 3 $s\ p\ d$	N 4 $s\ p\ d\ f$	O 5 $s\ p\ d\ f$	P 6 $s\ p\ d$	Q 7 s
1	H (hydrogen)	13.6	1						
2	He (helium)	24.5	2						
3	Li (lithium)	5.4	2	1					
4	Be (beryllium)	9.3	2	2					
5	B (boron)	8.3	2	2 1					
6	C (carbon)	11.3	2	2 2					
7	N (nitrogen)	14.5	2	2 3					
8	O (oxygen)	13.6	2	2 4					
9	F (flourine)	17.4	2	2 5					
10	Ne (neon)	21.6	2	2 6					
11	Na (sodium)	5.1	2	2 6	1				
12	Mg (magnesium)	7.6	2	2 6	2				
13	Al (aluminum)	6.0	2	2 6	2 1				
14	Si (silicon)	8.1	2	2 6	2 2				
15	P (phosphorus)	10.5	2	2 6	2 3				
16	S (sulfur)	10.4	2	2 6	2 4				
17	Cl (chlorine)	13.0	2	2 6	2 5				
18	Ar (argon)	15.8	2	2 6	2 6				
19	K (potassium)	4.3	2	2 6	2 6 .	1			

(Continued)

Z	Element	Ionization energy (eV)	K n:1 l:s	L 2 s p	M 3 s p d	N 4 s p d f	O 5 s p d f	P 6 s p d	Q 7 s
20	Ca (calcium)	6.1		2 6	2 6 .	2			
21	Sc (scandium)	6.5	2	2 6	2 6 1	2			
22	Ti (titanium)	6.8	2	2 6	2 6 2	2			
23	V (vanadium)	6.7	2	2 6	2 6 3	2			
24	Cr (chromium)	6.8	2	2 6	2 6 5	1			
25	Mn (manganese)	7.4	2	2 6	2 6 5	2			
26	Fe (iron)	7.9	2	2 6	2 6 6	2			
27	Co (cobalt)	7.9	2	2 6	2 6 7	2			
28	Ni (nickel)	7.6	2	2 6	2 6 8	2			
29	Cu (copper)	7.7	2	2 6	2 6 10	1			
30	Zn (zinc)	9.4	2	2 6	2 6 10	2			
31	Ga (gallium)	6.0	2	2 6	2 6 10	2 1			
32	Ge (germanium)	7.9	2	2 6	2 6 10	2 2			
33	As (arsenic)	9.8	2	2 6	2 6 10	2 3			
34	Se (selenium)	9.8	2	2 6	2 6 10	2 4			
35	Br (bromine)	11.8	2	2 6	2 6 10	2 5			
36	Kr (krypton)	14.0	2	2 6	2 6 10	2 6			
37	Rb (rubidium)	4.2	2	2 6	2 6 10	2 6 . .	1		
38	Sr (strontium)	5.7	2	2 6	2 6 10	2 6 . .	2		
39	Y (yttrium)	6.4	2	2 6	2 6 10	2 6 1 .	2		
40	Zr (zirconium)	6.8	2	2 6	2 6 10	2 6 2 .	2		
41	Nb (niobium)	6.9	2	2 6	2 6 10	2 6 4 .	1		
42	Mo (molybdenum)	7.1	2	2 6	2 6 10	2 6 5 .	1		
43	Tc (technetium)	7.3	2	2 6	2 6 10	2 6 6 .	1		
44	Ru (ruthenium)	7.4	2	2 6	2 6 10	2 6 7 .	1		

Z	Element	Ionization energy (eV)	K n:1 l:s	L 2 s p	M 3 s p d	N 4 s p d f	O 5 s p d f	P 6 s p d	Q 7 s
45	Rh (rhodium)	7.5	2	2 6	2 6 10	2 6 8 .	1		
46	Pd (palladium)	8.3	2	2 6	2 6 10	2 6 10 .	0		
47	Ag (silver)	7.6	2	2 6	2 6 10	2 6 10 .	1		
48	Cd (cadmium)	9.0	2	2 6	2 6 10	2 6 10 .	2		
49	In (indium)	5.8	2	2 6	2 6 10	2 6 10 .	2 1		
50	Sn (tin)	7.3	2	2 6	2 6 10	2 6 10 .	2 2		
51	Sb (antimony)	8.6	2	2 6	2 6 10	2 6 10 .	2 3		
52	Te (tellurium)	9.0	2	2 6	2 6 10	2 6 10 .	2 4		
53	I (iodine)	10.5	2	2 6	2 6 10	2 6 10 .	2 5		
54	Xe (xenon)	12.1	2	2 6	2 6 10	2 6 10 .	2 6		
55	Cs (cesium)	3.9	2	2 6	2 6 10	2 6 10 .	2 6 . .	1	
56	Ba (barium)	5.2	2	2 6	2 6 10	2 6 10 .	2 6 . .	2	
57	La (lanthanum)	5.6	2	2 6	2 6 10	2 6 10 .	2 6 1 .	2	
58	Ce (cerium)	5.6	2	2 6	2 6 10	2 6 10 1	2 6 1 .	2	
59	Pr (praseodymium)	5.5	2	2 6	2 6 10	2 6 10 3	2 6 . .	2	
60	Nd (neodymium)	5.5	2	2 6	2 6 10	2 6 10 4	2 6 . .	2	
61	Pm (promethium)	5.5	2	2 6	2 6 10	2 6 10 5	2 6 . .	2	
62	Sm (samarium)	5.6	2	2 6	2 6 10	2 6 10 6	2 6 . .	2	
63	Eu (europium)	5.7	2	2 6	2 6 10	2 6 10 7	2 6 . .	2	
64	Gd (gadolinium)	6.2	2	2 6	2 6 10	2 6 10 7	2 6 1 .	2	
65	Tb (terbium)	6.0	2	2 6	2 6 10	2 6 10 9	2 6 . .	2	
66	Dy (dysprosium)	6.8	2	2 6	2 6 10	2 6 10 10	2 6 . .	2	
67	Ho (holmium)	6.0	2	2 6	2 6 10	2 6 10 11	2 6 . .	2	
68	Er (erbium)	6.1	2	2 6	2 6 10	2 6 10 12	2 6 . .	2	
69	Tm (thulium)	5.8	2	2 6	2 6 10	2 6 10 13	2 6 . .	2	

(Continued)

Z	Element	Ionization energy (eV)	K n:1 l:s	L 2 s p	M 3 s p d	N 4 s p d f	O 5 s p d f	P 6 s p d	Q 7 s
70	Yb (ytterbium)	6.2	2	2 6	2 6 10	2 6 10 14	2 6 . .	2	
71	Lu (lutetium)	5.1	2	2 6	2 6 10	2 6 10 14	2 6 1 .	2	
72	Hf (hafnium)	7.0	2	2 6	2 6 10	2 6 10 14	2 6 2 .	2	
73	Ta (tantalum)	7.9	2	2 6	2 6 10	2 6 10 14	2 6 3 .	2	
74	W (tungsten)	8.0	2	2 6	2 6 10	2 6 10 14	2 6 4 .	2	
75	Re (rhenium)	7.9	2	2 6	2 6 10	2 6 10 14	2 6 5 .	2	
76	Os (osmium)	8.5	2	2 6	2 6 10	2 6 10 14	2 6 6 .	2	
77	Ir (iridium)	9.0	2	2 6	2 6 10	2 6 10 14	2 6 7 .	2	
78	Pt (platinum)	9.0	2	2 6	2 6 10	2 6 10 14	2 6 9 .	1	
79	Au (gold)	9.2	2	2 6	2 6 10	2 6 10 14	2 6 10 .	1	
80	Hg (mercury)	10.4	2	2 6	2 6 10	2 6 10 14	2 6 10 .	2	
81	Tl (thallium)	6.1	2	2 6	2 6 10	2 6 10 14	2 6 10 .	2 1	
82	Pb (lead)	7.4	2	2 6	2 6 10	2 6 10 14	2 6 10 .	2 2	
83	Bi (bismuth)	7.3	2	2 6	2 6 10	2 6 10 14	2 6 10 .	2 3	
84	Po (polonium)	8.4	2	2 6	2 6 10	2 6 10 14	2 6 10 .	2 4	
85	At (astatine)	9.5	2	2 6	2 6 10	2 6 10 14	2 6 10 .	2 5	
86	Rn (radon)	10.7	2	2 6	2 6 10	2 6 10 14	2 6 10 .	2 6	
87	Fr (francium)	4.0	2	2 6	2 6 10	2 6 10 14	2 6 10 .	2 6 .	1
88	Ra (radium)	5.3	2	2 6	2 6 10	2 6 10 14	2 6 10 .	2 6 .	2
89	Ac (actinium)	6.9	2	2 6	2 6 10	2 6 10 14	2 6 10 .	2 6 1	2
90	Th (thorium)	7.0	2	2 6	2 6 10	2 6 10 14	2 6 10 .	2 6 2	2
91	Pa (protactinium)		2	2 6	2 6 10	2 6 10 14	2 6 10 1	2 6 2	2
92	U (uranium)	6.1	2	2 6	2 6 10	2 6 10 14	2 6 10 3	2 6 1	2
93	Np (neptunium)		2	2 6	2 6 10	2 6 10 14	2 6 10 4	2 6 1	2
94	Pu (plutonium)	5.8	2	2 6	2 6 10	2 6 10 14	2 6 10 6	2 6 .	2

Z	Element	Ionization energy (eV)	K n:1 l:s	L 2 $s\,p$	M 3 $s\,p\,d$	N 4 $s\,p\,d\,f$	O 5 $s\,p\,d\,f$	P 6 $s\,p\,d$	Q 7 s
95	Am (americium)	6.0	2	2 6	2 6 10	2 6 10 14	2 6 10 7	2 6 .	2
96	Cm (curium)		2	2 6	2 6 10	2 6 10 14	2 6 10 7	2 6 1	2
97	Bk (berkelium)		2	2 6	2 6 10	2 6 10 14	2 6 10 8	2 6 1	2
98	Cf (californium)		2	2 6	2 6 10	2 6 10 14	2 6 10 10	2 6 .	2
99	Es (einsteinium)		2	2 6	2 6 10	2 6 10 14	2 6 10 11	2 6 .	2
100	Fm (fermium)		2	2 6	2 6 10	2 6 10 14	2 6 10 12	2 6 .	2
101	Md (mendelevium)		2	2 6	2 6 10	2 6 10 14	2 6 10 13	2 6 .	2
102	No (nobelium)		2	2 6	2 6 10	2 6 10 14	2 6 10 14	2 6 .	2
103	Lw (lawrencium)		2	2 6	2 6 10	2 6 10 14	2 6 10 14	2 6 1	2
104	Rf (rutherfordium)		2	2 6	2 6 10	2 6 10 14	2 6 10 14	2 6 2	2
105	Du (dubnium)		2	2 6	2 6 10	2 6 10 14	2 6 10 14	?	?
106	Sg (seaborgium)		2	2 6	2 6 10	2 6 10 14	2 6 10 14	?	?
107	Bh (bohrium)		2	2 6	2 6 10	2 6 10 14	2 6 10 14	?	?
108	Hs (hassium)		2	2 6	2 6 10	2 6 10 14	2 6 10 14	?	?
109	Mt (meitnerium)		2	2 6	2 6 10	2 6 10 14	2 6 10 14	?	?
110	Not yet named		2	2 6	2 6 10	2 6 10 14	2 6 10 14	?	?
111	Not yet named		2	2 6	2 6 10	2 6 10 14	2 6 10 14	?	?
112	Not yet named		2	2 6	2 6 10	2 6 10 14	2 6 10 14	?	?
114	Not yet named		2	2 6	2 6 10	2 6 10 14	2 6 10 14	?	?
116	Not yet named		2	2 6	2 6 10	2 6 10 14	2 6 10 14	?	?

Appendix D

Fundamental Physical Constants

This set of fundamental physical constants consists of selected values recommended by CODATA, the Committee on Data for Science and Technology of the International Council of Scientific Unions, resulting from the most recent (1998) compilation and computations. The digits in parentheses are the one-standard-deviation uncertainties in the last digits.

Quantity	Symbol	Value	Units
Universal constants			
Speed of light in vacuum	c	299,792,458	$\text{m} \cdot \text{s}^{-1}$
Permeability of vacuum	μ_0	$4\pi \times 10^{-7} = 12.566370614 \times 10^{-7}$	$\text{N} \cdot \text{A}^{-2}$
Permittivity of vacuum	ϵ_0	$1/\mu_0 c^2 = 8.854187817$	$10^{-12}\,\text{F} \cdot \text{m}^{-1}$
Newtonian constant of gravitation	G	6.673 (10)	$10^{-11}\,\text{m}^3 \cdot \text{kg}^{-1} \cdot \text{s}^{-2}$
Planck constant	h	6.62606876 (52)	$10^{-34}\,\text{J} \cdot \text{s}$
In electron volts, $h/\{e\}$		4.13566727 (16)	$10^{-15}\,\text{eV} \cdot \text{s}$
$h/2\pi$	$\hbar$	1.054571596 (82)	$10^{-34}\,\text{J} \cdot \text{s}$
In electron volts, $\hbar/\{e\}$		6.58211889 (26)	$10^{-16}\,\text{eV} \cdot \text{s}$
Planck mass, $(\hbar c/G)^{1/2}$	m_p	2.1767 (16)	$10^{-8}\,\text{kg}$
Planck length, $\hbar/m_p c = (\hbar G/c^3)^{1/2}$	l_p	1.6160 (12)	$10^{-35}\,\text{m}$
Planck time, $l_p/c = (\hbar G/c^5)^{1/2}$	t_p	5.3906 (40)	$10^{-44}\,\text{s}$
Electromagnetic constants			
Elementary charge	e	1.602176462 (63)	$10^{-19}\,\text{C}$
	e/h	2.417989491 (95)	$10^{14}\,\text{A} \cdot \text{J}^{-1}$
Magnetic flux quantum, $h/2e$	ϕ_0	2.067833636 (81)	$10^{-15}\,\text{Wb}$
Josephson frequency-voltage quotient	$2e/h$	4.83597898 (19)	$10^{14}\,\text{Hz} \cdot \text{V}^{-1}$
von Klitzing constant, $h/e^2 = \mu_0 c/2\alpha$	R_K	25,812.807572 (95)	Ω
Bohr magneton, $e\hbar/2m_e$	μ_B	9.27400899 (37)	$10^{-24}\,\text{J} \cdot \text{T}^{-1}$
In electron volts, $\mu_B/\{e\}$		5.788381749 (43)	$10^{-5}\,\text{eV} \cdot \text{T}^{-1}$
In hertz, μ_B/h		1.39962624 (56)	$10^{10}\,\text{Hz} \cdot \text{T}^{-1}$
In wave numbers, μ_B/hc		46.6864521 (19)	$\text{m}^{-1} \cdot \text{T}^{-1}$
In kelvins, μ_B/k		0.6717131 (12)	$\text{K} \cdot \text{T}^{-1}$
Nuclear magneton, $e\hbar/2m_p$	μ_N	5.05078317 (20)	$10^{-27}\,\text{J} \cdot \text{T}^{-1}$
In electron volts, $\mu_N/\{e\}$		3.152451238 (24)	$10^{-8}\,\text{eV} \cdot \text{T}^{-1}$
In hertz, μ_N/h		7.62259396 (31)	$\text{MHz} \cdot \text{T}^{-1}$
In wave numbers, μ_N/hc		2.54262366 (10)	$10^{-2}\,\text{m}^{-1} \cdot \text{T}^{-1}$
In kelvins, μ_N/k		3.6582638 (64)	$10^{-4}\,\text{K} \cdot \text{T}^{-1}$
Atomic constants			
Fine-structure constant, $\mu_0 ce^2/2h$	α	7.297352533 (27)	10^{-3}
Inverse fine-structure constant	α^{-1}	137.03599976 (50)	
Rydberg constant, $m_e c\alpha^2/2h$	R_∞	10,973,731.68549 (83)	m^{-1}
In hertz, $R_\infty c$		3.289841960368 (25)	$10^{15}\,\text{Hz}$
In joules, $R_\infty hc$		2.17987190 (17)	$10^{-18}\,\text{J}$
In eV, $R_\infty hc/\{e\}$		13.60569172 (53)	eV
Bohr radius	a_0	0.5291772083 (19)	$10^{-10}\,\text{m}$

Quantity	Symbol	Value	Units
Electron			
Mass	m_e	9.10938188 (72)	10^{-31} kg
		5.485799110 (12)	10^{-4} u
In electron volts, $m_e c^2/\{e\}$		0.510998902 (21)	MeV
Electron-muon mass ratio	m_e/m_μ	4.83633210 (15)	10^{-3}
Electron-tau mass ratio	m_e/m_τ	2.87555 (47)	10^{-4}
Electron-proton mass ratio	m_e/m_p	5.446170232 (12)	10^{-4}
Electron-deuteron mass ratio	m_e/m_d	2.7244371170 (58)	10^{-4}
Electron–α particle mass ratio	m_e/m_α	1.3709335611 (29)	10^{-4}
Specific charge	$-e/m_e$	-1.758820174 (71)	10^{11} C $\cdot$ kg^{-1}
Molar mass	$M(e)$	5.485799100 (12)	10^{-7} kg $\cdot$ mol^{-1}
Compton wavelength, $h/m_e c$	λ_C	2.426310215 (18)	10^{-12} m
$\lambda_C/2\pi = \alpha a_0 = \alpha^2/4\pi R_\infty$	λ_C	3.861592642 (28)	10^{-13} m
Classical radius, $\alpha^2 a_0$	r_e	2.817940285 (31)	10^{-15} m
Thomson cross section, $(8\pi/3)r_e^2$	σ_e	0.665245854 (15)	10^{-28} m^2
Magnetic moment	μ_e	-928.476362 (37)	10^{-26} J $\cdot$ T^{-1}
In Bohr magnetons	μ_e/μ_B	-1.0011596521869 (41)	
In nuclear magnetons	μ_e/μ_N	-1838.2819660 (39)	
Magnetic moment anomaly, $\mu_e/\mu_B - 1$	a_e	1.1596521869 (41)	10^{-3}
g-factor, $2(1 + a_e)$	g_e	-2.0023193043737 (82)	
Electron-muon magnetic moment ratio	μ_e/μ_μ	206.7669720 (63)	
Electron-proton magnetic moment ratio	μ_e/μ_p	-658.2106875 (66)	
Muon			
Mass	m_μ	1.88353109 (16)	10^{-28} kg
		0.1134289168 (34)	u
In electron volts, $m_\mu c^2/\{e\}$		105.6583568 (52)	MeV
Muon-electron mass ratio	m_μ/m_e	206.7682657 (63)	
Muon-tau mass ratio	m_μ/m_τ	5.94572 (97)	
Molar mass	$M(\mu)$	1.134289168 (34)	10^{-4} kg $\cdot$ mol^{-1}
Magnetic moment	μ_μ	4.49044813 (22)	10^{-26} J $\cdot$ T^{-1}
In Bohr magnetons	μ_μ/μ_B	4.84197085 (15)	10^{-3}
In nuclear magnetons	μ_μ/μ_N	8.89059770 (27)	
Magnetic moment anomaly, $[\mu_\mu/(e\hbar/2m_\mu)] - 1$	a_μ	1.16591610 (64)	10^{-3}
g-factor, $2(1 + a_\mu)$	g_μ	2.0023318320 (13)	
Muon-proton magnetic moment ratio	μ_μ/μ_p	3.18334539 (10)	
Tau			
Mass	m_τ	3.16788 (52)	10^{-27} kg
		1.90774 (31)	u
In electron volts		1777.05 (29)	MeV
Proton			
Mass	m_p	1.67262158 (13)	10^{-27} kg
		1.00727646688 (13)	u
In electron volts		938.271998 (38)	MeV
Proton-electron mass ratio	m_p/m_e	1836.1526675 (39)	
Proton-muon mass ratio	m_p/m_μ	8.88024408 (27)	
Specific charge	e/m_p	9.57883408 (38)	10^7 C $\cdot$ kg^{-1}
Molar mass	$M(p)$	1.00727646688 (13)	10^{-3} kg $\cdot$ mol^{-1}

(Continued)

Quantity	Symbol	Value	Units
Compton wavelength, $h/m_p c$	$\lambda_{C,p}$	1.321409847 (10)	10^{-15} m
$\lambda_{C,p}/2\pi$	$\lambdabar_{C,p}$	2.103089089 (16)	10^{-16} m
Magnetic moment	μ_p	1.410606638 (58)	10^{-26} J $\cdot$ T^{-1}
In Bohr magnetons	μ_p/μ_B	1.521032203 (15)	10^{-3}
In nuclear magnetons	μ_p/μ_N	2.792847337 (29)	
Diamagnetic shielding correction for protons			
(H_2O spherical sample, 25°C), $1 - \mu_p'/\mu_p$	σ_{H_2O}	25.687 (15)	10^{-6}
Shielded proton moment (H_2O spherical			
sample, 25°C)	μ_p'	1.410570399 (59)	10^{-26} J $\cdot$ T^{-1}
In Bohr magnetons	μ_p'/μ_B	1.520993132 (16)	10^{-3}
In nuclear magnetons	μ_p'/μ_N	2.792775597 (31)	
Gyromagnetic ratio	γ_p	26,752.2212 (11)	10^4 s^{-1} $\cdot$ T^{-1}
	$\gamma_p/2\pi$	42.5774825 (18)	MHz $\cdot$ T^{-1}
Uncorrected (H_2O, spherical sample, 25°C)	γ_p'	26,751.5341 (11)	10^4 s^{-1} $\cdot$ T^{-1}
	$\gamma_p'/2\pi$	42.5763888 (18)	MHz $\cdot$ T^{-1}
Neutron			
Mass	m_n	1.67492716 (13)	10^{-27} kg
		1.00866491578 (55)	u
In electron volts, $m_n c^2/\{e\}$		939.565330 (38)	MeV
Neutron-electron mass ratio	m_n/m_e	1838.6836550 (40)	
Neutron-proton mass ratio	m_n/m_p	1.00137841887 (58)	
Molar mass	$M(n)$	1.00866491578 (55)	10^{-3} kg $\cdot$ mol^{-1}
Compton wavelength, $h/m_n c$	$\lambda_{C,n}$	1.319590898 (10)	10^{-15} m
$\lambda_{C,n}/2\pi$	$\lambdabar_{C,n}$	2.100194142 (16)	10^{-16} m
Magnetic moment	μ_n	-0.96623640 (23)	10^{-26} J $\cdot$ T^{-1}
In Bohr magnetons	μ_n/μ_B	-1.04187563 (25)	10^{-3}
In nuclear magnetons	μ_n/μ_N	-1.91304272 (45)	
Neutron-electron magnetic moment ratio	μ_n/μ_e	1.04066882 (25)	10^{-3}
Neutron-proton magnetic moment ratio	μ_n/μ_p	-0.68497934 (16)	
Deuteron			
Mass	m_d	3.34358309 (26)	10^{-27} kg
		2.0135532127 (35)	u
In electron volts, $m_d c^2/\{e\}$		1875.612762 (75)	MeV
Deuteron-electron mass ratio	m_d/m_e	3670.4829550 (78)	
Deuteron-proton mass ratio	m_d/m_p	1.99900750083 (41)	
Molar mass	$M(d)$	2.01355321271 (35)	10^{-3} kg $\cdot$ mol^{-1}
Magnetic moment	μ_d	0.433073457 (18)	10^{-26} J $\cdot$ T^{-1}
In Bohr magnetons	μ_d/μ_B	0.4669754556 (50)	10^{-3}
In nuclear magnetons	μ_d/μ_N	0.8574382284 (94)	
Deuteron-electron magnetic moment ratio	μ_d/μ_e	0.4664345537 (50)	10^{-3}
Deuteron-proton magnetic moment ratio	μ_d/μ_p	0.3070122083 (45)	
Alpha particle			
Mass	m_α	6.64465598 (52)	10^{-27} kg
In electron volts		3727.37904 (15)	MeV
Physiochemical constants			
Avogadro constant	N_A, L	6.02214199 (47)	10^{23} mol^{-1}
Atomic mass constant, $m(C^{12})/12$	m_u	1.66053873 (13)	10^{-27} kg
In electron volts, $m_u c^2/\{e\}$		931.494013 (37)	MeV
Faraday constant	F	96,485.3415 (39)	C mol^{-1}

Quantity	Symbol	Value	Units
Molar Planck constant	$N_A h$	3.990312689 (30)	10^{-10} J $\cdot$ s $\cdot$ mol^{-1}
	$N_A hc$	0.11962656492 (91)	J $\cdot$ m $\cdot$ mol^{-1}
Molar gas constant	R	8.314492 (15)	J $\cdot$ mol^{-1} $\cdot$ K^{-1}
Boltzmann constant, R/N_A	k	1.3806503 (24)	10^{-23} J $\cdot$ K^{-1}
In electron volts, $k/\{e\}$		8.617342 (15)	10^{-5} eV $\cdot$ K^{-1}
In hertz, k/h		2.0836644 (36)	10^{10} Hz $\cdot$ K^{-1}
In wave numbers, k/hc		69.50356 (12)	m^{-1} $\cdot$ K^{-1}
Molar volume (ideal gas),			
RT/p (at 273.15 K, 101 325 Pa)	V_m	22.413996 (39)	10^{-3} m^3 $\cdot$ mol^{-1}
Loschmidt constant, N_A/V_m	n_0	2.6867775 (47)	10^{25} m^{-3}
Stefan-Boltzmann constant, $(\pi^2/60)k^4/\hbar^3 c^2$	σ	5.670400 (40)	10^{-8} W $\cdot$ m^{-2} $\cdot$ K^{-4}
First radiation constant, $2\pi hc^2$	c_1	3.74177107 (29)	10^{-16} W $\cdot$ m^2
Second radiation constant, hc/k	c_2	1.4387752 (25)	10^{-2} m $\cdot$ K
Wien displacement law			
constant, $\lambda_{max}T = c_2/4.96511423\ldots$	b	2.8977686 (51)	10^{-3} m $\cdot$ K
Conversion factors and units			
Electron volt, (e/C)J $= \{e\}$J	eV	1.602176462 (63)	10^{-19} J
Atomic mass unit (unified), $m_u = m(C^{12})/12$	u	1.66053873 (13)	10^{-27} kg
Standard atmosphere	atm	101,325	Pa
Standard acceleration of gravity	g_n	9.80665	m $\cdot$ s^{-2}

Source: P. J. Mohr and B. N. Taylor, *Physics Today,* August 2000.

Appendix E

Conversion Factors

Conversion factors are written as equations for simplicity; relations marked with an asterisk are exact.

Length
1 km = 0.6215 mi
1 mi = 1.609 km
1 m = 1.0936 yd = 3.281 ft = 39.37 in
*1 in = 2.54 cm
*1 ft = 12 in = 30.48 cm
*1 yd = 3 ft = 91.44 cm
1 light-year = 1 $c \cdot$ y = 9.461×10^{15} m
*1 Å = 0.1 nm

Area
*1 $m^2 = 10^4$ cm^2
1 $km^2 = 0.3861$ $mi^2 = 247.1$ acres
*1 $in^2 = 6.4516$ cm^2
1 $ft^2 = 9.29 \times 10^{-2}$ m^2
1 $m^2 = 10.76$ ft^2
*1 acre = 43,560 ft^2
1 $mi^2 = 640$ acres = 2.590 km^2

Volume
*1 $m^3 = 10^6$ cm^3
*1 L = 1000 $cm^3 = 10^{-3}$ m^3
1 gal = 3.786 L
1 gal = 4 qt = 8 pt = 128 oz = 231 in^3
1 $in^3 = 16.39$ cm^3
1 $ft^3 = 1728$ $in^3 = 28.32$ L = 2.832×10^4 cm^3

Time
*1 h = 60 min = 3.6 ks
*1 d = 24 h = 1440 min = 86.4 ks
1 y = 365.24 d = 31.56 Ms

Speed
1 km/h = 0.2778 m/s = 0.6215 mi/h
1 mi/h = 0.4470 m/s = 1.609 km/h
1 mi/h = 1.467 ft/s

Angle and angular speed
*π rad = 180°
1 rad = 57.30°
1° = 1.745×10^{-2} rad
1 rev/min = 0.1047 rad/s
1 rad/s = 9.549 rev/min

Mass
*1 kg = 1000 g
*1 metric ton = 1000 kg = 1 Mg

1 u = 1.6606×10^{-27} kg
1 kg = 6.022×10^{26} u
1 slug = 14.59 kg
1 kg = 6.852×10^{-2} slug
1 u = 931.50 MeV/c^2

Density
*1 g/cm^3 = 1000 kg/m^3 = 1 kg/L
(1 g/cm^3)g = 62.4 lb/ft^3

Force
1 N = 0.2248 lb = 10^5 dyn
1 lb = 4.4482 N
(1 kg)g = 2.2046 lb

Pressure
*1 Pa = 1 N/m^2
*1 atm = 101.325 kPa = 1.01325 bars
1 atm = 14.7 lb/in^2 = 760 mmHg
  = 29.9 inHg = 33.8 ftH$_2$O
1 lb/in^2 = 6.895 kPa
1 torr = 1 mmHg = 133.32 Pa
1 bar = 100 kPa

Energy
*1 kW $\cdot$ h = 3.6 MJ
*1 cal = 4.1840 J
1 ft $\cdot$ lb = 1.356 J = 1.286×10^{-3} Btu
*1 L $\cdot$ atm = 101.325 J
1 L $\cdot$ atm = 24.217 cal
1 Btu = 778 ft $\cdot$ lb = 252 cal = 1054.35 J
1 eV = 1.602×10^{-19} J
1 u $\cdot$ c^2 = 931.50 MeV
*1 erg = 10^{-7} J

Power
1 horsepower = 550 ft $\cdot$ lb/s = 745.7 W
1 Btu/min = 17.58 W
1 W = 1.341×10^{-3} horsepower
  = 0.7376 ft $\cdot$ lb/s

Magnetic field
*1 G = 10^{-4} T
*1 T = 10^4 G

Thermal conductivity
1 W/m $\cdot$ K = 6.938 Btu $\cdot$ in/h $\cdot$ ft^2 $\cdot$ F°
1 Btu $\cdot$ in/h $\cdot$ ft^2 $\cdot$ F° = 0.1441 W/m $\cdot$ K

Appendix F

Nobel Laureates in Physics

Listed are the names and a brief quotation from the award citation for all Nobel laureates in physics. Included, too, are a few Nobel laureates in chemistry whose work was very closely related to physics, this latter with a (C) following their names. (The Royal Swedish Academy of Sciences, which awards the prizes, has generally considered the discovery of new elements to be chemistry, rather than physics.)

Year	Nobel laureate		Citation for
1901	Wilhelm Konrad Roentgen	1845–1923	Discovery of x rays
1902	Hendrik Antoon Lorentz	1853–1928	Their researches into the influence of magnetism upon radiation
	Pieter Zeeman	1865–1943	phenomena
1903	Antoine Henri Bequerel	1852–1908	His discovery of spontaneous radioactivity
	Pierre Curie	1859–1906	Their joint researches on the radiation phenomena discovered by
	Marie Sklowdowska-Curie	1867–1934	Henri Bequerel
1904	Lord Rayleigh (John William Strutt)	1842–1919	Investigations of the densities of the most important gases and his discovery of argon
	Sir William Ramsay (C)	1851–1939	His discovery of the inert gaseous elements in air and his determination of their place in the periodic system
1905	Philipp Eduard Anton von Lenard	1862–1947	His work on cathode rays
1906	Joseph John Thomson	1856–1940	His theoretical and experimental investigations on the conduction of electricity by gases
1907	Albert Abraham Michelson	1852–1931	His optical precision instruments and the spectroscopic and metrological investigations carried out with their aid
1908	Gabriel Jonas Lippmann	1845–1921	His method of reproducing colors photographically based on the phenomena of interference
	Ernest Rutherford (C)	1871–1937	His investigations into the disintegration of the elements and the chemistry of radioactive substances
1909	Guglielmo Marconi	1874–1937	Their contributions to the development of wireless telegraphy
	Carl Ferdinand Braun	1850–1918	
1910	Johannes Diderik van der Waals	1837–1923	His work on the state of equations of gases and liquids
1911	Wilhelm Wien	1864–1928	His discoveries regarding the laws governing the radiation of heat
	Marie Curie (C)	1867–1934	Her services to the advancement of chemistry by the discovery of the elements radium and polonium, and by the isolation of radium and the study of its nature and compounds
1912	Nils Gustaf Dalén	1869–1937	His invention of automatic regulators for use in conjunction with gas accumulators for illuminating lighthouses and buoys

(Continued)

Year	Nobel laureate		Citation for
1913	Heike Kamerlingh Onnes	1853–1926	His investigations of the properties of matter at low temperatures, which led, *inter alia*, to the production of liquid helium
1914	Max von Laue	1879–1960	His discovery of the diffraction of x rays by crystals
1917	Charles Glover Barkla	1877–1944	His discovery of the characteristic x rays of the elements
1918	Max Planck	1858–1947	His discovery of energy quanta
1919	Johannes Stark	1874–1957	His discovery of the Doppler effect in canal rays and of the splitting of spectral lines in electric fields
1920	Charles-Édouard Guillaume	1861–1938	The service he has rendered to precise measurement in Physics by his discovery of anomalies in nickel steel alloys
1921	Albert Einstein	1879–1955	His services to Theoretical Physics, and especially for his discovery of the law of the photoelectric effect
	Frederick Soddy (C)	1877–1956	His contributions to our knowledge of the chemistry of radioactive substances, and his investigations into the origin and nature of isotopes
1922	Niels Bohr	1885–1962	His investigation of the structure of atoms and the radiation emanating from them
	Francis W. Aston (C)	1877–1945	His discovery, by means of his mass spectrograph, of isotopes in a large number of nonradioactive elements, and for his enunciation of the whole-number rule
1923	Robert Andrews Millikan	1868–1953	His work on the elementary charge of electricity and on the photoelectric effect
1924	Karl Manne Georg Siegbahn	1886–1978	His discoveries and researches in the field of x-ray spectroscopy
1925	James Franck	1882–1964	Their discovery of the laws governing the impact of an electron
	Gustav Hertz	1887–1975	upon an atom
1926	Jean-Baptiste Perrin	1870–1942	His work on the discontinuous structure of matter, and especially for his discovery of sedimentation equilibrium
1927	Arthur Holly Compton	1892–1962	His discovery of the effect named after him
	Charles Thomson Rees Wilson	1869–1959	His method of making the paths of electrically charged particles visible by condensation of vapor
1928	Owen Willans Richardson	1879–1959	His work on the thermionic phenomenon, and especially for the discovery of the law named after him
1929	Prince Louis-Victor de Broglie	1892–1987	His discovery of the wave nature of electrons
1930	Sir Chandrasekhara Venkata Raman	1888–1970	His work on the scattering of light and the discovery of the effect named after him
1932	Werner Heisenberg	1901–1976	The creation of quantum mechanics, the application of which has, *inter alia*, led to the discovery of the allotropic forms of hydrogen

Year	Nobel laureate		Citation for
1933	Erwin Schrödinger Paul Adrien Maurice Dirac	1887–1961 1902–1984	Their discovery of new productive forms of atomic theory
1934	Harold C. Urey (C)	1893–1991	His discovery of heavy hydrogen
1935	James Chadwick	1891–1974	His discovery of the neutron
1936	Victor Franz Hess Carl David Anderson Peter Debye (C)	1883–1964 1905–1991 1884–1966	His discovery of cosmic radiation His discovery of the positron His contributions to our knowledge of molecular structure through his investigations on dipole moments and on the diffraction of x rays and electrons in gases
1937	Clinton Joseph Davisson George Paget Thomson	1881–1958 1892–1975	Their experimental discovery of the diffraction of electrons by crystals
1938	Enrico Fermi	1901–1954	His demonstrations of the existence of new radioactive elements produced by neutron irradiation, and for his related discovery of nuclear reactions brought about by slow neutrons
1939	Ernest Orlando Lawrence	1901–1958	The invention and development of the cyclotron and for results obtained with it, especially with regard to artificial radioactive elements
1943	Otto Stern	1888–1969	His contributions to the development of the molecular ray method and his discovery of the magnetic moment of the proton
1944	Isidor Isaac Rabi Otto Hahn (C)	1898–1988 1879–1968	His resonance method for recording the magnetic properties of atomic nuclei His discovery of the fission of heavy nuclei
1945	Wolfgang Pauli	1900–1958	His discovery of the Exclusion Principle, also called the Pauli Principle
1946	Percy Williams Bridgman	1882–1961	The invention of an apparatus to produce extremely high pressures and for the discoveries he made in the field of high pressure physics
1947	Sir Edward Victor Appleton	1892–1965	His investigations of the physics of the upper atmosphere, especially for the discovery of the Appleton layer
1948	Patrick Maynard Stuart Blackett	1897–1974	His development of the Wilson cloud chamber method and his discoveries therewith in nuclear physics and cosmic radiation
1949	Hideki Yukawa	1907–1981	His prediction of the existence of mesons on the basis of theoretical work on nuclear forces
1950	Cecil Frank Powell	1903–1969	His development of the photographic method of studying nuclear processes and his discoveries regarding mesons made with this method

(Continued)

Year	Nobel laureate		Citation for
1951	Sir John Douglas Cockcroft	1897–1967	Their pioneer work on the transmutation of atomic nuclei by artificially accelerated atomic particles
	Ernest Thomas Sinton Walton	1903–1995	
	Edwin M. McMillan (C)	1907–1991	Their discoveries in the chemistry of the transuranium elements
	Glenn T. Seaborg (C)	1912–1999	
1952	Felix Bloch	1905–1983	The development of new methods for nuclear magnetic precision measurements and discoveries in connection therewith
	Edward Mills Purcell	1912–1997	
1953	Frits Zernike	1888–1966	His demonstration of the phase contrast method, especially for his invention of the phase contrast microscope
1954	Max Born	1882–1970	His fundamental research in quantum mechanics, especially his statistical interpretation of the wave function
	Walter Bothe	1891–1957	The coincidence method and his discoveries made therewith
1955	Willis Eugene Lamb, Jr.	b. 1913	His discoveries concerning the fine structure of the hydrogen spectrum
	Polykarp Kusch	1911–1993	His precision determination of the magnetic moment of the electron
1956	William Shockley	1910–1989	Their investigations on semiconductors and their discovery of the transistor effect
	John Bardeen	1908–1991	
	Walter Houser Brattain	1902–1987	
1957	Chen Ning Yang	b. 1922	Their penetrating investigation of the parity laws, which led to important discoveries regarding elementary particles
	Tsung Dao Lee	b. 1926	
1958	Pavel Alekseyevich Cherenkov	1904–1990	Their discovery and interpretation of the Cherenkov effect
	Ilya Mikhaylovich Frank	1908–1990	
	Igor Yevgenyevich Tamm	1895–1971	
1959	Emilio Gino Segrè	1905–1989	Their discovery of the antiproton
	Owen Chamberlain	b. 1920	
1960	Donald Arthur Glaser	b. 1926	The invention of the bubble chamber
	Willard F. Libby (C)	1908–1980	His method to use ^{14}C for age determination in several branches of science
1961	Robert Hofstadter	1915–1990	His pioneering studies of electron scattering in atomic nuclei and for his discoveries concerning the structure of the nucleon achieved thereby
	Rudolf Ludwig Mössbauer	b. 1929	His researches concerning the resonance absorption of γ rays and his discovery in this connection of the effect that bears his name
1962	Lev Davidovich Landau	1908–1968	His pioneering theories of condensed matter, especially liquid helium
1963	Eugene Paul Wigner	1902–1995	His contributions to the theory of the atomic nucleus and the elementary particles, particularly through the discovery and application of fundamental symmetry principles
	Maria Goeppert Mayer	1906–1972	Their discoveries concerning nuclear shell structure
	J. Hans D. Jensen	1907–1973	

Year	Nobel laureate		Citation for
1964	Charles H. Townes Nikolai G. Basov Alexander M. Prokhorov	b. 1915 1922–2001 1916–2002	Fundamental work in the field of quantum electronics, which has led to the construction of oscillators and amplifiers based on the maser-laser principle
1965	Shin'ichiro Tomonaga Julian Schwinger Richard P. Feynman	1906–1979 1918–1994 1918–1988	Their fundamental work in quantum electrodynamics, with profound consequences for the physics of elementary particles
1966	Alfred Kastler	1902–1984	The discovery and development of optical methods for studying Hertzian resonance in atoms
1967	Hans Albrecht Bethe	1906–2005	His contributions to the theory of nuclear reactions, especially his discoveries concerning the energy production in stars
1968	Luis W. Alvarez	1911–1988	His decisive contributions to elementary particle physics, in particular the discovery of a large number of resonance states made possible through his development of the techniques of using the hydrogen bubble chamber and data analysis
1969	Murray Gell-Mann	b. 1929	His contributions and discoveries concerning the classification of elementary particles and their interactions
1970	Hannes Alfvén Louis-Eugène-Félix Néel	1908–1995 b. 1904	Fundamental work and discoveries in magnetohydrodynamics with fruitful applications in different parts of plasma physics Fundamental work and discoveries concerning antiferromagnetism and ferrimagnetism, which have led to important applications in solid-state physics
1971	Dennis Gabor	1900–1979	His invention and development of the holographic method
1972	John Bardeen Leon N. Cooper J. Robert Schrieffer	1908–1991 b. 1930 b. 1931	Their theory of superconductivity, usually called the BCS theory
1973	Leo Esaki Ivar Giaever Brian D. Josephson	b. 1925 b. 1929 b. 1940	His discovery of tunneling in semiconductors His discovery of tunneling in superconductors His theoretical predictions of the properties of a supercurrent through a tunnel barrier
1974	Antony Hewish Sir Martin Ryle	b. 1924 1918–1984	The discovery of pulsars His observations and inventions in radio astronomy
1975	Aage Bohr Ben R. Mottleson L. James Rainwater	b. 1922 b. 1926 1917–1986	The discovery of the connection between collective motion and particle motion in atomic nuclei and for the theory of the structure of the atomic nucleus based on this connection
1976	Burton Richter Samuel Chao Chung Ting	b. 1931 b. 1936	Their pioneering work in the discovery of a heavy elementary particle of a new kind
1977	Philip Warren Anderson Nevill Francis Mott John Hasbrouck Van Vleck	b. 1923 1905–1996 1899–1980	Their fundamental theoretical investigations of the electronic structure of magnetic and disordered systems

(Continued)

Year	Nobel laureate		Citation for
1978	Pyotr L. Kapitza	1894–1984	His basic inventions and discoveries in the area of low-temperature physics
	Arno A. Penzias	b. 1933	Their discovery of cosmic microwave background radiation
	Robert Woodrow Wilson	b. 1936	
1979	Sheldon Lee Glashow	b. 1932	Their contributions to the theory of the unified weak and electromagnetic interaction between elementary particles, including, *inter alia*, the prediction of the weak neutral current
	Abdus Salam	1926–1996	
	Steven Weinberg	b. 1933	
1980	James W. Cronin	b. 1931	The discovery of violations of fundamental symmetry principles in the decay of neutral K-mesons
	Val L. Fitch	b. 1923	
1981	Nicolaas Bloembergen	b. 1920	Their contributions to the development of laser spectroscopy
	Arthur L. Schawlow	1921–1999	
	Kai M. Siegbahn	b. 1918	His contribution to the development of high-resolution electron spectroscopy
1982	Kenneth G. Wilson	b. 1936	His theory for critical phenomena in connection with phase transitions
1983	Subrahmanyan Chandrasekhar	1910–1995	His theoretical studies of the physical processes of importance to the structure and evolution of the stars
	William A. Fowler	1911–1995	His theoretical and experimental studies of the nuclear reactions of importance in the formation of the chemical elements in the universe
1984	Carlo Rubbia	b. 1934	Their decisive contributions to the large project, which led to the discovery of the field particles W and Z, communicators of the weak interaction
	Simon van der Meer	b. 1925	
1985	Klaus von Klitzing	b. 1943	The discovery of the quantized Hall effect
1986	Ernst Ruska	1906–1988	His fundamental work in electron optics and for the design of the first electron microscope
	Gerd Binnig	b. 1947	Their design of the scanning tunneling microscope
	Heinrich Rohrer	b. 1933	
1987	J. Georg Bednorz	b. 1950	Their important breakthrough in the discovery of superconductivity in ceramic materials
	Karl Alex Müller	b. 1927	
1988	Leon M. Lederman	b. 1922	The neutrino beam method and the demonstration of the doublet structure of the leptons through the discovery of the muon neutrino
	Melvin Schwartz	b. 1932	
	Jack Steinberger	b. 1921	
1989	Hans G. Dehmelt	b. 1922	Their development of the ion trap technique
	Wolfgang Paul	1913–1993	
	Norman F. Ramsey	b. 1915	The invention of the separated oscillatory fields method and its use in the hydrogen maser and other atomic clocks
1990	Jerome I. Friedman	b. 1930	Their pioneering investigations concerning deep inelastic scattering of electrons on protons and bound neutrons which have been of essential importance for the development of the quark model in particle physics
	Henry W. Kendall	1926–1999	
	Richard E. Taylor	b. 1929	

Year	Nobel laureate		Citation for
1991	Pierre-Gilles de Gennes	b. 1932	His discovery that methods developed for studying ordered phenomena in simple systems can be generalized to more complex forms of matter, in particular, to liquid crystals and polymers
1992	Georges Charpak	b. 1924	His invention and development of particle detectors, particularly multi-wire proportional counters
1993	Joseph H. Taylor, Jr.	b. 1941	Their discovery of rare binary pulsars
	Russell A. Hulse	b. 1950	
1994	Bertram N. Brockhouse	b. 1918	Their pioneering contributions to the development of neutron scattering techniques for studies of condensed matter
	Clifford G. Shull	1915–2001	
1995	Martin Perl	b. 1927	His discovery of the tau lepton
	Frederick Reines	1918–1998	His discovery of the neutrino
1996	David Lee	b. 1931	Their discovery of the superfluid phase of ^{3}He
	Douglas Osheroff	b. 1945	
	Robert Richardson	b. 1937	
1997	Steven Chu	b. 1948	Their development of techniques to chill atoms to millionths of a kelvin above absolute zero and to trap them with laser light
	Claude Cohen-Tannoudji	b. 1933	
	William Phillips	b. 1948	
1998	Robert B. Laughlin	b. 1950	Their discovery of a new form of quantum fluid with fractionally charged excitations
	Horst L. Störmer	b. 1949	
	Daniel C. Tsui	b. 1939	
1999	Gerardus 't Hooft	b. 1946	Elucidating the quantum structure of electroweak interactions in physics
	Martinus J. G. Veltman	b. 1931	
2000	Zhores I. Alferov	b. 1930	Basic work on information technology
	Herbert Kroemer	b. 1928	
	Jack S. Kilby	b. 1923	His part in the invention of the integrated circuit
2001	Eric A. Cornell	b. 1961	The achievement of Bose-Einstein condensation in dilute gases of alkali atoms and early fundamental studies of the properties of the condensates
	Wolfgang Ketterle	b. 1957	
	Carl E. Weiman	b. 1951	
2002	Raymond Davis, Jr.	b. 1914	Their pioneering contributions to astrophysics, in particular the detection of cosmic neutrinos
	Masatoshi Koshiba	b. 1926	
	Riccardo Giacconi	b. 1931	His pioneering contributions to astrophysics, which have led to the discovery of cosmic x-ray sources
2003	Alexei A. Abrikosov	b. 1928	For pioneering contributions to the theory of superconductors and superfluids
	Vitaly L. Ginzburg	b. 1916	
	Anthony J. Leggett	b. 1938	

Answers

These results are usually rounded to three significant figures. Differences in the third significant figure may result from rounding and are not important.

Chapter 1

1-1. (14.2 km, 16 km, 0.5 km)

1-5. (a) At $t = 2$s, a bright circle reflected from great circle perpendicular to the motion. (b) At $t = 2$s, entire interior lights up.

1-9. 4.63×10^{-13} s

1-13. (a) $x' = -9.54 \times 10^3$ m, $y' = 18$ m, $z' = 4.0$ m, $t' = 3.76 \times 10^{-5}$ s
(b) $x = 75.8$ m, $y = 18$ m, $z = 4.0$ m, $t = 2.0 \times 10^{-5}$ s

1-17. (b) 6 s

1-21. $0.14\,c$

1-25. $0.527\,c$ or 1.58×10^8 m/s

1-29. (a) in S': $V' = 16$ m³, in S : $V = 12.2$ m³

1-33. 657.0 nm, 662.9 nm, 725.6 nm

1-37. 3.0 m

1-41. 9.6 ms

1-45. (b) $v = 1.44 \times 10^8$ m/s   (c) 4.39 μs   (d) 4.39 μs

1-49. (a) $v = 0.5\,c$ in $-x$ direction   (b) 0.58 y   (c) $0.866\,c \cdot$y   (d) spacelike   (e) $0.866\,c \cdot$y

1-53. $\theta' = 0.494\,v_y/c$

1-57. (a) 120 min   (b) 240 min   (c) identical

1-61. (a) $A \rightarrow B$: $T/2 + 2vL/(c^2 - v^2)$; $B \rightarrow A$: $T/2 - 2vL/(c^2 - v^2)$ (b) $4vL/(c^2 - v^2)$

Chapter 2

2-5. (a) 1.1×10^{-16} kg; increases

2-9. (a) $0.999999999717\,c$ (b) 3.94×10^4 GeV/c (c) 3.31×10^9 GeV; -3.31×10^9 GeV/c

2-13. (a) $0.866\,c$ (b) $\sqrt{3}mc$

2-17. 6.26 MeV

2-21. 280 MeV

2-29. $u = 0.286\,c$; $m = 1673$ MeV/c^2

2-33. (c) is correct

2-37. 8.62 ms

2-41. (a) 1.73×10^5 m/s   (b) 1.5×10^5 m/s   (c) 155 kg

2-49. (a) muon: 4.12 MeV, 29.8 MeV/c
neutrino: 29.8 MeV, 29.8 MeV/c
(b) muon: 109.8 MeV, 29.8 MeV/c
neutrino: 29.8 MeV, 29.8 MeV/c

2-53. (a) $u/c = [1 - (2mc^2/Mc^2)^2]^{1/2}$ (b) $u/c = [1 - (Mc^2/4mc^2)^2]^{1/2}$

Chapter 3

3-1. proton 6.5×10^{-2} m, electron 3.6×10^{-5} m, deuteron 0.13 m, H_2 0.13 m, He 0.26 m

3-5. (a) 2.2 mm   (b) 9.1×10^9 Hz; 1.1×10^{-10} s

3-13. 5.67×10^{-8} W/m^2 K^4

3-17.   16

3-21.   278.3 K (5.3°C)

3-25.   (a) 255 nm   (b) 1.4×10^{-4}

3-29.   (a) 1.24×10^4 eV   (b) 1.24 GeV   (c) 3.75×10^{-7} eV

3-33. 4.14×10^{-3} nm, 5.8%

3-37.   0.243 nm

3-41.   (a) electron: 0.00243 nm, proton: 1.32 fm   (b) electron: 0.510 MeV, proton: 939 MeV

3-45.   (a) 2.08 eV   (b) 4.95×10^{14} Hz   (c) 4.19×10^{-15} eV/Hz

3-57.   (a) 0.0309 nm, 0.1259 nm   (b) 20.04 keV

Chapter 4

4-1.   Lyman: 91.16 nm, Balmer: 364.6 nm, Paschen: 820.4 nm

4-5.   4103 nm

4-9.   45.5 fm; 29.5 fm; 19.0 fm

4-13.   (a) 1.91 nm   (b) 0.95 nm

4-17.   (a) $n = 6$ to $n = 2$ (b) Balmer series

4-25.   (a) 19.0 μm   (b) 3.65×10^3 m/s

4-29.   680 fm

4-33. 1.90×10^{-8} Hz$^{-1/2}$

4-37.   10.2 V

4-41.   (a) 1.054×10^{-3} A   (b) 9.28×10^{-24} A · m^2

4-45.   (a) Lyman α: $n = 6$ to $n = 3$; Lyman β: $n = 9$ to $n = 3$ (b) $\Delta\lambda = 0.056$ nm

4-49.   (b) $I_0 R^2 \cos^2(\theta/2)$

4-53.   For $n = 1$: $v = 2.25 \times 10^6 \times Z^{1/2}$ m/s; $E = -14.4 Z$ eV

4-57.   10; 1042

Chapter 5

5-1.   (a) 2.1×10^{-23} m   (b) 2.1×10^{-21} m/y

5-5.   0.0276 nm

5-9.   (a) 0.445 fm   (b) 6.18×10^{-3} fm

5-13. 3.0×10^{-3} eV

5-17.   (b) 50 m/s   (c) 50 m/s   (d) $\Delta x = 5\pi$ m; $\Delta k = 0.4$ m^{-1}

5-21. 3.2×10^{-5} s

5-25.   (a) $A^2\, dx$ (b) $0.61 A^2\, dx$ (c) $0.14 A^2\, dx$ (d) $x = 0$

5-29. 1.99×10^{-21} eV

5-33.   (a) 5.3×10^{-10} (b) $\Delta E_T = 1.32 \times 10^{-7}$ eV

5-37. $\Delta f = 1.18 \times 10^{-9}$ Hz; $\Delta f/f = 3.9 \times 10^{-11}$

5-41. 5.27×10^{-34} J

5-45.   proton: 1.40×10^{-8} fm; bullet: 2.1×10^{-31} m

5-49. 1.04×10^{-44} kg

Chapter 6

6-9.   (a) 0.021 eV   (b) 205 MeV

6-13.   (a) 10^{-16} kg · m/s   (b) 9×10^{11}

6-17. 3.8×10^{14}

6-21. Use trig identity $2 \sin A \sin B = \cos(A - B) - \cos(A + B)$.

6-29. (b) $\langle x \rangle = L/2$ $\langle x \rangle^2 = L^2/3$

6-33. $m\hbar\omega/2$

6-37. (a) $\hbar/2A$ (b) [1] $E_0 = 4E_k$, [2]$E_0 = 2E_k$

6-41. (a) $k_2 = k_1/(2)^{1/2}$ (b) 0.0294   (c) 0.971   (d) 9.71×10^5; classically, 100% continue on

6-49. (a) 1/2   (b) 0.19   (c) 0.90

Chapter 7

7-1. $11 E_0, 12 E_0, 14 E_0$. The 1st, 2nd, 3rd, and 5th excited states are degenerate.

7-5. (b) 1, 1, 4 and 1, 2, 2

7-9. (a) 0, 1, 2   (b) $l = 0$, m $= 0$; $l = 1$, m $= -1, 0, 1$; $l = 2$, m $= -2, -1, 0, 1, 2$ (c) 18

7-13. (a) $2\hbar^2$ (b) $6\hbar^2$ (c) $5\hbar^2$ (d) 3

7-17. (a) $n = 6, l = 3$ (b) -0.38 eV   (c) $(12)^{1/2}\hbar$ (d) $-3\hbar, -2\hbar, -\hbar, 0, \hbar, 2\hbar, 3\hbar$

7-25. (a) $0.606a_0^{-3/2}(32\pi)^{-1/2}$ (b) $0.368a_0^{-3}/(32\pi)$ (c) $0.368/(8a_0)$

7-33. (a) 4   (b) 3

7-37. 1 or 2

7-45. (a) $1s^2 2s^2 2p^6 3s^2 3p^5$ (b) $1s^2 2s^2 2p^6 3s^2 3p^6 4s^2$ (c) $1s^2 2s^2 2p^6 3s^2 3p^6 3d^{10} 4s^2 4p^2$

7-49. (a) silicon   (b) calcium

7-53. similar to H: Li, Rb, Ag, Fr
similar to He: Ca, Ti, Cd, Ba, Hg, Ra

7-57. $D_{5/2} \rightarrow P_{1/2}$ forbidden

7-61. (a) 2.90×10^{-5} eV   (b) 7.83×10^{-3} nm   (c) 0.0638 T

7-65. (a) 1.67×10^6 m/s^2 (b) 1.95 cm

Chapter 8

8-1. (a) 1930 m/s   (b) 1.01×10^4 K

8-5. (a) 3400 J   (b) One mole of any gas has the same translational kinetic energy at the same temperature.

8-13. $C_V = R, C_P = 2R, \gamma = 2$

8-17. $N(E_2)/N(E_1) = 5.5 \times 10^{-9}$; $N(E_3)/N(E_1) = 2.8 \times 10^{-10}$; $N(E_4)/N(E_1) = 1.3 \times 10^{-10}$

8-21. (a) 0.347 eV   (b) 3660 K

8-25. 0.895 K (much lower than freezing temperature)

8-29. Al: 8.97×10^{11} Hz; Si: 2.46×10^{12} Hz

8-33. E_F(protons): 516 MeV; $\langle E \rangle$(protons): 310 MeV
E_F(neutrons): 742 MeV; $\langle E \rangle$(neutrons): 445 MeV

8-37. 10.3 eV

8-41. (a) $C = \sqrt{A/\pi kT}$ (b) $kT/2$

8-45. (b) as $T \rightarrow 0$ $\langle E \rangle \rightarrow 0$; as $T \rightarrow \infty$ $\langle E \rangle \rightarrow \epsilon/2$

Chapter 9

9-1. (a) 1 eV/molecule = 23.06 kcal/mol   (b) 98.5 kcal/mol   (c) 1.08 eV/molecule

9-5. (a) -5.39 eV   (b) 4.83 eV   (c) 0.46 eV

9-9. for KBr: 0.19 eV;   for RbCl: 0.23 eV

9-13. 2.63×10^{-29} C·m

9-17. (a) 0.67 nm   (b) 55 nm   (c) no

9-21. 1.78×10^{-4} eV

9-25.   (a) 18.6 u (b) 0.280 nm

9-29. 0.04×10^{-5} eV

9-33.   at 273 K: 2.4×10^{-4};   at 77 K: 1.4×10^{-13}

9-37.   2.81 km

9-41.   (a) 5.39 eV   (b) 4.66 eV   (c) 0.23 eV at r_0

9-49.   (a) 5.64×10^{-31} (b) 1273 W/cm^3

Chapter 10

10-1.   0.315 nm

10-5.   4.09 eV/atom

10-9.   (a) $1.23 \times 10^{-7} \Omega \cdot$ m   (b) $7.00 \times 10^{-8} \Omega \cdot$ m

10-13.   (a) 8.62×10^{28}/m^3 (b) 13.1×10^{28}/m^3

10-17.   (a) for Ag: 5.50 eV;   for Fe: 11.2 eV
    (b) for Ag: 6.38×10^4 K;   for Fe: 13.0×10^4 K

10-21. 4.98×10^3 K

10-29.   (a) 5.01×10^7 Si atoms   (b) 6.5×10^{-8} eV

10-33.   116 K

10-37.   47.6/1

10-41.   (a) 0.0011 eV   (b) 2.07×10^{-3} m

10-45.   (b) 1.386

10-49.   37 nm (Cu: 39 nm)

10-53.   (c) -0.0195 eV

Chapter 11

11-9.   (a) 52.8 MeV; 6.46 MeV/nucleon
    (b) 91.1 MeV; 7.47 MeV/nucleon
    (c) 499.9 MeV; 8.77 MeV/nucleon

11-13.   (a) 2.70 fm; 3.53 fm   (b) 4.26 fm; 5.57 fm
    (c) 6.34 fm; 8.30 fm

11-17.   (a) $t_{1/2} = 5.21$ h   (b) 3.11×10^6 atoms

11-21.   33.2 min

11-25. $A = 191, B = -72.2$

11-29.   1.00 MeV

11-33.   Lower energy configuration is 2α particles.

11-37.   789 MeV/c^2

11-41. ^{36}S, ^{53}Mn, ^{82}Ge, ^{88}Sr, ^{94}Ru, ^{131}In, ^{145}Eu

11-45. ^{30}Si $j = 0$, ^{37}Cl $j = 3/2$, ^{55}Co $j = 7/2$, ^{90}Zr $j = 0$, ^{107}In $j = 9/2$

11-49. 2.09×10^{15} y

11-53.   for ^{3}He: 7.72 MeV;   for ^{3}H: 8.48 MeV

11-57.   (b) ^{29}Si, ^{59}Co, ^{78}Se and ^{78}Kr, ^{119}Sn, ^{140}Ce

11-61.   (a) 1.189 MeV/c (b) 0.753 keV   (c) 0.0963%

Chapter 12

12-1.   (a) 4.03 MeV   (b) 18.4 MeV   (c) 4.78 MeV

12-5. 1.18×10^{10}/s

12-9. 1.56×10^{19} fissions/s

12-13. 1.26×10^{22} ^{238}U atoms; 1.26×10^{4} ^{239}U atoms

12-17. (a) 1.10×10^{3} MeV   (b) This reaction is not likely.

12-21. 1.31×10^{5} counts in 5 minutes

12-25. 16,800 y

12-29. 1.14×10^{8} kg

12-33. 3.22×10^{10} J

12-37. $E_{\text{He}} = 3.56$ MeV; $E_n = 14.1$ MeV

Chapter 13

13-1.   (b) Each photon's energy equals the rest energy of a π.   (c) 8.88 fm

13-5.   (a) A single photon cannot conserve both energy and momentum.
(b) 938.28 MeV   (c) 1.32 fm   (d) 2.27×10^{23} Hz

13-9. π^0 decays more quickly than the π^-.

13-17. (a) $T = 1$ (b) $T = 1$ or 0   (c) $T = 3/2$ (d) $T = 3/2$ (e) $T = 1/2$ or 3/2

13-21. (a) conserved   (b) not conserved   (c) conserved   (d) not conserved   (e) not conserved

13-25. (a) $T_3 = 0$ (b) $T = 1$ or 0   (c) $B = 1, C = 0, S = -1$

13-33. (a) $\mathbf{c\bar{d}}$ (b) $\mathbf{\bar{c}d}$

13-37. (a) Energy is not conserved.   (b) Angular momentum is not conserved.
(c) Angular momentum is not conserved.

13-41. (a) yes   (d) no

13-45. (a) no

13-49. (c) 40.3 s

Chapter 14

(This chapter is available on the W. H. Freeman Physics Web Site
at www.whfreeman.com/modphysics4e.)

14-1.   25.3 days

14-5.   16.9 eV

14-9.   (a) 3300 K, 1.93×10^{25} W   (b) 13,500 K, 3.85×10^{28} W
(c) 2.09×10^{8} m, 2.09×10^{9} m

14-13. (a) 2.9×10^{3} m   (b) 2.8 m   (c) 8.9×10^{-3} m

14-17. 9.5×10^{4} AU

14-21. 1.062 mm

14-25. (a) 170,000 BP   (b) 149,000 $c \cdot$ y; no

14-33. 676 °C (sufficient to boil oceans); $v = 11.2$ (H$_2$O stays in atmosphere)

Index

boldface indicates a definition
italics indicates a figure
t indicates a table
w(1a) indicates the first More section for Chapter 1, on the home page; *w*(1b) indicates the second More section for Chapter 1; and so forth.
w(AP) indicates material that appears in Appendix B3 on the home page. *w*(Ch14) indicates material in Chapter 14 on the home page.